Literature Criticism from 1400 to 1800

Guide to Gale Literary Criticism Series

For criticism on	Consult these Gale series
Authors now living or who died after December 31, 1999	*CONTEMPORARY LITERARY CRITICISM (CLC)*
Authors who died between 1900 and 1999	*TWENTIETH-CENTURY LITERARY CRITICISM (TCLC)*
Authors who died between 1800 and 1899	*NINETEENTH-CENTURY LITERATURE CRITICISM (NCLC)*
Authors who died between 1400 and 1799	*LITERATURE CRITICISM FROM 1400 TO 1800 (LC)* *SHAKESPEAREAN CRITICISM (SC)*
Authors who died before 1400	*CLASSICAL AND MEDIEVAL LITERATURE CRITICISM (CMLC)*
Authors of books for children and young adults	*CHILDREN'S LITERATURE REVIEW (CLR)*
Dramatists	*DRAMA CRITICISM (DC)*
Poets	*POETRY CRITICISM (PC)*
Short story writers	*SHORT STORY CRITICISM (SSC)*
Black writers of the past two hundred years	*BLACK LITERATURE CRITICISM (BLC)* *BLACK LITERATURE CRITICISM SUPPLEMENT (BLCS)*
Hispanic writers of the late nineteenth and twentieth centuries	*HISPANIC LITERATURE CRITICISM (HLC)* *HISPANIC LITERATURE CRITICISM SUPPLEMENT (HLCS)*
Native North American writers and orators of the eighteenth, nineteenth, and twentieth centuries	*NATIVE NORTH AMERICAN LITERATURE (NNAL)*
Major authors from the Renaissance to the present	*WORLD LITERATURE CRITICISM, 1500 TO THE PRESENT (WLC)* *WORLD LITERATURE CRITICISM SUPPLEMENT (WLCS)*

ISSN 0740-2880

Volume 78

Literature Criticism from 1400 to 1800

Critical Discussion of the Works
of Fifteenth-, Sixteenth-, Seventeenth-, and
Eighteenth-Century Novelists, Poets, Playwrights,
Philosophers, and Other Creative Writers

Michael L. LaBlanc
Project Editor

GALE®

THOMSON
™
GALE

Detroit • New York • San Diego • San Francisco • Cleveland • New Haven, Conn. • Waterville, Maine • London • Munich

Literature Criticism from 1400 to 1800, Vol. 78

Project Editor
Michael L. LaBlanc

Editorial
Jenny Cromie, Kathy D. Darrow, Elisabeth Gellert, Madeline S. Harris, Edna M. Hedblad, Jelena O. Krstovi, Michelle Lee, Jessica Menzo, Thomas J. Schoenberg, Lawrence J. Trudeau, Russel Whitaker

Research
Nicodemus Ford, Sarah Genik, Tamara C. Nott, Tracie A. Richardson

Permissions
Kim Davis

Imaging and Multimedia
Dean Dauphinais, Robert Duncan, Leitha Etheridge-Sims, Mary K. Grimes, Lezlie Light, Dan Newell, David G. Oblender, Christine O'Bryan, Kelly A. Quin, Luke Rademacher

Composition and Electronic Capture
Carolyn Roney

Manufacturing
Stacy L. Melson

LIBRARY OF CONGRESS CATALOG CARD NUMBER 94-29718

ISBN 0-7876-5992-4
ISSN 0740-2880

Contents

Preface vii

Acknowledgments xi

Literary Criticism Series Advisory Board xiii

Thomas Campion 1567-1620 1
  English poet, playwright, composer, and critic.

George Etherege 1636-1692? 95
  English playwright and poet.

Picaresque Literature of the Sixteenth and Seventeenth Centuries
Introduction 223
Representative Works 223
Context and Development 224
Genre 271
The Picaro 299
The Picara 326
Further Reading 353

Literary Criticism Series Cumulative Author Index 357

Literary Criticism Series Cumulative Topic Index 447

LC Cumulative Nationality Index 457

LC-78 Title Index 459

Preface

*L*iterature Criticism from 1400 to 1800 (*LC*) presents critical discussion of world literature from the fifteenth through the eighteenth centuries. The literature of this period is especially vital: the years 1400 to 1800 saw the rise of modern European drama, the birth of the novel and personal essay forms, the emergence of newspapers and periodicals, and major achievements in poetry and philosophy. *LC* provides valuable insight into the art, life, thought, and cultural transformations that took place during these centuries.

Scope of the Series

LC provides an introduction to the great poets, dramatists, novelists, essayists, and philosophers of the fifteenth through eighteenth centuries, and to the most significant interpretations of these authors' works. Because criticism of this literature spans nearly six hundred years, an overwhelming amount of scholarship confronts the student. *LC* organizes this material concisely and logically. Every attempt is made to reprint the most noteworthy, relevant, and educationally valuable essays available.

A separate Gale reference series, *Shakespearean Criticism,* is devoted exclusively to Shakespearean studies. Although properly belonging to the period covered in *LC*, William Shakespeare has inspired such a tremendous and ever-growing body of secondary material that a separate series was deemed essential.

Each entry in *LC* presents a representative selection of critical response to an author, a literary topic, or to a single important work of literature. Early commentary is offered to indicate initial responses, later selections document changes in literary reputations, and retrospective analyses provide the reader with modern views. The size of each author entry is a relative reflection of the scope of the criticism available in English. Every attempt has been made to identify and include the seminal essays on each author's work and to include recent commentary providing modern perspectives.

Volumes 1 through 12 of the series feature author entries arranged alphabetically by author. Volumes 13-47 of the series feature a thematic arrangement. Each volume includes an entry devoted to the general study of a specific literary or philosophical movement, writings surrounding important political and historical events, the philosophy and art associated with eras of cultural transformation, or the literature of specific social or ethnic groups. Each of these volumes also includes several author entries devoted to major representatives of the featured period, genre, or national literature. With volume 48, the series returns to a standard author approach, with some entries devoted to a single important work of world literature and others devoted to literary topics.

Organization of the Book

An *LC* entry consists of the following elements:

■ The **Author Heading** cites the name under which the author most commonly wrote, followed by birth and death dates. Also located here are any name variations under which an author wrote, including transliterated forms for authors whose native languages use nonroman alphabets. If the author wrote consistently under a pseudonym, the pseudonym will be listed in the author heading and the author's actual name given in parenthesis on the first line of the biographical and critical information. Uncertain birth or death dates are indicated by question marks. Topic entries are preceded by a **Thematic Heading,** which simply states the subject of the entry. Single-work entries are preceded by the title of the work and its date of publication.

■ The **Introduction** contains background information that introduces the reader to the author, work, or topic that is the subject of the entry.

- A **Portrait of the Author** is included when available.

- The list of **Principal Works** is ordered chronologically by date of first publication and lists the most important works by the author. The genre and publication date of each work is given. In the case of foreign authors whose works have been translated into English, the title and date (if available) of the first English-language edition is given in brackets following the original title. Unless otherwise indicated, dramas are dated by first performance, not first publication. Lists of **Representative Works** by different authors appear with topic entries.

- Reprinted **Criticism** is arranged chronologically in each entry to provide a useful perspective on changes in critical evaluation over time. The critic's name and the date of composition or publication of the critical work are given at the beginning of each piece of criticism. Unsigned criticism is preceded by the title of the source in which it appeared. All titles by the author featured in the text are printed in boldface type. Footnotes are reprinted at the end of each essay or excerpt. In the case of excerpted criticism, only those footnotes that pertain to the excerpted texts are included. Criticism in topic entries is arranged chronologically under a variety of subheadings to facilitate the study of different aspects of the topic.

- Critical essays are prefaced by brief **Annotations** explicating each piece.

- A complete **Bibliographical Citation** of the original essay or book precedes each piece of criticism.

- An annotated bibliography of **Further Reading** appears at the end of each entry and suggests resources for additional study. In some cases, significant essays for which the editors could not obtain reprint rights are included here. Boxed material following the further reading list provides references to other biographical and critical sources on the author in series published by Gale.

Cumulative Indexes

A **Cumulative Author Index** lists all of the authors that appear in a wide variety of reference sources published by the Gale Group, including *LC*. A complete list of these sources is found facing the first page of the Author Index. The index also includes birth and death dates and cross references between pseudonyms and actual names.

A **Cumulative Nationality Index** lists all authors featured in *LC* by nationality, followed by the number of the *LC* volume in which their entry appears.

A **Cumulative Topic Index** lists the literary themes and topics treated in the series as well as in *Nineteenth-Century Literature Criticism, Twentieth-Century Literary Criticism,* and the *Contemporary Literature Criticism* Yearbook, which was discontinued in 1998.

An alphabetical **Title Index** accompanies each volume of *LC*. Listings of titles by authors covered in the given volume are followed by the author's name and the corresponding page numbers on which the titles are discussed. English translations of foreign titles and variations of titles are cross-referenced to the title under which a work was originally published. Titles of novels, dramas, nonfiction books, and poetry, short story, or essay collections are printed in italics, while individual poems, short stories, and essays are printed in roman type within quotation marks.

Citing *Literature Criticism from 1400 to 1800*

When writing papers, students who quote directly from any volume in the Literary Criticism Series may use the following general format to footnote reprinted criticism. The first example pertains to material drawn from periodicals, the second to material reprinted from books.

Eileen Reeves, "Daniel 5 and the *Assayer*: Galileo Reads the Handwriting on the Wall," *The Journal of Medieval and Renaissance Studies,* 21, no. 1 (Spring 1991): 1-27; reprinted in *Literature Criticism from 1400 to 1800,* vol. 45, ed. Jelena Krstović and Marie Lazzari (Farmington Hills, Mich.: The Gale Group, 1999), 297-310.

Margaret Anne Doody, *A Natural Passion: A Study of the Novels of Samuel Richardson* (Oxford University Press, 1974), 17-22, 132-35; excerpted and reprinted in *Literature Criticism from 1400 to 1800,* vol. 46, ed. Jelena Krstović and Marie Lazzari (Farmington Hills, Mich.: The Gale Group, 1999), 20-2.

Suggestions are Welcome

Readers who wish to suggest new features, topics, or authors to appear in future volumes, or who have other suggestions or comments are cordially invited to call, write, or fax the Project Editor:

Project Editor, Literary Criticism Series
The Gale Group
27500 Drake Road
Farmington Hills, MI 48331-3535
1-800-347-4253 (GALE)
Fax: 248-699-8054

Acknowledgments

The editors wish to thank the copyright holders of the excerpted criticism included in this volume and the permissions managers of many book and magazine publishing companies for assisting us in securing reproduction rights. We are also grateful to the staffs of the Detroit Public Library, the Library of Congress, the University of Detroit Mercy Library, Wayne State University Purdy/Kresge Library Complex, and the University of Michigan Libraries for making their resources available to us. Following is a list of the copyright holders who have granted us permission to reproduce material in this volume of *LC*. Every effort has been made to trace copyright, but if omissions have been made, please let us know.

COPYRIGHTED MATERIAL IN *LC*, VOLUME 78, WAS REPRODUCED FROM THE FOLLOWING PERIODICALS:

COPYRIGHTED MATERIAL IN *LC*, VOLUME 78, WAS REPRODUCED FROM THE FOLLOWING BOOKS:

Literary Criticism Series Advisory Board

The members of the Gale Group Literary Criticism Series Advisory Board—reference librarians and subject specialists from public, academic, and school library systems—represent a cross-section of our customer base and offer a variety of informed perspectives on both the presentation and content of our literature criticism products. Advisory board members assess and define such quality issues as the relevance, currency, and usefulness of the author coverage, critical content, and literary topics included in our series; evaluate the layout, presentation, and general quality of our printed volumes; provide feedback on the criteria used for selecting authors and topics covered in our series; provide suggestions for potential enhancements to our series; identify any gaps in our coverage of authors or literary topics, recommending authors or topics for inclusion; analyze the appropriateness of our content and presentation for various user audiences, such as high school students, undergraduates, graduate students, librarians, and educators; and offer feedback on any proposed changes/ enhancements to our series. We wish to thank the following advisors for their advice throughout the year.

Thomas Campion
1567-1620

English poet, playwright, composer, and critic.

INTRODUCTION

Campion is best known for his work as a poet and as a composer of songs for voice and lute. He is also recognized for his poetry in Latin and for his work in the masque form of poetic drama, which is considered of some importance in the evolution of the genre. In addition to his creative works, Campion wrote a significant study on poetic theory, *Observations in the Art of English Poesie* (1602). In this controversial work, he argued that verse written in English should emulate classical meters. The influence of classical literatures, primarily Latin, are found throughout the work of Campion, whose reputation as a writer and composer has steadily improved over time.

BIOGRAPHICAL INFORMATION

Born on February 12, 1567, in St. Andrew's Holborn, England, Campion was the son of John Campion, a clerk of the Court of Chancery, property owner, and vestryman of St. Andrew's Church, and his wife Lucy (maiden name, Searle). Campion was orphaned by the time he was a teenager: his father died in 1576 and his mother in 1580. After the death of his mother, who had remarried, Campion was raised by his stepfather, Augustin Steward. At the age of fourteen, Campion entered Cambridge University, but did not attain a degree before he left in 1584. While there, he studied classical literature, an interest that would later influence his writing. In 1586, Campion decided to pursue a career in law and was admitted to Gray's Inn for his education in the field. According to his biographers, he probably did not complete this course and most likely left Gray's Inn before the end of the decade. During this part of Campion's life, he almost certainly began writing poems and songs. In 1591, Campion also gained experience as a soldier, and was likely part of a military operation lead by the Earl of Essex to Normandy to assist Henri IV. Campion's first published work, *Thoma Campiani Poemata,* appeared in 1595. His first work of significance was *A Book of Ayres,* which was published in 1601 and also contained works by Philip Rosseter. Because of the dedication of the book to Sir Thomas Monson, biographers surmise that Campion was writing primarily under the patronage of this significant musical benefactor. Their relationship would have both a positive and negative effect on Campion's career. Campion's next publication of note was his study of poetic theory, *Observations in the Art of English Poesie.*

At the same time that Campion was engaged in literary pursuits, he was also studying medicine, earning an M.D. degree from the University of Caen. After his return to England, Campion practiced as a physician amd continued to write, composing poetry, songs and masques. Through the influence of Monson, Campion was commissioned to write a masque on the occasion of the wedding of Princess Elisabeth, the daughter of King James I, in 1612. However, the king's son, Prince Henry, died before the wedding was to take place, and Campion's masque, entitled *The Lords' Masque* was not performed until the following year. Upon Prince Henry's death, Campion composed *Songs of Mourning* (1613). Throughout the remainder of his life, Campion composed and published poetry and songs, including *The Third and Fourth Bookes of Ayres* (c. 1617). This collection was also dedicated to Monson, who was involved in legal troubles in which Campion was implicated. Although Monson was exonerated of all charges, Campion's association with his literary patron lead to a decline in prestige. His last publication was *Thoma Campiani Epigrammatum Libri II,* another collection Latin poetry which appeared in 1619. The following year, on March 1, Campion died. He was buried in London at St. Dunstan's in the West.

MAJOR WORKS

Campion's important works consist primarily of poetry, written in both Latin and English; songs including musical accompaniment composed by the author; and masques. *Thoma Campiani Poemata,* Campion's first collection of poems in Latin, includes sixteen elegies and 129 epigrams on a number of topics, including friends, women, love, his days at Gray's Inn, his military experience, and the defeat of the Spanish Armada ("Ad Theamesin"). Campion's next work, *A Book of Ayres,* featured a number of his songs written for voice and lute. Among these compositions is "My Sweetest Lesbia," which was influenced by the Latin poet Catullus. The influence of classical Latin poetry is underscored in Campion's next work of note, *Observations in the Art of English Poesie.* In this work of poetic theory, Campion advanced his view that verse written in English should take as its model the metrical rules of Latin literature. He also condemns the use of rhyme as it had been employed in English poetry, discusses which verse forms would best suit English, and outlines a method for establishing the number of syllables in lines of English poetry. Campion then focused on the masque tradition, combining poetry, music, dance, and drama. His first work in the genre, *The Lord Hay's Masque,* was written for the wedding of Lord Hay, a Scottish man, to an English woman. The marriage had political overtones, as it occurred during the reign of James I, when Scotland and England were being united as Great Britain. Campion used mythological elements to tell his story. Diana, the goddess of chastity, incarcerates nine Knights of Apollo in trees because otherwise they will seduce her nymphs. Venus (Hesperus) intercedes to placate Diana, who releases the Knights. The Knights then join the marriage celebration. The masque was written to illustrate symbolically the importance of political harmony between the conflicting powers of Scotland and England. Campion's next masque, *The Lords' Masque,* is more multifaceted than his previous work. Again using mythological imagery, eight lords representing stars are brought to earth by Prometheus. Jove turns eight ladies into statues because of Prometheus's actions. Ultimately, Jove changes his mind and by fours the women come to life and dance with the stars. At the end of the masque, Sibylla, a prophet, materializes with the statues of the bride and groom and predicts the couple will live happily. In 1613, Campion wrote two more masques, *The Caversham Entertainment* and *The Somerset Masque,* both of which were less elaborate in structure and theme than his previous masques. The former was composed as an entertainment for Queen Anne during her stay at Caversham on her progress to Bath. Campion's second masque of the year, *The Somerset Masque,* was written for the wedding of the Earl of Somerset to the daughter of the Earl of Suffolk, and is based on a narrative of Catullus concerning the marriage of Peleus and Thetis. After this point, Campion's output consisted of songs and poems. In 1613, he published *Two Bookes of Ayres,* which contains devotional music and poetry as well as love songs and poems. Around 1617, he published *The Third and Fourth Bookes of Ayres.* Campion's last work was similar to his first, a collection of Latin poetry entitled *Thoma Campiani Epigrammatum Libri II* and dedicated to King James I. It contains 453 epigrams, thirteen elegies, and one epic poem.

CRITICAL RECEPTION

Significant critical study of Campion's works did not occur until the late nineteenth century. At that time, critics wrote favorably of his poetry but did not consider his work as a composer of songs. In general, Campion has been relegated him to the ranks of minor poets. By the mid-twentieth century, many critics began looking at Campion as a poet and composer. In terms of his songs, critics looked at issues related to how the poetry and the music worked or did not work together. Some contended that there was an aesthetic balance between his poetry and music, while others denied that musical accompaniment enhanced his poetry. Nonetheless, many critics believe these compositions show his versatility as a writer, if only because they demonstrate that he could use a variety of metrical forms successfully. Despite the fact that many of his poems were written as song lyrics, most critics still look at his poetry divorced from his music. A number of critics have compared his output in English to his Latin

poems, with the former sometimes regarded as less personal and revealing than the latter. Campion's work has also been analyzed in relation to the poetic theories presented in *Observations in the Art of English Poesie.* A number of critics regard this as an important work and have discussed the role it played in the development of English poetry. While contemporaries considered Campion's masques inferior to those by Ben Jonson, the master of the form in that era, some modern critics discern value in these works. For example, *The Lord Hay's Masque* has been examined in terms of Campion's symbolic commentary on matters of British politics during his lifetime.

PRINCIPAL WORKS

Thoma Campiani Poemata (poetry) 1595

A Book of Ayres, Set foorth to be song to the Lute, Orpherian, and Base Violl [with Philip Rosseter] (songs) 1601

Observations in the Art of English Poesie (criticism) 1602

The Lord Hay's Masque (play) 1607; published as *The Description of a Maske, Presented before the Kings Maiestie at White-H— on Twelfth Night last, in honour of the Lord Hayes, and his Bride, Daughter and Heire to the Honourable the Lord Dennye* 1607

A New Way of Making Fowre parts in Counter-point, by a most familiar, and infallible Rule. Secondly, a necessary discourse of Keyes, and their proper Closes. Thirdly, the allowed passages of all Concords perfect, or imperfect, are declared. Also . . . the nature of the Scale is expressed, with a briefe Method teaching to Sing. (nonfiction) 1610

The Lords' Masque (play) 1613

The Caversham Entertainment (play) 1613; published as *A Relation of The Late Royall Entertainment given By The Right Honourable The Lord Knowles, at Cawsome House neere Redding: to our most Gracious Queene, Queene Anne in her Progresse toward the Bathe, upon the seven and eight and twentie dayes of April 1613. Whereunto is annexed the Description, Speeches and Songs of the Lords Maske, presented in the Banqueting House on the Mariage night of High and Mightie, Count Palatine, and the Royally descended the Ladie Elizabeth* 1613; published as *The Description of a Maske. Presented in the Banqueting roome at Whitehall on Saint Stephens Night last, at the Mariage of the Right Honourable the Earle of Somerset: And the right noble the Lady Francis Howard* 1614

The Somerset Masque (play) 1613

Songs of Mourning (songs) 1613

Two Bookes of Ayres (songs) 1613?

The Third and Fourth Bookes of Ayres (poetry) 1617?

Thoma Campiani Epigrammatum Libri II (poetry) 1619

The Works of Dr. Thomas Campion [edited by A. H. Bullen] (songs, poetry, criticism, and plays) 1889

Campion's Works (songs, poetry, criticism, and plays) 1909

CRITICISM

Thomas MacDonagh (essay date 1913)

SOURCE: MacDonagh, Thomas. "Introductory," "Campion's Life and Works," and "The Beginnings of English Prosody: Campion's 'Observations'." In *Thomas Campion and the Art of English Poetry*, pp. 1-21. Dublin: Hodges, Figgis & Co., Ltd., 1913.

[*In the following excerpt, MacDonagh provides an overview of Campion's literary output and his importance in the history of English literature.*]

> *A man of faire parts and good reputation.*
>
> Samuel Daniel.

"The great period of English poetry," says Arthur Symons, "begins half-way through the sixteenth century, and lasts half-way into the seventeenth. In the poetry strictly of the sixteenth century, before the drama had absorbed poetry into the substance of its many energies, verse is used as speech, and becomes song by way of speech. Music had come from Italy, and had found for once a home in England. It was an age of music. Music, singing, and dancing made then, and then only, the 'Merry England' of the phrase. And the words, growing out of the same soil as the tunes, took equal root. Campion sums up for us a whole period, a perfect craftsman in the two arts."

Thomas Campion was a contemporary of William Shakespeare, and his equal in age from birth to death—Shakespeare, 1564-1616; Campion, 1567-1620. Others of his equals, in this sense, were his opponents in the metrical controversy, Samuel Daniel (1562-1619); Joshua Sylvester (1563-1618), to whom one of his most beautiful songs was for long attributed; Michael Drayton, born in 1563; Christopher Marlowe, born in 1564; and Thomas Nashe (1567-1601), his friend and admirer, honoured by him in his Latin verses. Ben Jonson and John Donne, great poets, the powerful influences of the next generation, were six years younger than Campion. This matter of dates may at first sight seem to count for little, but, to draw a comparison from the main part of this dissertation, the unit, the essential, is the period; the poet articulates the period. This was a period of music and power, and each good poet of it was the higher and stronger for the height and strength of his contemporaries. The phenomenon occurred again in England at the beginning of the nineteenth century, and then the wave came double-crested—Wordsworth (b. 1770), Scott (b. 1771), Coleridge (b. 1772), Byron (1788-1824), Shelley (1792-1822), Keats (1795-1821).

Two or three other such lists include all but a few of the great writers of the English language. There are some that are heard like a single word in the night, but in general the history of literature is like a line of verse, "a succession of sounds and silences," each sound syllabled, vowelled.

Campion was, then, a close contemporary of Shakespeare; yet in only one contemporary record that we know of are the two poets mentioned together. In no record of their time they have been mentioned with greater honour, "laudati a laudato viro." Camden, in his *Remaines of a Greater Worke concerning Britaine,* published in 1605, passes from "some Poeticall descriptions of our auncient Poets" to his contemporaries: "If I would come to our time, what a world could I present to you out of Sir Philipp Sidney, Ed. Spencer, Samuel Daniel, Hugh Holland, Ben. Jonson, Th. Campion, Mich. Drayton, George Chapman, John Marston, William Shakespeare, and other most pregnant witts of these our times, whom succeeding ages may justly admire." With the exception of Hugh Holland, who reminds one of the Hugh O'Lara of Lady Gregory's *Image,* one succeeding age or another has admired them indeed. With that one exception, Thomas Campion is last to receive his meed. From 1619 to 1814 there is a blank in his bibliography. The first edition of Palgrave's *Golden Treasury* knew him not. Later editions have wronged him by the inclusion of some of his inferior work and by the exclusion of some of his most lovely songs.

In 1814 he had appeared in Sir Egerton Brydges' *Excerpta Tudoriana.* The following year saw the first modern reprint of his ***Observations in the Art of English Poesie,*** in Hazlewood's *Ancient Critical Essays.* Then again a long blank till 1887, which gave us *Lyrics from the Song Books.* The year 1889 brought the *editio princeps* of his collected works, edited by Mr. A. H. Bullen. Campion had then been dead two hundred and sixty-nine years. There are at present two important editions of his works—Mr. Bullen's and Mr. Percival Vivian's—and three or four minor cheap editions. Now that after such long waiting he has won the admiration of a succeeding age, his fame is certain to stand, poised delicately on slight, graceful, strong foundations of beauty. We recognise in Campion a true poet, as truly a poet for his age as was his contemporary Shakespeare for all time. He is a poet of the Elizabethan song-books. His highest praise is that he is the best poet of the song-books.

For students of the art of English poesy his work has a further rare interest and value. He was a metrist in theory and practice. Here again, in theory, he was of his age; in practice he was a precursor. He was a scholar in an age of much wrong-headed learning. He was a sweet singer in an age of song. He wrote more poems in Latin than in English. He wrote of English verse as if it were imitation Latin verse. He tried to train himself to a foreign mode of poetic speech. He strove to write by rule and not by ear. He "whose commendable rimes had given to the world the best notice of his worth,"[1] was at much pains to show that the natural graces of English verse were vain and unworthy. He became, as Daniel laments, "an enemy of rime." He railed against "shifting rime, that easy flatterer," against "the fatnes of rime"—he, whose rimes and cadences, composed both before and after his railing, are unsurpassed in English song. But his ear triumphed. He followed his rule only a little way. Soon again he "tuned his music to the heart." He was too true a lyric poet to tune it to the false tones of the erring schoolmen.

And even in his railing and in his error his acute perception gives him glimpses of truth. His **Observations** is by far the ablest of the Elizabethan treatises on quantitative verse.[2] If the Elizabethan age was the greatest in matter of poetic achievement, it was so because it was free from self-consciousness. Campion, thinking much more highly of his English sapphics and of his Latin epigrams, referred to his lovely "Airs" as "after the fashion of the time, ear-pleasing rimes without art." Shakespeare's notes were to the greatest poet of the next age "native wood-notes wild," ear-pleasing, without art. But Campion and Milton sang native wood-notes too, in spite of what they thought to be their knowledge of higher things, in spite of the Renaissance and its sequel. Shakespeare the dramatist spoke through his masks the nervous, eager, living language of his tongue. Shakespeare unlocked his heart—or did not[3]—with the sonnet key which he found to his hand, imported and adapted by his immediate predecessors. Shakespeare, the lover of music, "warbled his native wood-notes wild," careless, most probably ignorant, of quantity, and stress, and "isochronous periods," and all the rules of English metrics—of all but what makes the best knowledge and creates earpleasing rimes without art, concealing art.

Campion, like Milton, was a musician. It would be interesting to trace the effect of Milton's musical knowledge on his verse, not merely on his verse of organ voice, but on the lyric measures of *Arcades* and *Comus* and *Samson Agonistes*. In Campion the effect is obvious and evident. His verse suggests music. All his lyrics are "airs," songs set to music, published with their tunes. Always in his verse he "chiefly aimed," as he says, "to couple words and music lovingly together." He is essentially a craftsman of the two arts.

CAMPION'S LIFE AND WORKS

Sweet Master Campion.

Marginal in a copy of William Covell's *Polimanteia*
(1595).

We ought to maintain as well in notes as in action a manly carriage.

Campion.

I have relegated to an appendix my detailed account of the life of Thomas Campion. Here, before proceeding to treat of the poet's works, I deal in passing with two points which do not fit into a chronological enumeration of the facts of his life. Very little is known with certainty of the grandson of John Campion of Dublin. I hope that further investigations will throw some new light on his ancestry. Mr. Percival Vivian, his most recent and most thorough biographer, brushes aside the Irish connection of his family, and fixes John Campion the elder as a Hertfordshire man, who "may have visited Ireland on some venture, commercial or otherwise, or held a paltry office there."

The minutes of the Parliament held in the Middle Temple in 1565 do not give colour to this surmise. Therein the poet's father, John Campion, is described as "son and heir of John Campion of Dublin, Ireland, deceased." There were Campions in Ireland at the time. The name, which appears to have been formerly pronounced Champion in Ireland and England, was one of the English forms of the Irish name O'Crowley, in Gaelic O Cruaidhlaoich, the descendant of the Hard Warrior, or Champion. It is quite common to the present day in Kilkenny and Queen's County. This, however, is not the place to go into the question of the poet's pedigree or to examine in detail Mr. Vivian's conclusions and inferences concerning his family. In the appendix I have given in chronological order the accepted facts.

The poet was born on Ash Wednesday, 12th February, 1567, and christened the following day at St. Andrew's Church, Holborn, of which parish his father was assistant or vestryman. Dr. Jessop in *The Dictionary of National Biography,* Mr. A. H. Bullen in his editions of Campion, and Mr. Vivian in his small "Muses' Library" edition, have been at some pains to prove the poet a Catholic. They have drawn inferences from the religion of his most intimate friends, the Mychelburnes, Sir Thomas Monson, and others; from the possibility of relationship between him and Edmund Campion, the Jesuit martyr, "the Pope's Champion"; from the fact that he did not proceed to a degree in Cambridge, though he was known to have been of the university;[4] and from his attacks on the Puritans. Researches made by Mr. Vivian or at his instance have now made it known that he belonged to Peterhouse, Cambridge; his not taking a degree argues nothing as to his faith. It is certain that his family adhered to the religion by law established. While satirising the Puritans—in itself no proof at the time of Catholicism—he hailed Elizabeth as "Faith's pure shield, the Christian Diana," and in his Latin poem **"Ad Thamesin (de Hyspanorum fuga)"** wrote:

"Nec Romana feret purgatis Orgia fanis
Reffluere, aut vetitas fieri libamen ad aras.
O pietas odiosa deo, sclerataque sacra,
Quae magis inficiunt (damnosa piacula) sontes."

Mr. Vivian in his complete edition of Campion recants his former pleading, and writes the poet down a moderate Anglican.

In the very first poem that we know for certain to be his, Campion is already "a curious metrist," in the phrase of W. E. Henley. This poem, **"Canto Primo"** of *Poems and Sonets of Sundry Other Noblemen and Gentlemen,* printed with a surreptitious edition of Sidney's *Astrophel and Stella* in 1591, and reprinted in *A Book of Airs,* 1601, is indeed amongst the best examples in English of the beauty of hovering or wavering rhythms. **"Canto Secundo"** of the same set is an experiment in classical rhythms:

"Whát faíre / pómpe haue I spíde / óf glitteríng / Ladíes,"

an accentual imitation of the Latin Asclepiad Minor. Of these I shall treat in the body of this dissertation. Here they are worth noting as indicating already the double bent of the poet—to classical theorising and imitation on the one hand, and on the other to freedom of lyric singing, won from practice of music and the lute.

Campion was twenty-four when these first-fruits of his genius appeared. It is probable that other poems of his were well known in the literary circles of London, for in 1593, eight years before the publication of *A Book of Airs,* George Peele had already addressed him as:

> "Thou
> That richly cloth'st conceite with well made words,
> Campion."

In 1595 was published his first acknowledged work, *Thomœe Campiani Poemata,* Latin poems which established him, in the opinion of his contemporaries, as one of the greatest "Englishmen being Latine poets."

In 1601 came *A Booke of Ayres, set foorth to be song to the Lute, Orpherian, and Base Violl, by Philip Rosseter, Lutenist.* The book is dedicated by Rosseter, on the authority of Master Campion, to Sir Thomas Monson; and in the dedicatory epistle half the airs are spoken of as of Campion's "own composition, made at his vacant houres, and privately emparted to his friends, whereby they grew both publicke, and (as coine crackt in exchange) corrupted." The words of all the songs are Campion's, and by these alone he takes rank as the first poet of the Elizabethan song-books. The singing quality of most of these songs, the grave, solemn music and earnest poetry of some, the metrical originality, the lovely grace and variety of the rime, mark their author as the friend and master of this kind of poetry.

And yet his next work showed him an enemy of rime. In 1602 he published his *Observations in the Art of English Poesie,* dedicated, strangely enough, to the famous author of the Induction to the *Mirrour for Magistrates,* one of the finest masters of English rimed verse.[5]

In 1607 appeared Campion's *Masque in Honour of Lord Hayes and his Bride.* This is followed by a comparatively long silence, broken only by an occasional complimentary reference to the "rare Doctor." The silence ends in 1613, his *annus mirabilis.* The *Masque for Lord Knowles,* the *Lords' Masque, Songs of Mourning, Two Books of Airs,* and the *Masque for the Marriage of the Earl of Somerset,* are the harvest of that year. The masques are full of good things, always of songs that take one with lovely first lines. Few poets have excelled Campion in winning openings of song. "Advance your choral motions now," in the *Lords' Masque,* sings itself; other measures dance themselves, heel and toe:

> "Come ashore, come, merry mates,
> With your nimble heels and pates."[6]

The first of the *Two Books of Airs* contains "Divine and Moral Songs." "His devotional poetry," says Mr. Bullen, "impresses the reader by its sincerity. To fine religious exaltation Campion joined the true lyric faculty, and such a union is one of the rarest of literary phenomena. In richness of imagination the man who wrote **'When thou must home to shades of underground'** and **'Hark, all you ladies that do sleep'** was the equal of Crashawe; but he never failed to exhibit in his sacred poetry that sobriety of judgment in which Crashawe was sometimes painfully deficient."[7] And in this poetry of his again is the sound of the harp with the words; and, like David's harp in Bacon's fine phrase, it has "as many hearse-like airs as carols." The poem **"Where are all thy beauties now, all hearts enchaining?"** with its solemn three-lined stanzas and double rimes, has something of the fall of the "Dies Iræ," and the great, earnest music of doom.

> "Thy rich state of twisted gold to bays is turnéd!
> Cold, as thou art, are thy loves, that so much burnéd!
> Who die in flatterers' arms are seldom mournéd."

Of even a higher mood are **"Never weather-beaten sail"** and **"Come, cheerful day, part of my life to me,"** while **"To music bent is my retiréd mind"** and **"Tune thy music to thy heart"** have the grace of simple singing rhythm that gave to the lyrics of that age a great part of their ineffable charm.

The second of the two books, the *Light Conceits of Lovers,* has some things for which Campion thought it right in the dedication to apologise, but enough of unsullied song to outshine all the rest. **"What harvest half so sweet is,"** **"The peaceful western wind," "There is none, O none but you,"** are masterpieces of melody.

In 1614 Campion published the *Masque for the Marriage of the Earl of Somerset,* composed and produced in the previous year. During the two following years he was in trouble, implicated in the plot for the murder of Sir Thomas Overbury, though quite innocent of guilt. In 1617, the *Third and Fourth Books of Airs.* In these again is an ever new variety of rhythm and rime and colour, if we may call it so. It is impossible ever to speak of the "subject" of a poem of Campion's; it is never with him a matter of theme and treatment, as modern reviewers would have it. His gift was song—"to sing and not to say," as Swinburne claimed of Collins—and his achievement, "full-throated ease." Mr. Bullen has drawn attention to the extraordinary and ever-recurring "difference" of Campion. On opposite pages of his *Third Book of Airs* are **"Now winter nights enlarge"** and **"Awake, thou spring of speaking grace! mute rest becomes not thee!"** and again, **"Shall I come, sweet love, to thee?"** and **"Thrice toss these oaken ashes in the air."**

The finest songs of these two books are also the most interesting metrically.[8] And yet, when one has said so, the thought of some others, simple and uncarved, gives one pause.[9]

Here may be mentioned poems which are with good reason attributed to him, and some occasional verses. The most interesting of the latter is the hymn to Neptune—**"Of Neptune's empire let us sing"**—with its one strange sliding line in each verse. Of the former class, and almost certainly his, is an exquisite poem published by Richard Alison in his *Hour's Recreation in Music* (1606), **"What if a day, or a month, or a year?"** For the rest, complimentary verses, dedicatory verses, verses prefixed to the works of the poet's friends, and the like, though always graceful and occasionally distinguished, are to us less interesting than one little poem attributed to Campion by Mr. Bullen on grounds of style alone—a poem which brings for the first time into English verse a cadence which in our age, joined to an artifice of rime not unknown to Campion,[10] has won, or largely helped to win, for one poem a place in a most select class, beside Gray's *Elegy* and Coleridge's *Ancient Mariner*.[11] One hears the music of Fitzgerald's *Rubaiyat* in these lines:

> "The rarer pleasure is, it is more sweet,
> And friends are kindest when they seldom meet.
> Who would not hear the nightingale still sing,
> Or who grew ever weary of the spring?"

In 1618 was published *The Airs that were sung and played at Brougham Castle in the King's Entertainment,* almost certainly written by Campion, though composed by others. The song for a dance, **"Robin is a lovely lad,"** has all his quaintness and musical dexterity. It was probably in the same year that he issued *A New Way for making Four Parts in Counterpoint,* a very technical treatise, long a standard book, and frequently reprinted. It afforded a rule of thumb for the harmonisation of tunes with simple concords.

In 1619 Campion published a splendid volume of Latin verse, containing four hundred and fifty-three epigrams, thirteen elegies, and one long poem. Judging from his prefaces, Campion considered these Latin poems his great work. To us their interest lies in their introducing us to the poet's literary circle. He addresses epigrams to William Camden, Charles Fitzgeoffrey, the three Mychelburnes, William Percy, Thomas Nashe, John Dowland, Edmund Spenser, Sir John Davies, and others.

In the second book of the *Epigrams,* No. 23, we get a description of the poet himself—a lean man, envious of the fat:

> "Crassis invideo tenuis nimis ipse, videtur
> Satque mihi felix qui sat obesus erit . . ."

On one day, March 1st, 1620, Campion made his will, died, and was buried. His sole legatee was his lifelong friend, Philip Rosseter; his place of burial, St. Dunstan's in the West, Fleet Street.

THE BEGINNINGS OF ENGLISH PROSODY: CAMPION'S *OBSERVATIONS*

How now Doctor Champion, musicks and poesies stout
  Champion,
Will you nere leave prating?
From MS. commonplace book of a Cambridge student
                    (*circa* 1611).

Is this faire excusing? O, no, all is abusing.

                                        Campion.

Campion's *Observations in the Art of English Poesie,* which appeared in the year 1602, is the third in order of time among the metrical treatises of importance published in English. It is, in the opinion of that most competent judge, Mr. T. S. Omond, by far the ablest of the Elizabethan treatises on quantitative verse. In 1575 had appeared George Gascoigne's *Certayne Notes of Instruction in English Verse,* and in 1589 George (or Richard) Puttenham's (or another's) *The Art of English Poesie.* Other works, half a dozen or so, had looked in at the door of prosody, but only these two had entered and stayed. Even they scarcely affect Campion's work and the matter in hand; they affect it, indeed, rather less than some of the minor works, such as William Webbe's *Discourse of English Poetrie,* from which he takes points, or the famous correspondence between Gabriel Harvey and Edmund Spenser about English accent and quantity. Nearly all the writers of the age who interested themselves in the grammar of the craft were infected with a passion for the "reform" of English verse, to remake it nearer to the heart's desire of classical schoolmen. And as the schoolmen in both France and England, ignorant of scientific philology, blundered at almost every step in their spelling reforms, so these prosodists, ignorant of the true nature of quantity and accent, blundered. The reformation failed because poets sing by ear and not by rule. The language was true to itself in its poetry. It is a joy to find Campion's worthy antagonist, the poet Samuel Daniel, proclaiming in his *Defence of Ryme* the duty of a literature to the genius of its language.[12] Yet Campion himself is a greater joy. He writes, now shrewdly, incisively, suggestively, of English verse, now all wrongly, led astray by his reverence for accent and his love of quantity, as he understood it. Always he writes with energy and earnestness, always with the zeal and ardour of a poet with music in him. The voice that breaks into those exquisite lyric openings of song after song in his *Book of Airs* is the same voice that presses so eloquently another business in the *Observations*—in the prose arguments of his treatise. For what are these "versings" of his, quoted as examples (or, indeed, as I suspect, the first springs of the whole train)—what are they to his rimed songs:

> "There is none, O, none but you,"

or:

> "Awake, thou spring of speaking grace!—

How can one choose among them?

I can well believe that Campion, in his youth certainly just the poet to be quickly responsive to all the influences of his age, wrote some at least of the unrimed poems printed by him in his *Observations,* before he thought of settin up as a prosodist. It must always be a strong temptation to poets of metrical originality to show their contemporaries that their innovations are not due to ignorance of the conventional ways of verse, and are not arbitrary irregularities. This is not to say that such innovations and such matrical irregularity are conscious, studied, arranged beforehand. One cannot repeat often enough the truth that the true poet sings by ear and not by rule, his ear no doubt formed by the music of the verse of his language, but his own, hearing that music in his own way, directing his tongue to utter his music in his own way. Afterwards, the rule. The good conventional critics of all the ages have reproved poets who made new music, have declared it no music. It must always be a strong temptation to the poets of the new melody to reply, to explain, to lay down rules of justification. If they do so, they probably will leave unsaid more than they say; they will easily give wrong explanations. If he is to make a new music, the poet in a man must be far in advance of the grammarian. In some men the poet and the grammarian have little to do with each other. Such a man was Edgar Allan Poe;[13] such a man was Wordsworth;[14] such a man was Campion. In him the poet had much to do with Master Campion, who "in his vacant hours" composed music, who "neglected these light fruits as superfluous blossoms of his deeper studies."[15] He "chiefly aimed," as he said, "to couple words and notes lovingly together." He never published a lyric without its musical setting. In him the grammarian, the author of the *Observations,* had to do with "sweet Master Campion" of Cambridge, the "scholarly learned," the "gentlemanlike qualified,"[16] with Thomas Campianus who had "attained renown and place among Englishmen, being Latine poets."[17] Thomas Campion, student of Gray's Inn, was one or the other at different times. Thomas Campion, doctor in physic, scarcely intruded into either personality.

Notes

1. Samuel Daniel, *A Defence of Ryme,* 1603.

2. T. S. Omond, *English Metrists.*

3. Wordsworth: ". . . With this key Shakespeare unlocked his heart." Browning: "Did Shakespeare? If so, the less Shakespeare he!"

4. "It was quite usual at this period for Englishmen who had conscientious objections to the religious tests enforced at both universities to abstain from matriculating or taking a degree."—Percival Vivian in *"Muses' Library"* Edition.

5. Thomas Sackville, Lord Buckhurst and Earl of Dorset (1536-1608), part author of the first English tragedy, *Gorboduc* or *Ferrex and Porrex.* The "Induction" is a stately poem, a solemn monotone pealing in a sombre hall. "It forms," says Hallam, "a link which unites the school of Chaucer and Lydgate with *The Faery Queen.* Mr. Saintsbury styles Sackville the "author of some of the finest rime-royal in the language."

6. *Masque for Marriage of Earl of Somerset.*

7. I give this as I find it. "Sobriety" generally produces dulness, but "sobriety" is not really a quality of Campion's poetry.

8. "Kind are her answers," "Break now my heart and die," "Fire, fire," "Every dame affects good fame," "To his sweet lute," "Love me or not."

9. "Sleep, angry beauty," "Never love unless you can," "Turn all thy thoughts to eyes."

10. The inclusion of an unrimed line in a rimed stanza.

11. It is difficult to find a definition to cover the *Elegy,* the *Ancient Mariner,* and the *Rubaiyat;* yet for other reasons than comparative similarity of length they must occupy a place together in English poetry.

12. I have made a special appendix (Appendix D) for Daniel and his *Defence.* He was not only "a good poet in his day," but a splendid master of prose. I give some excerpts from his book.

13. See Poe's *Rationale of Verse* and some of his essays and "marginalia." He resembles Campion not a little, in his incisiveness when right, and in his ingenuity when wrong.

14. See the famous preface to the *Lyrical Ballads.* "Most of our attempted explanations of artistic merit (which contains elements non-moral and non-intellectual) are incomplete and misleading. Among such explanations must be ranked Wordsworth's essays. It would not be safe for any man to believe that he had produced true poetry because he had fulfilled Wordsworth's conditions."—F. W. H. MYERS.

15. Rosseter's dedication to *A Book of Airs.*

16. William Covell's *Polimanteia.*

17. Meres' *Palladis Thamia.*

R. W. Short (essay date 1944)

SOURCE: Short, R. W. "The Metrical Theory and Practice of Thomas Campion." *PMLA* 59, no. 4 (December 1944): 1003-18.

[*In the following essay, Short examines Campion's poetry, his theories on meter as expressed in* Observations in the Art of English Poesie, *and the importance of his contribution to the theories of metrical poetry of his time.*]

Most of the scant attention paid by critics to the poetry of Thomas Campion has been sidetracked by two considerations which, however interesting in themselves, have little to do with his real poetic accomplishments. One of these considerations is that he was a musician and almost alone among his contemporaries composed settings for his own poems; the other is that he played some part in the guerilla warfare waged by a few Elizabethan writers against rhyme. Before we can make a fresh adjustment to his poetry, we must dispose of the first and reckon with the second.

The usual thing to say about Campion's poetry is that it was beautifully "married" to his music, and with the exception of some studies tracing his indebtedness to classical authors, almost all criticism that surmounts the obstacle of his attack upon rhyme merely extends or embellishes this popular opinion. As E. H. Fellowes implied in reviewing a book that considers Campion both as poet and musician, this makes too much of Campion's music, his lesser gift. Mr. Fellowes stated:

> It must also be pointed out, though Mr. Kastendieck does not seem to have done so, that the musical side of Campion's work was slight as compared with that of Dowland or Morley, for example.

Furthermore—

> A man may be both a poet and a musician; others less famous than Campion have, since his day, set their own words to music; but in every case the words must inevitably come first, even if the musical melody should occasionally have been designed when no more than a single stanza of the lyric has been written.[1]

Mr. Fellowes may have meant only that the words come first in point of time; if so, it should be further stipulated that, to Campion at least, the words also came first in importance. Far too much has been made of Campion's honest effort to write music that would not wholly betray the purposes of his lyrics. He avoided the violation of the lyric form wreaked by the writers of madrigals, motets, and other more elaborate musical compositions, but so did the other "lutenists" or writers of airs. To have achieved all the aptness with which he has been credited, Campion would have had to write separate music for each stanza of the songs he set, or as a poet, to write in an unvarying fixity of metre. This was far from his intention or practice; the stresses and cadences of his poetry are richly plastic, varying from stanza to stanza and from meaning to meaning. Frequently, it is true, in the first stanza of a song, which alone was printed in combination with the musical notation, a felicitous identity of musical and verbal accent appears to bear out the notion of unique harmony between words and music, but if the reader will observe where the same musical accent falls in the second and subsequent stanzas, he will find that in most cases no such extreme propriety exists.

There is, moreover, another and more compelling reason for studying Campion's poetry, or any other poetry, apart from the music with which it has become associated. A musical setting is so overpoweringly, determinatively sensuous that in its presence the subtleties of lyric poetry have little chance of making themselves felt. However various music itself may be, it dogmatizes upon any words that accompany it; it dictates one reading and precludes the hearing of any other, whereas for much great poetry there is no one right reading, but several which must be simultaneously apprehended. Drama furnishes an apt analogy. Though we may reject certain of the multitudinous interpretations of *Hamlet,* or of a line from *Hamlet,* the tantalizing wealth of the play doubtless inheres partly in the certainty of our retaining more than one. Yet if an actor is to succeed, he must make up his mind strongly to project a single interpretation, or at least a combination of interpretations much simpler than the combination we carry along in a silent reading. Like the expository resources of the actor, those of music are simple and sensuous, and impose limitations upon the expressiveness of the words.

Campion's tunes rig out his lyrics in pretty but concealing finery; his best poems mean more, as poems, when silently read than when sung or intoned. For this reason, whoever aims at justly appreciating his poetry had best forget his music.

In 1602 Campion published his ***Observations in the Art of English Poesie,*** a treatise having three parts: an introduction establishing the importance of numbers, especially over rhyme; a discussion of eight verse-forms deemed suitable to the genius of the English language; and a set of rules for determining the quantities of English syllables. The next year, Samuel Daniel's response, *A Defence of Ryme,* drew across Campion's track a red-herring that has in some degree distracted the attention of every subsequent commentator on his treatise.

With considerable indignation, Daniel set himself against what he considered to be an unpatriotic attack, by a man of "faire parts and good reputation,"[2] upon rhyme. It is true that Campion uttered a few rash denigrations of rhyming: as in his reference to the "vulgar and unarteficiall custome of riming," which had "deter'd many excellent wits from the exercise of English Poesy,"[3] but in his first chapter he described quite clearly the principal subject of his discourse, which was the nature and art of "numbers," a convenient term embracing both rhythm and metre. In the second chapter he touched upon "the unaptnesse of Rime in Poesie," but mainly from the point of view that the easiness of rhyming had led to the abasement of numbers: "there is growne," he wrote, "a kind of prescription in the use of Rime, to forestall the right of true numbers, . . . the facilitie and popularitie of Rime creates as many Poets as a hot sommer flies."[4] These bad poets he called Rimers, meaning as much to condemn their limping rhythms as their use of rhyme.[5] If it were not for the occasional rash statement, his point would have been quite clear, and quite tolerable, as he stated it: "The eare is a rationall sence and a chiefe judge of proportion; but in our kind of riming what proportion is there kept where there remains such a confused inequalitie of sillabies?"[6] Daniel himself, in the course of his famous defence, made reservations about the use of rhyme as serious as Campion's, though less vehemently stated.

The samples of unrhymed verse with which Campion illustrated his eight verse-forms further the misconception that his main point was mistrust of rhyme. They are so bad that nothing in them except the absence of rhyme attracts attention. The very first example, of Licentiate Iambick, begins with one of the rash statements:

> Goe, numbers, boldly passe, stay not for ayde
> Of shifting rime, that easie flatterer,
> Whose witchcraft can the ruder eares beguile.
> Let your smooth feete, enur'd to purer arte,
> True measures tread.[7]

Even the widely-anthologized "Rose-cheekt Lawra" smacks unfortunately of the *exercice à thèse*. But we misread our author's purpose if we think his essential preoccupation to have been with anything other than the principles of English rhythms. If we make allowances for the few overstatements, we can sum up his position in some such words as these: jingling in rhyme is so easy that our poets give us little else, neglecting rhythmical control, which though more difficult, is so important that when it is present the lack of rhyme will not be missed.

Rightly understood, Campion's packet of criticism makes two contributions to English numbers: the first is a recognition of the true place in English poetry of the classical principles of quantity.

Campion's predecessors in the long conflict over quantitative and accentual verse, Ascham, Drant, Harvey, Spenser, Stanyhurst, Sidney, and Webbe, apparently felt called upon to choose between quantity and accent. Even when Sidney, after having experimented with quantitative verse, decided that English was "fit for both sorts,"[8] he did not say for both sorts at one time, or if he had the notion that this was true, anything about how a mixture of the two should be ordered. In summing up the conflict, J. E. Spingarn wrote as follows:

> Drant's and Harvey's rules therefore constitute two opposing systems. According to the former, English verse is to be regulated by Latin prosody, regardless of accent; according to the latter, by accent regardless of Latin prosody. By neither system can quantity be successfully attempted in English; and a distinguished classical scholar of our own day has indicated what is perhaps the only method by which this can be accomplished. This method may be described as the harmonious observance of both accent and position; all accented syllables being generally accounted long, and no syllable which violates the Latin law of position being used when a short syllable is required by the scansion. These three systems, with more or less variation, have been employed throughout English literature. Drant's system is followed in the quantitative verse of Sidney and Spenser; Harvey's method is that employed by Longfellow in *Evangeline*; and Tennyson's beautiful classical experiments are practical illustrations of the method of Professor Robinson Ellis.[9]

The above passage approaches the subject from a limited and hence misleading point of view, having in mind, as it does, only the problem of making use of classical metres in English poetry, so that the author's comment upon Campion quite misses the mark: "With Campion's *Observations* (1602) the history of classical metres in England may be said to close, until the resuscitation of quantitative verse in the present century."[10] Campion's *Observations* were not upon classical, but upon English metres, and he regarded quantity not as a factor of classical superiority to be substituted for accent, but as a natural condition of well-written accentual verse and as an important element in all English measures.

He realized that both accent and quantity exist in English verse, frequently independently of each other. In this he was broader and more realistic than Ellis, who according to Professor Spingarn tried for combinations in which all accented syllables would be long and all unaccented syllables short. Campion pointed out that although accented syllables in English words are normally long, many unaccented syllables take equally long to pronounce, therefore, must also be considered long, As an example, he offered the word "Trumpington," the second syllable of which is "naturally long, and so of necessity must be held of every composer."[11] One easily perceives that a normal, careful pronunciation of this word dwells nearly as long, though not so sharply, upon the second syllable as upon the first; the first is distinguished from the last by stress, pitch, and length, from the second merely by stress and pitch. In a verse of poetry, the word would be scanned Trumpĭngtŏn.

Conversely, certain short syllables may bear the accent without thereby adding to their length.[12] We find an example in the line—"Some trade in Barbary, some in Turky trade"[13]—in which Campion called the second "some" short, though it is obviously distinguished from the syllables on either side of it both by stress and pitch. He also gave a list of words, "misery," "any," "pretty," "holy," etc., no syllables of which are to be construed as long, regardless of the fact that we "accent" a syllable in each word. Certain crucial places in a line demand syllables that are both long and accented, but in other places accents and long syllables may be used independently of each other.

In Campion's reasoning, the facts of pronunciation were no invitation to disregard the force either of accent or quantity and build metres solely upon one of them; instead, realizing that both are normal to English poetry, he attempted to regularize the use of quantities by rules corresponding in importance to the accepted rules for the use of accents. As a basis for this undertaking, he felt it necessary to come to a better understanding of the principles regulating English quantities than his predecessors or contemporaries had displayed. This accounts for his compilation of rules, which must have impressed many readers as discouragingly compendious, yet at the same time, too meager to be authoritative. It is difficult otherwise to account for the persistency with which they have been misunderstood.

Their empiricism, also, may put off the reader, yet it is our surety that they were devised in no spirit of classical pedantry. Although Campion started from the classical rule of position (a vowel is long when followed by two consonants), he stood out against the rigid application of position to English syllables. His greatest concern seemed to be to modify this canon in accordance with the vagaries of English pronunciation. His directions tried to exclude surds and liquids ("sliding and melting consonants"),[14] doubled consonants and other freaks of spelling, from the consonantal combinations that lengthen precedent vowels. He considered the influence of meaning upon pronunciation. In three lists of monosyllables, short ones, long ones, and ambiguous ones, words occur that must owe their appearance in different lists to their meanings, since they are alike in structure: "fly" and "die" for example may be either long or short, but "thy" is always short; "no," "go," and "so" are always short, but "flow" and "grow," though pronounced like them, are always long. Like many of Campion's discriminations, this one was not thoroughly worked out in his hasty compilation of examples; nor was the informing principle articulated. We must be content that it passed through his mind and found its way into his poetry. When we find the word "true" in two lists, one of short, one of ambiguous words, we may conclude, not that his lists are utterly irresponsible, but that different senses of the word occurred to him, and that he wished these differences to be reflected in the sound-texture of others' verses, as in his own: "For they are good whom such true love doth make"[15] and—"I cannot call her trūe that's false to me."[16]

Thus far Campion's contribution, though a real one, was mainly to Elizabethan theory or criticism. He cut the famous knot of controversy that troubled many of his fellow poets by giving critical standing to their normal poetic practice of combining both accents and quantities in English verse. What may be called his second contribution, though it stemmed logically from the first, involved an important refinement in poetic practice. He sought to bring back into English lyric verse the idea of conscious control over the time element of the verse as an essential quality of rhythm. This is the purpose to which all else in the ***Observations*** is subsidiary.

Campion believed that each verse of a poem should occupy the same amount of time in pronunciation, the only exception being of poems composed of lines of different metrical length. That is, in a stanza of alternating pentameter and dimeter lines, the pentameter lines should occupy equal amounts of time, as should the dimeter lines. Many of his apparently pedantic strictures are thence seen to aim at insuring each line's having the proper amount of syllabic material to fill it out.

From the treatise alone, it is difficult to ascertain beyond question that Campion held this belief.[17] Twice he seems almost to make the point, but each time fails to clinch it beyond doubt. The treatise gives us, as it were, clues for understanding Campion's poetics, but to interpret the clues

we must go to his poetry, where the rules were put into practice. Far from ignoring his own poetry, as has sometimes been suggested, the treatise is narrowly based upon it. The experimental material for the most valuable portions of the ***Observations*** can be found, not in the crude samples of verse it contains, but in the poems published the previous year (***A Booke of Ayres,*** 1601) and throughout his later songs. But until we turn to the poems, we can be sure only that he had the habit of listening for the length of each line as well as for the judicious disposition of its weak and strong syllables. Upon the line, "Was it my desteny, or dismall chaunce," he commented as follows:

> In this verse the two last sillables of the word *Desteny,* being both short, and standing for a whole foote in the verse, cause the line to fall out shorter then it ought by nature.[18]

From the fact that his objection is to a defective line rather than to a defective foot, the direction, if not the conclusion of his thought may be inferred. Also, we infer that the only possible "nature" a line might have prescribing its proper length would be derived from its context of other lines having a certain length. The same inference may be less certainly drawn from a later passage comparing the length of Latin with English lines:

> I have observed, and so may any one that is either practis'd in singing, or hath a naturall eare able to time a song, that the Latine verses of sixe feete, as the *Heroick* and *Iambick,* or of five feete, as the *Trochaick,* are in nature all of the same length of sound with our English verses of five feete; for either of them being tim'd with the hand, *quinque perficiunt tempora,* they fill up the quantity (as it were) of five sem'briefs;[19]

Rhythm in poetry is based on differences in syllabic value. To understand the aims and achievements of Campion, the usual distinction in value, accented against unaccented syllables, must be refined upon. Four classes of syllables must be noted: weak or neutral syllables, and three other kinds distinguished from the first by one of three qualities, by stress, by pitch, or by length. In practice, we tend to merge these qualities, to pronounce a stressed syllable higher in pitch and longer in time than surrounding weak syllables, but this merging is by no means invariable. Length and pitch frequently occur separately, and either may occur without stress.

Stress, a force of voice denoting rhythmical or grammatical importance, is almost always a rhythmical determinative, but neither pitch nor length can be so regarded.[20] Hence the common habit of regarding rhythm as any regular pattern of weak syllables, marked with the breve, and other syllables, marked with the macron or accent regardless of the quality that distinguishes them from the weak syllables, has no basis in fact. Rhythm is a time-pattern in a span of time; pitch has no time-value; length may equally create or destroy either the pattern or the span.

The time-span must be longer than the unit of the pattern, for it must, naturally, include recurrence of this unit. Commonly the line is regarded as the time-span, but actually the rhythm continues only as long as the feet continue to be equal in time-value. A source of difficulty in understanding rhythm is in the interpretation of "variation." The only allowable variation in such a measure as has just been described is in the total number of syllables within the feet. If a pyrrhic foot follows a spondaic foot, it is not strictly speaking a variation, but a breaking of the rhythm. This need not be displeasing. Experience shows that we demand very little rhythm. We are customarily satisfied by a quick succession of various rhythms, or by a rhythm that disappears for a time to crop up later in the same line or the same poem. Traditionally, we describe a destruction of rhythm as a rhythmical variation.

The foregoing account of rhythm supposes the ability of the mind to register the length of a foot of verse retentively enough to be aware of its recurrence in subsequent feet. There seems no reason why this awareness should not extend beyond the foot to the line itself, apprehending the line in turn as a unit of rhythm in the time-span of the whole stanza. Campion's habit of listening for equality of line-lengths directs our attention to this larger possibility, and his poems show that he composed according to this principle. In the examples that follow shortly, two points should be noted: first, that the lines are remarkably equivalent in length, and second, that far from making for rigidity or monotony of cadence and emphasis, the principle permits greater freedom within the line. That is, greater liberties may be taken without destroying rhythm. If the larger pattern is adhered to, interruptions in the basic pattern, that based upon the foot, do not affect the continuous, over-all rhythm of the poem. The interruptions then constitute or become absorbed in true variations.

In order to give some substance to my earlier statement that the poems in *A Booke of Ayres* closely illustrated the more important ideas of the *Observations,* I have taken from this book the three following examples of Campion's care in equalizing the quantities, hence the time-spans, in his lines. One finds the same care throughout the book; also in his later poems. The syllabic markings on the poems here given follow as closely as possible Campion's own rules for determining quantities. The macron indicates a long syllable, the breve a short one. When a given syllable seems not to be covered by Campion's rules, or when his rules permit that syllable to be regarded as either long or short, both markings have been used. Since his rules do not in any direct way regulate the position or accents, these have not been marked.

Let us look first at two poems in iambic pentameter.

> Thŏu ārt nŏt fāire fŏr āll thy rĕd ănd white,
> Fŏr āll thōse rōsĭe ōrnămēnts ĭn thĕe,
> Thŏu ārt nŏt swēet, thŏugh māde ŏf mēer dĕlight,
> Nŏr fāire nŏr swēet, ŭnlēsse thŏu pītĭe mĕe.
> I will nŏt sōoth thў fāncĭĕs: thŏu shālt prŏve
> Thăt bĕauty Is nŏ bĕautĭe wĭthōut lōve.
>
> Yēt lōve nŏt mĕ, nŏr sēeke thŏu tŏ āllūre
> My thŏughts wĭth bĕautĭe, wĕre Ĭt mōre dĕvine,

Thў smiles ănd kissĕs Ĭ cănnōt ĕndūre,
I'le nŏt bĕ wrăpt ŭp Ĭn thōse ārmes ŏf thine,
Nōw shēw ĭt, if thŏu bĕ ă wōman right,—
Ĕmbrāce, ănd kisse, ănd lōve mĕ, ĭn dĕspight.[21]

Each line of the above poem has ten syllables, five of which are long, except that the presence of ambiguous syllables in lines 5, 6, and 8 might seem to stretch out those lines by an extra long syllable, whereas lines 9 and 12 might seem to fall a bit short. It must be remembered, however, that this ambiguity is not an absolute quality but merely a sign of some uncertainty in the marker. In reading, we could and probably would make a decision about the ambiguous syllables and read them in a way that produced regularity exact enough to satisfy our ear. Campion seemed to value a certain amount of this quantitative ambiguity, possibly as making it easier for the reader to achieve the experience of true measure. "Every man," he said, "may observe what an infinite number of sillables both among the *Greekes* and *Romaines* are held as common."[22] In our next poem, one much finer than this, a greater proportion of the syllables are ambiguous, or common.

> Whĕn thŏu mūst hōme tŏ shādes ŏf ūndĕr grōund,
> Ănd thēre ărīv'd, ă nēwe ădmīrĕd gūest,
> Thĕ bĕautĕŏus spīrīts dŏ īngīrt thĕe rōund,[23]
> Whīte Ĭŏpĕ, blīth Hēllĕn, ănd thĕ rēst,
> Tŏ hēare thĕ stōriĕs ŏf thў fīnīsht lōve
> Frŏm thăt smōothe tōong whŏse mūsĭcke hēll căn mōve;
>
> Thĕn wīlt thŏu spĕake ŏf bānquĕtīng dĕlīghts,
> Ŏf māsks ănd rĕvĕls whĭch swēete yōuth dĭd māke,
> Ŏf Tūrnĭes ănd grĕat chāllēngĕs ŏf knīghts,
> Ănd āll thĕse trīūmphes fŏr thў bĕautĭĕs sāke:
> Whĕn thŏu hăst tōld thĕse hōnoūrs dōne tŏ thĕe,
> Thĕn tĕll, Ŏ tĕll, hŏw thŏu dīdst mūrthĕr mĕ.[24]

In this, as in the preceding poem, each line has ten syllables and it is reasonable to conclude that each also has five long syllables. Yet the situation is obviously not quite the same, since here there are many more ambiguous syllables to account for, so many that if one should insist on construing them all as long, lines 10 and 11 would have no less than seven long syllables. That, however, would be unreasonable. Probably few syllables, whether marked long or not, have exactly the same time-duration; our auditory interpretation of the must be subjective *within certain limits,* and it is those limits that Campion wished not to transgress. Readers sharing his demanding ear, reading these lines against a metronomic hand marking the end of each line, could without "a ridiculous and unapt drawing of their speech,"[25] make them fall out as they should by nature—equal in length. In the above poem, lines 2, 4, and 12 have exactly five long syllables; all the others have the possibility of more than five. We may explain this by quoting a sentence Campion used to explain another case:

> The causes why these verses differing in feete yeeld the same length of sound, is by reason of some rests which either the necessity of the numbers or the heaviness of the sillables do beget.[26]

The three lines which have five and no more long syllables are distinguished from the others by more sharply marked rests, required by grammar as well as by necessity of the numbers or heaviness of the syllables. It would seem, then, that the lines of this poem are stabilized at 5-plus long syllables, instead of five, as in the first example. This of course gives it slightly more density and slower pace than the other, characteristics which are reinforced and exaggerated by such other considerations as diction and subject.

The third specimen of Campion's poetry shows some interesting, intentional variations on the principle of equivalent lines. Only the second of three stanzas is here given.

        7   Ĭf ī lŏve Ămărīllĭs,   4
        7   Shĕ gīves mĕ frūit ănd flōwĕrs,   3
        7   Bŭt īf wĕ lōve thēse Lādiĕs,   4
        7   Wĕ mūst gīve gōldĕn shōwĕrs,   4
        6   Gīve thĕm gōld thăt sēll lōve,   5
        6   Gīve mĕ thĕ Nūtbrōwne lāsse.   4
        6   Whŏ whēn wĕ cōurt ănd kīss,   4
        6   Shĕ crīes, fŏrsōoth, lĕt gō.   4
        8   Bŭt whēn wĕ cōme whēre cōmfŏrt īs, 5
        6   Shĕ nēvĕr wīll sāy nō.[27]   4

For convenience, I have given the number of syllables, both long and short, in the left hand column of figures, and the number of long syllables in the right hand column. To obtain these figures, I have passed judgment upon the ambiguous syllables.

In the stanza proper, lines 5 and 6 have only six syllables, as against seven in the others. Campion, I think, would have marked their accents and quantities as follows:

        Gīve thēm gōld thăt sēll lōve,
        Gīve mĕ thĕ Nūtbrōwne lăsse.

The purpose of this syllabic variation is readily felt. The first of these lines has greater syllabic density (five, or 5-plus, long syllables), which adequately compensates for the missing short syllable; this density appropriately slows down the reader just where the nub of the meaning comes. In the second of these lines, an accent falls upon short "me," which is distinguished by pitch, not by length. The line, in time-value, acts as a transition to the livelier movement of the refrain, a movement which, I feel, somewhat curtails the value of the long syllables, so that there is an actual time-difference between the lines of the stanza and the lines of the refrain not reflected in my figures. Then we reach the unique second from last line, with its eight syllables, at least five of which are long. This line may be taken to echo the time-span of the first six lines; in order that it may do this effectively, the extra syllables are necessary, for the faster pace of reading established for the refrain naturally carries over to this line, so that it needs slightly more syllabic material to make it fill out the time-span of the lines it echoes.

The following examples,[28] given in less detail, show the degrees of intricacy achieved by Campion in contrasting lines of different lengths within a single stanza. The first figure represents the syllables, the second the long syllables, in each line.

> XII of *A Booke of Ayres* [Shall I come, if I swim? wide are the waves, you see][29] has this scheme, the second stanza being identical with the first:

12-6, 11-6, 11-6, 8-4, 12-6

> VII of *The Third Booke of Ayres* [Kinde are her answeres] has this scheme, the second stanza being identical except that the lines corresponding to 5 and 6 are transposed:

5-3, 8-5, 5-3, 8-5-plus, 8-5-plus, 5-3, 11-5-plus, 7-5-plus, 6-4

> VI of *The Fourth Booke of Ayres* [There is a Garden in her face] has the following normal scheme, the famous first line being defective with only four long syllables, and the lines corresponding to three and four transposed in the third stanza:

8-5, 8-5, 8-5, 8-6, 8-6, 8-5

In the stanza quoted above, "If I love Amarillis," the disposition of long syllables, in addition to helping regulate the time-span of the lines, comes to the support of the meaning of the poem. This is the rule, not the exception, in Campion's best poetry. The infractions of strict alternation between long and short syllables almost invariably supply grammatical emphasis (as well as rhythmical variety) where it is needed. Notice, for instance, the meanings expressed by all the collocations of long syllables in the first poem quoted: "all those rosie," "unlesse thou pitie," "thou shalt prove," "without love," and "Now shew it." Such effects are not, of course, peculiar to Campion; they can probably be found in the work of every good poet. But there is this distinction between such effects as found in Campion's poetry and in the poetry of many other poets whom we would not think of callingless "good." In Campion's poems, the quantities create the time-span of the line along with any contribution they may make to grammatical emphasis; in most other poets, they seem to exist for the latter purpose alone. The emphasis is secured, but whatever the rhythmical effect may be, it is of a different order from Campion's. It is not, in his sense, "measure."

The importance of Campion's contributions to metrics is confirmed by the use he made of them in his own poems. To a surprising extent, their superb vitality comes from controlled richness of rhythm. Sprinkled here and there throughout his work, we find happy examples of the sharply imaginative imagery, the teasing metaphor, and the startling employment of words so characteristic of his period. But felicities of this kind are not the rule. For the most part, his imagery and vocabulary are calm, often routine. But the cadences rise to unsurpassed heights of rhythmical flexibility, of firm, musical quality that enhances a characteristic natural, speech-like vigor.

His less successful songs suffer from a variety of defects we need not consider here. Some of them, banal in subject and language, nevertheless display the rhythmical regularity for which he stood. One stanza will amply represent this type.

8 Fāst tŏ thĕ rōofe clēave măy my tōngue, 4
8 Ĭf mīndelĕsse Ī ŏf thĕe bĕ fōund: 3-4
8 Ŏr īf, whĕn āll my jōys ăre sūng, 4
8 *Jĕrūsălĕm* bĕ nōt thĕ grōund.[30] 4

Probably, in addition to other defects, the rhythm is here too regular; Campion has not taken advantage of the possibilities for rich and emphatic variation offered by his principles. This suggestion is made because many times his utterly charming effects seem to owe almost everything to rhythm, being commonplace in diction, imagery, and subject-matter.

In the bad poems, however, we find more departures from strict measure than in the good ones. The following triplet illustrates the extent, by no means great, to which Campion sometimes departed from his own strictures:

13 Why prĕsūmes thy prīde ŏn thāt that mūst sŏ prīvăte bĕ, 6-7
13 Scārce thăt ĭt cān gōod bĕ cāl'd, thŏugh ĭt sēemes bēst tŏ thēe, 6-7
13-14 Bēst ŏf āll that Nātŭre frām'd ŏr cūrĭŏus ēye căn sĕe?[31] 8-10

"Curious," in the third line, may be two or three syllables. However we interpret the ambiguous syllables, our efforts to read the lines in equal time are not aided by equal numbers of long syllables.

The pentameter couplets that Campion used for the dramatic portions of his masques show no signs that he attempted to make their lines equivalent in value. They vary from line to line, apparently without plan. If their variations are less great than those of Shakespeare's dramatic passages in blank verse, a weaker feeling for dramatic effect, more than a sharper ear for equivalence, is doubtless responsible.

In conclusion, let us glance at some lines by other Elizabethan poets,[32] not with the intention of proving them inferior to Campion's work, but at least with the hope of hearing them as Campion did, of understanding better the grounds of his inordinate contempt for other lyricists of the period. First, the opening stanza of an Elizabethan poem by Robert Greene.

10 Swēet āre thĕ thōughts thăt sāvŏur ŏf cŏntēnt; 4-5
10 Thĕ quīĕt mīnd ĭs rīchĕr thăn ă crōwn; 4
10 Swēet āre thĕ nīghts ĭn cārelēss slūmbĕr spēnt; 6
10 Thĕ pōor ĕstāte scōrns fōrtūne's āngry frōwn; 7
10 Sŭch swēet cŏntēnt, sŭch mīnds, sŭch slēep, sŭch blīss, 9-10
10 Bēggărs ĕnjōy, whĕn prīncĕs ōft dŏ mīss. 5-6

However we take the ambiguous syllables in this stanza, the time-spans of the verses are necessarily different.[33] Equivalence could only be attained by a wrenched pacing

and pronunciation that would offend any ear. Furthermore, to establish the iambic pentameter metre, "of" in the first line and "than" in the second have to be accented; "scorn" in the fourth line must be unaccented. Rather than do this, the reader will prefer to read the first two lines as irregular tetrameter and the fourth as iambic pentameter with a spondee (which Campion would allow); he will also wish further to drag out the fifth line by reading it as a succession of spondees or near-trochees. Campion permitted many variations in what he called "licentiate iambick," but not such untutored variations as these. According to his views, the stanza is metrically confused and disorganized.

The next poem, by Dekker, embodies other qualities especially associated with the Elizabethan lyric. The first two stanzas only are given here.

11 Ō, thĕ mōnth ŏf Māy, thĕ mĕrry mōnth ŏf Māy, 5-6
12 Sŏ frōlīc, sŏ gāy, ănd sŏ grēen, sŏ grēen, sŏ grēen! 6
11 Ō, ănd thĕn dĭd Ĭ ūnto my trūe lōve sāy, 5-7
9 Swēet Pēg, thŏu shălt bĕ my Sūmmĕr's Quēen. 6-7

11 Nŏw thĕ nīghtĭngāle, thĕ prĕtty nīghtĭngāle, 4-5
11 Thĕ swēetēst sīngĕr ĭn āll thĕ fōrest quīre, 7
12 Ĕntrēats thēe, swēet Pēggy, tŏ hēar thy trūe lōve's tāle: 7-9
12 Lō, yōndĕr shĕ sīttĕth, hĕr brēast ăgaīnst ă brīer. 7-8

In this poem the metrical license far exceeds that in Greene's, amounting to what Campion called a "confusd inequalitie of sillables." Yet we must not overestimate the extent to which it is marred, or made, by lack of measure. In other qualities as well, it is "abandoned"—full of unrealized potentialities, parts setting off in indiscriminate directions from a vaguely located center, as for example the untied-in implications of the last quoted line. Nevertheless its effect of pretty chaos, of heedless exuberance, has great charm. Its spontaneity may be achieved by, or in spite of, the poet's prodigal expenditure of material. The disorganized metrics, however, probably actually impede, by constantly forcing the attention to start over, the expression of abundance and license. Whatever our final judgment of it may be, the poem certainly owes none of its success to measure, or to an established rhythm, if that term be correctly understood. The aesthetic effect of definite but different rhythms, following each other in quick succession, comes within the scope of the present paper but to this extent: it is abundantly clear that effects so produced gave only pain to the ear of Thomas Campion.

Notes

1. *RES* [*Review of English Stories*], (Jan., 1939), p. 100, reviewing M. M. Kastendieck, *England's Musical Poet. Thomas Compion* (Oxford, 1938).

2. *Elizabethan Critical Essays,* ed. G. Gregory Smith (Oxford, 1904), II, 358.

3. *Campion's Works,* ed. Percival Vivian (Oxford, 1909), p. 33. All quotation of Campion have been taken from this edition of his works.

4. *Op. cit.,* p. 36.

5. "*Iambick* and *Trochaick* feete, which are opposd by nature, are by all Rimers confounded." *Op. cit.,* p. 36.

6. *Op. cit.,* p. 36.

7. *Op. cit.,* p. 40.

8. *Elisabethan Critical Essays,* 1, 205.

9. *A History of Literary Criticism in the Renaissance* (New York, 1912), pp. 301, 302.

10. *Ibid.,* p. 304.

11. *Op. cit.,* p. 53.

12. It should perhaps be emphasized that Campion's postulate: "But above all the accent of our words is diligently to be observ'd, for chiefly by the accent in any language the true value of the sillables is to be measured" (*Op. cit.,* p. 53), refers mainly to the determination of "value" within words rather than within lines. As shown, Campion was clear that accenting a short syllable in a line of poetry did not necessarily increase its quantity.

13. *Op. cit.,* p. 41.

14. *Op. cit.,* p. 54.

15. *Op. cit.,* p. 29.

16. *Op. cit.,* p. 132.

17. G. Gregory Smith, however, had no doubt that this point was expressed in the *Observations*: "If he is aiming at anything tangible it is at equality in the reading length of the lines, and his rules to this end assume the propriety of syllabic equivalence." *Op. cit.,* 1, liv.

18. *Op. cit.,* p. 37.

19. *Op. cit.,* p. 39.

20. "Pitch, as William Thompson has strenuously maintained, has nothing whatever to do with rhythm, but one of its many functions is the heightening of logical emphasis, for we frequently elevate the pitch of a syllable when we give it heavy stress. In those cases, not altogether infrequent in modern English verse, when we are obliged to reduce the stress of a logically emphatic syllable in order to preserve the metre, we often allow it to keep the higher pitch, thus saying, in effect: 'I cannot stress this syllable as fully as its meaning requires, because the metre demands that I give accentual precedence to its neighbor. Take note, however, that it is logically superior'." John Collins Pope, *The Rhythm of Beowulf* (New Haven, 1942), p. 13n.

21. *Op. cit.,* p. 12.

22. *Op. cit.,* p. 55.

23. This line presents a special question: "beauteous" might be divided into three syllables and "spirits" considered as having only one. My treatment seems preferable, because Campion usually indicated by spelling which of the two current forms, "spirits" or "sprites," he intended. *Cf. esp.,* "With a Spirit to contend," *Op. cit.,* p. 185, where there can be no doubt that two syllables are needed.

24. *Op. cit.,* p. 17.

25. *Op. cit.,* p. 37.

26. *Op. cit.,* p. 39.

27. *Op. cit.,* p. 7.

28. *Op. cit.,* p. 26, 163, 178.

29. Ralph W. Berringer, arguing that Rosseter rather than Campion composed the lyrics of *A Booke of Ayres, Part II,* cites this poem as a climax of ineptitude. "Finally, it is almost impossible to believe that the author of 'Thou art not faire for all thy red and white' could have had anything to do with such a confused and faitering appeal as 'Shall I come, if I swim?'" *PMLA,* LVIII (Dec., 1943), 943. I concur rather with T. S. Eliot's estimate of the poem. In "Swinburne as Poet," from *Selected Essays* (Faber and Faber, 1932), p. 311, Mr. Eliot refers to the poem, then after quoting a lyric by Shelley, comments: "I quote from Shelley, because Shelley is supposed to be the master of Swinburne; and because his song, like that of Campion, has what Swinburne has not—a beauty of music and a beauty of content."

30. *Op. cit.,* p. 124.

31. *Op. cit.,* p. 163.

32. Random samplings of *Paradise Lost* suggest that the musician's ear of Milton also sought lines of the same time-value. Groups of lines, from four to ten in number, were found to possess a given number of long syllables. The groups vary considerable in density.

Great variation was found in Shakespeare's highly dramatic and highly colloquial passages of blank verse, much less variation in the "set pieces" of sustained splendor. A good example occurs in the *Tempest,* IV, i, l. 146, through Prospero's famous speech. The opening lines addressing Ferdinand are irregular in time-span. The first three lines of the "set piece" have 5 long syllables each; then beginning with "And like the baseless fabric of this vision," the next five lines have 6 long syllables. Three more lines of 5 long syllables each conclude the incomparable dirge. In the last five lines, Prospero addresses Ferdinand and present reality. These lines have 7, 5, 3, 6, and 7 long syllables respectively.

33. The "fairness" of subjecting others' poetry to Campion's rules for determining quantity might be questioned. The rules are especially deficient in meeting

the problem, merely hinted at, of the influence of meaning on quantity, a defect more apparent when scanning other poetry than when scanning Campion's own marvellously controlled harmonies. Yet whereas a more complete system might ascribe different values to some individual syllables, it is doubtful if the conclusions would be different. The troublesome empiricism of the rules is their best guarantee of approximate accuracy. We may apply them with no more humble an apology than Campion's own: "Others more methodicall, time and practise may produce. In the meane season, as the Grammarians leave many sillables to the authority of Poets, so do I likewise leave many to their judgments; and withall thus conclude, that there is no Art begun and perfected at one enterprise." *Op. cit.*, p. 56.

Wilfrid Mellers (essay date 1965)

SOURCE: Mellers, Wilfrid. "Thomas Campion and the Solo Ayre." In *Harmonious Meeting: A Study of the Relationship between English Music, Poetry and Theatre, c. 1600-1900*, pp. 70-80. London: Dennis Dobson, 1965.

[*In the following excerpt, Mellers looks at how poetry and music interact in selected music by Campion. Mellers also speculates on how Campion composed such pieces.*]

> *Author of light*
> *When to her lute Corinna sings*
> *Follow thy fair sun*
> *It fell on a summer's day*

We have seen how, in the madrigals of Ward and still more of Wilbye, a new kind of musical structure, apposite to a new kind of experience, was in process of evolution. This new technique often implied, and sometimes literally involved, instrumental resources; ultimately it was to seek fulfilment in the humanistic (rather than divine) ritual of opera. But in order to provide the basic elements of operatic music there had to be, alongside the development in ensemble techniques, a complementary development in solo song. Such a development was in any case natural in a society that stressed the humanly expressive power of words. Thomas Campion, equally celebrated as both poet and composer, and the leading theorist among the writers of ayres, emphasized the solo song with lute accompaniment precisely because in pieces for a solo voice music and sweet poetry could agree without the absurdities sometimes occasioned, in the madrigal, by contrapuntal treatment. At the most rudimentary level, the words in a solo song could be heard, not merely by the singer, but also by others who cared to listen. The lute, a sensitive but quiet instrument, could add its expressive commentary on the words as sung by the soloist. But there was no danger that the lute would become too obtrusive. The words would be immediately comprehensible; their human significance would be perhaps more directly 'realized' when they were sung rather than spoken.

In conformity with the spirit of the humanist movement Campion—like the Pléiade group associated with Ronsard in sixteenth century France, and like the Italian experimenters who worked for Count Bardi in the early years of the seventeenth century—imagined that in thus making music the overflow of poetry he was reviving the principles of classical antiquity. He even went so far as to try to systematize the setting of words by a literal equation of long and short syllables with long and short notes. Yet though his theory may seem pedantic, his practice is another matter. Basically he followed traditional notions of the relation between music and words. He resembled the French in that he wanted the musical rhythm to derive directly from the inflexions of the text as spoken, since music was 'la soeur puisnée de la poésie'. He resembled the Italians in that he wanted the lyricism of the musical line to be convincing in itself. When the complete fulfilment of this ideal was achieved—in the later work of Dowland and to a lesser degree Danyel—it entailed, as we shall see, some sacrifice in theoretic consistency. We should, however, start with Campion, if only because he was equally talented as poet and composer and perhaps for that reason the most conscious experimenter in the possibilities of music for a solo voice. From his work we can obtain an idea of the general principles by which Elizabethan composers tackled the setting of a text. We will begin with the simplest, because most 'systematic', example; proceed to some subtler cases from Campion's own work; and so lead on to the fulfilment of the ayre—which is also to some degree the relinquishment of Campion's theory—in the mature work of Dowland.

Unlike the madrigal, the ayre was normally strophic, the same music serving for several verses of the poem. Of course we do not know precisely how a man such as Campion set about writing an ayre. We may guess, perhaps, that he wrote the first stanza of his poem and then composed the music for it: unless, indeed, the music grew almost simultaneously with the words. This music must reflect the meaning of the text, so that thus far the music has been moulded by the poem. It is probable, however, that the poem will be incomplete in one stanza; and any further stanzas the poet writes must now fit the conventions of the already existing music. In the first verse the music is conditioned by the poetry. In the second verse the poetry must be conditioned by the music.

The song, which is of a religious nature, is in two stanzas.[1]

> Author of light, revive my dying sprite;
> Redeem it from the snares of all confounding night.
> Lord, light me to thy blessed way,
> For blind with worldly vain desires I wander as
>   a stray.
> Sun and moon, stars and underlights I see,
> But all their glorious beams are mists and darkness
>   being compared to thee.
>
> Fountain of health, my soul's deep wounds recure.
> Sweet showers of pity rain, wash my uncleanness
>   pure.

One drop of thy desired grace
The faint and fading heart can raise, and in joy's
        bosom place.
Sin and Death, Hell and tempting Fiends may rage;
But God his own will guard, and their sharp pains
        and grief in time assuage.

The first stanza depends on a characteristic Renaissance equivocation between World and Spirit. What the long sweeping rhythm suggests is a powerful awareness of the glories of the visible universe: 'confounding night' and 'worldly vain desires' turn out to be symbolized by the splendours of sun, moon, stars and underlights. It would seem to be pious duty, rather than inner conviction, that says these wonders are mists and darkness in the sight of God. In the second stanza the religious element is much stronger, because Campion is now thinking of the purgatorial process, in personal terms. This immediacy is conveyed, for instance, in the beautiful rise in rhythmic impetus as the fading heart is 'raised'. So in this stanza the ambiguous equation of the glories of the cosmos with worldly vanity disappears; the opposition is now unequivocally the powers of evil, sin, death, hell, and the fiends. This shift in emphasis provides Campion with his only problem in setting the poem strophically.

The opening apostrophe to the divinity is set to the noble interval of the falling fifth—the most stable of all interval relationships after the octave. The bass line rises to suggest the revivifying process of the flooding of light: but rises chromatically, so that light leads inevitably to its polar opposite, darkness and death. The highest note of the bass (E flat) makes a harsh dissonance with the lute's suspended seventh; above it, 'dying' is expressed by a drooping phrase, syncopated across the bar-line to create a little catch in the breath, with a tremulous semiquaver melisma. Thus this first line is a beautiful example of music's power to convey, through inherently musical means, two contradictory ideas—birth and death—at the same time.

In the next line, the reference to redemption suggests a clear diatonic phrase, built on a firmly rising fourth, in the relative major; whereas 'all confounding night' is set again to a strained syncopation and a perturbing melisma. 'Lord, light me to thy blessed way', is set in hopefully rising thirds, with a cross rhythm that carries the movement eagerly forward. But the cross rhythm then becomes, not hopeful impetus, but broken hesitancy; the melody really does 'wander as astray', swayed by worldly vain desires, fumbling and stumbling like a blind man. 'Sun and Moon' significantly recalls the opening address to the Author of Light, being a decorated version of the falling fifth. Thus it is at once a point of musical structure and illustrative: obscurely revealing, indeed, because it seems to equate the Author of Light with the Sun and so makes the ostensible identity between the sun and earthly error still odder. The leaping sixth and the cross rhythm of 'but all their glorious beams' convey the poet's rising excitement, prancing up to the high D with what we might take for resplendent affirmation. Then the line descends an octave when the

'glorious beams' turn out to be mists and darkness, which are set chromatically, of course, because chromaticism destroys tonal stability and the natural order. But the passage begins low and rises, because it is an ascent from the uncertainty of the mists to the certainty of God's love. The major triad at the end is thus, though conventional, also symbolic.

Having created this music, flowing so inevitably from the text, Campion then writes another stanza which nearly fits the music. Instead of 'Author of light' we have, for the noble fifth; 'Fountain of health'. For the syncopation, melisma and dissonance we have 'deep wounds' instead of 'dying sprite'. 'Sweet showers of pity' take the place of redemption; and 'uncleanness' that of confounding night. The faint and fading heart serves the same purpose as the blind wandering eyes; the heart-beat threatens to stop before it presses up through the sharpened seventh to the major triad on 'raise'. The only snag comes in the next line, when sin and hell are so inappropriately identified with the sun and moon: unless one thinks that this is in the profoundest sense logical, since only through the agency of the devil is the purgatorial process possible. In any case the chromatic ascent and major triad is perfect for the last line's assuaging of 'sharp pains and grief'.

The technique of musical allegory that Campion uses in this song harks back at least as far as the fifteenth century. With Campion, however, musical allegory is being translated into emotional realism. It is significant that the element of rather naive systematization is not present in his secular songs even when—as in **"When to her lute Corinna sings"**[2]—both the poetic and musical imagery are based on a conscious stylization.

When to her lute Corinna sings,
Her voice revives the leaden strings,
And doth in highest notes appear
As any challenged echo clear.
    But when she doth of mourning speak,
    E'en with her sighs the strings do break.

And as her lute doth live or die;
Led by her passion, so must I.
For when of pleasure she doth sing,
My thoughts enjoy a sudden spring;
    But if she doth of sorrow speak,
    E'en from my heart the strings do break.

The two stanzas of this poem bear much the same relationship to one another as do the two stanzas of **"Author of light"**: the first makes a general statement, the second reveals its personal application. Each stanza is based on a dichotomy between the opening quatrain, which is positive, and the concluding couplet, which is negative. The first two lines carry the music—as Corinna's singing revives the leaden strings—from G minor into the relative major, and then sharpward into the dominant, with an ornamental resolution to make the revival more reviving. A dancing lilt appears with the words 'and doth in highest notes appear', with repeated quavers prancing up through an octave. The phrase about the challenged echo excites this merry confidence by way of a cross rhythm; and the section ends, after eight symmetrical bars, with a clear modulation to the dominant major. The second half of the musical structure, which sets the couplet with some verbal repetition, is asymmetrical, as broken and disturbed as the quatrain is assured. The change comes with the chromatic E flat that enters the lute part on the word 'mourning', taking us back to the tonic minor. Then the sighs are set in a fragmentary dialogue between voice and lute, the verbal inflexion being literally broken as we pant for breath, yet in *rising* sequences, so that our agitation cumulatively increases. At the climax the strings 'break' in a descending arpeggio, echoed by the lute. In the excitement, a bar is dropped out of the eight-bar period. After an empty silence the voice rounds off with an ornamental cadence, repeating the words 'the strings do break'. The ornament is a quiver, almost a literal break in the voice.

The second stanza repeats this poetic and musical pattern exactly. The word 'passion' has the ornamental arabesque that in the first verse suggested revival. The cross rhythm for the challenged echo becomes the spring of joyful thoughts, prepared by the octave leap on 'pleasure'. In the second stanza the word 'heart' gets the stress that her sighs had originally. The music is not different; but we hear it more sympathetically because we now know that the conceit is not merely musical. It is not just the lute strings that are breaking, but also the strings of my heart.

This song is a fairly direct, if in effect subtle, example of poetic-musical form. Campion's lyrics are sometimes much more complex in their apparent simplicity; and when the verse's equivocations are complex the musical imagery is likewise richer in effect.

Like so many Elizabethan lyrics **"Follow thy fair sun"**[3] is based upon a paradox.

> Follow thy fair sun, unhappy shadow.
>   Though thou be black as night,
>   And she made all of light,
> Yet follow thy fair sun, unhappy shadow.
>
> Follow her whose light thy light depriveth.
>   Though here thou liv'st disgraced,
>   And she in heaven is placed,
> Yet follow her whose light the world reviveth.
>
> Follow those pure beams whose beauty burneth,
>   That so have scorched thee,
>   As thou still black must be
> Till her kind beams thy black to brightness turneth.
>
> Follow her while yet her glory shineth.
>   There comes a luckless night,
>   That will dim all her light;
> And this the black unhappy shade divineth.
>
> Follow still, since so thy fates ordained.
>   The sun must have his shade,
>   Till both at once do fade,
> The sun still 'proved, the shadow still disdained.

The basic idea is that the beloved is compared to the sun, which is the source of light and life; she is great creating Nature and therefore not so far from God (compare **"Author of light"** and Raleigh's **"What is our life?"**) The lover is the shadow. He is black and melancholy, presumably because the sun is indifferent to him: and also because apart from her, the sun, he has no existence. She is made all of light, and even if she is not God would seem to be a god: whereas in his blackness there is a taint of sin too, perhaps a suggestion of lost innocence. She is beyond moral judgment, he is a miserable sinner. She is in heaven and her light brings life to the world; but he, as shadow, lives 'disgraced', cut off from both heaven (her) and earth.

In the third stanza, however, there is a shift in the metaphor. Her 'pure beams' have burned him up, blackened him, not like a shadow but like charcoal. At least he now has material existence; and there is a further suggestion that black charcoal may turn to bright diamond, which is a treasure, solid and real, not an illusory shadow. So in the fourth stanza the shadow grows stronger. For a moment we even think he might *be* stronger, last longer, than the sun: for he points out that she is not really impervious to time and change; the sun's glory will be dimmed by night, when she and he will be equal. His final thrust is that the 'sun must have his shade, till both at once do fade'; they need one another, just as good cannot be conceived except in reference to evil. This is true despite conventional estimates of the relative worth of sun and shadow. There is a slightly sinister smugness, perhaps, in the shadow's turning of the tables.

This equivocal quality comes out in the music, which is again strophic. The first phrase is set simply and diatonically; a gentle arch that suggests how inevitable it is that the shadow should follow the sun. The long notes on 'though thou' stress the conditional clause; the slowly declining scale landing on the chromatic F sharp on the word 'black' has a resigned, inevitable pathos, rather than intensity. The answering phrase for 'and she made all of light' rises up the scale, to balance the shadow's descent. But it rises not diatonically but chromatically; and from the chromaticism springs an equivocation parallel to that of the words. Though we aspire towards the light, the aspiration is also a perturbation; and when we get to the high D we immediately fall through an octave. Abruptly, the sharp third of the cadence is cancelled by the minor third; and the rising chromatic scale literally 'follows' us through the instrumental bass, giving a nervous tremor to the harmony, culminating in a stress on the word 'unhappy'. The cadential resolution, as the phrase declines, has a trembling ornamental dissonance on the word 'shadow'.

The words of the other stanzas fit the musical images provoked by the first stanza, though sometimes with ironic implications. In stanza 2 the chromatic F sharp on 'black' appears on the word 'disgraced'. The ascending chromatic scale goes up to heaven. Here the words do not seem to be equivocal, but the music tells us that they are, and thus prepares us for the subsequent stanzas. By the time we get to stanza 4 the rising chromatic scale has become a *dimming* of light: which is what it really was from the start, since, though it rises upwards, its chromatic nature implies uncertainty rather than fulfilment. The long note and melisma on the word 'shade' beautifully convey the touch of self-satisfaction at the end of this stanza. The uncertainty thus admitted to remains in the last stanza, where the ascent becomes a fading. We are left with the shadow, as at the beginning, faintly self-indulgent.

A no less subtle example of the strophic song, with an equation between the poetic and musical image, is an apparently light piece, **"It fell on a summer's day"**:[4]

> It fell on a summers day,
> While sweet Bessy sleeping lay
> In her bower on her bed,
> Light with curtains shadowed,
> Jamie came. She him spies,
> Opening half her heavy eyes.
>
> Jamie stole in through the door;
> She lay slumbering as before.
> Softly to her he drew near;
> She heard him, yet would not hear.
> Bessy vowed not to speak;
> He resolved that dump to break.
>
> First a soft kiss he doth take;
> She lay still and would not wake.
> Then his hands learned to woo;
> She dreamt not what he would do,
> But still slept, while he smiled
> To see love by sleep beguiled.
>
> Jamie then began to play;
> Bessy as one buried lay,
> Gladly still through this sleight
> Deceived in her own deceit.
> And since this trance begun,
> She sleeps every afternoon.

Superficially, this looks like a ballad; but its slightly arch wit is poles apart from the folk spirit. Since the poem is highly sophisticated, the music is appropriately artful. Though it begins with a simple, folk-like phrase for the conventional opening gambit, there is artifice even here: for the second half of the vocal phrase is in canon (a love-pursuit?) with the bass; while the flattened F that harmonizes sweet Bessy gives us, as it were, an unobtrusive, delicate nudge or wink. The little shock of the false relation is sweetly sensuous (she's a gentle creature); yet there is a tang, too, of pleasurable excitement. In the next phrase the dancing, hesitant, irregular rhythm creates the chequered shadows and Bessy's playful sleepiness, the hazy summer's afternoon; this is a case where the musical rhythm complements, rather than intensifies, the extremely subtle verbal rhythm. In the poem these exploratory subordinate clauses lead with a bump into the trenchant words *Jamie came*. So in the music he comes after a double bar. His rhythm is regular; pressing onwards, with little imitative points: for it is a chase, albeit a love-chase.

On the word 'came' there is a false relation exactly similar to the earlier one for 'sweet Bessy'. The pleasurable excitement exists, after all, for them both, for she's in the game, and 'spies' him as part of the imitative chase. When she 'opens half her heavy eyes', however, we are taken back to the dreamy heat of the afternoon. There is a most delicate cross rhythm to stress the word 'half' and a lovely arabesque—at once drowsy and knowing—on the word 'heavy'.

This pattern of imagery is repeated with delicate precision in each stanza. In stanza 2 the F natural in the bass of bar 3 refers compassionately to the deceit in Bessy's 'slumbering'. The hesitant cross rhythm that had been the chequered shade becomes Jamie's cat-like approach, Bessy's hearing and not hearing. The imitative passage conveys her 'vow', his resolution. The cross rhythmed stress comes on the word 'resolved'; while the arabesque becomes the breaking of the dump. In stanza 3 the F natural suggests both the shock of the kiss and Bessy's quivery stillness. The hesitant rhythm becomes Jamie's wooingly exploratory hands, Bessy's dreaming and not dreaming. The regular movement of the imitative passage becomes the deceptive quiet of sleep; the archly stressed word is 'love', the arabesque becomes a beguiling. In the last stanza the F natural false relation deliciously buries Bessy in sleep, in bed, in love, while the cross rhythm acts the being deceived in her own deceit. The imitative phrase becomes associated with the development of delightful habit, with a tender chuckle, too. The stressed word is 'every': which points the joke to round the song off. The arabesque on 'afternoon' becomes a cooing; it is impossible to sing it other than comically.

In all these songs the poems are devised so that both imagery and rhythm can be complemented in musical terms, and the parallelism works in each stanza. The strophic convention would seem to imply rigid stylization; yet the songs are remarkable for the unexpectedly rich meanings that emerge from the interlocking of words and music. Though the songs are generalized, lyrical and narrative rather than dramatic, they reveal a personal situation beneath the generalizing convention. This mating of the general with the particular is more potently evident in the work of a much greater composer than Campion, John Dowland. It is significant that the ayres of Dowland are less dependent than those of Campion on the words; and that the texts he set were often, though not always, of inferior poetic merit. In a piece like **"It fell on a summer's day"** Campion has written a poem that is charming, subtle, and complete in itself. He has created musical images and rhythms which precisely parallel the delicacies of the poem, making a complementary experience; but the music does not 'improve' the poem, and is not intended to. Campion is, above all, the poet-composer.

Notes

1. Stainer and Bell, The English School of Lutenist Song Writers. Thomas Campion's *First Book of Ayres*. Edited by E. H. Fellowes.

2. Stainer and Bell, The English School of Lutenist Song Writers. Thomas Campion's *Songs from Rosseter's Book of Ayres,* Part I. Edited by E. H. Fellowes.

3. ibid.

4. ibid

Catherine Ing (essay date 1968)

SOURCE: Ing, Catherine. "The Lyrics of Thomas Campion." In *Elizabethan Lyrics: A Study in the Development of English Metres and Their Relation to Poetic Effect,* pp. 151-77. London: Chatto & Windus, 1968.

[*In the essay that follows, Ing examines six poems of Campion's in terms of his poetic theories. Ing also looks at the importance of the accompanying music to Campion's poems in determining their form and content.*]

It will be illuminating to take six, very varied, poems by Campion, examine each in the light of his own theories, and then consider whether there are in them elements of versification not mentioned in his theories.

1 "Rose-Cheekt LAWRA"

(from the *Obseruations in the Art of English Poesie,* 1602)

> Rose-cheekt *Lawra,* come
> Sing thou smoothly with thy beawties
> Silent musick, either other
>   Sweetely gracing.
>
> Lovely formes do flowe
> From concent devinely framed;
> Heav'n is musick, and thy beawties
>   Birth is heavenly.
>
> These dull notes we sing
> Discords neede for helps to grace them;
> Only beawty purely loving
>   Knowes no discord,
>
> But still moves delight,
> Like cleare springes renu'd by flowing,
> Ever perfet, ever in them-
>   selves eternall.

It should be easy to decide what is the intended effect of this poem, for '**Rose-Cheeket LAWRA**' occurs in the *Obseruations* as the example of the second kind of English Sapphic. Campion says that it 'consists of *Dimeter,* whose first foote may either be a *Sponde* or a *Trochy*'. The Dimeter he has described earlier as being 'of two feete and one odde sillable. The first foote may be made either a *Trochy,* or a *Spondee,* or an *Iambick,* at the pleasure of the composer, though most naturally that place affects a *Trochy* or *Spondee;* yet, by the example of Catullus in his *Hendicasillables,* I adde in the first place sometimes an *Iambick* foote. In the second place we must ever insert a *Trochy* or

Tribrack, and so leave the last sillable (as in the end of a verse it is alwaies held) common'. 'The two verses following are both of them *Trochaical,* and consist of foure feete, the first of either of them being a *Spondee* or *Trochy,* the other three only *Trochyes.* The fourth and last verse is made of two *Trochyes.*' It seems quite clear that Campion is here using the names of feet in the strict sense, and therefore expects us to look for a quantitative pattern independent of stress.

The first line of each stanza agrees punctiliously with the pattern described for the dimeter. He does not even allow himself the freedom of using an iamb in the first place. At first sight this foot in the last stanza might seem to be an iamb but, according to his rules of position, the 'but' is lengthened by the following three consonants in the combined words 'but', 'still'; the foot must therefore be accepted, so long as we accept his terms, as a spondee.

Even for those readers who cannot automatically apply the detailed rules of syllable length given at the end of the *Obseruations,* it is quite easy to read this poem as a trochaic measure. Campion has used a large number of adjectival and adverbial forms ending in '-y', and these forms are certainly always pronounced with a length in the first syllable much greater than that in the second. 'Smoothly', 'Sweetely', 'Lovely', 'beawty', 'purely', are words which come probably as near as possible to the strict trochaic shape of a long followed by a short in the ratio of two to one. It is therefore perfectly simple to scan a line like—

> Sing thou smoothly with thy beawties

as consisting of trochees from beginning to end, and this is probably how any unprepared reader would scan it. Campion, however, would probably call the first foot a spondee as it seems likely that he would consider 'thou' lengthened by position. The last syllable of 'beawties' he certainly considered long: 'The last sillable of all words in the plurall number that have two or more vowels before *s* are long, as *vertues, duties, miseries, fellowes.*' These liberties are in complete accord with his instructions; so this line and, in fact, all the lines on this pattern in the poem, can be read in a manner satisfying to the ear, and still theoretically agree with his rules about individual syllables. The only difficulty that is likely to arise is that the satisfactory reading of the line will omit some of his points of detail, and therefore not quite achieve his intended effect.

On the whole, however, the poem in reading, even by a comparatively careless reader, will come very near to the poem that Campion wrote, for it is noticeable that nearly all his long syllables have their length reinforced by the natural stress of English speech.

2 "Come, Let Us Sound with Melody"

(No. XXI of the First Part of *A Booke of Ayres,* 1601)

> Come, let us sound with melody, the praises
> Of the kings king, th'omnipotent creator,

Author of number, that hath all the world in
                   Harmonie framed.

Heav'n is His throne perpetually shining,
His devine power and glorie, thence he thunders,
One in all, and all still in one abiding,
                 Both Father and Sonne.

O sacred sprite, invisible, eternall
Ev'ry where, yet unlimited, that all things
Canst in one moment penetrate, revive me,
                 O holy Spirit.

Rescue, O rescue me from earthly darknes,
Banish hence all these elementall obiects,
Guide my soule that thirsts to the lively Fountaine
                 Of thy devinenes.

Cleanse my soule, O God, thy bespotted Image,
Altered with sinne so that heav'nly purenes
Cannot acknowledge me, but in thy mercies,
                 O Father of grace.

But when once thy beames do remove my darknes,
O then I'le shine forth as an Angell of light,
And record, with more than an earthly voice, thy
                 Infinite honours.

In his scrupulous determination to join words and notes lovingly together, Campion has given us, in the music for this poem, a definite indication of the scansion. The notes are:

♩♩♩♩♩♩♩♩♩♩♩♩
♩♩♩♩♩♩♩♩♩♩♩♩
♩♩♩♩♩♩♩♩♩♩♩♩
        ♩♩♩♩.

This gives us, in the terms of prosody, three lines of the pattern, - ˘ - - - ˘ ˘ - ˘ - -, followed by a short fourth line, - ˘ ˘ - -. These lines are easily divisible into strict classical feet, the long ones consisting of trochee, spondee, dactyl, trochee, spondee, or: - ˘ / - - / - ˘ ˘ / - ˘ / - - ; and the short one of a dactyl followed by a spondee, or: - ˘ ˘ / - -.

Now it is easy to keep to this line in singing, when the notation indicates the precise value to be assigned to each syllable, and comparison of the syllables with the rules given in the *Obseruations* makes it clear that Campion has taken great care to give each long of the musical and metrical pattern a syllable, either long in itself or lengthened by position. In some cases the pattern shows itself instantly through the words: the line—

And record, with more than an earthly voice, thy

would usually be spoken in an arrangement of longs and shorts corresponding to the indicated feet; the lengthening of 'And', which he ascribes to the effect of massed following consonants, would almost certainly be supplied, as most readers hesitate to run too many short syllables together, and the short 're-' tends to give length to the preceding word. This is, indeed, a kind of 'lengthening by

position', but not quite in the same sense as Campion understands it. It is, however, difficult to see how the reading voice, if it is unrestrained by musical exigencies, is to be dissuaded from precipitating itself off 'thy' on to 'Infinite', before the metre is ready for it.

Difficulties of this kind are more evident in other parts of the poem. 'Of' occurs twice in a position requiring a long syllable, and it is lengthened only by a following 'th-'. Again, two words, 'Both Father', are intended to make up a dactyl, and it requires strong self-discipline to read 'Both' as though it were twice as long as the first syllable of 'Father'. It is clear, then, that he has remembered his rule that 'position . . . can alter the accent of any sillable in our English verse' more strongly than the principle that 'above all the accent of our words is diligently to be observ'd, for chiefely by the accent . . . the true value of the sillables is to be measured'. Given a carefully trained reader, Campion himself, for instance, the rules would provide sufficient guide for overriding the accent. With an untrained reader, the question is bound to arise whether the form of the poem is adequately held together by Campion's rules alone.

3 "The Man of Life Upright"

(No. II in the First Part of *Two Bookes of Ayres,* c. 1613)

The man of life upright,
   Whose chearfull minde is free
From waight of impious deedes
   And yoake of vanitee;

The man whose silent dayes
   In harmless ioyes are spent,
Whom hopes cannot delude
   Nor sorrowes discontent;

That man needes neyther towres,
   Nor armour for defence:
Nor vaults his guilt to shrowd
   From thunders violence;

Hee onely can behold
   With unaffrighted eyes
The horrors of the deepe
   And terrors of the Skies.

Thus, scorning all the cares
   That fate or fortune brings,
His Booke the Heau'ns hee makes,
   His wisedome heav'nly things;

Good thoughts his surest friends,
   His wealth a well-spent age,
The earth his sober Inne,
   And quiet pilgrimage.[1]

The music set for this poem, if translated into the long and short signs of prosody, gives us a series of impossible lines, impossible, that is, from the classical point of view; it is difficult to imagine any Greek or Roman poet writing entirely in a series of tribrachs strung together. The notes are nearly all of exactly the same length, with an occasional lingering on one, followed by a hurried movement on the next. It is, therefore, useless to look to the music for an indication of any of the feet described in the *Obseruations.*

Yet the music gives no impression of formlessness, and the poem as read has a very clear form. The most conventional prosodists would agree that it was written entirely in an iambic or 'rising-stress' metre, according to whether they were using terms derived from classical prosody or names invented to agree as nearly as possible with the accepted theory of English utterance. Now, the music, showing as it does no trace of iambic structure, and the words, which can be satisfyingly read by anyone, actually agree as happily as Campion could have hoped. It follows that he has thrown over all his stated desires to write English poems on classical principles, and on those principles only.

This self-contradiction is underlined by his firm and unmistakable use of rime in the poem. According to his own views, this should mean that the poem is a rickety structure concealed under the fatness of ornament. He would hardly have published it if he himself really agreed with this verdict; certainly, no reader of this and other English verses can agree with the verdict. The poem does hold together; but if we are to find the integrating principle of its structure, we must look elsewhere than in the detailed instructions to versifiers with which he concludes the *Obseruations.*

4 "Never Weather-Beaten Saile"

(No. XI in the First Part of *Two Bookes of Ayres*)

Never weather-beaten Saile more willing bent to shore,
Never tyred Pilgrims limbs affected slumber more,
Than my wearied spright now longs to flye out of my
    troubled brest.
    O come quickly, sweetest Lord, and take my soule
    to rest.
Ever-blooming are the ioyes of Heav'ns high paradice,
Cold age deafes not there our eares, nor vapour dims
    our eyes:
Glory there the Sun outshines, whose beames the
    blessed only see;
    O come quickly, glorious Lord, and raise my spright
    to thee.

The music of this poem, again, gives us lines which are apparently metrically impossible. Once more, the notes are for the most part of equal length, and no prosodist can make classical feet out of a collection of tape-measured inches. There is a further difficulty here: the first phrase of the fourth line of each stanza, 'O come quickly', is made by the music to occur three times. Campion never published the poem without the music, and therefore, presumably, thought of the verse-form as having always this lengthened last line. Modern editors of the words alone give the phrase only once. In either form the stanza gives the impression of being well-balanced. If it were

written on a strict arrangement of classical feet, according to Campion's principles, this change of form would be impossible; the slight necessary change in the order of the feet would break down the form altogether and make it unrecognizable.

Manifestly, the form does not fall apart. Yet an attempt to scan the poem in terms of rising or falling stresses provides almost as many difficulties. The first phrase of the first line, 'Never weather-beaten Saile', would at first sight instantly be put down as a group of falling-stress feet; the second half of the line, 'more willing bent to shore', would, if treated by itself, be called a collection of rising-stress feet. There is no suggestion in the first half of the line that the poet is deliberately producing an effect of clash between words and ideal pattern. Unless we are to say simply that a syllable has been omitted at the beginning or the end, which is the usual explanation of this kind of line, or that there has been indecision in the creation of the line, we must look for an explanation in different terms. If there were any doubt that the first half of the line coincides instead of clashing with the pattern, it should be necessary only to look at the corresponding line,

Ever-blooming are the ioyes of Heav'ns high paradice,

in the second stanza. It cannot be supposed that this line is intended to give an impression of restlessness and difficulty. In fact, the whole poem is obviously constructed of words chosen to clarify the pattern and not to obscure it. Campion himself gives no description of the pattern we find here.

5 "Now Winter Nights"

(No. XII in the *Third Booke of Ayres*)

Now winter nights enlarge
    The number of their houres;
And clouds their stormes discharge
    Upon the ayrie towres.
Let now the chimneys blaze
    And cups o'erflow with wine,
Let well-tun'd words amaze
    With harmonie divine.
Now yellow waxen lights
    Shall waite on hunny Love
While youthfull Revels, Masks, and Courtly sights,
    Sleepes leaden spels remove.

This time doth well dispence
    With lovers long discourse;
Much speech hath some defence,
    Though beauty no remorse.
All doe not all things well;
    Some measures comely tread;
Some knotted Ridles tell;
    Some Poems smoothly read.
The Summer hath his ioyes,
    And Winter his delights;
Though love and all his pleasures are but toyes,
    They shorten tedious nights.

Once again, we are faced by the fact that the notes lovingly joined to the words of this poem are no help to anyone searching for Campion's practice of Campion's theories. Once again, the notes translated into metrical terms would give a fantastic collocation of tribrachs, divided impossibly at times into half-shorts. Some lines, in fact, will not provide the right number of syllables to be divided into an arrangement of any complete feet. 'Now winter nights enlarge', for instance, is given by the music the pattern ˘ ˘ ˘ ˘ - ; any good Roman would agree that this is ridiculous.

A prosodist adhering to any other system would find some difficulty in deciding where he was to divide the lines, not only internally into feet, but among themselves. The first line of each stanza must run without a pause into the second, and the third into the fourth, unless reason is to be denied. The decided rimes, however, cannot be denied. There is obviously some structural intent in the division of lines. It is an intent appearing clearly in most of the poems, and occasionally bursting its way into the well-mannered ranks of classical rules in the *Obseruations*.

6 "Follow Your Saint"

(No. X in the First Part of *A Booke of Ayres*)

Follow your Saint, follow with accents sweet;
Haste you, sad noates, fall at her flying feete:
There, wrapt in cloud of sorrowe pitie move,
And tell the ravisher of my soule I perish for her love.
But if she scorns my never-ceasing paine,
Then burst with sighing in her sight and nere returne
    againe.

All that I soong still to her praise did tend,
Still she was first; still she my songs did end.
Yet she my love and Musicke both doth flie,
The Musicke that her Eccho is and beauties simpathie;
Then let my Noates pursue her scornfull flight:
It shall suffice that they were breath'd and dyed for
    her delight.

By this time it must be obvious that we shall find no undeviating adherence to classical rules in many of the songs, least of all perhaps in this. The music makes no recognized classical metrical shape; rime is made very obvious by the early appearance of the second of each pair of riming words; there is never the slightest need to wrest a syllable from its customary form in the pronunciation of everyday speech. None of the rules of lengthening by position, length from spelling, or arbitrary length or short-ness ascribed to any monosyllable, appears to indicate a form not at once apparent. The form is apparent. The most insensitive reader could be dared to do his worst with this poem and a sense of shape would still emerge.

As in the fourth example, the first line may at first sight give an impression of indecision in the choice between rising-stress and falling-stress rhythms. Nobody can read **'Follow your Saint'** as a phrase in pure rising stress; if he wishes to do so he had better emend to 'Pursue your Saint'. Nobody, on the other hand, can read 'with accents sweet' as a phrase in falling-stress rhythm. Yet the whole line—

    Follow your Saint, follow with accents sweet;

fits into its place in the construction of the stanza as a whole, with a sense not only of ease, but of perfection. This is the more remarkable when we find one line at least—

    The Musicke that her Eccho is and beauties simpathie;

constructed in perfect rising-stress rhythm from beginning to end. Obviously, Campion has not decided arbitrarily on a novel shape for a single line, and made all other lines agree with the first; the relationship of syllables and lines is something more complex.

Neither classical theory nor music fully explains the structure of these poems. There are in them, however, other elements emphasizing structure.

In **'Rose-Cheekt LAWRA'** and **'Come, let us sound with melody,'** Campion is attempting to prove that English can be persuaded into providing relationships of length suf-ficiently strict to form a staple of pattern, and it therefore seems unlikely that any of these extra marks of shape will be used, though they may, of course, appear accidentally from time to time. Rime certainly is rigorously excluded, as might be expected from the fierce denunciation of this *figura verbi* in the **Obseruations**. Echoes and repetitions of vowel and consonant sounds, on the other hand, occur so frequently in both poems that they begin to enforce an examination of the reasons for their presence; and that examination soon shows that sounds of a similar nature are always closely grouped.

In **'Rose-Cheekt LAWRA,'** the first stanza has four words—'sing', 'smoothly', 'silent' and 'sweetely'—beginning with the latter 's'. The same sound, or a sound closely related to it, occurs internally in the words 'rose', 'musick' and 'gracing', while 'beawties' ends with a sound belonging to the same group. Next in frequency to these come the liquids and nasals, in 'rose', 'Lawra', 'come', 'sing', smoothly', 'silent', 'musick', 'sweetely' and 'gracing'. The next stanza employs this last group more obviously, only the words 'do', 'is' (which occurs twice), 'thy' and 'birth' showing no examples; in this stanza, too, the related sounds 'd' and 't' put in an appearance, occur-ring six times. In the third stanza, they come to the fore with nine appearances, while the background is quietly filled in by the unobtrusive work of the sibilants, liquids and nasals that have been more evident in the earlier stanzas. Finally, the fourth stanza rests upon all these sounds together, 's' having six entries, 'd' and 't' six, and 'l', 'm' and 'n' fourteen between them. In these four lines, moreover, the hard 'k' sound, which has come six times into the first twelve lines, is suddenly emphasized by be-ing used twice in the adjacent words 'like' and 'cleare'.

The arrangement of vowels, though not so obvious, is quite as interesting as the grouping of consonants. Vowels related, by pronunciation as well as spelling, appear in 'come', 'smoothly', 'beawties', 'musick' and 'other', while 'ee' occurs in both 'cheekt' and 'sweetely', in the course of the first stanza. Stanza two has the same sounds, though less frequently, and a new one in 'concent', 'heav'n' and 'heavenly'. The third stanza adds to these an emphasized use of the sound which has appeared in 'Lawra' and 'formes' by repeating the word 'discord'. Both the 'o' and the 'e' groups are used impartially in the last stanza.

'Come, let us sound with melody' moves straight into a bold collection of hard consonant-sounds in 'come', 'kings', 'king' and 'creator', supporting them with frequent 's's, 'l's and 'm's or 'n's. Stanza two abandons the 'k' sound in favour of 'p' in 'perpetually' and 'power', and 'th' in 'throne', 'thence', 'thunders' and 'Father', with an undercurrent similar to that in the first stanza. In the next stanza this undercurrent comes to the surface, in every word except 'O' (twice), 'yet', 'that', while 'k' and 'p' are present, though subdued, in 'sacred', 'spite', 'canst', 'penetrate' and 'Spirit'. The following stanza has the same sounds with the addition of 'th' and 'v' or 'f' in 'earthly', 'three', 'that', 'thirsts', 'lively', 'Fountaine' and 'devineness'. The fifth stanza uses all the sounds that have yet appeared without any apparent preference, while stanza six disregards 'p', and has 'k' only twice, sunk in the middle of the words 'darkness' and 'record'.

The vowels grouped in stanza one are the rounded 'oo', 'u' and 'o' sounds in 'come', 'us', 'omnipotent', 'author', 'of', 'number', 'all', 'world' and 'harmonie', while the second and fourth lines both end in words containing the same sound, 'creator' and 'framed'. Their placing in this position creates something like the shadow of a rime, and the shadow is deepened by the use of the same trick in all but the last two stanzas, stanza two having 'thunders' and 'Sonne' in the corresponding places, stanza three 'things' and 'Spirit', and stanza four 'objects' and 'devinenes'; these last two words have the syllable containing 'e' long, according to its place in the quantitative pattern indicated by the music. Stanza two even repeats the effect by closing the first and third lines in 'shining' and 'abiding'; stanza three uses this sound again in 'sprite' and 'revive', and adds the group in 'invisible', 'unlimited', 'things', 'in' and 'Spirit'; stanza four has chiefly the sound of its semi-rime ('-iects', '-nes'), in 'rescue' (twice), 'darknes', 'hence', 'elementall', 'obiects' and 'devinenes'; the fifth stanza, though keeping this sound, returns to a fuller use of rounded vowels in 'soule', 'O', 'God', 'bespotted', 'altered', 'so', 'purenes', 'cannot', 'acknowledge', 'O', 'Father'; while the characteristic trick of the last stanza is to repeat any one sound very soon after its first appearance in the stanza, line one having 'do' and 'remove' next to each other, line two 'I'le' and 'shine' next to each other, with 'light' at the end of the line, and line three picking up, from 'forth' in line two, the sound repeated in 'record' and 'more', with only a single intervening syllable.

Now, whether or not Campion's choice of all these linked sounds drawing out a pattern was deliberate, the fact remains that the linking of both vowels and consonants in these two poems is so close and complex that it compels the ear to sense some connection other than semantic between the parts of a group and between the groups themselves. The succession of vowels and the succession of consonants almost give the impression of two melodic lines in the older music going their independent but companionable ways, and between them supporting and emphasizing, after the fashion of the old music, the rational meaning of the words. In any case, the arrangement of actual sound in these poems makes it quite impossible for the verse to fall apart. **'Rose-Cheekt Lawra'** has always had its beauty admitted; and **'Come, let us sound with melody,'** though in official disgrace in both Bullen's and Vivian's editions of Campion, seems to me to have a beauty both rich and delicately subtle when it is read aloud with a due care for the intricate weaving of the two threads of vowels and consonants. It is not, after all, very difficult to notice and perhaps slightly emphasize sounds which the poet thought important enough to repeat; and the slight effort has in this case the tremendous reward of an increased facility in ascribing to difficult syllables their right length, for words like 'of' and 'with' and 'thy', by joining more obviously important words in their scheme of sound, emerge quite naturally to take their position as 'long' syllables where the pattern requires it. The possibility begins to arise that these *figuræ verbi*, as Campion himself would almost certainly have called them, have some structural function in the verse.

Now the figure most evident in the other four poems is, of course, rime. Number three in the six poems examined has a simple abcb scheme, number four has aabb, number five has ababcdcdefef and number six aabbcc. All these schemes are quite unmistakable; it is impossible to suppose that at the moment of writing these songs Campion was in the least ashamed of rime or had any desire to conceal it. **'The man of life upright,'** indeed, positively hammers its rimes, either by repeating a part of the rime-sound at the end of one of the strictly unrimed lines, as in stanza one, where 'deedes' occurs between 'free' and '(vani)tee', or by giving these lines a half-rime, as in stanza three, where lines one and three end in 'towres' and 'shrowd' respectively. In **'Never weather-beaten Saile'** the rimes are made to stand out with almost startling clarity in the first two lines through the two facts that the rime-words are literally the only possible points of repose in restless lines of thirteen syllables each, and that the rime is on a sound '-ore', completely different in character from the thin 'e's and 'i's of the rest of the words in the lines. This introduction to the scheme makes the ear unconsciously expectant of the rimes which are to come, and ready to pick them out in high relief. A different method makes the rimes equally obvious in **'Now winter nights enlarge,'** where they thrust their heads into some positions where nobody would expect a point of rest. It is natural to say 'Now winter nights enlarge the number of their houres' and 'And clouds their stormes discharge upon the ayrie towres' as phrases with hardly a pause; yet the insistent 'enlarge-discharge' chime makes some division inevitable. The refusal to provide a rime for 'lights' in the first stanza and 'ioyes' in the second until the expected interval has been increased by nearly half as much again makes a continuous run of the voice equally inevitable for the lines 'While youthful Revels, Masks, and Courtly sights' and 'Though love and all his pleasures are but toyes'. After the boldness and occasional shock of some of these uses of rime, it is impossible to find anything but a natural use of speech in the practice in **'Follow your Saint'**; it is sufficient to say that the rimes are neither obtrusive nor hesitant, but occur with the quiet confidence of perfect art.

Rime, however, though far the most important, is not the only device of sound used even in these poems. It is noticeable that each stanza of number three tends to use a clearly defined vowel-group of its own: 'e's and 'i's in the first stanza, 'o's and 'a's in the second, 'e's or 'i's and 'ow' in the third, 'e's and 'o's in the fourth, full round 'o's in the fifth, and in the sixth a mingling of nearly all the vowels of the preceding stanzas. Moreover, alliteration, repeated words and strong echoes like 'horror' and 'terror' occur within each stanza. This last device occurs at the beginning of number four, where 'never' and 'weather' stand side by side. There is also unobtrusive alliteration on 'beaten' and 'bent' in line one, 'deafes' and 'dims' in line six, and a more obvious use in the placing of 'beames' and 'blessed' with only 'the' intervening in line seven. The two stanzas of **'Now winter nights enlarge'** are differentiated from each other by the avoidance until the end of the first of hard consonants likely to create even a short pause, and the early and frequent employment in the second of 'p', 't' and 'k' sounds. This, and all other devices, are, like rime, less obvious in **'Follow your Saint'** than in any of the other poems; it can be remarked, however, that the whole poem tends to move on swift sibilants and liquids, pausing only in the middle of stanza two with the combined weight of 'k', 'p' and 't'.

Now it is obvious that the devices of repetition and echo in speech sounds can be used never for dividing, but always for connecting, the parts of verse. An extensive use of these devices must indicate a desire on the part of the poet to emphasize the larger units of his form rather than the small elements which are grouped to make those units. This, surely, is what Campion is doing throughout his poetry. Whether he does it deliberately or unconsciously it is impossible to determine. The use of the devices is so sure and sensitive that it seems to argue a deliberate craftsmanship, specially from a poet so scrupulous and so determined as he in maintaining the principle, unwelcome to many would-be artists, that artistic creation involves training and effort. On the other hand, those remarks in the *Obseruations* which suggest this very attitude, of looking for large organized units, appear to be the spontaneous utterance of impulse, and are different in tone from the careful reports of his conscious reflections on the structure of individual feet. In any case, these unreasoned remarks have proved more permanently interesting than the theories which the essay formally sets out to prove; and the ele-

ments of his practice which seem to bear the closest relationship to those remarks promise to be more fruitful than the painstaking performance of his imagined duties as a poet.

In **'Rose-Cheekt Lawra,'** for instance, the trochees demanded by his stated ideal pattern are contrived out of English material with remarkable ingenuity, and a very brief inspection will reveal them. Each one stands by itself in something like the ideal shape of a long syllable followed by a syllable half the length of the first. Yet when we compare one of these feet with another, it is sometimes difficult to find a real correspondence between them: 'smoothly' does not seem to have quite the same shape as 'either'; even more obvious is the discrepancy between 'either' and 'other', which stand side by side in the first stanza and are supposed to represent exactly the same foot. Surely 'smoothly' occupies in utterance a greater length of time than 'either', and 'either' than 'other'. Yet no whole line gives the impression of being out of balance with other lines, still less any whole stanza with other stanzas. In fact, it is almost impossible to feel certain that a stable unit has been found until a stanza has been completed. This sounds dangerous: if the correspondence between feet is really erratic, it seems unsafe to depend on the organization of those feet into a larger whole to secure a sense of form. But in this, perhaps the most surely and exquisitely satisfying of Campion's attempts at classical metres, he has been very much wiser than his critics. Bullen and Saintsbury, for instance, admitting the poem's beauty, sigh, 'But how much more beautiful would it have been with rime'!

Now rime would have exercised precisely the wrong function here: it would have suggested a division into strictly proportionate pairs of lines, whereas Campion needs, and secures, an irresistible run-on from beginning to end of at least the first stanza, which must indicate the form. If there were any doubt about this, it would be set at rest by a glance at the deliberate use of a single word to connect the last two lines of the poem. Having secured this movement, Campion proceeds to control it by that use of connecting sounds, varied from stanza to stanza, which has already appeared. The result is never rigid, always sure; for in the end the unit certainly is one of quantity, but it is a *quantitas discreta* into so many and such variable parts, through lines which differ slightly among themselves, to feet which preserve recognizable shapes together with incalculable proportions, that the effect is one of safety quite unmixed with boredom. The length of the stanza as a whole is dependable.

The same principle holds good throughout **'Come, let us sound with melody,'** and here perhaps it is even more interesting to watch. The acid comments which have been made about this poem, and about its music in the article by Janet Dodge 'On Campion's Music', in the introduction to Bullen's edition of Campion's Works, suggest that it is some enormity. A generation which has seen the return of music, since the time of Miss Dodge's article, to some of the methods of free barring used by Campion and his contemporaries probably has an advantage in the ability to see that the lack of four-square rhythm in this song certainly does not rob it of form; the phrases which accompany each line of the verse are balanced mathematically and there can be no doubts as to their outline. In fact, it is much easier to see and understand than the outline of the words; for Campion, relying no doubt on the fact that the music will always be able to settle disputes, has allowed himself a greater dependence on arbitrary rules of length in his syllables. According to the music, this poem is stricter than **'Rose-Cheekt Lawra.'** According to the natural utterance of speech, it is much less strict. Yet words and music are in a comfortable alliance, and the fact that moderately careful reading can make the words alone sound shapely is due once more to instinctive trust in the principle of making sure of the length of the line, which is itself stable in this poem, each long line corresponding to any other long and each short to any other short, and allowing the feet to vary among themselves. Once more the shape is held together by unobtrusive linking of letters; and if the voice is led by the prepared importance of certain sounds to linger over some syllables more than in normal speech, the effect is the very suitable one of imparting a kind of impassioned gravity to the whole poem.

Now these principles, though probably a sound basis for the treatment of quantity in English, are certainly far removed from the true principles of classical prosody, and it is as well to remember, in reading Campion's supposed examples of classical metres, that they are certainly examples of very subtle quantitative verse, and therefore require a slightly different approach from that required by the commoner English measures, but that the ordinary approach to Latin verse is equally useless. With the poems which frankly jettison most of the classical rules, there is, of course, no temptation to use this approach, but it is still sometimes necessary to be prepared for slight variations from straightforward stressed measures.

In **'The man of life upright'** the necessity for open-minded alertness is, perhaps, not very evident. Campion is quite simply using stresses to mark out a regular beat compatible with the mood of steady decision pervading the whole poem. He never deviates from rising-stress rhythm, but it is worth observing from the evidence of his accompanying music that he did not in this case intend stress to induce length, for the notes are all, with a very few exceptions, of the same length. It is certain, too, that he was not attempting to produce the foot that some prosodists apparently regard as possible, an 'iamb' with stress substituted for length, for the music gives at the beginning of each line a rest equivalent to the note used as the normal unit for each syllable, while the last syllable of each line is given a note lasting for two of these units; this makes hay of an attempt to scan on any 'iambic' basis, however licentiate. In fact, the prosodist is left in his usual precarious position of having to decide for himself where he is to divide one foot from the next. If he chooses the better part

of valour, he will probably accept no divisions except those indicated through rimes by the poet himself. This particular poem may seem temptingly easy to deal with when it offers a disarming regularity of stress, but the fact that its author gave eight musical units to each line of six syllables should be an indication that he neither worked nor desired to work on the idea of a strict mathematical value for each syllable.

Such an idea would be impossible for the next poem. **'Never weather-beaten Saile'** asks for, and is given by the music, a lingering on the last syllable of the first two and the last lines of each stanza; it is absolutely essential that these rather long and unpausing lines should have a decided rest on the rime-word. The third line of each stanza, which has two more syllables than the other lines, is allowed only the same aggregate in notes, and it will be found that in reading, the voice, hurrying to the resolution of the last line, actually allows this line no more time than the others. If the last line is read as it is usually now printed, it is exactly commensurate with the others. The music, by repeating 'O come quickly' twice, makes it half as long again. In either case, all the lines are in a remarkably simple ratio to each other. The syllables, on the contrary, fluctuate considerably; the phrase, 'more willing bent to shore', for instance, seems to demand at least four different syllable-lengths, for 'more', 'will-' and 'bent', '-ing' and 'to' and 'shore'. Stress changes from falling to rising in so many lines that the change can hardly be considered as variations on a pattern based on one stress-order. In fact, the only calculable unit is the line.

The next poem seems at first sight to demand a grouping of lines for its unit, for the music prefixes to some of them a rest which brings the first of several pairs of lines into the curious relationship with the second of seven and a half units to six and a half. This seems absurd to the Euclidean mind, but the phenomenon occurs so often that the ear becomes accustomed to it, and appreciates the delicate variety lent by this refusal to march with plantigrade steps. It learns, too, to move with an absolute trust in the placing of the rimes, which occur, as always in Campion's poetry, at intervals exactly calculated to give an effect of balance without solidity. The lines are short but, as they rime alternately and not in couplets, the effect is not that of the battering-ram. It is the dependable use of rime throughout ten lines bearing a repeated proportion to each other that makes the eleventh line, which is nearly twice as long as any of the others, run on its way without an awkward break at the point where the other lines end.

If all these poems show how securely a sensitive poet can move in the dangerous freedom of large units, **'Follow your Saint'** makes this freedom seem the only possible condition for poetry. Only one line in the whole poem has a regular rising-stress movement from beginning to end, and the way is so subtly prepared for this movement that it comes with that sense of combined freshness and inevitability that has sometimes been described as the essence of poetry. The first three lines of each stanza end with a rising-stress movement definite enough to give a suggestion of flight by the metre and pursuit by the words to the earlier part of the lines, though it would be rash to put forward the theory that the whole line is based on that movement. There must be a pause on 'Saint', 'noates', 'soong' and 'first' that will involve hurrying elsewhere, and so rule out the possibility of a regular, stress-marked arrangement of feet. Obviously, it is the stable proportion of lines, varying only between ten and fourteen syllables and indicated by rimes, that must provide the unit. But the persistent scrupulous use of this unit gives Campion the right suddenly to shape a line on a more definitely modelled pattern and so introduce a sense, not of the banal, but of the perfection of freshness. The exquisite coincidence of material and ideal pattern in the line 'The Musicke that her Eccho is and beauties simpathie' might occur in the midst of a series of lines on a regular foot-basis and lose half its breath-catching loveliness. Coming as it does among minutely fluctuating but highly organized groups of feet, it is perfect.

Even a casual glance at the matter of Campion's poetry will reveal characteristics of subject and imagery that themselves illumine the effect on some Elizabethan poetry of preoccupation with the means of establishing metrical form. Any reader of Campion's poetry will find that all Campion's subjects are neatly listed for him in the index of every other anthology of Elizabethan poetry. For it is evident that he—like Shakespeare—had no shyness or hesitation in drawing from the common poets' storehouse. The first complete book of English songs published by himself bears on the title-page his own division into 'Divine and Morall Songs' and 'Light Conceits of Lovers', and that is as good a classification as any of Elizabethan subjects. Campion's religious songs are all characterized by a quite simple reverence that may sometimes appear naïve, as in **'Tune thy Musicke to thy hart'**; but that reverence embraces complexities of religious experience that, perhaps more than anything else in his poetry, remind us of the fact that he lived through twenty years of the seventeenth century. Sometimes he reveals a personal vision of heaven with a luminous clarity that looks forward to Vaughan.

> Ever-blooming are the ioys of Heav'ns high paradice,
> Cold age deafes not there our eares, nor vapour dims
> our eyes;

and that Heaven evidently marches with the 'country far beyond the stars'. Sometimes Campion sees himself in personal relationship with God:

> View mee, Lord, a worke of thine:
> Shall I then lye drown'd in night?

and then he seems to 'surfet On the poysoned baytes of sinne' with Donne. And then he can forget them, with Herbert, to—

> Rise now and walke the waies of light;
> 'Tis not too late yet to begin.

Always, whether he is writing a version of one of the Psalms or crystallizing his own view of the world as—

> thou masse of meere confusion,
> False light, with many shadowes dimm'd,
> Old Witch, with new foyles trimm'd,
> Thou deadly sleepe of soule, and charm'd illusion,

there is something describable only as tone, which declares that he means what he says.

In 'Light Conceits of Lovers' we should hardly expect him always to mean what he says. With very few exceptions, as in **'When the God of merrie love,'** the lightness of his love-poems is always enchantingly delicate, amused and amusing. He can play the devout lover with just sufficient solemnity to be suspect, swearing with lying hand on heart that his pallor comes—

> not with poring on my booke:
> My Mistris cheeke, my bloud hath tooke,
> For her mine owne hath me forsooke.

He can admit placidly that—

> Though Love and all his pleasures are but toyes,
> They shorten tedious nights,

and assign them to their proper place in the gay list of 'harmonie divine, yellow waxen lights, youthfull revels, Masks, and Courtly sights' that 'give Winter his delights'. He will recognize and simultaneously pity the folly of love-lorn man or woman—and then turn in his tracks to confound us with the delicate sincerity of **'And would you see my Mistris face or Followe thy faire sunne.'** For his love is not always light or, in any sense, conceited, and he is capable of sounding with implacable sureness the deep note whose grave harmonies affect the whole key of that perfect lyric, **'When thou must home to shades of under ground.'**

In all these the balance of occasion and feeling, import and response, is preserved with finished poetic tact. Campion was sensitive enough to reflect nearly all the sides of Elizabethan alertness to the multitudinous delights of earth and the happiness of heaven, the pains of life and the darkness of death—and he reflected nothing else. It is useless to search him for *aliquid novi,* and there is no need to do so.

Yet there is a newness about the forms which many of his reflections take. His Corinnas and Lesbias and Bessies may be related to the Delias and Chloes and sweet Kates, but they have their individuality, and it arises partly from the fact that Campion draws attention to qualities in them hardly noticed by other poets. They may have golden wires for hair and pearls for teeth, but he is not particularly interested if they have. Yet if they move or speak or sing, his awareness quickens at once. Poem after poem reveals an almost total disregard for visual imagery in its usual forms. Colour, for instance, except in the dubious form of black, appears less than half a dozen times in all the songs, and when the mention of it is as general as 'thy red and white', it argues a decided lack of interest. Colour in itself seems to him too static to be stimulating, and he evidently passed the same disapproving verdict on unchanging shapes: his 'lovely formes do flowe'.

One of the few places where he presents a picture beautiful in its very freedom from change is in the description of 'heav'ns high paradice', and at that point, obviously, he has turned his back on his interests in the world; the beauties of heaven are *ipso facto* unsuitable for the earth. So when he descends from the rarefied atmosphere of Paradise he looks instantly and instinctively for something either in movement or capable of it. Darkness and light are so much relative terms that each implies the possibility of changing into the other, and he varies the lighting of his poems with sun and shadow, day and night and, occasionally, life and death. Natural description appears only through the varying forms of the seasons, when the 'peacefull westerne winde' tames the winter storms only to let the delights of winter replace the joys of summer; or in flowing sea and river; or in the lightly poised shapes of eagle or dove. Everything, in fact, is at the point of that 'sweete delicious morne' in his 'Mistris' face, 'Where day is breeding, never borne'. Love dies or flames like a fire. Human beings hardly seem alive to him until they begin to move or speak or sing. His saints and his wantons alike must be flying, his suns must flee their shadow, his ladies moving swiftly and lightly from raging to kindness.

> Awake, thou spring of speaking grace, mute rest
>   becomes not thee;
> The fayrest women, while they sleepe, and Pictures,
>   equall bee.

Naturally, then, he delights to think of anything which seems in itself the essence of movement. Winds blow through his fields and gardens, and the abstract word 'flight' occurs over and over again. Above all, he loves and praises and calls upon music in all he does, music which cannot exist without movement. 'Heav'n is Musick', 'To Musicke bent' is his mind, the beloved's voice 'is an Eccho cleare which Musicke doth beget', she has a 'smoothe toong whose musicke hell can move', God—

> hath all the world in
>   Harmonie framed.

Music sounds through his poetry as it probably sounded through all his existence; the reader cannot escape it if he would. It is significant that when he wishes to suggest, in **'The man of life upright,'** the complete absence of bustle and hurry with their possible attendant distresses, he speaks, not of 'quiet' days, which ninety-nine poets out of a hundred would have said, simply because the general term 'quiet' seems more inclusive than any other; but of 'silent' days, as though he could not make the idea immediate to his imagination unless he reached it through his hearing. It has exactly the same awakening effect on the mind as the use of the word 'crocus', by any other poet, instead of the more general 'yellow'.

Here is a poet in whom the sense through which the majority of men and women receive their clearest impressions is, by comparison with other senses, dormant. Campion simply is not interested in keeping his eye on the object; if he must use his eyes, he prefers to have to search, and follow movement. He likes the feel of air. But above all he loves the sound of things. His aural imagination is developed so much more fully than other perceptions in him, or than hearing in other poets, that it sometimes seems a will-o'-the-wisp fancy that he has consented to live anywhere but in the world of pure sound. But the poems are here as evidence of his wider human sympathies, and they are a sufficient proof of the rare rewards of that aural sensitiveness. Again, it seems impossible that anyone who disregards the sense of sight, the most generally and highly developed of the human senses, should succeed in conveying any of his auditory experiences. He is handicapped from the beginning by the fact that the technical terms of music are unfamiliar to most readers: either he must give up the idea of exact description, or he must create a musical-poetic diction of his own. Campion never seems to feel the need of technicalities; he does not go even as far as Jonson, who writes, 'Woe weeps out her division when she sings'. Campion is content with the general word 'music' and the occasional use of 'melody' and 'harmony'. He makes no attempt to translate his experience through analogies from other activities. There seems no solution to his problem of communication.

There is a solution, and it is the same as the answer to the earlier question. The study of Campion's versification is important, because without it a sharing of his experience is impossible. To examine subject alone leaves us with no means of distinguishing him from Anon.; to examine imagery alone is to find ourselves abandoned on an interesting road without a signpost. His matter as a whole remains meaningless until it has been defined and clarified by the sympathetic moulding of verbal form.

The six examples chosen from his poems, differing so widely as they do among themselves, do not nearly exhaust the variety of his metrical forms. It never seemed to occur to him that it was possible to write many songs in exactly the same measure. He knew instinctively that form affects mood; in the *Obseruations* he is obviously interested in the emotional effect of different forms of verse. But he never attempted to depend on the usually accepted effects of single feet; that left no room for subtlety. Always his ear was alert for the balance of groups, just as the ear of the musicians of the day was listening for balanced phrasing. The effort to relate one note or one syllable rigidly to the rest has been for the moment abandoned, and the result in the music and poetry of this period is an impression of directness and, deceptively, simplicity. The sureness of handling in those larger groups, a sureness setting the hearer's mind at rest and satisfying his rhythmical sense, gave room within the groups for a flexibility of utterance, for shifts of stress and complex syncopation, for resting and hurrying, for flying almost silently through the air-like movement of the 'f's and 'l's and 's's of a poem like **'Fol-**

low your Saint,' till something very like the complete re-creation of the artist's experience has been achieved. Campion's verse gives us a sense of sharing the completed mood of his poetic experience that no description could have conveyed, and it is the essence of a poem that its form should work on the emotions through the ear till it awakens the exact mood fitted for the reception of its matter.

Perhaps the hints given to us by Campion's practice will now enable us better to understand the poetry of his contemporaries.

Note

1. This song occurs also as No. XVIII in the First Part of *A Booke of Ayres,* 1601. There is another printed version of it in Alison's *An Houres Recreation in Musick,* 1606, and manuscript versions in Sloane MS. 4218; Harl. MS. 4064; MS. 17 B.L.; Rawl. MS. Poet. 31; Chetham MS. 8012.

   MSS. Sloane and B.L. state that the verses are by Fra. Bacon.

   Harl. MS. omits Stanza 4 and not, as Percival Vivian says, Stanza 5. Its variants are: line 2, life for minde; line 6, ioy for ioyes; line 9, tower for towres; line 17, But scorning all the chaunce: Vivian gives this line's variants for line 21.

   Variants in Sloane MS. are: line 17, care for cares; line 22, life for wealth.

   MS. B.L. has: line 8, fortune for sorrowes; line 17, care for cares; line 22, life for wealth.

Ian Spink (essay date 1968)

SOURCE: Spink, Ian. "Campion's Entertainment at Bougham Castle, 1617." In *Music in English Renaissance Drama,* pp. 57-74. Lexington: University of Kentucky Press, 1968.

[*In the following essay, Spink discusses Campion's sometimes disputed authorship of a masque given at a Brougham Castle in 1617 for King James I.*]

King James I spent the summer of 1617 in Scotland. Crossing the border on his return to London, he left Carlisle on August 6 and traveled south to Brougham Castle in Westmoreland, where he was to be the guest that night of Francis Clifford, Earl of Cumberland. Nichols says that the royal progress continued on to Appleby Castle the following day, but we shall see that the King must have stayed at least two nights at Brougham.[1]

The following year was published *The Ayres that were sung and played, at Brougham Castle in Westmerland, in the Kings Entertainment: Given by the Right Honourable the Earle of Cumberland, and his Right Noble* *Sonne the Lord Clifford. Composed by Mr. George Mason, and Mr. John Earsden. London: Printed by Thomas Snoham. Cum Privilegio. 1618.*[2]

No mention is made of the author of the entertainment, and (apart from these songs) neither a text nor a description ever seems to have been published. Vivian attributed it to Campion on the strength of a letter from the Earl to his son, which mentioned Campion in a likely connection; he also adduced some internal evidence in support of this theory—notably the similarity of image and occasion between the "Kings Good-night" (III) and one of Campion's Latin epigrams, **"De regis reditu e Scotia,"** written about the same time.[3] The original of the letter seems to have disappeared, for the time being at any rate, but Vivian's source was no doubt Whitaker's *History of Craven,* where the letter is quoted rather more extensively.[4]

> Sonn, I have till now expected y'r l'res, according to your promis at y'r departure: so did Geo. Minson [Mason] y'r directions touching the musick, whereupon he mought the better have writt to doctor Campion. He is now gone to my L'd President's, and will be redy to do as he heares from yo'. For my own opinion, albeit I will not dislyke y'r device, I fynde plainly, upon better consideration, the charge for that entertaynment will grow very great, besyde the musick; and that, instead of less'ning, my charge in gen'all encreaseth, and newe paim'ts come on, w'ch, without better providence hereafter, cannot be p'formed.

The letter continues to preach economy without referring again to the entertainment. As it stands, it is hardly positive proof of Campion's authorship. If Mason did consult Campion (as he "mought"), was it merely for advice from a more experienced musician, or for directions from the author? In any case, the Earl seemed dissatisfied with the plan at this stage, and it cannot be assumed that the version alluded to here, or Campion's connection with it, was unaltered before performance. But whatever revision may have been made, Campion certainly seems to have remained associated in some capacity. Among the Clifford household accounts, the following entry dated July 18, 1617, is significant: "It^m given this day in Reward to Sr Wm Constable his coachman who came to knowe what day he could be readie wth his Coach to Carrie Doctor Campion from Londsbrough to Brawhum ij^s and to ye Stewards boy whoe brought a letter to Doctor Campion from M^r Jo: Tailor—vi^d."[5]

These records, few though they are, suggest that the entertainment may have been written in some such manner as follows. The Earl's letter indicates that he had trusted his son with preparing it, and the reference to "y'r device" suggests that the basic conception was Lord Clifford's also. But for the actual text a poet was required, and Campion was chosen. Apart from his obvious experience, there were other reasons for this choice. The Earl and his son had been the dedicatees of Campion's *Two Bookes of Ayres* (*ca.* 1613), the dedicatory poem of which indicates a relationship already established.

What patron could I chuse, great *Lord,* but you?
Grave words your years may challenge as their owne,
And ev'ry note of Musicke is your due,
Whose House the *Muses* pallace I have knowne.[6]

The first draft of the entertainment was possibly too extravagant, and perhaps it was subsequently pruned in deference to the Earl's protest. Campion did not himself set the songs but dispatched them to the Earl's musician, George Mason, who was joined by John Earsden in composing the music. Sometime after July 18, Campion traveled to Brougham Castle to supervise preparations and to be on hand if required.

Of John Earsden we know nothing at all—not even which of these songs are his. George Mason was a musician in the Earl's household at least as early as 1610, when his name occurs among the accounts for Christmas of that year (at a salary of £7.13.4 *p.a.*).[7] But Anthony Wood complicates matters by saying that he graduated Mus. B. from Cambridge in 1601, and J. E. West states that he was organist of Trinity College, Cambridge, from 1612 to 1629.[8] However, recent investigations have been unable to support these statements, so for the moment they must be discounted.[9] The only mention of Mason in the Clifford accounts that might relate to preparations for the entertainment occurs on the same day as the reference to Campion quoted above. "Item paid this day to a man of Hull wch was sent for to Londsbrough to play on the Lute at Brougham by Mr George Mason but was sent back, their being noe occasion to use him—vi^s."[10] However, there would seem little point in trying to make much of this entry, though it deserves quoting.

The Entertainment

Brougham Castle is now a ruin. The Earl's niece and eventual heiress, Lady Anne Clifford, restored it and inscribed her work thus: "This Brougham Castle was repayred by the Ladie Anne Clifford, Countesse Dowager of Pembrooke, Dorsett, and Montgomery . . . in the yeares 1651 and 1652, after it had layen ruinous ever since about August 1617, when King James lay in it for a time in his Journie out of Skotland towards London, until this time."[11] However, it was sold for its stone early in the eighteenth century. The great hall and great chamber were both on the first floor and measured 41 by 21 feet, and 54 by 23 feet, respectively.[12] This was quite small by Whitehall standards, but not too small to prevent the Earl from putting on quite a spectacular show. The printed edition of the songs provides some hints as to the circumstances of their performance, and it is clear that there were in all three separate musical entertainments. The first consisted of **"A Dialogue sung the first night, the King being at Supper"** (I), **"Another Dialogue, to be sung at the same time"** (II), **"The Lords Welcome, sung before the Kings Good-night"** (X), and **"The Kings Good-night"** (III). As it appears, these items were sung at supper and before retiring on the night of the King's arrival, August 6. The reason **"The Lords Welcome"** was printed last in the collection, when it should obviously have been third, is not

clear; but possibly it was because this was John Earsden's only contribution (an inferior one, it must be admitted) and was kept separate for that reason. The second entertainment comprised items IV to VIII, evidently belonging to a masque, and this must have been celebrated on the second night, since the last chorus ends:

So humbly prostrate at thy sacred feet,
Our nightly sports and prophesies wee end.

And finally, **"The Farewell Song"** (IX) was no doubt sung at some brief entertainment given just before the King's departure on August 8.

This timetable has been set out in detail because of Nichols' assertion that the King stayed one night at Brougham. The text of the songs and the accompanying rubrics do not support him in this, however, for if the King stayed one night, what is the significance of the phrase, "sung the first night"? And the final couplets of both **"The Kings Good-night"** and the last masque song imply an end to a separate night's entertainment. That the King did in fact stay on at Brougham until the eighth is proved by a royal warrant enabling the Privy Council of Scotland to bring to summary justice any "declairit outlaw or notorious malefactour . . . Gevin at Broome Castell, the aucht of August 1617."[13]

The first night's entertainment was merely complimentary table music, larded (no doubt) with a few speeches, the gist of which can easily be imagined. The general drift of the following night's masque is fairly clear from the text of the songs. In subject matter it seems to have been the usual sort of thing; an anti-masque combining exotic and rustic elements, culminating in the main masque with an apotheosis of the King as the embodiment of all virtue. A wandering band of gypsies arrives on the scene—a hallowed spot which they recognize as the dwelling place of Honour and Grace. They break into an "anticke dance" and then give place to a crowd of country lads and lassies. A ballad is sung, then follows a rustic dance. A gypsy steps forward and sings a song invoking "a chaine of prophecies." At this point, or hereabout, the scene may have been transformed, revealing the kingly attributes of Truth, Peace, Love, Honour, Long-life, and Illustrious Posterity in a tableau or procession, to the accompaniment of a final hymn of praise.

Despite the similarity of occasion between this and Campion's earlier *Cavendish House Entertainment* (1613), it is by no means a reworking of the same formula. It is true that both have rustic interludes (the rural setting of both dwellings was no doubt the reason for this), but the treatment seems Jonsonian rather, and generally dissimilar from Campion's four authentic masques. Indeed, consciously or unconsciously, Jonson may have been influenced by reports of the Brougham Castle entertainment in his *Gipsies Metamorphosed,* performed almost exactly four years later, while the King was again in progress. Greg's outline of Jonson's masque shows the extent of the similarity.

The masque itself opens with the appearance of the Gipsies, and after some introductory speeches the Jackman invites the spectators to have their fortunes told. The Captain tells the King's. . . . These concluded, enter eight country clowns and wenches, who supply what may be called an antimasque. . . . After this . . . is sung the ballad of Cock Lorel. . . . The rest of the company now reappear, "changed" from their Gipsy disguise to their own fashion of lords and gentlemen of the court. . . . The conclusion in praise of King and Prince consists of verses by the metamorphosed Gipsies alternating with songs by the Jackman.[14]

It can be seen that both masques have three stages in common. First, the arrival of the gypsies; second, the rural interlude or anti-masque; and third ("unmasked now and cleare" as the Brougham Castle text expresses it) the gypsies' praise of the King in terms that are impressive enough, but all the more so because of the gypsies' supposed supernatural powers of divination. Jonson's masque is a work of considerable intricacy, more so than Campion's is likely to have been; but reduced to essentials, the relationship between the two seems quite pronounced and may indicate some sort of influence on Jonson by Campion.

Tuneful and Declamatory Ayres

Elsewhere I have suggested that the origins of the English declamatory ayre are to be found primarily in the songs written for the court masques performed between 1609 and 1613.[15] The idea that English composers began imitating Italian monodists and opera composers within a few years of 1600 seems hard to justify, in my opinion. For one thing, by the date of the earliest English declamatory songs (*ca.* 1609), only a handful of monodic collections had been published even in Italy, and although a few manuscripts may have penetrated England during the first decade of the century, so little indication of this now survives that it cannot have represented much of an influence at the time. Two songs by Caccini were printed in Robert Dowland's *Musicall Banquet* (1610), and a manuscript of his songs dating from before 1618 or so is extant at St. Michael's College, Tenbury. The emigrant Italian Angelo Notari, who arrived from Venice about 1610, was aware of the monodic style, as his *Prime Musiche Nuove* (London, 1613) shows; but apart from the queen's Italian musician, Giovanni Maria Lugaro, no other important Italian musician is known to have visited England during the early years of James I's reign. On the other hand, Italian music and musicians were certainly in fashion. John Cooper (alias Giovanni Coperario) affected an Italian version of his name, possibly after a visit to Italy about 1600; and Campion's patron, Sir Thomas Monson, is reported to have been "at infinite charge in breeding some [singers] in Italy."[16] John Dowland had been there in 1595, but without an immediately noticeable change in the style of his songs. Constantijn Huygens, while in London, refers to a visit to the house of the Ambassador of Savoy, Giovanni Francesco Biondi "ou il y a un collège de musiciens touts Italiens," but this was not

until 1618.[17] It is true that the works of many Italian madrigalists were well known, but monodic publications do not seem to have been in demand at all. And had they exerted any influence, it might be expected that the general style of the English ayre would show some change before or about 1610, whereas in fact this tendency is only traceable in a dozen or so of the more than 550 lute songs published up to 1622. Significantly, most of the dozen can be classified as masque songs.

It seems more likely that the peculiar conditions of masque performance affected the style of song and singing, reinforced perhaps by a vague awareness of what was happening in Italy. The English ayre, as practiced by Dowland and his school, was either semicontrapuntal in conception—almost madrigalian—with the lute accompaniment simulating a polyphonic texture, or else purely melodic. In either case, it was essentially chamber music of a most intimate kind. It was too exquisite in style for the stage, especially for the bombast of the court masque in which the demands of audibility necessitated a more rhetorical and exaggerated type of declamation, with a simpler harmonic accompaniment in support. Such an inflated, heroic style was very different from the beguiling subtleties of the English lute song.

Declamatory traits can be observed increasingly in Alfonso Ferrabosco II's surviving masque songs for Jonson's *Masque of Blackness* (1605), *Lord Haddington's Masque* (1608), *Masque of Beauty* (1608), *Masque of Queens* (1609), *Oberon* (1611), and *Love freed from Ignorance and Folly* (1611);[18] in John Dowland's ceremonial "Far from the triumphing court" and the two songs "Welcome black night" and "Cease these false sports," probably written for a masque celebrating the wedding of his patron, Theophilus, Lord Howard de Walden, to Lady Elizabeth Home in March 1611/12;[19] and still more so in Nicholas Lanier's "Bring away this sacred tree" from Campion's *Squire's Masque* (1613).[20] If anything, the style is even more developed in some of Mason's songs for the Brougham Castle entertainment. It might have been supposed that his isolated position in the border country would have prevented his being acquainted with the latest musical trends at court. But in fact, such an important household as the Cliffords' could hardly be regarded as provincial. The estates may have been more than three hundred miles from London, but though the Earl was naturally retiring, his son was very much a man about town, and both were forced to play the courtier because of their position.

Some of the differences between the two styles of ayre have already been suggested. The declamatory style sought to make the rhythm and melody of the voice part dependent on the accents, quantities, and inflections of the verse, at the expense of purely musical considerations. Hand in hand with this went a continuo type of bass that was realized on a lute or theorbo in chordal style. Written-out tablature became rarer, and the bass part was not even figured, as a rule.

A clear contrast is provided between the melodic and declamatory styles in the following examples.[21]

At the beginning of the second verse of **"The shadowes dark'ning our intents"** (VII), the declamation clearly follows and exaggerates the rhetorical qualities of the verse. The extent to which the music depends on the words can be gauged by considering for a moment the music without them—it becomes meaningless. On the other hand, the beginning of **"Welcome, welcome king of guests"** (III) shows no such dependence: rhythmically and melodically the music exists in its own right. It was at the dramatic climaxes of these sorts of entertainments that the declamatory style came into its own. Indeed, to a great extent it was the supernatural and triumphal aspects of the Jacobean masque that called the style into being. The gypsy's invocation, **"The shadows dark'ning our intents,"** and the ensuing pageant of Truth, Peace, Love, Honour, etc., which concludes the masque, are more or less highly declamatory in style; so too is the second and more serious of the first night's dialogues, and also the final **"Farewell Song."** Apart from the bass "character-song" **"Come follow me my wandring mates"** (IV), the music of the anti-masque is essentially tuneful, as indeed one would expect from the titles of the songs—**"A Ballad"** (V) and **"The Dance"** (VI).

Although the accounts for the entertainment have disappeared, the score gives some indication of the musical resources required. The structure of the ensemble numbers (VI and VIII) indicates the need for six singers; solo episodes being allotted to two basses, three tenors, and a treble—or more likely four tenors, one reading from a treble clef at the octave below.[22] The three solo songs are shared between a bass and two tenors, one song each. In addition, there were undoubtedly speaking parts and probably a troup of dancers as well as supers for the final tableau. So far as instruments are concerned, the printed tablature indicates a lute accompaniment (in two instances a bass lute), but other instruments of similar type were probably available, since a single instrument would hardly have been able to support the full chorus. The second dialogue (II) is the only song actually supplied with an instrumental bass part (that is, a bass part without words underlaid), but the omission elsewhere was perhaps an economy in the printing. Bass chorus parts almost certainly would have been doubled by the bass viol, especially since one seems to have been available. If the Carlisle waits were employed (or the musicians of some other town or nobleman), as they had been on previous occasions, the full chorus parts may have been doubled by instruments.[23] At Caversham, cornets, violins, and other "divers Instruments" had been available; and the instrumental resources used in Campion's court masques were, of course, extremely lavish.[24]

THE FIRST NIGHT'S MUSIC

The music for the first night consisted of four items; two dialogues sung at supper (I-II), **"The Lords Welcome"** (X) and **"The Kings Good-night"** (III). The dialogues are sharply contrasted in style. The first, in C major, is pleasantly tuneful and (like the words) rather banal—"Melodie now is needfull here, / It will helpe to mend our cheare." The second is much more impressive. C major turns to C minor, and the voices declaim:

Now is the time, now is the hower
When joy first blest this happy Bower.

Although in dialogue form, apparently the singers do not represent dramatic personages. Both dialogues end with a three-part chorus.

It has already been suggested that **"The Lords Welcome"** was Earsden's solitary contribution, a fact that caused it to be printed out of order at the back of the book. At any rate, Mason would seem to have been the senior partner (his name was printed on the title page in larger type), and the other songs show a certain consistency in style. For example, the striking similarity of cadence figure in numbers I, III, and VIII suggests a single composer, and in their turn these three songs are perfectly representative in style of the others, apart from **"The Lords Welcome."** This, with its uneasy changes in meter and general inexpertness, stands apart and may therefore be ascribed to the second composer, John Earsden.

"The Kings Good-night" is for tenor (treble clef) and bass, the last line of each verse being treated as a chorus in common time, echoing the phrase "Good-night" between voices rather charmingly. It is the imagery of the second verse of this song that Vivian found reflected in the epigram "De regis reditu e Scotia"—the King's return to England being a "northern dawn" outshining the usual "Roses of the East."[25]

THE SECOND NIGHT'S MUSIC: THE "ANTI-MASQUE"

The following night the main entertainment was presented. The first part or anti-masque, traditionally of a somewhat bizarre nature, featured gypsies and rustics. Reference to "our right Aegyptian race" is made explicit later on, but the popular conception of gypsies as a nomadic, clairvoyant, dusky, moon-worshiping race, is expressed in the first song (IV).

Come follow me my wandring mates,
Sonnes and daughters of the Fates:
Friends of night, that oft have done
Homage to the horned Moone.

Alone of the solo songs, this one is set for bass. As such it belongs to an interesting genre of early seventeenth-century "character songs"—usually play-songs expressing madness or the possession of supernatural powers, and sometimes of a humorous nature. The tone quality of the low voice and the dramatic style of declamation combine to conjure up the particular atmosphere required, in this case a mixture of the sinister and the exotic. Often, the voice merely "divides" the thorough-bass; that is, it fits syllables to the instrumental bass part with little attempt at melodic independence. Some idea of the general style, as well as particular details of expression, can be gained from Figure 9. The song suggests that an "anticke dance" followed.

Then comes the ballad of **"Queen Dido"** (V). Whether this is sung by one of the gypsies, or one of the rustics (who enter hereabout), or some other character, is not clear. Nor is the reason clear for the doubtful moral lesson of the last verse—it preaches rank infidelity without a hint of irony. And whatever the covert practices of the court might have been, it is unlikely that overt approval of such a doctrine could have been tolerated. Possibly the missing text makes clear that a contrast is intended between this heartlessness and the idyllic country lovers of the following dance. "Sib is all in all to me, / There is no Queene of Love but she."

Despite its title, it is doubtful that this song was really a traditional ballad, though it may be said to have become one later. There certainly was a "Dido Ballad" as early as 1565, known under various names such as "The Wanderynge Prince," "Queen Dido," "Troy Town" (after its first line, "When Troy Town for ten-years wars"), and the tune was very popular.[26] But the stanzas of "Troy Town" have six lines, each of eight syllables. Campion's ballad has ten lines to each verse and is rather more intricate metrically. They are obviously related in subject matter, but no version of "Dido was the Carthage Queen" earlier than Mason's *Ayres* is known at present. Stafford Smith, however, observed in a note on this item that "the last verse of the famous Ballad 'Dido Queen' was on this occasion, added to the more ancient song. The editor [Smith] has in his possession an older copy, without it."[27] If Smith was not mistaken, then of course Campion's authorship must be questioned and the traditional nature of the ballad asserted. But he may have confused the two ballads in his mind, intending to point out that the "moral" of the last verse is not to be found in the older and (as it happens) different version. Campion's "ballad" was printed again (without music, and with a few textual variants) in *Love's Court of Conscience* (1637), and again in D'Urfey's *Wit and Mirth; Or Pills to Purge Melancholy*, V (1714), also VI (1720), to a new tune.

It is more than likely that here we have an imitation of the ballad style on the part of both the poet and the composer. The tune is forthright in character and admirably suited to dancing. The **"Dance"** (VI) that follows continues in the same vein, employing similar melodic phrases and cadence figures. The first section is divided between six soloists, each of whom sings a couplet in praise of one of their number, though not necessarily of the opposite sex, since a bass sings:

> Tommy hath a looke as bright,
> As is the rosie morning light.

Each having sung his piece, they all sing together:

> Let us in a lovers round,
> Circle all this hallowed ground,

breaking into three time at "Softly, softly, trip and goe, trip and goe." A description of the dance follows:

> Forward then, and backe again;
> Here and there, and every where;
> Winding to and winding fro;
> Skipping hye and lowting low.
> And like lovers hand in hand
> March around, and make a stand.

The final couplet is marked "*Chorus*," but (as in the case of the previous four lines, marked "*All*") only a treble part and lute accompaniment is provided. Possibly, chorus parts were not printed, in this instance, but condensed into the accompaniment.

THE MAIN MASQUE

Country sports and all pretense are set aside, and the solemn moment has arrived when the gypsy ushers in "a chaine of prophecies" (VII):

> And Heaven-borne Truth our Notes shall guide,
> One by one, while wee relate
> That which shall tye both Time, and Fate.

It is here that the dramatic capabilities of the declamatory ayre are seen at their best, for no other style could create the sense of awe and pregnant anticipation of this moment. The change to a bass lute accompaniment also adds to the effect. Verbal and musical ideas unfold together, reaching a pitch at the words "Unmasked now and cleare." At this moment of climax the scene was probably transformed from what was presumably a rural setting to some nobler prospect appropriate to a pageant of kingly virtues. Whether Truth, Peace, Love, Honour, and the rest actually sing, or whether they only form a procession or tableau, cannot be said for certain. Each "virtue" has a solo verse, the last phrase of which is echoed in a four-part chorus, like a kind of vocal ritornello between verses. But since the solo voices required are the same as in the previous ensemble number (VI), perhaps they merely constituted an off-stage chorus in both, the "rustics" in VI and the "virtues" in VIII being masquers. A final chorus concludes the night's entertainment:

> Truth, Peace, Love, Honour and Long-life attend
> Thee, and all those that from thy loynes descend.
> With us the Angels in this *Chorus* meet:
> So humbly prostrate at thy sacred feet,
> Our nightly sports and prophesies wee end.

THE FAREWELL

The circumstances of this final show are more difficult to establish. Presumably, it was given sometime on August 8 before the King's departure as part of a farewell entertainment such as Campion had provided at Caversham House four years previously. This had taken place in "an Arbour in the lower Garden" and the sentiments of "a mournefull parting song" are closely paralleled.[28] But despite the appalling, sycophantic hyperbole of the words, which must surely have sickened even in 1617, **"The Farewell Song"** (IX) achieves an effect of genuine pathos through its music. Again a declamatory style is employed, smoother and more sustained in movement than before but nevertheless looking forward to Henry Lawes rather than back to the Elizabethans. As with **"The shadowes dark'ning our intents"** (VII), the solemnity of the occasion is underlined by the use of a bass lute accompaniment. The music for both verses is substantially the same, but the second verse has been written out in full since certain declamatory features of the first verse would not have fitted the second. These necessary modifications are interesting, for they show the composer's concern over such details—incidentally, it reveals an incipient tendency to compose "from the bass up."

These *Ayres* have been understandably disregarded by musical historians up to now. Being in the new, anti-lyrical, early seventeenth-century declamatory style, for the most part, and displaying an inferior technique in the traditional sense, they failed to excite either the interest or the admiration of Fellowes and Warlock in the 1920's—Warlock said that they "contain no music of any particular interest except one very robust tune, **'Dido was the Carthage Queen.'"**[29] At least he had looked at them, as had Parry (in Stafford Smith's edition). But they are not unimportant when considered as a representative and remarkably complete example of Jacobean masque songs. In them, more so perhaps than in any previous surviving masque music, we find an attempt at musical characterization and a sense of dramatic atmosphere conveyed by musical means. Some of the effects may be naive by later standards, but the music is not less interesting for that reason.

A full appreciation of these songs really depends on one's ability to view them within their dramatic context, and it has been one of the purposes of the present study to fill in this background. But it is a reciprocal process, and an enhanced knowledge and understanding of certain aspects of the drama—in this case the development of the Stuart masque—follows almost inevitably.

Notes

1. John Nichols, *The Progresses of King James I* (London, 1828), III, pp. 390-92.

2. These songs were edited by J. Stafford Smith in his *Musica Antiqua* (London, 1812), pp. 150-65, but without the original lute part and with other deficiencies. The present writer has recently edited them for Stainer & Bell, Ltd., in *The English Lute-Songs*, 2nd Ser., Vol. XVIII (London, 1962), pp. 23-48. The words are included in Percival Vivian's edition of *Campion's Works* (Oxford, 1909), pp. 227-34, and in E. H. Fellowes' *English Madrigal Verse* (Oxford, 1920), pp. 553-58.

3. Vivian, *Campion's Works,* p. li.

4. T. D. Whitaker, *The History and Antiquities of the Deanery of Craven* (London, 1805), pp. 263-64. The source may possibly have been one of the letters referred to under the date June 6, 1617, as "Copies of letters from the Earl to his son" in the appendix to *The Third Report of the Royal Commission on Historical Manuscripts* (London, 1872), p. 38, but which Mr. T. S. Wragg, the Keeper of the Duke of Devonshire's Collection at Chatsworth, informs me can no longer be traced. I am very grateful to Mr. Wragg for his kindness in answering my inquiries and for transcribing certain entries in the Bolton MSS.

5. Bolton MSS, Vol. XCVII.

6. Vivian, *Campion's Works,* p. 113.

7. W. L. Woodfill, *Musicians in English Society* (Princeton, 1953), p. 257.

8. Bodleian Library, Oxford, MS Wood, D. 19 (4), fol. 89v., and J. E. West, *Cathedral Organists Past and Present* (2nd ed.; London, 1921), p. 127.

9. The words of an anthem by George Mason are given in James Clifford's Divine Services and Anthems (2nd ed.; 1664), p. 281, and BM Add. MS 30826-28 includes some "Pavanes" attributed to "Mr. Mason" (Nos. 3-10). It may be significant that the same MS contains an anonymous "Trinitye Colledg Pavan" (No. 17), but to draw any conclusion from this would be exceedingly hazardous. The source of West's information is obscure and does not appear to be in any likely publication prior to 1899, the date of the first edition of his *Cathedral Organists.* It may have been communicated to him privately. Eitner was able to use West's note on Mason in the *Quellen-Lexicon* (Leipzig, 1901), VI, p. 369, since when it has been repeated frequently. However, it is not impossible that Mason (who might have been a Cambridge Mus. B.,—in 1601 an unnamed candidate graduated in that degree, according to C. Abdy Williams' *Degrees in Music* [London, 1893], p. 124) left the earl's employment in 1611 (his name does not seem to occur in the accounts between then and 1617) and was commissioned to compose the Brougham Castle music while in some other employment, perhaps as organist of Trinity College. But there is no evidence of this.

10. Bolton MSS, Vol. XCVII, dated July 18, 1617.

11. Nichols, *The Progresses of King James I,* p. 391.

12. See *An Inventory of the Historical Monuments in Westmoreland,* Royal Commission on Ancient and Historical Monuments, England (London, 1936) pp. 60-66, for plans and description.

13. *The Register of the Privy Council of Scotland, 1616-1619,* ed. David Masson (Edinburgh, 1894), XI, p. 217. Nichols' dates are derived from "Coles MSS (Brit. Mus.) Vol. XLVI; transcribed by him [Coles] . . . from the original drafts found among the papers

of Mr. Martin, the Suffolk Antiquary. Another copy of these Gests is among the MSS of Gonville and Caius College, Cambridge, No. 123" (Nichols, *The Progresses of King James I,* pp. 257, 389). However, these dates can be shown to be wrong in respects other than the Brougham Castle visitation.

14. W. W. Greg, *Jonson's Masque of Gipsies* (London, 1952), pp. 2-3.

15. In "English Cavalier Songs, 1620-1660," *Proceedings of the Royal Musical Association,* 86th session (1959/60), pp. 61-64.

16. Article on Monson in DNB, XII (1921), p. 646.

17. W. J. A. Jonckbloet and J. P. N. Land, *Corréspondance et ouvres musicales de Constantin Huygens* (Leyden, 1882), p. 1.

18. Those from masques before 1609 were printed in his *Ayres* (1609), see Nos. 3, 11, 18-23; those from the masques of 1611 are in St. Michael's College, Tenbury, MS 1018, fols. 36-37v. E. H. Fellowes edited the *Ayres* in *The English School of Lutenist Song Writers,* 2nd ser., Vol. XVI (London, 1927), and J. P. Cutts transcribed those from MS in "Le Rôle de la Musique dans les Masques de Ben Jonson," *Les Fêtes de la Renaissance,* ed. J. Jacquot (Paris, 1956), pp. 285-302. See also A. J. Sabol, *Songs and Dances for the Stuart Masque* (Providence, R.I., 1959), pp. 34-50, and the present author's edition of "Alfonso Ferrabosco II: Manuscript Songs," *The English Lute-Songs,* 2nd ser., Vol. XIX (London, 1966), pp. 14-25.

19. The first of these songs was printed in Robert Dowland's *Musicall Banquet* (1610), No. 8; the other two in John Dowland's *A Pilgrimes Solace* (1612), Nos. 20-21. Modern editions of all three are in E. H. Fellowes, *The English Lute-Songs,* 1st Ser., Vol. XIV (London, 1925), pp. 90-108.

20. Printed at the back of Campion's *The Description of a Maske . . . at the Mariage of . . . the Earle of Somerset* (1614) and reprinted in Stafford Smith's *Musica Antiqua,* p. 60, where it is falsely assigned to Davenant's *Luminalia* (1637). C. H. H. Parry quoted this version in "The Music of the XVIIth Century," *Oxford History of Music* (2nd ed.; London, 1938), p. 200. See also Sabol, p. 20, n. 35.

21. The figures are from *The English Lute-Songs,* 2nd Ser., Vol. XVIII (London: Stainer & Bell, Ltd., 1962). Reproduced by permission of the publishers.

22. But in the *Caversham House Entertainment* occurs the following direction, *"the* Robin-Hood-*men faine two Trebles"* (Vivian, *Campion's Works,* p. 80).

23. Numerous payments to waits are recorded in the Clifford account books, see Woodfill, *Musicians in English Society,* pp. 257-58, and there are many references to household instruments. An inventory of the musical instruments in one of the houses of the late Earl of Cumberland, compiled about 1644, includes "In the great hall . . . one pair of organs, one harpsicon. . . . In the gallery . . . one viol chest with six stringed instruments," see *ibid.,* p. 279.

24. *Ibid.,* pp. 192-93.

25. *Tho: Campiani Epigrammatum Liber Primus* (1619), No. 188; see Vivian, *Campion's Works,* pp. li, 263, 372.

26. See *Bishop Percy's Folio Manuscript, Ballads and Romances,* ed. J. W. Hales and F. J. Furnivall (London, 1868), III, pp. 260-62 and 499-506. Also W. Chappel, *Popular Music of the Olden Time* (London, 1859), I, pp. 370-72. I must thank Mr. David Greer for first drawing my attention to these (and other) references.

27. Stafford Smith, *Musica Antiqua,* p. 10.

28. Vivian, *Campion's Works,* pp. 86-87.

29. P. Warlock, *The English Ayre* (London, 1926), p. 122.

J. W. Binns (essay date 1974)

SOURCE: Binns, J. W. "The Latin Poetry of Thomas Campion." In *The Latin Poetry of English Poets,* edited by J. W. Binns, pp. 1-25. London: Routledge & Kegan Paul, 1974.

[*In the essay that follows, Binns evaluates Campion's major poems written in Latin.*]

About one-third of Thomas Campion's poetical output is written in Latin. It is customary by and large to ignore this in any assessment of his poetry. Yet a study of his Latin poetry is sufficient to modify the traditional view of Campion as a poet memorable chiefly for his agreeable but minor Elizabethan lyrics. Campion's two longest poems are both in Latin, and in these he forsakes the brief lyric and writes kinds of poetry which he never attempted in English. The Latin elegies are an important part of the corpus of his love poetry, whilst in his numerous epigrams he displays his abilities as a writer of short poems in other than lyric mould. The first publication by Campion of a volume of Latin poetry in 1595, and the second revised and augmented edition of 1619, are important landmarks planted near the beginning and end of his poetical career.

The first collection of poems to be published under Campion's name was the *Poemata* of 1595. This contains the poem **"Ad Thamesin"** celebrating the defeat of the Spanish Armada, the first 231 lines of the mythological poem **"Umbra,"** a book of sixteen elegies, principally amatory ones, and 129 epigrams. In the 1619 collection of Latin poems entitled *Epigrammatum Libri II,* the mythological poem **"Umbra"** was completed, most though not all of the elegies were reprinted with slight revisions and the addition of two new ones, whilst of the 453 epigrams in two books, over 360 appeared for the first time. Thomas Campion's Latin poetry thus falls conveniently into three main types: the elegies, the poems conceived on a more grandiose and extensive pattern, and the epigrams.

In his own day Campion's Latin poetry did not pass unnoticed, and several testimonies survive from the late 1590s onwards to bear witness to the impression he made on his contemporaries. The poet William Vaughan writes in a poem in his *Poematum Libellus* (London, 1598) that the Muses have taken up residence in England, and, praising amongst other poets, both Latin and English, Gager, More, Camden, Spenser, Daniel, Breton, and Drayton, he says of Campion:

> Hic cui cognomen tribuit Campana, volutas
>   O Thoma rectis metra ligata modis.

> (sig. C4r.)

(Here you, O Thomas, to whom Campania herself gives a surname, roll out rhythms bound by strict measures.)

Campion was also praised, along with other English writers of Latin poetry, by Francis Meres in his *Palladis Tamia* (London, 1598): 'these English men being Latine Poets, *Gualter Haddon, Nicholas Car, Gabriel Haruey, Christopher Ocland, Thomas Newton* with his *Leyland, Thomas Watson, Thomas Campion, Brunswerd* and *Willey,* haue attained good report and honorable aduancement in the Latin Empyre.'[1] It is clear from the context of Meres's remarks—he has just been speaking of continental neo-Latin poets who had 'obtained renown and good place among the auncient Latine Poets'—that by his use of the term 'the Latin Empyre', Meres believes that Campion is one of those who merit comparison with the classical Roman poets. Campion's friend Charles Fitzgeffrey praised both his epigrams and elegies in a volume of verse, the *Affaniae,* published at Oxford in 1601:[2]

> Primus apud *Britones* Latiis Epigrammata verbis,
>   More, tuo scripsit nomine notus *Eques*:
> Huic aetate quidem, sed non tamen arte secundus,
>   Cui *Campus* nomen, *Delius* ingenium.

(The first Briton to write epigrams in Latin was that famous knight More, who had the same name as you [i.e. Thomas]. Second to him in point of time, yet not in art, comes the man whose name comes from 'camp' [*lit.* field] but whose talent from Apollo.)

> O cuius genio *Romana* Elegia debet
>   Quantum *Nasoni* debuit ante suo!
> Ille, sed invitus, *Latiis* deduxit ab oris
>   In *Scythicos* fines barbaricosque *Getas,*
> Te duce caeruleos invisit prima *Britannos*
>   Quamque potest urbem dicere iure suam:
> (Magnus enim domitor late, dominator et orbis
>   Viribus effractis *Cassivelane* tuis
> Iulius *Ausonium* populum Latiosque penates
>   Victor in hac olim iusserat urbe coli.)
> Ergo relegatas *Nasonis* crimine Musas
>   In patriam revocas restituisque suis.

(O thou to whose talent Roman elegy is as much indebted as she was previously to her own Ovid! He, albeit unwillingly, left the shores of Italy for the lands

of the Scythians and the barbarous Getae. Under your guidance Elegy now visits the blue-dyed Britons for the first time, and the city which she can rightly call her own. (For the great Julius, a conqueror far and wide, and the ruler of the world, when he had broken your power, Cassivellaunus, had once victoriously ordered that the Italian people and the Latin gods should be revered in this city.) Thus you call back to your native land the Muses banished by the crime of Ovid, and restore them to their devotees.)

Campion is in this latter poem seen as an Ovid returned to life, and his Latin elegies do indeed form a substantial portion of his amatory verse. His eighteen elegies are with only two exceptions devoted to erotic themes. In the elegy which introduces the group of elegies contained in the 1595 edition of his poems, which was, however, omitted from the 1619 revision, Campion appeals for a sympathetic audience, and regards himself as the first British writer of elegy:[3]

> Ite procul, tetrici, moneo, procul ite severi,
>   Ludit censuras pagina nostra graves,
> Ite senes nisi forte aliquis torpente medulla
>   Carminibus flammas credit inesse meis.
> Aptior ad teneros lusus florentior aetas,
>   Vel iuvenis, vel me docta puella legat.
> Et vatem celebrent Bruti de nomine primum
>   Qui molles elegos et sua furta canat.

> (1a.1-8)

(Away with you, I say, you harsh and crabbed old men, away with you, my page mocks your stern censures. Away with you, old men, unless perchance some one of you with sluggish marrow believes that there is fire in my poems. A more flourishing age is more suitable for tender dalliance. May either a young man or a learned girl read me, and may they praise me as the first poet of the Britons to compose tender elegies telling of the stratagems of love.)

Campion's use of this topos of Roman love elegy suggests that he regarded his poetry as light-hearted, written for youth and laughter rather than for censorious old age, for the *tetrici* and *severi* of Latin poetry (cf. Martial 11.2.7, Catullus 5.2, Ovid, *Am.* 2.1.3 ff). Campion here makes deliberate use of the vocabulary of Latin amatory poems, *teneros lusus* (cf. Ovid, *Am.* 3.1.27), *docta puella* (cf. *A.A.* 2.281), *sua furta* (cf. *Her.* 18.64).

Campion's amatory elegies delineate various situations in the course of a love affair: falling in love at first sight, the fickleness of a former mistress, the folly of a friend in leaving his mistress in the poet's charge, the desire for hindrances which will add spice and allurement to a love affair, the joys of successful love, a complaint that wealth has more power than beauty to attract women's love, protestations of fidelity, accounts of assignations, advice to a lover. Three different women appear in the love elegies: Sybilla (elegies 1, 8) Caspia (6, 13a), and Mellea (5, 9, 4a). In the other poems the name of the woman involved is not given. But no clear picture emerges of a woman vibrant with individuality. Campion drew much of the inspiration for his verse from Roman amatory poetry, some perhaps from life, but the object of his affections remains shadowy. The force of his mistress's personality, whether real or imaginary, does not impress itself on the verse.

Nonetheless Campion builds up a convincing amatory landscape: he depicts a world in which the mistress is physically beautiful. Typically she is described as a *lauta puella* (an elegant girl) (5.18); she is *speciosa* (dazzling) (6.31). In a passage of advice to a lover, a range of imaginary charms is sketched:

> Quod pulchrum varium est; species non una probatur,
>   Nec tabulis eadem conspicienda Venus.
> Sive lepos oculis, in vultu seu rosa fulget,
>   Compositis membris si decor aptus inest,
> Gratia sive pedes, leviter seu brachia motat;
>   Undique spectanti retia tendit Amor.

                                                    (11.5-10)

(Beauty is manifold; it is not just one facet which is approved. We see different representations of Venus in paintings. Whether a girl's eyes sparkle with charm, roses gleam in her cheeks, or there's a becoming grace in her shapely limbs, whether she moves her feet daintily, or her arms gently, Love lays his snares on all sides for the beholder.)

The many forms in which the ideal woman of Campion's dreams may manifest herself are adumbrated in 8.39-42:

> Candida seu nigra est, mollis seu dura, pudica
>   Sive levis, iuvenis sive adeo illa senex;
> Qualiscunque datur, modo sit formosa, rogare
>   Non metuam, et longa sollicitare prece.

(Whether she is fair or dark, complaisant or unyielding, modest or shameless, young or even quite an old woman—whatever kind of woman comes my way, so long as she's beautiful, I shan't be afraid of approaching her and imploring her with a long entreaty.)

There is in this a clear echo of Ovid's stated willingness to fall in love with women of all types in *Am.* 2.4. The joys of Caspia's surrender are also described in physical, tactile terms, which again echo Ovid closely (*Am.* 1.5):

> Quas ego, quam cupide vidi tetigique papillas!
>   Quam formosa inter brachia molle latus!
> Qualia inhaerenti spiravit basia labro!
>   Qualia, sed castis non referenda viris!

                                                    (13a.9-12)

(How eagerly did I see and touch those breasts of hers! How soft her side between those shapely arms! What kisses did she breathe with clinging lip! What—! But chaste men should not be told such things.)

The rewards of love are the *suaves . . . horas, delicias, lusus, basia docta, iocos* (7.3-4) (sweet hours, voluptuousness, dalliance, experienced kisses, lasciviousness).

An antithesis is suggested between the polished cultivation of the town and the boorish rusticity of the country (cf. Tibullus 2.3.1ff):

> Ergo meam ducet, deducet ab urbe puellam
>   Cui rutilo sordent ora perusta cane?
> Mellea iamne meo valedicere possit amori,
>   Urbeque posthabita vilia rura colet?

                                                    (9.1-4)

(Will a man whose face is basely burnt by the heat of the summer sun marry my girl, and lead her away from the city? Could Mellea now say farewell to my love, and dwell in the vile countryside, despising the city?)

> Horrida rura virum, sed non metuenda, tenebant;
>   Tutum rivali fecit in urbe locum.

                                                    (8.9-10)

(The uncouth countryside detained your husband, but there was no reason for me to fear it. It made a safe place for his rival in the city.)

A bedchamber is the setting for an assignation (elegies 8 and 10), whilst an idealized vernal or floral landscape provides the backcloth for love in elegies 1 and 4a.

In the revised and augmented 1619 edition of Campion's poems, we have thirteen elegies, of which two, nos 1 and 3, appear for the first time. The other eleven had appeared in the 1595 edition, though a few slight alterations to the text were made in the new edition, whilst five elegies contained in the earlier edition were not reprinted. The number of lines was thus reduced from 578 to 440. The arrangement of the poems in the 1619 edition was considerably different. Thus, of the thirteen elegies in the 1619 edition, nos 1 and 3 were new to the volume, no. 2 in the 1619 edition had previously appeared as no. 8 in the 1595 edition, whilst nos 4-13 of the 1619 edition had appeared as nos 3, 5, 7, 10, 11, 12, 2, 15, 6, and 9 respectively in the earlier edition. Campion probably regrouped the elegies in the later edition so as to bring the poems into a closer thematic relationship. Thus after the new poem beginning:

> Ver anni Lunaeque fuit; pars verna diei

                                                    (1.1)

(It was the Springtime of the year and of the Moon, the vernal part of the day)

(cf. Lucretius 1.10) which, since it describes love at first sight, is an appropriate one for beginning the collection, there follow elegies 2 and 3, not dissimilar in length (32 and 24 lines respectively), each dealing with a similar theme, **"La Ronde,"** elegy 2 telling of the poet's abandonment by his mistress in favour of Ottalus, whom she will in turn abandon, whilst no. 3 recounts the abandonment of Calvus by Calvus' mistress in favour of the poet.

The final elegy of the 1619 edition concludes with a non-amatory poem addressed to Campion's friend Edward Michelborne consoling him on the death of his sister, a poem which ends on a note of hope. The two preceding poems, nos 11 and 12, form an antithetical pair of almost equal length (18 and 20 lines). Poem 11 opens with a recommendation that love should be shunned:

> Qui sapit ignotas timeat spectare puellas

> (A wise man should be afraid of looking at unknown girls)

whilst poem 12 concludes with a recommendation that advantage should be taken of the amatory opportunities that present themselves:

> Mane rosas si non decerpis, vespere lapsas
> Aspicies spinis succubuisse suis.

> (12.17-18)

> (If you don't pluck roses in the morning, you will see them drooping at eventide, sunk down on their thorns.)

Elegy 5 (28 lines) complains of the fickleness of women, who can be bought by any man who chances to be wealthy, and it ends with the ironic complaint:

> verum si olfecerit aurum
> Mulcebit barbam Mellia nostra tuam.

> (5.27-8)

> (If my Mellea smells true gold, she will stroke your beard.)

This poem is immediately matched by elegy 6 (38 lines) which demonstrates the constancy of the lover, elaborating the query of the opening line:

> Caspia, tot poenas meruit patientia nostra?

> (Caspia, has my patience deserved such punishment?)

Poems 8 (52 lines) and 10 (48 lines) form a contrasting pair: in poem 8 the lover gains access to the bedchamber of the lady with whom he is in love. Though he fails to take full advantage of the situation, he enjoys the sight of the lady in bed. In poem 10 the situation is reversed; here the lover is in bed waiting for his mistress to join him:

> Adieci porro plumas et lintea struxi
> Mollius ut tenerum poneret illa latus.

> (10.9-10)

> (Moreover I added feathers and piled up linen so that she could rest her delicate side more gently.)

But his solicitude is in vain, since his mistress fails to keep the assignation. The seventh elegy is a protestation of the poet's fidelity to his mistress, the ninth shows the poet as the victim of his mistress's infidelity. The fourth elegy seems to stand alone, set apart by its greater length, 60 lines. It contains within itself, however, the elements of an antithetical situation, in which the lover is dominated by his mistress during the day, to dominate her in turn during the night. The elegy starts with a general maxim,

> Ille miser faciles cui nemo invidit amores,
> Felle metuque nimis qui sine tutus amat.

> (He's an unfortunate fellow whose love affair runs smoothly with no one to envy him; who loves in excessive security without any fear and bitterness.)

In itself this echoes an attitude of Ovid:

> quod licet et facile est quisquis cupit, arbore frondis
> carpat et e magno flumine potet aquam.

> (*Am.* 2.19.31-2)

> (Whoever desires what is permissible and easily attainable, let him pluck branches from a tree, and drink water from a great river.)

Campion follows this maxim with advice to the mistress:

> Imperet et iubeat quae se constanter amari
> Expetit: utcunque est, obsequium omne nocet. . . .
> Discite, formosae, non indulgere beatis,
> Fletibus assuescat siquis amare velit.
> Nec tristes lachrimae, cita nec suspiria desint,
> Audiat et dominae dicta superba tremens.

> (7-18)

> (Let a woman who longs to be loved constantly be imperious and commanding. All complaisance of whatever kind is detrimental. . . . Learn, O beautiful girls, not to indulge your fortunate lovers. If anyone wants to be in love, let him grow accustomed to tears. Let sad tears and hasty sighs be his constant companions, let him hear in trembling the proud commands of his mistress.)

The situation is seen in general terms—any lover, any mistress. The poem develops the theme of servitude to a mistress, seeing love as a ritualized game. Cruelty helps to keep love strong.

This is Campion's most sensual poem, with its undertones of sado-masochism. Although the lover is to weep and sigh during the day, at night he should dominate her, bite her lips, draw blood from the nipples of her breasts, triumph like a horse in rich pastureland. But when day returns, he is to be submissive to his mistress, to help her with her toilette.

Campion seems then to have an interest in exploring certain amatory themes, in working out the variations of a conventional situation. He is a commentator on certain aspects of love. Thus general maxims or *sententiae* abound in his poetry, and many of the elegies are written to exemplify these maxims, which frequently occur in the opening lines of the elegy. Poems 4 and 11 simply develop the generalization of their opening lines already quoted above. Poem 5 illustrates the generalization of its opening couplet:

> Prima suis, Fanni, formosis profuit aetas,
> Solaque de facie rustica pugna fuit.

(Fannius, in the first age of men, the handsome reaped the rewards of their handsomeness, and the only rustic contest was about beauty.)

General maxims can indeed be found throughout the elegies (e.g. 6.9-10; 8.43-4; 11.3-4 and 15-16; 12.1-4, 11-12, and 17-20). In particular the poems end on a strong line which embodies a summarizing conclusion, e.g.:

> Nam perii, et verno quae coepit tempore flamma,
> Iam mihi non ullo frigore ponet hyems.
>
> (1.19-20)

(For I am undone, and no winter with its cold will quench the flame which fired me in the spring.)

> Dum iuvat, et fas est, praesentibus utere; totum
> Incertum est quod erit; quod fuit, invalidum.
>
> (12.19-20)

(Take advantage of the present whilst it gives you pleasure and it's right to do so. The future is entirely uncertain, the past irrelevant.)

But all the elegies end in an emphatic and pointed, almost epigrammatic manner, which helps to give the poetry a detached, ratiocinative tone. The same emphatic endings are observable in Campion's English lyrics:

> Thinke that thy fortune still doth crie,
> Thou foole, to-morrow thou must die.

> But when we come where comfort is
> She neuer will say no.

> But if she doth of sorrow speake,
> Eu'n from my hart the strings doe breake.
>
> (poems 2, 3, and 6 of *A Booke of Ayres*)

Campion's mood in his love elegies is one of lightness and detachment, the result of his easy and graceful style, which derives above all from Ovid. The mistresses who appear in Campion's erotic elegies are not placed in any particular identifiable social or historical setting. There are no allusions which would enable us to say that they are set in the world of Campion's own day—no reference to ruffs or farthingales—neither is the world recognizably Roman. There is no mention of chariots and games, or the witty social world of Rome. The setting is timeless and place-less, not specific. Nonetheless, the atmosphere of Campion's elegies is that of Ovidian love elegy, somewhat cynical, portraying a love that is concerned with physical beauty and attraction rather than a spiritual and transcendent love. There are, too, many close echoes of Ovid. (The verbal humour of 1.5-6 and 15-16, cf. *Met.* 3.380-92; the personification of Elegy, 13.9-10, cf. *Am.* 3.1.; the desire for rivals in love, 4.1-2 and 57-60, cf. *Am.* 2.19; the advice to beware of women seen at night, under the influence of drink, 9.13-16, cf. *A.A.* 1.243-52; the sensuality of 13a.9-13, cf. *Am.* 1.5.19-22.)

The vocabulary of Love too is drawn from Ovid, e.g. *perii* (1.19; cf. *Her.* 12.33); *flamma* (1.19; cf. *Am.* 2.1.8); *insidiosa* (1.12; cf. *Rem.* 148); *laedor* (1.15; cf. *Her.* 5.102);

speciosa (2.1; cf. *Met.* 11.133); *calores* (2.3; cf. *A.A.* 1.237); *ignes* (2.5; cf. *Am.* 1.15.27); *regna* (2.14; cf. *Am.* 1.1.13); *levitate* (2.28; cf. *A.A.* 2.429); *ocellis* (3.11; cf. *Am.* 2.19.19); *nec bene sanus* (3.16; cf. *A.A.* 3.713); *Cupidinis arte* (3.17; cf. *Am.* 2.4.30 and 1.11.11); *faciles . . . amores* (4.1; cf. *Her.* 11.29 and *A.A.* 3.27); *amica* (4.3; cf. *A.A.* 1.465); *dominam* (4.5; cf. *Am.* 3.4.43); *docta* (4.10; cf. *A.A.* 2.281); *ussit* (4.11; cf. *Am.* 3.1.20); *callida* 4.13; cf. *Am.* 1.2.6); *formosae* (4.15; cf. *Am.* 1.9.43); *lachrimae* (4.17; cf. *Am.* 1.4.61); *labella* (4.21; cf. *A.A.* 1.667); *delicias* (7.4; cf. *Am.* 3.15.4); *blandus . . . Amor* (8.16; cf. *T.*1.3.49); *Cassibus meis* (8.38; cf. *A.A.* 1.392); *faces* (8.36; cf. *Am.* 1.1.8); *amator* (8.50; cf. *A.A.* 1.722); *fides* (10.3; cf. *Am.* 2.9.50); *improba* (10.4; cf. *Her.* 10.77). The verse-style likewise is indebted more to Ovidian love elegy than to any other Latin poetry. At the end of each elegiac couplet is a strong break which marks the end of a sentence or at least a major pause within the sentence. The structure of the sentences is simple and graceful, with many of the repetitions and exclamations so characteristic of Ovid.

From Ovid too derive the mythological figures whom Campion uses as studied *exempla* in his love elegies—Theseus, Dido, Cephalus and Procris in elegy 7, Thisbe in elegies 10 and 12, Phaedra in elegy 11, and Leander in elegy 12. Campion's most successful use of mythology as an extended *exemplum* is the dramatic citation of Paris in elegy 4 as an illustration of the pleasure to be derived from the successful winning of a woman in the teeth of rivals:

> Quove animo Troiae portas subiisse putatis
> Cum rapta insignem coniuge Priamidem?
> Aurato curru rex, et regina volentes,
> Accurrunt; fratres, ecce, vehuntur equis;
> Et populus circum, iuvenesque, patresque, globantur
> Aemula spectatum multa puella venit.
>
> (4.47-52)

(In what spirits do you suppose that the famous son of Priam arrived at the gates of Troy with the wife whom he had abducted? The king and queen hasten gladly in a golden chariot; behold, his brothers ride on horses; the people, young men and old, throng around him; many an envious maiden comes to watch.)

In his English lyrics Campion shows himself to be simple, lucid and graceful. His Latin elegies are longer, more complex, written on a greater scale; in them he shows a gift for exploring a wide range of amatory situations, for analysing the emotions of love, and in certain poems, such as elegies 8 and 10, for creating a vivid and dramatic atmosphere as the setting of the poem. We see in the Latin elegies aspects of Campion as a poet which a consideration only of his English poems would not reveal to us.

In common with most neo-Latin poets, Campion wrote Latin epigrams, which enjoyed an enormous vogue in the sixteenth century. Latin, a terse and laconic language, is ideally suited for the mordant and trenchant qualities of the epigram—suited too for the pedantic and somewhat heavy-handed humour displayed by so many sixteenth-century writers of epigram, including Campion. Campion wrote nearly five hundred epigrams. The 1595 collection of Latin poems, *Poemata,* had contained 129 epigrams; of the two books of epigrams published in the second edition of Campion's poetry in 1619, the first book consisted entirely of 225 new epigrams, whilst of the 228 epigrams in the second book nearly a hundred were reprinted, sometimes with revisions, from the earlier volume.

Campion was interested in the theory of the epigram:

> What Epigrams are in Poetrie, the same are Ayres in musicke, then in their chief perfection when they are short and well seasoned.
>
> (Preface to *A Booke of Ayres*)

He believed that his own collection was unpretentious and witty:

> At tenues ne tu nimis (optime) despice musas;
>   Pondere magna valent, parva lepore iuvant.
>
> (*Epigrams,* 1.1.5-6)

(O best of men, don't be too contemptuous of my trifling Muses. Great poetry prevails by its grandeur, light-hearted poetry by its charm.)

He also claimed a didactic purpose for the epigram in its castigation of human folly:

> Sicut et acre piper mordax epigramma palato
>   Non omni gratum est: utile nemo negat.
>
> (*Epigrams,* 1.34.1-2)

(A mordant epigram, like pungent pepper, doesn't please every palate. But no one denies its utility.)

In another epigram Campion praises his exemplars Catullus and Martial:

> Cantabat Veneres meras Catullus;
> Quasvis sed quasi silva Martialis
> Miscet materias suis libellis,
> Laudes, stigmata, gratulationes,
> Contemptus, ioca, seria, ima, summa;
> Multis magnus hic est, bene ille cultis.
>
> (2.27)

(Catullus composed pure love poetry. But Martial like a wood houses all sorts of lumber in his little books, praise, blame, congratulations, scorn, jokes, weighty matters; he touched the depths and the heights. Martial is a great man to the many, Catullus to those of refined taste.)

The subject of his epigrams is described as *lusus . . . mollis, iocus . . . levis* (pleasant mockery, light-hearted joking) (*Epigrams,* 2.2.1). Campion, like Martial, wrote epigrams of one line in length (*Epigrams,* 1.53, 2.213; cf. Martial 7.98, 8.19). His longest epigram is 59 lines long.[4] The majority are, however, shorter than 16 lines, and many of them are couplets or quatrains.

Sixteenth-century theorists, such as Julius Caesar Scaliger, debated how long an epigram should be. Scaliger believed that 'Breuitas proprium quiddam est. Argutia anima et quasi forma. . . . Breuitatem vero intelligemus, non definitam, nam et monostichon est apud Martialem, et aliquot satis longa, si alia spectes.'[5] ('Brevity is a characteristic of the epigram. Wit is its soul, its form, as it were. . . . We will understand that there is no definition of brevity, for we find a monostich in Martial, and if you look at others, several are quite long.') Scaliger goes on to discuss the versatile nature of the epigram. It can embrace all types of poetry, dramatic, narrative, and mixed, can be written in all metres, and its subject matter can be unlimited.[6]

It would be easy enough to take a superficial view of the epigram, to believe that it is simply a short poem with a sting in the tail which will hardly stand up to discussion. Yet in its long history the epigram has been capable of a surprising degree of development. Originally a poetic inscription (as Scaliger was aware), often on a tomb, in the Alexandrian period the epigram had come to be a brief poem, usually in elegiacs, on a single event, either great or trivial. In the post-Alexandrian period it was not usually intended for funereal inscriptions, and the genre embraced other themes. Epigrams survive which deal with love, wine, works of art, famous men, natural beauties, sketches of women or animals. After the publication by Meleager of an anthology of six centuries of poems in the first century B.C., Philippus of Thessalonica published in A.D. 40 a 'garland' of poets writing after Meleager, in which are found poems which have a 'sting in the tail'. By developing this latter trait Martial made his own contribution to the development of the epigram, which became predominantly satirical.

Epigrams continued to be written after the decline of the antique world, and the introduction of the Planudean and Palatine Anthologies to the Latin West in the sixteenth and seventeenth centuries gave the epigram a new lease of life in the hands of the neo-Latin poets of Europe at that time. In his discussion of 'English Trochaik verse' in *Observations in the Arte of English Poesie* Campion gives examples of twelve English epigrams, mainly amatory and satirical, which make fun of human foibles:

> I have written diuers light Poems in this kinde, which for the better satisfaction of the reader I thought conuenient here in way of example to publish. In which though sometimes vnder a knowne name I haue shadowed a fain'd conceit, yet it is done without reference or offence to any person, and only to make the stile appeare the more English.
>
> (*Works,* ed. Vivian, p. 44)

Campion's Latin epigrams are very varied. We find amongst them poems addressed to the mistresses of the love elegies—Caspia, Mellea, and Sybilla—in the collection which had first appeared in the 1595 *Poemata.* In these the amatory situation is overlaid with irony:

> Anxia dum natura nimis tibi, Mellea, formam
>   Finxit, fidem oblita est dare.
>
> (*Epigrams,* 2.18)

(Whilst solicitous nature made you excessively beautiful, Mellea, she forgot to give you loyalty.)

In these amatory epigrams it is the negative and sterile
aspects of a love affair which are stressed, particularly in
the epigrams addressed to Caspia. Thus the poet complains
that Caspia holds herself remote from love (2.15), that she
is unstable (2.37), that she remains aloof and rejects his
advances (2.50), that she is contrary (2.53). In 2.56 the
lover is wretched, in 2.66 he bitterly dwells on the punishment in the underworld of the beloved who does not
requite the lover's love. In 2.89 the poet complains that he
is excluded from Caspia's affections, in 2.92 he longs for
one night of love. In 2.109 we are informed that Caspia
loves no one, whilst in 2.113 we hear of her *feritas*,
savageness. In 2.124 Caspia is stigmatized as an angry
woman who repels lovers; she is also constant in hatred
(Vivian, p. 342).

Mellea does not appear in any more favourable light. In
2.10 the poet feels an insane jealousy towards her; in 2.12
he tricks her with a kiss. 2.18 is a laconic reflection upon
her fickleness, whilst in 2.48 he bids her, 'Circe, in aeter-
num vale!' ('Enchantress, farewell for ever!') The poet is
afraid of Mellea's compliments (2.63); and Mellea loves
many men (2.109). The epigrams addressed to women
bearing different names from those of the women in the
elegies are similarly bitter.

> Qui te formosam negat haud oculos habet; at te
> Nauci qui pendet, Pasiphyle, cor habet.
>
> (*Epigrams*, 2.190)

(The man who says you are not beautiful is blind; but
the man who doesn't care two straws for you, Pasi-
phyle, is discerning.)

That mood of bitter disillusion pervades Campion's amatory epigrams. However, the bulk of his epigrams are written in a low key, drawing attention to some trait of human
folly or weakness. They lack the mordant vehemence of
satire, the 'sting in the tail' is slight. A good many of them
are addressed to unidentifiable individuals who are referred
to by such names as Nerva, Eurus, Haedus, Cacculus,
Sabellus, Lycus—Roman names, in the manner of Martial,
who adopted the same practice of stigmatizing the vice,
not the identifiable practitioner of the vice. And so we find
poems about the avariciousness of lawyers, the pretentiousness of poets; poems ridiculing quacks, bad singers,
cuckolds, false prophets; poems against the vogue for
tobacco and against other human frailties or notable
peculiarities: the man whose nose makes a loud noise
when he speaks (1.117), the man who is indifferent to debt
(1.78), the English fashion for wearing too many clothes
in the summer (1.144). Many of these seem to be only
mildly amusing today, to be low-powered and laboured,
lacking the neat and biting conclusion necessary to make
them memorable. Campion has toned down the final
emphasis characteristic of the epigrams of Martial.

A number of encomiastic epigrams addressed to men of
note partake of the qualities of the epigram only in their
conclusion. The attribution of praise or blame is, as

Scaliger had noted,[7] one of the properties of the epigram.
In the epigram praising the achievements of Sir Robert
Carey (1.46), the epigrammatic effect lies in the antithesis
of the concluding line,

> Qui novit iuvenem, noscet itemque senem.
>
> (Whoever knew the youth will likewise know him in
> his dotage.)

Likewise in the conclusion of the poem praising Drake's
Golden Hind (1.94):

> Cuius fama recens tantum te praeterit, Argo,
> Quantum mortalem Delia sphaera ratem.
>
> (The recent fame of this ship excels yours, O Argo, as
> much as the globe of the sun excels a man-made ship.)

There are finally a number of formal and controlled poems,
elegiac rather than 'epigrammatic' in mood, which com-
memorate the deaths of various famous men, among them
Prince Henry (1.96), Walter Devereux (2.9), and Sir Philip
Sidney (2.11). Campion thus demonstrated his ability as a
writer of epigrams which embrace most of the traditional
types and subjects.

In **"Umbra,"** a work which spans Campion's poetical
career, we have his most sustained poetical work. In the
1595 ***Poemata,*** the first 231 lines appeared, the poem
breaking off in mid-sentence after 'Et quid ait' in line 232.
The poem was reprinted and completed in the 1619 collection, and part at least of the conclusion must have been
written after the marriage in 1613 of Princess Elizabeth to
the Count Palatine of the Rhine, to which there is a reference in l. 343.

"Umbra" is a mythological poem of 404 lines which falls
into two almost exactly equal parts. The first section, lines
1-201, tells of the love of Apollo for the nymph Iole,
daughter of Cybele. Apollo desires the nymph, but she is
unwilling to receive his advances. Apollo drugs Iole to
sleep, then rapes her and makes her pregnant. The nymph
then begins to suffer the symptoms of pregnancy in
ignorance of what they portend. At last she gives birth to a
son, Melampus, who is black save for the image of the
sun, his father, on his breast. Apollo visits Jupiter to ward
off any possible anger on the latter's part. Jupiter laughs at
the complaints of Iole's mother, Cybele, whose anger
gradually fades away with the passing of time. The second
part of the poem centres upon the youth of Melampus.
Whilst Melampus is asleep, Morpheus the god of sleep
chances upon him, and is entranced by his beauty. Morpheus tries to attract Melampus' interest by transforming
himself into many different shapes, but to no avail. He
then decides to make a journey to the underworld, where
the shades of the most beautiful women are to be found, in
order to fashion for his purposes a composite figure of
ideal beauty. He then returns thus disguised to the sleeping
Melampus, who welcomes him and falls in love with the
vision. But day dawns, and the vision vanishes. Melampus
can nowhere find the object of his affections. He wastes
away and dies, and his shade wanders in darkness for ever.

Both halves of the poem are thus united by a thematic similarity. Both deal with the love of a god, unrequited at first, until he uses his superhuman powers. Moreover, in both stories the god escapes unpunished, whilst the mortal is ruined. Mythological *epyllia* were popular in England in the late sixteenth century (e.g. Marlowe's *Hero and Leander*, Shakespeare's *Venus and Adonis* and others).

Campion is, however, unusual in that he seems to have invented a story, rather than to have adapted an already existing myth. I am not aware of any previous treatment of the figures of Apollo and Morpheus dealing with the story which Campion relates, although Apollo was of course known from Ovid's *Metamorphoses* as a god addicted to the pursuit of nymphs.

Campion incorporates into his poem much of the machinery of previous philosophical epic. He describes two *loci amoeni,* pleasant and remote places which embody an ideal pastoral landscape. The first of these is the home of the nymphs:

> Est in visceribus terrae nulli obvia vallis,
> Concava, picta rosis, variaque ab imagine florum;
> Fontibus irrorata, et fluminibus lapidosis:
> Mille specus subter latitant, totidemque virenti
> Stant textae myrto casulae, quibus anxia turba
> Nympharum flores pingunt, mireque colorant.
>
> (17-22)

(There is a valley hollowed out in the bowels of the earth, which no one can enter, decorated with roses and different types of flowers, watered by fountains and rivers full of stones. Beneath it a thousand grottoes are hidden away; there are the same number of bowers woven from the myrtle in bloom, for which a sedulous band of nymphs adorns the flowers, and decorates them in a wondrous manner.)

The second is the home of Persephone in the second part of the poem:

> Luce sub obscura procul hinc telluris in imo
> Persephones patet atra domus, sed pervia nulli;
> Quam prope secretus, muro circundatus aereo.
> Est hortus, cuius summum provecta cacumen
> Haud superare die potuit Iovis ales in uno.
> Immensis intus spaciis se extendit ab omni
> Parte, nec Elisiis dignatur cedere campis,
> Finibus haud minor, at laetarum errore viarum
> Deliciisque loco longe iucundior omni.
>
> (255-63)

(In the dim light, far from here, in the depths of the earth lies the black home of Persephone, accessible to no one. Near is a secret garden, surrounded by a wall of bronze; the bird of Jupiter could not surmount its topmost peak in a day's flight. Inside, the garden extends in all directions, covering an immense area, and disdains to yield to the Elysian fields. It extends over an area just as great, but it is far pleasanter than any other place, both in the wandering of its happy byways and in its delights.)

In both instances the inaccessibility of the place described is stressed. In the latter the garden is surrounded by a high wall. Both are *nulli obvia* and *pervia nulli*. Morpheus alone can enter the most exclusive part of the latter when he has performed a curious ritual:

> Non huc fas cuiquam magnum penetrare deorum;
> Soli sed Morpheo, cui nil sua fata negarunt,
> Concessum est, pedibus quamvis incedere lotis. . . .
> Primo fons aditu stat molli fultus arena,
> Intranti. . . .
> Morpheus hac utrumque pedem ter mersit in unda,
> Et toties mistis siccat cum floribus herbis;
> Inde vias licitas terit.
>
> (276-88)

(It is not right for any of the great gods to enter this region—only Morpheus, whose destiny has denied him nothing, may enter when he has bathed his feet. . . . On the threshold as you enter there is a fountain resting on the soft sand. . . . Morpheus dipped each foot three times in its waters, and three times dried it with mingled grass and flowers. Then he treads the permitted path.)

In the second part of the poem, Campion envisages an elaborate underworld which owes something to Vergil. His underworld is a feminine one, presided over by Persephone, as the invocation to her at the beginning of the poem makes clear (ll. 1-12). The invocation similarly presents Campion's theory of immortality in the poem—that souls leave the underworld for their sojourn on earth, to return to it on death. But Campion has in mind principally the shades of women. He speaks in Vergilian language (*caelo ostentans*—cf. *Aeneid* 6.869) of Persephone manipulating the *Foemineos . . . manes* (shades of women).

In the high-walled inaccessible garden of which the description has been quoted above dwell the shades of beautiful women, past, present, and still to be born. Most of them rest in a valley, admiring their reflections in water, or weaving flowery garlands. But those who are destined to live in the town rather than in the country are engaged in less rustic pursuits. Finally, a special region situated on a hill is reserved for those who are to be heroines in this world. At the entrance to this region is a fountain where the returning shades wash off impurities contacted in the upper world. In this special region are to be found the shades of famous heroines of classical times, such as Antiope, Helen of Troy and Hippodamia, together with certain contemporary gentlewomen of note, such as the Princess Elizabeth. From these Morpheus fashions his ideally beautiful composite figure with which to enchant Melampus:

> capiunt hae denique formae
> Formarum artificem, nec se iam proripit ultra.
> Gratia, nec venus ulla fugit, congesta sed unam
> Aptat in effigiem.
>
> (344-7)

(And then these forms attract the shaper of forms, and he goes no further. None of the grace, none of the loveliness escapes him, in fact he gathers it all together and moulds it into a single figure.)

It may be that Campion is trying to make some sort of statement about beauty. Morpheus creates the shape of an ideally beautiful woman, an amalgam of the charms and beauties of the most beautiful women in the underworld. Zeuxis, the Greek painter, in adorning the walls of the temple of Juno at Croton, had similarly produced a composite of ideal beauty by modelling his portrait of Helen on five beautiful girls[8]—a story often quoted by Renaissance theorists.[9]

Earlier in the poem Campion shows his interest in creation theory. The nymphs paint (externally adorn) flowers for their bowers, and Cybele protects and guides the flowers on the earth above, whilst:

> Forma rosis animos maiores indidit, ausis
> Tollere purpureos vultus, et despicere infra
> Pallentes odio violas, tectasque pudore.
>
> (32-5)

(Beauty supplies the roses with greater spirit, as they dare to uplift their faces brightly coloured and to look down upon the violets beneath them pale with loathing and covered with shame.)

Campion here perpetuates an old tradition common in medieval Latin poetry, that violets are inferior to roses.[10]

"Umbra" is a strange poem. It contains many elements which suggest that the poem has a serious purpose and an inner meaning—the *loci amoeni,* the interest in the creative powers of Cybele, the impregnation by Apollo, identified with the sun and with light, of Iole, the daughter of Cybele; the birth from this union of the beautiful child, black save for the image of the sun on his breast, Morpheus' journey to the underworld, the mysterious fountain, the fashioning of the vision of ideal feminine beauty, the transformation of Melampus into a shadow. But it is not easy to divine what this meaning is. It is possible that Campion started to write this long poem and then found that his talents lay in other directions, that the writing of large-scale poetry was not for him, and that he quickly abandoned the attempt. Nonetheless he thought highly enough of the poem to print even an incomplete version of it in his 1595 collection of *Poemata*; for the poem does break off at a most inappropriate place in that edition, and the poem is advertised even on the title page as being **"Fragmentum Umbrae."** Campion did anyway complete the poem for the 1619 edition of his poetry. Yet he need not necessarily have had a serious purpose in mind. He might have found in the poem simply an opportunity for colourful description and fluent speeches. Certainly his own statements suggest a simple interpretation of the poem:

> insidias, et furtivos hymenaeos,
> Et Nympham canimus.
>
> (14-15)

(I tell of treachery and a stolen marriage, and a Nymph.)

In an **"Argumentum"** which is prefixed only to the 1595 version of the poem, he simply provides a précis of the narrative. The nearest he comes to suggesting a meaning for the poem is to say that Melampus 'falsa pulchritudinis specie deceptus in miserrimum amorem dilabitur' ('deceived by the false image of beauty slips into a most wretched love'). **"Umbra"** remains then an enigmatic poem, a decorative *epyllion.*

Campion's other long Latin poem, **"Ad Thamesin,"** is less lucid and interesting than *Umbra.* It appears only in the 1595 *Poemata,* and Campion probably did not esteem it highly enough to have it reprinted in 1619. An **"Argumentum"** sums up the ostensible subject of the poem:

> Totum hoc poema gratulationem in se habet ad Thamesin de Hyspanorum fuga, in qua adumbrantur causae quibus adducti Hyspani expeditionem in Angliam fecerint. Eae autem sunt, avaritia, crudelitas, superbia, atque invidia. Deinde facta Apostrophe ad Reginam pastoraliter desinit.

(This whole poem is a congratulation towards the river Thames on the flight of the Spaniards, in which are outlined the reasons which induced the Spaniards to make an expedition against England. Those reasons are avarice, cruelty, pride, and envy. Then, after an Apostrophe to the Queen, the poem ends in pastoral vein.)

After an address to the *Nympha potens Thamesis* (powerful Nymph of the Thames) the poet explains that Jupiter and Neptune did not tolerate the Spaniards as they followed their cruel banners. Jupiter will protect his Britons, and not allow the rites of the Roman Church to flourish again.

There follows a description of a region sacred to Dis (identified in a marginal note as America) in an inversion of the *locus amoenus* topos, introduced by the traditional words *Est locus* (there is a place). But here all is dark, the abode of Furies and monsters. These Dis urges to summon up anger in their hearts, and then urges Oceanus, the god of the Ocean, to provide a smooth passage for the invading Spanish fleet (ll. 38-61). Oceanus reminds Dis that the latter does not hold sway over the sea, and praises the piety and martial prowess of the Britons. Dis rails against Oceanus, who, frightened, departs to fulfil Dis's request, delighted however at the vengeance which Drake and Frobisher will inflict upon the Spaniards (ll. 91-3). Dis holds council with the Spaniards; Avarice in her brazen tower, Slaughter, and Pride, who are present, are described. The Stygian nymphs sing a mournful, miserable song (ll. 143-5), and then follows an account of the Fountain of Envy. Whoever looks into this fountain sees an image of all that the world contains. In this fountain the Spaniards see a representation of England, its white cliffs, fields, cities, rivers, and fountains, and are consumed with envy. The Spaniards are then entertained by Dis (ll. 201 ff) and depart to launch their invasion of England (ll. 240-1). But the river Thames disturbed the waters of the sea (l. 250) and the Armada was defeated. The poet wishes ruination upon the survivors and the poem concludes (ll. 266-83) with a prayer that Queen Elizabeth should flourish in her prime.

The narrative progress of the poem is certainly interrupted by the static descriptions of the House of Avarice and the Fountain of Envy. England and Elizabeth, rather than the river Thames, as the **"Argumentum"** had promised, are praised, and the speeches even of Dis are used to reflect credit upon them: thus Dis in his speech to Oceanus reminds him that England has never been conquered (ll. 56-8). Oceanus reinforces this in his speech:

> Sunt Angli, sunt Troiana de gente Britanni
> Qui pacem, numenque colunt, et templa fatigant.
>
> (65-6)

(They are Englishmen, they are Britons of Trojan origin, who worship peace and the Godhead, and weary the temples with their worship.)

In lines 159-62, the Spaniards too praise England:

> longe omnibus eminet una
> Cincta mari tellus, celeberrima rupibus albis,
> Hanc spectant, et agros, urbes, vada, flumina, fontes
> Laudant inviti.[11]

(One land surrounded by the sea far excels all others, a land most renowned for its white cliffs; this do they look upon, and unwillingly praise its fields, its cities, its streams, rivers, and fountains.)

This praise of England is, however, hardly that of 'the whole poem' which the **"Argumentum"** had promised. It is strange too that *crudelitas* and *superbia,* singled out for mention in the **"Argumentum,"** are sketched so briefly. Campion remarks that the poem ends *pastoraliter.* The praise of great persons is a feature of Vergilian pastoral—e.g. of Octavian and Pollio in *Eclogues* I and IV—so doubtless Campion is here referring to his apostrophe to Queen Elizabeth which concludes the poem. The whole poem, however, seems to strive for the grandeur of epic, only to be overburdened by its pretension.

"Ad Thamesin" is a patriotic poem of the type to be written in the immediate aftermath of a great national victory. It presents to us in what may be one of his very first poems (if the poem was indeed written immediately after the defeat of the Armada) the nascent poet making trial of his abilities as a poet, and learning, perhaps, that it was as a writer of shorter poems that his talent could best find expression.

Two conventional poems praising Queen Elizabeth and the Earl of Essex which are to be found only in the 1595 edition of his poems complete the corpus of Campion's Latin poetry.

It must be acknowledged that Campion is not a great writer of Latin poetry. Nonetheless his Latin poetry shows that he is a more versatile poet than he reveals himself to be in the English lyrics for which he is chiefly remembered. In his Latin poetry he demonstrates a competent command of the Latin styles of Vergil, Ovid, and Martial, and displays an interest in mythological and allegorical epic. His most interesting Latin poems are, I believe, his love elegies, in which he develops a range of erotic situations wider than that of his English poems. Campion will no doubt always be remembered chiefly as the delicate poet of *A Booke of Ayres,* but those who like to explore lesser known Elizabethan literature could well do worse than turn to Thomas Campion's Latin poetry.

Notes

1. Sig. Nn8r.

2. *Affaniae, sive Epigrammatum Libri tres* (Oxford, 1601), sigs F7r. and D5v. Campion is called a *vates* on sig. B6v.

3. Quotations from Thomas Campion are from *Campion's Works,* ed. Percival Vivian (Oxford, 1909, reprinted 1967). I adopt, however, the modern usage of *v* and *u* and transcribe *j* as *i* in quotations from the Latin poems. When referring to elegies which were printed only in the 1595 edition of Campion's poetry (these are given in an appendix by Vivian), I add for convenience of reference the suffix *a* to their number.

4. Appearing only in the 1595 edition of Campion's poetry, it is included in the Appendix to Vivian's edition, pp. 342-3.

5. *Poetics* (Lyon, 1561), III.cxxvi, p. 170. References are to book, chapter, and page of this edition.

6. *Ibid.*

7. *Ibid.*

8. See Cicero, *De Inventione* II.i.

9. E.g. by Thomas Nash in *The Anatomie of Absurditie* (see George Gregory Smith, ed., *Elizabethan Critical Essays* (Oxford, 1904), I.321); by Alberico Gentili in his Oxford, 1593, critical treatise (see my 'Alberico Gentili in defense of poetry and acting', *Studies in the Renaissance* 19 (1972), pp. 231 and 252); by Walter Haddon, *Lucubrationes* (London, 1567), sig. L14v.

10. See, e.g. Venantius Fortunatus, *Carmina* 8.6., ed. F. Leo, *Monumenta Germaniae Historica, Auctores Antiquissimi,* IV.i (Berlin, 1881; reprinted 1961).

11. In l. 160, I read *cincta,* the reading of the 1595 edition, for Vivian's erroneous *cuncta.*

David Lindley (essay date 1979)

SOURCE: Lindley, David. "Campion's *Lord Hay's Masque* and Anglo-Scottish Union." *Huntington Library Quarterly* 43, no. 1 (winter 1979): 1-11.

[*In the following essay, Lindley analyzes the masque Campion wrote for the wedding of James Hay and Honora Denny, a union of a Scotsman and Englishwoman, focus-*

ing on how the masque reflected the tensions and problems faced by the union of England and Scotland into Great Britain under King James I.]

When James VI of Scotland succeeded to the English throne, one of his most fervent ambitions was to see the two countries fully united in the single realm of Great Britain. To that end he forced his unwilling parliaments to devote a great deal of their time to the matter and encouraged, directly or indirectly, a substantial flow of propaganda which supported his endeavor.[1] It is not surprising, therefore, that two major court masques, Jonson's *Hymenaei*[2] and Campion's celebration of the marriage of James Hay and Honora Denny, should concern themselves with this issue.

It has generally been assumed, without any great thought, that the poems with which Campion prefaced the published masque, praising James and his endeavor in enthusiastic tone, are accurate indicators of the attitude to the Union embodied in the work itself. But a careful examination of the masque and proper attention to the context of discussion and prejudice within which it must be placed reveal that Campion, much more clearly than Jonson, articulates a view of the Union and the steps necessary for its achievement which reflects the real difficulties faced by the project.

Campion's task was to fashion a device appropriate to the Anglo-Scottish marriage which was its specific occasion, and also to the greater Union for which it made an apt and obvious metaphor.[3] In order to show how the masque's dramatic action and symbolic pattern fulfill this commission it is necessary first to outline the structure of the work.

The action of the masque is dependent on the resolution of two related disputes between the gods. The first begins when Night interrupts Flora and Zephyrus in their celebration of the marriage and chastises them for their effrontery in so gracing Venus' removal of a virgin from the service of the chaste goddess Diana. After a brief exchange, Night continues with Diana's second grievance. She has been further provoked by the profanation of her forests by Knights of Apollo, intent upon seducing her nymphs. For their effrontery they have been turned into trees. Flora and Zephyrus are prepared to contest Night's first charge, but for the second they offer no defense. There is an argument to be made about the relative merits of matrimony and celibacy, but for simple lust's assaults on chastity there is no excuse.

The entry of Hesperus resolves both conflicts. He announces first that

> *Cynthia* is now by *Phoebus* pacified,
> And well content her Nymph is made a Bride.[4]

He continues with Diana's command that the Knights be released from their trees. But, as befits their greater crime, they have to work for their restoration. First, still encased

in their trees, they must dance, then they are released; but only when they have surrendered the "greene leaved robes" in which they entered the forest at the tree of Diana are they fully restored to their "former shapes." After this the revels take place.

The mythological scheme which underlies this design is elegantly appropriate to marriage. It rests upon the resolution of the elemental discord between the three jarring planets. Diana (cold and moist) and Venus (warm and moist) need the hot dryness of Apollo to resolve the first dispute, and it is Venus' temperateness which provides the link that conjoins the otherwise incompatible deities of the sun and moon.[5]

In the masque itself this scheme is not only implied in the words, it is demonstrated spatially as Hesperus stands centrally between the tree of Diana at one end of the hall and the throne of James, identified with Apollo, at the other. Hesperus, the evening star, mediating between night and day, is of course the planetary Venus.[6] The emphasis which is placed on Hesperus as mediator (he is the only one of the three deities who actually speaks in the masque) is especially suited to the larger theme of the Union of the countries of England and Scotland. For just as he, representative of the goddess of love, stands between Diana, patroness of the female side of the marriage (and therefore of the English), and Apollo, patron of the male (Scottish side), so it was insisted repeatedly that a prerequisite of Union was the necessity for love to replace the historic Anglo-Scottish hostility.

James sounded the characteristic note himself, in the announcement of his succession to the throne of England made to his Scottish subjects, so that:

> it may not onlie be knawin to all his Hienes guid subjectis within this realme, bot lykwayis may kendile and steir up in the hartis of all his Hienes Scottis subjectis . . . ane loveing and kyndlie disposition towardis all his Majestis subjectis inhabitantis of England . . . that thai represent and acknawledge thame as thair deirest bretherein and freindis, and the inhabitantis of baith his realmes to obliterat and remove out of thair myndis all and qhatsumever quarrellis, eleistis or debaitis qhilk hes mentenit discord or distractioun of effectioun amangis thame in tyme past, and with ane universall unanimitie of hartis conjoine thameselffis as ane natioun under his Majesteis authoritie.[7]

Campion neatly combines political and matrimonial symbolism right at the beginning of his masque, to suggest the simultaneous relevance of his theme to both private and public ventures. As Flora and Zephyrus descend into the acting area they are accompanied by Sylvans who strew flowers "all about the place," and sing:

> Now hath *Flora* rob'd her bowers
> To befrend this place with flowers:
>   Strowe aboute, strowe aboute,
> The Skye Rayn'd never kindlyer Showers.
> Flowers with Bridalls well agree,

Fresh as Brides, and Bridegromes be:
   Strowe aboute, strowe aboute,
And mixe them with fit melodie.
   Earth hath no Princelier flowers
Than Roses white and Roses red,
But they must still be mingled.

(p. 215)

Red and white roses are the conventional attributes of Venus, goddess of love and marriage, and therefore "with Bridalls well agree." At the same time, the conjunction of red and white roses, which "must still be mingled," alludes to the Tudor Rose, emblem of the union of the houses of York and Lancaster achieved by Henry VII, which was seen and used as precedent and preparation for James's greater project.[8] For the spectator, then, the link between the specific occasion and its larger significance is made clear by this single dramatic symbol.

But if the masque's beginning and ending present an ideal picture of an Anglo-Scottish union in love, the working out of the final resolution pointedly alludes to the difficulties which impeded the progress of the scheme. Where the overall pattern of the masque shows the goal to be attained, the action and incident within it demonstrate the qualities necessary to achieve the desired end.

It is the restoration of Apollo's Knights which supplies most of the masque's drama. Night describes their crime and punishment:

Her holy Forrests are by theeves prophan'd,
Her Virgins frighted; and loe, where they stand
That late were *Phoebus* Knights, turned now to trees
By *Cynthias* vengement for their injuries
In seeking to seduce her Nymphes with love:
Here they are fixt, and never may remove
But by *Dianaes* power that stucke them here.
Apollos love to them doth yet appeare,
In that his beames hath guilt them as they grow,
To make their miserie yeeld the greater show.

(p. 218)

Later, as the Knights approach their final transformation, Night tells them to go up to Diana's tree, and

These greene leaved robes, wherein disguisde you
   made
Stelths to her Nimphes through the thicke forrests
   shade,
There to the goddesse offer thankfully,
That she may not in vaine appeased be.

(p. 224)

Their crime, as the words "theeves" and "stelths" indicate, is one of insidious attack.

When James faced a hostile English Parliament in 1607, he sought to allay the suspicions which he accurately diagnosed them to entertain: "There is a conceipt intertained, and a double jelousie possesseth many, wherein I am misjudged. First, that this union will be the *crisis* to

the overthrow of England, and setting up of Scotland: England will then bee overwhelmed by the swarming of the Scots, who if the Union were effected, would raigne and rule all." He expanded upon this grievance: "It is alleadged, that the Scots are a populous Nation, they shall be harboured in our nests, they shall be planted and flourish in our good Soile, they shall eate our commons bare, and make us leane."[9] The king here himself catches something of the tone of those who feared that Union was a synonym for surreptitious take-over, and it is exactly the atmosphere of that fear which Campion expresses in his depiction of the Knights.

The second English fear, which James also recognized, was of "my profuse liberalitie to the Scottish men more then the English, and that with this Union all things shalbe given to them, and you turned out of all."[10] There is a superabundance of evidence to show that James interpreted his subjects' attitudes correctly, from the moderate "Loyal Subjectes Advertisement," which stated "It is said that respecte, at the court of the Scott by all the attendant officers, theer is so parciall, as the Englishe find them selves muche disgraced . . . Manie offices have been taken from the Englishe and geven to the Scott," to the poem "In Scotos," which begins "They begg our Landes, Liveinges, and Lives / They switch our Nobillitie & lye with our wives."[11] There was some justice in the English accusation,[12] and the bridegroom, James Hay, was one of the most conspicuous recipients of the royal generosity. It is difficult to avoid the feeling that, in this context, the description of Apollo (later identified explicitly with King James) gilding the trees of his Knights, making their crime the occasion of splendor, is meant to hint at the excessive munificence of the king.[13]

If the nature of the crime of the Knights is deliberately depicted in terms which associate them firmly with English fears which obstructed the Union, then the course of their restoration describes action which will help to allay the disquiet.

The lesson they have to learn is the lesson of temperance and moderation. Their progress toward the regaining of their former shape is only completed when they do homage at Diana's tree. As they do so, a solemn motet is sung to the words:

With spotles mindes now mount we to the tree
   Of single chastitie.
The roote is temperance grounded deepe,
Which the coldjewc't earth doth steepe:
   Water it desires alone,
   Other drink it thirsts for none.

(p. 225)

The same message is contained in the song which concludes the masque:

Life is fullest of content
Where delight is innocent.
Pleasure must varie, not be long.

(p. 227)

James's liberality to the Scots was but one part of the general extravagance of his court, which brought him into conflict with sterner moralists and with his parliaments.[14] Since the search for the Union was universally regarded as the king's personal crusade,[15] the intemperance and indecorum of his court, fueling as it did the English antipathy to their Scottish monarch, made a convenient pretext for objecting to the proposed joining of nations. Harington's well-known letter describing the disastrous entertainment of Christian IV at Theobald's in 1606 expresses with great clarity the kind of disgust which the court's conduct provoked:

> I have much marvelled at these strange pegeantries, and they do bring to my remembrance what passed of this sort in our Queens days; of which I was sometime an humble presenter and assistant; but I neer did see such lack of good order, discretion, and sobriety, as I have now done . . . the gunpowder fright is got out of all our heads, and we are going on, hereabouts, as if the devil was contriving every man shoud blow up himself, by wild riot, excess, and devastation of time and temperance.[16]

Campion's masque, by presenting the celebration of the marriage as dependent upon the Knights' learning the value of temperance, clearly warns the king and court that the greater marriage of the two countries will only be celebrated if the reckless liberality and loose behavior which characterized the first years of the new reign are curbed.

The audience's sense of the importance of the virtue of temperance is generated not only through the process of the Knights' restoration, but also by the insistence throughout the masque on the dominant position of the temperate goddess, Diana. Her tree is the focal point of the stage setting, it is she who transformed the Knights into trees, and it is only by the operation of her influence, transmitted through the "vertuous gem" she sends with Hesperus that they are freed.[17] By comparison her mythological opponent Apollo has little power to influence the course of events.

This is surprising, since it is the identification of James with Apollo which provides the opportunity for the praise of the monarch which every masque required. Indeed, if Orgel's assertion that "Campion considered blatant flattery indispensible to the form"[18] were true, then we should surely expect to see the figure of James/Apollo, patron of the Union and of the Scottish side of the marriage, assume a much more vigorous role within the masque. In fact, the relative powerlessness of Apollo, and the choice of Diana as his more potent adversary, show more clearly than anything else Campion's freedom from servility and his success in representing the realities of the debate about the Union; for in fashioning a myth which included the figure of Diana, Campion chose as the guardian of the female, English side of the match the goddess most often associated with the late Queen Elizabeth. The choice was not fortuitous, and the resonances which this association made available are used deliberately and explicitly to sharpen the masque's message and intensify its impact.

Such bald statement needs proof of its plausibility if it is not to seem an arbitrary whim. It might be argued that by 1607, four years after Elizabeth's death, the old image would have lost its force, or that no particular purpose is served in making the identification at all. But justification there is, and it is to be found in the confluence of a number of factors which taken together make the conclusion inescapable.

There is precedent for the pairing of the figures of Apollo and Diana to represent the two monarchs in a number of poems written at the time of James's accession. Robert Fletcher's conceit may be taken as typical:

> Our *Cynthia* in the evening set
> or after midnight took her rest:
> Dan *Phoebus* straight did not forget
> to thinke his mansion must be blest.[19]

Much more significant is the fact that by 1607 the memory of Queen Elizabeth was being revived. Plays and poems reenacted the events of her reign.[20] This revival was not a simple matter of recalling times past, but had frequently the specific purpose of contrasting the present reign of James unfavorably with the age of Elizabeth. Harington in his letter already quoted makes this comparison, and Robert Niccols in his bitter satire on James's court, *The Cuckow* (1607), uses the figure of the moon-goddess explicitly to stand for the late queen, embodiment of the chastity and purity which were things of the past.[21] Goodman later described the phenomenon: "But after a few years, when we had experience of the Scottish government, then in disparagement of the Scots, and in hate and detestation of them, the Queen did seem to revive; then was her memory much magnified."[22]

This explanation for the revival, accurate though it is, leaves out one element which played a significant part in coloring the remembered portrait of the queen. For the English had expected much of James. The same Harington who in 1606 was looking back nostalgically to the previous reign had written a treatise welcoming the prospect of being governed by a "man of spirit and learning" instead of "a ladye shutt up in a chamber from all her subjectes and most of her servantes."[23] When James arrived, the French ambassador reported with some disgust the haste with which people forgot the queen and turned to their new sovereign: "C'est un miracle de voir ce peuple si sage et si peu esmeu et que la memoire de la Reine soit déja esvanouye en son coeur."[24] This joy in the new king evaporated with astonishing speed, and in its wake came a feeling of guilt. As early as June 1603 M. de Rosny reported to King Henry that: "chacun blasme maintenant quasy publiquement la faute qui a eté fait de n'avoir porté le deuil de la mort d'une si excellente Princesse que la feue Reine Elisabeth."[25] It is the presence of this feeling which accounts for some of the passion in the recalling of the queen. It is this feeling, furthermore, which allows Campion to use the figure of Diana not just as a stick to beat the Scots, but as a reminder to the English also of their responsibility.

There is ample evidence, then, that in 1607 the memory of Elizabeth was very much alive, a focus for English discontent, and therefore available for a poet to use. It remains to demonstrate that Campion was in fact using this potential symbol in his depiction of Diana.

In general terms the figure of Diana, incensed at the marriage of one of her train and furious with those who approached her nymphs, recalls well-known characteristics of Elizabeth. In 1606 Harington remembered: "She did oft ask the ladies around hir chamber, if they lovede to thinke of marriage? And the wise ones did conceal well their liking hereto; as knowing the Queene's judgment in this matter."[26] She frequently interfered with the marriages of her courtiers and punished those who made off with her ladies. As Stone remarks, "things were not easy for lovers at the Court of Elizabeth."[27]

Much more significant is Campion's presentation of the reconciliation of Diana and Venus by Phoebus. Hesperus announces the resolution in these terms:

> *Cynthia* is now by *Phoebus* pacified,
> And well content her Nymph is made a Bride,
> Since the faire match was by that Phoebus grac't
> Which in this happie Westerne Ile is plac't
> As he in heaven, one lampe enlightning all
> That under his benigne aspect doth fall.
> Deepe Oracles he speakes, and he alone
> For artes and wisedomes meete for *Phoebus* throne.
> The Nymph is honour'd and *Diana* pleas'd.
>
> (pp. 218-219)

The marriage is the metaphor for Union, so at its superficial level the speech says only that the English side should be content to accept the project desired by their wise king. But at the same time the speech emphasizes the role of Diana—the marriage may go ahead because *she* is content. Because it is at this point in the masque that the identification of James with Apollo is made specific for the first time; so if Elizabeth is shadowed by Diana, it ought to be here, where the specific political application of the work emerges clearly, that Campion should be using his myth to particular purpose.

Elizabeth's part in making the Union possible is stressed by a number of writers on the subject. Two of them are of particular interest because they are Scots. The first, John Russell, who wrote in his "Ane treatise of the happie and blissed Union":

> Certanelie thair is nathying doun in this be chance, fortune, or humaine pouer and counsall, bot immediatlie be the great providence of god. Using that happie and blissed Quene Elizabeth of uorthie memorie . . . to be the instrument to mak this mater sua suietlie to end: . . . in hir last gasp, to utter sic uisdome, sua profitablie, and effectuallie, persuading hir subjectis to acknauledge and embrace his M; qhom scho knew to be the laufull and undoubtit air of Ingland, France and Ireland, be richt of consanguinitie and laufull succes- sioun.[28]

Thomas Craig, one of the Commissioners for the Union, wrote of the late queen: "her hand was sought by many of the most powerful princes of Europe. But she persistently rejected them all, and was in the habit of saying, when she was urged to marry, that the union of the two realms was the alliance she looked for."[29] James himself, in his *Basilikon Doron,* had earlier advised his son that the union would be secured by true amity between the races, and cited as "a good beginning" to the project "the long and happy amitie beteene the Queene my dearest sister and me."[30]

It is this awareness of Elizabeth's role which underlies Hesperus' speech. Its didactic purpose is twofold. First to remind the English that, whatever their discontent with their king and his project, Elizabeth had given it her blessing when she acknowledged James as her heir. The flattery of James which the speech contains is therefore not merely an obligatory exercise but, coming as it does from Diana, an injunction with particular force. But the second effect of the speech is to insist, for the benefit of king and Scots alike, on the fact that it was the English queen who had made the Union possible. John Russell after describing the queen's part in securing James's succession continued: "Sould evir this depairt out of his G mynd? the lord mak his M. thankfull for his great benefittis, and for this honor, to the qlk he is sua heichlie advancit." There were many who felt that James had indeed forgotten Elizabeth. In the first years of his reign in particular he showed scant respect for her memory. Rosny reported that at dinner "an opportunity offering for the King to speak of the late Queen of England, he did it, and, to my great regret, with some sort of contempt."[31] Scaramelli similarly stated that "His Majesty has ordered the funeral of the Queen to take place without waiting his arrival, and they say he wishes to see her neither alive nor dead, . . . Elizabeth's portrait is being hidden everywhere, and Mary Stuart's shown instead."[32] Though James later attempted to repair the damage, yet there was particular point in using the figure of a powerful Diana specifically recalling the queen to act as a reminder to James and the Scots of the need to be sensitive to English feelings if the Union was to be acceptable.

The double address of this speech is typical of the balanced attitude which the masque as a whole takes toward the Union. It is presented, through the image of marriage, as a highly desirable ideal. Indeed, in a sense, since Diana objects after the marriage has taken place, the work accepts that Union of some sort has necessarily been achieved by virtue of James's accession. But the celebration of that Union can only be possible if certain conditions are met, chief among them a greater moderation of life, and greater respect for the English values symbolized by the late Queen Elizabeth.

Campion in this masque, then, shows himself sensitive to the climate of the debate about the Union, and reflects in his devised myth an awareness of the stumbling blocks which the project needed to surmount. He admirably fulfils the prescription which Chapman made for the court masque: "all these courtly, and honoring inventions . . . should expressively arise out of the places, and persons for and by whome they are presented; without which limits, they are luxurious, and vaine."[33]

Notes

1. An excellent summary of the course of the Union debate is D. H. Willson, "King James I and Anglo-Scottish Unity," in *Conflict in Stuart England,* ed. W. A. Aiken and B. D. Henning (London, 1960).

2. See D. J. Gordon, "Hymenaei: Ben Jonson's masque of Union," *JWCI* [Journal of the Warburg and Courtauld Institutes], 8 (1945).

3. Robert Wilkinson, in his sermon *The Merchant Royall* (London, 1607), addressed the couple: "Right Honourable in both sexes, the cause of this meeting, the joy of this day, yea the mysterie and little image of this great intended Union" (p. 35).

4. *The Works of Thomas Campion,* ed. Walter R. Davis (London, 1969), pp. 218-219. All quotations are from this edition.

5. Primaudaye's interpretation of Roman nuptial rites illustrates the same idea, "as fire and water are cleane contraries as well in the first as in the second qualities, so are man and wife, the one being hot and dry, of the nature of fire, and the other cold and moist, of the nature of water: which contrarieties being joined together make a harmonie and temperature of love": *The French Academie,* trans. T. B. (1586), P. 499.

6. "Lowest of the five planets and nearest to the earth is the star of Venus, called . . . in Latin Lucifer when it precedes the sun, but when it follows is Hesperus": Cicero, *De Natura Deorum,* ed. and trans. H. Rackham (London, 1933), p. 174.

7. *The Register of the Privy Council of Scotland,* VI, 514.

8. See D. H. Willson, *King James VI and I* (London, 1956), p. 250. Robert Fletcher in *A Briefe and Familiar Epistle* (1603) expressed the idea simply, "Like Lancaster and Yorke in love, / Must *England* now and *Scotland* joyne."

9. *The Workes of King James* (1616), pp. 514, 518.

10. *Workes,* p. 514.

11. "Loyal Subjectes Advertisement," ed. J. D. Mackie, *SHR,* [Scottish Historical Review] 23 (1925), p. 3; "In Scotos," Bodl. MS Malone 23, fol. 4[v].

12. See Lawrence Stone, *The Crisis of the Aristocracy* (Oxford, 1965), p. 476.

13. The double meaning of the word "guilt" intensifies this feeling. Compare Chapman's description of Leander swimming away after seducing Hero:

> And as amidst th' enamoured waves he swims,
> The god of gold of purpose gilt his limbs,
> That this word gilt including double sense,
> The double gilt of his incontinence
> Might be expressed.

Hero and Leander, Sestiad III, 23-27, from *Christopher Marlowe: The Complete Poems and Translations,* ed. Stephen Orgel (Harmondsworth, 1971).

14. James's ingenuous defense was that "my first three yeeres were to me as a Christmas, I could not then be miserable" (*Workes,* p. 515).

15. See, for example, the Scottish Council, writing to James of "that Union, . . . so little affected by us, except in that religious obedyence we aucht to your Majestie not to dislike onything that lykis you" (*Register of the Privy Council of Scotland,* VII, p. 512).

16. Sir John Harington, *Letter and Epigrams,* ed. N. E. McClure (Philadelphia, 1930), p. 120.

17. Campion is drawing on the talismanic magic by which the stone of one planet is employed to modify the astrological dominance of another. Thus the Knights are freed by tempering their Apollonian natures with lunar characteristics. See Cornelius Agrippa, *De Occulta Philosophia* (Basle, 1533), I, 98f.

18. Stephen Orgel, *The Jonsonian Masque* (Cambridge, Mass. 1965), p. 110. His argument is much weakened by the fact that the lyric he offers in evidence formed no part of the masque itself. It was written later (to fit a tune used only for dancing in the performance) so that purchasers of the published volume might sing it "to the Lute or Viol."

19. *A Briefe and Familiar Epistle* (1603), sig. B2[r].

20. E.g., Dekker, *The Whore of Babylon* (1607); Heywood, *If You Know Not Me* (1605), and *The Second Part* (1606); Christopher Lever, *Queene Elizabeths Teares* (1607). Lever speaks of "your Lordships regarde, even to the very name of your late soveraigne, approved by the generall applause and acclamation of all good people" (sig. A3[v]). This last source is especially interesting since it is dedicated to Robert Cecil, who (as I suggest in an article in *Notes & Queries,* N.S. 26 [1979], 144-145, helped to arrange the marriage and probably patronized the masque.

21. See Hoyt H. Hudson, "John Hepwith's Spenserian Satire upon Buckingham: With Some Jacobean Analogues," *Huntington Library Bulletin,* 6 (1934), 40-71.

22. Godfrey Goodman, *The Court of King James I,* ed. John S. Brewer (London, 1839), I, 98.

23. *A Tract on the Succession to the Crown,* ed. Clements R. Markham (London, 1880), p. 51.

24. BL, Kings MS 123, fol. 38[r].

25. Kings MS 123, fol. 258[v]. That this feeling persisted is evidenced by the 1621 "most humble peticion of . . . the Commons of England" to "the blest Saint Elizabeth":

When Heaven was pleasd (blest saint) to call thee
hence
. . .
Oh had Wee then the Kingdom drownd with
teares
And in the flood covered our soules, To heaven
to wait on thyne, wee had not now bin driven
to cry and call thee from thy fellow saintes
to heare and pitty these our sad complaintes
Oh pardon (blest) then these our grosse omissions

and Elizabeth's answer:

You lusted for a King, heavens King releeive you
And give you pardon, as I heere forgive you
You tooke a surfeit of my happy reigne
And paid my well deserving with disdeigne.

(Bodl. MS Rawlinson 398, fols. 222ᵛ, 227ʳ)

26. *Letters and Epigrams,* p. 124.

27. *Crisis of the Aristocracy,* p. 606.

28. National Library of Scotland, Advocates MS 31.4.7., fol. 2ʳ⁻ᵛ.

29. Thomas Craig, *De Unione Regnorum Brittanniae 1605,* ed. and trans. C. Sanford Terry (Edinburgh, 1909), p. 258

30. *The Workes,* p. 188.

31. Quoted in Beatrice White, *Cast of Ravens* (London, 1965), pp. 11-12.

32. *Calendar of State Papers (Venetian), 1603-7,* p. 9.

33. *The Memorable Masque,* in *The Plays of George Chapman: The Comedies,* ed. Allan Holaday and Michael Kiernan (Urbana, 1970), p. 569.

Stephen Ratcliffe (essay date 1981)

SOURCE: Ratcliffe, Stephen. "'*Silent Musick*': The Aesthetics of Ruins." In *Campion: On Song,* pp. 3-15. London: Routledge & Kegan Paul, 1981.

[*In the essay that follows, Ratcliffe attacks how critics have written about Campion as a composer and poet, arguing they do not address why he is good. Ratcliffe then offers his own analysis of Campion's works.*]

Praised in his own lifetime, largely forgotten by the eighteenth and most of the nineteenth centuries, resurrected in A.H. Bullen's *Lyrics from the Song-Books of the Elizabethan Age* (1887), Thomas Campion now enjoys a secure but minor reputation as one of the finest poets of the English Renaissance. His verse is valued chiefly for its technical mastery, its management of sound, syntax, rhythm and meter, formal and logical structure. Its virtue—a smoothly polished precision, a gracefully delicate charm which has become synonymous with his name—has most often been accounted for by remembering that Campion himself was a poet-composer who wrote

"ayres," or songs, the music as well as the words: "In these *English* Ayres, I have chiefly aymed to couple my Words and Notes lovingly together, which will be much for him to doe that hath not power over both."[1]

The unfortunate result of this tendency to explain Campion's literary excellence in terms of his talent, his "double gift of music and poetry,"[2] has been that for the last eighty-five years Campion criticism has paid surprisingly little attention to either his words by themselves or his words together with their music. Indeed, if Pound is correct ("You can spot the bad critic when he starts by discussing the poet and not the poem"[3]), Campion has attracted more than his share of offenders. Bullen himself set the precedent by implying that Campion's "lyrics" were good because of his unique abilities: "At least one composer, Thomas Campion, wrote both the words and the music of his songs; and there are no sweeter lyrics in English poetry than are to be found in Campion's song-books."[4] Percival Vivian, instead of pursuing what he took to be the distinguishing feature of Campion's verse, was also satisfied to point to its source in Campion's skill as a trained and sensitive musician: "Campion's verse was from the beginning free and musical. This musical quality is indeed the one which distinguishes the whole of his poetry; it is undoubtedly connected with the practice of musical composition and due to a feeling for musical effect, to which, with his trained musical ear, he was peculiarly susceptible."[5] Miles Kastendieck proposed that Campion comes closest to representing the ideal of the lyric poet, again "because he had the talent for both music and poetry."[6] While managing to focus upon certain key attributes of Campion's verse, Roy Fuller still found in his "ingenious mixture of meters" and his "marvellous rhythmic subtleties" the "evidence of an extraordinarily free and beautiful rhythmic talent."[7]

The fact is that by concentrating upon this "talent" as an unusual and remarkable phenomenon, people have made Campion into something of a *wunderkind*, a sacred cow, or, rather, a sacred calf. For his consignment to the rank of minor poet, and the scant critical attention he has received therein, confirms the apparent accuracy of John Irwin's complaint that "the musical qualification which his reputation bears . . . remains a form of special pleading which, whatever its judicious surface appearance, has the effect of protecting Campion from having to compete on the highest poetic levels."[8] People have accorded to Campion a privileged status, Irwin argues, because we have assumed that words originally written for music cannot achieve as much "metaphysical" weight and density of meaning as words originally written by themselves. He discovers, in what is probably the best piece of Campion criticism to date, that this assumption is incorrect at least as applied to Campion, whose verse reveals "a balanced, multi-level meaning other than the metaphysical," one that offers a reader more than enough of its own kind of pleasing complexity.

The claim Irwin makes, that Campion's "richness of meaning" lends itself to analysis as well as that of some of his more widely read contemporaries, has nonetheless been effectively denied by the fact that editors and critics alike, while agreeing that Campion's poems are indeed good, have been generally reluctant or unable to say precisely why. Whether or not Hallet Smith's simple rationalization is true ("Campion is the finest of the Elizabethan poets who wrote for music, and the reason is the obvious one that he was a composer at the same time"), it tells us little about exactly what in the poems makes them so good; nor is the matter so obvious, as Smith himself shows when he confesses that the relation between Campion's verse and music is "difficult to explain for the reason that he wrote both, and quite possibly there was interaction between them in the process of composition."[9] Most critics have headed in the same direction, fixing upon Campion's "musical qualification" as the original mark of his success. The need to return that success back to its source is typified by W.H. Auden's admission that though Campion's words can be enjoyed by themselves, "they would not be what they are or sound as they do if he had not, when he wrote them, been thinking in musical terms."[10]

I do not mean to suggest that these efforts have been entirely misguided. They have not; on the contrary, the fact that it has proved so much easier to discover causes than to describe effects itself suggests something important about the uniqueness of Campion's excellence. It was Pound's conviction that "poetry begins to atrophy when it gets too far from music."[11] The Symbolists before him tried to find a "pure poetry," one which would come as close to music as writing could. Campion himself has been recently named "the greatest master in English poetry of what the French symbolists called la poesie pure,"[12] and if the musical qualification that Campion's reputation carries has discouraged a true estimate of his work, as Irwin claims, the fact still remains that Campion did write songs, did "couple [his] Words and Notes lovingly together." If for no other reason, though Campion may perhaps be "minor" in comparison with certain of his contemporaries (Shakespeare, Jonson, Donne), as a composer of words *and* music he nonetheless stands alone in a lyric tradition that includes not only Shakespeare, Jonson and Donne, but Wyatt, Sydney, Herrick, Blake and Tennyson.

The history of Campion's curious reputation is itself curious. With little or no precedent for the criticism of Elizabethan lyrics except that of Hazlitt ("[they] as often wore a sylph-life form with Attic vest, with faery feet, and the butterfly's gaudy wings"),[13] one can certainly excuse an editor like Bullen for his full-blown account of Campion's famous disclaimer that his poems in *A Book of Ayres* were "eare-pleasing rimes without Arte": "'Ear-pleasing' they undoubtedly are; there are no sweeter lyrics in English poetry than are to be found in Campion's song-books. But 'without art' they assuredly are not, for they are frequently models of artistic perfection. . . . what a wealth of golden poetry . . . !"[14] Nor is it surprising, with the *fin de siecle* appetite for the "sweet" lyric whetted by such poets as Tennyson, Rossetti and Swinburne, to find that Bullen's *Lyrics from the Song-Books*, which included the words to

forty songs by Campion, and his privately printed edition of *The Works of Dr. Thomas Campion* three years later, received the highest acclaim. What is surprising, though, is that from this modest debut Campion's popularity should have increased to the point where, only sixteen years after his initial discovery, Bullen felt it necessary to prefix this summary and warning note to his 1903 *Muses' Library* edition: "In 1887 Campion's admirers were few indeed. By critics and by anthologists he had been persistently neglected. I pleaded that the time had come for him to take his rightful place among our English poets; and the plea was so successful that he now runs the risk of becoming the object of uncritical adulation."[15] Ironically enough, Bullen's adjectival enthusiasm in introducing what another early editor called "a poet that he had almost made his own"[16] had made Bullen himself the chief source of the danger he feared.

Even more remarkable is the fact that Campion criticism has continued to employ the kind of adulatory but hollow labels that Bullen first cautioned against. Instead of offering a close and systematic investigation of exactly what in the poems have made them so highly admired and valued by so many readers, when they talk about Campion even good critics begin to sound like dutiful sophomores paying special lip service. To Kastendieck, "Campion was an individualistic artist whose fastidious taste in the combination of words and notes brought to his ayres a certain grace and rare sense of perfection charactristic of all Elizabethan song and, of course, the secret of its spontaneity."[17] Claiming that "his poems can be divided only into the good and the better, or else into the more and less characteristic," C.S. Lewis praised Campion as "the one poet whose loss would leave a chasm in our literature."[18] To Douglas Bush, the poems are "jewels of pure art or artifice which carry no trace of the everyday world."[19] Auden elevates them one step higher, calling the poems "a succession of verbal paradises in which the only element taken from the world of everyday reality is the English language."[20] Though often enough suggestive, these attempts to define Campion's excellence have generally avoided testing his poems with the kind of critical scrutiny exercised on other poets. Campion criticism to date has remained enthusiastically imprecise and, therefore, inadequate.

More than its enthusiasm or its imprecision, however, the main inadequacy of twentieth-century Campion criticism has been its failure to perceive that Campion's excellence is embodied in the principal relationship of his verse to his music as complex parts of an even more complex whole. This failure is reflected in modern criticism's wide disagreement on the question of whether Campion's words should be considered with or without his music. The problem and its implications are serious, and need to be examined more closely.

From what I have said earlier a reader might guess that Bullen and the other great English editors, whose work at the end of the nineteenth century brought to light material which to that time had been largely unknown, considered Campion's music secondary to his words. And he would be correct. The praise which these first editors heaped upon their discovery seems clearly to indicate that they viewed him primarily as a poet—indeed, as a literary ancestor of those late Victorian poets whom they themselves most admired. While they paid token recognition to the fact that Campion's "poems" were actually songs that could be sung, to them the music was more or less unimportant. Bullen himself, whose monumental literary efforts included editions of Marlowe, Shakespeare and numerous other dramatists, as well as a long list of verse anthologies (*England's Helicon, An English Garner, Lyrics from the Dramatists of the Elizabethan Age, Speculum Amantis, Musa Proterva*), was described by Yeats as "a fine scholar in poetry who hates all music but that of poetry, and knows of no instrument that does not fill him with rage and misery."[21] Ernest Rhys, whose own work included editions of Ben Johnson, Dekker, Vaughan and Keats, indicated a similar literary bias:

> Campion was all but a lost poet when Mr. Bullen so fortunately came to his rescue six years ago. His lyrics, with the exception of the very few turned to account by modern musicians, or given a place in the anthologies, lay buried in the old music books in which they were first published. And yet, if they had been left to the famous obscurity of the British Museum, we had lost perhaps the one poet who came nearest to fulfilling, in the genre and quality of his work, the lyric canon in English poetry.[22]

Percival Vivian's attitude toward music is revealed in this small note to the fourth song in *A Booke of Ayres*: "the air to which this song is set *does duty* also for 'Seeke the Lord and in his wayes persever'"[23] (my italics). The implication here—altogether justified on the evidence Vivian presents—is that music is secondary, subservient, to the poem, the words.

In fact it was. Though Campion's poems had been originally conceived of as songs, and published as a text of words embedded in a musical score (the usual practice for the lute-song was to print the words of the first stanza of each ayre beneath the notes to which they were to be sung; the second and subsequent stanzas were then printed out in metrical form as stanzas beneath the music[24]), modern editors from Bullen on had effectively divorced his words from his music by printing the words only. This was more than a matter of convenience, though it was that too. With both Bullen's and Vivian's editions of Campion containing the words to all of his songs, his four masks, his *Observations in the Art of English Poetry, A New Way of Making Fowre Parts in Counterpoint* (omitted by Bullen), and his Latin epigrams and elegies, and already running to four hundred pages, neither can be blamed for not choosing to include all of Campion's music as well. Nevertheless, Bullen, Rhys and Vivian were primarily literary scholars, editors who made it their business to rescue poets lost "in the famous obscurity of the British Museum"—poets like Campion.

It was against this background, twelve years after publication of the complete Campion song-books in Fellowes' *English School of Lutenist Song-writers* series, that Miles Kastendieck first proposed his radically alternative view. Reacting against the consideration of Campion's songs as poems only, a perspective encouraged by the fact that Campion's early editors had printed only his words, Kastendieck claimed that the lack of attention paid to the music by literary scholars and critics had resulted in a peculiarly limited point of view. Bringing a musical as well as literary background to the first full-scale study of Campion, *England's Musical Poet,* Kastendieck proposed an historically more accurate approach to the matter of Campion's words and music. The fact that Campion was a composer of both words and music, he argued, forces us to extend the meaning of "lyric" back to its etymological origin:

> Campion, then, is to be considered *more* than a poet. He was both a poet *and* a musician. He must, therefore, be introduced again as a *musical poet* in the true meaning of the words. The music that swayed so many poets was part of his creative work. He did not write poems, but "ayres." If, in writing these ayres, he excelled as a lyric poet, that is all the more to his credit. To call him a lyric poet while recognizing only his literary achievement is to present half an artist.[25]

Unfortunately, however much his novel critical perspective may have gained him, Kastendieck's argument proved to be little more than another attempt to make Campion's music responsible for what everyone had already perceived to be the excellence of his words. The idea that, because he was a musician, Campion's skill as a poet is "all the more to his credit" is a perfect example of that familiar kind of lip service which gives in to the temptation to locate beauty and excellence in its cause, or means, rather than effects. Even so, while the consensus had in fact always been that Campion's musical skill was very much "to his credit," was even somehow directly responsible for the high literary quality of his work, Kastendieck carried the matter a logical step further by arguing that the appreciation of Campion's poetic texts must be broadened to include a consideration of those musical texts with which they had first been conceived and executed. The measure of the musical poet's success was to be found only in this "perfect union of words and notes":

> The full charm of this relationship in the ayres can be appreciated only when they are considered in their original settings. When read, the lyrics, however refreshing and delightful they may be, are nevertheless incomplete without the musical setting. The music brings an added daintiness, a resonant melody, and, most significant of all, a series of little changes in meanings and subtle connotations.

(p. 70)

Though both the timeliness of his revaluation and the significance of his reinterpretation should not be denied, the general imprecision that characterizes these remarks points to the limited success that Kastendieck had in coming any closer to determining what specifically in Campion's songs makes them so good. Both his description of the lyrics by themselves ("refreshing," "delightful") and his explanation of what a musical setting adds to them ("daintiness, a resonant melody. . . . a series of little changes in meanings and subtle connotations") are nearly as vague and unhelpful as they seem. Like Bullen and the rest, Kastendieck had come not to anatomize and dissect Campion but simply to praise him.

The reaction to Kastendieck followed quickly. Six years after the appearance of *England's Musical Poet,* Ralph W. Short published an article directly opposed to the idea that Campion's poems cannot be fully appreciated without their original settings. On the contrary, Short argued, music can only be an obstacle to the full appreciation of any poem:

> A musical setting is so overpoweringly, determinatively sensuous that in its presence the subtleties of lyric poetry have little chance of making themselves felt. However various music itself may be, it dogmatizes upon any words that accompany it; it dictates one reading and precludes the hearing of any other, whereas for much great poetry there is no one right reading, but several which must be simultaneously apprehended. . . . Campion's tunes rig out his lyrics in pretty but concealing finery; his best poems mean more, as poems, when silently read than when sung or intoned. For this reason, whoever aims at justly appreciating his poetry had best forget his music.[26]

Obviously cast in the wake of Empson's celebration of ambiguity as the main criterion of poetic excellence, which was itself the product of what Walter R. Davis has referred to as Eliot's "domination of the literary scene of the 1920's,"[27] Short's defense of the necessary independence of words and music, and, what is more, of the real necessity of taking words by themselves, has found a far greater following than Kastendieck's argument to the contrary. If critics like Lowbury, Salter and Young admit that "in becoming words for music, poetry, complete in its own right, changes its shape and acquires an apparent incompleteness,"[28] they do not seem to be disturbed by that music's absence. If others admit that by not knowing a Campion song's music they may well be missing a vital part of its wholeness, they justify their ignorance by also admitting that the task of appreciating Campion's words by themselves—however much their music may add to one's appreciation—is more than enough. Indeed, as Catherine Ing explains it, there is good reason why the study of Campion's words without their music is sufficient in its own right, why critics have been willing to accept a part of their subject for the whole:

> hundreds of readers have recognized as poetry, and loved and admired, the verse for songs, who not only have not known the music, but have for various reasons failed to enjoy the music when known. It is, I think, justifiable to look for the causes of such enjoyment of the poetry alone in elements of the poetry alone. There is in this poetry a structure, which contributes to enjoy-

ment, made in words alone, words which cannot do all that music can do, but can in themselves make a purely poetic (or literary) beauty that it is not music's function to make.[29]

Ing's statement is important, first for its attempt to locate the cause of that pleasure which a song's words have given to readers who neither know nor like its music, and second for its effort to distinguish the separate value that verse by itself can have. What she says here needs to be said because it is true. Because it is obvious it needs to be said all the more. Poetry and music *are* two different kinds of things, one made in words and one in notes, each one built upon and exhibiting its own particular structures and beauties which themselves contribute particular pleasures to those who experience them. At the same time, Ing's statement clearly stands in opposition to Kastendieck's assertion that Campion's words cannot be fully appreciated without their original settings, and to that extent it is like Short's defense of studying words and notes separately. But it is a better and stronger argument than Short's, whose somewhat provincial attitudes kept him from granting any but a negative virtue to a song's music. It is a better argument because it reaches further and comprehends more of the essential differences between poetry and music. It therefore is and should be the standard argument, if one is needed, for justifying a consideration of Campion's words apart from his music.

As it turns out, the justification has not been needed. While the fact that Campion "coupled . . . Words and Notes lovingly together" is most certainly crucial to our understanding and appreciation of the unique excellence of his songs, as Kastendieck insisted, most of the admiration and attention that they have continued to receive has been willingly directed toward the words only. This is not really surprising. From Williams to Wordsworth, from Creeley to Campion, modern readers take their poetry sitting down, in their classrooms and libraries and studies, from magazines, textbooks, chapbooks, anthologies, edited selections and complete editions. From Bullen's *Lyrics from the Song-Books* on, the modern reader has come to Campion's songs as "poems,"[31] as words—and words only—on the page. He has found them in either of the two currently available complete editions (Vivian's and Davis') or, more probably, in the standard anthologies in which Campion is usually given a generous representation (thirty selections in the *Oxford Book of Sixteenth Century Verse,* sixteen in the *Norton Anthology of Poetry*). He has not known Campion's music, nor has he needed to know it in order to enjoy the words. Indeed, as Ing suggests, most people who have praised Campion have probably done so without ever having heard or seen his music. They have not heard it because it is not easily available; as far as I know the only recording that gives anything close to a representative sample of Campion (*Deutsche Grammophon Archive Production,* ten songs on one side only) is long out of print. They are even less likely to have seen it in either Fellowes' *Lutenist Song Writers* series or in the Scolar Press facsimile reproductions. What is more, if they have, they probably have not understood it. It was one thing for Kastendieck to call for attention to the original settings of Campion's songs, quite another to give those settings the wide circulation or the direct and familiar intelligiblity that his words alone can have.

This was not always the case. Everyone knows that the Elizabethan Age was also an age of song. The standard reference books and histories are full of facts, figures, and stories documenting the musical spirit that pervaded England at the turn of the seventeenth century:

> Tinkers sang catches; milkmaids sang ballads; carters whistled; each trade, and even the beggars, had their special songs; the base-viol hung in the drawing room for the amusement of waiting visitors; and the lute, cittern, and virginals, for the amusement of waiting customers, were the necessary furniture of the barber's shop. They had music at dinner; music at supper; music at weddings; music at funerals; music at night; music at dawn; music at work; music at play.[31]

However much a cliché, Chappell's description is remarkable for two reasons. First, this kind of general history was itself largely the product of a mid or late nineteenth-century view of England's romantic past, a view that stands immediately behind people like Kastendieck, people who have taken the truism as their excuse to ground the excellence of Campion's songs in its historical and biographical necessity rather than in the songs themselves. "In the heart of this world of music and poetry lived Thomas Campion.—poet, musician":[32] the talented byproduct of a talented Age. Second, as far as it goes, Chappell's description of the situation is probably accurate.

The weight of evidence indicating the wide popularity of ballads, folk songs, psalms, madrigals and ayres gives substance to the notion that the Elizabethans knew their music. Music actually seems to have been as important to them as Chappell would have had us believe. More likely than not a musical education *was* an essential ingredient in the making of the complete gentleman, as Peachman required: "there is no one Science in the world, that so affecteth the free and generous spirit, with a more delightful and in-offensive recreation; or better disposeth the minde to what is commendable and vertuous."[33] Lute songs and madrigals really *were* printed so that they could be brought out for the guests to sing after supper, and Philomates' often cited inability either to discuss the art or to carry a tune probably *did* make him an uncomfortable member of the party:

> Among the rest of the guests, by chance master Aphron came thither also, who, falling to discourse of music, was in an argument so quickly taken up and hotly pursued by Eudoxus and Calergus, two kinsmen of Sophobulus, as in his own art he was overthrown; but he still sticking in his opinion, the two gentlemen requested me to examine his reasons and confute them; but I refusing and pretending ignorance, the whole company condemned me of discourtesy, being fully persuaded that I had been as skilful in that art as they took me to be learned in others. But supper being ended

and the music books (according to the custom) being brought to the table, the mistress of the house presented me with a part earnestly requesting me to sing; but when, after many excuses, I protested unfeignedly that I could not, every one began to wonder; yea, some whispered to others demanding how I was brought up, so that upon shame of mine ignorance I go now to seek out mine old friend Master Gnorimus, to make myself his scholar.[34]

Thus Philomates. But while he did seek out his Master Gnorimus, and made himself "his scholar," the point is that we in the twentieth century have not. Few of us have heard Campion's music, fewer still have seen it, and one wonders of those who have how many were willing or able to sing or discourse upon it. We are simply not equipped to make the kind of total appreciation called for by Kastendieck a general possibility.

I want to conclude this chapter with a proposition that opens up a whole sub-subject in aesthetic theory: "Heard melodies are sweet, but those / Unheard are sweeter." Keats was not thinking of Campion when he wrote that line. Nevertheless, it may be that our ignorance of Campion's music has had something to do with the popularity that Campion's words without music have enjoyed for the last one hundred or so years. Consider cathedrals. Their murals and frescoes are chipped and faded, the whole of their past is clamoring to speak through them. Mayan temples have gone back to the jungle. The Venus de Milo has no arms. The tapestries at the Cloisters in New York are partially rotted. No one alive has heard the sound of Old English. There are some things so good that we are willing to adore fractions of them. Indeed, by their very incompleteness they are enhanced. Since we are forced to imagine the whole from its part—forced to become artists as audience—and since ruins and fragments include the ideal as nothing else can, whatever is wrong must be the remains of a former right, whatever missing perfect beyond imagining. The Parthenon can never have been as beautiful as it must have been when it was new.

According to Valéry, "Hearing verse set to music is like looking at a painting through a stained glass window."[35] One is suddenly aware of another dimension, a whole new set of impinging complexities and possibilities. As if the painting itself were not enough, there is suddenly the added complication of muted colors, subtly transformed figures and patterns, new surfaces, new light, new shades of meaning. There is suddenly a new painting. But what if to begin with the painting were made in the light of a stained glass window; what if it were made to be hung in the window, made to be seen through thousands of pieces of leaded glass, thousands of colored pieces which themselves were integral parts of the whole: wouldn't the painting in natural light become, however beautiful, a fragment, a fraction of the whole? Wouldn't we find ourselves forced to imagine the glass which was missing? Wouldn't we find ourselves artists as audience?

However beautiful, Campion's words without their music are also fragments, ruins, puzzles with missing pieces. Our experience of them is like our experience of old tapestries,

Old English, old cathedrals. When we read them beneath a small block of print that tells us these exquisite poems were really the word-half of songs, we are forced to become artists as audience. We are forced to imagine what is missing, the thousands of pieces of colored glass, the unknown complexities of figures and patterns and surfaces. We are forced to include what we do not hear in what we do. The absence of music where music is known to exist has an effect comparable not only to the absence of Venus' arms but the effects of allusion, echo, and non-comic parody; when he comes to the first song in Campion's *A Booke of Ayres,* for example, what reader does not hear in the background *Vivamus, mea Lesbia, atque amemus* and *Come my Celia, let us prove?* Similarly, knowing that Campion's music is missing, what reader does not feel the need to supply it, to fill in the empty space behind Campion's words on the page? Who does not hear in the disorder that the absent, but allowed-for, missing order shows us—in Campion's metrical flexibility, his shifting rhythms, his beautifully realized stanzaic patterns—who does not hear the music he does not hear, that silent music whose beauty is indeed perfect and smooth:

> Rose-cheekt *Lawra,* come
> Sing thou smoothly with thy beawties
> Silent musick. . . .

Notes

1. Thomas Campion, Preface to "Two Bookes of Ayres," *The Works of Thomas Campion,* ed. Walter R. Davis (New York: W. W. Norton & Co., 1970), p. 55. I quote Campion throughout from this edition.

2. A. H. Bullen, *Elizabethans* (London: Chapman and Hall Ltd., 1925), p. 127.

3. Ezra Pound, *A B C of Reading* (New York: New Directions, 1960), p. 84.

4. A. H. Bullen, ed., *Lyrics from the Song-Books of the Elizabethan Age* (London: John C. Nimmo, 1887), p. vi.

5. Percival Vivian, ed., *Campion's Works* (1909; rpt. Oxford: Oxford Univ. Press, 1966), p. 1v.

6. Miles Kastendieck, *England's Musical Poet* (New York: Oxford Univ. Press, 1938), p. 199.

7. Roy Fuller, "Fascinating Rhythm," *The Southern Review,* IX (1973), 857-872.

8. John T. Irwin, "Thomas Campion and the Musical Emblem," *SEL* (Winter 1970), 121-124. Irwin's article, which begins to suggest some of the complexity I find in "Now Winter Nights Enlarge," in effect justifies my own further attention to that song.

9. Hallet Smith, *Elizabethan Poetry* (Cambridge: Harvard Univ. Press, 1966), pp. 287, 281.

10. W. H. Auden, ed., *Selected Songs of Thomas Campion* (Boston: David R. Godine, 1972), p. 9.

11. Pound, p. 14.

12. Auden, p. 11.

13. William Hazlitt, *Lectures on the Literature of the Age of Elizabeth* (London: George Bell, 1899), p. 174.

14. A. H. Bullen, ed., *The Works of Dr. Thomas Campion* (London: The Chiswick Press, 1889), p. xvi.

15. A. H. Bullen, ed., *Thomas Campion, Songs and Masques with Observations in the Art of English Poetry* (London, 1903).

16. Ernest Rhys, ed. *The Lyrical Poems of Thomas Campion* (London: J. M. Dent & Co., 1895), p. xxv. It is interesting to note the praise which Bullen himself received for his discovery. Swineburne, for instance, to whom Bullen sent every edition he put out, had this to say about the importance of the Chiswick Press Campion: "In issuing the first edition of Campion's *Works* you have added a name to the roll of English poets, and one that can never be hence forward overlooked or erased. Certainly his long neglected ghost ought now to be rejoicing in Elysium. (*Letters from Algernon Charles Swineburne to A.H. Bullen,* London, 1910, p. 21.) See also these stanzas by Edmund Gosse:

> Bullen, well done!
>   Where Campion lies in London-land,
>   Lulled by the thunders of the Strand,
> Screened from the sun,
>
> Surely there must
>   Now pass some pleasant gleam
>   Across his music-haunted dream,
> Whose brain and lute are dust.

(Quoted by Amy Cruse, *The Elizabethan Lyrists and their Poetry* [London, 1913].)

17. Kastendieck, p. 70.

18. C. S. Lewis, *English Literature in the Sixteenth Century* (Oxford: Oxford Univ. Press, 1954), pp. 552-553.

19. Douglas Bush, *English Literature in the Earlier Seventeenth Century* (New York: Oxford Univ. Press, 1962), p. 102.

20. Auden, p. 11

21. Quoted by Kastendieck, p. 44.

22. Rhys, p. viii.

23. Vivian, p. 355.

24. See Bruce Pattison, *Music and Poetry of the English Renaissance* (London: Methuen & Co., 1970). For an account of a modern editor's difficulty in separating and arranging in metrical form the madrigal lyric from its music, see also Edmund Fellowes, ed., *English Madrigal Verse, 1588-1632* (Oxford: Oxford Univ. Press, 1967), pp. xxi-xxiv.

25. Kastendieck, pp. 46-47.

26. Ralph W. Short, "The Metrical Theory and Practice of Thomas Campion," *PMLA,* LIX (1944), 1004.

27. Walter R. Davis, ed., *The Works of Thomas Campion,* p. xiii. Davis argues that Campion's reputation was forced into decline because of Eliot's "elevation of John Donne and the other 'metaphysical' poets to major status as the really important poets of the English Renaissance, and of metaphysical wit and the complex image as the major evidences of literary worth." This does not seem to be entirely true. Witness Short's article. Eliot's own remarks on Campion deserve notice: "I should say that within his limits there was no more accomplished craftsman in the whole of English poetry than Campion. I admit that to understand his poems fully there are some things one should know: Campion was a musician, and he wrote his songs to be sung. We appreciate his poems better if we have some acquaintance with Tudor music; and we want not merely to read them, but to hear some of them sung, and sung to Campion's own settings" ("What is Minor Poetry?" *On Poets and Poetry* [rpt. New York: Farrar, Straus, 1957]).

28. Edward Lowbury, Timothy Salter, and Alison Young, *Thomas Campion, Poet, Composer, Physician* (London: Chatto & Windus, 1970), p. 32.

29. Catherine Ing, *Elizabethan Lyrics* (London: Chatto & Windus, 1951), p. 150.

30. Borrowing a question from Bertrand Bronson, "When is a ballad not a ballad?" (answer: when it does not have its music), one sees the logic of calling Campion's songs without their music "poems."

31. W. Chappell, *Popular Music of the Olden Time* (London, 1855), quoted by Kastendieck, p. 31.

32. Kastendieck, p. 42.

33. Quoted by Kastendieck, pp. 32-33.

34. Thomas Morley, *A Plaine and Easy Introduction to Practical Music* (1957: rpt. New York: W. W. Norton & Company, 1973), p. 9.

35. Quoted by Lowbury, Salter, and Young, p. 32.

David Lindley (essay date 1986)

SOURCE: Lindley, David. "The Poetry." In *Thomas Campion,* pp. 1-61. Leiden: E. J. Brill, 1986.

[In the essay that follows, Lindley examines Campion's poetry in English, focusing on his love poetry.]

> 'The Apothecaries have Bookes of Gold, whose leaves being opened are so light as that they are subject to be shaken with the least breath, yet, rightly handled, they serve both for ornament and use; such are light *Ayres.'*
>
>   (p. 168)

Campion's prefatory remarks to *The Fourth Booke of Ayres* make an apt initiation of the discussion of his poetry. Apt in that they present quite clearly the crucial problems for any critic or reader who tries to articulate his delight in these lyrics.

The first difficulty arises from the avowed 'lightness' of Campion's poems. For many years established literary criticism held ambiguity, density and complexity to be necessary qualities for elevation to the literary pantheon, requiring at the same time seriousness of moral engagement and, preferably, some clear signs of rebellious originality. Faced with Campion the alternatives, in this climate, are three: to ignore him (as Douglas Peterson does); to accept the fundamental lightness of the poetry but to divert attention to the skill of his versification (as does Hallett Smith); or else to recuperate him by locating his excellence in the pregnant plainness of part of his output (as Yvor Winters argues, and, to a certain extent, Walter Davis after him).[1]

The existence of this book is self-evidently a denial of the first alternative, but Campion's remarks also prompt a challenge to the other approaches. For though his technical skill is a vital ingredient in his claim upon a reader's attention, he yet suggests that airs have a *useful* function as well as an ornamental one. This variation on the standard Renaissance justification of all literature must be taken to indicate that the matter of his collections as well as their manner was significant to him, and should be to the reader.

While Winters and Davis do accept that Campion's meaning is of importance, their praise is bought at some cost. In Davis's Introduction a developmental history of Campion's career is generated, and all that is most worthy is found at the end, in *The Third Booke of Ayres.* Not only is his view based on a rather dubious chronology,[2] but it rests for its persuasiveness on an assumption that the 'ornamental' (or 'light' in Davis's terminology) is necessarily inferior to the 'plain' (or 'solid'). This valorisation runs counter to the implication of Campion's statement. He does not distinguish one category from the other; both ornament and use inhere in the aery thinness of the lyrics, provided that they are 'rightly handled'.

This qualification is, of course, the key element in Campion's claim, and chief source of critical difficulty. At its simplest it poses a problem of decorum for the critic. The image of gold leaf suggests that delicacy is required in handling the poems, a delicacy that some might feel is contravened when John T. Irwin or Stephen Ratcliffe[3] unleash the full weight of their critical armoury on the single lyric 'Now winter nights enlarge'.

The question of 'right handling' goes, however, deeper than this. At the end of his address to the reader Campion, following Martial, asserts:

> To be brief, all these Songs are mine if you express them well, otherwise they are your owne.

This comment directs our attention back to an ambiguity in the opening image. For one can either take the books of gold as standing for the books of airs and the apothecaries for the audience who must handle with care, or else the apothecary figures the poet carefully treating his golden material to produce ornamental and useful ware. Both possibilities are clearly present as Campion expresses the dual responsibility of author and reader in constructing and construing his poetry.

The aim of this chapter is to take up these implications as they affect the reader and describe the management of the poems themselves. There will be no attempt to construct a picture of the poet apart from the text, or to try, as Davis does, to validate a view of the poetry's worth by creating a teleological model of the poet's 'development'.

I

It is appropriate first to consider how a reader might approach Campion's *Works* as a whole. Since they were published in separate books it is useful to enquire whether the individual collections have any integrity, and whether the ordering of the lyrics within each book has any part to play in the generation of significance.

In one collection it is self-evident that the sequence of the lyrics is significant. The *Songs of Mourning*, published in 1613 with music by Coprario as part of the flood of poetry engendered by the death of Prince Henry, contains a prefatory poem (in Latin) addressed to Frederick, Count Palatine; 'An Elegie' on Prince Henry; and seven lyrics addressed in turn to King James, Queen Anne, Prince Charles, Princess Elizabeth, Frederick, Great Britain and The World.

'An Elegie' is structured according to the conventions of the classical elegy,[4] offering praise of the departed and lamentation at the harshness of Fate, with consolation coming at the end of the poem. The lyrics which follow it are not rigorously tied to the elegiac form, but develop and amplify topics of grief and of consolation in ways determined by the character and social position of each addressee.

The composition of seven lyrics might have been suggested in part by the conventional association of the number seven with mutability and change,[5] but the external control on their sequence is most obviously a principle of hierarchical decorum. They begin with a poem addressed to the King, move down the order of precedence of the Royal family, admit nobles and commons in the sixth lyric, and everyone else in the last.

The poetic success of this collection derives from an interplay between conventional constraints on subject matter on the one hand, and on the other the need to shape each lyric in a fashion appropriate to the figure to whom it is addressed. As poem follows poem the reader becomes aware of a delicate and purposeful manipulation of the poet's stance. The first two poems, to the King and Queen, are marked by formal language, a high incidence of apostrophe, and a decorous distance maintained between the poet and the addressee. The poems speak *about* the King and Queen, not directly *to* them. In the first, a stanza meditating on the diverse shapes of grief is followed by an apostrophe to Fate:

> O Fate, why shouldst thou take from KINGS their joy
>   and treasure?
>   Their Image if men should deface,
>   'Twere death; which thou dost race
>   Even at thy pleasure.
>
>   (p. 120)

Sympathy for the King's plight is indirect, and the reader is invited only to wonder from a distance at the tragedy of Prince Henry's death.

In rather similar vein, the second lyric creates a role for the Queen as 'mother':

> 'Tis now dead night, and not a light on earth
>   Or starre in heaven doth shine:
> Let now a mother mourne the noblest birth
>   That ever was both mortall and divine.
>
>   (p. 121)

As it continues with heaped-up apostrophe, the reader's sense of the Queen's grief is not immediate. Her feelings are heroic, and promote only respectful compassion.

The next poem, to Prince Charles, takes advantage of his tenderer years and lesser dignity to speak directly to him, and to offer good advice:

> Follow, O follow yet thy Brothers fame,
> But not his fate: lets only change the name,
>   And finde his worth presented
>   In thee, by him prevented.
>
>   (p. 122)

This marks the first appearance in the lyrics of the chief topic of consolation offered in 'An Elegie'—the conventional hope fixed on those who live after the Prince's death. The standard topic is revivified here by the personal address of the lyric. In the first stanza Charles's feeling for his brother is characterised:

> What can to kinde youth more despightfull prove
>   Then to be rob'd of one sole Brother?
>   Father and Mother
> Aske reverence, a Brother onely love.

The tone is a development from the previous lyric, less detached, but still couched in a generalised sententiousness that preserves the poet's proper distance from the heir to the throne.

The poem to Princess Elizabeth which follows takes up the presentation of a loving relationship, but, by further dismantling the distance between poet and addressee, allows for the first time a sense of the poet speaking as grieving individual, rather than public spokesman, to emerge. It is perhaps the finest lyric in the set, and deserves to be quoted in full:

> So parted you as if the world for ever
>   Had lost with him her light:
> Now could your teares hard flint to truth excite,
>   Yet may you never
>   Your loves againe partake in humane sight:
> O why should love such two kinde harts dissever
> As nature never knit more faire or firme together?
>
> So loved you as sister should a brother,
>   Not in a common straine,
> For Princely blood doeth vulgar fire disdaine:
>   But you each other
>   On earth embrac't in a celestiall chaine.
> Alasse for love, that heav'nly borne affection
> To change should subject be, and suffer earths infec-
>   tion.
>
> (p. 123)

Part of the force of this poem derives from exquisite control of the relationship between rhythm, rhyme structure and sense units, especially in the manipulation of feminine line-endings. . . . But major constituents in this lyric's success are the delicacy of its address to the Princess, and the power its simplicity derives from the context of the poem in the sequence.

Where, in the third lyric, Prince Charles had been addressed in a formal 'thou', the increased intimacy of this poem is signalled by its use of the 'you' form. At the same time the opening lines dramatise the Princess's grief by their suggestion that the poet is an eye-witness of her sorrow, speaking from first-hand knowledge of the nature of her parting from her brother.

The creation for the poet of a posture involving him as sympathetic spectator gives a tenderness to the fourth and fifth lines, as tentative consolation is offered in a context of marvelling at such passionate sorrow. The apostrophe with which the stanza concludes then becomes a personal response to the plight of the Princess.

The warmth of the first stanza owes much to its hinting at the vocabulary and style of love-lyric. These hints are taken up in the second stanza, to be qualified and converted into praise of the Prince and his sister, before the poet delivers his final verdict, integrating this poem into the sequence of meditations on cruel fate.

This is not only a fine poem in its own right, but it also occupies a central place in the sequence in more than a simply numerical sense. The decorum required of the poet in his address to royal personages here permits him to approach most nearly to the poem's addressee, and, in so doing, to suggest fully his own sorrow at the death of the Prince. After this fourth poem, the poet gradually moves back to a position of detachment, making possible different perspectives upon the Prince's death.

Frederick, Elector Palatine, the addressee of the fifth poem, was betrothed to Elizabeth, but had only met Prince Henry some three weeks before his death. It is therefore appropriate that the tone of grief, dominant in the lyrics to immediate family, should be much more subdued, and the poetry should look to a positive future:

> Such the condition is of humane life,
> Care must with pleasure mixe, and peace with strife:
>   Thoughts with the dayes must change; as tapers
>   waste
>   So must our griefes; day breakes when night is
>   past.
>
> (p. 124)

Formally the last two poems, since they are not directed to individuals, act as a kind of concluding couplet, recapitulating and generalising the matter presented in the first five poems. So the ample mourning of Great Britain is narrated, testifying to universal regard for the Prince. Perhaps the rather flat tone of this poem is apt enough after the more personal lyrics which precede it, but that does not really save it from being the weakest of the set.

The last poem completes the sequence both in its further movement away from the poet's deepest involvement expressed in the fourth poem, and also by rounding out the external pattern of hierarchically ordered address. Its terminal function is also signalled by its return to the frequent use of apostrophe which marked the first two lyrics, making a kind of stylistic 'rhyme' which binds the collection together.

At the same time the poem concentrates on Prince Henry's role as a champion of Protestant Christianity, lamenting the fact that death prevented him from completing the unification of Christendom already begun by his father's polemic efforts. The concluding lines of the poem are interesting.

> O princely soule, rest thou in peace, while wee
> In thine expect the hopes were ripe in thee.
>
> (p. 126)

This first direct mention of the Prince's final rest is appropriate as the conclusion of an elegiac sequence, but at the same time it recapitulates the consolation offered at the end of **'An Elegie'**:

> Curst then bee Fate that stole our blessing so,
> And had for us now nothing left but woe,
> Had not th'All-seeing providence yet kept
> Another joy safe, that in silence slept:
> And that same Royall workeman, who could frame
> A Prince so worthy of immortall fame,
> Lives; and long may hee live, to forme the other
> His exprest image, and grace of his brother.
>
> (p. 119)

Concentration on the hope that lives on in James and Charles helps to unify the collection of lyrics. Encouragement was first offered to Charles to imitate his brother, and then consolation in rather general terms to Frederick. In the final lyric hope for the future is given specific direction in a Christian crusade. By suggesting that consolation for the Prince's death is only fully to be achieved when the heirs to his concerns take up the work he begun, the sequence as a whole assumes an exhortatory quality.

Scaliger suggested that elegy should

> be closed with exhortations; it is not so much a matter of their being mourned as it is that their present felicity, which shelters their survivors, be treated with due gravity, to further the emulation of their virtues, minds and deaths.[6]

The book is specifically offered to Frederick, and the work as a whole is designed to urge him to fulfil Henry's destiny as Protestant champion.

In this set of lyrics, then, an external linear ordering enables the development of a pattern of feeling which reaches its peak of intensity in the central poem. The whole is sustained by the topoi of the classical elegy, and given its focus by its direction to Frederick as dedicatee. Such a degree of integration is not to be found in any of Campion's other books, but in all of them there is evidence of care in the placing of lyrics, and in most an attempt to give an overall shape to the collection.

A range of organisational devices is exhibited in the five **Bookes of Ayres.** In order to build up a picture of the kinds of connections made between poems, and, more important, to establish how such connections are significant for the reader's experience of Campion's work, it is convenient to begin with the simplest relationships between individual lyrics and then to move on to consideration of patternings that inform the structure of the **Bookes** as whole units.

Perhaps the most obvious way of grouping poems together is to connect adjacent lyrics by some form of verbal or thematic repetition. In **A Booke of Ayres** three poems, Nos. 14-16, are linked by the presence of Cupid in each of them, and by play on the conventional notions of heat and cold associated with the God of Love. In these poems a common image functions principally as a kind of rhyme. A link is made, but the link is formal rather than generative of meaning; it does little more than reassure the reader that he is reading an articulated collection of poems.

In order for the reader to feel that connections have more substantial function he must be challenged by the poems to account for the fact of their juxtaposition on some higher level. A relationship of similarity between poems invites the reader to construct a context enabling them to be taken together, and it is then the nature of the variation between them that defines the kind of context that is appropriate and the deductions that may properly be made from it.

The first two lyrics of the **Third Booke** illustrate this reading process. In the opening poem a woman complains of desertion by her lover; in the second a man records his

reaction to a mistress who has left him. The similarity of situation, albeit a conventional one, asks the reader to consider them together. Since there are two different speakers they cannot be construed as expressing a single consciousness, and the fact that both speakers have been deserted precludes the creation of a narrative context in which the second poem might be an answer to the first. The reader is therefore directed to consideration of the situational parallel between the poems.

Taken together the lyrics generalise, suggesting that the situation of desertion is common to male and female (and, of course, commonplace in love poetry). The individual speakers move closer to being-taken as types, and the reader adds to his response to each individual poem the possibility of interpreting them as characteristic of female and male responses to a stock situation. The female response is seen as passive and resigned, the male as more active and forceful. Furthermore, since these are the first two poems in the book, there is also the possibility that they are defining a thematic area—of unfaithfulness and alternative responses to it—that will be explored further in the collection as a whole. To that possibility we will return later.

Another example of a pair of lyrics spoken by a man and a woman occurs in **The Second Booke,** and, in a more comic vein, their pairing also directs the reader's attention to thematic parallels. No. 14 is built on bawdy innuendo. It begins:

> Pin'd I am, and like to die,
> And all for lacke of that which I
>   Doe ev'ry day refuse.

                                                        (p. 103)

As the poem proceeds it becomes clear that the cause of his distress is uncertainty about what to do with his penis. 'It' interrupts his poetic composition and disturbs his sleep, and the lyric concludes:

> Would I had the heart and wit
> To make it stand, and conjure it,
>   That haunts me thus with feare.
> Doubtless tis some harmlesse spright,
> For it by day, as well as night,
>   Is ready to appeare.
> Be it friend, or be it foe,
> Ere long Ile trie what it will doe.[7]

That the speaker is youthfully naive is indicated by his puzzled failure to understand his own sexuality. His bewilderment is mimed by his failure to name the offending object, a device which at the same time creates the humour of the poem, as he is slow to solve a riddle for which poet and reader are only too easily able to provide an answer.

> So many loves have I neglected
>   Whose good parts might move mee,
> That now I live of all rejected,

There is none will love me.
Why is mayden heate so coy?
   It freezeth when it burneth,
Looseth what it might injoy,
   And having lost it, mourneth.

(p. 105)

The situational parallel is much less complete than in the first pair of poems, but there is sufficient similarity for the reader to be made aware that this is not a chance juxtaposition. Where the youth suffered from failure to understand the sexual source of his distress, the woman looks back on a youth when convention dictated that she must appear not to acknowledge or understand her sexual passion. Once this basic similarity is established, the main consequence of the pairing is to point up the dissimilarities of male and female roles in sexual conduct. Where a man can come to terms with his sexuality by trying 'what it will do', a woman is prisoner to her sexual role. In the third stanza she makes this difference explicit:

O happy men, whose hopes are licenc'd
   To discourse their passion,
While women are confin'd to silence,
   Loosing wisht occasion.

Presenting the male-female difference as one of opportunity for speech introduces a witty dimension to the relationship between the two poems. For it is the male speaker of the first poem who is presented as incapable of articulating his sexual nature directly, though finally he is permitted to solve his problem through action, whereas the articulate woman, who does not evade her sexual problem in language, is inhibited by custom from translating desire into performance.

Thus far the relationship between these two lyrics has been seen as very similar in kind to the first pairing, employing a degree of comparability to enable a little exploration of differences between male and female characteristics. But in this second pair there is a hint of a relationship of a different kind, where the order of the poems also contributes to the reader's understanding. The first poem is spoken by an untried youth, the second by a woman who looks back on past failure. He has a simple hope that, having recognised the source of his discontent, he will be able to cure it by action. She, however, representing the woman upon whom he must try his power, speaks, albeit repentantly, of the 'strangenesse' enjoined on the female sex. The first poem is therefore qualified by the second as the reader constructs a potential narrative sequence out of the pairing, where the optimistic youth is to be thwarted by conventionally chaste lady. Taken together they contribute to the study of frustration which, as will be seen, runs throughout ***The Second Booke.***

The desire to bring poems together by constructing a narrative frame in which to place them is deeply embedded in any reader's mind. A number of pairs and short runs of poems throughout Campion's work explicitly invite such a reading.

A straightforward example is to be found in ***The First Booke.*** This little sequence begins with one of Campion's better-known poems:

Never weather-beaten Saile more willing bent to shore,
Never tyred Pilgrims limbs affected slumber more,
Then my weary spright now longs to flye out of my
   troubled brest.
   O come quickly, sweetest Lord, and take my soule
to rest.

Ever blooming are the joyes of Heav'ns high paradice,
Cold age deafes not there our eares, nor vapour dims
   our eyes;
Glory there the Sun outshines, whose beames the
   blessed only see;
   O come quickly, glorious Lord, and raise my spright
to thee.

(p. 70)

This lyric elaborates the simple statement 'I am old and ready for death'. Its force derives in part from the quiet appropriateness of the amplificatory imagery in the first stanza, derived from journeying in the three elements of sea, earth and air and sanctioned by conventional association with the voyage and pilgrimage of life.

The next lyric begins:

Lift up to heav'n, sad wretch, thy heavy spright;
What though thy sinnes thy due destruction threat?
The Lord exceedes in mercy as in might;
His ruth is greater, though thy crimes be great.

(p. 72)

The first line signals a relationship with the previous poem, in the correspondence of 'heavy spright' with the 'weary spright' previously encountered, and in the recapitulation of desire for heaven and of the image of ascent. The second line, however, takes the reader in a new direction. Whereas **'Never weather-beaten Saile'** is built upon a desire for death seen as rest from labour, this poem presents death as destroyer, as just punishment for sin.

At first it might seem that this is no more than a gestural link between two largely independent lyrics presenting alternative visions of our ultimate destiny. But the reader invited by initial similarity to meditate further on the relationship between the poems looks back with a different awareness to the first poem, and realises that a line at first passed over assumes a new prominence. In its second stanza the reader was told that 'Glory there the Sun outshines, whose beames the blessed only see'. The second part of the line asserts a basic Christian truth—heaven is for the righteous—but the exclusive force of the word 'onely' barely registers in a context where the blessed are primarily presented as witnesses to God's supreme brightness, and inversion of natural word-order itself contributes to suppression of the adjectival status of the word. The reader then might supply a connection between the poems by 'filling in the gap' between them by a conjectured narrative. The poet desires death, but then begins, like Hamlet, to ask himself what dreams may haunt his eternal rest if he is not of the company of the 'blessed'. The second poem exposes that fear in order to allay it. That some such narrative conjecture is not merely wild supplementation of the text is further demonstrated by the second poem's conclusion.

> Remorce for all that truely mourne hath place;
> Not God, but men of him themselves deprive:
> Strive then, and hee will help; call him, hee'll heare:
> The Sonne needes not the Fathers fury feare.

In **'Never weather-beaten Saile'** the poet had called upon the Lord to come quickly. The injunction here in the penultimate line invites him to call again, but with a more instructed faith and a clearer sense of his dependence upon the Lord's mercy

The third poem in this little set also establishes immediately a relationship with the previous two poems:

> Loe, when backe mine eye,
>   Pilgrim-like I cast,
> What fearefull wayes I spye,
> Which, blinded, I securely past.
>
> But now heav'n hath drawne
>   From my browes that night;
> As when the day doth dawne,
> So cleares my long imprison'd sight.[8]

(p. 73)

The image of pilgrimage links it with the first poem, as does the picture of heaven (where no 'vapour dims our eyes') clearing the sight of the poet. Narratively the link with **'Lift up to heav'n'** is much closer to the surface than had been the narrative connection between the first two poems. The poet, reassured in the second poem, has had the confidence to strive with God's help, and has lifted his heart to heaven. His prayer has been answered, and he may look back at the Hell he has passed and see it for what it is with regenerated spiritual sight.

That these three lyrics trace a narrative progression is emphasised by the distance between first and third poems manifest in the final stanzas:

> Straight to Heav'n I rais'd
>   My restored sight,
> And with loud voyce I prais'd
> The Lord of ever-during light.
>
> And since I had stray'd
>   From his wayes so wide,
> His grace I humbly pray,
> Henceforth to be my guard and guide.

In place of crying for the Lord to come is a calling out of praise; instead of a demand to be released from pilgrimage is an acquiescence in continuing life supported by the grace of God. The three poems, then, trace a little spiritual path from weariness through repentance to security in faith.

In **The Second Booke** the first four poems may similarly be taken together as reflecting a sequence of attitudes in the mind of a lover. The first poem has a moralising flavour:

> Vaine men, whose follies make a God of Love,
> Whose blindnesse beauty doth immortall deeme:
> Prayse not what you desire, but what you prove,
> Count those things good that are, not those that seeme:
> I cannot call her true that's false to me,
> Nor make of women more then women be.
>
> How faire an entrance breakes the way to love;
> How rich of golden hope and gay delight;
> What hart cannot a modest beauty move?
> Who, seeing cleare day once, will dreame of night?
> Shee seem'd a Saint that brake her faith with mee,
> But prov'd a woman, as all other be.
>
> So bitter is their sweet, that true content
> Unhappy men in them may never finde;
> Ah, but without them, none; both must consent,
> Else uncouth are the joyes of eyther kinde.
> Let us then prayse their good, forget their ill:
> Men must be men, and women women still.

(p. 85)

This is a much more complex and elusive poem than it seems at first. Certain features contributing to its complexity may be picked out for their particular relevance to the present discussion of sequence.

Taken as a whole the poem's three stanzas form a pattern where the first and last, of sententious cast, frame a stanza of retrospective narrative. In the first the poet encourages the reader to adopt a realistic attitude to love. In the second he looks back to a time when his illusions about his mistress were shattered. Thus far the reader, as he 'unpacks' the poem, has little difficulty. In narrative terms the second stanza precedes the first, and the reader accepts the reversal of their order as reflecting the poet's desire to assert 'this is what I think, and this is why I think it'. But the third stanza, for all that it appears to return to the manner of the first and by its verbal reminiscence in the last two lines to be echoing its sentiments, in fact presents attitudes significantly different from those of the opening. Where that had advocated a stern realism, here we are encouraged to edit experience, to forget women's ill. In seeking to explain the modification of attitude the reader must look back to the second stanza, and see the third as a response not so much to the experience it recollects, as to the experience of recollection itself. In remembering a time full of 'golden hope' the poet realises that, however miserable he might have been, future happiness will still depend upon some contact with womankind. A way must be found of accommodating this realisation; and the final stanza, somewhat uneasily, suggests that selective response might be the answer.

In order to see the significance of the placing of the second stanza, one only has to imagine what sort of poem one might have had if the order of the first two stanzas were reversed. The lyric would then have been perfectly satisfactory without any continuation, since the order 'I experienced that, and hence I conclude this' is both more conventional and also aligns the sequence of experience with the sequence of expression that the reader follows in the poem.

The inversion of narrative order makes possible a double time-scheme. Super-imposed upon the sequence of event and reflection on it that the reader reconstructs from the poem is the time of the poem's composition as reflected in the order of words on the page. This double time-scheme helps to generate the richness of effect of the poem, as it involves the reader in responding both to the report on experience and to the experience of the poem itself. The last stanza makes sense only if he has understood that the second stanza is both a characterisation of an experience that is past, and at the same time a poetic present provoking immediate reaction in the third stanza.

The sequence of poems which follow can best be understood as a kind of clearer re-writing of the narrative of this lyric. The next poem, **'How easl'y wert thou chained'**, develops a picture of the time when 'shee seem'd a Saint'. At the end of the first stanza the lover writes:

> Yet 'tis no woman leaves me,
> For such may prove unjust:
> A Goddesse thus deceives me,
> Whose faith who could mistrust?
>
> (p. 87)

He has here not attained the detachment to recognise his literary characterisation of his Goddesse as the self-sustaining fantasy that it is.

The opening of the third lyric shows that the lover has now gained the kind of bitter understanding recorded in the first stanza of **'Vaine men'**:

> Harden now thy tyred hart with more then flinty rage;
> Ne'er let her false teares henceforth thy constant grief
>   asswage.
>
> (p. 88)

These two poems have an implied narrative that matches the terms the opening lyric of the book established for the illusion of love and the reality of rejection.

The fourth poem suddenly changes direction, as the lady relents, and the poet exults:

> O what unhop't for sweet supply!
>   O what joyes exceeding!
>
> (p. 89)

There is little overt connection between this poem and those which precede it. The reason for accepting it as part of a sequence is primarily that, after three poems having a reasonably overt relationship, the 'law of good continuation'[9] suggests that, unless there is decisive

evidence to the contrary, the pattern of connection will be continued. Furthermore, the pattern it makes, once accepted, is very much sanctioned by literary convention. The irruption of joy in Sidney's *Astrophil and Stella* at Sonnet 69, where, after long rejection the lover suddenly feels 'I, I, O I may say that she is mine',[10] is but one obvious analogue. In any case, once a reader has responded to the invitation to generate a narrative or quasi-narrative relationship between this poem and those immediately before it, his instinct is then validated by the realisation that this poem fleshes out the suggestion of the last stanza of the opening lyric. Here indeed are the joys that ensue when 'both consent'.

In this group, then, the complex pattern of the first poem is unpicked and clarified by the three poems that follow it, each treating one of its parts without complication. At the same time their effect is modified by the ironies which the opening lyric generates.

Thus far it is relationships between adjacent poems that have been considered. It is obviously also the case that in a collection of lyrics relationships between poems separated one from the other can and do carry structural weight. (Such is the case in many sonnet sequences, for example).

A Booke of Ayres, however, does not, in fact, offer a particularly rich coherence. The run of Cupid poems has already been mentioned;[11] a number of lyrics deal with sexual conquest (Nos. 3, 5, 7, 8, 11), but such motifs and images are so commonplace that it would be inappropriate to make much of them. The only exception is, perhaps, lyrics dealing with death as the end of love. It figures in the first two poems and the fourth, is alluded to in the ninth and surfaces again in the nineteenth and twentieth poems. It is significant particularly in that the first poem, **'My sweetest Lesbia'**, with its triumph of love in death contrasts with the bitterness of the murdered lover and dead lady in **'When thou must home'**. The recollection and revaluation of mortality makes a satisfying frame for the collection before the religious coda of the final poem 'Come let us sound'. But in general, *A Booke of Ayres* is a collection of poems loosely related, rather than a coherent whole.

The First Booke of Ayres, by contrast, seems much more fully controlled. In part this is an inevitable by-product of its exclusive concentration on religious subjects, in part also, a consequence of the restriction of stylistic range that the subject matter suggests as appropriate.

The proper style for religious verse was frequently a matter for debate in this period, as Barbara Lewalski has shown.[12] Campion's position is clearly set out in two adjacent poems. In **'To Musicke bent'** he writes:

> To Musicke bent is my retyred minde,
> And faine would I some song of pleasure sing:
> But in vaine joyes no comfort now I finde:
> From heav'nly thoughts all true delight doth spring.

Thy power, O God, thy mercies to record
Will sweeten ev'ry note, and ev'ry word.

(p. 66)

The beauty of devotional verse inheres in the subject, not in the treatment given to it, so that the effort to speak of the mercies of God will of itself 'sweeten' the words for the reader. Consequently, as the next lyric states:

Strive not yet for curious wayes:
Concord pleaseth more, the less 'tis strained.

(p. 66)

Campion's style, therefore, throughout the collection is, as Davis suggests, 'typically that of pithy literal statement . . . concentrating on clarity of outline and terseness'. But though the restricted style and subject matter of the collection give the reader an initial sense of its sameness, closer attention reveals both greater variety and at the same time a more profound unity than might at first be supposed.

The opening two lyrics define the territory, thematic and stylistic, within which the greater part of the book operates. **'Author of Light'** is a passionate prayer uttered by the poet from a sense of his own sinfulness. It is concerned with the life of the spirit, and belongs with the Biblical kind represented by the more introspective Psalms.

The second poem in the book, **'The man of life upright'**, in contrast, concerns life in the world rather than the life of the spirit, is classical rather than Biblical in its inspiration (though it is very much a Christianised version of the Horace *Ode* which is its starting point).[13] The poet here speaks as a public and moralising voice, rather than as an introspective individual.

The story of the book they initiate is in no small measure an elaboration and investigation of the double perspective upon Christian life they present. In the process the marked distinctiveness of their mode of address is eroded. The detached moralist's voice of **'The man of life upright'** becomes, in some poems, more urgent and exhortatory, though still preserving a sententiousness which functions as a guarantee of the speaker's wisdom. **'Tune thy Musicke to thy heart'** is one such poem, gravely answering the more personally expressed opening of the previous poem, **'To Musicke bent is my retyred minde'**.

'Awake, awake, thou heavy spright' blurs the two voices in an interesting fashion. It can be taken as dramatising the poet's internal consciousness of his own spiritual lethargy (so placing the reader in the same relationship to it as he occupies for **'Author of Light'**). But the reader can also take the second-person pronoun as being addressed to himself, so that he is the recipient of the lyric's exhortation in the same way as he had been for **'The man of life upright'**.

'Seeke the Lord' separates the two modes of address. The first two stanzas are unambiguously aimed at the reader, but in the last two the poet speaks in his own voice. The

effect of this shift is to give dramatic energy to the poem, as the poet seems to be persuaded by the beginning of his own lyric to abandon the ways of the world.

This is one direction that the collection takes to bring together the private and public voices of its opening. In quite a different fashion the public voice of **'The man of life upright'** is expanded in its range to take on a role as spokesman not for an individual, but for the whole people of God. This voice, like the voice of **'Author of Light'**, has its original in the Psalms, but Psalms of a different kind from the introspective meditation of **'Out of my soules deapth'**. **'Sing a song of joy'**, made up of a tissue of scriptural echoes, principally from the Psalms (see below pp. 33-35), is a clear example of the type, and has explicit connection with the content of **'The man of life upright'**. It celebrates the deliverance of the people of God from bondage (a function clarified by its juxtaposition with a paraphrase of the Psalm of the Babylonian captivity, **'As by the streames of *Babilon*'**), and ends:

Let us then rejoyce,
   Sounding loud his prayse:
So will hee heare our voyce,
And blesse on earth our peacefull dayes.

(p. 75)

The peaceful life figures at the end of this poem as it had at the end of **'The man of life upright'**. There it was the reward for personal integrity, here the consequence of the faithfulness of the people of God. **'Sing a song of joy'** is in its turn linked to an earlier poem that springs rather surprisingly upon the reader, the ode on the fifth of November, **'Bravely deckt'**. In retrospect the reader understands it as a hymn of praise spoken by the British as God's 'chosen Nation' for a deliverance as spectacular in evidencing God's mercy as the deliverance of Israel from Babylon. Both these poems present an ideal public life of peace and content corresponding to the individual prescription of 'The man of life upright'.

But this personal ideal of a quiet pilgrimage achieved by virtuous conduct, is significantly at odds with the attitude expressed in **'Author of Light'**. There a clear opposition is set up between the way of the world and the way of the spirit:

Lord, light me to thy blessed way:
  For, blinde with worldly vaine desires, I wander as a stray.

(p. 59)

Thus, though the order of the first two poems implies that the journey of the spirit necessarily precedes the possibility of a peaceful earthly life, their juxtaposition does not indicate any way of translating a negative view of life as a dark wandering into a positive espousal of life's 'quiet pilgrimage'. We have already seen one exploration of the image of pilgrimage in the poems which follow **'Never weather-beaten Saile'**, but it is only in a later sequence that the tensions set up by the first two poems in the book are fully resolved. This group begins:

Awake, awake, thou heavy spright,
That sleep'st the deadly sleepe of sinne;
   Rise now, and walke the wayes of light,
   'Tis not too late yet to begin.
     Seeke heav'n earely, seeke it late,
     True Faith still findes an open gate.

Get up, get up, thou leaden man:
Thy tracks to endlesse joy or paine
   Yeelds but the modell of a span;
   Yet burnes out thy lifes lampe in vaine.
     One minute bounds thy bane, or blisse,
     Then watch, and labour while time is.

(p. 76)

Here the twin aspects of the journeying image are brought together in a single poem. The spiritual journey to the 'wayes of light' can only be made as man treads the 'tracks' of his earthly life from birth to death. This introduces a sharply temporal dimension into the image, an awareness reinforced by the next poem, **'Come chear-full day'**, with its sombre refrain 'soe ev'ry day we live, a day wee dye' (p. 76). In turn it gives much greater urgency to the following poem **'Seeke the Lord'** than had obtained in the earlier **'Loe when backe mine eyes'** to which it is closely related. Here there is a sense of struggle, rather than of wonder at God's grace. The awareness that we must 'watch and labour' is then carried over to the beginning of the final poem in the group, **'Lighten heavy hart'**, a moralistic lyric condemning sloth. In this little group of poems, then, the image of journeying is used to suggest, neither the peacefulness of life's pilgrimage, nor the abandonment of the world for the ways of God, but rather the immediate and urgent necessity to turn the journey of life itself into a time for the pilgrimage of grace.

This brief discussion of some of the poems that manipulate a standard Christian image demonstrates how Campion explores and tests its resonance and implication. For the reader it means that an idea so conventional as to be easily passed over is revitalised and its suggestiveness is heightened, if he is prepared to consider the poems together rather than singly.

Something of the same is true of the rhyming and chiming of images of light which figure in over half the poems in the book. Light is a property of God and heaven. It is available to man as an illumination for his path (**'Author of light'**), or as a metaphor for the path itself (**'Awake, awake, thou heavy spright'**). Light may shine through man when he is infused by divine grace (**'View mee, Lord'**), or else represent the new light of perception that becomes his when he has gained his spiritual goal (**'Never weather-beaten saile'**, **'Loe, when backe mine eye'** and **'Seeke the Lord'**). Used in this context its opposite is either the world's false light (**'Seeke the Lord'**) or, in many poems, the darkness and opacity of the world. It may also be opposed more specifically to the darkness of sin (**'Bravely deckt'**). The poems also explore the possibilities of the opposition 'light' and 'heavy' (especially **'Awake, awake, thou heavy spright'** and **'Lighten, heavy**

heart thy spright'**), often using the punning possibility of playing with both senses of the word.

The play of these images from poem to poem adds up to a network of connection that brings the various poems in which they occur into relationships of mutual enrichment, and at the same time goes some way to ensure that the reader gives proper attention to images that are so commonplace as to run the risk of seeming merely mechanical.

The First Booke is perhaps the least regarded of Campion's collections. While it would be silly to pretend that he is the equal of Donne or Herbert as a religious poet, yet it does seem to me that, if the lyrics are taken as a whole, they are rich in suggestion and dexterous in their craft.

Some of the effect of ***The First Booke*** derives from the uniformity of its subject matter and the limited range of its style. ***The Second Booke,*** published with it, is much more varied. The poems are all love lyrics, but, as Puttenham observed, variety is part of the decorum of love poetry.[14] Nonetheless it is possible to discern in the collection as a whole a purposeful and structured selection from the huge available repertory of amatory topics.

The key to the book's structure is offered in its dedication to the young Henry, Lord Clifford. The poet distinguishes the book from its predecessor in these terms:

   Pure Hymnes, such as the seaventh day loves, doe leade;
Grave age did justly chalenge those of mee:
   Those weeke-day workes, in order that succeede,
Your youth best fits, and yours, young Lord, they be.

(p. 84)

Obviously the basic pattern is 'religion for age, love for youth', but the selection of the love poems is dictated by an attempt to make them especially appropriate to the youth of their dedicatee. The opening poem, **'Vaine men, whose follies'**, is the only one which sounds any note of detachment from the business of love. It acts as a kind of ironic preface from an older poet who knows that 'men must be men, and women women still', and that no amount of aged wisdom will prevent youth from treading the circular path from despair to hope and back again. The basic order of the poems reflects a loose narrative sequence telling a familiar 'story' of a hopeful lover, thematically appropriate to youth in its varied but continuous concentration on frustration, a frustration that grows ever more intense as the sequence proceeds.

After the opening run of four poems, already sufficiently discussed, the apparent triumph of **'O, what unhop't for sweet supply'** is swiftly undermined in the next poem, which concludes:

But, from her bowre of Joy since I
   Must now excluded be,
And shee will not relieve my cares,
   Which none can helpe but shee:

My comfort in her love shall dwell,
　Her love lodge in my brest;
And though not in her bowre, yet I
　Shall in her temple rest.

(p. 91)

This lady, like Stella in Sidney's sequence, clearly offers her love conditionally on the lover's chaste behaviour. The poet, at the same time, leaves little doubt of the specifically sexual 'relief' he seeks.

In the poems that follow the lover retreats from the lady, and diminishes the extent of his sexual demands upon her. In the sixth poem he wonders whether he dare declare his love, and thereby gain 'pity' which would satisfy the desire he tries vainly to repress. In the eighth, **'O deare, that I with thee might live'** he offers a mingling of minds, in the tenth asks only for kisses, since 'That which kinde and harmlesse is, / None can deny us'.

The retreat halts when, in **'Sweet, exclude me not'** the lover's sexual demands surface again. He pleads before the closed door of his betrothed to anticipate their wedding night. The next two poems see the lover once more in retreat but with the innuendo of **'Pin'd I am, and like to die'** (discussed above) the temperature rises. In two poems which follow (after the interlude of **'Though your strangenesse'**, to which we will return) sexual ambition is most explicitly declared.

They are interesting poems, for in both there is a subtle modification of the reader's understanding of the situation they imply as the poems proceed, suggesting that gratification of desire is in the mind of the speaker only, not in the likely conduct of the lady who is addressed.

The first begins confidently:

Come away, arm'd with loves delights,
　Thy sprightfull graces bring with thee:
When loves longing fights,
　They must the sticklers be.

(p. 108)

But then a note of uncertainty creeps into the poem:

Come quickly, come, the promis'd houre is wel-nye
　spent,
And pleasure, being too much deferr'd, looseth her
　best content.

The time during which the lady promised to turn up is almost gone—and we wonder whether she had any intention of keeping her appointment. In the second stanza the lover begins to share that apprehension, as anxious questions and a shift to the third person pronoun mime his anxiety:

Is shee come? O, how neare is shee?
　How farre yet from this friendly place?
How many steps from me?
　When shall I her imbrace?

These armes Ile spred, which onely at her sight shall
　close,
Attending as the starry flowre that the Suns noone-tide
　knowes.

We end in the future tense, as the lover vainly tries to salvage something out of the lusty hopes he entertained so securely at the beginning of the poem.

Almost exactly the same revaluation occurs in **'Come you pretty false-ey'd wanton'**, as a boastfully confident apprehension of the lady in the first stanza turns into emptily conditional threats in the second.

A very significant dimension of the patterning of the book is created by the poems in the collection spoken in whole or in part by women. The first of them, **'Good men, shew, if you can tell'**, as we have seen, initiates the parallel consideration of men and women. **'So many loves have I neglected'** has also been discussed earlier, but it may be added that it connects directly with a comment made by the uncertain male lover of the sixth poem:

Women, courted, have the hand
To discard what they distaste:
But those Dames whom none demand
Want oft what their wils embrace.

(p. 92)

The regret of the female speaker of **'So many loves'** seems to endorse what this male wishes women would understand—that they will be sorry they did not offer him the 'grace' he euphemistically demands.

The next poem, **'Though your strangenesse'**, presents a picture of a woman putting off her lover with ingenious excuses, while being friendly to other men. In this lyric there is a clear gap between the woman's experience and her lover's naiveté. Its effect is to undermine masculine self-confidence, boosted by the immediately preceding picture of a woman regretting her missed opportunities.

The last of this set, **'A secret love or two'**, continues the progression from innocent maid to experienced woman, as a married woman justifies her infidelity to her husband. He has no cause for complaint, since, no matter how many lovers she takes, 'His owne he never wants, but hath it duely'. The effect of this cynically witty poem is, in its context, rather subtler than its comic tone suggests. For in the frustrated mind of the young man, characterised with increasing intensity in the latter part of the book, the object he most desires is a female willing and able to answer to his desires. But the pattern of increasingly experienced and liberal ladies, at one level corresponding to his dreams, suggests that a woman ready to co-operate would also be a woman able to deceive him and exercise power over him. If, as the opening poem suggests, 'men must be men, and women women still', it is perhaps safer for the male if they stick to their literary sexual stereotypes of hopeless lover and chaste beauty.

The Second Booke, then, has a structure which enables the poems to be read as a loose quasi-narrative sequence. The sequential pattern in turn enables the reader to come to an ironic perspective upon youthful frustration as male and female poems are juxtaposed. The ironic perspective is prefigured in the opening lyric, but is only fully available if the set of poems are taken as a whole.

The three books so far discussed have each displayed structures of different kinds. The loosely associative pattern of *A Booke of Ayres* is different from the thematic and stylistic exploration of *The First Booke* and that in its turn is different from the quasi-narrative structure of *The Second Booke. The Third Booke* is patterned according to yet another principle. It is dedicated to Thomas Monson, recently released from the Tower where he had been confined on suspicion of complicity in the Overbury affair, and is offered to him explicitly as tribute to his patience and fortitude, and at the same time as an aid in dispelling the gloom of his misfortune. Unless the reader is aware of this external control on the book's shape and tone, he will miss a good deal of its impact.

The occasional nature of the collection is reflected, as Davis suggests, in the overall pattern of the book, which he describes thus:

> it takes Monson through a definite tonal progression from grief to light-heartedness. The first half is very dark: its dominant emotions are negative ones (as the reiterated word 'distaste' implies), such as complaint, disappointment, anger and cynical disenchantment. Suddenly with 'Now winter nights' the tone rises to gay conviviality, a tone which is sustained in the rest of the volume, where if cynicism exists, it is the gay cynicism of the coquettes who sing 'Silly boy', 'If thou longst', or 'So quicke, so hot, so mad', or where male disenchantment is spiced with comic acceptance.
>
> (pp. 128-9)

This characterisation of the volume needs to be qualified in one important respect. 'Tonally' the progression may be ever upward from gloom to cheerfulness, but this pattern plays against an arched structure of the poems' subjects. The first part of the collection deals with disappointed love; the three central poems, **'Now winter nights'**, **'Awake thou spring'** and **'What is it all'** speak of contentment in love; thereafter, with only two exceptions, we return to the opening territory of thwarted love. It is seen differently, is accepted more patiently than had been the case in the first part of the book—but that is the point of the central pivot. It makes possible an exercise in revaluation. Awareness of the presence of this arched, ABA thematic pattern also means that the reader is alert to the possibility that deeper notes are sounded in the latter part of the book than he might expect if he were armed only with Davis's pattern of progressive lightness.

The volume's relationship to Monson is most obvious in those lyrics not directly concerned with topics of love. **'O griefe, O spight'**, with its litany of complaint against a corrupt society, is the most striking, but **'So tyr'd are all my thoughts'**, depicting a state of dejection growing from an idle mind, has obvious application to the plight of an imprisoned man. **'Were my hart'** contains the clearest reference to the circumstances that caused Monson's imprisonment in the line 'Hidden mischiefe to conceale in State and Love is treason', since it was precisely the concealment of a murder for love for three years that had occasioned the whole business.

These poems draw attention to themselves by their departure from the amatory subjects of most of the poems. The reader accepts their presence because of their relationship with the book's occasion, and then, in turn, feeds them back into his reading of the love poems. The reader is enabled, without distorting the character of the love lyrics, to see them also as standing in a metaphoric relationship to Monson's imprisonment and release.

Once this perspective is accepted, then several significant patterns become apparent. The first is an insistence on truth and falsehood that is particularly marked in the earlier part of the book. The eighth poem opens:

> O griefe, O spight, to see poore Vertue scorn'd,
> Truth far exil'd, False art lov'd, Vice ador'd.
>
> (p. 142)

And the note sounded here is reflected in almost all the adjacent love lyrics. In the opening poem a woman complains of 'His faithlesse stay' and of her lover's readiness to 'breake vowes'. The second remarks 'True love abides to th'houre of dying; / False love is ever flying'. (p. 134) **'Maydes are simple'**, the fourth poem, opens its second stanza 'Truth a rare flower now is growne', and woman is advised in the sixth lyric to 'prove true' to one man. Finally the eleventh lyric opens with the sad comment 'If Love loves truth, then women doe not love'.

The applicability to Monson's position of so stressing the elements of faith and truth in love relationships is not hard to understand. He must have felt, as he languished in prison though he had never been convicted of any offence, that he had been betrayed by those of high position he should have been able to trust.

The book does more than describe a problem; it also explores the range of possible responses to a world where trust is liable to be misplaced. Reactions might take the form of passive lament (as in **'Oft have I sigh'd'**), despair (in **'O griefe'**), resolve to have nothing to do with the whole business (in **'Maydes are simple'**), or bitterness (in **'Now let her change'**). In a few poems the difficulties are more directly confronted.

'Could my heart more tongues imploy' comes near the end of the collection, and presents a complex reaction to betrayal (not at all the 'convivial' or 'light' tone that Davis would have us see throughout the latter part of the book).

Could my heart more tongues imploy
Then it harbours thoughts of griefe,
 It is now so farre from joy
That it scarce could aske reliefe.
  Truest hearts by deedes unkinde
  To despayre are most enclin'd.

Happy mindes, that can redeeme
Their engagements how they please,
 That no joyes or hopes esteeme,
Halfe so pretious as their ease!
  Wisedome should prepare men so
  As if they did all foreknow.

Yet no Arte or Caution can
Growne affections easily change;
 Use is such a Lord of Man
That he brookes worst what is strange.
  Better never to be blest
  Then to loose all at the best.

(p 160)

Some of the haunting quality of this lyric derives from the near suppression of the implied situation to which it is a response. It is only with the second line of the last stanza that the plight of the speaker, as one betrayed by a woman, is allowed unambiguously to the surface.

This is only one aspect of its indirectness. The statement of the opening stanza is that the speaker, because of the quality of his love, suffers the more keenly. At first it seems that the second stanza offers a preferred alternative of disengagement. But that possibility is then rejected in the third stanza, not on any moral grounds, but on grounds of simple observation and truth to experience. The despair of the ending excludes the positive alternative that the second stanza had entertained.

Other possible attitudes to betrayal are offered in the collection. A cynical realism, accepting the deceitfulness of women in **'If Love loves truth'** or the faults of man in **'Never love unlesse you can'** is one response; the fatalism of **'Kinde are her answers'** is another. The last poem in the book, **'Shall I then hope when faith is fled'** might seem at first sight to be nothing more than a cynical acceptance of woman's faithlessness, but in its final stanza there is complex play with the idea of freedom:

So my deare freedome have I gain'd
Through her unkindnesse and disgrace;
 Yet could I ever live enchain'd
As shee my service did embrace
  But shee is chang'd, and I am free:
  Faith failing her, Love dyed in mee.

At first glance the beginning of this stanza seems highly appropriate for the end of a collection offered to the newly freed Monson. In a way its resigned acceptance of unfaithfulness is an apt termination of the discussion of truth, faithfulness, and the response to its absence that has figured throughout the book. But the poem also exposes quite emphatically the limits of the metaphorical transfer-

ability of poems of love to Monson's situation. Obviously there are no circumstances in which he would wish 'really' to live imprisoned for ever. So, after teasing the reader throughout the book with the possibility of allowing the occasional nature of the collection to affect his understanding of love poems, at the end the poetry returns us firmly from that reality to the world of literary lovers.

There are other poems in the book which diversify this main sustaining theme; there are other ways in which the reader recognises an appropriateness to Monson's situation (the fact that the central poems all share a joy in human conversation, for example, is ideally suited to Monson's return to society). But enough has been said to demonstrate that this book, like its two predecessors, gains immeasurably in richness if the source and nature of the relationships between its individual poems are allowed to become part of the reader's awareness as he moves through it.

No such claims can be made for *The Fourth Booke*. Beyond the placing of the bawdier poems at the end, I can discover no other real structure in the work as a whole. It is not necessarily any the worse for that. In its delighted espousal of the variety of love poetry it offers an appropriate contrast to the more serious tone of *The Third Booke* with which it was published.

II

The preceding discussion of sequence and of relationships between poems making up Campion's six collections of airs, apart from suggesting that the 'right handling' of his poems should involve attention to the books as whole units, also serves as preparation for the discussion of individual lyrics which makes up the rest of this chapter. For in two important respects the problems raised in considering larger structures are analogous to those facing the reader of a single lyric.

In the first place, the process whereby a reader, teased with similarities between adjacent poems, constructs a framework which makes that similarity yield meaning, is identical to the effort he will make to construct from the evidence a single poem offers some situation which holds together its various elements in a shape that answers to the promise of coherence held out by the organised nature of its formal components. He might, for example, supply a situation to which the lyric can be construed as a response, or derive a pattern of feeling which makes psychological sense in terms of his own experience.

Secondly, just as in reading a sequence of poems the reader's understanding of one text depends upon another, so, as recent criticism frequently insists, the reading of all texts is controlled by a reader's sense of their literary relationships. In what follows relationships of subject matter, of generic kind or of linguistic 'code', will be brought to bear in discussing the way individual lyrics present themselves to the reader. These relationships, like those that subsist between adjacent lyrics, may be more or less closely controlled by the text itself. Some poems declare their affiliations very specifically as translations and imitations, while others manipulate a much less determined range of reminiscence. The thread on which the ensuing discussion is strung is a movement from one end to the other of that scale.

Imitation of texts was, of course, fundamental to the Renaissance view of the poet's craft. By diligent perusal of other men's writings the poet stocked his mind with topics, learnt the arts of writing, and, if his sources were classical or Biblical, conferred upon his own composition the authority borrowed from their status. At the same time slavish repetition was condemned—since a mere copy must necessarily be inferior to an original. Renaissance authors recognised that the imitator stamped himself upon his original even in the act of translation, and required therefore that the writer be self-consciously aware of his creative role, and not shirk the responsibility it laid upon him.[15]

From the reader's point of view, imitation poses a rather different set of problems. In the case of a poem whose original is so well-known as to be universally available he has comparatively little difficulty in accepting that the relationship of text and source is necessarily part of its explicit meaning. When the source of a poem is only revealed by scholarly investigation, and especially when it is not at all clear that a contemporary would have been likely to have known the original, then it might be felt that the information is relevant to a study of the transforming power of the imagination, but not to the effect or understanding of the poem before him.

The best place to begin the discussion is with two imitations where there is no doubt about the source, no question of its status, and no problem about the significance of its relationship to Campion's version. These are two of the Psalm paraphrases from *The First Booke*, **'Out of my soules deapth'** and **'Sing a song of joy'**.

To facilitate comparison I quote in full the first of these lyrics and the version in the *Book of Common Prayer*. (Campion might well have used the Geneva version, but it does not seem in this case to be significantly different.)

> Out of my soules deapth to thee my cryes have sounded:
> Let thine eares my plaints receive, on just feare grounded.
> Lord, should'st thou weigh our faults, who's not confounded?
>
> But with grace thou censur'st thine when they have erred,
> Therefore shall thy blessed name be lov'd and feared:
> Ev'n to thy throne my thoughts and eyes are reared.
>
> Thee alone my hopes attend, on thee relying;
> In thy sacred word I'le trust, to thee fast flying,
> Long ere the Watch shall breake, the morne descrying.

In the mercies of our God who live secured,
May of full redemption rest in him assured;
Their sinne-sicke soules by him shall be recured.

(p. 62)

1. Out of the deep have I called unto thee, O Lord: Lord hear my voice.

2. O let thine ears consider well: the voice of my complaint.

3. If thou, Lord, wilt be extreme to mark what is done amiss: O Lord, who may abide it?

4. For there is mercy with thee: therefore shalt thou be feared.

5. I look for the Lord; my soul doth wait for him: in his word is my trust.

6. My soul fleeth unto the Lord: before the morning watch, I say, before the morning watch.

7. O Israel, trust in the Lord, for with the Lord there is mercy: and with him is plenteous redemption.

8. And he shall redeem Israel: from all his sins.

In a Biblical paraphrase of this sort it is self-evident that modifications of and departures from the original register as an important element in directing the reader's understanding of what the poet is concerned to say. There was plenty of precedent for Campion's activity in providing a metrical version of the Psalm, and, in case of this, one of the Penitential Psalms, a long tradition sanctioning the writing of descants and free paraphrases upon it, where the poet absorbs the Psalmist's voice entirely into himself.[16]

Campion's version is quite close to the original. This in itself implies a more obedient posture before the sacred text than do the elaborations of a poet like Wyatt. It does not, however, preclude the reader's realisation, when the two texts are compared, of consistent and coherent adaptation.

The structure of the original is tidied up in the poem's division into four stanzas. In general the first and third express the prayers and promises of the poet, the second and fourth describe the merciful qualities of the Lord which guarantee that the prayer will be received. As a consequence of this arrangement some expansion of the Biblical text is needed in the second stanza. The nature of this additional material, in its turn, clarifies two of the significant ways in which the poem as a whole modifies its original.

In the sixth (new) line the posture of the poet is quiescent before the Lord's throne. This humble attitude typifies the consistent softening of the tone of the Psalmist throughout the lyric. In the first line 'cryes' becomes the subject of the verb, not 'I', and the preremptory 'Lord, hear my voice' is omitted; in the seventh, the Psalmist's 'I look for the Lord' becomes the more prayerful 'Thee alone my hopes attend'. The future tense of line eight suggests a petitionary posture compared with the self-justification of the original.

The second significant modification is the addition, in the fifth line, of the word 'lov'd' to the Biblical 'feared'. This signals that the poet is aware, as the Psalmist could not be, of the Christian revelation of the Lord of Love, and ties in with an unobtrusive but very significant Christianization of the original throughout the poem. In the fourth line 'mercy' becomes 'grace'. This apparently trivial alteration is in fact heavily loaded, marking not only the transition from Old Testament to the New Dispensation, but also placing this version of the Psalm securely in the Protestant camp. Both Luther and Calvin in their commentaries on this Psalm use it as evidence of the primacy of grace, as distinct from the Papists' 'mingling their own merits, satisfaction and worthy preparation . . . with the grace of God'.[17] (If this is taken in conjunction with the modification in line eight which adds the adjective 'sacred' to the 'word', suggesting a characteristically Protestant emphasis on the Bible, then this poem alone tends to indicate that Campion was not, at least at this time, a Catholic, as has been argued.[18])

The last significant modification is in the final stanza, where exhortation to the Israelites is turned into statement of God's mercy. The gloss on this verse in the Geneva Bible says: 'he sheweth to whom the mercie of God doth appertaine: to Israel, that is, to the Church and not to the reprobate'. Something of this standard Christian interpretation of Israel as type of the Church is apparent in Campion's final stanza, but he incorporates the idea within the generally individual and prayerful posture of his version. The recollection of the Psalm's opening in the phrase 'sinne-sicke soules', not only gives a nicely contained quality to the lyric's form, but also emphasises how the initial expansion of the Psalm's opening phrase has suited, even conditioned, the personal meditative stance that is maintained throughout.

In this poem, then, there is plenty of evidence of what one might call, in fashionable phrase, 'intertextual dialogue' between the poem and its original. The reader's knowledge of the text and status of the original not only sharpens his sense of Campion's poetic skill in a general sort of way, but enables him properly to take the force and implication of the modifications that the poet makes.

'Sing a song of joy' is rather different in that it is not a straightforward paraphrase of a single Psalm. Davis suggests that it is a 'free paraphrase of the first five verses of Psalm 104', but that is far too simple. The lyric opens:

> Sing a song of joy,
>   Prayse our God with mirth:
> His flocke who can destroy?
> Is hee not Lord of heav'n and earth?

> (p. 75)

The context of the poem in Campion's book, answering the Psalm of captivity which precedes it, clearly colours the address to God as a protector of his chosen people. It is quite unlike the opening of Psalm 104:

> Praise the Lord, O my soul: O Lord my God, thou art become exceeding glorious; thou art clothed with majesty and honour.

In its tone it is far more like the Mosaic song of deliverance from Egypt (Exodus, 15: 1-20), and verbally much closer to the beginnings of Psalms 95, 96 and 98. The details of the Lord's power in stanzas three to five of the lyric also owe their detail to more than the single source of Psalm 104. The third stanza runs:

> First who taught the day
>   From the East to rise?
> Whom doth the Sunne obey
> When in the Seas his glory dyes?

The last two lines recall Psalm 104 v. 19:

> He appointed the moon for certain seasons:
> And the sun knoweth his going down.

The first two lines, however, may derive from Psalm 74 v. 17 (v. 16 in the *AV*) 'thou hast prepared the light and the sun'. The opening of the next stanza is close to Ps. 147 v. 4 'He telleth the number of the stars'.

The point of this is not just to correct scholarly detail, but to show that this is not a poem aiming to re-present a well-known Biblical text, but rather to recall a general manner and matter common to many Psalms of praise.

But just as in the previous Psalm paraphrase there were details that marked the poet's attempt to give coherence and consistency of direction to his version, so here the note sounded in the opening stanza, of praise to the Lord for his protection of his people, is picked up and amplified in the fifth stanza:

> Angels round attend,
>   Wayting on his will;
> Arm'd millions he doth send
> To ayde the good or plague the ill.

Perhaps it was the fourth verse of Psalm 104 which provided the starting point for this stanza. It reads: 'He maketh his angels spirits: and his ministers a flaming fire'. The reader of this Psalm in the Geneva Bible is directed to a concordance in the New Testament, Hebrews 1: 14. 'Are they not all ministering spirits, sent forth to minister for them who shall be heirs of salvation?' Calvin's commentaries cite two other parallel texts, Psalm 34: 7, and Psalm 91: 11. So this stanza, like the earlier part of the lyric, is a composite of a number of scriptural texts. This has two major implications for the reader. First, by recalling a New Testament text, the applicability of a Jewish Psalm to the Christian church is made explicit. Secondly, the poem, in its synthesis of scriptural echoes, does not so much imitate an original as reenact the way a Christian should read his Bible, marking the similarities between dispersed texts that are the sign of the hand of God at work in its composition.[19]

Because of the special status of the Bible there is no question in these poems, or in any of others in **The First Booke** bearing a heavy scriptural imprint, of the poet 'overgoing his original. He may define himself, his thoughts and feelings, in relation to the Biblical material, but for him and his readers there is no doubt that the imitation stands in a subservient relationship.

The same is not the case when a poet imitates classical models. For all the authority of the ancients, for all the modesty that Renaissance writers were likely to feel about their own abilities or about the capabilities of their language, a poet was not inhibited from sporting with an original in a way that would have been unthinkable in the case of scripture.

A poem with a clear and direct relationship to a classical original is **'If any hath the heart to kill'** from **The Fourth Booke.** This narrative of an unfortunate case of impotence is based on Ovid, *Amores* III.6. Since the Elegies were well-known, we may assume that many of Campion's readers would have recognised the source.

The lyric is one of the 'vaine Ditties' which Campion tells his more squeamish readers they may ignore if they wish.

> If any hath the heart to kill,
>   Come rid me of this wofull paine.
> For while I live I suffer still
>   This cruell torment all in vaine:
>   Yet none alive but one can guess
>   What is the cause of my distresse.
>
> Thanks be to heav'n no grievous smart,
>   No maladies my limbes annoy;
> I beare a sound and sprightfull heart,
>   Yet live I quite depriv'd of joy:
>   Since what I had, in vaine I crave,
>   And what I had not, now I have.
>
> A Love I had, so fayre, so sweet,
>   As ever wanton eye did see.
> Once by appointment wee did meete;
>   Shee would, but ah, it would not be:
>   She gave her heart, her hand shee gave;
>   All did I give, shee nought could have.
>
> What Hagge did then my powers forspeake,
>   That never yet such taint did feele?
> Now shee rejects me as one weake,
>   Yet am I all compos'd of steele.
>   Ah, this is it my heart doth grieve:
>   Now though shee sees, shee'le not believe!

(p. 189)

All the details of the last two stanzas are taken from Ovid: the willing lady, the suspicion of witchcraft, and the belated return of capability. But where Ovid's poem is an explicit eighty-nine line story, Campion's lyric poem of only twenty-four lines compresses all its narrative detail into the last twelve. These are the facts, but the question is how they affect our response to a poem perfectly self-sufficient, and wittily successful.

At the very lowest level any correspondence self-consciously made between one work and another invites the reader who discerns it to indulge in self-congratulation, and in his election to an élite company of knowledgeable readers. It may not be the most important of literary responses, but it is a legitimate and deep-seated source of pleasure.

At another level, recognition of the source enables the reader to flesh out the lyric's sparse narrative with his awareness of Ovid's much more specific and luxuriant detail. So, for example, the poet's statement in line 20 of the uniqueness of his failure, conjures up the memory of Ovid's much more expansive boast:

> Yet boarded I the golden Chie twice,
> And Libas, and the white cheeked Pitho thrice.
> Corinna craved it in a summer's night,
> And nine sweet bouts we had before daylight.[20]

More significant still is the way the lyric's structure turns the moment when the reader recognizes its source into a constituent in his understanding of, and response to its meaning. The opening two stanzas are couched in conventional Petrarchan idiom, and the reader at first understands them, because of the pressure of that relationship, as deriving from a situation of disappointed love. The Ovidian narrative of the last two stanzas then revises the reader's first answer to the riddle of lines 11-12.

The reader, therefore, is faced with a poem whose underlying situation is recreated as the work proceeds. He imagines first a lover frustrated by a heartless mistress, but then realises that the opening stanzas' evasiveness signals the poet's reluctance to speak openly of his humiliation. The first stage is couched in Petrarchan generalities, the second signalled by Ovidian explicitness. But even then the reader recognises that the retold story is less explicit, less detailed than the source, and, in its condensation of the original, apt to the poet's general unwillingness to make his impotence public.

Looked at as a literary construct, however, the poem is assured in its organisation. It sets the reader a riddle, and a riddle implies that the poet knows the answer and is delighting in teasing his audience. There is, in other words, a tension between the narrative 'I' of the poem, insecure, humiliated and evasive, and the poet, secure in his manipulation of his texts. The paradox is explicit in the conclusion of the first stanza, where the couplet both expresses a sense of relief that only the lover's mistress knows of his failure and at the same time invites the reader to 'guess' what the source of his misery is. By making the story public the lyric undermines the truth of its own statement.

In this context, the literariness of the poem takes on added significance. Its goal, the answer to its puzzle, is a literary text. That text represents a way of talking about love that stands in direct opposition to the Petrarchan, good-mannered evasiveness with which the poem opens. So the lyric is, to a large extent, a poem about ways of writing love poetry, exposing the inadequacies of one code by juxtaposing it with another. This layer of implication is only fully available to the reader who recognises its specific literary affiliation.

In short, this poem does not merely abbreviate Ovid's Elegy, it redirects it. For the reader the nature of that conversion becomes part of the play of the poem's meaning. In the case of a more famous lyric, the act of conversion is much more complex, as more than one source is brought into play.

> My sweetest Lesbia, let us live and love,
> And, though the sager sort our deedes reprove,
> Let us not way them: heav'ns great lamps doe dive
> Into their west, and strait againe revive,
> But soone as once set is our little light,
> Then must we sleepe one ever-during night.
>
> If all would lead their lives in love like mee,
> Then bloudie swords and armour should not be,
> Nor drum nor trumpet peaceful sleepes should move,
> Unless alar'me came from the campe of love:
> But fooles do live, and wast their little light,
> And seeke with paine their ever-during night.
>
> When timely death my life and fortune ends,
> Let not my hearse be vext with mourning friends,
> But let all lovers, rich in triumph, come,
> And with sweet pastimes grace my happie tombe;
> And Lesbia, close up thou my little light,
> And crowne with love my ever-during night.

(p. 18)

The first stanza is based on Catullus's best-known poem:

> Vivamus, mea Lesbia, atque amemus,
> rumoresque senum severiorum
> omnes unius aestimemus assis.
> soles occidere et redire possunt:
> nobis cum semel occidit brevis lux,
> nox est perpetua una dormienda.

(Let us live, my Lesbia, and love, and value at one farthing all the talk of crabbed old men. Suns may set and rise again. For us, when the short light has once set, remains to be slept the sleep of one unbroken night.)[21] The relationship of these two poems has been discussed frequently.[22] The most significant modifications are three.

First, the potential critics are not 'old' but 'sage'. The poem is not a contest between age and passionate youth, but between false and true wisdom. This modification is cemented in the poem by the last two lines of the second stanza, which retrospectively 'justifies' the initial adaptation of the original.

Second is the expansion of the image of the setting and rising sun. This, while not changing the 'meaning' of the original in its contrast of night's temporariness with the permanent end of life, does significantly alter the reader's response to that meaning. Where in Catullus the statement's matter-of-factness gives a sober urgency to the poet's persuasive aim, Campion's version seems so to celebrate the revolution of night and day, as it endows the 'great lampes' with active desire in the verb 'dive', that the positive attitude lingers in the reader's mind as powerfully as the negative alternative.

The third, and most obvious change, is that the second half of Catullus's poem, demanding innumerable kisses, is simply omitted. At the simplest level this means that the reader who knows the original is briefly surprised that the poem does not continue in the direction he anticipated. He then realises that this lyric is a kind of descant on its classical initiator, explicitly creative and meditative. But though the poem departs from the original, it returns in the refrain at the end of each stanza to the point where it abandoned Catullus. This means that formally the poem consists of three ways of arriving at a single, Catullan statement. **'My sweetest Lesbia'** begins as a paraphrase of another poem, but ends as a three-fold exploration of a single image from it.

The matter of the stanzas which replace Catullus's continuation is itself derived from other classical originals. Davis, following Cunningham, points to the second stanza's dependance on Propertius II. 15, lines 41 and 43.[23] But the contrast between the life of war, and the life of love's more agreeable battles is a common one in all the Latin love poets. R.O.A.M. Lyne collects many examples.[24] Furthermore it is a conceit thoroughly absorbed in Renaissance love poetry. The relationship between the poem and a particular source is therefore nowhere near so determined in this stanza as the first.

It is possible that the third stanza also owes something to two classical sources, Tibullus, I.i, lines 59-68, and the opening of Propertius II.xiii (A). But where Tibullus asks that his death should not be the signal for mourning because grief would wound his ghost, and where Propertius dismisses the panoply of mourning because his books are the only companion he desires, Campion asks instead that his funeral should be the occasion for a triumph of love.

The poem as a whole, then, is an example of that kind of imitation where sources are fully digested by the poet and become the basis of a new poem. **'My sweetest Lesbia'** is sufficiently close to Catullus for its departures to be felt as part of its meaning, though its other classical references are much less significant. In other poems it scarcely matters that details may be traced back to a classical original.

A poem that nicely illustrates the point at which awareness of specific sources begins to merge with the less specific control exerted by generic expectation is **'It fell on a sommers day'** (p. 31). This narrative of Jamy's seduction of

Bessie in her feigned sleep fuses and recasts two classical sources, Propertius's description of his drunken return to a sleeping Cynthia (I.iii), and Ovid's *Amores,* I.vi where a sleeping man is disturbed by a woman. But these specific sources are not as significant to the reader's response as is the lyric's relationship to the whole genre of poems where a man approaches a sleeping lady. For the pleasure one takes in its humorous narrative is supplemented by the contrast between its plebeian participants and the mythological or aristocratic figures in other examples and by the way Bessie is merely pretending to the passive role that literary tradition ordains for the female participant. Perhaps the Ovidian source is significant here, for Bessie seems to take over from it a 'male' response—she delights in sex. Taken as a whole the poem is mildly and humorously subversive in its view of female lustiness. The subversiveness is not merely a matter of what the poem says, but is enacted and engendered in the reader by its subversive relationship to the genre in which he places it.

The control exerted on a reader by generic relationships of subject matter is, of course, much less precise than that sparked by recognition of an imitative relationship between a poem and a single ascertainable source. What is provided, for poet and reader, is a kind of narrative 'core' which makes easy the construction of a lyric's basic situation. What then matters is how creatively the poem descants upon its *cantus firmus.*

Two poems derived from a conventional situation related to that of **'It fell on a sommers day'**, where a lover contemplates his sleeping lady, make convenient examples of some of the different ways a single topos may be exploited.

The first is:

> Sleepe, angry beauty, sleep, and feare not me,
> For who a sleeping Lyon dares provoke?
> It shall suffice me here to sit and see
> Those lips shut up that never kindely spoke.
>   What sight can more content a lovers minde
>   That beauty seeming harmlesse, if not kinde?
>
> My words have charm'd her, for secure shee sleepes,
> Though guilty much of wrong done to my love;
> And in her slumber, see! shee close-ey'd weepes!
> Dreames often more then waking passions move.
>   Pleade, sleepe, my cause, and make her soft like thee,
>   That shee in peace may wake and pitty mee.
>
>   (p. 161)

The subtlety of this enchanting lyric derives from its playful exploitation of a conventional poetic situation on a number of levels. In the first stanza the poet establishes an attitude to his beloved by distinguishing himself from figures such as Astrophil,[25] or the speaker of Pilkington's song 'Now peep, boe peep',[26] or Jamy in 'It fell on a sommers day'. For the reader can only understand the significance of the injunction not to 'feare' in the first line,

or the statement 'it shall suffice me' in the third, if he realises they imply that this speaker, unlike others in a similar situation, intends to make no amorous advances.

The poet adopts a slightly self-mocking tone, as he timidly refuses to do what the convention expects him to do, and this is maintained in his passive hope that sleep will do for him what he cannot do for himself—persuade the mistress to kindness. Our sense of the lyric's self-awareness, however, derives also from the way the poem's development causes the reader to revise his initial formulation of the situation to which it may be construed as a response.

At first it seems as if the poet is addressing an already sleeping lady. This is the situation that literary convention would persuade the reader to construct, and it is reinforced by the particularity of the third line, where the adverb 'here' nicely solidifies the picture. The imperatives of the opening line are understood as meaning 'sleep on now', partly at least because in 'real life' one does not often order anyone to sleep.

The opening words of the second stanza, however, demand a recasting of this interpretation. If his 'words have charm'd her', then the imperatives must in fact have been giving instructions, and the lyric therefore does have a narrative development. The lady passes from wakefulness to sleep, then to weeping. Again in this stanza there is a particularity that enforces on the reader a sense of the poem's situation. The matter of fact opening line, and the exhortation of the third both work to make a poetically conventional situation seem vivid.

The process of reading is not, however, quite so simply one of discarding a provisional construction in favour of another which seems to fit better. For the initial impression remains present in the mind, the elements that persuaded the reader that it was not actually giving present-tense orders to a lady still stand. What happens is rather that a reader faced with the difficulty of reconciling the two stanzas moves towards another possibility—that the narrative happens in the mind of the poet, rather than in the reality it seems at first to be reporting.

In this light the line 'my words have charm'd her' assumes extra significance, for it draws attention to the literariness of the preceding stanza, and to the persuasive, quasi-magical nature of its content. We then understand that, at least in part, the vividly presented narrative situation of the opening is a picture drawn in the poet's imagination. It is not so much a statement of 'this is what is' as of 'I wish this might be so'.

One way of looking at this poem, then, is to regard it as that fashionable object, a literary fiction which draws explicit attention to its fictional status, undermining the 'realism' it seems on the surface to be offering to the reader. No doubt this is part of the truth, as it is of all literature that challenges its audience. But at the same time the poem stands as a convincing picture of the way the human mind tries to persuade itself by imagining a desired object with sufficient solidity to make it seem truly present, and therefore truly obtainable.

Part of this effort of self-persuasion is evidenced in the lyric's gradual shift of address. It opens with speech directed to the lady as the object of the speaker's love, then moves through a report of the poet's actions, embraces the audience of the poem as they are addressed in the imperative 'see' of line nine, and finally ends with the most obviously literary speech of all, an apostrophe to sleep. This pattern emphasises the rhetorical, persuasive character of the lyric. At the same time its shift towards increasingly abstract and literary objects of address mimics the process through which our sense of the reality of the poem's situation is undermined.

This lyric is delightfully elusive. Though underpinned by convention, it manipulates the reader's pre-set knowledge of its literary stereotype in a subtle, dislocatory fashion so that what seems on one level to be revivification of a standard topos by the application of solidifying detail and by an initial distancing of himself from the convention on the part of the speaker, turns into a witty example of the way a man trapped in one conventional situation (of frustrated love) tries to work himself out of it by imagining another (of addressing his sleeping lady).

The second lyric makes a nice contrast with **'Sleepe, angry beauty'** in several ways.

> Awake, thou spring of speaking grace, mute rest
>   becomes not thee;
> The fayrest women, while they sleepe, and Pictures
>   equall bee.
>   O come and dwell in loves discourses,
>   Old renuing, new creating.
>   The words which thy rich tongue discourses
>   Are not of the common rating.
>
> Thy voyce is as an Eccho cleare which Musicke doth
>   beget,
> Thy speech is as an Oracle which none can counterfeit:
>   For thou alone, without offending,
>   Hast obtain'd power of enchanting;
>   And I could heare thee without ending,
>   Other comfort never wanting.
>
> Some little reason brutish lives with humane glory
>   share;
> But language is our proper grace, from which they
>   sever'd are.
>   As brutes in reason man surpasses,
>   Men in speech excell each other:
>   If speech be then the best of graces.
>   Doe it not in slumber smother.
>
> (p. 148)

The basic situation of this lyric is the same as that of the preceding poem, but where **'Sleepe angry beauty'** used it to give a poem of pleading a quasi-narrative direction, here it acts as no more than a frame for a lyric that combines a little standard philosophy with another lyric type, the praise of a lady. At the simplest level the poem animates the conventions it employs precisely through the device of combining topoi of address and of situation, so that a not untypical celebration of a lady's voice is given a dramatic context, and solidified by being embedded in a quasi-logical argument.

This is not the only way that manipulation of a standard situation contributes to the reader's response, for the lyric generates some of its exuberance through control and qualification of deep-seated resonances attached to its conventional situation.

The picture of two figures, one sleeping, the other awake, was popular in the poetry and prose fiction of the period because the narrative opposition it offers could so readily be assimilated to the largerscale codes of love poetry. To explore fully the range of associations of the opposition of sleep and wakefulness would be a disproportionate indulgence, but some of the patterns more obviously relevant to these poems may be singled out.

Sleep is 'death's second self', and opposed therefore to life's vitality. The coldness of death and warmth of light are easily assimilated to the stereotype of cold chastity opposed to fiery passion, female to male. This is the pattern reflected in **'Harke, al you ladies'**, which opens:

> Harke, al you ladies that do sleep:
>   the fayry queen Proserpina
> Bids you awake and pitie them that weep.
>
> (p. 44)

In this scheme a woman's sleeping is a metaphor for her heartless neglect of her lover.

But sleep is also a 'care-charmer', and is then opposed to the toils of waking existence. This polarity surfaces most frequently in an individual lover's complaint at his own inability to sleep, as in **'The Sypres curten of the night is spread'** (p. 32), but it figures also in lyrics based on the opposition of sleeping and waking figures, as, for example, **'Sleep wayward thoughts'** from Dowland's *First Book.*[27] In this scheme the valorization of the two terms is reversed—sleep is desired, wakefulness lamented.

The attraction of narratives such as **'It fell on a sommers day'** lies in the way a dramatic situation plays with these associations. The chastity of the lady is figured in her sleeping, but narratively sleep renders her a quiescent and available victim, where awake she is antagonistic and tyrannical. The piquancy of the first stanza of **'Sleepe, angry beauty'** derives from its explicit denial of this potential, and its exploitation instead of the possibility that the positive power of sleep will itself dismantle the lady's coldness.

In the case of **'Awake, thou spring'**, the reader's sense of the poem's sunniness derives in part from its vigorous espousing of all the positive associations of the situation.

The mistress is bidden to awake, to enter into the living world of love. Moreover, where in **'Sleepe, angry beauty'** the lady's sleep had come as a respite for the lover from her unkind speech, in this poem he begs her to 'dwell in love's discourses'. At the same time a potential negative association is explicitly denied. For the lady's sleep is not an image of her habitual indifference to her lover (as it is in **'Harke, al you ladies'**), but a temporary cessation of her usual delightful speech. In the context of the associations potentially available to poet and reader once the situation of sleeping lady-wakeful lover is broached, **'Awake, thou spring'** defines itself by allowing no room for any negative associations to emerge.

The 'tonal complexity' which Davis sees as Campion's characteristic strength is in no small measure attributable to the flexibility with which he combines different generic conventions and manipulates the 'pre-packed' resonances that each brings with it.

One further set of poems may be considered to demonstrate this characteristic artfulness. The itemised description of a lady known as a 'blazon' is endemic in medieval and Renaissance poetry. Its conventional procedure is to begin at the head and work down the body, with many traditional images associated with each anatomical feature. In three lyrics Campion explores the convention creatively.

Perhaps the best-known is this one:

> There is a Garden in her face,
> Where Roses and white Lillies grow;
>   A heav'nly paradice is that place,
> Wherein all pleasant fruits doe flow.
>   There Cherries grow, which none may buy
>   Till Cherry ripe themselves doe cry.
>
> Those Cherries fayrely doe enclose
> Of Orient Pearle a double row,
>   Which when her lovely laughter showes,
> They looke like Rose-buds fill'd with snow.
>   Yet them nor Peere nor Prince can buy,
>   Till Cherry ripe themselves doe cry.
>
> Her Eyes like Angels watch them still;
> Her Browes like bended bowes doe stand,
>   Threatning with piercing frownes to kill
> All that attempt with eye or hand
>   Those sacred Cherries to come nigh,
>   Till Cherry ripe themselves doe cry.

(p. 174)

The conventionality of imagery in this lyric is obvious. Indeed its predictability is emphasised by the way the first two stanzas do not even name the objects of the similes—skin, cheeks, lips and teeth. The reader knows what is meant as he supplies the sense from his memory of innumerable other examples. The delicacy and delightfulness of this poem derives instead from its variation on the standard aim of a blazon—to praise a lady, supplying instead a more active and dramatic valuation of the nature of the woman described.

In the first stanza the reader receives a warm impression of the lady. The slightly odd fourth line, with its unusual verb, 'flow' fits the lubricious picture that the reader may readily construct with the appetitive associations of 'fruit' to aid him. This reading is endorsed when the refrain's ostensible setback to lusty imagining is overridden by the rapid resumption of the conventional image of lips as kissable cherries at the beginning of the second stanza. But the promise is shortlived. As the stanza moves towards its refrain the lady's choosiness becomes clearer. In place of an indeterminate 'none may buy' comes a more exclusive 'nor Peere nor Prince may buy'. The lady has become much less accessible. In the third stanza this distancing is completed, as we realise that she not only has the power to deny access to her 'cherries', but is temperamentally likely to use it. The cherries have become 'sacred', subsumed by that word into the divinely appointed charge of the Hesperides, and therefore unlikely ever to come to the touch of the poet or his readers. The finality of this last stanza is signalled to the reader by the sudden appearance of the lady herself in the poem—her eyes and brows have a physical presence by being named that the features earlier gestured to merely through their conventional substitutes did not.

In this lyric, then, the reader sees a lady delightedly and lustfully contemplated turn into a tyrant, and takes pleasure in this manipulation of a standard poetic subject. The refrain itself, which seemed at first promisingly 'earthy' (in Davis's term) with its associations with the marketplace, ends up as a demonstration of the lady's Petrarchan disdain.[28]

The next two poems to be considered are rather more straightforward variations on standard procedures. **'Mistris, since you so much desire'** begins by reversing the direction of conventional description, moving from breast up to lips, cheeks and eyes. The aim of the lyric seems at first to be to answer the mistress's implied question 'where is Cupid's fire?', but the upward movement of the catalogue of her beauties does not end, as we might expect, with the location of the deity in her 'starrie pearcing eyes', for the poet continues:

> Those eyes I strive not to enjoy,
> For they have power to destroy;
> Nor woe I for a smile, or kisse,
> So meanely triumph's not my blisse;
> But a little higher, but a little higher,
> I climbe to crowne my chast desire.

(p. 41)

The poet's protestation of his desire for the beauty of mind of his mistress is, of course, the standard talk of neo-Platonism lightly touched. It works wittily into the poem primarily because it is presented as a dimension supplied by the male speaker rather than, as would be more usual, being demanded by the lady. In the conventional context of love poetry the mistress might have asked her question for a variety of motives, but we must imagine her to have been surprised by the upward continuation of the catalogue that, in one way, denies the significance of the very praise that the first part of the poem offers. This indeed is why the poem succeeds in bringing its conventionality to life. For on one level the poetry of physical praise is opposed to the spiritual aspiration of neo-Platonic love. At another, their juxtaposition means that a poem which begins as praise of the loved object turns into a poem of self-congratulation on the part of the poet. It is this activity prompted in the reader's understanding that makes even a fairly slight lyric delightful.

In *The Fourth Booke* Campion rewrote this poem:

> Beauty, since you so much desire
> To know the place of *Cupids* fire:
> About you somewhere doth it rest,
> Yet never harbour'd in your brest,
> Nor gout-like in your heele or toe;
> What foole would seeke Loves flame so low?
> But a little higher, but a little higher,
> There, there, o there lyes *Cupids* fire.
>
> Think not, when *Cupid* most you scorne,
> Men judge that you of Ice were borne;
> For, though you cast love at your heele,
> His fury yet sometime you feele;
> And where-abouts if you would know,
> I tell you still, not in your toe:
> But a little higher, but a little higher,
> There, there, o there lyes *Cupids* fire.

(p. 190)

In this version the blazon element is much suppressed, but still has some part to play in generating and defining the reader's response. For in locating Cupid's fire in the female pudenda Campion is doing more than earth the aspiration of his own earlier poem. He is taking on that part of the blazon tradition which (in England at least) dictated a modest hop from belly to thighs. Pyrocles, in Sidney's *Arcadia,* laments this necessity as he enumerates Philoclea's beauties.

> Loth, I must leave his [Cupid's] chief resort,
> For such a use the world hath gotten,
> The best things still must be forgotten.[29]

Donne, in 'Love's Progress' (a poem that Campion may have had in mind when composing this lyric), banishes Cupid entirely, but asserts:

> Although we see celestial bodies move
> Above the earth, the earth we till and love:
> So we her airs contemplate, words and heart,
> And virtues; but we love the centric part.[30]

There was, then, precedent for Campion's drawing attention to forbidden territory. But the sense of vulgar realism that the poem gives to the reader yet derives in no small measure from its repudiation of the dominant tradition.

The wit of the poem lies in the way this denial is reinforced by the second stanza's direction to the woman with the implication that, contrary to all Petrarchan habit, she too feels sexual desire. It is the suggestion that the poet sees through female pretence that gives added force to the poem's denial of blazon convention. The lyric mounts a frontal assault on the tradition, denying the attitudes it enshrines by pointing to the truth of the desire it conventionally figures, but evades.

In each of these three poems, then, Campion manifests a fertile activity in his manipulation of a single literary convention. Wherever one might wish finally to place him in the poetical league tables, it is rarely that he can be accused of that vice most characteristic of the truly minor poet—complacency in the conventions he employs.

A poem which finely illustrates Campion's dexterity in manipulating the reader's response through the recollection both of specific texts and of generic convention is **'When thou must home'**:

> When thou must home to shades of underground,
> And there ariv'd, a newe admired guest,
> The beauteous spirits do ingirt thee round,
> White Iope, blith Hellen, and the rest,
> To heare the stories of thy finisht love,
> From that smoothe tongue whose musicke hell can move:
>
> Then wilt thou speake of banqueting delights,
> Of masks and revels which sweete youth did make,
> Of Turnies and great challenges of knights,
> And all these triumphes for thy beauties sake:
> When thou hast told these honours done to thee,
> Then tell, O tell, how thou didst murther me.

(p. 46)

The piquancy of this exquisite lyric is derived in no small measure from the sudden reversal brought about in the last line. In order that a surprise ending may work upon the reader he must feel both a shock of astonishment and yet, at the same time, a recognition of appropriateness. If the first were not successfully engineered then the poem would fall flat, but if the second quality were not also present, the reversal would seem merely adventitious.

Campion ensures this double effect in a number of complementary ways. Basically, as in other lyrics we have considered, the reader is forced into making a revision of his reading. At first he takes it as a poem of praise, where the inevitable mortality of a mistress is softened by the adulatory audience of classical beauties, and by the recollection of her own previous triumphs. This celebration is carefully engineered as the indirect compliment of the first stanza shifts into the more emphatic tribute of the second, where the honours recalled by the lady are arranged in ascending order of magnitude, topped by the appropriately summary 'triumphs' of line ten. The two stanzas are neatly interconnected, the first depicting an audience waiting to hear the narratives that the second supplies. They hinge upon the suppressed tribute of the sixth line, which compares the lady's voice to the legendary Orpheus. Thus far the poem suggests a traditionally adoring posture on the part of the poet, a suggestion reinforced if the reader recollects the Propertian text which underlies the first stanza:

> Haec tua, Persephone, maneat clementia, nec tu,
>   Persephone coniunx, saevior esse velis.
> Sunt apud infernos tot milia formosarum:
>   pulchra sit in superis, si licet, una locis.
> Vobiscum est Iope, vobiscum candida Tyro,
>   vobiscum Europa nec proba Pasiphae
> et quot Troia tulit vetus et quot Achaia formas, . . .

> (Persephone, may thy mercy endure, nor mayest thou, that hast Persephone for spouse, be over-cruel. There are so many thousand beauties among the dead; let one fair one, if so it may be, abide on earth. With you is Iope, with you snowy Tyro, with you Europa and impious Pasiphae, and all the beauties that Troy and Achaea bore of old . . .)[31]

It is not perhaps crucial to the poem's effect that this specific text be known to the reader, but yet, if it is recalled then the differences between them assume some significance. Where Propertius pleads for the soul of his beloved to be left on earth, Campion acknowledges the inevitable, though making every effort to ameliorate its harshness, thus reinforcing the feeling that he is attempting to convert a potentially sad subject into an occasion for celebration.

The opening of Propertius's poem, however, cements a connection between **'When thou must home'** and the poem that precedes it in *A Booke of Ayres*, **'Harke, al you ladies'**, which had been concerned with 'The fairie queen Proserpina'. In the first instance the relationship of these two lyrics seems primarily to point up the dissimilarity between them, and thereby to reinforce the 'optimistic' reading of **'When thou must home'**. The last stanza of **'Harke, al you ladies'** runs:

> All you that love, or lov'd before,
>   the Fairie Queene Proserpina
> Bids you encrease that loving humour more:
>   they that yet have not fed
> On delight amorous,
>   she vowes that they shall lead
>   Apes in Avernus.

(p. 44)

Here it is old maids who are consigned to Proserpina's other kingdom, and the reader proceeding to the next lyric, though teased by the obvious connection between them, quickly decides that the lady of **'When thou must home'**, with her stories of 'finish love', stringing along a train of classical beauties, does not belong with the tormented virgins.

Until the twelfth line of the lyric, then, the reader is persuaded directly and indirectly to construe the poem one way. With the surprise of that last line he is suddenly forced to view it entirely differently. It becomes, as Rosemond Tuve puts it, 'a perception, subtle and only half-smiling, of the general ironic discrepancy between Beauty's triumphs and Beauty's proud cruelty'.[32] It is the understanding of the poet's relationship to his lady that is most significantly revised, and, as a consequence, the reader looks back over the poem and constructs a second reading. The subtlety of the poem is that its various elements are capable of sustaining both readings. The change of direction is thereby made both surprising and satisfying.

The euphemism of the first stanza, at first understood as part of the poem's strategy of praise, comes to seem disquieting. For how can anyone be but a 'guest' in their own home? So too, Helen's blitheness cannot, now, override our knowledge of her dubious morality. The sly associations of the epithet 'smoothe' take over from the merely mellifluous meaning at first attributed to it, and the disproportion of attributing Orphic power to a voice engaged only in female gossip surfaces to enforce the suggestion that it is only the lady's vanity that can hope that she, like Orpheus, will be but a temporary 'guest' in her long home.

In the second stanza the poet's urgent and ironic plea that the lady will tell of her conduct towards him highlights the boastfulness of the narratives she has been prepared to offer, and makes us aware, as we were not on the first reading, where the tributes offered to her seemed to suit with an intention to praise, of the fact that she has only ever received, and never given.

Once this 'new' poem has been made, then its relationship with **'Harke, al you ladies'** is also revised. For in that poem it was comfortingly assumed that amiable ladies were rewarded with beauty, and only those who were indifferent to their lovers were tormented and ultimately consigned to hell. In **'When thou must home'** it is disconcertingly recognised that though this lady is equally heartless and also bound for Hell, it is not she who suffers for her cruelty. What the poems share, the reader now understands, is a male desire for vengeance on icy and unresponsive women.

The relationship between the two poems is therefore significant for the enriching of implication it engenders, but the most important literary relationship of all is that which subsists between **'When thou must home'** and a characteristic sonnet theme. In countless sonnets poets remind their ladies of the inevitable approach of decay and death. As Campion's poem begins, that whole tradition is recalled. As it proceeds it differentiates itself from the usual development of the topos. On first reading this difference seems to consist of an absence of any note of fear or warning. The lyric, therefore, establishes its apparently comforting note partly through this modification. The ending, however, generates a more complicated dialogue with characteristic sonnet treatment of the theme. For where most sonnets set against encroaching decay either encouragement to present loving action or else a promise that in the poet's praise the lady (or young man in Shakespeare's *Sonnets*) will be rendered eternal and inviolate, Campion's lyric vengefully records his mistress's obduracy, and clearly wishes all the torment of hell to punish her.

The relationship of this poem to the sonnet is not a matter only of theme, for in its structure too it reads like a variation upon sonnet form. The two stanzas are related by a 'when-then' pattern, and this is repeated in the pattern of the last two lines, giving them the feel of a sonnet's concluding couplet. Once the reader perceives this relationship two things follow. First, the repetition of the 'when-then' pattern integrates the final two lines firmly with the lyric they conclude. This means that the surprise effect is made more forceful, but also that the reader does not feel it comes out of nowhere. Secondly, though he is cheated of the summary function the couplet at first seems likely to perform, there is sufficient precedent in the sonnet form generally, and specifically in sonnets on the theme of decay for a change of direction in the final couplet, for him to feel that this lyric conforms to his formal expectations, however surprising it might be in its meaning and implication.

In short, this masterly lyric uses all its resources to achieve 'a combination of surprise and fulfilment that gives the last phrase its wit and the poem its point'.[33] That comment was made by Barbara Smith, not about Campion's poem, but about a modern epigram. Its appropriateness demonstrates how **'When thou must home'**, in addition to descanting on texts and conventional thematic material, also brings into play resonances that derive from a less specific cross-fertilisation of the lyric by other genres—sonnet and epigram.

The mixing of kinds, as Rosalie Colie has pointed out in *The Resources of Kind,* was particularly fruitful in the Renaissance. She directs attention, in passages of particular relevance here, to the mingling of epigram and sonnet, and 'the poet's capacity to enliven generic styles, to animate, confront and intertwine lyric and epigrammatic styles'.[34] **'When thou must home'** can be seen as combining the characteristic poses of sonnet and epigram in a single lyric, for, as she writes, 'one would expect that of a loving lover the poet properly writes sonnets, of an unloving lover epigrams',[35] and it is precisely the revision of one view of the lady into the other that, as we have seen, complicates and enriches the reader's response to that poem.

Of Campion's interest in the epigram as a genre there can be no doubt. In his publications of Latin verse at the beginning and the end of his career there are hundreds of epigrams. Furthermore he wrote, in the preface to *A Booke of Ayres*: 'What Epigrams are in Poetrie, the same are Ayres in musicke, then in their chief perfection when they are short and well seasoned', and 'as *Martiall* speaks in defence of his short Epigram, so may I say in th'apologie of Ayres, that where there is full volume, there can be no imputation of shortness'. (p. 15)

In seeking to demonstrate the effect and consequence of the importation of epigram into lyric we have immediately to confront the elusive nature of generic description. For two different streams, one Roman, the other Greek, fed into the Renaissance poet's sense of what constituted epigrams, and meant that a wide range of possibilities could be included under the title.[36] Nonetheless it is possible to establish certain features central to the genre. Briefly these might be characterised as brevity and pointedness; a fondness for aphorism and sententia; a detached and public posture on the part of the poet; and, finally, a tendency to see the plainness of epigrammatic style and sharpness of attitude as particularly appropriate to certain kinds of subject matter.

The pithy pointedness of epigram means that it is 'a pre-eminently teleological poem, and in a sense a suicidal one, for all of its energy is directed towards its own termination'.[37] In more recent times it has usually been felt that this urgently desired ending should involve some witty reversal of expectation, but, as Hudson demonstrates, this was not necessarily so. 'For the point of an epigram . . . does not always depend upon a *turn* of thought: the thought may go straight forward, and the point may be merely an emphatic summary of what has already been presented, or a distillation from it'.[38] In poems of this sort, aphorism, sentence or proverb are frequently found to serve particularly well. **'When thou must home'** does exemplify an epigrammatic conclusion involving a 'turn of thought', but it is not in fact very characteristic of Campion's lyrics of an epigrammatic cast, most of which are closer to Hudson's alternative pattern.

The importance of endings to epigrams predicates a certain kind of structuring of material. Barbara Smith refines upon Lessing's often quoted description of the two-part structure of epigram, suggesting that

> We may think of the characteristic structure of the epigram . . . as a thematic sequence which reaches a point of maximal instability and then turns to the business of completing itself.[39]

Such sharpening of a poem's direction by building continuously towards a pointed conclusion is a very useful means of overcoming the 'special problem of strophic verse intended for musical rendition . . . that the repetitive structure which is most effective with respect to musical demands is least effective with respect to closure'.[40] It is perhaps in this respect that the example of the epigram was formally most useful to Campion, overriding the potential fragmentation of stanzaic lyrics sung to repeated music. (I do not here imply that it was the only way of coping with the situation—other responses to the difficulty and equally successful solutions will figure in a later chapter).

A convenient example of the way these features of epigram are translated into lyric form is supplied by **'It fell on a sommers day'**, for Campion also wrote two epigrams on the same subject.[41]

The lyric and longer epigram share the same ending (the seduced lady's determination to sleep every afternoon in the hope of more such experiences). In the epigram, however, the conclusion is sprung upon the reader with little preparation. Its narrative concentrates exclusively on the male actor, and gives no sense of the girl's conspiracy in her own seduction. It is, indeed, the reader's sudden realisation of her complacence that is the 'point' of the epigram. In the lyric, by contrast, the reader is aware throughout of both participants, and therefore of irony at the expense of Jamy's inflated sense of his own daring as Bessy wilfully pretends quiescence. The ending clarifies and focusses implications wittily and ambiguously suggested in the course of the narrative and fixes the reader's stance towards the poem as a whole.

The shapeliness of many other lyrics is ensured by aphoristic conclusion. **'So tyr'd are all my thoughts'** sets up a series of questions answered in the final stanza; **'So many loves have I neglected'**, **'Beauty is but a painted hell'** and **'Thus I resolve'** are straightforward examples. In all of them a solid, forward-directed form is generated and assured by an ending that, in Hudson's earlier-quoted phrase, acts as a 'distillation from' the matter of the poem.

The influence of epigram is also to be found in lyrics where the stanza-form is reinforced, rather than subordinated to a larger design. **'Could my heart'**, for example, is made up of three stanzas each of which offer self-contained epigrammatic statements arranged as thesis, antithesis and conclusion. **'I must complain'** combines material divided into two epigrams in *Epigrammatum Liber II*, its two stanzas related by question and answer. **'Thou art not faire'** has a similar structure, though it is much less successful.

More significant is the kind of double perspective the linking of genres makes possible. By it our arrival at a sententia as the goal of a lyric's striving suggests that for the poem's speaker security is to be found when the private dilemmas of a lyrical world of love can be placed and fixed by reference to the public wisdom that aphorism encodes. Rosemond Tuve long ago pointed out that Renaissance poems frequently seek to generalise, rather than simply to express a state of mind.[42]

The fiction of the lyric mode is, even in the Renaissance, primarily an individual and introspective one. Astrophil, in Sidney's sequence, writes to 'paint the blackest face of woe' but also 'to ease a troubled mind'. The epigram, however, is a public mode, and its writer 'holds the reader at a distance, addressing him directly, but not inviting him to share experiences'. Where the writer of lyric mimes the fluctuation of thought and feeling, the epigrammatist 'writes a poem not when he is moved, but when he ceases to be. He records the moment of mastery—not the emotion, but the attitude that conquered it'.[43] This last comment is a particularly useful one in describing the effect of **'So tyr'd are all my thoughts'**. Its first three stanzas do seem to record a present state, made urgent by rhetorical question and apostrophe. If the poem ended at its twelfth line it would belong with numberless lyrics representing a disconsolate poet. With the last stanza all this is pushed

back in time and space, placed under a perspective of later wisdom that imparts a touch of retrospective irony to our picture of the somewhat self-indulgent figure of the first three stanzas.

The vital point to recognise here is that the epigrammatic mode is used by Campion with the same purpose as his variation upon conventional themes or classical source texts; to test and explore standard literary formulations of experience. But it must also be recognised that the roles may be reversed, and that the proud arrogance that the epigram's style generates through its assumption of wisdom can also be tested and found wanting.

Proverbial statement is mocked in **'A secret love or two'**, where the libertine female marshals any amount of public wisdom to justify her conduct. In poems such as **'Kinde are her answers'** or **'Faine would I my love disclose'** the reader feels that the poet reaches for the comfort of sententiae that signally fail to be adequate to his distress. Elsewhere epigrammatic conclusions are offered with a conscious irony, exposing their limitedness as prescriptions for living. **'Vaine men whose follies'** and 'If love loves truth' are poems of this kind.

Aphorism is particularly suitable to epigram since by its nature it suggests agreed, public truth. Bacon's observations on aphoristic writing are of interest here.

> But the writing in Aphorisms hath many excellent virtues, . . . For first, it trieth the writer, whether he be superficial or solid: for Aphorisms, except they should be ridiculous, cannot be made but of the pith and heart of sciences; for discourse of illustration is cut off: recitals of examples are cut off; discourse of connection and order is cut off; descriptions of practice are cut off. So there remaineth nothing to fill the Aphorisms but some good quantity of observation: and therefore no man can suffice, nor in reason will attempt to write Aphorisms, but he that is sound and grounded.

He suggests the effect of aphoristic writing on the reader:

> Aphorisms, representing a knowledge broken, do invite men to inquire farther.[44]

In the lyric poem aphorism functions very much as Bacon suggests, producing a lapidary effect as sentence is laid upon sentence, giving weight to the poet's utterance and inviting the reader to supply the connections, illustrations and situations that will fill out the experience of which he assumes they are a distillation. Frequently this leads to a paradoxical result—that language seeming weighty and full of compressed matter yet makes up a poem elusive and enigmatic.

Two examples may serve to illustrate this side of Campion's poetic personality. The first comes from his book of religious lyrics.

> Where are all thy beauties now, all harts enchayning?
> Wither are thy flatt'rers gone with all their fayning?
> All fled; and thou alone still here remayning.

Thy rich state of twisted gold to Bayes is turned;
Cold as thou art, are thy loves that so much burned:
Who dye in flatt'rers armes are seldome mourned.

Yet, in spight of envie, this be still proclaymed,
That none worthyer then thy selfe thy worth hath
    blamed:
When their poore names are lost, thou shalt live
    famed.

When thy story, long time hence, shall be perused,
Let the blemish of thy rule be thus excused:
None ever liv'd more just, none more abused.

                                              (p. 61)

This lyric has a sombre power, deriving in no small measure from the way simple language issues a string of summary pronouncements, mainly coincident with single line-units. Its structure is balanced, as two stanzas of dispraise are followed by two qualifying and ameliorating their severity. The reader's problem is to translate this general response into a more particular picture.

The opening lines of the poem suggest that the addressee is a conventional sonneteer's lady grown old; the flatterers, then, are taken as being those poets who have written emptily in her praise. One could imagine this beginning turning into one of Drayton's harsher sonnets. The fourth line, however, implies that the poet is speaking to a royal figure, an idea which then suggests a rather different understanding of the 'flatt'rers' of the sixth line. Matters are made more difficult by the apparent contradiction between the endings of these two stanzas. In the first we assume that the lady is solitary, but alive. In the second the word 'dye' is ambiguous; it might be fact, or merely prophecy. In turn this raises questions about the word 'cold' in the fifth line—is it the cold of heartlessness, or is it the lasting chill of death? In the rest of the lyric such problems are compounded, and we are left uncertain as to the 'story' that the envious might tell, and unsure whether the poem as a whole is more about rule and government than about beauty and love.

These uncertainties and doubts arise because the lyric's plain, emphatic style invites us to look towards a figure it refuses to disclose. In this respect the poem as a whole rests on a collision between the manner of the love lyric— where the conventionality of postures allows a poet to do no more than gesture towards the lady addressed, and epigram, which demands precise anatomy of those it characterises. The sententious style invites us, in Bacon's term 'to enquire farther', but its unconnectedness denies the means to do so.

In some ways this is Campion's oddest poem, made so by its presence in a book of religious lyrics, as well as by its internal complexities. Perhaps there is an answer to its riddling if some classical, Biblical or contemporary figure should be found who answered to its varied description. The other poem to be considered is not opaque in quite the same way, but it too offers teasing challenge to the reader.

Were my hart as some mens are, thy errours would
    not move me:
But thy faults I curious finde, and speake because I
    love thee;
Patience is a thing divine and farre, I grant, above
    mee.

Foes sometimes befriend us more, our blacker deedes
    objecting,
Then th'obsequious bosome guest, with false respect
    affecting:
Friendship is the glasse of Truth, our hidden staines
    detecting.

While I use of eyes enjoy, and inward light of reason,
Thy observer will I be, and censor, but in season:
Hidden mischiefe to conceale in State and Love is
    treason.

                                              (p. 137)

It is no doubt a coincidence that this poem of judicious reproof is, like the previous example, cast in three-line stanzas and placed third in its book, but there is a similarity of tone and style between the two. This poem, like the last, opens with a sentiment that suggests a straightforward love-lyric situation, but then takes the reader in an unexpected direction.

While the direction of the poem is less ambiguous than that of the previous example and its basic statement—'as a friend I must tell you of your faults'—is much more directly conveyed, there is still a degree of uncertainty about the nature of those faults. They begin merely as 'errors', move through 'blacker deedes' to 'hidden staines' which in turn becomes 'hidden mischiefe'. In retrospect one wonders whether the increasing severity of these terms undermines the tone of sweet reasonableness that the poet adopts at the beginning.

But this is not as significant to the ambiguity of the lyric as the way successive proverbial conclusions to each stanza raise questions about the view we are to take of the poet-speaker. At the simplest level, the three sententiae are carefully arranged in a pattern of increasing objectivity, as 'I' becomes 'our', and then there is no personal pronoun. This gives an epigrammatic solidity to the ending of the poem. But at the same time there is an opposition between the personal motivation for writing suggested in the second line, and the abstract moral imperative that the last line of the lyric puts forward. The implied questions this raises about the speaker's motivation are reinforced, first by his own admission in the third line, that Patience (and therefore silence) is the ideal, and secondly by the note of self-congratulation that creeps in to the seventh line.

It is, in the end, a matter of tone. It is possible to read the poem as Davis does, seeing the lover as 'an honest man' who reaches 'final balance of critic, servant ("observer"), and detached though tender wellwisher'. In my reading, however, it is not so much the poet who presents 'a complex and responsible attitude', as the reader who realises that a poet pretending well-motivated concern is sheltering a rather vindictive wish to broadcast failings and injuries under the hypocritical cloak of public and proverbial moralising. In other words, where Davis takes the detachedness of this lyric's epigrammatic posture as assured, it seems to me that Campion has taken the proverbial matter which forms the basis of the second stanza and subjected its wisdom to scrutiny by placing it within a lyric mode which permits the reader to question a speaker's motivation as it stands revealed in evolving dramatic speech.

My difference with Davis here is a mark of a more fundamental disagreement about the final verdict to be delivered on Campion's poetry. For him the epigrammatic quality of some of Campion's verse enables 'a full and sententious exploration of reality', and those poems have 'the true ring of the classical tone he had sought in vain during his early classicist imitations'. In part my own contentment with many of those 'classicist imitations' is as much the product of buried prejudices as Davis's preference for plain style. But in the end it seems to me that Campion did not accept quite so readily that the stylistic devices of the epigram, the detachment it encoded and the wisdom it professed, were any more 'real' than any other literary version of reality.

Auden offered a view diametrically opposed to Davis's:

> What he has to offer us is succession of verbal paradises in which almost the only element taken from the world of everyday reality is the English language. Since words, unlike musical notes, are denotative, his songs have to be 'about' some topic like love or religion, but the topic is not itself important.[45]

Campion himself would, in the light of his comments quoted at the beginning of this chapter, have been surprised if not offended by this attitude. It seems to me that it is too simply a prelude for what Auden wanted to say about Campion's metrical skill, and does not recognise that Campion's poetry, in its continual play with texts, conventions and styles, though it may not confront 'reality' directly, does by its questioning confront and test the perspectives that lyric poetry offers upon reality. Something of his skill as a metrical craftsman will be discussed later. It is the hope of this chapter that it offers a picture of a poet intellectually active himself, and offering to the reader a mental stimulus as well as sensual pleasure in sound.

Notes

1. Douglas L. Peterson, *The English Lyric from Wyatt to Donne* (Princeton, 1967); Hallett Smith, *Elizabethan Poetry* (Cambridge, Mass., 1952), pp. 279-87.

2. Campion in the dedication speaks of 'These youth-borne *Ayres*', implying early composition.

3. John T. Irwin, 'Thomas Campion and the Musical Emblem', *SEL* (Winter, 1970), pp. 121-141; Stephen Ratcliffe, *Campion: On Song* (London, 1981).

4. See O.B. Hardison, Jr., *The Enduring Monument* (Chapel Hill, 1962), pp. 113-62.

5. Alastair Fowler, *Spenser and the Numbers of Time* (London, 1964), p. 248, notes the significance of the number seven for Spenser's elegy *Daphnaida*.

6. Quoted by Hardison, p. 114.

7. Cf. Montaigne's 'Upon some verses of Vergil' in Florio's translation ed. Saintsbury (London, 1893) III, p. 84: 'The Gods (saith Plato) have furnished man with a disobedient, skittish and tyrannical member, which like an untamed furious-beast, attempteth by the violence of his appetite to bring all things under his becke.'

8. Compare the experience of Christian in Bunyan's *The Pilgrim's Progress*: 'Now was Christian much affected with his deliverance from all the dangers of his solitary way, which dangers, though he feared them more before, yet he saw them more clearly now, because the light of the day made them conspicuous to him'. ed. Roger Sharrock (Harmondsworth, 1965), p. 99.

9. 'A shape or pattern will, other things being equal, tend to be continued in its initial mode of operation.' Leonard B. Meyer, *Emotion and Meaning in Music* (Chicago, 1956), p. 92.

10. *The Poems of Sir Philip Sidney,* ed. William A. Ringler, Jr. (Oxford, 1962), p. 200.

11. The same juxtaposition was preserved in the revision of these poems in *The Fourth Booke* (pp. 190, 192).

12. Barbara Kiefer Lewalski, *Protestant Poetics and the Seventeenth Century Religious Lyric* (Princeton, 1979), pp. 213-50.

13. Horace, *Odes,* I. xxii. It also reflects something of Psalm I.

14. 'And because loue is of all other humane affections the most puissant and passionate . . . it requireth a forme of Poesie variable, inconstant, affected, curious and most witty of any others, whereof the ioyes were to be vttered in one sorte, the sorrowes in an other, and by the many formes of Poesie, the many moodes and pangs of louers, thoroughly to be discovered'. *The Arte of English Poesie* (London, 1589), p. 36.

15. See R. L. Peterson, *Imitation and Praise in the Poems of Ben Jonson* (New Haven and London, 1981), Ch. 1, and a stimulating discussion in Terence Cave, *The Cornucopian Text* (Oxford, 1979) pp. 35-77.

16. Lewalski, *Protestant Poetics,* pp. 237-8.

17. Martin Luther, *A Commentarie up in the 15 Psalmes,* translated by Henrie Bull (London, 1577) p. 240.

18. By L. Bradner, 'References to Chaucer in Campion's *Poemata*', *RES* xii (1936), pp. 322-3. I am assured by Professor McConica that recent research has produced no evidence of Campion's recusancy.

19. Cf. Herbert's 'Holy Scriptures'.

20. Marlowe's translation, in *The Complete Poems and Translations,* ed. Stephen Orgel (Harmondsworth, 1971), p. 172.

21. *Catullus, Tibullus and Pervigilium Veneris,* Loeb Classical Library (Revised ed., London, 1962) pp. 6-7.

22. See Gordon Braden, '*Vivamus mea Lesbia* in the English Renaissance', *ELR* [English Literary Renaissance] ix (1979), pp. 199-224.

23. For Campion and Propertius see J. V. Cunningham, 'Campion and Propertius', *PQ* [Poetry Quarterly] xxxi (1952), p. 96 and L. P. Wilkinson, 'Propertius and Thomas Campion', *London Magazine* vii (1967), pp. 56-65.

24. R. O. A. M. Lyne, *The Latin Love Poets* (Oxford, 1980), pp. 74-8.

25. In the 'Second Song' of *Astrophil and Stella.*

26. Edward Doughtie, ed., *Lyrics from English Airs 1596-1622* (Cambridge, Mass., 1970), p. 223.

27. Doughtie, p. 77.

28. John Hollander arrives at a similar conclusion by a different route in *Vision and Resonance* (New York, 1975), pp. 78-9.

29. ed. Maurice Evans (Harmondsworth, 1977), p. 289.

30. *The Complete Poems,* ed. A. J. Smith (Harmondsworth, 1971), p. 123.

31. II. xxviii, 49-52. Loeb edn. pp. 146-9.

32. Rosemond Tuve, *Elizabethan and Metaphysical Imagery* (Chicago, 1947), p. 16.

33. Barbara Herrnstein Smith, *Poetic Closure* (Chicago, 1968), p. 200.

34. Rosalie L. Colie, *The Resources of Kind* (Berkeley, 1973), p. 75.

35. Colie, p. 69.

36. See H. H. Hudson, *The Epigram in the English Renaissance* (Princeton, 1947), pp. 6-9.

37. Smith, p. 176.

38. Hudson, p. 4.

39. Smith, p. 199.

40. Smith, p. 67.

41. The first of these epigrams exists in two versions. See Davis, p. 505.

42. 'These songs show writers irresponsibly, blithely addicted to arriving at conclusions of the general nature usually considered proper to reasonable discourse'. Tuve, p. 18.

43. Smith, p. 208.

44. Francis Bacon, *The Advancement of Learning,* ed. G. W. Kitchen (London, 1915), p. 142.

45. W. H. Auden and John Hollander, *Selected Songs of Thomas Campion* (Boston, 1972), p. 11.

Abbreviations

ELR English Literary Renaissance

ELS The English School of Lutenist Song Writers, ed. E. H. Fellowes (London, 1920-32). Revised ed. by Thurston Dart and others, as *The English Lute-Songs* (1959-)

PQ Philological Quarterly

RES Review of English Studies

SEL Studies in English Literature

I have used two editions of Campion, those by Davis (London, 1969), and Fellowes, in *ELS.* Where reference is primarily to the text I give page references to Davis, where to the music I use B.A.; I; etc. (For *A Booke of Ayres, The First Booke* etc.,) followed by the song numbers. In Chapter 3 both are given; Though the musical examples are based on Fellowes's edition I give the text in Davis's old-spelling form.

Walter R. Davis (essay date 1987)

SOURCE: Davis, Walter R. "Masques." In *Thomas Campion,* pp. 118-53. Boston: Twayne Publishers, 1987.

[*In the following excerpt, Davis argues that masques bring together Campion's diverse skills, discusses how they were staged, and surveys critical responses to them.*]

THE LORD HAY'S MASQUE

James I and his Revels Office took an old form that had existed in England for at least a century and made it serve a new and intense political purpose, that of solidifying James's kingdom, which, by the Act of Union, was to combine England, Scotland, and Wales into Great Britain. Campion was chosen to compose the masque celebrating the first of the major political weddings James was to sponsor between Scots lords and English ladies; it took place 6 January 1607, it being Twelfth night, and it was between his favorite, James Hay, first earl of Carlisle and Baron Hay, and Honora Denny, daughter of the high sheriff of Hertfordshire who had welcomed James to England back in 1603. There seems to have been some difficulty in arranging the match, for James had to create Denny a baron and grant his daughter Strixton Manor in order to gain his consent. But it must have seemed worth the trouble, for James's full intention—as it was lauded both by Campion and by Robert Wilkinson in the wedding sermon—was to strengthen the ties between his two kingdoms (see [*The Works of Thomas Campion,* ed. Walter R Davis; hereafter cited as] *D,* 204).

The published souvenir program moves from the visual to the auditory: it contains an engraving of one of the knights masquers as a frontispiece and five pieces of music—two songs and three dances (to which Campion wrote new words for singing)—at the back. The art of writing out an account of a masque for publication was something quite new: Daniel in *The Vision of the Twelve Goddesses* (1604) did it in two parts, a description with explanations and comments, then the script with the speeches; Jonson tended to start with his idea, then the "body" as he called it, a physical description, then the "soul" or the words. Campion sees the piece as narrative and takes his model from military history, first describing the place and then the action:

> As in battailes, so in all other actions that are to bee reported, the first, and most necessary part is the discription of the place, with his opportunities, and properties, whether they be naturall or artificiall. The greate hall (wherein the Maske was presented) received this division and order: The upper part, where the cloth and chaire of State were plac't, had scaffoldes and seates on eyther side continued to the skreene; right before it was made a partition for the daunping place . . . eighteene foote from the skreene, an other Stage was raised higher by a yearde then that which was prepared for dancing. This higher Stage was all enclosed with a double vale, so artificially painted, that it seemed as if darke cloudes had hung before it: within that shrowde was concealed a greene valley, with greene trees round about it, and in the midst of them nine golden trees of fifteene foote high, with armes and braunches very glorious to behold. From the which grove toward the State was made a broade descent to the daunting place, just in the midst of it; on either hand were two ascents, like the sides of two hilles, drest with shrubbes and trees; that on the right hand leading to the bowre of *Flora,* the other to the house of *Night*; which bowre and house were plac't opposite at either end of the skreene, and betweene them both was raised a hill, hanging like a cliffe over the grove belowe, and on the top of it a goodly large tree was set, supposed to be the tree of *Diana*; behind the which toward the window was a small descent, with an other spreading hill that climed up to the toppe of the window, with many trees on the height of it, whereby those that played on the Hoboyes at the Kings entrance into the hall were shadowed. The bowre of *Flora* was very spacious, garnisht with all kind of flowers, and flowrie braunches with lights in them; the house of *Night* ample, and stately, with blacke pillors, whereon many starres of gold were fixt: within it, when it was emptie, appeared nothing but cloudes and starres, and on the top of it stood three Turrets underpropt with small blacke starred pillers, the middlemost being highest and greatest, the other two of equall proportion: about it were plac't on wyer artificiall Battes and Owles, continually moving: with many other inventions, the which for brevitie sake I passe by with silence.

(D, 211-12)

It was the great hall at whitehall Palace (the usual Banqueting House was being reconstructed). At one end was James's throne providing the point of view from which it

will all be seen in perspective, before it the dancing area that filled the bulk of the hall; at the other end a curtain or "skreene" painted as dark clouds. The stage behind the curtain had two levels: on the lower, a yard above the dancing area, the main stage of a green valley; then above that (connected by ramps) three small stages, the bower of Flora on the right, the house of Night on the left, and between them the hill of Diana with her sacred tree.[1] From the place Campion proceeds to the persons: four speaking parts and nine dancers, including the powerful Howards: Theophilus Howard, Lord Walden; Sir Thomas Howard; and others of the king's officers:[2] "Their number Nine, the best and amplest of numbers, for as in Musicke seven notes contain all varietie, the eight being in nature the same with the first, so in numbring after the ninth we begin again, the tenth beeing as it were the Diappason in Arithmetick. The number of 9 is famed by the Muses and Worthies, and it is of all the most apt for chaunge and diversitie of proportion. The chiefe habit which the Maskers did use is set forth to your view in the first leafe: they presented in their fayned persons the Knights of Apollo, who is the father of heat and youth, and consequently of amorous affections" (*D,* 213). Now for the action. It begins with music and song: Flora and Zephirus the West Wind (a pair immortalized in Botticelli's "Primavera") are plucking and strewing flowers all over the stage while a tenor and a soprano clothed as "Silvans" or fauns and Zephirus sing a three-part song accompanied by three lutes and a bandora. It is a lovely song, in dance form of AABAAB though they are not dancing.[3] It directs the action, its refrain being the command to "strowe aboute" (*D,* 215); and it links spreading flowers to singing, as if the two can blend: "Strowe aboute, strowe aboute, / And mixe them with fit melodie." The song is about the marriage this action prepares for, and marriage is related to the political mingling of the "princely" white and red roses—the flowers of York and Lancaster that Henry VIII and then Elizabeth brought together, and that James, in seeking to unite England and Scotland, continues together.[4] The song being ended, Flora speaks of the sacred occasion of marriage marked by flowers "figuring" beauty and youth, and explains that these flowers are not subject "To winters wrath and cold mortalitie" (*D,* 216). Zephirus echoes her in the male mode, relating marriage to the time when Venus brings "Into the naked world the greene-leav'd spring" and promising fertility. Then the Silvans sing a three-part dialogue-song on maidenhood versus marriage, ending on a classical wedding chorus, **"Sing Io, Hymen: Io, Io, Hymen"** (*D,* 217).

The masque begins with a mythological version, by female and male deities of nature, of a wedding preparation. But it is ruddely interrupted by a sudden spectacular revelation: "This song being ended the whole vale is sodainly drawne, the grove and trees of gold, and the hill with *Dianas* tree, are at once discovered. *Night* appears in her house with her 9 houres" (*D,* 217). Night threatens to take over the plot and thwart the marriage: she represents Diana "The Moone and Queen of Virginitie," who forbids that one of her chaste nymphs be pressed into marriage and further magnifies the depredation by pointing to the nine golden trees that are Apollo's knights transformed because they tried to seduce Diana's nymphs:

> Here they are fixt, and never may remove
> But by *Dianaes* power that stucke them here.
> *Apollos* love to them doth yet appeare,
> In that his beames hath guilt them as they grow,
> To make their miserie yeeld the greater show.
> But they shall tremble when sad *Night* doth speake,
> And at her stormy words their boughes shall breake.
>
> (*D*, 218)

Speech and stasis, things as they are resisting change, threaten to take over from lively song and fertile movement in this debate. The strife is soon resolved, however, by a god from the machine, Hesperus, "The Evening starre foreshews that the wisht marriage night is at hand." He explains to Night that Apollo has pacified Diana who is now

> well content her Nymph is made a Bride,
> Since the faire match was by that *Phoebus* grac't
> Which in this happie *Westerne Ile* is plac't
> As he in heaven, one lampe enlightning all
> That under his benigne aspect doth fall
>
> (*D*, 219)

—that is, King James has sponsored the marriage. He further commands that the nine knights be released from their spell.

Night will obey, and rather suddenly changes her tune:

> If all seeme glad, why should we onely lowre?
> Since t'expresse gladnes we have now most power.
> Frolike, grac't Captives, we present you here
> This glasse, wherein your liberties appeare:
> *Cynthia* is pacified, and now blithe *Night*
> Begins to shake off melancholy quite.
>
> (*D*, 219)

The interruption has been conceived as a clash in tone or feeling, Night at first complaining that the tragic loss of a virgin has become "sport" for Flora, Zephirus responding by words that seem to her "wanton." Now with this change of heart (like Kafka's leopards in the temple) Night becomes (naturally) the friend to lovers and will direct the remaining action of the masque, as if she were its dancing-master.[5] She asserts a wonder: the trees will dance, for "joy mountaines moves," and it is joy that will cause dancing, while "Dancing and musicke must prepare the way" for their retransformation into living, sentient beings:

> Move now with measured sound,
>   You charmed grove of gould,
> Trace forth the sacred ground
>   That shall your formes unfold.
>
> (*D*, 221)

The song accompanies the dance in question—probably the "measures" or a slow pavane—and directs its movement, impelling the nine golden trees toward King James and the couple:

> Yet neerer *Phoebus* throne
>   Mete on your winding waies,
> Your Brydall mirth make knowne
>   In your high-graced *Hayes.*

The song is set to the same music as **"The peacefull westerne winde"** (*Second Booke,* 12), and beneath both one hears the traditional "Westron wynde" melody that alludes to Zephirus and his power to revive natural heat.[6] The dancing long wished-for is beginning: first dance of trees setting life in motion, then transformation:

> Presently the *Silvans* with their foure instruments and five voices began to play and sing together the song following, at the beginning whereof that part of the stage whereon the first trees stoode began to yeeld, and the three formost trees gently to sincke, and this was effected by an Ingin plac't under the stage. When the trees had sunke a yarde they cleft in three parts, and the Maskers appeared out of the tops of them; the trees were sodainly convayed away, and the first three Maskers were raysed againe by the Ingin. They appeared then in a false habit, yet very faire, and in forme not much unlike their principall, and true robe. It was made of greene taffatie cut into leaves, and laid upon cloth of silver, and their hats were sutable to the same.
>
> (*D*, 221-22)

Campion's marginal note indicates that they had some difficulty removing the trees: apparently a stage hand had forgotten to reattach the trees to an engine after displaying them to the nobility the day before (see *D*, 222, n. 44). At any rate, the transformation proceeds by stages. First Night's feelings and the nature of her involvement were changed, then the trees by her natural magic become more human, in the intermediate appearance of leafy men. The second stage is accomplished by a **"Song of transformation"**:

> *Night* and *Diana* charge,
>   And th' Earth obayes,
> Opening large
>   Her secret waies,
> While *Apollos* charmed men
>   Their formes receive againe.
> Give gratious *Phoebus* honour then,
> And so fall downe, and rest behinde the traine.
>
> (*D*, 222)

This song is repeated three times, as Night transforms trees into leafy men three by three (in doing so breaking down the mystic 9 into the "best of numbers . . . contained in three"), ending in a great chorus to James: "Againe this song revive and sound it hie: / Long live *Apollo*, Brittaines glorious eye" (*D*, 223). To song succeeds dancing: "as soone as the *Chorus* ended, the violins, or consorte of twelve, began to play the second new daunce, which was taken in form of an Eccho by the cornetts, and then catch't in like manner by the consort of ten; sometime they mingled two musickes together, sometime plaid all at once; which kind of ecchoing musicke rarely became their *Silvan* attire, and was so truely mixed together, that no daunce could ever bee better grac't then that, as (in such distraction of musicke) it was performed by the maskers" (*D,* 223-24). The dance is a slow measure, probably the same sort of dance as **"Move now with measured sound"** was.[7]

The third stage of transformation must be achieved by human action of the nine men themselves, who must make obeisance to Diana's tree and make an offering of their leaves to her. This religious procession is accompanied by "a sollemne motet" in six parts sung by six "Chappell voices" with six cornets. It is a new kind of music in the masque, sacred polyphonic music, the text celebrating chastity and temperance, its movement appropriately upward:

> With spotles mindes now mount we to the tree
>   Of single chastitie.
> The roote is temperance grounded deepe,
> Which the coldjewc't earth doth steepe:
>   Water it desires alone,
>   Other drinke it thirsts
> for none:
> Therewith the sober branches it doth feede,
>   Which though they
> fruitlesse be,
> Yet comely leaves they breede,
>   To beautifie the tree.
> *Cynthia* protectresse is, and for her sake
> We this grave procession make.
> Chast eies and eares, pure heartes and voices
> Are graces wherein *Phoebe* most rejoyces.
>
>   (*D,* 225)

This interprets allegorically as it expresses purposeful human action. In its religious moment it fully reestablishes the wedding context, as something both in nature (as it was before the interruption) and now, also, above it in transcendence. The men can now appear in their proper ceremonial attire as Knights of Apollo in crimson satin doublets and robes "layd thicke with broad silver lace" (*D,* 224), inserted spangles reflecting the light, which was centered in the sparkling jewel of their elaborate helmets with turrets and plumes, all light and feathers swaying.[8] After a third "lively" dance, with the strong trochaic beat characteristic of a galliard,[9] they move out to blend audience and pageant: "they tooke forth the Ladies, and danc't the measures with them" (the measures being a slow and stately dance, probably a pavane: see *D,* 225, n. 55).

The piece ends with Hesperus defining "this golden dreame which I report" (*D,* 210) as a moment of "new birth," after which an elaborate farewell is given to Hesperus, the evening vanishing while full night takes over with her revels, "That th'ecclipst revels maie shine forth againe" (*D,* 226). The social occasion takes over with common dancing of pavanes, galliards, courantes, allemandes, la voltas, etc., after which Night announces an end, the chorus closes with music meant to recall the song of transformation, and all go off: "This *Chorus* was performed with severall Ecchoes of musicke and voices, in manner as the

great *Chorus* before. At the end whereof the Maskers, putting off their visards and helmets, made a low honour to the King, and attended his Majestie to the banquetting place" (*D,* 227).

There survive three masques that preceeded Campion's in the new reign, one per year, it seems, each Twelfth Night. Samuel Daniel's *Vision of the Twelve Goddesses* (1604), a tentative effort in the masque form, is little more than a pageant like those performed before Elizabeth I in the 1570s: he first sets a frame for his vision by having Night rouse Somnus to create a dream, then presents the dream, Sybilla first seeing the twelve goddesses with their gifts far off and then having them appear and dance while presenting their gifts to her and the kingdom, as at Christmas. There is no conflict, and very little music or dance. Daniel in his description is concerned that his speeches be printed because attention to the spectacle might have distracted the viewers, and he is concerned to establish only one extended sense for each goddess, as Thetis is meant to symbolize only power by sea.[10]

Jonson's *Masque of Blackness* (Twelfth Night, 1605) is much more theatrical, and in it Jonson shows that he had incorporated the model of Davison and Campion's **Masque of Proteus and the Adamantine Rock** at Gray's Inn back in 1594. That masque, we may remember,[11] helped set the form exploited in King James's reign: an introductory song and dialogue that lays out the myth or "device," the entry of the masquers amid spectacle, a debate ending in a song to the monarch. *Blackness* is built on this frame: the appearance of twelve Ethiopian nymphs in their seashell, the song, Niger's explanation to Oceanus that they are seeking a land that will turn them white, their landing and presenting of gifts, and their dance and the revels. There is no transformation, for *Blackness* was to be completed by *Beauty* two years later (Jonson was already thinking in terms of antimasque and masque). Speeches take up the bulk of the text, while song and dance are not integrated into the action.

Hymenaei derives its great unity from its occasion, that being the wedding of the earl of Essex and Frances Howard (the same woman whose scandalous second marriage Campion was to celebrate in 1613) on Twelfth Night, 5 January 1606. It begins as a Roman wedding ritual, with personated bride and groom, that is broken by the eruption of eight men "out of a microcosm, or globe, figuring man,"[12] representing the four humors and four affections. Reason quells the disturbance and explicates the wedding ceremony (with an extensive disquisition on the number 5 as the union of odd and even), at which point the great world dominated by Juno or order appears, the eight men join in dance with eight women representing marital virtues, and the ceremony resumes and proceeds to its end (which blends with the participants in the wedding going to bed). Here ceremony derived from the occasion creates a total form for the action.

Campion derived many elements of his first masque from these previous productions. We can trace a direct line from Daniel's procession of twelve goddesses with their gifts to

Jonson's twelve Ethiopian nymphs to Campion's nine male masquers making offering to Diana. Jonson's *Hymenaei* influenced Campion especially, with its device of the interrupted ritual and its reestablishment as beginning and end, its matching of knights and ladies, even its number symbolism—Campion's disquisition on 9 almost seems a self-conscious answer to Jonson's on 5. But when compared with Campion's predecessors, three elements of difference stand out: the great increase of ritual interest, the predominant use of music and with it dance, and the considerable extension of significance into allegorical senses.

The Lord Hay's Masque develops from *Hymenaei* the device of a wedding preparation first interrupted and finally reestablished, and here and there we can even hear an echo.[13] The descent of Hesperus performs the same function of harmonizing as Reason's descent in Jonson. But in Campion's masque the forces are those of nature—flowers, night, the evening star—and so the action becomes expressive of natural change; when Hesperus descends we see at one time a message from the god and the simple coming of evening. On this natural change is founded ritual, and Campion's masque develops a full sense of ritual as the human reproduction of natural forces; it becomes, in fact, one large ritual. The progress from interruption to reestablishment is accomplished by ritual: the song of transformation that brings green men out of the shell of golden trees, and then the ceremony of dedication to Diana that brings them further into full human shape. The device is permeated by transformation, and that transformation becomes the central action of the whole masque, which finally demonstrates how we achieve our proper humanity and harmonize our universe by means of religious dedication.

It is music and dance, rather than speech, that belong to ritual, and that in fact bring about transformation. The action Night sets out starts with joy producing the external movement of dance (by analogy and by cause from the internal increased flow of blood in joy), dance leading to song of transformation, the accomplishment of which is marked by a new dance. It is not so much that music and dance are integrated into the device, as that they carry it through, they are the main vehicles. **The Lord Hay's** is a musician's masque. When we quoted Campion's opening description earlier, we left out a portion. Here it is restored:

> The upper part, where the cloth and chaire of State were plac't, had scaffoldes and seates on eyther side continued to the skreene; right before it was made a partition for the daunceing place; on the right hand whereof were consorted ten Musitions, with Basse and Meane lutes, a Bandora, double Sackbott, and an Harpsicord, with two treble Violins; on the other side somewhat neerer the skreene were plac't 9 Violins and three Lutes; and to answer both the Consorts (as it were in a triangle) six Cornets, and six Chappell voyces, were seated almost right against them, in a place raised higher in respect of the pearcing sound of

those Instruments; eighteen foote from the skreene, another Stage was raised higher by a yearde then that which was prepared for dancing.

(*D*, 211)

Eleven violins, six cornets, at least five lutes strung low and high, a pandora (a flat-backed instrument like a guitar), a double sackbut or bass trombone, a harpsichord: this is a large orchestra; later we hear of oboes (or "hoboys"), and Campion tells us that he employed a total of forty-two voices and instruments (*D*, 223). We do not know whether or not it was typical because no other masque composer mentions it. The musicians are made an integral part of the set: they are placed directly on stage to the left, right, and front of the dancing area, and they carry through the numerological design of the piece by being set in three.

Moreover, the music carries through the theme of the masque. Andrew Sabol points out that "the most effective musical devices he describes in **Lord Hay's Masque** are those used to gain contrast."[14] One form contrast takes is the three dialogue songs where two, three, or four voices come together. Another is antiphonal music, when choirs of voices and instruments in different parts of the hall echo each other. This is suggested by the account of the chorus at the end of the song of transformation:

> This *Chorus* was in manner of an Eccho seconded by the Cornets, then by the consort of ten, then by the consort of twelve, and by a double *Chorus* of voices standing on either side, the one against the other, bearing five voices a peece, and sometime every *Chorus* was heard severally, sometime mixt, but in the end altogether; which kinde of harmony so distinguisht by the place, and by the severall nature of instruments, and changeable conveyance of the song, and performed by so many excellent masters as were actors in that musicke (their number in all amounting to fortie two voyces and instruments) could not but yeeld great satisfaction to the hearers.

(*D*, 223)

It is not difficult to see how these antiphonal pieces (that accompanying the dance following this song being another example: *D*, 223-24) and dialogues mime out the theme of the diverse coming together in the masque. Moreover, it is echo that takes a part in binding the whole together, the final chorus after the revels being in itself an echo of the echoing music of transformation (*D*, 227, 223).

An unusual feature is to mark the final stage action—before it moves off stage into the audience in the common measures—by the solemn six-part motet sung by the chapel choir that was normally heard in church services (*D*, 225). The text is allegorical, it interprets the religious goal while it directs the dancers to it. The music is religious, that is, church music; we may recall that Campion thought of the motet as the musical equivalent of the epic poem, for "in Musicke we yeeld the chiefe place to the grave and well invented Motet" (*D*, 15-16). The action of the masque moves to the religious level as the masquers make offering to Diana, and it is the motet that takes them there. Here toward the end we see religious ritual as the base of dramatic ritual, expressed in the music.

Finally, Campion is unusual and influential as well in making the symbolic media that comprise a masque—traditional iconography, number symbolism, the use of music to transform emotion, and dance as an emblem of order—come together to produce a variety of significances. Daniel had been quite insistent on establishing one meaning only in 1604: "And though these images have oftentimes diverse significations, . . . we took them only to serve as heiroglyphics for our present intention, according to some one property that befitted our occasion, without observing other their mystical interpretations." Pallas was for him "armed policy" and nothing else, and he bound in his single interpretations by his verse descriptions.[15] Similarly Jonson in *Blackness* chose to label his twelve nymphs pair-by-pair by means of having each pair carry "a mute hieroglyhic" or a single symbol, such as the golden tree carried by Euphoris and Aglaia signifying fertility.[16] Though Jonson moved toward the polyseimous in *Hymenaei*,[17] it was Campion who first brought it out fully.

We know of his early admiration of *The Faerie Queene* with its multiple allegorical extensions of significance, and his use of Spenser in the allegorical houses of his early Latin poem **"Ad Thamesin."** In his more mature Latin poem **"Umbra"** he imitated the Garden of Adonis in book 3, canto 6, of *The Faerie Queene* where form and substance, male and female, the changing and the permanent come together in the various senses of exposition. And perhaps from that Spenserian moment he derived his own myth in that poem of the paradoxical union of the cold, dark, wet female center of earth and the hot, dry, male inseminating principle in the sky.[18] Later, too, in 1609 he was to express admiration for Francis Bacon's similar exfoliation of natural myth in moral and cosmological interpretations in *The Wisdom of the Ancients* (**D,** 418-19). That is the background to his creation of a myth for the Lord Hay and his wife with its many extensions of significance. On stage we have the action of Flora and Night; but Flora is the agent of Apollo, Night of Diana, and such agency immediately suggests extended meanings, each visible deity being an agent of an invisible deity that is both natural and transcendent.

Most immediately, we understand this action as a psychological figure that exploits the minds of the bride and groom, who see in the masque a heightened image of their moment in time: the wedding day itself, betokening joy and fruitfulness with its scattered flowers; the coming of cool, chaste Night, which seems to destroy the aura of goodness around the wedding (perhaps because the virgin bride is fearful); and, finally, the transformation of night by the light of the occasion into a time of joy and fruitfulness. When Hesperus departs, the golden moment of the masque will dissolve and the bride and groom will depart from the hall to begin that night that will be unlike any

other. To this sense belong the transformations—the change of Night herself, the reduction of discord to concord by harmonious music, and the gradual change of the masquers from golden trees to green leafy men to Knights of Apollo resplendent in crimson.

In the most general sense, Campion asks his audience to enter a "golden dreame" in which marriage is seen as the human analogue of cosmic creation, for his myth, like his **"Umbra,"** deals with the original opposition of principles in nature, female potential (the earth, dark, cold and wet, governed by Diana the moon, tending to stasis) and male passion (the heavens, light, hot and dry, governed by Apollo the sun, eager to move), the act of mutual love and grace by which they are reconciled, and the cosmic growth that results. Over this union rules the divine triad and its self-multiple nine, the first union of the female-even and the male-odd.

The uppermost sense of the masque in the minds of the general audience (if not the bride and groom) was the Anglo-Scottish Union James was arguing in Parliament that very year. The fact that James, the "Phoebus" of this Western Isle, has sponsored this wedding is enough to pacify Diana and Night; the fact that his nine knights have to embrace the values of chastity and temperance indicates something like advice to the Scots of his entourage. He has united chastity and love by the ceremony of marriage. He has reconciled two kingdoms—that of the hot male daylight and that of the cool female darkness that is reluctant to enter the ceremony but eventually does. If Night and night represent England in one sense, Flora and daylight Scotland, then, too, historical continuity is suggested. David Lindley reminds us that Elizabeth I throughout her career was associated with Diana goddess of chastity, and if in this masque Diana and Apollo reach concord, so too their kingdoms form a continuity that helps solidify in the minds of the audience this new reign, with all its problems and desires.[19]

THE LORDS' MASQUE

When, in **The Lords' Masque** of 1613, Entheus is released from the crowd of madmen, there is a strong suggestion that the palates of the masque audience have been cloyed with vanity for a while and that Entheus the poet, having regained his "libertie and fiery scope againe," will create "Inventions rare" to repair the lack. This smacks of a composer's advertisement, a heralding of Thomas Campion's return to the stage after six years' absence, with the fiery scope of his genius intact (there may even be a suggestion that his immersion in the practice of medicine was like being tossed to and fro by madmen). We know nothing of the reasons why he stayed away from the court stage for so long. His self-advertisement may have irritated Ben Jonson, who from 1607 to 1613 had dominated the masquing scene with his *Beauty* (1608), *Queens* (1609), *Oberon* (1611), *Love Freed from Ignorance and Folly* (1611), and *Love Restored* (1612). We do not know the circumstances, nor the nature and degree of rivalry, that might have been involved, but we do know that Jonson made fun of Campion's next masque with his *Irish Masque*.[20]

The suggestion surrounding Entheus seems a little uncharitable of Campion, for when he returned to the court stage after his six years of absence, the form had advanced tremendously, and he took full advantage of it. Under the hands of Jonson and Jones, it had acquired the structure of antimasque (which both contrasted and gave a foundation to the masque), masque, and revels; and it had accumulated a vast amount of theatrical technique in the forms of stage sets, machines, lighting effects, and such. Into *The Lords' Masque* Campion incorporated these elements. If in his first masque he had been a musician facing the masque, here he appears as a masque composer, in full control of the idiom that was emerging in this new genre itself.

If you were a typical Englishman, the performance on St. Valentine's Day 1613 for the wedding of the Princess Elizabeth and the Elector Palatine would have given you occasion for rejoicing. It was true that the groom was ruler of a tiny kingdom within Germany, and it might have been difficult for you to locate on a map the place along the Rhine where the borders of the Palatinate began, or its center in Heidelberg. But the Elector Palatine or the Palgrave (the name derives from *palatium,* and is related to "paladin" or palace guard) had a power that far exceeded his physical realm, having traditionally supervised the election of the Holy Roman Emperor who governed Germany and much of central Europe, and having recently become a leader of continental Protestantism. That was important. Ever since the 1580s advisors had been trying to persuade first Elizabeth and then James to make common cause with their co-religionists across the channel, joining them militarily to create something of a Protestant league against Spain and her allies. Sidney got in trouble trying to dissuade Elizabeth from marrying a French Roman Catholic, and he had died defending the Dutch against Spain. Now, after more than thirty years' delay, James was seen by many as making that much-desired move. From the eleventh century the Palgrave had been the Holy Roman Emperor's closest aide; but the role was no longer proper for Protestants, and the groom's father, Frederick IV, who ruled from 1583 to 1610 (his early death hastened by that common disease of royalty, acute alcoholism), had cast himself in the role of leader of the Protestants, establishing the Evangelical Union to combat the aggressive tendencies of Catholics within the Empire. The young Frederick V, whose uncle was the powerful Dutch Protestant leader Maurice of Nassau, continued his father's work.[21]

The masque celebrating the marriage begins as a double consort strikes up a lively tune and the curtain is raised to reveal the lower half of a perspective setting. It is a forest in deep perspective, the sides slanting inward painted with trees, the trees at the back in relief or whole round. On the left is the entrance to a cave, on the right an artificial thicket. Suddenly there emerges from the thicket the figure of Orpheus followed by tame animals. He is dressed in an antique cuirass with bases, with a robe over his shoulder, his hair long and curled with a laurel wreath on his head and a small silver bird in his hand (see *D,* 249). The consort ceases and he speaks, calling "Mania" from her dark and earthy den. The consort sounds again, and she appears out of the cave, a wild and mad old crone dressed in black, a long robe with double sleeves and a petticoat, gesturing wildly in antic fashion.[22]

He tells her that Jove (read "James," the Jove mentioned throughout as ordering the action these people accomplish for him on stage) has ordered that she set free one "Entheus" or "Poetic Fury" from the crowd of the insane she has in her charge, and that he will control the babble with the music he commands: "Let Musicke put on *Protean* changes now; / Wilde beasts it once tam'd, now let Franticks bow" (*D,* 250). And suddenly, to the tune of strange music on high wind instruments, twelve lunatics tumble out of the cave: "there was the Lover, the Selfelover, the melancholicke-man full of feare, the Schooleman over-come with phantasie, the over-watched Usurer, with others that made an absolute medley of madnesse" (*D,* 250). With a change in the music, the madmen fall into a frenzied dance that exhausts them, but after a while Orpheus raises his hand and the music changes again into a soft and solemn air which quiets them. Orpheus is raising and quelling madness in them by music, and it ends when they meekly trail off the stage, back to the cave. While they were whirling about they were jostling a thirteenth figure, "*Entheus* (or Poeticke furie)," one classically dressed and very bewildered, as if he were not one of them. As they leave, he is left on stage with Orpheus. His costume shows the relation he bears to the great singer of civilization: he wears a close cuirass of the antique fashion like Orpheus's, the skin-tight sculpted cuirass that reveals the musculature of chest and shoulders like a Greco-Roman bust; he has a robe fastened to his shoulders and hanging down behind. Like Orpheus his head is encircled with laurel, but out of that wreath grows a pair of wings, and at its front it has a clasp in the shape of a star. His left arm encircles a large book, a bound folio, while he raises his right hand with a quill pen in it.[23]

These two figures face each other like person and mirror across the stage. There is a feeling of great dignity in their speeches as Orpheus explains that he has called Entheus forth at Jove's (James's) request to compose an invention to celebrate this night. Entheus replies,

> *Orpheus,* I feele the fires
> Are reddy in my braine, which *Jove* enspires.
> Loe, through that vaile, I see *Prometheus* stand
> Before those glorious lights, which his false hand
> Stole out of heav'n, the dull earth to enflame
> With the affects of Love, and honor'd Fame.
>
> (*D,* 251-52)

The singers burst into a song, **"Come away,"** and after the first strophe the upper part of the curtain falls away suddenly to reveal the heavens—eight huge stars fiery on top and silver in the middle burning in the midst of varicolored clouds, in front of the scene Prometheus standing attired in cuirass, greaves, and plumed helmet like an antique hero.

Orpheus and Entheus have provided a frame. What the audience is witnessing is the process of inventing a wedding masque: what is happening on the upper stage is what those on the lower stage are imagining. The masque proper, presided over by these three great classical figures that image eternity, now begins. Prometheus has actually ordered the stars to dance. As a song urging the "musick-loving lights" to dance in honor of the confluence of the Rhine and the Thames and then to descend to human shape is sung, apparently the stars do dance: "According to the humour of this Song, the Starres mooved in an exceeding strange and delightful maner; and I suppose fewe have ever seene more neate artifice then Master *Innigoe Jones* shewed in contriving their Motion, who in all the rest of the workmanship which belong'd to the whole invention shewed extraordinary industrie and skill; which if it be not as lively exprest in writing as it appeared in view, robbe not him of his due, but lay the blame on my want of right apprehending his instructions for the adoring of his Arte" (*D*, 254).

The stars then vanish, as if drowned among the colored clouds, and eight masquers appear from the wings of the upper stage, while a curtain behind them resembling clouds is drawn up to reveal circles of light in motion further off in the heavens. The masquers are the transformed stars. They are dressed in cloth of silver, combining the classical cuirasses of the three presiding heroes with the more modest contemporary round breeches with bases. Around their waists are flame-shaped green leaves. What seem flames sprout from the wrists and shoulders and around their small ruffs. But their heads seem on fire, for they wear crowns of gold plate and orange enameling that seem to blend in with their hair, and a silken feather that looks like smoke emerges at the top.[24]

These are the lords who will give this entertainment its name: Lord James Hay, the king's former favorite; Philip Herbert, Sidney's nephew, now earl of Montgomery (and to be honored with his brother William as patron of Shakespeare's First Folio); and William Cecil, earl of Salisbury, son of Elizabeth's and James's secretary of state and married to one of the powerful Howard women.

Prometheus speaks again of sparks from the earth to attend the lords, and suddenly sixteen pages dart out on the lower stage. They seem half naked and all aflame, being clothed only in skin-tight cuirasses with skirts colored orange tawney like flames, wings of flame, a circlet with flames about their heads.[25] They carry large wax torches which they swing about rather dangerously, as they break into a wild and vigorous dance. Light and fire fill the room and smoke rises to the rafters.

Now a new wonder: a cloud that covers the whole stage, top to bottom, appears, and Prometheus leads the masquers down on stairs concealed within it, at the end of which

procession the cloud splits in two. The lower scene has suddenly been changed, and instead of the woods there is now a two-dimensional architectural flat. It is a gorgeous facade, all gold set with rubies, sapphires, emeralds, and opals. It is Greco-Roman architecture, as if a space Orpheus and the other two have finally evoked for their exclusive use (and it may also form a compliment to the Holy Roman Empire of which Frederick is a part). There are four niches separated by gold pilasters, their capitals of the Roman composite order. Over them runs a mixed order featuring reverse scrollwork, and at the top a cornice arched slightly and touching every pilaster. In the niches stand four female statues of silver, and above each is a bas-relief in gold that seems to present part of the history of Prometheus. The statues are transformed ladies who must be awakened to love and life by the men.

The action is once more directed to the throne, where the earthly Jove sits and nods approval. Prometheus, Entheus, and Orpheus invoke Jove to release the ladies, in a brief hymn; the statues move slightly, and the men pantomime courtship of them in a galliard. It is danced to a courtly syncopated song, a rather popular contemporary cavalier piece that gives a nice sophistication to the usually less open matters of female coyness and male aggression:

> Wooe her, and win her, he that can:
>   Each woman hath two lovers,
> So shee must take and leave a man,
>   Till time more grace discovers;
> This doth *Jove* to shew that want
>   Makes beautie most respected;
> If faire women were more skant,
>   They would be more affected.
>
> Courtship and Musicke suite with love,
>   They both are workes of passion;
> Happie is he whose words can move,
>   Yet sweete notes helpe perswasion.
> Mix your words with Musicke then,
>   That they the more may enter;
> Bold assaults are fit for men,
>   That on strange beauties venture.

(*D*, 257)

The four women are transformed, and four more statues appear in their places; another invocation and courting, and all is complete. It is like rhyme. The eight ladies transformed from statues wear beautiful loose, silver dresses, with flowing gossamer veils, large fluffy ruffs, and mantles looped up on one side at the shoulder.[26]

The entertainment is moving out of the land of classical myth into the audience's world: the song is a contemporary courtly song in the meter of a galliard, and the masquers wear costumes like the clothes the fashionable audience is wearing. It becomes directed at the wedding party at this stage, for while the lords and ladies rest between dances a dialogue song with chorus wishes good luck to the bride and groom (*D*, 258-59). Also, the dancing has moved down the ramp into the dancing area of the banqueting room.

The staged entertainment starts to blend with its viewers. The eight lords and eight ladies take partners from the audience, and the revels begin.

An hour passes in this social dancing. Then a brief song calls a halt, and the curtains that had been closed during the dancing rise to reveal a whole new scene—a long Greco-Roman perspective with porticos receding into the distance, in its center a large silver obelisk whose top is lost in clouds with its lights, on either side statues of the bride and groom, now mirrored in gold (*D*, 259). Now that love has been celebrated, it is time for fame. A sage old woman, the Roman Sybil, in a golden robe, and veiled, pulls the obelisk forward on the stage with a single thread of gold. She chants in a high voice after the fashion of the time a long poem in Latin about joining Great Britain and Germany in unity (*D*, 260). Then a dance, and she prophesies again, in Latin; this time Orpheus and Prometheus paraphrase her blessing of bride and groom with a large progeny. There is a song (reminiscent of one of the corontos in the revels) and a final new dance as all sixteen masquers go out (*D*, 262).

James went to great expense for his daughter's wedding. The cloth for wedding and masque was extensive, over 700 yards of satin, over 230 pounds of lace, 204 yards of copper stuffs, 318 yards of tinsel, etc. It is known that Campion was paid slightly over sixty-six pounds for his libretto, Jones fifty pounds for his designs, thirty or forty pounds each to the dancing masters Jerome Herne, Thomas Giles, one Buchan, and one Confess, ten or twenty pounds apiece to the composers Giovanni Coperario, Robert Johnson, and Thomas Giles for music, a pound apiece to the ten members of the king's violins, a pound apiece to the twelve "Madfolkes" and the five speakers of parts.

Sir John Finett, master of the ceremonies, thought that the masque "was performed with exceeding charge and commendable discharge, . . . the devyse was ingeniously cast, the dances well figured." But John Chamberlain was impatient: "That night was the Lords maske whereof I heare no great commendation, save only for riches, theyre devises beeing long and tedious, and more like a play than a maske"—he liked dancing more than dialogue. But the Venetian ambassador Antonio Foscarini focussed on the sets; for him the masque "was very beautiful, with three changes of scene. . . . certain stars danced in the heavens by a most ingenious device."[27]

It is Stephen Orgel's opinion that "the effects that Jones created for this production comprise almost an anthology of scenic machinery of that time,"[28] and we have heard how much the Venetian ambassador, who must have witnessed much sophisticated staging in his native Italy, admired its changes of setting and the "most ingenious device" by which stars were made to dance in the heavens. The first setting is divided in half horizontally, and the antimasque takes place against the lower half alone, that being a setting in depth, "a wood in prospective, the innermost part being of releave or whole round, the rest

painted" (*D*, 249). It is all horizontal. When Entheus is freed from the limited perspective of madness and imagines for his poem the presiding figure of Prometheus, his vision is both literally and metaphorically true. The veil of imagination is the curtain of the stage, because after the first strophe of the song of invocation, "In the end of the first part of this Song, the upper part of the Scene was discovered by the sodaine fall of a curtaine; then in clowdes of severall colours (the upper part of them being fierie, and the middle heightned with silver) appeared eight Starres of extraordinarie bignesse, which so were placed as that they seemed to be fixed betweene the Firmament and the Earth; in the front of the Scene stood *Prometheus*, attyred as one of the ancient Heroes" (*D*, 252). Prometheus is the surrogate figure of the poet within his fiction, the stars a reification of his fiery brain. It is a mirror and a complement. The release of imagination with its light and fire completes the lower world of earth by evoking the upper world of the heavens in imagination and then producing it.

The world is now whole. The triad of power and poetry sets out the ceremony whose essence is bringing the stellar into human life. The Orphic song first makes the "musick-loving lights" of eight stars dance in the heavens "in an exceeding strange and delightful maner" that so impressed the Venetian ambassador. Then—probably on flats—the scene of clouds was drawn aside to reveal "an Element of artificiall fires, with severall circles of lights, in continuous motion, representing the house of *Prometheus*" (254); this scenic change accompanies the transformation of the stars into eight masquers in costume that recall their wedding apparel.

Action now turns vertical. Prometheus from above invokes fiery spirits that "Breake forth the earth like sparks" from below (*D*, 255), and the fires of heaven and earth now combine as the fiery masquers descend to join with the fires of earth on a huge transparent cloud that fills the stage from top to bottom. The cloud—probably composed of a flat surrounded by smoke from a cloud machine—breaks in two and reveals the second setting. In place of the woods in the lower half of the set we now have classical architecture with four female statues in niches. The set is glittering and two-dimensional. The geography is deliberately ambiguous, for this should be the House of Prometheus in the heavens but it seems to have been transferred to earth, in order to be palpable. This is the scene of corresponding transformation, when eight female statues and eight male stars become human and dance together.

The varied and ingenious scenes have taken us from wild nature to civilization with its complex and harmonious architecture; it is here that the revels of the court take place. When the revels are ended we have our third setting. Gone are the divisions between upper and lower, for now the scene is one from floor to ceiling. It is a perspective scene signifying unity, "a prospective with Porticoes on each side, which seemed to go in a great way" as had the woods before (*D,* 259). It is about depth, reaching into the past—a Palladian perspective on a Roman piazza with the obelisk of Egypt and Rome at its center. It is here that Sybilla prophesies in Latin, evoking fame, continuity, and the permanent values.

The structure of the masque, formed on the Jonsonian model, likewise stresses evolution. It begins with Mania, a nightmare vision of mankind dominated by a chaos of passions and delusions. This antimasque is the basis of the rest, so it is not so much dispersed as purified. For Entheus or "poetic fury" or "the imagination" is filtered out of the crowd. Orpheus the primordial poet and orderer of nature purges from the primordial flux of emotions the most valuable passion placed in mankind. "Poetic Fury" creates a fiction that comes to life (as the fire in his brain leads to stars and lights): Prometheus the man of fire and power is the reification of his words, it is he who is imagined to unite heaven and earth, to bring down ethereal virtuous man from heaven and unite him with the earthly art of the beautiful female element. Gone is the original opposition of Mania-earth-low-dark and Orpheus-heaven-high-light, for they are now united in a fertility imaged as constructing a world. The poet having had a vision of reasonable, virtuous, and loving mankind and then created it as real, his work is over; it is taken up and given permanence by a female, the prophetess Sybilla, under whose aegis the masque moves from its social revels to its transcendent conclusion out of time.

What is this about? It is about language; it is about poetry; it is about civilization. It builds on the ancient myth of Orpheus to show the magical language of the poet divinely inspired bringing about a progressively more continuous and permanent civilization. It moves from the dim past to a classical present, out to a deep-resounding future. It is an ever-fuller evocation of completeness: "The number's now complete," cries Entheus (*D,* 258). A. Leigh DeNeef presents this masque as "a formal celebration of the nature and function of poetry."[29] For him, the four central characters represent an analysis, as in a spectrum, of four elements of poetry. Orpheus, mover of trees and tamer of beasts, represents the form-giving or shaping power of poetry, the way it makes the chaos of life's experiences yield a vision of order. Entheus, who has been released from flux by this shaping activity, is poetic inspiration, the divine spark from above that gives life to shape. His creature Prometheus represents ornament, by which DeNeef means not only the attractive surface but the principles of symmetry, completeness, and measure that control the actual poem with its encapsuled vision.[30] Finally, Sybilla represents the prophetic function of poetry when all three previous elements are in place, the power of poetry not only to embody but to extend life. From form to inspiration to a formed whole that has prophecy as its most ambitious function: this is what Elizabeth Sewell in *The Orphic Voice* calls "poetry thinking about itself,"[31] and in tracing such thought it is also tracing the progress

of the civilization it sponsors. The element of ritual is strong though less overt than it was in the Lord Hay piece, but now it is shown to have power. Ritual speech creates things.

THE CAVERSHAM ENTERTAINMENT

When he came to publish his description of *The Lords' Masque* later in the spring, Campion included with it an account of the outdoor entertainment given to Queen Anne by Lord Knollys at Caversham near Reading on 27 and 28 April. It forms a fitting conclusion to the festivities of the wedding, for it marks the royal lady's return to private life. Two months after the marriage, Anne and James bade farewell to Elizabeth and Frederick at Gravesend; and ten days later, on 24 April, Queen Anne began her progress toward Bath, which she repeatedly visited for the gout. Of this progress, John Chamberlain wrote, "The King brought her on her way to Hampton Court; her next move was to Windsor, then to Causham, a house of the Lord Knolles not far from Reading, where she was entertained with Revells, and a gallant mask performed by the Lord Chamberlain's four sons, the Earl of Dorset, the Lord North, Sir Henry Rich, and Sir Henry Carie, and at her parting presented with a dainty coverlet or quilt, a rich carrquenet, and a curious cabinet, to the value in all of 1500 l" (*D,* 234).[32]

It is a much simpler piece than the masque, naturally employing no theatrical effects, having no governing device but only a continued cast of characters. Instead of an opening description of the scene, there is a brief description of the estate, and the bulk of the text is taken up with the speeches that were presented. Campion's goal seems to have been to surround the two-day visit with a light fiction. It falls into three parts: an outdoor piece performing a ceremony of welcome on Tuesday, an indoor piece celebrating the queen's transforming presence in a revels after supper, and a farewell ceremony with gifts on Wednesday morning.

The first piece takes Queen Anne through three stages, with pauses at the approach, at the park gate, and at the gardens before the house. For the first: "it shall be convenient, in this generall publication, a little to touch at the description and situation of *Cawsome* seate. The house is fairly built of bricke, mounted on the hill-side of a Parke within view of *Redding,* they being severed about the space of two miles. Before the Parke-gate, directly opposite to the House, a new passage was forced through earable-land, that was lately paled in, it being from the Parke about two flight-shots in length, at the further end whereof, upon the Queenes approach, a *Cynick* appeared out of a Bower" (*D,* 235). The Cynic presents a speech in favor of solitude, which is countered by "a fantastick Traveller" who has been secretly inserted into the queen's party on horseback. After the Traveller has converted the Cynic to the values of society, they go on together with the party to the park gate, where two Keepers and two "Robin-Hood-men in sutes of greene" (*D,* 237) meet the queen and offer her formal greeting, with a five-part song and a "Silvan-dance of six persons." Song and dance have succeeded to dialogue and involve the queen, and when she and her party are met in the lower garden by the Gardener and his boy language flourishes. There has been a progression in language: the Cynic had been plain and boorish—"Naked I am, and so is truth; plaine, and so is honestie" (*D*, 236)—the Traveller fantastic in his mock-logic. The Keeper and Robin-Hood-men had been plain but well intentioned—"accept such rude intertainment as a rough Wood-man can yeeld" (*D*, 238). The Gardener speaks in a homespun country version of the Euphuism that had been popular back in the 1580s: "Most magnificient and peerelesse Diety, loe, I the surveyer of Lady *Floras* workes, welcome your grace with fragrant phrases into her Bowers, beseeching your greatnesse to beare with the late woodden entertainment of the Wood-men; for Woods are more full of weeds then wits, but gardens are weeded, and Gardeners witty, as may appeare by me" (*D*, 240).

As language becomes more "flowery," it traces a rustic vision of the progress of civilization, from wilderness to forest to garden, whence Anne is guided to the door of the house. The second part of the entertainment takes place in the hall of the estate, the seat of its full civilization, and it is a miniature masque. The antimasque collects the characters of the welcoming ceremony: Traveller, Gardener, and Cynic appear, all appropriately drunk, and utter ridiculous speeches. The Traveller's mock-logic turns in on himself—"if we presse past good manners, laugh at our follies, for you cannot shew us more favour, then to laugh at us" (*D*, 243)—the Gardener becomes fulsomely self-satisfied, the Cynic rubbing his eyes in wonder at the combined effects of wine and the royal personage (*D*, 243-44). The three harmonize in a song betokening fellowship and the union of the different, and then they disperse—"Let us give place, for this place is fitter for Dieties then us" (*D*, 245). The indoor scene dominated by the presence of the queen resets rustic harmony as ridiculous.

What caused them to disperse was the appearance of a deity, the god "*Silvanus,* shapt after the description of the ancient Writers. His lower parts like a Goate, and his upper parts in an anticke habit of rich Taffetie, cut into Leaves" (*D*, 244-45). He represents myth, perhaps the myth of the world like Bacon's Pan, the lower parts linking him to earth while the upper parts reach to the sky.[33] It is his duty to present transcendence, and in his speech we observe for the first time a change from prose to verse. He praises the power of Queen Anne that transcends his, and then presents the masquers. They enter to "a great noise of drums and phifes" (*D*, 245), dance their entry, and then proceed to the little masque's third part, the revels that consume the rest of the night, the gouty queen deigning "graciously to adorne the place with her personall dancing" (*D*, 246).

The third part of the entertainment consists of a brief farewell speech by the Gardener, now speaking dignified verse about his "flowrie incantation" (*D*, 247), and the presentation of gifts, while a final three-part song is performed by three handsome country maidens. The action of transcendence that took place within the house the evening before leaves everything simple, dignified, and generous at its threshold.

The two pieces of this publication came out together printed in reverse chronological order, first *The Caversham Entertainment* of April, then *The Lords' Masque* of the preceding February. That arrangement seems designed to highlight a progression in tone from clowning in the country to stately action at court. These two tones (each of which rises, within its limitations, by deliberate modulations of style, one from rustic pretentiousness to the high style in verse, the other from mad babble to Latin verse) correspond to their respective occasions. The entertainment is designed to raise the spirits of a queen who has just lost her daughter to a husband, while the masque celebrates great affairs of state. What the two have in common is the theme of language and its power to trace and influence the evolution of civilization. The way they go together redoubles that evolution.

THE SQUIRES' MASQUE

In the court masque, that form that pulled together the skills he was master of, Campion was exploring questions of meaning or significance: his technique settled, he could plumb the problems of what it all meant. In his first masque he was an interpreter of nature: by evoking the allegorical senses he unfolded for his audience the nature of nature as conjunctions of opposites in the cosmic, human, and political realms. In *The Lords' Masque* he used the nature of poetic creation as its own scaffolding, the foundation of a suggestive device about the power of poetic language to create and make stable. His progress is analogous to what Michel Foucault finds as a great turn from sixteenth-century interpretation of a divinely ordered world by finding analogies, to the seventeenth-century representation of a world in which differences and distinctions play a major part.[34] And in his final masque he assays a direct representation of this-our-world as it exists, first in appearance and then in reality. This was a bold stroke: masques never before had been dedicated to mimesis.

Campion begins his description of *The Squires' Masque* with a theoretical statement:

> In ancient times, when any man sought to shadowe or heighten his Invention, he had store of feyned persons readie for his purpose, as *Satyres, Nymphes,* and their like: such were then in request and beliefe among the vulgar. But in our dayes, although they have not utterly lost their use, yet finde they so little credit, that our moderne writers have rather transfered their fictions to the persons of Enchaunters and Commaunders of Spirits, as that excellent Poet *Torquato Tasso* hath done, and many others.

> In imitation of them (having a presentation in hand for Persons of high State) I grounded my whole Invention upon Inchauntments and several transformations.

> (*D*, 268)

For him, the age of myth and fiction was over—as it was for Donne, who, Carew asserted, had banished the Ovidian trains of gods and goddesses from verse.[35] He is making a statement about Jacobean society: it is much more likely to be confused by rumor and false appearance than it is to be raised to a level of vision by myth as in Elizabeth's day. Enchantment and illusion are false myths; they distort rather than ennoble life. What is needed is an accurate rendering of the life we experience—as well as the necessary appreciation of such a rendering. The change involves a stress on the psychological perception of reality rather than interpreting reality in absolute metaphysical terms.

The realism of this masque consists in its depiction of myth as falsehood and in its coasting so near the actual occasion it celebrates: for the device of the twelve Knights enchanted by the evil illusions of Rumor and freed by the sufferance of Queen Anne seems deliberately designed as a tactful attempt to lift opprobrium from the countess of Essex's remarriage. We have recounted the sordid background to the occasion before, in the murder of Sir Thomas Overbury.[36] Rumors about the actual murder did not surface until the following spring and summer, but as of 26 December 1613 there was suspicion enough. People knew that the wedding was a culmination of the attempt of the Howard family to gain influence over Robert Car, earl of Somerset, the successor to James Hay as King James's favorite. To that end they encouraged Car's passion for Frances Howard and finally even managed to have her marriage to Essex annulled in order to pave the way for Car. The annulment proceedings, which concluded on 25 September, were a messy business: it had to be proved that Essex was impotent. Furthermore, court gossips knew that the two had been sleeping together since the previous spring: no matter of cool chaste Diana opposing Flora, this. The Yuletide wedding was an unabashed and even shameless Howard triumph: four of the dancers were Howards, and four others may have been pressed into duty in order to guarantee legitimacy, since they had danced in Jonson's *Hymenaei* celebrating the countess's first marriage, that had just been so scandalously dissolved, back in 1606 (see **D,** 264, 284).

For a masque, the setting is doggedly mundane. Instead of bowers of goddesses or the heavens with moving stars which become the House of Prometheus, we have a triumphal arch as proscenium with a familiar landscape or seascape within it:

> The place wherein the Maske was presented, being the Banquetting house at White Hall, the upper part, where the State is placed, was Theatred with Pillars, Scaffolds, and all things answerable to the sides of the Roome. At the lower end of the Hall, before the Sceane, was made an Arch Tryumphall, passing beautifull, which enclosed the whole Workes. The Sceane it selfe (the Curtaine being drawne) was in this manner divided.
>
> On the upper part there was formed a Skye with Clowdes very arteficially shadowed. On either side of the Sceane belowe was set a high Promontory, and on either of them stood three large pillars of golde; the

one Promontory was bounded with a Rocke standing in the Sea, the other with a Wood. In the midst betwene them apeared a Sea in perspective with ships, some cunningly painted, some arteficially sayling. On the front of the Sceane, on either side, was a beautifull garden, with sixe seates a peece to receave the Maskers; behinde them the mayne Land, and in the middest a payre of stayres made exceeding curiously in the form of a Schalop shell. And in this manner was the eye first of all entertayned.

(**D,** 268-69)

This is representation. It is notable that the setting is made to include the auditorium, the pillars near the chairs of state partaking of the architectural motif set by the arch, all "Theatred." That is important, for Queen Anne will take a central part in the masque, and that will signify to the onlookers that she has overcome her initial opposition to the wedding. And instead of a ceremony—or any music or dance—the piece opens with a bare narrative report. Four Squires (hence the alternative title, **The Squires' Masque,** as well as **The Somerset Masque**) who have narrowly escaped shipwreck tell how twelve Knights who had set sail to attend the wedding have been baffled by a storm at sea caused by Error, Rumor, Curiosity, and Credulity: six of the Knights vanished into the air at sea, while the other six were transformed into the pillars the audience sees on land (and sees reflected about them in the "theatred" room). The relation is dramatized: the first Squire can scarcely finish his account to King James because of exhaustion, while the fourth breaks out in fear at the arrival of Error and his train.

The antimasque is a bit unusual in that it is concluded entirely in pantomime. The four enchanters the Squires have mentioned—Error like a serpent (from book 1 of *The Faerie Queene*), Rumor clothed in tongues, Curiosity in eyes, and Credulity in ears—enter and whisper a while "as if they had rejoyced at the wrongs which they had done to the Knights" (**D,** 271) and then begin to dance. They are joined by three quaternities: "strait forth rusht the foure Windes confusedly," "After them in confusion came the foure Elements," "Then entred the four parts of the earth in a confused measure" (**D,** 271). The antimasque of the world in mute confusion is dispersed by the arrival of the delegation of value: Eternity, the three Destinies carrying a golden tree, and Harmony with nine musicians. Mere bodily action is replaced by song, song moreover that has as its goal direction of purposeful action:

CHORUS.

> Vanish, vanish hence, confusion;
> Dimme not *Hymens* goulden light
>   With false illusion.
> The Fates shall doe him right,
> And faire Eternitie,
>   Who passe through all enchantements
>   free.

Eᴛᴇʀɴɪᴛɪᴇ Sɪɴɢᴇs Aʟᴏɴᴇ.

> Bring away this Sacred Tree,
> The Tree of Grace and Bountie,
>   Set it in Bel-Annas eye,
> For she, she, only she
>   Can all Knotted spels unty.
> Pull'd from the Stocke, let her blest Hands convay
>   To any supliant Hand, a bough,
>   And let that Hand advance it now
> Against a Charme, that Charme shall fade away.

Toward the end of this Song the three destinies set the Tree of Golde before the Queene.

(*D*, 272)

Eternity's solo song is a celebrated piece: it was set by Nicholas Lanier in the new declamatory or monodic style, thus making the music partake of the realism of this masque by being reduced to heightened unmelodic speech.[37] The musical setting gives the song a feeling of personal urgency (one that contrasts with the dance melody of the next song when the purpose has been happily achieved), and so in brief space we have shifted, from a choric exorcism in the ceremonial mode, to a feeling personal persuasive lyric, to the action of setting the tree before the queen.

When "the Queene puld a branch from the Tree and gave it to a Nobleman, who delivered it to one of the Squires" (*D*, 273), the enchantments dissolve to a new melodic song in dance meter, **"Goe, happy man, like th'Evening Starre"**: six Knights appear in a cloud, the other six are suddenly transformed out of the pillars of gold. And the wedding can now be celebrated in a combination of song and dance: the masquers perform their first dance in three sections, between them appearing three strophes of a hymn **"While dancing rests"** (*D*, 274). That hymn, deliberately separate from the dance mode in its religious elements, expresses marriage by an echo-effect signifying meeting and bringing in other voices that modulate from nature's meetings to the religious chorus **"Io, Io Hymen."** The main masque is very short, little more than an interlude between the grotesque antimasque of illusion that the world has no order, and the revels with their planned combination of social order and disorder.

The revels conclude with the entrance of twelve sailors who dance a hornpipe and then convey the twelve Knights away to their waiting ships. It is notable that the revels are brought to an end by a set of characters from the lower classes who would normally be part of the antimasque, and they have come not for a ceremonial but a practical purpose, to row people back to their ships before the tide turns. Their music, like that of **"Bring away this Sacred Tree,"** is close to sounds the audience actually heard in life: heightened speech, a sailor's dance.[38]

The Golden Bough that is the pivot of the plot does not merely dissolve enchantments; it was the traditional guide through the underworld, but as **"Grace and Bountie"** it also guides us through an upper world that often seems confusing. It brings the audience into the actual world they inhabit, for at the moment when the Knights appear, "on the sodaine the whole Sceane is changed: for whereas before all seemed to be done at the sea and sea coast, now the Promontories are sodainly remooved, and London with the Thames is very arteficially presented in their place" (*D*, 273). To dissolve enchantment is not only to release the Knights but also to release us, to bring us into reality and activate the wedding celebration. In place of the confusion of the elements, we now have the natural cycle of the seasons—"Sweete springs, and *Autumn's* fill'd with due increase" (*D*, 275)—that frames love's ceremony. What had been miraculous elements become mundane: in a wedding dialogue the miraculous golden tree of Destiny is caught up in an image and becomes a natural tree serving as an emblem of fertility: "Set is that Tree in ill houre / That yeilds neither fruite nor flowre" (*D*, 275). And "Eternity" becomes a matter of blessing the couple with hopes of children so as to leave "a living Joy behind" (*D*, 275). The sailors who announce the end of the revels are ordinary sailors—"Straight in the Thames appeared foure Barges with skippers in them" (*D*, 275)—and they sing a colloquial song—"Come a shore, come, merrie mates"—while dancing a hornpipe. It ends as realistic representation: the myth was the illusion.

This is the bare bones of a masque entertainment. The text we have is one of the shortest of those publications, yet we know that it began at 11:00 P.M. and ended at 2:00 A.M.[39] One reason for its slightness is that the bulk of the action is contained and carried by music and dance, which are indicated rather than narrated in full. Another is that it is compressed, because much of the action is not explained in speeches but incorporated into the song and dance. For example, we know from their song that the sailors have come to tell the Knights it is time to embark. It was so compressed as to cause misunderstanding. The agent of Savoy attended, and to him the four Squires were merely "four men dressed poorly" who spoke in a funereal accent unsuited to a wedding, the tree "signifying the olive" of peace, the confused antimasque "a masque of twelve devils."[40] It was not simply that the agent Gabaleoni's English was at fault, for he did not attend to the visual iconography of the antimasque (iconography being in fact a science that grew up in his native Italy). The antimasque is compressed, and demands interpretation. The four enchanters form a solipsistic pattern among themselves. Credulity's ears lie open to receive the messages of Rumor's tongues, Curiosity's eyes are dazzled by the serpent Error, and the four form two couples, two men and two women for completeness. The elements of the world that enter to dance to their dance, Gabaleoni's twelve devils, represent Error's distortion of reality as something confused and chaotic. Error and Rumor not only throw one off course, but make the world seem frightening and threatening. The personified values that disperse them are abstract, but they are not so much virtues of the mind as representatives of what is—Eternity or how things have always been and will be, the three Destinies or how things must be, Harmony with nine musicians the elements of nature as it really exists with the nine spheres, and so forth. Number symbolism is involved as it was in 1607; 4 as the mundane sphere superseded by the divine number 3 and its multiples, then 12 Knights the product of their multiplication, and so on. Land and sea are disjoined by Error and his troop and rejoined by Queene Anne, under whose aegis the symbolism of 3 continues into the three sections of the wedding hymn.

The masque celebrates the reality it represents on many planes. But reality, we say, is a tricky business, by definition beyond our control. One thing Campion did not count on was the incompetence of the Florentine designer Constantine de Servi: as Gabaleoni recounts it with the relish of an Italian rival state, the device for lowering the cloud with six of the Knights in it was constructed as one makes a portcullis, and when the cloud came down the audience could see the ropes and hear the pulleys groaning away as they do when you raise the mast of a ship. The Savoyard concludes, "Apart from having seen their Majesties in good order and with great majesty, and also the great number of ladies, one could see nothing that came anywhere near meriting the inconvenience of the thousands of people who waited twelve hours without dinner."[41] Then of course the whole occasion blew up next autumn, when Campion was examined and his great patron Monson imprisoned under suspicion of having taken part in the conspiracy to murder Overbury.

Campion's big year was 1613: it was the year he published three books of songs in two volumes and composed three masque entertainments. It was marked, as we have seen, by an embracement of the psychological, of perception, of the actual. In the texts of the songs of that year he developed contrast, the literal and factual, and he was developing a style that would culminate in a dry realistic tone that encouraged a vibrant complexity of attitude. In his music he was incorporating many different voices, and was moving toward heightened speech rather than suggestive dance melody as a model for what music should be. These tendencies were to flower in his last song book in 1617. In the masques he kept throughout the overall theme of chaos yielding to order, but his means became progressively more spare, from the complex allegory of **The Lord Hay's Masque** to a naked presentation of the civilizing power of language to make a masque or a world in **The Lords' Masque**. Here in **The Squires' Masque** he stripped down the form to a spare diagram consisting of little more than an antimasque in pantomime followed by a spectacular but brief transformation scene. But the transformation did not catapult him or his audience into the wonderful; rather, it landed them in the world. What they all saw at the beginning was a tumult of elements, continents, and other personifications of the world—an illusion—and what they saw at its end was a crew of sailors coming up the Thames, disembarking, dancing a hornpipe. The masque became for Campion a means of clarifying what in fact quotidian London life was, rather than an ennoblement of it. And when the year of reality, 1613, was over, he had seen enough of it. He left the stage.

Notes

1. See the conjectural diagram in Orgel and Strong, *Inigo Jones,* 1:120.

2. For details, see *Works,* ed. Davis, 212-13.

3. For the music, see Sabol, *Four Hundred Songs,* no. 2.

4. See *Works,* ed. Davis, 207, for the epigram to James prefixed to the masque, in which he is compared to King Arthur, as Henry VIII was.

5. See Franz Kafka, *Parables and Paradoxes* (New York: Schocken Books, 1947), 92-93.

6. See Sabol, *Four Hundred Songs,* no. 3.

7. I assume that this is the third piece of music printed with the masque, the first being a song, the second the first new dance with its lyrics, the third, fourth, and fifth being the second, third, and fourth new dances; for the music, see ibid., no. 4.

8. See the illustration in Orgel and Strong, *Inigo Jones,* 1:121.

9. See Sabol, *Four Hundred Songs,* no. 5.

10. See Joan Rees, ed., "Samuel Daniel, *The Vision of the Twelve Goddesses,*" in *A Book of Masques in Honour of Allardyce Nicoll* (Cambridge: Cambridge University Press, 1967), 26, 33-35.

11. See chapter 1, above.

12. Jonson, *Complete Masques,* ed. Orgel, 79.

13. "This sacred place, let none profane" (*Works,* ed. Davis, 216) and "Bid all profane away" (Jonson, *Complete Masques,* 77), for example.

14. Sabol, *Four Hundred Songs,* 25.

15. See Rees in *A Booke of Masques,* 26, 36.

16. Jonson, *Complete Masques,* ed. Orgel, 56-57.

17. See D. J. Gordon, "*Hymenei*: Ben Jonson's Masque of Union," *Journal of the Warburg and Courtauld Institutes* 8 (1945):107-45.

18. See chapter 5, above.

19. See David Lindley, "Campion's *Lord Hay's Masque* and Anglo-Scottish Union," *Huntington Library Quarterly* 43 (1979):1-11.

20. See *Works,* ed. Davis, 264, 267, n., 269, n., 270, n.

21. On Elizabeth and Frederick, see Josephine Ross, *The Winter Queen: The Story of Elizabeth Stuart* (New York: St. Martin's Press, 1979).

22. See Orgel and Strong, *Inigo Jones;* 1:242.

23. See the illustration in ibid., 1:248.

24. See the illustrations in ibid., 1:249, and color plate of no. 80.

25. See the illustrations in ibid., 1:250, and color plate of no. 81, reproduced as the frontispiece to the present text.

26. See ibid., 1:44, and illustrations on 1:247, 251.

27. These accounts of expenses and opinions appear in ibid., 1:241-42.

28. Jonson, *Complete Masques,* ed. Orgel, 22.

29. A. Leigh DeNeef, "Structure and Theme in Campion's *Lords Maske,*" *Studies in English Literature* 17 (1977):95.

30. Ibid., 101.

31. Elizabeth Sewell, *The Orphic Voice* (New Haven: Yale University Press, 1960), 60.

32. On the entertainment as a genre, see Mary Ann McGuire, "Milton's *Arcades* and the Entertainment Tradition,"*Studies in Philology* 75 (1978):451-71.

33. Francis Bacon, *De Sapientia Veterum,* chap. 6, "Pan sive Natura," in *The Works of Francis Bacon,* ed. James Spedding, R. L. Ellis, and D. D. Heath, 15 vols. (Cambridge: Riverside Press, 1863), 13:92-101.

34. Michel Foucault, *The Order of Things: An Archaeology of the Human Sciences* (New York: Random House, 1970), 17-76.

35. Thomas Carew, "An Elegie on the death of the Deane of Pauls, Dr. Iohn Donne," in *The Poems of Thomas Carew,* ed. Rhodes Dunlap (Oxford: Clarendon Press, 1949), 71-74.

36. See chapter 1, above.

37. For the music, see Sabol, *Four Hundred Songs,* no. 20; on the song, see *Works,* ed. Davis, 266.

38. See ibid., no. 23.

39. John Orrell, "The Agent of Savoy at *The Somerset Masque,*" *Review of English Studies,* n.s. 28 (1977):304.

40. Ibid.

41. Ibid., 304-5.

Select Bibliography

Orgel, Stephen, and Strong, Roy. *Inigo Jones: The Theatre of the Stuart Court.* 2 vols. London: Sotheby Park Bernet Publications, Ltd., 1973. Collects all of Jones's designs and other documents for *The Lord Hay's Masque* and *The Lords' Masque.*

FURTHER READING

Criticism

Eldridge, Muriel T. *Thomas Campion: His Poetry and Music (1567-1620).* New York: Vantage Press, 1971, 165 p.
    Considers Campion primarily as a composer of airs and places his work in this genre in a historical context.

Hart, Joan. "Introduction." In *Ayres & Observations: Selected Poems of Thomas Campion,* edited by Joan Hart, pp. 7-24. Cheshire: Fyfield Books/Carcanet Press, 1976.
    Summarizes Campion's life and analyzes his major works.

Kastendieck, Miles Merwin. *England's Musical Poet: Thomas Campion.* New York: Russell & Russell, 1963, 203 p.
    Examines the inter-relationship between Campions's works as a poet, musician, and composer.

Loughlin, Marie H. "'Love's Friend and Stranger to Virginitie': The Politics of the Virginal Body in Ben Jonson's *Hymenaei* and Thomas Campion's *The Lord Hay's Masque.*" *ELH* 63, no. 4 (Winter 1996): 833-49.
    Compares how Johnson and Campion's masques portray the virginal body, an important, politically significant idea in post-Elizabethan England.

George Etherege
1636-1692?

English playwright and poet.

INTRODUCTION

Etherege has been credited as a principal founder of the comedy of manners tradition in English drama. This dramatic genre represents the satirical exploitation of the manners and fashions of the aristocratic class on the stage for their own amusement. Critics have acknowledged Etherege as an accomplished writer of wit, speculating that his comedic voice was shaped by his experiences as a young traveler in France, where he likely witnessed the pioneering social comedy of Molière as well as the ostentatious display of Parisian court fashion and manners. Based on these experiences, Etherege wrote comedies in which he affectionately, yet incisively parodied Carolinian attitudes toward a vast array of ideological concerns, including sexuality, naturalism, fashion, and social class. Etherege's peers revered his easy wit and his portraits of French-aping fops, gamely embracing the dramatist's social satire which poked fun at their class as a whole. As John Dryden wrote in the Epilogue to *The Man of Mode; or, Sir Fopling Flutter* (1676): "Yet none Sir Fopling him, or him can call; / He's Knight o' th' Shire, and represents ye all."

BIOGRAPHICAL INFORMATION

Etherege was likely born in London in 1636, to Captain George Etherege and Mary Powney. Little is known about his formative years, other than the fact that his father, who was a royalist during the Civil War, fled to France in 1644 and died in exile six years later. Placed in the care of his grandfather, Etherege was apprenticed to attorney George Gosnold of Beaconsfield in 1654. Five years later, he was admitted to Clements Inn to study law, during which time he was involved in a lawsuit between his uncle and grandfather over a disputed inheritance. Literary scholars have noted that Etherege exhibited neither the aptitude nor the inclination to study law; instead, he began writing poems and bawdy verse that earned him some notoriety in academic and courtly circles. Indeed, commentators have discovered little evidence to indicate the substance of Etherege's activities as a young man, but some have argued that he traveled to Flanders and France at this time and became highly influenced by French comedy and manners. Also during this period, Etherege became acquainted with Charles Sackville, Lord Buckhurst and later the earl of Dorset, who would become a close friend and patron.

Back in London by 1664, Etherege became an instant celebrity when his *The Comical Revenge; or, Love in a Tub* debuted to widespread popular acclaim at the Duke's Playhouse. Apparently taking advantage of his newfound fame, Etherege embraced a lifestyle of drinking, gambling, and seducing women, earning the nicknames "Gentle George" and "Easy Etherege" for his devotion to free living. He also became acquainted with a group of court wits known as the "merry gang," which included Buckhurst, Sir Charles Sedley, and John Wilmot, earl of Rochester. Rochester in particular shared Etherege's libertine proclivities and the two became fast friends. In fact, many scholars contend that the rake Dorimant in *The Man of Mode* was modeled on Rochester and his real-life antics.

In 1668 Etherege's *She Would If She Could* premiered at the Duke's Playhouse. Based on Samuel Pepys's eyewitness account, the audience was disappointed with the play, and Etherege himself placed the blame for the play's failure on the actors' uninspired performances. The failure of the play did not affect Etherege's court preferment; in fact, he was granted gentleman status and assigned as a secretary to the Turkish ambassador, Daniel Harvey. Etherege followed Harvey on a diplomatic mission to Constantinople in late 1668, and after some three years there, he made his way to Paris and then back to London. In London, Etherege resumed his life of dissolution, occasionally circulating poems and songs but more often pursuing libertine activities with his "merry gang." By 1676 Etherege had written his third and final play, *The Man of Mode,* which was staged at the Dorset Garden Theatre. That same year, Etherege and other members of the "merry gang" were involved in a fracas with a watchman at Epsom which left a man dead.

In the years that followed, Etherege was knighted and he married a rich widow named Mary Arnold. In fact, some biographers have posited that Etherege married Arnold for her fortune in order to pay off his gambling debts and to purchase a knighthood. Based on Etherege's own letters, the union was not happy, and when he was appointed by James II as ambassador to Ratisbon, Germany, in 1685, Arnold did not join him at his new post. By all accounts, Etherege missed his life of ease at the English court. He despised living in conservative, provincial Germany, and he became embroiled in several gambling and sex scandals. Nevertheless, he remained at his post in Ratisbon until he learned of James II's ouster in the Glorious Revolution in late 1688. The following year, Etherege joined James and the exiled court in Paris, where it is believed that he died in 1691 or 1692.

MAJOR WORKS

While most commentators have censured Etherege's insubstantial plots and the lack of dramatic action in his comedies, they nearly all acknowledge the brilliance of his brisk and witty dialogue. It is this element, critics have contended, which invigorates his characters and creates humorous scenes that resonated with Carolinian audiences. Because of their lack of technical sophistication, Etherege's plays have often been viewed as prototypes of the later, more refined Restoration comedies of William Wycherley, William Congreve, and John Vanbrugh.

In *The Comical Revenge,* critics have mainly focused on Etherege's experimentation with four plot schemes ranging from high drama to low comedy. Dismissing as inferior the serious high plot written in heroic rhyming couplets, commentators instead have focused on the comic plot featuring Sir Frederick Frolick. They have posited that Frolick is the embryonic representation of a character type known as the Restoration rake, a libertine aristocrat with a sharp wit who subscribes to free living, drinking, gambling, and pursuing women for romantic trysts. Despite the flashes of humor in the scenes featuring Frolick, critics have pointed out how Etherege's maladroit handling of the various unconnected plots creates a sense of ambiguity and lack of structural unity in the comedy.

In *She Would If She Could,* critics have contended that Etherege displayed marked improvement in developing a cohesive dramatic structure and in polishing his witty dialogue. Further, commentators have noticed that Etherege initiated a more complex exploration of sexual politics between his characters, especially Courtall and Lady Cockwood. They have argued that Courtall represents Etherege's ideal libertine of easy morals and fine wit who defies social convention, whereas Lady Cockwood embodies the playwright's disdain for those who succumb to sensual, naturalistic impulses but who hide behind social pretense to manipulate and seduce others.

According to most critics, Etherege demonstrates the full power of his dramatic genius in *The Man of Mode.* They have maintained that the comedy deftly combines witty dialogue, superbly drawn characters, and Etherege's trademark social satire to produce a work which had no small influence on subsequent Restoration comedies. Commentators have regarded Dorimant, the central character, as the consummate Restoration rake, still given to liberal excess, but also exhibiting a worldly cynicism which suggests a more complex perception of the character than the farcical, one-dimensional Sir Frederick Frolick. Critics have added that Harriet provides another layer of complexity to the play in that she complements Dorimant as no other female character had complemented a rake in Etherege's earlier dramas. Harriet is considered a strong and intelligent heroine who proves to be Dorimant's equal in verbal banter and who shares his distain for social artifice; moreover, of all of Etherege's women characters, Harriet comes the closest to outmaneuvering the rake in the end. The significance of Sir Fopling Flutter himself as the foil to Dorimant has not been lost on commentators: he is the epitome of the vain, superficial man of mode, who is wholly involved in his affectation of courtly manners and fashion. In fact, Sir Fopling initiated the popular stage convention of the foppish imitator of flamboyant French courtly manners who is oblivious to the mocking ridicule of the other characters.

CRITICAL RECEPTION

During his lifetime, Etherege's comedies met with general approbation by his peers and audiences, and he was eulogized in numerous contemporary poems and pamphlets. A generation later, the comedies were disdained as vulgar products of a licentious and immoral age.

Writing in 1711 about *The Man of Mode,* Sir Richard Steele asserted that: "This whole celebrated piece is a perfect contradiction to good manners, good sense, and common honesty." Theophilus Cibber in 1753 affirmed Steele's sentiments, writing that while he found merit in Etherege's wit, nevertheless "his works are so extremely loose and licentious, as to render them dangerous to young, unguarded minds." Throughout the remainder of the eighteenth century and well into the nineteenth, Etherege and his comedies remained in a state of general neglect. In the late nineteenth century, commentators began to reexamine Etherege as a leading innovator in the English comedy of manners, but still generally dismissed his works as superficial showpieces intended merely to appease the degenerate tastes of Carolinian theatergoers. This opinion prevailed well into the twentieth century.

Writing in 1924, Bonamy Dobrée maintained that "Etherege was not animated by any moral stimulus, and his comedies arose from a superabundance of animal energy that only bore fruit in freedom and ease, amid the graces of Carolingian society." Dobrée concluded that Etherege "rarely makes an appeal to the intellect." Etherege's literary reputation suffered another blow in 1937 when L. C. Knights wrote an essay condemning Restoration comedies as "trivial, gross, and dull" written by dramatists with a "miserably limited set of attitudes." Knights's essay ignited a critical controversy in which literary scholars set out to restore the reputation of Restoration drama. Thomas H. Fujimura was one of the first critics to challenge Knights's censure of Etherege in particular, arguing that the playwright was in fact a literary and intellectual genius who masterfully synthesized such cultural influences as naturalism, libertinism, and skepticism into multilayered social satires. Critics such as Robert Markley and Lisa Berglund examined the language of Etherege's comedies in an effort to understand the cultural and historical circumstances that influenced their composition. Markley explored the playwright's experimentation with dialogue and dramatic form in his plays to examine the ideological dislocation of aristocratic culture in Restoration England. Berglund discussed the dramatist's construction of a "libertine language" of extended metaphors and analogies in *The Man of Mode* to subvert conventional morality. Despite these complex interpretations of Etherege's works, modern scholars nevertheless have remained divided in their opinion of the level of his literary achievement. To some, the playwright has been redeemed as a brilliant satirist of the ideological turbulence of the Restoration period; to others, he remains an unsophisticated dramatist who merely intended to amuse and delight his peers by lampooning their court manners on the stage.

PRINCIPAL WORKS

The Comical Revenge; or, Love in a Tub (play) 1664
She Would If She Could (play) 1668
The Man of Mode; or, Sir Fopling Flutter (play) 1676
The Works of Sir George Etherege: Containing His Plays and Poems (plays, poetry) 1704
The Works of Sir George Etherege: Plays and Poems (plays and poetry) 1888
The Dramatic Works of Sir George Etherege 2 vols. (plays) 1927
The Letterbook of Sir George Etherege (letters) 1928
The Poems of Sir George Etherege (poetry) 1963
Letters of Sir George Etherege (letters) 1974
The Plays of Sir George Etherege (plays) 1982

CRITICISM

Samuel Pepys (diary date 1666)

SOURCE: Pepys, Samuel. Diary entry dated October 29, 1666. In *The Diary of Samuel Pepys: A New and Complete Transcription,* Vol. 7, edited by Robert Latham and William Matthews, pp. 346-47. London: G. Bell and Sons, 1972.

[*In the following journal entry, Pepys judges* The Comical Revenge *to be "a silly play."*]

[29 October 1666:] About 5 a-clock I took my wife (who is mighty fine, and with a new fair pair of locks, which vex me, though like a fool I helped her the other night to buy them), and to Mrs. Pierce's; and there staying a little, I away before to White-hall and into the new playhouse there, the first time I ever was there, and the first play I have seen since before the great plague. By and by Mr. Pierce comes, bringing my wife and his, and Knipp. By and by the King and Queen, Duke and Duchesse, and all the great ladies of the Court; which endeed was a fine

sight—but the play, being *Love in a Tubb,* a silly play; and though done by the Duke's people, yet having neither Baterton nor his wife—and the whole thing done ill, and being ill also, I had no manner of pleasure in the play. . . .

Samuel Pepys (diary date 1668)

SOURCE: Pepys, Samuel. Diary entry dated February 6, 1668. In *The Diary of Samuel Pepys: A New and Complete Transcription,* Vol. 9, edited by Robert Latham and William Matthews, pp. 53-4. London: G. Bell and Sons, 1976.

[*In the journal entry below, Pepys recounts viewing* She Would If She Could, *noting that Etherege himself attended the production and afterwards was unhappy with how the actors portrayed the characters.*]

[6 February 1668:] . . . [My] wife being gone before, I to the Duke of York's playhouse, where a new play of Etheriges called *She would if she could.* And though I was there by 2 a-clock, there was 1000 people put back that could not have room in the pit; and I at last, because my wife was there, made shift to get into the 18*d* box—and there saw; but Lord, how full was the house and how silly the play, there being nothing in the world good in it and few people pleased in it. The King was there; but I sat mightily behind, and could see but little and hear not all. The play being done, I into the pit to look my wife; and it being dark and raining, I to look my wife out, but could not find her; and so stayed, going between the two doors and through the pit an hour and half I think, after the play was done, the people staying there till the rain was over and to talk one with another; and among the rest, here was the Duke of Buckingham today openly sat in the pit; and there I found him with my Lord Buckhurst and Sidly and Etherige the poett—the last of whom I did hear mightily find fault with the Actors, that they were out of humour and had not their parts perfect, and that Harris did do nothing, nor could so much as sing a Ketch in it, and so was mightily concerned: while all the rest did through the whole pit blame the play as a silly, dull thing, though there was something very roguish and witty; but the design of the play, and end, mighty insipid. . . .

Edward Phillips (essay date 1675)

SOURCE: Phillips, Edward. "The Modern Poets: George Etherege." In *Theatrum Poetarum,* Vol. 2, p. 53. London: Charles Smith, 1675.

[*In the following excerpt, Phillips briefly identifies Etherege as a popular contemporary dramatist.*]

George Etheridge [is] a Comical writer of the present Age; whose Two Comedies, *Love in a Tub,* and *She would if She could,* for pleasant Wit, and no bad Oeconomy, are judg'd not unworthy the Applause they have met with.

Gerard Langbaine (essay date 1691)

SOURCE: Langbaine, Gerard. "Sir George Etherege." In *An Account of the English Dramatick Poets,* pp. 186-88. 1691. Reprint. New York: Garland Publishing, 1973.

[*In the essay below, Langbaine provides a favorable account of Etherege and his plays.*]

A Gentleman sufficiently eminent in the Town for his Wit and Parts, and One whose tallent in sound Sence, and the Knowledge of true Wit and Humour, are sufficiently conspicuous: and therefore I presume I may with justice, and without envy, apply *Horace*'s Character of *Fundanus,* to this admirable Author;

> *Argutâ meretrice potes, Davoque Chremet,*
> *Eludente senem, comis garrire libellos,*
> *Unus vivorum, Fundani.——*

This Ingenious Author has oblig'd the World by publishing three Comedies, *viz.*

Comical Revenge, or Love in a Tub, a Comedy, acted at his Royal-Highness the Duke of *York*'s Theatre in *Lincolns-Inn-fields:* printed quarto *Lond.* 1669. and dedicated to the Honourable *Charles* Lord *Backhurst.* This Comedy tho' of a mixt nature, part of it being serious, and writ in Heroick Verse; yet succeeded admirably on the Stage, it having always been acted with general approbation.

Man of Mode, or Sir Fopling Flutter, a Comedy acted at the Duke's Theatre printed 40. *Lond.* 1676. and dedicated to her Royal Highness the Dutchess. This Play is written with great Art and Judgment, and is acknowledg'd by all, to be as true Comedy, and the Characters as well drawn to the Life, as any Play that has been Acted since the Restauration of the *English* Stage. Only I must observe, that the Song in the last Act written by *C.S.* is translated from part of an Elegy written in *French* by *Madame la Comtesse de la Suze,* in *Le Recüeil des Pieces Gallantes, tom.* 1. *p.* 42.

She wou'd if she cou'd, a Comedy Acted at his Highness the Duke of *York*'s Theatre, and printed quarto *Lond.* 1671. This Comedy is likewise accounted one of the first Rank, by several who are known to be good Judges of Dramatick Poesy. Nay our present Laureat says, 'Tis the best Comedy written since the Restauration of the Stage. I heartily wish for the publick satisfaction, that this great Master would oblidge the World with more of his Performances, which would put a stop to the crude and indigested Plays, which for want of better, cumber the Stage.

Richard Steele (essay date 1711)

SOURCE: Steele, Richard. "No. 65, Tuesday, May 15, 1711." In *The Spectator,* Vol. 1, edited by Donald F. Bond, pp. 278-80. Oxford: Clarendon Press, 1965.

[*In the following essay originally published in* The Spectator, *Steele deems Etherege's wit immoral in* The Man of Mode, *concluding that the "whole celebrated piece is a perfect contradiction to good manners, good sense, and common honesty."*]

> *. . . Demetri, teque, Tigelli,*
> *Discipularum inter Jubeo plorare cathedras.*
>
> Hor.[1]

After having at large explained what Wit is, and described the false Appearances of it, all that Labour seems but an useless Enquiry, without some Time be spent in considering the Application of it. The Seat of Wit, when one speaks as a Man of the Town and the World, is the Play-house; I shall therefore fill this Paper with Reflections upon the Use of it in that Place. The Application of Wit in the Theatre has as strong an Effect upon the Manners of our Gentlemen, as the Taste of it has upon the Writings of our Authors. It may, perhaps, look like a very Presumptuous Work, tho' not Foreign from the Duty of a *Spectator,* to tax the Writings of such as have long had the general Applause of a Nation: But I shall always make Reason, Truth, and Nature the Measures of Praise and Dispraise; if those are for me, the Generality of Opinion is of no Consequence against me; if they are against me, the General Opinion cannot long support me.

Without further Preface, I am going to look into some of our most Applauded Plays, and see whether they deserve the Figure they at present bear in the Imaginations of Men, or not.

In reflecting upon these Works, I shall chiefly dwell upon that for which each respective Play is most celebrated. The present Paper shall be employed upon *Sir Foplin Flutter.*[2] The Received Character of this Play is, That it is the Pattern of Gentile Comedy. *Dorimant* and *Harriot* are the Characters of Greatest Consequence, and if these are Low and Mean, the Reputation of the Play is very Unjust.

I will take for granted, that a fine Gentleman should be honest in his Actions, and refined in his Language. Instead of this, our Hero, in this Piece, is a direct Knave in his Designs, and a Clown in his Language. *Bellair* is his Admirer and Friend, in return for which, because he is forsooth a greater Wit than his said Friend, he thinks it reasonable to perswade him to Marry a young Lady, whose Virtue, he thinks, will last no longer than 'till she is a Wife, and then she cannot but fall to his Share, as he is an irresistible fine Gentleman. The Falshood to Mrs. *Loveit,* and the Barbarity of Triumphing over her Anguish for losing him, is another Instance of his Honesty, as well as his good Nature. As to his fine Language; he calls the Orange Woman, who, it seems, is inclined to grow Fat, *An Overgrown Jade, with a Flasket of Guts before her*; and salutes her with a pretty Phrase of, *How now, Double Tripe?*[3] Upon the Mention of a Country Gentlewoman, whom he knows nothing of, (no one can imagine why) he *will lay his Life she is some awkard, ill-fashioned Country Toad, who not having above four Dozen of Hairs on her Head, has adorned her Baldness with a large white Fruz, that she may look Sparkishly in the Fore-front of the King's Box at an old Play.* Unnatural Mixture of senseless Common Place!

As to the Generosity of his Temper, he tells his poor Footman, *If he did not wait better*—he would turn him away, in the insolent Phrase of, *I'll Uncase you.*

Now for Mrs. *Harriot:* She laughs at Obedience to an absent Mother, whose Tenderness *Busie* describes to be very exquisite, for *that she is so pleased with finding* Harriot *again, that she cannot chide her for being out of the Way.*[4] This Witty Daughter, and Fine Lady, has so little Respect for this good Woman, that she Ridicules her Air in taking Leave, and cries, *In what Struggle is my poor Mother yonder? See, See, her Head tottering, her Eyes staring, and her under Lip trembling.*[5] But all this is atoned for, because *she has more Wit than is usual in her Sex, and as much Malice, tho' she is as Wild as you would wish her, and has a Demureness in her Looks that makes it so surprising!*[6] Then to recommend her as a fit Spouse for his Hero, the Poet makes her speak her Sense of Marriage very ingeniously. *I Think,* says she, *I might be brought to endure him, and that is all a reasonable Woman should expect in an Husband.*[7] It is, methinks, unnatural that we are not made to understand how she that was bred under a silly pious old Mother, that would never trust her out of her Sight, came to be so Polite.

It cannot be denied, but that the Negligence of every thing, which engages the Attention of the sober and valuable Part of Mankind, appears very well drawn in this Piece: But it is denied, that it is necessary to the Character of a Fine Gentleman, that he should in that manner Trample upon all Order and Decency. As for the Character of *Dorimant,* it is more of a Coxcomb than that of *Foplin.* He says of one of his Companions,[8] that a good Correspondence between them is their mutual Interest. Speaking of that Friend, he declares, their being much together *makes the Women think the better of his Understanding, and judge more favourably of my Reputation. It makes him pass upon some for a Man of very good Sense, and me upon others for a very civil Person.*

This whole celebrated Piece is a perfect Contradiction to good Manners, good Sense, and common Honesty; and as there is nothing in it but what is built upon the Ruin of Virtue and Innocence, according to the Notion of Merit in this Comedy, I take the Shoomaker to be, in reality, the fine Gentleman of the Play: For it seems he is an Atheist, if we may depend upon his Character as given by the Orange-Woman, who is her self far from being the lowest in the Play. She says of a Fine Man, who is *Dorimant's* Companion, There *is not such another Heathen in the Town, except the Shoe-maker.* His Pretention to be the Hero of the *Drama* appears still more in his own Description of his way of Living with his Lady. *There is,* says he, *never a Man in Town lives more like a Gentleman with his Wife than I do; I never mind her Motions; she never enquires into mine. We speak to one another civilly, hate one another heartily; and because it is Vulgar to Lye and Soak together, we have each of us our several Settle-Bed.* That of *Soaking together* is as good as if *Dorimant* had spoken it himself; and, I think, since he puts Humane Nature in as ugly a Form as the Circumstance will bear, and is a staunch Unbeliever, he is very much Wronged in having no part of the good Fortune bestowed in the last Act.

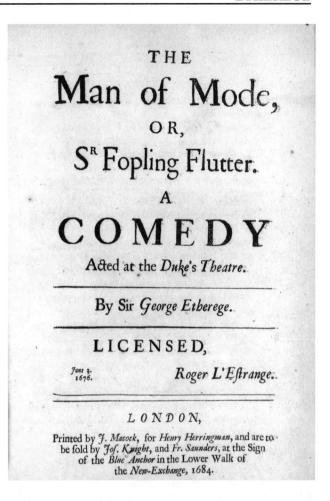

THE
Man of Mode,
OR,
S[R] Fopling Flutter.
A
COMEDY
Acted at the *Duke's Theatre.*

By Sir *George Etherege.*

LICENSED,

June 3.
1676.   *Roger L'Estrange.*

LONDON,

Printed by *J. Macock,* for *Henry Herringman,* and are to be sold by *Jos. Knight,* and *Fr. Saunders,* at the Sign of the *Blue Anchor* in the Lower Walk of the *New-Exchange,* 1684.

Title page from a 1676 edition of The Man of Mode; or, Sir Fopling Flutter.

To speak plainly of this whole Work, I think nothing but being lost to a Sense of Innocence and Virtue can make any one see this Comedy, without observing more frequent Occasion to move Sorrow and Indignation, than Mirth and Laughter. At the same time I allow it to be Nature, but it is Nature in its utmost Corruption and Degeneracy.[9]

Notes

1. *Motto.* Horace, *Satires,* 1. 10. 90-91:

   Demetrius and Tigellius, know your place;
   Go hence, and whine among the school-boy race.

2. Etherege's comedy, *The Man of Mode, or Sir Fopling Flutter* (1676), had been given at Drury Lane on 20 Apr., with the following cast: Sir Fopling, Cibber; Dorimant, Wilks; Medley, Mills; Old Bell-Air, Penkethman; Young Bell-Air, Bullock Junior; Shoemaker, Bowen; Loveit, Mrs. Oldfield; Belinda, Mrs. Rogers; Harriet, Mrs. Santlow; Emilia, Mrs. Porter.

3. The quotations in this paragraph and the next are all from the opening scene.

4. Act III, scene iii.

5. Act IV, scene i.

6. Act I, scene i.

7. Act III, scene i.

8. Bellair. The remaining quotations are again from the opening scene.

9. Dennis replied to this paper in his *Defence of Sir Fopling Flutter* in 1722 (*Critical Works,* ed. Hooker, ii. 241-50), arguing that while Dorimant might not be 'the Pattern of Gentile Comedy' by present-day standards, Etherege was writing according to Restoration standards of conduct and hence 'was oblig'd to accommodate himself to that Notion of a fine Gentleman, which the Court and the Town both had at the Time of the writing of this Comedy' (ii. 244).

John Dennis (essay date 1722)

SOURCE: Dennis, John. *A Defence of Sir* Fopling Flutter, *a Comedy Written by* Sir *George Etherege.* London: T. Warner, 1722, 24 p.

[*In the following essay, originally published as an anonymous pamphlet, Dennis conducts a thoroughgoing defense of* The Man of Mode *from Richard Steele's condemnation of the play in the* Spectator.]

A Certain Knight, who has employ'd so much of his empty Labour in extolling the weak Performances of some living Authors, has scurriously an inhumanly in the 65th Spectator, attack'd one of the most entertaining Comedies of the last Age, written by a most ingenious Gentleman, who perfectly understood the World, the Court, and the Town, and whose Reputation has now for near thirty Years together, surviv'd his Person, and will, in all Probability, survive it as long as Comedy shall be in vogue; by which Proceeding, this worthy Knight has incurr'd the double Censure, that *Olivia* in the plain'd Dealer has cast upon a certain Coxcomb *Who rather,* says she, *then not flatter, will flatter the Poets of the Age, whom none will flatter, and rather then not rail, will rail at the Dead, at whom none besides will rail.*

If other Authors have had the Misfortune, to incurr the Censure of ill-nature with unthinking deluded People, for no other so much as pretended Reason, than because to improve a noble Art, they have expos'd the Errors of popular Writers, who ow'd their Success, to the infamous Method of securing an ignorant or corrupt Cabal; when those Writers were not only living, but in full Prosperity, and at full Liberty to answer for themselves; what Appellation must he deserve, who has basely and scurrilously attack'd the Reputation of a Favourite of the comick Muse, and of the Darling of the Graces, after Death has for so many Years depriv'd him of the Means of answering for himself.

What the Knight falsely and impudently says of the Comedy, may be justly said of the Criticism, and of the whole 65th Spectator, that 'tis a perfect Contradiction to good Manners and good Sense. He allows this Comedy, he says, to be in Nature, but 'tis Nature in its utmost Corruption and Degeneracy.

Suppose this were true, I would fain know where he learnt, that Nature in its utmost Corruption and Degeneracy, is not the proper Subject of Comedy? Is not this a merry Person, who after he has been writing what he calls Comedy for twenty Years together, shews plainly to all the World, that he knows nothing of the Nature of true Comedy, and that he has not learnt the very first Rudiments of an Art which he pretends to teach? I must confess, the Ridicule in *Sir Fopling Flutter,* is an Imitation of corrupt and degenerate Nature, but not the most corrupt and the most degenerate; for there is neither Adultery, Murder, nor Sodomy in it. But can any Thing but corrupt and degenerate Nature be the proper Subject of Ridicule? And can any Thing but Ridicule be the proper Subject of Comedy? Has not *Aristotle* told us in the Fifth Chapter of his Poeticks, that Comedy is an Imitation of the very worst of Men? Not the worst, says He, but in every Sort of Vice, but the worst in the Ridicule. And has not *Horace,* in the Fourth Satyr of his First Book, reminded us, that the old *Athenian* Comick Poets made it their Business to bring all Sorts of Villains upon the Stage, Adulterers, Cheats, Theives, Murderers? But then they always took Care, says a modern Critick, that those several Villanies should be envelop'd in the Ridicule, which alone, says he, could make them the proper Subjects of Comedy. If this facetious Knight had formerly li'vd at *Lacedemon* with the same wrong turn'd Noddle that he has now among us, would he not, do you think, have inveigh against that People, for shewing their drunken Slaves to their Children? Would he not have represented it as a Thing of most pernicious Example? What the *Lacedemonians* did by Drunkenness, the Comick Poet does by that and all other Vices. He exposes them to the View of his Fellow Subjects, for no other Reason, than to render them ridiculous and contemptible.

But the Criticism of the Knight in the foresaid Spectator, is a contrary to good Manner, as it is to good Sense. What *Aritotle* and his Interpreters say of Tragedy, that 'tis infallibly good, when it pleases both the Judges and the People, is certainly as true of Comedy; for the Judges are equally qualify'd to judge of both, and the People may be suppos'd to be better Judges of Comedy then they are of Tragedy, because Comedy is nothing but a Picture of common Life, and a Representation of their own Humours and Manners. Now this Comedy of *Sir Fopling Flutter,* has not been only well receiv'd, and believ'd by the People of *England* to be a most agreeable Comedy for about Half a Century, but the Judges have been still more pleas'd with it then the People. They have justly believ'd (I speak of the Judges) that the Characters, and especially the principal Characters, are admirably drawn, to answer the two Ends of Comedy, Pleasure, and Instruction; and that the

Dialogue is the most charming that has been writ by the Moderns: That with Purity and Simplicity, it has Art and Elegance; and with Force and Vivacity, the utmost Grace and Delicacy. This I know very well, was the Opinion of the most eminent Writers, and of the best Judges contemporary with the Author; and of the whole Court of King *Charles* the Second, a Court the most polite that ever *England* saw.

Now, after this Comedy has pass'd with the whole People of *England,* the knowing as well as the Ignorant, for a most entertaining and most instructive Comedy, for fifty Years together, after that long Time comes a Two Penny Author, who has given a thousand Proofs thro' the Course of his Rhapsodies, that he understands not a Tittle of all this Matter; this Author comes and impudently declares, that this whole celebrated Piece, that has for half a Century, been admir'd by the whole People of *Great Britain,* is a perfect Contradiction to good Sense, to good Manners, and to common Honesty. *O Tempora! O Mores!*

The Knight certainly wrote the fore-mention'd Spectator, tho' it as been writ these ten Years, on Purpose to make Way for his fine Gentleman, and therefore he endeavours to prove, that **Sir Fopling Flutter** is not that genteel Comedy which the World allows it to be. And then, according to his usual Custom, whenever he pretends to criticise, he does, by shuffling and cutting and confounding Notions, impose upon his unwary Reader; for either Sir *George Etherege,* did design to make this a genteel Comedy, or he did not. If he did not design it, what is it to the Purpose, whether 'tis a genteel Comedy or not? Provided that 'tis a good one: For I hope, a Comedy may be a good one, and yet not a genteel one. The *Alchimist* is an admirable Comedy, and yet it is not a genteel one. We may say the same of *The Fox, and the silent Woman,* and of a great many more. But if Sir *George* did design to make it a genteel one, he was oblig'd to adapt it to that Notion of Gentility, which he knew very well, that the World at that Time had, and we see he succeeded accordingly. For it has pass'd for a very genteel Comedy, for fifty Years together. Could it be expected that the admirable Author, should accomodate himself, to the wrong headed Notions of a would be Critick, who was to appear fifty Years after the first Acting of his Play: A Critick, who writes Criticism, as Men commit Treason or Murder, by the Instigation of the Devil himself, whenever the old Gentleman owes the Knight a Shame.

To prove that this Comedy is not a genteel one, he endeavours to prove that one of the principal Characters is not a fine Gentleman. I appeal to every impartial Man, if when he says, that a Man or a Woman are genteel, he means any Thing more than that they are agreeble in their Air, graceful in their Motions, and polite in their Conversation. But when he endeavours to prove, that *Dorimont* is not a fine Gentleman, he says no more to the Purpose, then he said before, when he affirm'd that the Comedy is not a genteel Comedy; for either the Author design'd in *Dorimont* a fine Gentleman, or he did not. If he did not, the Character is

ne'er the less excellent on that Account, because *Dorimont* is an admirable Picture of a Courtier in the Court of King *Charles* the Second. But if *Dorimont* was design'd for a fine Gentleman by the Author, he was oblig'd to accommodate himself to that Notion of a fine Gentleman, which the Court and the Town both had at the Time of the writing of this Comedy. 'Tis reasonable to believe, that he did so, and we see that he succeeded accordingly. For *Dorimont* not only pass'd for a fine Gentleman with the Court of King *Charles* the Second, but he has pass'd for such with all the World, for Fifty Years together. And what indeed can any one mean, when he speaks of a fine Gentleman, but who is qualify'd in Conversation, to please the best Company of either sex.

But the Knight will be satisfy'd with no Notion of a fine Gentleman but his own. A fine Gentleman, says he, is one who is honest in his Actions, and refin'd in his Language. If this be a just Description of a fine Gentleman, I will make bold to draw two Consequences from it. The first is, That a Pedant is often a fine Gentleman. For I have known several of them, who have been Honest in their Actions, and Refin'd in their Language. The second is, That I know a certain Knight, who, though he should be allow'd to be a Gentleman born, yet is not a fine Gentleman. I shall only add, that I would advise for the future, all the fine Gentlemen, who travel to *London* from *Tipperary,* to allow us *Englishmen* to know what we mean, when we speak our native Language.

To give a true Character of this charming Comedy, it must be acknowledg'd, that there is no great Mastership in the Design of it. Sir *George* had but little of the artful and just Designs of *Ben Johnson*: But as Tragedy instructs chiefly by its Design, Comedy instructs by its Characters; which not only ought to be drawn truly in Nature, but to be the resembling Pictures of our Contemporaries, both in Court and Town. Tragedy answers to History-Painting, but Comedy to drawing of Portraits.

How little do they know of the Nature of true Comedy, who believe that its proper Business is to set us Patterns for Imitation: For all such Patterns are serious Things, and Laughter is the Life, and the very Soul of Comedy. 'Tis its proper Business to expose Persons to our View, whose Views we may shun, and whose Follies we may despise; and by shewing us what is done upon the Comick Stage, to shew us what ought never to be done upon the Stage of the World.

All the Characters in **Sir Fopling Flutter,** and especially the principal Characters, are admirably drawn, both to please and to instruct. First, they are drawn to please, because they are drawn in the Truth of Nature; but to be drawn in the Truth of Nature, they must be drawn with those Qualities that are proper to each respective Season of Life.

This is the chief Precept given for the forming the Characters, by the two Great Masters of the Rules which Nature herself dictated, and which have [gap in original] in every Age, for the Standards of writing successfully, and of judging surely, unless it were with Poetasters, and their foolish Admirers. The Words of *Horace*, in his *Art of Poetry*, are these, *v.* 153.

Tu, quid ego & populo mecum desideret, audi.
Si sessoris eges aulæa manentis, & usque
Sessuri, donec cantor, vos plaudite, dicat;
Ætatis cujusque notandi sunt tibit mores,
Mobilibúsque decor naturis dandus, & annis.

And thus my Lord *Roscommon* has translated it:

Now hear what ev'ry Auditor expects,
If you intend that he should stay to hear
The Epilogue, and see the Curtain fall;
Mark how our Tempers alter with our Years,
Then give the Beauty proper to each Age,
And by this Rule form all your Characters.

And now see the Character that *Horace* gives of a Person who is in the Bloom of his Years.

De Arte Poetica, v. 161

Imberbis tandem juvenis custode remoto,
Gaudet equis, canibúsque, & aprici gramine campi;
Cereus in vitium flecti, monitoribus asper,
Utilium tardus proviso, prodigus æeris,
Sublimis, cupidúsque, & amata relinquere pernix.

And thus the 'foresaid Noble Poet translates it:

A Youth that first casts off his Tutor's Yoke,
Loves Horses, Hounds, and Sports, and Exercise,
Prone to all Vice, impatient of Reproof,
Proud, careless, fond, inconstant, and profuse.

Now, *Horace,* to shew the Importance of this Precept, as soon as he has done with the Characters of the four Parts of Life, returns to it, repeats it, and enforces it.

————Ne forte seniles
Mandentur juveni partes, pueróque viriles,
Semper in adjunctis, ævóque morabimur aptis.

That a Poet may never be guilty of such an Absurdity, says he, *as to give the Character of an Old Man to a Young Man, or of a Boy a Middle Ag'd Man, let him take Care to adhere to those Qualities, which are necessarily or probably annexed to each respective Season of Life.*

If a Dramatick Poet does not observe this Rule, he misses that which gives the Beauty, and the Decorum, which alone can make his Characters please.

As *Horace* is but an Epitomizer of *Aristotle*, in giving Rules for the Characters; that Philosopher gives us more at large the Character of a Person in his early Bloom, in the 14th Chapter of the Second Book of his Rhetorick.

Young Men, says he, *have strong Appetites, and are ready to undertake any thing, in order to satisfy them; and of all those Appetites which have a Relation to the Body, they are most powerfully sway'd by Venereal ones, in which they are very changeable, and are quickly cloy'd. For their Desires are rather acute than lasting, like the Hunger and Thirst of the Sick. They are prone to Anger, and ready to obey the Dictates of it. For by Reason of the Concern which they have for their Honour, they cannot bear the being undervalu'd, but resent an Affront heinously. And as they are desirous of Honour, they are more ambitious ov Victory: For Youth is a Sort of Excellency.* Thus far *Aristotle.*

And here it may not be amiss to shew, that this Rule is founded in Reason and in Nature: In order to which, let us see what *Dacier* remarks upon that Verse of *Horace,* which we cited above.

Mobilibúsque decor naturis dandus, & annis.

Behold, says he, a very fine, and very significant Verse; which tells us, if we render it Word for Word, *That we ought to give to moveable Natures and Years their proper Beauty. By moveable Natures,* (says *Dacier*) Horace *means Age, which still runs on like a River, and which, as it runs, gives different Inclinations to Men; and those different Inclinations make what he calls* Decor, *the Beauty proper to the Age. For every Part of Man's Life has its proper Beauties, like every Season of the Year. He that give to Manly Age the Beauties of Youth, or to Youth the Beauties of Manly Age, does like a Painter, who should paint the Autumn with the Ornaments of Summer, or the Summer with the Ornaments of Autumn.*

A Comick Poet, who gives to a Young Man the Qualities that belong to a Middle Ag'd Man, or to an Old Man, can answer neither of the Ends of his Art. He cannot please, because he writes out of Nature, of which all Poetry is an Imitation, and without which, no Poem can possibly please. And as he cannot please, he cannot instruct; because, by shewing such a young Man as is not to be seen in the World, he shews a Monster, and not a Man, sets before us a particular Character, instead of an allegorical and universal one, as all his Characters, and especially his principal Characters, ought to be; and therefore can give no general Instruction, having no Moral, no Fable, and therefore no Comedy.

Now if any one is pleased to compare the Character of *Dorimont*, to which the Knight has taken so much absurd Exception with the two forementioned Descriptions, he will find in his Character all the chief distinguishing Strokes of them. For such is the Force of Nature, and so admirable a Talent had she given Sir *George* for Comedy, that, tho' to my certain Knowledge he understood neither *Greek* nor *Latin*, yet one would swear, that in drawing his *Dorimont*, he copy'd the foresaid Draughts, and especially that of *Aristotle*. *Dorimont* is a young Courtier, haughty, vain, and prone to Anger, amorous, false, and inconstant. He debauches *Loveit*, and betrays her; he *Belinda*, and as soon as he enjoys her is false to her.

But 2dly, The Characters in **Sir Fopling** are admirably contriv'd to please, and more particularly the principal ones, because we find in those Characters, a true Resemblance of the Persons both in Court and Town, who liv'd at the Time when that Comedy was writ: For *Rapin* tells us with a great deal of Judgment, *That Comedy is as it ought to be, when an Audience is apt to imagine, that instead of being in the Pit and Boxes, they are in some Assembly of the Neighbourhood, or in some Family Meeting, and that we see nothing done in it, but what is done in the World. For it is,* says he, *not worth one Farthing, if we do not discover our selves in it, and do not find in it both our own Manners, and those of the Persons with whom we live and converse.*

The Reason of this Rule is manifest: For as 'tis the Business of a Comick Poet to cure his Spectators of Vice and Folly, by the Apprehension of being laugh'd at; 'tis plain that his Business must be with the reigning Follies and Vices. The violent Passions, which are the Subjects of Tragedy, are the same in every Age, and appear with the same Face; but those Vices and Follies, which are the Subjects of Comedy, are seen to vary continually: Some of those that belonged to our Ancestors, have no Relation to us; and can no more come under the Cognisance of our present Comick Poets, than the Sweating and Sneezing Sickness can come under the Practice of our contemporary Physicians. What Vices and Follies may infect those who are to come after us, we know not; 'tis the present, the reigning Vices, and Follies, that must be the Subjects of our present Comedy: The Comick Poet therefore must take Characters from such Persons as are his Contemporaries, and are infected with the foresaid Follies and Vices.

Agreeable to this, is the Advice which *Boileau,* in his *Art of Poetry,* gives to the Comick Poets:

> *Etudiez la Cour, & connoissez la ville,*
> *L'une & l'autre est tousoers en modeles fertile,*
> *C'est par lá que Moliere illustrant ses evrits,*
> *Peutetre de son Art eut remporté la prix, & c.*

Now I remember very well, that upon the first acting this Comedy, it was generally believed to be an agreeable Representation of the Persons of Condition of both Sexes, both in Court and Town; and that all the World was charm'd with *Dorimont*; and that it was unanimously agreed, that he had in him several of the Qualities of *Wilmot* Earl of *Rochester,* as, his Wit, his Spirit, his amorous Temper, the Charms that he had for the fair Sex, his Falshood, and his Inconstancy; the agreeable Manner of his chiding his Servants, which the late Bishop of *Salisbury* takes Notice of in his Life; and lastly, his repeating on every Occasion, the Verses of *Waller,* for whom that noble Lord had a very particular Esteem; witness his imitation of the Tenth Satire of the First Book of *Horace:*

> *Waller, by Nature for the Bays design'd,*
> *With Spirit, Force, and Fancy unconfind,*
> *In Panegyrick is above Mankind.*

Now, as several of the Qualities in *Dorimont*'s Character were taken from that Earl of *Rochester,* so they who were acquainted with the late Sir *Fleetwood Shepherd,* know very well, that not a little of that Gentleman's Character is to be found in Medley.

But the Characters in this Comedy are very well form'd to instruct as well as to please, especially those of *Dorimont* and of *Loveit*; and they instruct by the same Qualities to which the Knight has taken so much whimsical Exception; as *Dorimont* instructs byt his Insulting, and his Perfidiousness, and *Loveit* by the Violence of her Resentment and her Anguish. For *Loveit* has Youth, Beauty, Quality, Wit, and Spirit. And it was depending upon these, that she repos'd so dangerous a Trust in *Dorimont,* which is a just Caution to the Fair Sex, never to be so conceited of the Power of their Charms, or their other extraordinary Qualities, as to believe they can engage a Man to be true to them, to whom they grant the best Favour, without which they can never be certain, that they shall not be hated and despis'd by that very Person whom they have done every Thing to oblige.

To conclude with one General Observation, That Comedy may be qualify'd in a powerful Manner both to instruct and to please, the very Constitution of its Subject ought always to be Ridiculous. Comedy, says *Rapin,* is an Image of common Life, and its End is to expose upon the Stage the Defects of particular Persons, in order to cure the Defects of the Publick, and to correct and amend the People, by the Fear of being laugh'd at. That therefore, says he, which is most essential to Comedy, is certainly the Ridicule.

Every Poem is qualify'd to instruct, and to please most powerfully by that very Quality which makes the Fort and the Characteristick of it, and which distinguishes it from all other Kinds of Poems. As *Tragedy* is qualify'd to instruct and to please, by Terror and Compassion, which two Passions ought always to be predominant in it, and to distinguish it from all other Poems. *Epick Poetry* pleases and instructs chiefly by Admiration, which reigns throughout it, and distinguishes it from Poems of every other Kind. thus *Comedy* instructs and pleases most powerfully by the Ridicule, because that is the Quality which distinguishes it from every other Poem. The Subject therefore of every Comedy ought to be ridiculous by its Constitutions; the Ridicule ought to be of the very Nature and Essence of it. Where there is none of that, there can be no Comedy. It ought to reign both in the incidents and in the Characters, and especially in the principal Characters, which ought to be ridiculous in themselves, or so contriv'd, as to shew and expose the Ridicule of others. In all the Masterpieces of *Ben Johnson,* the principal Character has the Ridicule in himself, as *Morose* in *The Silent Woman, Volpone* in *The Fox,* and *Subtle* and *Face* in *The Alchimist:* And the very Ground and Foundation of all these *Comedies* is ridiculous. 'Tis the very same Thing in the Master-pieces of *Moliere.* The *Mis-Antrope,* the *Impostor,* the *Avare,* and the *Femmes Secuanter.* Nay, the Reader will find, that in most of his other Pieces, the principal Characters are ridiculous; as *L'Etoardy, Les precieuses Ridicules, Le Cocu Imaginaire, Le Fascheux,* and *Monsieur de pousceaugnac, Le Bourgeois Gentilhomme, L'Ecole de Maris, L'Ecole des Femmes, L'Amour Medicis, Le Medicin Magré luy, La Mariage Forcé, George Dandin, Les Fourb-*

eries de Scapin, Le Malade Imaginaire. The Reader will not only find, upon Reflection, that in all these Pieces the principal Characters are ridiculous, but that in most of them there is the Ridicule of *Comedy* in the very Titles.

'Tis by the Ridicule that there is in the Character of Sir *Fopling,* which is one of the principal ones of this *Comedy,* and from which it takes its Name, that he is so very well qualify'd to please and instruct. What true *Englishman* is there, but must be pleas'd to see this ridiculous Knight made the Jest and the Scorn of all the other Characters, for shewing, by his foolish aping foreign Customs and Manners, that he prefers another Country to his own? And of what important Instruction must it be to all our Youth who travel, to shew them, that if they so far forget the Love of their Country, as to declare by their espousing foreign Customs and Manners, that they prefer *France* or *Italy* to *Great Britain,* at their Return, they must justly expect to be the Jest and the Scorn of their own Countrymen.

Thus, I hope, I have convinc'd the Reader, that this Comical Knight, Sir *Fopling,* has been justly form'd by the Knight his Father, to instruct and please, whatever may be the Opinion to the contrary of the Knight his Brother.

Whenever *The Fine Gentleman* of the latter comes upon the Stage, I shall be glad to see that it has all the shining Qualities which reommend *Sir Fopling,* that his Characters are always drawn in Nature, and that he never gives to a young Man the Qualities of a Middle-aged Man, or an old one; that they are the just Images of our Contemporaries, and of what we every Day see in the World; that instead of setting us Patterns for our Imitation, which is not the proper Business of *Comedy,* he makes those Follies and Vices ridiculous, which we ought to shun and despise; that the Subject of his *Comedy* is comical by its Constitution; and that Ridicule is particularly in the Grand Incidents, and in the principal Characters. For a true Comick Poet is a Philosopher, who, like old *Democritus,* always instructs us laughing.

Theophilus Cibber (essay date 1753)

SOURCE: Cibber, Theophilus. "Sir George Etherege." In *The Lives of the Poets of Great Britain and Ireland,* Vol. 3, pp. 33-9. 1753. Reprint. Hildesheim: Georg Olms Verlagsbuchhandlung, 1968.

[*In the essay below, Cibber appraises Etherege's life and works, maintaining that the poet "possessed a springly genius," but that "his works are so extremely loose and licentious, as to render them dangerous to young, unguarded minds."*]

A celebrated wit in the reign of Charles and James II. He is said to have been descended of an ancient family of Oxfordshire, and born about the year 1636; it is thought he had some part of his education at the university of Cambridge, but in his younger years he travelled into

France, and consequently made no long stay at the university. Upon his return, he, for some time, studied the Municipal Law at one of the Inns of Court, in which, it seems, he made but little progress, and like other men of sprightly genius, abandoned it for pleasure, and the gayer accomplishments.

In the year 1664 the town was obliged with his first performance for the stage, entitled the **Comical Revenge, or, Love in a Tub,** the writing whereof brought him acquainted, as he himself informed us, with the earl of Dorset, to whom it is by the author dedicated. The fame of this play, together with his easy, unreserved conversation, and happy address, rendered him a favourite with the leading wits, such as the duke of Buckingham, Sir Charles Sedley, the earl of Rochester, Sir Car Scroop. Being animated by this encouragement, in 1668, he brought another comedy upon the stage, entitled **She Would if She Could**; which gained him no less applause, and it was expected, that by the continuance of his studies, he would polish and enliven the theatrical taste, and be no less constant in such entertainments, than the most assiduous of his cotemporaries, but he was too much addicted to pleasure, and being impelled by no necessity, he neglected the stage, and never writ, 'till he was forced to it, by the importunity of his friends. In 1676, his last comedy called the **Man of Mode, or Sir Fopling Flutter,** came on the stage, with the most extravagant success; he was then a servant to the beautiful duchess of York, of whom Dryden has this very singular expression, 'that he does not think, that at the general resurrection, she can be made to look more charming than now.' Sir George dedicates this play to his Royal Mistress, with the most courtly turns of compliment. In this play he is said to have drawn, or to use the modern cant, taken off, some of the contemporary coxcombs; and Mr. Dryden, in an Epilogue to it, has endeavoured to remove the suspicion of personal satire, and says, that the character of Flutter is meant to ridicule none in particular, but the whole fraternity of finished fops, the idolaters of new fashions.

His words are,

> True fops help nature's work, and go to school,
> To file and finish God Almighty's fool:
> Yet none Sir Fopling, him, or him, can call,
> He's Knight o'th' Shire, and represents you all.

But this industry, to avoid the imputation of personal satire, but served to heighten it; and the town soon found out originals to his characters. Sir Fopling was said to be drawn for one Hewit, a beau of those times, who, it seems, was such a creature as the poet ridiculed, but who, perhaps, like many other coxcombs, would never have been remembered, but for this circumstance, which transmits his memory to posterity.

The character of Dorimant was supposed to represent the earl of Rochester, who was inconstant, faithless, and undertermined in his amours; and it is likewise said, in the character of Medley, that the poet has drawn out some sketch of himself, and from the authority of Mr. Bowman, who played Sir Fopling, or some other part in this comedy, it is said, that the very Shoemaker in Act I. was also meant for a real person, who, by his improvident courses before, having been unable to make any profit by his trade, grew afterwards, upon the public exhibition of him, so industrious and notable, that he drew a crowd of the best customers to him, and became a very thriving tradesinan. Whether the poet meant to display these characters, we cannot now determine, but it is certain, the town's ascribing them to some particular persons, was paying him a very high compliment, and if it proved no more, it at least demonstrated, a close imitation of nature, a beauty which constitutes the greatest perfection of a comic poet.

Our author, it seems, was addicted to some gay extravagances, such as gaming, and an unlicensed indulgence in women and wine, which brought some satirical reflexions upon him. Gildon in his *Lives of the Dramatic Poets,* says, that upon marrying a fortune, he was knighted; the circumstances of it are these: He had, by his gaming and extravagance, so embarrassed his affairs, that he courted a rich widow in order to retrieve them; but she being an ambitious woman, would not condescend to marry him, unless he could make her a lady, which he was obliged to do by the purchase of a knighthood; and this appears in a Consolatary Epistle to captain Julian, from the duke of Buckingham, in which this match is reflected on. We have no account of any issue he had by this lady, but from the information of Mr. Bowman we can say, that he cohabited, for some time, with the celebrated Mrs. Barry the actress, and had one daughter by her; that he settled 5 or 6000 l. on her, but that she died young.

From the same intelligence, it also appears, that Sir George was, in his person, a fair, slender, genteel man, but spoiled his countenance with drinking, and other habits of intemperance. In his deportment he was very affable and courteous, of a generous disposition, which, with his free, lively, and natural vein of writing, acquired him the general character of gentle George, and easy Etherege, in respect of which qualities, we often find him compared to Sir Charles Sedley. His courtly and easy behaviour so recommended him to the Duchess of York, that when on the accession of King James II. she became Queen, she sent him ambassador abroad, Gildon says, to Hamburgh; but it is pretty evident, that he was in that reign a minister at Ratisbon, at least, from the year 1686, to the time his majesty left this kingdom, if not later, but it appears that he was there, by his own letters wrote from thence to the earl of Middleton.

After this last comedy, we meet with no more he ever wrote for the stage; however, there are preserved some letters of his in prose, published among a collection of Familiar Letters, by John earl of Rochester; two of which, sent to the duke of Buckingham, have particular merit, both for the archness of the turns, and the acuteness of the observations. He gives his lordship a humorous description of some of the Germans, their excessive drunkenness;

their plodding stupidity and offensive indelicacy; he complains that he has no companion in that part of the world, no Sir Charles Sedleys, nor Buckinghams, and what is still worse, even deprived of the happiness of a mistress, for, the women there, he says, are so coy, and so narrowly watched by their relations, that there is no possibility of accomplishing an intrigue. He mentions, however, one Monsieur Hoffman, who married a French lady, with whom he was very great, and after the calamitous accident of Mr. Hoffman's being drowned, he pleasantly describes the grief of the widow, and the methods he took of removing her sorrow, by an attempt in which he succeeded. These two letters discover the true character of Etherege, as well as of the noble person to whom they were sent, and mark them as great libertines, in speculation as in practice.

As for the other compositions of our author, they consist chiefly of little airy sonnets, smart lampoons, and smooth panegyrics. All that we have met with more than is here mentioned, of his writing in prose, is a short piece, entitled ***An Account of the Rejoicing at the Diet of Ratisbon,*** performed by Sir George Etherege, Knight, residing there from his Majesty of Great Britain, upon Occasion of the Birth of the Prince of Wales; in a Letter from himself, printed in the Savoy 1688. When our author died, the writers of his life have been very deficient; Gildon says, that after the Revolution, he followed his master into France, and died there, or very soon after his arrival in England from thence. But there was a report (say the authors of the *Biograph. Brit.* which they received from an ingenious gentleman)

> that Sir George came to an untimely death, by an unlucky accident at Ratisbon, for, after having treated some company with a liberal entertainment at his house there, when he had taken his glass too freely, and, being through his great complaisance too forward, in waiting on his guests at their departure, flushed as he was, he tumbled down stairs, and broke his neck, and so fell a martyr to jollity and civility.

One of the earliest of our author's lesser poems, is that addressed to her Grace the Marchioness of Newcastle, after reading her poems, and as it is esteemed a very elegant panegyric, we shall give the conclusion of it as a specimen.

> While we, your praise, endeavouring to rehearse,
> Pay that great duty in our humble verse;
> Such as may justly move your anger, now,
> Like Heaven forgive them, and accept them too.
> But what we cannot, your brave hero pays,
> He builds those monuments we strive to raise;
> Such as to after ages shall make known,
> While he records your deathless fame his own:
> So when an artist some rare beauty draws,
> Both in our wonder there, and our applause.
> His skill, from time secures the glorious dame,
> And makes himself immortal in her fame.

Besides his Songs, little panegyrical Poems and Sonnets, he wrote two Satires against Nell Gwyn, one of the King's mistresses, though there is no account how a quarrel happened between them; the one is called **Madam Nelly's Complaint,** beginning,

> If Sylla's ghost made bloody Cat'line start.

The other is called the **Lady of Pleasure,** with its Argument at the Head of it, whereof the first line is,

> The life of Nelly truly shewn.

Sir George spent a life of ease, pleasure, and affluence, at least never was long, nor much, exposed to want. He seems to have possessed a sprightly genius, to have had an excellent turn for comedy, and very happy in a courtly dialogue. We have no proof of his being a scholar, and was rather born, than made a poet. He has not escaped the censure of the critics; for his works are so extremely loose and licentious, as to render them dangerous to young, unguarded minds: and on this account our witty author is, indeed, justly liable to the severest censure of the virtuous, and sober part of mankind.

Horace Walpole (essay date 1775-76)

SOURCE: Walpole, Horace. "Thoughts on Comedy." In *The Works of Horatio Walpole, Earl of Oxford,* Vol. 2, pp. 315-22. London: G. G. and J. Robinson and J. Edwards, 1798.

[*In the following excerpt, originally written between 1775 and 1776, Walpole ranks Etherege's* The Man of Mode *among the best English comedies.*]

The [Restoration] age dealt in the intricacies of Spanish plots, enlivened by the most licentious indecency. Dryden and the fair sex rivalled each other in violating all decorum. Wycherley naturalized French comedy, but prostituted it too. That chaste stage blushed at our translations of its best pieces. Yet Wycherley was not incapable of easy dialogue. The same age produced almost the best comedy we have, though liable to the same reprehension: **The Man of Mode** shines as our first genteel comedy; the touches are natural and delicate, and never overcharged. Unfortunately the tone of the most fashionable people was extremely indelicate; and when Addison, in the *Spectator,* anathematised this play, he forgot that it was rather a satire on the manners of the court, than an apology for them. Less licentious conversation would not have painted the age.

Thomas Davies (essay date 1784)

SOURCE: Davies, Thomas. *Dramatic Miscellanies,* p. 101. 1784. Reprint. New York: Benjamin Blom, 1971.

[*In the excerpt below, Davies praises Dorimant as one of the best creations of the "fine gentleman" on the English stage.*]

The only dramatic writer, in all Charles's reign, who wrote with some decency of manners and modesty of language, was Sir George Etheridge. His **Man of Mode** is the original of that species of dramatic writing called genteel comedy. The second Duke of Dorset assured a gentleman, as greatly esteemed for his learning and abilities as his humanity and integrity [Mr. Thomas Sheridan], that Dorimant was formed from two originals: his father, the witty Earl of Dorset, and Wilmot Earl of Rochester. This character is properly the first fine gentleman of the English stage; a more gay and spirited man of pleasure has not been drawn since, unless we except the Sir Harry Wildair of Farquhar. . . .

S. T. Coleridge (essay date 1812)

SOURCE: Coleridge, S. T. "Sir George Etherege, & c." In *Omniana; or Horae Otiosiores,* by Robert Southey and S. T. Coleridge, edited by Robert Gittings, pp. 185-88. Carbondale: Southern Illinois University Press, 1969.

[*In the following essay from a collection that was originally published in 1812, Coleridge discusses the immoral nature of Etherege's works, censuring the playwright for "lampoon[ing] the noblest passions of humanity in order to pander for its lowest appetites."*]

Often and often had I *read* Gay's *Beggar's Opera,* and always delighted with its poignant wit and original satire, and if not without noticing its immorality, yet without any offence from it. Some years ago, I for the first time saw it represented in one of the London Theatres; and such were the horror and disgust with which it imprest me, so grossly did it outrage all the best feelings of my nature, that even the angelic voice, and perfect science of Mrs Billington, lost half its charms, or rather increased my aversion to the piece by an additional sense of incongruity. Then I learnt the immense difference between reading and seeing a play . . . no wonder, indeed. For who has not passed over with his eye a hundred passages without offence, which he yet could not have even *read* aloud, or have heard so read by another person, without an inward struggle? In mere passive silent reading the thoughts remain mere thoughts, and these too not our own . . . phantoms with no attribute of place, no sense of appropriation, that flit over the consciousness as shadows over the grass or young corn in an April day. But even the sound of our own or another's voice takes them out of that lifeless, twilight realm of idea, which is the confine, the *intermundium,* as it were, of existence and non-existence. Merely that the thoughts have become audible, by blending with them a sense of *outness* gives them a sort of reality. What then when by every contrivance of scenery, appropriate dresses, accordant and auxiliary looks, and gestures, and the variety of persons on the stage, realities are employed to carry the imitation of reality as near as possible to perfect delusion? If a manly modesty shrinks from uttering an indecent phrase before a wife or sister in a private room, what must be the effect when a repetition of such treasons (for all gross and libidinous allusions are emphatically treasons against the very foundations of human society, against all its endearing charities, and all the mother virtues) is hazarded before a mixed multitude in a public theatre? When every innocent female must blush at once with pain at the thoughts she rejects, and with indignant shame at those, which the foul hearts of others may attribute to her!

Thus too with regard to the comedies of Wycherly, Vanburgh, and Etherege, I used to please myself with the flattering comparison of the manners universal at present among all classes above the lowest with those of our ancestors even of the highest ranks. But if for a moment I think of those comedies, as having been acted, I lose all sense of comparison in the shame, that human nature could at any time have endured such outrages to its dignity; and if conjugal affection and the sweet name of sister were too weak, that yet Filial Piety, the gratitude for a Mother's holy love, should not have risen and hissed into infamy these traitors to their own natural gifts, who lampooned the noblest passions of humanity in order to pander for its lowest appetites.

As far, however, as one bad thing can be palliated by comparison with a worse, this may be said, in extenuation of these writers; that the mischief, which they can do even on the stage, is trifling compared with that style of writing which began in the pesthouse of French literature, and has of late been imported by the *Littles* of the age, which consists in a perpetual tampering with the *morals* without offending the *decencies*. And yet the admirers of these publications, nay, the authors themselves, have the assurance to complain of Shakespear (for I will not refer to one yet far deeper blasphemy)—Shakespear, whose most objectionable passages are but *grossnesses* against lust, and these written in a gross age; while three fourths of *their* whole works are *delicacies* for its support and sustenance. Lastly, that I may leave the reader in better humour with the name at the head of this article, I shall quote one scene from Etherege's **Love in a Tub,** which for exquisite, genuine, original humour, is worth all the rest of his plays, though two or three of his witty contemporaries were thrown in among them, as a make-weight. The scene might be entitled, "the different ways in which the very same story may be told, without any variation in matter of fact": for the least attentive reader will perceive the perfect identity of the Footboy's account with the Frenchman's own statement in contradiction of it.

Scene IV.

Scene, Sir Frederick's Lodging.

Enter Dufoy and Clark.

CLARK.

I wonder Sir *Frederick* stays out so late.

DUF.

Dis is noting; six, seven o'clock in the morning is ver good hour.

CLARK.

I hope he does not use these hours often.

DUF.

Some six, seven time a veek; no oftiner.

CLARK.

My Lord commanded me to wait his coming.

DUF.

Matré *Clark,* to diverstise you, I vill tell you, how I did get be acquainted vid dis Bedlam Matré. About two, tree year ago me had for my convenience discharge myself from attending [*Enter a Foot boy*] as Matré D'ostel to a person of condition in *Parie*; it happen after de dispatch of my little affairé———

FOOT-B.

That is, after h'ad spent his money, Sir.

DUF.

Jan foutré de Lacque; me vil have de vip and de belle vor your breeck, rogue.

FOOT-B.

Sir, in a word, he was a *Jack-pudding* to a Mountebank, and turned off for want of wit: my master picked him up before a puppit-show, mumbling a half-penny custard, to send him with a letter to the post.

DUF.

Morbleu, see, see de insolence of de foot-boy English, bogre, rascale, you lie, begar I vil cutté your Troaté.

[Exit Foot-boy].

CLARK.

He's a rogue; on with your story, Monsieur.

DUF.

Matré *Clark,* I am your ver humble serviteur; but begar me have no patience to be abusé. As I did say, afte de dispatché of my Affairé, van day being idele, vich does producé de mellanchollique, I did valké over de new bridge in *Parie,* and to devertise de time, and my more serious toughté, me did look to see de marrioneté, and de jack-pudding, vich did play hundred pretty trické, time de collation vas come; and vor I had no company, I vas unvilling to go to de Cabareté, but did buy a darriolé, littel custardé vich did satisfie my appetite ver vel: in dis time young Monsieur de *Grandvil* (a jentelman of ver great quality, van dat vas my ver good friendé, and has done me ver great and insignal faveure) come by in his caroché, vid dis Sir *Frolick,* who did pention at the same academy, to learn de language, de bon mine, de great horse, and many oder trické; Monsieur seeing me did make de bowe, and did beken me come to him: he did tellé me dat de Englis jentelman had de Letré vor de posté, and did entreaté me (if I had de oppertunity) to see de letré deliver: he did tellé me too, it vold be ver great obligation: de memory of de faveur I had received from his famelyé, beside de inclination I naturally have to servé de strangeré, made me to returné de complemen vid ver great civility, and so I did take de letré and see it deliveré. Sir *Frolick* perceiving (by de management of dis affairé) dat I was man d'esprit, and of Vitté, did entreaté me to be his serviteur; me did take d'affection to his personé, and vas contenté to live vid him, to counsel and advisé him. You see now de lie of de bougre de lacque Englishe, Morbleu.

Robert Bell (essay date 1865)

SOURCE: Bell, Robert. "The Comedies of Etherege." *The Fortnightly Review* 3, no. 15 (15 December 1865): 298-316.

[*In the essay below, Bell acknowledges Etherege as the inventor of the comedy of manners and favorably surveys his dramatic works.*]

It has been said of the comedies of Etherege that they are mere Conversation Pieces, with barely enough of plot in them to thread the scenes together—a capital defect which weakens their whole foundations; and that the characters are shadows speaking a common language, so little marked by individuality that the dialogue might be shuffled like a pack of cards. The stage literature of the Restoration having long ceased to be either read or acted, nobody has thought it worth while to disturb a verdict, in the justice or injustice of which the world takes little interest; and Etherege has accordingly come down to us as a loose, easy dramatist, who was master of a certain airy way of making his characters talk, but who was altogether wanting in the power of putting them into action.

This judgment has been too hastily adopted. Etherege's comedies are essentially comedies of manners. They seize the fleeting colours on the surface of society, and dispose them on the canvas with a corresponding gaiety of tint and lightness of hand. A weightier treatment would be inconsistent with the aims of those brilliant and volatile productions. There is not much bustle in any of them; but there is everywhere a progressive movement which, worked out with quiet skill in its attenuated details, always rises to a climax at the close. Modern audiences, spoiled by coarser excitements for the carte and tierce of wit, would, probably, consider the dialogue tedious and languid; and the disorderly episodes that delighted the Londoners of the seventeenth century, who recognised their fidelity, would now be endured with impatience, if, indeed, they would be endured at all. Compared with the more advanced comedy of later times, which embraces a wider range of life, presented in more active development, the romping, dissipated comedy of Etherege must be admitted to be diffuse and tame. It has no startling effects. There are no violent transitions or unexpected situations. It never deals in sentiment; and wherever a scrap of serious-

ness crops up it generally looks like a sly touch of burlesque. The plot, slender as it is, sometimes stands still for half a scene together to let the scapegraces have full swing for their wicked pleasantries; and the current foibles and vices are often lashed in a round of repartees to the suspension of an intrigue, for the certain issue of which the audience are quite willing to be kept waiting on such agreeable terms. Now all this prodigality of the animal spirits, this trusting to impulse rather than to rule, and the setting up of headlong enjoyment above the canons of art, which would be fatal to a comedy of our day, if there were nothing more solid to depend upon, are vital elements in a comedy of manners of the age of Charles II. We must test such plays by the contemporary standard; and, tried by that test, Etherege is at the head of his class.

But it is a mistake to suppose that these comedies are deficient in plot. They have as much plot as they want, or as they could bear. They abound in sprightly incidents, are constructed with considerable ingenuity, considering the fragility of their texture, and are remarkable for the unity and compactness of such action as there is. If the scenes do not always advance the story, they never fail to heighten the colouring; and it would not be easy to retrench them without doing injury to the general effect. Nor should it be overlooked that the story is, by intention, of minor importance in these pieces. In that sense at least they fulfil one of the severest conditions of dramatic art by relying upon Expectation, which is the highest source of interest, in preference to Surprise, which is the lowest. Mysteries or sudden turns of fortune never enter into their design. There are no secrets in them to be kept from the audience. Everything that is done is clear, and everything that is coming is the obvious sequel of what has gone before. The audiences, consequently, who witnessed these plays, knowing what was going to happen quite as well as the author, were not impatient about the catastrophe, and, therefore, could afford to listen at ease to the dialogue.

Sir George Etherege wrote three comedies, the first of which, *The Comical Revenge; or, Love in a Tub,* was produced at the Duke's Theatre, in Lincoln's Inn Fields, in 1664. He was then about twenty-eight years of age, had not long returned from a tour in France, and had just relinquished the study of the law for the more dazzling attractions of fashionable life. The date of the production of *The Comical Revenge* determines his position as the founder of English comedy. During the four years that had elapsed since the re-opening of the theatres, the plays acted were nearly all revivals; and the few new pieces produced, such as *The Adventures of Five Hours,* either owed their origin to foreign sources or were composed of mixed and heterogeneous materials. *The Comical Revenge* was the first prose comedy that embodied living manners, and reflected back from the stage the habits of the people. Shadwell did not produce his first comedy, *The Sullen Lovers*—a piece adapted to English modes rather than drawn from them—till 1668, after Etherege's second comedy had appeared; nor did Shadwell acquire distinction as a writer of comedies, notwithstanding the success of his *début,* for three or four years afterwards, when Etherege was at the height of his reputation. Wycherley's first comedy, *Love in a Wood,* came out in 1672, eight years after *The Comical Revenge*; Congreve's *Old Bachelor* in 1693; and Vanbrugh did not appear as a writer for the stage till 1697. These dates are important, as enabling us to trace to its source that form of pure English comedy whose descending stream has been enriched by the contributions of Wycherley, Congreve, Vanbrugh, Farquhar, and Sheridan. "The dawn," observes Mr. Hazlitt, speaking of this style of comedy, "was in Etherege, as its latest close was in Sheridan;" and with this passing recognition he dismisses a claim to priority which a little closer examination would have led him to acknowledge with a larger measure of justice.

Etherege's second comedy, **She Would if She Could,** was produced at the same theatre, and played by the same actors, in 1668. It was not so successful as the first, although it exhibits some structural improvement.

His third comedy, **The Man of Mode; or, Sir Fopling Flutter,** was brought out at Dorset Gardens in 1676. Wycherley had produced all his comedies, except *The Plain Dealer*; Sedley had launched his *Mulberry Garden*; Shadwell had followed up *The Sullen Lovers* with three pieces, including the *Epsom Wells*; and this form of drama had by this time become familiar to the public. In the school which Etherege had himself founded, skilful competitors had appeared, and become established favourites; and it is, therefore, the more worthy of note that this, his last production, was not only his best, but, as a picture of existing society, the most perfect comedy of the age. It is in this particular excellence that Etherege is to be distinguished above all other writers who attempted to transfer the living manners to the stage. He is excelled by Wycherley in greater attributes; but he is incontestably superior to him in the closeness and high finish of his contemporary portraiture. In those qualities none of the dramatists of the Restoration will bear comparison with him. Shadwell's comedies are more crowded with local allusions; but they belong to a lower and ruder order of dramatic writing. Remarkable for audacious invention and prodigious variety, they are no less remarkable for want of symmetry and glaring defects of judgment. They served the fugitive purpose, however, for which they were written, and the very disorder that runs through them was probably one of the secrets of their popularity. But they made no permanent impression on the literature of the stage, supplied no models for study or imitation, and are now never read, except when some industrious antiquary consults their pages for the curious light they throw on extinct habits and fashions. Etherege, on the other hand, although he produced only three comedies—about a fifth of the number bequeathed to us by Shadwell—imparted a permanent character to that form of composition, and created materials out of which many subsequent reputations have been built without acknowledgment. Even Farquhar lies under large obligations to Etherege; and the lineage of most of the fine gentlemen of modern comedy may be distinctly traced back to the **Man of Mode.** Much of the special merit of these pieces, their comparative refinement in an age of grossness, their disciplined taste, and authentic tone of high breeding, may be referred to the fact that Etherege lived in the circles whose modes he described, and was himself one of the most accomplished men of fashion at the Court of Charles II.

Following the order of production, for the sake of showing the course of Etherege's genius, from its first step to its highest point of development, we will begin with the **Comical Revenge; or, Love in a Tub.** This comedy offers a striking contrast to the other two, in so far as it is addressed to a different phase of society. We have not to deal here merely with fine ladies and gentlemen. The main interest lies in an opposite direction, the intention being to exhibit in a broad light the roarers, scourers, cheats, and gamblers who infested the town, and made the taverns ring day and night with their riots. Mixed up with these rampant scenes is a pure love story, treated more gravely and earnestly than usual. This love story is the weakest part of the comedy. Etherege was out of his element in a true passion, and, as if he were conscious of the defect, he endeavours to make up for the want of real emotion by turgid declamation. There are two sisters, with romantic names to help them through their tender difficulties—Graciana and Aurelia. Colonel Bruce, a gallant cavalier, is in love with Graciana, who has bestowed her affections upon Lord Beaufort, a walking gentleman of the seventeenth century. The rivals fight a duel on the stage, and the Colonel is disarmed. Resolved not to survive the loss of his mistress, he falls on his sword, and is severely wounded. Carried in bleeding to the house of the lady's father, he discovers that Aurelia, who had magnanimously urged his suit with her sister, has all the time secretly loved him; whereupon he displays a nobility of soul worthy of Bayard himself, by at once relieving Graciana from his importunities, and transferring his affections to Aurelia. The passage in which this evolution is performed, affords a fair sample of that spurious coinage which passed current for the true metal with audiences to whom honourable love was little more than a myth.

BRUCE.

> Graciana, I have lost my claim to you,
> And now my heart's become Aurelia's due;
> She all this while within her tender breast,
> The flame of love has carefully suppressed,
> Courting for me, and striving to destroy
> Her own contentment to advance my joy.

AURELIA.

> I did no more than honour pressed me to;
> I wish I'ad wooed successfully for you.

BRUCE.

> You so excel in honour and in love,
> You both my shame and admiration move.
> Aurelia, here, accept that life from me,
> Which heaven so kindly has preserved for thee.[1]

This meretricious glitter, lacquering such remarkably shabby verse, would have been intolerable from sheer dreariness, but for a humorous underplot, crowded with absurdities, to which it acts as a foil. Sir Nicholas Cully, one of Oliver's knights, is the hero of the low comedy life, or more properly, the broad farce, of the play. He is an unmistakable gull, with a sufficient touch of cunning in him to make him a rogue when occasion serves; a genuine sot of the old, absolute stamp—a swilling, vapouring, country fool; the type of a class of sensual, sweltering ninnies, that abounded at the time, and were remorselessly choused and fleeced by town sharpers through their egregious vanity and love of drink. Whenever he appears, this consummate ass throws the stage into an uproar, kicks the drawers before him with monstrous oaths, is perpetually bellowing out for more wine and music, and is altogether so outrageous and contemptible a wittol, that when Sir Frederic Frolic dupes him into a marriage with his cast-off mistress, under pretence that she is his sister, and then, the cheat being disclosed, advises him to take her down into the country, where she will be sure to pass current amongst his neighbours for a very honest, well-bred woman, one cannot help feeling that the wife, with all her drawbacks, has the worst of the bargain.[2]

The Sullen of Farquhar is a lineal descendant of Sir Nicholas Cully, and closely resembles him—with a difference. Sullen lacks the active principle that makes Cully turbulent and uproarious. His constitution is not so robust. With Sullen all the vigour is soaked away in tobacco and sleep. Cully is a harder drinker, although he, too, sometimes sinks under it, as when he talks of marrying a widow whom, in his cups, he has mistaken for another woman. "Widow, Sir Frederic shall be one of our bride men; I will have none but such mad fellows at our wedding;—but before I marry thee, I will consider upon it," and then, by way of considering upon it, he sits down and falls asleep. But his faculties, as far as he has any, are wide awake up to the last moment of speech, and he is no sooner roused than he bursts out as tempestuous as ever. He never complains, like Sullen, of headache and nausea. He is superior to such infirmities. He has not stupefied himself with ale; and seems to have got something of the ruddy sunshine of the grape into his nature, only rendered a little muddy now and then by the lees. He is more genial than Sullen; is subject to none of his moods of spleen and brutality; and, although his notions about women are barbarous enough, he regards them through a bacchanalian medium which, at least, makes him treat them more hilariously. In nervous energy he is the representative of the great profligates of the time: his frame is capable of sustaining an incessant round of dissipation, and his animal spirits are inexhaustible. However offensive such a portrait would be on the modern stage, we can easily imagine the popularity that attended it two hundred years ago. There was a provocation to enjoyment even in the name of this boisterous fool, which was much the same as if we were now to put a rich country booby into a play, and call him Sir Nicholas Goose.

The brawls of Cully and his companions are set off by the more fashionable licentiousness of Sir Frederic Frolic, the fine gentleman of the piece—an inferior variety of the *genus* Dorimant, which was to be brought to full perfection in a future comedy. The first scene plunges at once into the town life, introducing the hero with a flourish of preliminaries, which has been imitated with sundry modifications by subsequent dramatists. Sir Frederic is a pattern rake. He passes his days in adventures with ladies, and his nights in the taverns, seldom finding his way home before six or seven o'clock in the morning. The play begins at noon in his lodgings. He had been out as usual, the night before, carousing after the play. From the tavern he had proceeded to knock up a frail acquaintance at the unseasonable hour of two o'clock, and, being denied admittance, he finished his exploits by breaking the windows and fighting the constables. When the scene opens, his French valet comes into the ante-chamber with a plaister on his head, complaining of his master's conduct; when presently Sir Frederic makes his appearance in a morning gown. This is a key to the whole play; 'and it makes a capital dramatic opening, which has been appropriated in several modern comedies. But the age of window-breaking and constable-beating is at an end; and the pictures of extinct manners we find in this piece, although very curious to the reader, no longer possess any interest for the spectator.

Notwithstanding his "sorrow and repentance" in the first act, Sir Frederic knocks up a respectable widow in the third, with a rout of link-boys and fiddlers; and the widow, who is not disinclined towards him, lets him in rather than alarm the neighbours and bring a scandal on the house. It is a choice of evils, and she risks her honour to save her reputation. But the adventure leads to nothing; for the lady has no sooner got him into the house, and appeased the uproar, than she very coolly dismisses him to the streets again. This oscillation between impetuous pursuit on the one side, and encouraging repulses on the other, keeps up the movement of the play to the end, when it settles down into the usual contract, with stringent stipulations for future good behaviour.

The second title of **Love in a Tub** is taken from a single scene, of a thoroughly farcical kind, which has so little to do with the plot that it might be advantageously left out. The French valet makes love to a chambermaid, and after drinking himself asleep is put into a tub with a hole in it for his head, and in this helpless condition he ramps about the stage, swearing and sputtering, to the infinite merriment of the Abigails who have put the trick upon him. Devices of this absurd description are common to this whole class of plays, and are generally so preposterous that one wonders how they could have been endured.

Upon the whole, this comedy is not very artistically put together. The scenes are too detached, and do not always help the progress of the action. There are two hostile meetings on the stage—one serious, and the other humorous. In the former, a duel is fought out before the audience, and the vanquished man and his second, after being fairly overcome, attempt to fall upon their swords—rather too grim an effect for comedy; and in the latter, the coward yields to the bully, and grants his conditions rather than engage. But although the scenes are strongly contrasted, the repetition of the same incident, however varied in treatment, is a blemish in art.

Pepys, whose judgment in these matters is not always so critical, had a poor opinion of *The Comical Revenge.* He describes it as "very merry, but only so in gesture, not wit at all." At another time, seeing it played at Whitehall by the Duke's people, he speaks of it as "a silly play," and adds, "the whole thing being done ill, and being ill also, I had no manner of pleasure in it." As it is one of those plays that materially depend for their effects on the free humours and high spirits of the actors, the flatness of its performance may, possibly, be attributable to the restraint the players felt themselves under in the presence of the Court, for the cast was exactly the same that had unprecedented success at Lincoln's Inn Fields, the comedy having brought no less than £1,000 to the house in the course of a month. The play was, indeed, so great a "hit," that it raised the popularity of all the actors concerned in it, especially of Nokes, whose Sir Nicholas Cully was considered his masterpiece. All the parts were in skilful hands; Betterton was the Lord Beaufort (a character much beneath his subsequent reputation), Harris Sir Frederic Frolic, Prince the French valet, and Mrs. Betterton and Mrs. Davis were amongst the ladies.

The Comical Revenge was followed four years afterwards by *She Would if She Could,* which was not successful, although it had the advantage of the same excellent actors. The idea attempted to be developed in this play is indicated clearly enough in the title. The wife of a country knight, who has outlived her attractions, but not her vanity (to express the lady's weakness inoffensively), lays open siege to a young town gallant, who humours her wishes only to disappoint them, while he prosecutes his designs in another quarter. There is more grossness in the language and conduct of this play than in either of Etherege's other comedies; but in invention it is superior to both, The broad humour is contributed by two country knights, who are resolved to make the most of their visit to London, and are detected in their unlawful indulgences by the ladies of their families. The ladies are themselves engaged in similar courses, and, in order to avert exposure, they adroitly turn the tables on the gentlemen. There is an ingenious situation where they all meet at the "Bear" in Drury Lane, which, unknown to each other, they had selected for their rendezvous; and another, where Lady Cockwood, perpetually frustrated in her object by Courtal, writes notes in the names of her young kinswomen to make an appointment in Spring Gardens with Courtal and his friend Freeman, and then surprises them together. Lady Cockwood's character is abominable enough, but it is full of humour. Her method of managing her husband, and persuading him that she is a woman of exemplary virtue and devoted affection, is irresistibly comical. The imbroglio in the last

scene, with the two gallants shut up in a closet (a situation often borrowed, and altered to suit circumstances), and the audacity of the explanations by which the honour of the wife is saved, all suspicions cleared up, and everybody enabled to come off handsomely at the conclusion, are happily contrived.

Some of the usual extravagances are interwoven with the plot to amuse the galleries. Of this description is the stratagem resorted to by Lady Cockwood to keep her husband at home, while she goes out to an appointment with Courtal. The trick consists in locking up his clothes, and leaving him only what she calls his "penitential suit," a ridiculous costume she forces him to wear, by way of punishment for having been drunk the night before, just as a fool's-cap is put upon a naughty boy at school. The husband, however, is persuaded by his friend, the other tipsy knight, to go to a tavern, and his appearance abroad in this ludicrous dress is a source of infinite mirth to the rest of the characters.

Altogether, we have few examples in English comedy of so much clever mechanism wrought out of such slender materials; but unfortunately the play is so saturated with licentiousness as to render all this constructive skill mere waste and abuse. The laxity of public morals is here presented with startling candour. The whole business of the scene is illicit pleasure. There is not a single person concerned, from the young ladies who come up to town with roses in their cheeks, to the experienced rake-hells into whose arms they are ready to throw themselves, that is not engaged in the same pursuit. The ordinary comedy of intrigue has generally some relief; there is none in *She Would if She Could.* It is intrigue from first to last. Even the young ladies enter into it with avidity, although it must be admitted to their credit that they betray a little fright when they find matters growing serious.

Pepys was present at the first representation of this comedy, and it appears from his account of its reception that the audience, who came in great crowds to see it, went away disappointed both with the play and the actors.[3] This was on the 6th February, 1667-8:—

> My wife being gone before, I to the Duke of York's playhouse, where a new play of Etherege's, called *She Would if She Could*; and though I was there by two o'clock, there was one thousand people put back that could not have room in the pit; and I at last, because my wife was there, made shift to get into the 18*d.* box, and there saw; but, Lord! how full was the house, and how silly the play, there being nothing in the world good in it, and few people pleased in it. The king was there; but I sat mightly behind, and could see but little, and hear not all. The play being done, I into the pit to look for my wife, it being dark and raining, but could not find her, and so staid going between the two doors and through the pit an hour and half, I think, after the play was done; the people staying there till the rain was over, and to talk with one another. And, among the rest, the Duke of Buckingham to-day openly sat in the pit; and there I found him with my Lord Buckhurst,

and Sedley, and Etherege, the poet; the last of whom I did hear mightily find fault with the actors, that they were out of humour, and had not their parts perfect, and that Harris did do nothing, nor could so much as sing a ketch in it;[4] and so was mightily concerned; while all the rest did, through the whole pit, blame the play as a silly, dull thing, though there was something very roguish and witty; but the design of the play, and end, mightily insipid.[5]

This passage is interesting in two or three points of view. It lets us into the interior of the playhouse, and enables us to see what sort of place it was, with all the celebrities "assisting" at the inauguration of the new piece, and the fine company flocking down from the boxes into the pit when the play was over, weather-bound and waiting for their "Flemish barbs," and glad of an excuse for a lounge amongst the wits, to pick up stray crumbs of scandal, and a little criticism. It shows us also something of the life of the stage; the imperfect study and ill-humours of the actors—Harris especially, who had a leading part, one of the ramping, uproarious country knights, yet could not sing a catch in it; the excitement of a first representation, drawing so great a concourse to the house that a thousand people were turned away from the doors, and Pepys himself, although he went so early as two o'clock, being obliged to put up with a back seat in the 18*d.* box, where he could see little and hear nothing; and, still more characteristic of a scene repeated often enough from that time to this, the mortification of the author condemned to see his play spoiled in the acting. And here, too, we have Etherege in his true position amongst the men of taste and fashion, who gave a tone to the literature of the day, and were themselves the principal persons to whom the stage held up its mirror.

The next, and last, is the greatest of Etherege's works. All the characters in *The Man of Mode* are now the common property, under different modifications, of many plays. But here these stock figures are for the most part new, and contain the germs of suggestions which later writers have expanded and adapted to other circumstances. Dorimant, the universal gallant of the piece, the prince of intriguers, dashing, handsome, irresistibly impudent, and adding to the rest of his fascinations the prestige of a most dangerous reputation, is the progenitor of the Belcours, Doricourts, and a score of brilliant heroes of modern comedy, lacking only those sentimental qualities which were considered necessary some sixty years ago to balance the recklessness of youth, but which would have taken off all its piquancy in the days of the Restoration. Dorimant is not wholly unredeemed, however, by a touch of grace, for after betraying two ladies, he settles down in marriage with a third, the sting of the moral being that the ladies he has undone are reconciled to his desertion by the consideration that he has abandoned them, not for a mistress, but a wife. This desperate refuge of a profligate philosophy lets us a little into the social ethics of the time. When a man married, instead of being shut out from the wild pleasures of the town, he became a sort of licensed libertine, and was more in favour than ever, especially when it was

thought desirable, which was seldom the case, to consult appearances. The last woman in the world a mistress would be jealous of was the wife of her lover. It seemed, indeed, to be quite true, as a married *roué* says in one of these comedies, when he is following up an amour, that "marriage is the least engagement of all, for that only points out where a man cannot love."[6]

This lax doctrine was carried down traditionally in our popular comedies long after, it is to be hoped, the practice of it had gone into disuse, and was last openly proclaimed under the *régime* of Garrick, subsequently to which it appears to have given way before a stricter code of domestic morality.

The other characters are a couple of young fellows about town, an old gentleman from the country, and the usual supply of ladies at cross-purposes, and bent upon adventures, with a dash of reserve and prudence thrown in amongst them in the persons of a suspicious mother and, what must have been regarded by most people as an anomalous hybrid, a respectable woman of fashion.

The old gentleman, although he has very little to do, stands out prominently from the rest. We are now so familiar with the portrait of prurient senility on the stage that we must keep in view the chronology of these plays in order to do full justice to the merits of the conception. But with a hundred copies of Old Bellair before us, the rich colouring of the original eclipses them all. Not wanting in sense, he betrays the folly of age only in the dawdling imbecility of a liquorish tooth; and this constitutional weakness is brought into play by his taking a violent fancy to a young girl, and making love to her with an hysterical gusto which has often been imitated, but rarely without degenerating into caricature. His delight is to chirp up to her, and then retreat from her, chuckling and pretending to chide her with a "Go—you're a rogue, you're a rogue;—dod, I can't abide you—I can't abide you!" When he is suddenly called off the scene, he cries out to one of the young sparks who are paying court to her, and laughing in their sleeves at him, "A-dod, what does she say? Hit her a pat for me there!" A vice so ludicrously peccant, and so liable to be overcharged, must have run into mere drivelling grossness in the hands of most of these dramatists—of which we have, indeed, plenty of examples; but it is restrained by Etherege within such careful limits, and regulated with such a judicious regard for the more rational features of the character, as to become a perfectly natural bit of genuine comic humour.

The great part is Sir Fopling Flutter, who gives the title to the play. Upon this elaborate fribbler Etherege has bestowed infinite pains, and the result is the most consummate coxcomb in the repertory of an age when the species were as common as flies in summer. All our stage fops and male coquets trace their lineage to this early exquisite, who overshadows the whole tribe by the costliness of his style and the surpassing self-satisfaction of his bearing. Sir Fopling is a special product of the period; the type of that class of travelled popinjays that brought home to England, in the train of Charles II., the most egregious follies and vanities of France. He has just arrived from Paris, and presents in his person a complete reflection of the extremity of the mode. His costume is a picture of the newest fashions carried to the height of the prevailing extravagance; and its details, which are enumerated with scrupulous minuteness, reveal all the secrets of a fine gentleman's toilet. His periwig is "more exactly curled than a lady's head newly dressed for a ball;" he wears a pair of fringed and perfumed gloves that stretch up to his elbows; every article upon him is of Paris make—the suit by Barroy, the garniture by Le Gras, the shoes by Piccar, the mountainous periwig by Chedreux,[7] and the gloves by Orangerii, always to be detected by their peculiar odour; knots, tassels, and ribbons stream from every available point of his body; he is literally steeped in scents; he carries his head on one side with the languishing air of a lady lolling in her coach, or angling for admirers from her box at the play; and his mincing conversation, which is the moral counterpart of his dress and action, acquires zest from a pretty lisp which he has studied and practised till it has become indispensable to the expression of his thoughts. Dryden, in his admirable epilogue to the comedy, gives a sketch of Sir Fopling, which, for what it is, is as good as the character itself. He describes him as the representative of the whole race of fops, and as being composed of features selected from a variety of originals.

> Yet none Sir Fopling him, or him, can call,
> He's knight o' th' shire, and represents ye all.
> From each he meets he culls whate'er he can,
> Legion's his name, a People in a Man.
> His bulky folly gathers as it goes,
> And, rolling o'er you, like a snow-ball grows.
> His various modes from various fathers follow;
> One taught the toss, and one the new French wallow.
> His sword-knot this, his cravat this designed,
> And this the yard-long snake he twirls behind.
> From one the sacred periwig he gained,
> Which wind ne'er blew nor touch of hat profaned.
> Another's diving bow he did adore,
> Which with a shog casts all the hair before;
> 'Till he with full decorum brings it back,
> And rises with a water-spaniel's shake.

This illustrious fop brings before us in colours that will never fade one of those portraits of bygone manners which are entitled to be received as valuable contributions to the gallery of history.

Sir Fopling's share in the action of the comedy is not much. He is merely made use of as a set-off to promote the intrigues of others, he being allowed, all the time, to flatter his vanity with the belief that he is achieving conquests on his own account. It clearly would never have answered the purpose of the dramatist to suffer such a butterfly to carry off the *éclat* of a successful amour from any of the lusty wooers, who, in their sweeping licentiousness, represented the ascendant spirit of the time. Poor Sir Fopling, therefore, after parading his equipage in the Mall, with a retinue of six footmen and a page, for the purpose

of making an impression on a lady who affects to be smitten by him merely to pique the triumphant Dorimant, is unceremoniously dismissed with contempt in the end. But he bears his humiliation like a gentleman, and consoles his wounded pride by resolving henceforth to dedicate himself, not to one woman, but to the whole sex. There is a grandeur in this view of the matter which was, probably, designed to appease the boxes, and reconcile the courtly part of the audience to the discomfiture of a character drawn from living originals in Whitehall.

In this comedy we have an example of that intrigue upon intrigue literally taking place, so to speak, in the open air, and conducted with the most peremptory frankness, which may be accepted as the express image of the scenes that were enacted every day in Spring Gardens, the Mall, the New Exchange, the China-houses, and other favourite places of resort. From the nature of the incidents, the scenes are unavoidably tinged with licentiousness; but they are singularly free from the gratuitous grossness which stained the bulk of the contemporary drama. Etherege threw into his dialogue a tone of society that gave it a certain softening air of refinement. He wrote upon the most dangerous themes like a gentleman.

The following scene will show how complete a master he was of stage art. The situation is constructed with remarkable skill. Old Bellair and Lady Woodvil having determined to force their son and daughter into a marriage, the young people plot together to contrive an escape from it, and have just hit upon the expedient of pretending to be in love with each other for the purpose of deceiving their tormentors and gaining time, when the father and mother make their appearance. The girl, although she professes to be a novice in such matters, falls into the plan with facility, and discovers an aptitude for improvised coquetry which must have been highly piquant in the acting.[8] The whole scene is played aside.

Y. Bell.

 Can you play your part?

Harriet.

 I know not what 'tis to love; but I have made pretty remarks by being now and then where lovers meet. Where did you leave their gravities?

Y. Bell.

 In the next room. Your mother was censuring our modern gallant.

   Enter Old Bellair and Lady Woodvil.

Har.

 Peace! Here they come. I will lean against this wall, and look bashfully down upon my fan, while you, like an amorous spark, modishly entertain me.

Lady Wood.

 Never go about to excuse 'em; come, come, it was not so when I was a young woman.

OLD BELL.

A-dod; they're something disrespectful.

LADY WOOD.

Quality was then considered, and not rallied by every fleering fellow.

OLD BELL.

Youth will have its jest, a-dod it will.

LADY WOOD.

'Tis good breeding now to be civil to none but players and exchange women; they are treated by 'em as much above their condition, as others are below theirs.

OLD BELL.

Out a-pize on 'em,[9] talk no more, the rogues ha' got an ill habit of preferring beauty, no matter where they find it.

LADY WOOD.

See your son and my daughter, they have improved their acquaintance since they were within.

OLD BELL.

A-dod, methinks they have! Let's keep back and observe.

Y. BELL.

Now for a look and gestures that may persuade 'em I am saying all the passionate things imaginable———

HAR.

Your head a little more on one side; ease yourself on your left leg, and play with your right hand.

Y. BELL.

Thus; is it not?

HAR.

Now set your right foot firm on the ground, adjust your belt, then look about you.

Y. BELL.

A little exercising will make me perfect.

HAR.

Smile, and turn to me again very sparkish!

Y. BELL.

Will you take your turn, and be instructed?

HAR.

With all my heart.

Y. BELL.

At one motion play your fan, roll your eyes, and then settle a kind look upon me.

HAR.

So?

Y. BELL.

Now spread your fan, look down upon it, and tell the sticks with a finger.

HAR.

Very modish.

Y. BELL.

Clap your hand up to your bosom, hold down your gown, shrug a little, draw up your breasts, and let 'em fall again gently, with a sigh or two.

HAR.

By the good instructions you give, I suspect you for one of those malicious observers who watch people's eyes, and from innocent looks make scandalous conclusions.

Y. BELL.

I know some, indeed, who out of mere love to mischief are as vigilant as jealousy itself, and will give you an account of every glance that passes at a play, and in the circle.

HAR.

'Twill not be amiss now to seem a little pleasant.

Y. BELL.

Clap your fan then in both your hands; snatch it to your mouth, smile, and with a lively motion fling your body a little forwards. So—now spread it; fall back on the sudden, cover your face with it, and break out into a loud laughter—take up! look grave, and fall a fanning of yourself. Admirably well acted!

HAR.

I think I am pretty apt at these matters.

OLD BELL.

A-dod I like this well.

LADY WOOD.

This promises something.[10]

A fuller flavour of the comedy may be obtained from a scene of higher pretensions, in which Dorimant comes out in all the glory of his inconstancy. Wearied of his mistress, Mrs. Loveit, whose violent temper and inconvenient jealousy have worn out his patience, he prevails upon Belinda, her successor in his vagrant affections, to enter into a scheme for getting rid of her. The two ladies are intimate acquaintances, but love cancels all other considerations in the heart of Belinda, who is easily persuaded to accept Dorimant's sacrifice of her friend as a proof of his devotion to herself. It is arranged that Belinda shall pay a visit to Mrs. Loveit, and inflame her jealousy by a story of Dorimant's infidelities with another (who is in reality Belinda herself), and that Dorimant shall break in upon them when the lady is at the height of her fury, and make a pretext of her invectives to discard her on the spot. The conspiracy is sufficiently base; but we must take these people in their own way. We must not look to their conduct for instances of fidelity, nor to their professions for maxims of love. On the other hand, there was no assumption of that "sentimental French plate," which Joseph Surface substitutes for the "silver ore of pure charity," and which, he tells us, "makes quite as good a show, and pays no tax." Everybody knew what they had to trust to in matters of this kind, and took the risk of the issue. Engagements such as that of Dorimant and Mrs. Loveit were regulated by an understood license, which greatly relieves our conscience in contemplating their ruthless violation. The lady could have expected nothing better from a man whose indiscriminate gallantries were so notorious; and, considering the general laxity to which he might have appealed for precedents, it is rather a sign of latent grace in Dorimant, that instead of outraging her pride by open desertion, he pays her the artful compliment of affecting to find in her own actions an excuse for his perfidy. A woman is naturally inclined to extract from such a situation whatever solace it may be made to yield; and the lover who throws upon her the sole responsibility of their separation leaves with her at least the miserable consolation, true or false, that she might have kept him if she had tried.

The scene is sustained with unflagging spirit and energy. The jealous rage of Mrs. Loveit, finding vent in torrents of abuse and despair, and the coolness and gaiety of Dorimant, floating triumphantly above the storm, present a striking opposition of temper, character, and circumstance. But this is merely the dramatic side of the picture. So mean a stratagem, conducted to so successful a close, would utterly revolt our better feelings, were it not that the moral which creeps out at the end, when Belinda expresses her fear that the lover who has acted so cruelly to another may one day act as treacherously to herself, goes some way, if not to redeem a little of the turpitude of the proceeding, at least to deprive it of complete impunity. In a more artificial age, when it would be necessary to propitiate the moral scruples of the audience, Belinda would have been made to exhibit remorse at the barbarous treatment she had brought upon her friend; but there is no affectation in these plays, and the only regret of which she is conscious, and to which she honestly confesses, is purely selfish—a slight, but significant, indication of the predominant sentiment that entered into such incidents in real life.

Etherege's intimate association with the Buckinghams, Dorsets, and Rochesters gives a special value to his comedies. He lived the life he painted, and represented in his own person all the experiences which other dramatists derived at second-hand. His plays have the direct impress of the lax high-breeding of the circles in which he moved. . . .

Notes

1. Act v., sc. 5.

2. In the last scene we have one of the numerous illustrations to be found in the Restoration comedies, of the indiscriminate mixture of women of character with others of tainted reputation. No less than two of these graceless ladies are brought in married to wind up the play, and join in the general wedding festivities with which it closes, the peculiar antecedents of the brides furnishing a characteristic joke to tag the whole.

3. Dennis says that, although it was esteemed by men of sense for the trueness of some of its characters, and the purity, freeness, and easy grace of its dialogue, yet, on its first appearance, it was *barbarously* treated by the audience. Shadwell, it will be seen, ascribed its failure to the negligence of the actors, an opinion strongly expressed by Etherege himself.

4. Harris played Sir Joslin Jolly, to whom nearly all the catches or snatches of song were given. Nokes, who had done wonders in Cully, was again fitted with a country knight; but, like most reproductions of a good thing, the second country knight was very inferior to his predecessor. Songs and dances were always introduced into the comedies of this period, and, being highly popular, often retrieved the credit of a new piece. Shadwell attributes the redemption of the *Humourists* from total condemnation to the success of a favourite *figurante*, "who, for four days together, beautified it with the most excellent dancings that had ever been seen upon the stage."

5. Others, it should be noted, held a different opinion. Shadwell, in his preface to the *Humourists,* threw the whole blame of its ill-success upon the actors. "The imperfect action," he says, "had like to have destroyed *She Would if She Could,* which I think (and have the authority of some of the best judges in England for it) is the best comedy that has been written since the restoration of the stage; and eventually, for the imperfect representation of it at first, received such prejudice that, had it not been for the favour of the Court, in all probability it had never got up again; and it suffers for it, in a great measure, to this very day." Philips, Gildon, and Langbaine also pronounce *She Would if She Could* one of the best comedies of the age.

6. Shadwell's *Epsom Wells.*

7. Extravagant periwigs were by no means the exclusive mark of the fribbler and the coxcomb, nor were they even confined to the laity. They were worn by vain

clergymen. Pepys was horribly scandalised at seeing the Earl of Carlisle's curate preach in a flowing peri-wig.

8. The name of the actress who played Harriet, at Dorset Gardens, is omitted from the cast, although the names of all the other performers are given. Jevon played Young Bellair; Betterton was the original Dorimant.

9. Equivalent to "plague on 'em!"

10. Act II., sc. 3.

Edmund W. Gosse (essay date 1881)

SOURCE: Gosse, Edmund W. "Sir George Etherege: A Neglected Chapter of English Literature." *Cornhill Magazine* 43, no. 255 (March 1881): 284-304.

[*In the following essay, Gosse considers Etherege a principal founder of modern English comedy, particularly focusing on Molière's influence on the dramatist. The critic also provides an intimate glimpse of the author's later years through an examination of his personal and official correspondence in a recently discovered* Letterbook.]

That Sir George Etheredge wrote three plays which are now even less read than the rank and file of Restoration drama, and that he died at Ratisbon, at an uncertain date, by falling down the stairs of his own house and breaking his neck after a banquet, these are the only particulars which can be said to be known, even to students of literature, concerning the career of a very remarkable writer. I shall endeavour to show in the following pages that the entire neglect of the three plays is an unworthy return for the singular part they enjoyed in the creation of modern English comedy; and I shall be able to prove that the one current anecdote of Etheredge's life has no founda-tion in fact whatever. At the same time I shall have the satisfaction of printing, mainly for the first time, and from MS. sources, a mass of biographical material which makes this dramatist, hitherto the shadowiest figure of his time, perhaps the one poet of the Restoration of whose life and character we know the most. The information I refer to has been culled from two or three fields. Firstly, from the incidental references to the author scattered in the less-known writings of his contemporaries; secondly, from an article published in 1750, and from MS. notes still un-printed, both from the pen of that "busy, curious, thirsty fly" of polite letters, the antiquarian Oldys; but mostly, and with far the greatest confidence, from a volume in the Manuscript Room of the British Museum, entitled *The Letterbook* of Sir George Etheredge, while he was Envoy Extraordinary at Ratisbon. This volume, which is in the handwriting of an un-named secretary, contains drafts of over one hundred letters from Etheredge, in English and French, a certain number of letters addressed to him by famous persons, some of his accounts, a hudibrastic poem on his character, and, finally, some extremely caustic let-ters, treacherously written by the secretary, to bring his

master into bad odour in England. I cannot understand how so very curious and important a miscellany has hitherto been overlooked. It was bought by the British Museum in 1837, and, as far as I can find out, has been never referred to, or made use of in any way. It abounds with historical and literary allusions of great interest, and, as far as Etheredge is concerned, is simply a mine of wealth. Having premised so much, I will endeavour to put together, as concisely as possible, what I have been able to collect from all these sources.

On January 9, 1686, Etheredge addressed to the Earl of Middleton an epistle in octosyllabics, which eventually, in 1704, was printed in his *Works.* Readers of Dryden will recollect that a letter in verse to Sir George Etheredge by that poet has always been included in Dryden's poems, and that it begins:—

> To you who live in chill degree,
> As map informs, of fifty-three,
> And do not much for cold atone
> By bringing thither fifty-one.

That Etheredge was fifty-one at the date of this epistle has hitherto been of little service to us, since we could not tell when that letter was composed. *The Letterbook,* however, in giving us the date of Etheredge's epistle, to which Dry-den's poem was an immediate answer, supplies us with an important item. If Etheredge was fifty-one in the early spring of 1686, he must have been born in 1634 or the first months of 1635. He was, therefore, a contemporary of Dryden, Roscommon, and Dorset, rather than, as has always been taken for granted, of the younger generation of Wycherley, Shadwell, and Rochester. Nothing is known of his family. Gildon, who knew him, reported that he belonged to an old Oxfordshire family, and, therefore, may probably have been a descendant of Dr. George Etheredge, the famous Greek and Hebrew scholar, who died about 1590, and whose family estate was at Thame. Oldys very vaguely conjectures that our dramatist was educated at Cambridge. Gildon states that for a little while he studied the law, but adds, what external and internal evidence combine to prove, that he spent much of his early man-hood in France. My own impression is that from about 1658 to 1663 he was principally in Paris. His French, in prose and verse, is as fluent as his English; and his plays are full of allusions that show him to be intimately at home in Parisian matters. What in the other Restoration playwrights seems a Gallic affectation seems nature in him. My reason for supposing that he did not arrive in London at the Restoration, but a year or two later, is that he appears to have been absolutely unknown in London until his *Comical Revenge* was acted; and also because he shows in that play an acquaintance with the new school of French comedy. He seems to have possessed means of his own, and to have lived a thoroughly idle life, without aim or ambition, until, in 1664, it occurred to him, in his thirtieth year, to write a play.

At any critical moment in the development of a literature, events follow one another with such headlong speed, that I must be forgiven if I am a little tiresome about the sequence of dates. According to all the bibliographers, old and new, Etheredge's first play was **She Would if She Could,** 1668, immediately followed by **The Comical Revenge,** first printed in 1669. If this were the case, the claim of Etheredge to critical attention would be comparatively small. Oldys, however, mentions that he had heard of, but never seen, an edition of this latter play of 1664. Neither Langbaine, Gildon, or any of their successors believe in the existence of such a quarto, nor is a copy to be found in the British Museum. However, I have been so fortunate as to pick up two copies of this mythical quarto of 1664, the main issue of which I suppose to have been destroyed by some one of the many accidents that befell London in that decade, and Etheredge's precedence of all his more eminent comic contemporaries is thus secured. The importance of this date, 1664, is rendered still more evident when we consider that it constitutes a claim for its author for originality in two distinct kinds. **The Comical Revenge, or Love in a Tub,** which was acted at the Duke of York's Theatre in Lincoln's Inn Fields, in the summer of 1664, is a tragicomedy, of which the serious portions are entirely written in rhymed heroics, and the comic portions in prose. The whole question of the use of rhyme in English drama has been persistently misunderstood, and its history misstated. In Mr. George Saintsbury's new life of Dryden, for the first time, the subject receives due critical attention, and is approached with the necessary equipment. But while I thoroughly agree with Mr. Saintsbury's view of the practice, I think something may be added from the purely historical side. The fashion of rhyme in the drama, then, to be exact, flourished from 1664 until Lee and Dryden returned to blank verse in 1678. Upon this it suddenly languished, and after being occasionally used until the end of the century, found its last example in Sedley's *Beauty the Conqueror,* published in 1702. The customary opinion that both rhymed dramatic verse and the lighter form of comedy were introduced simultaneously with the Restoration is one of those generalisations which are easily made and slavishly repeated, but which fall before the slightest historical investigation. When the drama was reorganised in 1660, it reappeared in the old debased forms, without the least attempt at novelty. Brome and Shirley had continued to print their plays during the Commonwealth, and in Jasper Mayne had found a disciple who united, without developing, their merits or demerits. During the first years of the Restoration the principal playwrights were Porter, a sort of third-rate Brome, Killegrew, an imitator of Shirley, Stapylton, an apparently lunatic person, and Sir William Lower, to whom is due the praise of having studied French contemporary literature with great zeal, and of having translated Corneille and Quinault. Wherever these poetasters ventured into verse, they displayed such an incompetence as has never before or since disgraced any coterie of considerable writers. Their blank verse was simply inorganic, their serious dialogue a sort of insanity, their comedy a string of pothouse buffooneries and preposterous "humours." Dryden, in his *Wild Gallant,* and a very clever dramatist, Wilson, who never fulfilled his extraordinary promise, tried in 1663 to revive the moribund body of comedy, but always

in the style of Ben Jonson; and finally, in 1664, came the introduction of rhymed dramatic verse. For my own part, I frankly confess that I think it was the only course that it was possible to take. The blank iambics of the romantic dramatists had become so execrably weak and distended, the whole movement of dramatic verse had grown so flaccid, that a little restraint in the severe limits of rhyme was absolutely necessary. It has been too rashly taken for granted that we owe the introduction of the new form to Dryden. It is true that in the 1664 preface to *The Rival Ladies,* a play produced on the boards in the winter of 1663, Dryden recommends the use of rhyme in heroic plays, and this fact, combined with the little study given to Dryden's dramas, has led the critics to take for granted that that play is written in rhyme. A glance at the text will show that this is a mistake. *The Rival Ladies* is written in blank verse, and only two short passages of dialogue in the third act exhibit the timid way in which Dryden tested the ear of the public. Of course lyrical passages in all plays, and the main part of masques, such as the pastorals of Day, had, even in the Elizabethan age, been written in decasyllabic rhymed verse; but these exceptions are as little to the point as is the example which Dryden shelters himself under, *The Siege of Rhodes.* This piece was an opera, and therefore naturally in rhyme. As a point of fact Dryden was the first to propose, and Etheredge the first to carry out, the experiment of writing ordinary plays in rhyme. Encouraged by the preface to *The Rival Ladies,* and urged on by the alexandrines he was accustomed to listen to on the French stage, Etheredge put the whole serious part of his **Comical Revenge** into dialogue of which this piece from the duel scene is an example:—

BRUCE.

> Brave men! this action makes it well appear
> 'Tis honour and not envy brings you here.

BEAUFORT.

> We come to conquer, Bruce, and not to see
> Such villains rob us of our victory;
> Your lives our fatal swords claim as their due,
> We'ed wronged ourselves had we not righted you.

BRUCE.

> Your generous courage has obliged us so,
> That to your succour we our safety owe.

LOVIS.

> You've done what men of honour ought to do,
> What in your cause we would have done for you.

BEAUFORT.

> You speak the truth, we've but our duty done;
> Prepare; duty's no obligation. [*He strips.*]
> None come into the field to weigh what's right,
> This is no place for counsel, but for fight.

And so on. The new style was at once taken up by the Howards, Killegrews, and Orrerys, and became, as we have seen, the rage for at least fourteen years.

But the serious portion of *The Comical Revenge* is not worth considering in comparison with the value of the prose part. In the underplot, the gay, realistic scenes which give the play its sub-title of the "Tale of a Tub," Etheredge virtually founded English comedy, as it was successively understood by Congreve, Goldsmith, and Sheridan. The Royalists had come back from France deeply convinced of the superiority of Paris in all matters belonging to the business of the stage. Immediately upon the Restoration, in 1661, an unknown hand had printed an English version of the *Menteur* of Corneille. Lower had translated the tragedies of that poet ten years before, and had returned from his exile in Holland with the dramas of Quinault in his hand. But the great rush of Royalists back to England had happened just too soon to give them an opportunity of witnessing the advent of Molière. By the end of 1659 the exiled Court, hovering on the Dutch frontier, had transferred their attention from Paris to London. A few months before this, Molière and his troop had entered Paris, and an unobtrusive performance of *L'Étourdi* had gradually led to other triumphs and to the creation of the greatest modern school of comedy. What gave *The Comical Revenge* of Etheredge its peculiar value and novelty was that it had been written by a man who had seen and understood *L'Étourdi, Le Dépit Amoureux,* and *Les Précieuses Ridicules.* Etheredge loitered long enough in Paris for Molière to be revealed to him, and then he hastened back to England with a totally new idea of what comedy ought to be.

The real hero of the first three comedies of Molière is Mascarille, and in like manner the farcical interest of *The Comical Revenge* centres around a valet, Dufoy. When the curtain went up on the first scene, the audience felt that a new thing was being presented to them, new types and an unfamiliar method. Hitherto Ben Jonson had been the one example and theoretical master of all popular comedy. The great aim had been to hold some extravagance of character up to ridicule, to torture one monstrous ineptitude a thousand ways, to exhaust the capabilities of the language in fantastic quips and humours. The comedian had been bound to be in some sort a moralist, to lash himself into an ethical rage about something, and to work by a process of evolution rather than by passionless observation of external manners. Under such a system wit might flourish, but there was no room for humour, in the modern acceptation of the word, for humor takes things quietly, watches unobtrusively, and is at heart sublimely indifferent. Now, the Royalists had come home from exile weary of all moral discussion, apt to let life slip, longing above all things for rest and pleasure and a quiet hour. It was a happy instinct that led Etheredge to improve a little on Molière himself, and simply hold up the mirror of his play to the genial, sensual life of the young gentlemen his contemporaries. The new-found motto of French comedy, *castigat ridendo mores,* would have lain too heavy on English shoulders, the time of castigation was over, and life flowed merrily down to the deluge of the Revolution. The master of Dufoy, Sir Frederick Frollick, is not a type, but a portrait; and each lazy, periwigged fop in the pit clapped hands to welcome a friend that seemed to have just strolled from the Mulberry Garden. He is a man of quality, who can fight at need with great spirit and firmness of nerve, but whose customary occupation is the pursuit of pleasure without dignity and without reflection. Like all Etheredge's fine gentlemen, he is a finished fop, although he has the affectation of not caring for the society of fine ladies. He spends hours at his toilet, and "there never was a girl more humorsome nor tedious in the dressing of her baby." It seems to me certain that Etheredge intended Sir Frederick as a portrait of himself. Dufoy gives an amusing account of his being taken into Sir Frederick's service. He was lounging on the new bridge in Paris, watching the marionettes and eating custard, when young M. de Grandville drove by in his chariot, in company with his friend, Sir Fred. Frollick, and recommended Dufoy as a likely fellow to be entrusted with some delicate business, which he carried out so well, that Sir Frederick made him his valet. *The Comical Revenge* is a series of brisk and entertaining scenes strung on a very light thread of plot. Sir Frederick plays fast and loose, all through, with a rich widow who wants to marry him; a person called Wheedle, with an accomplice, Palmer, who dresses up to personate a Buckinghamshire drover, plays off the confidence-trick on a stupid knight, Sir Nicholas Cully, quite in the approved manner of to-day. This pastime, called "coney-catching" a century earlier, was by this time revived under the title of "bubbling." By a pleasant amenity of the printer's the rogues say to one another, "Expect your Kew," meaning "cue." Meanwhile high love affairs, jealousies, and a tremendous duel, interrupted by the treachery of Puritan villains, have occupied the heroic scenes. The comedy grows fast and furious; Sir Nicholas rides to visit the widow on a tavern-boy's back, with three bottles of wine suspended on a cord behind him. Sir Frederick frightens the widow by pretending to be dead, and Dufoy, for being troublesome and spiteful, is confined by his fellow-servants in a tub, with his head and hands, stuck out of holes, and stumbles up and down the stage in that disguise. A brief extract will give a notion of the sprightly and picturesque manner of the dialogue. A lady has sent her maid to Sir Frederick's lodgings to capitulate with him on his boisterousness.

BEAUFORT.

Jenny in tears! what's the occasion, poor girl?

MAID.

I'll tell you, my Lord.

SIR FRED.

Buzz! Set not her tongue a-going again; she has made more noise than half a dozen paper-mills; London Bridge at low water is silence to her; in a word, rambling last night, we knocked at her mistress's lodging, they denied us entrance, whereat a harsh word or two flew out.

MAID.

These were not all your heroic actions; pray tell the consequences, how you marched bravely at the rear of an army of link-boys; upon the sudden, how you gave defiance, and then, having waged a bloody war with the constable, and having vanquished that dreadful enemy, how you committed a general massacre on the glass windows. Are not these most honourable achievements, such as will be registered to your eternal fame by the most learned historian of Hicks's Hall?

Sᴉʀ Fʀᴇᴅ.

Good, sweet Jenny, let's come to a treaty; do but hear what articles I propose.

The success of **The Comical Revenge** was unprecedented, and it secured its author an instant popularity. While it was under rehearsal, it attracted the attention of the young Lord Buckhurst, then distinguished only as a Parliamentary man of promise, but soon to become famous as the poet Earl of Dorset. To him Etheredge dedicated his play, and by him was introduced to that circle of wits, Buckingham, Sedley, and the precocious Rochester, with whom he was to be associated for the rest of his life.

Four years later he produced another and a better play. Meanwhile English comedy had made great advances. Dryden and Wilson had proceeded; Sedley, Shadwell, the Howards, had made their first appearance; but none of these, not even the author of *The Mulberry Garden,* had quite understood the nature of Etheredge's innovation. In **She Would if She Could** he showed them more plainly what he meant, for he had himself come under the influence of a masterpiece of comedy. It is certain to me that the movement of **She Would if She Could** is founded upon a reminiscence of *Tartuffe,* which, however, was not printed until 1669, "une comedie dont on a fait beaucoup de bruit, qui a esté longtemps persecutée." Etheredge may have been present at the original performance of the first three acts, at Versailles, in May 1664; but it seems to me more probable that he saw the public representation at Paris in the summer of 1667, and that he hastened back to England with the plot of his own piece taking form in his brain. The only similarity between the French and English plays is this, that Lady Cockwood is a female Tartuffe, a woman of loud religious pretensions, who demands respect and devotion for her piety, and who is really engaged, all the time, in the vain prosecution of a disgraceful intrigue. Sir Oliver Cockwood, a boisterous, elderly knight, has come up to town for the season, in company with his pious lady, who leads him a sad life, with an old friend, Sir Jocelyn Jolly, and with the wards of the latter, two spirited girls called Ariana and Gatty. These people have taken lodgings in St. James's Street, at the "Black Posts," as Mrs. Sentry, the maid, takes pains to inform young Mr. Courtall, a gentleman of fashion in whom Lady Cockwood takes an interest less ingenuous than she pretends. The scene, therefore, instead of being laid in Arcadia or Cockayne, sets us down in the heart of the West End, the fashionable quarter of the London of 1668. The reader who has not studied old maps, or the agreeable books of Mr. Wheatley, is likely to be extremely ill-informed as to the limits and scope of the town two hundred years ago. St. James's Street, which contained all the most genteel

houses, ran, a sort of rural road, from Portugal Street, or Piccadilly, down to St. James's Park. One of Charles II.'s first acts was to beautify this district. St. James's Park, which then included Green Park, had been a sort of open meadow. The King cut a canal through it, planted it with lime-trees, and turned the path that led through St. James's Fields into a drive called Pall Mall. In St. James's Street rank and fashion clustered, and young poets contended for the honour of an invitation to Mr. Waller's house on the west side. Here also the country gentry lodged when they came up to town, and a few smart shops had recently been opened to supply the needs of people of quality.

Such was the bright scene of that comedy of fashionable life of which **She Would if She Could** gives us a faithful picture. In a town still untainted by smoke and dirt, with fresh country airs blowing over it from all quarters but the east, the gay world of Charles II.'s court ran through its bright ephemeral existence. There is no drama in which the physical surroundings of this life are so picturesquely brought before us as that of Etheredge. The play at present under discussion distinguishes itself from the comic work of Dryden, or Wycherley, or Shadwell, even from that of Congreve, by the little graphic touches, the intimate impression, the clear, bright colour of the scenes. The two girls, Sir Jocelyn's wards, finding life dreary with Lady Cockwood and her pieties, put on vizards, and range the Parks and the Mall without a *chaperon.* This is an artful contrivance, often afterwards imitated—as notably by Lord Lansdowne in his *She Gallants*—but original to Etheredge, and very happy, from the opportunity it gives of drawing out *naïve* remarks on familiar things; for in the second act the girls find their way to the Mulberry Garden, a public place of entertainment, adjoining Lord Arlington's mansion of Goring House, afterwards Buckingham Palace, and much frequented by a public whom Cromwell's sense of propriety had deprived of their favourite Spring Garden. Here Ariana and Gatty meet Lady Cockwood's recalcitrant spark Courtall, walking with his friend Freeman, and from behind their masks carry on with them a hazardous flirtation. The end of this scene, when the two sprightly girls break from their gallants and appear and reappear, crossing the stage from opposite corners, amid scenery that reminded every one in the theatre of the haunt most loved by Londoners, must have been particularly delightful and diverting to witness; and all these are circumstances which we must bear in mind if we wish the drama of the Restoration to be a living thing to us in reading it. It was a mundane entertainment, but in its earthly sincerity it superseded something that had ceased to be either human or divine.

The two old knights are "harp and violin—nature has tuned them to play the fool in concert," and their extravagances hurry the plot to its crisis. They swagger to their own confusion, and Lady Cockwood encourages their folly, that she herself may have an opportunity of meeting Courtall. She contrives to give him an appointment in the New Exchange, which seems to have been a sort of arcade leading out of the Strand, with shops on each side. When the curtain rises for the third act, Mrs. Trinkett is sitting in the door of her shop inviting the people of quality to step in: "What d'ye buy? What d'ye lack, gentlemen? Gloves, ribbands, and essences? ribbands, gloves, and essences?" She is a woman of tact, who, under the pretence of selling "a few fashionable toys to keep the ladies in countenance at a play or in the park," passes letters or makes up rendezvous between people of quality. At her shop the gallants "scent their eyebrows and periwigs with a little essence of oranges or jessamine"; and so Courtall occupies himself till Lady Cockwood arrives. Fortunately for him, Ariana and Gatty, who are out shopping, arrive at the same moment; so he proposes to take them all in his coach to the "Bear" in Drury Lane for a dance. The party at the "Bear" is like a scene from some artistically mounted drama of our own day. Etheredge, with his singular eye for colour, crowds the stage with damsels in sky-blue, and pink, and flamecoloured taffetas. To them arrive Sir Oliver and Sir Jocelyn; but as Sir Oliver was drunk overnight, Lady Cockwood has locked up all his clothes, except his russet suit of humiliation, in which he is an object of ridicule and persecution to all the bright crowd who—

> Wave the gay wreathe, and titter as they prance.

In this scene Etheredge introduces a sword, a velvet coat, a flageolet, a pair of bands, with touches that remind one of Metzu or Gheraerdt Douw. Sir Oliver, who is the direct prototype of Vanbrugh's Sir John Brute, gets very drunk, dances with his own wife in her vizard, and finally brings confusion upon the whole company. The ladies rush home, whither Freeman comes to console Lady Cockwood; a noise is heard; and he is promptly concealed in a cupboard. Courtall enters, and then a fresh hubbub is heard, for Sir Oliver has returned. Courtall is hurried under a table just in time for the old knight to come in and perceive nothing. But he has brought a beautiful china orange home to appease his wife, and as he shows this to her it drops from his fingers, and runs under the table where Courtall lies. The maid, a girl of resource, promptly runs away with the candle, and, in the stage darkness, Courtall is hurried into the cupboard, where he finds Freeman. The threads are gradually unravelled: Courtall and Freeman are rewarded, for nothing in particular, by the hands of Ariana and Gatty, and Lady Cockwood promises to go back to the country and behave properly ever after. The plot of so slight a thing is a gossamer fabric, and scarcely bears analysis; but the comedy was by far the most sprightly performance at that time presented to any audience in Europe save that which was listening to Molière.

Etheredge had not dedicated **She Would if She Could** to any patron; but the grateful town accepted it with enthusiasm, and its author was the most popular of the hour. It was confidently hoped that he would give his energies to the stage; but an indolence that was habitual to him, and against which he never struggled, kept him silent for eight years. During this time, however, he preserved his connection with the theatres, encouraged Medbourne the actor to translate *Tartuffe,* and wrote an epilogue for

him when that play was first produced in England in 1670. He wrote, besides, a great number of little amatory pieces, chiefly in octosyllabics, which have never been collected. Oldys says, in one of his MS. notes, that he once saw a *Miscellany,* printed in 1672, almost full of verses by Etheredge, but without his name. I have not been able to trace this; but most of the numerous collections of contemporary verse contained something of his, down to the *Miscellany* of 1701. If anyone took the trouble to extract these, at least fifty or sixty poems could be put together; but they are none of them very good. Etheredge had but little of the lyrical gift of such contemporaries as Dryden, Rochester, and Sedley; his rhymed verse is apt to be awkward and languid. This may be as good an opportunity as any other of quoting the best song of his that I have been able to unearth:—

> Ye happy swains, whose hearts are free
> From love's imperial chain,
> Take warning and be taught by me
> To avoid th' enchanting pain;
> Fatal the wolves to trembling flocks,
> Fierce winds to blossoms prove,
> To careless seamen, hidden rocks,
> To human quiet—love.
>
> Fly the fair sex, if bliss you prize—
> The snake's beneath the flower;
> Who ever gazed on beauteous eyes
> And tasted quiet more?
> How faithless is the lovers' joy!
> How constant is their care!
> The kind with falsehood do destroy,
> The cruel with despair.

We learn from Shadwell, in the preface to *The Humorists* of 1671, that the success of **She Would if She Could** was endangered by the slovenly playing of the actors. This may have helped to disgust the fastidious Etheredge. At all events, the satirists began to be busy with the name of so inert a popular playwright; and, in 1675, Rochester expressed a general opinion in the doggerel of his *Session of the Poets:*—

> Now Apollo had got gentle George in his eye,
> And frankly confessed that, of all men that writ,
> There's none had more fancy, sense, judgment, and wit;
> But i' the crying sin, idleness, he was so hardened
> That his long seven years' silence was not to be pardoned.

"Gentle George" gave way, and composed, with all the sparkle, wit, and finish of which he was capable, his last and best-known piece, *The Man of Mode, or Sir Fopling Flutter,* brought out at the Duke's Theatre in the summer of 1676. Recollecting his threatened fiasco in 1668, Etheredge determined to put himself under powerful patronage, and dedicated his new play to Mary of Modena, the young Duchess of York, who remained his faithful patroness until fortune bereft her of the power to give. Sir Car Scroope wrote the prologue, Dryden the epilogue, and the play was acted by the best company of the time—Betterton, Harris,

Medbourn, and the wife of Shadwell, while the part of Belinda was in all probability taken by the matchless Mrs. Barry, the new glory of the stage.

The great merit of **The Man of Mode** rests in the brilliance of the writing and the force of the characterisation. There is no plot. People of the old school, like Captain Alexander Radcliffe, who liked plot above all other things in a comedy, decried the manner of Etheredge, and preferred to it "the manly art of brawny Wycherley," the new writer, whose *Country Wife* had just enjoyed so much success; but, on the whole, the public was dazzled and delighted with the new types and the brisk dialogue, and united to give Sir Fopling Flutter a warmer welcome than greeted any other stage-hero during Charles II.'s reign. There was a delightful heroine, with abundance of light brown hair, and lips like the petals of "a Provence rose, fresh on the bush, ere the morning sun has quite drawn up the dew;" there was a shoemaker whom everyone knew, and an orange-woman whom everybody might have known—characters which Dickens would have laughed at and commended; there was Young Bellair, in which Etheredge drew his own portrait; there was the sparkling Dorimant, so dressed that all the pit should know that my Lord Rochester was intended; there was Medley, Young Bellair's bosom friend, in whom the gossips discovered the portrait of Sir Charles Sedley; above all, there was Sir Fopling Flutter, the monarch of all beaux and dandies, the froth of Parisian affectation—a delightful personage, almost as alive to us to-day as to the enchanted audience of 1676. During two acts the great creature was spoken of, but never seen. Just arrived from France, all the world had heard about him, and was longing to see him, "with a pair of gloves up to his elbows, and his periwig more exactly curled than a lady's head newly dressed for a ball." At last, in the third act, when curiosity has been raised to a fever, the fop appears. He is introduced to a group of ladies and gentlemen of quality, and when the first civilities are over he begins at once to criticise their dress:—

LADY TOWNLEY.

Wit, I perceive, has more power over you than beauty, Sir Fopling, else you would not have let this lady stand so long neglected.

SIR FOPLING

(*to Emilia*). A thousand pardons, Madam! Some civilities due of course upon the meeting a long absent friend. The *éclat* of so much beauty, I confess, ought to have charmed me sooner.

EMILIA.

The *brilliant* of so much good language, sir, has much more power than the little beauty I can boast.

SIR FOPLING.

I never saw anything prettier than this high work on your *point d'Espagne*.

EMILIA.

'Tis not so rich as *point de Venise*.

SIR FOP.

Not altogether, but looks cooler, and is more proper for the season. Dorimant, is not that Medley?

DORI.

The same, sir.

SIR FOP.

Forgive me, sir, in this *embarras* of civilities, I could not come to have you in my arms sooner. You understand an equipage the best of any man in town, I hear!

MEDLEY.

By my own you would not guess it.

SIR FOP.

There are critics who do not write, sir. Have you taken notice of the *calèche* I brought over?

MEDLEY.

O yes! it has quite another air than the English make.

SIR FOP.

'Tis as easily known from an English tumbrel as an inns-of-court man is from one of us.

DORI.

Truly there is a *bel-air* in *calèches* as well as men.

MEDLEY.

But there are few so delicate as to observe it.

SIR FOP.

The world is generally very *grossier* here indeed.

LADY TOWNLEY.

He's very fine (*looking at Sir Fop*).

EMILIA.

Extreme proper.

SIR FOP.

O, a slight suit I had made to appear in at my first arrival—not worthy your admiration, ladies.

DORI.

The pantaloon is very well mounted.

SIR FOP.

The tassels are new and pretty.

MEDLEY.

I never saw a coat better cut.

SIR FOP.

It makes me look long-waisted, and, I think, slender.

LADY TOWNLEY.

His gloves are well-fingered, large, and graceful.

SIR FOP.

I was always eminent for being *bien-ganté.*

EMILIA.

He must wear nothing but what are originals of the most famous hands in Paris!

SIR FOP.

You are in the right, Madam.

LADY TOWNLEY.

The suit?

SIR FOP.

Barroy.

EMILIA.

The garniture?

SIR FOP.

Le Gras.

MEDLEY.

The shoes?

SIR FOP.

Piccat.

DORI.

The periwig?

SIR FOP.

Chedreux.

LADY TOWNLEY AND EMILIA

(*together*). The gloves?

SIR FOP.

Orangerie (*holding up his hands to them*). You know the smell, ladies?

The hand that throws in these light touches, in a key of rose-colour on pale gray, no longer reminds us of Molière, but exceedingly of Congreve. A recent critic has very justly remarked that in mere wit, the continuity of brilliant dialogue in which the action does not seek to advance, Moliere is scarcely the equal of Congreve at his best, and the brightest scenes of **The Man of Mode** show the original direction taken by Etheredge in that line which was more specially to mark the triumph of English comedy. But the author of *Love for Love* was still in the nursery when **The Man of Mode** appeared, as it were, to teach him how to write. Until Congreve reached manhood, Etheredge's example seemed to have been lost, and the lesson he at-

tempted to instil to have fallen on admiring hearers that were incapable of repeating it. The shallowness, vivacity, and vanity of Sir Fopling are admirably maintained. In the scene of which part has just been quoted, after showing his intimate knowledge of all the best tradesmen in Paris, some one drops the name of Bussy, to see if he is equally at home among literary notabilities. But he supposes that Bussy d'Ambois is meant, and is convicted of having never heard of Bussy Rabutin. This is a curiously early notice of a famous writer who survived it nearly twenty years; it does not seem that any French critic has observed this. Sir Fopling Flutter is so eminently the best of Etheredge's creations that we are tempted to give one more sample of his quality. He has come with two or three other sparks to visit Dorimant at his rooms, and he dances a *pas seul.*

YOUNG BELLAIR.

See! Sir Fopling is dancing!

SIR FOP.

Prithee, Dorimant, why hast thou not a glass hung up here? A room is the dullest thing without one.

Y. BELL.

Here is company to entertain you.

SIR FOP.

But I mean in case of being alone. In a glass a man may entertain himself,———

DORI.

The shadow of himself indeed.

SIR FOP.

Correct the errors of his motion and his dress.

MEDLEY.

I find, Sir Fopling, in your solitude you remember the saying of the wise man, and study yourself!

SIR FOP.

'Tis the best diversion in our retirements. Dorimant, thou art a pretty fellow, and wearest thy clothes well, but I never saw thee have a handsome cravat. Were they made up like mine, they'd give another air to thy face. Prithee let me send my man to dress thee one day. By heavens, an Englishman cannot tie a ribband.

DORI.

They are something clumsy fisted.

SIR FOP.

I have brought over the prettiest fellow that ever spread a toilet, he served some time under Merille, the greatest *génie* in the world for a *valet de chambre.*

DORI.

What, he who formerly belonged to the Duke of Candolle?

SIR FOP.

The very same—and got him his immortal reputation.

DORI.

You've a very fine brandenburgh on, Sir Fopling!

SIR FOP.

It serves to wrap me up after the fatigue of a ball.

MEDLEY.

I see you often in it, with your periwig tied up.

SIR FOP.

We should not always be in a set dress; 'tis more *en cavalier* to appear now and then in a *deshabille*.

In these wholly fantastical studies of manners we feel less than in the more serious portions of the comedy the total absence of moral purpose, high aim, or even honourable instinct which was the canker of the age. A negligence that pervaded every section of the upper classes, which robbed statesmen of their patriotism and the clergy of their earnestness, was only too exactly mirrored in the sprightly follies of the stage. Yet even there we are annoyed by a heroine who is discovered eating a nectarine, and who, rallied on buying a "filthy nosegay," indignantly rebuts the accusation, and declares that nothing would induce her to smell such vulgar flowers as stocks and carnations, or anything that blossoms, except orange-flowers and tuberose. It is a frivolous world, Strephon bending on one knee to Cloe, who fans the pink blush on her painted cheek, while Momus peeps, with a grin, through the curtains behind her. They form an engaging trio, *mais ce n'est pas la vie humaine*.

The Man of Mode was licensed on June 3, 1676; it enjoyed an unparalleled success, and before the month was out its author was flying for his life. We learn this from the Hatton Correspondence, first printed in 1879. It seems that in the middle of June, Etheredge, Rochester, and two friends, Captain Bridges and Mr. Downes, went down to Epsom on a Sunday night. They were tossing some fiddlers in a blanket for refusing to play, when a barber, who came to see what the noise was, as a practical joke, induced them to knock up the constable. They did so with a vengeance, for they smashed open his door, entered his house, and broke his head, giving him a severe beating. At last they were overpowered by the watch, and Etheredge having made a submissive oration, the row seemed to be at an end, when suddenly Lord Rochester, like a coward as he was, drew his sword on the constable, who had dismissed his men. The constable shrieked out "Murder!" and the watch returning, one of them broke the skull of Downes with his staff. The others ran away, and the watchmen were left to run poor Downes through with a pike. He lingered until the 29th, when Charles Hatton records that he is dead, and that Etheredge and Rochester have absconded. Four years afterwards the Hatton Correspondence gives us another glimpse of our poet, again in

trouble. On January 14, 1680, the roof of the tennis-court in the Haymarket fell down. "Sir George Etheridge and several others were very dangerously hurt. Sir Charles Sidley had his skull broke, and it is thought it will be mortal." Sidley, or Sedley, flourished for twenty years more; but we may note that here, for the first time, our dramatist is "Sir George." It is evident that he had been knighted since 1676, when he was plain "George Etheredge, Esq." In an MS. poem called *The Present State of Matrimony,* he is accused of having married a rich widow to facilitate his being knighted, and with success. The entries in ***The Letterbook*** give me reason to believe that he was not maligned in this. But he seems to have lived on very bad terms with his wife, and to have disgraced himself by the open protection of Mrs. Barry, after Rochester's death in 1680. By this famous actress, whose name can no more be omitted from the history of literature than that of Mrs. Gwynn from the history of statecraft, he had a daughter, on whom he settled five or six thousand pounds, but who died young.

The close of Etheredge's career was spent in the diplomatic service. When this commenced is more than I have been able to discover. From ***The Letterbook*** it appears that he was for some time envoy of Charles II. at the Hague. It would even seem that he was sent to Constantinople, for a contemporary satirist speaks of

Ovid to Pontus sent for too much wit,
Etheredge to Turkey for the want of it.

Certain expressions in ***The Letterbook*** make me suspect that he had been in Sweden. But it is not until the accession of James II. that his figure comes out into real distinctness. In this connection I think it would be hard to exaggerate the value of ***The Letterbook,*** which I am about to introduce to my readers. After reading it from end to end I feel that I know Sir George Etheredge, hitherto the most phantasmal of the English poets, better than I can know any literary man of his time, better than Dryden, better, perhaps, than Milton.

In February 1685 James II. ascended the throne, and by March, Mary of Modena had worked so assiduously for her favourite that this warrant, for the discovery of which I owe my best thanks to Mr. Noel Sainsbury, was entered in the Privy Signet Book:—

Warrant to pay Sir Geo. Etheredge (whom his Maj. has thought fit to employ in his service in Germany), 3*l.* per diem.

On March 5 ***The Letterbook*** was bought, and Etheredge and his secretary started for the Continent. Why they loitered at the Hague and in Amsterdam does not appear, but their journey was made in so leisurely a manner that they did not arrive in Ratisbon until August 30. It does appear, however, that the dissipated little knight behaved very ill in Holland, and spent one summer's night dead drunk in the streets of the Hague. On his arrival at Ratisbon, he had two letters of recommendation, one from Barillon to the French ambassador, the other from the Spanish ambassador to the Burgundian minister. The first of these he used at once, and cultivated the society at the French Embassy in a way that would have been extremely impolitic if it had not, without doubt, been entered upon in accordance with instructions from home. It was doubtless known to Etheredge, although a secret at the German court, that James had commenced his reign by opening private negotiations with France. The poet settled in a very nice house, with a garden running down to the Danube, set up a carriage and good horses, valets, and "a cook, though I cannot hope to be well-served by the latter" in this barbarous Germany. On December 24 he wrote two letters, parts of which may be quoted here. To Lord Sunderland he writes:—

> Since my coming here I have had a little fever, which has been the reason I have not paid my duty so regular as I ought to do to your Lordship. I am now pretty well recovered, and hope I am quit at a reasonable price for what I was to pay on the change of climate, and a greater change in my manner of living. Is it not enough to breed an ill habit of body in a man who was used to sit up till morning to be forced, for want of knowing what to do with himself, to go to bed in the evening; one who has been used to live with all freedom, never to approach anyone without ceremony; one who has been used to run up and down to find variety of company, to sit at home and entertain himself in solitude? One would think the Diet had made a *Reichsgut-achten* to banish all pastimes in the city. Here was the Countess of Nostitz, but malice would not let her live in quiet, and she is lately removed to Prague. Good company met at her house, and she had a little *hombre* to entertain them. A more commode lady, by what I hear, never kept a basset [table] in London. If I do well after all this, you must allow me to be a great philosopher; and I dare affirm Cato left not the world with more firmness of soul than I did England.

And to a friend in Paris, on the same date:—

> Le divertissement le plus galant du pays cet hiver c'est le traîneau, où l'on se met en croupe de quelque belle Allemande, de manière que vous ne pouvez ni la voir, ni lui parler, à cause d'un diable de tintamarre des sonnettes dont les harnais sont tous garnis.

In short, he very soon learned the limitations of the place. His letters are filled with complaints of the boorish manners of the people, the dreary etiquette which encumbers the Court and the Diet, and the solitude he feels in being separated from all his literary friends. The malice of the secretary informs us that Sir George soon gave up his precise manner of living, and adopted a lazier style. He seldom rose until two or three P.M., dined at five or six, and then went to the French ambassador's for three or four hours. Finding time hang heavy on his hands, he took to gaming with any disreputable Frenchman that happened to pass through the town. Already, early in 1686, a scoundrel called Purpurat, from Vienna, has got round him by flatteries and presents of tobacco, and has robbed him of 10,000 crowns at cards. When, however, things have come to this pass, Etheredge wakes up, and on the suggestion of M. Purpurat, that he will be going back to Vienna, detains him until he has won nearly all his money back again, and finally escapes with the loss of a pair of pistols, with his crest upon them, which Purpurat shows in proof of his ascendency over the English ambassador.

These matters occupy the spring and summer of 1686, but there is nothing said about them in the letters home. These letters, however, are cheerful enough. In January he encloses, with his dispatches to the Earl of Middleton, a long squib in octosyllabic verse, which the English minister, who is ill at these numbers, gets Dryden to answer in kind. A cancelled couplet in the first draft of the former remarks:—

> Let them who live in plenty flout;
> I must make shift with sour kraut.

In June 1686 he writes to Middleton that he has "not this week received any letter from England, which is a thing that touches me here as nearly as ever a disappointment did in London with the woman I loved most tenderly." Middleton comforts him by telling him that the king, after a performance of *The Man of Mode,* remarked to him that he expected Etheredge to put on the sock, and write a new comedy while he was at Ratisbon. Once or twice, in subsequent letters, the poet refers to this idea; but the weight of affairs, combined with his native indolence, prevented his attempting the task. Meanwhile, he does not seem to have neglected his duty, as it was understood in those days. He writes, so he says at least, twice every week about state matters to Middleton, and, notwithstanding all the spiteful messages sent home about him, he does not seem to have ever lost the confidence of James and his ministers. These latter were most of them his private friends, and in his most official communications he suddenly diverges into some waggish allusion to old times. His attitude at Ratisbon was not what we should now demand from an envoy. The English people, the English Parliament, do not exist for him; his one standard of duty is the personal wish of the king. By indulging the bias of James, which indeed was his own bias, an excessive partiality for all things French, he won himself, as we shall see, the extreme ill-will of the Germans. But the only really serious scrape into which he got, an affair which annoyed him throughout the autumn and winter of 1686, does not particularly redound to his discredit. It is a curious story, and characteristic of the times; *The Letterbook,* by giving Etheredge's own account, and also the secretary's spiteful rendering, enables us to follow the circumstances pretty closely. A troop of actors from Nuremburg came over to Ratisbon in the summer of 1686, with a star who seems to have been the leading actress of her time in South Germany. This lady, about whom the only biographical fact that we discover is that her Christian name was Julia, seems to have been respectability itself. Even the enemies of Etheredge did not suggest that any immoral connection existed between them, and on the last day of the year, after having suffered all sorts of annoyance on her behalf, he still complains that she is as *fière* as she is fair. But actors were then still looked upon in Germany, as to some extent even in France, as social pariahs, vagabonds whom it was disgraceful to know, except as servants of a high order; artistic menials, whose vocation it was to amuse the great. But England was already more civilised than this; Etheredge was used to meet Betterton and his stately wife at the court of his monarch, and even the sullied reputation of such lovely sinners as Mrs. Barry did not shut them out of Whitehall. Etheredge, therefore, charmed in his Abdera of letters by the art and wit and beauty of Julia, paid her a state visit in his coach, and prayed for the honour of a visit in return. Ratisbon was beside itself with indignation. Every sort of social insult was heaped upon the English envoy. At a fête champêtre the lubberly Germans crowded out their elbows so as to leave him no place at table; the grand ladies cut him in the street when their coaches met his, and it was made a subject of venomous report to England that, in spite of public opinion, he refused to quit the acquaintance of the *comédienne*, as they scornfully named her. At last, on the evening of November 25, a group of students and young people of quality, who had heard that Julia was dining with the English ambassador to meet the French envoy and one or two guests, surrounded Etheredge's house in masks, threw stones at the windows, shouted "Great is Diana of the English envoy!" and, on Etheredge's appearing, roared to him to throw out to them the *comédienne*. The plucky little poet answered by arming his lacqueys and his maids with sword-sticks, pokers, and whatever came to hand, and by suddenly charging the crowd at the head of his little garrison. The Germans were routed for a moment, and Etheredge took advantage of his success to put Julia into his coach, jump in beside her, and conduct her to her lodging. The crowd, however, was too powerful for him; and though she slept that night in safety, next day she was thrown into prison by the magistrates, for causing a disturbance in the streets.

Etheredge, not knowing what to do, wrote this epistle to the ring-leader of the attack on his house, the Baron von Sensheim:—

> J'estois surpris d'apprendre que ce joly gentil-homme travesty en Italien hier au soir estoit le Baron de Sensheim. Je ne savois pas que les honnetes gens se mêloient avec des lacquais ramassez pour faire les fanfarons, et les batteurs de pavéz. Si vous avez quelque chose à me dire, faites le moy savoir comme vous devez, et ne vous amusez plus à venir insulter mes Domestiques ni ma maison, soyez content que vous l'avez échappé belle et ne retournez plus chercher les récompences de telles follies pour vos beaux compagnons. J'ay des autres mesures à prendre avec eux.

To this he received a vague and impertinent reply in German. Opinion in the town was so strongly moved, that for some time Etheredge never went out without having a musketoon in his coach, and each of his footmen armed with a brace of pistols ready charged. Eventually the lady was released, on the understanding that she and her company should leave the town, which they did, proceed-

ing in the last days of 1686 across the Danube to Bayrischenhoff, where Etheredge visited them. It was in the midst of this turmoil that Etheredge composed some of his best occasional verses. I do not think they have ever been printed before:—

> Upon the downs when shall I breathe at ease,
> Have nothing else to do but what I please,
> In a fresh cooling shade upon the brink
> Of Arden's spring, have time to read and think,
> And stretch, and sleep, when all my care shall be
> For health, and pleasure my philosophy?
> When shall I rest from business, noise, and strife,
> Lay down the soldier's and the courtier's life,
> And in a little melancholy seat
> Begin at last to live and to forget
> The nonsense and the farce of what the fools call
>   great.

There is something strangely Augustan about this fragment; we should expect it to be dated 1716 rather than 1686, and to be signed by some Pomfret or Tickell of the school of Addison.

On New Year's Day, 1687, he encloses in a letter to the Earl of Middleton a French song, inspired by Julia, which may deserve to be printed as a curiosity. I give it in the author's spelling, which shone more in French than English:—

> Garde le secret de ton ame,
>   Et ne te laisse pas flatter,
> Qu'Iris espargnera ta flamme,
>   Si tu luy permets d'éclater;
> Son humeur, à l'amour rebelle,
>   Exile tous ses doux desirs,
> Et la tendresse est criminelle
>   Qui veut luy parler en soupirs.
>
> Puis que tu vis sous son empire,
>   Il faut luy cacher ton destin,
> Si tu ne veux le rendre pire
>   Percé du trait de son dédain;
> D'une rigeur si delicate
>   Ton cœur ne peut rien esperer,
> Derobe donc à cette ingrate
>   La vanité d'en trionfer.

In February a change of ministry in London gives him something else to think about; he hears a report that he is to be sent to Stockholm; he writes eagerly to his patrons for news. On the eleventh of the month he receives a tremendous snub from the treasury about his extravagance, and is told that in future his extra expenses must never exceed fifty pounds every three months. He is, indeed, assailed with many annoyances, for his wife writes on the subject of the *comédienne* from Nuremburg, and roundly calls him a rogue. Upon this Etheredge writes to the poet, Lord Mulgrave, and begs him to make up the quarrel, sending by the same post, on March 13, 1687, this judicious letter to Lady Etheredge:—

> My Lady,
>
> I beg your pardon for undertaking to advise you. I am so well satisfied by your last letter of your prudence

and judgment that I shall never more commit the same error. I wish there were copies of it in London that it might serve as a pattern to modest wives to write to their husbands; you shall find me so careful hereafter how I offend you that I will no more subscribe myself your loving, since you take it ill, but,

> Madam,
>
> Y^r. most dutyfull husband,
>
> G. E.

His letters of 1687 are very full of personal items and scraps of literary gossip. It would be impossible on this, the first introduction of **The Letterbook,** to do justice to all its wealth of allusion. He carefully repeats the harangue of the Siamese ambassadors on leaving the German court; he complains again and again of the neglect of the Count of Windisgrätz, who represents the Prince of Nassau, and is all powerful in the Palatinate; he complains still more bitterly of the open rudeness of the Countess Windisgrätz; he is anxious about the welfare of Nat Lee, at that time shut up in a lunatic asylum, but about to emerge for the production of *The Princess of Cleve,* in 1689, and then to die; he writes a delightful letter to Betterton, on May 26, 1687, asking for news of all kinds about the stage. He says that his chief diversion is music, that he has three musicians living in the house, that they play all the best operas, and that a friend in Paris sends him whatever good music is published. One wonders whether Etheredge knew that Jean Baptiste Lully had died a week or two before this letter was written. News of the success of Sedley's *Bellamira* reaches him in June 1687, and provokes from him this eloquent defence of his old friend's genius:—

> I am glad the town has so good a taste as to give the same just applause to S^r. Charles Sidley's writing which his friends have always done to his conversation. Few of our plays can boast of more wit than I have heard him speak at a supper. Some barren sparks have found fault with what he has formerly done, only because the fairness of the soil has produced so big a crop. I daily drink his health, my Lord Dorset's, your own, and all our friends'.

A few allusions to famous men of letters, all made in 1687, may be placed side by side:—

> Mr. Wynne has sent me *The Hind and the Panther,* by which I find John Dryden has a noble ambition to restore poetry to its ancient dignity in wrapping up the mysteries of religion in verse. What a shame it is to me to see him a saint, and remain still the same devil [myself].

> Dryden finds his *Macfleknoe* does no good: I wish him better success with his *Hind and Panther.*

> General Dryden is an expert captain, but I always thought him fitter for execution than council.

> Remind my Lord Dorset how he and I carried two draggled-tailed nymphs one bitter frosty night over the Thames to Lambeth.

> If he happens in a house with Mr. Crown, John's songs will charm the whole family.

A letter from Dryden, full of pleasant chat, informs Etheredge in February that Wycherley is sick of an apoplexy. The envoy begs leave, later in the year, to visit his friend, the Count de Thun, whose acquaintance he made in Amsterdam, and who is now at Munich, but permission is refused. In October the whole Electoral College invites itself to spend the afternoon in Sir George Etheredge's garden, who entertains them so lavishly, and with so little infusion of Danube water in the wine, that next morning he is ill in bed. His indisposition turns to tertian ague, and towards the end of the month he asks to be informed how quinine should be prepared. He compares himself philosophically to Falstaff, however, and by Christmas time grows pensive at the thought of the "plum-pottage" at home, and is solicitous about a black-laced hood and pair of scarlet stockings which he has ordered from London. In January 1688 he laments that Sedley has grown temperate and Dorset uxorious, but vows that he will be on his guard, and remain foppish. The last extract that has any literary interest is taken from a letter dated March 8, 1688:—

> Mrs. Barry bears up as well as I myself have done; my poor Lord Rochester [Wilmot, not Hyde] could not weather the Cape, and live under the Line fatal to puling constitutions. Though I have given up writing plays, I should be glad to read a good one, wherefore pray let Will Richards send me Mr Shadwell's [*The Squire of Alsatia*] as soon as it is printed, that I may know what is being done. . . . Nature, you know, intended me for an idle fellow, and gave me passions and qualities fit for that blessed calling, but fortune has made a changeling of me, and necessity now forces me to set up for a fop of business.

Three days after this he writes the last letter preserved in **The Letterbook,** and, but for an appendix to that volume, we might have believed the popular story that Etheredge fell down stairs at Ratisbon and broke his neck. But the treacherous secretary continues to write in 1689, and gives us fresh particulars. He states that his quarrel with Sir George was that he had been promised 60*l.* per annum, and could only get 40*l.* out of his master. He further declares that to the last Etheredge did not know ten words of Dutch (German), and had not merely to make use of a French interpreter, but had to entrust his private business to one or other of his lacqueys; and that moreover he spent a great part of his time "visiting all the alehouses of the town, accompanied by his servants, his *valet de chambre,* his hoffmaster, and his dancing and fighting master, all with their coats turned inside outwards." In his anger he lets us know what became of Etheredge at the Revolution, for in a virulent Latin harangue at the close of **The Letterbook** he states that after a stay at Ratisbon of "tres annos et sex menses," accurately measured, for the secretary's cry is a cry for gold, Etheredge fled to Paris. This flight must therefore have taken place early in March 1689. "Quando hinc abijt ad asylum apud Gallos quærendum," the poet left his books behind him, a proof that his taking leave was sudden and urgent. The secretary gives a list of them, and it is interesting to find the only playbooks mentioned are Shakespeare's *Works* and the *Œuvres de Molière,* in 2 vols., probably the edition of 1682. I note also the works of Sarrazin and of Voiture.

At this point, I am sorry to say, the figure of Etheredge at present eludes me. There seems no clue whatever to the date of his death, except that in an anonymous pamphlet, written by John Dennis, and printed in 1722, Etheredge is spoken of as having been dead "nearly thirty years." Dennis was over thirty at the Revolution, and is as trustworthy an authority as we could wish for. By this it would seem that Etheredge died about 1693, nearer the age of sixty than fifty. But Colonel Chester has the record of administration to the estate of a Dame Mary Etheredge, widow, dated Feb. 1, 1692. As we know of no other knight of the name, except Sir James Etheridge, who died in 1736, this was probably the poet's relict; and it may yet appear that he died in 1691. He was a short, brisk man, with a quantity of fair hair, and a fine complexion, which he spoiled by drinking. He left no children, but his brother, who long survived him, left a daughter, who is said to have married Aaron Hill.

G. S. Street (essay date 1893)

SOURCE: Street, G. S. "Etherege." In *Miniatures and Moods,* pp. 34-9. London: David Nutt, 1893.

[*In the essay below, Street praises Etherege's display of comedic talent in* The Comical Revenge, She Would If She Could, *and* The Man of Mode.]

When you read Wycherley, you recognise a master of theatrical effects, the able exponent of a robustly vile humanity; then you feel a trifle sickened, and anon are downright bored. He is no cynic, not held by any ethical convention; if in his pages the world be a thing grotesque, obscene, it is because to a modern apprehension the man was even so: honest he was, as well, and, therefore, with little satisfaction for a splenetic mood. Congreve, of course, is pre-eminent in wit and diction; and because there is a malicious subtlety in the wickedness of his world, and his way is to see evil in everything, while you are aware, all the time, that your author has in reality as clear a perception of what is otherwise as your own, he suits your occasional spite against dull circumstance. But this convention—that there is nothing good under the sun, that desire is the whole of life—grows, in spite of Elia, tedious to minds that have outgrown the counter convention of Puritan propriety too long for constant militancy against it.

If this be so with you, Etherege should find place in your appreciations. If he lack the scenic sense of Wycherley, he lacks also his brutality; if the wit of Congreve, Congreve's conscious narrowness. He is more apt to distinguish than either; the passions of his men take an individual air; his women, honest or not, show degrees and differences. A

most readable play is his last, **The Man of Mode, or Sir Fopling Flutter.** It seems to show you 'Gentle George's' world, as he saw it. A world gayer and more wanton than our own, but not immersed in (what you would call) immoral pursuits, not unknowing of the charm of frank innocence and virile friendship. It is an obvious criticism to say, with Lamb, that the whole business of this world is intrigue. But these plays are frankly of intrigue, and in what age have idle young men of the town not given the most of their attention to one or other sort of the world of women? The Dorimant is said to be sketched from Rochester, and it may well be the case, though it is curious that a song in the play, said to be by Dorimant, is by Sir Charles Sedley. Dorimant is of profligate habit and ironical temper, a 'fine gentleman,' a man of parts withal, and fascinating at will. 'I know he is a devil,' says poor Mrs. Loveit; 'but he has something of the angel yet undefac'd in him.' Now when he would cast off this Mrs. Loveit—a woman 'in society'—it is to be noted that, vain and unfeeling though he be, he yet sets about it with a regard for outward decency, bears him in fact more as a gentleman than in a like case the hero of *The Story of the Gadsbys.* And his friend Medley, 'the spirit of scandal'— said to be Sedley or Etherege himself—and young Bellair are possible. Old Bellair would be no doubt accounted coarse in his speech to-day, but he is neither a brute nor a bully, and his heartiness (that most difficult quality to portray) has a certain engaging sincerity. Sir Fopling Flutter was said by Dean Lockitt to be Etherege, which can hardly be the case; the foundation for the idea is that in him French modes and predilections are ridiculed, and Etherege had lived in Paris. He may or may not be drawn from one Beau Hewit, but in any case he is drawn with art, effectively. Dryden can say with truth in his epilogue that 'Sir Fopling is a fool so nicely writ, the ladies 'would mistake him for a wit.' His folly is absurd but not extravagant; his conceit immense but not abnormal. Supposed to have birth and breeding, he is no clown: and because it is comedy, the satire is not a whit less mordant. The women are, one passionate and reckless, one amorous and discreet, besides two lightly sketched match-makers. Their superficial coarseness is of the time, hardly more pronounced than you find it a hundred years later.

Of the other two plays, **She Would if She Could** is merely farcical on broad lines, diverting sometimes, sometimes wooden; and **Love in a Tub** is a compound of serious scenes in verse, and of buffoonery dragged in by the heels. They deserve a word: the 'Poems' do not, and one may pass to a general and somewhat noticeable consideration. The girls in Etherege are commonly charming. In the first play, **Love in a Tub,** they are on a poetical plane, and, it may be, dull; but at least you must credit their author with a not ignoble conception. Aurelia, who pleads with her sister to accept the love of a man herself loves secretly, may be unconvincing, but is not, surely, the creation of a narrowly base nature. This play, it is to be observed in the connection, benefited the house by a thousand pounds in a month. In *She Would if She Could* are 'two young ladies' neither prudes nor hussies, neither sticks nor unnaturally witty. Wild by our notions, they are provocative, human, delightful.

> This is sly and pretty,
> And this is wild and witty;
> If either staid
> 'Till she dy'd a maid,
> I' faith 'twould be great pity.

And you feel, as you read, that the catch is in the right. And Harriet, in the best play, is likewise natural and frank and charming. All are unaffectedly aware of the lives of their suitors, but they are open with their knowledge, and sin not with innuendo or pretence. And the writers who can show, convincingly, innocence which is not mere ignorance are sufficiently uncommon.

Etherege, then, has distinction as a writer. He is fanciful, life-like, and sometimes even fine, and is further notable among his contemporaries for an effective restraint in satire. A touch of feeling here and there and a suggestion of romance come pleasantly upon you. His grossness—ah, there we come on an old friend in this connection. 'Chastity,' says Sterne, 'by nature the gentlest of the affections, 'give it but its head—'tis like a ramping and 'a roaring lion.' But it must really spare this lamb without the argumentative interference of a champion. Of Etherege the man our ramping lion has better right to make a meal. Horace Walpole tells a tale of a king's mistress discarded, who was insulted by the rabble. '*Messieurs,*' she said, '*puis-que vous me connoissez, priez Dieu pour moi.*' Etherege was the friend of Rochester, and had to retire with my lord from the public eye. Sent to the Hague by Charles, and to Ratisbon by James, he was a scandalous ambassador given to gaming and other vice. But he had the grace to be ruined by the Revolutions which ruined his master. *Priez Dieu pour lui,* though he himself would not have thanked you.

Bonamy Dobrée (essay date 1924)

SOURCE: Dobrée, Bonamy. "Etherege (? 1635-91)." In *Restoration Comedy, 1660-1720*, pp. 58-77. 1924. Reprint. Westport, Conn: Greenwood Press, 1981.

[*In the following essay, Dobrée characterizes Etherege's comedies as lighthearted, unsophisticated works intended mainly to delight and amuse Carolinian audiences.*]

> *The air rarefied and pure, danger near, and the spirit full of a gay quickedness: these agree well together.*
>
> —ZARATHUSTRA.

Seen through the haze of time, Etherege appears as a brilliant butterfly, alighting only upon such things as attract him; a creature without much depth, but of an extraordinary charm and a marvellous surety of touch.

He was professedly no student. 'The more necessary part of philosophy', he once wrote to Dryden, 'is to be learn'd in the wide world more than in the gardens of Epicurus'; and again, to Lord Dover, 'The life I have led has afforded me little time to turn over books; but I have had leisure sufficient, while I idly rolled about the town, to look into myself'. What he found in himself was that he was infinitely delighted in the delicate surface of things, and that not for the world would he have had anything changed. All was entertaining to 'gentle George' or 'easy Etherege', to that 'loose wand'ring Etherege, in wild pleasures tost', of whom Southern wrote. All, except hard work.

Thus his is a perfectly simple, understandable figure in Restoration court society; he is in tune with it. His friends were Buckingham, Sedley, Rochester, Buckhurst—with the last of whom he 'carried the two draggle-tailed nymphs one bitter frosty night over the Thames to Lambeth'[1]— and, above all, Dryden. He was the intimate of lords and wits, of actors (perhaps he used to spend musical evenings with the Bettertons) and of actresses. It was said he had a daughter by Mrs. Barry. He had friends at the *Rose,* and there was a lily at the *Bar,* for he was never absent from a new play, nor behindhand with a pretty woman.

Between his last two comedies he went on some diplomatic mission to Constantinople;

> Ovid to Pontus sent for too much wit,
> Etherege to Turkey for the want of it,

they said. When he came back he resumed his gay life, rioted at Epsom with Rochester, and wrote his best play. Then he married for money so as to get a knighthood, or got a knighthood so as to marry for money, which it was is not quite clear. In any case he does not appear to have been fortunate:

> What then can Etherege urge in his defence,
> What reason bring, unless 'tis want of sense.
> For all he pleads beside is mere pretence . . .
> Merit with honour joined a crown to life,
> But he got honour for to get a wife.
> Preposterous knighthood! in the gift severe,
> For never was a knighthood bought so dear.

Etherege apparently agreed, for when in the year 1685 he was sent as envoy to Ratisbon, he left Dame Etherege behind. One of his letters to her remains:

> I beg your pardon for undertaking to advise you. I am so well satisfied by your last letter of your prudence and judgement that I shall never more commit the same error. I wish there were copies of it in London; it might serve as a pattern for modest wives to write to their husbands. You shall find me so careful hereafter how I offend you, that I will no more subscribe myself your loving since you take it ill, but
>
> > Madame,
> > Your most dutiful husband, G. E.

We see that he liked things to be clear cut.

And if he is perfectly simple to understand, so are his plays. They are pure works of art directed to no end but themselves, meant only, in Dryden's phrase, 'to give delight'. For Etherege was not animated by any moral stimulus, and his comedies arose from a superabundance of animal energy that only bore fruit in freedom and ease, amid the graces of Carolingian society. He was a hothouse product, and knew it. 'I must confess', he once wrote, 'I am a fop in my heart. I have been so used to affectation, that without the help of the air of the court, what is natural cannot touch me.' So what was the use of Dryden urging him to 'scribble faster' when he was abroad? 'I wear flannel, sir,' he wrote to another friend, 'wherefore, pray, talk to me no more of poetry', for his comedy was a gesture not very different in impulse from the exquisite tying of his cravat, or the set of his wig; 'poetry' to him was essentially an affair of silks and perfumes, of clavichord music and corrants.

His plays then are lyrical, in the sense of being immediate reactions to things seen around him, pondered only as works of art and not as expositions of views. He was a true naïf, 'too lazy and too careless to be ambitious', as he wrote to Godolphin. He had no ethic to urge him to produce the laughter of social protection. His laughter, on the contrary, is always that of delight at being very much alive in the best of all possible societies, and is only corrective, here and there, by accident. There was, for instance, no move in the sometimes graceful sex-game he did not enjoy. 'Next to the coming to a good understanding with a new mistress', says Dorimant, whom, we may remember, he perhaps designed as a portrait of himself, 'I love a quarrel with an old one; but the Devil's in it, there has been such a calm in my affairs of late, I have not had the pleasure of making a woman break her fan, to be sullen, or forswear herself these three days.' Or again, in the words of Courtal, 'A single intrigue in love is as dull as a single plot in a play, and will tire a lover worse than t'other does an audience'. The motto of life is gaiety at all costs, the first duty the defeat of dulness.

Indeed, there is no lack of plots in his first play; there are no less than four—and a curious mixture they are. There is a romantic Fletcherian plot, that of Lord Beaufort and Graciana, Bruce and Aurelia, written in rhymed couplets; a Middletonian one, with cheats and gamesters, and a great deal of noise and drinking; a number of completely farcical scenes centring about the French valet Dufoy; and finally the Sir Frederick-Widow tale, which, from both the historical and artistic points of view is the most interesting. It set the whole tone of Restoration comedy, and gave out the chief theme, which was never relinquished. At his first trial, with amazing intuition, Etherege had laid his finger upon the most promising material of his time.

The Comical Revenge, or Love in a Tub need not be taken very seriously. It is on the whole a sheer ebullience of high spirits, full of joyous pranks, practical joking, and charming but not very real sentiment, in which the shrewd witty observer of the later plays is almost entirely absent.

Yet his alertness for a telling simile, or for bringing all London upon the stage, is apparent in the first act.

Lᴏʀᴅ Bᴇᴀᴜғᴏʀᴛ.

How now, cousin! What, at wars with the women?

Sɪʀ Fʀᴇᴅᴇʀɪᴄᴋ.

I gave a small alarm to their quarters last night, my lord.

Lᴏʀᴅ Bᴇᴀᴜғᴏʀᴛ.

Jenny in tears! What's the occasion, poor girl?

Mᴀɪᴅ.

I'll tell you, my lord.

Sɪʀ Fʀᴇᴅᴇʀɪᴄᴋ.

Buzz; set not her tongue going again (*clapping his hand before her mouth*). She has made more noise than half a dozen paper mills! London Bridge at low water is silence to her.

This is clever drawing, but most of this comedy is the purest tomfoolery. The valet, while drugged, is locked in a tub which he has to carry about on his shoulders. 'Vat are you?' he cries, as he awakes. 'Jernie! Vat is dis? Am I Jack in a box'? Begar, who did putté me here?' Disguise is the order of the day, and there is high-spirited burlesque, as when Sir Frederick dresses up his fiddlers as bailiffs, and Dufoy, released from his tub, thinks his master is in danger. He enters, therefore, 'with a helmet on his head, and a great sword in his hand, "Vare are de bougres de bailié! Tête-bleu, bougres rogues"', he cries, and 'falls upon the fiddlers'.

This is not comedy, but roaring, rollicking farce—that is, the fun depends upon incident. Our author had not found himself; there was small promise in all this of what was to come, little of the 'sense, judgement, and wit' for which Rochester was later to praise him. Yet in the Sir Frederick-Widow plot there are portions that treat most deliciously of the duel of the sexes.

Sɪʀ F.

Widow, I dare not venture myself in those amorous shades [of the garden]; you have a mind to be talking of love, I perceive, and my heart's too tender to be trusted with such conversation.

Wɪᴅᴏᴡ.

I did not imagine you were so foolishly conceited; is it your wit or your person, sir, that is so taking?

Isn't it delightfully boy and girl? And later:

Sɪʀ F.

By those lips,———

WIDOW.

Nay, pray forbear, sir———

SIR F.

Who is conceited now, widow? Could you imagine I was so fond to kiss them?

WIDOW.

You cannot blame me for standing on my guard, so near an enemy. . . .

SIR F.

Let us join hands then, widow.

WIDOW.

Without the dangerous help of a parson, I do not fear it, sir.

The whole play, even to the romantic scenes, is just a youngster's game. It is tentative, full of action and boisterousness, alive with gaiety indeed, but the method is not perfected.

In *She Would if She Could* Etherege was much more certain of what he wanted to do. He had begun to see what elements to reject, and in consequence devoted a great deal of space to that delightful quartette, Ariana and Gatty, Courtal and Freeman. The passages where these are involved read like directions for a ballet; it is all a dance; the couples bow, set to partners, perform their evolutions, and bow again; and indeed their value consists in their ability to create this sort of atmosphere. Here is the first meeting of the principal dancers:

COURT.

Fie, fie! put off these scandals to all good faces.

GATTY.

For your reputation's sake we shall keep 'em on. 'Slife, we should be taken for your relations if we durst show our faces with you thus publicly.

ARIANA.

And what a shame that would be to a couple of young gallants. Methinks, you should blush to think on't.

COURT.

These were pretty toys, invented, first, merely for the good of us poor lovers to deceive the jealous, and to blind the malicious; but the proper use is so wickedly perverted, that it makes all honest men hate the fashion mortally.

FREE.

A good face is as seldom covered with a vizard-mask, as a good hat with an oiled case. And yet, on my conscience, you are both handsome.

COURT.

Do but remove 'em a little, to satisfy a foolish scruple.

ARIANA.

This is a just punishment you have brought upon yourselves by that unpardonable sin of talking.

GATTY.

You can only brag now of your acquaintance with a Farendon gown and a piece of black velvet.

COURT.

The truth is, there are some vain fellows whose loose behaviour of late has given great discouragement to the honourable proceedings of all virtuous ladies.

FREE.

But I hope you have more charity than to believe us of the number of the wicked.

And here is another figure:

GATTY.

I suppose your mistress, Mr. Courtal, is always the last woman you are acquainted with.

COURT.

Do not think, madam, I have that false measure of my acquaintance which poets have of their verses, always to think the last best—though I esteem you so in justice to your merit.

GATTY.

Or if you do not love her best, you always love to talk of her most; as a barren coxcomb that wants discourse is ever entertaining company out of the last book he read in.

COURT.

Now you accuse me most unjustly, madam; who the devil that has common sense will go birding with a clack in his cap.?

ARIANA.

Nay, we do not blame you, gentlemen; every one in their way; a huntsman talks of his dogs, a falconer of his hawks, a jockey of his horse, and a gallant of his mistress.

GATTY.

Without the allowance of this vanity, an amour would soon grow as dull as matrimony.

The very words foot it briskly, taking their ease among horsemen's terms. When Courtal and Freeman first sight Ariana and Gatty in the Mulberry Garden, Freeman says, ''Sdeath, how fleet they are! Whatsoever faults they have they cannot be broken-winded.' And Courtal takes it up, 'Sure, by that little mincing step they should be country fillies that have been breathed a course at park and barley-break.[2] We shall never reach 'em.' Sir Joslin Jolley, the young ladies' kinsman, describes Gatty as 'a clean-limbed wench, and has neither spavin, splinter nor wind-gall', while Sir Joslin himself is straight from the kennels, and evidently hunts his own hounds. 'Here they are, boys, i' faith', is his method of introducing 'that couple of sly skittish fillies', his wards, to the young gallants, 'heuk! Sly girls and madcap, to 'em, to 'em boys, alou!'

Though full of charm and vivacity, the play was not a success when first acted. Pepys wrote that he heard 'Etheredge, the poet . . . mightily find fault with the actors, that they were out of humour, and had not their parts perfect, and that Harris (who played Sir Joslin) did do nothing', and Shadwell supports the view that it was badly acted. But, indeed, it was difficult for the actors to be *in* humour, for Etherege had fallen between two stools. He had not quite fused the elements of art and life, for side by side with Ariana's fragile world we have the full-blooded boisterousness of Sir Joslin Jolley and Sir Oliver Cockwood. With those boon companions the play could hardly fail to partake of rough and tumble. They are bold, desperate old fellows among women and wine, and Sir Joslin is ever bursting into song which for frankness would not have disgraced our armies in Flanders. The two atmospheres are mutually destructive. Etherege had not yet broken away from the late Elizabethan tradition.

The Cockwoods and Sir Joslin are, for the matter of that, would-be Jonsonian, but they have all the grittiness of Jonsonian characters without their depth. What are we to make of this scene, where Lady Cockwood is in company with the young ladies and their gallants, Sir Joslin, and Sentry, her 'gentlewoman'?

SIR OLIVER

> (*strutting*). Dan, dan, da, ra, dan, & c. Avoid my presence! the very sight of that face makes me more impotent than an eunuch.

LADY COCK.

> Dear Sir Oliver (*offering to embrace him*).

SIR OLIVER.

> Forbear your conjugal clippings; I will have a wench; thou shalt fetch me a wench, Sentry.

SENTRY.

> Can you be so inhuman to my dear lady?

SIR OLIVER.

> Peace, Envy, or I will have thee executed for petty treason; thy skin flayed off, stuffed and hung up in my hall in the country, as a terror to my whole family.

It is no wonder that after the scene in the Mulberry Garden the actors were a little puzzled; it is too brutal, and the punishment that follows upon Sir Joslin's misdemeanour

is humorous fantasy, certainly, but a little crude in idea. His clothes are locked up, with the exception of his 'penitential suit', an old-fashioned, worn-out garment in which he dare not stir abroad.

Lady Cockwood, who gives the play its title, is an unpleasant character, not clearly conceived. The 'noble laziness of the mind', of which Etherege was so proud, forbade him to deal ably with things he did not like. Since he was no satirist (until he went to Ratisbon), and did not feel impelled to criticize manners—which after all suited him admirably—he could only touch well what he could touch lovingly. And he did not love Lady Cockwood. She was a woman eager for amorous adventure, and equally eager to preserve her 'honour'; so far good. But Courtal, whom she pursued ferociously, found her 'the very spirit of impertinence, so foolishly fond and troublesome, that no man above sixteen is able to endure her'. Alas! the poor soul had not got the technique of the Restoration game; she could not pretend to deny.

On the other hand, there is plenty of fun to be got out of her, and Courtal's evasions of her addresses are full of ingenuity. The figure of the man who, as his name implies, was not over selective, pursued by a woman he cannot endure, provides a good case of the Meredithan comic. But the best scene of all, where she is concerned, takes place in an eating-house. She has gone there with Courtal, Freeman, and the two young ladies, leaving Sir Oliver safe at home in his penitential suit. But though he had 'intended to retire into the pantry and there civilly to divert himself at backgammon with the butler', Sir Joslin lures him forth with the promise of good wine, and women not so good, to the very place where Lady Cockwood has gone. Her ladyship outmanœuvres her husband, and bursts upon him with all the colours of offended virtue flying bravely. After a counterfeited swoon she breaks out:

> Perfidious man; I am too tame and foolish. Were I every day at the plays, the Park and Mulberry Garden, with a kind look secretly to indulge the unlawful passion of some young gallant; or did I associate myself with the gaming madams, and were every afternoon at my Lady Brief's and my Lady Meanwell's at ombre and quebas, pretending ill-luck to borrow money of a friend, and then pretending good luck to excuse the plenty to a husband, my suspicious demeanour had deserved this; but I who out of a scrupulous tenderness to my honour, and to comply with thy base jealousy, have denied myself all those blameless recreations which a virtuous lady might enjoy, to be thus inhumanly reviled in my own person, and thus unreasonably robbed and abused in thine too!

Such admirable prose from a lady so little able to manage her affairs astonishes Courtal. 'Sure she will take up anon, or crack her mind, or else the devil's in it', he remarks. And here we see the value of the restraint Etherege had learned; the Elizabethan scene might have romped away with him to the regions of farce, but seeing the danger he pulled it together with some neat phrasing. The *jeunes premiers* and their partners are calming Lady Cockwood after her outburst against her husband:

Aria.

> How bitterly he weeps! how sadly he sighs!

Gatty.

> I daresay he counterfeited his sin, and is real in his repentance.

Court.

> Compose yourself a little, pray Madam; all this was mere raillery, a way of talk, which Sir Oliver, being well bred, has learned among the gay people of the town.

Free.

> If you did but know, Madam, what an odious thing it is to be thought to love a wife in good company, you would easily forgive him.

What charming wit! and how naïvely Etherege seems to believe in the argument himself!

The above may show how Etherege laughed with delight at the entertaining thing life was. Neither it nor his plays were to be taken too seriously. Both were vastly amusing things, and sex comedy like the frolicking of lambs. He rarely makes an appeal to the intellect. Yet there are two or three notes in this play that, wittingly or not, cause that deeper laughter, provoked by man's realization of his own helplessness against his desires, the laughter at the triumph of man's body over his mind Schlegel found at the root of all comedy. Thus when the young ladies are finally engaged, Sir Joslin asks, 'Is it a match, boys?' and Courtal replies, 'if the heart of man be not very deceitful, 'tis very likely it may be so'.

After this play Etherege was silent for eight years, and in the interval two things had happened; he had become less boisterous, his pleasures were becoming those of the intellect rather than those of the healthy animal seeking 'wild pleasures' as an outlet for his energies; and at the same time he had begun to weary a little of the game, so that here and there we have a display of sheer bad temper. He was no longer so young as he had been, and perhaps the life led by 'gentle George' was beginning to tell on his nerves. But if in his weariness he would have liked solitude, he could not endure dullness. If it can be said he was afflicted by any sort of *Weltschmierz,* he knew of no method to dissipate it other than a brawl, such as the one which, in the year *The Man of Mode* appeared, culminated in the death of one of the participators. So, as already in the rough and tumble of his earlier comedies we find a spice of brutality underlying the laughter, in his last play there is now and again a harshness that is in danger of spoiling it. When he writes such a sentence as 'I have of late lived as chaste as my Lady Etherege', we get a hint of the state of mind that produced the Dorimant-Mrs. Loveit scenes in *The Man of Mode.* We may take the first, where Dorimant, determined to break relations with his mistress for the sake of her 'friend' Belinda, sets to work:

Loveit.

> Faithless, inhuman, barbarous man!

Dor.

> Good, now, the alarm strikes—

Loveit.

> Without sense of love, of honour, or of gratitude, tell me—for I will know—what devil, masked she, were you with at the play yesterday?

Dor.

> Faith, I resolved as much as you, but the devil was obstinate and would not tell me.

Loveit.

> False in this as in your vows to me! You do know.

Dor.

> The truth is, I did all I could to know.

Loveit.

> And dare you own it to my face? Hell and furies— (*tears her fan in pieces*)

Dor.

> Spare your fan, madam; you are growing hot, and will want it to cool you.

Loveit.

> Horror and distraction seize you, sorrow and remorse gnaw your soul, and punish all your perjuries to me (*Weeps*).

Dor.

> > So thunder breaks the clouds in twain
> > And makes a passage for the rain.

This is no longer in comedy vein; it is too cruel. It was no wonder that Belinda, herself the 'devil, masked she', declared:

> > He's given me the proof I desired of his love:
> > > But 'tis a proof of his ill-nature too;
> > > I wish I had not seen him use her so.

But the ill-nature does not stop there, and Dorimant becomes an outrageous bully. He gets Belinda to induce Loveit to walk in the Mall that he may cause her to make a fool of herself with Sir Fopling. Even Belinda protests, 'You persecute her too much', but the excuse is that 'You women make 'em (the afflications in love), who are commonly as unreasonable in that as you are at play; without the advantage be on your side, a man can never quietly give over when he is weary'. This is sex-antagonism with a vengeance; we are down to bedrock here, and thus expressed it is not very laughable. There is too much spite in it.

At the same time Mrs. Loveit is an amazingly natural presentation of a jealous woman, struggling fiercely against her fate. She did not deserve to be told in public by Harriet, her successful rival, a charming coquette full of womanly wisdom, that 'Mr. Dorimant has been your God Almighty long enough', and that she must find another lover, or, better still, betake herself to a nunnery! Yet this only harshness in an otherwise admirable comedy may not have appeared a flaw to the audiences of those days. Those scenes may have induced the laughter of common sense which the writer of comedy can rarely escape, but for us they spoil the delight. After all, Etherege could do better on the theme:

> It is not, Celia, in our power
> To say how long our love will last;
> It may be we within this hour
> May lose those joys we now do taste;
> The blessed, that immortal be,
> From change in love are only free.
>
> Then since we lovers mortal are,
> Ask not how long our love will last;
> But while it does let us take care
> Each minute be with pleasure pass'd:
> Were it not madness to deny
> To live, because we're sure to die?

the perfect expression of Etherege's philosophy of love—and life. For even in this comedy he could keep the sentiment on the lyric level, as when Emilia says, 'Do not vow—Our love is frail as is our life and full as little in our power; and are you sure you shall outlive this day?'

To turn to Dorimant. He is a marvellous erotic, with 'more mistresses now depending than the most eminent lawyer in England has causes'. 'Constancy at my years!' he cries. 'You might as well expect the fruit the autumn ripens in the spring.' He has, moreover, the courage of his philosophy. 'When love grows diseased the best thing we can do is to put it to a violent death; I cannot endure the torture of a lingering and consumptive passion.' He is master of all the technique of feminine conquest; he can pique as well as caress and insinuate, and his method of attack on Harriet is blunt. Loving her to the distraction of marriage—though even here he must excuse himself on the plea that it will 'repair the ruins of my estate'—he attempts the satiric. He tells her:

> I observed how you were pleased when the fops cried,
> She's handsome, very handsome, by God she is, . . .
> then to make yourself more agreeable, how wantonly
> you played with your head, flung back your locks, and
> look'd smilingly over your shoulder at 'em.

Temerarious man, she was more than a match for him, and retorted with an admirable little sketch of what we cannot but think an odious gallant:

> I do not go begging the men's, as you do the ladies'
> good liking, with a sly softness in your looks and a
> gentle slowness in your bows as you pass by 'em—as
> thus, sir—(*acts him*).

For Etherege was a master of witty description: the fat orange-woman is an 'overgrown jade with a flasket of guts before her', or an 'insignificant brandy-bottle'; Medley, as Amelia tells him, is 'a living libel, a breathing lampoon', and he is at times 'rhetorically drunk'. This is the bright current coin of lively description, but Etherege, with his vivid imagination, can give us wonderful set pieces of brilliant mimicry. Long before we see Sir Fopling Flutter, we know exactly what he looks like:

> He was yesterday at the play, with a pair of gloves up
> to his elbow and a periwig more exactly curled than a
> lady's head newly dressed for a ball. . . . His head
> stands for the most part on one side, and his looks are
> more languishing than a lady's when she lolls at stretch
> in her coach, or leans her head carelessly against the
> side of a box in the playhouse.

He delighted to observe every pose and gesture, each revealing intonation. Here, for instance, are Young Bellair and Harriet instructing one another how to appear charmed by each other's company, so as to deceive their parents about their real sentiments. First Bellair has his lesson from Harriet:

HAR.

> Your head a little more on one side, ease yourself on
> your left leg, and play with your right hand.

BEL.

> Thus, is it not?

HAR.

> Now set your right leg firm on the ground, adjust your
> belt, then look about you . . . Smile, and turn to me
> again very sparkish.

Then it is her turn to be instructed:

BEL.

> Now spread your fan, look down upon it, and tell the
> sticks with a finger . . .

HAR.

> 'Twill not be amiss now to seem a little pleasant.

BEL.

> Clap your fan then in both your hands, snatch it to
> your mouth, smile, and with a lively motion fling your
> body a little forwards. So—now spread it; fall back on
> the sudden, . . . take up! look grave and fall a-fanning
> of yourself—admirably well acted.

Could anything be written with a surer touch, a greater descriptive acumen?

Occasionally he touches farce in a manner we must admit is Molièresque:

MEDLEY.

> Where does she live?

ORANGE-W.

> They lodge at my house.

MEDLEY.

> Nay, then she's in a hopeful way.

ORANGE-W.

> Good Mr. Medley, say your pleasure of me, but take heed how you affront my house. God's my life, in a hopeful way!

Finally, the character of his observation may be seen in Dorimant's remark:

> I have known many women make a difficulty of losing a maidenhead, who have afterwards made none of a cuckold.

Or in this letter from Molly:

> I have no money, and am very mallicolly, pray send me a guynie to see the operies.

This is life, and its placing makes it art.

The ostensible hero of the play, Sir Fopling Flutter, has little to do with the action. He is the most delicately and sympathetically drawn of all the fops in the great series of coxcombs. He is in himself a delight, presented from pure joy of him, and is not set up merely as a target for the raillery of wiser fools. Unlike Vanbrugh's Lord Foppington, he has no intellectual idea behind his appearance. He exists by his garments and his *calèche*; there is, as it were, no noumenal Flutter. We have his picture:

LADY TOWN.

> His gloves are well fringed, large and graceful.

SIR FOP.

> I was always eminent for being *bien ganté*.

EMILIA.

> He wears nothing but what are originals of the most famous hands in Paris. . . .

LADY TOWN.

> The suit?

SIR FOP.

> *Barroy.*

EMILIA.

> The garniture?

SIR FOP.

> *Le Gras.*

MEDLEY.

> The shoes?

SIR FOP.

> *Piccat.*

DORIMANT.

> The periwig?

SIR FOP.

> *Chedreux.*

LADY T. EM.

> The gloves?

SIR FOP. ORANGERIE.

> You know the smell, ladies.

Moreover, all the people around him enjoy him as much as Etherege himself so evidently did. Life would be the duller without him, and so his existence is justified. He must even be encouraged:

SIR FOP.

> An intrigue now would be but a temptation to throw away that vigour on one, which I mean shall shortly make my court to the whole sex in a ballet.

MEDLEY.

> Wisely considered, Sir Fopling.

SIR FOP.

> No one woman is worth the loss of a cut in a caper.

MEDLEY.

> Not when 'tis so universally designed.

It is exquisite. Etherege never oversteps the bounds. Sir Fopling is not for a moment the fatuous ass Vanbrugh's Lord Foppington becomes. Should he say, 'I cannot passitively tell whether ever I shall speak again or nat', our attitude would at once become critical. But this one cannot be with Sir Fopling, who so obviously enjoys himself without any affectation whatever. He is not like Sir Courtly Nice in Crowne's comedy, who when challenged declared, 'It goes against my stomach horribly to fight such a beast. Should his filthy sword but touch me, 'twould make me as sick as a dog.' Etherege was too good an artist for that kind of exaggeration. He presented, and avoided awakening the critical spirit. Sir Fopling was to him what a rare orchid is to an enthusiastic gardener, a precious specimen, and the finger of satire must not be allowed to touch him. We should be fools to take the trouble to think Sir Fopling a fool, and to weary of him would be to show ourselves 'a little too delicate', like Emilia. It is not as an universal abstract that he exists, but as a fantasy. To him, and perhaps to him only, Charles Lamb's remarks are applicable. No disharmonies of flesh and blood disturb this delicate creation: no blast of reality dispels the perfumery, or ruffles the least hair on the inimitable perruque. No acrimony guided the pen that described him, no word of common sense reduced him to a right proportion among 'les gens graves et sérieux, les vieillards, et les amateurs de vertu'. To attempt to deduce a lesson from him is as fruitful as to seek a symbol in a primrose, a meaning in the contours of a cloud.

But Etherege was writing comedy, and he could not quite escape the presentment of the happy mean, or an indication of the most comfortable way to live. Bellair, 'always complaisant and seldom impertinent', is to be our model; but even he errs on the side of sentiment, and does not escape the comic censor:

BEL.

I could find in my heart to resolve not to marry at all.

DOR.

Fie, fie! that would spoil a good jest, and disappoint the well natured town of an occasion of laughing at you.

Indeed, Etherege, from the 'free' comedy point of view, was slightly tarnished by experience. 'When your love's grown strong enough to make you bear being laughed at, I'll give you leave to trouble me with it', Harriet tells Dorimant. She was in the right of it there, but it has a serious note, and Medley is ever and anon a little tiresome. To him Sir Fopling is 'a fine-mettled coxcomb, brisk and insipid, pert and dull', but one would weary of Medley sooner than of Sir Fopling. These, however, are only occasional lapses, and even the most sententious remarks are relieved in a spirit of tomfoolery, or lightened with a happier wisdom. When Harriet says 'beauty runs as great a risk exposed at Court as wit does on the stage', she would have pleased Collier, until she added, 'where the ugly and the foolish all are free to censure', and the sound truths enunciated by Loveit and Dorimant are only by way of weapons against each other. They would be the last to live by their own precepts.

For some reason Etherege has been much neglected. Leigh Hunt did not include him in his famous edition—it was thus his none too blameless life escaped the misrepresentations of Macaulay—nor does he grace the Mermaid collection. But Mr. Gosse and Mr. Palmer have done much to remedy this, and the former has done him full justice as a delicate painter who loved subtle contrasts in 'rose-colour and pale grey', who delighted in grace and movement and agreeable groupings. It is a frivolous world, Strephon bending on one knee to Chloe, who fans the pink blush on her painted cheek, while Momus peeps with a grimace through the curtains behind her. They form an engaging trio, 'mais ce n'est pas la vie humaine'. Well it is not *la*

vie humaine to us nowadays, but if it was such to Dennis ('I allow it to be nature'), how much more so must it have been to the Sedleys, the Rochesters, and the Beau Hewitts! Even Langbaine stated it to be 'as well drawn to the life as any play that has been acted since the restoration of the English stage'. And if Steele said that 'this whole celebrated piece is a perfect contradiction of good manners, good sense, and common honesty', we must remember that such a play could never appeal to the 'good sense' of the confectioner of the sentimental comedy.

Etherege, if you will, is a minor writer, in his exuberance nearer Mrs. Behn than to Congreve with his depth. But from another point of view he is far above all the other playwrights of his period, for he did something very rare in our literature. He presented life treated purely as an appearance: there was no more meaning in it apart from its immediate reactions than there is in a children's game of dumb-crambo. This sort of comedy, while it is realistic in semblance, and faithfully copies the outward aspects of the time, creates an illusion of life that is far removed from reality. Here is no sense of grappling with circumstance, for man is unencumbered by thoughts or passions. Life is a merry-go-round, and there is no need to examine the machinery or ponder on the design. It is not play for the sake of exercise, but play for its own sake, and the game must not be allowed to become too arduous. Nor is it life seen at a distance, but the forms of those known and liked seen intimately from a shady arbour in an old, sunny garden. Butterflies hover against the wall, and the sound of the *viol da gamba* floats serenely over the scent-laden atmosphere, while the figures, absorbed in their own youth, bend gracefully to the movements of the bourrée or sarabande. *Eheu fugaces!* Yes, now and again: but the idle thought passes in the ripples of laughter, and the solemn motto on the sundial is hidden beneath the roses.

Notes

1. An episode of which he reminded Dorset in a letter from Ratisbon. Etherege, Letter-book, Brit. Mus. MS.

2. A game not unlike Prisoner's Base.

Ashley H. Thorndike (essay date 1929)

SOURCE: Thorndike, Ashley H. "The Restoration, 1660-1680." In *English Comedy*, pp. 269-303. New York: Macmillan, 1929.

[*In the excerpt below, Thorndike maintains that Etherege's comedies reflect a combination of cynicism and wit which springs from an intellectual mind.*]

The initiation of that particular type of the comedy of manners which reaches its height in Congreve has been universally attributed to Sir George Etherege. "The dawn," said Hazlitt, "was in Etherege, as its latest close was in Sheridan."[1] His three plays possess therefore a certain historical as well as inherent interest, and the last, *The Man of Mode,* has long served as an archetype of the Restoration comedy both for the admirers and the detractors of that species. Of Etherege's life little is known; he apparently lived in France long enough to gain an intimate knowledge of things Parisian; he was a gay man about town, the companion of Rochester and Sedley, married a fortune, was knighted and at fifty left England for a diplomatic career at Ratisbon. French literature and manners perhaps helped to form his style and dramatic method, but his plays are manifestly a reflection of the manners and the wit of the London circle of which he was thought one of the ornaments.

His first play, *The Comical Revenge or Love in a Tub* (1664) has little to distinguish it from other plays of that date. The serious plot in which love and honour appear in their loftiest mien is written in rhymed couplets, then a novelty; and the realistic scenes are in prose which is at least vastly superior to the verse. The confusion of heroics, humours and intrigues gives little hint of a new dramatic development, unless in the occasional wit and gaiety of Sir Frederick Frollick and his impudent French valet, borrowed from Molière.

The Comical Revenge appears to have excited so much interest that the second play *She Wou'd if She Cou'd* (1668) was greeted with extraordinary excitement, Pepys finding the theater crowded and "1000 people put back that could not have room in the pit." The piece did not at first meet the public expectations, but it soon won general admiration, Shadwell declaring it "the best comedy that has been written since the restoration of the stage." It shows indeed a marked improvement over the earlier play. Sentiment and heroics have disappeared, and though both intrigue and humours are commonplace, they are brightened by wit, with enough hints of characterization to give verisimilitude to the clever dialogue. Courtal, the self-contained and cynical gentleman, directs the tricks and the wit, frees himself from the seductions of the middle-aged Lady Cockwood and captures for himself and his friend Freeman the two young heiresses, "sly girl and madcap." This seems to have been the epitome of life and the triumph of wit as understood by Restoration comedy.

The Man of Mode or Sir Fopling Flutter was not produced until eight years later, after Dryden's *Marriage à la Mode* and all four of Wycherley's comedies. It is, however, nearer to Congreve and Sheridan than any of those plays, and unquestionably a fine example of the pure comedy of manners. It is free from sentimentality or heroics and from practical jokes or impossible tricks, while its humours are confined to the affected Sir Fopling Flutter, the first of a long line of stage fops airing French styles on the English stage. Five gentlemen encounter six gentlewomen in various drawing-rooms or on the Mall, and both action and conversation move nimbly and naturally without any excess unless it be of wit. The chief personage is the arrogant, clear-headed and cold-hearted Dorimant, thought at the time to have been patterned after Rochester. His manners are admirable when he wishes them to be; his wit equal to any occasion and master over his emotions or even his vanity. He coldly insults and discards one mistress, the ardent and hysterical Mrs. Loveit, as coolly dismisses her successor, the timid but amorous Belinda, and carries off the heiress, overcoming by his politeness and self-control the alarms of her mother and her own sharp-tongued defense.

A few lines may be enough to recall the exquisite finish and the dramatic point of the dialogue. The stage has filled for the closing scene. The two cast mistresses have intruded on the company but have failed in their purpose to injure Dorimant. The mother of the heiress graciously accepts him.

LADY WOODVIL.

> Mr. Dorimant, every one has spoke so much in your behalf that I can no longer doubt but I was in the wrong.

Then Mrs. Loveit speaking to Belinda, the other cast mistress, fires her parting shot.

MRS. LOVEIT.

> There's nothing but falsehood and impertinence in this world, all men are villains or fools; take example from my misfortunes, Belinda; if thou wouldst be happy, give thyself wholly up to goodness.

Harriet, the heiress, now hastens to take a shot at her retreating rival.

HARRIET

> (to *Loveit*). Mr. Dorimant has been your God Almighty long enough; 'tis time to think of another.

LOVEIT.

> Jeered by her! I will lock myself up in my house and never see the world again.

HARRIET.

> A nunnery is the more fashionable place for such a retreat, and has been the fatal consequence of many a belle passion.

LOVEIT.

> Hold, heart! till I get home; should I answer, 'twould make her triumph greater.

> > [*Is going out.*

Dorimant does not speak to the furious lady, or even escort her to the door, but in two words he completes her humiliation by passing her over to the odious fop.

DORIMANT.

> Your hand, Sir Fopling—

SIR FOPLING.

Shall I wait after you, madam?

LOVEIT.

Legion of fools, as many devils take thee!

[*Exit.*

But the lovers do not now rush into each other's arms. That is not the fashion. Lady Woodvil invites Dorimant to visit them in the country, and the last words of the lovers before the final dance are as follows:

HARRIET.

To a great rambling lone house that looks as if it were not inhabited, the family's so small; there you'll find my mother, an old lame aunt, and myself, sir, perched up on chairs at a distance in a large parlour, sitting moping like three or four melancholy birds in a spacious volery. Does not this stagger your resolution?

DORIMANT.

Not at all, madam. The first time I saw you, you left me with the pangs of love upon me, and this day my soul has quite given up her liberty.

HARRIET.

This is more dismal than the country, Emilia; pity me who am going to that sad place. Methinks I hear the hateful noise of rooks already—Knaw, knaw, knaw. There's music in the worst cry in London. *My dill and cucumbers to pickle.*

Everyone has admired the wit that distinguishes all the persons of the play, but there has been difference of opinion as to how far it presents a natural or an artificial view of society. Etherege has been denied skill in characterization; and Dryden's criticism, extravagant if applicable at all, has been sometimes echoed in regard to his masterpiece—"being too witty himself, he could draw nothing but wits in a comedy of his; even his fools were infected with the disease of the author. They overflowed with smart repartee, and were only distinguished from the intended wits by being called coxcombs though they deserved not so scandalous a name."[2] Etherege anticipates such criticism when he makes Emilia say of Sir Fopling, "However you despise him, gentlemen, I'll lay my life he passes for a wit with many." But really his pseudo wit and affected asininity are made apparent, although without exaggeration or horseplay. And the gentlemen and ladies are sufficiently individualized in spite of the fact that they all exhibit skill in dialogue and repartee. They do not attempt to lay bare their souls, but they never speak out of character, and we have some satisfaction in knowing that such superior gentlemen as Dorimant and Bellair find ladies who match them in wit. Superior wit is, of course, always artificial in comparison with the dulness of ordinary conversation, but the dialogue in *The Man of Mode* presents a real society and real persons. "I allow it to be nature," cried Steele in *The Spectator,* "but it is nature in its utmost corruption and degeneracy."[3] Well, Etherege's view of human nature is assuredly not that of the sentimentalists or idealists, but he holds up for admiration neither corruption nor degeneracy but good manners and good dialogue. He sees the comedy of life, not through sentiment or fancy, nor with either malice or kindness, nor with any emotional prepense whatever, but with a cynicism and wit that both spring from the intellect. This is something new in our dramatic art, and it is not, I think, without a refreshing moral stimulus.

Notes

1. Hazlitt, quoted from *The English Comic Writers.*

2. Dryden's criticism. See A. W. Ward, Vol. III, p. 444.

3. Steele, *Spectator,* No. 65. See also No. 51 for further criticism of Etherege.

Thomas H. Fujimura (essay date 1952)

SOURCE: Fujimura, Thomas H. "Sir George Etherege." In *The Restoration Comedy of Wit*, pp. 75-116. Princeton, N. J.: Princeton University Press, 1952.

[*In the essay below, Fujimura discusses how Etherege employs wit in his plays to reflect Restoration intellectual attitudes toward such topics as naturalism, skepticism, and libertinism.*]

Sir George Etherege is generally credited with having originated a new type of comedy, and this belief need not be challenged, though there is reason to question modern opinion as to the type of comedy he inaugurated. To determine the nature of his contribution, however, we should first find out what sort of man he was. And here we are fortunate in having the **Letterbook,** the epistolary record of his last years at Ratisbon. From these letters, both personal and official, and also from contemporary records, there emerges a clear picture of Etherege as a Truewit—libertine, skeptical, naturalistic, and more concerned with wit than with morality or "manners."

Unfortunately, Etherege has suffered the same misinterpretation as have his comedies, and at present his true features are obscured by the descriptions of the censorious and of the "manners" critics. On the one hand, he is called "the most irresponsible rake of all," "an atrocious libertine" who could be fierce and vindictive under passion, and a man whose life is "a sordid story."[1] On the other hand, he is described by the "manners" critics as "a brilliant butterfly, alighting only upon such things as attract him; a creature without much depth, but of an extraordinary charm and a marvellous surety of touch."[2] He is called "a delicate painter who loved subtle contrasts in 'rose-colour and pale grey'";[3] and he is said to have encountered gracefully the one problem of his generation, that of style, "whether it was fighting the Dutch, defeating the policy of Achitophel, tying a riband, or writing a play."[4] The world of his plays is described as a frivolous one, where Strephon bends on one knee to Chloe fanning the pink blush on her painted cheek, while Momus peeps out at them—"an engaging trio, *mais ce n'est pas de la vie humaine.*"[5]

Of these two schools, the moralistic critics have at least a more colorful conception of Etherege than his apologists, who emasculate both the man and his art. But neither gives a credible nor faithful picture of the witty dramatist who created such intelligent and convincing people as Harriet and Dorimant. What is needed is an examination of Etherege's ideas and personality to determine to what extent he was affected by the currents of naturalism, skepticism, and libertinism, and how his comedies are an aesthetic expression of the Truewit's attitude toward life. Once we have a clear picture of Etherege as a human being, and of the connection between the man and his art, we shall not dismiss him casually as a brilliant butterfly or a mere rake, nor regard his plays as creating only the illusion of life.

The accounts of his contemporaries do not harmonize with either of the descriptions given above of Etherege. By Oldys he was called "a celebrated Wit," and he was praised by Langbaine as "a Gentleman sufficiently eminent in the Town for his Wit and Parts, and One whose tallent in sound Sence, and the Knowledge of Wit and Humour, are sufficiently conspicuous."[6] The Earl of Rochester, in "A Trial of the Poets for the Bays," credited Etherege with "fancy, sense, judgment and wit"—virtues which are not all suggested in the "manners" description. The charming, yet rather malicious, character of his wit is evident from his comedies (particularly in such passages as the raillery between Dorimant and Harriet), the rallying letter to Buckingham, and some "smart lampoons" on Nell Gwynn with which Theophilus Cibber credited him.[7] In his writings there was a grace, delicacy, and courtly air that made them attractive;[8] and this, with his affable and courteous deportment, and his sprightly and generous temper, gained him the character of "Gentle" George and "Easy" Etherege.[9] By virtue of these qualities, he gained ready access to the best company, and soon became a popular companion of aristocratic Wits like Buckingham, Rochester, Sir Car Scroope, Sedley, and Henry Savile.[10] They constituted an intimate circle with similar tastes: they were all men of wit and pleasure, all naturalistic, libertine, and skeptical; they were occasionally amateur men of letters, now and then diplomats, and sometimes rakes, but always Truewits. With them Etherege had his share of writing, diplomacy, and dissipation. He wrote three plays and some verse, served as secretary to the English ambassador at Constantinople, created some scandal, and in late life found himself the King's envoy at Ratisbon.

There is not much need to linger over the more scandalous events of his life, such as his part, with Rochester, in the notorious Downes affair in which Downes was killed,[11] his squabble with Buckley,[12] his championing of the actress Julia which upset the staid citizens of Ratisbon,[13] or his keeping a wench and getting diseased.[14] He was, as Cibber

said, as great a libertine "in speculation as in practice."[15] Such libertinism was the product of an unsettled age, when the Civil Wars created political and social chaos, and the "new philosophy" induced skepticism among thinking men. Etherege belonged to a younger generation, described by Clarendon as having no respect for authority or religion, which had seen conventional notions discarded and family relations destroyed.[16] He passed through an unsettled youth in unsettled times, and though of gentle birth, he seems to have had little or no university training, and went early into France to escape the Civil Wars in England.[17]

The libertinism of Etherege consisted of a witty, naturalistic attitude born of such conditions, rather than of settled principles arrived at through speculation. There is a poem by him entitled **"The Libertine"** which sums up the easy *carpe diem* philosophy by which he lived:

> Since death on all lays his impartial hand,
> And all resign at his command,
> The Stoic too, as well as I,
> With all his gravity must die:
> Let's wisely manage the last span,
> The momentary life of man,
> And still in pleasure's circle move,
> Giving t'our friends the days, and all our nights to
>   love.

CHORUS

* * *

> Thus, thus, whilst we are here, let's perfectly live,
> And taste all the pleasures that nature can give;
> And fill all our veins with a noble desire.

In this and the remaining stanzas, there is a touch of disillusionment and cynicism, a sense of the brevity and vanity of this "momentary life of man"; but this is buoyed up by the witty irreverence for conventional notions, and a zestful relish for "all the pleasures that nature can give," such as friendship, gaming, wine, women, and wit.

His easy libertinism and his naturalistic bias are expressed also in his letters from Ratisbon. Like his friend the Earl of Rochester, Etherege pursued the pleasures of "wine and women,"[18] and he found himself "often very hearty" with a "plain Bavarian,"[19] though he complained that the handsome young ladies were difficult because "their unconscionable price is marriage."[20] To a man who had been "bred in a free nation / With liberty of speech and passion,"[21] it must have been extremely painful to curtail the natural indulgence of sexual passion, which he believed good and necessary. "'Tis a fine thing," he exclaimed, "for a Man, who has been nourish'd so many Years with good substantial Flesh and Blood, to be reduc'd to Sighs and Wishes, and all those airy Courses which are serv'd up to feast a belle Passion."[22] But at least there was the divertissement of "le traîneau où l'on se met en croupe de quelque belle Allemande,"[23] and for a time there was also Julia, "a comedian no less handsome and no less kind in Dutchland than Mrs. Johnson was in England."[24] At times, after over-indulgence, he confessed himself more epicurean than libertine: "tout d'un coup je suis devenu disciple d'Épicure, je me tien, dans ma petite retraite, et je me suis établi pour maxime que la plus grand volupté consiste dans une parfaite santé."[25]

His philosophy was a worldly and sensible one arrived at through experience and observation, and he was never overly interested in anything transcendental or theoretical. Speaking of his epicureanism, he declared: "je n'ai pas le loisir de m'étendre sur un si digne sujet; pour ces atomes ils ne me rompent guère la tête." Metaphysics and the atoms of Democritus were beyond his scope: "Par la grâce de Dieu je sais où mon esprit est borné et je ne me mets guère en peine de savoir de quelle manière ce monde ici a été fait ou comment on se divert dans l'autre."[26] Like the skeptical St. Evremond, Etherege regarded such metaphysical speculations as futile and sterile.

His skeptical and naturalistic temper is evident also in his references to religion. In such matters he confessed, "'tis indifferent to me whether there be any other in the world who thinks as I do; this makes me have no temptation to talk of the business."[27] As the boon companion of free-thinkers like Sedley and Rochester, Etherege probably had a commonsensical, and perhaps deistic, attitude toward religion, and he no doubt accepted the hereafter as another of the possible hazards of existence. In a letter to a friend he said that the only quarrel that Mme. de Crecy had with them was that they were "heretics,"[28] and Hughes reported the Count to have said of Etherege, "Ce que je trouve de plus pire en lui que toutes ses débauches est, qu'il est profane et voudrait persuader tout le monde d'être de son sentiment."[29] There is no proof that Etherege was atheistic, but he was at least anticlerical and as Erastian as Hobbes, for he wrote of the clergy: "The mischief they daily do in the world makes me have no better an opinion of them than Lucian had of the ancient philosophers; their pride, their passion, and their covetousness makes them endeavour to destroy the government they were instituted to support, and, instead of taking care of the quietness of our souls, they are industrious to make us cut one another's throats."[30]

As a Truewit he accepted the vicissitudes of this life with equanimity, and without too much anxiety about the future. Of his attitude toward life he wrote:

> Humble to fortune, not her slave,
> I still was pleas'd with what she gave;
> And, with a firm, and cheerful mind,
> I steer my course with every wind,
> To all the ports she has design'd.[31]

He accepted life as it is, without complaint, because he had experienced enough of it to know what its limitations are. After all, this life is brief, and there is the disillusionment of knowing that "our Gayety and Vigour leaves us so soon in the lurch, . . . Feebleness attacks us without giving us fair Warning, and we no sooner pass the Meridian of Life but begin to decline."[32] He was not dazzled by the sham prizes of this world; and when James Fitzjames, the king's natural son, received a dukedom, Etherege wrote him that such honors are of no intrinsic value—"nevertheless the glittering favours of fortune are necessary to entertain those who, without examining any deeper, worship appearances."[33] This is the wisdom of a Truewit who has seen enough of the world to know that titles are baubles, of no intrinsic value to men of sense, yet useful in impressing the foolish, with whom the world abounds. When Etherege was praised too highly by Lord Dover, he wrote back: "The life I have led has afforded me little time to turn over books, but I have had leisure sufficient while I idly rolled about the town to look into myself and know when I am too highly valued."[34] He was not swayed by popular opinion or rumor, and upon hearing that Prince Herman of Baden, who was coming to Ratisbon, was an intolerably proud person, Etherege wrote to his superior in London, "I know the injury report generally does to mankind and therefore will not give you his character by hearsay, but stay till I have seen him and know him a little myself."[35] He showed manliness and generosity, if not prudence, in defending the actress Julia against the irate citizens of Ratisbon,[36] and he remained loyal to King James to the end of his life.

This is hardly the superficial "butterfly" depicted by the "manners" critics. Though never profound in his thinking, Etherege had the sensible worldliness of an Augustan like Horace. He was not overly interested in speculative matters like religion and philosophy, and he lived for this world in an epicurean spirit, in accordance with his naturalistic bias; but he was tolerant of others' beliefs, affectionate toward his friends, and capable of loyalty. He accepted this life, according to his judgment, without illusions, and he lived it as sensibly and pleasantly as a Truewit could, suffering neither envy at the fortunes of others nor regret for his libertine existence.

Toward women he had the naturalistic bias of most Truewits: he regarded them as affected, hypocritical, vain, and dissembling creatures, useful principally for venereal pleasures. From Constantinople, during his secretaryship there, he wrote of the Sultana: "though women here are not so polite and refin'd as in Christendome, yet shee wants not her little arts to secure her Sultan's affections, shee can dissemble fondness and jealousy and can swoone at pleasure."[37] He probably agreed with Dryden when the latter wrote to him from London, "Ask me not of love, for every man hates every man perfectly and women are still the same bitches."[38] To Buckingham he wrote a witty account of how a grief-stricken widow, a "Pattern of Conjugal Fidelity," had eloped with a young ensign, after being persuaded that immoderate sorrow would be ruinous to her beauty, and had thus proved herself a modern example of the Widow of Ephesus.[39] Toward matrimony he could scarcely be charitable in view of his own unhappy marriage to a widow, gently described by an anonymous writer as "a Bitch, / A Wizard, wrincled Woman, & a Witch."[40] In a poem **"To a lady, asking him how long he would love her,"** he declared that a man and woman should be constant to each other, freely and naturally, only so long as love endured between them; any such yoke as marriage was an unnatural imposition on human nature, and a commitment to love one another when love had ceased to exist.

Being a Truewit, he was opposed not only to marriage but to business; and as the King's envoy at Ratisbon he conducted himself more like a Wit than a diplomat, though he discharged his duties creditably. He was encouraged in this attitude by his superior and friend Lord Middleton, who wrote, "I hope in a little time we may hear something of your diversions as well as your business, which would be much pleasanter, and perhaps as instructive."[41] Following such advice, Etherege referred lightly to political matters, and to a friend he wrote, "The business of the Diet for the most part is only fit to entertain those insects in politics which crawl under the trees in St. James's Park."[42] Yet, to the Duke of Buckingham he confessed to a greater aptitude for business than he had suspected,[43] and his lucid reports of the political situation in the Empire and of its relations with France show his mastery of affairs. Though he challenged Dryden's title to the province of idleness,[44] he turned out a voluminous official correspondence, as well as many personal letters, three comedies, and some verse. One suspects that his "noble laziness of mind" was a pretense, especially when he described himself ironically as an idle fellow at the end of a lengthy official communication that runs to some three printed pages.[45] Etherege was closer to the truth when he said, "I am too lazy and too careless to be ambitious."[46]

At Ratisbon, he longed for cheer, company, and late hours—some such evening as Dryden described so happily in his dedication of a play to Sedley: "We have, like them our genial nights, where our discourse is neither too serious nor too light, but always pleasant, and, for the most part, instructive; the raillery, neither too sharp upon the present, nor too censorious on the absent; and the cups only such as will raise the conversation of the night, without disturbing the business of the morrow."[47] But at Ratisbon, Etherege found that the men were so addicted to drinking that it destroyed the pleasures of conversation.[48] The ceremony of the place also made convivial gatherings rare; and often he was condemned "To make grave legs in formal fetters, / Converse with fops, and write dull letters."[49] Wittily Etherege exposed the absurd formality with which the Diet conducted even the trifling business of arranging to see a farce that had come to town,[50] and he exercised his wit in a malicious portrait of the Count de Windisgratz, the most pompous of them all.[51] He kept the wittiest and easiest company he could find—the French ambassador the Count de Crecy, described by Etherege as "a *bel esprit*"; the Count de Lamberg, a gentleman who knew how to live; and Monsieur Schnolsky, so much a Wit that no one could distinguish "between his jest and earnest."[52] He remembered with regret the bitter frosty night when he and Dorset carried "two draggle-tailed nymphs" over the Thames to Lambeth,[53] and in his letters he asked to be remembered to all his friends at the Rose

and "the lily at the bar."[54] He was cheered to hear that his friend Sedley, who "had always more wit than was enough for one man," had produced a successful play in *Bellamira*.[55] Himself he compared to Ovid at Pontus,[56] and epigrammatically he dismissed the bourgeois society in which he was stranded: "London is dull by accident but Ratisbon by nature."[57] The person mirrored in these letters is, indeed, a Truewit—genial, witty, skeptical, worldly, and easy.

As a writer, Etherege displayed the same careless, playful attitude, and of his literary success he wrote to Dryden: "Though I have not been able formerly to forbear playing the fool in verse and prose I have now judgment enough to know how much I ventured, and am rather amazed at my good fortune than vain upon a little success; and did I not see my own error the commendation you give me would be enough to persuade me of it. A woman, who has luckily been thought agreeable, has not reason to be proud when she hears herself extravagantly praised by an undoubted beauty. It would be a pretty thing for a man who has learned of his own head to scrape on the fiddle to enter the list with the greatest master in the science of music."[58] Yet, Etherege was the man of whom Dryden said in 1687, "I will never enter the lists in prose with the undoubted best author of it which our nation has produced."[59] That this high praise is merited is evident if we compare the rather heavy and labored wit of Dryden's letter with the sprightly ease and wit of Etherege's reply.[60] There was ease and carelessness in Etherege's attitude toward writing, but he was by no means an artless writer. In his library at Ratisbon he had copies of *Critiques sur Horace* (5 volumes), Rymer's *Tragedies of the Last Age,* and *Reflections on Aristotle's Treaty of Poesy*;[61] and as a Truewit, Etherege was also committed to the principle of decorum (wit), which called for naturalness, an easy elegance, and propriety. What he objected to was the labored writing that savored of the pedant or the professional writer, as one may gather from his censure of the Count de Crecy for meticulously polishing and repolishing the expressions in his memorial.[62]

As a writer Etherege seems to have been interested in wit in all its manifestations. In the prologue he wrote for Dryden's *Sir Martin Mar-all,* he lamented the fact that the age was no longer content with wit, but wanted gaudy sights. From Ratisbon, he requested a copy of Shadwell's *Squire of Alsatia* that he might know what fools were prevalent.[63] In his own comedies, what contemporaries praised was the witty, naturalistic depiction of coxcombs and Truewits, and Dryden wrote in "MacFlecknoe":

> Let gentle George in triumph tread the stage,
> Make Dorimant betray, and Loveit rage;
> Let Cully, Cockwood, Fopling, charm the pit,
> And in their folly show the writer's wit.

Oldys, in fact, attributed Etherege's success as a dramatist to his witty dialogue and to his naturalistic representation of Truewits: "These applauses arose from our Author's changing the study after old copies, and chimerical

draughts from ungrounded speculation, which is but painting with dead colours, for those, taken directly from the
freshest practise and experience in original life. . . . He
has also spirited his dialogues, especially in the courtship
of the fair sex, for which he is distinguished by Mr. Dryden
and others, with a sparkling gaiety which had but little appeared before upon the stage, in parts pretending to the
character of modish Gallants; and to judge his figures according to the rules of true resemblance, he will appear a
masterly hand; but strictly to examine them, by the rules
of honour, morality, and the principles of virtue, where
none are seriously professed . . . would be a severity."[64]

This is as clear a statement as one can find anywhere of
what constitutes the salient features of Etherege's comic
writing: witty dialogue, especially between the gallant and
his mistress in raillery and "proviso" scenes, a naturalistic
view of man (and a consequent disregard of conventional
morality), and realistic technique. These are the points in
which Etherege excelled as a writer, though not every
critic approved, as one gathers from Captain Alexander
Radcliffe's censure of Etherege for being too photographic
in his realism, "So what he writes is but Translation /
From Dog and Partridge conversation."[65] What we should
look for in Etherege's comedies, then, is not interest in
"manners," but such features of wit comedy as witty
dialogue, naturalistic content, and realistic technique. We
should also expect malicious laughter at fools, and the
expression of a skeptical and libertine philosophy in witty
form.

His first comedy, *The Comical Revenge, or Love in a Tub*
(1664),[66] has most of these elements, though in rather
rudimentary form. Evelyn described the play as "a facetious comedy," and Pepys observed that it was "very merry,
but only so by gesture, not wit at all, which methinks is
beneath the House."[67] Both Langbaine and Downes record
that the play was a success,[68] and we have Oldys' statement that "the fame of this play," dedicated to the witty
Lord Buckhurst, helped Etherege gain the friendship of the
aristocratic Wits.[69]

But despite its warm reception, the play reveals an ambiguity of purpose on Etherege's part, and a consequent lack
of unity; and at best, it represents only a groping toward
what later became the comedy of wit. In the prologue,
Etherege lamented the fact that political bias, and not wit,
determined the merit of a play. Yet one cannot say that he
succeeded in writing a witty play, nor in wholly excluding
political bias. The title of the play suggests an outwitting
situation; and the three comic plots are indeed of this
nature: Wheadle and Palmer setting plots against Sir
Nicholas Cully, only to be outwitted themselves by the
Truewit; Betty exposing Dufoy; and Sir Frederick and the
Widow trying to outwit each other in a series of "comical
revenges." But in these situations, the comical element is
more in evidence than the witty; and the opening scenes
could hardly have impressed the audience. In the first
scene, Dufoy, with a plaster on his head, is complaining
that his master Sir Frederick has broken his head:

DUFOY:

> dis Bedlamé, Mad-cape, diable de matré, vas drunké de
> last night, and vor no reason, but dat me did advisé
> him to go to bed, begar he did striké, breaké my headé,
> Jernie.

CLARK:

> Have patience, he did it unadvisedly.

DUFOY:

> Unadvisé! didé not me advise him justé when he did
> ité?

> (I, i)

When Sir Frederick appears, the wit is not much better.
Upon Dufoy's showing his plastered head, Sir Frederick
remarks lamely, "Thou hast a notable brain" (I, ii).

The embryonic character of this first comedy of wit by
Etherege is most apparent from an examination of the
Truewits in the play. Sir Frederick, who dominates the
outwitting situations, is such a man as is described in *The
Character of a Town-Gallant*—a drinker of wine, an as-
sailer of the watch, and a breaker of windows.[70] His wildness reminds us of the author's own frolics. The night
prior to the first scene, Sir Frederick has been out drinking, crying "whore" at the door of a kept mistress, and he
has come home drunk and broken Dufoy's head. There are
coachmen, link-boys, and fiddlers to be paid after the
night's debauch. There is a rather sophomoric quality about
his escapades; and by the standards of Dorimant or Mira-
bell, Sir Frederick could hardly qualify as a Truewit. Noise,
bustle, the breaking of windows, and the beating of the
watch gradually came to be regarded as signs of false wit;
and in later wit comedies, these came to be the marks of
Witwoud rather than of the Wit. Sir Frederick conforms to
a rather callow conception of the Truewit, though Etherege
distinguished between his gallant wildness and the stupid,
witless wildness of Sir Nicholas (IV, iii).

Though he is a poor specimen of a Truewit by comparison
with Dorimant, Sir Frederick satisfies the Widow's taste
for "the prettiest, wittiest, wildest Gentleman about the
Town." He has traveled abroad in France; he has the easy
courage of a Truewit who does not take life, death, or love
too seriously; and he can bear with "the inconveniences of
honest Company," if there is freedom of conversation. He
speaks lightly of virtue, and is inclined to be cynical about
women and matrimony. He believes that "Women, like
Juglers-Tricks, appear Miracles to the ignorant; but in
themselves th' are meer cheats" (I, ii); and when he
disposes of his kept mistress Lucy to Sir Nicholas, he tells
the cully: "And, give her her due, faith she was a very
honest Wench to me, and I believe will make a very honest Wife to you" (V, v). As a Truewit he also shares the
naturalistic belief that love is only lust, and when informed
by Beaufort that the Widow loves him, he exclaims,
"What? the Widow has some kind thoughts of my body?"
(I, ii). He has honesty enough to save Sir Nicholas from

being cheated by Wheadle, but he has malice enough to marry off Sir Nicholas to his own kept mistress, and to couple Wheadle with Grace, and Palmer with Grace's maid.

There is no doubt that Sir Frederick possesses vivacity, some degree of perspicacity, and malice—all marks of the Truewit. But he hardly conforms to the standard of decorum, nor displays much novelty or fineness of fancy. In fact, he can even be gross in his *double-entendre,* as on the occasion of his disturbing the Widow's household late at night:

MAID:

> Sir *Frederick,* I wonder you will offer this; you will lose her favour for ever.

SIR FRED:

> Y'are mistaken; now's the time to creep into her favour.

MAID:

> I'm sure y'ave wak'd me out of the sweetest sleep. Hey ho—

SIR FRED:

> Poor girl! let me in, I'le rock thee into a sweeter.

(III, ii)

In his solitary efforts he is seldom striking, and for the Widow he has this rather jejune similitude: "Some Women, like Fishes, despise the Bait, or else suspect it, whil'st still it's bobbing at their mouths; but subtilly wav'd by the Angler's hand, greedily hang themselves upon the hook" (I, ii).[71] Again, the double hyperbole of his remark on Jenny the maid lacks novelty: "Sh'as made more noise than half a dozen Paper-mills: *London*-bridge at a low water is silence to her" (I, ii). Even the most frequently quoted of his witticisms comes off poorly when read in its context:

MAID:

> Unhand me; are you a man fit to be trusted with a woman's reputation?

SIR FRED:

> Not when I am in a reeling condition; men are now and then subject to those infirmities in drink, which women have when th' are sober. Drunkenness is no good Secretary, *Jenny;* you must not look so angry, good faith, you must not.

(I, ii)

The author spoils the wit by not knowing when to stop; and Sir Frederick, after a witty stroke at women, tumbles into a feeble apology to a maid. Sir Frederick's wit splutters now and then, but is never sustained.

The liveliest wit is to be expected in the courtship scenes, but here again, we usually find tricks rather than comic wit. Part of this defect is due to the fact that the heroine

suffers under the handicap of being a widow. Sir Frederick assumes that her marital experiences have only sharpened her sexual appetite, and the Widow Rich conforms to his expectations by betraying more eagerness than a witty woman should. She is obviously in love with him from the beginning; and when he pretends to be dead, in order to trick a confession of love from her, she weeps with genuine grief and exclaims in blank verse: "Unhappy woman! why shou'd I survive / The only man in whom my joys did live? / My dreadful grief!" (IV, vii). Though she laughs at Sir Frederick a moment later to prove she saw through his trick, her show of emotion is too genuine to be laughed away so easily. She is too warm and generous for a Truewit: she feels sorry for Dufoy and orders him released from the tub, and she also sends money to free Sir Frederick when she hears he has been arrested for his debts. In these episodes she shows a lack of perspicacity which makes her the dupe of others. It is evident that the Widow lacks the perspicacity and the malice of a Truewit, so that she is no ready match for Sir Frederick. Because of this initial disadvantage under which the Widow labors, there can be no real wit combat between her and Sir Frederick such as we find in later comedies by Etherege. Furthermore, the combats between the two very often degenerate into tricks ("comical revenges"), such as Sir Frederick's having himself borne in on a bier or his sending word that he has been arrested. It is then up to the Widow to penetrate his trick, and thus expose him.

It is in these encounters, however, that we have the best repartee in the play. There is not a great deal of wit in these exchanges, but they do show some spirit. On their first meeting the two are wary of each other but amiable, and they rally one another sharply, though with more humor than wit:

SIR FRED:

> Widow, I dare not venture my self in those amorous shades; you have a mind to be talking of Love I perceive, and my heart's too tender to be trusted with such conversation.

WID:

> I did not imagine you were so foolishly conceited; is it your Wit or your Person, Sir, that is so taking?

SIR FRED:

> Truly you are much mistaken, I have no such great thoughts of the young man you see; who ever knew a Woman have so much reason to build her Love upon merit? Have we not daily experience of great Fortunes, that fling themselves into the arms of vain idle Fellows? Can you blame me then for standing upon my guard?

(II, i)

Sir Frederick and the Widow are too good-natured for sharp raillery, and his disparagement of himself at the same time that he rallies the Widow shows a man of humor as much as a man of wit. On another occasion, when he pounds her door at night to prove his wit, we have this characteristic passage of repartee:

SIR FRED:

> Can you in conscience turn a young man out of doors at this time o'th' night, Widow? Fie, fie, the very thought on't will keep you waking.

WID:

> So pretty, so well-favour'd a young man; one that loves me.

SIR FRED:

> Ay, one that loves you.

WID:

> Truly 'tis a very hard-hearted thing. (She sighs.)

SIR FRED:

> Come, come, be mollifi'd. You may go, Gentlemen, and leave me here; you may go. (To the Masquers.)

WID:

> You may stay, Gentlemen; you may stay, and take your Captain along with you: You'l find good Quarters in some warm Hay-loft.

SIR FRED:

> Merciless Woman! Do but lend me thy Maid; faith I'le use her very tenderly and lovingly, even as I'd use thy self, dear Widow, if thou wou'dst but make proof of my affection.

(III, iii)

The Widow's wit is sarcasm of no very high order, and her speech, with its "Hay-loft," is too homely for a city Wit. The raillery lacks polish and point; and Sir Frederick can be smutty but not very witty. Now and then the Widow may bristle up and exclaim, "I have seen e'ne as merry a man as your self, Sir *Frederick,* brought to stand with folded arms, and with a tristful look tell a mournful tale to a Lady" (II, ii); but more often, Sir Frederick adopts a domineering tone toward her, and cries, "Widow, May the desire of man keep thee waking till thou art as mad as I am" (IV, vii).

It is evident that Pepys's criticism of the play as "merry by gesture, not wit," is largely justified. The play has occasional flashes of wit, but they are never sustained. The two Truewits lack the polish and brilliance of a Dorimant and Harriet. They are promising young fledglings not yet come of age, and their wit necessarily shows a somewhat callow quality. Sir Frederick at least has the buoyancy and carefree attitude toward life characteristic of the Truewit, but his interests are still too physical, such as playing tricks on the Widow, creating disturbances at night, and chasing maids. He has not yet arrived at a refined taste in women or in wit.

The naturalistic temper in the play is much more consistently maintained than the wit, particularly in the comic scenes involving the minor figures. There are such naturalistic passages as Dufoy jesting about being "clap'd":

CLARK:

> Methinks the wound your Master gave you last night, makes you look very thin and wan, Monsieur.

DUFOY:

> Begar you mistake, it be de voundé dat my Metresse did give me long agoe.

CLARK:

> What? some pretty little English Lady's crept into your heart?

DUFOY:

> No, but damn'd littel English whore is creepé into my bone begar, me could vish dat de Diable vould také her vid allé my harté.

(II, i)

In appreciating such scenes, we need not be as squeamish as some modern critics are,[72] for such witticisms are to be expected from characters naturalistically conceived. The saucy, impertinent Dufoy is also ridiculous as an incipient Witwoud who claims he was hired for being a "man d'esprit, and of vitté," and is consequently exposed to the malicious laughter of his superiors.

The strength of the naturalistic temper is evident, too, in the Wheadle-Sir Nicholas plot. This has been described as Middletonian in spirit,[73] but Etherege probably did not go back to his literary predecessor when he could copy directly from the life about him. A book published in the reign of Charles, *Proteus Redivivus: or the Art of Wheedling, or Insinuation* (1675), gives a very complete account of the contemporary practice of wheedling, and describes such persons as Wheadle and Sir Nicholas. "Wheadle" is defined as a term in the "Canting Dictionary" which "imports a subtil insinuation into the nature, humours and inclinations of such we converse with, working upon them so effectually, that we possess them with a belief that all our actions and services tend to their pleasures and profit, whereas it is but seemingly so, that we may work on them our real advantage"; and the town Wheadle is described as living off fops, whom he entices to a tavern for the purpose of swindling them.[74] He has also laid up a store of choice things to say, and has wit enough to please in conversation.[75] This picture corresponds to Sir Frederick's description of Wheadle: "one whose trade is Trechery, to make a Friend, and then deceive him; he's of a ready Wit, pleasant Conversation, throughly skill'd in men" (I, ii). Like Dufoy, Wheadle has a dry, hard wit that is part of his naturalistic make-up. When outwitted by the Truewit and forced to marry the mistress he has been keeping, he says: "Come hither, *Grace*; I did but make bold, like a young Heir, with his

Estate, before it came into his hands: Little did I think, *Grace,* that this Pasty, (Stroaking her belly.) when we first cut it up, should have been preserv'd for my Wedding Feast" (v, iv). Wheadle has many of the characteristics of the Witwoud; and at the same time, he is a realistic portrayal of a familiar figure from contemporary low-life.

Sir Nicholas Cully is obviously the Witless in the play, but like Wheadle, he is an imperfect copy of what eventually became a type figure in wit comedy. He is ridiculous not only because of his stupidity and boorishness but because he has Puritan antecedents. He is described by Sir Frederick as "one whom *Oliver,* for the transcendent knavery and disloyalty of his Father, has dishonour'd with Knighthood; a fellow as poor in experience as in parts, and one that has a vain-glorious humour to gain a reputation amongst the Gentry, by feigning good nature, and affection to the King and his Party" (I, ii).

Though neither Sir Nicholas nor Wheadle are perfect examples of Witless and Witwoud, they fit into the normal pattern of wit comedy. Wheadle, as Witwoud, plays with Sir Nicholas Cully; but he overrates his wit (cleverness), and is exposed at the end by Sir Frederick, the Truewit, who forces him to marry Grace. Wheadle and Sir Nicholas, along with Dufoy, are naturalistically conceived, and they contribute to the comic side of the play, since they are all exposed to the malicious laughter of the Truewits.

Of the main plot, which is heroic and serious, I have said nothing, because it is out of keeping with the rest of the play. Aurelia puts her finger on the essential difference between it and the rest of the play when she says: "But we by Custom, not by Nature led, / Must in the beaten paths of Honour tread" (II, ii). The characters in the comic portion follow nature because of their naturalistic bias, and a person like Sir Frederick never considers honor; but the people of the Graciana-Beaufort world act according to custom and honor. Yet the heroic world is not insulated against the currents of skepticism and naturalism; and even Graciana recognizes the fact that men admire women who can conceal their love, and contend with them on equal terms (II, ii), though she herself is incapable of profiting from this knowledge, as the Widow Rich does. The two worlds in the play are irreconcilable; and Etherege, perhaps unintentionally, shows the absurdity and artificiality of the code by which the honorable, custom-bound half lives and suffers.

Etherege's second play, **She Would it She Could,** opened on February 6, 1668, to a capacity audience which included Wits like Charles, Buckingham, Buckhurst, and Sedley. Pepys, who was also there, wrote in his *Diary,* "Lord! how full was the house, and how silly the play, there being nothing in the world good in it, and few people pleased in it"—to which he added, "all the rest did, through the whole pit, blame the play as a silly, dull thing, though there was something very roguish and witty; but the design of the play, and end, mighty insipid." Dennis observed many years later that despite its poor reception on the first

performance, "it was esteem'd by the Men of Sense, for the trueness of some of its Characters, and the purity and freeness and easie grace of its Dialogue."[76]

The story of the overeager woman frustrated is not very original, and is familiar to us from pre-Restoration plays like Shirley's *Lady of Pleasure* (1635). But the picture of the lustful woman in Lady Cockwood is an extremely fine naturalistic study. She serves several purposes in the play: first, she exemplifies the author's naturalistic belief that women are, at bottom, as sensual as men; second, she gives pleasure to the audience by serving as the butt of its malicious laughter; and third, through her, the dramatist wittily exposes the conventional notion of honor. It is a mistake to think of her as "a woman of social pretensions whose attempted illicit amours are wrecked by the pressure of a social standard which she lacks intelligence to comprehend."[77] She has no social pretensions because she is evidently on good terms with the modish people of her group. Nor is she "a female Tartuffe, a woman of loud religious pretensions, who demands respect and devotion for her piety, and who is really engaged, all the time, in the vain prosecution of a disgraceful intrigue."[78] Neither the "manners" nor the moralistic interpretation can explain her character and her role in the play. She is actually an unhappily married woman whose strong sexual desires are frustrated because her unmanly husband shuns his marital duties.

In the naturalistically conceived role of the frustrated wife, Lady Cockwood becomes ridiculous only because of her overeager efforts to satisfy her sexual desire, and, at the same time, her refusal to recognize the natural fact that she has physical needs. Since she has other faults such as impertinence, inordinate fondness, vanity, and jealousy—all marks of the female Witwoud—she is also ridiculed for aspiring to the love of a Truewit. But her chief flaw is her pretending to the principles of conventional morality: she declares that she loves her husband fondly, and she professes to be the very soul of honor. Since she is at the same time striving to satisfy her desires extramaritally, she speaks euphemistically, from hypocrisy or self-delusion, of Courtall's "generous passion." Even in her relations with her maid Mrs. Sentry, she cannot put off her tarnished dress of honor; and following an interview alone with Courtall, which she desired, Lady Cockwood admonishes her maid:

LA. COCK:

> What a strange thing is this! will you never take warning, but still be leaving me alone in these suspicious occasions?

SEN:

> I was but in the next room, Madam.

LA. COCK:

> What may Mr. *Courtall* think of my innocent intentions? I protest if you serve me so agen, I shall be strangely angry: you should have more regard to your Lady's Honour.

(II, ii)

This is not social satire, as the "manners" critics would suggest, for Lady Cockwood is not criticized because of her failure to conform to a social mode: she is ridiculed because of her self-delusion, her hypocrisy, and her cant about honor. On the other hand, this is not conventional moral satire; for though Etherege may prefer sincerity to hypocrisy, he is not concerned with virtue or with exposing vanity and hypocrisy for the usual moral reasons. In fact, Lady Cockwood will undoubtedly take Courtall's advice at the end to "entertain an able Chaplain," as the best means of satisfying her sexual appetite circumspectly. She remains as obdurate as ever in her lust and reforms only so far as to solace herself with a chaplain rather than a gallant; and there is no suggestion that Etherege condemns her for having adulterous desires. As her name implies, she is a naturalistically conceived woman who would follow nature and fornicate, if she could stop pretending that she lives by honor. Through her, Etherege wittily exposes the conventional notion of honor, since it is only a ridiculous female coxcomb like her that professes it.

In this naturalistic world, Sir Oliver Cockwood and Sir Joslin Jolly are quite at home: they are a pair of Witlesses who set off each other's folly and expose themselves to the malicious laughter of the Truewits. Sir Oliver and Lady Cockwood, in the familiar role of Witless and Witwoud, are also involved in an outwitting situation in which the more stupid is exposed to laughter. Sir Oliver pretends to be a "taring Blade" but is cowardly at heart, and as a husband, he is not only uxorious and hen-pecked, but lacks the wherewithal to satisfy his wife. Above all, he is a stupid oaf who believes in his wife's fidelity, and says fatuously, "Never man was so happy in a vertuous and loving Lady!" (v, i). Sir Joslin Jolly is equally a Witless. His merriment smacks of the coarse boisterousness of the country, and his speech is larded with sexual references, horse and hare similitudes, and country snatches; and he thinks that low creatures like the pimp Rake-hell and the whores that Rake-hell brings to their parties are the finest company in the world. These two Witlesses are ridiculous because they lack sense and judgment, they are boorish in their fun, and they lack perspicacity to see through the deception of others.

Pepys's comment on the mediocrity of the plot and the unoriginal ending applies to the pursuit of the young girls by the gallants as much as to the Cockwood story, for the courtship is left pretty much to chance, and the final agreement among the lovers is due principally to accident and opportunity. The outwitting plot serves as a framework, however, for the wit play of a quartet of Truewits consisting of the two gallants and their mistresses.

Courtall and Freeman are "two honest Gentlemen of the Town" in pursuit of wine, women, and wit. Of the two, Courtall is not only the wittier and more perspicacious but the bolder, and he takes the lead in the intrigue to outwit Lady Cockwood and gain the favors of the young women. When Freeman fears that the girls mistrust them, Courtall exclaims, "Never fear it; whatsoever women say, I am sure they seldom think the worse of a man, for running at all, 'tis a sign of youth and high mettal, and makes them rather piquee, who shall tame him" (III, i). With his ready tongue, he rallies the Exchange women, who are fond of him for his wit; and he plays with Lady Cockwood, wittily pretending that it is his virtue and her honor that stand in the way of their affair:

COUR:

> Oh, 'tis impossible, Madam, never think on't now you have been seen with me; to leave 'em upon any pretence will be so suspitious, that my concern for your honour will make me so feverish and disordered, that I shal lose the taste of all the happiness you give me.

LA. COCK:

> Methinks you are too scrupulous, heroick Sir.

> (III, i)

This is Truewit using Lady Cockwood's own cant about honor to outwit a hypocritical woman for whom he has no real taste. Courtall rallies her ironically at times: "The truth is, Madam, I am a Rascal; but I fear you have contributed to the making me so" (IV, ii). He is cynical about marriage, and exclaims, "a Wife's a dish, of which if a man once surfeit, he shall have a better stomach to all others ever after" (III, iii). In a conversation with Sir Oliver, he also expresses his libertinism and skepticism:

SIR OLIV:

> Well a pox of this tying man and woman together, for better, for worse! upon my conscience it was but a Trick that the Clergy might have a feeling in the Cause.

COUR:

> I do not conceive it to be much for their profit, Sir *Oliver,* for I dare lay a good wager, let 'em but allow Christian Liberty, and they shall get ten times more by Christnings, than they are likely to lose by Marriages.

> (I, i)

Freeman is less witty than his friend, and is less inclined to indulge in skeptical wit, though now and then he can handle a witty antithesis cleverly: "I have an appointment made me without my seeking too, by such a she, that I will break the whole ten Commandments, rather than disappoint her of her breaking one" (IV, ii). But more often he plays second fiddle to his friend:

COUR:

> I have been so often balk'd with these Vizard-Masks, that I have at least a dozen times forsworn 'em; they are a most certain sign of an ill face, or what is worse, an old Acquaintance.

FREE:

> The truth is, nothing but some such weighty reason, is able to make women deny themselves the pride they have to be seen.

> (II, i)

In the witticisms of these two gallants, there is nothing very striking, aside from an occasional hit at matrimony and Courtall's ironical pretense to virtue. Sometimes they even fall into such labored similitudes as the following, when they meet unexpectedly:

COUR:

> What unlucky Devil has brought thee higher?

FREE:

> I believe a better natur'd Devil then yours, *Courtall,* if a Leveret be better meat then an old Puss, that has been cours'd by most of the young Fellows of her country: I am not working my brain for a Counterplot, a disappointment is not my bus'ness.

COUR:

> You are mistaken, *Freeman:* prithee be gone, and leave me the Garden to my self, or I shall grow as testy as an old Fowler that is put by his shoot, after he has crept half a mile upon his belly.

FREE:

> Prithee be thou gone, or I shall take it as unkindly as a Chymist wou'd, if thou should'st kick down his Limbeck in the very minute that he look'd for projection.

(IV, ii)

The wit play of the two gallants alone, though spirited, shows no great merit: not only is there an absence of original similitudes, but there is little of the elegance and epigrammatical quality of fine wit. What chiefly distinguishes the two as Truewits is their carefree attitude, their naturalistic temper, and their contempt for Witlesses like Sir Oliver and Sir Joslin.

Of the two girls, Gatty is the only real Truewit: she is almost as fine a figure as Harriet, and she is superior to Courtall. On their first appearance, Gatty reveals herself as a Truewit, and Ariana as something less. Gatty cries, "How glad am I we are in this Town agen," while Ariana regrets the pleasures of the country—"the benefit of the fresh Air, and the delight of wandring in the pleasant Groves" (I, ii). Gatty is also rebellious against the restraints imposed by their "grave Relations," and wants to partake freely of the pleasures of the town. She is wild and free, and has the freshness of the country about her; if she does not always show the decorum of a fine town lady, she has the verve of a young filly romping about the pasture. She is not above a homely country simile: to the young gallants she says, "Our Company may put a constraint upon you; for I find you daily hover about these Gardens, as a Kite does about a back-side, watching an opportunity to catch up the Poultry" (IV, ii). But this is part of her carefree, witty attitude toward life. She likes freedom and sincerity, and when Ariana reproves her for singing a wanton love-song, she exclaims, "I hate to dissemble when I need not." With true naturalistic bias, she ridicules Platonic love, and she rallies her sister for being melancholy out of love: "Now

art thou for a melancholy Madrigal, compos'd by some amorous Coxcomb, who swears in all Companies he loves his Mistress so well, that he wou'd not do her the injury, were she willing to grant him the favour, and it may be is Sot enough to believe he wou'd oblige her in keeping his Oath too" (v, i). To a woman, nothing can be more serious than love, but she will jest about it nevertheless. Gatty has the virtue of maintaining the character of a Truewit throughout the play, without falling into flat similitudes or ever losing her witty attitude toward life.

It is hardly sound, then, to suggest, as Dobrée does, that "the full-blooded boisterousness of Sir Joslin Jolly and Sir Oliver Cockwood" is incompatible with "Ariana's fragile world."[79] Actually there is no such fragile and artificial world of the sort the "manners" critics imagine, for the world of Ariana and Gatty is full-blooded and naturalistic. The two girls are happy-go-lucky in their attitude toward life; and after so serious an episode as Sir Oliver and Courtall fighting, the girls are next door, "laughing and playing at Lantre-lou." Though Ariana expresses too much sentiment in her earlier appearances, neither of the girls weeps and trembles over the future, as do Graciana and Aurelia in the preceding play. They are a charming pair of Truewits, with a touch of naïveté, but with sufficient perspicacity to see through the hypocrisy of Lady Cockwood and the coxcombry of Sir Oliver. There is more good-nature than malice in their raillery, and their frank delight in the pleasures of courtship is unspoiled by satiety or experience.

Separately, the four young Truewits do not approach the highest wit. The courtship scenes, however, provide passages that Pepys found "very roguish and witty." When the quartet meet, they usually engage in what Gatty calls "a little harmless Raillery betwixt us." Their first encounter is marked by a long passage of sustained repartee which has the character of a tour de force:

COUR:

> By your leave, Ladies—

GATTY:

> I perceive you can make bold enough without it.

FREE:

> Your Servant, Ladies—

ARIA:

> Or any other Ladys that will give themselves the trouble to entertain you.

FREE:

> 'Slife, their tongues are as nimble as their heels.

COUR:

> Can you have so little good nature to dash a couple of bashful young men out of countenance, who came out of pure love to tender you their service?

GATTY:

'Twere pity to baulk 'em, Sister.

ARIA:

Indeed methinks they look as if they never had been slip'd before.

FREE:

Yes faith, we have had many a fair course in this Paddock, have been very well flesh'd, and dare boldly fasten.

(II, i)

The speeches are quick and short, and the repartee has verve. Despite the absence of balanced epigrams and of real malice, the remarks are witty, and Freeman's *double-entendre* is superior to anything in the preceding play.

As they grow more familiar and develop a little pique toward each other, the comic wit improves; and when the girls encounter the men, who they believe have audaciously forged letters from them, there is some sharp repartee:

GATTY:

I suppose your Mistress, Mr. *Courtall,* is always the last Woman you are acquainted with.

COUR:

Do not think, Madam, I have that false measure of my acquaintance, which Poets have of their Verse, always to think the last best, though I esteem you so, in justice to your merit.

GATTY:

Or if you do not love her best, you always love to talk of her most; as a barren Coxcomb that wants discourse, is ever entertaining Company out of the last Book he read in.

COUR:

Now you accuse me most unjustly, Madam; who the Devil, that has common sense, will go a birding with a Clark in his Cap?

ARIA:

Nay, we do not blame you, Gentlemen, every one in their way; a Huntsman talks of his Dogs, a Falconer of his Hawks, a Jocky of his Horse, and a Gallant of his Mistress.

GATTY:

Without the allowance of this Vanity, an Amour would soon grow as dull as Matrimony.

(IV, ii)

Here are fine "turns" and some pointed rejoinders. Finally, in an incipient "proviso" scene, there is one fine passage, at once balanced and paradoxical, when Courtall says to Gatty: "Now shall I sleep as little without you, as I shou'd do with you" (v, i).

She Would if She Could is superior to the first play in every respect. Yet the wit is not always of the highest: there is often a lapsing into flat similitudes; there is not much of the malicious and skeptical wit that gives so much vitality to wit comedy; and there is little of the elegance and fine balance of language which is the mark of high wit. The comic wit sparkles at times, but principally because of the zest and high spirit of the young Truewits rather than because of an original play of ideas. The Truewits are, in fact, extremely young, and display more fancy than judgment in their speech and conduct. Finally, the wit in the play does not always spring from the dramatic action, nor is the wit of the different characters often distinguished, since the witticisms are assigned somewhat indiscriminately to the several Truewits. The best thing in the play is the naturalistic portrait of Lady Cockwood, and Etherege's witty use of her to deflate the notion of honor.

His last play, *The Man of Mode, or Sir Fopling Flutter* (1676), is one of the best examples of the comedy of wit. In the prologue Sir Car Scroope implied that one would find "Nature well drawn and Wit" in this comedy; and Langbaine commended its naturalism: "This Play is written with great Art and Judgment, and is acknowledg'd by all, to be as true Comedy, and the Characters as well drawn to the Life, as any Play that has been Acted since the Restauration of the *English* Stage."[80] The contemporaries of Etherege noted particularly this fact of realistic portraiture, and there was much speculation as to the originals of characters like Dorimant, Sir Fopling, and Medley.

It is a failure to appreciate the realistic technique and the naturalistic basis which has led to an underestimation of the play's true merits. On the one hand, we have Steele's moralistic censure of the play, in the *Spectator* #65, as "a perfect contradiction to good manners, good sense, and common honesty," and of Dorimant as "a direct knave in his designs, and a clown in his language." On the other hand, we have the "manners" view that the play is "a more exquisite and airy picture of the manners of that age than any other extant."[81] Neither of these estimates does justice to the comedy, for they both fail to appreciate the essential character of the play and the two main elements in it—the wit and the naturalistic characterization. *The Man of Mode* is a comedy of wit, with the usual outwitting situations involving naturalistically conceived characters.

Among the major figures, Dorimant is perhaps the least appreciated by modern readers, largely because the naturalistic characterization is not recognized. He is too often dismissed as a cruel and selfish rake; whereas he is actually a superb portrait of a Truewit. Dennis, in his defence of the play, pointed out that "*Dorimont* is a young Courtier, haughty, vain, and prone to Anger, amorous, false, and inconstant," because this is the true nature of young men as described by Aristotle in his *Rhetoric,* and the dramatist must be true to life (that is, be a naturalistic writer).[82] Dennis also pointed out that Rochester was the model for the part: "all the World was charm'd with *Dorimont*; and . . . it was unanimously agreed, that he had in him several of the Qualities of *Wilmot* Earl of *Rochester,* as, his Wit, his Spirit, his amorous Temper, the Charms that he had for the fair Sex, his Falshood, and his Inconstancy; the agreeable Manner of his chiding his Servants . . . ; and lastly, his repeating, on every Occasion, the Verses of *Waller,* for whom that noble Lord had a very particular Esteem."[83] Jacob says further that "the Character of *Dorimant* was drawn in Compliment to the Earl of *Rochester.*"[84]

Dorimant embodies all the virtues of the masculine Truewit, and he is what Dean Lockier called "the genteel rake of wit."[85] Every term of this description deserves emphasis: Dorimant is genteel, as a Truewit who observes decorum ought to be; he is a rake, because his principles are libertine; and above all, he is a Wit, for he values intellectual distinction above other virtues. This is a far better description than Hazlitt's, which makes Dorimant "the genius of grace, gallantry, and gaiety"[86]—and sacrifices accuracy to alliteration. The gallantry of Dorimant is more predatory than courtly, in keeping with his naturalistic bias; and his gaiety is subdued, for there is a dark streak in his nature, compounded of the intellectuality, cynicism, and passion of his original. He is not easy to understand because he has considerable depth, and unlike Courtall and Freeman, he is not open and frank about his inner life. He is a man of strong passions, but is Wit enough to have control over them; his fancy is tempered by judgment; and he possesses higher intellectual qualities than the average Truewit.

On the more superficial side, he is the embodiment of elegant ease—a ready Wit, a cultivated man who has Waller on his lips, and an easy conversationalist with "a Tongue . . . would tempt the Angels to a second fall." He has histrionic talents, and can adopt the proper tone for every occasion: with Lady Woodvill, he ironically plays the role of the formally courteous Mr. Courtage; with his fellow Wits he is the railler; with Belinda he is gallantly amorous and ardent; and with the Orange Woman and the Shoemaker, he adopts a tone of rough raillery and easy superiority. Possessing the superior perspicacity and cleverness of a Truewit, Dorimant can see through the devices of others, and at the same time, dissemble well enough so that others cannot see through him. His histrionic talents are also displayed in mimicry of others, a talent which Harriet shares with him. He does it grossly and sarcastically with Loveit, in his imitation of Sir Fopling, or ironically and maliciously, as in his mimicry of Harriet. Dorimant can please anyone when, and if, he wishes to do so, because he possesses the virtues of versatility, ease, and perspicacity.

As a Truewit, he also has a tongue as sharp as a rapier—and the raillery of Dorimant is seldom gentle, since he has malice enough to be cutting. Yet it has point and originality enough to be pleasing. It can be as fine as his repartee with Harriet on their first encounter:

DOR:

> You were talking of Play, Madam; Pray what may be your stint?

HAR:

> A little harmless discourse in publick walks, or at most an appointment in a Box bare-fac'd at the Play-House; you are for Masks, and private meetings, where Women engage for all they are worth, I hear.

DOR:

> I have been us'd to deep Play, but I can make one at small Game, when I like my Gamester well.

HAR:

> And be so unconcern'd you'l ha' no pleasure in't.

DOR:

> Where there is a considerable sum to be won, the hope of drawing people in, makes every trifle considerable.

HAR:

> The sordidness of mens natures, I know, makes 'em willing to flatter and comply with the Rich, though they are sure never to be the better for 'em.

DOR:

> 'Tis in their power to do us good, and we despair not but at some time or other they may be willing.

HAR:

> To men who have far'd in this Town like you, 'twoud be a great Mortification to live on hope; could you keep a Lent for a Mistriss?

DOR:

> In expectation of a happy Easter, and though time be very precious, think forty daies well lost, to gain your favour.

> (III, iii)

His raillery can also be as sarcastic as his retort to Pert, "Oh Mrs. *Pert,* I never knew you sullen enough to be silent" (II, ii); or as good-naturedly rough as his remark to his servant, "Take notice henceforward who's wanting in his duty, the next Clap he gets, he shall rot for an example" (I, i).

As a Truewit, Dorimant professes naturalistic principles, and he is cynical about women. He has known enough women to be certain that they are vain, hypocritical, and affected creatures; most complaisant when they seem most to resist; and jealous and demanding when won. A striking example of his raillery, malice, his libertinism, frankness, and wit is his passage with Mrs. Loveit:

LOVEIT:

> Is this the constancy you vow'd?

DOR:

> Constancy at my years! 'tis not a Vertue in season, you
> might as well expect the Fruit the Autumn ripens i'the
> Spring.

LOVEIT:

> Monstrous Principle!

DOR:

> Youth has a long Journey to go, Madam; shou'd I have
> set up my rest at the first Inn I lodg'd at, I shou'd
> never have arriv'd at the happiness I now enjoy.

LOVEIT:

> Dissembler, damn'd Dissembler!

DOR:

> I am so, I confess; good nature and good manners cor-
> rupt me. I am honest in my inclinations, and wou'd
> not, wer' not to avoid offence, make a Lady a little in
> years believe I think her young, wilfully mistake Art
> for Nature; and seem as fond of a thing I am weary of,
> as when I doated on't in earnest.

LOVEIT:

> False Man!

DOR:

> True Woman!

LOVEIT:

> Now you begin to show your self!

DOR:

> Love gilds us over, and makes us show fine things to
> one another for a time, but soon the Gold wears off,
> and then again the native brass appears.
>
> (II, ii)

He is professedly libertine, and lives according to
naturalistic principles.

If there is any fault in Dorimant as a Truewit, it is his
over-sophistication, which makes his wit a little too self-
conscious; for now and then his wit is a trifle forced, as in
his raillery on the young woman whom the Orange Woman
reports to him: "This fine Woman, I'le lay my life, is some
awkward ill fashion'd Country Toad, who not having
above Four Dozen of black hairs on her head, has adorn'd
her baldness with a large white Fruz, that she may look
sparkishly in the Fore Front of the Kings Box, at an old
Play" (I, i). Harriet, who is a keen judge of wit, observes
of Dorimant, when Young Bellair praises him for his ease
and naturalness, "He's agreeable and pleasant I must own,
but he does so much affect being so, he displease me" (III,
iii). Dorimant has too much judgment to indulge in franci-
ful wit, so that he does not provide the most natural and
spontaneous display of wit. But he is a Truewit because he
is libertine in his principles, perspicacious and malicious,
he observes decorum in his speech and conduct, and he
detests coxcombs like Sir Fopling.

His friend Medley has the more fanciful wit of the two,
and he serves, therefore, as a foil to Dorimant's more solid
wit. When he is "rhetorically drunk," he is a great elabora-
tor of fancies; and he rallies the ladies with a pleasant account of a fictitious book, "written by a late beauty of
Quality, teaching you how to draw up your Breasts, stretch
up your neck, to thrust out your Breech, to play with your
Head, to toss up your Nose, to bite your Lips, to turn up
your Eyes, to speak in a silly soft tone of a Voice, and use
all the Foolish French Words that will infallibly make your
person and conversation charming, with a short apologie
at the end, in behalf of young Ladies, who notoriously
wash, and paint, though they have naturally good Complexions" (II, i). Medley rallies everyone, but with much less
malice than Dorimant, and he lets his tongue run freely on
everyone and everything.

It is also he, rather than Dorimant, who voices most of the
skeptical wit in the play; and this is done with a much
more natural, if less fine, carelessness than Dorimant is
capable of. He is a skeptic in matrimony as well as
religion, and he rallies Young Bellair on his intended marriage: "You have a good strong Faith, and that may
contribute much towards your Salvation. I confess I am
but of an untoward constitution, apt to have doubts and
scruples, and in Love they are no less distracting than in
Religion; were I so near Marriage, I shou'd cry out by Fits
as I ride in my Coach, Cuckold, Cuckold, with no less
fury than the mad Fanatick does Glory in *Bethlem*" (I, i).
When Dorimant gets a letter from Molly the whore asking
for a guinea to see the "Opery," Medley exclaims, "Pray
let the Whore have a favourable answer, that she may
spark it in a Box, and do honour to her profession" (I, i).
He also gives the rallying advice to the witty Shoemaker:
"I advice you like a Friend, reform your Life; you have
brought the envy of the World upon you, by living above
your self. Whoring and Swearing are Vices too gentile for
a Shoomaker" (I, i). Though Dorimant is the finer Wit,
with more malice, perspicacity, and judgment, Medley,
with his fanciful and skeptical wit, is often more original
and entertaining.

The one other important Truewit in the play is Harriet,
who has much in common with Dorimant. Compared to
her sisters Gatty, Ariana, and the Widow Rich, Harriet is
endowed with a much more solid wit; and her perspicacity, sound sense, and fine self-control make her a formidable person. She is, as Dorimant says, "Wild, witty, lovesome, beautiful and young," but tempering these qualities
is sound judgment and sincere feeling. Her exceptional
physical beauty is the least part of her merits, and it speaks
well for Dorimant that he is interested in her wit (I, i).

Like Dorimant, she has histrionic talents and the ability to
dissemble, and there are excellent scenes of comic with
when she and Dorimant take each other off on their first

meeting, and when she and Young Bellair dissemble before their parents, by pretending to be in love. She displays a roguish wit, as when she tells Young Bellair, "I know not what it is to love, but I have made pretty remarks by being now and then where Lovers meet" (III, i). Or when she is merry at her mother's expense, by exclaiming in the presence of Dorimant, who is unknown to Lady Woodvill, "I would fain see that *Dorimant,* Mother, you so cry out of, for a monster; he's in the *Mail* I hear" (III, iii). But there is goodnature at bottom in Harriet, and the occasional malice of her tongue is due to some deeper feeling which she wishes to conceal. She is a Truewit with sufficient self-control to treat her lover and her emotion playfully; and if her emotion breaks through, it is perceptible only in her sharper and more malicious wit:

HAR:

I did not think to have heard of Love from you.

DOR:

I never knew what 'twas to have a settled Ague yet, but now and then have had irregular fitts.

HAR:

Take heed, sickness after long health is commonly more violent and dangerous.

DOR:

I have took the infection from her, and feel the disease spreading in me—(Aside.)

Is the name of love so frightful that you dare not stand it? (To her.)

HAR:

'Twill do little execution out of your mouth on me, I am sure.

DOR:

It has been fatal—

HAR:

To some easy Women, but we are not all born to one destiny; I was inform'd you use to laugh at Love, and not make it.

DOR:

The time has been, but now I must speak—

HAR:

If it be on that Idle subject, I will put on my serious look, turn my head carelessly from you, drop my lip, let my Eyelids fall and hang half o're my Eyes— Thus—while you buz a speech of an hour long in my ear, and I answer never a word! why do you not begin?

(IV, i)

Such raillery is a fine weapon in her capable hands.

Her wit is charming because it springs from sincere feeling and sound judgment. She has sensible views, untainted by cynicism; and though she may say of a husband, "I think I might be brought to endure him, and that is all a reasonable Woman should expect in a Husband," she adds significantly, "but there is duty i'the case," implying thereby that were not duty involved (as there must be in an arranged marriage), a woman might reasonably dote on her husband (III, i). As a Truewit she is an enemy of all that is affected, dull, and formal, and speaking of Hyde Park, she says, "I abominate the dull diversions there, the formal bows, the Affected smiles, the silly by-Words, and amorous Tweers, in passing" (III, iii). She has passions, and will not conceal them under an affected softness (IV, i). In fact, she loves naturalness so much that she criticizes even Dorimant for not being natural enough in his wit (III, iii). And she exclaims against all pretenders—"That Women should set up for beauty as much in spite of nature, as some men have done for Wit!" (III, i). At its best, her wit is first-rate because it is unpretentious: her witticisms are never forced, and her speech is free of labored similitudes. Only she is capable of wit at once so sensible and whimsical as the following:

DOR:

Is this all—will you not promise me—

HAR:

I hate to promise! what we do then is expected from us, and wants much of the welcom it finds, when it surprizes.

DOR:

May I not hope?

HAR:

That depends on you, and not on me, and 'tis to no purpose to forbid it.

(V, ii)

It must be her speeches in particular that Dennis had in mind when he said of ***The Man of Mode:*** "the Dialogue is the most charming that has been writ by the Moderns: That with Purity and Simplicity, it has Art and Elegance; and with Force and Vivacity, the utmost Grace and Elegance; and with Force and Vivacity, the utmost Grace and Delicacy."[87]

As foils to the three Wits discussed so far, there are the several characters who fall short of being Truewits. Of these Emilia and Young Bellair are the most attractive, but like Graciana and Beaufort in the first play, they belong to an honorable world which is out of harmony with the dominantly naturalistic temper of the play. Young Bellair is described by Dorimant as "Handsome, well bred, and by much the most tolerable of all the young men that do not abound in wit" (I, i); and Emilia, according to Medley, "has the best reputation of any young Woman about Town, who has beauty enough to provoke detraction; her Carriage is unaffected, her discourse modest, not at all censorious, nor pretending like the Counterfeits of the Age" (I, i). What alone makes them tolerable to the Truewits is their naturalness and lack of affectation; as lovers, they lack fire and spirit, and theirs is a conventional affair, with the usual obstacles and hazards of honorable courtship and marriage.

Aside from Bellinda, who is a rather foolish young woman, the other foils to the Truewits are all objects of malicious laughter in the play. Mrs. Loveit has some beauty and wit, but she is absurd because of her unnatural jealousy and affectation. Lady Woodvill and Old Bellair, "their Gravities" of a past age, are minor objects of ridicule. Old Bellair is laughable because of his unnatural love for a young girl, for such fond love at his age is a sure sign of dotage or impotent lechery. Lady Woodvill is "a great Admirer of the Forms and Civilities of the last Age," when beauties were courted in proper form, with a due regard for the conventions of Platonic love. "Lewdness is the business now," she says with regret, "Love was the bus'ness in my Time" (IV, i). She does not realize that the new world in which she is so out of place is naturalistic in its principles, and that young couples like Emilia and Young Bellair who carry on in the approved fashion of her age are passé.

The chief foil to the Truewits is Sir Fopling, but so much has been said about him by critics that further commentary seems superfluous. It is important, however, to note that he is not chiefly an object of social satire, as is commonly supposed: he is laughed at principally because he is deficient in wit. His pretension to fashion and taste in clothes reveals the poverty of his mind, and it is this mental defect that exposes him to laughter. He is such a person as the Marquess of Halifax described—a superfine gentleman whose understanding is so appropriated to his dress that his fine clothes become his sole care.[88] After the Truewits have ironically ridiculed his supposed fine taste in clothes, they mercilessly condemn him as a fool:

MED:

   a fine mettl'd Coxcomb.

DOR:

   Brisk and Insipid—

MED:

   Pert and dull.

EMILIA:

   However you despise him, Gentlemen, I'le lay my life he passes for a Wit with many.

DOR:

   That may very well be, Nature has her cheats, stum's a brain, and puts sophisticate dulness often on the tasteless multitude for true wit and good humour.

                                        (III, ii)

Undoubtedly there is some element of social satire in the ridicule of the fop, but the "manners" approach which makes Sir Fopling a mere conglomeration of fine clothes misses the whole point of his being Witwoud. Furthermore, the "manners" view which finds him a superfluous accessory to the plot fails to grasp the unity of the play. It is quite evident that in this comedy of wit he occupies the role of the Witwoud who is exposed by his intellectual superiors, and that he is not only a foil to the Truewits but the butt of their malicious laughter.

In his three wit comedies, Etherege shows a progressive development in his art. *The Comical Revenge,* his first attempt at the comedy of wit, shows an uncertain mastery: the heroic-moral world is not properly subordinated, Wheadle and Dufoy are not perfect Witwouds, and Sir Nicholas is not a very amusing Witless. The Truewits are also deficient: Sir Frederick, with his callow interest in frolics, and the Widow, with her over-ready show of feeling, are not yet capable of the brilliant comic wit to be found in later plays. But the naturalistic temper is prominently displayed. In the second comedy, *She Would if She Could,* Etherege successfully poked witty fun at the conventional notion of honor, in the person of Lady Cockwood, and he brought together a quartet of spirited Truewits. The wit in the play, however, seldom reaches a very high level: the repartees are characterized more by high spirits than by an original exchange of ideas; there is a preponderance of wit play over comic wit; and the Truewits are not properly distinguished in their wit, for the difference between Courtall and Freeman, for example, is that the former is the bolder of the two.

The last play, *The Man of Mode,* is superior in every respect. Not only does it have a fine Witwoud in Sir Fopling Flutter, but it has three notable Truewits, in Dorimant, Harriet, and Medley, who are carefully distinguished by Etherege in terms of their wit: Dorimant is characterized by malice and judgment, Medley by fanciful and skeptical wit, and Harriet by natural, spontaneous wit. In Dorimant and Harriet, we see to what an extent Etherege succeeded in making the wit significant and dramatic: not only does the wit of Harriet probe deeper into human absurdities; it is more thoroughly a part of the dramatic action, as well as an expression of her true character. Dorimant and Harriet also have an intellectual solidity and depth of feeling which make them far more human and substantial than their predecessors. These two Truewits are both lovers of fine wit; they have penetration enough to see through the affectation and folly of others, and wit enough to dissemble with the world; enough judgment to act sensibly at all times; a sufficiently playful attitude toward life not to be swept away by their own emotions; and an easy and elegant superiority to everyone else by virtue of these qualities. They are intelligent without being over-intellectual, worldly without being disillusioned with life, and witty without being superficial or frivolous.

Dorimant and particularly Harriet represent the finest expression of Etherege's witty attitude toward life—his good sense, elegance, and libertinism; and his scorn of fools, ceremony, and artificiality. As Truewits they belong to a free world—and a world which is neither corrupt as the moralistic critics affirm, nor superficial as the "manners" critics would have us believe. It may not have the breadth of Dante's universe because the supernatural is excluded, but there is much in this world of the Truewit that is valuable, such as elegance, intellectual distinction, clarity of thought, absence of artificial formality, freedom from cant about honor, and a graceful and natural acceptance of this life on earth.

Notes

1. Elwin, *The Playgoer's Handbook to Restoration Drama,* pp. 12-13; Dr. Doran, *"Their Majesties' Servants": Annals of the English Stage, from Thomas Betterton to Edmund Kean,* New York, 1865, I, 140; Felix E. Schelling, *English Drama,* London and New York, 1914, p. 259.

2. Dobrée, [Bonamy.] *Restoration Comedy [1660–1720.* Oxford University Press, 1925], p. 58.

3. *Ibid.,* p. 76.

4. Palmer, [John.] [*The*] *Comedy of Manners* [London, G. Bell and Sons, 1913], p. 91.

5. Edmund Gosse, "Sir George Etheredge," in *Seventeenth Century Studies,* New York, 1897, p. 283.

6. John Oldys, "Sir George Etherege," in *Biographia Britannica,* London, 1747-1766, III, 1841. Gerard Langbaine, *An Account of the English Dramatick Poets,* Oxford, 1691, p. 186.

7. Theophilus Cibber, *The Lives of the Poets of Great Britain and Ireland to the Time of Dean Swift,* London, 1753, III, 37-38.

8. Dennis, *Original Letters, Familiar, Moral and Critical,* London, 1721, p. 52.

9. Oldys, "Sir George Etherege," *Biographica Britannica,* III, 1844.

10. *Ibid.,* III, 1841. Cf. also, Cibber, *The Lives of the Poets,* III, 33; Charles Gildon, *The Lives and Characters of the English Dramatick Poets,* London, 1699, p. 53.

11. *Correspondence of the Family of Hatton,* 1878, ed. Edward M. Thompson, I, 133-134.

12. *The Rochester-Savile Letters, 1671-1680,* ed. John Harold Wilson, Columbus, Ohio, 1941, p. 52.

13. Etherege, *The Letterbook,* ed. Rosenfeld, pp. 388-389.

14. *Ibid.,* pp. 383-384.

15. Cibber, *The Lives of the Poets,* III, 37.

16. Clarendon, [Edward Hyde.] [*The*] *Life, [of Edward Earl of Clarendon,* 3 vols. Oxford, 1759], II, 39-49.

17. Cibber, *op. cit.,* III, 33.

18. *Letterbook,* p. 304.

19. *Ibid.,* p. 190.

20. *Ibid.,* p. 304.

21. *Ibid.,* pp. 62-63.

22. *Ibid.,* p. 422.

23. *Ibid.,* p. 55.

24. *Ibid.,* p. 328.

25. *Ibid.,* p. 264.

26. *Ibid.*

27. *Ibid.,* p. 305.

28. *Ibid.,* p. 310.

29. *Ibid.,* pp. 386-387.

30. *Ibid.,* p. 337.

31. *Ibid.,* p. 63.

32. *Ibid.,* p. 415.

33. *Ibid.,* p. 187.

34. *Ibid.,* pp. 301-302.

35. *Ibid.,* p. 284.

36. *Ibid.,* p. 119.

37. *Ibid.,* p. 406.

38. *Ibid.,* p. 357.

39. *Ibid.,* pp. 417-421.

40. Quoted by H. F. Brett-Smith, intro. to [Etherege, Sir George.] *The Dramatic Works of Sir George Etherege,* [ed. H. F. Brett-Smith, 2 vols. Oxford, Basil Blackwell, 1927], I, xxix.

41. *Letterbook,* p. 344.

42. *Ibid.,* p. 210.

43. *Ibid.,* p. 413.

44. *Ibid.,* p. 167.

45. *Ibid.,* p. 67.

46. *Ibid.,* p. 139.

47. Dryden, Dedication of *The Assignation, or Love in a Nunnery,* in [Dryden, John. *The*]*Works, [of John Dryden,* ed. Sir Walter Scott and George Saintsbury, 18 vols. Edinburgh, 1882–1893], IV, 351.

48. *Letterbook,* p. 414.

49. *Ibid.,* p. 62.

50. *Ibid.,* p. 117.

51. *Ibid.,* pp. 103-104.

52. *Ibid.,* p. 290, p. 142, p. 309.

53. *Ibid.,* p. 240.

54. *Ibid.,* p. 325.

55. *Ibid.,* p. 227, p. 212.

56. *Ibid.,* p. 293.

57. *Ibid.,* p. 278.

58. *Ibid.,* p. 168.

59. *Ibid.,* p. 355.

60. Dryden to Etherege, February 16, 1687; Etherege to Dryden, March 10/20, 1686/7. Letters 13 and 14, in *The Letters of John Dryden,* ed. Charles E. Ward, Durham, 1942.

61. *Letterbook,* pp. 376-378.

62. *Ibid.,* p. 289.

63. *Ibid.,* p. 338.

64. Oldys, "Sir George Etherege," *Biographia Britannica,* III, 1842.

65. Radcliffe, "News from Hell," in Dryden, *Miscellany Poems,* London, 1716, II, 101.

66. The edition used for this and subsequent plays is *The Dramatic Works of Sir George Etherege,* ed. H. F. Brett-Smith, 2 vols., Oxford, 1927.

67. Evelyn, [John. *The*] *Diary* [*of John Evelyn,* 3 vols. London, Macmillan, 1906], April 27, 1664; Pepys, [Samuel. *The*] *Diary* [*of Samuel Pepys,* ed. by Hendy B. Wheatley, 2 vols. New York, Random House, 1946], January 4, 1664/5.

68. Langbaine, *An Account of the English Dramatick Poets,* p. 187. Rev. John Downes, *Roscius Anglicanus, or, an Historical Review of the Stage,* London, 1789, p. 35.

69. Oldys, *op. cit.,* III, 1841.

70. *The Character of a Town-Gallant*[; *Exposing the Extravagant Fopperies of some vain Self-conceited Pretenders to Gentility and Good Breeding.* London, 1675], p. 6.

71. Cf. Etherege's use of the same figure in Act I, sc. iii, where Wheadle is speaking of Sir Nicholas Cully: "How eagerly did this half-witted fellow chap up the bait? Like a ravenous Fish, that will not give the Angler leave to sink his Line, but greedily darts up and meets it half way." This reveals a somewhat indiscriminate distribution of wit among the characters in the play.

72. Cf. Palmer: "To-day the scenes in which the plight of Dufoy is for comic purposes exploited are wholly disgusting" (*Comedy of Manners,* p. 75).

73. Lynch, *The Social Mode of Restoration Comedy.* [University of Michigan Publications, III, New York, Macmillan, 1926], p. 143.

74. [Richard Head], *Proteus Redivivus: or the Art of Wheedling, or Insinuation,* London, 1675, pp. 2, 4, 198.

75. *Ibid.,* p. 149.

76. Dennis, "A Large Account of the Taste in Poetry" (1702), in *The Critical Works,* I, 289.

77. Lynch, *op. cit.,* p. 154.

78. Gosse, "Sir George Etheredge," p. 271.

79. Dobrée, *Restoration Comedy,* p. 65.

80. Langbaine, *An Account of the English Dramatick Poets,* p. 187.

81. Hazlitt, *Lectures on the English Comic Writers,* in *The Collected Works,* VIII, p. 129.

82. Dennis, "A Defence of Sir *Fopling Flutter,*" *The Critical Works,* II, 245-247.

83. *Ibid.,* p. 248.

84. Giles Jacob, *The Poetical Register,* London, 1719, p. 96.

85. Rev. Joseph Spence, *Anecdotes, Observations, and Characters, of Books and Men,* London, 1858, p. 47.

86. Hazlitt, *op. cit.,* VIII, 68.

87. Dennis, "A Defence of Sir *Fopling Flutter,*" *The Critical Works,* II, 243.

88. Halifax, [Marquess of.] "Some Cautions offered to the Consideration of those who are to chuse *Members* to serve for the Ensuing *Parliament,*" in *The Complete Works* [*of George Savile, First Marquess of Halifax,* ed. Walter Raleigh. Oxford, Clarendon Press, 1912], p. 153.

Norman N. Holland (essay date 1959)

SOURCE: Holland, Norman N. "*The Comical Revenge; or, Love in a Tub,*" "*She Wou'd If She Cou'd,*" and "*The Man of Mode; or, Sir Fopling Flutter.*" In *The First Modern Comedies: The Significance of Etherege, Wycherley and Congreve,* pp. 20-7, 28-37, 86-95. Cambridge, Mass.: Harvard University Press, 1959.

[*In the essays below, Holland analyzes the plot, main characters, themes, and structure of each of Etherege's comedies in an effort to trace his artistic maturation.*]

THE COMICAL REVENGE; OR, LOVE IN A TUB

By March 1664 the theaters had been open for well over four years following the so-called dramatic interregnum. Yet scarcely a half-dozen new comedies had emerged to interrupt the revivals of Fletcher, Shakespeare, and Jonson that filled the stages, and none of these had caught the fancy of Restoration audiences enough to set a new style.

There survived only Dryden's device of witty lovers from *The Wild Gallant* (February 1663), probably suggested by Nell Gwyn and her then lover, Charles Hart, of the Theatre Royal. The first new comedy to provoke real imitation was Sir George Etherege's *The Comical Revenge.*

Of Etherege the man, little is known. A gay, handsome individual, who spoiled his looks with drinking, he was a wit of the court circle who turned his hand to playwriting as a gentlemanly thing to do and wrote no more than the gentlemanly number of three plays. James II appointed him envoy to the Diet in Ratisbon, where he misbehaved in a gentlemanly manner, complained of Lady Etherege (apparently a shrew whom he had married for money), and found solace with a young comedienne stranded in the Low Countries. After the Glorious Revolution, he was, of course, replaced. He cast his lot with the Stuarts, went to France, and apparently never returned to England. He died in the early nineties; neither the date nor the place are known. Although to modern eyes his first play looks anything but promising, "The clean and well performance of this Comedy," wrote the prompter, John Downes, "got the Company more reputation and profit than any preceding Comedy; the Company taking in a month's time at it 1000£."[1]

The Comical Revenge has three plots, high, low, and middle. The high plot, in neat couplets and even neater patterns of love, honor, and confidants, follows the crossed loves of Lord Beaufort and Colonel Bruce for Graciana, and the unrequited love of Graciana's sister, Aurelia, for Bruce. In the middle plot, Sir Frederick Frollick, Beaufort's cousin, lackadaisically pursues the Widow Rich, Graciana and Aurelia's aunt. The low plot shows Wheadle, a rogue acquaintance of Sir Frederick's, and Palmer, a card-sharper, swindling a Cromwellian knight named Sir Nicholas Cully. In the incident—one cannot call it a plot—that gives the play its title, Betty, the widow's maid, lures and locks Sir Frederick's valet, the Frenchman Dufoy, into a tub. (A sweating-tub was the usual seventeenth-century remedy for Dufoy's "French disease.")

Most commentators on this play dismiss the heroics of the high plot as irrelevant—"obviously out of the picture," or "out of keeping with the rest of the play." "We turn from one to the other," says one critic of a similarly bifurcated play, "as a music-hall audience will welcome the alternation of bawdry and sentiment."[2] More important, however, is the fact that the high heroic drama and the low farce interact, each making the other more meaningful. "The clash," Mr. Empson notes of Dryden's similarly hybrid *Marriage à la Mode,* "makes both conventions less unreal; . . . it has a more searching effect, almost like parody, by making us see they are unreal."[3] Certainly the high plot is not the main plot, as many writers seem to think. On the contrary, more than twice as many scenes and two and a half times as many lines are given to the low plots as to the romantic, heroic plot. The play opens and closes with Sir Frederick.[4]

The high plot of *The Comical Revenge* idealizes and exaggerates in pure heroic style. The story concerns Cavalier bravery and romance. Both Lord Beaufort and Colonel Bruce love Graciana, while Graciana's sister Aurelia loves Colonel Bruce. The colonel returns from imprisonment by the Roundheads to find Graciana in love with Beaufort. He therefore challenges Beaufort; on the field, these gallant enemies unite to drive off some treacherous Cromwellian assassins pursuing Bruce and then return to their fight. Beaufort wins the duel but spares the colonel's life. The colonel, then, despairing of Graciana, falls on his sword and the doctor pronounces him certain to die. Graciana decides she ought to be in love with Colonel Bruce and therefore spurns Beaufort, who despairs. Meanwhile Aurelia reveals her love for Bruce and he reciprocates, at which point "the wound / By abler Chyr'gions is not mortal found," and confessions match the proper pairs.

It is somewhat puzzling that a man of "easie" George Etherege's urbanity could write this sort of thing. Etherege was a comic writer, and nothing could be farther from the multiple perspectives of comedy than the single-minded admiration of the heroic manner. Possibly, as I suggested in the preceding chapter, Etherege and his friends found the heroic manner funny in and of itself. But whether they did or not, Etherege plays the high plot of *The Comical Revenge* off against the lower plots to develop Sir Frederick Frollick's role as a realistic but golden mean.

Frollick, being somewhat of a roisterer, beats up the widow's quarters with a drunken serenade by way of showing his affection; she puts him off, however. He acts as second for Beaufort in the high-plot duel, and has himself carried in as though dead to make the widow reveal her love, but she sees through his ruse in time. He then pretends to be arrested for a debt and the widow pays it, thus committing herself. After much verbal play and pretended indifference, Sir Frederick and the widow are finally matched. As a ludicrous parallel to their courtship, Betty, the widow's maid, locks the neck of Sir Frederick's valet into a great tub, which Dufoy must then carry about with him like a snail's shell.

Strange as it may seem, Sir Frederick is the one breath of common sense in the high plot, as, for example, when, after Colonel Bruce has fallen on his sword, he prevents Bruce's second from doing the same so as to complete the stylized heroic pattern. Sir Frederick says simply, "The Frollick's not to go round, as I take it" (55).[5] "I mistrust your Mistresses Divinity," he answers to one of Beaufort's exalted love-speeches. "You'l find her Attributes but Mortal: Women, like Juglers Tricks, appear Miracles to the ignorant; but in themselves th'are meer cheats" (7). "What news from the God of Love?" he cries to Beaufort's servant, "he's always at your Master's elbow, h'as jostl'd the Devil out of service; no more! Mrs. *Grace!* Poor Girl, Mrs. *Graciana* has flung a squib into his bosome, where the wild-fire will huzzéé for a time, and then crack; it fly's out at's Breeches" (3). The hint that Beaufort knew the wench Grace somewhat better than his high-flown heroics warrant (see also 7) and these various contrasts—physical sex as opposed to spiritual love, the devil as opposed to the god of love, firecrackers as opposed to the flames of love, Grace the wench as opposed to Graciana the heroine—run throughout the play and make up the antiheroic humor.

Sir Frederick is also the one who straightens out the complexities of the low plot. Wheadle, an acquaintance of Frollick's, and Palmer, another crony, disguised as a sheep-farmer, cheat Sir Nicholas Cully at cards. Cully refuses to pay his losses, and Palmer challenges him. In the field, Cully's cowardice forces him to sign a judgment for the amount. Wheadle, at this point, promises to mend his fortunes by introducing him to the Widow Rich (actually Wheadle's mistress Grace in disguise). Cully, however, blunders in on the real Widow Rich, roaring like Sir Frederick. The real Sir Frederick rescues both her and Sir Nicholas by blackmailing the sharpers out of the debt and into marrying: Wheadle to Grace, and Palmer—and Sir Nicholas—to his own ex-mistresses.

Just as Sir Frederick is contrasted by his common sense and earthiness to Beaufort, his counterpart in the high plot, he is, as an urbane, brave, amorous Cavalier, the opposite of the countrified, Cromwellian knight Cully, the fake Frollick of the low plot. Just as Sir Frederick wittily reveals the unreality of the high plot with his skepticism, he brings to the intrigues of the low characters a semblance of honor and mercy. "'Tis fit this Rascal shou'd be cheated; but these Rogues will deal too unmercifully with him: I'le take compassion upon him, and use him more favourably my self" (73), he says, as he decides to marry Cully off to his ex-mistress. The fact that it is Sir Frederick who puts Cully in his place, Professor Underwood points out, establishes a sense of "degree" between "hero and dupe, wit and fool, gentleman and fop." The applicability of the word "degree" here shows how this typical trick of Restoration comedy relates to traditional medieval and Renaissance values.[6]

Even so, lest Sir Frederick be taken too seriously, there is always his own ludicrous counterpart, Dufoy, who puts a comic perspective on even the golden mean. Not all the antiheroic contrasts are channeled through Sir Frederick, moreover. Palmer ironically pretends to be a virtuous Loyalist like Colonel Bruce (32), and Wheadle compares the dueling-field to a sheep-field (29). Palmer can speak the heroic cant of the high plot as he complains of his lack of business:

> I protest I had rather still be vicious
> Then Owe my Virtue to Necessity.
>
> (9)

The widow (who "must needs have furious flames," 16) is a comic compromise between the virginal heroines of the high plot and the wenches of the low—a woman sexually experienced, but not immorally so. High and low scenes are contrasted individually: III. v, the cowardly duel, to III. vi *et seqq.*, the honorable duel; the incident of a letter supplies a bridge between low I. iii and heroic I. iv; the

mention of love-wounds brings the audience from Aurelia's unrequited worship in I. iv to Dufoy's syphilis in II. i.

As all this talk of wounds suggests, the whole play is a set of variations on the theme of hostility. Sir Frederick's debauches set the keynote; as described in the opening scene they consist of brawls with watchmen and constables, "beating up" a lady's quarters, breaking windows, and the like. Counterattacks take place in the morning: "De divil také mé," announces Dufoy in his French dialect, "if daré be not de whole Regiment Army de Hackené Cocheman, de Linke-boy, de Fydler, and de Shamber-maydé, dat havé beseegé de howsé" (3). Love, in particular, is compared over and over to fighting. In the high plot, the metaphor takes the form of a stale Petrarchanism—the victory of the mistress' eyes over the lover (17, 34, 46, 56, 57, 63). "Beauty's but an offensive dart; / It is no Armour for the heart" (76). In the low and middle plots, however, the metaphor becomes an anti-ideal, a reference to the sexual duel: "I have not fenc'd of late," says Sir Frederick, "unless it were with my Widows Maids; and they are e'en too hard for me at my own weapon" (47). Grace, when she is trapping Sir Nicholas, must "lye at a little opener ward" (78). Sir Frederick mocks the convention when he raids the widow's home in the middle of the night: "Alas, what pains I take thus to unclose / Those pretty eye-lids which lock'd up my Foes!" (31). In the high plot, love is the heart-wound inflicted by the mistress' conquering eyes (63, 64), but Dufoy's wound is far more realistic. He expains it in a dialogue with Beaufort's servant:

Dufoy.

> . . . it be de voundé dat my Metresse did give me long agoe.

Clark.

> What? some pretty little English Lady's crept into your heart?

Duf.

> No, but damn'd little English Whore is creepé into my bone begar.
>
> (14)

This colloquy is immediately preceded by a soliloquy in the high plot in which Aurelia mourns the wounds Bruce has inflicted on her heart (13), wounds she later refers to as her "disease" (22).

Hostility exists not just between lovers: love itself and all passions are essentially hostile influences, flaming arrows (63) or flames (46) that burn and torture the heart (63). Passions assault (19); they raise a tempest in the mind (44) that tosses and tumbles the individual until difficulties are resolved and love reaches its expression in marriage:

> Thus mariners rejoyce when winds decrease,
> And falling waves seem wearied into Peace.
>
> (82)

Nor is dueling the only metaphor in the lower plots for the hostilities associated with love. Sir Frederick describes his courtship of the widow as fishing (8) and the sharpers in the low plot use exactly the same metaphor for their swindle (11) and refer to it also as trapping (9, 78). The ideas of tricking and courtship are linked again when Sir Frederick disguises fiddlers as bailiffs and tricks the widow into bailing him out thereby swindling her: "Nay, I know th'art spiteful," he laughs, "and wou'dst fain marry me in revenge; but so long as I have these Guardian Angels about me, I defie thee and all thy Charms: Do skilful Faulkners thus reward their Hawks before they fly the Quarry?" (82). (The pun on "angels" as coins is only one of many parodies of the religious imagery in the high plot.) Instead of revenge taking the form of a duel, as in the high plots, in the middle plot the widow retains her estate when Sir Frederick marries her for it; that is one "comical revenge" (Epilogue) and Betty's locking Dufoy into a tub is another.

With marrying for money in mind, Etherege supplies his characters with gambling, as well as swindling, as a metaphor for courtship and marriage. "Do you imagine me so foolish as your self," the widow asks of Sir Frederick, referring to the money of which he has cheated her, "who often venture all at play, to recover one inconsiderable parcel?" (83) Sir Frederick's debt is a parody of the obligations ("debts," 64, 65, 77, 85) of love and honor in the high plot. Just as Beaufort can speak of his "claim" or "title" to Graciana (45), so Wheadle can call his illicit relationship with Grace, making "bold, like a young Heir, with his Estate, before it come into his hands" (80). This "conversion downward" of abstractions to matter, of people to things—Sir Frederick's former mistresses to furniture (84) or old gowns (85), the soul to body (42), reputation to a possession (5), and the like—becomes a major component of the antiheroic jokes of Restoration comedy, a metaphorical form of hostility.

Love, in the high plot, is divine, a kind of religious devotion to the loved one (45), directed by the god of love (12, 45, 81), for passion is too much for mere mortals to control (43). By contrast to this febrile neoplatonism, the low plot takes place in the "Devil" inn (10), using the "Devil's bones" (27), i.e., dice. The "hell" of the low plot is dramatized as complete pretense. One disguise follows another and the basest motives are tricked out as love, friendship, or honor. The high plot lacks any pretense. Every emotion is on the surface, to be talked about, analyzed, displayed. It is as though Etherege were trying "to express the motions of the spirits, and the affections or passions whose center is the heart," trying "in a word, *to make the soul visible.*" (These phrases come from a treatise on painting that Dryden translated for its insights into poetry.)[7] In the high plot, there is no body; the fact that "the Parenchyma of the right lobe of the lungs, near some large branch of the *Aspera arteria,* is perforated" must never intrude upon "Those flames my tortur'd breast did long conceal" (63). As opposed to the low plot, the heroics are only a different kind of incompleteness.

Between this bodiless heaven and soulless hell stands Sir Frederick Frollick, complete because he partakes of both sides. He cuts through the pretenses of both high and low, but is in turn capable of both kinds of conduct, honorable dueling or drunken battles with constables and bailiffs, which are called his "Heroick actions" (6).

Thus, an elaborate set of contrasts and parallels establishes the somewhat doubtful merits of Sir Frederick Frollick as a golden mean and casts a comic perspective on the doings of all the characters, both high and low. There are the parallel duels, one the paragon of honor, the other of dishonor. There are the parallel near-deaths, Bruce's real and Sir Frederick's pretended one, both of which result in declarations of love later recalled. There are the parallel "revenges": Betty the maid taunts Dufoy the valet for his disease as the widow taunts Sir Frederick for his promiscuity; the maid drugs the valet and locks him in a tub, while the mistress makes her admirer fall in love, and locks him into marriage. All four plot lines are united by the faintest hint of a comic version of death and resurrection. Each one of the men must be laid low before the final matches can take place: Sir Frederick has himself brought in as though dead; Sir Nicholas falls into a drunken stupor and wakes to find himself about to receive Sir Frederick's Lucy in marriage; Dufoy is drugged so Betty can lock him into the tub; and Colonel Bruce is nearly killed before Aurelia declares her love. These absurd deaths-and-rebirths fit into what Professor Underwood sees as the basic comic action of Restoration comedy, which, he says, Etherege developed in this play: the protagonist (Sir Frederick—or Sir Nicholas or Colonel Bruce or Dufoy) aspires to a love or libertinism beyond his "degree," falls (dies) through this pride, and is regenerated by compromise.[8] We might say the hero dies and is reborn at a more reasonable level.

Thus, in the much-maligned scene (IV.vii) where Sir Frederick pretends to be dead to trick the widow into declaring her love, the action runs the whole gamut from utter heroic down to utter antiheroic and comes up again to the middle note. The intrigue is admittedly not very sophisticated, but the scene is central to the structure of the play. In the scene immediately preceding it, Betty locked the drugged Dufoy into the tub. A messenger from the field of honor goes before Sir Frederick's corpse to announce in solemn poesy the "bloody consequence" of the duel. The widow drops social restraint and reveals her love. "The World's too poor to recompense this loss," she cries, but just as Sir Frederick is about to be elevated to the role of Everyman, Dufoy enters, grotesquely locked in his tub, and frightens everyone away with *his* cries of distress at his master's death. Sir Frederick starts up, and the fact of death against which the widow's pretense of indifference had collapsed shrinks again to comic size: "Farewell, Sir;" laughs the widow, "expect at night to see the old man, with his paper Lanthorn and crack'd Spectacles, singing your woful Tragedy to Kitchin-maids and Coblers Prentices," and the love-duel resumes. The scene ranges in fifty-six lines from high plot to low.

As this sample shows, the play seems neither overpoweringly funny, nor startlingly new. It uses a number of Restoration devices developed before 1664: the witty lovers, the concentration upon the upper class, and the cynical, competent rake-hero. In many ways, moreover, it stands closer to Tudor-Stuart dramatic techniques than to those of the Restoration, particularly in the religious imagery of the high plot and the extended use of parallelism and analogy. Nevertheless, the play did, for those who first saw it, define a new comedy. Although the dominant humor of this new comedy was to be antiheroic, its techniques grow from the same sense of schism that shows in the rigid patterns of love and honor in heroic drama and the antithetical structure of heroic verse. Its cynicism is that of a disappointed idealist. Things are either perfect or awful: the hero, if he cannot be a heroic Cavalier, becomes a rake.

This antiheroic comedy found three characteristic devices of language and action. First, love is shown with a strong component of hostility or reluctance (a comic and truer version of the artificial love-honor conflicts of heroic drama). The lovers engage in a verbal duel, pretending indifference and comparing themselves to adversaries. Second, abstractions and ideals are converted downward into physical realities: love into sex, reputation into a possession, and so on. Finally, the outer appearance of a thing or person and its inner nature are shown as separate, indeed, inconsistent, and this division is seen as usually true, not an aberration that the action of the play corrects. The cuckold is not given justice as he would be in an Elizabethan play; rather Cully must set out to pass Frollick's ex-mistress off as an honest lady to his country neighbors.

Although *The Way of the World,* written nearly forty years later, is a far more subtle and complex piece, these three elements of Etherege's first play still pervade it. "The Coldness of a losing Gamester lessens the Pleasure of the Winner," says the villain in what is almost the opening speech, "I'd no more play with a Man that slighted his ill Fortune than I'd make Love to a Woman who undervalu'd the Loss of her Reputation." First, there is the sarcastic sense of hostility: love is a winning against the woman-opponent. Second, the speaker converts reputation downward into something monetary that can be priced and wagered. Third, he tacitly assumes that reputation (an appearance) is normally inconsistent with the woman's "natural" desires. Unpromising as it is, *The Comical Revenge* sounded the authentic triad.

. . . . .

SHE WOU'D IF SHE COU'D

It was nearly four years before Etherege brought out his second play. In his entry for February 6, 1668, Pepys describes the opening run:

> I to the Duke of York's playhouse; where a new play of Etherige's, called "She Would if she Could;" and though I was there by two o'clock, there was 1000

people put back that could not have room in the pit: and I at last, because my wife was there made shift to get into the 18 *d.* box, and there saw; but, Lord! how full was the house, and how silly the play, there being nothing in the world good in it, and few people pleased in it. The King was there; but I sat mightily behind, and could see but little, and hear not at all. The play being done, I into the pit to look [for] my wife, and it being dark and raining, I to look my wife out, but could not find her; and so staid going between the two doors and through the pit an hour and half, I think, after the play was done; the people staying there till the rain was over, and to talk with one another. And, among the rest, here was the Duke of Buckingham to-day openly sat in the pit; and there I found him with my Lord Buckhurst, and Sidly, and Etherige, the poet; the last of whom I did hear mightily find fault with the actors, that they were out of humour, and had not their parts perfect, and that Harris did do nothing, nor could so much as sing a ketch in it; and so was mightily concerned: while all the rest did through the whole pit, blame the play as a silly, dull thing, though there was something very roguish and witty; but the design of the play, and end, mighty insipid.[9]

A rival playwright, though, Thomas Shadwell, wrote in the preface to his own *The Humorists* (1671), "I think (and I have the Authority of some of the best Judges in *England* for't), [it] is the best Comedy that has been written since the Restauration of the Stage."[10] Even though Shadwell was writing before Restoration comedy had reached a very high level, I fear that Pepys, for once in his life, was right in his critical judgment.

Nevertheless, Etherege had come a step closer to what was to become the final Restoration style. That is, **She wou'd if she cou'd** does not make its point by the contrast between high and low plots as Elizabethan or Jacobean drama—or **The Comical Revenge**—did. Instead, it concentrates on the one plot of matching two pairs of witty lovers. Further, **She wou'd if she cou'd** presupposes a fundamental split in human beings between appearance and nature, between social requirements and "natural" desires. The basic theme of the play, its sense of humor, thus becomes the contrast between liberty and restraint. "The Town" in the play stands for a place big enough, offering enough opportunities for anonymity, so that social restrictions do not really interfere with natural desires. Conversely, the country stands for a place where close observation makes social restrictions impinge directly on natural desires. In the town, private self and social self can be quite separated; in the country they cannot. The town thus suggests liberty, and the country, restraint. Similarly, gallantry and flirtation are associated with the town and liberty; marriage becomes associated with confinement and the country. Country restraints are permanent; one only lends oneself to such town requirements as clothing, conversation, or disguise. Thus, plot, symbols, and action all grow from the fundamental assumption that there is a deep division between social and "natural" man.[11]

As the play opens, two young gallants, Courtall and his friend Freeman, are interrupted in their search for "new game" by Mrs. Sentry, who tells Courtall that her mistress,

Lady Cockwood, has come back to town and is eagerly looking forward to seeing him. Courtall has so far managed to avoid satisfying the lady's importunities, and to escape her attentions this time he pleads an engagement to meet her henpecked husband, Sir Oliver Cockwood, and his drinking companion, Sir Joslin Jolly, both of whom are eager to run riot after their release from the country. While Courtall and Freeman are on their way, they meet and are charmed by two witty and handsome girls in masks. When the two gallants are brought to Lady Cockwood's by the two drunken country knights, they find these young ladies are Sir Joslin's nieces Ariana and Gatty, who, also feeling suddenly liberated from the restraints of the country, had been taking the liberty of the town. After a number of meetings during Sir Oliver's alternate drinking bouts and penances and Lady Cockwood's schemes to consummate her relation with Courtall, the two gallants become thoroughly enamoured of the girls. Lady Cockwood sees that they are and angrily realizes why she and Courtall never seem to find an opportunity. She sends forged letters to antagonize the couples, meanwhile assuring Sir Oliver that Courtall has made her dishonorable proposals. Despite the confusion, Courtall adroitly figures out what is going on, and maneuvers Lady Cockwood into a position where she is forced to let the young romances take their course. The girls finally agree to accept their suitors on a month's probation.

As one might surmise from the plot, there is one "natural" desire which is constant for every character—almost the only one: the desire for sexual gratification. And this desire is constant regardless of outward differences between town people or country people, between Lady Cockwood's pretenses to honor or Sir Joslin's frank vulgarity. It is conspicuously true of all the women in the play, to any one of whom the title *She wou'd if she cou'd* applies. Moreover, each character assumes that sexual desire is the major motive in any action by another. Ariana and Gatty suspect Lady Cockwood's affair with a gallant as she does theirs; Sir Oliver assumes Lady Cockwood is motivated by desire—his only mistake is that he thinks he is to be the instrument of her gratification; Sir Joslin introduces the lovers to each other on strictly physical terms; Lady Cockwood even suspects Sentry of trying to take Courtall away from her. The characters express this indiscriminate sexuality in animal terms. A lover is to his mistress as a spaniel (155) or as horses are to a coach (98).[12] A jealous woman is like a bloodhound (142). "I was married to her when I was young, *Ned*," sighs the restless Sir Oliver, "with a design to be baulk'd, as they tye Whelps to the Bell-weather; where I have been so butted, 'twere enough to fright me, were I not pure mettle, from ever running at sheep again" (137).

Birds are the most common symbol for this animality. Thus, Courtall describes himself as an "old Fowler" (151), and Gatty compares him to a kite looking for poultry (154). The belligerent little oldsters, Sir Oliver and Sir Joslin, think of themselves as game-cocks (101, 131) and Sir Joslin even swears: "If I ever break my word with a Lady,

. . . she shall have leave to carve me for a Capon" (100). Like Courtall, Lady Cockwood pursues and is a "kite" (59), and "old Haggard" (122), even an old hen, to whom the girls are chicks (130). The girls themselves are birds in a cage (103), whereas whores are "ravenous Cormorants" (140). Courtall calls the pursuit of Ariana and Gatty going "a birding" (155); "Are you so wild," asks Freeman, comparing the masked girls in the park to falcons, "that you must be hooded thus?" (107). The play makes this one joke over and over—its theme, insofar as this play has a satirical theme: the absurdity of a two-legged animal's pretending its animal desires are something better. A curious comparison presents itself at this point. As Professor G. Wilson Knight points out in an entertaining appendix called "The Shakespearian Aviary," Shakespeare also uses birds frequently.[13] "Such images and impressions," writes Professor Knight, "occur mainly in direct relation to all essences which may be, metaphorically, considered ethereal and volatile. Bird-life suggests flight and freedom and swiftness: it also often suggests pride." For Etherege, birds are just another two-legged animal. The difference, in a sense, epitomizes what had happened to English drama.

Etherege portrays love in this play, as in *The Comical Revenge,* as various antagonisms. Thus, the love-chase is a naval battle (106) or land war (118): the gallants are military strategists (105) and the girls mere soldiers (105) to whom they ultimately surrender (109). Even Sir Oliver and Sir Joslin are "mighty men at Arms" ready to "charge anon to the terrour of the Ladies" (132), for whoring requires courage (138). In this terminology, a billet-doux is a challenge, an assignation a duel (156), and so on. In another form of sex-antagonism, the pursuit of the opposite sex is "hunting" (91, 101, 104, 106, 107) or hawking or horsebreaking (92) or fishing, the girls being "young Trouts" (121). In a set of monetary comparisons, sex is a "trade" (91, 119, 131, 175), "gambling" (98, 128, 168), swindling (104), or lawsuits (150): thus, Courtall speaks of Lady Cockwood's sexual forwardness as trying to arrest him for debt (153). Etherege so proliferates this kind of unfavorable comparison that it almost seems to lose any kind of pattern or direction: love (or sex) is acting a part in a play (121), alchemical projecting (151), an execution (131), a stain (168), or a fever (169); a woman is something to be eaten (153, 178), or even read (155). The same disparagement applies to marriage: it is a duel (176) to which the proposal is the challenge. It is a business enterprise (103, 174), a mortgaging of one's person to acquire an estate; courtship is simply negotiating the contract (174). Nevertheless, these comparisons, even as varied and as proliferated as they are, do show a pattern. In every case, the basis for the comparison is that the individual is about to accept an apparent restraint in order to satisfy his real natural desires. In a sense, he must obey "the rules of the game" to achieve satisfaction: in this respect, love and marriage can be thought of as acting or bargaining or lawsuits, even as alchemy. Etherege is simply saying metaphorically that a fine gallant hates falling in love, for then he must restrain his liberty: "All the happiness a Gentleman can desire, is to live at liberty" (174).

This theme of liberty and restraint—the most basic theme of the play—is organized about various contrasts. One such contrast is that between sexual animality and falling in love. Another such contrast is that between town and country. Indeed, the action of **She wou'd if she cou'd** is simply that of country people (the Cockwoods, Jolly, and his nieces) adventuring into the wider scope and complexity of London. The difference between town and country shows itself in the form of intrigue. "There is some weighty affair in hand, I warrant thee: my dear *Ariana,* how glad am I we are in this Town agen," cries Gatty as she infers an intrigue from Lady Cockwood's behavior (102). "A man had better be a vagabond in this Town, than a Justice of Peace in the Country," says Sir Oliver, summing up the difference between them. "If a man do but rap out an Oath, the people start as if a Gun went off; and if one chance but to couple himself with his Neighbours Daughter without the help of the Parson of the Parish, . . . there is presently such an uproar, that a poor man is fain to fly his Country" (93). The difference, in other words, is that the country allows little or no scope for a personal life. There is no privacy: observation is so close that one's nature cannot be given free play, but is bound in tightly by social restrictions. Petty pretenses, like a child's, are the only escape.

In the town, on the other hand, pretenses become large and graceful responses to convention, ends in themselves because the town is large enough and anonymous enough for a person's outward appearance and private life to be quite separated. By being separated, each becomes important in and of itself. Clothing, for example, assumes a new importance in the town. Lady Cockwood can severely restrict Sir Oliver's activities by locking up all but his "Penitential Suit" (127ff.) A face is like a hat (107); an affair to Freeman is like putting on a new suit (97); and a lover, to the girls, runs in one's head like a new gown (168). A woman is known simply as her mask and her petticoat (103, 131). In the town, appearances, because they are separated from the private self, have a separate existence all their own.

The humor of the play lies in the contrast between what the young people do with the liberty of the town and what their elders do with it. Lady Cockwood makes herself ridiculous by pursuing Courtall, and Sir Oliver and Sir Joslin make themselves ridiculous by their sophomoric debauches, while the young people use their liberty to fall in love. Their doing so does not mean they are wiser. On the contrary, they have simply used their freedom to exchange it for confinement; they have ceased being "Tenants at Will" and have bound themselves to a "Lease for life" (174). Accepting confinement means letting oneself in for pretense, because confinement creates a tension between the "natural" self and the outward, social self, and that tension in turn creates a need to deceive others. Thus, Ariana and Gatty disguise themselves to flirt in the Mulberry Garden and resent the social rules that deny them the same liberties as men. Thus, too, Sir Oliver pretends fidelity to escape and resents Lady Cockwood

who, by restraining him, creates the need for pretense. In this way, the Cockwood marriage operates not by love but power politics. Sir Oliver tries to establish himself as a monarch (114, 115) or "tyrant" (96) controlling the "politicians," his wife and Mrs. Sentry. Sentry's name, of course, is significant and Sir Oliver's might be a reminiscence of the Civil War. At any rate, domestic altercations are called "civil war" (137) and infidelities, whether Sir Oliver's or Courtall's, "treason" (139, 144). They are put down, however, and in the finale Lady Cockwood is cast as a restored monarch bestowing an "Act of Oblivion" (176) and marching Sir Oliver off to bed where "we'll sign the Peace" (179). Even the young lovers at this early stage of their relation are subject to power politics. Courtall and Freeman are to Gatty and Ariana as subjects are to rulers, or indeed to "absolute Tyrants" (103).

The play, however, develops one important difference between the old pretenders and the young. Sir Oliver and Lady Cockwood have been pretending so long and so hard that the inconsistency between their inner natures and outer appearances has confused them and corrupted the expression of their real selves. The two overtones in their name suggest this confusion, Cockwood, expressing sexual desire, and "woodcock," the bird proverbial for stupidity. Lady Cockwood, even in her private interviews with Courtall, cannot put aside her pretenses to honor (as in II.ii, for example.) Even when they are alone, she scolds Sentry for neglecting to chaperone her, and Sentry apologizes for her: "This is a strange infirmity she has, [but] custom has made it so natural, she cannot help it" (113). Sir Oliver's continual pretense of affection and respect to his lady has mixed his inner and outer selves, too, so that he can no longer satisfy his desires for other game. His riots are tainted with the impotency that his relations with Lady Cockwood bring out ("The very sight of that face makes me more impotent than an Eunuch"—114). Thus, his amours in the play are uniformly failures; even his desires are limited: "When we visit a Miss, / We still brag how we kiss, / But 'tis with a Bottle we fegue her" (141). He pretends to his wife (to whom he should not have to pretend at all) that he is more virtuous than he is and to the world that he is more vicious.

This, then, is what is laughable about the older people: that they let their social pretenses creep into private affairs where they do not belong. The difference between them and the young people shows in the two "hiding" scenes. In the first (I.i), Mrs. Sentry, who has come to tell Courtall of the Cockwoods' arrival, is forced to hide when Sir Oliver comes, and overhears him invite the young men to a wild evening. Only confusion results from Lady Cockwood's learning of this, because, since both Cockwoods are pretending to each other, she cannot admit to her knowledge. In the later hiding scene (V.i), when Courtall and Freeman overhear the girls solving the problem of the forged letters, the result is to give both sides the knowledge to break down the barriers Lady Cockwood put between them. The lovers can use their knowledge because they are completely aware of the line where social pretense leaves off and plain dealing begins. The young people use pretense without being dominated by it, and their sense of appropriateness is the screen against which most of the wit sallies are projected. The young people are as aware of their double selves as an actor in a part and, indeed, Gatty uses the metaphor: "I hate to dissemble when I need not; 'twou'd look as affected in us to be reserv'd now w'are alone, as for a Player to maintain the Character she acts in the Tyring-room" (170). "A single intrigue in Love," says Courtall, "is as dull as a single Plot in a Play, and will tire a Lover worse, than t'other does an Audience." "We cannot be long without some under-plots in this Town," replies Freeman, "let this be our main design, and if we are anything fortunate in our contrivance, we shall make it a pleasant Comedy" (121). Two acts of frankness in friendship are what break through the outer barriers of pretense and resolve the intrigue, such as it is. "Let us proceed honestly like Friends, discover the truth of things to one another," says Freeman, and the two gallants find to their good fortune that they are pursuing different women (152). Similarly, it is Ariana's and Gatty's frank talk (168) that clears up the business of the forged letters. In broader terms, the lovers know that appearance and nature are necessarily different; they know when one's inner nature can be converted into a social, outer fact and when it cannot be, and that is the key to their competence. The difference between old and young, then, is simply that pretense has taken over the old folks' personalities, but not the young lovers'—at least not Courtall's and Gatty's.

The lesser lovers, however, Freeman and Ariana, have begun to show the same confusion of selves that mars the actions of the older people. Freeman's explanation to Courtall of his beginning an intrigue with Lady Cockwood is not convincing (173), and suggests that he is playing his friend false. Similarly, Ariana rejects Gatty's frankness; Gatty demands, "Hast thou not promis'd me a thousand times, to leave off this demureness?" and Ariana answers, "If your tongue be not altogether so nimble, I may be conformable," suggesting that she, like Lady Cockwood, carries social pretense into a relationship where it ought not to be (102, see also 170).

The denouement resolves these contrasts between town and country, gallantry and marriage, old and young, liberty and restraint, by compromise. Early in the play, when Gatty and Ariana successfully trick Courtall, they speak of turning him into a "Country Clown" (126). At the end of the play, Gatty, speaking of marriage as a kind of confinement, ironically remarks, "These Gentlemen have found it so convenient lying in Lodgings, they'll hardly venture on the trouble of taking a House of their own." "A pretty Country-seat, Madam," replies Courtall gallantly, "with a handsom parcel of Land, and other necessaries belonging to't, may tempt us; but for a Town-Tenement that has but one poor conveniency, we are resolv'd we'll never deal" (174). The young men accept their confinement and agree to a month's trial before their final satisfaction: For Courtall, the ways of intrigue seem almost to have passed: "If the heart of man be not very deceitful, 'tis very likely it

may be [a match]." For Freeman, however, the lesser lover, "A month is a tedious time, and will be a dangerous tryal of our resolutions; but I hope we shall not repent before Marriage, whate're we do after" (176). The month's trial, of course, continues the pattern of the various unfavorable metaphors for love and marriage: that one must obey "the rules of the game" to achieve satisfaction, submitting to a restraint to win in the end. There is a hint in Freeman's remark that these marital confinements will give rise eventually to the same pretense and hostility that mar the Cockwood marriage. The older people at the end of the play continue their pretenses unchanged. "I am resolv'd," piously says Lady Cockwood, "to give over the great bus'ness of this Town, and hereafter modestly confine my self to the humble Affairs of my own Family." "Pray entertain an able Chaplain," replies Courtall dryly (178). Sir Joslin and the unwitting Sir Oliver are just as restless as at the opening of the play as they prepare to return to country life, a morass of crabbed pretenses forced on them by the binding effect of social restrictions on natural desires.

Etherege's second play is quite different from his first, and the change measures his capacity for growth as a dramatist. Gone are the old devices of parallel plots and character groups. The entire action is built on a series of contrasts, each of which grows from one central idea: the felt conflict between social restraints and "natural" desires. The conception is thoroughly un-Elizabethan, and the form of the play his grown to meet the conception. While there is an occasional heroic note in Lady Cockwood's hypocritical cant about her honor, the highness of the high plot of *The Comical Revenge* is almost wholly gone, too. The supernatural element, present in a half-serious way in his first play, has now been almost eliminated. The Devil appears: everyone in the play is called a devil at one time or another (126, 129, 150, 151, 157, 158); Lady Cockwood, in particular, is an "Old Devil" (153, 158) or a "long-Wing'd devil" (121). But the epithet is not meant in any traditional religious way and there is hardly any heavenly counterpart in the finale; marriage is taken as a penance for the sins of the gallants (174), Lady Cockwood is urged to entertain an able chaplain, and that is about all. The new play is saturated with realism, real taverns, real parks, real stores, contrasted implicitly to the outlandish atmospheres of heroic drama. The play is antiheroic, but to heroics heard only in the mind's ear. So too, the low plot has been absorbed into the single, unified dramatic situation. Folly, in this play, has risen to the upper class, though it still is, as it was for Sir Nicholas Cully, allowing one's pretenses to take the place of one's real nature.

She wou'd if she cou'd is a study, still somewhat crude, of this kind of folly. The young people of the play face constantly the risk that their necessary and proper social pretenses, whether to honor or to vice, may obstruct their real feelings; they face, too, the warning example of the Cockwoods. Their success in avoiding this pitfall defines an ethic of pretense. Etherege's second play has little of the sheer doings of his first—there are neither duels nor slapstick—and this suggests a growing awareness on the part of the characters and their author that "*talk* is a very important kind of action."[14] Conversation is a performance; speech, clothing, manners, and other forms of appearance have importance in themselves because they are separate from the private life of the individual, his "nature." These appearances constitute the visible, apparent acquiescence to social and other restraints and are thought of as separate from the nature that rebels against restraint. But even the purely private actions of an individual—sexual conversation as opposed to verbal, for example—are felt to have this double nature, a visible, external performance and a personal, internal satisfaction.

The talk Etherege gives his characters bodies forth this sense in linguistic form. "Now shall I sleep as little without you," cries Courtall, in his curtain speech, as he is parting from his betrothed, "as I shou'd do with you: Madam, expectation makes me almost as restless as Jealousie." These comparisons, a late-seventeenth-century version of Donne's conceits, let a man be passionate but discuss his passion at the same time, as Donne's do. Impersonally, whimsically, the observer talks about things which he, by an odd coincidence, happens to be doing.[15] In later Restoration comedies, this figure of speech becomes a rhetorical device of extraordinary complexity: the speaker hides his feelings by the comic comparison at the same time that by discussing them at all he makes them more visible and himself transparent in the heroic manner. In *She wou'd if she cou'd* the device is not yet used with skill. When the events of the play move quickly, metaphor drops out. Where characters are acting or planning action, they speak normally, as when Sir Oliver or Sir Joslin plan their parties or Lady Cockwood an assignation or when the gallants hide in the Cookwood house. Figurative speech is reserved for the obvious occasions when talk is an action itself, such as the time in the park when the two young men meet the girls or when the final matches are made. Metaphor is still felt as a frothy formality opposed to the "weighty affairs" of the play, not yet a part of them. Nevertheless, Etherege has begun to weld action and language into a way of seeing. Town and country symbolize opposite poles of experience, liberty and restraint. Etherege uses this division to split his characters, to show how in response to the pressure to conform some respond by dissimulation and affectation, and some evolve a golden mean of a restraint, the acceptance of which is an expression of self—marriage for love. Both language and action represent human conduct split under the pressure of conformity into a visible, social appearance and a personal, private nature. Folly is the confusion of the two; wisdom is their separation and balance. *She wou'd if she cou'd* is a quasi-scientific exploration of divided man, and this was to be the Restoration comic mode.

. . . . .

THE MAN OF MODE; OR, SIR FOPLING FLUTTER

There have been few audiences in history as lucky as the one that in 1676 braved the March weather of London and the crowding at Dorset Garden to see Etherege's new play,

destined to be his last. *The Man of Mode* was a tremendous success; its easy, witty dialogue was the finest yet to appear, and its hard, brilliant portrait of the Restoration rake was never to be equaled. Etherege, however, had not taken over the sense of good and evil that Wycherley had begun to develop in *The Country Wife*. *The Man of Mode* still treats cleverness as the ultimate virtue.

The play develops its theme and humor from the contrast between two parallel lines of intrigue, one "high" and one "low." The high intrigue involves Harriet, Young Bellair, and Emilia. The low involves Mrs. Loveit, Dorimant, and Bellinda. In each, a young man is involved with two women, one he wants and one he does not want but who pursues him: Dorimant wants Bellinda, but is pursued by Mrs. Loveit; Young Bellair wants Emilia, but is pursued by Harriet, or, more properly, she is forced on him by their families who wish the match. In each line, the young man uses another young man to decoy the extra woman away: Dorimant uses Sir Fopling for Mrs. Loveit, and Bellair helps Dorimant's relationship with Harriet along. Dorimant thus occupies a pivotal position in both lines of intrigue: he is the decoy for the "high" line and he is the man pursued in the "low."

In more detail, Dorimant, at the beginning of the play, has begun the exchange of an old mistress, Mrs. Loveit, for a new and younger one, Bellinda. To do the business Bellinda uses Dorimant's attention to a masked lady (actually Bellinda herself) to work Mrs. Loveit into a jealous rage, while Dorimant accuses her of flirting with Sir Fopling Flutter, the "man of mode." In the second intrigue, young Bellair, one of Dorimant's friends, is in love with Emilia, but his father is forcing him to marry Harriet. Dorimant falls in love with Harriet, but she pretends to be in love with Young Bellair just long enough to let him fool his father and marry Emilia, and, unknown to her, long enough to let Dorimant consummate his affair with Bellinda. Finally, however, Dorimant succumbs to Harriet's charms and agrees to go off to the country (no less!) to court her.

Etherege contrasts the characters as he does the two plot lines. Most critics agree that the play sets off the sleek competence of Dorimant against the strained effects of Sir Fopling. Actually, however, not just these two, but all the principal characters are ranged on a scale. For the men, affectation is the negative value and the worst offender is, of course, Sir Fopling, who absurdly and magnificently incarnates the idea. He has no inner personality, only externals—clothes, attendants, and mannerisms. For example, he criticizes Dorimant for not having a mirror in his drawing room, for "In a glass a man may entertain himself." "The shadow of himself," remarks Dorimant. Medley, Dorimant's gossipy friend, ironically adds: "I find, Sir *Fopling*, in your Solitude, you remember the saying of the wise man, and study your self" (260-261).[16] Sir Fopling's self is totally outside: there is neither inner man nor inner desires.

Medley, Dorimant's confidant, slightly older than the other young men of the play, is almost as bad. He too remains always a spectator of the action, never a participant (255).

For his natural self, he has substituted the gossip the ladies enjoy, so much so that Emilia calls him "a living Libel, a breathing Lampoon" (225), and Dorimant, "the very Spirit of Scandal" (226). Medley is also rather effeminate, the only character who indulges in "the filthy trick these men have got of kissing one another," or who calls Dorimant, "my Life, my Joy, my darling-Sin" (191). Young Bellair is next to Medley in the scale of affectation. "By much the most tolerable of all the young men that do not abound in wit," "ever well dress'd, always complaisant, and seldom impertinent," are the judgments of his peers (201-202). Harriet, more subtle, says of him: "The man indeed wears his Cloaths fashionably, and has a pretty negligent way with him, very Courtly, and much affected; he bows, and talks, and smiles so agreeably, as he thinks. Varnish'd over with good breeding, many a blockhead makes a tolerable show" (220). He is to Dorimant what the heroic people of **The Comical Revenge** were to Sir Frederick Frolick, but Etherege has developed: the contrast is much subtler.

The cynical, witty Dorimant is far more "wild" and "bewitching" (213) than earnest Young Bellair, but even he, as Harriet sets him out, has some affectation. His reputation as a lover is as important to him as clothing is to Sir Fopling. Thus, Dorimant speaks of his long affair with Loveit as old clothes (194) and compares his own person to a bauble or a fashion (229). This play has not just one "man of mode," but two: Dorimant, as well as Sir Fopling, both occupying similar places in the structure. Etherege is laughing at the hero as well as the fop.

There is, then, a second pattern on which the men are ranked: sexual success, an alternative kind of affectation. Thus, the ladies laugh at Sir Fopling; Medley achieves some popularity, but no particular successes; Young Bellair reaches consummation, but only within the framework of marriage, while Dorimant has two successful illicit affairs and one matrimonial courtship. This scale parallels the other; modishness is a sublimation of sexuality, or replaces it. Sir Fopling thus sees men and women simply as clothes, equipage, or the like (230); he treats his own gown as a person (253). In short, he is one of "the young Men of this Age" who are "only dull admirers of themselves, and make their Court to nothing but their Perriwigs and their Crevats, and would be more concern'd for the disordering of 'em, tho' on a good occasion, than a young Maid would be for the tumbling of her head or Handkercher" (245). Sir Fopling's importance is not so much that he is affected about clothes and "manners," but that his affectation supplants his sexuality, indeed, his very self.

Etherege sets up this relation between Sir Fopling and Dorimant in his brilliant post-seduction scene (IV.ii); the dialogue contains some appalling insights into the ways of womankind. Critics have complained of the frank stage direction calling for Dorimant's manservant "*tying up Linnen.*" His inconspicuous, useful presence, however, is a meaningful realistic note, an ironic comment on the fancy speeches of Dorimant and Bellinda downstage. She escapes just as Sir Fopling enters. He, by way of contrast to Dorimant's sexual affectation, immediately starts to dance by himself and to talk of mirrors and clothes. The juxtaposition of the fop's affectations with the hero's, like the juxtaposition of the false courtship of Bellinda and the "real" courtship of Harriet, reveals Dorimant's Don Juanism for what it is, simply another kind of affectation.

Etherege puts the ladies of the play into a pattern based on the opposite of affectation: "Wildness," which shows itself mostly as sexual promiscuity. Just as Dorimant displays a permissible, or at least curable, kind of affectation, so a woman must be only "as wild as you wou'd wish her," and should have "a demureness in her looks that makes it so surprising" (193). Mrs. Loveit is far from this ideal. Her affair with Dorimant is the common gossip of London. At the slightest provocation she tears a passion to tatters with a welter of invective (out of Restoration tragedy): "Insupportable! insulting Devil! this from you, the only Author of my Shame!" and so on. Her inner self is always on the surface. She has virtually no concern with appearances, no "affectation," as that word applies to the men. Bellinda is next in the scale. Although she conceals her affair with Dorimant, she lets her passionate, private self burst the outer restraint of reputation. She cannot control herself, even though she sees how Dorimant used Loveit (274). Emilia does not hide her affectations so adeptly as Bellinda, but she is considerably more chaste. Yet even her virtue is not above suspicion: Dorimant cynically hints that once she is married he might have better luck with her (202). Harriet alone is so completely in control of her passions as to confine her wildness to the dressing table (219). She is outraged that anyone should think her "easy" to marry, let alone to be seduced (279). Yet to Dorimant she can say: "My Eyes are wild and wandring like my passions, / And cannot yet be ty'd to Rules of charming" (248). She is hardly passionless: she simply does not allow her wildness any unfitting expression.

The comedy opens with two brilliantly drawn characters who appear only once: Foggy (i.e., puffy) Nan the orange-woman and Swearing Tom the shoemaker who call on Dorimant at his levée. They introduce, the critics say, a touch of low life and suggest vices among the lower classes like those of the aristocracy. While they certainly do these things, they occupy a good deal of valuable space at the beginning of the play for purely gratuitous bits of local color. One must, I think, find some sort of keynote they represent, or else conclude that Etherege erred seriously in starting with two irrelevancies instead of exposition. Actually, they serve as "sign-post characters." They establish the two scales along which the other characters are ranged. Nan's business is fruit, something appropriate to one's natural self as opposed to one's social front. (The rest of the ladies in the play face chiefly this problem, expressing their "natural" desires within the limits of society.) Thus, fruit is used later in the play (267) as a *double-entendre* for Bellinda's misbehavior: "She has eaten too much fruit, I warrant you." "'Tis that lyes heavy on her Stomach." "I was a strange devourer of Fruit when I was young, so ravenous—" says Mrs. Loveit's ingenuous maid. Harriet's mother criticizes the appetite of the age for "green Fruit," instead of ladies like herself, "kindly ripen'd" (246). Swearing Tom, on the other hand, deals in shoes, and the men in the play are ranked by clothing or other factors of appearance. Secondarily, he is concerned with his own inner vices "too gentile for a Shoomaker." "There's never a man i' the town," he says, "lives more like a Gentleman, with his Wife, than I do" (198). Just as Medley and Dorimant are called atheists by Bellair, the orange-woman calls Tom an atheist, religious devotion being a continued metaphor in the play for love (278ff.). Tom's chief attribute, swearing, reflects Dorimant's pretended loves and broken vows.

Besides the main characters and these "sign-post" characters, there are three older people. Harriet's mother and Old Bellair (who falls in love with Emilia) make themselves ridiculous by their flirtatious efforts to impose their outmoded selves on the young. Lady Townley, however, Young Bellair's aunt, is urbane and sophisticated, wise enough to accept her role as elder stateswoman, a charming instance of the wisdom "the Town" offers: how to express one's inner nature in outward forms that will withstand time.

To the satirical contrasts between the two plots and the characters associated with them, Etherege adds further contrasts; for example, the differing treatments of love in the two plots. To Loveit, in the low plot, love is subject to disease and death (217), for which jealousy is the best medicine (239). Dorimant, before Harriet brings him from the low plot to the high, calls love a sickness (242), a disease, a "settled Ague" or "irregular fitts" (249), for which intercourse is the cure (260); an appetite, though one can very quickly get one's "belly full" (257). It is a deception: "Love gilds us over," says Dorimant, "and makes us show fine things to one another for a time, but soon the Gold wears off, and then again the native brass appears" (216). To the people in the low plot, love seems a kind of adversary proceeding, a duel (201), no different for people than for "game-Cocks" (224), for an affair is "a thing no less necessary to confirm the reputation of your Wit, than a Duel will be to satisfie the Town of your Courage" (231). Love affairs are lawsuits (208), carried on with ladies who are "practising Lawyers" (228). Love is a game, in which a woman ought to lose her reputation fairly (269): "The deep play is now in private Houses" (228). Sex, in the low plot, is thoroughly animal: poaching (190), hunting (207, 217), or fishing (242). Only while Dorimant is still in the low plot can he think of Harriet as a business enterprise, requiring "Church security," or speak of their relation as gambling (235). In the high plot, however, the loves of Harriet, Emilia, and Young Bellair are described in half-serious religious images, "Faith" as opposed to "sence" or "reason" (198-199).

Etherege contrasts the two plots further by their use of acting and dissembling. In the Bellinda-Loveit intrigue, all the affairs are illicit and must be concealed. The whole atmosphere is one of dissimulation. In the Emilia-Harriet plot, acting is a mere *jeu d'esprit*. The orange-woman sets the tone when she describes Harriet's playful imitation of Dorimant (191), for Harriet does indeed enjoy "the dear pleasure of dissembling" (222), as do Emilia and Lady Townley when they mimic Old Bellair (233). They and Harriet and Young Bellair, however, play-act only to "deceive the grave people" outside the threesome. In the Bellinda-Loveit intrigue, the pretenses are to deceive the people within the threesome: Bellinda and Dorimant conceal their affair; Mrs. Loveit feigns an interest in Sir Fopling. In the low plot, Loveit can say: "There's nothing but falsehood and impertinence in this world! all men are Villains or Fools" (286); "Women, as well as men, are all false, or all are so to me at least" (265). Dorimant sees "an inbred falshood in Women" (269). Acting is not sport but deadly earnest, to hurt, as when Dorimant imitates Sir Fopling (267) or pretends indifference to Loveit (238), or to deceive and manipulate—Bellinda's pretenses (V.i) or Loveit's feigned indifference to Dorimant (242).

Etherege provides still a third contrast. In the low plot, everyone—Loveit, Bellinda, even Medley—is a "Devil" (193, 208, 210, 214, 218, 270), though Dorimant "has something of the Angel yet undefac'd in him" (210), and is charming enough to "tempt the Angels to a second fall" (237), as indeed he does. True love and the high plot, on the other hand, represent Heaven, at least linguistically. Dorimant establishes the metaphor in the opening speech of the play when he compares his being forced to write a billet-doux "after the heat of the business is over," to a "Fanatick" paying tithes. Medley and Young Bellair also discuss in the first scene the contrast between the "Heaven," "Faith," and "Salvation" of true love and the "doubts and scruples" of the rakes (199). But in the end, the most cavalier of Cavaliers gives up his skepticism for "repentance" and "the prospect of . . . Heav'n" (278).

In this, as in most Restoration comedies, the action involves a cure or therapy for one of the characters, and the important therapy of this play is to tame Dorimant. He must be brought out of the "hell" of the low plot where pretense is the normal order of business, "good nature and good manners" (216); where it is laughable when one's emotions show (as Mrs. Loveit's or Young Bellair's do); and where sex comes not from love, but from hostility. "There has been such a calm in my affairs of late," says Dorimant, summing up this stormy way of life, "I have not had the pleasure of making a Woman so much as break her Fan, to be sullen, or forswear her self these three days" (195). He must be brought into the "heaven" of the high plot in which the emotional, natural desire can be made a social fact. The critics' sympathies for Loveit and Bellinda in this situation are simply wasted words. By Restoration, or for that matter Victorian, standards these ladies are irretrievably lost, condemned to an endless series of pretenses. The fault in the situation is not that Dorimant gives up his mistresses in favor of a wife, but that the ladies wrongfully succumbed to his blandishments. Neither of them expects Dorimant to marry her; all they ask is that he continue his illicit relationships. Surely Dorimant is more to be praised than censured for preferring the honorable course of matrimony.

It is, of course, Harriet who performs the cure. She very quickly realizes what is wrong with Dorimant: affectation in a much broader sense than the other characters conceive it—for example, Young Bellair in the dialogue quoted above. She knows that Dorimant concerns himself too much with superficial sexual affairs that answer only his vanity: "begging . . . the Ladies Good liking, with a sly softness in your looks, and a gentle slowness in your bows, as you pass by 'em—as thus, Sir—[*Acts him*] Is not this like you?" (236). She realizes that Dorimant is used to a group that keeps appearance from revealing the private self, to whom dissembling is the normal condition. She therefore refuses to have anything to do with the oaths that Bellinda and Loveit had regarded as such important tokens, and that Dorimant had broken so lightly (216, 227, 259): "Do not speak it, if you would have me believe it; your Tongue is so fam'd for falsehood 'twill do the truth an injury" (278). Before she will let him come over to the way of life she shares with Young Bellair and Emilia, she puts him through a sort of initiation:

Harriet.

> I was inform'd you used to laugh at Love, and not make it.

Dorimant.

> The time has been, but now I must speak—

Har

> If it be on that Idle subject, I will put on my serious look, turn my head carelessly from you, drop my lip, let my Eyelids fall and hang half o're my Eyes—Thus—while you buz a speech of an hour long in my ear, and I answer never a word!

This is, of course, exactly the same kind of play-acting she fell into so naturally with Bellair. But while that was to "deceive the grave people," this is to achieve a catharsis in Dorimant. Dorimant, however, resists.

Har

> . . . why do you not begin?

Dor

> That the company may take notice how passionately I make advances of Love! and how disdainfully you receive 'em.

Har

> When your Love's grown strong enough to make you bear being laugh'd at, I'll give you leave to trouble me with it. Till when pray forbear, Sir.

(249-250)

Submitting to being laughed at is only the beginning.

Dorimant's final submission or "initiation" comes in Act V. It is marked by the transition from Act V, scene i, at Mrs. Loveit's, where all the characters of the low plot are treacherously deceiving each other, to Act V, scene ii, Lady Townley's house, where all the pretenses are broken down and all is camaraderie and good fellowship. (In both scenes, three women work on Dorimant, in each case, two ladies and a maid. Not much is made of the parallel in the text; it is more in the director's realm, to be brought out in the grouping of the players.) Whereas the earlier scene is a study in continued deception, Dorimant having betrayed both the ladies, the initiation scene moves from deception to truth. At first, Harriet quite consciously plays Dorimant's game to make him play hers; she makes herself appear indifferent to force him to commit himself;

Har

> [*Aside turning from* Dorimant.] My love springs with my blood into my Face, I dare not look upon him yet.

Dor

> What have we here, the picture of a celebrated Beauty, giving audience in publick to a declar'd Lover?

Har

> Play the dying Fop, and make the piece compleat, Sir.

Dor

> What think you if the Hint were well improv'd? The whole mystery of making love pleasantly design'd and wrought in a suit of Hangings?

Har

> 'Twere needless to execute fools in Effigie who suffer daily in their own persons.

(277)

Half-serious religious imagery marks Dorimant's progress toward the "heaven" of the high plot:

Har

> In men who have been long harden'd in Sin, we have reason to mistrust the first signs of repentance.

Dor

> The prospect of such a Heav'n will make me persevere, and give you marks that are infallible.

Har

> What are those?

Dor

> I will renounce all the joys I have in friendship and in Wine, sacrifice to you all the interest I have in other Women—

Har

> Hold—Though I wish you devout, I would not have you turn Fanatick—

(278-279)

Because she knows Dorimant is in the habit of hiding or suppressing his emotions, Harriet insists now, in effect, that he train himself into the habit of letting his actions reflect his state of mind. If Dorimant is to love Harriet, she laughingly insists, not only must he submit to being mocked, he must pursue her into the country: "To a great rambling lone house, that looks as it were not inhabited, the family's so small; there you'l find my Mother, an old lame Aunt, and my self, Sir, perch'd up on Chairs at a distance in a large parlour; sitting moping like three or four Melancholy Birds in a spacious vollary—Does this not stagger your Resolution?" (287). As in Etherege's earlier plays, the country was to be understood by his audience as a place highly unpleasant because close observation forces the inner self to conform to visible mores; it is therefore a suitable House of Holiness for Dorimant's penance:

HAR

> What e're you say, I know all beyond *High-Park's* a desart to you, and that no gallantry can draw you farther.

DOR

> That has been the utmost limit of my Love—but now my passion knows no bounds, and there's no measure to be taken of what I'll do for you from any thing I ever did before.

HAR

> When I hear you talk thus in Hampshire, I shall begin to think there may be some little truth inlarg'd upon.

　　　　　　　　　　　　　　　　　　　　(279)

Dorimant, Professor Underwood points out, is undergoing the conflict between reason and passion which is traditional for comic heroes, though in this case the "reason" is that of the libertine and Machiavellian school of naturalism.[17] The passion, moreover, is antirational and fideistic.

Harriet has forced Dorimant from the finite loves of the low plot to a love nominally, at least, infinite. Appropriately enough, she can now sneer at Mrs. Loveit, "Mr. *Dorimant* has been your God Almighty long enough, 'tis time to think of another—" and suggest a nunnery as the fashionable place for her retreat. Harriet has made it quite clear she does not want Dorimant to abandon his naturalistic desires, but to translate them into marriage: "Though I wish you devout, I would not have you turn Fanatick." In the play's terms, she does not want a permanent residence in the country which would stifle Dorimant's energy and competence. What she does want is to teach him to bring his natural desires to the social framework of marriage. Only "this dear Town," as Harriet calls it, admits the full expression of self.

This, then, is the action of the comedy and its sense of humor: to bring Dorimant—and through him the audience—from the low plot where the private self fights social restrictions by deception to the high plot where one can realize his private life in viable social forms. Old Bellair, in these last few lines of the play, hails Sir Fopling indignantly, "What does this man of mode do here agen?" as though Etherege wanted to underline his point: that Dorimant has left that status in favor of a richer kind of "modishness."

In other words, the play is nothing more nor less than the old sentimental story of the rake reformed, indeed redeemed, by the love of a good woman. At least that *would* be the basic form of the action, were it not so variously undercut by irony. One very basic irony is the fact that Harriet (the good woman) occupies a position in the plot structure that corresponds to Mrs. Loveit's; similarly Dorimant functions as a decoy like Sir Fopling. Harriet's making Dorimant court her in the country, in fact, her whole "holding out" for marriage is nothing but a more elaborate and safer form of the oaths and conditions Bellinda required from Dorimant. The entire first scene of the play makes Dorimant look arrogant and arbitrary by showing him as he berates and badgers his servants in his slovenly, helter-skelter household. In general, the opening scene provides a variety of episodes running the gamut of love from the poor whore's trade to Young Bellair's neo-platonic adoration; all these episodes serve to strip the conventions and formalities from life and lay bare the naturalistic substratum at the core of every social pretense. There is still more ironic crossfire in the final scene: at the very moment when Dorimant is agreeing to go off to the country to court Harriet, he is deftly assuring Loveit (out of one side of his mouth, as it were) that he is only marrying Harriet for her money and (out of the other side) trying to make another assignation with Bellinda.[18] The play bristles with so many ironies, all undercutting one another, that it is difficult to say what, if anything, Etherege wants us to take seriously. Virtually every action of every character becomes a gambit in a great and meaningless social game.

One thing is clear, however. The comedy does not simply laugh at those who do not have "manners." There are two absurdities. One lies in substituting arbitrary formalism for the inner self, as Sir Fopling does. He lists some French rules of courtship and Medley drily comments, "For all this smattering of the Mathematicks, you may be out in your Judgment at Tennis" (251). The opposite kind of absurdity is Loveit's ranting, an attempt to impose her unformalized inner self on others: "Horrour and distraction seize you, Sorrow and Remorse gnaw your Soul," and so on (215). "Ill customs," wrote Etherege from his diplomatic post at Ratisbon, "affront my very senses, and I have been so used to affectation that without the help of the air of the court what is natural cannot touch me. You see what we get by being polished, as we call it."[19] Precisely this kind of "affectation" is the value the comedy half-seriously puts forward: to express the private self in a social form which is decorous, natural, and even redeeming, or, as Old Bellair somewhat crudely puts it (280): "To Commission a young Couple to go to Bed together a Gods name."

Notes

1. John Downes, *Roscius Anglicanus* (London, 1708), p. 25. *The Letterbook of Sir George Etherege,* ed. Sybil Rosenfeld (Oxford: Oxford University Press, 1928), pp. 1-28.

2. John Palmer, *The Comedy of Manners* (London: Bell, 1913), p. 67. Thomas H. Fujimura, *The Restoration Comedy of Wit* (Princeton: Princeton University Press, 1952), p. 95. Clifford Leech, writing of *Marriage à la Mode* in "Restoration Tragedy: A Reconsideration," *Durham University Journal,* XLII (1950), 109.

3. William Empson, *English Pastoral Poetry* (New York: Norton, 1938), p. 47.

4. John Wilcox, *The Relation of Molière to Restoration Comedy* (New York: Columbia University Press, 1938), p. 73n.

5. My references are to page numbers in *The Dramatic Works of Sir George Etherege,* ed. H. F. B. Brett-Smith, 2 vols. (Oxford: Basil Blackwell, 1927), I, 1-88. They may be related to other editions by the following table:

   Act I, sc. i: 1-2; sc. ii: 2-8; sc. iii; 9-11; sc. iv: 11-13.

   Act II, sc. i: 13-16; sc. ii: 17-22; sc. iii: 22-29.

   Act III, sc. i: 29-30; sc. ii: 30-33; sc. iii: 33-34: sc. iv: 35-36; sc. v: 36-40; sc. vi: 40-44; sc. vii: 44-46.

   Act IV, sc. i: 46-47; sc. ii: 48-49; sc. iii: 49-51; sc. iv: 52-56; sc. v: 56-57; sc. vi: 58-59; sc. vii: 60-62.

   Act V, sc. i: 62-66; sc. ii: 66-75; sc. iii: 76-78; sc. iv: 78-81; sc. v: 81-86.

6. Dale Underwood, *Etherege and the Seventeenth-Century Comedy of Manners,* Yale Studies in English, vol. 135 (New Haven: Yale University Press, 1957), p. 56.

7. Du Fresnoy, "Observations on the Art of Painting," trans. John Dryden, *Works,* ed. Sir Walter Scott and George Saintsbury, 18 vols. (Edinburgh, 1882-1893), XVII, 363.

8. Underwood, *Etherege* (n. 6), chap. iii.

9. *The Diary of Samuel Pepys,* ed. Henry B. Wheatley, 8 vols. (London: Bell, 1926), VII, 287.

10. Thomas Shadwell, "Preface to *The Humorists, A Comedy*" (1671), reprinted in Joel E. Spingarn, *Critical Essays of the Seventeenth Century,* 3 vols. (Oxford: Oxford University Press, 1908), II, 152.

11. Dale Underwood, *Etherege and the Seventeenth-Century Comedy of Manners,* Yale Studies in English, vol. 135 (New Haven: Yale University Press, 1957), chap. iv, discusses the form and structure of the play at length and with considerable subtlety. This chapter also has a number of insights into the imagery and significance of the play. Though Professor Underwood's approach differs from mine, our conclusions, not unsurprisingly, sometimes agree.

12. My references are to pages in *The Dramatic Works of Sir George Etherege,* ed. H. F. B. Brett-Smith, 2 vols. (Oxford: Basil Blackwell, 1927), II, 89-180. They may be applied to other editions by means of the following table:

    Act I, sc. i: 91-98; sc. ii: 99-104.

    Act II, sc. i: 104-110; sc. ii: 110-118.

    Act III, sc. i: 118-126; sc. ii: 126-129; sc. iii: 129-143.

    Act IV, sc. i: 143-149; sc. ii: 149-159.

    Act V, sc. i: 160-179.

13. G. Wilson Knight, *The Shakespearian Tempest,* 3d ed. (London: Methuen, 1953), p. 293.

14. Cleanth Brooks and Robert Heilman, *Understanding Drama* (New York: Holt, 1948), p. 442. The quotation refers to *The Way of the World* but is widely applicable to Restoration comedy.

15. Andrews Wanning, "Some Changes in the Prose Style of the Seventeenth Century," (Cambridge, Eng., 1938, unpub. diss. on deposit in the Harvard College Library), p. 313. This statement also refers to *The Way of the World* but applies equally to Etherege's language. Professor Wanning's chapter is entitled "The Language of Split-Man Observation," a useful term generally for the language of Restoration comedy, and one to which we shall have frequent reference.

16. My references are to pages in *The Dramatic Works of Sir George Etherege,* ed. H. F. B. Brett-Smith, 2 vols. (Boston and New York, 1927), II, 182-288. They may be related to other editions by means of the following table:

    Act I, sc. i: 189-204.

    Act II, sc. i: 205-210; sc. ii: 210-218.

    Act III, sc. i: 219-224; sc. ii: 225-233; sc. iii: 233-244.

    Act IV, sc. i: 244-257; sc. ii: 258-263; sc. iii: 264.

    Act V, sc. i: 265-274; sc. ii: 274-287.

17. Dale Underwood, *Etherege and the Seventeenth-Century Comedy of Manners* Yale Studies in English, vol. 135 (New Haven: Yale University Press, 1957), p. 79.

18. Professor Underwood (*ibid.,* pp. 90-91) goes so far as to say that Dorimant is following Harriet to the country more for a "ruin" than a romance.

19. Letter to Mr. Poley, January 2/12, 1687/8, *The Letterbook of Sir George Etherege,* ed. Sybil Rosenfeld (Oxford: Oxford University Press, 1928), p. 309.

Virginia Ogden Birdsall (essay date 1970)

SOURCE: Birdsall, Virginia Ogden. *"The Man of Mode, or Sir Fopling Flutter."* In *Wild Civility: The English Comic Spirit on the Restoration Stage,* pp. 77-104. Bloomington: Indiana University Press, 1970.

[*In the essay below, Birdsall explores the contrast of lifestyles between Sir Fopling Flutter's rule-bound world of social pretense and Dormant and Harriet's natural, honest, and self-deterministic world. The critic posits that Sir Fopling's milieu is "a dead world . . . being exposed by juxtaposition to a living one."*]

FASHION n. A despot whom the wise ridicule and obey.

REASON, v.i. To weigh probabilities in the scales of desire.

—AMBROSE BIERCE, *The Devil's Dictionary*

If Etherege's third and last play (1676) is by common consent his best, it is also his most insistently tough-minded and unremittingly open-eyed and honest. The comic challenge which the chief protagonists Dorimant and Harriet hurl at their self-consciously polished, rule-bound world is one which draws its vitality from a full awareness of their own deeper, more demonic natures and from their absolute refusal of all illusions. Knowing and accepting themselves for what they are, they *will* be free to be themselves; and they will play the game of life with the bravado and the ruthless skill of born gamblers. The gaiety and zest for life of Etherege's earlier protagonists is still theirs, but they suffer fools less gladly, and they both pursue their Hobbesian "power and pleasure and appetite" with aggressive artistry.

In a more than superficial sense the theme of ***The Man of Mode*** is, as its title indicates, fashion or "modishness," and the world in which Dorimant and Harriet move is one of "modes"—both of behavior and dress. A man or woman of "quality" (a term which occurs again and again in the play) acts and dresses by the rules—rules sufficiently solidified so that books of instructions have appeared. Asked by Emilia about "any new Wit come forth, Songs or Novels?" Medley replies: "there is the Art of affectation, written by a late beauty of Quality, teaching you how to draw up your Breasts, stretch up your neck, to throw out your Breech, to play with your Head, to toss up your Nose, to bite your Lips, to turn up your Eyes, to speak in a silly soft tone of a Voice, and use all the Foolish French Words that will infallibly make your person and conversation charming, with a short apologie at the latter end, in the behalf of young Ladies, who notoriously wash, and paint, though they have naturally good Complexions." The deeper suggestion here is that the "new Wit" is a far cry from the imaginative expansiveness to be expected from "Songs or Novels"; and indeed "rules" and "modishness" become in the play the central metaphor used to define artificiality, effeteness, sterility as these qualities stand opposed to the natural, the robust, the creative possibilities

exemplified by Dorimant and Harriet. Again, as in Etherege's earlier comedies, a dead world is being exposed by juxtaposition to a living one.

At the center of the world of artificiality and so-called wit stands that walking rule-book for social and sartorial affections Sir Fopling Flutter. If Dorimant is "the Prince of all the Devils in the Town" (237), Sir Fopling enjoys an equally supreme status as "the very Cock-fool of all those Fools" (217). Both are "men of Mode," but with a significant difference that is repeatedly underlined by the dialogue of the play. Being himself made up of "Pantaloon," "Gloves . . . well fring'd," and "Perriwig," Sir Fopling is never happier than when characterized as a "shape" that "Ladies doat on" (231), and the only fault he can find with Dorimant is in the matter of "Crevats": "*Dorimant,* thou art a pretty fellow and wear'st thy cloaths well," he cries condescendingly, "but I never saw thee have a handsom Crevat. Were they made up like mine, they'd give another Aire to thy face. Prithee let me send my man to dress thee but one day. By Heav'ns an English man cannot tye a Ribbon" (261).

For their part neither Dorimant nor Harriet is indifferent to fashion and neither is lacking in his share of vanity, but both reject impatiently Sir Fopling's brand of artifice. "Varnish'd over with good breeding," says Harriet, "many a blockhead makes a tolerable show" (220). For her as for Dorimant the morning toilet is a necessary preliminary to the adventure of living, but clothes do not "make the man." Rather, they must be made to fit him. Thus Dorimant's complaint about his "Shooe" that it "Sits with more wrinkles than there are in an Angry Bullies Forehead" is stoutly denied by the shoemaker (who clearly knows his customer): "'Zbud, as smooth as your Mistresses skin does upon her" (198). But both Dorimant and Harriet firmly refuse to allow themselves to be turned into manikins. "Leave your unnecessary fidling;" Dorimant says testily to Handy, "a Wasp that's buzzing about a Mans Nose at Dinner, is not more troublesome than thou art" (199). And Harriet exclaims to Busy, "How do I daily suffer under thy Officious Fingers!" (219) Both hero and heroine have planted themselves in indignant opposition to the empty modishness of the world in which they live. "That Women should set up for beauty as much in spite of nature, as some men have done for Wit!" deplores Harriet. "That a man's excellency should lie in neatly tying of a Ribbond, or a Crevat!" protests Dorimant.

Clearly the difference between Dorimant and Harriet on the one hand and Sir Fopling on the other has to do in part with style as a manifestation of self. For Dorimant and Harriet style *expresses* the natural man. For Sir Fopling style *replaces* nature. Or, to put the matter another way, Dorimant and Harriet control and determine their own modes of dress and behavior according to their own individualities, while every piece of clothing donned by Sir Fopling and every move he makes is dictated by his conception of what polite society demands. Sir Fopling's comicality, in fact, may be regarded as an instance of the

Bergsonian "covered" having turned into the "covering."[1] Hopelessly bound by social rules, he has no real *life,* no "living suppleness" left. He has acted the part of the "Compleat Gentleman" for so long that no vestige of spontaneity has survived; every motion is made by the book, and the imitation has stifled and obliterated the reality. As Medley says, "He has been, as the sparkish word is, Brisk upon the Ladies already; he was yesterday at my Aunt *Townleys,* and gave Mrs. *Loveit* a Catalogue of his good Qualities, under the Character of a Compleat Gentleman, who according to Sir *Fopling,* ought to dress well, Dance well, Fence well, have a genius for Love Letters, an agreeable voice for a Chamber, be very Amorous, something discreet, but not over Constant" (200, 201).[2]

Sir Fopling, in short, invariably behaves as the rules say he "ought to," and in this respect he is clearly identified with that other slave to form and model of rigidity, Lady Woodvil. If she is "a great admirer of the Forms and Civility of the last Age" (193), Sir Fopling is just as irrevocably committed to the forms and rules of the new age. And if she is an egregious social snob in her constant concern for "women of quality," he is equally snobbish in his desire to parade himself as a "man of Quality" (268)—"in imitation of the people of Quality of France." "It might be said," remarks Bergson, in an observation which is peculiarly applicable to both Lady Woodvil and Sir Fopling, "that ceremonies are to the social body what clothing is to the individual body. . . . For any ceremony, then, to become comic, it is enough that our attention be fixed on the ceremonial element in it, and that we neglect its matter . . . and think only of its form."[3]

Significantly Dorimant has occasion in the course of the action to play the fop in both Lady Woodvil's and Sir Fopling's senses and thus to supply a fully conscious parody of both kinds of empty affectation. For the old lady's benefit he appears as Mr. Courtage—"That foppish admirer of Quality, who flatters the very meat at honourable Tables, and never offers love to a Woman below a Lady-Grandmother!" (244) "You know the Character you are to act, I see!" comments Medley, and not even the guarded Harriet can deny that he delivers a convincing performance: "He fits my Mothers humor so well, a little more and she'l dance a Kissing dance with him anon" (245). But the contrast between a Mr. Courtage and Dorimant himself is later underlined heavily:

HAR.

Lord! how you admire this man!

L. WOOD.

What have you to except against him?

HAR.

He's a Fopp.

L. WOOD.

He's not a *Dorimant,* a wild extravagant Fellow of the Times.

HAR.

He's a man made up of forms and common places, suckt out of the remaining Lees of the last age.

(254)

And subsequently the difference between Dorimant and Sir Fopling is made equally plain in the brief and angry exchange between Dorimant and Loveit:

DOR.

Now for a touch of Sir *Fopling* to begin with. Hey— Page—Give positive order that none of my People stir—Let the Canaile wait as they should do—Since noise and nonsence have such pow'rful charms,
 I, that I may successful prove,
 Transform my self to what you love.

LOV.

If that would do, you need not change from what you are; you can be vain and lewd enough.

DOR.

But not with so good a grace as Sir *Fopling.* Hey, *Hampshire*—Oh—that sound, that sound becomes the mouth of a man of Quality.

(267, 268)

Several years had elapsed between Etherege's second play and his third, and during that period he had, it would seem, recognized the emergence of a fresh challenge for the comic spirit. In effect, Sir Fopling's modishness represents to the younger aristocratic generation a new kind of affectation which was replacing the *précieux* mode of an earlier time and which had gradually developed to the point where it was, in its own way, equally far removed from the realities of human experience. The trouble with Sir Fopling is that he has taken over a social mode which had originally grown out of the emancipating libertine convictions of Charles II's courtiers and out of the needs of the Hobbesian "natural man," and he has turned it into a social pretense quite lacking its original life-giving force and hence as empty of meaning as Lady Woodvil's *précieux* mode. Oscar Wilde remarks in one of his essays that "Costume is a growth, an evolution, and a most important, perhaps the most important, sign of the manners, customs, and mode of life of each century."[4] But it is a truism to observe that both manners and costume can easily become hollow externals when the real human needs that originally inspired them are lost or forgotten, and it is then that "a man's excellency" comes to "lie in neatly tying of a Ribbond, or a Crevat."

In Dorimant's and Harriet's world the mode has spread so far down the social scale as to include even Tom the Shoemaker (significantly a dealer in "costume"), who prefers the word "Tope" to the word "drunk" and who exclaims: "'Zbud, there's never a man i'the Town lives more like a Gentleman, with his Wife, than I do. I never mind her motions, she never inquires into mine; we speak to one another Civilly, hate one another heartily, and because 'tis vulgar to lie and soak together, we have each of us our several Settlebed" (198). Artificiality and sterility have extended even into Tom's world. Yet it is the real function of this entire little scene to emphasize, with a kind of sly comic inversion, that for all their affectations there is no essential difference between a Sir Fopling and a Tom nor, for that matter, between a "vulgar" and illiterate "Molly" and a "woman of quality" like Lady Woodvil or Mrs. Loveit. Thus when simple Molly writes to Dorimant: *"I have no money and am very Mallicolly; pray send me a Guynie to see the Operies,"* Medley remarks, "Pray let the Whore have a favourable answer, that she may spark it in a Box, and do honour to her profession." And Dorimant assures him "She shall; and perk up i'the face of quality" (204).

To define Young Bellair and Emilia as the "golden mean" in this modish society, as does Norman Holland, is not only to make use of a term which has no validity in the Etheregean comic world unless as a standard to be rejected, but also to ignore the patent tendency of both characters to sentimentality and to what the play repeatedly defines as "unreasonable" behavior and to overlook their commitment to the courtly tradition of love and honor. Bellair, as measured against the positive standards of daring and defiance established by Etherege, emerges as a conservative nonentity. It is he who warns Harriet against the "Mail" as a rather dangerous place for nice young ladies; and earlier Medley has recognized his own and Dorimant's company as equally dangerous for nice young men like Bellair: "how will you answer this visit to your honourable Mistress?" he demands tauntingly, "'tis not her interest you shou'd keep Company with men of sence, who will be talking reason" (198).

The most Dorimant can say of Bellair is that "He's Handsome, well bred, and by much the most tolerable of all the young men that do not abound in wit," a judgment reinforced by Medley's subsequent characterization: "Ever well dress'd, always complaisant, and seldom impertinent . . ." (201, 202). In Lady Townley's gay social groups, he fades rather colorlessly into the background, and although he is not quite so much in love with Emilia as to marry her while there is a serious risk of losing his inheritance (he is "reasonable" enough about money if not about love) and is not above a contrivance with Harriet "to deceive the grave people," he inspires in Harriet herself nothing more than the lukewarm approbation: "I think I might be brought to endure him" (220). Lacking Dorimant's ruthless aggressiveness, he is also lacking in the vitality, virility, and excitement which contribute to making Dorimant the overwhelmingly dominant figure that he is, and he represents finally only a more subtle foil than Sir Fopling in bringing out the fact of the hero's evident superiority.

Much the same can be said also of the role of Emilia vis-à-vis Harriet, and again it is Medley—serving at once as Dorimant's confidant and as the chorus of the play—who sums her up: "her Carriage is unaffected, her discourse modest, not at all censorious, nor pretending like the Counterfeits of the Age" (202). There is, moreover, a special irony in Dorimant's marking her out as a likely prospect for a future conquest ("I have known many Women make a difficulty of losing a Maidenhead, who have afterwards made none of making a cuckold"), since he is thereby not only underscoring his own skeptical attitude toward every "discreet Maid," but in the process suggesting that the pedestal on which she stands is more than a little precarious and that she is, in her elemental nature, no more civilized and no less appetitive than a Mrs. Loveit, a Bellinda, or a Molly.

On more than one occasion, in fact, Etherege seems to be pointedly asking us to recognize in Emilia something of the same overrefined preciousness that belongs to Sir Fopling. When, for example, Lady Townley says in talking of Dorimant and Mrs. Loveit: "We heard of a pleasant Serenade he gave her t'other Night," and Medley describes it as "A Danish Serenade with Kettle Drums, and Trumpets," Emilia exclaims, "Oh, Barbarous!" and Medley chides, "What, you are of the number of the Ladies whose Ears are grown so delicate since our Operas, you can be charm'd with nothing but Flute doux, and French Hoboys?" (208, 209) And in the next Act Lady Townley feels prompted to tax Emilia with being "a little too delicate" after she has remarked stuffily: "Company is a very good thing, Madam, but I wonder you do not love it a little more Chosen" (228, 229).

Neither exchange by itself may seem to possess much importance, but when placed in juxtaposition with certain of Sir Fopling's scenes, an evolving theme becomes apparent, and it is one which has had its roots in the opening scene of the play. Thus to Sir Fopling's question, "Have you taken notice of the Gallesh I brought over?" Medley replies, "O yes! 't has quite another Air, than th'English makes" and Dorimant adds, "Truly there is a bell-air in Galleshes as well as men." Whereupon Sir Fopling responds approvingly, "But there are few so delicate to observe it" (230, 231). Dorimant and Medley are, of course, playing with Sir Fopling, and their delicacy is only make-believe. The word "delicate," however, has at this point already been used twice about Emilia, and Dorimant's choice of the word "bell-air" is certainly suggestive. In the following scene Sir Fopling makes another statement reminiscent of Emilia when he declares, in response to Bellinda's observation about "all the rabble of the Town" gathered in the Mail, "'Tis pity there's not an order made, that none but the Beau Monde should walk here" (240). A few lines later we hear him exclaiming, "there's nothing so barbarous as the names of our English Servants" (242). And finally, in the fourth act, Sir Fopling invades Lady Townley's drawing room with a group of masqueraders whom he describes as "A set of Balladins, whom I pickt out of the best in *France* and brought over, with a Flutes deux or two" (253).

In effect, then, two life styles are being repeatedly contrasted with each other throughout the play—a contrast variously expressed in terms of the "barberous" versus the "delicate," the English versus the French, the inclusive versus the exclusive, Dorimant versus Sir Fopling. Sir Fopling, as the embodiment of an effete society which has cut itself off almost wholly from its life-giving roots, defines a mode of life which threatens to overtake Emilia as well. His snobbishness and exclusiveness—"I was well receiv'd in a dozen families, where all the Women of quality us'd to visit" (251)—is set against the "universal taste" which Lady Townley advocates. Her house, representing along with the "Mail" the "green world" of the play, is described as "the general rendevouze, and next to the Playhouse is the Common Refuge of all the Young idle people." It is itself, indeed, a kind of "play-house" and "new world," and Dorimant, in his role as Mr. Courtage, succinctly defines its difference from the old for the benefit of Lady Woodvil: "All people mingle now a days, Madam. And in publick places Women of Quality have the least respect show'd 'em. . . . Forms and Ceremonies, the only things that uphold Quality and greatness, are now shamefully laid aside and neglected" (244, 245). And Lady Woodvil goes on to summarize the case more accurately than she knows in lamenting: "Lewdness is the business now, Love was the bus'ness in my Time," for in the terms of the play love has become an empty word and "lewdness" a vital reality (and precisely the quality in which Sir Fopling and his ilk are deplorably lacking).

In Sir Fopling's world every judgment as to a man's "excellency" is made in terms of modishness. Strolling in the Mail with Mrs. Loveit, Sir Fopling comments upon the *"four ill-fashioned Fellows"* who have passed singing across their path: "Did you observe, Madam, how their Crevats hung loose an inch from their Neck, and what a frightful Air it gave 'em?" To a man of his refined and "delicate" sensibilities, the smell of such dirty fellows is almost unbearable:

Lov.

> Fo! Their Perriwigs are scented with Tobacco so strong—

Sir Fop.

> It overcomes our pulvilio—Methinks I smell the Coffeehouse they come from. . . .

Sir Fop.

> I sat near one of 'em at a Play to day, and was almost poison'd with a pair of Cordivant Gloves he wears—

Lov.

> Oh! filthy Cordivant, how I hate the smell!

(240, 241)

Sir Fopling's own gloves, of course, are delicately perfumed: "Orangerie! You know the smell, Ladies!" (231) And to an educated nose like his, even a burning candle is "filthy" and scarcely endurable: "How can you breathe in a Room where there's Grease frying!" (252) To such foppery, Dorimant's impatient opposition has been expressed early in the play:

Hand.

> Will you use the Essence or Orange Flower Water?

Dor.

> I will smell as I do to day, no offence to the Ladies Noses.

(199)

Only in the last act of the play, however, does the full thematic significance of this kind of emphasis become apparent. The act opens with a conversation which offers a clear parallel with the opening scene of Act I. Again it is early morning and again the talk is about "Markets" and "Fruit," and the earlier conversation between Dorimant and the Orange-woman as well as that already quoted between Sir Fopling and Mrs. Loveit ought to echo in our ears as Bellinda confronts Mrs. Loveit:

Bell.

> Do you not wonder, my Dear, what made me abroad so soon?

Lov.

> You do not use to be so.

Bell.

> The Country Gentlewomen I told you of (Lord! they have the oddest diversions!) would never let me rest till I promis'd to go with them to the Markets this morning to eat Fruit and buy Nosegays.

Lov.

> Are they so fond of a filthy Nosegay?

Bell.

> They complain of the stinks of the Town, and are never well but when they have their noses in one.

Lov.

> There are Essences and sweet waters.

Bell.

> O, they cry out upon perfumes they are unwholsome; one of 'em was falling into a fit with the smell of these narolii.

Lov.

> Methinks in Complaisance you shou'd have had a Nosegay too.

Bell.

> Do you think, my Dear, I could be so loathsome to trick my self up with Carnations and stock-Gillyflowers? I begg'd their pardon and told them I never wore any thing but Orange Flowers and Tuberose. That which made me willing to go was a strange desire I had to eat some fresh Nectaren's.

Lov.

And had you any?

Bell.

The best I ever tasted.

(265, 266)

If any doubt exists as to the sexual implications of "fruit" in the opening scene of the play, it can scarcely survive now. Since Bellinda has just come from her assignation with Dorimant, the double-entendre of her concluding remarks here becomes obvious and is even more insistently underscored a few lines later as Bellinda pretends illness:

Pert.

She has eaten too much fruit, I warrant you.

Lov.

Not unlikely!

Pert.

'Tis that lyes heavy on her Stomach.

Lov.

Have her into my Chamber, give her some Surfeit Water, and let her lye down a little.

Pert.

Come, Madam! I was a strange devourer of Fruit when I was young, so ravenous—

(267)

The special irony of the scene lies in the fact that both women are explicitly denying their identity with the "Country Gentlewomen" and, in effect, their own physical, appetitive natures at the same time that they implicitly acknowledge them. Throughout the play the gap between artificiality and naturalness is expressed in terms of "Orange Flower Water" or "Orangerie" on the one hand and "oranges" (or "peaches" or "Nectarens") on the other. In the broader context of the play, it is the difference between Sir Fopling and Dorimant, between a suit of clothes and a man, between sterility and fertility.

The Orange-woman is, of course, by profession both a seller of fruit and a bawd, and the peach which she offers to Dorimant ("the best Fruit has come to Town t'year") has a clear identity with Harriet ("a young Gentlewoman lately come to Town"). Dorimant cynically begins by expressing a disbelief in the "freshness" of both, calling the peach the "nasty refuse of your Shop" (190) and the gentlewoman "some awkward ill fashion'd Country Toad" (191), but the description Medley supplies is enough to make Dorimant's mouth water with anticipation. He first describes her as being "in a hopeful way" (192)—a phrase which the Orange-woman chooses to interpret according to her own earthy lights—and then goes on to lyricize:

Med.

What alteration a Twelve-month may have bred in her I know not, but a year ago she was the beautifullest Creature I ever saw; a fine, easie, clean shape, light brown Hair in abundance; her Features regular, her Complexion clear and lively, large wanton Eyes, but above all a mouth that has made me kiss it a thousand times in imagination, Teeth white and even, and pretty pouting Lips, with a little moisture ever hanging on them that look like the Province Rose fresh on the Bush, 'ere the Morning Sun has quite drawn up the dew.

By the time Medley has concluded his eulogy, he has Dorimant exclaiming: "Flesh and blood cannot hear this, and not long to know her" (193). It is in this connection that Bernard Harris, commenting on Etherege's prose, points out that "his similitudes from the natural life offer a relationship to the human, not a distinction or even a parallel. In ***The Man of Mode*** . . . there is a persistent relationship effected between the forms of life. . . . The simile is perfectly absorbed and absorbing."[5]

Sir Fopling's senses, however, have, in contrast to Dorimant's, virtually lost touch with flesh-and-blood, sensuous reality. Not only is his nose offended by natural smells but his ears are offended by harsh sounds. Preferring delicate flute notes to Dorimant's "barbarous" trumpets and kettle drums, he also finds the name John Trott "unsufferable" and changes it to the more euphonious (and pretentious) "Hampshire." "The world is generally very grossier here, indeed," he remarks, comparing England to France (231), and Dorimant's vigorous masculinity is continually set off against his preciousness and effeminacy:

Med.

He was Yesterday at the Play, with a pair of Gloves up to his Elbows, and a Periwig more exactly Curl'd then a Ladies head newly dress'd for a Ball.

Bell.

What a pretty lisp he has!

Dor.

Ho, that he affects in imitation of the people of Quality of *France.*

Med.

His head stands for the most part on one side, and his looks are more languishing than a Ladys when she loll's at stretch in her Coach, or leans her head carelessly against the side of a Box i'the Playhouse.

(200)

In a later scene, when the group gathered at Lady Townley's tries to persuade Sir Fopling to dance, Medley remarks: "Like a woman I find you must be struggl'd with before one brings you to what you desire." But there is no persuading Sir Fopling, and when he apologizes to Harriet

("Do not think it want of Complaisance, Madam"), she returns, "You are too well bred to want that, Sir *Fopling*. I believe it want of power." To which he smugly assents: "By Heav'ns and so it is. I have sat up so Damn'd late and drunk so curs'd hard since I came to this lewd Town, that I am fit for nothing but low dancing now, a Corant, a Boreè, or a Minnuét; but St. *André* tells me, if I will but be regular in one Month I shall rise agen. Pox on this Debauchery" (253). Sir Fopling, as it proves, can only "endeavor at a caper" and then be content to dance by proxy—throwing out instructions to his "set of Balladins" from his position seated among the ladies. And his "want of power" turns out to include a strong suggestion of sexual impotence when at the end of the play he is all too easily discouraged from continuing his pursuit of Mrs. Loveit: "An intrigue now would be but a temptation to me to throw away that Vigour on one, which I mean shall shortly make my Court to the whole sex in a Ballet" (285).

Even Old Bellair possesses more animal vigor than does Sir Fopling, and indeed it is he who is the true heir to the role of Sir Joslin Jolley of **She wou'd if she cou'd.** Forever dancing, singing, drinking, and "bepatting" the ladies, he is the high-spirited, irrepressible Dionysian clown at Lady Townley's revels and is always in the forefront of the exuberant country dances, which contrast so sharply in their energetic natural rhythms with the mannered "French air" imposed by Sir Fopling on his own little "equipage." Like Sir Joslin, Old Bellaire seems to be constantly in motion ("You are very active, Sir," says Emilia. He views the male-female relationship in coarsely physical terms and acts as good-natured matchmaker at the end of the play. ("Please you, Sir," he bids the Chaplain, "to Commission a young Couple to go to Bed together a Gods name?")

Dorimant, for all his refinement and ironic detachment, possesses the masculine vigor which identifies him with Old Bellair's rather primitive spontaneity and virility, but Sir Fopling has lost touch almost completely with such earthy, natural behavior. Even his carelessness is studied: "We should not alwaies be in a set dress, 'tis more en Cavalier to appear now and then in a dissabillée" (261). And he writes his love songs, as he does everything else, by the rules so that the end product sounds like something straight out of the heroic plot of **The Comical Revenge**—a pretty pastoral with appropriate references to "my wounded heart" and to sighs and languishings. Boasting of having learned singing from Lambert in Paris, he has to acknowledge: "I have his own fault, a weak voice, and care not to sing out of a ruél," whereupon Dorimant comments: "A ruél is a pretty Cage for a singing Fop, indeed" (262).

Dorimant himself refuses categorically to live like a songbird in a cage. Just as he takes over the form of the pastoral love song and uses it to express what Underwood calls his own "'satanic' posture,"[6] so he takes over the vows and protestations of the *précieux* mode and uses them to his own aggressive ends. Always the comic artist, adapting every form and rule to his particular needs, he sings and versifies his way through the play with supreme

confidence in his own superior knowledge of the ways of the world and of the women in it, and Young Bellair pays him the ultimate tribute by remarking: "all he does and says is so easie, and so natural" (234).

To him as to Harriet the first requirement of the game of life is freedom to follow one's own inclinations, however arbitrary they may be. "We are not Masters of our own affections," he says to Mrs. Loveit, sounding like an echo of Courtall, "our inclinations daily alter; now we love pleasure, and anon we shall doat on business; human frailty will have it so, and who can help it?" (214) The greatest enemy to the élan vital is restriction of the kind Mrs. Loveit would impose on Dorimant and Lady Woodvil on her daughter, and Dorimant's defiance of Mrs. Loveit in Act I, scene ii, has its counterpart in Harriet's defiance of her mother in Act II, scene i. Harriet too has her own "inclinations," and she confides to her waiting woman her real objection to marrying Bellair:

HAR.

> I think I might be brought to endure him, and that is all a reasonable Woman should expect in a Husband, but there is duty i'the case—and like the Haughty *Merab*, I
> *Find much aversion in my stubborn mind,*

> Which,
> *Is bred by being promis'd and design'd.*

> (220)

And a few lines later, when Young Bellair asks: "What generous resolution are you making, Madam?" Harriet retorts, "Only to be disobedient, Sir."

In terms of the highly civilized world to which Dorimant and Harriet belong, they are both "barberous" (a word which recurs repeatedly in indignant references to Dorimant)—possessed of no illusions about the "native brass" which lies at the bottom of their own natures. Egotistically cognizant of their own value, they shake off impatiently any attempt to reduce them to a civilized formality. Thus, when Busy pleads with Harriet, "Dear Madam! Let me set that Curl in order," Harriet exclaims, "Let me alone, I will shake 'em all out of order" (219). In short, they are both "sons of the morning"—the time of day when they first appear on stage in all their rebellious individuality—armed for their encounter with the world with the freshness and vigor of free spirits but also with a tough skepticism that will take nothing on faith.

Neither harbors any undue respect for "quality" and both are merciless mockers of both the foppish and the *précieux* affectations which surround them. When, for example, Dorimant taunts Harriet by making a jeering comment about ladies' eyes ("Women indeed have commonly a method of managing those messengers of Love! now they will look as if they would kill, and anon they will look as if they were dying. They point and rebate their glances, the better to invite us"), she promptly retorts: "I like this variety well enough; but hate the set face that always looks as it would say *Come love me*. A woman, who at Playes makes the Deux yeux to a whole Audience, and at home cannot forbear 'em to her Monkey" (248). Both hero and heroine can, like their comic predecessors, play a tongue-in-cheek part in the social game and at the same time detach themselves from it either as highly entertained onlookers or as sardonic commentators.

Possessing flexibility of response and a keen eye for the false and the ridiculous in human behavior, they delight in their own superior ability to control the world around them and are consummate Hobbesian "gloriers." And dissembling represents one of their methods of having their own way with the world and of remaining wild and free in a society bent on reducing its members to a common mold. Toward the end of the play Lady Townley observes that "Men of Mr. *Dorimants* character, always suffer in the general opinion of the world," and Medley corroborates her view: "You can make no judgment of a witty man from common fame, considering the prevailing faction, Madam—" (283). The same might be said of the social response to the comic spirit in any age. Representing as they do the rebellious, freewheeling play spirit dedicated to the art of living well on their own terms, the Dorimants of the world will always find people to brand them as "Devil" and "ingrate" with a wholly negative implication.

Sinner and devil are, of course, the names invariably given by a conventional or Christian society to indulgers of the natural instincts, especially sexual, and to indulgers of the truth-speaking instincts as well. But a comic hero such as Dorimant will always in effect contend with Oscar Wilde, "What is termed sin is an essential element of progress"; and he will thus rejoice in and pride himself on his own sinfulness. Medley, in his opening greeting to Dorimant, calls him "my Life, my Joy, my darling-Sin" (191), and Tom the Shoemaker accuses both men of belonging among those "men of quality" who "wou'd ingross the sins o'the Nation" (197). And in a later passage Medley remarks concerning Mrs. Loveit's jealousy of Dorimant: "She cou'd not have pick'd out a Devil upon Earth so proper to Torment her" (208). In fact the language of the play repeatedly associates "that wicked *Dorimant,* and all the under debauchees of the Town" (246) with both sin and the devil; and Lady Woodvil recognizes Dorimant as an exceedingly dangerous tempter: "Oh! he has a Tongue, they say, would tempt the Angels to a second fall" (237). In short, not only is the comic hero himself a rebel against divine authority, but he has so charming and persuasive a way about him that he threatens to carry some segments of the angelic group along with him.

Closely associated with the devil imagery, moreover, is the religious terminology frequently used by the "devils" themselves as one means of defining their own nature and their irreverent attitude toward both orthodox religion and marriage as a sacred institution. The play opens, for example, with Dorimant complaining of the difficulty of writing a love letter with all passion spent: "It is a Tax upon good nature which I have here been labouring to

pay, and have done it, but with as much regret, as ever Fanatick paid the Royal Aid, or Church Duties." And later, when Bellmour is discussing with Medley and Dorimant the subject of his approaching marriage, we witness the following exchange:

BELL.

> You wish me in Heaven, but you believe me on my Journey to Hell.

MED.

> You have a good strong Faith, and that may contribute much towards your Salvation. I confess I am but of an untoward constitution, apt to have doubts and scruples, and in Love they are no less distracting than in Religion; were I so near Marriage, I shou'd cry out by Fits as I ride in my Coach, Cuckold, Cuckold, with no less fury than the mad Fanatick does Glory in *Bethlem*.

BELL.

> Because Religion makes some run mad, must I live an Atheist?

MED.

> Is it not great indiscretion for a man of Credit, who may have money enough on his Word, to go and deal with Jews; who for little sums make men enter into Bonds, and give Judgments?

BELL.

> Preach no more on this Text, I am determin'd, and there is no hope of my Conversion.

> (199)

Clearly Medley is quite as capable as Dorimant of doing witty violence to the religious view of marriage, and in his talk about "Faith" and "Salvation," "doubts and scruples," as well as his glib mixing of religious and economic metaphors, he is following Dorimant's lead and emphasizing his devilish inclination to regard nothing as sacred.

And Dorimant's dialogues with Mrs. Loveit suggest a similar pattern. Mrs. Loveit belongs wholeheartedly to the world of sacred convention, and it has been argued by more than one critic that Dorimant treats her with such calculating cruelty that in our sympathy with her we lose all admiration for him. But although such may be Bellinda's reaction, it can hardly have been the audience reaction expected or intended by Etherege, and the play can certainly be acted so as to call forth quite a different response. If Sir Fopling's rule-bound modishness is sterile, her uncontrolled passion for dominance is actively destructive, and her relationship with Dorimant is actually very much like Lady Cockwood's with Courtall. She wants to possess him wholly, to make his vows and oaths eternally binding, to deny him all his liberty. In a world of human relationships characterized by power politics, she wants absolute dominance where only a balance of power is tolerable.

Like Lady Cockwood, moreover, she is masculine in her aggressive pursuit of Dorimant and would reduce him to the submissiveness of fools like Sir Fopling who, as she says with satisfaction, "are ever offering us their service, and always waiting on our will" (268). And like Lady Cockwood too, her thirst for power, when frustrated, leads finally to a wholly destructive rage. In her fury she is even more the heroine of melodrama than is Lady Cockwood: "Death! and Eternal darkness! I shall never sleep again. Raging feavours seize the world, and make mankind as restless all as I am" (274). She expresses her destructiveness actively by tearing her fan into shreds and "flinging" chaotically about the stage, while Dorimant remarks with a coolness designed to madden her still further: "I fear this restlessness of the body, Madam, proceeds from an unquietness of the mind" (214).

Yet in the devilish terms of the play and of a Hobbesian world, Dorimant is quite "reasonable" in expecting his freedom once he has discovered his "decay of passion," and Mrs. Loveit is wholly "unreasonable" in her jealous possessiveness. (Both words appear repeatedly in the dialogue and always with these same implications.) When Emilia reminds him sentimentally of "afflictions in Love," he retorts, "You Women make 'em, who are commonly as unreasonable in that as you are at Play; without the Advantage be on your side, a man can never quietly give over when he's weary!" (228) To be "reasonable" in Etherege's comic world is simply to be realistic about the appetitive and inconstant nature of man and to comport oneself accordingly. Thus when Mrs. Loveit accosts Dorimant with: "Is this the constancy you vow'd?" he replies, "Constancy at my years! 'tis not a Vertue in season, you might as well expect the Fruit the Autumn ripens i'the Spring." Again "fruit" and naturalness are identified, and the passion-versus-reason exchange continues:

Lov.

Monstrous Principle!

Dor.

Youth has a long Journey to go, Madam; shou'd I have set up my rest at the first Inn I lodg'd at, I shou'd never have arriv'd at the happiness I now enjoy.

Lov.

Dissembler, damn'd Dissembler!

Dor.

I am so, I confess; good nature and good manners corrupt me. I am honest in my inclinations, and wou'd not, wer't not to avoid offence, make a Lady a little in years believe I think her young, wilfully mistake Art for Nature; and seem as fond of a thing I am weary of, as when I doated on't in earnest.

Lov.

False Man!

Dor.

True Woman!

Lov.

Now you begin to show your self!

Dor.

Love gilds us over, and makes us show fine things to one another for a time, but soon the Gold wears off, and then again the native brass appears.

Lov.

Think on your Oaths, your Vows and Protestations, perjur'd Man!

Dor.

I made 'em when I was in love.

Lov.

And therefore ought they not to bind? Oh Impious!

Dor.

What we swear at such a time may be a certain proof of a present passion, but to say truth, in Love there is no security to be given for the future.

Lov.

Horrid and ingrateful, begone, and never see me more!

(216)

Like all his kindred comic protagonists, Dorimant matter-of-factly accepts men for the fallen creatures they are and is quite ready (maddeningly so, in Mrs. Loveit's view) to regard himself as more fallen than most. Thus he blandly accepts her cries of "False" and "Impious" and opposes to such passion his own reasonable and realistic analysis of the human condition. The analysis constitutes a highly effective method of verbal attack, both against Mrs. Loveit herself and against the whole religious-moral-social framework which stands behind her abstractions concerning "Constancy," "Oaths," "Vows," "Protestations." Beneath their innocently logical exterior, Dorimant's remarks are patent insults—insults compounded by the smugly condescending tone in which he coolly sets forth the truths that explain his outrageous behavior. Each lengthy, deliberate speech is clearly designed to enrage further an already angry woman, and each is a little exercise in logic which arraigns by implication her stupidity. Not only is the subject of the dialogue passion as opposed to reason, but so also is the dialogue itself.

Only a Harriet can finally successfully challenge a Dorimant, because only she can meet him on his own ground of controlled reasonableness. As aware as he of the ridiculous posturings of the human animal, she is as ingenious as he in deceits and contrivances which will allow her to have her own way. When her waiting woman reproaches her with eluding her mother ("the Extravagant'st thing that ever you did in your life"), Harriet rejoins, "Hast thou so little wit to think I spoke what I meant when I over-joy'd her in the Country, with a low

Courtsy, and *What you please, Madam, I shall ever be obedient?"* And poor, baffled Busy can only answer, "Nay, I know not, you have so many fetches" (220). Harriet—like Dorimant although more ingenuously—is overwhelmingly in love with life—with "this dear Town" and with "the dear pleasure of dissembling" (222). Taking nothing for granted, she stubbornly refuses to be taken for granted herself—or to fit docilely into any predetermined mold. "I am sorry my face does not please you as it is," she says defiantly to Dorimant, "but I shall not be complaisant and change it" (248).

Her hatred of life in the country, which she can "scarce indure . . . in Landskapes and in Hangings" (222), suggests a hatred of repose equal to Dorimant's own, and she is as exuberant a contriver and prankster as he is. At one point Medley explains to Lady Townley the reason for Mrs. Loveit's rage by remarking: "*Dorimant* has plaid her some new prank" (225); and later Dorimant reveals to Medley his reason for acting the part of Mr. Courtage with the words: "This is *Harriets* contrivance" (244). Always a sworn enemy of "gravity," Harriet has "so many fetches" that even Dorimant has a difficult time keeping pace. When she makes him a mock curtsey, he protests: "That demure curt'sy is not amiss in jest, but do not think in earnest it becomes you," and in the ensuing dialogue it is clear that for her the curtsey is tantamount to flinging a challenge:

HAR.

> Affectation is catching, I find; from your grave bow I got it.

DOR.

> Where had you all that scorn, and coldness in your look?

HAR.

> From nature, Sir, pardon my want of art:
> I have not learnt those softnesses and languishings
> Which now in faces are so much in fashion.

DOR.

> You need 'em not, you have a sweetness of your own,
> if you would but calm your frowns and let it settle.

HAR.

> My Eyes are wild and wandring like my passions, And
> cannot yet be ty'd to rules of charming.

> (248)

It is Harriet's wit which dominates here, and she is in effect giving Dorimant a taste of his own medicine. She too can appeal to "Nature" and to her "wild and Wandring Passions," and her witty technique inevitably recalls that which Dorimant himself has used in "handling" Mrs. Loveit. Like Dorimant's words in the earlier scene, hers here are also sweetly reasonable and constitute at once a defense and an attack. While remaining, with her wryly spoken "Sir" and "pardon," ostensibly within the bounds

of good manners, she is actually insulting and defying and making fun of Dorimant. Etherege's most brilliant stroke in the language of the passage, however, has to do with the rhythms he here imparts to Harriet's speeches, for at the very moment when she is impudently apologizing for her "want of art," she is speaking in blank verse and thus at once parodying such "art" and suggesting the special quality of her own artistic control, organic to her own essentially poetic nature.

Here, as always, Harriet is an indefatigable player (both of roles and of the exciting and even dangerous game of life) and one who delightedly welcomes any challenge. When the respectable young Bellair, escorting her in the Mail a few minutes earlier, has remarked: "Most people prefer *High Park* to this place," she has had an instant response ready: "It has the better reputation I confess: but I abominate the dull diversions there, the formal bows, the Affected smiles, the silly by-Words, and amorous Tweers, in passing; here one meets with a little conversation now and then." And to Bellair's warning: "These conversations have been fatal to some of your Sex, Madam," she has replied, "It may be so; because some who want temper have been undone by gaming, must others who have it wholly deny themselves the pleasure of Play?" Upon which the always reasonable Dorimant has sounded the familiar note of approbation: "Trust me, it were unreasonable, Madam" (234, 235).

In our softer, more optimistic moods we may all prefer, as so many critics have preferred, a Bellair to a Dorimant, an Emilia to a Harriet, but the comic spirit at its best has no patience with our softer moods, and if the cruelty of Dorimant has often proved a stumbling block to critical appreciation, it has been due to a continuing propensity to regard him as a romantic rather than a comic hero. English comic laughter has always contained a strong vein of cruelty, and no honest study of laughter and comedy has been able to avoid some acknowledgment of the strain. James Sully defines it as an "unfeeling rejoicing at mishap," to be found "in the laughter of the savage and of the coarser product of civilisation at certain forms of punishment, particularly the administration of a good thrashing to a wife," but he reluctantly admits that even "'polite society' seems to have a relish for this form of amusement."[7] The fact is that neither Hobbes, nor Etherege following in his footsteps, was willing to recognize any essential difference between the members of a polite society and those of a primitive or savage one. Presumably man, in either setting, laughed from a feeling of his own superiority in which he "gloried," and such laughter is, more often than not, something less than kind.

In Dorimant's and Harriet's world, as in Hobbes's, life is a struggle for power. In more universal comic terms, it is a game involving a battle for self-assertion and self-definition from which the comic hero emerges victorious because he possesses superior mental agility and because he never deceives himself. He is always a disruptive force, challenging a complacent world which would repress his vigorous individuality in the name of civilization. Dorimant's philosophy in matters of both friendship and love is a hard-headed one of mutual advantages or pleasure to be reaped. To Medley's observations about his having "grown very intimate" with Bellair, he explains reasonably: "It is our mutual interest to be so; it makes the Women think the better of his Understanding, and judge more favourably of my Reputation; it makes him pass upon some for a man of very good sense, and I upon others for a very civil person" (202). And when Bellinda, at the conclusion of her assignation with Dorimant, sighs, "Were it to do again—" he replies, "We should do it, should we not?" (258)

Like most of his comic ilk, he is a charming cad, reveling in his own powers of conquest, and he delights in a spirited fight like that with Mrs. Loveit and even seeks it out because it offers him additional opportunity to display his own superiority. Thriving on trouble and excitement, he declares with customary self-confidence: "next to the coming to a good understanding with a new Mistress, I love a quarrel with an old one; but the Devils in't, there has been such a calm in my affairs of late, I have not had the pleasure of making a Woman so much as break her Fan, to be sullen, or forswear her self these three days" (195). The full import of such a statement can perhaps best be appreciated by setting it against an observation made by Faure: "Is not repose the death of the world?" he asked. "Had not Rousseau and Napoleon precisely the mission of troubling that repose? In another of the profound and almost impersonal sayings that sometimes fell from his lips, Napoleon observed with a still deeper intuition of his own function in the world: 'I love power. But it is as an artist that I love it. I love it as a musician loves his violin, to draw out of it sounds and chords and harmonies. I love it as an artist.'"[8]

Dorimant too finds "repose the death of the world" and loves power "as an artist," and it is precisely because Mrs. Loveit lacks his artistic control that her counterplot against him is foredoomed. Possessing passion without wit, she can only shout "Hell and Furies!" in response to his taunt, "What, dancing the Galloping Nag without a Fiddle?" (214) Much in the manner of Courtall in his struggle with Lady Cockwood, Dorimant is momentarily defeated and has to endure Medley's jibes at his expense, but in the final scene he again gathers all the reins into his own competent hands, and Medley declares: *"Dorimant!* I pronounce thy reputation clear—and henceforward when I would know any thing of woman, I will consult no other Oracle" (286). In a world of power-hungry, passion-driven people, it takes a clearheaded, self-aware, resilient manipulator like Dorimant to keep his balance. And, as already stated, it takes a woman of Harriet's wit and cunning to counter him effectively.

In her own way she is as proud and egotistical as her opponent, and the game they play is one in which she is on the offensive as often as he is. She is, indeed, as Medley once calls her, the "new Woman" (244). Wholly aware of her own power and possessed of both "wit" and "malice," she enters the playground attracted by its perils and ready to take on the very "Prince of all the Devils" himself. In fact Lady Woodvil's attitude creates for her recalcitrant daughter sufficient provocation to drive her precipitately into his arms. "Lord," exclaims the Orange-woman to Dorimant, "how she talks against the wild young men o'the Town; as for your part, she thinks you an arrant Devil; shou'd she see you, on my Conscience she wou'd look if you had not a Cloven foot" (193). Harriet corroborates the statement by explaining to Young Bellair: "She concludes if he does but speak to a Woman she's undone; is on her knees every day to pray Heav'n defend me from him." But when Bellair asks, "You do not apprehend him so much as she does?" Harriet, who is "wild" and "extravagant" enough in her own right, replies confidently, "I never saw any thing in him that was frightful" (233, 234). And the very fact that Dorimant is a man of "no principles" (226) only serves to increase her interest. Rejecting the safety and security of an arranged marriage, she insists on living dangerously, whatever the chances of being "ruined" and "undone."

Both Dorimant and Harriet constantly refer to the love game in terms of fighting and gambling. "These young Women apprehend loving, as much as the young men do fighting, at first;" says Dorimant, "but once enter'd, like them too, they all turn Bullies straight" (201). Mrs. Loveit has, in effect, "turned bully," but Harriet seeks an excitement and adventure in her relationship with Dorimant which is quite opposed to Mrs. Loveit's desire for absolute dominance; and the rules by which she plays the game can be reduced to two: play your cards close to the chest and never trust your opponent even for a minute.

Neither Sir Fopling's rule-bound unimaginativeness nor Bellair's and Emilia's complacency will do for either Dorimant or Harriet. Life is for them a continual conflict, and as spectators we are invited to watch the struggle with a full knowledge of the prevailing tensions. "I love her, and dare not let her know it," mutters Dorimant in an aside. "I fear sh'as an ascendant o're me and may revenge the wrongs I have done her sex" (249). "I feel . . . a change within," says Harriet aside, "but he shall never know it" (235). Their self-control is as complete as their self-awareness, and every witty exchange between them pulsates with the resulting rhythmic energies. Both are artists at the game of life, with a pride in their own imaginative and attractive powers which determines them to challenge each other as a part of their refusal to submit to dull and repressive conventionality. "You were talking of Play, Madam;" remarks Dorimant, "Pray what may be your stint?" "A little harmless discourse in publick walks," comes Harriet's rejoinder, "or at most an appointment in a Box bare-fac'd at the Play-House; you are for Masks, and private meetings, where Women engage for all they are worth, I hear." And the battle is on:

Dor.

> I have been us'd to deep Play, but I can make one at small Game, when I like my Gamester well.

HAR.

And be so unconcern'd you'l ha' no pleasure in't.

DOR.

Where there is a considerable sum to be won, the hope of drawing people in, makes every trifle considerable.

HAR.

The sordidness of mens natures, I know, makes 'em willing to flatter and comply with the Rich, though they are sure never to be the better for 'em.

DOR.

'Tis in their power to do us good, and we despair not but at some time or other they may be willing.

HAR.

To men who have far'd in this Town like you, 'twould be a great Mortification to live on hope; could you keep a Lent for a Mistriss?

DOR.

In expectation of a happy Easter, and though time be very precious, think forty daies well lost, to gain your favour.

HAR.

Mr. *Bellair!* let us walk, 'tis time to leave him, men grow dull when they begin to be particular.

DOR.

Y'are mistaken, flattery will not ensue, though I know y'are greedy of the praises of the whole Mail.

HAR.

You do me wrong.

DOR.

I do not; as I follow'd you, I observ'd how you were pleased when the *Fops* cry'd *She's handsome, very handsome, by God she is,* and whisper'd aloud your name; the thousand several forms you put your face into; then, to make your self more agreeable, how wantonly you play'd with your head, flung back your locks, and look'd smilingly over your shoulder at 'em.

HAR.

I do not go begging the mens as you do the Ladies Good liking, with a sly softness in your looks, and a gentle slowness in your bows, as you pass by 'em—as thus, Sir—[*Acts him.* Is not this like you?

                                                    (235, 236)

In such a passage, typical of the witty exchanges between the two protagonists, language becomes in Dorimant's case a substitute for a more open aggressiveness and in Harriet's a substitute for that elusive female maneuver involving the "no" which suggests "yes." Words take on a decidedly dramatic quality, with physical activity on the

stage giving way to an activity of mind of such intensity that we feel as if we were watching two skilled fencers with mind instead of hand in control. As Harriet repeatedly alters her tactics by a facile change of metaphors (from gaming to the flattery of the rich and thence to religion), Dorimant adjusts his own with scarcely a pause for breath, and the sexual implications are invariably and forcefully present beneath the polite metaphorical surface, whether the reference be to "deep Play," to the "power" of the wealthy "to do us Good," or to the following upon "Lent" of "a happy Easter." And presumably the use of religious terminology in connection with sex suggests again, as in earlier passages and in earlier plays, a defiant irreverence of attitude toward both Christianity and the religious stance of the *précieux* mode. At this point, however, Dorimant breaks the unspoken rules by shifting from the impersonal third person to the "particular" second, and Harriet is quite justified in walking off the playground—pausing only to throw back with good measure at the piqued Dorimant the insult which he has resentfully flung and to restore the comic perspective with her pantomime. But we have only to observe the way the evenness of the back-and-forth exchange has been interrupted to know that the rhythmic balance of the game has been broken. Short, sharp sallies have abruptly given way to Dorimant's diffuseness.

Whatever their rivalry on their own playground, however, they are partners on the larger social playground, both "contriving" to "make a little mirth" (276) by turning their world into a vastly entertaining spectacle, both mocking at "gravity" and "Rules" by means of parody, and both glorying none too kindly in their triumphant superiority. "Mr. *Dorimant* has been your God Almighty long enough," cries Harriet to Mrs. Loveit, "'tis time to think of another—" (286). Seizing upon the affections of their mannered world, both Harriet and Dorimant turn them into a spirited comedy of which they are at once the authors and the principal actors. And they play with language as they play with life, controlling it with a masterful skill and putting it to use for their own purposes of challenge and aggression.

In the end Harriet has won. Or has she? And Dorimant has won. Or has he? In the last analysis both have won out against the larger world. Mrs. Loveit has been outplotted; Lady Woodvil has been brought around. But on their own playground neither has finally either won or lost, and the game goes on. Superficially, of course, a bargain has been struck: Harriet's money in exchange for Dorimant's promise of marriage. Yet all the important questions remain unanswered, and all the dangers are as threatening as ever. "Do all men break their words thus?" asks Bellinda of Dorimant in the final scene. And he replies, "Th' extravagant words they speak in love; 'tis as unreasonable to expect we should perform all we promise then, as do all we threaten when we are angry—" And, never one to succumb to the "unreasonable," he adds, "We must meet agen" (283). And to Mrs. Loveit he has testily remarked in the same scene: "I must give up my interest wholly to my

Love; had you been a reasonable woman, I might have secur'd 'em both, and been happy—" (282, 283). The exchanges ironically undercut all the "extravagant words" which Dorimant has been speaking to Harriet, and those words thus take on the nature of a dare, which she at once recognizes and proceeds to counter with a dare of her own. Thus when Dorimant declares his delight in the "prospect of such a Heav'n" and promises to "renounce all the joys I have in friendship and in Wine, sacrifice to you all the interest I have in other Women—" Harriet cuts him short with, "Hold—Though I wish you devout, I would not have you turn Fanatick—Could you neglect these a while and make a journey into the Country?" (278, 279) Again she is making insinuatingly irreverent use of religious metaphors as an indication of her distrust of his "Heav'n" references and is thereby rejecting the possibility of sinking into any stultifying orthodoxy of the *précieux* kind. But in effect she is also asking Dorimant, in terms of her own earlier metaphor, to "keep a Lent for a Mistriss."

If it is the Country which is to constitute the ultimate testing-ground of their relationship, it is also love, and Etherege significantly seems to ask us to equate one with the other. Both represent, paradoxically, at once the source of life and the threat of repression and sterility. Harriet, who cannot "indure the Country . . . in Hangings," rejects with equal vehemence the thought of representing "the whole mystery of making love . . . in a suit of Hangings," which has become the subject of one of her last witty rallies with Dorimant:

Dor.

> What have we here, the picture of a celebrated Beauty, giving Audience in publick to a declar'd Lover?

Har.

> Play the dying Fop and make the piece compleat, Sir.

Dor.

> What think you if the Hint were well improv'd? The whole mystery of making love pleasantly design'd and wrought in a suit of Hangings?

Har.

> 'Twere needless to execute fools in Effigie who suffer daily in their own persons.

> (277)

The passage suggests that what Harriet finally cannot endure is any pressure to reduce her to a formalized pattern of behavior and thus to turn her into just another docile fool. When Dorimant utters his last declaration to the effect that his "soul has quite given up her liberty," she at once seems to associate his words with the sterility suggested both by "the dying Fop" and by "the hateful noise of Rooks" in Hampshire ("Hampshire" being incidentally the sound Sir Fopling has found so pleasing); and she declares, "This is more dismal than the Country!" In short,

she turns off the threat of such a death by turning it into yet another challenge, and the play ends with both protagonists still in tense and rhythmic comic motion.

Notes

1. Bergson speaks of the source of the comic as "*some rigidity or other* applied to the mobility of life, in an awkward attempt to follow its lines and counterfeit its suppleness," and he goes on to say: "It might almost be said that every fashion is laughable in some respect. Only, when we are dealing with the fashion of the day, we are so accustomed to it that the garment seems, in our mind, to form one with the individual wearing it. We do not separate them in imagination. The idea no longer occurs to us to contrast the inert rigidity of the covering with the living suppleness of the object covered: consequently, the comic here remains in a latent condition. It will only succeed in emerging when the natural incompatibility is so deep-seated between the covering and the covered that even an immemorial association fails to cement this union: a case in point is our head and top hat." "Laughter," *Comedy,* ed. Wylie Sypher (Garden City, N.Y.: Doubleday Anchor Books, 1956), p. 85.

2. In view of Etherege's patent insistence on these differences between Sir Fopling and Dorimant, it is astonishing that so many recent critics have largely denied the existence of any such distinction. Jocelyn Powell has actually reversed the differences, making an observation about Dorimant and his world which can in reality only be justified with specific reference to Sir Fopling: "in the society Etherege portrays manners have become not a means to an end, but an end in themselves . . . that which was intended to express feeling, now dictates to it, and manners prevent the intercourse they were designed to aid." She then goes on to suggest quite rightly that the "energy of love and of living is expressed in the communication between human beings," but denies, in effect, that Dorimant and Harriet manage to express any such "energy," hamstrung as they are by "the lightness and elegance of fashion." And the issue becomes further confused when Sir Fopling is seen as the heir to the "lyrical and musical life and energy" of Sir Frederick Frollick and Sir Joslin Jolly—"picking up the realism of the play and turning it into a dance," and when the example of Dorimant is held up as one in which "form has become a substitute for feeling." "George Etherege and the Form of Comedy," *Restoration Theatre,* Stratford-upon-Avon Studies 6 (London: Edward Arnold, 1965), 66-68.

3. Bergson, "Laughter," *Comedy,* p. 89.

4. Oscar Wilde, "The Truth of Masks," *Intentions* (New York: Modern Library, n.d.), p. 241.

5. Harris, "The Dialect of those Fanatic Times," *Restoration Theatre,* Stratford-upon-Avon Studies 6 (London: Edward Arnold, 1965), 29, 30.

6. Dale Underwood, *Etherege and the Seventeenth-Century Comedy of Manners* (New Haven: Yale Univ. Press, 1957), p. 88. The song, of which Underwood says that there is a "'satanic' posture embedded in the verses' synthetic pastoralisms," includes the lines:

> *The threatning danger to remove*
> *She whisper'd in her Ear,*
> *Ah Phillis, if you would not love,*
> *This Shepheard do not hear.*

> *None ever had so strange an Art*
> *His passion to convey*
> *Into a listning Virgins heart*
> *And steal her Soul away.*

7. James Sully, *An Essay on Laughter: Its Forms, Its Causes, Its Development, and Its Value* (New York: Longmans, Green, 1907), p. 97.

8. Quoted in Havelock Ellis, *The Dance of Life* (Boston and New York: Houghton Mifflin, 1923), pp. 11, 12.

Jean Gagen (essay date 1986)

SOURCE: Gagen, Jean. "The Design of the High Plot in Etherege's *The Comical Revenge.*" *Restoration and Eighteenth-Century Theatre Research* 1, no. 22 (winter 1986): 1-15.

[*In the essay below, Gagen discusses* The Comical Revenge, *focusing on how Etherege's satirical treatment of the high plot differs from the more conventional approach of other early Restoration playwrights.*]

The tremendous success which Etherege's *The Comical Revenge, or, Love in a Tub*[1] received when it was first performed (c. March, 1664) is a matter of theatrical history. Later critics, however, have often accused Etherege of incongruously mixing two dramatic modes—a high plot written in heroic couplets and dealing seriously and sedately with love and honor conflicts among aristocrats and several low or comic plots written in prose and concerned with characters who never seriously consider honor.[2] The heroic rimed drama of the high plot "modeled on Davenant and Lord Orrery" has been said to conflict in "spirit and style" with the "realistic comedy and farce" of the low plots,[3] which have been the major focus of the critical attention and praise that the play has received.

With the increasing awareness, however, of the compatibility that can exist between comic and serious plots embodying differing themes and sets of conventions, *The Comical Revenge*—as well as plays apparently similar to it in structure, such as James Howard's *All Mistaken* (1665), Charles Sedley's *The Mulberry Garden,* and Dryden's *Secret Love* (1667) and *Marriage Ala-Mode* (1671)—has been absolved of the charge of thematic disunity. Virginia Birdsall,[4] Laura Brown,[5] Norman Holland,[6] Jocelyn Powell,[7] Arthur Scouten,[8] and Dale Underwood,[9] have all discussed the many ways in which the comic and serious plots of *The Comical Revenge* interact through situational parallels and contrasts. Robert Hume, moreover, cites such plays as *The Comical Revenge,* Tuke's *Adventures of Five Hours* (1663) and Dryden's *The Rival Ladies* (1664?) as evidence that it was certainly possible in the 1660s to present exemplary and even heroic characters in works regarded as comedies—that comedy was obviously not thought of exclusively in terms of ridicule of fools or low characters.[10]

Nevertheless, reputable scholars have continued to express disagreement, disapproval, and downright bewilderment about Etherege's intentions in the high plot. Norman Holland confesses frank puzzlement that a man of Etherege's "urbanity" could write a plot "in pure heroic style" since "nothing could be further from the multiple perspectives of comedy than the single-minded admiration of the heroic manner" (21). Jocelyn Powell accuses Etherege of dallying half-heartedly "with conventional problems of 'platonic' love that neither his imagination nor technique" were fitted to handle (46-47). Dale Underwood, on the other hand, maintains that the serio-comic division of *The Comical Revenge* is fundamental to Etherege's intention—namely, the presentation of "two contrasting worlds of values, attitudes, and action." In the comic world, libertine attitudes prevail; in the heroic world a "totally virtuous love and honor" regulates the attitudes and actions of all the characters, and honor invariably triumphs in the love and honor conflicts (46-50). Underwood and Holland, moreover, have suggested that in the context of the play as a whole, the staunchly heroic high plot has comic implications. Because the heroic values of the high plot are constantly qualified and undercut by the libertine values of the low plots, both sets of values are negated, and a comic perspective is cast over both the higher and lower worlds of the play (Underwood 49-50; Holland 25).

Virginia Birdsall agrees that the values of the heroic plot constantly suffer an undercutting in comparison with the low comic plots. Yet she insists that we are meant to accept the honor-bound world of the high plot seriously as one of the possible interpretations of reality according to which men may still choose to live (44-45). Hume likewise believes that the leading characters in Etherege's top plot are clearly meant to be "exemplary models of propriety" (44) and that Etherege could enjoy and admire the "high-blown flummery" of the heroic love and honor conflicts even though this pleasure may have been mixed with a "little ironic skepticism" (77).

The very expression "high-blown flummery" suggests, of course, that heroic plots are apt to *seem* exaggerated and somewhat ridiculous to modern readers. But because of convincing evidence that heroic dramas were originally intended to be taken seriously,[11] critics have continued to assume that Etherege's heroic plot was meant to be taken about as seriously[12] as other similar plots in plays contemporary with his. Nevertheless, a close examination

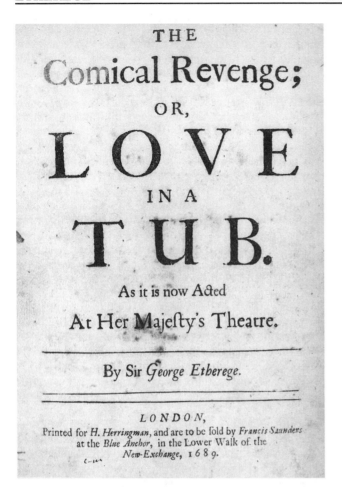

THE
Comical Revenge;
OR,
LOVE
IN A
TUB.

As it is now Acted
At Her Majesty's Theatre.

By Sir *George Etherege*.

LONDON,
Printed for *H. Herringman*, and are to be sold by *Francis Saunders*
at the *Blue Anchor*, in the Lower Walk of the
New-Exchange, 1 6 8 9.

Title page from a 1689 edition of The Comical Revenge; or, Love in a
Tub

of Etherege's high or heroic plot reveals that, unlike heroic dramas or the heroic plots in multi-plot plays with which **The Comical Revenge** is frequently associated, Etherege's high plot is *not* meant to be taken seriously. Those critics who have conjectured that the high plot, although serious in itself, has comic implications within the total context of the play—or that Etherege's treatment of love and honor conflicts is mixed with a "little ironic scepticism"—are certainly on the right track. They have simply not gone far enough. The ironic contrasts and parallels between the high and low plots may contribute to the humor of the play. But there are more direct sources of humor within the high plot itself, and there is more than a tincture of "ironic scepticism" in Etherege's handling of the intense concern over honor exhibited by the supposedly exemplary characters. In fact, the essence of the comedy of the high plot is the fact that it is an ironic parody rather than an exemplification of the heroic ethos involving love and honor. Its apparent seriousness is a mock-seriousness, its "staunchly heroic" tone is parodic rather than real, and neither its love nor its honor is invariably "totally virtuous."

Perhaps the fact that modern readers have to exercise their historic imaginations rather more strenuously than usual in order to react seriously to heroic love and honor conflicts has contributed to the failure to notice the difference between Etherege's treatment of the heroic ethos involving love and honor and that of playwrights who had no parodic intent. An even more likely reason is that readers and critics alike have tended to slight the high plot in favor of the robust and obviously amusing low plots which, according to some critics, occupy a crucial position in the evolution of the Restoration comedy of manners.[13] Without very careful attention to precisely how Etherege manipulates his love and honor conflicts, the reader inevitably misses the rich humor implicit in the apparently solemn and decorous high plot. It is true, however, that Etherege cleverly "traps" his readers and auditors into assuming that they are about to become involved in serious dilemmas over honor: at first his dignified aristocrats do indeed seem to be thoroughly dedicated to the romantic ethos of love and honor. Even when they are flagrantly violating it, they still profess their ardent devotion to it.

This code of gallantry,[14] which had become an international literary phenomenon and had found its way into a variety of literary forms, had already infiltrated Cavalier drama and had begun to infiltrate heroic drama by the time Etherege composed **The Comical Revenge.** Although the code was concerned with the proper conduct of lovers in a variety of circumstances, it had much to say about how an honorable gentleman should behave when he finds that he has a rival in love.

Ideally, each lover should behave with courtesy and generosity to the other. Both of them should scrupulously honor sacred vows and promises. And eventually one of the lovers should renounce his claim to the love of his lady. *Which* lover should surrender in deference to his rival depended on a number of factors. But this self-renunciation, when motivated by a genuine sense of honor, was regarded as an act of magnanimity, worthy of praise and glory.

Cavalier[15] and earlier heroic drama, as well as other forms of popular drama, had already provided Etherege and his audience with numerous instances of rival lovers, one of whom heroically surrenders his love in favor of his rival. The Earl of Orrery in *The General* (Dublin, 1662; London, 1664) presented a lover who twice saves the life of his rival and at the close surrenders the lady he loves to his rival because she herself prefers the rival. In later heroic plays by Orrery—*Henry the Fifth* (1664), *Mustapha* (1665), *The Black Prince* (1667), and *Tryphon* (1668)—similar renunciations occur. For example, in *The Black Prince,* Lord Delaware gallantly yields his love for the beautiful widow Plantagenet to his friend and royal master Prince Edward. In *Tryphon,* Seleucus surrenders his love for Cleopatra to his friend and king Aretus, whom Cleopatra prefers.

Dryden's heroic dramas carry on the tradition of glorifying magnanimity and self-sacrifice in situations involving rivalry in love.[16] Moreover, in his tragicomedy *The Rival*

Ladies Dryden dramatizes a conflict arising from rivalry in love which has so many analogies to the situation which Bruce faces in Etherege's high plot that some critics are convinced that Dryden's play influenced Etherege's, even though this belief necessitates dating *The Rival Ladies* earlier than its first known performance in the early summer of 1664.[17] What has heretofore not been noted, however, is that Dryden's Don Gonslavo eventually behaves in an exemplary fashion as a rival lover while Etherege's Bruce does not. Dryden's Don Gonsalvo allows himself to be affianced to a woman whose love he knows has already been won by a rival. But he never deludes himself into believing that it is a matter of honor for him to marry Julia against her will. Moreover, after a sharp struggle, he yields to the hard demands of honor, exercises heroic generosity, and surrenders Julia to the man she loves. It is important to note that when Don Gonsalvo makes this magnanimous surrender, he is completely unaware that he will soon be consoled by a new love. Bruce, on the other hand, magniloquently surrenders Graciana to his rival only after his love for Graciana has been replaced by a new love, and he no longer *wishes* to marry Graciana. In fact, Bruce's conduct as a rival lover repeatedly falls short of the magnanimous ideal that Don Gonsalvo represents once he has won the victory over his dishonorable impulses.

Initially, however, there is nothing reprehensible in Bruce's reaction to the news that a rival has won the love of Graciana, the sister of his friend Lovis. During Bruce's absence at war, Graciana has fallen in love with Beaufort, a virtuous nobleman, and Graciana's father Lord Bevill has consented to their marriage. Only in the first shock of his disappointment does Bruce momentarily blame Graciana. But when Lovis closely questions him, Bruce's honesty compels him to admit that Graciana has not been at fault except in having had too much compassion for him. Bruce freely admits that Graciana had never plighted a promise to him and had even made her distaste for him plain. But because she grieved for the pain she knew that she was inflicting on him, she promised to *try* to return his love. Unfortunately, this promise encouraged Bruce excessively. He banished despair and allowed his hopes to grow to undue proportions. But after he learns that his hopes have proved false, he sadly remarks, "There is a fate in love, as well as war; / Some though less careful more successful are" (III. vi. 100-101). The latter line suggests "sour grapes" and some self-pity, but there is no serious suggestion that Graciana and Beaufort have actually wronged him.

It is the hot-headed Lovis who precipitates the conflict between Bruce and Beaufort. Though Lovis has been bred "in the school of honour," in his distress over the plight of his "gen'rous friend," Lovis' sense of honor becomes thoroughly perverse. Stubbornly determined that Graciana marry his friend Bruce in accordance with his own wishes and Bruce's, Lovis refuses to recognize that Bruce has no rightful claim to Graciana's love. At one point Lovis' anger is so explosive that he rashly exclaims that he wishes Graciana were dead! He declares that the honor of their family is imperiled. He even insists that Lord Bevill *order* Graciana to marry Bruce. As he is increasingly carried beyond reason, Lovis completely ignores the fact that his father's gracious approval of Bruce's courtship of Graciana had been strictly qualified by his "sacred vow / Never to force what love should disallow" (II. ii. 96-97). In other words, Bruce had to *win* Graciana's love.

Unfortunately, Lovis is abetted in his resentment against Beaufort and Graciana by his other sister Aurelia. Secretly in love with Bruce herself, she is so tenderly sympathetic to him that she loathes to see him suffer. She accordingly allows her love for Bruce to distort her own sense of honor. She presents the courtship of Beaufort and Graciana in the most derogatory terms possible, as if there had been something almost criminal about it! Lord Bevill, however, knows that there has been nothing amiss in the courtship of Beaufort and Graciana nor in his permission for them to marry. In fact, he becomes so angered by Lovis' outcries over the "threat'ning stain" to the honor of their house that he orders Lovis to "forbear" his "wicked insolence" (III. vi. 2-3) and abruptly leaves him.[18]

Lovis, however, is now so thoroughly in the grip of pride and anger that he urges Bruce to challenge Beaufort's right to Graciana in a duel. At first Bruce excuses the suggestion because even he realizes that Lovis' behavior is excessive and that Lovis' friendship for him has incited him to speak rashly. Finally, however, Bruce is infected by Lovis' impassioned urgency. As Lovis continues to taunt Bruce for "tamely" surrendering, Bruce suddenly decides that Graciana was indeed at fault in not instantly putting a damper on his "flame." Once his pride and anger have clouded his reason and corrupted his sense of honor, Bruce views his despair over gaining Graciana's love as "ignoble" and cowardly. Nevertheless, he makes the damaging admission that his love has become "so wild a fire" that he fears it will conspire to both their ruins. Now whipped into a frenzy of anger, Bruce confronts Beaufort and Graciana with the announcement that he has come to make his lawful claim on Graciana (III. vi. 16). Beaufort has previously expressed a generous compassion for the plight of his rival Bruce. But he has recognized that Bruce has no justifiable claim to Graciana. Had Bruce and Beaufort been friends, or had Bruce been Beaufort's royal master, Beaufort might have felt some compulsion to surrender his right to Graciana. But no such situation exists. Consequently, both he and Graciana are in the right when they remind Bruce that Graciana belongs to the man whom she loves and to whom she is avowed. Bruce, however, is by now deaf to all reason and justice and challenges Beaufort to a duel. Despite Graciana's protests, Beaufort accepts the challenge, convinced that the sacredness of his reputation is at stake.

So far there is nothing inherently comic about the crisis which has developed. There is irony, of course, in the fact that courtly characters earnestly devoted to honor find themselves as deeply embroiled in conflicts as those whose sense of honor is much more casual, if it exists at all. It is also ironic that Bruce continues to consider his conduct honorable after he has become as self-deceived in this respect as his friend Lovis. It is doubtful, however, that the irony of the situation in which Bruce, Lovis, and Beaufort find themselves would *seem* to have comic implications if subsequent events in the plot were handled differently. What actually happens, however, is that from this point on, Etherege's satiric intent emerges much more openly.

Except for Sir Frederick's cynical jesting at Beaufort's exalted ideal of love in the first act, the first unmistakable intrusion of comedy into the high plot occurs at the end of the duelling scene. But from the moment the participants in the duel assemble on the duelling field, we are increasingly prepared to accept the burst of laughter with which this scene concludes.

Before the duel even begins, Beaufort rescues Bruce from an unexpected attack by five villains. Out of gratitude to Beaufort, Bruce now claims that his honor will not permit him to draw his sword against the life that has just saved his own. Beaufort, however, quite rightly refuses to accept Bruce's surrender because Bruce has failed to express any contrition for the unruly pride and passion which induced him to challenge Beaufort's right to Graciana.[19] Still suffering from orgies of gratitude to Beaufort, Bruce next offers to allow Beaufort to plunge his sword into his bosom. Again Beaufort, in perfect accord with the rationale and protocol of the duel,[20] refuses: to accept Bruce's offer would make him guilty of an appalling lack of courtesy, to say nothing of cruelty. In spite of Bruce's melodramatic display of gratitude, none of this noble posturing absolves him in the least from the blame of provoking a totally unjust duel.[21]

Finally, when Bruce seems intent on halting the duel for reasons other than the fact that he has no just cause to dispute Beaufort's claim to Graciana, Beaufort becomes so exasperated that he decides to goad the reluctant Bruce into fighting: Beaufort then proceeds to taunt Bruce by asserting that the man who stands before him is the very man who "robb'd" Bruce of Graciana. At this juncture, Etherege directs the shafts of his comic irony at Beaufort instead of Bruce. In order to redeem his honor by defeating Bruce in the duel, Beaufort untruthfully convicts himself of behaving dishonorably in winning Graciana as his prospective bride. With the issues surrounding this "duel of honor" now finely scrambled, Bruce declares that the mere mention of Graciana's name has aroused his "lazy courage," and he proceeds to strip for action, confident that he is obeying his "scrup'lous honour."

Beaufort quickly disarms Bruce, then hands Bruce his sword and bids him live. His life saved a second time by his rival, Bruce salutes Beaufort for his honor, courage, and nobility of mind. Though he no longer disputes Beaufort's right to Graciana, Bruce declares that he does not wish to live without Graciana and promptly falls on his

sword. He is about to be followed by his friend Lovis when Sir Frederick intervenes with the comment which prevents an orgy of desperate deaths and underscores the essential comedy of the situation. "Forbear, sir; the frolic's not to go round, as I take it," Sir Frederick remarks. Sir Frederick himself has few scruples about honor. He would never die for love or honour. But he is clear-sighted enough to see the ludicrousness of Bruce's and Lovis' behavior, and he belittles it humorously as a "frolic" rather than a display of heroism as these elegant victims of passion and folly suppose.

From the conclusion of the duelling scene to the end of the play, the comically ironic perspective in which the "heroic" activities of the high plot are placed becomes increasingly apparent. When Graciana learns from her father that the "gen'rous Bruce" has given himself a supposedly mortal wound because he scorned to live without her, the stage is set for another elegant muddle over honor. Graciana's common sense is positively shattered by the prospect of Bruce's imminent death. In bewilderment, she asks "Which is path that doth to honour lead?" and vows not to be misled by love. So confused is she over what the demands of honor are that when Beaufort enters, confident that Graciana will applaud his victory in the duel, she condemns him as a perfidious man—as the only man she hates. As Graciana sweeps off the stage and leaves the astonished Beaufort to lament his cruel fate, surely the audience was intended to smile, at least, at the lengths to which Graciana's excessive pity for Bruce have finally driven her.

Meanwhile Graciana's sister Aurelia, who throughout the play has concealed her love for Bruce out of regard for custom and honor and even pled Bruce's cause to Graciana, decides that she would be justified in disclosing her love to the dying Bruce. Immediately after the surgeon has confessed that he despairs of Bruce's recovery and has left the room, Aurelia enters. Kneeling by Bruce's chair and weeping copiously, she confesses the suffering she has undergone because of her unrequited love. Aurelia's beauty, together with her confession of love for him, instantaneously banishes the love Bruce once had for "proud Graciana." In fact, he expresses regret that Aurelia concealed her love until this moment when all he is able to do in return is "sigh away" for her what breath still remains to him. For the first time, he repents his rashness in falling on his sword and in some wonderment remarks, "I ne'er thought death till now a punishment" (V. i. 65).

At this moment, Graciana enters begging Bruce not to talk of death. Then on her knees she confesses that she has childishly refused "the gold" of Bruce's love and accepted "the dross" of Beaufort's. Graciana's self-renunciation, motivated by her mistaken sense of honor, is presented in a thoroughly ironic context, since she does not know what the audience knows—that Bruce no longer *seeks* her love. As the scene progresses, irony is piled on irony. The situation hovers on the edge of farce and escapes falling into actual farce only because of the courtly language and manners of the participants. Bruce tactfully does not reveal that he now loves *Aurelia*. Instead he commends Graciana for choosing Beaufort instead of him and affirms that only Beaufort's "great soul" is worthy of her love. Graciana, however, protests that if her love is due to the most deserving, it is due to Bruce. Bruce replies that this is mere flattery. "By honour," she owes her love to the generous Beaufort and to forget this debt would be unjust, for "Honour with justice always does agree" (V. i. 89). Then, as if the effort to dissuade Graciana were too much for him, Bruce declares that his spirits faint within his wearied breast, and the servants enter and convey him to his bed.

Throughout this scene, Bruce has assumed the heroic manner of the magnanimous lover like Don Gonsalvo, who surrenders his love to his worthy rival without any prospect of finding consolation elsewhere for his loss. Bruce, however, never admits that he has no claim on Graciana's love until after he has fallen in love with Aurelia and is no longer interested in Graciana. Consequently, Bruce's renunciation of Graciana's love has no ethical substance. Bruce's mock renunciation and the solemn prattle about honor which accompanies it is as comically ironic as Graciana's unwelcome gesture of self-renunciation.

As long as Graciana has been in Bruce's presence, she has played the part that she believes her honor requires of her with faultless propriety. Yet when she is alone with her maid she confesses that she is pursuing her honor too rigidly—something is due her love. Eventually she decides that her honor will allow her to marry Beaufort if Bruce lives. Only if Bruce dies will she be forever "contracted to his memory" (V. iii. 52-58). When Beaufort enters unexpectedly and overhears Graciana's remarks, he rejoices that "fortune joins with love" to be his friend, for abler surgeons have pronounced Bruce's wound "not mortal."

In the final scene, in the presence of Lord Bevill, Beaufort, Lovis, Graciana, and Aurelia, Bruce announces that he has lost his claim to Graciana. He conveniently ignores that he never *had* any legitimate claim to her. Instead he declares that his heart is due to Aurelia because of her selflessness in courting Graciana for him while her own heart yearned with love for him. In fact, he asserts that Aurelia so excels "in honour and in love" that she has inspired in him both shame and admiration. Bruce then bestows Graciana, who was never his to bestow, on his "gen'rous Rival" Beaufort, to whom she has belonged all along.

Bruce gives no indication that he realizes that his conduct has ever fallen short of complete virtue or that his attitude towards Beaufort's right to Graciana has undergone a radical change. Etherege apparently intended to show that, at least in matters of the heart, Bruce is so accustomed to allowing his passions or emotional inclinations to determine what is honorable and what is not that he can see nothing faulty, inconsistent, or ridiculous in his behavior at any point in the play. In so doing, Etherege has made a beautifully ironic commentary on the self-deception of this "honor-bound" aristocrat from the moment he first insists that Graciana rightfully belongs to him until he surrenders his "right" to the noble Beaufort. At any rate, once Bruce is no longer an obstacle to their love, Beaufort and Graciana—as well as Lord Bevill—are willing to play their parts flawlessly in the elegant game of honor in which Bruce takes the lead, probably without even realizing that his gestures of honor are ostentatious and meaningless.

Graciana demurely confesses that since Bruce has recovered and declined his claim to her, she can "with honour" resign her heart to Beaufort. She does not mention that she had already decided that if Bruce recovered, her honor would allow her to marry Beaufort. Nor does she allude to the fact that until Bruce's flamboyant suicide attempt had thoroughly unsettled her emotionally, she had clearly realized that Bruce never *had* any claim on her love. Though Beaufort knows that Graciana had already decided to marry him if Bruce recovered, and he has consistently defended the honor of his right to Graciana, he lavishly praises Graciana for her refusal to give herself to him as long as Bruce made any claim on her love. "Such honour and such love," he asserts with a flourish which must have brought a smile to a sophisticated audience, have not heretofore been known. He then asks and receives Lord Bevill's consent to marry Graciana (a consent he already had), and this segment of the plot is finally concluded with rejoicing on the part of all who have been involved in it.

The scene has allowed every one to save face. Surely it was meant to be played with mock-seriousness, in which laughter is rippling just below the surface, or with a smiling geniality which acknowledges the irony of what is going on and in which both the actors and the audience are bound together in their enjoyment of a performance in which they are all participating.[22] There is no indication in this final episode that anyone's behavior has been foolish or anything but totally virtuous. Etherege, however, knew better, and so very possibly did his original audiences, at least some members of it. John Evelyn, who saw the play on April 25, 1664, described it as a "facecious Comedy."[23] Pepys, who was present at a performance on Jan. 4, 1664/1665, referred to it as "very merry."[24]

While these comments do not in themselves prove that Restoration audiences regarded the high plot as well as the low plots as comic in the sense of being laughter-provoking, they point in that direction. They provide evidence that at least two note-worthy theatre goers of the day felt the impact of the play as a whole was sprightly and amusing. At a time when dramatically sophisticated members of the audience could be counted on to understand the niceties of the code of honor which should govern the behavior of courtly rivals in love, we have every right to believe that at least some members of Etherege's original audiences realized that Etherege was comically manipulating and often reducing to essential meaninglessness the heroic ethos which the plot is supposedly demonstrating. After beginning his tale involving a conflict between love and honor by following the proper ethical guidelines in this matter, Etherege allows courtly personages schooled in the precepts of honor to succumb in the name of honor to some of the same naturalistic passions as characters who make no pretense to honor. Then as the plot progresses the issues centering on honor become so deftly scrambled that they are virtually emptied of all ethical substance.

When the intent of Etherege's high plot is properly understood, it can be enjoyed instead of merely tolerated—perhaps with some patronizing amusement—until portions of the comic plot recur. In this high plot, Etherege has presented a delightfully clever and light-hearted satire on a number of the conventions and ideals which had already pervaded Cavalier and early heroic drama and would continue to characterize many later heroic plays. Etherege has mocked the glorification of self-renunciation by ironically praising it in the approved manner while showing that it is empty, in Bruce's case, and foolish and unwelcome in Graciana's. He has shown how easily passion can dictate what "honor-bound" characters consider honorable or dishonorable. In both the aristocratic world of the high plot and the libertine world of the low plots, Etherege has found targets for laughter. Etherege's achievement in his next two plays was far greater than in his first play. But his accomplishment in **The Comical Revenge** is more complex and sophisticated than has been realized, and it deserves to be recognized.

Notes

1. Edition used: *The Plays of George Etherege,* ed. Michael Cordner (Cambridge: UP, 1982). Act and scene will be given in text in Roman numerals, line or lines in Arabic.

2. Thomas Fujimura in *The Restoration Comedy of Wit* (Princeton: Princeton UP, 1952) is one of a number of critics who have considered the high and low plots "irreconcilable" 45.

3. H. F. B. Brett-Smith, introduction, *The Dramatic Works of Sir George Etherege,* 2 vols. (Oxford: Basil Blackwell, 1927) I:xvi, lxxi, and John Palmer, *The Comedy of Manners* (London: Bell and Sons, 1913) 67.

4. *Wild Civility: The English Comic Spirit on the Restoration Stage* (Bloomington: Indiana UP, 1970) 42-57.

5. *English Dramatic Form, 1660-1760: An Essay in Generic History* (New Haven: Yale UP, 1981) 31, 36-37.

6. *The First Modern Comedies* (Cambridge, Mass: Harvard UP, 1959) 20-27.

7. "George Etherege and the Form of a Comedy," *Restoration Theatre,* ed. John Russell Brown and Bernard Harris, Stratford-upon-Avon Studies, No. 6 (London: Edward Arnold, 1965) 46-48.

8. "Plays and Playwrights," vol. 5 of *The Revels History of Drama in English: 1600-1750,* gen. ed. T. W. Craik (London: Methuen, 1976) 178-181.

9. *Etherege and the Seventeenth-Century Comedy of Manners* (New Haven: Yale UP, 1957) 46-50.

10. *The Development of English Drama in the Late Seventeenth Century* (Oxford: Clarendon P, 1976) 45.

11. See Geoffrey Marshall, *Restoration Serious Drama* (Norman: U of Oklahoma P, 1975).

12. Among such references are the relatively recent ones by Laura Brown 31; Arthur Scouten 181; and Hume 44; 48, n. 2; 77.

13. Bonamy Dobrée, for example, in *Restoration Comedy, 1660-1720* (1924; London: Oxford UP, 1966) 66, declared that the comic plot centering on Sir Frederick and his wooing of the Widow "set the whole tone of Restoration comedy." Alfred Harbage in *Cavalier Drama* (New York: Modern Lang. Assoc. of America, 1936) also accords *The Comical Revenge* a supremely high place in the development of Restoration comedy, as does Virginia Birdsall (4). Fujimura, however, disagrees (87) and so does Hume, who insists that such a view ignores crucial evidence about comic modes which were firmly established before Etherege and on which he and other playwrights drew (238).

14. D'Urfé's *L'Astrée* was the single most popular source of the intricacies of this code and for this reason was highly valued by Henrietta Maria and her coterie, who helped popularize the code in England. See, for example, Harbage, chs. 1 and 2 and Kathleen Lynch, *The Social Mode of Restoration Comedy* (New York: MacMillan, 1926), ch. 3 for discussions of the ethical ideals which this code embodied.

15. In Walter Montague's *The Shepherd's Paradise* (London, 1629), Prince Basilino relinquishes Fidamira because her "faith" has been given to another. In Thomas Killigrew's *The Princesse* in *Comedies and Tragedies* (London, 1644), Lucius surrenders Sophia to his brother because of his brother's prior claim to her.

16. Derek Hughes in *Dryden's Heroic Plays* (Lincoln: U of Nebraska P, 1981) represents a minority view in contending that Dryden's heroic plays "reveal profound scepticism about the utility and practicability of heroic endeavour" (Preface viii).

17. C. V. Deane in *Dramatic Theory and the Rhymed Heroic Play* (1931; New York: Barnes and Noble, 1968) 168; John Harrington Smith, "The Dryden-Howard Collaboration," *SP,* 51 (Jan. 1954) 56; and Frank Harper Moore, *The Nobler Pleasure: Dryden's Comedy in Theory and Practice* (Chapel Hill: U of North Carolina P, 1963) 237, n, 11 all argue for 1663 as the date when *The Rival Ladies* was written and believe that Etherege's play was influenced by Dry-

den's. Similarly, Judith Milhous and Robert Hume in "Dating Play Premieres from Publications Data, 1660-1700," *Harvard Library Bulletin* 22 (1974) consider it likely that *The Rival Ladies* was performed in the fall of 1663 or early in 1664 (380) and thus could have influenced *The Comical Revenge.*

18. Not only would Bruce's behavior be considered dishonorable in accordance with the heroic ethos, but even seventeenth century plays relatively uninfluenced by this code of gallantry regarded the belief that the rejection of a lover's suit justified the taking of revenge as a perversion of the code of honor. See Elizabeth Mary Brennan, "The Concept of Revenge for Honour in English Fiction and Drama between 1580 and 1640," diss., U of London, 1958.

19. Sir William Segar in *The Booke of Honor and Armes* (London, 1590) would allow the injured to accept satisfaction for an injury in place of a duel if the injured expresses contrition, yields himself into the hands of the one he has injured, and stands at his mercy (41). Bruce *does* place himself at Beaufort's mercy, but out of gratitude for the fact that Beaufort saved his life, not out of contrition for the wrong he has done Beaufort. *Vincent Savioli, his Practice* (London, 1595) took a dim view of even a man who expresses genuine contrition but waits until he has his weapons in hand to recant. The man who pursues an unjust quarrel to the very zero hour dishonors himself and reveals "a most vile and wicked mind" (n.p.).

20. According to Segar, when a man in genuine contrition for a wrong he has done places himself at the mercy of one he has injured, he is following a very doubtful course of action, "For if the injured with his own hand shall doe anything to his satisfaction, in so doing he sheweth no courtesie" (41).

21. To consider this duel a "paragon of honor" which is contrasted with "the tricksters' mock . . . duel of dishonour" in the low plot (Powell 47 and Holland 25) is to see only half of Etherege's satire. The duel in the low plot is conducted in broadly farcical terms. When honor or reputation or conscience is invoked by Wheadle, Palmer, or Sir Nicholas, these words are such thinly disguised cloaks for cowardice or deceit that they provoke outbursts of laughter. The satire on the duel in the high plot is much more subtle. Nevertheless, Etherege makes it clear that despite Bruce's edifying display of gratitude, his motives for challenging Beaufort are nearly as discreditable as those which have generated the projected duel between Cully and Palmer.

22. Peter Holland in *The Ornament of Action: Text and Performance in Restoration Comedy* (Cambridge: UP, 1979) presents the thesis that to discover how a Restoration audience understood a play, one must examine carefully the nature of the performance that they witnessed. Holland, however, does not discuss how Restoration audiences would have understood *The Comical Revenge* in performance, although he does allude briefly to the fact that in the early 1660s Thomas Betterton played "quasi-heroic roles in comedy" like the role of Beaufort in *The Comical Revenge* (80).

23. *The Diary of John Evelyn,* ed. E. S. DeBeer (London: Oxford, 1959) 460, entry for April 27, 1664.

24. *The Diary of Samuel Pepys,* eds. Robert Latham and William Matthews, 6 vols. (London: G. Bell and Sons, 1972) 6:4, entry for Jan. 4, 1664/1665.

Robert Markley (essay date 1988)

SOURCE: Markley, Robert. "'A Way of Talk': Etherege and the Ironies of Wit." In *Two-Edg'd Weapons: Style and Ideology in the Comedies of Etherege, Wycherley, and Congreve,* pp. 100-37. Oxford: Clarendon Press, 1988.

[*In the following essay, Markley discusses how Etherege experiments with dialogue and dramatic form in his plays to examine the ideological dislocation of aristocratic culture in Restoration England.*]

> Shakespeare and Jonson did herein [in comic language] excel,
> And might in this be imitated well;
> Who refined Etherege copies not at all,
> But is himself a sheer original.[1]

Rochester's praise of his friend (implicitly at Dryden's expense) might sum up three centuries of critical reaction to the dramatic stylist Dryden called the 'best author of [prose] which our nation has produced'.[2] Etherege's comic style, particularly in *The Man of Mode,* has been praised since his own day, but often only in broad and effusive terms.[3] As the first of the 'major' Restoration dramatists, Etherege is usually considered as 'sheer' an 'original' as one finds after 1660, the inventor of an elegant prose style which faithfully emulates the conversation of gentlemen. But this ahistorical characterization, besides overlooking Dryden's stylistic experiments in the 1660s, praises Etherege's style at the expense of studying it. His first play, *The Comical Revenge* (1664) sifts through a variety of stylistic options, offering its audience a kind of capsule history of early Restoration comic dialogue. Its originality lies not, as Rochester suggests, in its neglect or rejection of Shakespeare and Jonson but in its complex response to the stylistic traditions of Renaissance drama, the linguistic innovations of his own era, and the problems of 'restoration' itself. Etherege does not simply refurbish the comic forms he has inherited. More deliberately than any of his contemporaries, he explores the ironies and tensions inherent in the Cavalier ideals of wit and carriage. He is, in this regard, a 'sheer original' in adapting the linguistic conventions of comedy to unconventional ends.

In *The Comical Revenge* Etherege selectively rewrites several decades of experimentation with comic language. If Dryden tries to reconcile the demands of comedy and fashionable stylistic theory, Etherege demystifies the ideal of a stable, conversational medium by employing a variety of theatrical languages, ranging from heroic verse to farcical prose. In one sense, the play fragments Fletcherian tragicomedy into its components: debunking comedy and obstreperous idealism. It offers both an ironic critique and an imaginative reworking of traditional forms, exaggerating the tendencies of satiric and heroic languages and exploiting the discrepancies between them for comic effect.

Each of the play's four plots has its own language: the dilemmas of love and honour are cast in heroic couplets; Sir Frederick and the Widow speak in fashionably witty prose; Wheadle and Palmer are given a language reminiscent of Jacobean city comedy; and Dufoy speaks the broken English of an earlier generation of travestied foreigners. These idioms reflect different influences and parody different languages, from the rhetoric of contemporary tragedy to the morally revealing prose of Jonsonian intrigue and gulling. Yet the boundaries separating these styles often seem to exist solely to be transgressed, particularly by the play's comic hero. As Etherege's first incarnation of the wit, Sir Frederick works both to unify disparate elements of the plot and to call into question the ideological presuppositions underlying the hierarchical arrangement of styles, including the notion that we are supposed to admire and identify with those characters who speak in tub-thumping couplets. The dialogical competition among the languages of wit, pretence, and honour subverts simple notions of the play's 'aesthetic' coherence or 'dialectical unity' by rendering in dramatic form the contradictions within its 'restored' Cavalier ideology. As *The Comical Revenge* violates narrow conceptions of dramatic decorum, it also leads us to ask whether its various styles represent the 'natural' expressions of fundamentally different outlooks or whether they enforce idiomatic distinctions without demonstrating any substantive ideological differences. This question is complicated because the play's ideological—as opposed to political—values resist precise formulation and because comedy, for Etherege, is an affective process rather than merely a formal arrangement of stylistic effects.[4]

The play's discrete languages call attention self-consciously to those parodic strategies that complicate the relationship of verbal wit to aristocratic privilege. *The Comical Revenge* is cavalier about defining the social status, though not the political allegiances, of its characters. Sir Frederick is Beaufort's cousin and the Widow Lord Bevill's sister, but the two of them seem more at home in the company of low comic characters than in the heroic world of the romantic lovers; the hero apologizes early in the play for his wit by telling Beaufort, 'my Conversation has not been amongst ceremonious Ladies' (I. ii. 189-90).[5] The butt of the play's farcical satire is Sir Nicholas Cully, 'knighted by Oliver'. Wheadle and Palmer are identified simply as 'gamesters' in the dramatis personae but demonstrate their ill nature by hiding their schemes under the pretence of plotting for the King's return; and Dufoy

tries to obscure his past by insisting that he is a gentleman temporarily forced into the role of servant. The play's stage-aristocracy exists, in this regard, under a comic state of siege; and one of the challenges facing Etherege is to redesign comic idioms to disclose both the conservative and radical tendencies of libertine wit in the 1660s. If Dryden reasserts the values of wit and carriage, Etherege's first comedy distances itself from defensive justifications of the social order which returned to power after 1660. Its wit does less to celebrate the mythos of the Restoration than to investigate the tensions inherent in the play's formal disjunctions; it acknowledges implicitly that the civil war had radically challenged the presumptions of aristocratic culture.[6] The seeming haphazardness of Etherege's dramatic form, then, may be seen as a working out of the ideological divisiveness of the 'restored' conventions of wit and honour.

The most destabilizing of the play's idioms results from Dufoy's mangling of English. The Frenchman wreaks havoc with grammar and syntax: oaths, mispronunciations, added syllables, inverted word order, hammering repetitions, and syntactic confusion characterize his speech. His favourite oath 'begar' punctuates most of his speeches of more than a few words; it indicates his frustration with English. He uses it frequently when he wants to stress his sense of being victimized by others: 'Begar, I do not care two Soulz if de Shamber-maid ver hangé; be it not great deal better pretendé d'affection to her, dan to tellé de hole Varldé I do take de Medicine vor de clapé; begar it be de ver great deale better' (II. i. 102-5). Other linguistic features emphasize Dufoy's role as a pretender to wit and fashion. His accent—stage mock-French—is no doubt intended to get laughs by itself. The typographical substitutions ('d' for 'th', 'v' for 'f' and 'w') and the dropped and added syllables should be taken as cues for the actor rather than as linguistic evidence about speech patterns in 1664. Dufoy is fond of derogatory epithets, either stringing them into a series ('dis Bedlamé, Mad-cape, diable de matré') or doubling them. Synonymous verbs are also frequently doubled ('to beaté and abusé'). Almost as a matter of course Dufoy takes the final words of others' speeches and repeats them as introductions to his own:

CLARK.

Have patience, [Sir Frederick beat you] unadvisedly.

DUFOY.

Unadvisé! didé not me advise him justé when he did ité?

CLARK.

Yes; but he was in drink you say.

DUFOY.

In drinké! me vishé he had ben over de head and de ear in drinké . . .

(I. i. 13-18)

Dufoy's repetitions turn these words and phrases into brief comic routines that fuel his exasperation and emphasize his role as a satiric butt.

Etherege uses the Frenchman's mangling of English to emphasize the self-serving nature of language in ***The Comical Revenge.*** When characters speak, they usually intend either to deceive others or to justify their actions. The prose given to Dufoy, Wheadle, Palmer, and Sir Frederick, in this regard, is often as deceptive as the heroic verse of Bruce and Beaufort is compulsively transparent. Dufoy's account of being hired by Sir Frederick turns the rhetoric of compliment into hyperbolic self-praise:

> . . . young Monsieur de *Grandvil* (a Jentleman of ver great Quality[)] . . . did tellé me dat de Englis Jentleman had de Letré vor de Posté, and did entreaté me (if I had de oppertunity) to see de Letré deliver; he did tellé me too, it vold be ver great obligation: de memory of de faveur I had receive from his Famelyé, beside de inclination I naturally have to servé de strangeré, made me retourné de complemen vid ver great civility, and so I did take de Letré, and see it deliveré. Sir *Frollick* perceiving (by de management of dis affairé) dat I vas man d'esprit, and of vitté, did entreaté me to be his Serviteur, me did take d'affection to his Personé, and vas contenté to live vid him, to counsel and to advisé him.

(III. iv. 33-52)

Syntactically, Dufoy's speech is marked by frequent parentheses and involved dependent clauses that slow its progress to a near standstill. His attempts to narrate a chronological sequence of events are side-tracked by his efforts to glorify his past. His pretence to chivalry, like his pretence to logic, is undercut by his rambling exaggerations and verbal quirks. It is not merely what Dufoy says that is comically suspect but how he says it. His prose is inherently, if ineptly, deceptive; it allows the audience to judge satirically his pretence to being something more than Sir Frederick's lackey.

Dufoy's speech, however, is neither pure fantasy nor, in a Jonsonian sense, a precise measure of his moral failings; it is rather a parodic travesty of the language of '*Birth & Quality*', of aristocratic presumptions to absolute moral and political authority. For Etherege, it seems a strategy for controlling (or suppressing) the tendencies of comic language towards Bakhtinian heteroglossia, towards displaying itself as the site of class antagonism, ideological conflict, and festive misrule. By reducing the discourse of the servant to a parody of gentlemanly speech, Etherege implicitly promotes the fiction that the former is an imperfect version of the latter, that it exists parasitically on its refined host. In this regard, Dufoy's speech raises the question which I posed about *The Wild Goose Chase*: is the language of ***The Comical Revenge*** self-consciously dialogical or merely, as Bakhtin puts it, 'dramatistic', a dividing up of a dominant, authoritative speech among several characters? I would argue that Etherege arrives at a historically significant compromise between these theoreti-

cal—and evaluative—extremes: he foregrounds the parodic, subversive, and destabilizing tendencies of comic discourse but exploits them as strategies to dramatize the ironies *within* dominant modes of discourse—wit and the idealized language of heroic passion—rather than to display the opposition of class-specific languages. The parodic ironies and competing voices in ***The Comical Revenge*** make it difficult for the audience to latch on to any stable values or immutable truths of the sort articulated by the Queen in *Secret Love*. Dufoy's language, then, encourages a double-take: he undermines himself satirically by appropriating the language of gentlemanly compliment to deny the Footboy's claim that 'he was *Jackpudding* to a Mountebank' (III. iv. 16); yet his language also serves as an ironic commentary on polite discourse by demonstrating its susceptibility to parody and solipsistic farce. It is suggestive, in this regard, that the play's wits, sharpers, and pretenders to wit often upstage those characters who proclaim their devotion to the values of heroic absolutism.

Etherege's undermining of affected compliment in Dufoy's prose is indicative of the ways he subverts hierarchical distinctions between 'low' and 'high' forms of dramatic discourse. In one sense the verse of Beaufort and Graciana is a naïvely idealized form which isolates its speakers from the naturalistic world of Dufoy and Sir Frederick; in another, however, it represents an extreme articulation—to the point of self-parody—of the values underlying the Restoration settlement: loyalty, propriety, honour, and class privilege. Abstract and often morbidly self-centred, Beaufort's, Graciana's, Lovis's, and Aurelia's verse parodies the excesses of *précieuse* sentiment. Its tensions and inconsistencies are heightened by Etherege's antithetical couplets:

> Small is the difference that's between our grief:
> Yours finds no cure, and mine seeks no relief:
> You unsuccessfully your Love reveal;
> And I for ever must my Love conceal:

(I. iv. 62-5)

> [Beauty] like the glow-worm, only cast'st a light
> To them whose Reason Passion does benight.
> Thou art a Meteor, which but blazing dies,
> Made of such vapours as from us arise.

(III. vi. 7-10)

To make sure that his audience hears the contradictions in his characters' verse, Etherege repeats several of these rhymes throughout the play. These pairings are one measure of the dilemmas which plague the heroic figures. The rhyme scheme which brings 'grief' and 'relief' together also calls attention to the discrepancies that underlie their similar sounds. Each end word embodies an emotion or attitude to which the speaker is passionately committed; its rhyme word counters that passion with its own absolute statement. Etherege's verse, in this respect, does not progress from emotion to emotion so much as it parades its contradictory verbal postures. These contortions of aristocratic idealism register not as ironic wit but as the language of baffled absolutism.

The self-parodying verse of *The Comical Revenge* represents an ideaological dislocation, a de-centring of the values of nobility and honour on which aristocratic conceptions of order and identity are based. Etherege does not directly attack aristocratic love and honour so much as he subverts their claims to unquestioned moral authority and dramatizes the dilemmas which these values create. The 'heroic' characters are united by their expressions of steadfast loyalty to the exiled King and his cause. When Bruce is ambushed by disguised Commonwealth 'slaves', Beaufort, his rival for Graciana's love, and Sir Frederick come to his rescue. As soon as the common enemy has retreated, however, Beaufort and Bruce are no longer bound by their transcendent loyalty to the King and revert to form, declaring their convictions and proceeding with their duel. Bruce's honour—his unassailable political virtue as a Cavalier hero of the Battle of Naseby[7]—becomes a liability when he tries to apply its dictates to his love life. After he has lost the duel, his response to Beaufort's offer of friendship is to attempt suicide. The conflicts between love and honour that all of the heroic characters, to some degree, experience demonstrate that they are verbally and ideologically incapable of exploring the conditions of their existence; they can neither analyse their behaviour nor question the ideology of aristocratic privilege and obligation that is ultimately the source of their problems. Graciana, for example, who has previously rejected Bruce, feels bound by her honour to him after he tries to kill himself: she jilts Beaufort and vows to remain unmarried if her unsuccessful suitor dies. Her honour, like Bruce's, is a form of self-inflicted torture.

Because the language of moral absolutism can only state and restate its contradictions, it verges on becoming a parody of the hero's wit, an unsuccessful strategy for coping with the demands of upper-class existence. Before the audience has heard a single couplet, Jenny (Grace's maid) offers a mock-heroic account of Sir Frederick's previous night's 'Heroick actions': 'tell the Consequence, how you march'd bravely at the rere of an Army of Link-boys; upon the sudden, how you gave defiance, and then wag'd a bloody war with the Constable; and having vanquish'd that dreadful enemy, how you committed a general massacre on the glass windows' (I. ii. 117-23). Jenny's speech does not, however, end in a satiric condemnation of Sir Frederick but in an appointment for him to come to her lodgings. By setting the play sometime before the Restoration, Etherege is able to imply that Sir Frederick's violations of 'all order', his 'Heroick actions', are a form of Cavalier 'resistance' to the hypocrisy and moralistic rigour of the Commonwealth. The order that the hero disrupts is, in a sense, paradoxically that of both the 1650s and the 1660s. It becomes difficult for the audience to condemn moralistically Sir Frederick's excursions because his actions represent a comic fifth column within Puritan London. Wit becomes part of a political dialectic with

royalist honour, a comic version of the 'dear loyalty' which Beaufort and Bruce embody. Yet although wit has loyalist overtones, its oppositional force goes beyond defying Puritan pieties. It allows Sir Frederick to out-negotiate and out-plot the Jennys, Wheadles, and Palmers of the world, and to avoid the excessive zeal of those characters who are committed to idealistic but self-defeating actions. Ideologically and theatrically, wit thrives where honour fails.

The prose which Etherege creates for Sir Frederick and the Widow is akin to Dryden's comic language in its use of similes, comparatives, antitheses, and evocations of the fashionable world of chasing women and beating fiddlers. Yet it seems closer, in some respects, to the language which Fletcher uses for his comic renegades. Etherege's success in revitalizing the wit-hero after the Restoration lies in his evoking those traditional values which his hero comically subverts and which had been under attack during the 1640s and 1650s. Sir Frederick comes close to being as 'sheer' an original as one finds on the stage in the early 1660s: a Fletcherian defier of all order, protected from harsh condemnation by his royalist good nature, negotiating his way through the idealized mystifications of aristocratic absolutism. Paradoxically, Etherege's first hero represents both a vindication of Cavalier values and a displacement into libertine wit of the radical political energies—the potential hostilities of class and religious antagonism—that the restoration of Charles II had papered over but hardly eliminated.[8]

Sir Frederick's first speech displays the kinds of self-mocking, ironic verbal poses which the hero assumes throughout the play:

> I am of the opinion that drunkenness is not so damnable a sin to me as 'tis to many; Sorrow and Repentance are sure to be my first Work the next morning: 'Slid, I have known some so lucky at this recreation, that, whereas 'tis familiar to forget what we do in drink, have even lost the memory, after sleep, of being drunk: Now do I feel more qualms then a young woman in breeding.
>
> [*Enter* DUFOY *and* CLARK. DUFOY *goes out again*]
>
> Clark! What news from the God of Love? he's always at your Master's elbow, h'as jostl'd the Devil out of service; no more! . . . Mrs. *Graciana* has flung a squib into his bosome, where the wild-fire will huzzéé for a time, and then crack; it fly's out at's Breeches.
>
> (I. ii. 21-32)

The hero's cavalier consideration of his drunkenness accounts for much of the humour of his opening lines. Unlike Fletcher's Mirabel, Sir Frederick does not launch frontal assaults against accepted moral values. Instead he appropriates and parodies the diction of moral analysis—'sin', 'Sorrow', and 'Repetance'—to contemplate the effect of his drinking: he subverts both conventional pieties (the kind that the noble lovers voice) and merely cynical debunking and deception (the staples of Wheadle and

Palmer). Sir Frederick's wit is double-edged. It celebrates his libertine life-style yet reminds the audience that wild debaucheries have their consequences—whether hangovers or, as the image of the young woman implies, unwanted pregnancies; it makes explicit the reckonings which Fletcher's wit usually only implies. Sir Frederick, like Dorimant in *The Man of Mode,* is ironically both the perpetrator and object of his wit. His prose is not part of a dialectic, as Celadon's is in *Secret Love,* but a destabilizing counter-discourse. By mediating dynamically between the plays' high and low idioms, it registers the ambiguities of libertine existence. The hero's language, in effect, offers a partial solution to the dilemma which troubles Dryden: how to justify wit as a principle of dramatic structure without descending to 'fifth-rate' trivialities.

With Clark's entrance, Sir Frederick's speech changes from musingly witty to bluntly suggestive. His language becomes abrupt, almost fractured, given to contractions, exclamations, and rhetorical questions. It also gives over the imagery of sin and its consequences for sexual fireworks. His final image is a self-dramatizing parody of fashionable naysaying; it appropriates a diction traditionally associated with low-life characters, undermining the 'decorous' separation of styles to which Dryden, for example, scrupulously adheres. In one sense, Sir Frederick's wit is dialogical, although its subversive implications—those which might carry it towards a radicalizing heteroglossia—are subordinated to an ironic debunking of essentialist commonplaces. His wit is centred neither in a holistic notion of 'self' nor simply in a rejection of the stylistic excesses of love and honour; rather it is the protean, ambiguous nature of his wit that attracts our attention. Beaufort tells him early in the play that his 'careless carriage has done more / Than all the skill and diligence of love / Could e're effect' (I. ii. 200-2) to impress the Widow. Wit and carousing become the hero's erotic and theatrical attractions.

The hero has many comic voices. He prevents Lovis from falling on his sword, and interrupts a passage of high-flows verse, with 'Forbear, Sir; the Frollick's not to go round' (IV. iv. 101). With the Widow he is often more verbally aggressive, even brutal, than wittily seductive: 'Laugh but one minute longer I will forswear thy company, kill thy Tabby Cat, and make thee weep for ever after' (IV. vii. 33-5). Sir Frederick's punning on his name and mock-heroic threats are typical of his self-dramatizing wit. He is, at heart, an ironist who implicates himself in his debunking of others:

> his Name is *Wheadle*; he's one whose trade is Trechery, to make a Friend, and then deceive him; he's of a ready Wit, pleasant Conversation, throughly skill'd in men; in a word, he knows so much of Virtue as makes him well accomplish'd for all manner of Vice: He has lately insinuated himself into Sir *Nich'las Culley,* one whom *Oliver,* for the transcendent knavery and disloyalty of his Father, has dishonour'd with Knight-hood; a fellow as poor in experience as in parts, and one that has a vain-glorious humour to gain a reputation amongst the

Gentry, by feigning good nature, and an affection to the King and his Party. I made a little debauch th' other day in their Company . . .

(I. ii. 155-67)

Having satirically dissected Wheadle's deception and Sir Nicholas's traitorous lineage, the hero concludes by suggesting that they are worth carousing with. The basis of his satire is political rather than moral. In describing Sir Nicholas, Sir Frederick implies that aristocratic wit and carriage are functions of political loyalty: 'feigning good nature' is equated with the 'transcendent knavery and disloyalty' of opposition to the King. But if Sir Frederick allies himself with virtue and loyalty, he also provides the means for the audience to question these values by invoking a 'democratic' community of 'debauch'. Drinking, wenching, and gaming in *The Comical Revenge,* like the wit-battle between Rosalaura and Mirabel in *The Wild Goose Chase,* reduce man—aristocratic man—to his physical appetites, implying a 'natural' similarity underlying the differences of birth and politics.[9] Given this 'levelling' tendency of wit, it is significant that Etherege has Sir Frederick devote his energies to outwitting Wheadle and Palmer, to keeping them within their generically and politically foreordained places as 'low' comic villains who have pretensions to rank and ill-gotten privilege. Wheadles states his credo in a manner reminiscent of Massinger's Sir Giles Overreach: 'I was not born to ease or Acres; Industry is All my stock of living' (IV. iii. 78-9). Like Sir Nicholas, who claims that the regicide 'Colonel *Hewson* is my neighbour, and very good friend' (III. v. 7-8), Wheadle and Palmer fall outside the 'natural' aristocracy of loyalty, birth, and quality, and must be punished by being forced to marry sexually-compromised women. In this regard, the play works paradoxically both to validate a hierarchical ideology at the expense of the 'democratic' biology of 'debauch' and to demystify the values of rank and privilege on which the comic authority of wit ultimately depends. Neither function takes precedence over the other; they are dialectically bound as operations of a divided ideology.

Structurally as well as ideologically, Sir Frederick's language emphasizes disjunctions, ironies, and contradictions that work against our hearing it as an expression of a consistent, essentialist point of view. His 'characters' of Wheadle and Culley are cast in a language which does not progress from point to point so much as it seizes occasions to demonstrate its speaker's ingenuity. Logical transitions are often suppressed or ignored. The hero frequently begins sentences or independent clauses with 'Now' or 'But', words which separate the member from its predecessor and call attention to its self-sufficiency. As a result, his speech is assertive and aphoristic as well as ironic. The raw material for his wit is often a comic version of seventeenth-century misogyny:

> Women, like Juglers Tricks, appear Miracles to the ignorant; but in themselves th'are meer cheats.

(I. ii. 179-81)

> Some Women, like Fishes, despise the Bait, or else suspect it, whil'st still it's bobbing at their mouths; but

subtilly wav'd by the Angler's hand, greedily hang themselves upon the hook. There are many so critically wise, they'l suffer none to deceive them but themselves.

(I. ii. 207-11)

I'le have all the helps that may be to allay a dangerous fire; Widows must needs have furious flames; the bellows have been at work, and blown 'em up.

(II. i. 93-5)

Sir Frederick's images focus the audience's attention as much on his ingenuity as on the 'nature' of women. They are, in effect, double-edged utterances which serve both as commonplaces, ahistorical assertions of feminine sexual aggressiveness, and as strategies which allow him to avoid the excesses of passion displayed by the heroes of the high plot. His language stresses the socially acceptable antagonism between the sexes and acts as a safety valve to control this hostility by making it the subject of his self-dramatizing wit. Sir Frederick uses his characterizations of women to position himself ironically between Petrarchan idealism and misogynistic cynicism. In this regard, his libertine assertions about women articulate a patrilineal culture's ambiguous, tension-filled responses to feminine sexuality. It is significant that the object of Sir Frederick's desire is a sexually knowledgeable widow rather than, as in Fletcher's and Dryden's comedies, witty but virtuous virgins. As a sexually experienced woman, the Widow is less a cipher, less a paradox for the hero than the embodiment of his imagery—a woman already educated in the libertine verities of 'furious flames' and 'bellows'.

The Comical Revenge is ultimately a play of stylistic factions. Its hero's wit is not an icon of the dispassionate observation of human folly but a means of coping with and overcoming the tensions and ambiguities of seventeenth-century culture. Sir Frederick both embodies and travesties the fictions of aristocratic disinterest. His wit, as the final act makes clear, is extremely 'interested' in the pursuit of money, women, and land, in separating the rightful heirs of the King's party from the pretenders to fashion and privilege who are satirized in the figure of Sir Nicholas Cully. What intrigues Etherege is precisely this paradox of interested and disinterested wit. In his next two plays he explores the language of his heroes and heroines as historical responses to the ironies of libertine existence.

In its own way, the prose of *She Wou'd if She Cou'd* is as experimental as that of *The Comical Revenge.* In his second play Etherege abandons the variety of styles he experimented with in his first comedy in an effort to resolve within a single comic language the tensions of a divided dramatic form. If verbal wit in *She Wou'd* develops from the assumptions and practices that characterize Sir Frederick's speech, it is also stripped of its overt political implications—less given to dislocations of syntax and meaning and less dependent on its opposition to heroic verse. Outright burlesque, like Dufoy's broken English, gives way to more subtle forms of linguistic and social

satire. Yet in focusing on the language of wit, Etherege keeps the stylistic ideals celebrated by Sprat, Glanvill, and Dryden at arm's length. He remains as sceptical of the dictates of fashionable decorum as he seems to be of Restoration idealism. His stylistic motto for the play might be taken from Abercrombie's *A Discourse of Wit:* 'as the greatest *Wit* of Angels consists in knowing; the greatest *Wit* in Men consists in doubting'.[10] Like Rochester, Etherege elevates to a fine art the ironies of 'doubting', calling into question even the self-questioning wit that his heroes and heroines employ. The dialogical tensions and paradoxes of his language, then, emerge less as positive ideals than as necessary processes of self-scrutiny, the irony—at once limiting and transcendent—that he sees as essential to dramatic presentation.[11]

Comic prose in *She Wou'd* subsumes the functions that Etherege had divided among various forms of speech in his first play. In the mouths of different characters wit articulates, lampoons, perverts, and comments ironically upon its own ideals of gentlemanly decorum. All the characters try to live up to fashionable standards of wit and carriage; the ways in which they fail mark their own limitations and those of wit as a cultural ideal. Yet compared to the prose of *The Man of Mode,* the language of *She Wou'd if She Cou'd* seems inelastic, tied to a Fletcherian comedy of situation rather than to a satiric anatomy of society. Again and again in the play, Etherege returns to the antitheses, similes, stock images, and verbal tags that by 1668 are staples of comic language. The result, as Brown notes, is that the characters, particularly Courtall and Freeman, talk a better game than they play; there often seems to be less at stake than their verbal rejections of conventional morality imply. Their libertinism is a stylistic construct, a product of their wit that partially conceals the conventionality of their pursuit of Gatty and Ariana.[12] Like Dryden in *An Evening's Love,* Etherege creates an ironic language that is indebted to the values it mocks.

Polite discourse in Etherege's second play is characterized by frequent repetitions, agrammatical interjections, and varieties of proclitic and enclitic constructions that comically undermine its idealistic claims to rational, univocal communication. As in his first comedy, Etherege manipulates conventional verbal formulae for satiric effect. Using the familiar 'nay . . . but' structure, for example, he calls attention to the disruptions and contradictions inherent in the oppositional stance of Cavalier wit.

SIR JOSLIN.

Come, come, never talk of Cloaths, put on any thing, thou hast a person and a mind will bear it out bravely.

SIR OLIVER.

Nay, I know my behaviour will show I am a Gentleman; but yet the Ladies will look scurvily upon me, Brother.

(III. ii. 36-8)

Sir Oliver's 'but' emphasizes the lack of logical co-ordination between clauses, the distance between standards of gentlemanly behaviour and individual folly. It is, in this respect, typical of the abrupt syntactical changes and rhetorical dislocations that characterize Etherege's attempts to register the fragmentation and contentiousness that he hears in the raillery of fashionable society.[13]

The 'buts', 'nays', and negative constructions that qualify direct statements in *She Wou'd* are characteristic of a comic rhetoric that proceeds by indirection, that falls short in its attempts to pin language down to unequivocal meanings. As the syntactical structuring of Etherege's dramatic prose becomes more complex, it also becomes more precise in assigning causes and weighing effects. But these efforts at clarification demonstrate that the characters' actions and explanations need clarifying, that the dynamics of fashionable existence and speech are opaque and problematic, not morally unambiguous and ideologically pristine as the theorists in the Royal Society claimed. Even as it narrows interpretative possibilities, 'but' reminds the audience of the uncertainties and second-guessing that accompany all imperfect speech and that necessitate the circumlocutions that intrude between desire and articulation. At one point Courtall acknowledges the impression that Gatty has made on him: ''Tis impossible to be insensible of so much goodness, Madam' (IV. ii. 252-3). Even in the play's final scene, negative constructions and circumlocutions hedge in the traditional language of celebration:

SIR JOSLIN.

   . . . is it a match, Boys?

COURTALL.

   If the heart of man be not very deceitful, 'tis very likely to be so.

FREEMAN.

   A month is a tedious time, and will be a dangerous tryal of our resolutions; but I hope we shall not repent before Marriage, whate're we do after.

                            (v. i. 540-6)

Courtall's and Freeman's negative phrasings work against comic convention, distancing them not only from marriage but from the women they are to marry and from what we might suppose are their own sexual desires. Their constructions are indicative of a discourse that defines its speakers' interactions negatively. Positive values—love, for example—are encrypted in negative, awkwardly impassive, phrasings. Sentry justifies her role as go-between in this fashion: 'having reason to believe the young Ladies had no aversion to their inclinations, I was of opinion I shou'd have been ill natur'd, if I had not assisted 'em in the removing those difficulties that delay'd their happiness' (v. i. 567-72). This restrictive, affected propriety, hedged in by limiting adverbs and negative phrasings, suggests the limitations of a society 'naturally' given to pretence and hypocrisy.

The excessive verbal formality that marks the closing of the play, though, should be taken less as Etherege's attempt to re-create contemporary speech than as a stylized rendering of how language functions within social constraints. As in Dryden's comedies, the ideological restrictions of wit and carriage result in overdetermined systems of communication that paradoxically deny and reveal their characters' desires. Courtall and Freeman adopt libertine truisms to describe their existence in the language of aesthetic—not political—rebellion. They are wits as much out of fashion as conviction. Ironically, their libertine imperatives seem as demanding and confining as the conventional moral proprieties that they, like the other characters, verbally attack. If Lady Cockwood is a familiar type of hypocrite who tries to disguise lust with a show of respectability, her husband, by attempting to emulate the heroes' libertinism, becomes a pretender of a new sort. His 'counterfeited . . . sin, and real . . . Repentance' (III. iii. 375-6) are comically contrasted to his wife's real appetite and counterfeited honour. The complicated, overdetermined decorum of wit becomes, for Etherege, an object as well as a means of comedy; it exposes its practitioners to the same risks that it holds for its victims.

In this context, we should keep in mind that Etherege, writing in 1668 for the Duke's Company, does not have Charles Hart and Nell Gwyn to trade witticisms on stage. If Dryden uses the conventions of wit in *An Evening's Love* to showcase the abilities of Hart and Gwyn, Etherege makes a virtue of theatrical necessity by emphasizing the sceptical, self-mocking nature of his theatrical language. As Holland points out, *She Wou'd* comes out of a tradition of double-plot plays for the company (including *The Comical Revenge*) that produces a peculiar attitude toward wit and repartee.[14] Wit, for Etherege, is impure, polyvocal, and protean; it reflects his desire to resolve ideologically tensions that inhere in the discrete languages of tragicomedy. If wit in *An Evening's Love* is the language of holiday libertinism, it is more diffuse and paradoxical in *She Wou'd*—neither an end in itself nor an aberration that needs to be corrected in Act V but a stylistic strategy that doubles back upon and ironically questions the libertine premises that bring it into being. In this sense, Etherege's wit retains something of the radical energy of Fletcherian comedy; yet it is also more self-consciously structured: its ironies centre as much on its reflexive violations of decorum as they do on its challenges to patrilineal authority.

Courtall and Freeman open the play by commenting ironically on their participation in a comically corrupt society. Their language is part deception and part affection, a way to distance themselves from their environment and their own actions. Typically, they cast their lust for wine and women in a rationally impersonal form:

COURTALL.

   Well, *Franck,* what is to be done to day?

FREEMAN.

   Faith, I think we must e'ne follow the old trade; eat well, and prepare our selves with a Bottle or two of

good *Burgundy,* that our old acquaintance may look
lovely in our Eyes . . .

COURTALL.

Well! this is grown a wicked Town, it was otherwise in
my memory . . .

(I. i. 3-10)

Courtall's use of the passive makes him seem as much an
object as an actor in the opening tableau, disassociating
him from Freeman's description of the day's activities.
The verbs describe states of existence rather than actions.
The characters' speech registers changes in their surroundings—'this is grown a wicked Town'—as though 'what is
to be done' were more a function of custom or fashion—
that is, of a determinant ideology—than an individual
decision. For Courtall and Freeman, wit describes the
repetitive processes of drinking and wenching, the 'old
trade' of cavalier carousing. In this respect, their language
presents itself as a social form which can be consciously
assumed, imitated, and replicated, that celebrates the
anonymity of fashion. It is a means to acclimate themselves
to the repetitions of fashionable existence.

The anonymity of wit—the ease with which it may be
replicated or appropriated—ensures its perversion. In *She
Wou'd* wit is defined differentially as well as hierarchically. If characters are judged by how closely they approximate Cavalier ideals of wit and carriage, they are
also played off against each other to offer the audience a
variety of comic images: the rake as huntsman, the rake as
schemer, the rake as fool. Etherege's distinctions among
these aspects of the protean wit are both maintained and
ironically blurred. Sir Oliver, for example, appropriates the
stylistic forms of wit to present his libertine credentials:

> . . . a man had better be a vagabond in this Town, than
> a Justice of Peace in the Country: I was e'ne grown a
> Sot for want of Gentleman-like recreations; if a man do
> but rap out an Oath, the people start as if a Gun went
> off, and if one chance but to couple himself with his
> Neighbours Daughter, without the help of the Parson of
> the Parish, and leave a little testimony of his kindness
> behind him, there is presently such an uproar, that a
> poor man is fain to fly his Country: as for Drunken-
> ness, 'tis true, it may be us'd without scandal, but the
> Drink is so abominable, that a man would forbear it,
> for fear of being made out of love with the vice.

(I. i. 79-91)

Like Courtall, Sir Oliver affects a distance from his generic
catalogue of libertine pursuits, and, again like Courtall, he
defines himself by his speech rather than by his actions.
The personal pronoun 'I' (with one exception) is replaced
by the impersonal forms 'a man' and 'one'. The adverb
'but' ('but rap out', 'but to couple himself') makes violating country morality seem like chance incidents that
naturally befall men of wit. The transparent exaggerations
of Sir Oliver's derivative wit allow Courtall, Freeman, and
the audience to see through his verbal disguises. In Act III,
when Courtall defends Sir Oliver's 'Repentance', he sug-

gests that this 'was meer Raillery, a way of talk, which Sir
Oliver being well bred, has learned among the gay people
of the Town' (III. iii. 377-9). Although Sir Oliver may be a
fool, his social position offers him the opportunity to
reproduce 'a way of talk' that guarantees his entry into
fashionable society and confirms his pretensions to the
existence that Courtall and Freeman discuss in the opening
scene. The discrepancies in Sir Oliver's attack on country
life between a comically decorous language and the physical appetites it describes are, in this respect, exaggerations
of the tensions that mark the heroes' existence, the ironies
of being defiers of order in the ideologically sensitive
world of post-Restoration England. What labels Sir Oliver
as a fool is his lack of scepticism, his eager embrace of the
libertine forms that the play comically questions.

Like her husband, Lady Cockwood is a victim of her
speech, although her 'way of talk' is less a corruption of
fashionable wit than a prose version of heroic ranting.
Whether trying to deceive others or bewailing her
misfortunes, she speaks in stock phrases that trivialize her
passionate displays:

> Do not stay and torment me with thy sight; go, grace-
> less Wretch, follow thy treacherous resolutions, do, and
> waste that poor stock of comfort which I should have
> at home, upon those your ravenous Cormorants below:
> I feel my passion begin to swell again.

(III. iii. 356-60)

> How am I fill'd with indignation! To find my person
> and my passion both despis'd, and what is more, so
> much precious time fool'd away in fruitless expecta-
> tion: I wou'd poyson my face, so I might be reveng'd
> on this ingrateful Villain.

(IV. i. 57-61)

As Lady Cockwood's passion swells, her language wilts
into clichés. If her tirade against her husband is intended
to deceive him, her brief soliloquy becomes self-deceiving.
Her linking of her 'person' and 'passion' aptly and ironically suggests her lack of self-control: she acts like, and
sees herself as, the heroine of a graceless tragedy. The
stylistic similarities of the two speeches—particularly the
strong verb forms and hyperbolic diction—make her
hypocrisy and pretentiousness come close to being one
and the same. Regardless of her conscious motives, then,
her self-serving language becomes inherently deceptive; it
measures the parodic degradation of heroic passion to
mock-heroic rant. Her speech offers Etherege a means to
deflate verbally the ideology of 'passion', the kind of hu-
mourless absolutism caricatured more subtly in Bruce's
couplets in *The Comical Revenge.*

Lady Cockwood is the play's most linguistically subversive
character, a forerunner of the ladies of 'Honour' who flock
to Horner in *The Country Wife.* Her obsessive abuse of
'Honour' transcends simple hypocrisy, making it, in effect,
a pimp for her sexual appetite. She protests hypocritically
to Courtall, whom she is trying to seduce, 'I shall deny
myself the sweetest recreations in the world, rather than

. . . bring a blemish upon my spotless Honour' (III. i. 136-8). The workings of 'Honour', like those of all pimps, are as ambiguous as they are deceptive. The 'Honour' that Lady Cockwood abuses but cannot lose is both a verbal joke and a symptom of the play's semantic instability. In one respect, this instability seems a residue of Etherege's satire of heroic hyperbole; in another, it suggests the end to which all verbal pretence must come. When Lady Cockwood exclaims, 'Heaven knows my innocence', her assertion lays bare the arbitrary relationship between verbal signs and what they presume to signify. That she remains technically innocent despite her efforts makes her protest absurdly false and more absurdly true.

Lady Cockwood's inability to cuckold her husband calls attention to the discrepancies which exist throughout the play between the characters' libertine languages and their conventional actions. If Etherege has mastered the 'quickness of wit in repartees', he is faced with the problem of developing an action for his ironic, self-questioning wit to describe. In 'Timon' (1674) Rochester has Dingboy praise his friend's 'two talking plays without one plot' (l. 125), a telling assessment of Etherege's fascination in his first two plays with the articulation—rather than demonstration—of the ironies of libertine existence. All of the major figures in his second play would, if they could, violate prohibitions against adultery or premarital sex, but they are constrained by a code of conduct that allows them to voice challenges to traditional morality without offering them the opportunities to accomplish what they threaten. After complaining about the liberty that men enjoy and that women can only envy, Ariana concludes, 'But whatsoever we do, prithee now let us resolve to be mighty honest' (I. ii. 162-3). This resolution in their first scene on stage distinguishes what Gatty and Ariana say from what they do; they speak freely but act chastely. For their part, Courtall and Freeman talk as though the women of the town lay panting at their feet, but they devote themselves to pursuing only two. Throughout *She Wou'd* potentially disruptive actions are displaced into speech; talking about sex defers sexual experience to an unrealized future 'after' the end of the play, to the marriage conventions of festive comedy that the playwright chooses not to dramatize. In this respect, the language of wit disrupts conventional systems of signification without necessarily undermining the values they uphold.

This paradox of an ironic wit undercutting its pretences to a radical critique of social hypocrisy is particularly evident in the speech of the play's heroines. Gatty, like Fletcher's Rosalaura and Dryden's Isabelle and Jacinta, often speaks as cavalierly as the men around her. Her language signifies her desire to appear liberated from conventional morality; it is a strategic statement of her availability as a mate, a form of advertisement that both conceals and reveals her vulnerability as an unmarried woman. The wit duels between the two sets of lovers emphasize that verbal style, for Etherege, is not the man or woman but a self-conscious projection of the social self. 'Quickness of wit' is at once a challenge to the speakers' ingenuity and a testing of one another's verbal poses. The following exchange marks a crisis in the plot; Lady Cockwood's plan to discredit Courtall is apparently succeeding and colours the women's responses to the wits' advances:

GATTY.

I suppose your Mistress, Mr. *Courtall,* is always the last Woman you are acquainted with.

COURTALL.

Do not think, Madam, I have that false measure of my acquaintance, which Poets have of their Verses, always to think the last best, though I esteem you so, in justice to your merit.

GATTY.

Or if you do not love her best, you always love to talk of her most; as a barren Coxcomb that wants discourse, is ever entertaining Company out of the last Book he read in.

COURTALL.

Now you accuse me most unjustly, Madam; who the Devil, that has common sense, will go a birding with a Clack in his Cap?

ARIANA.

Nay, we do not blame you, Gentlemen, every one in their way; a Huntsman talks of his Dogs, a Falconer of his Hawks, a Jocky of his Horse, and a Gallant of his Mistress.

(IV. ii. 203-19)

The language of this exchange is almost self-generating. The heroes and heroines do not argue specific points—say, instances of Courtall's treachery—but trade generalizations about the vicissitudes of libertine behaviour. Wit becomes a circumscribed code that reduces language to the give and take of repartee triggered by the 'Or's', 'Now's', and 'Nay's' characteristic of Etherege's dialogue. Both Courtall and Ariana adopt the animal imagery that is prevalent throughout the play. The comparisons that she draws between the heroes' bragging and the 'Falconer' and 'Jocky' praising their animals degrade the relationship between the sexes into naturalistic images that reinforce structures of patriarchal authority: women become beasts, men their masters.

In this respect, the chase of wit is never far removed from the appetites that motivate it. Petrarchan idealizations of women as saints and whores are conflated and debased into images that stress their physicality and their subservience to men. For the male characters, women are 'Rook[s]' (II. i. 27), 'Deer' (II. i. 69), 'skittish Fillies' (II. ii. 132), 'Trouts' (III. i. 100), 'Chickens' (III. iii. 30), and 'Horse-flesh' (IV. ii. 152). Gatty and Ariana, for their part, see the men 'daily hover about these Gardens, as a Kite does about a back-side, watching an opportunity to catch up the Poultry' (IV. ii. 189-91). As these images suggest, the town's 'way of talk' is shot through with sexual hostility.

While the heroines' cold-shouldering of the men in Act IV is a result of Lady Cockwood's machinations, their language voices a basic antagonism between the rulers and the ruled that underlies their exchanges with their suitors: 'we cannot plague 'em enough', says Gatty, 'when we have it in our power for those priviledges which custom has allow'd 'em above us' (I. ii. 151-4). Verbally plaguing the heroes, then, becomes a way of rebelling against 'custom'—the ideological apparatus which asserts masculine 'priviledges' and restricts women to talk rather than action. Sexual encounters are transformed metaphorically into political struggles, naval battles, and hand-to-hand combat. Gatty and Ariana, politicizing Petrarchan convention, describe themselves as 'absolute Tyrants' to their 'lawless Subjects' (I. ii. 168, 165). When the women first glimpse their suitors in Mulberry Garden, Ariana hopes 'these should prove two men of War that are cruising here, to watch for Prizes', and Gatty confesses that she 'long[s] to be engag'd' (II. i. 73-6). Later Sir Joslin claims that he and Sir Oliver 'are both mighty men at Arms' who will 'charge anon to the terrour of the Ladies' (III. iii. 102-4). Like the animal imagery, these metaphors of conflict verbalize the sexual hostility that stricter notions of decorum might proscribe. They are a form of psychological release for the characters and the basis of a politically charged language that reasserts masculine, patriarchal values, even as it registers the volatile nature of sexual relationships.

The divorce of language and action in the play thus provides Etherege with an escape from the dialogical, 'revolutionary' implications of wit. He is wary rather than unaware of the destabilizing potential of libertine speech. Like *An Evening's Love*, *She Wou'd* tests the limits of how far wit can go without offending its audience. By having his characters verbalize rather than act, Etherege ensures that his wit manifests itself as a form of hyperbole that is comically overstated as well as ideologically overdetermined. By deliberately promising more than he delivers, he exploits and satirizes both the assertiveness of wit—its penchant for generalized observations—and its substitution of form for substance. In this respect, wit takes on connotations different from those it exhibited in his first play. In *The Comical Revenge* the characters suffer the consequences of their actions: hangovers, the pox, and various figurative and literal wounds; in *She Wou'd,* they suffer the indeterminacies of their language: at the end of the play Courtall and Freeman are given a probationary period of a month by their lovers and the game of wit continues. The heroes undergo no fifth-act conversion; they pledge their love in the same language that they have employed throughout the play. The antagonism that marks the wit duels of the first four acts does not disappear so much as it temporarily dissipates. The play has produced neither a radical critique of society nor a whole-hearted endorsement of the values of aristocratic wit. It has instead suspended the characters, and the audience, in comic irresolution.

Between the first performances of *She Wou'd if She Cou'd* in 1668 and the opening of *The Man of Mode* in 1676,

Etherege spent three years in Constantinople as secretary to the Ambassador, Sir Daniel Harvey, and then nearly five in London living what Bracher moralistically calls 'a life of dissipated idleness'.[15] During these eight years, a number of influential comedies were produced in London, among them *The Rehearsal,* Wycherley's first three plays, Dryden's *Marriage à la Mode,* Shadwell's *The Humorists* and *The Libertine,* Sedley's *Mulberry Garden,* and Behn's *The Dutch Lover.* These plays—particularly *The Rehearsal, The Country Wife,* and *The Libertine*—altered comic practice radically. In the latter two, Wycherley and Shadwell redefined the limits of the naturalistic comedy of aggression by exploiting dramatically what is implicit in the imagery of Etherege's first two comedies.[16] In *The Rehearsal* Buckingham travestied Dryden's verse, lambasting theatrical conventions and burlesquing the heroic ideals and rhymed couplets that Restoration tragedy tried to take seriously. The theatre to which Etherege returned was not, in short, the theatre he had left. Between aborted duels and drinking bouts, he apparently took stock of the theatrical successes of others, particularly the changes wrought in comedy by Wycherley's ironic attacks on wit and its pretensions. The result is that in his final play Etherege does not simply rehash his previous successes but breaks new ground stylistically and dramatically by offering an insider's appreciation of the dynamics of language and fashion in 'the Town'. Social satire gives way to an ironic rendering of upper-class society that implicates the audience in the ambiguities of fashionable pretense and deception.

If *The Comical Revenge* and *She Wou'd* parody the language of heroic passion, *The Man of Mode* registers the reflexive, parodic tendencies of gentlemanly wit. For the most part, Etherege dispenses with the naturalistic imagery and jagged antitheses of his earlier plays. The satiric languages of cant and mock-realism are limited to minor characters: Old Bellair, 'Foggy *Nan* the Orange Woman and swearing *Tom* the Shoomaker'. In place of straightforward linguistic satire, Etherege offers a hierarchical anatomy of wit: Dorimant and Harriet are truewits, Medley is the fashionable gossip and scandalmonger, Emilia and Young Bellair are lower-order redactions of the hero and heroine, Loveit is a caricature of the passionate woman, and Sir Fopling is the satirically gullible pretender to wit and fashion. But the action of the play blurs distinctions among these characters by calling into question the bases on which we judge them. In Act I, for example, Dorimant describes Young Bellair as 'by much the most tolerable of all the young men that do not abound in wit' (I. i. 424-6) and justifies their friendship as a matter of 'mutual interest': 'it makes the Women think the better of his Understanding, and judge more favourably of my Reputation; it makes him pass upon some for a man of very good sense, and I upon others for a very civil person' (I. i. 430-4). Harriet, Young Bellair's nominal fiancée, remarks of him that 'Varnish'd over with good breeding, many a blockhead makes a tolerable show' (III. i. 48-9). Yet as the play progresses, it becomes difficult to remember that this 'blockhead' is a mere pretender to wit: the scene that he plays with Harriet to deceive their parents puts him on an equal footing with her. 'By the good instructions you give', she tells him, 'I suspect you for one of those malitious Observers who watch peoples Eyes, and from innocent looks, make scandalous conclusions' (III. i. 167-9). Harriet's compliment elevates Young Bellair, at least for the moment, to the status of a Medley, if not a Dorimant. If he does 'not abound in wit', he is apparently an adroit reader of the semiotics of flirtation and capable of blending into the anonymous company of fashionable society. That at different times in the play he seems a blockhead and a worthy coconspirator is indicative of the shifting perspectives and competing assessments of character and situation that the audience encounters in *The Man of Mode*. The wit that Young Bellair may or may not have is less a register of social competence than an unstable sign of the ambiguity which characterizes the play's language.

Etherege's metaphors for the instability of wit and perception in the play are, as Hawkins notes, those of acting and game-playing.[17] The ironies of acting measure the distance between the actual and the ideal, between the ways characters appear to others and the ways they appear to themselves. Role-playing in *The Man of Mode* is presented as a given, morally neutral condition of society, an accepted expression of social character.[18] The audience is confronted by the difficulties that arise from trying to distinguish the original from the copy, true wit, emotion, and fashion from their various imitations. In the course of the play, Harriet acts Dorimant, Dorimant acts Sir Fopling, Harriet mimics Dorimant, he mimics Loveit's passionate outbursts, Harriet and Young Bellair act as though they are in love, Emilia and Young Bellair pretend they are not, Old Bellair feigns disinterest in his son's lover, Dorimant assumes the role of Courtage to fool Lady Woodvil, and is or pretends to be in love with Bellinda, Harriet, and Emilia. What the heroine calls 'the pleasure of dear dissembling' is not the province solely of Etherege's wits, although they are by definition more accomplished actors than Sir Fopling, the 'senceless Mimick' (v. i. 101). Dorimant warns Loveit that 'Fools can dissemble too—' (v. i. 118). The parodic language of wit destabilizes the relationships between actor and role, original and mimic, truewit and witwoud. Acting makes identity a *problem* rather than a Cartesian truism. As Bellinda, Dorimant, and Harriet discover, to play a role is to disturb relationships between self and social projection. The language of wit in the play, then, mediates between social forms and natural desires; it subverts conventional distinctions between nature and art by suggesting that language is both natural and artificial, a 'reflection' of character and a tool to be manipulated. In this manner, nature and affection—the staples of seventeenth-century satire—are dialogically related: they compete with and impinge on each other. Unlike Valentine and Angelica in *Love for Love*, Etherege's characters cannot 'think of leaving acting, and be [them] selves' (IV. i. 708)[19] because they have no 'selves' distinct from their acting.

The Man of Mode begins by setting competing comic idioms against each other. Dorimant and Medley in the opening scene insult 'Foggy *Nan*' and 'swearing *Tom*' unmercifully: she is a 'Jade', 'Cartload of Scandal', and 'Bawd' and he a 'Rogue', 'drunken sot', and 'Raskal'. Wit as detraction in these exchanges is based on a not-too-subtle class antagonism that springs from the pretensions and ambitions of Nan and Tom and the uneasiness of their 'betters'. Harriet and her mother, the audience soon learns, are lodgers at the Orange-woman's house, and Tom, Medley, and Dorimant are drawn into a discussion of libertine existence:

MEDLEY.

> I advise you like a Friend, reform your Life; you have brought the envy of the World upon you, by living above yourself. Whoring and Swearing are Vices too gentile for a Shoomaker.

SHOOMAKER.

> 'Zbud, I think you men of quality will grow as unreasonable as the Women; you wou'd ingross the sins o' the Nation; poor Folks can no sooner be wicked, but th'are rail'd at by their Betters.

DORIMANT.

> Sirrah, I'le have you stand i'the Pillory for this Libel.

SHOOMAKER.

> Some of you deserve it, I'm sure; there are so many of 'em, that our Journeymen now adays instead of harmless Ballads, sing nothing but your damn'd Lampoons.

DORIMANT.

> Our Lampoons, you Rogue?

SHOOMAKER.

> Nay, Good Master, why shou'd not you write your own Commentaries as well as *Caesar*?

> (I. i. 266-81)

Although the Shoemaker's oaths label him as a low comic character, he manages to live 'above [him]self' as much by his imitation of gentlemanly wit as by his 'Whoring and Swearing'. Dorimant and Medley rail at Tom for his 'Libel' precisely because he is able to replicate the patterns, if not the studied ease, of polite discourse. His jibe at the 'Commentaries' of the wits satirically reduces aristocratic privilege to mock-heroic pretensions, thereby both fulfilling and questioning conventional expectations about the language of wit.[20] Wit represents an 'ideal' standard of gentlemanly discourse, but it is an ideal which is itself dialogical, shot through with destabilizing forms, radical implications, and incipient challenges to authority. Its ideological divisiveness renders it capable of being imitated, appropriated, and turned back upon its aristocratic practitioners. Medley's lame follow-up to Tom's 'Commentaries' line—'The Raskal's read, I perceive'—emphasizes that, in this exchange at least, a shoemaker has proved more verbally adroit than the rakes who are baiting him. The Fletcherian equation of wit and breeding has been disrupted for comic effect.

Etherege's treatment of wit necessarily complicates our responses to Dorimant, a hero who embodies the ironies of libertine existence.[21] More subtly than Horner in *The Country Wife,* Dorimant exploits fashionable assumptions about wit, carrying its aesthetic implications to comic extremes in his quests for absolute grace and sexual mastery. But like Courtall and Freeman, he inhabits a world in which all ideals prove illusory. What distinguishes him from them and from Dryden's rake-heroes is his ability to modulate his voice, to assume different tones to fit his needs. His language attempts to bridge the chasm between the actual and the ideal—it is less an end in itself than a way of colouring experience to make it fit his image of how matters should be. Dorimant is a consummate actor, the Fletcherian wit metamorphosed from rebel to artist. The skill and irony with which he plays his roles are essential to his thriving in a world that, like his letter to Mrs Loveit, is often 'a Tax upon good nature' (I. i. 4-5).

Dorimant's language is unusually concise and controlled for a Restoration hero, always calculated for its theatrical effect. It shapes rather than passively reflects his involvement in the world. The audience first hears him, like Sir Frederick Frollick, speaking to his servants rather than to his peers:

DORIMANT.

Call a Footman.

HANDY.

None of 'em are come yet.

DORIMANT.

Dogs! Will they ever lie snoring a bed till Noon?

HANDY.

'Tis all one, Sir: if they're up, you indulge 'em so, they're ever poaching after Whores all the Morning.

DORIMANT.

Take notice henceforward who's wanting in his duty, the next Clap he gets, he shall rot for an example.

(I. i. 14-20)

Dorimant is both imperious and indulgent. His language, given to imperative verb forms and declarations, seems almost as assertive as the couplet of Waller's with which he begins the play. But his forcefulness, as Handy makes clear, is at least partially an act. Dorimant's indulging his servants reveals a tolerant, even undisciplined side to his character at odds with his vision of an aesthetically ordered world of punctual footmen and resounding couplets. His threat to let his men rot seems more a rhetorical display

than a means to discipline them. His wit serves as a release for the kind of frustration that Sir Frederick takes out physically on Dufoy.

As this exchange suggests, Dorimant's characteristic mode of expression is hyperbole, whether he is insulting the Orange-woman, bantering with Medley, or ordering about his servants. When he first hears about Harriet from the Orange-woman he imagines that she 'is some awkward ill fashion'd Country Toad, who not having above Four Dozen of black hairs on her head, has adorn'd her baldness with a large White Fruz, that she may look sparkishly in the Fore Front of the Kings Box, at an old Play' (I. i. 51-5). What distinguishes this comic portrait from the set pieces of satiric invective in *She Wou'd* is its dramatic function: Dorimant uses his wit to establish his social superiority to the Orange-woman, debunking her conception of a 'Fine Woman' and provoking her to prove that Harriet is all that the bawd says she is. His language is not simply fashionable detraction but a comic negation of the actual—Harriet—that allows him to create a free space in his mind for the play of irony and desire. For Dorimant, wit is invariably self-dramatizing. When he speaks, he calls attention not to what he is describing but to his verbal artifice, to whatever role he is playing at the moment. He perceives his existence as an aesthetic endeavour, an attempt to master the contradictions of social gamesmanship by the virtuosity of his performance.

Performance, for Dorimant, frequently takes the form of verbal parody. Like Harriet, the hero echoes, mimics, and assumes the voices of those around him to assert his control, not simply to travesty verbal affectations. He answers Loveit's passionate tirades with mock-heroic detraction; with Bellinda, he modulates his voice to counter her uncertainties. His speech to her in front of the distraught Mrs Loveit, is shot through with irony: 'here I vow revenge [for 'making discoveries' of his infidelity]; resolve to pursue, and persecute you more impertinently than ever any Loving Fop did his Mistress, hunt you i'the *Park,* trace you i'the *Mail,* Dog you in every visit you make, haunt you at the Plays, and i'the Drawing Room, hang my nose in your neck, and talk to you whether you will or no, and ever look upon you with such dying Eyes, till your Friends grow Jealous of me, send you out of Town, and the World suspect your reputation' (II. ii. 172-84). Dorimant's ironies work in several ways: they ridicule Loveit, implicate Bellinda in his scheme, even as they play off her insecurities, and distance the hero from both women by demonstrating his power over them. His hyperbole reduces Loveit's metaphoric fury earlier in the scene to the social dimensions of the Park and the Mall. His active verbs ('pursue', 'persecute') jar ironically with the actions they describe, emphasizing the discrepancies between the world as Loveit sees it and the social realities of the 'Drawing Room'. By making Bellinda his accessory, Dorimant forces her to assume the role that he creates for her: his mistress. She is trapped, by having to deceive Loveit, into putting herself in his power. Yet the exaggerations of his mock-heroic voice also emphasize that the hero, too, is part of a society that reduces passion to game-playing or ridicule. Dorimant's language becomes his means of controlling his attraction for Bellinda by placing it within the context of a created mock-reality. After he has seduced her, his subtler parodying of her seriousness (see IV. ii. 11-25) allows him to play an ambiguously double role: he becomes both her heartless seducer and concerned lover, an actor capable of erasing the line between parody and sincerity.

Dorimant's acting, then, does not resolve itself into thematic contraries: appearance versus reality or art versus nature. He does not appear to be one thing and then reveal himself to be another but incorporates several possibilities at once. In defending his inconstancy to Loveit, he revels in the ambiguities of his existence:[22]

LOVEIT.

> Dissembler, damn'd Dissembler!

DORIMANT.

> I am so, I confess; good nature and good manners corrupt me. I am honest in my inclinations, and wou'd not, wer't not to avoid offence, make a Lady a little in years believe I think her young, wilfully mistake Art for Nature; and seem as fond of a thing I am weary of, as when I doated on't in earnest.

LOVEIT.

> False Man!

DORIMANT.

> True Woman!

LOVEIT.

> Now you begin to show your self!

DORIMANT.

> Love gilds us over, and makes us show fine things to one another for a time, but soon the Gold wears off, and then again the native brass appears.

> (II. ii. 198-210)

Dorimant, as he admits, is a dissembler, but his dissembling is more complex than Loveit perceives. By linking 'good nature' and 'good manners', he initially implies that they work in similar ways to corrupt him. In the next sentence, however, Dorimant's refusal to offend against decorum drives a wedge between his 'nature' and his assumed 'manners'. 'Honest', then, becomes a loaded—and ambiguous—term. At first it seems to carry the conventional meaning of Dorimant's being true to his nature. Yet to avoid the social sin of giving 'offence', the hero does precisely what he says he would otherwise not do, 'wilfully mistake Art for Nature'. The double negative ('wou'd not . . . wer't not') hints at the complications underlying his antitheses. That Dorimant recognizes the necessity of dissembling—and willingly participates in the deceptions of others—undercuts the distinction that he then makes

between 'seem' and 'earnest'. This antithesis, like those contrasting 'nature' and 'manners' or 'Gold' and 'native brass', paradoxically implies similarities where the logic of the prose insists on differences. Dorimant's 'Nature' is his 'Art'; he takes Loveit's accusation—'damn'd Dissembler!'—as a compliment. Unlike Harriet, she fails to realize that his dissembling is a form of self-definition, an implicit acknowledgement of the radical contingencies of 'character' and 'identity'. Even as he speaks to her he is playing a role. Much of what he says in this exchange, like the gold-brass metaphor, condescends to Loveit's understanding. He is not, as she assumes, revealing his true 'self' by jilting her but merely taking on another role—that of the heartless ex-lover.

In Dorimant, then, Etherege demonstrates that verbal pretence and sexual deceit are forms of power that celebrate rather than suppress the contradictions of the dramatic 'self'. But by creating a hero who lives as well as speaks ironically, the dramatist hardly intends to produce mindless laughter among the would-be rakes in his audience. In contrast to Medley, a more conventional version of the simile-spouting wit ('a living Libel, a breathing Lampoon' as Emilia calls him (III. i. 6)), Dorimant performs less for the sake of others than as a condition of his existence. His acting is a form of dialogical actualization: it displays the tensions within traditional theatrical incarnations of the libertine wit and calls attention to the interplay among the roles that constitute Dorimant's fragmented and fragmentary 'nature'.

Among the roles that the hero finds himself playing is that of the fool. Once, when Loveit temporarily bests him by feigning an attraction to Sir Fopling, the role is forced on him, but several times Dorimant assumes it willingly. To gall Loveit after her 'triumph' in the Mall, Dorimant enters her house imitating Sir Fopling and quoting Waller: 'I, that I may successful prove, / Transform my self to what you love' (v. i. 94-5). At 'Harriets contrivance' he takes on the role of Courtage, a man he describes as a 'foppish admirer of Quality, who flatters the very meat at honourable Tables, and never offers love to a Woman below a Lady-Grandmother'. Medley responds, 'You know the Character you are to act, I see! (III. iii. 351-4). Harriet has cast the hero as a sycophant, a fop who is neither a wit nor an aristocrat, a socially-debased version of Sir Fopling. As Courtage, Dorimant slips easily into the mocking, dispassionate observations that Lady Woodvil eagerly accepts as genuine wit: 'the young Men of this Age . . . [are] generally only dull admirers of themselves, and make their Court to nothing but their Perriwigs and their Crevats, and would be more concern'd for the disordering of 'em, tho' on a good occasion, than a young Maid would be for the tumbling of her head or Handkercher' (IV. i. 20-5). Although Dorimant may be playing a role, his observation comes close enough to what the audience sees on stage—including his own fastidiousness (see I. i. 349-55)—to prevent his speech from being simply a cliché to gull Lady Woodvil. It becomes difficult to tell where Courtage leaves off and Dorimant begins. When Lady Woodvil asks her daughter what she has against Courtage, Harriet replies, 'He's a Fopp . . . a man made up of forms and common places, suckt out of the remaining Lees of the last age' (IV. i. 339, 342-3). Harriet's target may be Dorimant's performance, but her remark is similar enough to her other jibes as his affectations to be taken as a critique of the actor. Earlier, Harriet had exercised her wit on the synthetic qualities of Dorimant's social graces:

Y. BELLAIR.

> . . . have you not observed something extream delightful in his Wit and Person?

HARRIET.

> He's agreeable and pleasant I must own, but he does so much affect being so, he displeases me.

Y. BELLAIR.

> Lord, Madam, all he does and says is so easie, and so natural.

HARRIET.

> Some Mens Verses seem so to the unskilful, but labour i'the one and affectation in the other to the Judicious plainly appear.

(III. iii. 22-30)

On one level, Harriet's protestations are themselves a pretence to hide her attraction for Dorimant. Yet her criticism reveals the disturbing possibilities that exist in any culture which worships appearance. Dorimant, in effect, is already Courtage, or Courtage is a part of the protean 'self' waiting to be actualized, to be performed. What Young Bellair accepts as Dorimant's 'Person' Harriet sees as part of his self-willed performance.

The ease with which Dorimant slips into and out of his roles is contrasted to the naïveté with which Sir Fopling Flutter acts out his fantasies as the man of mode. Sir Fopling is a paradox. His presence in the play comically disturbs the hierarchical socio-political assumptions of Fletcherian comedy: the gentleman is displayed as 'the freshest Fool in Town' (III. ii. 140). Yet if, on one level, the play encourages the audience to see him playing the witwoud to Dorimant's truewit, on another it suggests that there are similarities between them. At times Sir Fopling seems less a foil for the hero, an inept imitation, than a simpler version of Dorimant, the man of mode uncontaminated by the deception of his society.

Sir Fopling's appeal lies in his innocence, in the paradox of a fool naïve enough to believe that his performance is being taken as he intends it. In one respect, he seems a later version of Cokes in *Barthol'mew Fair,* the wide-eyed man-child fascinated by all that he sees—women, crevats, French dances—who is protected by his lack of guile. This paradox, the fop as innocent, comes to the other characters' minds when they attempt to describe him:

DORIMANT.

> Brisk and Insipid—

MEDLEY.

> Pert and dull.

EMILIA.

> However you despise him, Gentlemen, I'le lay my life he passes for a Wit with many.

DORIMANT.

> That may very well be, Nature has her cheats . . . and puts sophisticate dulness often on the tasteless multitude for true with and good humour.

(III. ii. 261-7)

These paradoxical descriptions accurately sum up a character for whom the height of eloquence is reciting the names of his Parisian tailor, shoemaker, and wigmaker (see III. ii. 220-33). His obsession with fashion extends to his speech, unselfconsciously littered with Gallicisms: 'When thou wer't [in Paris] La corneus and Sallyes were the only habitudes we had, a Comedian would have been a bone fortune' (IV. i. 235-8). For Sir Fopling, French words and phrases are newly acquired playthings. Like his clothing, they are a projection of his vanity, evidence of his devotion to his idol, fashion.

Yet his concern with being 'bien gante', as exaggerated as it may be, is shared by the society he inhabits. Unlike Dufoy in *The Comical Revenge,* Sir Fopling does not wander through a farcical world of his own; his folly lies ironically in his eagerness to conform to the same dictates that the other characters recognize and observe. The more he seeks to conform, the more 'original' he appears. In creating him, Etherege works with and against the archetype of the fop as absolute fool. Sir Fopling's childlike devotion to playing the role of the man of mode travesties his society's preoccupation with style as an end in itself. As Emilia and Dorimant suggest, he is close enough to being a wit to pass for one among 'the tasteless multitude' who are aesthetically (and ideologically) unable to distinguish true wit from false. Medley, Lady Townley, and Dorimant encourage his folly, then, for two reasons: his 'Extravagancies' are entertaining and they provide a painless way for the play's wits to laugh at the follies to which they, in more subtle ways, are prone.

At the beginning of Act V, Pert tries to comfort her mistress by asserting that her new suitor, Sir Fopling, is 'as handsom a man as Mr. *Dorimant,* and as great a Gallant' (V. i. 4-5). Loveit finds Pert's comparison 'intolerable' and 'false', but her reaction is typical of the overdetermined satire directed against the fop throughout the play.[23] She is angry not because Pert's comparison is far-fetched but because it comes close to subverting the ideological distinctions between true and false wit that all the upper-class characters try rigorously to maintain. The proximity of true and false wit allows Sir Fopling to function as a convenient target to deflect from Dorimant the kind of criticism that can be levelled at a hero who admits, 'I would fain wear in Fashion as long as I can . . . 'tis a thing to be valu'd in men as well as Bawbles' (III. ii. 156-7). Sir Fopling represents that aspect of the man of fashion given to small vanities, self-dramatizing poses, and celebrations of style, that part of Dorimant susceptible to foolishness and fashion-mongering. After Sir Fopling's appearance in Act III, the hero's diction, for the first time in the play, shows symptoms of Gallic affectation:

DORIMANT.

> The Town has been very favourable to you this afternoon, my Lady *Townley,* you use to have an Ambara's of Chaires and Coaches at your Door, an uproar of Footmen in your Hall, and a noise of Fools above here.

> (III. ii. 122-5)

SIR FOPLING.

> Forgive me, Sir, in this Ambara's of Civilities, I could not come to have you in my Arms sooner.

> (III. ii. 187-8)

MEDLEY.

> What was *Bellindas* business with you at my Lady *Townleys*?

DORIMANT.

> To get me to meet *Loveit* here in order to have an Eclerisment; I made some difficulty of it, and have prepar'd this rancounter to make good my Jealousy.

> (III. iii. 168-72)

Although the semiotics of Restoration comedy encourage us to hear Sir Fopling's French as affectation and Dorimant's as a mark of sophistication, their use of 'Ambara's' a few moments apart is suggestive. Sir Fopling's 'Ambara's of Civilities' marks his sacrifice of common sense to far-fetched ingenuity, but it also casts the formalities of Lady Townley's house in a satiric light; like Dorimant's 'Ambara's of Chaires and Coaches', it reduces social ceremony to comic disorder. If Sir Fopling inadvertently mimics the hero, however, Dorimant falls into patterns of speech similar to those that his foolish counterpart affects. When he begins plotting his sexual intrigues, his diction—'Eclerisment', 'rancounter'—becomes that of a simpler, more conventional comic figure, the rake-hero as rake-fop. His French (like his recitation of Waller's verse) is a defence mechanism, insulating him from the effects of his machinations by turning his intrigues into a verbal game of artifice and exaggeration. Etherege's parody, then, works in both directions: the fool and the hero are of a world compact, distinguished not by their values but by the quality of their acting.

Harriet presents a different kind of challenge to Dorimant and to the decorum of wit. Although her language often masks her feelings for the hero, it is not in itself ambigu-

ous or inherently deceptive; it is less a pose than a projection of her determination to turn her powerlessness as a woman to her advantage. Her language is sparse, frequently epigrammatic, and given to bold, commonsensical declarations:

> I . . . hate the set face that always looks as it would say *Come love me.* A woman, who at Playes makes the Deux yeux to a whole Audience, and at home cannot forbear 'em to her Monkey.

> (IV. i. 126-30)

> Beauty runs as great a risque expos'd at Court as wit does on the Stage, where the ugly and the foolish, all are free to censure.

> (IV. i. 148-50)

Harriet's assertions achieve their authority by rigorously excluding doubts and second guesses and by emphasizing her distance from the objects of her satiric censure. If Dorimant, even by Loveit's admission, 'has something of the Angel yet undefac'd in him' (II. ii. 17-18), Harriet seems far removed from the angelic. Her constant upbraiding of the hero for his 'affectation' suggests that she is a more accurate judge of his character than Loveit or Young Bellair. Like the hero, she is an accomplished parodist, who '*Acts him*' (stage direction) to his face while asking, 'Is not this like you?' (III. iii. 106). Her mimicking of Dorimant is both a pleasure and a form of control; it reflects both her struggle to master her attraction to him and her desire to outwit and out-perform him. By playing the part of the disdainful beauty, she is able to force Dorimant into the role of the dutiful suitor. As Hawkins and Hume argue,[24] her success in winning his love results from outplaying him at his own game, even as she faces the temptations that she is quick to ridicule in others.

The wit duels between Dorimant and Harriet contrast two different epistemologies of language, two kinds of verbal tactics. The hero tries a variety of approaches, ranging from easy banter to fervent protestation; she consistently uses her wit to mock his assumed voices and deflate his hyperbole. Their languages represent male and female versions of libertinism: the first to depart from the rhetoric of wit—the first, in other words, to be forced into sincerity—loses. In a society in which pretence is the norm and romantic love ridiculed, the wit battles between Dorimant and Harriet become their only means to distinguish dissembling from 'genuine' emotion. Their exchanges, in this respect, have a dramatic purpose often absent from earlier versions of the wit duel.

Harriet's success in her verbal skirmishings with Dorimant results from her ability to parody his different voices: what he does successfully to Bellinda and Loveit, she does to him. She disrupts his performances and mocks his roles, responding to his 'grave bow', for example, with a 'demure curt'sy' and the line, 'Affectation is catching' (IV. i. 110). Harriet has mastered the semiotics of outright deception: her 'scorn' and 'coldness', which she claims are the natural signs of her 'want of art' (IV. i. 114), belie her confessed feelings for Dorimant. Her disdainfulness, her mocking of his pretensions to love, distinguish her deflating, mocking wit from both Loveit's passion and Bellinda's vacillation:

HARRIET.

> . . . I was inform'd you use to laugh at Love, and not make it.

DORIMANT.

> The time has been, but now I must speak—

HARRIET.

> If it be on that Idle subject, I will put on my serious look, turn my head carelessly from you, drop my lip, let my Eyelids fall and hang half o're my Eyes— Thus—while you buz a speech of an hour long in my ear, and I answer never a word! why do you not begin?

DORIMANT.

> That the company may take notice how passionately I make advances of Love! and how disdainfully you receive 'em.

HARRIET.

> When your Love's grown strong enough to make you bear being laugh'd at, I'll give you leave to trouble me with it.

> (IV. i. 169-82)

Harriet gains the advantage in this exchange by forcing Dorimant into the role of passionate lover while she acts out her feigned indifference to his 'Idle subject'. Her verbal wit becomes an erotic inducement that tempts the hero by challenging his rhetorical control of the scene.

If wit becomes the scene of their confrontations, however, what each of them invests in their verbal battles differs. For Dorimant, the stakes are his ironic scepticism and self-esteem as an actor. In an aside he admits, 'I have took the infection [love] from her, and feel the disease now spreading in me—' (IV. i. 161-2). The image of love as disease marks his retreat from ironic wit to a metaphoric language that threatens to become a self-conscious parody of *précieuse* sentiment. But Dorimant has no other language to deal with an emotion that he cannot express directly or master ironically. He may, as he claims, 'renounce all the joys I have in friendship and in Wine, sacrifice . . . all the interest I have in other Women', but his sacrifices are announced in a language of passionate intensity that Harriet recognizes as overwrought. 'Though I wish you devout', she responds, 'I would not have you turn Fanatick—' (v. ii. 143-7).

Harriet's risks in the wit duels—precisely because she is a woman—are qualitatively different from Dorimant's. Wit, for her (as it is for Fletcher's women), is a form of release, a means of expressing those desires which she cannot act upon. When Busy, her waiting-woman, counsels her to 'let

[Dorimant] know your mind,' Harriet responds, 'May he hate me, (a curse that frights me when I speak it!) if ever I do a thing against the rules of decency and honour' (v. ii. 167, 172-4). Her predicament is the opposite of Bellinda's. Bellinda must maintain a show of innocence after her seduction; Harriet must play the role of a wit to entice Dorimant into a relationship that is both sexual and honourable. Her verbal wit, therefore, is a displacement into language of the 'Rules of charming' (IV. i. 120) that she accuses other women of using to seduce men. If Dorimant's wit reflects the ironies of his existence, Harriet's is shaped by the ideological and moral constraints that determine its seductive and deceptive functions. The form of her wit is more assertive and conservative than her suitor's because she must still play the mating game by 'the rules of honour and decency'. No matter how witty she may be, her wit cannot obscure the fact that she is out to bring back a man—a potential patriarch—to an estate inhabited solely by women. In this respect, her wit is a means to lure an acceptable mate into marriage and fatherhood. As in *The Wild Goose Chase,* feminine wit becomes the vehicle for the comedy of patrilineal succession.

Feminine wit in **The Man of Mode,** then, operates in an inverse relationship to sexual experience: Harriet, like the heroines of **She Wou'd,** is witty but chaste; Loveit, the sexually-compromised woman, has lost her capacity to dissemble along with her virginity. When she forces herself to flirt with Sir Fopling, she is able—temporarily—to rekindle Dorimant's interest. But physical passion has robbed her of her ability to sustain her charade. Harriet, in contrast, keeps both her tongue and body inviolate. Her wit is itself an erotic display that entices Dorimant yet forestalls their sexual relationship to a future that exists only in the blank space 'after' the end of the play. Like the hero, Harriet has no language that can reconcile the demands of appearance and emotion. She can resolve only to try her suitor by forcing him to join her in the country.

Etherege's return to the device of a month's trial is instructive for what it suggests about the self-imposed limits of his final two comedies. Fifth-act marriage scenes in comedy—feasts, dances, nuptial celebrations—are both metaphors for and promises of fertility, assurances that the species will be propagated, that a son will be born who can inherit his father's land and wealth and continue the socio-economic stability that the marriage secures. In patrilineal cultures marriage signals the hero's passage from adolescence into political maturity, into history; yet it paradoxically testifies to a desire to overcome or deny history (think of the Cavaliers) by reproducing one's self— and one's place in society—in the person of a son and heir.[25] In this respect, fifth-act marriages mark the hero's ascension to patriarchal responsibility: there is, in effect, no need to dramatize what happens 'after' his marriage because his history has 'already' been inscribed in the self-perpetuating traditions of patrilineal succession. Etherege's deferrals of the expected weddings at the conclusions of his final two plays thus imply a retreat from marriage and the responsibilities it entails. Unlike the proviso scenes that mark the endings of *Secret Love* and *The Way of the World,* the ending of **The Man of Mode** forgoes the legalisms that seek to reintegrate the libertine into society. Dorimant retreats into passionate declarations which Harriet mocks by turning his new-found language of fanaticism against him: 'In men who have been long harden'd in Sin, we have reason to mistrust the first signs of repentance' (v. ii. 138-9). Significantly, it is the heroine who, at the end of the play, is still speaking the language of wit, still questioning Dorimant's sincerity, and still verbally resisting dwindling into a wife. If his claim that his 'soul has quite given up her liberty' parodies myths of the rake reformed, her reaction reasserts the sceptical irony of libertine wit: 'This is more dismal than the Country' (v. ii. 428-30). The ending of the play thus pits our expectations of a happy ending against our knowledge of the characters and the world they inhabit. The relationships of actors to their roles are not resolved linguistically or philosophically, as they are at the conclusion of *Love for Love,* but are ironically confirmed.

Harriet's final line might stand as an epitaph for sixty years of Fletcherian wit comedy. Like the heroes of *The Libertine* and *The Plain Dealer,* Dorimant ultimately runs out of stylistic options. The dialogical energy of Etherege's dramatic prose tends toward indeterminacy because his 'radical' wit is culturally and historically constrained: it dissipates rather than focuses (as Bakhtin assumes) its incipient political critique. Etherege has taken the language of wit as far as it can go toward an ironic discourse which celebrates the metaphysics of paradox and pretence without surrendering the parodic mythos of rebellion and restoration that shapes comedy from 1660 to 1676. His deconstruction of wit can be taken as a variety of mock-heroic, a questioning and subverting of one set of fashionable ideals that *The Rehearsal* had left untouched. But by exposing wit's seductiveness and limitations, its subversive ingenuity and stale pretensions, Etherege has effectively undermined its post-Fletcherian conventions, leaving his successors to restructure comedy as best they can. After Wycherley and he retired from the stage, the language of wit underwent a series of radical transformations that turned it into a vehicle for an exemplary, if not a sentimental, comic mode.[26] When wit comedy was revived in the 1690s by Southerne, Congreve, Vanbrugh, and Cibber, it developed new languages and modified existing ones. Rather than overtly challenging the traditions of Fletcherian wit, these playwrights search for ways to reinvest comedy with moral seriousness.

Notes

1. 'An Allusion to Horace', *The Complete Poems of John Wilmot, Earl of Rochester,* ed. David Vieth (New Haven, 1968), 122. All subsequent quotations from Rochester's works are from this edition.

2. *Letters of Sir George Etherege,* ed. Frederick Bracher (Berkeley, 1974), 276.

3. For an important exception see Dale Underwood, *Etherege and the Seventeenth-century Comedy of Manners* (New Haven, 1957), 94-110.

4. On the affective aspect of Etherege's plays see Jocelyn Powell, 'George Etherege and the Form of a Comedy', in *Restoration Theatre,* ed. John Brown and Bernard Harris (London, 1965), 43-69. For arguments for the thematic unity of the play see Norman Holland, *The First Modern Comedies: The Significance of Etherege, Wycherley, and Congreve* (Cambridge, Mass., 1959), 20-7; Underwood, *Etherege and Comedy,* pp. 43-58; and Virginia Birdsall, *Wild Civility: The English Comic Spirit on the Restoration Stage* (Bloomington, Ind., 1970), 41-56.

5. All quotations from Etherege's plays are from the edition of H. F. B. Brett-Smith, *The Dramatic Works of Sir George Etherege* (repr. St Clair Shores, Mich., 1977).

6. On the close connections between the theatre and the Court after the Restoration see Nicholas Jose, *Ideas of the Restoration in English Literature* (Cambridge, Mass., 1984), 37, 120-41.

7. The Battle of Naseby (June 1645) was a crippling defeat for the royalist forces. The chief of Bruce's attackers vows revenge for his father's 'murder' during this battle, but one of his 'hired slaves' remarks, 'I have heard [Bruce] kill'd him fairly in the Field at *Nasby*' (IV. iv. 8-9).

8. In *Some Considerations Touching the Style of the Holy Scriptures* (London, 1661), Robert Boyle explicitly yokes libertine wit to atheism, blasphemy, and sedition. In a series of rather clumsy satires of 'wits' he maintains that they appeal to 'our Corruptions' rather than to 'our Judgments' (see esp. pp. 175-86).

9. It is worth noting that Etherege, who went to London to study law at Clements Inn, ended up as one of Rochester's drinking companions. For Etherege and Wycherley, dramatic wit offered a means to advance socially as well as theatrically. In this respect, libertine wit ironically encourages the transgression as well as the maintenance of class barriers, a point which both playwrights exploit.

10. David Abercrombie, *A Discourse of Wit* (London, 1686), 106.

11. On the ironic aspects of the play see Holland, *First Modern Comedies,* pp. 28-37; Laura Brown, *English Dramatic Form 1660-1760* (New Haven, 1981), 38-40; Birdsall, *Wild Civility,* pp. 57-76; and Peter Holland, *The Ornament of Action* (Cambridge, 1979), 48-54.

12. See Brown, *Dramatic Form,* pp. 39-40.

13. 'But' appears as a connective over 100 times in the play; this frequency suggests something of the oppositional structure of Etherege's prose.

14. See Holland, *Ornament of Action,* p. 86.

15. Etherege, *Letters,* p. ix; see also Thomas Fujimura, 'Etherege at Constantinople', *PMLA* 62 (1956), 465-81.

16. For Etherege's praise of Shadwell's *The Squire of Alsatia* see Etherege, *Letters*, pp. 96, 186. See also Michael Neill, 'Heroic Heads and Humble Tails: Sex, Politics, and the Restoration Comic Rake', *The Eighteenth Century: Theory and Interpretation,* 24 (1983), 133.

17. Harriet Hawkins, *Likenesses of Truth in Elizabethan and Restoration Drama* (Oxford, 1972), 79-97.

18. See Holland, *Ornament of Action,* p. 55, and John Barnard, 'Point of View in *The Man of Mode*', *Essays in Criticism,* 34 (1984), 285-308.

19. All quotations from Congreve's plays are from Herbert Davis's edition, *Complete Plays of William Congreve* (Chicago, 1967), and will be cited parenthetically in the text.

20. See Neill, 'Heroic Heads and Humble Tails', pp. 134-5.

21. On Dorimant's role in the play see Hawkins, *Likenesses,* pp. 79-97; Powell, 'Etherege and the Form of a Comedy', pp. 58-69; Underwood, *Etherege and Comedy,* pp. 72-93; Holland, *First Modern Comedies,* pp. 86-95; Birdsall, *Wild Civility,* pp. 77-104; Brown, *Dramatic Form,* pp. 43-8; Robert Hume, 'Reading and Misreading *The Man of Mode*', *Criticism,* 14 (1972), 1-11; id., *The Development of English Drama in the Late Seventeenth Century* (Oxford, 1976), 92-7; Brian Corman, 'Interpreting and Misinterpreting *The Man of Mode*', *Papers on Language and Literature,* 13 (1977), 35-53; Rose Zimbardo, 'Of Women, Comic Imitation of Nature, and Etherege's *The Man of Mode*', *Studies in English Literature,* 21 (1981), 373-87; Derek Hughes, 'Play and Passion in *The Man of Mode*', *Comparative Drama,* 15 (1981), 231-57; Paul C. Davies, 'The State of Nature and the State of War: A Reconsideration of *The Man of Mode*', *University of Toronto Quarterly,* 39 (1969), 53-62; John G. Hayman, 'Dorimant and the Comedy of a Man of Mode', *Modern Language Quarterly,* 30 (1969), 183-97; Ronald Berman, 'The Comic Passions of *The Man of Mode*', *Studies in English Literature,* 10 (1970), 459-68; and Leslie Martin, 'Past and Parody in *The Man of Mode*', *Studies in English Literature,* 16 (1976), 363-76.

22. See Underwood, *Etherege and Comedy,* pp. 96-103 for another discussion of this passage.

23. See Susan Staves's discussion of the role of the fop, 'A Few Kinds Words for the Fop', *Studies in English Literature,* 22 (1982), 413-28.

24. See Hawkins, *Likenesses,* pp. 88-9 and Hume, 'Reading and Misreading', pp. 10-11.

25. On the significance of the Oedipal situation, see Norman O. Brown, *Life Against Death: The Psychoanalytical Meaning of History* (Middletown, Conn., 1959) and id., *Love's Body* (New York, 1966), esp. 3-12. On the political implications of patriarchal social structures see Gordon Schochet, *Patriarchalism in Political Thought* (Oxford, 1975).

26. On comedy between Etherege and Congreve see Robert Hume's valuable article, '"The Change in Comedy": Cynical versus Exemplary Comedy on the London Stage, 1678-1693', *Essays in Theatre,* I (1983), 101-18.

Lisa Berglund (essay date 1990)

SOURCE: Berglund, Lisa. "The Language of Libertines: Subversive Morality in *The Man of Mode*." *SEL: Studies in English Literature* 30, no. 3 (summer 1990): 369-86.

[*In the essay below, Berglund explores how Dorimant and his retinue use a "libertine language" of extended metaphors and analogies to subvert conventional morality in* The Man of Mode.]

When the practical but unhelpful maid Pert advises her mistress to renounce Dorimant, Mrs. Loveit defends her devotion by indicting her tormentor's paradoxical nature. "I know he is a devil," she cries, "but he has something of the angel yet undefaced in him, which makes him so charming and agreeable that I must love him, be he never so wicked" (II.ii.15-17).[1] Critics of Etherege's *The Man of Mode* suffer similar distress when faced with Dorimant, who, though the hero, is after all a damned libertine. He maintains three mistresses, treats them all shamefully, interrupts an evening with the woman he professedly loves for a sordid liaison, and sneers at his friend Bellair behind that "tolerable" young man's back (I.i.395). At the same time, he is witty, charming, and magnetic, and clearly deserves the love of the most fascinating woman of his world, Harriet.

Evading the need to address this contradiction, Harriett Hawkins argues, "The primary purpose of this comedy seems to be neither immoral nor moral, but rather spectacular—to exhibit, rather than to censure."[2] She suggests that the discomfort Dorimant provokes should not disturb us, because Etherege did not intend us to judge his hero, but merely to appreciate him. Jocelyn Powell, too, contends that "we are seeing [Etherege's libertines] in human, not in moral terms."[3] More persuasively, Laura Brown argues that our uncertain response to Dorimant derives from Etherege's deliberate attempt simultaneously to support and to condemn his hero's rakish values. She writes, "[T]he ambivalence toward the social status quo—or the disjunction between represented social reality and the implicit moral judgment upon the 'rightness' of that reality—represents an aesthetic expression of the ambiguous aristocratic attitude toward the subversive content of the libertine ideology."[4] Etherege and his peers, according to Brown, advocated freedom from a morality that had become identified with the monied middle class, but at the same time recognized that such subversiveness could destroy the society on whose stability, in the end, all depended. *The Man of Mode* and other "dramatic social satires," as she calls them, is "fundamentally conservative in its allegiance to traditional values and to the status quo, but daringly radical in its exposure of the hypocrisy, the immorality and the materialism of the society it must finally accept" (p. 42).

Despite her reasonable argument that Etherege's attitude toward his society is not amoral, but rather satirical, Brown fails to recognize that his impulse, like that of any responsible satirist, is to correct as well as to expose. She claims that "*The Man of Mode* is filled with actual and serious conflict—so serious that it does not submit to resolution" (p. 46). However, the evidence that she offers as Etherege's irresolute criticism of Dorimant is flawed, for it issues from characters who are outside Dorimant's society and who therefore neither adequately comprehend their target nor merit enough respect from either Dorimant or Etherege's audience to be credible witnesses. For example, Brown uses Mrs. Loveit's attack on Dorimant in V.i to conclude that "the force of her eloquence, joined with the force of moral judgment communicated more indirectly in the rest of the action, permits her to carry the day" (p. 45). But Mrs. Loveit does *not* carry the day, because her own moral failure (the publicly recognized affair with Dorimant) ultimately excludes her from society. Etherege cannot and does not present her as a successful critic of Dorimant's vices. When, at the end of the play, Harriet and the rest of the company at Lady Townley's laugh her from the room, Mrs. Loveit exits with none of the power of persecuted virtue or despised sense.

If we are to look to Etherege for an attack on Dorimant's libertine values, and I agree that we ought, then unlike Brown I believe that such criticism will come from *within* the society it condemns, from characters who, like Etherege himself, can both correctly appreciate the impulse to immorality and offer a solution tempting enough to convert the guilty. Brown wrongly concludes that Mrs. Loveit voices Etherege's censure of Dorimant, and identifies the Orange Woman and the Shoemaker as lesser moralists, because she neither allows for the extreme separation of Etherege's characters into two independent groups, nor recognizes on what principle this division exists. Dorimant, Medley, Young Bellair, Harriet, Emilia, and Lady Townley form an exclusive, witty society from which all other characters, whatever their social or financial lot, from Old Bellair to Molly the whore, are excluded. These six witty characters clearly differ from the rest of the dramatis personae because they alone use and understand extended metaphors, a speech pattern that I will call the "libertine language." Any character who attempts to influence, attack, or join the society of the wits, but does not speak its language, cannot possibly succeed because his inarticulateness betrays his ignorance of the code of libertinism, and exposes him to contempt. On the other hand, a critic who couches his censure in the metaphorical language of the wits is heard and approved because his targets recognize that his membership in their society gives him the authority to demand reform. In *The Man of Mode* two characters speak for true love and marriage, but maintain their aristocratic freedom: Young Bellair and Harriet. They

counter rakish antagonism to constancy, affection, and honor by demonstrating that conventional morality may be, like Harriet herself, "wild, witty, lovesome, beautiful" (III.iii.327-28).

Brown rightly points out that "libertinism is . . . viewed as a threat . . . even by the libertine himself" (p. 42). To reconcile with his moral sense his enjoyment of dangerous antisocial behavior, Etherege's libertine speaks a highly metaphorical language that conceals the true nature of his sexual activities. His use of analogy to discuss the institutions in which restrictive and conventional morality is most overwhelmingly embodied—love and marriage—disguises his rebellion against those institutions, and displaces both confession and criticism into an understood sub-text. (It is Etherege's removal of explicit moral debate from the play that provokes "spectacular" interpretations like that of Hawkins.) In other words, Dorimant and his peers avoid confession or judgment by perpetually speaking of other things.[5] They most usually cloak their licentiousness in allusions to health or to games of chance; their disdain for honest love is voiced as disdain for the church and "devotions." For example, Emilia, Medley, and Dorimant discuss the risks of illicit love, and Mrs. Loveit's tiresomeness, in terms of gambling:

EMILIA.

> There are afflictions in love, Mr. Dorimant.

DORIMANT.

> You women make 'em, who are commonly as unreasonable in that as you are at play: without the advantage be on your side, a man can never quietly give over when he's weary.

MEDLEY.

> If you would play without being obliged to complaisance, Dorimant, you should play in public places.

DORIMANT.

> Ordinaries were a very good thing for that, but gentlemen do not of late frequent 'em. The deep play is now in private houses.

> (III.ii.95-103)

Notice how much ground the conversation covers within the terms of the analogy of "play." Dorimant admits that he is tired of Mrs. Loveit; Medley recommends that he confine himself to prostitutes, who will not require him to be agreeable; and Dorimant rejects this suggestion because, as a rake, he finds it more stimulating to seduce women of quality. After Dorimant establishes the initial comparison, neither he nor Medley mentions the tenor of the simile, keeping the conversation strictly within the terms of the vehicle. The libertine language thus creates a polite fiction (that women are bad-mannered gamblers) which conceals the actual result of the libertine ethic (the destruction of Mrs. Loveit's honor).[6]

The wits also turn to metaphor when Bellair and Medley greet Dorimant after his tryst with Bellinda. They are perfectly aware of his activities, if not of the lady's identity, but wouldn't dream of being explicit:

YOUNG BELLAIR.

   Not abed yet?

MEDLEY.

   You have had an irregular fit, Dorimant.

DORIMANT.

   I have.

YOUNG BELLAIR.

   And is it off already?

DORIMANT.

   Nature has done her part, gentlemen. When she falls kindly to work, great cures are effected in little time, you know.

                                          (IV.ii.66-71)

Medley, by recalling the phrase "irregular fit," with which Dorimant himself had described his amorous dalliances (in his conversation with Harriet [IV.i.146]), inserts an entire scene between vehicle (illness) and tenor (sexual intercourse). This polite inquiry into Dorimant's health, in which Medley confirms that Dorimant has been entertaining a lady, and Bellair that she has departed, therefore even more successfully practices the art of displacement than the first example I quoted. It also illustrates how the discourse of the six wits separates them from the other characters. Speaking the libertine language confirms their mutual recognition that although libertinism is destructive, to give over their freedom for conventional morality would violate their aristocratic identities. The ends of their linguistic strategy become particularly clear as IV.ii continues, because Dorimant's activities are exposed through the obtuseness of Sir Fopling, who does not recognize that the practice of immorality requires the protection of a metaphor. Sir Fopling's gauche persistence forces Dorimant, against his will, to explain the nature of his "fit":

SIR FOPLING.

   We thought there was a wench in the case, by the chair that waited. Prithee, make us a *confidence*.

DORIMANT.

   Excuse me.

SIR FOPLING.

   Le sage Dorimant. Was she pretty?

DORIMANT.

   So pretty she may come to keep her coach and pay parish duties, if the good humor of the age continue.

                                          (IV.ii.72-77)

Dorimant's embarrassment and vexation in this scene, however, do not undercut the fact that those who speak the libertine language are the most powerful characters in the play—powerful because they use wit to disguise and transform their weaknesses and thus render themselves invulnerable to external criticism or pressure. Thus the key to Mrs. Loveit's unfitness for the society of the wits is her inability to mask her passion and challenge Dorimant in his own terms. The explicitness that convinces Brown of her critical "force" in fact undermines Mrs. Loveit's case, because it exposes her own moral blemish.

MRS. LOVEIT.

   Now you begin to show yourself.

DORIMANT.

   Love gilds us over and makes us show fine things to one another for a time; but soon the gold wears off, and then again the native brass appears.

MRS. LOVEIT.

   Think on your oaths, your vows, and protestations, perjured man!

                                          (II.ii.194-99)

The "*belle passion*" (V.ii.356) that prevents Mrs. Loveit from pursuing Dorimant's gilding metaphor, a response that would be proof of wit and self-control, is also the root of Dorimant's disgust for her, and, presumably, the flaw that made her susceptible to seduction. In other words, Mrs. Loveit's inability to speak the libertine language is a symptom of the ungoverned temperament that drives her to ostracism.

Like Mrs. Loveit, Old Bellair and Sir Fopling cannot speak the libertine language. Although, unlike her, they do not try to force the wits into plain dealing, the linguistic strategy they severally adopt nevertheless exposes them as incompetent imitators. Old Bellair and Sir Fopling set up rival languages whose shallowness betrays the dullness of the speakers; and their inferiority is emphasized by the glee with which the witty characters mockingly mimic them. Old Bellair's fancy that his constant snubs of Emilia conceal his senile passion for her suggests an impotent approximation of the displacement effected by the libertine language. The repetitive pattern of the insults—"You are ugly, you are ugly!" (IV.i.82)—carries over into the rest of his conversation, which he also interlards with ejaculations of "Out a pize!" and "A dod!" The latter, for example, appears four times in his first three speeches, and his first scene ends with the following flourish:

   Out, a pize o' their breeches, there are keeping fools enough for such flaunting baggages, and they are e'en too good for 'em. (*To* Emilia.) Remember night. (*Aloud.*) Go, y'are a rogue, y'are a rogue. Fare you well, fare you well. (*To* Young Bellair.) Come, come, come along, sir.

                                          (II.i.70-74)

This monotonous speech pattern identifies Old Bellair as an old fool, just as Mrs. Loveit's passionate outbursts illustrate her inability to control her desires.

Sir Fopling's conversation, too, is distinctive, in his case because he embellishes his remarks with French phrases, an affectation that Emilia parodies the moment they are introduced:

SIR FOPLING.

. . . The *éclat* of so much beauty, I confess, ought to have charmed me sooner.

EMILIA.

The *brillant* of so much good language, sir, has much more power than the little beauty I can boast.

(III.ii.163-66)

Emilia's pointed reference to the power of language should not be overlooked. Her sarcasm alerts the audience to the awareness of the libertines that language is the tool of those who would control their world. Characters who try but fail to create their own languages, on the other hand, betray their corresponding lack of a motive for metaphor; they reveal that they are sexually powerless. Old Bellair is a conventional *senex* figure, his son's unsuccessful rival, while Sir Fopling is husbanding his "vigor" in order to "make [his] court to the whole sex in a ballet" (V.ii.340-41). The two cannot understand the seriousness of the strategy of displacement because they do not participate in the antisocial intrigues it conceals.

Yet we cannot dismiss Sir Fopling as easily as we do Old Bellair, for the eponymous fop, with his equipage and his wig, his clothes and his capers, has a magnetism and *joie de vivre* as captivating as that of the witty lovers.[7] Like Harriet, as we shall see, Sir Fopling penetrates the metaphors of Dorimant and Medley and discloses their polite secrets; he does so, however, because he is sublimely unaware that anything has been concealed. For example, he sees through the reticence of the "half a dozen beauties" whom he meets in Whitehall:

DORIMANT.

Did you know 'em?

SIR FOPLING.

Not one of 'em, by heavens, not I! But they were all your friends.

DORIMANT.

How are you sure of that?

SIR FOPLING.

Why, we laughed at all the town—spared nobody but yourself.

(IV.i.244-49)

Sir Fopling's subsequent indiscretion at Dorimant's apartments already has been discussed; in both these cases, he ignores the super-texts of metaphor and, in the case of the "beauties," of discreet silence, because for him sex itself is part of the *garniture*. The energy that a Dorimant expends on intrigues, the fop channels into surface; where the rake hides behind metaphors and false names, the fop in disguise is instantly recognizable:

Enter Sir Fopling and *others in masks*. . . .

. . . . .

YOUNG BELLAIR.

This must be Sir Fopling.

MEDLEY.

That extraordinary habit show it.

(IV.i.168-75)

Sir Fopling has no patience with concealment. When a cloaking metaphor is too obscure, he protests (and exposes the libertine strategy to the audience):

SIR FOPLING.

Let her be what she will, I know how to take my measures. In Paris the mode is to flatter the *prude,* laugh at the *faux-prude,* make serious love to the *demi-prude,* and only rally with the *coquette.* Medley, what think you?

MEDLEY.

That for all this smattering of the mathematics, you may be out in your judgment at tennis.

SIR FOPLING.

What a *coq-à-l'âne* is this? I talk of women, and thou answer'st tennis.

MEDLEY.

Mistakes will be, for want of apprehension.

(IV.i.203-11)

Sir Fopling's vitality, therefore, derives from being purely extrinsic; he incorporates into his surface everything that the rakes wish to conceal. Dorimant may disdain mirrors because in them a man sees "[t]he shadow of himself" (IV.ii.88), but Sir Fopling is a very tolerable reflection of the libertine hero. He forces the rakes to look at themselves and, as Dryden notes in his epilogue, "Sir Fopling is a fool so nicely writ, / The ladies would mistake him for a wit" (lines 7-8). Although an object of derision, Sir Fopling in every gesture and remark belittles the character of Mr. Courtage—the polite surface—that Dorimant assumes, and implicitly diminishes the power of Dorimant's sexuality to a "ballet."

While Sir Fopling unconsciously undercuts Dorimant, Etherege locates in the wit of Young Bellair and Harriet informed criticism of the libertine code. It is no accident that, at the beginning of the play, Harriet and Young Bellair are all but betrothed; they are coupled to highlight the fact that their views of the world and morality are identical. That Etherege gave them similar Christian names—Harriet and Harry—also contributes to my sense of them as female and male versions of the same character: a character who accepts the institutions that the libertines reject. In the ante-contract scene, the two articulate their belief in true love:

HARRIET.

> There are some [ladies], it may be, have an eye like Bart'lomew, big enough for the whole fair; but I am not of the number, and you may keep your gingerbread. 'Twill be more acceptable to the lady whose dear image it wears.

YOUNG BELLAIR.

> I must confess, madam, you came a day after the fair.

HARRIET.

> You own then you are in love?

YOUNG BELLAIR.

> I do.

HARRIET.

> The confidence is generous, and in return I could almost find in my heart to let you know my inclinations.

(III.i.87-95)

Note that, although this conversation begins in the metaphorical manner of the witty set, Harriet then asks a direct question, and receives a direct answer. Neither she nor Bellair *needs* to speak in metaphor, because, unlike Dorimant or Emilia, they have embraced the institutions of love and marriage. They are both, however, sharp-eyed (as the love scene they stage for their parents confirms) and sensitive to the reasons for the concealment practiced by their peers; both therefore when conversing with the other wits speak the libertine language. They use it, however, to articulate their disagreement with the ideology of the rakes.

When Young Bellair first enters, Medley challenges his wish to marry. Their debate employs the metaphor of the church, and while Young Bellair contradicts Medley, he does so in Medley's terms:

MEDLEY.

> . . . may the beautiful cause of our misfortune give you all the joys happy lovers have shared ever since the world began.

YOUNG BELLAIR.

> You wish me in heaven, but you believe me on my journey to hell.

MEDLEY.

> You have a good strong faith, and that may contribute much towards your salvation. I confess I am but of an untoward constitution, apt to have doubts and scruples;

and in love they are no less distracting than in religion. Were I so near marriage, I should cry out by fits as I ride in my coach, "Cuckold, cuckold!" with no less fury than the mad fanatic does "Glory!" in Bethlem.

YOUNG BELLAIR.

> Because religion makes some run mad, must I live an atheist?

(I.i.303-16)

Bellair's retort is powerful because in itself it demonstrates that a man may be both a wit and a lover. Similarly, when Emilia, who at the beginning of the play, like Dorimant and Medley, puts no trust in emotions, substitutes the metaphor of health for matters of the heart, Bellair answers within the limits of her analogy, and his words only confirm his faith in true love:

YOUNG BELLAIR.

> My constancy! I vow—

EMILIA.

> Do not vow. Our love is frail as is our life, and full as little in our power; and are you sure you shall outlive this day?

YOUNG BELLAIR.

> I am not, but when we are in perfect health, 'twere an idle thing to fright ourselves with the thoughts of sudden death.

(II.i.26-30)

Young Bellair's fluency in the libertine language locates a voice of morality within, rather than without, society. The play ends with a celebration of his marriage in order to show that one may accept moral institutions without forfeiting wit and gaiety. When Old Bellair, who has been reconciled to his son's disobedience, tells the pit, "And if these honest gentlemen rejoice, / Adod, the boy had made a happy choice," Etherege asks approval not just for *The Man of Mode,* but in particular for the decision of one of his libertines to forsake profligacy for marriage (V.ii.399-400).

Within the restrictions of metaphor, Young Bellair warns Dorimant that Harriet will not abandon her principles—"You had best not think of Mrs. Harriet too much. Without church security, there's no taking up there" (IV.iii.179-80)—and Dorimant confesses that he "may fall into the snare, too" (line 181). Harriet fascinates him because she speaks the libertine language as effortlessly as he, and he therefore treats her as an equal, a fellow wit. Witness their first conversation, using the gaming analogy, in which they establish the limits of their courtship:

DORIMANT.

> You were talking of play, madam. Pray, what may be your stint?

HARRIET.

A little harmless discourse in public walks or at most an appointment in a box, barefaced, at the playhouse. You are for masks and private meetings, where women engage for all they are worth, I hear.

DORIMANT.

I have been used to deep play, but I can make one at small game when I like my gamester well.

HARRIET.

And be so unconcerned you'll ha' no pleasure in't.

(III.iii.62-70)

Because she has fallen in love, Harriet understands Dorimant even better than does Young Bellair. Her last remark in the dialogue quoted above confirms what Dorimant himself only hints (at I.i.189ff.): that he does not enjoy harmless flirtation ("small game"), but rather, as Mrs. Loveit later charges, takes "more pleasure in the ruin of a woman's reputation than in the endearments of her love" (V.i.183-84). But whereas Mrs. Loveit's direct accusation will provoke Dorimant to label her coquetry with Sir Fopling "an infamy below the sin of prostitution with another man" (V.i.188-89), Harriet's metaphorical criticism piques Dorimant's interest because it attacks his rakish career without threatening to violate the libertine code of indirection; and so he answers in kind with a compliment, albeit a lascivious one: "Where there is a considerable sum to be won, the hope of drawing people in makes every trifle considerable" (III.iii.71-72).

Harriet also recognizes that Dorimant is so much the rake, he calculates every word and movement, and she therefore confronts him with the charge of affectation with which she had earlier surprised Young Bellair (III.iii.23-29):

DORIMANT.

That demure curtsy is not amiss in jest, but do not think in earnest it becomes you.

HARRIET.

Affectation is catching, I find. From your grave bow I got it.

(IV.i.100-103)

Harriet's retort tells Dorimant that she finds his pose—that of the libertine—no more attractive than he finds her assumed prudery. She also reminds him of their first meeting, when she imitated his pleasure in "the ladies' good liking" (III.iii.95-96) and showed him that she knew he was vain.[8] In each conversation with him, although she confesses her love in asides, Harriet treats Dorimant the way he treats Mrs. Loveit: she demonstrates that she thoroughly understands his character, forces him to confess his love, and leaves him:

HARRIET.

To men who have fared in this town like you, 'twould be a great mortification to live on hope. Could you keep Lent for a mistress?

DORIMANT.

In expectation of a happy Easter; and though time be very precious, think forty days well lost to gain your favor.

HARRIET.

Mr. Bellair! Let us walk, 'tis time to leave him. Men grow dull when they begin to be particular.

(III.iii.78-84)

By turning the libertine language to her own ends, and making it a vehicle for honest avowals rather than a cloak for profligacy (see also her religious metaphors in V.ii), Harriet forces Dorimant to confront the libertine ideology to which he subscribes, and to recognize that she, like Young Bellair, unites wit with love, desire with constancy.[9] The Restoration heroine, as John Harrington Smith points out, *must* marry, but at the same time neither she nor the man she loves can "surrender . . . individuality" to matrimony.[10] Etherege makes Harriet woo Dorimant in the libertine language to prove to him that he will not forfeit his independence if he falls in love with her.[11]

In Harriet's use of the libertine language to criticize as well as to fascinate Dorimant, Etherege matures the flirtation of his earlier heroes and heroines into a moral, as well as a sexual, confrontation. His first play, *The Comical Revenge: Or, Love in a Tub,* set the stakes low. Within the limited space they occupy in this plot-heavy play, neither the roistering Sir Frederick Frollick nor the independent Widow Rich appears to regard their eventual union as demanding more than a token sacrifice. (Sir Frederick disposes of his mistress Lucy with daunting insouciance.) Only one brief exchange suggests the extended banter Etherege would write for *The Man of Mode.* Repulsing her suitor's advances, the Widow adopts a military analogy:

WIDOW.

You cannot blame me for standing on my guard so near an enemy.

SIR FREDERICK.

If you are so good at that, widow, let's see, what guard would you choose to be at should the trumpet sound a charge to this dreadful foe?

WIDOW.

It is an idle question amongst experienced soldiers; but if we ever have a war, we'll never trouble the trumpet; the bells shall proclaim our quarrel.

SIR FREDERICK.

It will be most proper; they shall be rung backwards.

WIDOW.

Why so, sir?

SIR FREDERICK.

> I'll have all the helps that may be to allay a dangerous fire; widows must needs have furious flames; the bellows have been at work, and blown 'em up.

WIDOW.

> You grow too rude, sir.

> (II.i.85-101)[12]

This conversation demonstrates that the Widow and Sir Frederick deserve one another—they speak the same language. Yet they employ extended metaphors not, like Dorimant, to disguise the nature of their sexual activities, but simply for the fun of it (I read the Widow's "Why so, sir?" as a rueful admission that she can't quite follow his analogy).

Similarly, Ariana and Gatty in **She Would if She Could** secure the love of Freeman and Courtall through metaphorical repartee, even before removing their black velvet masks. (As Freeman exclaims, "I perceive, by your fooling here, that wit and good humour may make a man in love with a blackamoor" [II.i.161-63]). Fluent use of metaphor, however, merely ranks with the young ladies' other accomplishments, as Sir Joslin Jolly makes clear:

> so, boys, and how do you like the flesh and blood of the Jollies—heuk, Sly-girl—and Mad-cap, hey—come, come, you have heard them exercise their tongues a while; now you shall see them ply their feet a little: this is a clean-limbed wench, and has neither spavin, splinter, nor windgall; tune her a jig and play't roundly, you shall see her bounce it away like a nimble frigate before a fresh gale—hey, methinks I see her under sail already.
>
> Gatty *dances a jig.*
>
> (II.ii.235-43+s.d.)

In his last and most sophisticated comedy, however, Etherege transforms metaphor from the "*garniture*" of carefree flirtation into the defensive language of a society aware of its willful moral degradation.[13]

Throughout **The Man of Mode,** Etherege uses the image of the mask to illustrate the metaphorical technique of the libertines. Since Restoration masks are shaped like faces, a masker not only conceals his or her identity, but substitutes another face for his own, just as the language of the libertines exchanges a dangerous subject for an innocuous one. When Harriet prevents Dorimant from declaring his love by pointing out that both amorous words and looks are suspect, she makes the analogy of countenance and language explicit:

HARRIET.

> Do not speak it if you would have me believe it. Your tongue is so famed for falsehood, 'twill do the truth an injury. (*Turns away her head*)

DORIMANT.

> Turn not away, then, but look on me and guess it.

HARRIET.

> Did you not tell me there was no credit to be given to faces—that women nowadays have their passions as much at will as they have their complexions, and put on joy and sadness, scorn and kindness, with the same ease they do their paint and patches? Are they the only counterfeits?

> (V.ii.118-26)

In a conversation I quoted earlier, Harriet compares her desire for sincerity to appearing "barefaced in the playhouse," while noting that Dorimant prefers "masks." When a masked Sir Fopling crashes the party at Lady Townley's, the lovers' responses to his disguise apply pertinently to their own situation:

DORIMANT.

> What's here—masquerades?

HARRIET.

> I thought that foppery had been left off, and people might have been in private with a fiddle.

DORIMANT.

> 'Tis endeavored to be kept on foot still by some who find themselves the more acceptable, the less they are known.

> (IV.i.169-73)

Harriet's contempt for "that foppery" recalls her mimicry of Dorimant's affectation, while the fact that Dorimant has appeared at the party pretending to be Mr. Courtage gives his explanation of masquerades double significance: he, like Sir Fopling, is attempting to appear "the more acceptable." Yet despite her criticism of masks here and in her conversation with Busy in III.i, Harriet bewitches Dorimant by playing his game better than he does himself; *she* never unmasks, or allows her language to grow too "particular," and their courtship ends by reversing the play's established relationship between Dorimant and women:

DORIMANT.

> Is this all? Will you not promise me—

HARRIET.

> I hate to promise. What we do then is expected from us and wants much of the welcome it finds when it surprises.

> (V.ii.149-51)

Compare Harriet's refusal to commit herself to Bellinda's capitulation:

DORIMANT.

Be sure you come.

BELLINDA.

I sha' not.

DORIMANT.

Swear you will.

BELLINDA.

I dare not.

DORIMANT.

Swear, I say!

BELLINDA.

By my life, by all the happiness I hope for—

DORIMANT.

You will.

BELLINDA.

I will.

(III.ii.69-76)

The most important mask in the play, of course, is the "vizard" with whom Dorimant has been seen at the theater. At different moments in the play she is identified as a prostitute, as Mrs. Loveit, as Bellinda, and as Harriet. This collection demonstrates that the mask, like the language of the libertines, really covers Dorimant's sexual appetite, and, ultimately, his willingness to reform, while the various interpretations offered by the characters spring from their own response to libertinism. Mrs. Loveit, who has been ruined by Dorimant, believes the "vizard" to be what she herself has become: an "unknown, inconsiderable slut" (V.i.159). Bellinda mendaciously asserts that she had taken the woman for Mrs. Loveit, a deliberate substitution that marks her plunge into illicit sexuality, and confirms to us that she has replaced Mrs. Loveit as Dorimant's mistress (II.ii.75-85). Medley, who bears too much allegiance to the libertine code to peek beneath the mask, is content to speak of "a vizard" (I.i.184), while Young Bellair recognizes Bellinda, and his accuracy disconcerts Dorimant into an insult (I.i.380ff.). Finally, when Dorimant himself claims to unmask the lady, a disclosure comparable to "growing particular," he names Harriet, and declares his wish to marry her (V.ii.261-66).

Etherege understood the attractions of the libertine ideology, and recognized that to conclude *The Man of Mode* with absolute capitulation from Dorimant would be as awkward as the reversal Colley Cibber did *not* resist at the end of *Love's Last Shift*. Instead, Dorimant's marriage to Harriet is left conditional, and it is up to the imagination of the pit to decide whether the "devil" or the "angel . . . undefaced" will prevail in the hero's heart. (By ending the play with a test ordered by the heroine to judge the hero,

Etherege recalls Shakespeare's strategy in *Love's Labors Lost*, where the constancy of the gentlemen goes on trial as the curtain falls.) Nevertheless, that Dorimant accepts Lady Woodvill's invitation to Hartly, a surrender set amid the nuptial rejoicings of the other lovers, shows that the corrective impulse embodied in Harriet and in Harry Bellair is more powerful than the drive to libertinism, and can reform the community of the wits without destroying it. Because Harriet, unlike Mrs. Loveit, speaks the language of the libertines, she demands no unreasonable metamorphosis or confession. Instead, she cuts short Dorimant's extravagant vows of temperance, saying, "Hold! Though I wish you devout, I would not have you turn fanatic" (V.ii.137-38). Her words recall Medley's comparison of a man bent on marriage to a "mad fanatic . . . in Bethlem" and therefore suggest that Bellair's response to the analogy may now apply to Dorimant as well; he, too, need no longer live an atheist. By bringing Dorimant to confess the pangs of the passion to which he has always been an enemy, without ever herself violating *his* standards, she resolves the libertine dilemma. Harriet offers honesty in indirection, and virtue beneath a vizard.

Notes

1. All references to *The Man of Mode* are from *The Man of Mode*, ed. W. B. Carnochan, Regents Restoration Drama Series (Lincoln: Univ. of Nebraska Press, 1966).

2. Harriett Hawkins, *Likenesses of Truth in Elizabethan and Restoration Drama* (Oxford Univ. Press, 1976), p. 94.

3. Jocelyn Powell, "George Etherege and the Form of a Comedy," *Restoration Theatre*, ed. John Russell Brown (New York: St. Martin's Press, 1965), p. 60. See also Thomas H. Fujimura, *The Restoration Comedy of Wit* (Princeton: Princeton Univ. Press, 1952); Norman Holland, *The First Modern Comedies: The Significance of Etherege, Wycherley and Congreve* (Cambridge, MA: Harvard Univ. Press, 1959); John G. Hayman, "Dorimant and the Comedy of a Man of Mode," *MLQ* 30 (1969):183-97; and Dale Underwood, *Etherege and the Seventeenth-Century Comedy of Manners* (Hamden: Archon Books, 1969).

4. Laura Brown, *English Dramatic Form, 1660-1760: An Essay in Generic History* (New Haven: Yale Univ. Press, 1981), p. 41.

5. In his essay "Language and Action in *The Way of the World, Love's Last Shift* and *The Relapse*," *ELH* 40, 1 (1973):44-69, Alan Roper makes a similar argument about metaphor in Vanbrugh's play. He writes, "Berinthia's 'Virtue is its own Reward' is also strictly ironic in its use of a cliché of moral congratulation as a means of self-deprecation. As such, it is defensive. The metaphor enables Berinthia to talk about the fact without, as it were, referring to it. The metaphor places a shield of language between her and the actuality of her deeds and motives" (p. 56). Unlike Berinthia's defensive strategy, however,

Etherege's extended metaphors are spoken and shared by a community of wits, not all of whom require a "shield of language." And whereas Vanbrugh locates a moral voice in the plain-speaking Amanda (as Roper notes, "Amanda insists in reading off the literal sense" [p. 59]), thus clearly separating wit from wisdom, Etherege harmoniously confuses the two qualities in Harriet and Harry Bellair.

6. John G. Hayman argues that the wits strive to preserve "the semblance of *l'honnêteté*" (p. 187), and he describes "the tempting strategy that offered itself to a wit such as Dorimant: he might conform to the superficies of courtesy and use them to cloak an essentially antisocial nature" (p. 186). The libertine language offers the cover Dorimant requires.

7. W. B. Carnochan points out that a 1965 revival of *The Man of Mode* "was announced as the first since 1793" (p. xi); when confined to the printed page, as it was for 170 years of readers, Sir Fopling's exuberance is muted.

8. For other interpretations of the roles of dissembling, mimicry, and playacting in *The Man of Mode,* see two articles in *Restoration: Studies in English Literary Culture, 1660-1700* 6 (1982): James Thompson, "Lying and Dissembling in the Restoration," pp. 11-19; and Katherine Zapantis Keller, "Re-reading and Re-playing: An Approach to Restoration Comedy," pp. 64-71.

9. J. Douglas Canfield, in "Religious Language and Religious Meaning in Restoration Comedy," *SEL* 20 (1980):385-406, writes that "the religious language associated with Harriet and Dorimant's love . . . suggests the *possibility* of transcendence" (p. 388). Canfield rightly addresses the play's copious allusions to Christian ceremonies and to scripture; but by failing to note that the libertine language relies as well on metaphors of health, gambling, and masquerades (among others), Canfield's reading disproportionately emphasizes religious language as the key to Dorimant's potential reformation. It is Harriet's witty use of *all* these metaphors that attracts and disarms the rake. I do agree with Canfield's argument that the prevalence of religious ejaculations and allusions "also serves in part to portray this world as one in which such language has become merely a manner of speaking" (p. 389). Since the libertines employ metaphors to disguise antisocial behavior, images drawn from a religion reduced to a mere "manner of speaking" are particularly useful, for they lack any power beyond that which the libertines choose to bestow.

10. John Harrington Smith, *The Gay Couple in Restoration Comedy* (Cambridge, MA: Harvard Univ. Press, 1948), p. 49.

11. Similarly, Derek Hughes remarks that "when Dorimant tries to convince Harriet of his earnest feelings he can find no reliable words . . . since he has playfully misused them all in the past. . . . Harriet's task, therefore, is not only to reconcile love and play but to reconcile love and language," ("Play and Passion in *The Man of Mode," CompD* 15 [1981]:231-257; 237). I differ from Hughes in finding serious motives for Dorimant's linguistic strategy. Sheer "playfulness," on the other hand, does characterize the metaphorical exchanges of Etherege's two earlier dramas.

12. All references to *The Comical Revenge* and *She Would if She Could* are from *The Plays of Sir George Etherege,* ed. Michael Cordner (Cambridge and New York: Cambridge Univ. Press, 1982).

13. Other Restoration comedies usually employ extended metaphors simply to separate the wits from the gulls, as in this exchange from Wycherley's *The Country Wife:*

DORILANT.

Ay, ay, a gamester will be a gamester whilst his money lasts, and a whoremaster whilst his vigor.

HARCOURT.

Nay, I have known 'em when they are broke and can lose no more, keep a-fumbling with the box in their hands to fool with only, and hinder other gamesters.

DORILANT.

That had wherewithal to make lusty stakes.

PINCHWIFE.

Well, gentlemen, you may laugh at me, but you shall never lie with my wife; I know the town.

(*The Country Wife,* ed. Thomas H. Fujimura, Regents Restoration Drama Series [Lincoln: Univ. of Nebraska Press, 1965], I.i.421-28).

By insisting on the tenor, rather than the vehicle, of the conversation, Pinchwife excludes himself from witty society; but Dorilant and Harcourt, unlike Dorimant and Medley, do not *require* indirection. They spin out the metaphor for its own sake and for the pleasure of needling Pinchwife.

Michael Cordner (essay date 1994)

SOURCE: Cordner, Michael. "Etherege's *She Would If She Could*: Comedy, Complaisance and Anti-Climax." In *English Comedy,* edited by Michael Cordner, Peter Holland, and John Kerrigan, pp. 158-79. Cambridge: Cambridge University Press, 1994.

[*In the following essay, Cordner maintains that Etherege deliberately utilized the device of anti-climax in the courtship and marital discord plotlines in* She Would If She Could *to allow his rake-heroes the ability to maneuver successfully through the courtship process.*]

The première of George Etherege's second comedy was an unhappy occasion. The triumphant success of its predecessor and the subsequent delay of four years before the unveiling of this sequel heightened expectations in advance of the first performance of *She Would If She Could* on 6 February 1668 at the Duke's Playhouse in Lincoln's Inn Fields. But, in the event, the new play pleased almost no one. Samuel Pepys, who was present at the première, reported how most spectators in the pit agreed with him in blaming 'the play as a silly, dull thing, though there was something very roguish and witty; but the design of the play, and end, mighty insipid'. He did, however, also observe an embryonic group of dissenters from this prevailing view: 'among the rest, here was the Duke of Buckingham today openly sat in the pit; and there I found him with my Lord Buckhurst and Sidly and Etherige the poett—the last of whom I did hear mightily find fault with the Actors, that they were out of humour and had not their parts perfect'.[1]

Dramatists whose plays have just failed are apt to blame the actors' inadequacy for the disaster. But, in this case, others appear to have echoed Etherege's frustration. In 1671, Thomas Shadwell noted how 'imperfect Action [i.e. poor performance], had like to have destroy'd *She would if she could,* which I think (and I have the Authority of some of the best Judges in *England* for't) is the best Comedy that has been written since the Restauration of the Stage: And even that, for the imperfect representation of it at first, received such prejudice, that, had it not been for the favour of the *Court,* in all probability it had never got up again, and it suffers for it; in a great measure to this very day.'[2] So, Etherege's scapegoating of the players has here hardened into established fact, and socially and aesthetically influential opinion—'some of the best Judges' and 'the favour of the *Court*'—is at work to enthrone *She Would* as the 'best Comedy' written since 1660. Those 'Judges', we may presume, included Buckingham, Sedley and Buckhurst, all of whom had sat with Etherege in his moment of angry disappointment after the premiere. A narrowly constituted élite was seeking to instruct the wider theatre audience in the incorrectness of its taste. Shadwell's remarks suggest that, although they had made real headway by 1671, their work was still far from complete.[3]

The expectations of *She Would*'s original audience must have been partly shaped by memories of *The Comical Revenge,* its enormously popular predecessor of four years earlier. Etherege's first comedy is a bravura piece of playmaking, intertwining and counterbalancing four socially and stylistically disparate plots with an agility astonishing for a début performance. Beside it, *She Would* must have seemed puzzlingly minimalist, with its much smaller cast of characters, narrower linguistic register and relatively uneventful action. Modern attempts to characterise it indeed often begin by listing all the fundamentals of his earlier comic practice which Etherege has here chosen to do without. For its first audience also, it must have been easier to catalogue what had been mislaid during this process of stripping down than to recognise what might have been gained by it.

She Would's 'tissue-thin plot'[4] narrates the progress of the visit to London of Sir Oliver Cockwood and his wife, who are accompanied by Sir Oliver's bosom friend, Sir Joslin Jolly, and the latter's two young kinswomen, Gatty and Ariana. All the country characters see the capital as offering a release from the confinements of rural existence. All, in different ways, find it more difficult than they had anticipated to avail themselves freely of metropolitan liberties. Their fortunes in London interwine at every point with the peregrinations of Courtall and Freeman, described in the 1668 quarto's dramatis personae as 'two honest gentlemen of the town' (p. 110).[5] By the comedy's end, gallants and country heiresses appear, unsurprisingly, to be moving towards a marriage bargain.

Simple though *She Would*'s materials undeniably are, Etherege's structural ingenuity in their deployment should not be underestimated. His design provocatively combines a courtship narrative with an anatomy of an irretrievably failed marriage. The stories are so closely interwoven as to constitute a single plot. The four characters who may themselves be about to contract new matches thus have before their eyes throughout the play a vision of the kind of domestic hell to which they risk consigning themselves. The audience too is positioned so as to look 'upon this picture, and on this', its perception and judgement of the young quartet's conduct of themselves being significantly focussed and shaped by the simultaneous spectacle of the marital mayhem inflicted on each other by the Cockwoods. It is an elegantly brilliant mingling of plot materials—and one for which Etherege could have found no exact precedent in English comedy of the 1660s or, indeed, earlier. Once devised, however, it is the kind of structural mechanism which is almost fated to prompt imitation-cum-adaptation from other dramatists. Over the next fifty years, a sustained dialogue on marriage and its attendant woes would be conducted in a series of comedies—by such dramatists as Shadwell, Otway, Vanbrugh, Cibber and Farquhar—which are all linked by their use of that close yoking of courtship and marital disharmony actions pioneered by *She Would* in 1668.

Whatever its formal inventiveness, however, 'the design of the play' and its 'end' appeared, as we have already seen, 'mighty insipid' to Pepys and many others at its premiere. The risk of such a response is aired in the dialogue of *She Would* itself. In 3.1, Courtall and Freeman are coping with the discovery that the two pairs of girls they have been hunting together have disappointingly turned out to be one and the same:

COURTALL

> . . . that which troubles me most, is, we lost the hopes of variety, and a single intrigue in love is as dull as a single plot in a play, and will tire a lover worse, than t'other does an audience.

FREEMAN

> We cannot be long without some underplots in this town, let this be our main design, and if we are anything fortunate in our contrivance, we shall make it a pleasant comedy.

She vvou'd if She cou'd,

A

COMEDY.

ACTED AT HIS HIGHNESS

THE

Duke of York's

THEATER.

WRITTEN

By *GEORGE ETHEREGE* Efq;

In the *SAVOT*:

Printed by *T. N.* for *H. Herringman,* at the Sign of the *Blew Anchor* in the Lower-walk of the *New Exchange.* 1671.

Title page from a 1671 edition of She Would If She Could.

COURTALL

Leave all things to me, and hope the best . . .

(lines 112-21)

Such writing positively flaunts the meagreness of the narrative materials from which Etherege is seeking to build a play. It also assumes in at least some of its potential spectators a lively interest in the laws and logics of playmaking and the games which individual dramatists can play in eluding or reinventing the constraints of the conventional rule-book. And, finally, it aligns dramatist, gallant and spectator along a rakish continuum. The playgoer's delight in multiple-plot actions is analogised to the roving gentleman's preference for pursuing several amours simultaneously; and the playwright, in devising such a 'fortunate . . . contrivance' as a multiple plot, is similarly seen as playing to his own, and his spectator's, relish for a diversity of pleasurable stimuli. By implication, playwriting and playwatching are as naturally part of a male libertine's round of eroticised urban pleasures as his

multiple sexual laisons. Paradoxically, however, this exchange also reminds the audience that it is precisely this mandatory variousness of stimulus which Etherege's play has so far conspicuously failed to provide. *She Would* seems teasingly to be offering itself to be read as a comedy by a rake playwright which obstinately refuses to deliver the rakish pleasures which might be anticipated from it.

Since Etherege presumably does not wish to convict his comedy of insipidity, the insinuation must be that the discerning gallant—first as dramatist, then as spectator—can ingeniously contrive a connoisseur's delight for himself and his fellows even from the straitened narrative circumstances in which his fictional twins perforce operate in *She Would.* Such an intricate game with the arousal, disappointment and redirection of expectation asks of the audience a highly specialised and self-aware sophistication of response—an ambitious, possibly even an arrogant, demand, and one which was clearly not met by most of those present at the first performance on 6 February 1668.

Twentieth-century commentary has often coped with the quirky elusiveness of the play's tactics by assigning to it a questionable clarity of thematic organisation. Norman Holland, for instance, identified a 'contrast between liberty and restraint' as one of its key motifs and aligned that antithesis with a recurrent opposition between town and country:

> 'The Town' in the play stands for a place big enough, offering enough opportunities for anonymity, so that social restrictions do not really intefere with natural desires. Conversely, the country stands for a place where close observation makes social restrictions impinge directly on natural desires.[6]

The certainty that 'among the masse of people in *London,* and frequency of Vices of all sorts' an individual's self-indulgence 'might passe in the throng'[7] is often voiced in writing, dramatic and non-dramatic, of the 1660s. That a matching polarisation of town against country is at work in Etherege's text is evident, for example, from Sir Oliver's complaint that in the country 'if a man do but rap out an oath, the people start as if a gun went off' (1.1.93-4) and Lady Cockwood's relish at the prospect of enjoying 'the freedom of this place [i.e., London] again' (1.1.54-5). But Norman Holland is too inclined to take the word for the deed, since anonymity is precisely what neither country spouse can secure during their urban misadventures. Their every move towards adultery is checkmated by the inhibiting proximity of a close acquaintance or relative. The London staged in *She Would* is, in practice, a place small enough for eight principal characters constantly to interfere, by accident and/or design, with each other's indulgence of their 'natural desires'. The play's events do not, in other words, actualise the contrast between urban liberties and country restrictions which some of its dialogue takes for granted.

As a result, Freeman's certainty that 'We cannot be long without some underplots in this town' is mistaken. *She Would* permits its lead gallants only a single 'main design' on which to exercise their talents—and, in addition, one which tends ineluctably towards marriage with two resolutely chaste girls. Even here disappointments are played out. In 4.2, for example, forged letters make the men think that Gatty and Ariana may defy 'the modesty' of 'their sex' (line 108) and surrender to them 'without assault or summons' (lines 286-7), but their resultant cock-a-hoop brashness is rapidly deflated by a bruising encounter with the indignant victims of this slander. Thus, the gallants are not simply denied the variety they covet, but tantalisingly offered the phantom possibility that chastity might accommodatingly be revealed to be mere masquerade, only to have their hopes once again abruptly dashed.

Sir Oliver endures a parallel, but grotesquer, sequence of sexual anti-climaxes. Thus, in 3.3, he dances with a masked woman he imagines to be a whore, drooling over her 'exact and tempting' body (lines 299-300), only to be immediately floored by the revelation that the titillating disguise conceals his own wife, whose comprehensive lack of sexual allure for him he has just been corrosively expounding. This incident epitomises his fortunes in the play as a whole. Although confidently anticipating the 'variety' (3.3.41) London will afford him, he is in the event comprehensively defeated in his attempts to turn the single plot of detested monogamy into an adulterous double action with the help of the fabled whore, Madam Rampant. The latter's climactic encounter with Sir Oliver is frequently anticipated and never accomplished. The comedy's repeated forestalling of her imminent arrival onstage—a game played with ingenious variations right through to the final moments of Act 5[8]—presses home its commitment to disappointment as a central principle of its dramatic action.

Overturning its subjects' most cherished hopes is, of course, one of comedy's favourite stratagems. But *She Would*'s addiction to the humour of anti-climax is, even so, remarkably persistent and emphatic. The parallel between the careers of the gallants and the country buffoon hints that anti-climax ultimately here means matrimony. Sir Oliver, frustrated in his would-be libertinism, must finally return to the marital boredom he etched so vividly in his 1.1 dialogue with Courtall (lines 133ff.). Equally, Courtall's aphorism that 'a single intrigue in love is as dull as a single plot in a play, and will tire a lover worse, than t'other does an audience' cannot but cast a shadow forwards to the concluding marriage negotiations.

Whatever constraints may bind its leading male characters, however, the play's flamboyant title centres attention on those which trammel its female characters.[9] Its most obvious and most unflattering reference is to Lady Cockwood—driven by adulterous cravings, but relentlessly impeded by circumstances and her own inhibitions from satisfying them. But an early exchange between the girls implicitly acknowledges its application to them also:

GATTY

> . . . how I envy that sex! well! we cannot plague 'em enough when we have it in our power for those privileges which custom has allowed 'em above us.

ARIANA

> The truth is, they can run and ramble here, and there, and everywhere, and we poor fools rather think the better of 'em.

GATTY

> From one playhouse, to the other playhouse, and if they like neither the play nor the women, they seldom stay any longer than the combing of their periwigs, or a whisper or two with a friend; and then they cock their caps, and out they strut again.

> (1.2.163-73)

The women confidently demystify the familiar double standard—it is a matter of mere arbitrary 'custom'—but Etherege does not allow them to envision any substantive rebellion against it. Indeed, Ariana's 'we poor fools rather think the better of 'em' toys with the proposition that female folly can be relied upon to accommodate women to custom's inequalities. For some limited periods—'when we have it in our power'—a mocking revenge may be exacted; but the absolute differentiation between male and female liberties remains for them an unbudgeable fact of their social existence, as their next speeches make clear:

ARIANA

> But whatsoever we do, prithee now let us resolve to be mighty honest.

GATTY

> There I agree with thee.

ARIANA

> And if we find the gallants like lawless subjects, who the more their princes grant, the more they impudently crave—

GATTY

> We'll become absolute tyrants, and deprive 'em of all the privileges we gave 'em—

> ARIANA Upon these conditions I am contented to trail a pike under thee—march along girl.

> (lines 174-83)

The bold talk of behaving like 'absolute tyrants', with its confident-sounding inversion of the conventional seventeenth-century male/monarch, female/subject analogies, only temporarily masks the girls' acceptance that in the contest between the sexes society decrees that the advantage finally lies with the men. This conclusion is underscored by their firm identification of the playhouse itself—in which their dialogue is, after all, written to be spoken—as an arena dedicated to the enactment of specifically male freedoms of behaviour. (Women are present there in this account only to catch the glance of the ranging gallant and possibly detain his interest for some short time.) Their exchanges thus chime revealingly with the automatic assumption of Courtall and Freeman in 3.1 that the natural spectator for the kind of comedy in which the gallants envisage participating is male.

Thus, Etherege gives Gatty and Ariana an eager desire to emulate male freedoms if they could, but also burdens them with the conviction that their society allows them no discreet or safe way of achieving this. In addition, he allows them to waste no time hankering after what they are told is unobtainable, but instead has them calmly resolve to play within the socially prescribed limits for their sex and class. The ease with which he has them accommodate themselves to those limits clearly works to ratify, not problematise, the double standard. As a result, neither of the girls has been positioned by him so as to be able to apply rigorously reformist pressure with conviction to the gallant she may marry. The women's resolution to be 'mighty honest' is an obeisance to social necessity, not a commitment to a moral imperative, while their imaginative sympathies still surreptitiously lie with the liberties permitted to, and enjoyed by, the rakes. They can thus provide the men with congenial sparring partners in their courtship combats, but can never be radically challenging interrogators of the gallants' way of life.

To all of this Lady Cockwood works as a formidable foil. Gatty and Ariana may imagine becoming 'absolute tyrants' if the men overstep the limits of modesty, but Lady Cockwood's behaviour is constantly imaged in terms of an indecorous and grotesque usurpation of power. Her manipulation and subjugation of Sir Oliver, for instance, are monarchical and absolutist. Emboldened by drink, he dares to berate her as 'a very Pharaoh', who 'by wicked policy . . . would usurp my empire' and is 'every night . . . a-putting me upon making brick without straw' (2.2.176-9). In a moment of guilt-stricken panic, on the other hand, he cravenly acknowledges the legitimacy of her enforced rule and foresees himself indicted for a 'premunire' (3.3.330), that is, an act in contempt of her royal prerogative. Even as she comprehensively unmans her husband and denudes him of authority, so she proves imperious and authoritarian in her conduct towards her targeted gallant. Courtall, her potential victim, regards her as 'the very spirit of impertinence', who 'would by her good will give her lover no more rest, than a young squire that has newly set up a coach, does his only pair of horses' (1.1.265, 278-81). In a text where the gallants repeatedly chart their erotic quests in analogies drawn from gentlemanly field sports, Lady Cockwood, in her usurping of male initiative, appears to Courtall as a 'ravenous kite' that 'will be here within this half hour to swoop me away' or a 'long-winged devil' that may 'truss me' before rescue intervenes (3.1.65-6, 87-8). The play thus portrays its embodiment of rampant female desire as comically grotesque and incipiently unnerving.

It also condemns her to a permanent, bathetic failure to find sexual fulfilment. Cheated by hostile circumstances, she is also incapacitated by 'a strange infirmity' (2.2.110) of mind. While invincibly addicted to the pursuit of

adulterous consummation, she has so totally internalised her society's insistence on the maintenance of the decorums of female honour that she cannot ever admit to herself the nature of the fleshly imperative which drives her. The wild contradictions and extremes of behaviour which result from this furnish a spectator-sport which the play invites its audience to relish. They also generate moments of passionate extravagance which turn genuinely enigmatic. During her frenzied denunciation of Sir Oliver in 3.3, for example, for attempting the crime she had herself also been set on, it is impossible to disentangle premeditation and bad faith from authentic, yet completely self-deceiving, outrage. As Courtall observes, 'Sure she will take up anon, or crack her mind, or else the devil's in't' (3.3.374-5). Sir Oliver's self-prostration in the same scene is similarly ambiguous. Ariana notes, 'How bitterly he weeps! how sadly he sighs!', and Gatty replies, 'I dare say he counterfeited his sin, and is real in his repentance' (lines 395-7). This total dissolution of self-knowledge and self-control in husband and wife is clearly intended to contrast with 'the skeptical, yet civil powerbroking of the young lovers'.[10] Yet the play's notion of clear-eyed prudence for a woman appears to prescribe that Gatty and Ariana must know the limits set down for them and eschew the imperial delusions which are so comprehensively discredited by Lady Cockwood's cavortings.

I recognise that many recent accounts of the play discern a quite different pattern at work in it—one which compels the rakes to relinquish substantial freedoms as the play proceeds. One of the most challenging of such readings, for instance, proposes that 'To be a rake, especially at the wrong time, is in this play to come close to being a fool', and also that 'As the play proceeds, the audience is shown that those areas which the rake-hero might reasonably expect to control, be they places in town or stage-devices, work against him until the rake must abandon his claim to social control.' In the play's concluding stages, the rake, 'made dupe-like', must as a consequence 'accept his fall into the state of grace', and central to that acceptance is 'his new distrust of himself'.[11] That Courtall and Freeman are at key moments wrongfooted and outwitted by one or more of the women is undeniable. It is also fundamental to my understanding of the play that there is a carefully calculated ill match between the rakes' instinct for variety and the single, marriage-destined action in which they are assigned to perform. None of this, however, makes it apparent to me that, in the longer run, the rake-hero's 'claim to social control' is itself seriously threatened in *She Would,* nor do I easily recognise the alleged 'new distrust of himself' in Courtall's concluding conduct.

A brief excursion into a comparison with other plays of the late 1660s can, I think, help here. Etherege was not the only Court Wit to have a premiere which flopped during the 1667-8 season. The first performance of Sir Charles Sedley's first play, *The Mulberry Garden,* at the King's Playhouse on 18 May 1668, was in many ways a re-run of *She Would*'s three months earlier. Pepys was once again present to report the audience's advance hopes and the ensuing sad anti-climax.[12] The two dramatists were close friends, and Sedley's modern biographer plausibly imagines the plays as being the product of 'some kind of friendly rivalry' between them.[13] A month before the première of **She Would,** Sedley's working title for his own comedy appears to have been *The Wandering Ladies,*[14] a choice which points up the play's similarities in plot, since in both virtuous country ladies, newly arrived in London and eager to enjoy the freedoms the capital offers, find their reputations at risk as a result of the misrepresentation of their conduct by others. In both **She Would** and *The Mulberry Garden,* this crisis breeds an Act 4 confrontation in one of London's pleasure gardens between the ladies and the gallants they blame for their discrediting. Sedley and Etherege were clearly not writing in total ignorance of each other's designs.

An interpretative context for Sedley's comedy is provided by his having designed the leading roles of Wildish and Olivia for the King's Company's star partnership of Charles Hart and Nell Gwyn. This duo had a formidable influence on innovative comic writing in the 1660s, and it might be expected that Sedley would tailor his invention to their established strengths. Their particular specialty was in playing 'witty, amoral, "mad couples"',[15] flamboyant freethinkers, exuberantly out of step with the straitlaced communities in which they find themselves. In early 1668, the finest play yet inspired by their partnership was undoubtedly John Dryden's *Secret Love, Or The Maiden Queen* (1667), in which Hart played the congenitally inconstant Celadon. His mercurial unreliability attracts Florimell (Gwyn's role), but she also sets herself to curb it. Ultimately, that means imposing marriage on him. In the play's early stages, none of his promises to her are fully earnest, his recidivism always predestined. Whatever his ruses, however, he can never keep his other loves secret from her, a pattern which climaxes with a joyous setpiece, in which Florimell, disguised as a dashing male courtier in the latest fashionable garb, diverts two girls Celadon is aiming to seduce into her/his own possession and right from under Celadon's nose. This total undermining of male braggadocio epitomises the play's consistent awarding of the superiority in wit to Florimell. In their concluding marriage-bargaining—the first great proviso scene of the post-1660 comedy—they devise agreed liberties to alleviate what each sees as wedlock's most troublesome and deadening constraints. It is clearly, however, Florimell who now has the negotiating initiative. When she asks him, 'is not such a marriage as good as wenching, *Celadon*?', he wistfully replies, 'This is very good, but not so good, *Florimell*' (5.1.560-2).[16]

Florimell's adoption of male dress to invade and colonise the rake's domain finds its corollary—in the play's other, heroic plot—in the Queen of Sicily's eventually confident manipulation of the conventionally male role of monarch. The Queen and Florimell are their respective 'plots' prime movers and most fully realized characters, authoritative, willful, single-minded, sometimes unscrupulous'. Both 'test their lovers without revealing their own feelings,

keeping their "secrets" intact'.[17] In the words of Rothstein and Kavenik, 'Dryden's feminizing of *Secret Love* puts women on an equal footing in nature with men'; the obstacles its principal female characters confront are 'the result of social constraints that bind women differently from men, rather than of a difference in nature'.[18] In this play, those constraints are never definitively eroded or defied. Just as Florimell has finally to lure the straying Celadon into the traditional 'safety' of marriage, so the Queen's climactic coup, in relinquishing her 'secret love' and resolving never to marry, is a concession to those 'social constraints that bind women', since her society effectively prescribes that she cannot enjoy power and the fulfilment of her love simultaneously. But the play leaves her supreme over her political world, as it leaves Florimell surefootedly dictating terms to Celadon. No earlier post-1660 play had awarded one woman, let alone two, so pre-eminent a role in its dramatic power-structure.

Echoes of *Secret Love* are discernible in *The Mulberry Garden.* But Sedley decisively redistributes the balance of power between his leading players. Rebuked by Olivia for his libelling of women, Wildish replies, 'Why, Madam, I thought you had understood Raillery', and then explains:

> . . . this is only the way of talking I have got among my Companions, where when we meet over a Bottle of Wine, 'tis held as great a part of wit to rallee women handsomly behind their back, as to flatter 'um to their Faces.
>
> (2.1.84-5, 87-91)[19]

So, style and content of discourse become entirely relative to company, the crucial distinctions being largely drawn on gender lines. Wildish's confession is also a challenge. If his language, chameleon-like, adapts itself to the company he is in, does that not reduce all his avowals of love to her to mere compliance with expected norms? Even as he accommodates himself to conventional decorums, he signals clearly, almost insultingly, that this is indeed what he is doing and thus initiates a far more elaborately knowing courtship game than in any earlier Hart/Gwyn pairing.

Although Sedley deals Olivia/Gwyn many telling put-downs and incisive challenges along the way, it is to Wildish/Hart that he awards the agenda-setting role. This is never clearer than in 4.1, a scene which invites comparison with Florimell's routing of Celadon in male disguise. Gwyn is again assigned a comic routine in which she becomes privy to male secrets which she can then use to devastating effect. But, this time, Hart is not the victim of the revelations, but the smug contriver of others' humiliation. Olivia and her sister listen from concealment while Wildish lures Modish and Estridge into boasting that they have enjoyed the two ladies' favours. The dupes are susceptible because of their sense of how kudos is acquired in all-male society: as Modish says, 'it sounds handsomly, to boast some familiarity' (lines 90-1). The incident Wildish stages thus demonstrates brilliantly his claim that company subdues men to its norms, since it is apparent that, without his temptation, neither Modish nor Estridge would have dared contemplate making such an outrageous allegation. It equally proclaims, of course, his capacity, as trickster, to manipulate the workings of company to his advantage and thus makes him an exception to his gener- alisation, since what distinguishes him from his victims is the difference between craven compliance with social norms and the capacity to use them as a tool for one's own ends.

Wildish's chameleon manipulativeness in this scene finds no equivalent in Olivia's narrower repertoire. Early in the play, she defines the love-game in a way which promises fireworks to follow:

> . . . the great pleasure of Gaming were lost, if we saw one anothers hands; and of Love, if we knew one an- others Hearts: there would be no room for good Play in the One, nor for Address in the other; which are the refin'd parts of both.
>
> (1.3.32-7)

But such fine phrase-making does not yield the expected dividends. For much of the play, Olivia's concealment of her true feelings is only nominal; Wildish is placed in no serious doubt. And the combat between them is often not, as the gaming simile here proposes, waged between two equal players. In *Secret Love,* Florimell invaded Celadon's world and unmasked his secrets. In *The Mulberry Garden,* Olivia merely witnesses Wildish's staging of the indiscre- tions of which he can make two pliable idiots capable. He himself eludes, and defies, unmasking. The Dryden scene feeds off, and celebrates, Gwyn's intense theatricality. Sedley's subdues her and gives centre-stage to Hart—and to the rake's capacity to remain almost infinitely flexible and manipulative. The two plays thus represent dia- metrically opposed responses to the challenge of creating a script for the Hart/Gwyn team. Theatrically, Sedley's looks, and proved, the riskier. Cramping the exuberant wildness which was Gwyn's trademark was unlikely to recommend itself readily to an audience which had ap- plauded her recent successes. That Sedley should, even so, have attempted it may simply reflect a misguided desire on his part to ring surprising changes on a renowned stage partnership. But his choice of tactics can clearly also be read as a reaction against Dryden's emphatic favouring of his two leading actresses in the contest between the sexes in *Secret Love.* Sedley and Etherege, writing in knowledge of each other's stage projects, seem to be at one in a desire to set limits to female freedoms.

As we have already seen, **She Would** also contains an Act 4 episode in which a pair of country ladies tongue-lash two gentlemen for having traduced them. In Etherege's version, however, the men under attack are the play's lead gallants, not second-string dupes. They are also innocent of the offence they are charged with. The acrimony is orchestrated by a revengeful Lady Cockwood, who has discovered not only that Courtall does not reciprocate her

passion for him, but that he has been concealing from her his designs on Gatty. The matching incident in *The Mulberry Garden,* like the scene of Florimell's male masquerade, finally resolves itself into a relatively simple display-piece in which one character demonstrates at length and without serious opposition the supremacy of his wit over other contenders. Etherege's scene charts a tenser struggle for control, from which, as yet, no certain victor emerges. Lady Cockwood, arriving to relish her handiwork, finds herself at risk of exposure from the gal- lants' quick-thinking deductions, and only the violent erup- tion of a drunken Sir Oliver to embroil Courtall in a sword- fight temporarily reprieves her. At the act's end, it remains unsettled whether the advantage will finally lie with her or with Courtall. Sir Oliver earlier pictured his marriage as a state of 'perpetual civil war' (3.3.283). The play's larger community seems at this point to be overtaken by a comparable fate. Yet, at the comedy's end, general reconciliation has been accomplished, and Lady Cockwood is once again 'in charity' with Courtall (5.1.417-18). Etherege here sets himself a larger dramatic problem than Sedley attempted. He solves it, however, by the same means—the improvisatory dexterity of the rake. In the process, he makes Courtall justify the name he bestowed on him.

In 1.1, an astonished and admiring Freeman watches from hiding the suppleness with which his friend adapts himself to dealing in quick and potentially disastrous succession with an unexpected visit from Sentry, Lady Cockwood's servant and confederate, and then the inopportunely overlapping arrival of Sir Oliver. Freeman's applause— 'the scene was very pleasant' (lines 230-1)—pinpoints the theatricality of the actions he has witnessed. He is also awed by the extreme skill of Courtall's performance: 'I admire thy impudence, I could never have had the face to have wheedled the poor knight so' (lines 231-3). Their subsequent exchanges draw from Courtall a revealing definition of gentlemanly conduct. In dealing with, and eluding, Lady Cockwood's advances, he tells Freeman, he has consistently 'carried it so like a gentleman, that she has not had the least suspicion of unkindness' (lines 263- 5). A gentleman thus secures his own interests without seeming to rebuff those whose aims threaten to collide with his. Indeed, he always seeks to maintain amity with the latter. To achieve that requires quasi-diplomatic skills of a high order.

As Susan Staves has observed, the flow of books from the presses on conduct and social interaction in the 1660s and 1670s presumed, and fed, a contemporary conviction 'that modes and manners were changing with unusual rapidity'.[20] The exposition of the arts of complaisance in some of these texts could easily be exemplified from Courtall's ac- tions in **She Would.** In this definition, complaisance is fundamentally a political skill, capable of application to either national or domestic challenges. According to a key text of the 1670s (derived in large part from an earlier French source), 'this admirable Art . . . by a secret and most powerful charm, calms the displeasures of tyrants, disarms or averts the fury of our enemies, & wrests the sword from the hand of vengeance, all this it does by its submissions, and by perswading them that we have devested our own enmity, and changed it into a true friendship'. It asks of its disciples a '*dexterity*, by means whereof we dispatch our affairs with the most happiness, rendring that which is difficult, easie and pleasant, receiving and representing all things without gall or bitterness'. It also requires '*Affability*', which 'consists . . . principally in the knowledge to give an obliging reception to all persons, to entertain them with freedom and kindness, to salute, honour and respect them, in short, by all outward signs, and Caresses that may assure them of our Courtesie and good will, giving them by these attractive wayes, all the assurance and confidence that may be'.[21]

The advocates of the civil virtues of complaisance tend to presume 'a threatening world in which considerable skill is needed to avoid giving offense'. Among its benefits, 'by making gentlemen slower to take affront, it avoids violence'. It is also a technique to ensure privacy, even secrecy: 'in a world increasingly filled with importuning but apparently genteel strangers, complaisance is a way to avoid unwanted intimate contact with them'.[22] Courtall's handling of the Cockwoods in *She Would*'s early acts illustrates his mastery of the art. Thus, Sir Oliver is convinced of his own intimacy with the gallant, while being allowed to discern no hint of the reserve and disdain with which Courtall actually regards him. Similarly, Lady Cockwood's designs on him are repeatedly disappointed, without her detecting his responsibility for this. She remains convinced that this 'heroic sir' (3.1.198) is as distressed as she is by their failure to consummate. Her emergence as 'Madam Machiavil' (4.2.305) in Act 4 is provoked by her belated recognition of how radically deceptive his anodyne behaviour has been. But, in a neatly punitive irony, her final accommodation with him is founded on her own need for his ready way with a lie. Her declaration of war produces a crisis in which even Sir Oliver is likely to register her double dealing. Only Courtall commands the required fluency in improvisation to rescue her with a comprehensive, fictitious explanation of all incriminating circumstances. He thus demonstrates complaisance's talent for devising 'lenitive Unctions' and 'Insinuating them sweetly into the spirit of those to whom we speak'.[23] In the process, he also covers his own tracks, by obscuring his previous association with Lady Cockwood from the girls. Whatever tactical reverses, therefore, he may have suffered during the action, Courtall's 'impudence' remains as limber in the final scene as when Freeman first admiringly witnessed it in action in 1.1. Etherege also makes that 'impudence' the indispensable constituent of the peacemaking with which *She Would* ends. In teaching him how to 'court all' with such agility, complaisance fulfils its claims to be '*an Art*' which can '*regulate our words and behaviour, in such a manner as may engage the love and respect of those with whom we Converse*'.[24]

Complaisance, with its resources of strategic reticence, is here the monopoly of the male gallant. In this play, it is

the men's prerogative to unmask the women's secrets, while much about the rakes' conduct and natures remains opaque to Gatty and Ariana. Etherege decrees a sequence of farcical coincidences in Act 5 which leads to the gallants being concealed in a closet in the Cockwoods' lodgings. There they overhear the girls talking privately. The latter's susceptibility to being wooed into an easy reconciliation with the men is first made clear:

GATTY

. . . time will make it out, I hope, to the advantage of the gentlemen.

ARIANA

I would gladly have it so; for I believe, should they give us a just cause, we should find it a hard task to hate them.

(lines 331-5)

Gatty then sings a song which she has come to love since meeting Courtall. It confesses to an overwhelming obsession with a man met in her 'rambles' (line 340) in town and concludes:

My passion shall kill me before I will show it,
And yet I would give all the world he did know it;
But oh how I sigh, when I think should he woo me,
I cannot deny what I know would undo me!

(lines 346-9)

The play's title has a double application here. In the first couplet, female modesty forbids her to voice the passion she wishes to declare. In the second, she imagines how, faced with Courtall's direct wooing, one part of her mind at least would wish, but be unable, to evade admitting her love. That such a weakness would lead to her undoing is the thought on which the song concludes.

By contriving their overhearing of this, Etherege has stacked the cards massively in the gallants' favour. In 1.2, referring to Lady Cockwood, Gatty wished this curse on herself: 'if she does not dissemble, may I still be discovered when I do' (lines 123-4). In 5.1, her capacity to dissemble in her courtship games with Courtall is taken from her at a stroke. She justifies the boldness of her song to an alarmed Ariana in this way:

I hate to dissemble when I need not; 'twould look as affected in us to be reserved now w'are alone, as for a player to maintain the character she acts in the tiring-room.

(lines 351-44)

But such frank speaking is allowable to her only because the two women think they are alone. If *The Mulberry Garden* built a scene around two country ladies overhearing the 'way of talking' native to all-male company, *She Would* reverses the situation to open the girls' privacy to the gallants' surveillance. Gatty's comparison of the girls to players 'in the tiring-room' gains piquancy from the recurrent association of the rakes—as playwrights, spectators and actors—with the world of the playhouse. Thus, in 3.1, they compare the pleasures offered by single and double plots, in 3.3 Courtall casually sends to the theatre for 'masking-habits' to enhance the plot 'design' (lines 242, 245) he is himself now crafting, and in 4.1 Sentry can sufficiently rely on their addictedness to the playhouse to be certain where they will be during performance time (lines 11-12). It is therefore logical that their moment of final emplowerment *vis-à-vis* the girls should also be implicitly analogised to their activities as playhouse habitués. In the 1660s theatres, gallants took to themselves total rights of access to actresses' dressing-rooms. Etherege accords the characters the privileges comparable command over the retirement of the girls they pursue.

That there is in **She Would** a male kingdom of discourse the girls never penetrate is equally apparent. In 3.3, the gallants try to appease his wife's fury by explaining that Sir Oliver's lewd swaggering is 'mere raillery, a way of talk, which Sir Oliver being well-bred, has learned among the gay people of the town' (lines 399-401). There are two levels of irony here: Sir Oliver is, in any case, only capable of talk, not action, and his notion of rakishness, with its wild boasts and flamboyant crudeness, is—far from 'being well-bred'—at best a parody of yesterday's theatrical model of the style. In **She Would,** the modern rake cultivates the composure and even affability of manner which complaisance recommends. Far from flaunting his libertine credentials, he aims to be seamlessly absorbed into civil society. His devotion to his own self-interest and empire-building, however, is not diminished by this. Nor is the ruthlessness with which he may treat the women who place themselves at his mercy. Speaking the dialect of their rakish tribe to Freeman in private, Courtall, for example, asserts that 'talk [i.e., boasting of one's dealings with a specific woman] is only allowable at the latter end of an intrigue, and should never be used at the beginning of an amour, for fear of frighting a young lady from her good intentions' (4.2.99-102). The two men may be innocent of slandering Gatty and Ariana, but we are thus instructed that they are indeed capable of similar actions, when it serves their purposes and pleasures. Their power-play also potentially pits them against each other. When Freeman suggests to his friend that he might 'with your good leave . . . outbid you for her ladyship's favour' (4.2.163-4), the steely limits of complaisance are briefly glimpsed in Courtall's reply:

> I should never have consented to that, Frank; though I am a little resty at present, I am not such a jade, but I should strain if another rid against me; I have ere now liked nothing in a woman that I have loved at last in spite only, because another had a mind to her.

> (lines 165-70)

The mask, thereafter, is immediately reassumed.

The girls are never vouchsafed a comparable revelation. At the comedy's end, they insist on 'a month's experience of your good behaviour' (5.1.567-8) before final agreement. But this is more a sop to their own self-esteem than a real testing of the gallants' mettle. Complaisance is, after all, an art precisely designed to assure others of 'your good behaviour', while you pursue your own agenda which may even be antagonistic to theirs. Etherege has designed the action so that the rakes, while stooping to the possibility of marriage, have in the process conceded nothing of substance to the girls they woo. Crucially, this is a play without a proviso scene. All that the girls propose to test in its imagined sixth act is whether, 'upon serious thoughts' (line 568), the men will still want 'to engage further'. Their right to retreat is therefore freely conceded. It is also clearly presumed that, if they prove resolute, the girls will, of course, take them. In addition, Gatty and Ariana have not been given the nerve or negotiating muscle to imitate Florimell's precedent and insist on a contract which stipulates penalties for post-marital recidivism by the husband. The extent to which the advantage is here being conceded to the men is further confirmed by the fact that Act 5 also marks Freeman's full coming-of-age. Despite Courtall's warning, he makes an abortive move towards adultery with Lady Cockwood and later meets his friend's suspicions about this with the suave and fraudulent explanation that his visit to her had been part of an innocent attempt to 'clear ourselves to the young ladies' (5.1.471). The erstwhile apprentice thus demonstrates that he too has mastered the arts of complaisance.

My exploration of **She Would** began by noting how it seemed to be offering itself to be read as a play by a rake playwright which was refusing to provide its spectators with the expected rakish pleasures. My subsequent interpretation has moved towards a related, but inverse, account of it. In this version, although the comedy may at first glance seem to relate the process whereby two gallants, used to richer liberties, are subdued to the anti-climax of marriage, a closer reading suggests that within theoretically uncongenial narrative circumstances the rakes contrive a showcase for the complaisant dexterities in which they most excel and in the process largely preserve their own freedom of action. Against the odds, therefore, rakish ingenuity proves that it can make 'a pleasant comedy' (3.1.120) for itself even out of a plot which is unrelievedly single.

There remains one final use of anti-climax to be noted in **She Would.** The confinement of Courtall and Freeman to a single plot heads them towards what for the rake, with his devotion to variety, threatens to be the ultimate anticlimax, matrimony. But its final pages defer that closure to beyond the play's own timespan, if ever. Having identified its likely ending as potentially anti-climactic, **She Would** then suavely cheats expectation yet again by preferring a conclusion which, in effect, does not conclude. The Cockwoods and the girls have been assigned fixed positions of passion, but the rakes are not similarly tethered. All their options remain theoretically open. Freezing the action at this point leaves them permanently poised at the moment before a decision which could begin to foreclose on some of those options.

Modern commentary has made much of a response Courtall makes to Sir Joslin:

SIR JOSLIN

   . . . and is it a match, boys?

COURTALL

   If the heart of man be not very deceitful, 'tis very likely it may be so.

                        (5.1.571-4)

Dale Underwood, for instance, detects here what he notates as the concluding stage of 'the typical curve of the comic hero—from conviction to experience to doubt'.[25] As the preceding pages will have made clear, I see no evidence that this allegedly 'typical curve' is followed by either Courtall or Freeman. Interrogating the 'heart' of either gallant has never been seriously on the agenda in *She Would.* Similarly, imputing self-doubt—or, indeed, bad faith—to Courtall at this point takes us far beyond what the text justifies. All the play presents us with in these concluding moments are further instances of his assuredly complaisant behaviour. That Gatty engages and stimulates him is evident. Anything beyond that remains mere surmise—as is surely teasingly implied by the conditionality of the form in which Courtall's reply to Sir Joslin is cast.

As Ted Cohen has reminded us, jokes possess 'the capacity to form or acknowledge a . . . community and thereby to establish an intimacy between the teller and the hearer'.[26] Such communities can be generous in the width of their embrace or very selectively constituted. All joking relationships work to exclude some potential participants who, for one reason or another, are not positioned so as to be able to understand and/or relish the joke. The principle that works for the single joke also applies to the more elaborate procedures of a five-act comic play. A persistent, but unfounded, myth would have it that audiences in the 1660s were overwhelmingly dominated by courtiers and courtly tastes.[27] *She Would*'s difficult progress into acceptance by its early audiences should in itself have suggested some of the problems this mythology left unaddressed. If my analysis of the play is on the right lines, then one deduction to be made from it is that Etherege partly brought that initial failure on his own head, since his play is designed to be fully savoured only by a relatively narrow community of laughers. The 'Model Spectator' anticipated by the text[28] is precisely the élite one defined by that exchange between the gallants in 3.1. If one cannot confidently locate oneself somewhere on that rakish continuum between lead character, author and imagined spectator, then some of the play's more intimate pleasures will always appear elusive, perhaps indeed inaccessible.

All this has one crucial consequence for Etherege's handling of his structural innovation in yoking so closely courtship and marital disharmony actions in a single comedy. One obvious extrapolation from such a fusion is clearly that the spectacle of a marriage on the rocks should spur those premeditating wedlock in the same play into attempting to ensure that their own prospective unions do not reproduce the catastrophes inflicted on themselves by their elders. Etherege's jealous preservation of his rakes' freedom of manoeuvre means that he does not seek to realise this possibility. What a marriage between Courtall and Gatty or Freeman and Ariana might be like is—as the absence of a proviso scene suggests—left essentially unaddressed in *She Would.* A consequence of this is that Etherege has, in effect, bequeathed this as a potentiality of the form to be developed by some of his successors. In doing so, as also in devising other ingenious and pertinent employment to which it can be put, some of them went on to develop very different notions of an Ideal Spectator or Spectators from that which guided the composition of *She Would.*

Notes

1. Samuel Pepys, *Diary,* eds. Robert Latham and William Matthews (London, 1970-83), IX, 54.

2. Thomas Shadwell, 'Preface to *The Humorists*', *Complete Works,* ed. Montague Summers (London, 1927), I, 183.

3. This concerted advocacy of the play's merits left a clear imprint on late seventeenth- and early eighteenth-century retrospects on early Restoration drama. Gerard Langbaine, for instance, recorded that *She Would* is 'accounted one of the first Rank, by several who are known to be good Judges of Dramatick Poesy', to which select number he now added Shadwell's name (*An Account of the English Dramatick Poets* (Oxford, 1691), 187). For John Dennis in 1702, the play was an example of the unreliability of popular taste, mistreated by 'the People at first, tho at the same time it was esteem'd by the Men of Sense, for the trueness of some of its Characters, and the purity and freeness and easie grace of its Dialogue', a critical judgement fully vindicated, he alleges, by its having been subsequently 'acted with a general applause' (*Critical Works,* ed. Edward Niles Hooker (Baltimore, 1939-43), I, 289). Six years later, however, John Downes put Dennis's claims into due perspective. In the end, he tells us, it 'took well', but always 'inferior to' Etherege's first play (*Roscius Anglicanus* (London, 1708), 29).

4. John Harold Wilson, *The Court Wits of the Restoration: An Introduction* (Princeton, 1948), 152-3.

5. References for *She Would If She Could* are taken from Sir George Etherege, *Plays,* ed. Michael Cordner (Cambridge, 1982).

6. Norman N. Holland, *The First Modern Comedies: The Significance of Etherege, Wycherley, and Congreve* (Cambridge, Mass. 1959), 29.

7. [James Heath], *Flagellum: Or The Life and Death, Birth and Burial of O. Cromwell The Late Usurper: Faithfully Described* (3rd edn: London, 1665), 9.

8. On the issues surrounding the staging of Madam Rampant's final near-arrival, see the note to the stage direction at 5.1.552, in my edition of Etherege's *Plays* (Cambridge, 1982), 205.

9. In 1711, the title drew this comment from Richard Steele: 'Other Poets have, here and there, given an Intimation that there is this Design, under all the Disguises and Affectations which a Lady may put on; but no Author, except this, has made sure Work of it, and put the Imaginations of the Audience upon this one Purpose, from the Beginning to the End of the Comedy' (*The Spectator,* ed. Donald F. Bond (Oxford, 1965), I, 217).

10. Michael Neill, 'Heroic Heads and Humble Tails: Sex, Politics, and the Restoration Comic Rake', *The Eighteenth Century,* 24 (1983), 127.

11. Peter Holland, *The Ornament of Action Text and Performance in Restoration Comedy* (Cambridge, 1979), 51, 53.

12. Samuel Pepys, *Diary,* IX, 203.

13. V. De Sola Pinto, *Sir Charles Sedley 1639-1701 A Study in the Life and Literature of the Restoration* (London, 1927), 104.

14. Samuel Pepys, *Diary,* IX, 203.

15. Katharine Eisaman Maus, '"Playhouse Flesh and Blood": Sexual Ideology and the Restoration Actress', *ELH,* 46 (1979), 599.

16. John Dryden, *Works* (Berkeley, Los Angeles, London, 1961-), IX, ed. John Loftis and Vinton A. Dearing, 200.

17. Eric Rothstein and Frances M. Kavenik, *The Designs of Carolean Comedy* (Carbondale and Edwardsville, 1988), 140.

18. Eric Rothstein and Frances M. Kavenik, *The Designs of Carolean Comedy,* 139.

19. References for *The Mulberry Garden* are from Sir Charles Sedley, *Poetical and Dramatic Works,* ed. V. De Sola Pinto (London, 1928), I.

20. Susan Staves, 'The Secrets of Genteel Identity in *The Man of Mode:* Comedy of Manners vs. the Courtesy Book', *Studies in Eighteenth-Century Culture,* 19 (1989), 120.

21. *The Art of Complaisance or The Means to Oblige in Conversation* (2nd edn: London, 1677), 5, 14, 34. W. Lee Ustick describes the work's provenance in 'The Courtier and the Bookseller: Some Vagaries of Seventeenth-Century Publishing', *Review of English Studies,* 5 (1929), 149-52.

22. Susan Staves, 'The Secrets of Genteel Identity', p. 122.

23. *The Art of Complaisance,* 15.

24. *The Art of Complaisance,* 2.

25. Dale Underwood, *Etherege and the Seventeenth-Century Comedy of Manners* (New Haven, 1957), 61.

26. Ted Cohen, 'Metaphor and the Cultivation of Intimacy', in Sheldon Sacks, ed., *On Metaphor* (Chicago and London, 1978), 9.

27. Recent scholarship has, one hopes, laid this ghost finally to rest. The key texts include Robert D. Hume and A. H. Scouten, '"Restoration Comedy" and its Audiences, 1660-1776', in Robert D. Hume, *The Rakish Stage Studies in English Drama, 1660-1800* (Carbondale and Edwardsville, 1983), 46-81; Harold Love, 'Who Were the Restoration Audience?', *Yearbook of English Studies,* 10 (1980), 21-44; Allan R. Botica, *Audience, Playhouse and Play in Restoration Theatre, 1660-1710* (University of Oxford, D.Phil thesis, 1985).

28. On this useful concept, see, for example, Marvin Carlson, 'Theatre Audiences and the Reading of Performance', in Thomas Postlewait and Bruce A. McConachie, eds., *Interpreting the Theatrical Past: Essays in the Historiography of Performance* (Iowa City, 1989), 84.

FURTHER READING

Bibliography

Mann, David D. *Sir George Etherege: A Reference Guide.* Boston: G. K. Hall & Co., 1981, 135 p.
Comprehensive bibliography of Etherege's life and works, ranging from 1664 to 1980.

Criticism

Barnard, John. "Point of View in *The Man of Mode.*" *Essays in Criticism* 34, no. 4 (October 1984): 285-308.
Examines the relationship between the text of *The Man of Mode* and how Restoration cultural milieu likely influenced the way it was staged in Etherege's time.

Boyette, Purvis E. "The Songs of George Etherege." *Studies in English Literature* 6, no. 3 (summer 1966): 409-19.
Discusses the significance of the songs included in Etherege's plays.

Brown, Laura. "Dramatic Social Satire." In *English Dramatic Form, 1660-1760: An Essay in Generic History,* pp. 28-65. New Haven: Yale University Press, 1981.
Explores the evolution of social satire in Etherege's plays, finding little criticism of social standards in his two early comedies and a more outspoken approach in *The Man of Mode.*

Davies, Paul C. "The State of Nature and the State of War: A Reconsideration of *The Man of Mode.*" *University of Toronto Quarterly* 39, no. 1 (October 1969): 53-62.

Argues that a "true understanding" of the relationship between Dorimant and Harriet is essential for understanding *The Man of Mode* as a whole.

Fisher, Judith W. "The Power of Performance: Sir George Etherege's *The Man of Mode.*" *Restoration and Eighteenth-Century Theatre Research* 10, no. 1 (summer 1995): 15-28.

Analyzes the text of *The Man of Mode* in an effort to reconstruct how the play might have been staged for Etherege's audience.

Hayman, John G. "Dorimant and the Comedy of *A Man of Mode.*" *Modern Language Quarterly* 30 (1969): 183-97.

Contends that the "comic movement" of *The Man of Mode* rests on Dorimant's "initial skill and subsequent failure in fulfilling the requirements of polite society and turning them to some ulterior end."

Hazlitt, William. "Lecture III: On Cowley, Butler, Suckling, Etherege, Etc." In *Lectures on the English Comic Writers, with Miscellaneous Essays*, pp. 49-69. 1819. Reprint, London: J. M. Dent & Sons, 1910.

Brief notice of Etherege, with a favorable description of *The Man of Mode* as a "more exquisite and airy picture of the manners of that age than any other extant."

Henshaw, Wandalie. "Sir Fopling Flutter, or The Key to *The Man of Mode.*" *Essays in Theatre* 3, no. 2 (May 1985): 98-107.

Contends that critics have underestimated Sir Fopling Flutter's significance to *The Man of Mode*, due to their emphasis on the characters of Dorimant and Harriet.

Hughes, Derek. "Play and Passion in *The Man of Mode.*" *Comparative Drama* 15, no. 3 (fall 1981): 231-57.

Analyzes game-playing and religious imagery in *The Man of Mode*, maintaining that the subtly shifting images reveal Etherege's attitudes toward game-playing and the losers in those games.

Hume, Robert D. "The Nature of Comic Drama." In *The Development of English Drama in the Late Seventeeth Century*, pp. 63-148. Oxford: Clarendon Press, 1976.

Takes exception to the claim that *The Man of Mode* is an intellectual showpiece on the manners and mores of Etherege's cultural milieu, arguing that the dramatist simply meant to create "a delightfully satiric entertainment."

Husboe, Arthur R. *Sir George Etherege*. Boston: Twayne Publishers, 1987, 143 p.

In-depth critical discussion of Etherege's life and works.

Knights, L. C. "Restoration Comedy: The Reality & The Myth." *Scrutiny* 6 (June 1937): 122-43.

Censures all Restoration comedy, including Etherege's, as inferior works of literature which depict social conventions artificially. The critic further argues that because these dramatists relied on "a miserably limited set of attitudes," not one "has achieved a genuinely sensitive and individual mode of expression."

Martin, Leslie H. "Past and Parody in *The Man of Mode.*" *Studies in English Literature, 1500-1900* 16, no. 3 (summer 1976): 363-76.

Posits that Etherege invented the character of Mrs. Loveit in *The Man of Mode* to parody heroic drama and other outmoded conventions.

Mignon, Elizabeth. "Etherege." In *Crabbed Age and Youth: The Old Men and Women in the Restoration Comedy of Manners*, pp. 36-47. Durham, N.C.: Duke University Press, 1947.

Examines Etherege's attitudes toward youth and old age in his comedies.

Morrow, Laura. "The Right Snuff: Dorimant and the Will to Meaning." *Restoration* 14, no. 1 (spring 1990): 15-21.

Psychological analysis of Dorimant and his relationships to women in *The Man of Mode.*

Muir, Kenneth. "Sir George Etherege." In *The Comedy of Manners*, pp. 28-40. London: Hutchinson University Library, 1970.

Broad survey of Etherege's comedies and their critical reception.

Palmer, John. "The Life and Letters of Sir George Etherege." In *The Comedy of Manners*, pp. 30-91. 1913. Reprint, New York: Russell & Russell, 1962.

Comprehensive biographical and critical account of Etherege.

Pepys, Samuel. *The Diary of Samuel Pepys*, Vols. IV-VI, edited by Henry B. Wheatley, p. 304. London: G. Bell and Sons, 1926.

Briefly recounts seeing Etherege's *The Comical Revenge*, describing it as "very merry, but only so by gesture, not wit at all."

Pinto, Vivian de Sola. "Sir George Etherege." In *The Restoration Court Poets*, pp. 33-40. London: Longmans, Green & Co., 1965.

Examines Etherege's role in the influential group of court poets which included John Wilmont, earl of Rochester, Charles Sackville, and Sir Charles Sedley.

Powell, Jocelyn. "George Etherege and the Form of Comedy." In *Restoration Theatre*, Stratford-upon-Avon Studies, no. 6, edited by John Russell Brown and Bernard Harris, pp. 43-69. London: Edward Arnold, 1965.

Argues that Etherege's comedies display a central problem of subjectivity in that they condone ridicule and vice rather than satirizing antisocial behavior.

Staves, Susan. "The Secrets of Genteel Identity in *The Man of Mode*: Comedy of Manners vs. the Courtesy Book." In *Studies in Eighteenth-Century Culture,* Vol. 19, edited by Leslie Ellen Brown and Patricia Craddock, pp. 117-28. East Lansing, Mich.: Colleagues Press, 1989.

Discusses the relationship between *The Man of Mode* and contemporary courtesy books, asserting that Etherege represents courtesy literature as "a threat to his ideology of gentility."

Traugott, John. "The Rake's Progress from Court to Comedy: A Study in Comic Form." *Studies in English Literature* 6, no. 3 (summer 1966): 381-407.

Explores the role of the rake in Restoration comedy, noting that Dorimant in Etherege's *The Man of Mode* nearly succeeds in making "a nasty character the vessel of value for the society and the aesthetic center of a proper comedy."

Underwood, Dale. *Etherege and the Seventeenth-Century Comedy of Manners.* New Haven, Conn.: Yale University Press, 1957, 165 p.

Comprehensive discussion of Etherege's comedies within the context of the seventeenth-century intellectual and cultural milieu. The critic maintains that Etherege's plays validate the genre of the comedy of manners in that they are works of "literary and comic art" which enhanced "the principal traditions of pre-Restoration drama."

Walsh, Paul. "Performance, Space, and Seduction in George Etherege's *The Man of Mode* (Dorset Garden Theatre, 1676)." *Essays in Theatre/Études Théâtrales* 11, no. 2 (May 1993): 123-31.

Proposes a possible seventeenth-century staging of *The Man of Mode,* exploring how "performance space"—the physical environment of the theater and the audience interaction with the actors—perhaps influenced the "dynamics of seduction and revelation" in the play.

Weber, Harold. "Charles II, George Pines, and Mr. Dorimant: The Politics of Sexual Power in Restoration England." *Criticism* 32, no. 2 (spring 1990): 193-219.

Examines the sexual dynamics in Etherege's *The Man of Mode,* arguing that the comedy affirms a patriarchal anxiety in the Restoration period about the power of female sexuality.

Wilkinson, D. R. M. "Etherege and a Restoration Pattern of Wit." *English Studies* 68, no. 6 (December 1987): 497-510.

Asserts that Etherege played a critical role in the development of the witty dialogue which is the hallmark of Restoration comedy.

Young, Douglas M. "The Play-World of Sir George Etherege." In *The Feminist Voices in Restoration Comedy: The Virtuous Women in the Play-Worlds of Etherege, Wycherley, and Congreve,* pp. 25-83. Lanham, Md.: University Press of America, 1997.

Discusses how Etherege innovated on Restoration attitudes toward women in his comedies, arguing that in each of the plays the virtuous heroine culminates the action in equal standing to her libertine male suitor.

Zimbardo, Rose A. "Of Women, Comic Imitation of Nature, and Etherege's *The Man of Mode.*" *Studies in English Literature* 21, no. 3 (summer 1981): 373-87.

Analyzes the comic function of the female characters in *The Man of Mode,* noting that Etherege was one of the last playwrights to utilize women to achieve proper comic perspective.

Picaresque Literature of the Sixteenth and Seventeenth Centuries

Predominantly Spanish narrative genre, 1550-1680.

INTRODUCTION

While scholars continue to debate the specifics of the picaresque as a genre, it is commonly accepted that the picaresque narrative originated in Spain in the 1550s. Picaresques are episodic first-person narratives, fictionalized autobiographies of lower-class roguish wanderers. This broad definition of the genre has sparked a considerable amount of controversy among modern critics, many of whom maintain that the form encompasses any work that features an antihero, adventures, and an inversion of traditional value systems, from the anonymously published early picaresque *La vida de Lazarillo de Tormes y de sus fortunas y adversidades* (1554) to modern films such as *Easy Rider* (1969).

Most scholars agree that *Lazarillo de Tormes* is the seminal work of the genre, though it does not feature all of the elements that came to be viewed as characteristic of this type of fiction. First published in 1554, it was revived towards the end of the sixteenth century, when it was attached to a Spanish translation of Giovanni della Casa's *Galateo,* an Italian example of Renaissance courtesy literature, which became popular in the Spanish court of Phillip III. This coupling of *Lazarillo de Tormes* with a courtesy book aimed at an elite audience points to the popularity the picaresque enjoyed among the aristocracy, who found diversion in the adventures and trials of characters belonging to the lower classes, especially those living outside the law.

Picaresque literature focuses on the adventures of a lower-class rogue, known as a picaro, from whose perspective the reader views the action of the story. Picaro is a slang term that appeared in the early sixteenth century and carried connotations of mischief, vagrancy, and low birth. The term also gives the genre its name, and Mateo Alemán's use of the term in *Guzmán de Alfarache* (1599) first identified the picaro as a literary type. The picaro is often portrayed as a petty criminal, living by his wits outside the law and conventional morality. A true picaro is an antihero; even if he wins the sympathy of his readers—usually as the victim of hypocritical or unjust superiors—he does not right any wrongs or gain any particular wisdom. The picaro sees himself as the clever hero of his narrative, but the events of his story belie this self-perception.

The picaro figure also has a female counterpart in the picara, a character type that scholars generally agree grew out of the female bawd of such earlier works as Alonso Jerónimo de Salas Barbadillo's *La hija de Celestina* (1499). Some scholars maintain that the picara developed alongside the picaro: the picaresque-like fiction *La lozana Andaluza,* by Francisco Delicado, was first published in 1528, well before *Lazarillo de Tormes,* and Francisco López de Ubeda's *La pícara Justina* (1605) followed shortly after *Guzmán de Alfarache.* Frank Chandler, one of the pioneering modern scholars on the picaresque, has suggested that the picara—whose physical attractiveness and her trade as a purveyor of sexual services gave her more autonomy as a character and thus more potential as a rogue—played an important role in the evolution of the genre. The picara also appears in many of the earliest picaresque novels in English, including Daniel Defoe's influential *Moll Flanders* (1722) and *Roxana* (1724).

Critical studies of the picaresque have tended to focus on the placement of picaresque narratives in the overall evolution of the novel as a literary form, and on the qualities that define the picaresque as narrative form in its own right. Scholars argue that picaresque narratives played an important role in the history of the novel; their colorful characters and often exotic subject matter closely relate to the romance, the immediate precursor to the novel, while their use of realistic detail anticipates the novel's emphasis on realistic detail. There is little agreement among scholars regarding which works truly fit the criteria of the picaresque, even when discussion is confined to early Spanish narratives. One of the major scholars of the picaresque, Ulrich Wicks, addresses the task of defining the picaresque by narrowing classifications of picaresque literature into the picaresque myth, picaresque fictions, picaresque-like fictions, and the picaresque as a formal literary genre. Some commentators, including Wicks and Claudio Guillén, maintain that from the publication of *Guzmán de Alfarache* a general notion of the genre shaped the picareques that followed. Others, such as Daniel Eisenberg, maintain that no such notion existed when early picaresque novels were being written and that the concept of genre was invented largely by literary critics. Scholars have also focused on the ambiguous morality of the picaresque, contextualizing picaresque values in early modern Spanish culture and discussing the phenomenon of the unreliable narrator.

REPRESENTATIVE WORKS

Anonymous
La vida de Lazarillo de Tormes y de sus fortunas y adversidades [*The Life of Lazarillo de Tormes: His Fortunes and Adversities*] (novel) 1554

Mateo Alemán

Guzmán de Alfarache. [*The Life and Adventures of Guzman D'Alfarache*; 2 vols.] (novel) 1599-1604

Francisco Delicado

La lozana Andaluza [*The Lusty Andalusian Woman*] (novel) 1528

Vicente Martinez Espinel

Relaciones de la vida y aventuras del escudero Marcos de Obregón (novel) 1618

Hans Jakob Christoffel von Grimmelshausen

Simplicius Simplicissimus (novel) 1668

Francisco Gomez de Quevedo

Historia de la vida del buscón [*The Sharper*] (novel) 1626

Alonso Jerónimo de Salas Barbadillo

La hija de Celestina [*The Daughter of Celestina*] (novel) 1612

Francisco Lopez de Ubeda

La pícara Justina (novel) 1605

CONTEXT AND DEVELOPMENT

Walter L. Reed (essay date 1981)

SOURCE: Reed, Walter L. "The Advent of the Spanish Picaresque." In *An Exemplary History of the Novel: the Quixotic Versus the Picaresque,* pp. 43-70. Chicago: University of Chicago Press, 1981.

[*In this essay, Reed discusses the development of the picaresque as an aspect of the development of the novel.*]

> He has chosen things low and contemptible, mere nothings, to overthrow the existing order.
>
> 1 Corinthians 1:28

Lazarillo de Tormes, published in three separate editions in 1554, appeared just before the onset of the Counter Reformation in Spain, and it shows some distinctive features as a picaresque novel. Most notably, it is closer to the spirit of humanistic satire, with its critique of ecclesiastical abuse, than the later Spanish novels were to be. Scholars have frequently suggested that the author of the anonymous *Lazarillo* was a Spanish follower of Erasmus. Although this hypothesis has been discredited,[1] one can see a number of structural and imaginative affinities between this first instance of the novel and a satirical encomium like Erasmus's *Praise of Folly.* Both works present an ambiguously colloquial address by a speaker of

doubtful integrity, a situation that Barbara Babcock calls the framing paradox of the Cretan liar.[2] Like Lazarillo's obviously self-serving apology, the praising of folly is done by "Folly" herself. Both works also pay special attention to the sins of the church, a critique which goes beyond medieval clerical satire by invoking the reforming authority of the New Testament. The attack on religious orders is oblique in *Lazarillo* and direct in *The Praise of Folly,* but it is an attack on the corruption of the office more than simply on the corruption of the officeholder. The protagonist's name in *Lazarillo* alludes to the biblical Lazaruses in the Gospels of Luke and John, both of whom are resurrected after death; Folly's claim that "all Christian religion seems to have a kind of alliance with folly and in no respect to have any accord with wisdom" more forcefully recalls Paul's first letter to the Corinthians.[3] In both these texts we see the alliance of a low secular spokesman with a high religious authority, an alliance that conspires against the authority, dignity, and self-sufficiency of the existing order, of church as well as of state. The spokesman is not himself (herself) religious; he or she alludes to the generic humility of the Christian vision without embodying it.

This autonomy of the speaker in Erasmus, grounded in the classical techniques of satire, helps prepare the way for the sudden and virtually accidental appearance of the kind of writing we now call the novel. Yet *Lazarillo de Tormes* moves in a different direction from *The Praise of Folly.* It gives the autonomous voice a more radical freedom. Erasmus insists on the traditional oratorical medium of his discourse, and dramatizes a particularly responsible audience by addressing an introductory letter to Sir Thomas More. He cites numerous classical precedents for his playful exercise—Homer, Democritus, Virgil, Ovid, Lucian, and others—at the beginning and alludes directly to numerous precedents in Scripture for valuing "folly" as the discourse proceeds. Indeed, the fiction that a pagan goddess named "Folly" is speaking becomes quite thin by the middle of the text. The author of *Lazarillo,* on the other hand, has his character address an anonymous "Vuestra Merced," an ambiguous character who seems himself implicated in Lazarillo's morally dubious situation. The arch-priest, to whose mistress Lazarillo is married, is the interlocutor's friend, and on one level Lazarillo is trying to defend himself against the rumors circulating against this ménage à trois. But Lazarillo also has his eye on a broader kind of audience when he cites Pliny's maxim that "there is no book, however bad it may be, that doesn't have something good about it" (23). He makes a gesture in the direction of classical literature by citing Pliny and Cicero, but these authorities are merely pretexts for his advertisements for himself. If anything, the allusions only serve to undermine the notion of the classics as morally improving literature; a little of such learning is a dangerous thing.[4] And where Folly increasingly reveals the biblical subtext behind her rhetorical pretext, Lazarillo shows his spiritual potential only fleetingly in his narrative, when he shares his food with his indigent *hidalgo* master. Thereafter he becomes more worldly, as he serves more venial and more reliable employers, which leads one critic to speak of his social success as his spiritual "death."[5] Such religious judgments are rendered secondary by the text, as I will show later on, but the narrative voice in *Lazarillo de Tormes* does detach itself from the scriptural chorus and speak of the low and humble world, the material and social realities, as things in and of themselves.

It is useful to compare *Lazarillo* in this regard with another prose fiction that comes out of the Erasmian matrix, the books of Rabelais's *Gargantua and Pantagruel*. In Rabelais's five books one can see a structure broadly similar to that of *Lazarillo* and *The Praise of Folly*: an alliance of high moral ideals and low secular clowning, of the spiritually elevated and the physically debased. High and low together attack a pretentious and inadequate middle, an established order that no longer mediates but rather, with its prohibitions and its nonsense, oppresses both mind and body. One can also see how Rabelais, like the author of *Lazarillo*, tips the Erasmian balance toward the realities of the lower world, where flesh is flesh and not merely a vehicle for the Incarnation, where folly is foolish and not merely a trope for God's truth. Food and drink have some sacramental associations in Rabelais but are more significant as a means of celebrating or sustaining the life of the physical man. And the spokesmen for these realities achieve a subversive freedom from all apparent rules, defeating the official hierarchy by appeal to popular culture.[6]

It is sometimes proposed, and has been increasingly of late, that *Gargantua and Pantagruel* be considered as an early example of the novel.[7] The terms of the previous chapter suggest why I do not agree with this view. While reacting in unprecedented ways to the revolution of the book, Rabelais's narratives are deeply committed to the humanist ideals of the Renaissance and are also deeply involved in the oral media of literary presentation. The critique in Rabelais is not so much of the institution of literature per se as of the official norms of academic scholastic culture in general. I will have more to say on the question of Rabelais and the novel in the following chapter on *Don Quixote*. But I would like here to insist on the important differences between the two types of innovation represented by Rabelais's *Oeuvres* and the anonymous *Lazarillo*.

The most obvious difference involves the physical and imaginative scale on which the two narratives operate. Gargantua and Pantagruel are giants, human in form but grossly larger than life, and although Rabelais is not consistent in his use of his fiction, even exploiting the incongruity of normal and gigantic proportions, the gigantic is the norm against which most of the actions and achievements are to be judged. Lazarillo is of ordinary stature; the attention to his childhood and the diminutive of his titulary name render his presence particularly unimposing. He is notable for his lacks rather than for his fulfillments, and his bouts with hunger and thirst contrast markedly with the surfeit of food and drink in Rabelais.

The contrast between excess and minimality functions on an intellectual level as well. The figure in Rabelais most like the picaro is Panurge, the trickster whom Pantagruel encounters begging and in rags, whom he takes on as his servant. But Panurge's quest for food is imaginatively redundant. He begs in twelve different languages, several of them literally unheard of, in a staggering display of erudition rather than a practical sharpening of the wits. Panurge becomes Pantagruel's comrade more than his menial; his tricks are exuberant and gratuitous, motivated by a sense of comic play, where Lazarillo's are calculating and constrained, motivated by physical and psychological needs. As Thomas Greene observes, the pranks of Panurge belong to a widespread Renaissance "art form," a traditional trickster behavior common in poetry and drama.[8]

The differences between these two fictions, then, are a function of the difference in ethos: of all-inclusiveness in *Gargantua and Pantagruel,* of deprivation in *Lazarillo de Tormes.* As Erich Auerbach puts it, "everything goes with everything" in Rabelais—high culture with low culture, the body with the spirit, modernity with antiquity. Auerbach's comments on Rabelais's humanism are particularly relevant to my argument on the origins of the novel:

> His humanistic relation to antique literature is shown in his remarkable knowledge of the authors who furnish him with themes, quotations, anecdotes, examples and comparisons; in his thought upon political, philosophical, and educational questions, which, like that of the other humanists, is under the influence of antique ideas; and particularly in his view of man, freed as it is from the Christian and stratified-social frame of reference which characterized the Middle Ages. Yet his indebtedness to antiquity does not imprison him within the confines of antique concepts; to him, antiquity means liberation and a broadening of horizons, not in any sense a new limitation or servitude; nothing is more foreign to him than the antique separation of styles, which in Italy even in his own time, and soon after in France, led to purism and "Classicism."[9]

Rabelais's fiction is thus prior to neoclassicism rather than being anti-neoclassical. It attacks the established order not from the excluded and humble viewpoint of the half-outsider, to use Guillén's phrase, but from the all-inclusive vision of the polymath and the polyglot, a vision that overwhelms structure, inverts hierarchy, and subverts significance in its sheer plenitude. It is the world in Pantagruel's mouth, not the world from Lazarillo's jaundiced eye. As we have been discovering, the novel is a critique of the neoclassical purification of literature; such a separation of the old and the new had not become a significant enough adversary for Rabelais.

As I shall argue in the next chapter, with *Don Quixote* the novel later developed its own strategies of inclusiveness, by channeling the multiplicity of literary forms through the consciousness of a character who is himself a reader of texts. But at this earlier point of departure it is fair to describe the difference between *Lazarillo de Tormes* and *Gargantua and Pantagruel* as a difference between novel and satire. Rabelais anticipates the novel in interesting ways, and he is reinterpreted novelistically by later writers like Sterne and Melville. But the ethos of his prose fiction is finally the ethos of satire, before his time and after. I would describe this as an ethos of exaggeration, as distinct from the ethos of displacement peculiar to the novel. The label of "satire" is certainly not definitive of Rabelais's work, but at the level of definition on which I have been discussing the novel so far, it is clearly the more appropriate term.[10]

The type of satire known as Menippean or Varronian includes many examples of narratives in prose, in which characters and incidents predominate and in which contemporary manners and morals are directly represented. *Gargantua and Pantagruel* shares many features with Lucian's dialogues and stories, with Petronius's *Satyricon,* with Erasmus's colloquies and with Swift's later *Gulliver's Travels* and *A Tale of a Tub.* Such satires resemble novels in many ways, not the least of which is their generally subversive and antinomian quality. As Alvin Kernan notes, satire seems to disregard the formal order and decorum of good literature so-called.[11] But it is in the question of literary rules that the difference between satire and the novel is most important. Satire deliberately violates the rules of literary decorum and of representational form; physical and moral faults are grossly exaggerated, while conventional aesthetic distinctions between one kind of form and another are deliberately confused. "The scene of satire is always disorderly and crowded, packed to the very point of bursting," writes Kernan.

> The deformed faces of depravity, stupidity, greed, venality, ignorance, and maliciousness group closely together for a moment, stare boldly out at us, break up, and another tight knot of figures collects, stroking full stomachs, looking vacantly into space, nervously smiling at the great, proudly displaying jewels and figures, clinking moneybags, slyly fingering new-bought fashions. The scene is equally choked with things: ostentatious buildings and statuary, chariots, sedan-chairs, clothes, books, food, houses, dildoes, luxurious furnishings, gin bottles, wigs.[12]

The effect of such formal confusion and proportional excess, paradoxically, is to affirm the validity of the formalities in question, to reaffirm the rules by dramatizing their necessity. Norms and ideals themselves are represented only fleetingly in the satiric fiction, and when they do appear at any length they often seem thin and inadequate. The real force of rules in satire, which belong more to the domain of custom than to the domain of ethics,[13] is only revealed in the flagrant violation of them that the satirist depicts. A kind of negative jurisprudence is thus entailed. A satire is an adversary system, a case for the prosecution, and the particular rule that is violated is given all the force of law—of the spirit of the law rather than its letter. Satire presents offenses against customs and mores as if they were violations of a legal covenant.

The legal sanction that satire lends to literary rules is by no means a simple one. There are innumerable reversals, dialectics, and shiftings of logical ground in the case

presented. In *Gargantua and Pantagruel,* for example, the exaggerated human scale of the giants is frequently itself the law by which the physical pettiness and false modesty of ordinary human beings are implicitly condemned—a complex equation of physical excess and moral largesse that Swift reproduces in the Brobdingnagians in *Gulliver's Travels.* Or there is the self-defense of Folly in Erasmus's *Encomium,* which impreceptibly turns into a defense of Christian humility and an attack on Stoic philosophical pride. In these early humanistic satires, the overestablished order of the medieval church is the chief offender, and the simpler virtues of Scripture, the classical authors, and folk tradition are the main sources of a countervailing principle or spirit of the law. Nevertheless, the relation of exceptional instance to normative standard is essentially judicial. A particular character, action, or expression is considered as if it were trying to live up to a particular standard of wisdom or virtue—which in point of fact it often is not—and failing miserably in the attempt.

Thus where the institution of literature is concerned, satire pretends to regard the rules of "good literature" as more legally binding than mere generic convention. To write bad epic verse is not simply to be an indifferent poet but to commit a crime against the literary community. Furthermore, satire pretends to regard other forms of human culture and behavior as if they were aspiring to the status of "good literature." The strategy of the mock-heroic is to look at a particular modern sub- or extraliterary phenomenon as if it were trying consciously to emulate canonical forms like the epic—as if it were trying to crash the cultural gate. The strategy of the carnivalesque in Rabelais is to regard medieval theology as if it were trying to take part in a classical symposium, as if scholastic logic, with its intricate formalities and terminologies, were trying to join the convivial colloquium, with its free speculation, drunken rapture, and popular laughter.

In the novel, on the other hand, exception and norm are placed in a different kind of relationship. The exception, like the excluded servant Lazarillo, is given a new autonomy and becomes *another* norm, a new law unto itself which to a significant extent eludes the embrace of the canonical law that would judge it and find it wanting. The relation between competing or conflicting forms is thus not judicial, rather it is diplomatic. The novel takes a stand outside a particular system of values, or between competing systems, and while its apparent norms are more visible than the norms of satire, they are also more problematic. The dialectical relationship of the novel to literary tradition entails a conflict of rules, a competition among values, and a general lack of codified precedent for the formal result. It seems to me that the term which best describes the relation of divergent forms in the novel is a diplomatic rather than a legal one; forms are arranged according to a *protocol.*

The word "protocol," in English, is used outside the general legal vocabulary. Coming from a Greek word meaning "a flyleaf glued to a manuscript describing its contents," it refers to an original record of a particular negotiation carried on outside the authority of a given system of law. It is a record that serves as the basis for further negotiations that may become more binding, as in a treaty. The term has been used in analytic philosophy to describe the syntax of basic statements of truth. Protocol sentences are models of verifiable scientific observation of the world. But I would like to use it in this study to define the kind of rules by which the novel, as distinct from other types of literature, tends to operate. A protocol is an agreement sui generis, but its terms are rendered formal and public. A novelistic protocol informs the text on a number of different levels, but it does not establish order or unity in any widely shared literary sense. A protocol is formal, but its form is not necessarily organic, harmonious, or logically coherent. The protocol of a particular novel is often adopted and adapted in subsequent novels, but it is also considerably less normative, as I will argue shortly, than what is generally understood by the term "genre" in literature more oriented toward tradition. If a genre is "a challenge to match an imaginative structure to reality," as Rosalie Colie suggests, a protocol may be said to reverse the definition: it is a warning against the attempt to match reality with a preexistent literary form.[14]

Finally, a secondary meaning of "protocol" helps to explain the way in which the original diplomacies of the novel may easily become highly conventionalized themselves. The term also refers to the rigid rules of ambassadorial precedence, behavior, and dress, which are necessary where no deeper, more organic system of rights and privileges obtains. As in the mass of "popular" novels which remain comfortably and predictably within the formulas of the detective story, science fiction, or the historical romance, a protocol, when it *is* followed, often produces a proliferation of examples in which even the dialectical tension of traditional literary genres is never achieved. The so-called "realism" of the novel is best seen as a series of protocols in which novels reach out to engage new areas of sign and structure beyond the domain of literary convention, beyond even the cumulative conventions of the novel itself. But the realism of one novel or group of novels may easily become a matter of convention or cliché in novels that exploit the original terms—plot formulas, settings, character types, manners of speech—on a superficial level. The concept of the protocol thus captures one of the paradoxes of the novel that this study had not yet dwelt on sufficiently, the paradox of a kind of writing inherently committed to innovation which at the same time seems so prone, in the mass of its examples, to the stereotypical and the formulaic.

One might say, then, that the novel and satire are opposing revaluations of the nature of literary rules. Satire is conservative and reactionary in the way it appeals to an earlier standard, to literary rule as a spirit of the law. The novel is liberal and progressive in the way it dramatizes a negotiation between new and old species of writing, juxtaposing rather than subordinating one kind to another. Such political labels, of course, can be misleading. One might put the contrast in terms of economics and say that satire affirms standards of value by radically bankrupting the currency of the modern, where the novel describes with more relativity the mechanics of devaluation and exchange. Or one might use categories of logic, as Julia Kristeva does, and say that the novel deals with the "non-disjunction" of logically opposite terms.[15] Whatever terminology is preferred, it should convey the idea that the novel is countersystematic: beyond a system, between systems, or against system altogether. Thus it is finally to the protocol of particular novels that one must turn, and to the way in which these protocols are renegotiated by subsequent novelistic texts.

Lazarillo de Tormes is a text that emerges from the matrix of satire, as I have already noted. It is in this sense not fully novelistic, and some critics have insisted that it is more a precursor than a true example of the picaresque.[16] There is no point in exaggerating its resemblances to later instances of the novel. As a narrative it is quite short; its precision and economy are effective but rarely expand either character or setting with the plenitude of *Guzmán de Alfarache* or even the relatively economical *El Buscón*. None of the other characters besides Lazarillo is given a proper name, and Lazarillo's masters are a gallery of social types familiar from the medieval satire of "estates": the conniving blind man, the miserly priest, the false pardoner.[17] Similarly, the language is not particularly committed to objective description; it is rather made up of conventional phrases and proverbs. As Lazarillo says of his first master, "He relied on the proverb which says that a hard man will give more than a man who hasn't anything at all" (32).

Nevertheless, there are subtle but important dislocations of this apparently traditional material. We have a character who is both knave and gull, who is exploited by others and who deceives them in turn, with no clear standard of virtuous conduct or superior wit. As Francisco Rico has argued, we have in *Lazarillo* a primary instance of novelistic "point of view," in which the individual perspective is a primary constituent of value and significance, placing rather than placed within the world.[18] The proverbial and conventional language is ironically twisted, recombined, and misapplied. "I think it's a good thing that important events which quite accidentally have never seen the light of day, should be made public and not buried in the grave of oblivion," the narrator says, slyly and pompously, of his own paltry *vida* (23). The wise words of the community are revealed as detachable clichés and can be manipulated to the speaker's advantage. "God (to grant me revenge) had blinded his good sense for that instant" (36), Lazarillo says of his success in luring his blind master to smash his head into the stone pillar. A major theme of *Lazarillo* is "the opposition of authentic and uniquely personal experience (resulting in this case from the hero's exposure to hunger, cold, blows and justice) and the commonplace terms which the community applies to experience and with which it hopes to dismiss experience," writes Stephen Gilman.[19]

Yet to call Lazarillo's experience "authentic" and "uniquely personal" is to miss the protocol of the novelistic text. In fact, *Lazarillo de Tormes* is a systematic exploration of the inauthentic; it is informed throughout by a protocol of the ersatz, in which a substituted object or experience is made to serve, provisionally, as a replacement for something else. The substitute is offered deliberately, with an awareness of its lesser value and reduced efficacy. But it serves as a challenge to the intrinsic worth of that which it replaces, a challenge to the status of the status quo.

The operation of the protocol can be seen most easily in the peculiar treatment of objects in the narrative. In a well-known incident, in which the hero is initiated into the picaro's way of life, Lazarillo is asked by his blind master to put his ear close to a stone animal that resembles a bull: "put your ear close to the bull, and you'll hear a loud noise inside it" (27). Lazarillo obeys and has his head smashed against it. In place of the promised sound, which suggests a special message or revelation, he discovers the brute materiality of the object, an object which is itself a replica of something else. The experience acts as an ersatz revelation, nevertheless: "at that moment I felt as if I had woken up and my eyes were opened. I said to myself: 'What he says is true; I must keep awake because I'm on my own and I've got to look after myself'" (27-28). His curiosity is satisfied in a way that he did not expect.

Lazarillo learns this lesson of substitution very well. He gives his blind master smaller coins than the ones actually donated by passersby, putting a *blanca* into his mouth and passing a half-*blanca* on to the beggar who has been saying the prayers. In a more complicated series of substitutions, he steals the blind man's sausage, takes the sausage from its pan and puts a thin rotten turnip in its place. When the blind man discovers the switch and suspects his servant, he pokes his long sausage- (and turnip-) like nose down Lazarillo's throat, which prompts Lazarillo to vomit "his property" back up: "his nose and the half-digested sausage came out at the same time" (34). Lazarillo has the last word in these exchanges when he lures the blind man to jump head-on into the pillar, as an appropriate reprisal for the stone bull. He jeers at the beggar as he runs away, "What! You smelled the sausage and you couldn't smell the post? Olé! Olé!" (37). Just as the physical objects can replace one another, they can also turn out to serve radically different functions. The blind man's wine jug brings Lazarillo pleasure when he sips through a straw from a hole he has made in the bottom of it, but it brings him pain when the blind man discovers the trick and smashes the jug down on his face: "the jug, which had been the source of pleasure and was now to be the instrument of pain" (30).

On the level of character as well, this protocol of the ersatz informs Lazarillo's relationships with his different masters. With the miserly priest he is forced to act like vermin by breaking into the chest that contains the priest's supply of bread. The priest finally catches him, beats him, and tells him, when he regains consciousness, "By God,

I've hunted down the mice and snakes that persecuted me" (48). With the impoverished *hidalgo*, his third master, the master changes places with his servant. The *hidalgo* ends up depending on Lazarillo for his food and it is finally he who runs away from Lazarillo. In Lazarillo's marriage to the archpriest's mistress in the last chapter, the husband becomes a knowing replacement for the lover, part-time.

Thus on the level of plot, in the interaction of characters and objects, we see a series of bad bargains being made, exchanges which are instrumental rather than ends in themselves and whose success is either temporary or highly ambiguous. Nevertheless, these exchanges are not purely ironic or absolutely devaluing. They involve dubious likenesses that dramatize the instability of life in the social and psychological world, but they do not reveal, even negatively, a clear otherworldly standard of truth. To speak of Lazarillo's success and dishonor simply as his spiritual "death," as Gilman and others do, is to overemphasize the vertical reference of the text and to overestimate the force of Christian precept in the horizontal relationships of society. The sympathy Lazarillo shows for the impoverished *hidalgo* is like Christian charity but it is finally not the same. As with the other forms of ersatz, a potential metaphoric identity keeps collapsing into metonymic proximity or juxtaposition. In fact, there is even a scriptural precedent for this frustration of religious message in the Lucan parable of Lazarus to which the novel alludes. In Luke the beggar Lazarus dies after being ignored by the rich man (*dives* in the Vulgate); the rich man also dies and finds himself in hell. When he sees Lazarus far off in the bosom of Abraham and is denied any relief for himself, the rich man asks Abraham to send Lazarus back to earth to warn his five brothers. "But Abraham said, 'They have Moses and the prophets; let them listen to them.' 'No, father Abraham,' he replied, 'but if someone from the dead visits them they will repent.' Abraham answered, 'If they do not listen to Moses and the prophets they will pay no heed even if someone should arise from the dead.'"[20] The idea of the resurrected beggar as a stand-in for the prophets is explicitly rejected here; Lazarus is a type for the rejection of new typologies.

Nor is it clear on a more practical level that, as some critics have tried to argue, Lazarillo's wits become less sharp as he becomes less hungry. Gilman describes the Prologue, delivered by the older man, as a dull performance, an "epilogue post-mortem,"[21] but it is equally possible to argue that Lazarillo is here, as elsewhere, the creator rather than the butt of the irony. Thus R. W. Truman considers that Lazarillo "comes before us as one who feels he had made substantial material progress in life and yet is so far conscious of the limited nature of what he has achieved that he enjoys the comedy of pretending to have achieved more than he has in fact done."[22] Even at the end of his narrative, when he accepts his wife's adultery with apparent unconcern, he shows that his wits are still alive and his tongue still sharp. When the archpriest has told him to ignore the gossip about his wife, he reports his reply: "'Sir,' I said to him, 'I made up my mind a long time ago to keep in with respectable people. It's quite true that my friends have said something to me about my wife. In fact they've proved to me that she had three children before she married me, speaking with reverence because she's here.' Then my wife began to swear such fearful oaths that I was sure the house was about to fall down about our ears" (78). What we see here is not so much an irony directed at Lazarillo, who remains too evasive to be anyone's dupe, but an irony directed at the social concept of honor itself. Lazarillo wears the manners of the socially respectable as a disguise, in a way that exposes the fictionality of these manners. Thus he says to anyone who would hint at his wife's infidelity, "I swear on the Sacred Host itself that she is as good a woman as any in Toledo. If anyone says the opposite I'll kill him" (79). The boundary between 'worse than' and 'as good as' is challenged, and the ersatz man of honor installs himself in the midst of respectability. "That was the same year as our victorious Emperor entered this famous city of Toledo and held his Parliament here. There were great festivities, as Your Honour doubtless has heard. At that time I was at the height of my good fortune" (79).

The reader, of course, is made a party to the protocol of the text. The book that he holds in his hands is a substitute for the letter to "Vuestra Merced"—a replacement underlined in Spanish by the general use of *Vd.* as the polite form of the second-person address. It is not a case of someone's private letters being presented to the world by an editor, as in the later fiction of the epistolary novel, but of a self-confessed public performance presenting itself as a private communication—and vice versa. Similarly, Lazarillo's life story or *vida* is a surrogate for the explanation of his dubious circumstances or *caso* that his fictional correspondent has supposedly requested: "And since Your Excellency has written to ask a full account of this subject I thought best not to begin in the middle but at the beginning, so as to present a complete narrative of myself." The idea of beginning at the beginning rather than in the middle implicitly disclaims any epic ambitions on Lazarillo's part, yet the final phrase of his prologue ironically presents him as an ersatz Aeneas: "how much more they have accomplished who have had Fortune against them from the start, and who have nothing to thank but their own labor and skill at the oars for bringing them into a safe harbor."[23]

The protocol of substitution in *Lazarillo de Tormes* thus suggests from the start a view of the novel as surrogate literature, as a humble yet arrogant pretender to cultural respectability. Its pretense, at the same time, lays the respectability of literature open to question. If there is no book however bad that does not have some good in it, as Lazarillo reminds us Pliny has said, it may be that the greatest of books have some bad in them as well, or—more to the point—can be used for morally dubious ends like self-advancement in the hands of a vulgar class of readers.

This is not to say that all its readers, especially the initial ones, responded to *Lazarillo* according to the terms of the protocol I have sketched out here. On the contrary, there is evidence that the book was read along quite different lines—for example, by the author of an anonymous and spurious "sequel," who went on to describe Lazarillo's transformation into a tuna fish in the manner of Apuleius and to report his scholarly disputations with the doctors of the University of Salamanca in the manner of Rabelais.[24] Though less popular than the original, which appeared in four separate editions within two years, parts of this spurious sequel found their way into translations from the Spanish for some time. Other evidence of the fact that Lazarillo was misunderstood—or rather read unsympathetically—is its appearance on the *Index Expurgatorius* in 1559 and the appearance of a censored edition in 1573, which cut out the chapters with the worldly friar and the false pardoner but left the chapter with the miserly priest. The Council of Trent itself abolished the granting of indulgences for offerings of money and thus got rid of pardoners, but the Inquisition was apparently most sensitive to criticism of the itinerant functionaries and mendicant orders. In spite of its initial popularity, *Lazarillo* had to wait until the end of the century until it was widely recognized as a new species of writing; until, that is, it became more than one of a kind.

The argument over the novelistic status of *Lazarillo de Tormes*—whether it belongs to the class of subsequent picaresque novels or whether it is merely a "prototype" of the genre—has been resolved, for all intents and purposes, by Claudio Guillén, who shows that historically considered, it is both.[25] Guillén traces the publication history of *Lazarillo* and observes that its popularity dwindled in the half-century after its publication, until the appearance of *Guzmán de Alfarache* in 1599. Then it went through nine editions in four years, and in most cases it was the editors of *Guzmán* who produced the new *Lazarillos*. The final seal was put on the process of recognition, Guillén argues, when Cervantes's character, Ginés de Pasamonte, speaks in the First Part of *Don Quixote* of his own life story, "so good . . . that Lazarillo de Tormes will have to look out, and so will everything in that style that has ever been written or ever will be" (176).[26] The form of the novel as a particular literary kind is constituted not by one example or even by two, but by a reader who singles out the kind (*género,* says Cervantes) and commits his recognition to the medium of print.

The term "genre," as applied to the picaresque in particular and the novel is general, is misleading, however. It implies a more stable set of rules than in fact ever pertained, and a greater commitment to the idea of such rules than can be discerned from the texts. As the spurious sequels to *Lazarillo, Guzmán,* and *Don Quixote* attest, the novel was from its inception a particularly open invitation to other authors; it encouraged expropriation more than imitation, a cashing in on the marketable material rather than an observation of literary decorum. Both *Guzmán* and *Don Quixote* were immediate and unprecedented best-sellers, and respect for tradition or rules seems to have played a small part in the proliferation of narratives "in that style." The novelistic protocol, as I have suggested, allows considerably more latitude in the observance of literary formalities than do poetic or dramatic genres. Similarly, the novelistic *series,* as I would prefer to call the succession of novels bearing family resemblances to one another, is a more open-ended affair than a generic tradition, however much genres might themselves have been combined or transformed. As Rosalie Colie argues, it was "the *concept* of generic form" that was important for the Renaissance humanists, much more than the definition of specific generic norms. And that concept had a "*social force and function,*" setting forth "definitions of manageable boundaries, some large, some small, in which material can be treated and considered."[27]

It is precisely the lack of such a shared belief in separable (and combinable) literary kinds that gives the novel its impetus in literary history. Instead of conforming to a generic type, a novel follows another novel in a historical series. The novelistic series may be a matter of explicit sequels: *The Second Part of the Life of the Picaro, Guzmán de Alfarache; Lazarillo de Manzanares; James Hind, the English Guzmán; The Spiritual Quixote; Sir Launcelot Greaves.* The changes are rung on a local habitation or a name.[28] Or the series may be made up of less explicit successor novels that exploit a plot and setting formula (the Gothic novel, the sea story, the Western), a character-type and professional role (the detective story, the *Bildungsroman,* the portrait of the artist). As I noted earlier, many of these series resemble genres in their tendency to the stereotypical and the formulaic, but the conventions have much more to do with their subject matter than with any formal characteristics—plot structure, mode of characterization, diction, or "point of view"—and have much less normative power than the rules of genre. Novelistic series are by nature more loosely defined, in part because of their focus on the "history" or "adventures" of a particular character or group. Such a focus promotes the idea of additive sequence. How can my book be finished, asks Ginés de Pasamonte, when my life isn't over yet? No matter what sense of an ending is given by a particular novel, there is an implicit "to be continued"—a promise that is explicit from *Lazarillo* onwards: "I will inform Your Honour of my future in due course"; "Something further may follow of this Masquerade."[29]

Recent scholarship on the picaresque novel has unfortunately blurred this distinction between novelistic series and poetic or dramatic genre. The most lucid and informed discussion of the subject is again that of Claudio Guillén, in "Toward a Definition of the Picaresque," where distinctions are drawn between (1) picaresque novels "in the strict sense," (2) "another group of novels [that] may be considered picaresque in a broader sense of the term only," and (3) "a picaresque myth: an essential situation or significant structure derived from the novels themselves." For the strict sense of the term, Guillén offers a list of seven shrewdly chosen characteristics. These however exclude a number of early Spanish successors to *Lazarillo* and *Guzmán* (such as Salas Barbadillo's *La hija de Celestina* and Espinel's *Marcos de Obregón,* both influential

abroad). Furthermore, these defining characteristics are somehow independent of "the picaresque genre," which Guillén identifies only as "an ideal type, blending, in varying degrees or fashions, *Lazarillo de Tormes* with *Guzmán de Alfarache . . .* with the addition of other novels according to the case." In other words, the normative genre, with its supposedly "stable features" is kept in isolation from specific criteria in Guillén's analysis, and has only a putative existence in the possible community of texts. In spite of his keen insight into the dynamics of literary history, Guillén here finally refuses the novel its full literary difference.[30]

At the other extreme of Guillén's historical flexibility lies the procrustean attempt of Stuart Miller in *The Picaresque Novel,* which frankly avows its model in Aristotle's *Poetics:* "a forthrightly systematic attempt to construct an 'ideal genre type' for the picaresque novel, showing how a number of coherent formal devices unite to produce a specific picaresque content and emotional response."[31] There is something deeply contradictory about Miller's desire to formalize the rules of a genre that he finds reflecting "a total lack of structure in the world, not merely a lack of ethical or social structure" (p. 131). He abstracts, or chooses examples, from eight different picaresque novels, from *Lazarillo* to *Roderick Random;* he sees 1550-1750 as the "classic period" of the picaresque (p. 4), and thus surreptitiously canonizes the anticanonical form.

Like attempts at a poetics of the novel discussed in Chapter 1, most definitions of the picaresque as a genre go astray in considering it on the model of poetry, of drama, or even of myth, rather than as an early instance of the novel. Ulrich Wicks is in fact specific on this point: "I suggest that . . . we leave out of consideration for the time being one half of our term, namely *novel,* a formidable job of definition itself."[32] Like so many of the nets cast by literary criticism, genre theory allows the novel, in its genuine yet not unlimited novelty, to escape.

It is more accurate, therefore, to think of *Lazarillo de Tormes* as a pretext for *Guzmán de Alfarache* and certain other novels than to think of it as a prototype for a genre. There is, in fact, little direct evidence that Alemán had *Lazarillo* foremost in his mind, or that he considered resemblances worth advertising. There are reminiscences in the form of the title and in the occasional references to "Guzmanillo"; there is an allusion to the trials of being a blind man's servant, although Guzmán never has a blind master. And there is a picaresque conversion that recalls Lazarillo's, though it lacks the specificity of the stone bull. "I plainly began to perceive," Guzmán says, "how Adversitie makes men wise: in that very instant, me thought, I discovered a new light; which as in a cleare Glasse, did represent unto mee things past, things present, and things to come" (Mabbe, I, 236). But as one critic puts it, Alemán's novel is most notable for the way it enlarges the scope of *Lazarillo*—its geography, its social spectrum, and its range of cultural reference.[33] Thus Ben Jonson wrote in a dedicatory poem to Mabbe's translation:

Who tracks this Authors, or Translators Pen
Shall finde, that either hath read Bookes, and Men;
To say but one, were single. Then it chimes,
When the old words doe strike on the new times,
As in this Spanish Proteus; who, though writ
But in one tongue, was form'd with the worlds wit.

(I,31)

The neoclassicizing rhetoric of Jonson's verse, the assumption that books and "old words" are a primary source for describing the "new times" and that Guzmán is a Proteus redivivus, misrepresents *Guzmán* as a novel, perhaps, but it does describe the greater bookishness and broader worldliness of Alemán's text.

The major problem for a modern reader, in fact, is in coming to terms with the overabundance of commentary on the simple story line of Guzmán's adventures. Instead of the spare understatement of *Lazarillo,* we have a voluminous moralizing on the part of the older narrator, a moralizing that takes off from the behavior of the picaro or of the characters he encounters, but extends itself into general expositions of doctrine, proverbs, *sententiae,* exemplary anecdotes, and other narrative digressions. The digressions are not made without a certain self-consciousness on the narrator's part; some of the asides anticipate *Tristram Shandy.* "O what a gentle disparate, what a pretty absurdity is this of mine, yet well grounded in Divinity? how am I leapt from the Oare to the Helme? What a Saint John the Evangelist am I become on the sudden that I reade you such a lecture?" (I, 83), Guzmán remarks ironically at one point. And at another: "I treat in this of mine owne life, and therefore will not meddle with other mens; but I doe not know, whether I shall be able, when a ball offers it selfe so fairly, to pull backe my hand or no? For there is no man that is Master of himselfe, when he is on horse-backe" (I, 103). English and French translations, particularly in the eighteenth century, frequently omit this homiletic material, but a historical reading of the novel must take it into account.[34]

If we cease to look for traditional literary form and search instead for the peculiar protocol of Alemán's narrative, however, we need not apologize for the lack of unity or symmetry. There is clearly a double structure or duality at least in the narrative, but it is not simply a "precarious equilibrium" in which both sides "lessen" or "weaken" one another.[35] There is a function and purpose in the pervasive dichotomy, a symbolic action that may best be identified as that of punishment, chastisement, or castigation. The edition of *Lazarillo* that was approved by the Inquisition was the *edición castigado.* Alemán, in effect, makes such "chastisement" an integral part of his text, the dominant protocol of his own version of the picaresque. As Guzmán says himself at one point, "It stood with me as with prohibited bookes" (II, 60). A new novelistic protocol is simply written over the older protocol of *Lazarillo de Tormes.*

The protocol of castigation is most obvious in the moralizing commentary, which functions almost as a gloss or marginalia on the primary narrative line of autobiography.

Indeed, the "discreet reader" is invited to collaborate: "In this Discourse, thou maist moralize things, as they shall be offered unto thee, Thou hast a large margent left thee to doe it" (I, 18). The *prodesse* is intrinsically separated from the *delectare* in the Horatian formula; moral "profit" is to be brought in from beyond any unified literary text.[36] A characteristic moralizing sequence in *Guzmán* is the report on an immoral act by the protagonist, followed by a criticism of that act, followed by a general condemnation of the offense as common to all mankind, followed by proverbs and a brief exemplum. It is this moral policing of literature that Cervantes mocks so brilliantly in his picaresque fantasia "The Dog's Colloquy": "All this is preaching, Scipio my friend," Berganza interrupts his canine companion. "I agree with you, and so I'll be quiet," Scipio replies—whereupon Berganza launches into a long moralizing digression of his own.[37]

Yet the chastisement is not merely extrinsic to *Guzmán de Alfarache.* It is also represented, vividly and realistically, in the psychology of the picaro himself. Realism in the novel, I have suggested, is simply a certain type of protocol, one that engages certain formalities of an extraliterary world. In *Lazarillo* it is most fully rendered in the attention to physical objects, to their manipulation and substitutability for one another. The thoughts and feelings of the character are more hidden, more ambiguous. In *Guzmán,* the world of objects is of less concern; the focus of novelistic realism is the emotional and cognitive experience of the corrected offender. We see clearly Guzmán's ambivalence toward morality, and his psychological dependence on the approval of others. He becomes addicted to certain gratifications beyond all physical need, as when he compulsively steals sweetmeats at the house of the Cardinal. He experiences humiliation and then struggles to assuage it. His response to correction is a mixed one, involving rationalization, self-condemnation, and criticism of the offense in other people. The older narrator, supposedly converted and redeemed at the end of his story, looks back on his earlier self and belabors it with moral truths, but the earlier self has internalized the psychic drama of crime and punishment as well.

It is important to see that the scene of this crime and punishment is the self rather than society; Guzmán is considerably less than a hardened criminal. Alexander Parker rightly insists that a picaro is a "delinquent" rather than a felon, a character whose social acts are more in the nature of misdemeanors than gross violations of the law. The law Guzmán is most concerned with is moral and religious, and when he is finally sent to the galleys it is for misappropriation of funds rather than robbery or murder. While he is in the galleys he is most severely punished for a theft he did not commit. There is considerable attention to Guzmán's family as causal factors in his delinquency—to his father, a converted Jew and a merchant of varying fortunes and shady practices; to his mother, who is a fortune hunter and a whore; and to his one-time wife, whose death causes him multiple hardships. He is often punished for and by the failings of those he depends on, yet Alemán conveys little sense of protest at the injustice.

Guzmán's own attitude might be called both pessimistic and masochistic. He even has some insight into the way his attitude limits his prospects. "I have learned long agoe couragiously to suffer and abide the changes of Fortune with an undaunted minde, for I alwayes suspect the worst, looking for the hardest measure she can give me, and prevent her better usage, by expecting no good at her hands" (III, 131-32). But in Alemán's imagination the precise justice of a particular punishment is less important than the rough justice of human suffering for human sinfulness. As one critic has suggested, the religious stress of the novel is less on the New Testament law of love and redemption than on the Old Testament law of persistent original sin.[38]

The castigation or chastisement that is so pervasive in Guzmán's experience is a means of preserving the intrinsically wayward self. As Guzmán says at one point, "All which I did, that by correcting my selfe, I might conserve my selfe" (II, 35). Dissipation is more than a metaphor; it becomes a threat to one's very identity. Or as Guzmán says to the reader, "My only purpose was (as I told thee before) to benefit thee, and to teach thee the way, how thou mightest with a good deale of content and safetie, passe thorow the gulph of that dangerous sea wherein thou saylest. The blowes I shall receive, thou the good counsels" (III, 28). Guzmán is a scapegoat for the self in Counter Reformation society, one in whose sacrifice every reader may vicariously participate, just as he, in his moral castigation of the sins widespread in that society, participates vicariously in the survival of the reader.

Thus we see in the structure of *Guzmán de Alfarache* the picaresque's characteristic alliance of the high and the low against the middle, but the alliance works in a different way than in *Lazarillo de Tormes*. Here high religious doctrine continually chastizes low secular practice, subjecting it to corrective punishment. Low practice does not insinuate itself into the honorable middle estate, as in the ironic upward mobility of Lazarillo; rather it drags this middle estate down with it, into its own abasement. Thus in *Guzmán* the picaro and the novel are allowed many of the trappings of humanistic dignity and culture. There are dedicatory poems and prefaces advertising the artistry of Mateo Alemán, and we are told in one of them that Guzmán has "(by his study) come to be a good Latinist, Rhetorician, and Grecian" (I, 19). Guzmán spends a good deal of time in cultivated Italy, and pursues a degree in the liberal arts at the University of Alcalá de Henares. Yet all this residual humanism is of little consolation as Guzmán continually experiences the collapse of his higher aspirations. He visits Florence at one point in his travels and marvels for a time at the beauty and fine artistic form of the city. But his aesthetic valuation is soon subjected to an economic one as he runs out of money; Florence "began now (me thought) to stinke, I could not endure the sent of it; every thing seemed so foule and filthy to my sight, that I did now long to be gone. . . . You may see (my masters) what wonders want of money can worke" (III, 213).

It is a similar case with the three interpolated romances that Alemán introduces into Guzmán's narrative, a device uncharacteristic of other picaresque novels. They are, in their mode, more idealizing and "entertaining" than Guzmán's picaresque adventures, but they also deal, thematically, with more cruel and unusual punishments. The first, a Moorish romance, allows the hero to convert to Christianity and escape his execution. The third, taken from Masuccio, involves a rape which revenges itself and leaves the husband in blissful ignorance of his wife's violation. The middle tale, "Dorido and Clorinia," is a macabre story in which a man cuts off the hand of a woman and has both his hands cut off in return. The hands are nailed to the dying woman's door with some verses in which the first offender proclaims the "sentence / . . . too small a punishment for my Offence" (II, 291). In effect, Alemán creates a fictional arm of the Inquisition itself through his protocol of corrective punishment. But like the irony of the impetus given to modern capitalism by the theology of Luther and Calvin, the irony of Alemán's project is that his didactic religious purpose considerably extended the developing secularity of the novel as a literary form.

The publication of a spurious Second Part of *Guzmán de Alfarache* by a certain Juan Martí apparently led Alemán to intensify and complicate, though not essentially to change, the protocol of the First Part. There is not the major transformation of the rules of the First Part that we see in the Second Part of *Don Quixote,* but like Cervantes, Alemán manages to incorporate the counterfeit sequel into his continuation of the novel while taking an imaginative revenge on its author. Alemán's revenge is indirect. He has Guzmán meet a character named Sayavedra (Martí's pseudonym) who identifies himself as Juan Martí's brother. Sayavedra first robs Guzmán, but then becomes his servant; he recounts his life to his master, which is a pure, unmoralized version of the picaresque. Finally, during a storm at sea, Sayavedra goes mad, claims that he is Guzmán de Alfarache, jumps overboard, and drowns. Guzmán laments his death with apparent sincerity, making Alemán's punishment of his rival seem an impersonal fate:

> It would have griev'd a mans heart and moved much compassion, to see the things that he did, and the fooleries which he uttered; . . . he would crye out in a loud voyce, I am Guzman de Alfarache's ghost, I am that ghost of his, which goes thus wandering up and downe the world; whereat he made me often both laugh and feare. . . . he would not leave his talking, but by flashes would fall a ripping up of my life, and bolt out by fits, all that which I had formerly recounted unto him concerning the courses I had taken, composing a thousand extravagancies.

> (IV, 38-39)

Whether Martí's sequel is the main cause of the change or not, we can see how Alemán's Second Part of *Guzmán* further criticizes and corrects the narrative energy of the simple picaresque *vida*. Guzmán is himself the master in this relationship, not the servant. The picaresque account of trickery and deceit is attributed to another character, and this understudy is then killed off. The picaresque scapegoat is given a picaresque scapegoat of his own. Alemán complains in the Second Part that he does not want his book to be known as the book of the picaro, but as "The Watch-Tower of mans life" (III, 127). The subtitle *Atalaya de la vida humana* (the "watchman" is borrowed from Ezekiel), appears on the title page, and though one may well question Guzmán's status as a latter-day prophet, there is a substantial increase in moralizing in this sequel. Whole chapters go by with only the briefest allusion to specific events from Guzmán's life story, and the narrator loses all self-consciousness about his digressions. As a character, Guzmán is also a more public and official figure than in the First Part—he is a courtier, a master of servants, a husband, a merchant, and a scholar. His final position is that of a convict in the galleys, but this dramatic degradation can also be seen as part of the heavier castigation of the picaresque in the Second Part. He does undergo a conversion in the galleys but, as Norval notes, "Guzmán's most spectacular conversion has been followed by his most hideous act of revenge," the entrapment and betrayal of Soto, a convict who had earlier borne false witness against him.[39] "Soto, and one of his Companions, who were the Ring-leaders of this rebellion, were condemned to be drawne in pieces with foure Gallies; and five others to bee hang'd: Which sentence was executed. And as many as were found to have a finger in this businesse, were confined to the Gallies for terme of life, being first publikely whipt, passing from Gally to Gally, till they had rounded the whole Fleete" (IV, 352-53). After this orgy of correction, Guzmán himself is pardoned and set free, and his narrative comes to an end. The clearest thing about his conversion is that it finally enables the old offender to join forces with the police. Alemán promises a third part of *Guzmán de Alfarache* but it seems never to have appeared. His only subsequent works were a book on spelling, a life of the archbishop of Mexico, and *San Antonio de Padua,* a saint's life.

There were many successors to *Guzmán,* however, in the series of picaresque novels that developed in Spain. The series became not a single line of development but a branching in several directions. Ignoring for the moment the picaresque novellas of Cervantes, which will be taken up in the following chapter, one can describe three different lines of succession. The first was inaugurated by *La Pícara Justina* (1605), more properly a parody of the picaresque. It is "an implicit satire on the aims and structure of *Guzmán de Alfarache,*" Parker notes, "whose appearance was, as the Prologue states, the spur of its own publication." "Its style . . . is a treasure-house of the language of burlesque, a riot of verbosity in which popular speech is given an exuberant ornamentation by being overladen with the language of polite literature."[40] But this parody was reclaimed by more straightforward picaresque novels, as Parker shows, like Salas Barbadillo's *Hija de Celestina* (1612) and Castillo Solorzano's *La Garduna de Sevilla* (1642), in which the protagonist is female, the narrative is in the third person, and there is little or no moral emphasis. As one critic points out, Salas Barbadillo tries

to give his version of the picaresque a unity of form and a coherence of effect that would bring it in line with neo-Aristotelian principles.[41]

A second line of succession tended to bypass *Guzmán de Alfarache* and hearken back to *Lazarillo de Tormes.* The ironic tone of *Lazarillo* becomes more playful and comic, and there is a notable lack of moral commentary. The lower-class rogue continues to survive on the fringes of society by his wits alone. Examples of this line include Jean de Luna's "corrected and emended" second part of *Lazarillo de Tormes* (1620), Tolosa's *Lazarillo de Manzanares* (1620), and the apparently eponymous *Estevanillo Gonzalez* (1646). In *Estevanillo* in particular, the hero becomes a more traditional jester, and the spirit of the Counter Reformation is conspicuously absent.

Finally, there are a number of Spanish texts that adopt certain forms or themes of the picaresque novel for essentially other kinds of writing: Espinel's *Marcos de Obregón* (1618), a largely autobiographical series of adventures with a minimal emphasis on deceptive transactions; Carlos García's *Desordenada Codicia* (1619), combining one rogue's confession with a general anatomy of thieves and thieving, extending to classical and biblical precedents; and Enríque Gómez's *El siglo pitagorico* (1644), probably based on a satire of Lucian, which deals with the transmigration of a picaro's soul. Though these last works clearly derive from the picaresque, they move well beyond the novel into the miscellaneous "literature of roguery," as Chandler calls it. The novel arose in Golden Age Spain, but it was perfectly capable of declining then as well, or of passing into other kinds of literature. *Estevanillo Gonzalez* was the last picaresque novel of any significance written in Spain until the nineteenth century. It is probably this curious loss of the novelistic initiative in Spanish literature itself that has led literary historians to underestimate its importance in the reorganization of the novel in France and in England, when the challenge of the novel to canonical literature was to become more permanently established.

The most brilliant of all the successors of the original *Lazarillo de Tormes* and *Guzmán de Alfarache* was Quevedo's *El Buscón—La vida del Buscón llamado don Pablos,* which may have been begun as early as 1604 but which was not published until 1626. What is most interesting about this version of the picaresque is that Quevedo appears quite hostile to the values and techniques of *Lazarillo* and *Guzmán,* indeed to the idea of the novel itself. He was one of the most learned classical scholars of his time and a virulent defender of aristocratic privilege. As far as editors can tell, he never authorized the publication of *El Buscón* as a book, but instead had it circulated in manuscript, in the older courtly manner of transmission.[42] The narrative is literarily self-conscious; its stylistic brilliance is heavily indebted to the baroque conceit rather than to literal description. The story is "The Life of the Swindler, Called Don Pablos," a generic rather than a specific title and one that calls attention to the hero's unreliability and social pretensions rather than to his proper name and birthplace. Quevedo's reception of the picaresque resembles that of Cervantes, who saw the emergent novel as a literary kind rather than as something unique.

Nevertheless, Quevedo's literary mimicry is such that he produces a novel of his own—not a parody like the *Pícara Justina,* nor a satire like his own *Sueños,* which freely mingle the natural and the supernatural in their visionary denunciation of human vice and folly. Unlike Cervantes, Quevedo did not create the broadly different counterfiction to the picaresque that *Don Quixote* represents, but, like Ginés de Pasamonte in Cervantes's novel, he turns out one of the best of the kind ever written.[43] To use a current theoretical term, Quevedo deconstructs the picaresque novel as he knew it, dismantles its formality and its ideology from within. Yet in the ongoing history of the novel as a form, this deconstruction is virtually indistinguishable from a new novel in the series, another novel informed by a different protocol. As we have seen, in the emergence of the novel such opposition became the rule rather than the exception.

The stance of *El Buscón* toward its predecessors can be seen most clearly in a preface "To the Reader," which is apparently not Quevedo's own but was added by the bookseller, Roberto Duport, who arranged for the first printed text.[44] If such is the case, Duport is an attentive reader of Quevedo, making explicit what the author leaves his audience to discover on its own: that the reader of this text will pick it up expecting entertainment but will find his pleasure quickly turning to embarrassment and pain. "Here you will find all the tricks of the low life or those which I think most people enjoy reading about," the preface advises. The admission of our pleasure becomes somewhat unsettling as we follow the list: "craftiness, deceit, subterfuge and swindles, born of laziness to enable you to live on lies." The pleasure principle becomes a still more disturbing kind of profit: "and if you attend to the lesson you will get quite a lot of benefit from it." Such benefits one would hardly want to acknowledge. The final humiliation comes as we are advised to reform ourselves, on the basis of something not even in the text: "Study the sermons, for I doubt if anyone buys a book as coarse as this in order to avoid the inclinations of his own depraved nature." The nonexistent "sermons" are a jibe at *Guzmán de Alfarache,* but the more serious accusation is leveled at the *hypocrite lecteur.*[45] It is not only the picaresque novel that Quevedo calls into question but the picaresque reader who would consume them, the "idle reader" treated so much more liberally by Cervantes.

Thus while there are many signs of Quevedo trying in *El Buscón* to outdo *Lazarillo* by presenting exaggerated versions of episodes in the earlier text,[46] and while there is much evidence that *El Buscón* is a thoroughgoing thematic rejection of the social and moral values of *Guzmán* (in the version of Juan Martí as well as of Alemán),[47] the most powerful assault is made on the expectations and the sensibilities of the reader. The protocol of this novel is a protocol of mortification, like the chastisement of *Guzmán* in some respects, but different in the means and the purpose of the punishment meted out. Where Alemán intends the punishment as corrective and finally beneficial to the self, Quevedo holds out little hope for anyone's reform. And where Alemán effects his chastisement by a heavy application of moral wisdom from outside and beyond, Quevedo mortifies the pleasure of the text by subversion from within. The focus of this protocol is not on objects in the world, nor is it on psychology of the main character as an actor in the world. It is rather on the vicarious experience of reading a first-person novel, where we experience objects and psychology through the medium of another self, or, more strictly speaking, through the medium of another's printed discourse. Pablos's first initiative in the novel is to reject the careers his parents envision for him—his father wants him to be a thief, his mother a male witch—and to pursue an education: "I told them I wanted to learn to be an honest man and that they ought to send me to school, because you couldn't do anything without knowing how to read and write" (87). Literacy is easily acquired, but honesty (virtue, *virtud* in the Spanish) is not. As readers we are quickly led to sympathize with Pablos's desire to escape his demoralizing origins, but we are repeatedly shown the impossibility of his doing so.

As recent critics of the novel point out, there is a persistent pattern in Pablos's adventures of the past returning to haunt him, humiliate him, and finally destroy him. "The structure of the *Buscón,* based on a repetition of motifs, is designed to block Pablos' exit from the family of which he is so ashamed," writes C. B. Morris.[48] Thus Pablos's moment of picaresque awakening comes from the realization that the insults other children have heaped on his mother—that she is a witch and a whore—are true. "When I realized the truth it was like a kick in the stomach" (89). Thus he is "paralyzed with shame" in the middle of his career by the fact that his uncle is a hangman (142) and he is forced to leave Madrid. And thus toward the end of the novel, when he is trying to pass himself off as a nobleman, his childhood friend Don Diego reappears and inadvertently reveals his antecedents. Speaking of the remarkably similar person he used to know, Don Diego exclaims, "You won't believe this, sir, but your mother was a witch, your father a thief and your uncle a public executioner, and he was the worst and most unpleasant man you ever saw" (189). Of course Don Diego soon discovers the truth of Pablos's identity.

Nevertheless, as Leo Spitzer observed long ago, it is difficult to maintain that a coherent moral judgment on Pablos is being elicited from us as readers.[49] In the first place, such a judgment is so easily passed as to be uninteresting. Pablos's wrongdoing and dullness are obvious and self-confessed, and his singular lack of success as a trickster can hardly evoke the indignation of satire. Secondly, the main impetus of his adventures is the emulation of someone else's example. Much more than Guzmán, Pablos is overanxious to please; he is less a servant of many masters than a student of many teachers. "I went to school," he says, "and the master greeted me very cheerfully, saying that I looked a quick bright lad. As I didn't want to disabuse him I did my lessons very well that day" (88). He adopts the role of picaro later on out of a similar desire to conform: "'when in Rome do as the Romans do,' says the proverb, and how right it is. After thinking about it I decided to be as much a tearaway as the others and worse than them if I could. I don't know if I succeeded but I certainly tried hard enough" (112). And even at the lowest moral point in his career, when he kills two policemen in Seville, he has been inspired by the example of others, in particular by a former classmate, Mattoral, whom he calls "the master of novices" (212). Pablos is an incurable reader of other persons' *vidas*. Conversely, the reader of his *vida* is continually and disarmingly solicited to identify with Pablos's emotions, rather than to pass judgment on his acts. "How can I explain my feelings?" he asks rhetorically (96). "You can imagine what sort of life we led under these conditions" (97). "You can't imagine how disgusted I was," he says of a meal with his uncle where the meat pies are made of human flesh—an understatement more effective than any exaggeration (143).

The ruling passion of Pablos as a character, and the dominant affect with which the reader finds himself involved, is the feeling of shame. With Guzmán, it is more proper to speak of a sense of guilt, of the internalization and partial grasp of the sense of wrongdoing and suffering for wrong. But in Pablos's case the sense of self is bound up with externals and surfaces, with the image reflected to the self by others. This personal shame-culture of the main character is reflected in the hyperbolic conceits and understated euphemisms that pervade the narrative style. As Parker puts it, "The exposure of human self-conceit is apparent . . . in a particular type of verbal witticism that is a constant thread running through the style. In describing people or objects connected with them, Quevedo uses an epithet or a phrase that ennobles them, and then, by word-play, shatters the illusion by turning it into its opposite."[50] For example, Pablos mentions his younger brother, who picks pockets in their father's barbershop. "He was caught in the act," Pablos says, "and the little angel died from a few lashes they gave him in prison. My father was very upset, because the child stole the heart of everybody who saw him" (85). We are mortified by our initial assent to the sentimental metaphors.

The focus on surfaces can also be seen in the emphasis on clothing in the novel, on disguises which dignify temporarily but which only heighten the sense of shame when they ultimately fail. Pablos dresses up as the "boy-king" in carnival time and ends up smeared with excrement. Don Torribio and his beggars' fraternity dress in bits and pieces of respectable attire, and their "honor" depends on only being seen from the right angle. Don Diego insists on trading cloaks with Pablos at the end, only to set him up for a beating and slashing by Don Diego's men. As a picaro, Pablos is for the most part a bad imitation, a parody of the more honest and honorable substance of the aristocrat. But as readers we are forced to identify with the

parodic figure; we are given no access to the character of authentic social value.[51]

This mortification of character and reader is intensified by Quevedo's specific denial of religious transcendence to this lowest of the low. The alliance of the high and the low found in *Lazarillo* and in *Guzmán* is explicitly rejected in *El Buscón,* as when Pablos is spat upon and beaten. "Please don't," Pablos protests; "I'm not Christ on the Cross, you know" (108). In a theological as well as an emotional sense, Quevedo's narrative is merciless. One might argue that the ultimate purpose of Quevedo's mortification of Pablos's flesh and of the reader's spirit is religious salvation, as in the *autos da fé* which allowed the heretic to recant. But such a prospect would be radically extrinsic to the text, which ends instead in a confirmation of mortal hopelessness. Like Lazarillo, Pablos ends his story joined up with a proven whore, but, unlike Lazarillo, Pablos is radically displaced from European society.

> When I saw that this situation was going to be more or less permanent and that bad luck was dogging my heels, I made up my mind, not because I was intelligent enough to see what was going to happen but because I was tired and obstinate in my wickedness, to go to America with Grajales. . . . I thought things would go better in the New World and another country. But they went worse, as they always will for anybody who thinks he has only to move his dwelling without changing his life or ways.
>
> (213-14)

The manuscript versions of the text promise that we will see this worsening in a "second part," but Quevedo apparently thought better of a sequel. It is perhaps proper to speak of *El Buscón* as a dead end of the Spanish picaresque, as it is hard to envision any sequel following its particular lead into any further negation.

Notes

1. See Marcel Bataillon, *Erasme et l'Espagne* (Paris: E. Droz, 1937), pp. 652-53; Francisco Marquez Villanueva, "La actitud espiritual del *Lazarillo de Tormes,*" *Espiritualidad y literatura en el siglo XVI* (Madrid-Barcelona: Alfarguana, 1968), pp. 67-137. Ann Wiltrout argues for the influence of one of Erasmus's satiric colloquies on *Lazarillo* in "The *Lazarillo de Tormes* and Erasmus' 'Opulentia Sordida,'" *Romanische Forschungen* 81 (1969), 550-64, and R. W. Truman suggests a confluence of motifs in "*Lazarillo de Tormes,* Petrarch's *De remediis adversae fortunae,* and Erasmus's *Praise of Folly,*" *Bulletin of Hispanic Studies* 52 (1975), 33-53.

2. "'Liberty's A Whore,'" *The Reversible World,* p. 108.

3. *The Praise of Folly,* trans. John Wilson (1688) (Ann Arbor: University of Michigan Press, 1958), p. 141. Cf. 1 Cor. 3:18: "Make no mistake about this: if there is anyone among you who fancies himself

wise—wise, I mean by the standards of the passing age—he must become a fool to gain true wisdom. For the wisdom of this world is folly in God's sight" (NEB).

4. The allusion to Cicero recalls an accusation that Cicero himself came from "low and obscure ancestors and from modest and unworthy parents," a piece of information retailed by Torquemada in Spain in 1553; see Harry Sieber, *The Picaresque,* The Critical Idiom (London: Methuen & Co., 1977), p. 15.

5. S. Gilman, "The Death of Lazarillo de Tormes," *PMLA* LXXI (1966), p. 161.

6. See in this regard Mikhail Bakhtin's broad and compelling study of Rabelais in the tradition of the folk carnival, *Rabelais and His World.* The more sparing, though still significant, folk elements of *Lazarillo* are noted in A. D. Deyermond, *Lazarillo de Tormes: A Critical Guide,* Critical Guides to Spanish Texts, no. 15 (London: Grant and Cutler, 1975), pp. 34-35, 81-87.

7. Bakhtin uses the term, for example. See also Barbara Babcock-Abrahams, "The Novel and the Carnival World: An Essay in Memory of Joe Doherty," *Modern Language Notes* 89 (1974), 911-37; Alice Fiola Berry, "'Les Mithologies Pantagruelicques': Introduction to a Study of Rabelais' *Quart livre*," *PMLA* 92 (1977), 471-80; and Gabriel Josipovici, "A Modern Master," *New York Review of Books,* 24, no. 16 (Oct. 13, 1977), 34-37.

8. *Rabelais: A Study in Comic Courage* (Englewood Cliffs, N.J.: Prentice-Hall, 1970), p. 30.

9. *Mimesis: The Representation of Reality in Western Literature,* trans. Willard R. Trask (Princeton: Princeton University Press, 1953), pp. 277-78.

10. Greene claims, for example, that the term satire "shrivels up" before Rabelais (*Rabelais,* p. 10), and Bakhtin insists on the broader and more integral humor of Gargantua and Pantagruel as distinct from the narrow and disintegrating quality of satire in the seventeenth and eighteenth centuries (*Rabelais and His World,* pp. 59-144, passim). Ronald Paulson, on the other hand, argues for the essentially satiric nature of Rabelais and extends the term to the Spanish picaresque novel and *Don Quixote* as well; see *The Fictions of Satire* (Baltimore: Johns Hopkins Press, 1967), pp. 58-73, 80-86, 98-104. The theory of satire is only slightly less vexed than the theory of the novel.

11. *The Cankered Muse: Satire of the English Renaissance,* Yale Studies in English, vol. 142 (New Haven: Yale University Press, 1959), pp. 3-4.

12. Ibid., pp. 7-8.

13. See Leonard Feinberg, *Introduction to Satire* (Ames: The Iowa State University Press, 1967), p. 11: "In actual practice, satirists usually apply a standard not of morality but of appropriateness—in other words a *social* norm. It is a norm concerned not with ethics but with customs, not with morals but with mores; and it may be accepted by an entire society, or only one class of that society, or just a small coterie."

14. *The Resources of Kind: Genre-Theory in the Renaissance,* ed. Barbara K. Lewalski (Berkeley: University of California Press, 1973), p. 7; she is paraphrasing Claudio Guillén here. As Colie goes on to argue, the *mimesis* of Aristotelian genre theory was often interpreted to mean the imitation of the formal models themselves, or as Alexander Pope put it in his *Essay on Criticism,* "Learn hence for Ancient *Rules* a just Esteem; / To copy *Nature* is to copy *Them.*"

15. *Le Texte du roman,* pp. 45 ff. Kristeva does not distinguish adequately, however, between the structure of the novel and the structure of satire ("la menippée").

16. See, for example, Parker, *Literature and the Delinquent,* pp. 28-31. Francisco Rico, on the other hand, regards *Lazarillo* and *Guzmán de Alfarache* as the prime examples of the picaresque novel and Quevedo's *El Buscón,* which Parker regards as the "zenith" of the picaresque, as a dead end; see *La novela picaresca y el punto de vista,* 2d ed. (Barcelona: Editorial Seix Barral, 1973), pp. 129 ff.

17. See Bataillon, Introduction, *Le roman picaresque* (Paris: Renaissance du Livre, 1931), p. 5.

18. *La novela picaresca y el punto de vista,* esp. pp. 45-55.

19. "The Death of Lazarillo de Tormes," p. 158.

20. Luke 16:28-31 (NEB). It is arguable that Lazarillo is an allusion as well to the Lazarus in John 11, who *does* arise from the dead and who does "bring glory to the Son of God"—as well as precipitating the Crucifixion. But the parabolic nature of the story in Luke and the way in which Lazarus is seen as inferior to Moses and the prophets is closer to the spirit of the Spanish novel than is the dramatic and compelling miracle described in John. Some biblical scholars suggest that the Johannine episode may in fact be a reshaping of the Lucan parable, though the borrowing may have proceeded in the other direction; see the commentary on John 11 in the Anchor Bible, *Gospel According to John* (i-xii), ed. Raymond E. Brown, S.S. (Garden City, N.Y.: Doubleday, 1966), pp. 428 ff.

21. "The Death of Lazarillo de Tormes," p. 153. See also Richard Hitchcock, "Lazarillo and 'Vuestra Merced,'" *Modern Language Notes* 86 (1971), 264-66, and L. J. Woodward, "Author-Reader Relationship in the *Lazarillo de Tormes,*" *Forum for Modern Language Studies* 1 (1965), 43-53, for different versions of this normative approach.

22. "Parody and Irony in the Self-Portrayal of Lázaro de Tormes," *Modern Language Review* 63 (1968), 605.

Cf. Frank Durand, "The Author and Lázaro: Levels of Comic Meaning," *Bulletin of Hispanic Studies* 45 (1968), 89-101, esp. p. 100: "To acknowledge specific social or clerical criticism, clearly stated moral observations, is to accept the obvious; to limit one's conclusions to the fact that Lázaro feels he has reached the ultimate heights of success when he has, in fact, descended to the lowest moral depths, is to remain on the surface of the work at the easiest ironic level."

23. I owe this allusion to my friend Alfred MacAdam, now of the Spanish Department of the University of Virginia. The quotation, and the previous one as well, are from W. S. Merwin's translation, *The Life of Lazarillo de Tormes: His Fortunes and Adversities* (Garden City, N.Y.: Doubleday, 1962), p. 39.

24. See Chandler, *The Romances of Roguery,* pp. 205-9. But by 1620 Jean de Luna had "corrected and emended" this sequel, making the tuna-fish transformation a trick rather than a metamorphosis and in general reproducing quite effectively the realism and irony of the original.

25. "Genre and Countergenre: The Discovery of the Picaresque," *Literature as System,* pp. 135-38. An earlier version of this essay appeared in 1966.

26. *Literature as System,* pp. 146 ff. The publication of what amounts to a parody of the picaresque novel, *La Pícara Justina,* in the same year as the First Part of *Don Quixote* should be mentioned as a further element in the recognition process.

27. *Resources of Kind,* pp. 12, 115 (her italics). Colie argues that some genres are defined by subject matter alone, but this is simply an overextension of the term. As Alistair Fowler claims, "Strictly speaking, only motifs with a formal basis, such as the singing contest, are securely genre-linked," although Fowler admits that there is a tendency for "genre" to become a more loosely defined "mode" ("The Life and Death of Literary Forms," *New Literary History* 2 [1971], 203, 214). For a stimulating Marxist critique of genre theory, see Fredric Jameson, "Magical Narratives: Romance as Genre," *New Literary History* 7 (1975), 135-63.

28. A precedent for such sequels was provided by the chivalric romances (*Amadis of Greece* following *Amadis of Gaul, Orlando Furioso* following *Orlando Innamorato*). It is interesting that Cervantes ends the First Part of *Don Quixote* with a line from *Orlando Furioso,* "Forse altri cantera con miglior plettro" ("Perhaps another will sing with a sweeter tone"), after promising to relate more of Quixote's adventures himself. He perhaps anticipated a worthier imitator than he got in Avellaneda. The idea of the novelist as "sole proprietor" of his fictional characters and terrain, as claimed by William Faulkner for his Yoknapatawpha County, has yet to be recognized by modern copyright law.

29. The endings of *Lazarillo* and Melville's *The Confidence-Man,* respectively—though modern editors of *Lazarillo* regard the promise of a sequel as the work of an interpolator.

30. *Literature as System,* pp. 71-106, passim.

31. *The Picaresque Novel* (Cleveland: Case Western Reserve University Press, 1967), p. 4.

32. "The Nature of Picaresque Narrative: A Modal Approach," *PMLA* 89 (1974), 240. Wicks does discriminate levels of generality and abstraction similar to Guillén's, however. And he advocates a hermeneutic circularity of interpretation, in which the reader moves from "the total picaresque fictional situation" (243) back to specific texts. Richard Bjornson's *The Picaresque Hero in European Fiction* (Madison: University of Wisconsin Press, 1977), which appeared too late for me to profit from in this chapter, proceeds under the aegis of Wicks's modal approach. It combines historical and critical commentary on a series of picaresque narratives from *Lazarillo* to *Roderick Random,* but avoids the question of the novel per se.

33. Sieber, *The Picaresque,* pp. 22-23.

34. Donald McGrady calculates that the moralizing alone makes up 13 percent of the First Part of *Guzmán* and 23 percent of the Second Part (*Mateo Alemán* [New York: Twayne Publishers, 1968], p. 74). Lesage's translation, Englished in turn by Motteux, is the clearest example of the paring away of the moralizing. On the other hand, translations like those of Barezzo Barezzi's Italian, Gaspar Ens's Latin, and even Mabbe's English add considerably to the so-called digressive material; see James Fitzmaurice-Kelly's introduction to Mabbe, *The Rogue,* pp. xxx-xxxvi, and Edmond Cros, *Protée et le gueux* (Paris: Didier, 1967), pp. 104-26. Cros, for his part, over-emphasizes the moralistic commentary. He treats *Guzmán* not as a picaresque novel but as a rhetorical anatomy of beggary, not "The Life of Guzman de Alfarache" but "The Book of the Beggar" (*Le livre du gueux*).

35. The phrases are J. A. Jones's in "The Duality and Complexity of *Guzmán de Alfarache*: Some Thoughts on the Structure and Interpretation of Alemán's Novel," in *Knaves and Swindlers: Essays on the Picaresque Novel in Europe,* ed. Christine J. Whitbourne, University of Hull Publications (London: Oxford University Press, 1974), p. 44.

36. See Lawrence Lipking, "The Marginal Gloss," *Critical Inquiry* 3 (1977), 609-55, for a useful discussion of literary marginalia, esp. pp. 621-25 on the gloss in the Renaissance and its dependence on biblical commentary.

37. *Exemplary Stories,* trans. C. A. Jones (Baltimore, MD: Penguin Books, 1972), p. 205.

38. M. N. Norval, "Original Sin and the 'Conversion' in the *Guzmán de Alfarache*," *Bulletin of Hispanic Studies* 51 (1974), 346-64.

39. Norval, "Original Sin," p. 363. He offers a detailed critique of Alexander Parker's position (in *Literature and the Delinquent*) that Guzmán has been psychologically changed by his conversion, though one must acknowledge the theological ambiguity of any conversion experience.

40. *Literature and the Delinquent*, pp. 50, 46. The only English translation, in *The Spanish Libertines,* trans. Captain John Stevens (London, 1707), unfortunately simplifies the diction and strips down the plot. Marcel Bataillon shows that the parody was a roman à clef for the society of the Court at Madrid ("Recherches sur la *Pícara Justina*," *Annuaire du Collège de France* 59 [1959], 567-69, and 60 [1960], 416-20).

41. Leonard Brownstein, *Salas Barbadillo and the New Novel of Rogues and Courtiers* (Madrid: Playor, S.A., 1974), pp. 85-94. Brownstein notes that a laudatory poem by a friend compares *La hija de Celestina* to "los Poemas" of Heliodorus and Achilles Tatius.

42. See the critical edition of Fernando Lázaro Carreter, Acta Salmanticensia, Filosofía y Letras, vol. XVIII, no. 4 (Salamanca, 1965), pp. lxv-lxvii.

43. The term "counterfiction" is used in an article on *El Buscón* by Michele and Cecile Cavillac, "A propos du *Buscón* et de *Guzmán de Alfarache*," *Bulletin Hispanique* 75 (1973), 124. But I would like to reserve it for the more independent antithesis of *Don Quixote,* as a substitute for what Guillén calls "countergenre." Cf. T. E. May, "Good and Evil in the *Buscón*: A Survey," *Modern Language Review* 45 (1950), 321: "Pablos shows the old *pícaro* of literature undergoing a transformation basically similar to that suffered by the knight of romance in becoming incarnate in Don Quixote."

44. This is the conclusion of Lázaro Carreter in his critical edition, pp. xv n., lxxviii.

45. The insult is compounded in the Spanish by the use of the second person singular rather than the polite and proper "Vuestra Merced." Carreter includes a brief "Carta Dedicatoria" that appears in two of the manuscripts and that he considers more likely to be by Quevedo himself, which does use the polite mode of address. Nevertheless, the self-presentation is peculiarly evasive and the politeness elaborately self-effacing, especially as compared to Lazarillo's prologue, on which it is most likely based. It reads, in its entirety: "Having known your honor's desire to hear the various discourses of my life, in order not to leave room that someone else (as in other cases) may lie, I have wanted to send you this account, which I hope will be not merely a small relief for your sad moments. And because I intend to be long in the telling of how short I have been of good fortune, I will cease to be so now." I am indebted to my colleague Ramón Saldívar for help with the translation.

46. E.g., the miserly priest who keeps the bread from Lazarillo becomes Dr. Cabra, "the High Priest of Poverty and Avarice Incarnate" (94) who actually starves boys to death; the poor *hidalgo*, Lazarillo's third master, becomes Don Torribio Rodriguez Valligo Gomez de Ampuero y Jordan, the nobleman-beggar, whose honor consists in his patchwork clothing. See R. O. Jones, *The Golden Age: Prose and Poetry, A Literary History of Spain* (London: Ernest Benn, 1971), pp. 135-36.

47. The most obvious element of *Guzmán* that *El Buscón* rejects is the lower-class critique of aristocratic honor; others include the ideas of social mobility, moral self-scrutiny, the need for social reform, and the possibility of the picaro's conversion. The critique is detailed by M. and C. Cavillac, who describe it as "une réaction *systématique* a l'encontre du modèle élaboré par Mateo Alemán avec la contribution abusive de Mateo Luján. . . . Son intention ne semble pas avoir été celle, positive, de rivaliser avec Alemán en fertilité d'invention et en puissance créatrice, mais bien celle, négative, de détruire la fiction alémanienne" ("A propos de *Buscón*," pp. 124-25). The fact that Quevedo does try to rival *Lazarillo* is perhaps a sign that he regards it as less of a threat than *Guzmán*.

48. *The Unity and Structure of Quevedo's Buscón*, Occasional Papers in Modern Languages, no. 1 (Hull: University of Hull Publications, 1965), p. 7. Cf. Parker, pp. 61.ff.

49. "Zur Kunst Quevedos in Seinem *Buscon*," *Archivum Romanicum* 11 (1927), 511-80.

50. *Literature and the Delinquent*, pp. 59-60.

51. May speaks of Pablos as the "shadow self" of Don Diego, and of Don Diego as the "conscience of Pablos, before which he is weaponless" ("Good and Evil in the Buscón," pp. 327-28). The doppelgänger effect is undeniable, although Quevedo's version of self-alienation is quite different from the nineteenth-century versions in such writers as Hoffmann, Gogol, Dostoevsky, and later in Kafka: the social definition of the self is both all-powerful and completely inaccessible, a kind of *societas abscondita*.

Ulrich Wicks (essay date 1989)

SOURCE: Wicks, Ulrich. "The Picaresque Genre." In *Picaresque Narratives, Picaresque Fictions: A Theory and Research Guide*, pp. 3-16. New York: Greenwood Press, 1989.

[*In the following essay, Wicks outlines the history of the picaresque narrative, and surveys current debates regarding the specific characteristics of the picaresque.*]

It has become a critical commonplace in generic theory to make an obligatory acknowledgment of vicious circularity before being forced to proceed within it. The frustration of this part of the hermeneutic task is succinctly put by Paul Hernadi (paraphrasing Günther Müller) in *Beyond Genre* (1972): "How can I define tragedy (or any other genre) before I know on which works to base the definition, yet how can I know on which works to base the definition before I have defined tragedy?" (2). Inside this circle is still another problem, which Alastair Fowler in *Kinds of Literature* (1982) calls "ineradicable knowledge": "In order to reconstruct the original genre, we have to eliminate from consciousness its subsequent states. For the idea of a genre that informs a reader's understanding is normally the latest, most inclusive conception of it that he knows. And unless he can unknow this conception, it seems that he cannot recover meanings that relate to the genre's earlier, 'innocent' states" (261). The first of these activities is essentially synchronic, seeking to create a paradigm or hypothetical *Ur*-type in the context of which individual works might be better understood. The second is primarily diachronic, aiming to trace the evolution of an identifiable genre or type in specific historical contexts. Together such literary activities only formalize theoretically and critically what is absolutely unsuppressible in even the most cursory acts of reading: trying to assimilate a new text into the familiar community of our accumulated reading experiences.

Even the child reading (or being read) her first stories gropes for connections, for the most rudimentary generic signals. In the act of reading, a text yields meaning only in the context of its co-texts from other acts of reading; these cotexts in turn alter their meanings and slightly rearrange themselves with the addition of every new text. The reading of each new text is therefore of necessity also a rereading of already familiar texts; the reading of the new and this rereading of the old often combine to form an extratext, a generic construct, or type, or kind against which the strangely new text can be familiarized while simultaneously reassessing the old texts. The reading experience is always implicitly and sometimes explicitly generic, and the whole of genre theory springs from this dynamic process, which T. S. Eliot in his "Tradition and the Individual Talent" (1917) captured in an assertion that itself resonates like the phenomenon it describes: "What happens when a new work of art is created is something that happens simultaneously to all the works of art which preceded it" (50). Fifty years later, Eliot's statement finds an echo in Julia Kristeva's description of the structuralist concept of *intertextuality,* as quoted in Jonathan Culler's *Structuralist Poetics* (1975): "Every text takes shape as a mosaic of citations, every text is the absorption and transformation of other texts" (139). Culler himself adds, "A work can only be read in connection with or against other texts, which provides a grid through which it is read and structured by establishing expectations which enable one to pick out salient features and give them a structure." Both Eliot's statement and the structuralist variations of it describe the creation and reception of literary texts as a process of continual generic readjustment, of constant reformulation of the literary frame of reference within which we read.

The very imprecision and circularity of Eliot's assertion ("what happens . . . is something that happens") are particularly appropriate to a phenomenon that is always process. Just when we think we have the "what" pinned down, the "something" proves elusive and forces us back to reformulate the "what," which in turn impels us to reassess the "something," and so on. The circle is not vicious after all, for it is hardly closed. As more texts are added to the collectivity of experienced texts, it resembles more an ever-expanding spiral, with each new text (or new reading of a previously read text) at its center for the duration of the reading. The centrifugal force of the new reading and the centripetal force of all accumulated readings (the "ineradicable memory") automatically—and dynamically—interact, creating the generic process that leads to an understanding of texts in the only way that we can understand them: in relation to other texts.

Or should lead. Genre theory, unfortunately, has more often than not in literary history been rigidly prescriptive rather than flexibly descriptive, for both maker and reader. When genre theory exists primarily as a pigeonholding or classification system for its own sake, it soon becomes tiresome to all but the hyperorganized reader, as individual literary works are coerced through formulaic reduction into available slots. Rigid genre theory actually undermines literature by squelching what we most admire in literary texts: the innovative, the unpredictable, the experimental—in short, the new, for which there may be no existing pigeonhole. When genre theory cannot or will not do what individual texts are constantly doing, then one of the two must make way for the other; either the new text is rejected as an unacceptable mutation, or genre theory must refine or expand its categories.

When literature thrives on experimentation, as it has in the twentieth century, prescriptive genre theory must make room or else make way. That the latter has been the case— that the theory of genres has not been at the center of literary study and reflection in this century—is diagnosed by René Wellek at the beginning of his "Genre Theory, the Lyric, and *Erlebnis*" (1967): "Clearly this is due to the fact that in the practice of almost all writers of our time genre distinctions matter little: boundaries are being constantly transgressed, genres combined or fused, old genres discarded or transformed, new genres created, to such an extent that the very concept has been called in doubt" (225). If genre theory adapted itself to what Wellek describes literature as doing—if, that is, it conceived of itself in Eliot's terms or along the lines of structuralist conceptions of intertextuality—it could again be at the heart of literary study, where in fact it should be, given that the act of reading is inherently generic.

If every act of reading is fundamentally, inherently, and inescapably generic and yet genre theory is not at the center of literary study, then somewhere theory must have gotten seriously out of whack with practice. It did so primarily by not changing as literature itself changes. This is precisely the point Fowler makes in refuting those who hold genre theory to be irrelevant because they misapprehend genres as simple and immutable permanent forms, established once and for all:

> But . . . genres are actually in a continual state of transmutation. It is by *their* modification, primarily, that individual works convey literary meaning. Frequent adjustments in genre theory are needed, therefore, if the forms are to continue to mediate between the flux of history and the canons of art. Thus, to expect fixed forms, immune to change yet permanently corresponding to literature, is to misunderstand what genre theory undertakes (or should undertake).
>
> (*Kinds of Literature,* 24; emphasis mine)

As Fowler suggests, genre theory must be conceived in rhythm with what actually happens in our individual acts of reading, which are only superficially guided by a genre theory that limits itself to the prescriptively taxonomic or the historically cartographic. When genre theory acknowledges the rudimentary generic groping of the reading experience itself, it can help us understand a text as the act of reading blends imperceptibly into interpretation. Here, too, generic identity is absolutely fundamental. It is also unavoidably consequential, as E. D. Hirsch points out in *Validity in Interpretation* (1967) when he says that "an interpreter's preliminary generic conception of a text is constitutive of everything that he subsequently understands, and that this remains the case unless and until that generic conception is altered" (74). It is this process of constant alteration that generic theory should concern itself with, as Thomas Kent proposes in *Interpretation and Genre* (1986) when he calls for a holistic theory of genre that will attempt to see each text as both an unchanging body of words and a continually developing cultural artifact: "The holistic genre critic, then, should see both the part and the whole, the synchronic and the diachronic conventional elements, constantly interacting together to form new patterns of meaning, and generating a descriptive model of this kind of activity requires a substantial shift in attitude about the critic's role in the study of literary texts" (27). Yet such a shift would only bring critical theory into line with literary practice; it would simply and rightfully acknowledge what actually happens to and in the text as it is being made and whenever it is being received. The term *holistic genre theory* ought to be something of a redundancy, but its necessity for Kent's purpose emphasizes how fragmenting and distancing our received concepts of genre have become when we bring them into our actual encounters with literary texts. Genre theory that has a healthy respect for how literature actually works should by its very nature be holistic, always keeping the text and its kind in a carefully balanced and mutually respectful relationship, which Rosalie Colie in her conclusion to *The Resources of Kind* (1973) captures in an almost aphoristic way: "Significant pieces of literature are worth much more than their kind, but they are what they are in part by their inevitable kindness" (128).

What concept of kind-ness was going through the mind of the reader in 1554 who picked up a slim volume called *La vida de Lazarillo de Tormes y de sus fortunas y adver-*

sidades? And what kinds of kind-ness had been at work in the mind and imagination of the anonymous author when he wrote it a year or two earlier? What prompted 1599 readers of the first part of *Guzmán de Alfarache* to make a conscious connection with *Lazarillo*? How aware were these readers of the generic newness of what they were reading, and how consciously did they have to sift through their accumulated reading experiences in order to assimilate these new texts? What generic signals were the texts themselves giving these readers? Was it only something as crude as mere content or subject matter? Who, in fact, were these first readers, and how did they respond interpretively to these fictions?

Unfortunately, the further back in literary history we go, the more elusively hypothetical the answers to such questions become. Thus far, we know relatively little about the actual readers of the fictions that soon came to be called picaresque. We know that *Lazarillo* was considered to be a subversive book. (In 1559 it was placed on the *Index Librorum Prohibitorum,* a list of books forbidden by Church authority to be read by Roman Catholics.) We know that *Guzmán* became an unprecedented best-seller. In the wake of the popularity of *Guzmán, Lazarillo* was reissued at least nine times in the four years between 1599 and 1603—as many editions as there had been in the whole forty-five years since its initial publication. King Philip II had died in 1598, and the new reign of his son Philip III resulted in some relaxation of censorship. For several years, then, until the publication of the first part of *Don Quixote* in 1605, *Lazarillo de Tormes* and *Guzmán de Alfarache* must have been the most talked-about books of the decade, if not of the century. But the actual composition of this sizable literate audience has not yet been explored. It seems reasonable to conclude that almost none of this large readership coincided with the lower class, among whom were the hordes of vagrants and beggars roaming the roads of Spain and congregating in some cities in such huge numbers that they had to be periodically expelled. The poor, as Lionel Trilling has said, do not read about the poor. One may imagine then, as Helen H. Reed does in *The Reader in the Picaresque Novel* (1984),

> a reading public comprised of aristocrats, courtiers, *conversos,* country gentry, the urban bourgeoisie, clergy, students, some women, and virtually no *pícaros.* . . . No doubt the individual novels varied in their appeal to different social groups as well as to different tastes, but the early picaresque novel might be described as a new genre in search of a readership, or a genre in the process of formation that created its own readership.
>
> (17-18)

That it was a democratic intended readership we know from the hypothetical readers set up in the prologues to both *Lazarillo* and *Guzmán*. Lazarillo not only addresses a specific narratee ("Vuestra Merced"), to whom he has been asked to explain his life, but he also invites a homogeneous readership to listen in, as it were, for "anybody can read my story and enjoy it." Alemán in *Guzmán* provides two direct addresses to readers—one "al Vulgo," the other "al discreto lector"—and then adds a "Declaration for the Understanding of this Book," which is addressed to all readers. No actual reader is going to admit belonging to the mob at whom the first prologue is aimed, and so Alemán shapes his readers by making them feel privileged, above the incorrigible rabble—a narrating strategy that justifies his subject matter by short-circuiting any objections to it. Ironically, the reader becomes part of an in-group looking at society's down and out. In both *Lazarillo* and *Guzmán,* all readers ("anybody") are discreet; this flattery aimed at the self-images of readers makes them paradoxically both willing and wary participants in a narrative confidence game that enables picaresque narration to function between author and reader.

In two of his three addresses to readers in the 1599 first part, Alemán uses *pícaro* (which does not occur in *Lazarillo*), a word choice he would come to regret by the time he published the second part of *Guzmán de Alfarache* in 1604, when he has Guzmán (in the sixth chapter of book 1) lament the epithet by which he has been known since writing the first part. The etymology of *pícaro* is troublesome. Corominas (1954-1957) dates its first appearance in 1525 in the expression *pícaro de cozina* ("kitchen boy," or "scullion"), a relatively neutral word with none of the associations Guzmán is complaining about. But around 1545, the meaning of *pícaro* shifted from designating a lowly profession to describing immoral and antisocial behavior. In Eugenio de Salazar's *Carta del Bachiller de Arcadia* (1548), *pícaros* are explicitly contrasted with courtiers. In a morality play of that time, the word is used in a context clearly of mischief and wrongdoing. Harry Sieber in *The Picaresque* (1977) suggests that the semantic shift may have had something to do with the vast armies of pike-men (*picas secas* and/or *piqueros secos,* from the verb *picar*) needed in Spain's defense of its territories. Some of them were recruited from among criminals, and many deserted. "Deserting soldiers . . . attempted to return home, begging and stealing on the way. It is possible that some of the deserters carried their previous military title of *piquero* with them into 'civilian' life" (6). Another explanation for the later meaning of *pícaro* is by association with Picardy, a region near Flanders where Spain was engaged in wars from 1587 to 1659. To a Spaniard, a Picard was a rogue. Whatever its precise origins, the word *pícaro* achieved wide currency by the end of the sixteenth century. In dictionaries compiled in 1570 and 1593, a *pícaro* is defined as a shabby man without honor. This was the popular meaning of the word when Alemán applied it to his literary creation, and from then on the meaning of the word has been inextricably bound up with the various literary characters who are called *pícaros.* A dramatic interlude called *Testamento del pícaro pobre,* which must have been written before 1605, when the author to whom it has been attributed (Pedro Láinez) died, has a sonnet in praise of the picaresque life; it begins, "Gozar de libertad, vivir contento" ("to enjoy freedom, to live content"), which emphasizes the picaro's outsider status positively as a freedom from responsibility and tiresome social obliga-

tions. A similar tone dominates a poem from about the same time, *La vida del pícaro,* in which "sólo el pícaro muere bien logrado, / que desde que nació, nada desea" ("only a picaro dies successful, because from birth he desired nothing"). By 1611 in Covarrubias's *Tesoro de la lengua castellana,* as Bjornson points out in *The Picaresque Hero in European Fiction* (1977), the word *pícaro* meant a vulgar, rootless person willing to perform menial tasks, but there begins to be associated with him "a characteristic freedom from duty and responsibility" (262).

A year after Guzmán de Alfarache complained of his epithet, Cervantes published the first part of *Don Quixote,* in the twenty-second chapter of which Quixote encounters the galley slave Ginés de Pasamonte, who says that he is writing a book:

> "It's so good," replied Ginés, "that Lazarillo de Tormes will have to look out, and so will everything in that style that has ever been written or ever will be. One thing I can promise you, is that it is all the truth, and such well-written, entertaining truth that there is no fiction that can compare with it."
>
> "And what is the title of the book?" asked Don Quixote.
>
> "*The Life of Ginés de Pasamonte,*" replied that hero.
>
> "Is it finished?" asked Don Quixote.
>
> "How can it be finished," replied the other, "if my life isn't? What is written begins with my birth and goes down to the point when I was sent to the galleys this last time."
>
> (Trans. J. M. Cohen, 176-77)

There are two allusions here: a direct one to Lazarillo and an indirect one to Guzmán de Alfarache, who writes while serving a sentence in the galleys. Not only is an explicit link made between *Lazarillo* and *Guzmán,* but a sense of genre distinctly emerges in Ginés's comparing his effort with "everything in that style" that has been or is yet to be written. Ginés de Pasamonte the writer is generically conscious of his narrative task, and the genre he is actively being shaped by and shaping is the emerging picaresque genre as thus far articulated in *Lazarillo de Tormes* and *Guzmán de Alfarache.* "One witnesses here," writes Claudio Guillén in "Genre and Countergenre" (1971), "the spontaneous discovery of a class by a reader-critic belonging to the most vast of the audiences. . . . Ginés, as a reader neither cultured nor ignorant, as a layman (or *ingenio lego*), combines a bold ability to recognize novelty with the generic mentality of his time, that is, with an immoderate fondness for classification, be it within or without the pale of traditional poetics" (*Literature as System,* 151-52). The essential point here is that Ginés is not merely expressing the imitative urge of a hack copycat; he is not spinning off *Lazarillo* but rather improving on the kind or "style" or class of which he sees *Lazarillo* as a specific example (Cervantes's word is actually *género,* but it did not then mean "genre" in the modern sense). Ginés has a strong, if rudimentary, sense of genre, both diachronically and synchronically, as he posits the future development of this kind of fiction. And Cervantes assumed that his own readers would catch the allusions and understand the implications without further explanation.

This passage from *Don Quixote* establishes as strongly as any contemporary evidence can a generic awareness of the emerging picaresque genre in both writers and readers. The passage also emphasizes major characteristics of the structure, content, style, and readership of works in that genre. A work of this kind is, first of all, a *vida,* and thus narrated by its protagonist; as such, it is true to life in the sense of being empirically valid, as compared to the chivalric romances, which were not and which the emerging picaresque must have dealt a considerable blow (when Cervantes has a friend in his prologue to part 1 of *Don Quixote* describe the book as "una invectiva contra los libros de caballerías," he may have been beating a dying or already dead horse). When Ginés insists on the need to live out his life before writing about it, he emphasizes the empirical impulse in this kind of writing. A *vida* is, moreover, chronological in structure. It should be entertaining and well written. Its content is determined by the shady, shifty—even criminal—behavior of characters like Ginés de Pasamonte himself (who later validates his status as a picaro by turning the galley slaves against Don Quixote, stealing Sancho's donkey, and robbing the priest and barber; in disguise as Maese Pedro in part 2, he reappears as a full-fledged trickster). And, finally, such *vidas* can be read—and indeed written—by everybody, including the Ginés de Pasamontes of the world: the "anybody" Lazarillo addresses in his prologue.

Even if we accept the by-now almost conventional interpretation of the Ginés de Pasamonte episode in *Don Quixote* as expressing Cervantine hostility against the new picaresque narrative form (as expounded perhaps most influentially in Carlos Blanco Aguinaga's 1957 article, "Cervantes y la picaresca. Notas sobre dos tipos de realismo"), we have to assume that in the dialogue between Ginés and Don Quixote, Cervantes is relying absolutely on a rudimentary generic awareness on the part of his readers. As reader Ginés converses with reader Quixote, their exchange is listened to by a third: the readers of *Don Quixote* who, whether they interpret the discussion as critical parody or not, are nevertheless expected to bring to it an intertextual and intergeneric awareness of the picaresque, which is as necessary for understanding this episode as an even more fundamentally assumed generic familiarity with the chivalric romances is for the whole of *Don Quixote.* Thus, by 1605, the emerging picaresque is already "defined"—implicitly, if not explicitly—as a distinctly recognizable kind of writing, and it is so defined by a picaro himself. By 1605, a huge (by any previous standard) audience has been responding to, and by that very response further engendering, a specific narrative type, if not a literary genre in the formal sense of a traditional literary kind familiar to educated Renaissance readers. A regulative concept must have been at work, though its "poetics" will remain informal for several more centuries, until literary historians in the nineteenth century begin to formulate it a posteriori.

Through Ginés de Pasamonte, Cervantes gives us the first theory of the picaresque, defining it aesthetically by its autobiographical form, sociologically by its democratic readership—and authorship, and even ideologically by its subject matter—which is clearly subversive, given Ginés's arrogant character, his past behavior, and his present and future behavior as revealed in the tricks he will play on Don Quixote. The seasoned criminal, reader of picaresques and would-be author of them, confronts the self-deluded *hidalgo,* reader of romances who anticipates an *historiador* writing his life even as he sets out on his first sally. Having read *Lazarillo,* Ginés must see in Quixote much of the equally deluded *hidalgo* in the third chapter of that work; reading *Don Quixote,* Cervantes's reader cannot avoid making the connection. Lazarillo sees through his *hidalgo* (though with a great deal of sympathy) as much as Ginés sees through his. In their stances, the two picaros represent a new order defying an old. Their upstart tone must have satisfied a need in what Guillén suggests was the core audience of the picaresque: "the discontented middle class" (*Literature as System,* 144).

With the appearance of López de Ubeda's *La pícara Justina* in that same year, the picaresque as a narrative genre is firmly established, for *Justina* is among other things a parody of picaresque fiction itself. Parody assumes its audience's familiarity with the conventions of the literary tradition or specific work that is its parodic object, and *Justina* works successfully only in contextuality with *Guzmán de Alfarache* and *Lazarillo de Tormes.* In addition to its conscious (and self-conscious) parody, which demands generic awareness in the reader, and its introduction of a picara, or female rogue, *Justina* is also significant in the picaresque tradition for a more or less extratextual contribution, which has been much reproduced and from which a number of critics have drawn important conclusions about the picaresque genre: the frontispiece to its first edition, which depicts "La nave de la vida picaresca" (the ship of picaresque life). On board, the principal figures are Guzmán, Justina, and Celestina (Justina's literary "mother"); Lazarillo is by himself in a little rowboat connected by a rope to the larger vessel. Classical divinities, proverbial sayings, allegorical figures, and pictorial emblems constituting the paraphernalia of the picaresque life complete the crowded scene. We can derive a number of moralistic readings from this interesting engraving, some of them mutually contradictory; and the perspective is such that we cannot be entirely sure if Lazarillo is towing the ship. But what is most significant in this picture is that Lazarillo, Guzmán, and Justina are all inside the same frame. In both this engraving and its text, *La pícara Justina* establishes its genre; by bringing two superficially unlike texts into contact with a third—itself—*Justina* forces readers into seeking out deeper similarities, in the course of which they cannot avoid constructing a generic type, or abstract extratext, which governs all three. Once the third text acknowledges as models the first and second texts, generic identity and awareness regulate both the writing and the reading of the fiction, and a genre exists.

The works belonging to this genre were not fully enumerated until the late nineteenth century, when Fonger de Haan and Frank Wadleigh Chandler published their doctoral dissertations on the picaresque. The generally accepted canon of Spanish picaresque fictions was established by Angel Valbuena Prat who in 1943 produced a two-thousand-page anthology, *La novela picaresca española.* This anthology, which has gone through more than a half-dozen editions, contains twenty-three works of fiction in their entirety. In addition to *Lazarillo, Guzmán,* and *Justina,* Valbuena Prat includes Juan de Luna's *Segunda parte de Lazarillo de Tormes* (1620) and Juan Martí's *Segunda parte de Guzmán de Alfarache* (1602), published under the pseudonym Mateo Luján de Sayavedra; and four *novelas ejemplares* by Cervantes: "La ilustre fregona," "Rinconete y Cortadillo," "El casamiento engañoso," and "Coloquio de los perros" (published in 1613 but written earlier). The other works anthologized are Salas Barbadillo, *Le hija de Celestina* (1612); Vicente Espinel, *Vida de Marcos de Obregón* (1618); Quevedo, *El Buscón* (1626); Carlos García, *La desordenada codicia de los bienes ajenos* (1619); Jerónimo de Alcalá, *Alonso, mozo de muchos amos* (*El donado hablador*) (1624, 1626); Alonso de Castillo Solórzano, *La niña de los embustes, Teresa de Manzanares* (1632), *Adventuras del Bachiller Trapaza* (1637), and *La garduña de Sevilla* (1642); María de Zayas, "El castigo de la miseria" (1637); Guevara, *El diablo Cojuelo* (1641); Antonio Enriquez Gomez, *Vida de don Gregorio Guadaña* (part of *El siglo pitagórico,* 1644); the anonymous *Vida y hechos de Estebanillo Gonzalez* (1646); Francisco Santos, *Periquillo el de las gallineras* (1688); and Torres Villarroel, *Su vida* (1743, 1752, 1758). There is considerable lack of consensus among scholars that this collection indeed constitutes a generic canon. Torres Villarroel's *Vida* and Santos's *Periquillo el de las gallineras,* for example, are almost universally rejected as picaresques, or just simply ignored, while Guevara's *El diablo Cojuelo* is, more properly speaking and as Valbuena Prat himself says in his introduction, a formal satire with picaresque characteristics. The critical emphasis among scholars has been and continues to be overwhelmingly on *Lazarillo, Guzmán,* and *El Buscón,* with *Justina* trailing behind, and even lesser attention to the other writers except, perhaps, for Cervantes. As the only collection of its kind in any language, *La novela picaresca española,* immensely useful and helpful as it is, has proved frustrating to critics looking there for a clear genre definition. Putting twenty-three works together inside the same covers does not yield as strong a sense of generic identity as did putting Lazarillo, Guzmán, and Justina inside the same frame in the frontispiece to *Justina,* which Valbuena Prat also uses as his frontispiece.

In his "Zur Chronologie und Verbreitung des spanischen Schelmenromans" (1928), Helmut Petriconi chronologically lists thirty-seven works of fiction published between 1528 (*La lozana andaluza*) and 1680 (*Trabajo del vicio*) and in a parallel chronology lists the thirty-one editions of *Lazarillo de Tormes* published between 1554 and 1664. With a basic definition of the picaresque guiding his selection of fictional works, Petriconi demonstrates that there is a thoroughly traceable development, which peaks around 1620. *Lazarillo* continues to be widely read as new picaresque fictions appear, reinforcing its position as generic prototype and suggesting a generic impulse in readers to connect with what must have been perceived even then as the earliest text in the tradition.

Among a certain group of readers, the picaresque even became what today we would call trendy. Bjornson says that picaresque life as viewed by the upper-class reader "exercised an undeniable appeal in the increasingly secular atmosphere at Philip III's court, where women even adopted the custom of disguising themselves in ragged clothes and claiming to be dressed 'a lo picaresco' (in picaresque fashion)" (*The Picaresque Hero in European Fiction,* 69). Works that parodied the picaresque, such as *La pícara Justina* and *El Buscón* (the latter already circulating in manuscript before *Justina* was published), were thus intended in large part as in-jokes for a highly select audience, and the more frivolous picaresques, like the adventure stories of Salas Barbadillo and Castillo Solórzano, were aimed at a leisure-class readership seeking vicarious excitement. It has therefore sometimes been argued that highly self-conscious, even precious, works such as *Justina* and *El Buscón* and superficially derivative works such as *La hija de Celestina* and *La garduña de Sevilla,* for example, cannot be considered genuine picaresques. Specifically targeted for an elite audience, such works either caricature their genre through clever exaggeration of its characteristics or seek to cash in on the genre's success by spinning off its most popular conventions. Such arguments, valid though they may be in some cases, are primarily value judgments of individual works rather than generic assessments. In the end, such a line of thinking leaves us with a genre comprised of a mere two or three works. But a new genre does not remain naive for long; after *Lazarillo* and *Guzmán,* generic self-consciousness itself becomes a major convention of the picaresque genre. A genre would be truly sterile if every work in it recapitulated the prototype. Genres evolve through the tension between generic constraints and the demands of the unique work, a tension that itself may become the center of interest, as it does in *Justina* and *El Buscón,* or that may be erased altogether in favor of emphasizing and embellishing those characteristics of the genre that were proving most popular, as it is in the superficial imitations. Both kinds of generic perpetuation rely on and in turn enhance the reader's generic awareness. A parody is probably one of the most revealing things that can happen to a genre. By their very act of expending clever literary force against a grouped body of literary works, parodies like *Justina* and *El Buscón* sharpen the reader's sense of the genre being spoofed—just as we have a better grasp, for example, of the gothic novel after reading Jane Austen's *Northanger Abbey* or just as through *Don Quixote* we get an excellent sense of what a *libro de caballería* is without ever having read one. The copycat works are equally revealing generically. By their formulaic reduction of generic conventions, they can give us a more coherent understanding of a genre than can the more complex and creative works in that genre.

When Guzmán de Alfarache becomes Justina's husband in *La pícara Justina* in 1605, the picaresque genre has fully emerged in Spanish literature. The frontispiece to the book explicitly connects both of them with Lazarillo. In that same year, readers were also meeting Ginés de Pasamonte, whose life closely resembles Guzmán's and whose literary goal is to surpass *Lazarillo de Tormes* when he finishes writing his own *vida*. In the course of the development of the picaresque genre, both *Lazarillo* and *Guzmán* remain exemplary fictions; they continue together to be the generic prototypes, providing the models against which many subsequent works measure themselves, no matter how freely they play variations on the genre through self-conscious parody, unauthorized continuation, exploitive mimicking, and epigonic imitation. In 1646, the picaro in *Vida y hechos de Estebanillo González, hombre de buen humor* still measures his work (albeit ironically) against the generic models when he claims to be writing a "true" story, not "la fingida Guzmán de Alfarache, ni la fabulosa de Lazarillo de Tormes."

The enormous popularity of the picaresque in Spain soon spread to other European countries as translations made the major works widely accessible to English, French, German, and Italian readers who could not read Spanish. By the middle of the seventeenth century, the picaresque was an international literary phenomenon as translations gave way to narrative attempts to perpetuate the genre while simultaneously integrating it with indigenous literary conditions and conventions. In 1655 in England there was Head's *The English Rogue*, with a dedicatory verse that mentions *Lazarillo*, *Guzmán*, and *El Buscón*. In 1669 Germany produced its own major contribution to the picaresque genre in Grimmelshausen's *The Adventurous Simplicissimus*, which was just as explicitly influenced by Alemán's work (through Albertinus's translation) and a year later spun off one of its minor characters into *The Runagate Courage*, with a formidable picara who is successor to Justina and predecessor of Moll Flanders and whose birth out of the pages of *Simplicissimus* is the obverse of Guzmán's absorption into the pages of *La pícara Justina*. In 1683 and 1690, respectively, according to A. A. Parker in *Literature and the Delinquent*, appeared *The Dutch Rogue, or Guzman of Amsterdam* and *Teague O'Divelly, or The Irish Rogue*. In the eighteenth century, the picaresque underwent a significant transformation as Lesage in France shaped the Spanish tradition his own way in *The Adventures of Gil Blas* (1715, 1724, 1735). It is his version of the picaresque that became normative throughout the rest of the century and well into the nineteenth, especially in English literature. Lesage's English translator was Smollett, who was primarily responsible for establishing *Gil Blas* as the picaresque prototype, although in his own *The Adventures of Ferdinand Count Fathom* (1753) he made explicit references to *Guzmán de Alfarache* and Petronius's *The Satyricon* in addition to *Gil Blas*. In the early nineteenth century, Sir

Walter Scott perpetuated the French model; he and Smollett were responsible for many of the major misconceptions of the picaresque that still haunt theory and criticism in English. The confusion was confounded by the English novelists' love for Cervantes, and in using both *Don Quixote* and *Gil Blas* as models for their own fiction, the eighteenth-century novelists created a case of literary mistaken identity that continues today in the misapprehension of *Don Quixote* as a picaresque novel even among well-read critics, an error that Hispanists (despite their own lack of unanimity about the nature of the Spanish picaresque genre) would never make. Although the original Spanish picaresques continue to be read—there is evidence that Defoe read them, and in Fielding's *The History of the Life of the Late Mr. Jonathan Wild the Great* (1743) Wild cites *The Spanish Rogue* (that is, *Guzmán*) as his favorite book—the indigenous narrative tradition of the criminal biography shapes whatever influence they may have had as distinctly as *Gil Blas* had shaped them.

Meanwhile, in 1822 there was *Der deutsche Gil Blas,* so titled by Goethe, and at midcentury there was even a *Russian Gil Blas,* by Vassily Narezhny. In the New World, Mexican writer José Joaquín Fernández de Lizardi wrote *The Itching Parrot (Vida y hechos de Periquillo Sarniento,* 1816, 1830), which alludes directly to *Periquillo el de las gallineras*; and a century later, also in Mexico, José Rubén Romero in *The Futile Life of Pito Pérez (La vida inútil de Pito Pérez,* 1938) alluded to both when Pito referred to himself as a Periquillo. Toward the end of the nineteenth century in the United States, William Dean Howells suggested that the picaresque might provide the appropriate narrative structure for rendering the American experience, but Howells read *Lazarillo* through *Don Quixote* and conjured up an image true to neither, like the earliest American attempt to mix the Cervantine and the picaresque, Brackenridge's *Modern Chivalry*, the first two volumes of which had appeared a century before (1792). Nonetheless, a stable sense of the historical Spanish picaresque genre persisted, even in otherwise casual and unpretentious fictions like, for example, *The Picaroons* (1904), by Gelett Burgess and Will Irwin, which is prefaced by this note:

> Picaroon—a petty rascal; one who lives by his wits; an adventurer. The Picaresque Tales, in Spanish literature of the beginning of the Seventeenth Century, dealt with the fortunes of beggars, imposters, thieves, etc., and chronicled the Romance of Roguery. Such stories were the precursors of the modern novel. The San Francisco Night's Entertainment is an attempt to render similar subjects with an essentially modern setting.
>
> (*The Picaroons*, p. v)

In the twentieth century, such self-conscious use of tradition continued. Mann's *Confessions of Felix Krull*, composed over a forty-year period, was written directly in the tradition of *Simplicissimus*. Oskar in Günter Grass's *The Tin Drum* (1959) is a direct descendant of the drummer boy Simplicissimus. Hans Schmetterling, the character in Alfred Kern's only peripherally picaresque *Le Clown*

(1957), is referred to by the circus performers as "our Simplicissimus" and runs into Felix Krull in Paris. John Hawkes has acknowledged Quevedo as a major influence on his fiction. Camilo José Cela continues Lazarillo's life almost four hundred years later, in his *Nuevas andanzas y desventuras de Lazarillo de Tormes* (1944). At midcentury in the United States, works such as Saul Bellow's *The Adventures of Augie March* (1953), Donlevy's *The Ginger Man* (1955), Ellison's *Invisible Man* (1952), Kerouac's *On the Road* (1957), Purdy's *Malcolm* (1959), and Pynchon's *V.* (1963) were linked back to Nathanael West's *The Dream Life of Balso Snell* (1931) and *A Cool Million* (1934) to signal the apparent emergence of a contemporary American picaresque as an assertive strand of twentieth-century narrative. In Canada, there is Mordecai Richler's *The Apprenticeship of Duddy Kravitz* (1959). In England, fictions like Kingsley Amis's *Lucky Jim* (1954), Malcolm Bradbury's *Eating People Is Wrong* (1959), and John Wain's *Hurry on Down* (1953) were grouped with such works as Evelyn Waugh's *Decline and Fall* (1928), eliciting similar speculations about a "neopicaresque" in contemporary British fiction. In Germany, *Felix Krull* and *The Tin Drum*, already linked extra- and intertextually with *Simplicissimus*, were compared to a whole roster of new fictions, including Heinrich Böll's *The Clown (Ansichten eines Clowns,* 1963). The new fiction there was studied under such titles as "Picaro Today," "The Return of the Picaros," and "The Eternal Simplicissimus." In Spanish literature itself, the persistence of the picaresque in twentieth-century fiction is demonstrated by the more than one hundred pages devoted to this topic in the proceedings of what billed itself as the First International Congress on the Picaresque (Madrid, July 1976), edited by Manuel Criado de Val as *La picaresca: Orígenes, Textos y Estructuras* (1979). In addition to Cela and Pio Baroja, writers like Ricardo León (*Los Centauros,* 1912), Juan Antonio de Zunzunegui (*La vida como es,* 1954), Sebastián Juan Arbó (*Martín de Caretas,* 1955), Darío Fernández-Flórez (*Lola, espejo oscuro,* 1950), and Juan Goytisolo (*Fiestas,* 1958) wrote fictions often explicitly rooted, through generic self-reference or indirect allusion, in the seventeenth-century Spanish picaresque narrative tradition. Among fictions written in French, Alfred Kern's *Le Clown* tries deliberately to be picaresque, and in France, too, there is talk of a *renaissance du roman picaresque* as critics look at Kern and at some of the new fictions being produced in Germany, England, and the United States.

Even this sketchiest of surveys over three and a half centuries of several major literatures makes it clear that the picaresque genre of *siglo de oro* Spain left a historically robust and geographically diverse narrative legacy. This culturally very coded narrative structure, which emerged, peaked, and declined under specific social, economic, political, religious, and literary conditions in Spain over the relatively short span of the first three decades of the seventeenth century (there being no genre until *Guzmán* and *Lazarillo* together created it in 1599), proved universally appealing to readers and writers outside Spain and has continued, despite a number of sea-changes,

with traceable continuity up to the present. Today book reviewers, literary critics, and even film critics call works "picaresque" with such frequency that any objective observer of the literary and film scenes cannot help but conclude that the picaresque is a thriving contemporary narrative form. Such an observer would also automatically assume that the term's ubiquity reflected unanimity about its meaning. But, in fact, disagreement about the precise nature of the Spanish picaresque genre, the definition of the concept *picaresque,* and the narratological usefulness of the term *picaresque novel* has never been more intense than it is now in the immediate wake of the perceived surge of contemporary picaresque fictions, as a brief survey of the picaresque in literary scholarship will illustrate.

BOOKS AND ARTICLES

Bjornson, Richard. *The Picaresque Hero in European Fiction.* Madison: University of Wisconsin Press, 1977.

Blanco Aguinaga, Carlos. "Cervantes y la picaresca. Notas sobre dos tipos de realismo." *Nueva Revista de Filología Hispánica* 11 (1957): 313-42. (Trans. and abr. as "Cervantes and the Picaresque Mode" in *Cervantes: A Collection of Critical Essays,* ed. Lowry Nelson, Jr. Englewood Cliffs, N.J.: Prentice-Hall, 1969.)

Guillén, Claudio. "Genre and Countergenre: The Discovery of the Picaresque." In *Literature as System: Essays toward the Theory of Literary History,* 135-58. Princeton, N.J.: Princeton University Press, 1971. Translation and expansion of "Luis Sánchez, Ginés de Pasamonte y los inventores del género picaresco," in *Homenaje a Rodríguez-Moñino: Estudios de erudición que le ofrecen sus amigos o discípulos hispanistas norteamericanos,* vol. 1, 221-31. Madrid: Castalia, 1966.

Reed, Helen H. *The Reader in the Picaresque Novel.* London: Tamesis, 1984.

Sieber, Harry. *The Picaresque.* The Critical Idiom 33. London: Methuen, 1977.

GENRE THEORY, NARRATIVE TECHNIQUE, LITERARY HISTORY, AND OTHER RELATED STUDIES

Colie, Rosalie L. *The Resources of Kind: Genre-Theory in the Renaissance.* Ed. Barbara K. Lewalski. Berkeley: University of California Press, 1973.

Culler, Jonathan. *Structuralist Poetics: Structuralism, Linguistics and the Study of Literature.* Ithaca, N.Y.: Cornell University Press, 1975.

Eliot, T. S. "Tradition and the Individual Talent." 1917. In *The Sacred Wood: Essays on Poetry and Criticism,* 47-59. 1928. University Paperbacks. New York: Barnes and Noble, 1960.

Fowler, Alastair. *Kinds of Literature: An Introduction to the Theory of Genres and Modes.* Cambridge, Mass.: Harvard University Press, 1982.

Hernadi, Paul. *Beyond Genre: New Directions in Literary Classification.* Ithaca, N.Y.: Cornell University Press, 1972.

Hirsch, E. D., Jr. *Validity in Interpretation.* New Haven, Conn.: Yale University Press, 1967.

Kent, Thomas. *Interpretation and Genre: The Role of Generic Perception in the Study of Narrative Texts.* Lewisburg, Pa.: Bucknell University Press, 1986.

Wellek, René. "Genre Theory, the Lyric, and *Erlebnis.*" In *Discriminations: Further Concepts of Criticism,* 225-52. New Haven, Conn.: Yale University Press, 1970. Orig. in *Festschrift für Richard Alewyn.* Ed. H. Singer and Benno von Wiese. Cologne: Böhlau, 1967.

Harry Sieber (essay date 1995)

SOURCE: Sieber, Harry. "Literary Continuity, Social Order, and the Invention of the Picaresque." In *Cultural Authority in Golden Age Spain,* edited by Marina S. Brownlee and Hans Ulrich Gumbrecht, pp. 143-64. Baltimore: Johns Hopkins University Press, 1995.

[*In the essay which follows, Sieber approaches the development of the picaresque tradition from a sociopolitical perspective, suggesting that this literary genre reflected issues relating to the court of Phillip III.*]

In the exploration of various interrelations between literature and history in the second half of the sixteenth century in Spain, my main interests are those points of contact between literature as a process of imitation and renewal, of "new" texts re-creating "old" texts on the one hand, and historical tradition on the other, or rather, tradition as a cultural force in history. "For the literary historian and critic"—and here I intentionally abuse a quotation from Robert Weimann in order to make it my own—the problem "is not whether to accept both worlds and points of reference, but rather, since each is so inevitable and necessary, how to relate them so as to discover the degree and consequences of their connections."[1] José Antonio Maravall's *La literatura picaresca desde la historia social* is a recent example of an attempt to articulate such relationships through the language of a social history of *mentalités* in an age of crisis and decline and in a world, defined in another context by Theodore K. Rabb, "where everything had been thrown into doubt, where uncertainty and instability reigned."[2]

For the purposes of this essay I focus more narrowly on Spain's cultural preoccupation with its origins in the process of exploiting continuation as a way of celebrating the empowering myths that serve as its self-legitimation. The manifestations of this reappropriation of the past are contingent with Pierre Bourdieu's general observation in *Outline of a Theory of Practice*: "If all societies that seek to produce a new man through a process of 'deculturation' and 'reculturation' set such store on the seemingly most insignificant details of dress, bearing, physical and verbal manners, the reason is that, treating the body as a memory, they entrust to it in abbreviated and practical, i.e.,

mnemonic form the fundamental principles of the arbitrary content of the culture."[3] Bourdieu's remarks seem especially relevant to the literature, history, and culture of late-sixteenth-century Spain when translations, adaptations, and imitations of Italian treatises of courtly conduct—of manners—coincided with debates over honor, status, and identity.

Courtesy literature, as Frank Whigham has written, must be viewed as "having an intricate social purpose combining poetry and politics, philosophical speculation and social combat, ritual pageantry and ambition," because the "court was simultaneously an arena of conflict and a mart of opportunity as well as a radiant center of order."[4] Whigham refers to Elizabethan England, but much of his argument can be applied to late-sixteenth-century Spain as well. Spain, like England, had its own "educational revolution," producing a surge of educated men in search of social mobility and ladders of opportunity in law, the church, the military, and governmental administration.[5] And as in England, "movement across the gap between ruling and subject classes was becoming increasingly possible, and elite identity came to be a function of action rather than of birth—to be achieved rather than ascribed."[6] In addition, Ruth Kelso (again writing of Elizabethan England) also reflects the Spanish scene: "Those who lacked the title [of gentlemen] were busy trying to acquire it . . . those who had it were anxious to resist encroachment."[7] One of the paths toward the achievement of such status was to embrace courtesy books as perceptive manuals, which Stephen Greenblatt has characterized as "handbooks for actors, practical guides for a society whose members were nearly always on stage, . . . offering an integrated rhetoric of the self, a model for the formation of an artificial identity."[8]

The extent to which the translations and adaptations of the works of Castiglione and his descendants—Guazzo, della Casa, Riminaldo—played a comparable role in the Spanish court is still unknown.[9] We do know that Castiglione's *Book of the Courtier* was reprinted at least fourteen times in Spain after being translated by Juan Boscán in 1534,[10] and that by 1591 Juan Benito Guardiola's *Tratado de la nobleza* had transformed Castiglione's *gentiluomo* into a Spanish *caballero.* By the late 1580s, strategies for advancement in the court had become a parlor game. Alonso de Barros's treatise *Filosofía cortesana moralizada* (1587), first introduced to its readers with a sonnet by a relatively unknown Miguel de Cervantes, was actually an instruction manual that accompanied a board game not unlike Monopoly, in which, with the throw of the dice and the right moves, one could land on a space called Good Fortune, arrange a meeting with the king's favorite, and win the pot. However, one could also land on spaces—called "casas"—such as the *Mudanza de ministros* or *La muerte del valedor* and lose what had been gained and be forced to begin the game again at the *Puerta de la opinión.*[11] For many at court, such activity was no trivial pursuit but rather a matter of life or death, as the famous case of Rodrigo Calderón would later attest.

It is also important to note that the historical situation in Spain had prepared the way for the reception of such treatises. Charles V, for instance, continued the practice of his predecessors by elevating those not born to nobility who rendered military and financial service to the crown. "Government service," as John Elliott has written, "could lead to dramatic social advancement, as the career of Charles V's secretary, Francisco de los Cobos, spectacularly demonstrated."[12] Some merchant families gained noble status through entry into the military orders, and by marriage into the ranks, as Ruth Pike has pointed out in her study of Genoese traders in Seville, and as Henri La Peyre has argued with regard to the Ruiz family of Medina del Campo.[13] While Philip II seems to have cast a suspicious eye on the nobility and their proximity to the sources of power in government service, the demand for honor and a place near the king reached a critical juncture at the end of his reign, perhaps as the result of increasing taxes levied throughout the century, taxes from which only those of noble status were exempt. Becoming a nobleman from mid-century on implied more than acquiring honorable status. Even with the introduction of the "Servicio de los millones" in 1590, a consumer tax placed on basic foodstuffs, those landowners of noble descent who lived in Madrid could import their own supplies of food without having to pay taxes, thus providing for themselves some financial buffer from all taxation policies imposed by both royal and local governments by the end of the sixteenth century.

After the king's death in September 1598, Francisco Gómez de Sandoval y Rojas, the Marquis of Denia who would soon become the Duke of Lerma, quickly began to consolidate his power over the new king and the court. Some three months later, in January 1599, the contemporary court historian Cabrera de Córdoba was able to report that "la privanza y lugar que el marques de Denia tiene con S. M. desde que heredó, va cada día en aumento sin conocerse que haya otro privado semejante, porque son muy estraordinarios los favores que se le hacen"[14] [the favor and position the Marquis of Denia has gained with His Majesty from the moment he became king is increasing every day unchallenged, as evidenced by the extraordinary favors with which the kind showers him]. Patronage, status and honor, lineage and wealth became matters of immediate concern and debate in a court in which a favorite held power. Lerma and the men he had appointed around him would virtually become the source of "royal" patronage as Philip III removed himself from the day-to-day affairs of government. Antonio Feros has recently demonstrated that "monopolio del favor, lisonja, interés privado y compraventa fueron . . . prácticas que socavaron la distribución del patronazgo real"[15] [monopoly of favor, flattery, personal interest, and venality were . . . practices that undermined the distribution of royal patronage] and characterized the regime of Lerma and his favorites. Thus Philip II, often distant and isolated at the Escorial monastery but obsessively in charge of his government, was succeeded by Philip III, who left government to others and whose court in Madrid provided a larger, more public space in which status, identity, and former codes of courtly conduct were subjects of debate.

Many of Philip II's ministers and court functionaries were exiled or expelled from service, and new men with relatively unknown backgrounds and experience, such as Pedro Franqueza (secretary to the queen), Rodrigo Calderón (secretary to the Cámara del Rey), and Silva de Torres (alcalde de casa y corte; corregidor of Madrid), found themselves with new power and authority. At the same time these men actively sought to control access to their ranks by neutralizing those who questioned their power. More significant for us is the fact that it was precisely at this moment that a little novel first published almost fifty years previously, *La vida de Lazarillo de Tormes,* was reprinted as an appendix to Lucas Gracián Dantisco's Spanish translation of Giovanni della Casa's *Galateo.*[16] Why the *Lazarillo,* principally known for its subtle irony and biting satire of a cruel beggar and priest, proud nobleman, fraudulent pardoner, hypocritical chaplain, and venal archpriest, reappeared at this moment to become part of such a volume is the question I hope to answer by placing it in the context of the literature of manners, the formation of a new court, and the invention of the picaresque novel.

Claudio Guillén has pointed out that *La vida de Lazarillo de Tormes* has been made an integral part of the history of the picaresque novel at the turn of the seventeenth century primarily by publishers and readers, and more specifically through Ginés de Pasamonte's famous reference to its title in *Don Quijote.*[17] The 1554 edition was placed on Inquisitor Valdés's 1559 *Index of Prohibited Books.* There is no evidence of the novel's being reprinted in Spain until 1573, and only then in the censored version of Juan López de Velasco, Philip II's cosmographer and principal chronicler, whose primary fame today is based on his authorship of *La geografía y descripción universal de las Indias.* Because Velasco's edition was most likely the version of the *Lazarillo* available to readers at the turn of the seventeenth century, I would like to identify him briefly and to outline the role he may have played in resurrecting the novel.

Juan López de Velasco was recommended for his position at the Escorial library by Juan de Ovando y Godoy, one of Philip II's trusted advisors and president of the Council of the Indies in the late 1560s.[18] Ovando was also a member of the Council of the Inquisition. Both Ovando and Velasco corresponded with Benito Arias Montano, who was in Antwerp during these same years on official business, presiding over a committee charged with compiling an updated list of prohibited and expurgated books.[19] The exchange of letters between Ovando, Velasco, and Montano also reveals that Montano was involved in the book market in general, buying and shipping great quantities of material for Ovando's personal library as well as for the library at the Escorial. Montano was thorough in his work. In his letter to Ovando, dated August 2, 1571, he was able to assure his superior that "el libro o índice expurgatorio se está imprimiendo: será una cosa de grande provecho; porque, de cuantos libros admitían expurgación no se ha dejado de ver y examinar cosa y darse sentencia sobre cada lugar dellos con toda equidad"[20] [the book, or index, of expurgated works is at press. It will be of great benefit, for among the books that could be expurgated, nothing has been left unscrutinized or unexamined, and the books have been judged with the utmost fairness]. It is possible that the *Lazarillo* was one of these "cuantos libros."[21]

Velasco for his part had a number of interests beyond writing and copying letters and compiling data for his history of the Indies. He was particularly fascinated with spoken and written Spanish, publishing his *Ortografía y pronunciación castellana* in 1582, and with educational reform, as indicated by his *Instrucción para examinar los maestros de escuela de la lengua castellana y enseñar a leer y escribir a los niños.*[22] His sensitivity to matters of language and style no doubt accounts for his interest in the *Lazarillo* and other Spanish texts that had already appeared in Valdés's catalog of prohibited books. The fact that Velasco's version is based on the 1554 Antwerp edition of the novel rather than on the Burgos or Alcalá editions of the same year suggests that communication between Ovando and Montano may have played an important role in supporting Velasco's efforts to obtain permission or even with the text that was printed in Madrid two years later, by itself or with other previously prohibited works,[23] as Velasco's prologue indicates:

> Aunque este tratadillo de la vida de Lazarillo de Tormes, no es de tanta consideración en lo que toca a la lengua, como las obras de Christóbal de Castillejo y Bartolomé de Torres Naharro, es una representación tan biva y propria de aquello que imita con tanto donayre y gracia, que en su tanto merece ser estimado, y assi fue siempre a todos muy acepto, de cuya causa *aunque estaba prohibido en estos reynos, se leya, y imprimía de ordinario fuera dellos.*

> [24] [Even though this short treatise on the life of Lazarillo de Tormes is not, when it comes to language, as worthy of consideration as the works of Christobal de Castillejo and Bartolomé de Torres Naharro, it is such a lively and fitting representation of what it charmingly and wittily imitates, that as a whole it is deserving of esteem; and as such everyone always found it appealing, which is why *despite being prohibited in this kingdom, it was commonly published and read outside of it.*]

Velasco's rescue of three Spanish "classics" coincided with the Inquisition's strategy: his newly available *Lazarillo* would eventually replace the relatively few surviving 1554 originals (if any) or manuscript copies made from them. Given the tone of mid-sixteenth-century Spanish censorship, it was more acceptable to have a "corrected" *Lazarillo* circulating at the time than to allow the continued reading of its original prohibited version.

After 1573—with the possible exception of a Tarragona edition of 1586—there is, according to Claudio Guillén and others, no explicit reference to *Lazarillo* the novel in Spain until 1599. It seems that perhaps earlier, however, our novel acquired new life as it began to circulate with the *Galateo español.*[25] Miguel Martínez, a Madrid bookseller with a somewhat tarnished reputation, added an anonymous translation from Italian of another courtesy book, Oracio Riminaldo's *Destierro de ignorancia,* obtaining permission to print and sell all three works in one volume "que *otras veces* con su licencia han sido impressos" (Medina del Campo, 1603) [which *on other occasions* have been printed with his license], indicating that the novel reached its audience perhaps earlier and was more widely distributed at the end of the century as part of a trilogy.[26] Here it is important to note that the project was initiated and financed by Martínez ("a costa de . . . ," the title page informs us), who would have hired Luis Sánchez to print all three *tratados* together. Martínez, then, was the one who clearly perceived a common thread linking the *Lazarillo* to the *Galateo,* and then to the *Destierro*: together they constituted a courtesy book aimed at a specific group of readers. Martínez's marketing strategy is revealing in this regard: the second edition containing all three treatises was published in Valladolid in 1603 and the third in Medina del Campo the same year.

These locations coincided with the movement of the court of Philip III at the beginning of the century. Despite considerable public protest, the court, through the Duke of Lerma's influence, was moved from Madrid to Valladolid in 1601. And to make room for the large bureaucracy that accompanied the court, nearby Medina del Campo was chosen as the place for the royal tribunal and its various judges, lawyers, and secretaries.[27] Only when Madrid regained royal favor with bribes and special real estate deals for Lerma, his family, and the men he had placed in office did the court return in 1606.[28] It seems evident that the readers Martínez had in mind were those literate courtiers, government bureaucrats, merchants, and hangers-on who followed the court and who, according to Madrid's city fathers, numbered in the hundreds.[29] Martínez's own travels during these years followed the same itinerary. He had operated a bookshop in the Patio of the Alcázar as early as 1591; in 1601, soon after pirating an edition of Mateo Alemán's *Guzmán de Alfarache,*[30] he too moved to Valladolid, where he opened another shop to serve his recently departed clients.

Without detailing all the appropriate forms of courtly behavior listed by Lucas Gracián, many of which are direct translations from della Casa's treatise, it is enough to point out that his manual is designed to communicate to his readers one of the potential sources of honor and privilege in the court: the art of winning the goodwill and favor of others through the use of proper language and behavior. Acceptable speech, forms of address, table manners, topics of conversation, dress, and ceremony are illustrated, often through negative examples. At one point Lucas Gracián seems to recall an incident that takes place in the squire episode of the *Lazarillo*:

> Muchas veces acaece . . . venir a reñir y enemistarse, . . . quando un ciudadano dexa de honrar a otro como es costumbre, no quitándole la gorra, ni hablándole con

crianza. . . . Y ansi quien llamasse de vos a otro, no siendo muy más calificado, le menosprecia y haze ultrage en nombralle, pues se sabe que con semejantes palabras llaman a los peones y travajadores.

(Morreale, p. 132)

[Many times it happens that citizens fight one another and become enemies . . . when one fails to honor the other as is customary, refusing to tip his hat or to speak properly. . . . And thus one who addresses the other as "vos," not being of higher rank, insults him and commits an outrage in referring to him in this way, because it is known that with such words one refers to common peasants and laborers.]

Then there is advice related to bearing and dress: "Y hay algunos de tal manera que ponen todo el gusto y su felicidad y cuidado en sus vestidos y compostura exterior . . . son fríos, inútiles y de poca sustancia en su trato y conversación, que no son más que para mirados, o topados en la calle" (p. 114) [There are some who put all pleasure, happiness, and care in their clothing and exterior demeanor . . . {but} are cold, useless, and of little substance in their behavior and conversation; they only want to be seen or encountered in the street]. He also refers to clearly unacceptable behavior when he narrates the following scene, again taken from della Casa, which would later be associated with the court satire of Quevedo:

Hase visto . . . otra mala costumbre de algunos que suenan las narizes con mucha fuerça y páranse delante de todos a mirar en el pañizuelo lo que se han sonado, como si aquello que por allí han purgado, fuesse perlas o diamantes que le cayessen del celebro.

(p. 109)

[You have seen another evil custom of those who blow their noses with great force and then stop in front of everyone to look in their handkerchiefs at the results, as if what they discharged were pearls or diamonds that have fallen from their brains.]

Unfortunately, searching for pearls or diamonds in the discharge of one's nostrils was not the place where wealth and power would be found in the court of Philip III.

It may be useful at this point to describe briefly some of the main differences between the *Lazarillo* of 1554 and Velasco's censored text because, as I have noted elsewhere, it was López de Velasco's version of the novel that was most likely read by Cervantes, Mateo Alemán, and Francisco de Quevedo, as well as by other writers of picaresque fiction during the first years of the seventeenth century. The excised fourth and fifth chapters and various sentences and words may seem at first glance to reflect little damage, but the sharp scissors wielded by the censor and approved by the Inquisition weakened the novel's anticlerical tone and suppressed central episodes, one of which, according to Raymond Willis, is artistically necessary for our modern understanding of the final half of the book.[31] Seventeenth-century readers learned that Lazarillo's father confessed but was not allowed to deny his crimes,

and while his father is still located in "heaven" ("la gloria") he is not called one of the "blessed" ("bienaventurados"). A paragraph that compares Lazarillo's stepfather to "clerics and friars" who steal from the poor to support their religious houses is conspicuously absent. The third chapter with the squire is left intact. The Mercedarian friar and the fraudulent pardoner in the fourth and fifth chapters never make an appearance. The structure of the novel also changed. The episode of the blind beggar was extracted to become a separate chapter, "Assiento de Lázaro con el ciego," and Lazarillo's adventures as a water seller, paint grinder, constable's assistant, and town crier are collapsed into one: "Lázaro assienta con un capellán y un alguazil y después toma manera de vivir" (fol. 278r).[32]

By the end of the sixteenth century, the *Lazarillo* would have been for its original author a different book, emphasizing primarily the lessons learned by Lazarillo about how to manipulate others through language, the lack of charity as exemplified by the episode with the priest, the shame of poverty and importance of honor of the squire, and the ironic success Lazarillo claims at the end of his life as he boasts of his position as town crier. The centerpiece of the new *Lazarillo* is the squire episode, which clearly attracted the attention of Miguel Martínez and the court with its critique of ritualized manners, proper speech, courtly dress, distinguished lineage, and powerful role of honor. We are told, for instance, that the squire was born in Valladolid. After he arrives in Toledo, he is described by Lazarillo as he leaves his rented house "con un paso sosegado y el cuerpo derecho, haciendo con él y con la cabeza muy gentiles meneos, echando el cabo de la capa sobre el hombro y a veces so el brazo, y poniendo la mano derecha en el costado"[33] [walking slowly, holding his body straight and swaying gracefully, placing the tail of the cape over his shoulder or sometimes under his arm, and putting his right hand on his chest]. When he attends mass, Lazarillo continues, his master wishes only to be seen by others, remaining through "los otros oficios divinos, hasta que todo fue acabado y la gente ida. Entonces salimos de la iglesia" (p. 73) [the other holy ceremonies very devoutly until they had ended and the people had gone. Then we left the church]. The squire carefully straps on his sword, proudly displaying it as if it were a fine piece of jewelry—and just as useless, Lazarillo implies, because it is used only as decoration. The squire embodies the proud and mannered nobleman whose rhetoric of courtly manners fails to provide him with that artificial identity to find a place in Toledo's closed society, an example that was unlikely to be lost on those who sought honor and privilege in the court of Philip III.

The Velasco/Martínez *Lazarillo* is "picaresque" in the narrowest historical sense because it is the version mentioned in all probability by Cervantes in the "Galley Slaves" episode of *Don Quijote* and is closely associated with the word *pícaro* in Mateo Alemán's *Guzmán de Alfarache*. Recall that Guzmán becomes a *pícaro* in Book 2 after he arrives in Madrid ("Trátase cómo vino a ser pícaro y lo que siéndolo le sucedió"[34] [{This second book} deals with how he became a *pícaro* and what happened to him]). The story continues through Chapter 8 with his journey to Toledo. Guzmán enters the city at night, but before appearing in public the next morning he quickly changes his attire, "vistiéndose muy galán" (1:329) [dressing like a gentleman]. More importantly, these chapters are shot through with references to honor, the same subject that obsessed the squire in the *Lazarillo de Tormes*. In Alemán's text Guzmán sermonizes against the vanity of honor: "¿Qué sabes o quién sabe del mayordomo del rey don Pelayo ni del camarero del conde Fernán González? Honra tuvieron y la sustentaron y dellos ni della se tiene memoria. Pues así mañana serás olvidado" (1:281) [What is known or who knows about King Pelayo's majordomo or of Count Fernan Gonzalez's servant? They acquired honor and lived by it and no one remembers them or their honor]. But it is not only honor that Guzmán criticizes; he also attacks its trappings and rituals. Attempting to sustain honor is self-effacing because it precludes the possibility of individualizing one's identity; instead the self is invented and sustained by others. "¡Oh . . . lo que carga el peso de la honra y como no hay metal que se le iguale! ¡A cuánto está obligado el desventurado que della hubiere de usar! ¡Qué mirado y medido ha de andar! . . . y cuán fácil de perder por la común estimación!" (1:266-67) [Oh . . . how heavy is the weight of honor and how no metal equals it! How obligated is he who uses it! How he must look and walk! . . . and how easy it is to lose it in the esteem of others!]. Honor demands a rule-governing form of behavior: costume, manners, proper forms of address, gaining the friendship and favor of others, and avoiding the apperance of poverty point to an imprisoned existence. This is precisely the problem of the squire in the *Lazarillo*: the artificiality of his studied manners and ostentatious dress are emphasized by his claims to be able to lie, flatter, laugh, and serve "titled gentlemen" better than anyone else despite his poverty and new identity.

Such mannered behavior for Guzmán, then, is seen as a form of imprisonment; he speaks of the "freedom" he has by not joining those who choose to live by the strict rules of honor. Like Lazarillo, he too becomes a beggar to feed himself and refers to crop failures as the reason for lack of charity in Toledo: "Dábase muy poco limosna y no era maravilla, que en general fue el año esteril y, si estaba mala la Andalucía, peor cuánto más adentro del reino de Toledo y mucha más necesidad había de los puertos adentro" (1:263) [Very few alms were given because of crop failures everywhere, and if it was bad in Andalucia it was worse in the kingdom of Toledo and even worse in the city itself]. Despite his use of flattering language, his dress and behavior broadcast his poverty and reputation and determine the role he will play in Madrid: "Viéndome tan despedazado, aunque procuré acreditarme con palabras y buscar a quien servir, ninguno se aseguraba de mis obras ni quería meterme dentro de casa en su servicio, porque estaba muy asqueroso y desmantelado. Creyeron ser algún pícaro ladroncillo que los había de robar y acogerme" (1:263) [Seeing myself in such rags, although I tried to gain confidence and look for someone to serve, no one could be certain about my deeds nor wanted to place me in his house as servant, because I was filthy and ruinous. They believed I was a thieving *pícaro* who would rob them and escape].

The more freedom he seeks, the further he alienates himself from the social hierarchy he hopes to join, until he becomes a "pícaro de cocina" (1:287). He is told by his master, however, that someday he might become a magistrate and enter "la casa real y que, sirviendo tantos años, . . . retirarme rico a mi casa" (1:287) [the royal household, and after serving a certain number of years . . . retire a wealthy man to my estate]. When he returns to Madrid after his journey to Italy, he initiates his strategy to gain admittance to the court in order to sell his stolen jewelry by choosing and wearing the proper clothes in order to associate with his gentlemen clients: "Comencé mi negocio por galas y más galas. Hice dos diferentes vestidos de calza entera, muy gallardos. Otro saqué llano para remudar, pareciéndome que con aquello, si comprase un caballo, que quien así me viera, y con un par de criados, fácilmente me compraría las joyas que llevaba" (2:320-21) [I began my trade with finery and courtly dress. I made two different outfits with long stockings, very elegant. I took out another pair to change into, appearing to me that if I were to buy a horse whoever would see me (and with a couple of servants) would reaidly buy the jewelry I had].

These hurried references to the *Guzmán* and the *Lazarillo* suggest an intertextual reading that announces the origins of the picaresque and its association with the court. Alemán closely follows the historical definition of the *pícaro* given to us by sixteenth-century texts: "pícaro de cocina," "pícaro vagabundo," that is, the *pícaro* who formed an integral part of the growing urban population that contributed to Madrid's demographic explosion at the end of the sixteenth century. He combines historical, immediate experience with the central problem of honor and its rituals as explored in the *Lazarillo*. His master tells him: "Aquí verás, Guzmán, lo que es la honra, pues a éstos la dan. El hijo de nadie, que se levantó del polvo de la tierra, siendo vasija quebradiza, llena de agujeros, rota, sin capacidad que en ella cupiera cosa de algún momento, la remendó con trapos el favor, y con la soga del interés ya sacan agua con ella y parece de provecho" (1:278) [Here you see, Guzman, what honor is, because to these it is given. The son of a nobody who raises himself up from the dust of the earth is like a leaking vessel full of holes, without the capacity to contain anything of substance; favor patched it with rags, and with the rope of interest others are able to bring it up filled with water and with profit too]. The shift from worthlessness and poverty to material gain and success through the "patchwork" of favors is a movement from the historical *pícaro* inherited by Alemán to the redefined *pícaro* of the court: the basic "vessel" remains the same. The power of goodwill and favor to win and maintain a position at court with flattering words and proper dress and behavior, central to Gracián Dantisco's project in the *Galateo español*, is the target of Alemán's critique of what he perceived to be the arbitrary nature of honor and privilege at the end of the sixteenth century in Spain.

In order to demonstrate how and why the *Galateo,* the *Lazarillo,* and the *Guzmán* found an enthusiastic audience in the first years of the seventeenth century, I must turn briefly to another novel—described variously as the zenith or nadir of the picaresque genre—Francisco de Quevedo's *La vida del Buscón,* written about 1604, according to the most recent authorities,[35] but not published until 1626. Quevedo's novel tells a story, a simple but grotesque story, about the son of a thief and a prostitute who seeks to deny his blood by falsifying his lineage in order to become a gentleman and to gain admittance to polite society, that is, to live an honorable life in the court. To use Alemán's metaphor, Pablos, the "son of nobody," a "broken vessel" made up of "dust of the earth," seeks honor and profit in the court through special favor and connections. He hopes to become part of Madrid's society by acting like a gentleman, by associating with others of rank, and by marrying into the right family. Quevedo's readers discover that Pablos's efforts to adopt the style of the court fail, that his true identity is discovered, that he abandons Madrid, traveling to Seville, where like many of his kind in the sixteenth and seventeenth centuries, he escapes to the Indies in the hope of improving his fortune.

But Pablos is not the only character who seeks to break through social barriers by speaking, behaving, and dressing like a gentleman. All characters in the *Buscón* pretend to be of higher rank than they are. Pablos's reputed father is a barber who insists that he be called a "tundidor de mejillas y sastre de barbas" ("shearer of cheeks and tailor of beards"). His mother is a prostitute whose surnames— "hija de Diego de San Juan y nieta de Andrés de San Cristóbal" [daughter of James of St. John and granddaughter of Saint Christopher]—are mentioned to prove that she is descended from the Litany of the Saints (pp. 73-74).[36] The licentiate Cabra, Pablos's schoolmaster, puts bacon in the soup "por no sé qué que le dijeron un día de hidalguía allá fuera" (p. 98) [for something they said to him one day out there about nobility], alluding to the purity of blood statutes that traditionally defined noble old Christian lineage. Pablos's uncle, the hangman from Segovia, refers to the "ocupaciones grandes desta plaza en que me tiene ocupado su Majestad" (p. 131) [the weighty affairs of this employment in which it has pleased His Majesty to place me]. In Madrid Pablos carefully dresses according to the style of the court and names himself "don Ramiro de Guzmán," telling others that he is "un hombre rico, que hizo agora tres asientos con el Rey" [a rich man, who has already gained three contracts from the king]. Nearly everyone in the *Buscón* except Don Diego de Coronel y Zúñiga, Pablos's childhood friend, appropriates courtly language and manners to create new identities to survive in Madrid, searching for honor and profit, the philosopher's stone that will transform them as if by magic from the margin to the center, from the fringes of the court to a place in its society.

Maurice Molho has noted that the narrator of the *Buscón* could just as easily have been Don Diego Coronel de Zúñiga.[37] When Quevedo writes in the first words of the novel that Pablos is from Segovia, his statement applies to Don Diego as well. And when he refers to Pablos's attempts to disguise his lineage and deny his blood, Quevedo cleverly alludes to Don Diego's family too. The name "Coronel" was taken by the converted Segovian Jew, Abraham Senior, in 1492 for himself and for his descendants.[38] Don Diego's second surname, "Zúñiga," may have made him doubly suspect to Quevedo's contemporary readers because in some minds it would have linked him to various noble families or even to Diego de Zúñiga, the first son of the president of the Council of Castile under Philip III, Pedro Manso de Zúñiga, whose meteoric rise to power was described at the time as an "estallido tal que a todos pareció de los milagros de la naturaleza"[39] [such an explosion that everyone thought it was a miracle of nature]. The major difference between Don Pablos and Don Diego, however, is that the latter appears in the novel already the son of a gentleman (no matter how tainted), whereas the former will never attain such status. Both apparently descend from converted Jews, but Quevedo allows Don Diego to remain at court as a *caballero* of a prestigious military order while he condemns Pablos to the life of a hardened criminal. If Don Diego is not as worthy a character as some have argued, why is he not exiled along with Don Pablos? Why is he perceived to be part of the dominant elite in the court of Philip III?

It is possible to begin to answer such questions by first going to another of Quevedo's works, written at about the same time that he was composing his novel. I refer to his satiric poem "Poderoso caballero es don Dinero."[40] Sir Money is the subject of a daughter's confession to her mother: "Madre, yo al oro me humillo; / él es mi amante y mi amado" [Mother, I humble myself before gold; / he is my lover and my beloved]. His genealogy is of supreme importance:

> Son sus padres principales,
> y es de nobles descendiente,
> porque en las venas de Oriente
> todas las sangres son reales;
> y pues es quien hace iguales
> al duque y al ganadero
> *poderoso caballero es don Dinero.*[41]

[His parents are illustrious, / and he is descended from noblemen, / because in veins {of gold/of blood} of the East / all blood is royal; / since he is the one who makes equals / of the duke and the rancher / *a powerful knight is Sir Money.*]

That Don Diego is meant to be perceived as a wealthy nobleman Quevedo leaves little doubt, locating his house on the Calle del Arenal, one of the most prestigious streets in early-seventeenth-century Madrid.[42] His neighbors would have been the Count of Oñate, the Count of Fuente Ventura, the Marquis of Salinas, and the Duke of Arcos, among others.[43] The power of Don Dinero, then, has no limits, and it is the relationship between money and power that turns profit into honor, rustic into nobleman, *converso* into *caballero*.[44] The language and manners of the court for Quevedo, when driven by ostentatious—if not illegitimate—wealth, were forms of deception that allowed those of questionable birth and tainted blood to live nobly and among noblemen in Madrid. Writers of picaresque fiction, if we base their role on Quevedo's example, were morally bound to expose through the language of satire the threat to social and political order that such behavior disguised.

The Coroneles were examples of noblemen by concession and not by blood: "de privilegio y no de sangre," a traditional pathway to nobility that suddenly was perceived to threaten the exclusivity and legitimacy of those who considered themselves to constitute the high elite and who were already in power. Within months of Philip III's accession to the throne, Cabrera de Córdoba reported that "hánse dado más hábitos de las tres órdenes, después que S. M. heredó, que no se dieron en diez años en vida del Rey su padre; porque pasan de cincuenta personas a los que se han dado, y que los más lo han alcanzado con poca diligencia"[45] [more military habits of the three orders were given after the king inherited {the throne} than were given in ten years during his father's reign, because there are more than fifty persons to whom they were given, and most of them obtained them with little effort]. The worst was to come. By 1605, the son of Rodrigo Calderón, less than a year old, was admitted to the prestigious Order of Alcántara. Reaction was swift against the king's wholesale creation of *caballeros*. The Order of Santiago met in 1603 and approved new entry qualifications: "Ordenamos que el que hubiere de tener el hábito de nuestra orden sea hijodalgo de sangre de parte de padre y de parte de madre y no de privilegio"[46] [It is ordered that whoever joins our ranks must be of pure blood on both the father's and mother's side; nobility based on concession is not allowed]. This and other restrictions came too late, and in the final analysis—as we have noted with regard to Rodrigo Calderón's son, and certainly with Don Diego Coronel—had little impact. Don Diego and his kind point to that powerful elite, already too entrenched and powerful to be attacked directly and by name. In sum, Don Diego, despite the tainted blood of his ancestors and his questionable behavior in the novel, is identified as the legitimate son of a Segovian nobleman, whereas Don Pablos is unmasked as the bastard son of a Segovian barber whose *oficio mecánico* alone was sufficient to deny his family noble status.

Quevedo was intimately aware of the strategies adopted by Don Diego and Don Pablos at the beginning of the seventeenth century. Those who would get ahead had to live nobly, forge strong political alliances, and be connected to the right families. Quevedo's own success was assured when he attached himself to the Duke of Osuna, who was appointed viceroy of Sicily in 1609, a year after he arranged the marriage of his oldest son to the second daughter of the Duke of Uceda, Lerma's son. Quevedo profited handily by associating himself with *hombres de*

bien; he insisted on maintaining the exclusivity of the legitimate elite through his picaresque novel by exiling Don Pablos and by pointing a finger at those like Don Diego who would falsify their lineage and deny their blood.[47]

Claudio Guillén is correct when he writes that the invention of the picaresque took place with the almost simultaneous publication of the rediscovered *Lazarillo* and the *Guzmán de Alfarache*. However, it may not have been because an enterprising printer named Luis Sánchez wanted to cash in on the popularity of a new literary genre, but rather because a politically and financially astute book publisher named Miguel Martínez had detected the signs of a new court, a court within which the values of the picaresque found a responsive audience. The social and political worlds of the *valido* both engendered and resisted the picaresque novel, a literary genre that questioned and sustained the arbitrary nature of identity, the power of money and courtly manners, family networks, and political favoritism.

Notes

1. Robert Weimann, *Shakespeare and the Popular Tradition in the Theater: Studies in the Social Dimension of Dramatic Form and Function* (Baltimore: Johns Hopkins University Press, 1978), p. xiii.

2. José Antonio Maravall, *La literatura picaresca desde la historia social* (Madrid: Taurus, 1986); Theodore K. Rabb, *The Struggle for Stability in Early Modern Europe* (New York: Oxford University Press, 1975), p. 33.

3. Pierre Bourdieu, *Outline of a Theory of Practice* (Cambridge: Cambridge University Press, 1977), p. 94.

4. Frank Whigham, *Ambition and Privilege: The Social Tropes of Elizabethan Courtesy Literature* (Berkeley: University of California Press, 1984), p. x.

5. See Richard L. Kagan, *Students and Society in Early Modern Spain* (Baltimore: Johns Hopkins University Press, 1974), and Janine Fayard, *Les membres du Conseil de Castille a l'époque moderne, 1621-1746* (Geneva: Droz, 1979).

6. Whigham, *Ambition and Privilege,* p. 5.

7. Cited ibid., p. 7.

8. Stephen Greenblatt, *Renaissance Self-Fashioning: From More to Shakespeare* (Chicago: University of Chicago Press, 1980), p. 162.

9. M. Morreale points out in her edition of Lucas Gracián's *Galateo español* (Madrid: Consejo Superior de Investigaciones Científicas, 1968), p. 2, that its first translator, Domingo de Becerra, remarked that "para notar una mala costumbre o crianza . . . se suele dezir como proverbio 'no manda esso el Galateo.'" Morreale adds that "una europa ansiosa de

afinar el trato social y difundir la urbanidad aun fuera de la clase aristocrática, no podía menos que apreciar los avisos del librito italiano, tan agudamente seleccionados y aplicables a las más variadas circunstancias."

10. See Margherita Morreale, *Castiglione y Boscán: el ideal cortesano en el renacimiento español, Boletín de la Real Academia Española,* Anejo 1 (1969).

11. Alonso de Barros, *Filosofía cortesana moralizada,* ed. Trevor J. Dadson (Madrid: Comunidad de Madrid, 1987).

12. John Elliott, *The Count-Duke of Olivares: The Statesman in an Age of Decline* (New Haven: Yale University Press, 1986), p. 9.

13. Ruth Pike, *Enterprise and Adventure: The Genoese in Seville and the Opening of the New World* (Ithaca: Cornell University Press, 1966), pp. 3-5; Henri La Peyre, *Une famille de Marchands les Ruiz* (Paris: A. Colin, 1955).

14. Cabrera de Córdoba, *Relaciones de las cosas sucedidas en la corte de España* (Madrid: J. Martín Alegría, 1857), p. 3.

15. Antonio Feros, "Gobierno de Corte y Patronazgo Real en el reinado de Felipe III (1598-1618)" (thesis, Universidad Autónoma de Madrid, 1986), p. 40.

16. I will cite Margherita Morreale's edition, *Galateo español.* Her preliminary study has been helpful in sorting out early editions, especially regarding the early texts of the *Lazarillo castigado* and Lucas Gracián's treatise.

17. See Claudio Guillén, *Literature as System: Essays toward the Theory of Literary History* (Princeton: Princeton University Press, 1971), pp. 135-58.

18. For Velasco, see María del Carmen González Muñoz, ed., *Geografía y descripción universal de las Indias* (Madrid: M. Atlas, 1971), "Estudio preliminar."

19. J. M. Bujanda et al., *Index des livres interdits,* vol. 7 (1988): 89-97. "Le comité présidé par Arias Montano semble avoir réalisé un travail de vérification, de compilation et de sélection" (p. 89).

20. Marcos Jiménez de la Espada, ed., "La correspondencia del Doctor Benito Arias Montano con el Licenciado Juan de Ovando," *Boletín de la Real Academia de Historia* 19 (1912): 488.

21. The Index of Antwerp (1570) reproduces the list of Valdés (1559) with one important change in the section beginning with the letter "L": the *Lazarillo,* which was sandwiched between *Las lamentaciones de Pedro* and the *Lengua de Erasmo en Romance, y en Latín, y en qualquier lengua vulgar* in Valdés, is missing in the Antwerp index. No longer completely prohibited, had the *Lazarillo* been withdrawn to be expurgated? This is difficult to ascertain because certain *comedias* of Torres Naharro remained. See Bujanda, pp. 696, 700.

22. Many of his autograph manuscripts remain in the Escorial library, including this one, L. I. 13. See J. Zarco Cuevas, *Catálogo de manuscritos castellanos en la Real Biblioteca de El Escorial,* 3 vols. (Madrid: El Escorial, 1924-29).

23. The royal privilege included in the Madrid 1573 edition of Cristóbal de Castillejo (BN R-1.485) was issued at San Lorenzo de El Escorial on August 5 for its circulation in Aragón, and includes a reference to the works of Torres Naharro and to the *Lazarillo:* "Por parte de vos Iuan Lopez de Velasco, nos ha sido hecha relación, que mandado y commission del Consejo de la Sancta Inquisicion haviades recopilado y corregido la *Propaladia* de Bartholome de Torres Naharro, y la vida de *Lazarillo de Tormes,* y las obras de Christobal de Castillejo, Secretario que fue del emperador don Hernando, . . . Y vos aveys suplicado, que atendido vuestro buen zelo que teneys del comun aprovechamiento y el trabajo que en esto abeys tenido fuessemos servido de dar licencia y facultad, para que vos y quien de vos tuviese poder para ello, y no otra persona alguna lo podays y puedan imprimir y vender . . . assi *todo junto en un volumen, como dividido en dos, o tres volumenes, o partes, de la manera que a vos os pareciere mas a convertir a la utilidad de los leyentes*" (my emphasis).

24. C. Pérez Pastor, *Bibliografía madrileña (Siglo XVI)* (Madrid: Tip. de los Huérfanos, 1891), p. 39. The work of Castillejo was apparently published separately.

25. Juan Berrillo, a Madrid bookseller, had received permission to publish both texts in one volume in April 1599, but a copy of this edition has never been located. Enrique Macaya Lahmann, *Bibliografía del Lazarillo de Tormes* (San José, Costa Rica: Ediciones del Convivio, 1935), notes that the edition of the *Lazarillo* now in the Hispanic Society of America is bound together with the "Coplas de Jorge Manrique, las de Mingo Revulgo y las Cartas de Refranes de Blasco de Garay" (p. 65).

26. Lucas Gracián died in July 1587; Juan López de Velasco had managed to retain his original permission to publish the *Lazarillo,* but the fact that the novel began appearing within a year of his death seems an odd coincidence. There remains some mystery about the various editions of the *Lazarillo* published at this time. See Enrique Macaya Lahmann, *Bibliografía del Lazarillo de Tormes,* who refers to an edition of 1599 printed by Luis Sánchez, which he was unable to locate for his study (p. 64).

27. In an entry for February 1601, Cabrera de Córdoba noted that "Mandan mudar la Audiencia y Chancillería, que allí [Valladolid] reside, a Medina del Campo, y las ferias que hasta agora se han hecho en Medina, las mandan pasar a Burgos" (p. 95). The *Lazarillo* was also published in Valencia in 1601 (remember that the court made a slow return to

Madrid from Valencia in late 1599) and in Alcalá de Henares in 1607.

28. The town council records of Madrid at this time are filled with references as to how the (bankrupt) city would fulfill its end of the agreement. The Duque de Cea, Lerma's son, was provided a house (formerly of Agustín Alvarez de Toledo) whose rent was to be paid by the city. Cea had built a "pasadizo" from the house to the Royal Palace "en conformidad del . . . ofrescimiento . . . para S. M. por razon de la buelta de la corte a esta villa" (Archivo Municipal de Madrid: Libros de Acuerdos, vol. 25, fol. 400r, 20 November 1606). Madrid had also agreed to pay the king the sixth part of rental houses, but found that it was "muy ynconbiniente para esta villa y sus vecinos" (fol. 418r, March 1607), and ordered that a committee be sent to Valladolid "a tratar deste servicio por razón de la buelta de la corte" (ibid.). The original agreement stipulated that the city would pay the king 250,000 ducats; the city managed to have the amount spread over ten years, and in addition, "los alquileres de las casas del Marques de Auñón y Agustín Albarez de Toledo en que vive y a de vivir el Sr. Duque de Cea" (fol. 451v, 5 May 1607).

29. See Claudia W. Sieber, "The Invention of a Capital: Philip II and the First Reform of Madrid" (Ph.D. diss., Johns Hopkins University, 1985).

30. See Donald McGrady, "A Pirated Edition of *Guzmán de Alfarache*: More Light on Mateo Alemán's Life," *Hispanic Review* 34 (1966): 326-28.

31. Raymond Willis, "Lazarillo and the Pardoner: The Artistic Necessity of the Fifth Tractado," *Hispanic Review* 8 (1959): 267-79.

32. I cited the Medina del Campo edition of 1603, housed in the Library of Congress, BJ 1981. G66 / 1603.

33. Francisco Rico, ed., *La vida de Lazarillo de Tormes* (Madrid: Cátedra, 1987), p. 82. All subsequent references are to this edition.

34. Benito Brancaforte, ed., *Guzmán de Alfarache,* 2 vols. (Madrid: Cátedra, 1979), p. 248. All references to the novel are to this edition.

35. See Pablo Jauralde's note in his edition of the *Buscón* (Madrid: Castalia, 1990), p. 18.

36. All references to the *Buscón* are to Pablo Jauralde, ed. (Madrid: Castalia, 1990).

37. See Molho's perceptive study, "Cinco lecciones sobre el 'Buscón,'" in *Semántica y poética (Góngora, Quevedo)* (Barcelona: Crítica, 1977), pp. 89-131.

38. See Carroll B. Johnson, "*El Buscón*: Don Pablos, don Diego y don Francisco," *Hispanófila* 51 (1974): 1-26; Agustín Redondo, "Del personaje de don Diego Coronel a una nueva interpretación del *Buscón*," *Ac-*

tas del Quinto Congreso Internacional de Hispanistas (Bordeaux: U. de Bordeaux, 1974 [1977]); Idalia Cordero, *El 'Buscón' o la vergüenza de Pablos y la ira de don Francisco* (Madrid: Playor, 1987). See also Angel G. Loureiro, "Reivindicación de Pablos," *Revista de Filología Española* 67 (1987): 225-44, and Henry Ettinghausen, "Quevedo's Converso Pícaro," *Modern Language Notes* 102 (1987): 241-54.

39. Vicente Andosilla Salazar, *A don Pedro Manso de Zúñiga, Patriarca de las Indias y Presidente del Consejo Real de Castilla* (place and year unknown), fol. 4v. This reference comes from Antonio Feros, p. 84.

40. James O. Crosby, *En torno a la poesía de Quevedo* (Madrid: Castalia, 1967), p. 157. This poem was first included in Pedro Espinosa's *Flores de poetas ilustres* (Valladolid, 1605). The collection, however, received official permission to be published almost two years later.

41. The text is taken from José Manuel Blecua, ed., *Francisco de Quevedo: Obra poética* (Madrid: Castalia, 1970), 2:175-76.

42. See the *Buscón,* p. 228.

43. See the *Planimetría general de Madrid,* facs. ed. (Madrid: Tabapress, 1988), 1:315-16.

44. See Cordero, p. 14, who cites Maravall, "La aspiración social de *medro* en la novela picaresca," *Cuadernos hispanoamericanos* 312 (1976): 595: "Muchos, aunque procedan de baja cuna, si consiguen reunir dinero en cantidad bastante, quieran disponer de placeres, comodidad, ociosidad, lujo, ostentación, consiguiente, de respeto social y, en fin, de poder y mayor riqueza."

45. *Relaciones de las cosas sucedidas en la corte de España desde 1599 hasta 1614,* pp. 4-5.

46. See Elena Postigo Castellanos, *Honor y privilegio en la corona de Castilla. El Consejo de las Ordenes y los caballeros de hábito en el siglo XVII* (Madrid: Valladolid: Junta de Castilla y León, 1988), p. 135. The *Diccionario de Autoridades* (Madrid: 1732) contains a useful definition of the "hidalgo de privilegio": "El siendo hombre llano [that is, he who pays taxes], por algun servicio particular o accion gloriosa, el Rey le concedio los privilegios exenciones, y prerogativos que gozan los hijosdalgo de casa y solar conocido: o aquel que compró este mismo privilegio a los reyes."

47. For Quevedo's ancestry and his early connection to the court, see Pablo Jauralde, ed., *El Buscón* (Madrid: Castalia, 1990), pp. 10-11. Jauralde points out that "la relación, bastante sinuosa, de Quevedo con la nobleza de su tiempo constituye uno de los capítulos más apasionados de su ya apasionante biografía" (pp. 10-11).

Giancarlo Maiorino (essay date 1996)

SOURCE: Maiorino, Giancarlo. "Picaresque Econopoetics: At the Watershed of Living Standards." In *The Picaresque: Tradition and Displacement,* edited by Giancarlo Maiorino, pp. 1-39. Minneapolis: University of Minnesota Press, 1996.

[*In this essay, Maiorino applies the insights of New Historicist scholarship to the picaresque, focusing on Lazarillo de Tormes.*]

I

At the divide between the waning of feudalism and the birth of capitalism, orations on human dignity, praises of folly, seafaring discoveries, and mercantile adventurism set off outbursts of human ingenuity. Merchants in Florence and elsewhere, Jules Michelet wrote at an early stage of Renaissance criticism, upheld a religion that found "in gold its real presence and in letters of exchange its eucharist."[1] It was the "other" Renaissance of commercial pursuits that made ambitious individuals proud, powerful, and appreciative of the advantages wealth could bestow on lineage and society.

At the beginning of early modern Europe, the sociology of wealth quantified its influence through an array of paintings, ledgers, account books, and art objects as well as literary, historical, and ecclesiastic texts. While "signifiers" such as "labor," "price," and "profit" are not just mercantile, concepts of value, utility, and effectiveness have been artistic and economic for the longest time. *Seme,* in fact, means "word" and "coin." Even people could be "of base coinage"; like gold, they could be adulterated.[2] As a matter of fact, the very word-concept "classical," which has set a major standard in Western culture, stems from the appropriate usage of language among educated citizens who belonged to the first-class taxpayers, whereas *proletarius* did not pay taxes (Aulus Gellius, *Noctes Atticae* xix, 8, 15). Canon-making and cultural standards were thus geared to economic and social criteria (Curtius 249-50).[3] In a significant way, therefore, mimesis was "econo-mimesis."[4] In the wake of studies on the Protean complexity of the Renaissance, scholarship has highlighted the impact of economics on the cultural syncretism of the age through such topics as "Venetian and Dutch *Elites,*" "Art and Accounting," "The Embarrassment of Riches," "The Poetics of Accumulation," and "Cultural Aesthetics."[5]

Antiquity favored affluence over indigence, and so did Humanism in Florence and elsewhere. Below the veneer of aristocratic wealth and mercantile prosperity, however, the majority of the population lived in abject poverty. Paganism and Christianity took the poor to be a familiar presence on street corners and in market-places. Because its social depth and range were significant, poverty was recognized, but no remedies were proposed. Throughout the early Middle Ages, society was entrenched along the divide between *maiores et potentiores* and *minores et infir-*

miores. After the tenth century, a tripartite structure ordered society into *oratores, bellatores,* and *imbelle vulgus.* Physical work and mechanical arts were held in low esteem vis-à-vis intellectual and moral strength. The humanists did not openly test that assumption. In Spain, the picaresque mindset did not either, but it did expose a society whose class divisions left no doubts about who was privileged and who was exploited. If the new novelistic mode did not call for open revolt, it nevertheless singled out an unfair state of things. To foster awareness was a first step toward provoking indignation, which in turn could lead to change. But it would take centuries for that process to shake the status quo (MacMullen 86-87, 118, 127). Economic power and class discriminations were thus crucial to marginality, picaresque or otherwise. *Popolo grasso* and *ricos hombres,* in fact, knew how to guard their wealth, and they did it with a vengeance (Huppert 17). At best, indigence was to be alleviated, but not eliminated.

Introductory remarks of this sort make it clear that *Homo ludens, Homo loquens,* and *Homo oeconomicus* shared a common vocabulary long before the Renaissance, and research could not but follow suit. Sociologists have explored the psychological and aesthetic range of the philosophy of money, and historians have found in consumerism a point of entry into processes of cultural change.[6] Along Mediterranean shores, the 'golden century' drew strength from the "cycle of gold" that financed it. Any golden age, in fact, must rest on gilded foundations if it is to have a lasting impact on society.[7] Since it became a marker of individual and collective "fashioning," wealth—or lack thereof—affected what could be called econopoetics, which this essay takes to describe deficient negotiations between economic signs and noneconomic verbal signifiers in *Lazarillo de Tormes* (1550-54?).

While focusing on the autobiographical life of a single individual from birth to adulthood, the picaresque text exposes bankrupt aspects of sixteenth-century culture in Spain, where the Christian Reconquest set up a mindset whose outlook on economics was substantially different from Italian or Dutch mercantilism. Once the Old Christians emerged victorious, the socioeconomic context of the Iberian peninsula retained Arabic and Jewish ascendancy on matters of agriculture, trade, and business. To them, one ought to add Italian merchants and bankers. And many Spanish businessmen who excelled at their trade used wealth to acquire estates and become noblemen in the manner of landed aristocrats. By so doing, they dried out the ranks and power of their own middle class. While the wealth coming from the New World kept dreams of grandeur alive, the ruling classes kept on despising any sort of manual or commercial labor. Their unproductive supremacy was bound to tumble. And it did. At the opposite pole of purity of blood and contempt of money and labor, there emerged the picaresque. To put it in terms of New Historicism, this study explores artworks embedded into a network of material practices which called on will, guts, and wits to face the relentless assaults of poverty.

In his lifelong study of the picaresque, Francisco Rico has found in the technique of "point of view" the "unifying principle" of plot, meaning, and narratology (91-92).[8] Likewise, my approach to *econopoetics* makes poetics primary to interpretation, while economics represents a distinctive "point of entry" into a reading of the text that pays equal attention to aesthetic and social relationships. Especially in the antiheroic mode of lifestyles at the margins of affluence, the picaresque borrowed from the traditions of chivalry and Humanism as much as it relied on parody to stir a better awareness of the societal makeup. Compromises and reversals of that sort reached depths that Italian texts never dared to probe, even though the Spanish art of thieving was paralleled on Italian shores by writings on the related "art of lying."

In spite of gold and goods coming from overseas, too many royal policies proved to be disastrous to commerce and agriculture. In their rubble, the ranks of beggars, *pícaros,* and vagrants grew almost out of control. Alongside the aristocracy, humanist elites, and a small middle class, there also thrived a "sub" or "under" culture of *pícaros,* thieves, and adventurers that would crowd Cervantes's *Novelas Ejemplares* and the Golden Age stage of Lope de Vega and Tirso de Molina. Even conservative estimates counted *pícaros* by the thousands everywhere. And among all Spanish cities, Mateo Alemán called Seville the *Babilonia de pícaros.*

In the empirical form of a novelistic journey from Salamanca, the city of law and learning, to Toledo, the city of business and trade, *Lazarillo de Tormes* presents the growth of a social outcast whose ambition is to build a better future for himself. Since picaresque "success" thrives more on standards of mediocrity than excellence, the text deals with a blindman's boy who succeeds in becoming town crier. His growth would not produce another tale of rags-to-riches in either the epic or the chivalric mode, but it would tell a story of human survival more typical of life-as-is.[9] The new genre thus presented urban paupers, alienated middle-class *conversos,* and individual stories whose self-preservation was spurred and defended by hook and by crook.[10] Although roguery was part of the European scene at large, the socioeconomic depth and artistic output of picaresque life in Spain was unique. Around the middle of the sixteenth century, the life of the underprivileged made inroads into the art and literature of Spain, where a *"crítica vulgar"* under the aegis of *"lo insignificante"* offset the traditions of epic and chivalry (Castro, *Cervantes* 121). As Sancho Panza later put it,

> "There are only two families in the world, my old grandmother used to say, the *Have* and the *Have-Nots.* She was always for the *haves,* and to this very day, my lord Don Quixote, the doctor would rather feel the pulse of a *Have* than a *Know.*"
>
> *(Don Quixote* II: Chapter 20)[11]

By setting forth ideas about poverty that already had concerned Erasmus, writings such as Juan Luis Vives's *De subventione pauperum* called for a sharing of basic goods with the poor. Contacts between economics and the picaresque quickly revealed gaps between the affluence of the aristocracy and the destitution of the working classes—not to mention the underemployed. Since the bourgeoisie had been disintegrating at the periphery of the other two groups,[12] the novel voiced long-standing contrasts that were socioeconomic at heart.[13] In their midst, Lázaro de Tormes spent much of his youth growing out of *lacería.*

With ease, *Lazarillo de Tormes* would validate the Bakhtinian emphasis on the "prosaic intelligence" and the "prosaic wisdom" of a vulgar discourse that stood as a counterpoint to more privileged genres (Morson and Emerson 308). Picaresque and Cervantine characters believed that "stealing was a free trade," much as they relished "gipsy language" and "thieves's slang."[14] And one need only add that, before the emergence of the picaresque, *La Celestina* gave tragicomic form to the concept of life as mere doing. In addition to literary precedents, picaresque literature included *poesía cancioneril, teatro primitivo, refranes glosados, diálogos,* as well as continuations and imitations of *La Celestina*; all in all, a *literatura desesperanzada* that fostered a rather pessimistic vision of human life (Villanueva 91, 136-37). At the periphery of ingrained privileges, poverty had spread as a social disease throughout Europe, and tales of utter destitution were popular everywhere around the middle of the sixteenth century. However bright the veneer of imperial grandeur, almost half of the population was poor in Spain (Herrero 876-79). While playing a role in the emergence of the picaresque, data of that sort quantified a dejected humanity whose presence was conspicuous throughout Europe. The poor had to remain poor, even though some attention was invested in turning a sympathetic eye toward them. After all, it was economically advantageous that they survive and be strong enough to work.

In the vocabulary of social distribution, the picaresque text was probably the first to call attention to the oppressed humanity of *infrahombres.*[15] The humanity, that is, of *mozos, pícaros,* and cheap manpower, not to mention thieves, criminals, *picardía,* and *vida buscona*; a low-life world where *jerigonza, nombres germanescos,* and slangs of all sorts gained currency. Picaresque novels, Michel Butor would remind us, exposed "les entrailles, les dessous, les coulisses de la société—the guts, the underside, the margins of society" (96). Hence the dilemma: what kind of language would such a humanity speak? It certainly was neither humanistic nor courtly, let alone chivalric. Instead, it was more likely a vernacular counterlanguage replete with colloquialisms, preliterate jargon, *refranes,* and the *vox populi* of proverbial phrases. The type of linguistic brew that was more Erasmian—from *Adagia* to *Colloquia*—than Ciceronian. This essay aims at reconciling the New Historicist emphasis on unheroic subjects with the uniquely Spanish notion of *intrahistoria.* Instead of a microhistory, however, I focus on the prototype of the picaresque. While centering on the economic marginality of poor Spaniards whose lives were shaped by survival, my approach sets out to balance the ever widening gyre of contextuality—which draws from New Historicism, cultural anthropology, and interdisciplinary approaches of sorts—with aesthetic matters of form.[16] From food and lodging to fashion, money, and manners, econopoetics brings together an array of different languages, which are reciprocally paraliterary and paraeconomic. For Barbara Hernnstein Smith, the traditional tendency to exclude economic factors from works of art and literature mystifies their very nature. And the picaresque could certainly prove that exclusions of that sort would have the effect of defining the genre out of existence (33).[17] My treatment of econopoetics in *Lazarillo de Tormes* centers on the waterseller chapter, whose threshold function will be highlighted through a comparison with Velázquez's painting of the same subject.

II

Lázaro becomes a waterseller in the sixth chapter of *Lazarillo de Tormes*. At first, he takes up the task of mixing colors for a painter. But he soon quits because that job made his life very hard. In the cathedral of Toledo a priest then gives him the job of water carrier. Lázaro discharges his duties successfully. He pays the priest an agreed amount of money and keeps the rest for himself. After four years, he has saved enough to buy clothes and a sword. At that point, he decides to quit his job and try for better luck. Age-wise, he is a restless youth whose socioeconomic ascent begins with the instruments of the trade: a whip, four jugs, and a donkey. So equipped, he sets out to carry water around town. Yet he never calls himself *aguador*. During those four years, however, the tempo of life picks up. The vaguely achronological "by now" and "one day" of the boy's earlier tasks echoed medieval practices, which divided the day along religious zones such as "at dawn," "about noon," or "toward sunset." That was the beggar's time at street corners familiar to blindmen and their servants. Neither time nor space could be of their choice, for they had to be "where" and "when" alms were more likely to be given. By contrast, the young water carrier pays the priest thirty *maravedís* every day, keeps the rest, and works for himself on Saturdays. His daily chore sets a money-yielding pace; time itself is about to become a clock-measured commodity. Lázaro thus learns to discipline talent, initiative, and the dynamics of his environment into a profitable routine. He saves money and gains confidence in himself; however meager his earnings, he can set ambitious goals. Money brings regularity to the narrative, while savings introduce some vestiges of wealth. Yet, the appearance of prosperity would not yield substantial possessions.

The job of waterseller gives Lázaro security. But security could not remain his life project. In the commercial city of Toledo, in fact, the *escudero* taught him that one's life had to be guided by a set of principles. Once Lázaro understood that he had to pursue a version of honor within reach of his *buena fortuna,* the economic makeup of the chapter turned around. Jugs and whips faded into the background:

> I did so well at the job that after four years of careful saving I had enough to dress myself very decently in second-hand clothes; I bought an old fustian jacket and a worn coat with braided sleeves and a vent. I also got a cloak which had had a fringe once, and an old sword made when they used to make them at Cuéllar.
>
> (76)[18]

If he still appreciates the fact that it took him four years of careful saving to buy second-hand clothes, one must surmise that Lázaro's ensuing prosperity has been rather limited. His experience points back to the *escudero,* whose pathetic demeanor carried the stamp of economic bankruptcy. The text thus brings to the fore disjunctions between "cost of living" and "standard of life." The former is meant to provide for basic needs. At the periphery of affluence most humanity kept on struggling with cost of living. Amid lowlife society, cost of living sets up compensations based on exploitation rather than fairness. And all sorts of political, psychological, and religious pressures were brought to bear on the acceptance of such a disparity. By contrast, standard of life points to a lifestyle that makes cultural values almost as primary as subsistence itself. In a minor—if not parodic—key, Lázaro reaches, or at least he thinks he has reached, that qualitative threshold at the end of the sixth chapter. Thereafter, he would try to convince himself that his good luck has drawn cost of living and standard of life into a profitable—if not honorable—equation.

For Lázaro de Tormes, standard of life represents the future. For the *escudero,* instead, it symbolizes loss. In fact, he enters the narrative long after his standard of life fell by the wayside. The economy he bodies forth is out of currency, and his rhetoric of wishful affluence folds under its own insubstantiality. Lázaro, instead, begins to invest in the future. Weekly earnings and weekend overtime draw a line between dependence and self-sufficiency. Yet, he could buy only second-hand clothes, a worn-out cloak, and an old sword. Earlier in the fourth chapter, he was given an old pair of shoes that lasted only one week. Nevertheless, he got to know what it meant not to walk barefooted and what it would take to wear shoes once again. Consumable items of that sort demanded a steady income. As always, advantage had a price. The symbolism of shoes in folklore and literature (*Libro de Buen Amor*) points to sexual favors, which would be given at the price of moral taxation by the end of the last *tratado*. If Lázaro gets old stockings from the archpriest, we can bet that the same provider would offer his wife plenty of shoes!

Increases and depletions of Lázaro's *buena fortuna* are part and parcel of a novelistic project that set much of the action within reach of water. Actually, he was born by the river Tormes—"mi nacimiento fue dentro del río Tormes." Having traded amniotic for fluvial waters, so to speak, the journey downstream transforms him neither into a leader of people nor a valiant knight. Along the way, however, he would learn just about everything one could want to know about matters of indigence.

To draw on current levels—if not kinds—of narrative, the picaresque text would fall outside the *grand récit* of a totalizing and idealized concept of history. Yet, it could be counted among those *petites histoires* that historians and cultural anthropologists—from Natalie Zemon Davis and Stephen Greenblatt to Carlo Ginzburg, Piero Camporesi, and Michel de Certeau—have linked to anecdotes and the practice of everyday life.[19] Amid artworks one would assign to the province of *grand récit,* Velázquez's *Las Lanzas* (or the *Peace of Breda*) stands out. Conversely, his *Waterseller* fits the unheroic context of *pequeño intrahistórico.*

Whereas Lázaro's ambulatory job takes water to people, youths and adults gather around Velázquez's old man. He bestows life-giving liquid in a room where two jugs are set on a table flanked by a bench. Since the composition is foreshortened, a sense of spatial closure draws viewers into a communal space at the edge of the large water jug. While it is just a commodity in the novel, water involves the archetypal transmission of life in the painting, where the waterseller stands out as the embodiment of an almost archetypal task.[20] His gaze does not betray senescence, and there is nothing temporary about him; above all, his posture projects the solemn stability of ritual. Whereas it serves commercial exchanges in the novel, water involves a higher form of transaction in the artwork. The old man holds the bottom of the goblet and the youngster secures his grip on its stem; generations thus join hands. Dictionaries of Renaissance symbols tell us that the purity of glass pointed to intellectual and spiritual clarity. The goblet stands as a transparent point of conjunction between young and old. A kind of eucharistic act is performed, if we only think of contemporary proverbs—"People of Toledo, people of God, water belongs to him, and we only sell it"—or Juan Luis Vives's words: "Your drink shall be . . . that natural liquor prepared by God for all living creatures in common—pure, clean water." While passages from Matthew and Psalms speak of water as fountain and source of human experience, Francisco de Quevedo and the moralist Damián de Vegas insisted that heaven was waiting for those who would give a glass of water to one who thirsts (Wind 103; Moffitt 10).

Velázquez's pot-bellied jug is of plain clay, and its shape introduces the waterseller's own figure. Correspondences of that kind make the human face itself appear to be "stilled from within" (Steinberg 282). Under somber lighting effects, the artwork reveals a subdued interplay of clay glazed and unglazed, of wrinkles and flesh, of wood and fabrics, and of a miracle-bestowing goblet. Carrier and vessel are bound together into the portrait of an activity that foregrounds the waterseller's story. By ignoring urban settings and commercial equipments, the artist has painted a rather bare and yet sheltering environment in which objects are as crucial to meaning as human presence itself; one is a function of the other, and both of them shoulder the representation of a humanized reality.

Whereas macrohistory acts out narratives which recount pasts of epic grandeur, microhistory is linked to the description of current events and prosaic, if not altogether petty, attitudes of mind. Emphasis is placed on situations that tend to "equalize" people and things. At their static worst, we confront texts that simplify individualism and edge on genre. By yielding an array of details in excess of what is appropriate to the economy of the narrative, texts of that sort create "still life" conditions. Velázquez's painting, however, avoids such a pitfall. Even a cursory comparison with his own *bodegones* makes it clear that *The Waterseller* foregrounds a view of human values bent on praising dignity rather than depravation, and intensity rather than insignificance. The pictorial economy of details is as axiomatic as it is crucial to the implied narrative. If one were to argue that description debases human beings to the level of inanimate things, then one could trust that Velázquez "redeemed" the descriptive mode; he did not start with *things,* but with *people.* At their most constructive, picaresque artworks take on a kind of "narrative grandeur," which one could indeed find typical of what has been called the epic of the *infrahombre.* Readers and viewers are thus moved to reflect on moral and ethical aspects of human existence.

Since it is full of water, the jug responds to external heat by exuding moisture. At spots where drops and runnels make its thick impasto seem almost transparent, the clay partakes of the goblet's brilliance. Condensation thus couches beauty in forms which call to mind the forthcoming passion (baroque or otherwise) for the evanescent—from snow flakes to air bubbles. At the same time, the jug's horizontal crevices echo the wrinkles on the old man's forehead, just as blemishes on the smaller jug repeat the rough texture of his cheeks. Man and jug meet through the handle, which makes the mimesis of reality more direct by foregrounding the utilitarian function of clay ware. At the same time, tears in the old man's cloak heighten fullness and consumption. In the painter's hands, even forms of stillness, Mikhail Bakhtin might agree, could be chronotopic. With ease but without banality, pictorial surfaces unfurl textures which weave a life-giving image.

The large jug rests on a bench that sets it apart from the rest of the composition. Its small neck and heavy size disqualify it as an object apt to expedite distribution. On the table, the smaller pitcher with a wider neck and a clay cup on its top proves to be a more practical dispenser of fluids. One vessel is unique in Velázquez's *oeuvre,* and it works as a pivot between here and there, quotidianity and archetype. The other is of a stock that appears on kitchen and dinner tables from *Christ in the House of Martha and Mary* (1618) and the *Old Woman Frying Eggs* (1618) to *Christ at Emmaus* (1620-21). The coarseness of the clay jug clashes with the elegant goblet he hands to the youngster. Task, thought, and posture are so transparently wholesome that the goblet seems to mirror a humane clarity of heart. That refined piece of craftsmanship is strikingly different from Velázquez's usual glassware. While *Three Men at the Table* (1618-19) and *Bacchus-Borrachos* (1628-29) show cheap tumblers, *The Waterseller* makes a qualitative leap. With pride, common laborers in Pedro de Guzmán's *Los bienes del honesto trabajo* (1614) could "drink from the work of their hands" (Wind 101-2). A daily task thus turns into an act that exudes wholesome maturity. It would be safe to guess that thoughts about wealth, profit, or career-oriented ambitions have never made a dent in the old *aguador*'s sense of social responsibility. Subtly, the artist has juxtaposed the economics of the trade, which demands efficient utensils, to an archetypal blueprint. The old man does not deal with merchandise, and he seems to have forsaken profit. For sure, he has relinquished the 'competitive' evil of goals and ambitions tailored after, and against, other people.

While focusing on expectation and magnanimity, the crystal-clear goblet heightens a still moment replete with past, present, and future. We look at a life-giving transparency. Liquidity itself has been dissolved into a mental contemplation on the meaning of water as the very sustenance of life. Silence enfolds a virtual narrative apt to pour wisdom into the naive emptiness of youth. Such a potential for story telling seems to make a case for ekphrasis in reverse. The picture, in fact, is emblematic in a literary sense, much as language has corporealized itself into the silent people of *intrahistoria*. Ordinary individuals of that sort are more familiar with facts than performances, much as they speak in songs, maxims, and legends of a kind which the old man would pass on to the youth.

Proverbial forms voice the ethical underpinning of folklore, which reflects the more stable aspects of popular culture (Gramsci 189-90).[21] It suffices to add that picaresque texts are studded with maxims. The *ciego* relies on the long-standing symbolism of wine and horns to set up the plot. Economics motivates his journey toward Toledo, and proverbial wisdom justifies it; a hard man in fact can give more than another who does not have anything to give. Selfishness of that kind is unknown to the old waterseller, and it points to that border line where the indigent humanity of *intrahistoria* edges on more affluent counterparts. On moral and economic grounds, proverbial wisdom tends to spur conformity, which would reinforce Lázaro's gregariousness.

As a literary image, the jug's full shape harks back to grain bins and maternal wombs at the beginning of the novel, which also highlights shoes, cloaks, bread, sausages, cow's feet, and the priest's glorious bunch of onions. Such an array of things and goods belongs to what the nomenclature of art has called "rhopography." Its etymon, *rhopos*, points to trifles and small wares that cultural aesthetics has parceled out to the realm of triviality.[22] By contrast, unimportant things are of little interest to artists interested in "megalography," which depicts objects symbolic of gods, heroes, and memorable deeds. With an eye to economic matters, "megalography" finds a parallel in Xenophon's *Oeconomicus,* which defines lavish public expenditures. The virtue of *megaloprepeia* is thus unthinkable in the picaresque, and Norman Bryson insists that rhopography ought to remind us that "all men must eat; there is a levelling of humanity, a humbling of aspiration before an irreducible fact of life, hunger" (61). Hunger makes objects functional; spoons, knives, glasses, and

plates imply touch, hands, and mouths. Activities of that sort would be just as familiar to Murillo's destitute youths, who are forever engaged in eating grapes and watermelons (*Two Boys Eating Fruit* [1670s]).[23] The world of rhopography was bound to proliferate. Laurence Sterne's *Tristram Shandy* includes a "chapter on things," and Honoré de Balzac would divide his human comedy into three categories: men, women, and things. Things thus began to take on human qualities; in turn, humans were ever more dependent on materialist goods. Realism, in fact, refers to *res*, that is to say, to things. Etymologically speaking, realism is "thing-ism" (Levin 33-34, 193).

Cow's feet, innards, and tripe punctuate the prosaics of *Lazarillo de Tormes,* which rejoices in the depiction of eating scenes known as *bodegones* and *bamboccianti* in contemporary painting. Usually, the *pícaro* was an errand boy—*esportillero* or *ganapán*—who hung around kitchens and other places of consumption, ready as he was to carry packages, take on odd jobs, and seize any opportunity—however underhanded—that might yield food or money.[24] Their world often was contained at the far edge of stoves and dinner tables, where darkness dimmed historical events and perspectival space. Velázquez's own *Old Woman Frying Eggs* is a *bodegón* in which the youth holds a watermelon and a water pitcher. Time is culinary, and the two frying eggs mark the seconds that separate the raw from the cooked. By contrast, stark details in *The Waterseller* deny the possibility of an "eating scene." Everybody stands as if expected to stage an event extraneous to the casualness of "dining time." The transfer of water is linked to acts that are passive for the youth, acquisitive for the adult, and dispensational for the old man. Such archetypal thematics, Miguel de Unamuno would comment, seem to draw from "los abismos sub-históricos, bajo la historia" (49-50). It is a ritual that outlasts human generations without changing people's lot.

At a higher pitch of privation, Velázquez's water jug calls to mind a literary counterpart in the third *tratado,* where Lázaro shared bread and cow's feet with his master:

> He asked me to get the water-jug and when I brought it
> it was as full as when I had come back from the river.
> That told me quite clearly that he hadn't eaten very
> much that day. We drank and went to bed very happily.
>
> (57)[25]

Toothpicks are in order after food consumption, and water is part of that activity. Food calls for a drink; starvation does not. Quickly, therefore, Lázaro understands that his master has not had a meal. At an earlier occasion and in spite of evidence to the contrary, Lázaro presumed that an *escudero*'s jug would contain wine: "'Agua es,—me respondió. Bien puedes beber.'—'You can drink this,' he said. 'It's water'" (52, 33). That correction foregrounded utter indigence, while the sword upheld an obsolete world of appearances at variance with life. In fact, Lázaro found in the *escudero*'s purse neither a copper coin "ni señal que la hubiese tenido mucho tiempo—any trace of one having been there for a very long time" (58, 39). The water's undisturbed stillness is of a kind akin to still lifes in the French and Italian sense of *nature morte* and *natura morta.* Actually, the ghostlike existence of the *escudero,* whose nobility is bygone and whose wealth is out of currency, is itself a kind of "lifeless nature." To that extent, swords, toothpicks, and water jugs could be read as *fragments ideologiques.*[26] The jug foregrounds an implied narrative; rather than denying human presence, it calls forth the *escudero*'s haunting insubstantiality. As a result, the tempo of the story slows down to motionlessness, which echoes the mental inanity of the *escudero*'s worn-out existence (Blanchard 276-77). The narrative thus moves from effects to causes. The jug is full because the empty purse could not buy food. For the *escudero,* description earmarks the breakdown of potential action, which is instead implicit in Lázaro's own surprise. In one case, water points to inanity and sterility; it is the stillness of the deathlike. For the boy, that very stillness is taken as a negative pause in the unfolding process of life's travails.

As a servant to the *escudero,* Lázaro gears his concept of time to hunger. Having met his new master in the morning, he measures time against the expected routine of "shopping" for lunch and dinner. Hours pass by, but neither lunch nor dinner is mentioned. Time thus stretches out hopes and delusions. To justify himself, the *escudero* reverses the orderly routine of food consumption: "Pues, aunque de mañana, yo había almorzado y, cuando así como algo, hágote saber que hasta la noche me estoy así. Por eso, pásate como pudieres, que después cenaremos—Well, although it was quite early, I'd already eaten. If I eat early, you'd better know that I don't have anything else until nighttime. You'll have to make do as well as you can. We'll have supper later on" (32, 51). Master and servant are playing cat-and-mouse. The "provider" tries to mask his inability to provide for his servant by "displacing" the time of biological needs. When stomachs are not fed, the narrative stealmates into an ominous silence. The very absence of sounds reduces existence itself to a kind of life-threatening wait that puts human potential on hold, as if the future could not come to pass. Hunger reduces time, space, and the world itself to nothing more than the expectation of food. Wits, honor, hopes, memories, and human personality lose all relevance vis-à-vis hoped-for food. At that point, Lázaro and his master are reduced to the animal-like state of predators whose whole being could respond to nothing but the call of hunger.

In the ontological nomenclature of the picaresque, eating time plays a major role, marking as it does the materialist heartbeat of existence. Once lack of nourishment is exposed, the ontology and stylistics of literary art strikes close equivalences between words and things. Whether it be the jug in the literary text or in Velázquez's painting, language thrives on forms of such simplicity that image, writing, and expression seem to defy the very concept of fiction. To that extent, goblet and jug offset the objectual deceptiveness of the stone-bull episode at the end of the first *tratado.* Whereas the mousetrap signals the presence

of goods, unused water denies them. Having reached a state of utter indigence, the text exposes the futility of people whose social standing has to deny starvation, however irrefutable its evidence. By the same token, such "descriptions by default" are quite typical of the picaresque parody of conspicuous consumption. With a passion, literary stylistics mixes taxonomic with rhetorical codes. The first selects items to be foregrounded for description's sake; the second chooses strategies of denotation, connotation, and significance that thicken the symbolism of the narrative. In the picaresque mode, exchanges between the two are at once effective and recurrent. Since men of honor would neither beg nor steal, the outcome is all the more predictable. Just as he wanted sex but could not buy it, so did the *escudero* end up eating a cow's foot his servant had begged for.

Recent scholarship has focused on the unsavory vicissitudes that hunger has imposed on the poor. Throughout the sixteenth century, a cluster of texts outlined the effects of famine from Italy to Poland. Behind the ambiguous and ominous term "refuse," in fact, there lurked instincts that preyed on corpses and dung; there were no limits to abomination, so much so that the remains of *Buscón*'s father were linked to the taking of the Holy Sacrament (Camporesi 86-87). Literally and symbolically, the economics of food consumption were an apt, if pitiless, barometer of societal conditions.[27] While the *escudero*'s toothpick is no more than a gestural afterthought in the wake of a meal he never consumed, Lázaro finds comfort in the memory of bits of food. Although no semantic field other than food and sex can claim a more euphoric vocabulary (Jeanneret 8-9), picaresque rhopography breaks down discourse through a rhetoric of loss; food and sex are equally deficient in it. However much hunger could not ennoble the praxis of life at its most basic, Marco Antonio de Camos resorted to human anatomy to justify social order (*Microcosmia* 1595). Faith was lodged in the head and royalty in the heart; veins and nerves stood for nobility; legs and feet carried merchants, artisans, and farmers. The poor, in turn, were reduced to nails, hair, and human debris that fed on edible waste (139-46).[28] Because food defines humanity in itself as well as in relation to life at large, picaresque diets are indicators of cultural status. After a reading not of Rabelais or Perrault but of picaresque poverty, one ought to surmise that Louis Marin's "food for thought" would be strictly verbal among most *pícaros* who never made it to Toledo. In Segovia, there were people who would gladly "breakfast" on nominatives by "swallowing the words" (95, 97). Instances of that sort are introduced in the third chapter of *Lazarillo de Tormes,* where the penniless *escudero* feeds Lázaro words instead of meals he craves for more than his servant.

Master and servant, in fact, inhabit a house apt to lodge the dead rather than the living.[29] We need only mention that Benedetto Croce called the picaresque "l'epica della fame," a label that set parodic correlations between megalography and rhopography, the epic and the novel.[30] On novelistic matters of *romanzi della fame,* onions as big as oranges constitute the staple diet of Sicilian fishermen in Giovanni Verga's *I Malavoglia* (*The House by the Medlar Tree* 1881). The nineteenth-century *verista* novel, in fact, updated picaresque toils.[31] They all shared stylistic and thematic traits that weighed on food intake, whether it be actually eaten or just conjured up by the imagination. And trade between what Italo Calvino has called the dialectic of *sapore* and *sapere* has been central to a genre as privative or cornucopian as the novel.

The ritual integrity of Valázquez's *aguador* stands out even more forcefully if one sets it against the literary narrative. In Toledo's cathedral, a greedy priest gives Lázaro the job of waterseller; with ease, men of the cloth would turn into dubious *mercaderes; hombres de negocio* and *hombres de iglesia* often were one and the same.[32] Just as easily waters were parted between business and religion. To make things worse, doubts have been shed on representations of "pristine" and good-natured watersellers. Equations between *aguadores* and *moriscos* were negative, and so they would remain in Lope de Vega's *El anzuelo de Fenisa* and Cervantes's *gente baja* (*Don Quixote* I: 21). Emphasis was placed on genealogical falsification, name changing, and efforts at furtive assimilation (Shipley, "Lazarillo de Tormes" 250). A Cervantine nobleman, Don Tomás de Avendano, took up "the trade of water-carrier" in Toledo. "With a single load of water he could wander about the city all day long, looking at the silly girls."[33] Prejudices aside, that menial job was just a few notches above begging.

By and large, watersellers were unsavory characters closer to Velázquez's own *Drinkers* (also called *Borrachos* 1626-28),[34] which José Ortega y Gasset has read as a Titianesque bacchanal that has been turned "into drunken debauch. Bacchus is a fraud. There is nothing more than what you can see and touch." To that extent, Velázquez paved the way for the "administrative era in which, in place of Dionysus, we speak of alcoholism" (Ortega y Gasset, *Velázquez* 97; Braudel, *Structure* 23-24, 27-29). Because he is not a fraud, the old *aguador* would keep on living the same way. He is a symbolic image of the enduring, and yet stagnant, "infra-economy" of material life. His time frame is one in which the reliability of ritual takes precedence over the instability of gains and losses.[35] In a substantial way, the *aguador* bodies forth a concept of personality rooted in a culture where individualism is equated with one's given role in society. Man could not yet conceive of himself as an individual except through communal "otherness" (Manrique de Aragon 42). Much as deities were trivialized, Velázquez bestowed dignity on common people; the heroic became common, and the ordinary grew into prominence. Although he lived at the fringe of the urban world he never thought of entering, the waterseller could not be found among the swelling ranks of Sevillian *picardía*, which rounded its beggars and cutpurses by the slaughterhouse or in nearby San Lucar de Barrameda. At that point in the narrative, old and young watersellers did not, and could not move away from the routine of everyday life; to borrow from Miguel de Un-amuno, "el suceso del día, de cada día, es para el hecho de siempre . . . el hombre de cada día esta naciendo diariamente." Measured against standards of social climb and conspicuous consumption, it was indeed the average life—*vidita*—of an ordinary man—*hombrecito* (Ortega y Gasset, "Sobre el cultivo" 9: 907; Braudel, *Mediterranean* 2: 740).[36]

In a way, Lázaro is forced to mystify his origins as much as he has to demystify reminiscences about the *escudero*'s ghostlike nobility and empty claims. Societal myths are measured down to the "realistic" potential of a dispossessed soul out to secure some sort of civilized living for himself. At that threshold, we ought to recall Claudio Guillén's comments on picaresque role-playing, which compels the *pícaro* to "compromise and live on the razor's edge between vagabondage and delinquency. . . . He becomes what I would call a 'half-outsider'" (80). Actually, that boundary condition unravels through stages. In the first two chapters, Lázaro lives at the edge of survival. Even though he has become street-wise, his lack of mental sophistication emerges in the third *tratado,* where he fails to conceptualize the literal reference to the "dark house" in the episode of the funeral cortege. Since he is determined to dress up his societal "other," Lázaro changes jobs and breaks away from the simple existence of Velázquez's waterseller. He reaches a point where economic choice and societal constraints lock horns, and the ensuing narrative would teach him the limits of both.[37] Once he invests his earnings in buying worn-out apparel, his hard-gained "affluence" turns into another form of poverty. As a result, existence shapes itself as a deficient, if not outright negative counterpart of affluence. Later, Miguel de Unamuno asked a significant question: "What zeal can a worker show as he fashions toys for the sons of the rich merely so as to earn bread for his own children, who have no such toys to play with?" (302). That was a rather middle-class question grown out of a world of production that remained quite foreign to picaresque parasitism. Survival could not, and did not, empower anybody to test the "destination" of goods. For most people, work was aimed at sustenance rather than improvement, much as zeal stemmed from need rather than competence. As a waterseller who provided a service as old as humankind, Lázaro could have lived comfortably at the fringe of bureaucracy and business. Because he rejected work limited to survival, the youth gave up a job and much of his upbringing with it. His father had been working at the mill for fifteen years, and only a transgression halted that routine. In his son's case, circumstances drove him out of agricultural milieus. Two processes converged: one of social integration and the other of moral debasement.

Part and parcel of Lázaro's growth is a new sense of monetary precision and critical judgment. In the first two *tratados,* time is linked to acts of theft, whether they involve a piece of sausage or a few breadcrumbs. The appearance of money, however, alters the *mozo*'s behavior: "cuanto le mandaban rezar y le daban blancas, como él carecía de vista, no había el que se la daba amagado con ella, cuando yo la tenía lanzada en la boca y la media aparejada; que por presto que él echaba la mano, ya iba de mi cambio aniquilada en la mitad del justo precio ("when people asked him to say prayers and gave him *blancas,* as soon as they offered the coin I grabbed it, popped it into my mouth and handed him a half *blanca.* However quickly he stretched out his hand I had already halved the value of the offering") (10, 29). First of all, half *blancas,* whole *blancas,* and *maravedís* immediately point to immaterial goods that could be gained by means of equally immaterial services. Unlike food, money could be halved, doubled up, stored, and exchanged with ever-varying speed.[38]

By paying the priest thirty *maravedís* every day, Lázaro the waterseller introduces a clock-paced concept of time, which quickly becomes a commodity linked to the sequence *ganancia-recaudo-ahorre-compre* (earning-collecting-saving-buying) (Sieber 76). However pedestrian its way, the picaresque echoes an eventful shift. Rather than being linked to living experiences, time is divided into measurable units. That development replaced events that could be framed by approximation—*à-peu-près*—with models of conduct that subordinated time, work, and money to precise standards of evaluation. Whether on pagan or Christian grounds, the Deity was assumed to have created through numbers, weights, and measurement. Before the Renaissance, however, nobody bothered to implement those principles in the world of material existence. Lázaro is thus able to discipline the dynamics of his environment into a profitable routine. He saves money and gains confidence in himself; however meager his earnings, he has grown to a point where he could entertain ambitious projects; chance gives way to plan. Money brings regularity to the narrative; a steady income calls for a stable job in a place where picaresque mobility comes to a halt. While saving rushes in some "potential" for wealth, the appearance of prosperity would not yield substantial benefits.

Individual growth under the aegis of economics thus pivots around the concept of self-reliance. Ironically, its point of origin could be traced back to Lázaro's experience with the stone bull in the first *tratado.* The very fact that a blind beggar would teach self-reliance set the "educational process" on a rather slippery footing. It was imperative that "el mozo del ciego un punto ha de saber más que el diablo" (8). Literally and symbolically, the blindman could not but refer to a world of darkness where survival itself is nestled in the "darkened" pit of loss and privation. Because the world of darkness is irremediable by definition, self-reliance teaches Lázaro to outwit his master, even though society will prove to be crowded with legions of people blind at heart whose standards of survival would be ever more difficult to meet. In the sixth *tratado,* self-reliance shifts toward income-yielding work. As such, the devil's standard is both pervasive and unspoken. Once work, service, and income steer Lázaro's socioeconomic lot toward a kind of primitive marketplace economy where the evil of exchange proves to be a blessing, Lázaro finds that work empowers him to pursue values at bay of any

ciego's reach. In a rather contradictory way, trade imposes the burden of regularity and efficiency on one's lifestyle; "in the name of work" is preferable to "in the service of." The power of earning money by means other than begging and theft belongs to a devil unknown to the *ciego.* The *hombre de bien* is good and respectable also because he is a money-earning individual. Steady work and a legitimate job free self-reliance from the scourge of both alms and gifts.

At this point, we ought to bear in mind that money makes its appearance in the picaresque text sooner than one might expect. The blindman, in fact, "destas sacaba el grandes provechos con las artes que digo, y ganaba más en un mes que cien ciegos en un año—made a lot of money from these tricks and earned more in one month than a hundred blind men usually do in a whole year" (9, 28). Yet, all that money has no impact on his lifestyle. Master and servant keep on fighting over crumbs by the wayside, and the canvas bag shows evidence of little food and nothing else. What about all that money? By counting money, master and servant activate a "battle of wits" at once attractive and inconsequential. Once he hires Lázaro, the *ciego*'s intake of *maravedís* dwindles because his *mozo* cheats him by switching half *blancas* for whole ones; and he gets away with it. Although theft as exchange succeeds, there is no evidence that money could change anyone's lot. Strife is between paupers; the biggest crust of bread is carried off by the one who begs best (Unamuno 409). Support for that downtrodden condition falls back on folkloristic *cuentos.* It is a pivotal moment in the narrative, one that would lead to Lázaro's appointment to the office of *pregonero.* His hopes come through, but at a price. Slowly, he would settle into a complacent routine whose goal is to maintain *el estatismo de su estado* (Prieto 30-33). Yet, the *caso* launched against him spurs the present toward a troublesome future. While updating adversities, the *Prólogo* also promises a follow-up. From an economic as well as a literary standpoint, the picaresque steered away from the indefinite, if not outright fabulous, past of romance.

To be a *hombre de bien,* Lázaro must avoid jobs that call for manual labor. Once he understands that words could earn him an income, Lázaro sets out to become a *Homo loquens.* Hence, he breaks free of archetypal models. Although he could flaunt only wornout clothes, his readers would not lose sight of him for generations to come. Once he makes it clear that his life's goal is other than his humble job, the economic makeup of the sixth *tratado* turns around. Jugs and whips fade in the background. The spatial gives way to the temporal, which sets up the value-loaded pace of "everyday—*cada día*" work. As soon as he adjusts to the pressures of money-yielding time, Lázaro's conduct becomes *cronoe-conómico.* While his daily routine is restricted to the socioeconomic confines of *intrahistoria,* no reference is made to the larger historical—if not macro-historic—framework. The nameless author, in fact, did not date his autobiographical experience, except for the final reference to Charles V's entrance in Toledo (either in 1525 or 1539).

Hard work aside, Lázaro can buy only second-hand clothes, a worn out cloak, and an old sword. New forms of investment are called for. Although weekly earnings and weekened overtime draw a line between freedom and dependence, all he could show for four years of hard work is old stuff. Selling water is neither profitable nor honorable. Means and goals are disjointed. Hypothetically speaking, the *escudero* predicted that minor noblemen would pay with a sweaty doublet for his services. The barter of things prevailed over the exchange of money. Lázaro, instead, earns wages and makes profits on the side. Determined as he is to seek prosperity, he sets out to change jobs and break the archetypal life cycle of Velázquez's waterseller. For the old *aguador,* selling water was not just a job; it gave him identity, personal pride, and social respect. For Lázaro, instead, it is an economic task that he judges in strictly economic terms. He wastes no time in sizing up the limits of that humble job, which allows him to buy clothes and a sword meant to sketch out an image appropriate to his wished-for role in society. Whip, jugs, and donkey give way to the purchase of objects apt to fill symbolic needs. Money thus trades the necessary for the aesthetic. If we think of Karl Marx's remarks that money changes "representation into reality and reality into mere representation," then we could agree that Lázaro is on his way to shift from the factual reality of waterseller toward the "representation" of himself in light of values he has inherited from the *escudero.* Whereas the *aguador*'s healthy activities at the level of cost of living are reflected in the unblemished condition of jug and goblet, the incipient pursuit of standards of life begins with the acquisition of old and worn-out items, which echo the ruinous state of the *escudero*'s alleged real estate back in Valladolid. Objects symbolic of a higher social standing betray the volatility—and vulnerability—of the very concept of standard, which could be neither defined with precision nor upheld with confidence. One variable was money, whose valuation and devaluation made the standard itself liable to continuous redefinitions. In a significant way, therefore, standards of life tend to measure frustration as well as success.[39] If we reflect on the analogy drawn between the novel's claim to represent reality and money's claim to represent things of enduring value, then we might agree that both claims shortchange fiction and reality alike. Lázaro's money, in fact, is invested at the periphery of the *aguador*'s reality as well as the periphery of the *escudero*'s anachronism. Much of Lázaro's earnings still are based on gifts and exchanges, his would-be *provecho* as a modern *mercader* turns out to be as misleading—if not outright fictitious—as the *escudero*'s land-based wealth of times past. In light of such precedents, his ambitious plans are uncertain. Money could not buy the future, and the past had become worthless.

At night, the town crier has plenty of time to think about moral payoffs which neither wine nor sleep could ease; nevertheless, everybody teaches him that money moves people. He is neither a critic nor a reformer of society, but a survivor and an opportunist. The final words in the seventh *tratado* tell us that the *pregonero* has reached the peak of his *buena fortuna.* The *Prólogo,* however, makes it clear that his luck has been called into question. Once the indictment is launched against him, Lázaro falls prey to the wider circularity of *Fortuna*'s rise and fall. At the top of the ladder, his steadfast growth stalls, and he begins to slip down.[40]

Yet, it is in the sixth *tratado* that Lázaro transcends the wanderer, the jester, and the have-not. He thus takes notice of his environment, whereas the Sevillan *aguador* of Velázquez did not (Alter 6). Segovia and Toledo were manufacturing towns, and it was through Seville that precious metals from the New World were pouring into Europe. While chapters of human history followed the migratory rhythm of gold and silver across the oceans, there were social enclaves which held on to the timelessness of archetypal lifestyles. Mythic resistance and economic adventurism stood side by side, much as the primeval stability of "material life" was set against the mercantile growth of "economic life." Material life is rooted in the steady pace of daily routines that have remained unchanged for centuries. For Américo Castro, that is the history that only needs to be "described;" it refers to the mere facts of living, the plain linen of life without embroidery. What is at stake here is the lives of people whose existence rests on elementary motivations—physiological, psychic, and economic.[41] Within boundaries of that sort, economic matters could not exceed the cost of living, which set strict limitations on the life of *pícaros,* beggars, millers, and water carriers old or new. Their menial tasks are typical of an economy that is oriented neither toward production nor surplus goods, but toward the satisfaction of elementary needs. As Antonio de Guevara wrote at that time, "It is a privilege of villages that those who dwell in them have flour to sift, a bowl for kneading, and an oven for their baking."[42] At such a basic level, existence relies on those economic institutions that restrict human potential to survival. As the third *tratado* unfolds, Lázaro's need to find a master tests the materialist core of cost of living. Quickly, the narrative makes it clear that the servant has to provide for himself as well as for his master, who is bound to play a twofold role in the youth's growth. While he introduces Lázaro to a world of values, the unity-duality of master and servant proves that utter poverty still treasures a kind of hierarchical order. Antona Perez, in fact, believed that his son would not stand a chance in life unless he served someone, even as hopeless a character as a blind beggar. To be himself, Lázaro needed a master, and his ascent in society traded one form of dependence for another. Medieval ideology called for man to earn only what was necessary to let him live in his given place. Any gain in excess of need was a sign of greed—*turpe lucrum.* In light of that doctrine, Lázaro's meager savings as waterseller foreshadow doom, exceeding as they do the cost of living.

Cost of living becomes problematic the moment it is linked to lifestyles that rest on cultural values. Lázaro reaches that threshold in the sixth *tratado.* Thereafter, he tries to convince himself that his *buena fortuna* has drawn cost of living and standard of life into a favorable equation; although needs measure the first and achievements the second, they are both materialistic. Yet, the latter gives goods a metaphorical depth which could be at once humanizing and dehumanizing. As a water carrier, Lázaro lived on the ground floor, as it were, of material life. But he found that the bottom level was neither comfortable nor satisfactory. Through care and calculation, he thus proceeded to set standards of life for himself. To set Lázaro's choice in historical perspective, we ought to turn to one of Don Quixote's "educational" axioms: "I tell you, Sancho, that no man is worthier than another unless he does more than another" (*Don Quixote* I: Chapter 18). That lesson may have fallen on deaf ears in the Cervantine text, where the *hidalgo* alone "did" more than most to "make himself"—*hacerse*—into a better Other. But such a self-creating impulse was absent in pre-Cervantine fiction. In the picaresque mode, however, the *mozo* from Tormes made himself into a better Other; if not as *pregonero*, certainly as author. That his "worth" was ultimately deficient should not diminish his achievement. Even the undistinguished Don Quijano the Good, after all, denied Don Quixote and regained sanity. Such different, and yet parallel, ascents shed light on Renaissance polarities; courtly versus picaresque, anachronistic versus contemporary. Whereas Lázaro espoused values that were concrete and led to specific actions, Don Quixote never stopped charging windmills. In the elementary marketplace of basic services, the waterseller, whether he be a pictorial image or a literary figure, operated within a socioeconomic enclave that ushered in a rather independent, though narrow, sense of self-reliance. The old *aguador* had always known that; young Lázaro, instead, was in search of social status. He based his future on the stability of societal structures whose authority was institutional. However pegged to a legitimate job, Lázaro's self-reliance would remain largely parasitic. It was the "Other" that validated the self, whose fortunes were bound to remain at risk.

In the immemorial time of myth, man thrives on nature; in the remembered time of human experience, he exploits the mechanisms of civilized society. Lázaro's surname—*sobrenombre*—stems from a river; it is a place-name. His roots are linked to water, which would yield temporary as well as permanent benefits. Whether it be in literary texts or ritual codes, water stands for life-sustaining values. By contrast, wine remains a carrier of shame, income, and punishment. Wine caused Lázaro's early beatings, but wine also healed him. From *El Buscón* to *La Hija de Celestina,* the antigenealogy of parental indignity often is linked to wine consumption. And the *ciego*'s prophecy about wine spells trouble for Lázaro.

With an eye to spatiotemporal coordinates, the chronotope of the road exhausts its itinerant potential in the sixth *tratado.* The *escudero*'s lesson at last bears fruit, even though the *pregonero* would not further his career amid the hypocrisy and corruption of Toledan society. By growing into a writer, however, he would break free of everyday mediocrity, reaching out toward that *sublime du quotidien*

that disrupts routine to the advantage of transcendence. Questions of meaning vis-à-vis picaresque quotidianity at last touch on central aspects of literary fictions somehow aimed at "realism." Tomé Gonzales's work as a miller who provided for his family year in and year out ended the moment he was caught stealing. Hence, "fue preso, y confesó, y no negó, y padeció persecución por justicia—they arrested him, and he confessed, denied nothing and was punished by law" (5, 25). The verbal sequence strings out three complementary actions whose conciseness points to John and Matthew. A tone of stoic endurance couples theft with a sense of inevitability that plagues the social landscape of poverty. In a rather parodic mode, the indignity of theft is diminished by the steadfast acceptance of punishment. Later on, Lázaro's own routine of waterseller exhausts the "literary potential" of such an insignificant practice. Miller and waterseller make it clear that transgression and transcendence are part and parcel of picaresque teleology. From the very beginning, the text mixes literalness with literariness.

At the fountainhead of picaresque textuality, sheer descriptions of life-as-is tend to be negative. Tomé, the *escudero,* the *fraile de la Merced,* and the *buldero* suggest that the praxis of life could not support itself without sliding toward degeneration one way or another. In Tomé's case, criminality edged on incredulity when Antona told the *ciego* that his son was "hijo de buen hombre, el cual por ensalzar la fe había muerto en la de los Gelves—the son of a good man, who had been killed for the greater glory of the Faith at the battle of Las Gelves" (7, 27). Before Cervantes, therefore, "mills" needed not be just mills. Like stone bulls and old stockings, they all upheld ambiguity. On Sanchopanzesque matters of unidealized existence, Miguel de Unamuno wrote that "fear and only fear made Sancho see—makes the rest of us simple mortals see—windmills where impudent giants stand . . . those mills milled bread, and of that bread men confirmed in blindness ate" (57). The sixth *tratado* thus ends with a self-aggrandizing, though wishful, sense of materialist transcendence, which glorifies the power of privilege and protection (Parret 18-19, 168-69). Although nurtured in poverty of body, aesthetic consciousness and literary creation could not fail to set Lázaro's mills of the mind in motion.

From beginning to end, Mateo Alemán insists that Guzmán de Alfarache began as a *pícaro* and ended as *maestro pícaro.* In his case, the writer tells his *discreto lector* "lo que hallares no grave ni compuesto, eso es el ser de un pícaro." As a matter of fact, the verb *picardear* calls for random appreciations on matters of literary taste, which the *pícaro* would just as well extend to conduct: "Las tales cosas, aunque seran muy pocas, picardea con ellas."[43] It is, in other words, a life deficient in direction as much as in ideology. Lázaro de Tormes reaches that stage in the sixth *tratado,* where the job of waterseller teaches him discipline and points to a safe harbor. He trades indigence for sufficiency. Perhaps unbeknownst to himself, Lázaro faces up to ideology. His decision to give up his job made of *pí-*

cardear an intransitive verb, which he replaced with ameliorative pursuits.

III

Velázquez's old waterseller wears a humble and tattered jerkin. Lázaro, instead, buys a second-hand cloak. Sinners and criminals, so we are told, wore a *jubón de azotes* as sign of punishment; and Lázaro's father had worn one. In light of the *caso* hanging over his head, one might wonder whether Lázaro would ever wear a new cloak or rather something more appropriate for a *pregonero* who had been Tomé Gonzales's son back in Tejares and who would walk criminals to their punishment in Toledo. Although the life of criminality was not a choice for Lázaro, the picaresque offered fertile grounds to the epidemic *humus* of delinquency.

Among people involved in some kind of economic service, the miller and the *buldero* body brought forth pathological aspects of work ethics; they cannot keep their greed under control. Amid picaresque *infrahumanidad,* honesty often is shortchanged. But one could bet that the old waterseller in Velásquez's painting is an exception. To borrow from Miguel de Unamuno on matters of lifestyles based on humility, there exists a sublime form of activity that converts work "into prayer" for "the greater glory of God." The painter captured that spiritual commitment when he painted his old *aguador.* Below that standard, Sancho is encouraged to be the first in "his craft," so as to make of work a point of honor that could dignify "the artisan." At that point in the narrative, we could surmise that Lázaro discharges his job with honesty and efficiency, but in the name of materialist profit rather than God's greater glory. At the fountainhead of picaresque textuality, sheer descriptions of life-as-is tend to be negative. And it could not be otherwise, since the social mimesis at stake here is the life of ethical and material poverty. Tomé the *escudero,* the *fraile de la Merced,* and the *buldero* suggest that the praxis of life could not support itself without degenerating one way or another. Perhaps the very notion of common men leading common lives under the guidance of ordinary values is itself a fiction. For sure, the picaresque test could not endorse that premise. Its socioeconomic structures, in fact, are based on strife between production and consumption, ingenuity and parasitism. It is thus indicative that as soon as the arts began to deal with econopoetics, Renaissance artists concerned themselves with the novel as well as with pastorals, utopias, romances, and fables. At the very time that economic concerns became ever more paramount, such "unnovelistic" textuality relished forms of socioeconomic escape against forms of socioeconomic success.

As a *pregonero,* Lázaro would stand at the right side of the law, even though he could not keep too far from criminals. Actually, they never lost sight of each other (Cros 178, 189).[44] Even more than his heir Buscón, Guzmán was privileged with formal education. It included "latino, retórico y griego—a good Latinist, Rhetorician,

and Grecian," and his goal was to become a churchman. But things turned out otherwise. He ended up in prison, where he set out to write his *memorias.* Learning was prominent in the *pícaro*'s *carrera de vivir.* Yet, it would not yield social and materialist benefits in the tradition of Florentine Humanism. Somehow, the more punishing circumstances of *vivir* had the best of education. Only the written texts of *pícaros*' lives survived. None of them grew to establish himself as either a scholar or a civic leader. Once human nature began to respond to the trials of growth, time castigated people to an extent that humanist treatises on merchants (Alberti) and courtiers (Castiglione) bypassed. Whereas the Italian humanists presented virtual figures whose potential was never tested by life, the picaresque put the learning of Guzmán and Buscón to the test of existence. They could never afford the leisure of scholarship in the *studiolo.* Instead, they had to write in prisons or lonely rooms where criminality and indignity afforded them a downgraded version of *otium*'s privileged idleness. None of them emerged victorious, but they all survived.

For sure, Lázaro was bound to dress up for better "employment." The elementary field of primeval facts made room for deeds that would yield greater profits. To put it in terms of Clemente Pablos, the barber who sired Buscón, Lázaro was about to trade a mechanical for a liberal art; at least he so believed. Yet, we all know that Clemente Pablos was executed by his own relative, Alonso Ramplón, the hangman. And Alonso never claimed that his trade was more than a mechanical art, whose equipment of "cordeles, lazos, cuchillos, escarpias y otras herramientas del oficio— rope, nooses, knives, meat-hooks and other tools of the public executioner's trade" (162, 142) made a compelling case for rhopography at its crudest.

When all is said, is Lázaro's divestiture as a waterseller an ominous premonition? Wine earned him the first beating. Would his rise to the *oficio* of town crier charged with the sale of wines be prophetic of greater punishments? While the bureaucratic title of *pregonero* refers to function rather than origin, Lázaro's surname is rooted in nature, which he tries to leave behind. Nominally at least, the town crier would be appointed by the king, who is mentioned at the end of the book. But Toledans would never forget that he came from Tormes. Short of either epiphanic or fateful rescues, his ascent would be bound to flow downstream amid muddled waters.

Notes

1. *Histoire de France* (Paris, 1898), vol. vii; as translated in Wallace Ferguson's *The Renaissance in Historical Thought: Five Centuries of Interpretation* (Cambridge: Houghton Mifflin Co., 1948) 176.

2. On classical precedents, see Victor Ehrenberg, *The People of Aristophanes: A Sociology of Old Attic Comedy* (219) and Fernand Braudel, *The Structure of Everyday Life: The Limits of the Possible* (3). On the more archetypal grounds of pre-verbal cultures, Gi-

ambattista Vico has made an observation whose semi-otic implications are important: "Since its has been demonstrated that the first gentile nations were all mute in their beginnings, they must have expressed themselves by gestures or by physical objects having natural relations with their ideas. They must have used signs to fix the boundaries of their estates and to have enduring witnesses of their rights. They all made use of money. All these truths will give us the origins of languages and letters, and thereby of hiero-glyphs, laws, names, family coats of arms, medals, money, and of the language and writing in which the first natural law of the gentes was spoken and writ-ten" (*The New Science* par. 434).

3. Having noted that such a standard was upheld by Sainte-Beuve, Curtius noted: "What a tidbit for a Marxist sociology of literature!"

4. In his exemplary study, Marc Shell writes that his "book seeks to understand dialectically the relation-ship between thought and matter by focusing—for reasons I shall now consider—on economic thought and literary and linguistic matters" (2).

5. See Peter Burke, *Venice and Amsterdam: A Study of Seventeenth-Century Elites;* Basil S. Yamey, *Art and Accounting*; Simon Schama, *The Embarrassment of Riches: An Interpretation of Dutch Culture in the Golden Age*; Richard Halpern, *The Poetics of Primi-tive Accumulation: English Renaissance Culture and the Genealogy of Capital*; Patricia Fumerton, *Cultural Aesthetics: Renaissance Literature and the Practice of Social Ornament*. Stephen Greenblatt finds the same complexity at work on more focused matters of Renaissance individualism: "There is no such thing as a single 'history of the self' in the sixteenth century, except as the product of our need to reduce the intricacies of complex and creative beings to safe and controllable order" (8).

6. On sociological grounds, I refer to the paradigmatic scholarship of Georg Simmel, *The Philosophy of Money*. Richard Goldthwaite writes that the historian ought "to look outside his discipline at some of the larger problems of cultural history—at the wellhead of demand and at the nature of material culture; and with a different perspective of this kind he can perhaps reorient his own research on purely economic problems to raise new questions that will—at last—get him out of the greatest gaps that divide the disciplines in Renaissance studies" (2: 39).

7. Within the province of cultural aesthetics, in fact, Fernand Braudel and the French school of the *An-nales* have set money and business at the core of historical studies. For a comprehensive analysis of the *monde Braudellien* vis-à-vis historiographical method and economic factors, see J. H. Hexter (61-148) and Hayden White's discussion of the *Annales* in *The Content of the Form: Narrative Discourse and Historical Representation* (32-45). On matters of Spanish historiography, Américo Castro has warned against Braudel's concentration on "economicomate-rialistic reasoning." Although important, the "histori-comaterialistic vision" could not account for the unifying forces that made the Reconquest possible. In fact, "the economic dimension came later; it was not the primary and unifying 'logos'" (*Spaniards* 5-6).

8. Peter Dunn takes structural elements such as "I," the various "others," and Vuestra Merced to "serve as points of entry into the text" (91). Susan Sniader Lanser has spearheaded an encompassing notion of point of view, and her detailed study of the matter opens with a chapter in which she proposes "A Philosophy of Point of View" (11-63).

9. With a Marxist outlook on the whole concept of the Renaissance, Agnes Heller has consistently set the ideal against the real within the humanist tradition itself: "Everyday life was at least as important a *theme* of Renaissance thought as the problems of ontology, epistemology, art, or ethics; more ac-curately, there was a constant and fruitful interaction between those 'technical' matters and the study and analysis of daily life. The former were, for the most part, an outgrowth of the examination of the latter" (157-58). For Heller, Montaigne, Bacon, and the development of science and technology were repre-sentative of the age's adherence to the practice of life.

10. I paraphrase here Elias L. Rivers, whose concise but clear pairing of two counter-genres, the pastoral and the picaresque, is worth quoting: "The two different sets of fictional conventions underlying these two works constitute a perfect binary opposition. The Spanish pastoral romance, deriving from Garcilaso's eclogues and Sannazaro's *Arcadia* (1504), present a utopian world of shepherds, who, with a readily ac-cessible and seldom-mentioned diet of natural foods such as acorns and cheese, devote themselves to a leisurely life filled with music and with dialogues about love; the shepherds are courtiers in disguise, placed in an idealized world of natural art, which is free of social and economic pressures. Conversely, the Spanish picaresque novel, with roots in exemplary (*ex contrario*) folktales about sly tricks and decep-tions, presents an urban society of paupers who, under the constant pressure of hunger and economic necessity, learn to defend themselves by hook and crook, trying to rise in a harsh world of free enterprise" (66-67).

11. "Dos linajes sólos hay en el mundo, como decía una abuela ma, que son el tener y el no tener; aunque ella al de tener se atenía; y el día de hoy, mi señor Don Quijote, antes se toma el pulso al haber que al saber."

12. For historical background, J. H. Elliott writes that Spain was unique because it lacked a "middling group of solid, respectable, hardworking *bourgeois*

to bridge the gulf between the two extremes . . . The contempt for commerce and manual labour, the lure of easy money from the investment in *censos* and *juros*, the universal hunger for titles of nobility and social prestige—all these, when combined with the innumerable practical obstacles in the way of profitable economic enterprise, had persuaded the *bourgeoisie* to abandon its unequal struggle, and throw in its lot with the unproductive upper classes of society" (305-6).

13. As Walter L. Reed puts it, "Thus in the literary history, the literary politics, and the literary sociology of sixteenth-century Spain one can see similar structures, structures of polarization with a relatively weak middle between the two extremes. I would argue not that these structures are a direct cause of the early Spanish novel but that they are homologous with the form of the novel in a culturally significant way. They both reflect and produce the structure of the Spanish picaresque, where divine transcendence and human degradation conspire against the middle estate of man. They also mirror and project the structure of *Don Quixote*, where an incorrigible idealistic imagination keeps colliding with an incontrovertibly material world. In these novels and in this society, it is a game of both ends against the middle. And it is in the book itself, that mechanically reproduced and privately consumed text of uncertain authority and value, that these extremes are brought most intriguingly together" (35). A while ago, a pioneer in the interdisciplinary study of the sociology of art, Arnold Hauser, wrote that Cervantes wavered "between the justification of unworldly idealism and of worldly-wise common sense" (2: 147).

14. I draw here from Cervantes's "Rinconete y Cortadillo," *Exemplary Novels* (New York: Penguin Books, 1982) 94-95.

15. The term has been popularized by Pedro Salinas in *Ensayos de literatura hispánica* (72). To set such a social level within the context of Renaissance society at large, it could be helpful to point to Stephen Greenblatt's *Renaissance Self-Fashioning: From More to Shakespeare,* which centers on a higher middle-class plateau, where none of the figures he analyzes "inherits a title, an ancient family tradition or hierarchical status that might have rooted personal identity in the identity of a clan or caste. With the partial exception of Wyatt, all of these writers are middle-class" (9).

16. On the subject of New Historicist criticism, I refer to the programmatic collection of essays assembled by H. Aram Veeser, *The New Historicism* (xi, xiv). On strictly picaresque matters, José Antonio Maravall recommended back in 1976 that "a study of the picaresque novel in relation to the rapidly advancing precapitalist spirit has yet to be done" (40).

17. The full passage reads: "The recurrent impulse and effort to define aesthetic value by contradistinction to all forms of utility or as the negation of all other measurable sources of interest or forms of value—hedonic, practical, sentimental, ornamental, historical, ideological, and so forth—is, in effect, to define it out of existence; for when all such utilities, interests, and other particular sources of value have been subtracted, nothing remains" (33).

18. Quotations from *Lazarillo de Tormes* are from the edition by Everett W. Hesse and Harry F. Williams; translations are from *Two Picaresque Novels* with page numbers indicated in the text.

"Fueme tan bien en el oficio que al cabo de cuatro años que le usé, con poner en la ganacia buen recaudo, ahorré para me vestir muy honradamente de la ropa vieja. De la cual compré un jobón de fustán viejo, y un sayo raído de manga tranzada y puerta, y una capa que había sido frisada, y una espada de las viejas primeras de Cuéllar."

19. Gene Brucker gives a retrospective overview on that historical school, to which he contributed his *Giovanni and Lusanna: Love and Marriage in Renaissance Florence*: "The story of Giovanni and Lusanna fits into a genre of historical writing, microhistory, that has recently achieved some notoriety in the discipline" (vii-viii). Other noteworthy examples of the genre that have recently appeared include Carlo Ginzburg's tale of the Friulian miller Menocchio (*The Cheese and the Worms,* 1980), Natalie Zemon Davis's account of the footloose peasant Martin Guerre, and Judith Brown's poignant story of the nun Benedetta and her tribulations in a Tuscan convent.

20. On more strictly literary grounds, Paul Julian Smith has drawn a parallel distinction between the inclusiveness of pictorialism and the fragmentariness of representation in *Writing in the Margin: Spanish Literature of the Golden Age* (78-88). The critic would consider Francisco Rico's *The Spanish Picaresque Novel and the Point of View* as one that enforces a humanistically unifying, validating, and authentic point of view (81). See also John F. Moffitt (5).

21. In his treatment of the "nocion del 'popular' en literatura," Maurice Molho refers to, and paraphrases, Gramsci on matters of popular literature (*Cervantes* 18-19).

22. Patricia Fumerton writes that "trivial" is "my general term for an analytic of the fragmentary, peripheral, and ornamental addressed at once to the context of historical fact and to the texts of aesthetic artifact" (1).

23. By way of contrast, such edible items were foreign to the geometric and textured theatricality of those untouchable still lifes that Francisco de Zurbarán or

Juan Sánchez Cotán have made us familiar with. For "spiritual" interpretations of these still lifes, see Edwin Mullins's comments (19-21) and Bryson (60-69).

24. Marcelin Defourneaux so describes such activities: "A degree above those who lived by begging came the *pícaros,* who, with the aid of a little work sufficient to keep them from the offence of vagabondage, applied themselves to scrounging and petty theft; such as the *pinches de cocina* (scullions), who could always find enough to feed themselves and their friends plentifully at the expense of the kitchens where they were employed, and the *esportilleros* (street porters and errand boys), who being responsible for delivering to the homes of customers goods of all kinds, pinched anything that could be hidden easily under their clothes. Alongside them were the peddlers (*buhonero*), a calling carried on for some time by Estebanillo after being, he says, 'degraded' from his status of pilgrim, and investing his capital in the purchase of knives, combs, rosaries, needles, and other shoddy wares, which he sold in the streets of Seville, an obligatory stage in every picaresque life" (219).

25. "Pidiome el jarro del agua, y díselo como lo había traído. Es señal que, pues no le faltaba el agua, que no le había a mi amo sobrado la comida. Bebimos, y muy contentos nos fuimos a dormir como la noche pasada" (38).

26. The French term was used by Louis Marin (*Etudes* 91).

27. On specific matters of literature, see Alban K. Forcione (98).

28. See also Javier Herrero, "Renaissance Poverty and Lazarillo's Family: The Birth of the Picaresque Genre" (882).

29. On hunger in the picaresque, see Pedro Salinas, *Ensayos de literatura hispánica.* Joaquín Casalduero wrote: "En los tres primeros tratados, la crueldad de la vida, la avaricia, el orgullo son solamente la modulación del mismo tema: el hambre. Lazarillo no es nada más que el punto donde a través de varias representaciones converge la misma necesidad de subsistencia, esa necesidad que siente la humanidad de conservarse" (65).

30. On Croce's comments on *Lazarillo de Tormes* and *La Celestina,* see Benito Brancaforte (118-24). Until 1948, Marcel Bataillon maintained a similar thesis in his lectures at the university, but then gave priority to the theme of *honor* (see *Pícaros y picaresca: La pícara Justina*).

31. On food in the Italian novel from Alessandro Manzoni to Primo Levi, see Gian Paolo Biasin, *I sapori della modernità: Cibo e romanzo.* D. H. Lawrence wrote a couple of essays on Verga, and he so commented on *I Malavoglia*: "There is too much, too much of the tragic life of the poor, in it. There is a sort of wallowing in tragedy: the tragedy of the humble. It belongs to a date when the 'humble' were almost the most fashionable thing. And the Malavoglia family are most humbly humble. Sicilians of the sea-coast, fishers, small traders—their humble tragedy is so piled on, it becomes almost disastrous. The book was published in America under the title of *The House by the Medlar Tree* (273).

32. See Maurice Molho, *The Politics of Editing* (*Introducción* 35, 42); George A. Shipley, "Lazarillo and the Cathedral Chaplain: A Conspiratorial Reading of *Lazarillo de Tormes,* Tratado VI" (231); Harry Sieber, *Language and Society in "La vida de Lazarillo de Tormes"* (78).

33. *The Illustrious Kitchen Maid,* in *Six Exemplary Novels* (Great Neck, N.Y.: Barron's Educational Series, 1961) 261.

34. An excellent essay on the sixth *tratado* is George Shipley's "Lazarillo de Tormes Was Not a Hardworking, Clean-Living Water Carrier" in *Hispanic Studies in Honor of Alan D. Deyermond: A North American Tribute.*

35. To put it in Georg Lukács's critical terms, such images of primeval simplicity would confirm that "biological and sociological life has a profound tendency to remain within its own immanence" (90).

36. To expand on the socioeconomic conditions of classes of manual workers, the *aguador* shared with many a lifestyle of subsistence, as Erich Fromm clarifies for us: "Although there were always some who had to struggle hard to earn enough to survive, by and large the guild member could be sure that he could live by his hand's work. If he made good chairs, shoes, bread, saddles, and so on, he did all that was necessary to be sure of living safely on the level which was traditionally assigned to his social position. He could rely on his 'good works,' if we use the term here not in its theological but in its simple economic meaning" (43-44).

37. On the relationship between economics and sociology, see Stephen R. G. Jones (10-11).

38. Having divided the text into two parts, each containing three *tratados,* Joaquín Casalduero made the fourth *tratado* pivotal inasmuch as it stressed "el aumento de movilidad, el tempo rápido que va a introducir en la segunda parte" (63).

39. On the connection between frustration and realism, see Jon Romano, *Dickens and Reality* (94). On the representation of objects in Balzac and Dickens, see John Vernon, *Money and Fiction: Literary Realism in the Nineteenth and Early Twentieth Centuries* (75-79).

40. George A. Shipley writes that Lázaro's story "is more exactly the chronicle of an initiation into a vile and degraded world. He represents as an arrival in

safe port and, later, as a rise to a pinnacle of satisfaction what is scarcely more than a lateral move of incorporation into the debased city of man in the fallen world" ("The Critic as Witness" 179-80).

41. It is worth quoting Castro's assessment of description: "This is life with a minimum of significance, devaluated life—when compared with the lives of those people who created the great cultures of the earth. In this, as in all questions of value, there is gradation. The lowest level corresponds to groups now called primitive, groups that have arrived at dead ends of human self-realization and who mark time down the centuries. For such life as this description is quite adequate . . . There are no deeds or triumphs of any sort to incite the children of the future. Such primitive peoples may, in effect, be thought of as residing at the end of blind alleys, as excluded from the broad avenues of future possibility available to others" (*Idea* 293).

42. *Menosprecio de corte y alabanza de aldea* (Madrid: Calpe, 1967) 71-72. I follow the translation and commentary in José Antonio Maravall, *Utopia and Counterutopia in the "Quixote"* (Detroit: Wayne State Univ. Press, 1991) 45.

43. *Guzmán de Alfarache* edición, introducción y notas de Francisco Rico (Barcelona: Planeta, 1983) 94.

44. Cros refers here to the social and moral frontiers of the picaresque.

Works Cited

Alter, Robert. *Rogue's Progress: Studies in the Picaresque Novel*. Cambridge: Harvard Univ. Press, 1965.

Bataillon, Marcel. *Pícaros y picaresca: La pícara Justina*. Madrid: Taurus, 1969.

Biasin, Gian Paolo. *I sapori della modernità: Cibo e romanzo*. Bologna: Il Mulino, 1991.

Blanchard, Marc Eli. "On Still Life." *Yale French Studies* 61 (1981): 276-277.

Brancaforte, Benito. *Benedetto Croce y su crtica de la literatura española*. Madrid: Gredos, 1972.

Braudel, Fernand. *The Structure of Everyday Life: The Limits of the Possible*. New York: Harper and Row, 1979.

———. *The Mediterranean and the Mediterranean World in the Age of Philip II*. Vol. 2. New York: Harper and Row, 1972.

Brucker, Gene. *Giovanni and Lusanna: Love and Marriage in Renaissance Florence*. Berkeley: Univ. of California Press, 1986.

Bryson, Norman. *Looking at the Overlooked: Four Essays on Still Life Painting*. Cambridge: Harvard Univ. Press, 1990.

Burke, Peter. *Venice and Amsterdam: A Study of Seventeenth-Century Elites*. London: T. Smith, 1974.

Butor, Michel. *Essais sur le roman*. Paris: Gallimard, 1969.

Calvino, Italo. *Sotto il sole del giaguaro*. Milan: Garzanti, 1986.

Camporesi, Piero. *Bread of Dreams: Food and Fantasy in Early Modern Europe*. Cambridge: Basil Blackwell, 1989.

Casalduero, Joaquín. *Estudios de literatura española*. Madrid: Gredos, 1973.

Castro, Américo. *The Spaniards*. Berkeley: Univ. of California Press, 1971.

———. *Hacia Cervantes*. Madrid: Taurus, 1967.

———. *An Idea of History: Selected Essays of Américo Castro*. Ed. S. Gilman and E. D. King. Columbus: Ohio State Univ. Press, 1977.

Cros, Edmond. *Mateo Alemán: Introducción a su vida y a su obra*. Salamanca: Anaya, 1971.

Curtius, Ernst Robert. *European Literature and the Latin Middle Ages*. New York: Harper and Row, 1953.

Defourneaux, Marcelin. *Daily Life in Spain in the Golden Age*. New York: Praeger Publishers, 1970.

Dunn, Peter. "Reading the Text of *Lazarillo de Tormes*." *Studies in Honor of Bruce Wardropper*. Ed. D. Foz, H. Sieber, R. TerHorst. Newark: Juan de la Cuesta, 1989.

Ehrenberg, Victor. *The People of Aristophanes: A Sociology of Old Attic Comedy*. New York: Schocken Books, 1962.

Elliott, J. H. *Imperial Spain, 1469-1716*. New York: St. Martin's Press, 1963.

Ferguson, Wallace. *The Renaissance in Historical Thought: Five Centuries of Interpretation*. Cambridge: Houghton Mifflin Co., 1948.

Forcione, Alban K. *Cervantes and the Mystery of Lawlessness: A Study of El casamiento engañoso y El coloquio de los perros*. Princeton: Princeton Univ. Press, 1984.

Fromm, Erich. *The Fear of Freedom*. London: Routledge and Kegan Paul, 1950.

Fumerton, Patricia. *Cultural Aesthetics: Renaissance Literature and the Practice of Social Ornament*. Chicago: Univ. of Chicago Press, 1991.

Goldthwaite, Richard. "The Economy of Renaissance Italy. The Preconditions for Luxury Consumption." *I Tatti Studies. Essays in the Renaissance*. Vol. 2. Florence: La Nuova Italia, 1987.

Gramsci, Antonio. *Antonio Gramsci: Selections from Cultural Writings*. Ed. D. Forgacs and G. Nowell-Smith. Cambridge: Harvard Univ. Press, 1985.

Greenblatt, Stephen. *Renaissance Self-Fashioning: From More to Shakespeare*. Chicago: Univ. of Chicago Press, 1984.

Guevara, Antonio de. *Menosprecio de corte y alabanza de aldea*. Madrid: Calpe, 1922.

Guillén, Claudio. *Literature as System: Essays towards the Theory of Literary History.* Princeton: Princeton Univ. Press, 1971.

Halpern, Richard. *The Poetics of Primitive Accumulation: English Renaissance Culture and the Genealogy of Capital.* Ithaca: Cornell Univ. Press, 1991.

Hauser, Arnold. *The Social History of Art.* Vol. 2. New York: Vintage Books, 1951.

Heller, Agnes. *Renaissance Man.* London: Routledge and Kegan Paul, 1978.

Herrero, Javier. "Renaissance Poverty and Lazarillo's Family: the Birth of the Picaresque Genre." *PMLA* 94 (1979): 876-79.

Hexter, J. H. *On Historians.* Cambridge: Harvard Univ. Press, 1979.

Huppert, George. *After the Black Death: A Social History of Early Modern Europe.* Bloomington: Indiana Univ. Press, 1986.

Jeanneret, Michel. *A Feast of Words: Banquets and Table Talk in the Renaissance.* Chicago: Univ. of Chicago Press, 1991.

Jones, Stephen R. G. *The Economy of Conformism.* Oxford: Basil Blackwell, 1984.

Lanser, Susan Sniader. *The Narrative Act: Point of View in Prose Fiction.* Princeton: Princeton Univ. Press, 1981.

Lawrence, D. H. *Selected Literary Criticism.* New York: Viking Press, 1956.

Lazarillo de Tormes. Ed. Everett W. Hesse and Harry F. Williams. Madison: Univ. of Wisconsin Press, 1969.

Lazarillo de Tormes. Two Picaresque Novels. Trans. Michael Alpert. Baltimore: Penguin Books, 1969.

Levin, Harry. *The Gates of Horn: A Study of Five French Realists.* New York: Oxford Univ. Press, 1963.

Lukács, Georg. *The Theory of the Novel.* Cambridge: MIT Press, 1971.

MacMullen, Ramsay. *Roman Social Relations: 50 B.C. to 284 A.D.* New Haven: Yale Univ. Press, 1974.

Manrique de Aragón, Jorge. *Peligrosidad social y picaresca.* San Antonio de Colonge: Hijos de J. Bosch, 1977.

Maravall, José Antonio. *La literatura picaresca desde la historia social (siglos XVI y XVII).* Madrid: Gredos, 1986.

———. *Utopia and Counterutopia in the "Quixote."* Detroit: Wayne State Univ. Press, 1991.

Marco Antonio de Camos. *Microcosmia: Gobierno universal del hombre cristiano, para todos los estados y cualquiera de ellos.* Madrid, 1595.

Marin, Louis. *Etudes Semiologiques.* Paris: Klincksieck, 1971.

———. *Food for Thought.* Baltimore: Johns Hopkins Univ. Press, 1989.

Marx, Karl. "Economic and Philosophical Manuscripts," in Erich Fromm, *Marx's Concept of Man.* New York: F. Ungar Publisher, 1968.

Moffitt, John F. "Image and Meaning in Velázquez's Water Carrier of Seville." *Traza y Baza* 7 (1979): 5.

Molho, Maurice. *Cervantes: Raíces Folklóricas.* Madrid: Gredos, 1976.

———. *Introducción al pensamiento picaresco.* Salamanca: Anaya, 1972.

Morson, Gary Saul, and Caryl Emerson. *Mikhail Bakhtin: Creation of a Prosaics.* Stanford: Stanford Univ. Press, 1990.

Mullins, Edwin. *Great Paintings.* New York: St. Martin's Press, 1981.

Ortega y Gasset, José. "Sobre el cultivo de la demótica." *Obras completas.* Vol. IX. Madrid: Revista de Occidente, 1971.

———. *Velázquez, Goya, and the Dehumanization of Art.* New York: W. W. Norton, 1972.

Parret, Herman. *Le sublime du quotidien.* Paris: Hades, 1988.

Prieto, Antonio. *Ensayo semiológico de sistemas literarios.* Barcelona: Planeta, 1972.

Reed, Walter R. *An Exemplary History of the Novel: The Quixotic versus the Picaresque.* Chicago: Univ. of Chicago Press, 1981.

Rico, Francisco. *The Spanish Picaresque Novel and the Point of View.* Cambridge: Cambridge Univ. Press, 1984.

Rivers, Elias L. *Quixotic Scriptures: Essays on the Textuality of Hispanic Literature.* Bloomington: Indiana Univ. Press, 1983.

Romano, John. *Dickens and Reality.* New York: Columbia Univ. Press, 1978.

Salinas, Pedro. *Ensayos de literatura hispánica.* Madrid: Aguilar, 1958.

Schama, Simon. *The Embarrassment of Riches: An Interpretation of Dutch Culture in the Golden Age.* New York: Knopf, 1987.

Shell, Marc. *The Economy of Literature.* Baltimore: Johns Hopkins Univ. Press, 1978.

Shipley, George. "Lazarillo and the Cathedral Chaplain: A Conspiratorial Reading of Lazarillo de Tormes, Tratado IV." *Symposium* 37 (1983): 231.

———. "Lazarillo de Tormes Was Not a Hardworking, Clean-Living Water Carrier." *Hispanic Studies in Honor of Alan D. Deyermond: A North American Tribute.* Ed. S. Miletich. Madison: Univ. of Wisconsin Press, 1986. 247-56.

———. 'The Critic as Witness for the Prosecution: Making the Case against Lázaro de Tormes." *PMLA* 97 (1982): 179-80.

Sieber, Harry. *Language and Society in "La vida de Lazarillo de Tormes."* Baltimore: Johns Hopkins Univ. Press, 1978.

Simmel, Georg. *The Philosophy of Money.* London: Routledge and Kegan Paul, 1978.

Smith, Barbara Herrnstein. *Contingencies of Value: Alternative Perspectives for Critical Theory.* Cambridge: Harvard Univ. Press, 1988.

Smith, Paul Julian. *Writing in the Margin: Spanish Literature of the Golden Age.* Oxford: Clarendon Press, 1988.

Steinberg, Leo. "José López-Rey, Velázquez: A Catalogue Raisonné of His Oeuvre, with an Introductory Study." *Art Bulletin* 47 (1965): 282.

Unamuno, Miguel de. *Our Lord Don Quixote.* Princeton: Princeton Univ. Press, 1976.

Veeser, H. Aram. *The New Historicism.* London: Routledge and Kegan Paul, 1989.

Vernon, John. *Literary Realism in the Nineteenth and Early Twentieth Centuries.* Ithaca: Cornell Univ. Press, 1984.

Villanueva, Francisco Márquez. *Espiritualidad y literatura en el siglo XVI.* Madrid: Alfaguara, 1968.

White, Hayden. *The Content of the Form: Narrative Discourse and Historical Representation.* Baltimore: Johns Hopkins Univ. Press, 1987.

Wind, Barry. *Velázquez's Bodegones: A Study in Seventeenth-Century Spanish Genre Painting.* Fairfax: George Mason Univ. Press, 1987.

Yamey, Basil. *Art and Accounting.* New Haven: Yale Univ. Press, 1989.

GENRE

W. M. Frohock with Gregory Fitz Gerald and Eric Steel (interview date 1971)

SOURCE: Frohock, W. M., Gregory Fitz Gerald, and Eric Steel. "Picaresque and Modern Literature: A Conversation with W. H. Frohock." Edited by Philip L. Gerber and Robert J. Gemmett. *Genre* 13, no. 2 (1971): 187-97.

[In this interview, Frohock discusses the characteristics of the picaresque novel and the possibility of a modern picaresque.]

[Steel:] Mr. Frohock, you have said that you feel the term picaresque *has been used for too loosely in describing modern fiction. At the same time you admit that many modern works contain features that can be legitimately classified as picaresque. Since some modern works of fiction exhibit characteristics of the old picaresque it might be a good procedure for the critic to indicate the picaresque features in the novels that he's criticizing and then proceed from there to a further discussion of the novel.*

[Frohock:] That's the only way you can proceed when you're talking about literature: from what you know to what you don't know. And this process is going to call very often for the use of old terms, digging them up sometimes out of the scrap heap and applying them where they'll do the most good. I don't really feel, though, that this is a justification for being sloppy with the old terms, for using them to mean something that they actually didn't mean in the first place.

[Fitz Gerald:] How then would you define the term picaresque?

[Frohock:] I tend not to define it very closely. I'd much rather describe than define. Let's say that when I say picaresque, I'm thinking of a kind of fiction that began to flourish in Spain in the 1550's. It's a fiction which takes the form of pseudo-autobiography, the narrator being the hero, telling his own story. It always assumes the form of a journey; the hero gets out on the road, goes from place to place, has various adventures, works for various masters and thereby sees a great deal of society. It uses the road-novel pattern. You know, we go here and something happens; we pack up and go to the next town and something else happens; one town, one episode; and on we go. It may be that we no longer appreciate the road novel because we no longer appreciate the road. We no longer have roads in the sense that the Spaniards did; we have records that show that in 1550 they were accustomed, many of them, to walking eighty kilometers a day—they must have trotted, that's fifty miles! When they went out on the road, they weren't going to get home soon. They were changing their way of life; all sorts of things were going to happen to them. Nowadays, when you go out on the road—the New York Thruway—everything is so beautifully regulated to keep you away from adventure. That is not a road in the Spanish sense. No picaro could go very far on the Thruway!

For a novel to be picaresque, the hero himself has to be a picaro, that is a rogue, not a born criminal, but somebody who has to live by his wits, by thinking faster than the rest of the world does; he will steal, play tricks on people, do various things that we would probably call immoral, and his fortunes will go up and down. Along with this, an essential feature is that the hero has to have a "worm's eye view" of society, looking up from the very bottom. No matter how low somebody else is, he's always above the picaro on the social scale.

Then too, there are the overt ironies drawn from the contrasts that the old Spanish picaro discovers between what established society assumes life to be and what it turns out to be in actual fact. In recent interpretations, not much is made of the character of the picaro either as a social type or as the unwilling product of a society bemused by its own concept of *honora*, that outrageously unrealistic kind of self-esteem. We find today almost nothing of the inherent interest in life on the criminal fringes that the old picaresque shares with many patently unpicaresque works. In short, attention has been immeasurably diverted from the "plot, character, and verisimilitude" of the picaresque.

[Fitz Gerald:] Would you give us a few examples of some genuinely picaresque novels?

[Frohock:] Well, there are the four great Spanish novels. *The Life of Lazarillo de Tormes* was the first, though some people say that it isn't really picaresque, but *proto*-picaresque. Then *The Life of the Rogue (La vida del buscon)* by Quevedo, *Guzmán de Alfarache* by Mateo Alemán, and a fourth, *Marcos de Obrégon*, which was written by Vincente Espinel.

[Fitz Gerald:] And how does Don Quixote *fit into this picture?*

[Frohock:] Very poorly, because it's not narrated in the first person. Furthermore, the hero is not a rogue or a villain. The old man is a knight, which is well up the social scale; he's not worried about eating. The great motivation of the picaro, after all, is to keep the wrinkles out of his belly.

[Fitz Gerald:] Then you would not consider Sancho as a picaro either?

[Frohock:] He would come nearer in some ways. He has the right social level; he has a very realistic attitude toward existence. But even Sancho isn't out making his way by stealing or by playing tricks on society. Certainly not the kind of thing we find in *Lazarillo de Tormes*. Poor Lazarillo becomes the serving boy of an old blind man. The old blind man won't give the young hero any wine with his supper, so Lazarillo bores a hole in the wine gourd and plugs it with wax. The wax plug is in the bottom of the gourd and as the old man holds it in his lap, covering the gourd with his hands, Lazarillo slides down under the blind man, pries out the wax and gets his wine that way every night until, of course, the blind man catches him doing it and breaks the container on Lazarillo's head.

[Fitz Gerald:] Is there any modern fiction that you would classify as picaresque?

[Frohock:] If we identify recent fiction as any fiction published since 1930, I would say that we do have some works which attempt to be self-consciously picaresque. *Felix Krull* and *The Adventures of Augie March* are

examples which come immediately to mind. In both cases, we know that the author intended a picaresque novel because he said so beforehand. We also know that both Mann and Bellow are very literate men who have read their Spaniards and know the picaresque tradition.

[Fitz Gerald:] Would you include Huckleberry Finn *in the same group?*

[Frohock:] I don't know how much Mark Twain had in mind doing anything self-consciously picaresque, but I really doubt that his book belongs in the same category as, say, *Felix Krull.*

[Fitz Gerald:] It occurs to me that Mark Twain's A Connecticut Yankee *shows an example of a shrewd man coming from a less than middle section of society, a man who has some of the characteristics of the picaro even though, perhaps, we might not be willing to assent to defining the whole work as picaresque.*

[Frohock:] I think you're probably right. In fact, you're really heading toward a solution to the critical dilemma by using this adjective *picaresque* about aspects of the fiction and not about the whole of the fiction itself. The fundamental question is how well any critical term—such as picaresque—characterizes the writing it's applied to. In other words, the criterion is usefulness. I have not read all the works that have been called picaresque by one critic or another. But I've read enough to be afflicted with some enduring doubt as to the usefulness of assigning these books to the picaresque category, particularly when insistence on real or imagined picaresque elements in the story obscures the presence of some other element which more accurately defines its type. You can find several traits of the picaresque hero in *A Connecticut Yankee*, though not as many as in the traditional European picaresque novels. You know picaresque spread over Europe very fast. There were translations of *Guzmán de Alfarache* out within a year after the original publication. The picaresque emerged in Germany in a fine way at the end of the seventeenth century with the publication of *Simplicissimus*. By this time picaresque novels were already appearing in England. Now I've taken you away from the question about *A Connecticut Yankee*, but in so doing I've tried to suggest a ploy for getting at the meaning of this word.

[Fitz Gerald:] Actually, I was leading up to the following question: Do you see any essential differences between the American picaresque as it has developed and the European tradition which you've just described?

[Frohock:] I would prefer to narrow that question down a bit before attempting an answer. Could we take it this way? How does American picaresque compare with what is called picaresque in Germany? Focusing on books contemporary with each other, such as Bellow's *Augie March* and Heinrich Böll's *The Clown* or Günter Grass' *The Tin Drum*, I would say that the obvious split between the two has to do with the American's being more a comic novel. Bellow obviously strives to be funny in places and sometimes he succeeds in being funny when he doesn't necessarily intend it. Whereas, the Germans' works in the picaresque vein tend to be less humorous and much more deeply and violently satiric.

[Steel:] The word picaresque *was used recently to characterize a new American novel,* Setting Free the Bears. *You may be familiar with it.*

[Frohock:] I am, and I would have brought that novel into the conversation sooner or later it you hadn't, because I like it so well. It's the first novel by a young man named John Irving. He is a thoroughly American writer, who chooses to place his story in Vienna and make it the adventures of two Europeans. He has modernized the picaresque, if this *is* picaresque, by setting his main characters on the road on a tremendous Enfield motorcycle and sending them off on a wild adventure across country. Most unfortunately, this part of the story ends with the death of one of the heroes, which is not in the picaresque tradition.

But then the story becomes almost a fantasy, when the remaining hero attempts to realize a long-cherished desire of letting loose all the animals in the Vienna zoo. Thus the rest of the novel deals mostly with this and the first chap's autobiography, a very interesting one, and one that is in the picaresque tradition. The book is actually brought together into one very closely laced-up thing, and the element of picaresque will be evident to everyone who reads it. *Time* magazine chose to give it quite a long review. The reviewer liked it because he said it took advantage of what was already strong among Americans, a sort of picaresque tradition.

[Fitz Gerald:] Mr. Frohock, in 1950 you published a book called The Novel of Violence in America; *it seems to me that if we don't too strictly adhere to the term* picaresque, *but talk about the* picaro *instead, we might find him in some of the novels of violence: I have in mind such characters as Sam Spade in Dashiell Hammett's* The Maltese Falcon, *or the protagonists of James M. Cain and Raymond Chandler, especially the latter's private detective, Marlowe—the whole hard-boiled school, including some of Hemingway's characters.*

[Frohock:] I was hoping you'd mention one other writer. It seems to me that the best picaros in that generation can be found in Steinbeck's work. Steinbeck's best known novel, *The Grapes of Wrath,* does take the form of a road novel in which people who are on the very bottom of society get out on the road in their jalopies on Highway 66, after they've been driven out of Oklahoma. There are even some of the old picaro's tricks in this book, especially when the characters get hard up for food. The tough detective type you mention, the fellow who always gets beaten up or who beats somebody else up, does not have the comic element about him that a good picaro always seems to have. Also—and this seems to be particularly true of Cain's heroes—they're not very clever.

[Fitz Gerald:] But Spade and Marlowe are very clever. Would you still say the application of the term picaresque *to these detective novels is incorrect?*

[Frohock:] Yes. It would be misleading.

[Steel:] For that matter, The Grapes of Wrath *is outside the tradition in that it is not autobiographical.*

[Frohock:] That's true, it's not.

[Fitz Gerald:] What works in your opinion give the truest picture of the picaresque tradition in contemporary literature?

[Frohock:] Probably the most legitimate use of the word would be with reference to Böll's *The Clown* and Grass' *The Tin Drum.*

[Fitz Gerald:] Would you include Catch 22 *with these two works?*

[Frohock:] *Catch 22* shows a good deal of what's in the picaresque tradition. But it's not autobiographical, and it's strangely taken up with some pretty serious stuff about the war. Yet, I think everyone who talks about our moment as one when the picaresque seems to be coming back will mention this novel.

[Fitz Gerald:] In describing the picaro *as character type, you've mentioned several characteristics. One that occurs to me as we talk about* Catch 22 *is the* picaro's *enormous amatory success. Not, of course, the idealistic kind of love that we're accustomed to find in Wordsworth or Coleridge.*

[Frohock:] Oh, it's a long way from Wordsworth to Heller! But, actually, when you go back to the old picaresque novels, there is not a great deal of love in them, in the Spanish ones, for instance, or in *Simplicissimus,* or even in *Moll Flanders.* Although Moll Flanders is amorously active, as we're all aware, there is very little attention to love as such. You know, there are a couple of picaresque stories that have women in the major role. I don't mean just *Moll Flanders.* There's *La picara Justina* in Spanish, for example. The picaro, when he meets a lady, assumes that he can expect from her in the way of treatment what he would expect from any other person like himself. He understands only the "rogue character." A woman has one advantage over the male picaro in that she can also trick people with her attractiveness.

[Fitz Gerald:] There's an American cinema called Cat Ballou *that focuses on a real* picara—*a woman who lives by her wits and who is the leader of a gang of rogues.*

[Steel:] That makes me feel that Tom Jones *is a pretty good example of the male and female* picaro.

[Frohock:] Sooner or later, everyone wants to bring *Tom Jones* into the tradition, but it's very difficult. The problem is, of course, that *Tom Jones* is an eighteenth-century

English novel which was written by Henry Fielding. That's a bad combination for picaresque, because Fielding after all was as much a dramatist in his own mind as he was a novelist, and a comic dramatist at that. Fine, but English comedy always requires the happy ending. What are you going to do with your rogue? You have a nice girl like Sophia Western, but you can't have her marrying a cad; so you discover at the end that the picaro isn't really a picaro at all. Tom Jones is, we discover, a nice boy who comes from a nice family with plenty of money. He can support Sophia as she wants to be supported. He's no rogue, after all, but the equivalent of a college boy out on pranks. The same thing happens at the end of *Roderick Random*. Roderick is in love with a woman, but he can't rise to her social level. The reader doesn't see how this is all going to turn out until Roderick, while traveling in South America, meets a man in a hostelry who looks at him across the room and says "Roderick" and in Roderick's mind rings the man's name, which he's heard before: Rodrigo. "Father!" "Son!" "Money-bags! you're a nice guy after all; you can marry the girl." And your picaresque has gone out the window in a hand basket.

[Fitz Gerald:] Does Kerouac's On The Road *fit into the picaresque category at all?*

[Frohock:] Pretty well, as such things go. Kerouac finally managed to tell a story about the American road in which he kept off the main roads for his adventures. Besides being a road novel, it's a first-person narration, more or less pseudo-autobiographical, which lets in quite a lot of the tradition.

[Fitz Gerald:] The central character is certainly a roguish type of fellow, who has sexual prowess, and spends his time traveling back and forth in America.

[Frohock:] Yes. I think you've got to let in a great deal heavier admixture of sex in any formula for modern picaresque because we just see life that way. Americans wouldn't understand a sexless picaro. Then there are other novels, like Céline's *Journey to the End of the Night,* and *Invisible Man,* Ralph Ellison's lovely job. My reasons for thinking of these novels as picaresque are somewhat more compelling. They *are* road novels and autobiographies of heroes with appropriately low social origins, and the heroes move through a world that beats them about the ears with more brutal experience than they can bear. There is one towering difference. Céline's hero, Bardamu, and Ellison's man, who has no name that I can remember, are on the road because they want to get *away* from something, something either in themselves or in the ethos around them. Bardamu's a paranoid whose case is complicated because people actually do persecute him. Ellison's character carries about in his pocket a letter of introduction which tells recipients to keep this boy running.

[Steel:] Are there other instances you'd like to point out?

[Frohock:] Calling certain other recent novels picaresque has the double result of saying nothing significant about them and at the same time of blurring the term's meaning.

For example, James Purdy's *Malcolm* is a string of episodes in the life of a wealthy adolescent who somehow has been abandoned by his father. He meets a gallery of human types, most of them phonies, and finally lets himself be married to a nymphomaniac nightclub singer who shortly kills him by exhaustion. He does not tell his own story, he is not a criminal, he is almost completely passive, and he is, from one end of the story to the other, too naive to be capable of defending himself. And the atmosphere he moves in feels less like traditional picaresque than like the nightmares of the disciples of Nathaniel West. *Malcolm* is episodical and satirical and full of grotesques, but so have been many books over the ages that no one has thought of calling picaresque.

[Fitz Gerald:] Then Terry Southern's The Magic Christian *is not germane either.*

[Frohock:] No, *The Magic Christian* is not even in the genre. Guy Grand, the hero, is a very rich man who devotes wealth and great ingenuity to devising enormous tricks that are designed to reveal how much cheaper, viler, and more perverse humanity is than we have commonly thought. In one episode he builds a gigantic cesspool in the Chicago Loop, fills it with the most revolting slop he can concoct, strews the surface with bank notes, and chortles over the willingness of people to undergo, for a little money, what Dante once saw fit to make a punishment in hell. But Guy Grand—that *Grand Guy,* that's why he is named this, by the way—is much less like anything anyone ever took for a picaro, until these last years, than a member of a long line of tricksters and twisters that includes Falstaff, various medieval allegory types, characters in the old Folksbücher, and Eulenspiegel. It might be advisable to distinguish between the trickster who exists only for and by virtue of his tricks and merry pranks, and the picaro, whose roguery is at most the by-product of a way of life and no more.

[Fitz Gerald:] Considering these variant approaches to the picaresque, could you tell us something about your new book on the subject?

[Frohock:] It will involve a survey of present fiction written in Germany, France, America, England, Italy, and Spain. The book will try to say something, not so much about the old picaresque—that's been raked over a great deal—but actually about this present literature that we're trying to describe by calling it picaresque, but which is obviously something new, something different from what we've had in the past. We do have a new kind of fiction, a very interestingly new kind of fiction, being written around us. We've named a considerable number of its writers, but we've not named John Barth and Kurt Vonnegut and all the rest who are also contributing. It's a fiction that is richly, and sometimes wildly inventive, with alienated, withdrawn, or dropped-out heroes living in a world where only the neurotic—if even he—can feel at home, and often it is deeply, perhaps totally, subversive of institutions and basic cultural values. This is why it sells so well.

My book will be saying that this literature is new and different, and it will be trying to describe that difference, which is what I think criticism is largely about. Some of the traits in this literature, in some degree, can be found in the old picaresque literature. But it is different enough so that maybe we can't quite handle it with this awkward term that I've been using so much this morning. I doubt that taking over the concept of picaresque really helps much. What we have is a new kind of literature.

Claudio Guillen (essay date 1971)

SOURCE: Guillen, Claudio. "Genre and Countergenre: The Discovery of the Picaresque." In *Literature as System: Essays Toward the Theory of Literary History,* pp. 135-58. Princeton, N. J.: Princeton University Press, 1971.

[*In the essay below, Guillen reviews the development of the picaresque novel as a model for a theory of genre.*]

Bibliographical research, of which the works of Antonio Rodríguez-Moñino offer today an eminent example,[1] provides the student of literature with a very substantial problem: that of the relationship between a poem and its readers. As everyone suspects in the most generic way—*scripta manent*—art can and often does succeed in conquering time. But how does literature, in addition, traverse space? Is one of these dimensions a condition of the other? This is what a certain branch of the sociology of literature, of which Robert Escarpit is the persuasive advocate, attempts to clarify. These studies deal with the aftermath of poetic creation by examining the history of *books*. As a poet's words are published, multiplied, and distributed among other men, the main instrument of publication, the book, develops into the vehicle not of mere one-to-one communication but of broad social diffusion. A book, in this sense, "is neither more nor less than its diffusion," as Professor Escarpit explains:

> "Since, in a little space, it has a high density of intellectual and formal content, since it can easily be passed from hand to hand, since it can be copied and reproduced at will, the book is the simplest intrument which, from a given point, can liberate a multitude of sounds, images, feelings, ideas, facts, by opening the gates of time and space to them—and then, joined with other books, can reconcentrate those diffused data in countless other points scattered through the centuries and the continents in an infinity of combinations, each different from any other."[2]

These changing combinations require the passage of historical time. Moreover, they imply a temporal process on an aesthetic level. The publication of a poem is comparable to the performance of a drama or of a symphony only to the extent that it makes *possible* a series of future readers. A theatrical performance can bring about an immediate contact between author, director, actor, text, and audience. Where written literature is concerned, an extensive process unfolds that is both temporal and spatial.

The book requires certain intermediaries in order to make its appearance—the editor, the printer, the bookseller—but it can only presume or anticipate a reader. As the real readers multiply, a collective sort of communication begins to take place. A second printing, and a third, or a fifth, particularly if these spread out in space, tend to prove that the audience has ceased to be hypothetical. Thus, the publishing history of a book manifests a process of actualization that is both aesthetic and sociological. The "after-the-fact" sociology of literature does not show how poetry reflects or refracts social patterns (usually a circular issue). It highlights, rather, the power to affect those patterns, that is, the ways in which literature alters a society's awareness of itself.

Bibliographical data allow us to reconstruct decisive links in the process of actualization of single works. As an example, I will examine in the first part of this article the early career of *Lazarillo de Tormes*. The study of this career, which coincided with the birth of the picaresque narrative—a crucial step, in turn, in the rise of the modern novel—will draw us into the orbit of the theory of genres. In fact, it may very well be that of all the "combinations" and "reconcentrations" that Robert Escarpit indicates, the most stable and the most significant *is* the formal model usually called genre.

I

In 1554 three little books entitled *La vida de Lazarillo de Tormes, y de sus fortunas y adversidades* appeared in Antwerp, Burgos, and Alcalá de Henares. None of the three is in all certainty the *first* edition. The hypothesis that an earlier edition, now lost, was published in 1553, has been advanced but never proved. Modern critics concur in rejecting the Alcalá version, which deviates most often from the other two and is marred by no less than six interpolations, obviously spurious. This leaves Antwerp and Burgos—two notoriously mercantile towns in the sixteenth century.[3] It should not be forgotten that printers were good businessmen from the start. Two centuries later Voltaire would point out that Dutch booksellers earned millions because certain Frenchmen had been blessed with wit and intelligence ("les libraires hollandais gagnent un million par an parce que les Français ont eu de l'esprit").[4] Toward the middle of the sixteenth century there were witty Spaniards too, as well as discriminating Flemish merchants.

Lazarillo de Tormes has had a genuine audience since the end of the sixteenth century and the start of the seventeenth. Why not since 1554, one might ask, that is, since the beginning of its existence as a book? A most competent student of the subject, A. Rumeau, has shown how limited the popularity of *Lazarillo* actually was during the reign of Philip II (1556-1598).[5] Four editions were offered to the public within the span of two years: in Antwerp (by the printer Martín Nucio), Burgos (Juan de Junta), and Alcalá de Henares (Salcedo), in 1554; and a second time in Antwerp (Guillermo Simón) in 1555. An early success is evident. Hence the odd contrast with what follows, or rather, fails to follow. The anonymous *Segunda parte* (published in Antwerp in 1555 by Martín Nucio and Guillermo Simón) is immediately forgotten. (It will only be reprinted, together with the first part, in Milan in 1587 and 1615; in Spain it will be published for the first time in 1844. This Flemish sequel clearly has played no part whatsoever in the history of the Spanish picaresque novel.) And even *Lazarillo* itself, after the flare-up of popularity in 1554-1555, will be reprinted rather seldom during the second half of the century—five times, to be exact, twice in Spain: Madrid, 1573; Tarragona, 1586; Milan, 1587; Antwerp, 1595; and Bergamo, 1597.[6] Furthermore, Rumeau explains that the Italian edition of 1597 (Bergamo) owed its existence to the fact that the editor, Antonio de Antoni, was anxious to sell the remaining copies of the 1587 Milanese printing, which had not been doing well, even though the Bergamo dedication tried to suggest the very opposite; and that one should also not take at face value the publicity-minded declarations found among the preliminaries of the 1573 censored edition (*edición castigada*), brought out in Madrid by the royal chronicler, secretary, and cosmographer Juan López de Velasco, according to whom *Lazarillo* had always been well received, particularly abroad ("fue siempre a todos muy acepto, de cuya causa, aunque estaba prohibido en estos reinos, se leía y imprimía de ordinario fuera dellos)."[7]

The 1587 Milan edition opens with a dedication that is rather more honest. There the novel is presented as nearly forgotten, and worm-eaten with age: "la vida de Lazarillo de Tormes, ya casi olvidada, y de tiempo carcomida."[8] Thirty-three years, it is true, had passed. The censored edition was not being reprinted in Spain, actually, nor the uncensored text outside of the peninsula. Besides, I should like to call attention to yet another fact, which completes the picture without modifying it. The first French translation, published in Lyon in 1560, adds to the conclusion of the tale one more chapter—dealing with Lazaro's friendship with certain wine-loving Germans—which happened to be the first chapter of the *Segunda parte* or sequel published in Antwerp in 1555. The same addition can be found in the Antwerp editions of 1595 and 1602, by the heirs of the famous Plantinus, and in numerous later reprints (until Bordeaux, 1837). It would have been odd for the Flemish printers to decide to copy the innovation of a French translator (whose starting point had been the Antwerp original of 1554 or 1555). The opposite probably happened, as Gabriel Laplane suggests,[9] and one may postulate the appearance of an additional Flemish edition between 1555 and 1559, of which no copies are extant today, and to which the editor (perhaps Guillermo Simón) had added for the first time the opening chapter of the Antwerp sequel. We may also recall in passing that the Flemish original of *Lazarillo*—not the Burgos or the Alcalá text—was the basis for the 1573 *edición castigada*, the 1587 and 1597 reprints in Milan and Antwerp respectively, and the first French and English translations (the latter by David Rowland, in London, 1586). The version of *Lazarillo* which attained real temporal and spatial diffu-sion during the *Siglo de Oro* in Spain and Europe—and thus became really a "book"—was the Antwerp text, whether complete or truncated, of 1554. Everything suggests that the first "discoverers" of the novel were living in Flanders.[10]

In Spain, the book was banned and condemned by the Grand Inquisitor's *Cathalogus librorum qui prohibentur* (Valladolid, 1559). The story was consistently irreverent, of course, and one may surmise that it was enjoyed as such by its first readers: the longest interpolation we encounter in the Alcalá text (1554) offers still another false miracle by the swindling pardoner. But these components were not enough to make *Lazarillo* steadily popular anywhere. The touches of anticlerical satire were not new—in this sense, they were the least original parts of the novel[11]—and their effect was likely to be short-lived. López de Velasco's cuts in 1573 did not affect the essential structure of the tale, that is to say, the sequence of situations and the narrative method on which the future picaresque novel, and its immense European success, would ultimately be based.

Today we know that *Lazarillo de Tormes* marked a crucial moment in the rise of the European novel. We know that this tale of a small boy's partial but enduring disaffection with a scandalous world has lent itself to numberless variations from the sixteenth century to our time. In the passages where we see Lazarillo wandering from town to town, looking for a shelter and a master, we recognize easily enough an early figuration of the freedom and the quest that are the burden of modern novelistic heroes. There is no doubt but that *Lazarillo* inaugurated with singular skill, within the Spanish literary curve spanning *La Celestina* and *Don Quixote,* the presentation of the hopes and failures of men who, orphan-like but inquiring, far removed in practice from any abstract canon, test their knowledge as they grow older and confront or work out the compromises that will determine their lives.

Yet, as we return to the sequence of events in the sixteenth century, all such developments become virtual once more. The historical view forces us to conjecture that what did take place might not have happened at all. At best, we are justified in singling out the factors that were most favorable to a particular series of possibilities. During the decades of the *Siglo de Oro,* a Spanish novel, or any Spanish text, enjoyed exceptional conditions for influence and propagation. We have seen that the original Castilian text of *Lazarillo* was printed not only in Spain but in the Low Countries and in Italy—and shortly afterwards in France as well. This initial "space"—the dimensions of a publishing world—coincided with the mercantile support for the Hispanic conquest and colonization of America. Nevertheless, the rhythm of acceptance of *Lazarillo* was slow. A genuine audience, as Robert Escarpit will remind us, presupposes the convergence of the factors of space and time. To the spatial diffusion of our proto-picaresque novel, in other words, a certain temporal continuity was still to be added.

To decipher an absence is always hazardous. Why, one asks, was this rhythm of acceptance so slow? In its day, of course, the position of *Lazarillo* was truly singular. That is to say, in the middle of the sixteenth century, a novel, or a genuine pre-novel, was unusual and isolated indeed. The fact that an original work remains without immediate effect or consequences, surely is an ordinary occurrence in the history of the arts. (*Lazarillo*, as Marcel Bataillon has stated, was "un commencement absolu.")[12] Also, it often happens that a new work stimulates a great deal of interest at first, only to be forgotten just as quickly, for it has not been understood or assimilated. Thus, the first triumph of *Lazarillo* was followed by decades of relative indifference. Particularly in the career of the visual arts, there are a number of similar cases—for example, the delayed impact of Goya in the nineteenth century. The great Giotto, who died in 1337, remained without successors for almost a century in the midst of one of the most intense periods of creativity in the history of painting. "For a hundred years after Giotto," Berenson observed, "there appeared in Florence no painter equally endowed with dominion over the significant."[13]

The author of *Lazarillo* had no successor for nearly fifty years. In 1599 Mateo Alemán—the humanist, *cristiano nuevo,* and businessman from Serville—published his *Guzmán de Alfarache,* ending the isolation of the earlier novel. Today the thematic and formal differences between *Lazarillo* and its followers seem worthy of consideration. On a certain level, *Guzmán de Alfarache* (a didactic and dogmatic monolith) and *Lazarillo de Tormes* (compassionate and pluralistic) seem nearly antithetical. But the seventeenth-century reader very probably had his eye on another level, where the two works converged. The result of this convergence was a common *género picaresco,* which did not come into being until 1599, of course—just as the heroic couplet did not exist until Chaucer had enough admirers and imitators, as John Livingston Lowes once pointed out: "'The heroic couplet,' says Professor Manly, with the utmost truth, 'originated . . . suddenly. Chaucer wrote heroic couplets, and there they were.' But when Chaucer wrote heroic couplets, and there all at once they were, the heroic couplet did not thereby spring into existence as a convention. It became that later, when other poets, following Chaucer, looked upon it and saw that it was good, and wore it threadbare."[14] What matters to us here, likewise, is the reaction of Mateo Alemán's contemporaries. As we shall see in a moment, the acceptance of either *Lazarillo* or *Guzmán* was second to the main development: the surge of popularity of the model, the pattern, the genre, which they sustained not singly but conjointly.

Guzmán de Alfarache was one of the first authentic best sellers in the history of printing. Its huge success immediately transformed a narrative form—in Lowes's terms—into a convention. The evidence suggests that Luis de Valdés was not far from the truth when he affirmed, in the "Elogio" heading the *Segunda parte* of 1604, that twenty-six different editions and no less than fifty thousand copies had appeared in four or five years: "¿De cuáles obras en tan breve tiempo vieron hechas tantas impresiones, que pasan de cincuenta mil cuerpos de libros los estampados, y de veinte y seis impresiones las que han llegado a mi noticia?"[15] The success of *Guzmán de Alfarache* around 1600 is well known. But critics have not observed that it also resulted in the resurrection of *Lazarillo de Tormes*; and that it sparked a "combination" (to use Escarpit's word), a double acceptance, a convergence, from which there arose, during the years immediately following the publication of *Guzmán* (1599), the idea of a *género picaresco*—an idea which was formulated for the first time by Ginés de Pasamonte in a passage of *Don Quixote* (1605): "mal año," said Ginés in a defiant moment, "para *Lazarillo de Tormes,* y para todos cuantos de aquel género se han escrito o escribieren" (Part 1, Chap. 22). We shall return later to these provocative words.

Four editions of *Lazarillo* had appeared in 1554 and 1555. Then, for as long as a second phase lasted, from 1573 to 1595, the book had five reprintings. Now a third, very different phase begins: within four years, from 1599 to 1603, at least nine editions of *Lazarillo* will be published. Basically, its public will be the same as *Guzmán*'s. I cannot venture a guess as to its composition. But we do know that it was large. And a large literate audience of Spaniards around 1600 could not possibly coincide with the lower class. It was probably most akin not to the heroes of picaresque novels but to their authors, particularly Mateo Alemán. Its core, in other words, would have been the discontented middle class. (Generally speaking, the rise of the novel in sixteenth-century Spain seems to have been rooted not in the triumph but in the frustration of the bourgeoisie.)

The king, Philip II, had died in 1598. The start of a new reign had brought either fresh hopes or a greater degree of boldness to writers and printers. The *Primera parte de Guzmán de Alfarache* was published for the first time in Madrid, "en casa del Licenciado Várez de Castro," a printer's shop where it began to be sold around the first week of March 1599. The *tasa* (or right to charge a certain price) was fixed by Gonzalo de la Vega on March 4. (Curiously enough, the *aprobación*—or ecclesiastical license—had been granted on January 13 of the previous year.)[16] Now, exactly nine weeks later, the printing house of Luis Sánchez in Madrid offered to the public an edition of *Lazarillo de Tormes*. The *tasa* for it was authorized by Gonzalo de la Vega on May 11.[17] In the meantime, *Guzmán de Alfarache* had begun to appear in the other kingdoms of the peninsula, as several alert publishers outside of Madrid tried to capitalize on the success of the Castilian edition. Sebastián de Cormellas, "a costa de Angelo Tabano, mercader de libros," brought out Alemán's long novel in Barcelona, with a license delivered on April 27.[18] (By this time a certain specialization had taken place in the trade, with the printer and the bookseller becoming two separate persons with different functions.) A second businessman from Barcelona, Miguel Menescal, followed suit, working with the printers Gabriel Graells and Giraldo

Dotil.[19] In Aragon we find that it was Juan Pérez de Valdivielso, "a costa de Juan Bonilla, mercader de libros," who issued *Guzmán de Alfarache,* in Zaragoza, the *aprobación* having been granted on June 21, 1599. Besides, it seems that Sebastián de Cormellas proceeded to sell still more copies of the novel in his own printing shop; and that the original edition by Várez de Castro was immediately pirated in Madrid.[20]

We can now observe that *Lazarillo de Tormes* followed precisely the *same* itinerary. Luis Sánchez, as we just noted, brought it before the public in Madrid a few days after the initial success of *Guzmán de Alfarache.* Sebastián de Cormellas and Juan Pérez de Valdivielso, Alemán's editors in Barcelona and Zaragoza respectively, published *Lazarillo* too, also in 1599. (There is no *tasa* or *aprobación* in either printing, obviously because the edition by Luis Sánchez was pirated.)[21] These were not the sole occasions on which *Lazarillo* appeared to follow closely in the steps of the illustrious *Guzmán.* In Paris Nicolas Bonfons would print the latter in 1600, and *Lazarillo* in 1601; in Milan, Juan Baptista Bidelo brought both novels out in 1615, and so on.[22]

Yet—the story is not finished—*Lazarillo* was not reprinted between 1603 and 1607. This surprising pause may be attributed to the sudden advent of three competitors: the two sequels to *Guzmán de Alfarache* (the spurious continuation by Mateo Luján de Sayavedra in 1602, and Alemán's own *Segunda parte* in 1604); and, above all, the publication of *Don Quixote* in 1605. The success of Miguel de Cervantes' entry in the publishing race was so irresistible that *Guzmán de Alfarache,* the best seller, would not reappear until 1615, in Milan. If what most of these bibliographical data seem to indicate is the rise of a new genre, then an important consequence of this rise was the emergence of a diametrically opposed masterpiece, which itself was able to serve as seed for a "countergenre." Surely the facts of the case are unequivocal. On the editorial and literary levels, Cervantes' seminal novel was an inspired response to the challenge of the newborn picaresque genre.

II

These "negative" impacts or *influences à rebours,* through which a norm is dialectically surpassed (and assimilated) by another, or a genre by a countergenre, constitute one of the main ways in which a literary model acts upon a writer. Yet this is an aspect of genre theory we tend to overlook. Since the early nineteenth century and the breakdown of normative systems of poetics, the subject has become more and more a province of historical scholarship. Thus one neglects the equally historical fact that the life of poetic norms and models has involved above all the poets, the dramatists, and the storytellers themselves.

With this fact in mind, I have tried to discuss in another essay ("On the Uses of Literary Genre") three perspectives or distinctions of some relevance not only to theorists or critics but to writers and readers as well. Briefly, these distinctions can be reduced to three questions: Is the norm under consideration a model that could have affected the writer (exerted an influence upon the work in progress), or is it a critic's "afterthought" and an a posteriori category (though liable as time passes to become an a priori model)? Is it an explicit norm and an accepted part of the authoritative systems of the day, or does it belong to the "unwritten poetics" of the period? Has it come into being by means of a process of definition on the part of critics and theorists, or as a result of the *decisions* of writers, readers, and audiences?

Let us now return to our practical example. We have just seen that the parallel publication and success between 1599 and 1605 of two Spanish novels created the appropriate circumstances for the emergence of a new model and for its immediate impact on an incipient countergenre: *Don Quixote* (1605) and its successors. Curious though I am about those exact "circumstances," there is little I can add, unfortunately, to the bibliographical-historical data presented in the first section of this essay. I propose the following comments less as evidence for a real sequence of events than as illustrations of a theoretical approach toward the subject.

Our best clue, I think, is fictional—for we find it in *Don Quixote.* The problem at hand, after all, is literary; and it even has to do with fiction. It might be argued that no evidence could be truer than that of one of Cervantes' own characters (since he himself played the main role), or more likely to illuminate what actually took place in the minds of the "real" readers of *Lazarillo* and *Guzmán.* But it would complicate matters unduly to introduce here one of the main topics of *Don Quixote* itself.

In the chapter following the adventure of Mambrino's helmet, Don Quixote meets a chain of galley slaves on the road, engages them in conversation, and undertakes finally to liberate them (Part I, Chap. 22). Not the least articulate of the galley slaves is the famous Ginés de Pasamonte, otherwise known as Ginesillo de Parapilla:

> "Señor comisario," dijo entonces el galeote, "váyase poco a poco, y no andemos ahora a deslindar nombres y sobrenombres: Ginés me llamo y no Ginesillo, y Pasamonte es mi alcurnia, y no Parapilla como voacé dice, y cada uno se dé una vuelta a la redonda, y no hará poco."
>
> "Hable con menos tono," replicó el comisario, "señor ladrón de más de la marca, si no quiere que le haga callar, mal que le pese."
>
> "Bien parece," respondió el galeote, "que va el hombre como Dios es servido; pero algún día sabrá alguno si me llamo Ginesillo de Parapilla o no."
>
> "¿Pues no te llaman así, embustero?", dijo la guarda.
>
> "Sí llaman," respondió Ginés; "mas yo haré que no me lo llamen, o me las pelaría donde yo digo entre mis dientes. Señor caballero, si tiene algo que darnos, dénoslo ya y vaya con Dios, que ya enfada con tanto

querer saber vidas ajenas; y si la mía quiere saber, sepa que soy Ginés de Pasamonte, cuya vida está escrita por estos pulgares."

"Dice verdad," dijo el comisario, "que él mismo ha escrito su historia, que no hay más que desear, y deja empeñado el libro en la cárcel en doscientos reales."

"Y le pienso quitar," dijo Ginés, "si quedara en doscientos ducados."

"¿Tan bueno es?", dijo Don Quijote.

"Es tan bueno," respondió Ginés, "que mal año para *Lazarillo de Tormes,* y para todos cuantos de aquel género se han escrito o escribieren: lo que le sé decir a voacé, es que trata verdades, y que son verdades tan lindas y tan donosas, que no puede haber mentiras que se le igualen."

"¿Y cómo se intitula el libro?", preguntó Don Quijote.

"*La vida de Ginés de Pasamonte,*" respondió el mismo.

"¿Y está acabado?", preguntó Don Quijote.

"¿Cómo puede estar acabado," respondió él, "si aun no está acabada mi vida? Lo que está escrito es desde mi nacimiento hasta el punto que esta última vez me han echado en galeras."

("Señor Commissary," spoke up the prisoner at this point, "go easy there and let us not be so free with names and surnames. My just name is Ginés and not Ginesillo; and Pasamonte, not Parapilla as you make it out to be, is my family name. Let each one mind his own affairs and he will have his hands full."

"Speak a little more respectfully, you big thief, you," said the commissary, "unless you want me to make you be quiet in a way you won't like."

"Man goes as God pleases, that is plain to be seen," replied the galley slave, "but someday someone will know whether my name is Ginesillo de Parapilla or not."

"But, you liar, isn't that what they call you?"

"Yes," said Ginés, "they do call me that; but I'll put a stop to it, or else I'll skin their you-know-what. And you, sir, if you have anything to give us, give it and may God go with you, for I am tired of all this prying into other people's lives. If you want to know anything about my life, know that I am Ginés de Pasamonte whose life story has been written down by these fingers that you see here."

"He speaks the truth," said the commissary, "for he has himself written his story, as big as you please, and has left the book in the prison, having pawned it for two hundred reales."

"And I mean to redeem it," said Ginés, "even if it costs me two hundred ducats."

"Is it as good as that?" inquired Don Quixote.

"It is so good," replied Ginés, "that it will cast into the shade *Lazarillo de Tormes* and all others of that sort that have been or will be written. What I would tell you is that it deals with facts, and facts are so interesting and amusing that no lies could equal them."

"And what is the title of the book?" asked Don Quixote.

"*The Life of Ginés de Pasamonte.*"

"Is it finished?"

"How could it be finished," said Ginés, "when my life is not finished as yet? What I have written thus far is an account of what happened to me from the time I was born up to the last time that they sent me to the galleys.")[23]

If is of course impossible to know exactly what Ginés de Pasamonte means when he boastfully talks of a "género" of which *Lazarillo* is the prototype. We may notice, however, that the existence of such a genre was a matter of experience for him. Where theorists are inclined to "define," writers are rather more likely to "decide": Ginés de Pasamonte the writer (and Cervantes with him) is strongly determined not only to equal but to surpass *Lazarillo* and its successors ("It is so good . . . that it will cast into the shade *Lazarillo de Tormes* and all others of that sort"). In fact, the nature of his decision—that a group of works exists with which he proposes to compete— seems immeasurably less vague and more pertinent than the nature of the group itself ("all others of that sort that have been or will be written"). In this context, a genre is above all a challenge to the writer's will, and in that sense an inspiration or an influence. Ginés does not refer to it by means of any technical or cultured term (such as "especie," since "género" was usually reserved for the genus of imitation),[24] but with ordinary words ("all others of that *sort,*" Putnam correctly translates). One witnesses here the spontaneous discovery of a class by a reader-critic belonging to the most vast of audiences. This vastness is what Cervantes, in his perspectivistic, illusion-creating, and problem-producing fashion, is able to stress and even exaggerate through the fiction of Ginés de Pasamonte.

It is difficult to ascertain today whether it was feasible for a real thief or a real galley slave to identify, as Ginés does, with the fictional galley slave Guzmán de Alfarache and to begin writing a book comparable to the real Mateo Alemán's. As I noted earlier, a large literate audience in seventeenth-century Spain could not have coincided with the lower class, and those who identified with the *pícaro* must have been mostly members of the discontented middle classes. But on a fictional level, and especially in *Don Quixote,* where the hero imitates the romances of chivalry and where literature becomes not a separate art but the environment and condition of living, the fact that a certain character feels that the picaresque existence is very near his own appears credible and almost reasonable. In this case the "realistic" narrative genre based on *Lazarillo* is doubly worthy of imitation—by Ginés de Pasamonte in his fictional life as a thief and also by Ginés the writer, who is fictional too, but whose *Vida* is moreover a narrative within a narrative. Ginés de Pasamonte may be viewed as a Don Quixote who not only experiences (without losing his mind) but writes down his life (a life which, as Don Quixote finds out early in Part II, another wrote for him): hence the amusement Cervantes obviously derives from the dialogue between the two novel-imitators, which may justify his having cast here Don Quixote as the straight man. Between the man and the writer, besides, one finds the reader or the critic, who is called upon to determine the existence of the literary genre to be imitated. Ginés, as a reader neither cultured nor ignorant, as a layman (or *ingenio lego*), combines a bold ability to recognize novelty with the generic mentality of his time, that is, with an immoderate fondness for classification, be it within or without the pale of traditional poetics.

I might add that Cervantes presents here the operations of "unwritten" poetics. One can say that Ginés de Pasamonte, like many Spanish readers after 1599, of whom he could be considered a fictional symbol (both by ourselves and by Cervantes) establishes a category a posteriori (i.e., a category which did not exist when *Lazarillo* was written) when he speaks of a newly born genre ("todos cuantos de aquel género se han escrito"); while mentioning at the same time a class of books in the process of becoming an a priori model, to be imitated by others in the future ("todos cuantos . . . se . . . escribieren": "will be written"). From *Gil Blas* to *Felix Krull*, the evidence proves abundantly the correctness of Cervantes' guess, or rather of Ginés de Pasamonte's.

For the two are of course distinct, as the same dialogue makes clear. A dialogue in Cervantes is a joining of critical perspectives, and it would be impossible for him to embrace fully either the technical simplicity of Don Quixote, as far as the narrator's craft is concerned, or Ginés de Pasamonte's allegiance to the picaresque form. It is Ginés, not the real author, who imitates *Lazarillo* and *Guzmán de Alfarache*. For it must be realized that although this passage refers explicitly to the former, it tacitly alludes to the latter. Mateo Alemán's hero, at the end of the very long last part of *Guzmán de Alfarache* (1604), writes his autobiography while serving a sentence in the king's galleys, as Alemán had announced he would in one of the preliminaries to the first part (1599). "He himself writes his life in the galleys," Alemán had said, who went on to explain that this is quite proper, and not incompatible with the expression of moral doctrine:

> "El mismo escribe su vida desde las galeras, donde queda forzado al remo, por delitos que cometió, habiendo sido ladrón famosísimo, como largamente lo verás en la segunda parte. Y no es impropiedad ni fuera de propósito, si en esta primera escribiere alguna dotrina; que antes parece muy llegado a razón darla un hombre de claro entendimiento, ayudado de letras y castigado del tiempo, aprovéchandose del ocioso de la galera. Pues aun vemos a muchos ignorantes justiciados, que habiendo de ocuparlo en sola su salvación, divertirse della por estudiar un sermoncito para en la escalera."[25]

(He himself writes his life in a galley, where he has been forced to row as a consequence of the delinquent acts he had committed, having been a very famous thief, as the Second Part will copiously show you. And it is not improper nor untimely that he should write down matters of moral doctrine in the First Part; it seems quite reasonable, rather, for a man to do so who has a clear intelligence, some education and many years' experience, while taking advantage of his idle hours in the galley. We even know of ignorant men brought to justice who, instead of devoting those last idle hours to the salvation of their soul, spend their time studying a little sermon for use on the staircase to the gallows.)

Thus the adventures of Ginés de Pasamonte resemble Guzmán's much more than they do Lazarillo's, at least in their literal dénouement. On another plane, however, the differences are quite substantial. At the end of Part II Guzmán undergoes a sudden religious conversion, though not so profound a one as to prevent him from recounting his former existence with considerable sympathy for the rogue and the swindler he once was. Doubtless Cervantes does not miss an opportunity to remember ironically Mateo Alemán, that great and crucial opponent who is alluded to not only in *Don Quixote* but in several of the *Exemplary Novels*.[26] It may be that one of these ironies points to the questionble authenticity of Guzmán de Alfarache's religious conversion, since Ginés de Pasamonte appears to associate himself with Guzmán without the slightest intention of ceasing to be the genuine rogue and swindler that he is. A second allusion is quite explicit, and has to do with the narrative uses of the first- and third-person forms of the verb. Joaquín Casalduero is one of the few critics who has observed that Cervantes is stressing in this passage the pseudoautobiographical aspect of the picaresque genre,[27] while suggesting a basic polarity between this aspect and the techniques of the "countergenre" for which *Don Quixote* stands. With his well-known ambiguity, Cervantes both praises and ridicules *Lazarillo, Guzmán,* "and all others of that sort that have been or will be written."

The dialectics of genre and countergenre are essential to the understanding of a particular axiological structure. In the context of the dialogue between Don Quixote and Ginés de Pasamonte, *género* means essentially "fictional autobiography"—as implicitly opposed to the third-person narrative or "fictional history." (This is a polarity, I need not stress, that will dominate the poetics of the novel, from Alemán-Cervantes to Defoe-Fielding, *Werther*-Scott or Balzac, etc.) As such, *La vida de Ginés de Pasamonte* is supposed to exhibit indubitable virtues as well as defects. On the one hand, its title, like those of *Lazarillo* and *Guzmán* (*La vida de Lazarillo de Tormes, y de sus fortunas y adversidades* and *Primera parte de la vida del pícaro Guzmán de Alfarache*), begins with the words "La vida de." The novelist's task, to paraphrase Ginés, does indeed consist in prying into other people's *lives*. His purpose cannot be grasped by means of any pre-Renaissance emphasis on "character." For the novel presents, recounts, unfolds not characters but lives—even as Ginés refuses to identify himself independently from the *vida* that he has written down. (Hence the wonderfully loose and apparently inconsequential exchange concerning his name and surname: Ginés merely wishes to be as responsible for his name as he is for his identity as presented in *La vida de Ginés de Pasamonte*.) To this end, i.e., the presentation of *a* life, the autobiography or pseudoautobiography is most effective: it reproduces the original chronology of events ("from the time I was born up to the last time that they sent me to the galleys") and gives the impression of being truthful or true to life—in Ginés' words, "que trata verdades" ("that it deals with facts"). The use of the first-person form of the verb adapts itself singularly well to the concealment of all thematic deceptions and lies ("mentiras"). Since *Lazarillo,* the most eminent example of this is the picaresque genre, whose roguish hero need not respect the truth of other people's lives as a storyteller, any more than he does their property in everyday practice.

Should Ginés (if this is his name) the writer be more honest than Ginés the thief? The reader is led to ask himself this question, and to interpret in his own way the facts: *La vida de Ginés de Pasamonte* is presented by its author, with the commissary's consent, as a truthful autobiography. Nevertheless, Cervantes stresses most explicitly the problem of narrative structure. A dramatic or epic character possesses, to be sure, some sort of identity; but how does one shape a "life"? The supposed proximity to "life" of the autobiographer is exacted at a very high cost: that of formlessness—and perhaps, as a consequence, of meaninglessness. Any life that is narrated by its own subject must remain incomplete and fail to achieve artistic unity or, very simply, the status of art.

Narrative form demands a "second" or "third" person expressing a consciousness that is extrinsic to the sequence of events. Only such a consciousness can make possible the writing, in Aristotelian terms, of either "poetry" or "history." The saturation of the picaresque with the narrator's individual and willfully limited point of view is most remote from history. And it is one of the ironies of Cervantes that *Don Quixote,* as told by the Arabic chronicler Cide Hamete Benengeli, apparently emulates the structural and presentational virtues of history. It seems to me, to a large extent, that it actually *does*; and that this is an irony one cannot afford to take too lightly. The novel as it emerges in the sixteenth century, after the great Florentine historians and the chroniclers of the conquest of America, owes much to this crucial *rapprochement* between literature and history—to the organization and detailed recreation and tolerant understanding of the concrete wealth of experience by a "third" person. Cervantes, at any rate, penetrated deeply into these polarities. He quickly saw and judged that the most daring and characteristic feature of the picaresque story was its pseudoautobiographical nature, while his own work as a whole would prove that he had chosen to reject the techniques which Ginés de Pasamonte had so enthusiastically embraced.

The acceptance of a genre is normally an extended process, embracing several stages. The elevation of a single book or of a series of books to the rank of a formal model is secured above all by the readers (or by the writers and critics before they write, i.e., as readers). In our case, we may regard Ginés de Pasamonte as the representative or the fictional symbol of this reading public. Yet still another symbol would be needed for an earlier stage in the acceptance of the picaresque, that is to say, for the intermediaries who brought the novels to a particular audience: the printers. Toward the beginning of the sixteenth century, printers fulfilled all three of the functions that would subsequently be divided into a number of different specialties or professions: the selection, the printing, and the sale of books. In other words, they were editors and booksellers as well. Later in the sixteenth century, as I showed with regard to the editions of *Lazarillo* and *Guzmán,* printers would begin to delegate the actual sale of books to special dealers. But they did not relinquish as yet the crucial editorial or selective role. As Robert Escarpit stresses in his *Sociologie de la littérature,* "les premiers imprimeurs sont déjà des éditeurs-accoucheurs. Leurs choix ont un caractère créateur. Ainsi c'est à Caxton, qui les a imprimés parmi les premiers, que Chaucer, Gower, Lydgate, Malory, etc., auteurs déjà anciens, doivent une résurrection à la vie littéraire que leur maintien en manuscrit leur eût probablement interdite."[28]

In the Spanish context of my subject, the representative of this creative function could be Luis Sánchez, who was responsible not only for the resurrection of *Lazarillo* in 1599 but for its association in Madrid with *Guzmán*—a pairing that was imitated immediately in Barcelona, Zaragoza, Paris, and elsewhere[29]—thus grouping physically the two masterpieces and promoting the rise of a model. Unfortunately, we do not know enough about him. His father, Francisco Sánchez, had run a modest printing shop in Madrid during the second half of the sixteenth century. Luis, who inherited the shop, distinguished himself by publishing a number of very fine works. According to Pérez Pastor, he was said to employ the best craftsmen available: "tuvo en su imprenta los mejores oficiales en aquella época."[30] Luis Sánchez, moreover, was an educated person. We know that he composed Latin poems as preliminaries for some of the books he printed.[31] We may suppose that he possessed a measure of humanistic learning and an effective interest—whether critical or commercial—in the newer trends in writing. It was, at any rate, men like Ginés de Pasamonte and Luis Sánchez who made possible the birth of a genre.

Notes

1. This chapter is a translation (and a development) of "Luis Sánchez, Ginés de Pasamonte y los inventores del género picaresco," in *Homenaje al Prof. Rodríguez-Moñino* (Madrid, 1966), I, 221-231.

2. Robert Escarpit, *The Book Revolution* (London and Paris, 1966), p. 19.

3. Cf. J. Denucé, *Inventaire des Affaitadi, banquiers italiens à Anvers, 1568* (Antwerp, 1934); R. Doehaerd, *Etudes anversoises. Documents sur le commerce international à Anvers de 1488 à 1514,* 3 vols. (Paris, 1963); J. Finot, *Etudes historiques sur les relations commerciales entre la Flandre et l'Espagne*

au Moyen Age (Paris, 1899); J. A. Goris, *Etude sur les colonies marchandes méridionales à Anvers* (Louvain, 1925); V. Vazquez de Prada, *Lettres marchandes d'Anvers,* 4 vols. (Paris, 1960); R. Carande, *Carlos V y sus banqueros* (Madrid, 1943), vol. 1.

4. Quoted by Robert Escarpit, *Sociologie de la littérature* (Paris, 1966), p. 61.

5. Cf. A. Rumeau, "Notes au 'Lazarillo.' Des éditions d'Anvers, 1554-1555, à celles de Milan, 1587-1615," *Bulletin Hispanique,* LXVI (1964), 272-293.

6. These data are in E. Macaya Lahmann, *Bibliografía del Lazarillo de Tormes* (San José, Costa Rica, 1935). All bibliographical facts mentioned without a special footnote are to be found here.

7. Quoted by Rumeau, "Notes au 'Lazarillo,'" p. 274.

8. *Ibid.,* p. 284.

9. Cf. "Les anciennes traductions françaises du 'Lazarillo de Tormes' (1560-1700)," in *Hommage à Ernest Martinenche* (Paris, 1936), p. 148.

10. Cf. Rumeau, "Notes au 'Lazarillo,'" pp. 285-287; Laplane, "Les anciennes traductions," p. 149, note 10; *The Pleasant History of Lazarillo de Tormes,* ed. J.E.V. Crofts (Oxford, 1924), p. viii.

11. Suffice it to mention the names of Juan de Lucena, Juan Maldonado, Gil Vicente, Torres Naharro, Diego Sánchez de Badajoz, Cristóbal de Castillejo as links within "una tradición ininterrumpida de sátira anticlerical y antimonástica cuyo más celebre representante en España es el Arcipreste de Hita," in the words of Marcel Bataillon, *Erasmo y España* (Mexico, 1950), I, 251.

12. *Le roman picaresque,* ed. Marcel Bataillon (Paris, 1931), p. 5.

13. *The Florentine Painters of the Renaissance* (New York, 1909), p. 20.

14. John Livingston Lowes, *Convention and Revolt in Poetry* (Boston and New York, 1919), p. 48.

15. Mateo Alemán, *Guzmán de Alfarache,* ed. S. Gili Gaya (Madrid, 1953), III, 59. See R. Foulché-Delbosc, "Bibliographie de Mateo Alemán. 1598-1615," *Revue Hispanique,* XLII (1918), 481-556. Foulché-Delbosc did not see an edition in-4° of *Guzmán,* similar to the *princeps,* published by Várez de Castro in Madrid in 1600 (there is a copy in the Biblioteca Nacional in Madrid); nor a reprint by Sebastián de Cormellas in Barcelona, 1599, where one reads at the bottom of the title page not "A costa de Angelo Tabano," but "Véndense en la mesma Emprenta" (Biblioteca Menéndez y Pelayo, Santander); nor another by Juan Mommarté, Brussels, 1600, with a title page that is slightly different from the one in the Biblioteca Nacional or that in the British Museum. Counting these editions, then, in addition to those Foulché-Delbosc saw, I obtain a total of twenty-five editions (of the *Primera parte* alone) previous to 1605.

16. This *editio princeps* can be found in a number of libraries: the Biblioteca Nacional both in Madrid and Lisbon, the British Museum, Widener Library (Harvard University), the Hispanic Society (New York), and elsewhere.

17. Cf. Lahmann, *Bibliografía,* p. 64.

18. I have seen the copy in the Biblioteca Nacional in Madrid.

19. It has the same *aprobación* as the edition by Cormellas (copy in the Hispanic Society).

20. The Zaragoza edition has *aprobaciones* by Licenciado Mateo de Canseco (June 21, 1599) and by the Asesor Galván (June 22) (Biblioteca Nacional, Madrid; Wiener Hofsbibliothek).

21. Cf. Lahmann, *Bibliografía,* pp. 67-68. I owe the data concerning the edition by Cormellas (Hispanic Society) to the courtesy of Professor Homero Serís. Valdivielso's Zaragoza edition is in the Bibliothèque Nationale in Paris.

22. Cf. Lahmann, *Bibliografía,* pp. 69, 74.

23. I quote from the translation by Samuel Putnam (New York, 1949), I, 172-173.

24. Cf. above, p. 117.

25. *Guzmán de Alfarache,* ed. Gili Gaya, I, 36, "Declaración para el entendimiento deste libro."

26. As far as *Don Quixote* and *La ilustre fregona* are concerned, this is a problem that demands detailed study. I will limit myself here to a critical conjecture and a biographical fact: it seems that many of the literary-structural ironies and censures formulated in *El coloquio de los perros* (regarding the abuse of sermons and moral discourse, the tendency to digress, the lack of form, the wordiness, the fact that if the dogs in the story turn out to be *pícaros,* the *pícaros* themselves, *mutatis mutandis,* should be regarded as dogs, or rather, as mere "cynics") have *Guzmán de Alfarache* as their object. Secondly, it is suggestive that when Mateo Alemán emigrated to America in 1608, never to return to his native country, he read during the crossing and brought to Mexico with him a copy of the recently published first part of *Don Quixote*—which was confiscated upon arrival by the Inquisition. Cf., on the latter, A. S. Bushee, "The 'Sucesos' of Mateo Alemán," *Revue Hispanique,* XXV (1911), 421-422, note 2.

27. Cf. Joaquín Casalduero, "Notas sobre 'La ilustre fregona,'" *Anales Cervantinos,* III (1953), 6; and *Sentido y forma del Quijote* (Madrid, 1949), p. 113.

28. *Sociologie de la littérature,* p. 60.

29. Cf. above, p. 145.

30. Cristóbal Pérez Pastor, *Bibliografía madrileña* (Madrid, 1891), I, xxix.

31. Cf. *ibid.,* I, nos. 465, 670.

Daniel Eisenberg (essay date 1976)

SOURCE: Eisenberg, Daniel. "Does the Picaresque Novel Exist?" *Kentucky Romance Quarterly* 26, no. 2 (1979): 203-19.

[*In the following essay, presented in 1976, Eisenberg argues that "picaresque" as a literary term is so general as to be meaningless and proposes doing away with the classification.*]

The concept of the picaresque novel and the definition of this "genre" is a problem concerning which there exists a considerable bibliography;[1] it is also the subject of a bitter personal debate.[2] According to Fernando Lázaro Carreter, the picaresque novel is "escurridiza" and something which "se resiste enérgicamente a ser definida."[3] Claudio Guillén entitled a paper "Toward a Definition of the Picaresque,"[4] implying that a definition is a goal which we can perhaps reach at some time in the future; a recent dissertation bears the ambitious title "Hacia una evaluación exacta de lo que se entiende por literatura picaresca."[5] Samuel Gili Gaya tells us even that the picaresque novel can not be "lógicamente definida."[6] I would like to examine in this paper just what sort of genre it is that is impossible to define, and will suggest that if the picaresque novel can not be defined, the term has no validity and should not be further used.

Before proceeding I should state my views on the subject of genres in general, since the concept of genre is also a particularly confusing one.[7] Some genres, I believe, are real in at least some sense, and even those critics opposed to them speak of them;[8] therefore, I am not opposed to genres in general, provided that the classifications they represent are valid and meaningful ones, and not merely "simples étiquettes commodes."[9] "L'esprit humain a besoin d'ordre," stated Pierre Kohler;[10] the desire to classify things is at the very least a basic theme of our Western civilization, going back to those creators of literary genres, the Greeks,[11] and may be universal. We find it useful to speak of "dogs," though no two dogs are identical, and of cars and houses, which are all different—without classifications, language as we know it, much less the study of literature, would be impossible.[12] But it is easy to create vague or deliberately misleading classifications, with people or things just as much as with literary works.[13] The validity of terms referring to nationalities ("Americans," "Spaniards"), the old debate about national character,[14] has never been definitely settled. Whether the inhabitants of a smaller political or geographical division have anything in common besides the accident of their location—that is, whether they can be validly and usefully classified—is even more open to question.

It is necessary to state also that, like Lázaro Carreter, I am limiting my comments to those works originally written in Spanish. As both A. A. Parker and W. M. Frohock pointed out independently in 1967,[15] the term "picaresque" is used by non-Hispanists in a very different way, so loosely that, according to Frohock, for every new novel there is at least one critic waiting to find something picaresque in it;[16] the recent novels called picaresque are almost without number.[17] An attempt to study simultaneously the works of the Spanish Golden Age customarily called picaresque and the more recent novels sometimes labeled with this term is to invite further confusion.[18] That these even more diverse modern works, which have in common only a journey in which the protagonist comes into contact with low society,[19] could themselves constitute a genre seems to me just as indefensible a position, but this is not our problem today, and my position regarding those who feel the *need*[20] of a term to refer to these modern "picaresque" works is *allá ellos*. Certainly the validity of the concept of the picaresque novel in Spanish literature must be determined first.

The problem has its origin in the undisputed fact that although some similarities between the *Lazarillo* and the *Guzmán de Alfarache* were noted,[21] neither the term nor the concept "novela picaresca" existed in the Spanish Golden Age. Covarrubias tells us what *libros de caballerías* and *romances* are; he disserts at some length on *comedia* and *tragedia*, but he says not a word about the picaresque novel. Nor do contemporary literary theorists have anything to say about it, since the attention they gave to the novel was directed toward the Byzantine novel and the prose epic;[22] the term "picaresque novel," like the word "genre" itself, was in fact not used before the last half of the nineteenth century.[23]

Yet genres existed before the word "genre"; they were just called by different names. (López Pinciano called them "diferencias" or "especies.") Very clear-cut and specific genres are a familiar part of Renaissance literary theory; as Rosalie Colie has pointed out, the Renaissance writers, following classical models, took their genres seriously. Can we say that the picaresque novel existed unrecognized in this genre-conscious period, before the term, before even the idea, was created?

Such genres have been called genres *a posteriori*,[24] genres whose definitions can not be obtained from the statements of the authors of the works, or their contemporaries. Although *a posteriori* genres, now very much in vogue, are less useful to the literary critic or historian than genres which existed in the minds of the authors of the component works of the genre, it is not my intention to question the validity of all of them; even Aristotle, whose statements were later taken as prescriptive, was writing *a posteriori*.[25] I would, however, point out that in the case of genres such as these there must be a clearly identifiable and well-defined body of works which belong to the genre for a usable definition to be obtained, and the more works used in drawing the definition, the more validity it will have.[26] Furthermore, the similarities between the works must be more than coincidental: there must be some relationship between them, as it would otherwise be possible to create many hypothetical non-genres composed of unrelated works with some accidental similarities.[27]

Critics discussing the nature of the picaresque do start with the assumption that there exists a body of picaresque works. A. A. Parker tells us that beginning in 1605 there were "quite a large number" of picaresque novels (*Literature and the Delinquent,* p. 6). Unfortunately he neglects to tell us what they were, and in his book only mentions a few: *Guzmán de Alfarache, La pícara Justina, La hija de Celestina, Marcos de Obregón, Alonso, mozo de muchos amos, El buscón,* and *Estebanillo González.*[28] Lázaro Carreter, on the other hand, complains of the poverty of the genre, which "no constituyó una moda extensa" and has only "dos docenas escasas de títulos posibles" ("Para una revisión," p. 42). If there are twenty-four "possible" titles, how many "certain" titles are there? Which works can we all agree to be picaresque novels, from them to draw our definition?

The logical starting place in a search for picaresque novels is the influential collection of Valbuena Prat, which bears the unequivocal title of *La novela picaresca española;*[29] it is surely this set which Lázaro Carreter had in mind with his figure of two dozen possible works,[30] as it in fact contains twenty-three.[31] Of these, one, the life of Torres Villarroel, can surely be excluded, inasmuch as it is not a novel at all but the true autobiography of a professor of the University of Salamanca;[32] although Torres had read Quevedo and to a degree attempted to imitate him in his autobiography, he was not even born until long after the other works in the collection were written.[33] No one any longer defends its status as a picaresque novel; most writers on the topic, such as del Monte, scarcely mention it.[34]

Looking at Valbuena Prat's introductory material, we find that he himself questions his own selection of works. *El diablo cojuelo,* he tells us, "pertenece . . . a un género satíricosocial, más bien que picaresco" (II, 693); it, then, can not help us define the picaresque novel, and one wonders for what reasons it was included. Francisco Santos's *Periquillo el de las gallineras* has, according to Valbuena Prat, a curious quality: we find in it "un ambiente y técnica de picaresca sin pícaros" (II, 959), and it is "más una sombra de picaresca que una obra tal" (II, 961). Professor Parker concurs in excluding *Periquillo* from the list of picaresque works; it "is not, properly speaking, a picaresque novel because it has a saintly hero" (*Literature and the Delinquent,* p. 167).

Vicente Espinel's *Marcos de Obregón,* Valbuena Prat further tells us, is a "novela más de aventuras que picaresca" (I, 72), and in his *Historia de la literatura española* he says it is "más libro de memorias que novela propiamente picaresca."[35] Jerónimo de Alcalá Yáñez's *Alonso, mozo de muchos amos* is compared by Valbuena Prat with literature "a lo divino," and he suggests that the author might have been imitating Fray Luis de León's *De los nombres de Cristo* (I, 80-81; *Historia,* III, 170), whose relation to the picaresque is hard to see.

Other critics and literary historians support Valbuena's own doubts about whether works in his *Novela picaresca española* are properly called picaresque novels. Roy Jones, for example, tells us that *Alonso, mozo de muchos amos*

"is not a picaresque novel, though often called one. Alonso is not a rogue, simply a harmless and garrulous man who has seen a good deal of life."[36] *Marcos de Obregón,* "though commonly called a picaresque novel . . . is the story of a respectable and prudent man" (p. 139). Samuel Gili Gaya, besides emphasizing the autobiographical and deemphasizing the picaresque nature of *Marcos de Obregón,*[37] states of another work in Valbuena's collection, Carlos García's *La desordenada codicia de los bienes ajenos*—a strange title indeed for a novel—that "más que novela propiamente dicha, es una exposición acerca de la antigüedad y características del oficio de ladrón" (p. xii). Alberto del Monte agrees that "tampoco pertenece al género picaresco . . . *Marcos de Obregón*" (p. 108), and that "es arbitraria la inclusión en el género picaresco de *El diablo cojuelo*" (p. 149), but he questions yet another of the works in Valbuena Prat's volume, the *Vida de don Gregorio Guadaña,* in which we find only "huellas de la tradición picaresca" (p. 150), and in which the protagonist "no tiene un talento picaresco" (p. 151).

We could continue in this fashion, pointing out how one or another scholar questions the classification as "picaresque" of one or another of these twenty-three possible titles collected by Valbuena Prat. It is obvious, however, that in contrast with other genres, such as the epic, we have only a very limited number of works, agreed to be picaresque, from which to draw our inductive definition. These remaining works, moreover, have as many differences as similarities, for some, like the *Lazarillo,* are short, and others are extremely long, some, like the *Guzmán de Alfarache,* are serious, whereas others are frivolous, some are literarily sophisticated and still others are ingenuous. Under such circumstances, the choice of works from which to draw the definition of the picaresque becomes even more critical, for the inclusion or exclusion of a single work—as Parker has pointed out in the case of the *Lazarillo*—produces a quite different definition. One scholar has even stated that the definition of the picaresque depends on our interpretation of a single work (the *Buscón*),[38] but such a definition would surely have little validity for the other works making up the picaresque "genre."

This leads us to our first conclusion: since there is no body of similar works agreed to be picaresque novels, it is impossible to define this genre inductively; a large body of works would produce a very vague definition, and a more specific one could only be supported by an extremely limited number of works.

There is, in fact, only *one* work which all agree to be picaresque novel, Part I of the *Guzmán de Alfarache,* for Francisco Rico would exclude Part II of the *Guzmán,*[39] Parker,[40] and others before him,[41] the *Lazarillo,* and Edmond Cros would study only the *Guzmán,* excluding all others.[42] This is for a reason which is logical, consistent, and dramatically simple: the work contains a *pícaro.* Mateo Alemán used the word in the work, and the *Guzmán* was to contemporaries the *Libro del pícaro.*[43] Since the book is a novel, what better reason could there be for calling it a picaresque novel?

Yet no critic is willing to accept the consequences of defining the picaresque novel on the basis of the term *pícaro*, and most ignore the meaning the word had in Golden Age Spain,[44] even to the extreme of saying that *pícaros* are unnecessary to a picaresque novel.[45] For if one uses the *pícaro* as a means to identify and classify picaresque novels, how could one help but agree that *La pícara Justina* is one of the novels most worthy of being called picaresque? It is the only novel to use the word in the title; more clearly than any other, it imitates the *Guzmán,* the protagonist of which, whom she will eventually marry, is addressed by Justina in a prologue. In the well-known engraving which serves as frontispiece to the book,[46] used by some to demonstrate the existence of a picaresque genre, Justina rides in the "nave de la vida pícara," together with Guzmán and "la madre Celestina,"[47] while Lázaro, as if confirming Parker's thesis, goes in a rowboat which is separate from, though linked to, the picaresque ship.

No one, save Marcel Bataillon,[48] has devoted much attention to *La pícara Justina*; most treat the work as if it were merely an obstacle which makes a discussion of the picaresque more difficult, as, from their perspective, it surely does.[49] The work is in many ways different from the *Guzmán*: it is humorous, while the *Guzmán* is serious; Justina enjoys life and is cruel to others; the moralizing of the work, to which less attention is given than to the "muestrario de versos," is so superficial as to be obviously parodical. Rather than explaining an "estado de deshonor," which some have thought a characteristic of the picaresque,[50] the work moves toward an "estado de honor." Yet does this mean that *La pícara Justina* is not picaresque?[51]

Another example from a more prestigious author is even more clear-cut. Cervantes discusses the *pícaro* at greatest length in the opening pages of *La ilustre fregona.* Carriazo, one of the protagonists, was "llevado de una inclinación picaresca" and "sin forzarle a ello algún tratamiento que sus padres le hiziesen, sólo por su gusto y antojo, se desgarró, como dicen los muchachos, de casa de sus padres, y se fue por ese mundo adelante, tan contento de la vida libre, que en la mitad de las incomodidades y miserias que trae consigo, no echaba menos la abundancia de la casa de su padre, ni el andar a pie le cansaba, ni el frío le ofendía, ni el calor le enfadaba: para él todos los tiempos del año le eran dulce y templada primavera; también [tan bien] dormía en parvas como en colchones; con tanto gusto se soterraba en un pajar de un mesón como si se acostara entre dos sábanas de Holanda. Finalmente, él salió tan bien con el asumpto de pícaro, que pudiera leer cátedra en la facultad al famoso de Alfarache." Carriazo was a *pícaro*, although he was "virtuoso, limpio, bien criado y más que medianamente discreto." Carriazo "pasó por todos los grados de pícaro, hasta que se graduó de maestro."[52]

Here we have a character who is labeled by the author as a *pícaro*—as Lazarillo, of course, is not, as Pablos de Segovia is not, as in fact most of the characters in Valbuena Prat's collection are not. Yet, again, critics are reluctant to accept *La ilustre fregona* as a picaresque novel, dismissing it almost casually.[53] Carriazo does not suffer from hunger, he has known parents, who do not mistreat him, and he is a much more admirable figure than either Lázaro or Guzmán. The characteristics of the *Guzmán,* the autobiographical structure, the serving of a series of masters, the presentation of the world as cruel, all absent from *La ilustre fregona,* are seen more clearly in the *Coloquio de los perros,*[54] and to a lesser degree in *Rinconete y Cortadillo.* Yet to say that these works are picaresque, and that *La ilustre fregona* is not, is to ignore what *pícaro* and *picaresco* meant to Cervantes, and to assign to these words arbitrary new meanings of our own. This is just what Parker and Frohock criticized others for doing.

We arrive, then, at our second conclusion: although one valid approach to the definition of the picaresque novel is by means of the definition of the word "*pícaro*" in the seventeenth century, an attempt along these lines would be doomed to failure because the word is today used so loosely.

Scholars are, of course, aware of the difficulty of defining the picaresque by the means outlined above; the problem of a definition is one of the standard topics which is discussed repeatedly. Their response to this dilemma takes one of two forms, the first of which is to minimize the problem by attacking the concept of genre, or to suggest, as do Wicks and Guillén, that the picaresque must be defined in a different fashion. "Genres, as everyone knows [?], do not really exist," is the first sentence of Stuart Miller's *Picaresque Novel*; "un género . . . no puede definirse," roundly states Lázaro Carreter ("Glosas críticas," p. 469). The latter scholar has in fact gone a step further, and suggested that the picaresque novel was a genre with no fixed characteristics, but one in which the author chose which characteristics he wished to incorporate in his work ("Para una revisión," pp. 28-30).

These suggestions are circular ones, however, and I know of no other example of a genre, above all, one allegedly centuries old, without fixed characteristics nor in which traditional forms of definition (from contemporary literary documents or, failing that, by induction) are inadequate. To argue that the picaresque novel can not be defined in the ordinary way is to admit that it does not exist in the ordinary sense. Although there are works which are tangential or which share only isolated characteristics of other genres, even with the most controversial ones, such as tragedy, there is a larger "core" of works around which such tangential works group themselves.

The second response to the impossibility of a definition by traditional means is a positivistic suggestion that the picaresque should be defined in terms of one of its constituent elements: thus Parker's emphasis on the subject matter ("an examination of delinquency"), the attention given by Pfandl[55] and others to the social ideas and outlook of the authors, and the traditional emphasis on structure (the autobiographical narration, the service to many masters, and so on), now reaffirmed by Lázaro Carreter, Stuart Miller, and Wicks. The fallacy of this approach is that it is another version of the inductive method, even if not acknowledged as such. *Some* of the works called picaresque offer an examination of delinquency, and thus Parker suggests basing his definition on this feature. *Some* use one or another of the structural features enumerated by the various writers on the topic. But not *all* of them do either, and to exclude a work, such as *La ilustre fregona,* when drawing the definition, and then to justify the exclusion because the work does not share all of the characteristics of the remaining works, is also circular reasoning.

I wish I could offer a new definition of the picaresque novel, one that would be consistent, logical, and acceptable to all. Unfortunately, I can not do this, and if the debate about the definition of the picaresque seems likely to continue forever, it is precisely because it is impossible to ever arrive at a satisfactory one. A term which can mean anything, which is more than just "impreciso," as Parker called it, is scarcely an aid to communication. Should we not follow Edmond Cros's suggestion,[56] and abandon its use?

If we were dealing with a closely knit body of works with many features in common, and if the Spanish picaresque novel did become, in Guillén's term, an *a priori* genre, it would be imprudent to discard a label for these works. We do not have this, of course. When we have mentioned the influence of the *Guzmán* on López de Úbeda, a few *Novelas ejemplares,* the *Guitón Honofre,* and the *Buscón,* all written, by best guesses, within a very short time period,[57] and the influence of *Lazarillo* on Mateo Alemán and on the author of *Estebanillo González,* we have virtually exhausted the influence of the authors of Golden Age picaresque novels, most written at irregular intervals over a century or more,[58] on each other.

By saying this I am not taking the position of Croce, who, reacting against rigid nineteenth-century concepts of genre, insisted that all works of art are unique, and must be so studied.[59] I do think that the works called picaresque have something in common, a description of low society or lower-class life. But I would like to suggest that this feature is incidental to the works rather than a meaningful common element, a "semejanza" rather than a "diferencia significativa," in Parker's terms.[60] Likewise, I would also suggest that it is a distortion of the Golden Age literary scene and of some of the individual authors to take these works out of their context, for no other reason, in many cases, than their supposed realism, falsely concluded from the lower-class subject matter, and to give them such disproportionate attention as the picaresque has recently received. The error of seeing Spanish Golden Age literature in terms of its so-called realistic works was pointed out by Amado Alonso in 1929, a position also taken by Dámaso Alonso and Américo Castro shortly thereafter.[61] The *Guzmán* was surely a popular work, though no doubt more for its moral tone and didactic qualities than for its

"realistic" descriptions of Spanish life or its contributions to the development of the novel.[62] *Lazarillo* had a certain popularity, ambiguous enough for this point in itself to be a cause of debate,[63] since it was most known as the bowdlerized *Lázaro castigado*[64] and published together with other works; certainly it would have been less important to a contemporary reader than the *Araucana,* or Lope's *Arcadia,* or any one of a long series of more widely accepted and more influential books. The other titles collected by Valbuena Prat, and I include the *Buscón,* were works which disappeared from the Spanish literary scene shortly after their publication, with a small number of reprints, or none at all. Vicente Espinel was known for his poetry, not *Marcos de Obregón*; "El amante liberal" was held in higher esteem than "Rinconete y Cortadillo" or the "Coloquio de los perros";[65] Quevedo would surely be disappointed if he knew that he is remembered today for the *Buscón* and to a much lesser extent the *Sueños,* and that his philosophical and social works are read only by a handful of specialists.[66]

My final conclusion, then, is that we should not refer to the Spanish novels discussed in this paper by the term "picaresque," which has no exact meaning and which suggests close relationships between the works which in many cases do not exist. If we would cease to do so, we could better study each of the works for what it is, and see more accurately the contribution each makes to Spanish literature. I am not so naïve to think that this modest proposal will gain widespread approval, since the term "picaresque novel" is so widely used, but I do ask that those who continue to use the term specify which works they mean to refer to, and that they consider it in the same way that Croce considered all terms for genres, as a convenient modern label, one which would have been unfamiliar and perhaps unacceptable to the Golden Age authors in question.

Notes

1. Criticism prior to 1966 is competently reviewed by Joseph Ricapito in his dissertation, "Toward a Definition of the Picaresque. A Study of the Evolution of the Genre together with a Critical and Annotated Bibliography of *La vida de Lazarillo de Tormes, Vida de Guzmán de Alfarache,* and *Vida del Buscón,*" Diss. UCLA, 1966 (abstract in *DA,* 27 [1967], 2542A-43A); this dissertation will be published in a revised and updated version by Castalia. Meanwhile, the most important of the very substantial bibliography since that date, which has reopened the question of the definition of the picaresque, is: W. M. Frohock, "The Idea of the Picaresque," *YCGL,* 16 (1967), 43-52, and also his "The Failing Center: Recent Fiction and the Picaresque Tradition," *Novel,* 3 (1969), 62-69, and "Picaresque and Modern Literature: A Conversation with W. M. Frohock," *Genre,* 3 (1970), 187-97, Stuart Miller, *The Picaresque Novel* (Cleveland: Case Western Reserve, 1967; originally entitled, as Miller's dissertation at Yale, "A Genre Definition of the Picaresque"), on which see Harry

Sieber's comments in "Some Recent Books on the Picaresque," *MLN,* 84 (1969), 318-30, and the review by Hugh A. Harter, *Novel,* 3 (1969), 85-86, Edmond Cros, "De Lazarillo a Guzmán: Ensayo de definición del pícaro," in *Mateo Alemán: Introducción a su vida y a su obra* (Salamanca: Anaya, 1971), pp. 171-83, A. A. Parker, *Literature and the Delinquent* (Edinburgh: Edinburgh University Press, 1967), and the important introduction of Parker to the Spanish translation of his book, *Los pícaros en la literatura* (Madrid: Gredos, 1971), Ulrich Wicks, "The Nature of Picaresque Narrative: A Modal Approach," *PMLA,* 89 (1974), 240-49, and earlier his "Picaro, Picaresque: The Picaresque in Literary Scholarship," *Genre,* 5 (1972), 153-92, and his "Picaresque Bibliography" on pp. 193-216 of the same number; see also the items cited in the following notes. I would like to thank Donald McGrady for sending me a copy of his unpublished paper, "The Spanish Picaresque Novel from *Lazarillo* to Quevedo's *El Buscón,*" read before a MLA Seminar on "A Reevaluation of the Structure of the Picaresque," December 29, 1975, and Ulrich Wicks for a copy of his "The Romance of the Picaresque," also read at the Twenty-Ninth Annual Kentucky Foreign Language Conference.

A useful summary of attempts to define the picaresque, although unfortunately not employing Ricapito's dissertation, may be found in Chapter I, "Hacia un concepto de la novela picaresca," of the dissertation of Javier Sánchez-Díez, "La novela picaresca de protagonista femenina en España durante el Siglo XVII," Diss. North Carolina, 1972; abstract in *DAI,* 34 (1973), 286A.

2. Fernando Lázaro Carreter, "Glosas críticas a *Los pícaros en la literatura* de Alexander A. Parker," *HR,* 41 (1973), 469-97; Parker, "Sobre las *glosas críticas* de Fernando Lázaro Carreter," *HR,* 42 (1974), 235-39; Lázaro Carreter, "Contrarréplica," *HR,* 42 (1974), 239-41.

3. "Para una revisión del concepto 'novela picaresca,'" p. 27 of the original publication, which I use, in the *Actas del Tercer Congreso Internacional de Hispanistas* (Mexico: El Colegio de México, 1970). This paper was reprinted in Lazarillo de Tormes *en la picaresca* (Esplugues de Llobregat: Ariel, 1972), and is reviewed in laudatory fashion by Gonzalo Sobejano, "El *Coloquio de los perros* en la picaresca y otros apuntes," *HR,* 43 (1975), 33-35, who calls it "indispensable" and "'la' solución."

4. First published in the *Proceedings of the IIId Congress of the International Comparative Literature Association* (The Hague, 1962), pp. 252-66; reprinted in Guillén's *Literature as System* (Princeton: Princeton University Press, 1971), pp. 71-106. The book of Guillén is reviewed, together with those of Miller and Parker, by Maximillian E. Novak, "Liberty, Libertinism and Randomness: Form and Content in Pi-caresque Fiction," *Studies in the Novel,* 4 (1972), 75-85, reprinted with more documentation in *Racism in the Eighteenth Century,* ed. Harold E. Pagliaro (Cleveland and London: Case Western Reserve, 1973), 35-48. Guillén's book is more perceptively treated by Ciriaco Morón-Arroyo, "System, Influence and Perspective: Three Words in Search of a Definition," *Diacritics,* 3, No. 1 (Spring, 1973), 9-18.

5. This dissertation is by Antonio Burón, Minnesota, 1971, abstracted in *DAI,* 32 (1972), 6415A-16A.

6. *Diccionario de literatura,* 4th ed. (Madrid: Revista de Occidente, 1972), p. 709. For other writing of Gili Gaya on the picaresque, see the work cited below in n. 37.

7. For a discussion of modern discussions of genre, including a chapter on "The Genres of Genre Criticism," see Paul Hernadi, *Beyond Genre: New Directions in Literary Criticism* (Ithaca and London: Cornell University Press, 1972), who includes a bibliography. A briefer but valuable discussion of genre is found in René Wellek and Austin Warren's *Theory of Literature,* 3rd ed. (New York: Harcourt, Brace & World, 1956), pp. 226-37, and Margaret Newels's *Die dramatischen Gattungen in den Poetiken des Siglo de Oro* (Wiesbaden: Steiner, 1959; Spanish translation, London: Tamesis, 1974) is useful for background. Quite outdated is Wolfgang Kayser's *Interpretación y análisis de la obra literaria,* trans. María D. Mouton and V. García Yebra, "cuarta edición [no] revisada" (Madrid: Gredos, 1961); Wolfram Krömer, in his learned "Gattung und Wort *novela* im spanischen 17. Jahrhundert," *RF,* 81 (1969), 381-434, is concerned with the characteristics and evolution of the *novela* in the Italian sense of the word, particularly with reference to Cervantes's *Novelas ejemplares.*

8. Elias Schwartz, "The Problem of Literary Genres," *Criticism,* 13 (1971), 113-30.

9. Paul Van Tieghem, "La Question des genres littéraires," *Helicon,* 1 (1938), 99. In the short-lived *Helicon,* now reprinted by Brill, were published the acts of the IIIe Congrès International d'Histoire Littéraire (Lyon, 1939), which was devoted exclusively to a study of literary genres; the papers are stimulating even when not directly relevant to the present problem.

10. "Contribution à une philosophie des genres," *Helicon,* 1 (1938), 234.

11. Van Tieghem, p. 96; see also M. Gustave Cohen, "L'Origine médiévale des genres littéraires modernes," *Helicon,* 2 (n.d., but 1940), 129-33, and, particularly germaine to our study, Rosalie L. Colie, *The Resources of Kind. Genre-Theory in the Renaissance,* ed. Barbara K. Lewalski (Berkeley, Los Angeles, London: University of California Press, 1973).

12. This point was previously made by Alan Rodway, "Generic Criticism: The Approach through Type, Mode and Kind," in *Contemporary Criticism* (New York: St. Martin's, 1971), p. 89.

13. As an example of questionable literary classifications, responding perhaps to some need to create groupings, we have only to cite the controversial Spanish literary generations, that of 1898, whose members, Ricardo Gullón has said orally, had nothing more in common than their agreement that Benavente should not have received the Nobel prize, and that of 1936; surely another generation will soon be found between 1939 and the present. See Ricardo Gullón, *La invención del 98 y otros ensayos* (Madrid: Gredos, 1968), and *Spanish Writers of 1936,* ed. Jaime Ferrán and Daniel P. Testa (London: Tamesis, 1973). On the general problem see René Wellek, "Periods and Movements in Literary History," *English Institute Annual, 1940* (New York: Columbia University Press, 1941), 73-93, and Guillén, "Second Thoughts on Literary Periods," in *Literature as System,* pp. 420-69.

14. Itself relevant to literary studies; see Peter Brooks, "Romania and the Widening Gyre," *PMLA,* 87 (1972), 7-11. A similar point with regard to the study of "Spanish" literature, at least in the medieval period, was made by Keith Whinnom, *Spanish Literary Historiography: Three Forms of Distortion* (Exeter: University of Exeter, 1967). Nicholas Round's "The Myth of National Character and the Character of National Myth," *EMU* [Glasgow], No. 4 (1974), 7-22, which deals specifically with Spain, deserves to be reprinted in a more accessible form.

15. Parker, *Literature and the Delinquent,* pp. vi, 2-4; Frohock, "Idea," *passim.*

16. "Failing Center," p. 64. Another example of how loosely the term is used, by a critic who will not accept even Frohock's mild restrictions, is found in the article of Donald B. Sands, "Reynard the Fox as *Pícaro* and *Reinarts Historie* as Picaresque," *Journal of Narrative Technique,* 1 (1971), 137-45. The term is now being applied to films as well; see Robert L. Fiore, "The Picaresque Tradition in *Midnight Cowboy,*" *Literature and Film Quarterly,* 3 (1975), 270-76.

17. Miller, p. 133. Those familiar with Miller's book and the critical reaction to it will not be surprised to learn that he has left academia entirely, to publish the presumptuous *Hot Springs; The True Adventures of the First New York Jewish Literary Intellectual in the Human Potential Movement* (New York: Viking, 1971).

18. Parker attempted in his book to do this (see *HR,* 42 [1974], 235-56), but his definition has not been widely accepted. The scholar who has most recently attacked this problem is Wicks, who, in his *PMLA* article cited in n. 1, tries to find a definition of "picaresque" which will fit all the ways it has been used. Although I respect Wicks, who, like Saint Thomas, concientiously labors to harmonize the old and the new, I question why the definition of the picaresque should be so stretched, and wonder if this is not reducing the concept to its lowest common denominator.

19. Walter Allen, *The English Novel,* cited by Parker, *Literature and the Delinquent,* p. 3.

20. Miller, p. 4.

21. Claudio Guillén has pointed out that the printer Luis Sánchez reprinted the *Lazarillo* almost simultaneously with his edition of Part I of the *Guzmán,* certainly implying that he saw a relationship between the two works ("Luis Sánchez, Ginés de Pasamonte y los inventores del género picaresco," *Homenaje a Rodríguez-Moñino* [Madrid: Castalia, 1966], I, 221-31, translated and revised as "Genre and Countergenre: The Discovery of the Picaresque," in *Literature as System,* pp. 135-58). I can not accept, however, Guillén's conclusion that the obscure Sánchez "invented" the picaresque genre. Does his association of the two works count for more than Alemán's deliberate imitation of some aspects of the *Lazarillo?* And what are we to make of the fact that Sánchez in 1603 reprinted the Lazarillo together with Gracián Dantisco's *Galateo español* rather than the *Guzmán* (in which association he was followed by Cristóbal Lasso of Medina del Campo and the Viuda de Alonso Martín, of Madrid)? There is nothing in Ginés de Pasamonte's ambiguous comment to substantiate the hypothesis that by "género," which did not mean "genre" in the modern sense, he envisioned the picaresque novel, nor even that by mentioning the *Lazarillo* he was referring to a fictional autobiography (*Literature as System,* p. 155). (Were Golden Age readers aware that the *Lazarillo* was fictional?) Ginés seems to imply that he has in mind a numerous body of works ("todos cuantos de aquel género"), not the lone *Lazarillo,* with the anonymous second part of 1555, unknown in Spain, and the *Guzmán.* And the life of Gerónimo de Pasamonte, apparently the real-life model for Cervantes's "Vida de Ginés de Pasamonte," has no obvious relationship with either (see Martín de Riquer, "El *Quijote* y los libros," *PSA,* 54 [1969], 5-24, and Olga Kattan, "Algunos paralelos entre Gerónimo de Pasamonte y Ginesillo en el *Quijote,*" *CHa,* No. 244 [1970], 190-206).

22. See L. G. Salingar, *"Don Quijote* as a Prose Epic," *FMLS,* 2 (1966), 41-68, Alban Forcione, *Cervantes, Aristotle, and the* Persiles (Princeton: Princeton University Press, 1970), reviewed by the present author in *NRFH,* 23 (1974, publ. 1975), 419-20, Sanford Shepard, *El Pinciano y las teorías literarias del Siglo de Oro,* 2nd ed. (Madrid: Gredos, 1970), and Tilbert Stegmann, *Cervantes' Musterroman* Persiles (Hamburg: Lüdke, 1971), reviewed by Forcione in *MLN,* 88 (1973), 434-44.

23. Francisco Rico, in *La novela picaresca y el punto de vista* (Barcelona: Seix Barral, 1973), p. 100, n. 17, says, without explanation, that the term was "elaborada en el siglo XVIII." It could scarcely antedate the use of the word *novela* in the modern sense; even Ticknor, in his *History of Spanish Literature*, 6th ed. (Boston: Houghton Mifflin, 1891), III, *95, has to struggle for a term ("tales in the *gusto picaresco*").

24. Guillén, *Literature*, p. 152.

25. I believe this to be generally known; nevertheless, see *Classical Literary Criticism*, ed. T. S. Dorsch (Harmondsworth: Penguin, 1965), p. 18.

26. See on this point the important article of Charles E. Whitmore, "The Validity of Literary Definitions," *PMLA*, 39 (1924), 722-36, especially pp. 729-730.

27. Whitmore, p. 730; Hernadi, pp. 2-4.

28. On p. 111 Parker mentions in passing "three Spanish works from the picaresque canon" published in France, *La desordenada codicia de los bienes ajenos,* Hernando de Luna's second part of *Lazarillo,* and the *Vida de don Gregorio Guadaña,* without, however, offering us any further discussion or comment on these members of the "picaresque canon."

29. I use the seventh edition, in two volumes (Madrid: Aguilar, 1974). As with other volumes in the same series (see *HR,* 43 [1975], 428), the influence of this publication has not always been for the best. It has served to limit the attention of writers on the picaresque to those novels included (for example, Joseph L. Laurenti, in his *Bibliografía de la literatura* [*not novela*] *picaresca, desde sus orígenes hasta el presente* [Metuchen, N. J.: Scarecrow, 1973], without any explanation simply limits himself to precisely those works included in Valbuena Prat's collection), and it has discouraged examination of other works not included, such as the *Lazarillo de Manzanares,* now edited by Giuseppe Sansone, Clásicos Castellanos 186-187 (Madrid: Espasa-Calpe, 1974), the *Guitón Honofre,* published for the first time by Hazel Genéreux Carrasco ([Chapel Hill]: Estudios de Hispanófila, 1973), and the verse *Vida del pícaro* and *Testamento del pícaro pobre,* which might well be published and studied together with the other works called picaresque. (Both Alberto del Monte, in his *Itinerario de la novela picaresca española,* trans. Enrique Sordo [Barcelona: Lumen, 1971], and Helmut Petriconi, "Zur Chronologie und Verbreitung des spanischen Schelmenromans," *Volkstum und Kultur der Romanen,* 1 [1928], 324-42, reprinted in *Pikarische Welt,* ed. Helmut Heidenreich [Darmstadt: Wissenschaftliche Buchgesellschaft, 1969], pp. 61-78, include references to many lesser-known works related in content with the "picaresque.")

30. In the introduction to the Spanish translation of his book, p. 18, Parker states that he too had understood that the "género picaresco" would include all the works collected by Valbuena Prat, except *Periquillo el de las gallineras,* the life of Torres Villarroel, "y, en parte, el *Lazarillo.*"

31. *Lazarillo,* the second part of Luna, four *Novelas ejemplares, Guzmán de Alfarache* and the continuation of Mateo Luján, *La pícara Justina, La hija de Celestina, Marcos de Obregón,* the *Buscón, La desordenada codicia de los biene ajenos,* the *Donado hablador* of Alcalá Yáñez, three novels of Castillo Solórzano, *El castigo de la miseria* of María de Zayas, *El diablo cojuelo,* the *Vida de don Gregorio Guadaña, Estebanillo González, Periquillo el de las gallineras,* and the life of Torres Villarroel.

32. The term "autobiography" is nearly as recent as "picaresque novel," for it is not documented before 1796 in German and 1809 in English, the latter instance by the English Hispanist Robert Southey (Georg Misch, *A History of Autobiography in Antiquity* [Cambridge: Harvard University Press, 1951], I, 5). The autobiography is thus another *a posteriori* genre, but one which is, to me, a more valid one. However much the artistic and creative elements in autobiography are emphasized by critics, however vague the line between truth and fiction, all autobiographies share an obvious common ground: the desire of the author to communicate something about himself to the reader.

Barrett John Mandel, in an essay not irrelevant to a discussion of genres, has pointed out how the autobiography has often been scorned (*Literature and the English Department* [Champaign: National Council of Teachers of English, 1970], p. 9). Early studies are few, those dealing with Spanish works even fewer. (The latest [Frankfurt: G. Schulte-Bulmke, 1962-76] edition of the German original of Misch's *Geschichte der Autobiographie* publishes for the first time a posthumous chapter on the relationship between autobiographie and the Spanish picaresque.) While the 70's have seen the publication of at least five major books on autobiography in English, in Spanish we have only two recent volumes on Torres Villarroel, Eugenio Suárez-Galbán's *La Vida de Torres Villarroel: Literatura antipicaresca, autobiografía burguesa* (Chapel Hill: Estudios de Hispanófila, 1975) and Russell Sebold's *Novela y autobiografía en la Vida de Torres Villarroel* (Barcelona: Ariel, 1975), in both of which the label of "picaresque novel" for Torres's *Vida* is firmly rejected, and a study of Randolph D. Pope, *La autobiografía española hasta Torres Villarroel* (Bern and Frankfurt: Lang, 1974), in which the life of Gerónimo de Pasamonte (see note 21) is discussed. I have not been able to see Beverly Sue Jacobs, "Life and Literature in Spain. Representative Autobiographic Narratives from the Middle Ages to 1633," Diss. NYU 1975, of which an abstract is published in *DAI,* 36 (1975), 2243A-44A.

33. "It is far too remote to form a part of the literary movement initiated by *Guzmán de Alfarache*"

(*Literature and the Delinquent*, p. 167). "Se la relaciona con la vieja y gloriosa tradición de nuestra picaresca, lo cual sólo es exacto por lo que se refiere a algunas partes" (Juan Antonio Tamayo, in the *Diccionario de literatura*).

34. "No creemos que se pueda hablar de picaresca a propósito de la autobiografía de Diego Torres Villarroel" (del Monte, pp. 159-60).

35. 8th ed. (Barcelona: Gili, 1968), II, 151.

36. *A Literary History of Spain. The Golden Age: Prose and Poetry* (London: Benn, and New York: Barnes and Noble, 1971), p. 139.

37. "Apogeo y desintegración de la novela picaresca," in *Historia general de las literaturas hispánicas,* III, rev. ed (Barcelona: Vergara, 1968), p. xi. (This section is printed between pages 104 and 105.)

38. "It turns out that how one understands the meaning of picaresque depends on how one reads the ending of the *Buscón*," affirms W. M. Frohock, "The *Buscón* and Current Criticism," in *Homenaje a William L. Fichter* (Madrid: Castalia, 1971), p. 223.

39. "Por sólo la segunda etapa de su carrera [Part II of the *Guzmán*] pienso que nadie lo hubiera llamado pícaro" (*La novela picaresca,* p. 105).

40. Although this [*Lazarillo*] is generally considered the prototype of the picaresque novel, it is better called the precursor" (*Literature and the Delinquent*, p. 6); "Lázaro is not a *pícaro* at all" (p. 4). Parker's position is oversimplified by Maximillian Novak in his review article when he states that "Given Parker's view, every work after *Guzmán de Alfarache,* with the possible exception of Grimmelshausen's *Simplicissmus* [sic] must appear as a decline" (*Racism,* p. 39). Parker in fact includes at least the *Buscón* within his definition of the picaresque.

41. Parker has been attacked, most vehemently by Lázaro Carreter ("Glosas críticas," pp. 470-72), for limiting the *Lazarillo* to the position of precursor, but besides the predecessors cited by Parker himself (p. 144, n. 13), the same point was made by Américo Castro in *El pensamiento de Cervantes* (p. 231 of the second edition [Barcelona: Noguer, 1972]), and in an article, "Perspectiva de la novela picaresca," (*RABM,* 12 [1935], 123-38, reprinted in *Hacia Cervantes*; see p. 127 of the 3rd edition [Madrid: Taurus, 1967]), which Parker knew (it is cited in his "The Psychology of the 'Pícaro' in *El Buscón," MLR,* 42 [1947], 58-69, an article still worth reading and one which clearly prefigures his book); Miguel Herrero García also made this point in his his "Nueva interpretación de la novela picaresca," *RFE,* 24 (1937), 343-62, as did Ricapito in his dissertation, already cited, p. 636. Howard Mancing, in "The Deceptiveness of *Lazarillo de Tormes," PMLA,* 90 (1975), 426, says that the differences between the *Lazarillo* and the subsequent Spanish prose works called picaresque are "a critical commonplace."

42. *Protée et le gueux* (Paris: Didier, 1967), p. 16.

43. Rico, *La novela picaresca,* p. 100. On some of the early editions (though not the first), the title page identifies the book as the *Libro del pícaro Guzmán de Alfarache.*

44. Discussed by Bernardo Sanvisenti, "Alcuna osservazioni sulla parola *pícaro," BH,* 18 (1916), 237-46. It is instructive to note how the meaning of *pícaro* as "chistoso, alegre, placentero y decidor," found in the *Diccionario de Autoridades,* is missing from the current (19th) Academy dictionary, in which the meaning (of "picaresco," at least), is explicitly based on the interpretation of unspecified literary works. See also Parker, *Literature and the Delinquent,* p. 144, n. 10, who only cites the meaning from the *Diccionario de Autoridades* which serves his argument.

45. Castro, *El pensamiento de Cervantes,* p. 234. This position was also taken by José F. Montesinos in his "Gracián o la picaresca pura," *Cruz y Raya,* No. 4 (1933), 37-63 (reprinted in Montesinos's *Ensayos y estudios de literatura española,* ed. Joseph H. Silverman [Madrid: Revista de Occidente, 1970], pp. 141-58); also see the quote from Valbuena Prat, *supra,* p. 205. If the novels they refer to have some common, linking feature other than the *pícaro,* the name they are called by should be based on that feature rather than on the *pícaro* they claim is irrelevant.

46. Parker reproduces it, facing p. xii of his *Literature and the Delinquent.*

47. The association in the frontispiece of *Celestina* with the picaresque (an association also made by Justina herself, in the poem which introduces Book III, Chapter IV, Section 3, and apparently by Luis Sánchez as well, since he reprinted not only the *Lazarillo* but also the *Celestina* shortly after the publication of the *Guzmán*), illustrates well how our modern conceptions of genre—the *Celestina* as drama, *Lazarillo* as novel—have led us to minimize relationships which contemporaries may have felt to be present. The picaresque as an answer to the romances of chivalry, now correctly attacked by Wicks (in his paper "The Romance of the Picaresque," cited in n. 1), has been a commonplace for over a hundred years, and is found in so many discussions of the picaresque that even to list them would be impossible, but its debt in subject matter and *Weltanschauung* to that body of works which make up the "celestinesque" (on which see now Pierre Heugas, *La Célestine et sa descendance directe* [Paris: Institut d'Études Ibériques et Ibéro-Americaines de l'Université de Bordeaux, 1973], and my review in *NRFH,* 25[1976], 410-12 has scarcely been examined. (For some structural influence of Rojas's work [only] on *Lazarillo,* see Dorothy Sherman Severin, *Memory in* La Celestina [London: Tamesis, 1970], pp. 67-69; also see *Hacia Cervantes,* pp. 122-23, and Stephen Gilman, "The Death of Lazarillo de Tormes," *PMLA,* 81 [1966], 155, n. 25.)

48. Bataillon's various articles on *La pícara Justina,* some relatively inaccessible, are collected in Spanish translation in his volume *Pícaros y picaresca* (Madrid: Taurus, 1969).

49. For example, Parker, *Literature and the Delinquent,* p. 46; Rico, *La novela picaresca,* pp. 118-20; Maurice Molho, *Introducción al pensamiento picaresco,* trans. Augusto Gálvez-Cañero y Redal (Salamanca: Anaya, 1972), pp. 121-23; del Monte, pp. 121-24.

50. This in particular is the thesis of Rico; see *La novela picaresca y el punto de vista,* p. 116, and his *La novela picaresca española,* I (Barcelona: Planeta, 1968), xlii-lv.

51. Anticipating a possible objection, it will not do to simply dismiss *La pícara Justina* as parody of the *Guzmán,* although there is a great deal of parody in *Justina.* An attitude related to that of Justina can be found in other works, such as *Estebanillo González,* "hombre de buen humor," who refers in his prologue to the *Lazarillo* and the *Guzmán,* or in Luna's continuation of the *Lazarillo,* quoted by Guillermo Díaz-Plaja, *Las lecciones amigas* (Barcelona: Edhasa, 1966), p. 127. See also Bataillon's "'La picaresca.' A propos de *La pícara Justina,*" in *Wort und Text. Festschrift für Fritz Schalk* (Frankfurt: Klostermann, 1963), pp. 233-50, reprinted in *Pícaros y picaresca,* pp. 175-99.

52. Quoted from Rodríguez Marín's Clásicos Castellanos edition, I (1915; rpt.: Madrid: Espasa-Calpe, 1969), 221-22, 224, checked against the facsimile.

53. "La nada picaresca novela de *La ilustre fregona,*" is how Marcel Bataillon describes it, "Relaciones literarias," in *Suma cervantina,* ed J. B. Avalle-Arce and Edward C. Riley (London: Tamesis, 1973), p. 230. "*La ilustre fregona* [no es] en ningún sentido una novela picaresca," says Carlos Blanco Aguinaga, "Cervantes y la picaresca," *NRFH,* 11 (1957), 338.

54. On the "picaresque" nature of the *Coloquio de los perros,* see the review article of Gonzalo Sobejano cited in note 3.

55. *Historia de la literatura nacional española en la edad de oro,* trans. Jorge Rubió Balaguer (Barcelona: Sucesores de Juan Gili, 1933), pp. 291-321, especially pp. 300-01.

56. See note 42.

57. Although there is no firm evidence, Lázaro Carreter and the Cavillacs agree on the early composition of the *Buscón*; see Michel and Cécile Cavillac, "A propos du *Buscón* et de *Guzmán de Alfarache,*" *BH,* 75 (1973), 114-31.

58. Thus the comment of Parker on the *Lazarillo* and the *Guzmán, Literature and the Delinquent,* pp. 23-24.

59. On Croce's ideas about genre, see Benito Brancaforte, *Benedetto Croce y su crítica de la literatura española,* trans. Juan Conde (Madrid: Gredos, 1972).

60. Introduction to the Spanish translation of *Literature and the Delinquent,* p. 15.

61. Amado Alonso, "Lo picaresco de la picaresca," *Verbum,* 22 (1929), 321-38; Dámaso Alonso, "Escila y Caribdis de la literatura española," *Cruz y Raya,* No. 7 (1933), 78-101, reprinted in *Ensayos sobre poesía española* (Madrid: Revista de Occidente, 1944), pp. 9-27, and *Estudios y ensayos gongorinos,* 3rd ed. (Madrid: Gredos, 1970), pp. 11-28; Américo Castro, "Perspectiva de la novela picaresca," *RABM,* 12 (1935), 123-38, reprinted in *Semblanzas y estudios españoles* (Princeton: Princeton University Press, 1956), pp. 73-92, and *Hacia Cervantes,* 3rd ed. (Madrid: Taurus, 1967), pp. 118-42; see p. 122 of the latter version. Critics have repeatedly attacked the widespread assumption that the works called picaresque are realistic. Dámaso Alonso in the article cited argues against the realism of the *Buscón,* and Blanco Aguinaga, in "Cervantes y la literatura picaresca," against that of the *Guzmán de Alfarache;* on the *Lazarillo* see Angel González Palencia, "Leyendo el *Lazarillo,*" in *Del* Lazarillo *a Quevedo* (Madrid: CSIC, 1946), pp. 3-39 (first published in *Escorial,* 15 [1944], 9-46), Stephen Gilman, "Death," p. 151, and Gregorio Marañón, in his preface to the Colección Austral edition of the *Lazarillo* (15th edition, Madrid: Espasa-Calpe, 1966; reprinted, though with the date of its composition erroneously given as 1958, in Volume I, pp. 1019-27 of his *Obras completas,* Madrid: Espasa-Calpe, 1968).

62. I thus disagree completely with the superficial comment of Novak, "his book was read for its roguish adventures and romantic novellas," in *Racism,* p. 40.

63. Rico, *La novela picaresca y el punto de vista,* pp. 95-100. I agree with the arguments expressed by Alberto Blecua in the introduction to his edition of the *Lazarillo* (Madrid: Castalia, 1972 [publ. 1974]), pp. 46-47. See also on this point, and on Lazarillo's alleged realism and the Spanish "preference" for the same, Cyril Jones, "*Lazarillo de Tormes*: Survival or Precursor" in *Litterae Hispanae et Lusitanae,* ed. Hans Flasche (Munich: Heuber, 1968), p. 187. I am fascinated by Jones's Unamunian observation that *Lazarillo* is not an innovative but rather a medieval work, whose publication was similar in purpose to that of the contemporary collections of *romances.*

64. Neither this version, the one reprinted by Luis Sánchez (see note 21), nor that of Juan de Luna has received a modern edition. From these two censored versions we can tell that at least some contemporary readers of the original saw only the most obvious religious criticism.

65. See Ruth El Saffar, *Novel to Romance. A Study of Cervantes's* Novelas ejemplares (Baltimore and London: Johns Hopkins, 1974), reviewed by the present author in *NRFH,* 23 (1974), 420-22, for information on the relative popularity and contempo-

rary opinion of the *Novelas ejemplares.* James Mabbe, the first English translator, chose to translate precisely those novels least read today: *Las dos doncellas, La señora Cornelia, El amante liberal, La fuerza de la sangre, La española inglesa,* and *El celoso extremeño.*

66. For a welcome look at some of them, see Henry Ettinghausen, *Francisco de Quevedo and the Neostoic Movement* (Oxford: Oxford University Press, 1972), which I review in *NRFH,* 25 (1976), 150-51.

Ulrich Wicks (essay date 1978)

SOURCE: Wicks, Ulrich. "The Romance of the Picaresque." *Genre* 11, no. 1 (1978): 29-44.

[*In the essay below, Wicks defends the notion of a picaresque tradition, while acknowledging the difficulty in defining the characteristics of the genre.*]

I

—Es tan bueno—respondió Ginés—, que mal año para *Lazarillo de Tormes* y para todos cuantos de aquel género se han escrito o escribieren.

—*Don Quijote* (Part I, Chapter 22)

The awareness of picaresque fiction as a genre begins almost simultaneously with the first (though not universally accepted) prototype, *Lazarillo de Tormes* (1554). In an essay called "Genre and Countergenre: The Discovery of the Picaresque," Claudio Guillén has shown that with the publication of the first part of Mateo Alemán's best-selling *Guzmán de Alfarache* in 1599, a "common *género picaresco*" came into being. The success of Alemán's book resurrected *Lazarillo de Tormes* which, after its initial popularity, had been reprinted only five times during the second half of the century. From 1599 to 1603 at least nine editions of *Lazarillo* were published. The direct link, therefore, is that *Guzmán* sparked "a double acceptance, a convergence, from which there arose, during the years immediately following the publication of *Guzmán* (1599), the idea of a *género picaresco.* . . ."[1] The words of the rogue Ginés de Pasamonte in the first part of *Don Quixote* (1605) echo and affirm this awareness:

"It's so good," replied Ginés, "that Lazarillo de Tormes will have to look out, and so will everything in that style that has ever been written or ever will be. One thing I can promise you, is that it is all the truth, and such well-written, entertaining truth that there is no fiction that can compare with it."

"And what is the title of the book?" asked Don Quixote.

"*The Life of Ginés de Pasamonte,*" replied that hero.

"Is it finished?" asked Don Quixote.

"How can it be finished," replied the other, "if my life isn't? What is written begins with my birth and goes down to the point when I was sent to the galleys this last time."[2]

There are two allusions here, one direct (to Lazarillo), the other indirect (to Guzmán de Alfarache, who writes while serving a prison sentence in the galleys). (In "La ilustre fregona," one of his *Novelas ejemplares* [1613], Cervantes mentions Guzmán as the model of picaros.) Whether Ginés' use of the word *género,* as Guillén points out, is to be read in the technical sense of "literary genre" is impossible to say. In his edition of *Don Quixote* (New York: Las Americas Publishing Company, 1958), Martín de Riquer does in fact annotate the word as referring to the picaresque genre (p. 208). But the point is that Ginés (and, of course, Cervantes) is aware of another book that is dynamically influencing a book in progress (and perhaps influencing the book that contains the book—as Guillén goes on to show).

In his anthology *La novela picaresca española* (Madrid: Aguilar, 1968), Angel Valbuena Prat uses as frontispiece a famous illustration from the first edition of *La pícara Justina* (1605) in which we see Lazarillo and the bull of Salamanca in a small boat which appears to be towing a larger one called *La nave de la vida picaresca* whose passengers include Guzmán, Justina, and Celestina. A. A. Parker in *Literature and the Delinquent* (Edinburgh: University Press, 1967) uses this illustration to prove that Lazarillo, being separated from the others, is not a full-fledged pícaro and the book *Lazarillo de Tormes is* really a precursor, not a prototype, of the picaresque genre. Whether we agree with that thesis or not, the point is, again, that the picture is yet another contemporary indication of awareness of the picaresque as a distinct kind of narrative—if not a literary genre in the formal sense.

Further proof of this awareness is provided in an essay by Helmut Petriconi, "Zur Chronologie und Verbreitung des spanischen Schelmenromans."[3] Petriconi chronologically lists thirty-seven works of fiction published between 1528 (*La lozana andaluza*) and 1680 (*Trabajo del vicio*) and in a parallel chronology he lists the editions of *Lazarillo de Tormes*—thirty-one between 1554 and 1664. This bibliographical evidence convinces him that there is indeed a thoroughly traceable development, which peaks around 1620. While we may dispute some of the works he includes in his picaresque list, the point is, yet again, that historical evidence proves the existence of a body of works which were seen as belonging to a class or genre.

But we need not stop with external evidence. If we glance at some representative works generally considered picaresque, we find internal evidence of such generic awareness. The influence—through imitation, borrowing, or modelling—of the structure and pattern of a group of other works on the writer in the act of writing is sufficient evidence of a rudimentary generic awareness at work. *Guzmán de Alfarache* moves to another work and becomes Justina's husband; Estebanillo González claims, in *Vida y hechos de Estebanillo Gonzélez, hombre de buen humor* (1646), to be writing a "true" story, not "la fingida de Guzmán de Alfarache, ni la fabulosa de Lazarillo de Tormes" (Valbuena Prat, p. 1721); Jonathan Wild's favorite book was *The Spanish Rogue* (that is, *Guzmán*); Head and Kirkman's *The English Rogue* (1655, 1668, 1671) is a deliberate imitation; Lesage shaped the Spanish tradition his own way in *Gil Blas* (1715, 1724, 1735); Smollett acknowledged (and translated) Lesage: in *The Adventures of Ferdinand Count Fathom* (1753) there are explicit references to *Guzmán,* to Petronius, and to *Gil Blas* (Part I, Chapter 1); Grimmelshausen's Courage in *Die Landstörtzerin Courasche* (1670) is writing "trutz Simplex" to spite the portrayal of herself in *Der abenteuerliche Simplicissimus* (1669), which was clearly influenced by *Guzmán* (through Albertinus' translation); in 1822 we have *Der deutsche Gil Blas,* so titled and introduced by Goethe; there is a *Russian Gil Blas* (by Vassily Narezhny) and A. A. Parker mentions *The Dutch Rogue, or Guzman of Amsterdam* (1683) and *Teague O'Divelly, or The Irish Rogue* (1690); Pito Pérez, in *La vida inútil de Pito Pérez* by José Ruben Romero (1938), sees himself as a Periquillo, alluding to *Periquillo el de las gallineras* (1688) by Francisco Santos and to *Vida y hechos de Periquillo Sarniento* (1816, 1830) by José Joaquín Fernández de Lizardi; Hans Schmetterling, the picaroclown in Kern's *Le Clown* (1957), meets Thomas Mann's Felix Krull in Paris ("He's nothing but a crook!") and Hans himself is referred to as "our Simplicissimus"; Günter Grass' Oskar in *The Tin Drum* (1959) has as ancestor the drummer Simplicissimus (II,4). And so on. While some of these are no doubt the work of hacks copying formulas—like the TV writers of our own day, who give us spin-offs of spin-offs—there is a literary genetics at work here from the sixteenth century to our own day, and, however crude the course of influence may be, the awareness of writing within—or even against—a specific kind of narrative fiction is internally traceable, especially outside Spanish fiction.

These examples provide us with both external and internal evidence that a picaresque tradition, a normative sense of genre, however rudimentary, did—and continues to—exist. Whether this sense of genre was ever codified into a conscious poetics, whether it ever became a regulative—even prescriptive—genre concept or remained "unwritten," is another question. But we know that picaresque fictions were generating, influencing, and parodying other picaresque fictions. Both writers and reader, therefore, experienced these works in the context of other similar works, with generic awareness, however informal or unformulated. And every new work in a genre redefines our concept of that genre as a whole. T. S. Eliot said in "Tradition and the Individual Talent" that what happens when a new work of art is created is something that happens simultaneously to all the works of art which preceded it. A specific work not only signals its generic identity to us, directly or indirectly, but it also reshapes our concept of that very genre.

We can be reasonably sure that there was a specific picaresque genre, identified with a specific literature and a specific set of socio-cultural conditions at a particular time in history (*siglo de oro* Spain). The essential characteristics of this genre have become the core of an ahistorical

concept of a narrative type we continue to call "picaresque"—a term which, as we know, is often used to describe contemporary works of fiction (and even films) that have no direct link with Spanish fiction of the sixteenth and seventeenth centuries, but have instead a formal, generic link. Such contemporary works as Ralph Ellison's *Invisible Man* (1952), J. P. Donleavy's *The Ginger Man* (1955), Günter Grass' *Die Blechtrommel* (1959) and Jerzy Kosinski's *The Painted Bird* (1965) belong—and are illuminated by the reader's awareness of their belonging—within a generic tradition that is still recognizably picaresque in the strict sense of the term. And some modern writers proclaim direct links with the picaresque fiction of the seventeenth century: John Hawkes, for example, who names Quevedo,[4] and Thomas Mann, who composed *Felix Krull* in the tradition of *Simplicissimus*.[5] W. M. Frohock would protest that such conscious imitation is "self-conscious and dependent upon an established tradition. *Felix Krull* and *The Adventures of Augie March* are, in this sense, learned works."[6] No literary work, however, is created in a vacuum, and Frohock seems to equate generic continuity with lack of creativity—a criterion which, ultimately, denies literary genetics altogether.

II

. . . the romance of roguery, in fact, rather evolved negatively from the notion of the anti-hero.

—F. W. Chandler, *Romances of Roguery* (1899)

There seems to be no problem in accepting the existence of a picaresque genre.[7] But when we try to define that genre, the concept itself becomes problematic, especially when we expand the term ahistorically to include works outside the specific Spanish tradition. In his chapter "Originality: The New Literary Genres," Otis H. Green is sure that the picaresque is a new genre and that it is still being cultivated: "[*Lazarillo de Tormes*] is the protopicaresque novel, and its fruitful entrance into the world of books created what might be called a subgenre, which is still cultivated." Moreover, "it was necessary to surpass the ancients: . . . to create the picaresque novel, inferior in category to *Don Quixote,* yet a vehicle used by writers of many nations, and to our own day, for a certain type of satirical social analysis. . . ."[8] But he is not very helpful in specifying which more modern works carry on the picaresque genre. In fact, an increasing bibliography of critical works on the picaresque leaves us confused; the accumulating approaches, instead of refining the genre concept, complicate it, as *Lazarillo* is included here and thrown out there, as the works to be included expand or contract geographically and temporally. I am not here going to concern myself with a comprehensive definition of the picaresque genre.[9] Rather, I would like to focus on a recurrent aspect of the definition process—specifically, the tendency to define the picaresque negatively, by telling us what it is not, by comparing it to its antitype. Though this—like all genre theory—involves a good deal of vicious circularity (to define something by its opposite you have to know what that something "is"), I think we can make a case for the approach that the picaresque novel is most clearly defined when compared to romance.

Gerald Brenan in *The Literature of the Spanish People* (Cleveland and New York: World Publishing Company, 1957) describes the imaginative fiction of the *Siglo de Oro* as consisting of "two quite distinct kinds—that which deals in an ideal way with high life and that which deals in a realistic way with low life" (p. 167). George Tyler Northup in *An Introduction to Spanish Literature* (3rd ed. rev. and enlarged by Nicholson B. Adams; Chicago: University of Chicago Press, 1960) calls picaresque fiction "a salutary reaction against the absurdities of the idealistic fiction of the time," and adds that it "constantly reacts against, and often parodies, the idealistic fiction of the time, as when the anti-hero's family-tree is elaborated to ridicule the heroic genealogies in the romances of chivalry" (pp. 171-73). In "La picardía original de la novela picaresca," *Obras completas,* 6th ed. (Madrid, 1963), Ortega y Gasset talks about a literature of the noble classes and a literature of the plebians; the theme of "love and fantasy" was developed in chivalric fiction, and the theme of resentment and criticism in the picaresque novel. Stuart Miller in *The Picaresque Novel* (Cleveland: The Press of Case Western Reserve University, 1967) compares the plot of picaresque with the plot of romance, concluding: "The pattern and meaning of the romance plot contrast absolutely with the episodic plot of the picaresque novel" (p. 12). Robert Scholes and Robert Kellogg in *The Nature of Narrative* (New York: Oxford University Press, 1966) trace the evolution of narrative forms from the time of the epic, after which narrative tends to dissolve into two antithetical types: the *empirical* and the *fictional*. Where the epic storyteller's allegiance had been to a *mythos* or traditional plot, the empirical type of narrative replaces this allegiance to tradition with allegiance to reality. Empirical narrative can be either *historical,* which owes its allegiance to truth of fact, or it can be *mimetic,* which owes its allegiance to truth of sensation and environment. The fictional type of narrative replaces allegiance to the *mythos* with allegiance to the ideal, and it can be either *romantic,* which is determined by an aesthetic impulse to portray an ideal world of beauty in which poetic justice prevails, or it can be *didactic,* which is ruled by an intellectual and moral impulse. Picaresque narrative, they say, "is the comic antitype of the romance. It approaches the mimetic, but for comic and satiric purposes mainly. It sets the contemporary world and a first-person narrator up against the never-never world and impalpable narrator of romance . . ." (p. 75). Elsewhere, in *Elements of Fiction* (New York: Oxford University Press, 1968), Scholes presents the six major plot patterns in narrative fiction, one of which is "the anti-romantic (picaresque) quest" (p. 13). André Jolles theorizes that fiction offers us vicarious escape by way of "play" into fictional worlds above, below, and outside the social norm—romance, picaresque, and pastoral, respectively; we become heroes, rogues, or shepherds by imaginatively removing ourselves from the pressures of the everyday through a special kind of *travesty*

(in the original meaning of "dressing up") that allows us to gain a therapeutic distance from them.[10] And A. A. Parker in *Literature and the Delinquent* says that "The first Spanish novels can indeed be considered, historically, as reactions against pastoral novels and novels of chivalry, but as alternatives not as satires." The picaresque novel arose "as a reaction to the romances—not as satire or parody, but as a deliberate alternative, a 'truthful' literature in response to the explicit demands of the Counter-Reformation" (pp. 19, 22).

And, finally (but actually first chronologically), Chandler, whose work on the subject is still the most comprehensive, says: ". . . the romance of roguery, in fact, rather evolved negatively from the notion of the anti-hero," but "the picaresque novels in Spain had little direct invective against the romances of shepherds and of chivalry." The title of his 1899 book, *Romances of Roguery: An Episode in the History of the Novel* (New York: Burt Franklin, 1961), seems to complicate the matter: did he mean these are romances in the way we would use the term today? The phrase "romances of roguery" appears at least some seventy times and seems to be interchangeable with "picaresque novel" (which appears about thirty times). Chandler indiscriminately uses terms such as "picaresque fiction," "picaresque narrative," "picaresque tale," "novel of rogues," and others synonymously with "romances of roguery," making no generic distinctions between *novel* and *romance*. Though *romance* as a term once could have embraced all prose fiction (retained in the French *roman* and the German *Roman*), by Chandler's time a sharp distinction had developed. In fact, from Homer's gates of ivory and horn (*Odyssey,* Book XIX) to Clara Reeve's famous distinction between *novel* and *romance* in *The Progress of Romance* (1785) to Hawthorne's oft-cited preface to *The House of the Seven Gables* (1851), there has all along been a genuine distinction between fictions portraying ideal worlds and fictions portraying real worlds (ignoring, for our purposes, the difficulty of the term "real"). The term *romance* is itself problematic in its historical evolution as a critical term. In an essay called "The Romance of Novel / Novella"[11] Edith Kern points out: "'Novel' has become the generic term for all long fictitious prose narratives. Even retroactively, it has usurped the place of 'romance,' which now designates only a particular kind of long narrative, although it was once applicable to all of them. 'Romance' has been supplanted by 'novel' to such an extent that modern critics unflinchingly speak of chivalric and picaresque 'novels' where earlier critics would have used the term 'romance.'" Not only is the term problematic in its changing historical meanings, it is problematic as a *concept* as well. (In Spanish literature, of course, *romance* refers to a specific kind of ballad in the fifteenth and sixteenth centuries, but that usage does not concern us here.) As with the picaresque, *romance* is in the process of being defined. In contemporary generic usage, *romance* designates a particular kind of fictional world-vision or -construct. "In literature," says Northrop Frye in *The Educated Imagination* (Bloomington: Indiana University Press, 1964), "we always seem to be looking either up or down. It's the vertical perspective that's important, not the horizontal one that looks out of life" (p. 97). And in *The Anatomy of Criticism* (Princeton: Princeton University Press, 1957) Frye writes: "The romance is the nearest of all literary forms to the wish-fulfillment dream . . ." and the "perenially child-like quality of romance is marked by its extra-ordinarily persistent nostalgia, its search for some kind of imaginative golden age in time or space." At its naivest, "it is an endless form in which a central character who never develops or ages goes through one adventure after another until the author himself collapses" (p. 186).[12]

Like picaresque, which is used historically to designate a special episode in the historical evolution of fictional forms and ahistorically to designate a universal kind of narrative, *romance* refers both to a specific group of medieval and Renaissance fictions and to a universal kind of fiction with certain characteristics. We should probably call the broader uses of each term *modes,* and the narrower, historical uses *genres.* Mode designates a fictional construct characterized by the qualities of the world it renders. A fiction in the romance *mode* (though not necessarily of the romance *genre*) would offer a word-world-construct in which harmony, integration, and perfection prevail: dream-like wish-fulfillment. The picaresque *mode* would offer a word-world-construct in which disharmony, disintegration, and chaos prevail: nightmarish anxiety. Thus both modally and generically, both qualitatively and historically, romance and picaresque are antitypes.

III

La Vida de Guzmán, mozo perdido,
por Mateo Alemán historiada,
es una voz del cielo al mundo dada
que dice: Huid ser lo que este ha sido.

. . .

El delicado estilo de su pluma
advierte en una vida picaresca
cual deba ser la honesta, justa y buena.

Este ficción es una breve summa,
que, aunque entretenimiento no parezca,
de morales consejos está llena.

—*Guzmán de Alfarache,* II (1604)

But are they? Having looked at some substantial evidence, we can arrange the pieces in such a way that this traditional antithesis convinces us as self-evident. Is the picaresque really the inverse or converse of romance?—that is the question I would like to pose. My declarative title would seem to suggest that I've answered the question. But it is premature to prove anything just yet; rather, I would like to speculate about some aspects of picaresque narrative that prove troublesome if we accept the traditional definitions. Apart from the superficial structural similarities between romance and picaresque (episodes, adventures, journeys, unifying character, etc.) and the sometime inclusion of a romance *within* picaresque (the story of Daraxa

and Ozmin, for example, in Part I, Book I, Chapter 8 of *Guzmán de Alfarache*), how do we integrate the following into our genre concept?

(1) What do we do with the "communities of roguery" that appear recurrently in picaresque? These brotherhoods of thieves, like the ones in Brecht's *Dreigroschenoper* and Fritz Lang's *M,* may serve as parody of the social order: but, paradoxically, these brotherhoods are much more ordered and structured than the social order which they both parody and undermine. We know that beggar books were a popular sub-genre,[13] but when these structures become part of picaresque proper, what do they mean? In Rome, Guzmán tells about a charter concerning "The Laws and Ordinances that are inviolably to be observed amongst Beggers" (Part I, Book III, Chapter 2), the general and superintendent of whom is called "the Prince of Roguerie, and the Arch-begger of Christendome." Pablos in Quevedo's *El Buscón* (1626) joins a group of beggars who are just as rigidly ordered (Book II, Chapter 6, Book III, Chapters 1-3). We find a similar organization in Cervantes' "Rinconete y Cortadillo." In García's *La desordenada codicia* (1619) there is an elaborate genealogy of thieves which, like the lineage of the romance hero, is an outrageous justification of thieves, as the romance hero's lineage justifies his prowess and goodness. García traces thievery and thieves back to Adam (whose sin thieves partake of) and to Lucifer, the first thief, who stole from God (Chapter 5). In *The English Rogue* Meriton Latroon refers to his "comrogues" and talks about a brotherhood of rogues in which an elaborate hierarchy exists (Part II, Chapter 15). In Fielding's *Jonathan Wild* (1743) Wild can chastize one of his thieves on a point of honor: "He [Wild] said he was sorry to see any of his gang guilty of a breach of honour; that without honour *priggery* [thievery] was at an end; that if a *prig* had but honor he [Wild] would overlook every vice in the world" (III, Chapter 6). In Ellison's *Invisible Man* the hero joins a Brotherhood which "was a world within a world," and which orders existence: "Life was all pattern and discipline . . ." (Chapter 17). And in *The Tin Drum* Oskar Matzerath becomes the leader of a group of pranksters called "The Dusters," for whom he serves as an embodiment of Jesus. As a final example, we might note the parody of a battle in *Simplicissimus* (II, Chapter 28), where Grimmelshausen's hero juxtaposes a real battle with his own version of war against the fleas that are attacking him; and the dream in which Simplex sees a tree (I, Chapter 15) on which everyone has his designated place in a hierarchy of oppression which is all too metaphorically true of the Thirty Years' War landscape Grimmelshausen's character must cope with. Are these orders anti-societies, or perverse romance structures of orders within a disordered world?

(2) What about the larger pattern of picaresque, which A. A. Parker, connecting picaresque with pastoral and mystical writings, calls "the circle of existence"? Guzmán inherits original sin from his father and must find his way back to God the Father through a delinquent life. Simplicissimus begins life in total innocence in an Edenic forest

and ends it, converted, alone, on a paradisiacal island. Along the way he experiences a romance—not just as a story, as Guzmán does, but as an absorbing, dynamic event: the Mummelsee, a paradise below the earth (Book V, Chapters 10-16). We can find this circle in modern picaresque too—for example, in *Invisible Man,* where the picaro is ejected from college, "this Eden" (Chapter 5). In fact, the "circle of existence" as Parker describes it has a lot in common with what Frye in *The Anatomy of Criticism* calls the "Genesis-apocalypse myth" in the Bible, in which "Adam is cast out of Eden, loses the river of life and the trees of life, and wanders in the labyrinth of human history until he is restored to his original state by the Messiah" (p. 191). This is one of the central myths of quest romance, which leads us to our third point.

(3) Is not the essential picaresque pattern a quest for "home"—home in the sense of material and social success (as in *Lazarillo*), or in the spiritual sense of union with God (as in *Guzmán* and *Simplicissimus*), or even in the mythic sense of a return to Paradise? Hesse's minor novel *Knulp* (1915) deals with such a cosmic homesickness, and Karl in Kafka's *Amerika* (1913) finds "The Nature Theater of Oklahoma." Oskar in *The Tin Drum* wants to get back to the umbilical cord. It might even be said that contemporary picaresque, especially, is a fictional exploration of man's exile from and search for "home."[14]

(4) Is not the strong didactic or moral and intellectual impulse of picaresque a romance characteristic? Guzmán creates a deliberate tension between the appeal of personal experience and sensation and the allegiance to an ideal of moral conduct in a world shaped by God, which is also true of Simplicissimus. Alemán and Grimmelshausen are, on the narrative level, writing essentially philosophical works, pointing out directly the illustrative quality of the represented life. Mimetic portrayal of ugly life and moralizing ideals of conduct provide a continuous dualism and tension which, in modal-generic terms, means romance vs. picaresque.[15] In an introductory sonnet to Part II of *Guzmán* we read (in Mabbe's version):

> Poor Guzman's life, the mapp of Vice and Sinne,
>   Story'ed by Aleman, is as a Voyce
> From Heav'en, shewing how thou shouldst make thy
>   choise.
>   The word, *Shunne thou to be what I have bin.*
> Who stands here as a Marke; that thou maist see
> Where his ship was drown'd; How the same was split,
> More through lacke of Wisedome, then want of Wit.
>   Which was the cause of all his Misery.
> The dainty style of this his pleasing quill
> By Guzmans roguish life, adviseth thee
> What an upright and honest life should be.
>   How this, doth leade to good; how that, to ill.
> How slight so e're this fiction seeme to be,
>   None, can be fuller, of Morality.

And Otis H. Green points out (in the chapter from *Spain and the Western Tradition* referred to earlier) that in "all the works of the period there remains intact the belief in an over-all harmony—Christian with Platonic over-

tones—in the ultimate goodness of God's universe, the ultimate justice of His will. The paths trod by mankind have a destination which is none other than the chief end of man as defined by Christian doctrine in all centuries" (IV, 283). This would seem to be as true of the picaresque as it is of romance and pastoral.

(5) Isn't the picaro's impulse to tell his story itself a yearning for order? Shaping one's *vida* in words satisfies the form-completion impulse to impose aesthetic and moral order on the chaotic past which is re-membered now as a structure. The re-membering "I" tries to balance the chaos of experience-as-lived with the moral order-now-contemplated. In *Simplicissimus and Guzmán* we are suspended between two modes—romance and picaresque; the picaro's role in the actual narrating process is thus a kind of double-exposure—superimposing the shaping artist over the objectified character in the chaotic past. To some extent, the picaro "cosmeticizes" himself, a word which comes from the Greek *kosmos,* which means an "order." Robert Jay Lifton, in "Protean Man," *Partisan Review,* 35 (1968), describes two contemporary behavioral patterns, one of which is "the mode of transformation"—the need to disrupt all things and make them constantly new; and the other is "the mode of restoration"—the yearning for a mythical past of perfect harmony. To illustrate this, he in fact uses two modern picaresques, *The Tin Drum* and *The Ginger Man.* In our terminology Lifton's modes of transformation and restoration could be picaresque and romance.

(6) If we consider the picaro as a literary version of the trickster archetype in myth, what then is his role in the total scheme of things? According to Kerenyi, "Disorder belongs to the totality of life, and the spirit of this disorder is the trickster. His function in an archaic society, or rather the function of his mythology, of the tales told about him, is to add disorder to order and so make a whole, to render possible, within the fixed bounds of what is permitted, an experience of what is not permitted." And, "Picaresque literature has consciously taken over this function."[16] Jung says the trickster myth was "supposed to have a therapeutic effect. It holds the earlier low intellectual and moral level before the eyes of the more highly developed individual, so that he shall not forget how things looked yesterday." At the end of the trickster myth, "the savior is hinted at."[17] This notion is not unlike that of Jolles, or that of Robert Heilman, who, in "Felix Krull: Variation on Picaresque," *The Sewanee Review,* 56 (1958), points out that one of the main traits of the picaro is his ability to find willing victims; the picaro thus gratifies certain desires of ours to *be* tricked. Though the picaro's function is chaotic and disordered, his effect is healthful and therapeutic—certainly an effect associated with romance order.

(7) Finally, how has the picaresque merged with other narrative forms in the evolution of narrative types? There are some fictions that synthesize picaresque and romance visions, as *Guzmán* and *Simplicissimus* really do. Eichendorff's *Aus dem Leben eines Taugenichts* (*Memoirs of a Good-*

for-Nothing, 1826) is a curious synthesis of the picaresque fragmented world of wandering existence and its deceiving appearances on the one hand, and the ordered, harmonized and divine world of romance on the other. Picaresque is both parodied and contrasted with romance, and romance is parodied and contrasted with picaresque. That the random world of chance and disorder should turn out to have been ordered by an elaborately designed plot is romance's mockery of picaresque. Smollett's *Roderick Random* (1748) and *Ferdinand, Count Fathom* begin as picaresques and end, with marvelous coincidences, as romances. The tendency of picaresque and romance modes to blend into the genre known as the *Bildungsroman* in late eighteenth- and early nineteenth-century German fiction is another example. In the *Bildungsroman* what at first appears to be a disconnected picaresque world slowly takes shape as an emerging world of order and moral goodness, in short, as a world of romance. The picaresque, even in its "purest" form, often has an eye on romance; and, conversely, the *Bildungsroman* has an eye on picaresque.[18] For Felix Krull and for Gulley Jimson in Cary's *The Horse's Mouth* (1944) art itself provides a romance vision to counteract a world that is in flux. And in *The Tin Drum* two Oskars are telling stories about Oskar's two selves in the past—a frenzied blend of Dionysian and Apollonian visions that gives us perhaps the best recent example of the mixing of the modes of romance and picaresque.

Well, let us end with questions and turn to some speculative conclusions. Perhaps the picaro has more to do with Amadis and other romance heroes than being their negative image or antitype. Perhaps the picaro is very much like the romance hero, the difference being one of degree, not type. Let us return to Ginés de Pasamonte. In freeing the galley slaves, Don Quixote acts according to a higher concept of justice than that which operates in the "real" world. He says, "It seems to me a hard case to make slaves out of those whom God and nature made free." Quixote's romance vision and Ginés' picaresque stance are in sharp contrast here—but they also implicate each other: the picaresque episode of the galley slaves takes place within a structure of romance perceived and projected by Don Quixote on to it. Significantly, Ginés reappears in Part II as Maese Pedro, who performs a puppet-show romance which Don Quixote demolishes, a reversal of roles from their earlier encounter (Chapters 24-26). If the story of Ginés de Pasamonte is a picaresque inside a novel that is also a romance, then perhaps we ought to look more closely at the romances within the picaresque.[19]

It is not enough to treat romance and picaresque as a sharp antithesis generically, and to define picaresque as the antitype of romance. The make-up of picaresque narrative is more complex than our definitions perhaps admit (though we do frequently admit that our *definitions* are inadequate). Romance visions of order are integrated into the picaresque vision in a way that makes the concept of antitypes false. For Guzmán and Simplicissimus, in fact, the narrative

vehicle is in tone, stance, and temporal vantage point distinctly romance-like. Though the romance and the picaresque may, superficially, be the inverse or converse of each other, their relationship, as I have tried to suggest, is such that one *implies* the other rather than absolutely opposes it. The very chaos and fragmentation rendered in the world-vision of the picaresque actually direct our eyes toward an alternative. In this sense, every picaresque is romantic; every explicit picaresque contains within it an implicit romance. Perhaps Chandler said a good deal more than he consciously intended to when he titled his seminal study *Romances of Roguery.* In any case, we need to look more closely at the romance-picaresque dichotomy as our critical acts continue to refine the generic concept of the picaresque. That generic impulse to structure and order these fictions of disorder is itself a romance desire.

Notes

1. In *Literature as System: Essays Toward the Theory of Literary History* (Princeton: Princeton University Press, 1971), pp. 135-58. This is a translation and development of "Luis Sánchez, Ginés de Pasamonte y los inventores del género picaresco," in *Homenaje a Prof. Rodríguez-Moñino* (Madrid, 1966), I, 221-31. Compare Harry Sieber's observation, built on Guillén's essay, that "the picaresque novel as a genre emerges, as Cervantes clearly perceived, out of the confluence of the *Lazarillo* and of the autobiography of a criminal [Guzmán]" and "It was the combined popularity and publication of the *Lazarillo* and the *Guzmán* which generated imitations, emulations and parodies of the new genre"; Harry Sieber, *The Picaresque* (London: Methuen, 1977), p. 24.

2. Trans. J. M. Cohen (Baltimore: Penguin Books, 1950), pp. 176-77.

3. In *Volkstum und Kultur der Romanen,* 1 (1928), 324-42; reprinted in Helmut Heidenreich, ed., *Pikarische Welt: Schriften zum europäischen Schelmenroman* (Darmstadt: Wissenschaftliche Buchgesellschaft, 1969), pp. 61-78.

4. See Robert Scholes, *The Fabulators* (New York: Oxford University Press, 1967), Ch. 4, "Fabulation and Picaresque," pp. 59-94. Hawkes' remarks appeared originally in *Wisconsin Studies in Contemporary Literature.*

5. *Nachlese, Prosa 1951-1955* (Berlin and Frankfurt, 1967), pp. 194-95.

6. "The Idea of the Picaresque," *Yearbook of Comparative and General Literature* (1967), 43-52.

7. I am grateful to Daniel Eisenberg for supplying me a copy of his paper, "Does the Picaresque Novel Exist?"—presented at a session on the picaresque novel at the 29th Kentucky Foreign Language Conference, The University of Kentucky, Lexington, April 22-24, 1976. Eisenberg, with very persuasive arguments and

documentation, points out how impossible it is to define the picaresque genre inductively; moreover, it is equally impossible to define the genre in terms of the meaning *picaresque* may have had in the seventeenth century because subsequent use of the term has been so broad, especially outside the framework of Spanish literature. Eisenberg's precise delineation of the seventeenth-century Spanish literary situation is convincing and I can't help but agree with him. I am not, however, persuaded by his solution to the problem: dropping the term altogether, or at least de-emphasizing it in favor of specific works themselves, or at the very least qualifying the term when we do have to use it. Whatever the pitfalls of genre theory, surely common sense tells us that there must be *something* useful in a term which has had such widespread currency; there must be something which books like *Lazarillo* and *Felix Krull* have in common, for which the concept "picaresque" has been serving. My inclination, whatever the inadequacies of the term as applied to the historical situation of Golden Age Spanish fiction may be, would be to continue the *a posteriori* process of definition. The term has simply gone too far, either to abandon it or to stop pursuing it.

8. *Spain and the Western Tradition: The Castilian Mind in Literature from El Cid to Calderón* (Madison, Milwaukee, and London: University of Wisconsin Press, 1966), IV, 214, 283.

9. I have made an attempt in "The Nature of Picaresque Narrative: A Modal Approach," *PMLA,* 89 (1974), 240-49.

10. "Die literarischen Travestien: Ritter—Hirt—Schelm," *Blätter für deutsche Philosophie,* 6 (1932/ 33) [originally a lecture delivered in Holland, 1931], reprinted in Heidenreich, *Pikarische Welt,* pp. 101-18.

11. In *The Disciplines of Criticism: Essays in Literary Theory, Interpretation, and History,* ed. Peter Demetz, Thomas Greene, and Lowry Nelson, Jr. (New Haven and London: Yale University Press, 1968), pp. 511-30.

12. See also his "The Archetypes of Literature" [originally in *The Kenyon Review,* 13 (1951)] in *Fables of Identity: Studies in Poetic Mythology* (New York: Harcourt, 1963), pp. 7-20. For a historical survey of romance see Gillian Beer, *The Romance* (London: Methuen, 1970). See also C. S. Lewis, "On Myth" and "The Meanings of 'Fantasy'" in *An Experiment in Criticism* (Cambridge: Cambridge University Press, 1961), Chapters 5 and 6 respectively. For an excellent treatment of the romance mode see Kathryn Hume, "Romance: A Perdurable Pattern," *College English,* 36 (1974), 129-46.

13. See Claudio Guillén, "The Anatomies of Roguery: A Comparative Study in the Origins and the Nature of Picaresque Literature," Diss., Harvard University, 1953; and Parker, *Literature and the Delinquent,* pp. 10-13.

14. I've tried to explore this aspect in "Onlyman," *Mosaic,* 8 (1975), 21-47.

15. The didactic dimension of picaresque was first emphasized by Miguel Herrero, "Nueva interpretación de la novela picaresca," *Revista de Filología Española,* 24 (1937), 343-62. See also Enrique Moreno Baéz, *Lección y sentido del Guzmán de Alfarache* (Madrid, 1948).

16. Karl Kerenyi, "The Trickster in Relation to Greek Mythology," in Paul Radin, *The Trickster: A Study in American Indian Mythology* (London: Routledge and Kegan Paul, 1956), p. 185.

17. C. G. Jung, "On the Psychology of the Trickster-Figure," trans. R. F. C. Hull, in *The Collected Works of C. G. Jung,* ed. Sir Herbert Reade, Michael Fordham, and Gerhard Adler (London: Routledge and Kegan Paul, 1959), IX, 255-72. Originally published for the appendix of Paul Radin's *The Trickster* (see note 16).

18. See Ralph Freedman's theory of the novel based on the picaresque: "The Possibility of a Theory of the Novel," in *The Disciplines of Criticism,* pp. 57-77.

19. The integration of romance and picaresque conventions shows up as early as 1555, in the sequel to *Lazarillo,* but it is more prominent in later, non-Spanish fictions. In *The Picaresque Hero in European Literature* (Madison: University of Wisconsin Press, 1977), Richard Bjornson sees this as a recurrent characteristic of picaresque works outside the Spanish tradition: "The ambiguity of bourgeois attitudes toward individualism and social mobility is even suggested by the fact that romance conventions and aristocratic assumptions reappear in picaresque novels which depict real-seeming heroes, situations, and geographical locations" (p. 17). Bjornson goes on to perceive romance patterns in such works as Charles Sorel's *Histoire comique de Francion* (1623, 1626, 1633) (pp. 151-53, 160-61), in *Simplicissimus* (p. 167), in Alain-René Lesage, especially in his *Histoire de Gil Blas de Santillane* (1715, 1724, 1735) (pp. 210-13, 226), in Defoe's *Moll Flanders* (p. 192), and in Smollett's *Roderick Random* (1748) (p. 230). Bjornson concludes that because the original Spanish picaresque works were read "according to French genius and taste, they themselves came to be regarded as comic novels in which typically picaresque panoramas of representative vices and follies were superimposed upon romance patterns and adventure-story plots. It was in this form that many of them were introduced to English and German audiences" (p. 161).

THE PICARO

Alexander Parker (essay date 1967)

SOURCE: Parker, Alexander. "Zenith and Nadir in Spain." In *Literature and the Delinquent: the Picaresque in Spain and Europe, 1599-1753*, pp. 53-74. New York: Greenwood Press, 1989.

[*In the following excerpt, Parker focuses on* Historia de la vida del buscón *and the development of the character Pablo.*]

The first conscious attempt to find a middle-way solution to the problem of presenting delinquency in polite literature led the *genre* in a new direction. The next novel to appear was *Marcos de Obregón* (1618)[1] by the poet and musician Vicente Espinel (1550-1624), who, after an adventurous and peripatetic youth, took orders and became choir-master of a Madrid church. His novel is to a considerable extent a genuine autobiography and it has proved possible to disentangle the fact from the fiction.[2] Espinel cast his memoirs in the form of fiction in order to make them more palatable, for his story links up with *Guzmán de Alfarache* in being the tale of a repentant sinner. He does not therefore eschew a moral purpose, but he is very conscious that he must steer a path between two extremes. Thus he writes in the Prologue:

> It was my aim to see whether I could succeed in writing in prose something that would be of profit to the commonwealth by giving both pleasure and instruction, following the precept of my master Horace; for some books have been published by men of great literary learning and reputation who cling so exclusively to doctrine that they have no opportunity for the mind to recover breath and feel some pleasure; and other books have appeared, so intent on giving pleasure by jests and farcical tales, that after being stirred and sifted are found to be so vain and futile, that nothing substantial or profitable is left for the reader, and no credit is won for their authors.[3]

These are the extremes of an exclusively religious literature on the one hand and such works as *Justina* and *La hija de Celestina* on the other. It is legitimate to think that he included *Guzmán* among the former, for it is certain that Espinel would not have thought it fulfilled his own aim, which was to tune the right note between the too tightly stretched string of doctrine and the too loosely stretched string of entertainment. He is therefore consciously aiming at something different from any picaresque novel published till then, and this he succeeded in producing; for *Marcos de Obregón* is more discreet and restrained than its predecessors: the harshness and dark colours of Alemán, the exuberant burlesque of Úbeda, the flippant sensationalism of Salas Barbadillo—all these disappear. This necessitates an alteration in the conventions. The work is much more an adventure story than a picaresque novel, and Marcos is not a picaroon or delinquent at all;

he is an observer of low life, of adventures that are neither crude nor cruel. This detached position of the protagonist is achieved by a device that, from the start, establishes the gentler tone.

In the case of *Guzmán* I emphasized the difficulty Alemán had in avoiding incongruity between the tone of his comments on life and the tone in which the misdeeds of his delinquent had to be narrated, this incongruity arising from the novelistic inadvisability of revealing at the beginning that the man who was writing his life-story was a reformed character. Espinel's technique is different: at the beginning we see Marcos as he is when he is writing his story, a wise but not pedantic old man, one who, without condoning wrong-doing, has a sympathetic understanding of human weakness. When he begins his life story, we retain this impression of him all through the adventures of his youth; he thus appears as a detached observer, because behind the narrating voice we sense the calm experience of an old man. We see, too, a protagonist who is usually able to right wrongs or to give picaroons a taste of their own medicine, but who is never a picaroon himself. This new tone and this new technique really remove the work from the picaresque class, because there is no delinquency in the protagonist and what there is in the environment is very much watered down. In the endeavour to create profitable entertainment, Espinel, in fact, destroyed the special significance of the *genre*. Instead of a psychological, spiritual, and social tension between good and evil, he produced an agreeable enough, but rather commonplace, balance that points directly to the neo-classical world of Lesage, on whose *Gil Blas* he exercised the greatest single influence.

A similar result is obtained in the religious sphere, by exactly the same change of narrative technique, in the next so-called picaresque novel. This is *Alonso, mozo de muchos amos* (*Alonso, Servant of Many Masters*)[4] by Jerónimo Alcalá Yáñez (1563-1632), the First Part of which was published in 1624 and the Second in 1626. It is in dialogue form, Alonso narrating his life in answer to questions and comments from his interlocutor, who in Part I is the prior of the friary in which Alonso is an unprofessed lay-brother, and in Part II the parish priest of the district where Alonso is living as a hermit. The device of first presenting the narrator as he is at the end of the life he is describing has the same result as in *Marcos de Obregón*, that of providing detachment from a world that we know has been left behind. The fact that the narrator is attached to a religious house, and is later a hermit, gives the book a religious focus and aim throughout. Its main interest is its return to the point of departure of the picaresque *genre* with Alemán, and its attempt to do again what Úbeda had said was impossible: to place this novelistic material in a religious setting. Alemán's method, as regards his narrative plot, was the subtle one of keeping the religious doctrine implicit symbolically in the tension of the picaresque action, gradually making it show through until it becomes fully explicit in the act of submission to the divine law, the reader being involved, like the protagonist, in the picaresque action and in the painful process of climbing the mountain of misery in order to reach up to heaven.

In *Alonso, mozo de muchos amos,* however, the method is much simpler, and is, in fact, entirely obvious. The world of religion is explicit from the very start as the goal of the human journey, and from this safe vantage point both protagonist and reader watch mankind's procession through the world without taking part. This non-involvement and sense of security from first to last robs the story of any tension, of any suffering or anguish. For this reason it is not to my mind a genuinely religious book, or at least not significantly so, whereas *Guzmán de Alfarache* is; for in the former, religion is an escapist refuge, at life's beginning so to speak, while in the latter it is the meaning to life that emerges at the end out of the existential agony of having to act by the mere fact of being free, of *not* being in a refuge. Alcalá's vantage-point of the religious house, and later of the hermitage, colours the narrative: there is an atmosphere of peacefulness, an air of innocence in the adventures, and the work is very chaste, not because there is any real apprehension of the ideal of purity but merely because the women who appear are generally ugly. From the point of view of this book, which is to see whether picaresque literature could come to grips with the problem of delinquency, *Alonso, mozo de muchos amos* is an evasion of the issue.

None-the-less, despite these symptoms of decline, it is at this point, chronologically, that the *genre* reaches its zenith at the hands of a genius of the first order, Francisco de Quevedo Villegas (1580-1645), in the form of his only novel, *La vida del buscón.*[5] This appeared in 1626, but on the basis of a remark in the text indicating that Ostend is being besieged, it is generally thought to have been written in 1604, since the city was finally captured in September of that year. This would mean that Quevedo wrote it at the early age of twenty-four, which is very hard to believe even for a man of his genius, for the work has a depth of psychological insight and a mature control of a complex style beyond the capacity of a young man. A close comparison of its style with that of other satirical works of his whose dates of composition are known would not be likely, in my opinion, to point to a date much earlier than 1620.

The word *buscón,* which means 'thief' and 'swindler', has been variously rendered in translations of the novel as 'sharper', 'rascal', and (quite incorrectly) 'scavenger'. Although there are five different English translations[6] it must be emphasized that much of the work is untranslatable. For instance, the description of Cabra, the miserly schoolmaster, in cap. III contains the sentence *la nariz, entre Roma y Francia, porque se le había comido de unas bubas de resfriado, que aun no fueron de vicio, porque cuestan dinero;* which means, 'his nose [lay] between Rome and France, because it had been eaten away by sores from colds; they weren't even from vice, because those cost money.' *Roma* also means a flat or snub nose;

venereal disease was called 'the French illness'; therefore, 'his nose lay between Rome and France. . . .' The most recent translator renders this: 'His nose, which had once been a Roman one, had been worn flat by sores, from colds, but which one would have thought to come from the French disease except that that illness involves the price of a girl.' The startling geographical witticism evaporates. Consider this sentence from the same paragraph[7]: *Traía un bonete los días de sol, ratonado con mil gateras, y guarniciones de grasa.* The same translator has: 'On sunny days he wore a cap; it was riddled with holes and had a trimming of grease.' But *bonete* is the clerical biretta; it is also the bastion of a fortified wall (with protruding angles like the corners of a biretta); *ratonado* means riddled by mice, and the holes, *gateras,* are the openings in walls or roofs for cats to pass through, so that we have a momentary vision of cats and mice, chasing themselves in and out of the biretta; *guarniciones* does mean 'trimmings', but it also means 'garrison' and so connects with the 'bastion' of the biretta; it is garrisoned only by *grasa,* which in the sense of lard or bacon fat is suitable food for mice, who therefore 'riddle' it, but which in the sense of grease stains means that the wearer's unwashed head transfers to the biretta its only 'trimmings'. The novel is full of this complex playing on words, brilliantly sustained, which is either lost or falls flat in translation. For virtuosity of language, Quevedo has no equal in Spanish literature.

El buscón is essentially, in intention and execution, a humorous work. It represents the culmination, in the picaresque novel, of the 'low', or comic, style, doing to perfection what Úbeda had thought was demanded by the subject-matter. But, in contrast to *La pícara Justina,* Quevedo's humour is not inappropriate to, or incompatible with, a serious interest in delinquency, for it is not festive or sprightly but pungent and sardonic; rather than humour proper, it is wit of a sharp-pointed kind. It stretches and distorts realism into caricature, creating a grotesque world of surrealist fancy. When the two boys were carried home after being starved at Cabra's boarding-school, they were so emaciated that 'spies' had to be brought to search for their eyes 'all over their faces'; the dust had to be removed from inside their mouths with foxtail brushes as if they were the easily damaged statues on the retables of altars; the doctors forbade anyone to speak in more than a whisper in their bedroom so that the words should not echo in their hollow stomachs; their cheeks had become so wrinkled through lack of chewing that each day the inside of their mouths had to be slowly moulded back into shape with pestles.[8] Isolated examples like this would suggest an extravaganza for its own sake, but when wit and plot are interrelated and the novel looked at as a whole, it becomes clear that this world is made grotesque in order to reveal the distortions and unreality of human social life in the self-conceit and hypocrisy of men.

Thus, the grotesque description of the miserly Cabra concludes with the outward signs of his priesthood. First his biretta already referred to, then his cassock: this is called 'miraculous'. We think of Christ's garment which healed the woman who touched it and of Christ as the exemplar of the priestly life, but this first impression is immediately shattered. The cassock is miraculous because 'you couldn't tell what colour it was. Some, seeing it so threadbare, thought it was made of frogskin; others said that it was an illusion; close by it seemed black, from afar bluish; he wore it without a girdle.' In the literature of the time the sky was sometimes called a falsehood because its blue colour is illusory; the cassock, so worn as to be shiny, and so changing from black to blue as the light catches it, is an 'illusion' like the colour of the sky as it changes from night to day—in other words, Cabra's priesthood was a sham. The girdles round religious habits were used as 'disciplines', for doing penance by self-flagellation. Cabra's cassock is worn without a girdle because there is no penance in his priesthood. His description concludes: 'with his long hair and his short cassock, he looked like the lackey of death. Each shoe could have been the tomb of a Philistine.'[9] A priest should be the guide to salvation, but Cabra is the opposite—the guide to death. He is the opposite because a priest's head ought to be shaven and his garment long, but Cabra's hair is long (*largos*) and his cassock short (*mísera*); but *largo* also means 'generous' and *mísero* 'stingy': Cabra is generous to himself because he encourages his private interests by stinting his priesthood, which should be charity to others. Since he is turned into a guide to death (the death of the spirit), the last parts of him to be described are turned into gigantic tombs so that our final image may be that of the grave swallowing him and all men who are the opposite of what they should be. The wit is brilliant, but it is wit directed to a serious satirical end.

The exposure of human self-conceit is apparent also in a particular type of verbal witticism that is a constant thread running through the style. In describing people or objects connected with them, Quevedo uses an epithet or a phrase that ennobles them, and then, by word-play, shatters the illusion by turning it into its opposite. A simple example is the meal served at the miserly Cabra's boarding-school: the pupils, he says, 'ate an eternal meal'; but since the definition of eternity is that it has no beginning and no end, the food was conspicuous by its virtual absence: *comieron una comida eterna, sin principio ni fin*. This joke must be placed in the context of the clerical schoolmaster who is not a guide to salvation (eternity) but to death. At the end of the novel, the delinquent protagonist is enjoying a social prosperity that is illusory because it contradicts his moral condition; to ape the well-to-do by hanging tapestries on his walls, he buys cast-off armorial hangings from taverns; these, he says, 'were more worth seeing than those the King had'. But the idiom Quevedo uses for 'worth seeing' means literally 'for seeing', so: 'they were more for seeing than those the King had, for you could see through mine because they were so full of holes, while through his you would see nothing.'[10]

This type of joke is applied to every character in the novel except Don Diego Coronel (who is the symbol of reality and goodness contrasted with the illusory world of

Francisco Gomez de Quevedo, author of Historia de la vida del buscón.

delinquency). The picaroon's father 'came of a very good stock'—'and considering how he drank one can well believe it'; his brother 'stole everybody's hearts' and was 'a little angel', a term of endearment that would be justified by his being dead, were it not for the fact that he had died in prison because of his powers of attracting objects from other men's pockets. His mother 'had so much charm that she enchanted everybody she dealt with'—'only they said something about a he-goat and flying through the air. . . .'[11] Variants of this type of joke are euphemisms that characters apply to themselves in order to hide the mean reality. The picaroon's father 'was a barber by trade; although his thoughts were so elevated that he was ashamed to be called that, claiming that he was a shearer of cheeks and a tailor of beards.'[12]

So frequent are these jokes, so strong an impression is left on the reader by the phantasmagoria of Quevedo's grotesque world, that most critics have succumbed to the temptation to see nothing more in the plot and the characterization than the occasion for a prolonged display of flashing wit. But just as the grotesque descriptions disclose a serious satirical purpose below the surface of distortion, so, too, are these jokes directed to a similar end. They all show the same technique of pricking a bubble of illusion; since human beings have an infinite capacity for self-conceit, reality can only be reached by exposing their illusions. This is how Quevedo focuses the problem of the delinquent. He writes what is above all a sarcastically funny book, but the psychology of delinquency is seriously conceived and the wit has a structural pattern which harmonizes with the psychological presentation of the protagonist; and not only the wit, for the way the plot itself is constructed contributes to this over-all unity. In common with all other Spanish picaresque novels, *El buscón* has been accused of having no structure but only a jumble of disconnected incidents; C. B. Morris, however, has now demonstrated that it has a structural unity of a subtle and original kind, based on a series of recurring motifs, which, as it were, project the past into the present and the future, 'entrapping' the protagonist, who, seeking to escape from the past, is in effect constantly reenacting it.[13] The significance of this will be soon apparent.

Quevedo's characteristically laconic Prologue bluntly states the problem of hypocrisy, which, as we have seen, was raised as a crucial issue by Alemán's attitude to his material and by Úbeda's reactions to it. 'Here you will find', says Quevedo to the reader, 'every kind of roguery—which I think most people like—astuteness, deceptions, ingenuities and ways, born of idleness, of living by trickery; and you will be able to derive no little profit from this if you heed the moral lesson—and if you don't derive profit from this then go and listen to sermons, for I doubt whether anyone buys a jocular book to escape from the temptations of his depraved nature.'[14] Readers of novels do not turn to picaresque stories for sermons and Quevedo is not going to pretend that they do by offering them any. They want the excitement and the fun of picaresque knavery, and that is what he will give them. But this does not mean another ironical work like *La pícara Justina,* or another *Hija de Celestina,* because behind the fireworks of the wit there lies a profound insight into the character of a delinquent. Since this character is revealed as one that gradually empties itself of anything positive until only a void is left, and since the wit itself is so devised that it exposes an empty world behind the social self-assertion of men, the picaresque narrative carries its own moral within it and requires no sermons. The triumph of Quevedo—what helps to make *El buscón* the peak of the picaresque novel—is that the values of morality are intrinsic to the narrative, and that it is impossible to read it correctly without reading it as a profoundly moral story. But to be read correctly, it cannot be read superficially, as it often has been and still is.[15] For it is a novel rich in human truth, one that gives us a psychological study of a delinquent that is far in advance of its time, an analysis of the relationship between character and environment that reaches through the pressure of external circumstances into the heart of the conflict between the individual and society, and probes the inner, deep-seated motives that make a delinquent choose that manner of life rather than another.[16]

Quevedo's picaroon is called Pablos. His father is a thief and his mother a witch. They are notorious figures in Segovia. As a boy, Pablos suffers mercilessly from the taunts of the other boys in the town, who make constant mocking allusions to his parents:

I put up with everything, until one day a boy dared to shout after me that I was the son of a whore and a witch; because he said this so clearly—for I would not have minded had he said it darkly—I picked up a brick and broke his head. I ran to my mother for her to hide me . . . I asked her to tell me whether I could truthfully tell the boy he lied, or whether she had conceived me by giving many men a share, or whether I was the son of my father alone. She laughed and said: 'Gracious me! Do you know about those things already? You're going to be no fool; you've got a sense of humour; you did right in breaking his head, because such things, even though they be true, should never be said.'[17]

The cynicism of this answer is a cruel blow to the boy, leaving him with no defence against the mockery of his companions except flight. 'When I heard this I was as if struck dead; I determined to collect what belongings I could within the next few days and to leave my father's house, so strong was the shame I felt.'[18]

This shame and the accompanying fear of the hostility of society produce in Pablos a deep-seated feeling of inferiority. To cancel the superiority of others he takes refuge in an ideal world of fantasy, in which he eliminates the factor that oppresses him in real life. He lifts himself out of his actual situation as far as his fantasy can possibly take him.[19] Just as his inferiority feeling derives from shame at his parents' social standing and notoriety, so his dreams for the future take a social form, placing him in a social position as far removed as possible from theirs. 'My parents had long arguments about whose profession I was to follow; but I, who had always from childhood had the idea of becoming a gentleman, never applied myself to either.'[20] A pathetic ideal, indeed, harmless at this stage, but potentially dangerous.

The first step to becoming a gentleman is to be educated. 'I pacified them, saying that I was firmly determined to learn to live a virtuous life and to persevere in my good resolutions; I therefore asked them to put me to school, because if one couldn't read or write, one wouldn't be able to do anything.'[21] His entry into school brings to the fore another trait in his character which, together with his compensatory fantasy, is to be decisive for his future development. The timid Pablos, requiring the practical compensation of actual praise, goes out of his way to curry favour:

[The master] gave me a cheerful welcome, and told me I had the look of a sharp-witted and intelligent man. Because of this, in order not to prove him wrong, I learned the lessons well that morning. The master used to make me sit by his side; on most days, as a reward for being the first to arrive, I was given the cane to wield; and I was the last to leave because I ran errands for 'Madam', as we called the master's wife. I was in their good graces for being so obliging. They showed me too much favour, and this made the other boys envious.[22]

This pathetic attempt to compensate for his timidity and shame only accentuates the unpleasant behaviour of his schoolmates, who make cruel fun of him.

Pablos's first efforts to realize his goal of a gentleman, combined with this toadying, also bring failure. He abandons the boys of his own class and makes up to those of a higher:

> I sought out the sons of gentlemen and people of quality, and particularly a son of Don Alonso Coronel de Zúñiga, with whom I shared my lunches. On holidays I went to his house to play with him, and I kept him company every day. But the other boys, because I didn't speak to them, or because they thought I was being too snobbish, kept on giving me nicknames that recalled my father's profession.[23]

His failure here is not only social. Since he cannot approach this young gentleman on terms of equality—because of his class, but still more because of his timidity and shame—he makes up to him by a form of flattery, seeking to win his favour by always denying himself pleasure in order to give it to his friend:

> During all this period I was constantly visited by that son of Don Alonso Coronel de Zúñiga, who was called Don Diego; naturally he liked me, because I exchanged my tops for his if mine were better; I used to give him part of my lunch, never asking for any of his in return; I would buy him picture cards, I taught him to wrestle, I played at bull-fighting with him and kept him constantly amused.[24]

At last Pablos has won for himself affection, and affection from a person of high social standing, but at the cost of laying the seed of servility. This flattery is here natural enough, but it is pointing forward to what Quevedo will later make the decisive factor that plunges him into the career of a delinquent—the willingness to barter moral independence and self-respect for the praise of others.

Such conduct leads Pablos into a vicious circle. His efforts to compensate for the hostility of society serve only to increase it. One day the two boys see in the street a man called Pontius Aguirre, who was rumoured to be a Jew. 'Call him Pontius Pilate and run', says Diego, and Pablos does it 'to please him'; the result is a beating. Another such disaster, which immediately follows, is recounted with a remarkably subtle touch. At the Shrovetide carnival boys used to tilt at a hanging cock; one was chosen to be their leader, the 'Cock King', and was dressed up appropriately. The honour falls to Pablos, to whose timid and repressed spirit it provides a tremendous satisfaction; with ill-concealed pride he leads the procession 'bowing to one side and the other like a Pharisee on the march'. His horse seizes a cabbage as it passes a greengrocer's stall; the vendor sets up a hue and cry, Pablos is pelted by the market-women, his horse rears, and he is thrown into a privy. His self-satisfaction thus ends in a greater humiliation than any that he had previously suffered; but there is more in the episode than that:

> And I want to confess to you in passing that when they started throwing eggplants and turnips at me, since I was wearing feathers in my hat, I thought that they had mistaken me for my mother, and that they were throwing at her as they had done on other occasions. And so, being simple-minded and only a boy, I said: 'Sisters, although I am wearing feathers, I am not Aldonza de San Pedro, my mother', as if they couldn't see that from my clothes and face. The fear I felt excuses my ignorance, and the fact that this calamity befell me so suddenly.[25]

Witches were punished by being tarred and feathered, which is the reason for this strange confusion in Pablos's mind. The suddenness with which everything happens makes Pablos's reaction a purely spontaneous one; no defences are interposed, and fear—fear of the ill-treatment that society is constantly meting out to him—brings to the fore the dominant element in his character: his self-identification with his mother's guilt. This family guilt, he thinks, is what provokes the brutal hostility of society; it results in a humiliation and a shame so overpowering and so lasting in its effects ('even to recount it makes me feel afraid', he says), that the memory of it is later to influence him decisively at a critical moment in his moral development. For the time being, his only refuge is to escape from his family and his home town:

> I resolved never to return to school or to my parents' house . . . I wrote home saying that I no longer needed to go to school even though I couldn't write well, because the first requirement for my intention to become a gentleman was to write badly; and that I was therefore abandoning school to save them expense, and their house to save them displeasure.[26]

The hostility of society, in other forms, dogs his steps despite the change of environment. He follows Don Diego, as his servant, first to Cabra's boarding-school and later to the University of Alcalá; at the former he is all but starved to death; at the latter, hostility in the form of practical jokes reaches the extreme of heartless cruelty. In self-defence he is driven to assert himself, to decide on a course of action that will make life bearable. Since it is difficult for this timid youth, obsessed with a fear of society, to stand up to ill-treatment in a resolute or valiant way, he is more likely to adopt a weak than a heroic course. There are two weak courses: either he can evade coming to terms with his environment by shrinking into despair, or he can rise superior to it by excelling it according to its own standards. Pablos finds himself in the society of students; what they seem to admire most is roguery of the practical joker's kind. Among them, he can gain significance only by outrivalling them at their own game, and it is this decision that he comes to. He determines to develop that form of cunning and astuteness that consists in 'getting away with it'.[27] '"When in Rome do as the Romans do", says the proverb, and it says rightly. After turning it over and over in my mind, I eventually decided to be a rogue among rogues, and more of a rogue than all of them if I could.'[28]

This is the first of two major decisions that are to lead him along the path of delinquency. It is a further, and now a pernicious, example of the weakness that had made him curry favour as a child. Then his success had been only partial, now it is complete; for he wins from all sides the praise he has always yearned for. On the one hand his skill in thieving arouses the admiration of Don Diego for what he takes to be the faithfulness and honesty with which their money allowance is made to go so far; on the other hand, it delights and astonishes the rest of the students, whose applause spurs him on to ever more of these meretricious triumphs. But behind this self-assertion there lies a deeper motive than the quest for flattery—that of revenge for the humiliation of his childhood: 'In order not to be tedious I shall refrain from telling how I turned the town square into a forest, for from the boxes of the cloth-shearers and the silversmiths, and from the stalls of the fruiterers—*since I shall never forget the disgrace I suffered when I was the Cock King*—I fed the fire of our house all the year round.'[29] Pablos is thus revenging himself for the hostility of society by declaring war on it. His actions are antisocial, not by accident but of set-purpose; it is not only praise he seeks but vengeance.

Pablos makes the second major decision when Don Diego is forced to dismiss him from his service. With the newly-won self-confidence that would appear to make his social ambitions realizable, he rejects the offer of useful work befitting his station. Don Diego 'was distressed at dismissing me. He said he would find me a situation with another gentleman among his friends. I, laughing, said to him: "Sir, I am now another man with other ideas; I am aiming higher and need a more influential position."'[30] His own master, he will be a servant no longer: society will be made to accept him as a gentleman. Yet this presumptuousness is still a pathetic day-dream in whose smug and pleasant picture of himself he overcomes the hardness of reality: 'I kept on thinking how difficult it would be for me to live a life of honour and virtue, since it was first necessary to hide how little my parents had had, and then to have so much myself that no one would recognize in me what I had been. So much did I approve of these honourable thoughts that I was grateful to myself for them. I said to myself: "I, who have not had anyone from whom to learn virtue, or any virtuous person to imitate, shall deserve more thanks than one who has inherited virtue from his ancestors."'[31]

In his home town where, unrecognized, he passes himself off as 'a gentleman of rank', he is soon made to suffer agonies of shame from the patronage of his disreputable hangman uncle, whose brawls he is forced to witness: 'When I saw how honourable were the people who were conversing with my uncle, I confess that I blushed, unable to hide my shame . . . I was on tenterhooks to get the dinner over, collect my money and flee from my uncle.' 'All this abomination and depravity that I was witnessing made me ever more impatient to be among gentlemen and people of quality.' Pocketing his father's legacy, he therefore departs for Madrid, turning his back on his family shame: 'what most comforted me was the thought that I was going to the capital—where nobody knew me'. 'I must repudiate my kin', he writes in his farewell letter to his uncle.[32]

But it is precisely his kin—his ancestral stock—that makes his ambition impossible. He cannot consort with the upper classes on terms of equality, for he has neither birth nor wealth. Inevitably, therefore, he enters into association with those aristocrats who, through penury, have sunk to his own level, and who ludicrously strive by every manner of artful and dishonest deception to keep body and soul together while maintaining genteel appearances. Pablos's ambition, therefore, leads him into delinquency, and his special form of self-confidence confirms him in it. In no other sphere can he hold his own and excel. His cleverness brings him to the verge of success—he gets himself accepted as an equal by 'people of quality' and is about to marry an heiress—but the extravagance of his ambition is his undoing.

There is cruel, if poetic, justice in the manner in which his imposture is unmasked, for this is brought about by the very person to whom, as a boy, he first humbly turned in his efforts to rise above his family shame. It is Don Diego who exposes him—Don Diego who, before establishing his identity, recalls his social stigma when apologizing to the impostor for having thought him to be Pablos: 'You will not believe it: his mother was a witch, his father a thief, his uncle a hangman.' After exposure, Pablos meets his punishment at the hands of the gentlemen with whom he had tried so hard to consort. His arrogant but all too understandable endeavour to 'repudiate his kin' recoils upon him. Attempting to compensate himself for his sense of guilty inferiority, he had pitched his aims inordinately high and is, as a result, plunged into the depths of social disgrace. Because of a moral weakness that had begun as the fruit of ingrained fear and that had grown through indulgence in self-conceit into the pride of unscrupulous over-confidence, he attempts to impose himself upon a hostile society by cunning and fraud, and becomes a socially unadapted person, a moral reprobate. At the end he is one of a gang who, in a drunken brawl, murder two policemen. Hunted by the law, he can only go out at night disguised. Tiring of this harassing existence, he emigrates to the Indies with the whore who had shared his home, only to find, as he tells us in his closing sentence, that he fared even worse across the sea.[33] By letting the novel peter out in the hint of continuous decline Quevedo is going to disturb his French translator, but he is in fact giving it an ending that is perfectly fitted to his theme, for by pricking the bubble of the delinquent's inflated ambition, he makes him gradually, as it were, shrivel away into nothingness.

This analysis has been concerned only with the character of the protagonist, but there is still more to *El buscón* than that. No one has written more profoundly on its wider significance than T.E. May, and one of the points he adds to its interpretation should not be overlooked here.[34] Pablos is presented by Quevedo as bearing a burden of guilt and shame that seems to have been imposed upon him from without. The reality and meaning of a guilt of this kind, and its concomitant suffering, could not, says May, be imaginatively sought by Quevedo except in a context of religious belief. The crisis in Pablos's life is the persecution to which, as a freshman, he is subjected on arrival at the university. This brings him to the momentous choice whether he is to seek adjustment to society by accepting his suffering, or reject his suffering and so turn against the society that inflicts it. The form in which Quevedo presents this crucial experience and decision is seen by May as a kind of internally experienced allegory.

As the freshman Pablos makes his way to the lecture rooms on his first morning, the students gather round him, hold their fingers to their noses and say: 'This Lazarus is ready to be raised from the dead, he stinks so much.' They then follow up this mockery of Christ by spitting on Pablos. Christ, mockery and spitting symbolically recall the Passion: Pablos is thus thrust into a situation which parallels that of the suffering Christ. That the Crucifixion is reproduced as a possibility in his mind is revealed by the fact that when, after this torment, he returns to his lodging and to his landlord who looks with astonishment at his shocking appearance, Pablos says: 'I am not *Ecce Homo.*' 'Behold the Man' were the words spoken by Pilate as he brought out the scourged Christ to be shown to the people; and 'Ecce Homo' is the name traditionally given to pictures of Christ at that stage of the Passion. Pablos thus recalls the Crucifixion, but only to repudiate any connexion between himself and the suffering Christ. He then enters his room, goes to bed, and falls asleep. Since there is no reason why he should sleep in the middle of the morning, May sees this as symbolical of the entombment of Christ that precedes the Resurrection; and, in fact, his master, returning from lectures and astonished to find Pablos asleep in bed, wakes him with the words: 'This is now another life.' (Later, after Pablos has decided to seek revenge on society by becoming a delinquent, he says to his master: 'I am now another man.') This crisis in Pablos's life consequently takes a form which links his sufferings with those of Christ. Thus, according to May, Quevedo sees the supernatural as not only present in the delinquent's world but as actually thrust upon him. The grief of Pablos is the grief of humanity and this grief is apprehended in a Christian way. The words 'I am not *Ecce Homo*' preface the choice of delinquency and represent the rejection of Christ—Pablos's refusal to take up his cross. The new life to which he awakes is, in accordance with the mockery of the students, a travesty of spiritual resurrection: it is the life of the sinner, not of the saved.

This interpretation is so subtle that one accepts it only after an initial resistance, since the pointers to this symbolism seem too few and too undeveloped to carry so deep a seriousness. Such seriousness, also, might seem incompatible with the wit that describes the episode and the crudity with which the students enact it. But wit (especially in the seventeenth century) is not synonymous with irreverence; everything human, even jesting and depravity, has a bearing on the ultimate seriousness of life; further, this symbolism need not have been present to Quevedo's conscious mind at all—his imagination, the servant of an acute intelligence, could have seized on these images of the Passion for their inner appropriateness while the conscious mind saw their potential wit. It is not necessary to accept this symbolism in order to accept the character study of a delinquent, since the two are independent; but if it is accepted, then *El buscón* is linked, like *Guzmán de Alfarache,* to the religious conscience of the age (which is not to say that it is a religious work); that it is linked to it without any sermonizing, but only by the strength of Quevedo's imaginative vision, is a measure of the greater brilliance of his novel. The brilliance lies also in the way its satirical wit is harmonized with the theme, and above all in its insight into the psychology of a delinquent. The protagonist moves through a stylized world of caricature, but his character is human. Despite what has nearly always been repeated since Chandler, the individual character is here, as in *Guzmán de Alfarache,* more important than the society through which he moves. The character drawing in *El buscón,* though always concise, is consistent and complete. Because Pablos is a rounded character he can arouse our understanding and compassion, all the more so because of the unflinching hardness of the world in which he is placed.

For these reasons, *El buscón* must be considered the masterpiece of the picaresque tradition. It is the zenith to which *Guzmán* marked the rise. Both these two major Spanish picaresque novels show how misguided are those historians of the novel in France and England who dismiss the Spaniards for the incompatibility of their professed moral aims with the nature of their picaresque material. This shows both an ignorance of the historical causes of the picaresque *genre* in the Counter Reformation and a misunderstanding of the first approach to picaresque material. Alemán and Quevedo turned to this kind of material because they were profoundly interested in the causes of sin and crime. For Alemán, the causes of sin are explained by moral theology, but an interest in this theology leads him to an interest in practical psychology. Thus he shows insight into the clash between temptation and conscience, and he gives a moving analysis of the psychological and emotional factors behind the process of conversion. In Quevedo, the psychological insight is much more remarkable and it is autonomous; it explores the influence of environment upon the development of character without the intrusion of moral theology.

Both novels must be classed as significant explorations of the problem of the delinquent, and thus as novels that give the new *genre* of the picaresque both literary validity and human depth. What comes after *El buscón* marks only a decline in one or other of the two directions mapped out by *Marcos de Obregón* and *La hija de Celestina*—either that of toning down the harsh colours or that of facetiousness. The middle-of-the-road good-mannered treatment of picaresque material is continued by Alonso de Castillo Solórzano (1584-1648?), a fairly prolific novelist who is a contemporary of Quevedo's, but who is quite lacking in the latter's intelligence and passion. He attempts to make of the picaresque novel an artistic literary form. We find unity of plot and a style with pretentions to elegance.

There is no didactic moralizing, no acid wit; neither is there any crude farce or facetiousness; instead, the *genre* assumes an air of refinement in order to amuse polite upper-class readers without shocking them or touching their consciences on the raw. Castillo Solórzano does achieve a consistent level of artistry, but only one of polished mediocrity.[35] The world of criminal life thus becomes something to be treated with well-bred gentility.

The actual nadir of the *genre* in Spain is reached, appropriately enough, by the last work to exemplify the basic elements of the tradition, *Estebanillo González* (1646).[36] Although the end is now reached, forty-seven years after the beginning, and although the French realistic novel has come into existence, an independent picaresque novel, properly speaking, has not yet been born abroad. This last Spanish example is, however, a bridge that leads out of Spain into Europe, into a wider sphere of human delinquency—that of international warfare.

Notes

1. *Relaciones de la vida del escudero Marcos de Obregón* (Madrid 1618).

2. George Haley *Vicente Espinel and Marcos de Obregón: A Life and its Literary Representation* Brown University Series xxv (Providence, Rhode Island 1959).

3. 'El intento mío fue ver si acertaría a escribir en prosa algo que aprovechase a mi república, deleitando y enseñando, siguiendo aquel consejo de mi maestro Horacio; porque han salido algunos libros de hombres doctísimos en letras y opinión que se abrazan tanto con sola la doctrina, que no dejan lugar donde pueda el ingenio alentarse y recibir gusto; y otros tan enfrascados en parecerles que deleitan con burlas y cuentos entremesiles, que después de haberlos revuelto, ahechado y aun cernido, son tan fútiles y vanos que no dejan cosa de sustancia ni provecho para el lector, ni de fama y opinión para sus autores.'

4. A Madrid edition of 1804 changes the title to *El donado hablador, vida y aventura de Alonso,* etc.; the novel is now commonly called by this title, which means 'The Talkative Lay-brother'.

5. *Historia de la vida del buscón, llamado don Pablos, ejemplo de vagamundos y espejo de tacaños* (Saragossa 1626). It has been alleged by Felicidad Buendía that the Inquisition 'persecuted' *El buscón* after Quevedo's death, since she publishes a document of 1646 in which an official of the Inquisition reports that the novel is on sale at a bookshop, despite the fact that the latest Index has prohibited all Quevedo's works except those he has acknowledged to be his, which do not include this novel. (Quevedo *Obras completas,* ii, *Obras en verso,* Aguilar, Madrid 1960, 1103-4). While it is possible that Quevedo may have found difficulty in publishing *El buscón* as he did his *Sueños,* because some of his jokes were on the border-line of irreverence, once it was published the Inquisition never interfered with any of its numerous editions, either during Quevedo's lifetime or after his death. The only probable explanation of this document is the following. We know that on his release from captivity in 1643, Quevedo began to prepare an edition of his Collected Works, for which he obtained a licence in 1644. Since he had been often attacked for the alleged malice and virulence of his satires, he would now have been anxious, knowing himself to be near to death, to exclude any such works from his projected edition. He therefore 'repudiated' *El buscón*; but since he died in the following year, his repudiation had no effect.

6. In 1657 (from the French), 1707 (by John Stevens in *The Comical Works of Don Francisco de Quevedo*) and three modern ones: by Charles Duff *The Life of the Great Rascal,* included in the volume of Quevedo's *Choice Humorous and Satirical Works* in the Broadway Translations (London and New York 1926); by Frank Mugglestone (under the pseudonym Francisco Villamiquel y Hardin), *The Life and Adventures of Don Pablos the Sharper* (The Anglo-Spanish Library, Leicester 1928); and by Hugh A. Harter, *The Scavenger* (Las Americas Publishing Co., New York 1962).

7. Harter, op. cit., 32.

8. 'Trajeron exploradores que nos buscasen los ojos por toda la cara; y a mí, como había sido mi trabajo mayor y la hambre imperial—que al fin me trataban como a criado—en buen rato no me los hallaron. Trajeron médicos, y mandaron que nos limpiasen con zorras el polvo de las bocas, como retablos, y bien lo éramos de duelos . . . Mandaron los doctores que por nueve días no hablase nadie recio en nuestro aposento, porque como estaban huecos los estómagos, sonaba en ellos el eco de cualquier palabra. Con estas y otras prevenciones comenzamos a volver y cobrar algún aliento; pero nunca podían las quijadas desdoblarse, que estaban magras y alforzadas, y así se dió orden que cada día nos las ahormasen con la mano del almirez.' (Cap. iv, pp. 46-8. All references are to the edition by Américo Castro in Clásicos Castellanos; the current edition, 1960, has several printing errors which I have corrected from the first edition of 1927 in the passages I quote. The critical edition of Fernando Lázaro Carreter, *La vida del buscón, llamado don Pablos,* in Clásicos Hispánicos, Salamanca 1965, did not come to my notice until after the completion of this book.)

9. 'La sotana era milagrosa, porque no se sabía de qué color era. Unos, viéndola tan sin pelo, la tenían por de cuero de rana; otros decían que era ilusión; desde cerca parecía negra, y desde lejos entre azul; traíala sin ciñidor. No traía cuellos ni puños; parecía, con los cabellos largos y la sotana mísera, lacayuelo de la muerte. Cada zapato podía ser tumba de un filisteo' (Cap. iii; 34).

10. The joke is introduced through a pun on *real*: 'costáronme veinte o treinta reales, y eran más para ver que cuantos tiene el rey, pues por éstos se veía de puros rotos, y por esotros no se verá nada' (Cap. XXII; 245).

11. 'Dicen que era de muy buena cepa; y, según él bebió, puédese muy bien creer' (p. 16). 'Murió el angelito de unos azotes que le dieron dentro de la cárcel. Sintiólo mucho mi padre (buen siglo haya), por ser tal, que robaba a todos las voluntades' (p. 17). 'Un día alabandómela una vieja que me crió, decía que era tal su agrado, que hechizaba a cuantos la trataban; sólo diz que se dijo no sé qué de un cabrón y volar, lo cual la puso cerca de que la diesen plumas con que lo hiciese en público' (p. 17).

12. 'Su oficio fue de barbero; aunque eran tan altos sus pensamientos, que se corría que le llamasen así, diciendo que él era tundidor de mejillas y sastre de barbas' (p. 16).

13. C.B. Morris 'The Unity and Structure of *El buscón: desgracias encadenadas*', Occasional Papers in Modern Languages I, University of Hull, 1965.

14. 'Aquí hallarás en todo género de picardía—de que pienso que los más gustan—sutilezas, engaños, invenciones y modos, nacidos del ocio, para vivir a la droga, y no poco fruto podrás sacar de él si tienes atención al escarmiento; y, cuando no lo hagas, aprovéchate de los sermones, que dudo nadie compre libro de burlas para apartarse de su natural depravado.' The sentence 'cuando no lo hagas, aprovéchate de los sermones' can be taken to mean 'if you don't profit from my book's moral lesson, then profit from its sermons'. Since it contains none, this would be a wittier comment on *Guzmán de Alfarache* than interpreting it as a reference to the sermons preached in churches; none the less, it seems to me more natural to take it in this latter sense.

15. E.g. Fernando Lázaro Carreter, 'Originalidad del Buscón' in *Studia Philologica,* Homenaje ofrecido a Dámaso Alonso (Madrid 1961) II, 319-38. I find myself in disagreement with almost everything in this paper. It denies that there is any moral intention in the novel, seeing it as essentially a display of wit behind which there is a cold and impassive vision of a hard world. The author had not read any of the three earlier papers which offered abundant evidence to refute this interpretation: the papers by T. E. May and myself, mentioned below, and P. N. Dunn 'El individuo y la sociedad en *La vida del buscón*', in *Bulletin Hispanique,* LII (1960) 375-96.

16. In what follows I reproduce a substantial section of an early paper of mine, 'The Psychology of the "Pícaro" in "El Buscón"', in *Modern Language Review,* XLII (1947) 58-69. The validity of my thesis has been accepted by those critics who have read it, but these have been few. Lázaro Carreter, op. cit., did not have access to it; del Monte, op. cit., refers to it but gives

the wrong journal, and his treatment of *El buscón* shows no awareness of the existence of my interpretation; neither S. Serrano Poncela 'El buscón, ¿parodia picaresca?', in *Insula,* No. 154 (Sept. 1959) nor Fritz Schalk 'Über Quevedo und *El Buscón*', in *Romanische Forschungen,* LXXIV (1962) 11-30, refer to it, or to May or Dunn, and have really nothing new to say on the novel, repeating the conventional statements about its 'amorality' which have been refuted for the last twenty years. No writer on the picaresque novel in France, England or Germany, as far as I know, has shown any knowledge of my paper. Since my interpretation is cardinal for the revaluation of the Spanish picaresque novel offered in this book, I reproduce the relevant section here, together with the supporting quotations from the text of the novel.

17. 'Todo lo sufría, hasta que un día un muchacho se atrevió a decirme a voces hijo de una puta hechicera; lo cual, como me lo dijo tan claro—que aún si lo dijera turbio no me pesara—agarré una piedra y descalabréle. Fuime a mi madre corriendo, que me escondiese . . . Roguéla que me declarase si le podía desmentir con verdad, o me declarase si me había concebido a escote entre muchos, o si era hijo de mi padre sólo. Rióse y dijo: "¡Ah, noramaza! ¿Eso sabes decir? No serás bobo; gracia tienes; muy bien hiciste en quebrarle la cabeza; que esas cosas, aunque sean verdad, no se han de decir."' (Cap. II, 24-5).

18. 'Yo, con esto, quedé como muerto, determinado de coger lo que pudiese en breves días, y salirme de casa de mi padre: tanto pudo conmigo la vergüenza' (ibid.).

19. There is a correspondence between this psychological situation as presented by Quevedo and the findings of the school of Individual Psychology. According to these, the compensation by which the sufferer from an inferiority feeling strives to overcome it never takes the form of actual compensation, but always of over-compensation; the goal of perfection, which is never attainable in practice, becomes the aim, and the possibility of disaster looms large. 'This mechanism of over-compensation in the sphere of unreality, which plunges a man in the depths in direct proportion to the height of his aims for the future, plays a decisive rôle in abnormal development. If the child experiences situations that he interprets in terms of prejudice, oppression and inferiority, the mechanism of over-compensation proportionately raises his future aims to inordinate heights. . . . It is reality that decides whether the goals a man sets before himself are attainable . . .' (Rudolf Allers *The Psychology of Character,* Engl. trans. (London 1939) 89). Quevedo gives us exactly this situation in the case of Pablos. By setting himself an unattainable goal, he will land in disaster.

20. 'Hubo grandes diferencias entre mis padres sobre a quién había de imitar en el oficio; mas yo, que siempre tuve pensamientos de caballero desde chiquito, nunca me apliqué a uno ni a otro' (Cap. I, 19).

21. 'Metílos yo en paz, diciendo que quería aprender virtud, resueltamente, e ir con mis buenos pensamientos adelante; y así, que me pusiese en la escuela, pues sin leer ni escribir no se podía hacer nada' (ibid.).

22. '. . . recibióme muy alegre; díjome que tenía cara de hombre agudo y de buen entendimiento. Yo con esto, por no desmentirle, di muy bien la lección aquella mañana. Sentábame el maestro junto a sí; ganaba la palmatoria los más días por venir antes, e íbame el postrero por hacer algunos recados de "señora", que así llamábamos la mujer del maestro. Teníalos a todos con semejantes caricias obligados. Favorecíanme demasiado, y con esto creció la envidia de los demás niños' (Cap. II, 22).

23. 'Llegábame a los hijos de los caballeros y personas principales, y particularmente a un hijo de don Alonso Coronel de Zúñiga, con el cual juntaba las meriendas. Íbame a su casa a jugar las fiestas, y acompañábale cada día. Pero los otros, porque no les hablaba, o porque les parecía demasiado punto el mío, siempre andaban poniéndome nombres tocantes al oficio de mi padre' (ibid.).

24. 'En todo esto, siempre me visitaba aquel hijo de don Alonso Coronel de Zúñiga, que se llamaba don Diego; queríame naturalmente, porque trocaba con él los peones, si eran mejores los míos; dábale de lo que almorzaba, y no le pedía de lo que él comía; comprábale estampas, enseñábale a luchar, jugaba con él al toro y entreteníale siempre' (Cap. II, 25).

25. 'Y de paso quiero confesar a v.m. que cuando me empezaron a tirar las berengenas y nabos, que, como yo llevaba plumas en el sombrero, entendí que me habían tenido por mi madre, y que la tiraban, como habían hecho otras veces; y así, como necio y muchacho, dije: "Hermanas, aunque llevo plumas, no soy Aldonza de San Pedro, mi madre", como si ellas no lo echaran de ver por el traje y el rostro. El miedo me disculpa la ignorancia, y el sucederme la desgracia tan de repente' (Cap. II, 29-30).

26. '. . . determinéme de no volver más a la escuela ni a casa de mis padres . . . Escribí a mi casa que yo no había menester más ir a la escuela, porque, aunque no sabía bien escribir, para mi intento de ser caballero lo que primero se requería era escribir mal; y que así, yo renunciaba la escuela por no darles gasto, y su casa por ahorrarles pesadumbre' (Cap. II, 31).

27. Here, too, there is a clear parallel with the Adlerian psychologists' analysis of the effects of an ingrained inferiority feeling. See, for example, Rudolf Dreikurs *An Introduction to Individual Psychology* (Eng. trans., London 1935) 29-33.

28. '"Haz como vieres" dice el refrán, y dice bien. De puro considerer en él, vine a resolverme en ser bellaco con los bellacos, y más que todos, si más pudiese' (Cap. VI, 69).

29. 'Por no ser largo, dejo de contar cómo hacía monte la plaza del pueblo, pues de cajones de tundidores y plateros, y mesas de fruteras—*que nunca se me olvidará la afrenta de cuando fui rey de gallos*—sustentaba la chimenea de casa todo el año' (Cap. VI; 84; italics mine).

30. '. . . a él le pesaba de dejarme. Díjome que me acomodaría con otro caballero amigo suyo. Yo riyéndome, le dije: "Señor, ya yo soy otro, y otros mis pensamientos, más alto pico y más autoridad me importa tener"' (Cap. VII; 89-90).

31. 'Iba yo pensando en las muchas dificultades que tenía para profesar honra y virtud, pues había menester tapar primero la poca de mis padres; y luego tener tanta, que me desconociesen por ella; y parecíanme a mí tan bien estos pensamientos honrados, que yo me los agradecía a mí mismo. Decía a solas: "Más se me ha de agradecer a mí, que no he tenido de quién aprender virtud, ni a quién parecer en ella, que al que la heredó de sus abuelos"' (Cap. IX; 105-6).

32. 'Yo, que vi cuán honrada gente era la que hablaba con mi tío, confieso que me puse colorado, de suerte que no pude disimular la vergüenza . . . Yo rabiaba ya por comer y por cobrar mi hacienda, y huir de mi tío' (Cap. XI; 135). 'Con estas infamias y vilezas que yo veía, crecíame por instantes el deseo de verme entre gente principal y caballeros' (139). 'Consideraba yo que iba a la corte, donde nadie me conocía—que era la cosa que más me consolaba' (Cap. XII; 141). '. . . me importa negar la sangre' (142).

33. A MS version, which is the text published in Clásicos Castellanos, concludes with the promise of a Second Part which will show how he fared worse in America. The novel was, however, printed as being in two parts and the reference to a continuation was dropped. Whatever Quevedo's original intention might have been, the work was published as complete.

34. 'Good and Evil in the *Buscón*', in *The Modern Language Review*, XLV (1950). The section summarized is 331-3. Though this brilliant paper is mentioned by del Monte (who does not seem to have grasped its significance), it appears to have remained unknown to every one else who has dealt with *El buscón*.

35. See Peter N. Dunn *Castillo Solórzano and the Decline of the Spanish Novel* (Oxford 1952).

36. *La vida y hechos de Estebanillo González, hombre de buen amor. Compuesto por él mismo. Dedicada al Excelentísimo Señor Octavio Piccolomini, Duque de Amalfi . . .* (Antwerp 1646). Angel Valbuena Prat, in his anthology *La novela picaresca* (4th ed. Madrid 1962), includes two works later than this: *Periquillo el de las gallineras* (1688) by Francisco Santos and the autobiography by Diego de Torres Villarroel (1743, 1752, 1758). The former is not, properly

speaking, a picaresque novel because it has a saintly hero; the latter is far too remote to form part of the literary movement initiated by *Guzmán de Alfarache.*

Barbara A. Babcock (essay date 1978)

SOURCE: Babcock, Barbara A. "'Liberty's a Whore': Inversions, Marginalia, and Picaresque Narrative." In *The Reversible World: Symbolic Inversion in Art and Society,* edited by Barbara A. Babcock, pp. 95-116. Ithaca, N.Y.: Cornell University Press, 1978.

[*In the essay which follows, Babcock discusses the social role of the picaresque hero, focusing on early Spanish picaresques as well as the film* Easy Rider.]

In one of the most recent picaresque fictions, my colleague Zulfikar Ghose's *The Incredible Brazilian,* his picaro-narrator informs his reader in the prologue:

> I am aware of the danger of fantasies, of adding spice to situations which were no more memorable than a frugal meal of rice and beans. I am aware, too, that since the reader is inevitably going to consider some aspects of my narrative as unbelievably impossible, I have the temptation before me of straining incredibility still further by making incredibility a kind of literary convention, by suggesting, say, that the reader can only believe in my story if he first accepts the proposition that everything I say is unbelievable. This is an interesting notion, no doubt. But let me say it categorically once and for all: what ensues may seem incredible, but there is not one word of untruth in it.
>
> [1972:10]

This is precisely the problem faced by the writer of picaresque narrative that defines itself through dramatic inversions of social, moral, and literary orders: how to speak the truth about society, but from an ironic, inverse perspective. The writer wants to amaze and yet be believed at the same time, and so rather than talking for truths he must speak in double negatives of not untruths. This "not not" is the mainspring of the rogue's hit-and-run style; he maintains his position of constant mobility, his half-outsider stance, by being able to say to the reader-listener when asked "Is it *true*?", "Well, it's not *un*true, is it?"[1]

The picaro-narrator establishes this perspective by playing with the conventions of the travel book and the confessional, both of which rely upon the trustworthiness of the narrator. But we can seldom attribute this trait to the picaro, the unwitting traveler, the rogue and trickster who is forced onto the road. Thus his confessions have the ring of the lurid, the voyeuristic, and they can never be regarded as illustrating the moral insights of a reformed individual, despite his claims to that effect. To the contrary, it is precisely the amoral tone which marks the genre and provides it with its sense of the fantastical, or at best, ambiguous. The force of this ostracism may be lost on us today, for we have come to idealize gypsying as a symbolic

means of asserting our freedom from social constraints. But we haven't completely lost the sense of existence in a disapproved moral vacuum which is attendant upon such declassifying or dismembering moves; even Peter Fonda, who participated in the picaresque film of the 1960s, *Easy Rider,* noted that "my movie is about the lack of freedom, not about freedom. My heroes are not right, they're wrong" (Hardin and Schossberg 1969:28). But to us they are *both,* and it is how picaresque narrative creates this ambiguity, this "nondisjunction" of values, by inversions on various levels that I will examine in this essay.

The term *pícaro* was first documented in 1525 with the meaning of "kitchen boy" and the connotation of "evil living." In the first dictionary of the Spanish Academy of 1726, *pícaro* is defined as an adjective meaning "low, vicious, deceitful, dishonourable and shameless" (Parker 1967:4). By way of literary definition, it could be said that the *pícaro* is one of the first "low" characters in written narrative who is not just a supernumerary, but is a hero or antihero. The first protagonist of a novel to whom the word is applied in the novel itself is the title character of *Guzmán de Alfarache* (1599-1604). Since then *pícaro* has generally been translated as "rogue" or "delinquent," notably by A. A. Parker in his monograph on the picaresque novel, *Literature and the Delinquent.* The word, however, was first used in reference to a real social type rather than a literary one, and while it usually designates one who violates social and human norms, picaro always has the connotation of "prankster," and does not mean "criminal" in the serious sense in which we use that term.

The word "picaresque" was first used in English in 1810. It has since described a type of satirical novel, originating in Spain in the sixteenth century, whose hero is an amusing vagabond or rogue who tells of his life and adventures in a loose, episodic fashion. The "picaresque novel" is at best a problematic literary concept. In its narrowest sense the term refers only to certain novels of the Spanish Golden Age (ca. 1550-1650); in its broadest sense it is used to describe any first-person, episodic, on-the-road novel, and at times is erroneously used as a synonym for plotless, formless, or structureless.[2] In the hope of mediating these extremes, I will use the term to refer to a basic narrative form or pattern, that is, "an essential situation or significant structure derived from the novels themselves" (Guillén 1971:71), which can account both for a specific kind of literary narrative and for a general narrative pattern characteristic of a variety of expressive forms. I think this shift of focus toward viewing the picaresque synchronically as a particular narrative pattern is essential to any description of the distinctive features of the form and to an initial outline of generic distinctions.[3]

When performances define themselves primarily in terms of the inversion of social and moral order *and* of the form and content of accepted literary genres, the very act of inversion creates such confusion that these enactments are generally accused of being formless. This is, of course, the charge often leveled at the picaresque.[4] Yet on closer examination, this formlessness seems more apparent than real, more an initial impression created by somehow turning the world upside down than the actual embodiment of chaos.

In the first place, there is an order, almost a hierarchy, to the norms and institutions which are upended and thereby satirized—that is, to the masters the picaro serves or the collective conditions he observes. The order of inversions generally corresponds to (1) the relative importance of the norms and institutions in a given society, (2) the degree of "reality" or necessity of such social fictions in contrast to their artifice, and (3) the chronological development of the protagonist. And since the picaro is generally a social climber, this sequence also corresponds to his vertical movement through levels of society. Couple this with his horizontal movement through space and away from home, and you can also predict, as Guillén has pointed out, that his adventures will become increasingly cosmopolitan. Second, such unifying devices as recurrent images, thematic contrast sets, circular patterns, and a "dance pattern" of reappearing secondary characters superimpose an order on the picaro's seemingly random episodic adventures.[5] Third, episodes are frequently related through the structural mirroring or interior duplication of stories-within-the-story which reflect, duplicate, invert, and otherwise comment upon the episode within which they are told. Fourth, as the preceding implies, there are frequently causal or logical connections among two or more episodes even though the overall structure of the narrative may not be causal or developmental. Fifth, the antisocieties of rogues with whom the picaro associates are, contrary to assumptions about the motley state of the underworld, often more highly structured than the dominant society.

Underlying the episodic and antidevelopmental narrative of the picaresque is yet another important pattern of organization: the structure of the narrative genre (or genres) being parodied. While numerous critics have discussed the picaresque as "antiromance," as a "counter-genre" that develops dialectically as an inversion of the pattern of chivalric romance, few have realized that it embodies the structures or the romance at the same time as it inverts them. The code which is being broken is always implicitly there, for the very act of deconstructing reconstructs and reaffirms the structure of romance. This formal, generic nondisjunction is central to the picaresque's problematic ambiguity: the pattern of expectation created by the inverted form (i.e. the picaresque) competes with the still somewhat operant, formal constraints of the genre or genres that have been inverted. In other words, the reader receives at least two sets of competing formal meta-code signals: "this is a romance"; "this is a picaresque antiromance."[6] As a consequence, even a reader familiar with the tradition is somewhat confused and frustrated, and the narrative "message" has an initial appearance of chaos. These conflicting systems of formal constraints or inherent expectations create some specific problems with regard to the picaresque (especially its ending) which I will discuss later.

As both Wicks and Guillén have pointed out, parody of other fictional types (notably, romance, pastoral, travel book, and confession) and of the picaresque tradition itself is a distinctive feature of the genre. In addition to explicit inversions of accepted social norms and institutions, judgement and satire of a society is implicitly made through a critical lampooning of some of its favorite literature. The impulse to parody is fundamental to the satiric mode, for nothing comments so fully on hypertrophied and banal formalism as the overimitation of the form. The "as-if" quality of all our necessary social fictions is repeatedly expressed in the critical parody of our accepted literary ones. While we tend to dissociate criticism and satire, defining the former as literary critique and the latter as social critique, it is interesting to note with regard to the picaresque that Roman satire (*satura*), from which picaresque narrative ultimately derives, was the traditional vehicle for literary criticism. The *satura* or "plate of mixed fruit" consisted, like the picaresque, of an admixture of genres and their reciprocals.

Historically, the picaresque dialectically develops and distinguishes itself as an inversion of the patterns of the chivalric romance and the pastoral.[7] The base transformation of the romance is the substitution of a lowlife delinquent for a princely hero. This initial inversion is developed by a mocking perversion of the hero's career pattern. The romance hero is born into a firm place in society, usually noble. He is then forced because of circumstance (often the loss or questioning of patrimony—patrimony operating here as a symbol of social place) into a physical and spiritual exile, in which he faces at least two tasks (usually the defense of a lady and the killing of a beast) that he must and does complete through his courage, intelligence, and hard work. Thus endowed with special power, he returns from the wilderness to society and reachieves social status through marriage to a noble's daughter or some other ceremonial conferral of renewed status.[8]

This exile-and-return pattern emphasizes the necessity for the hero to go beyond the margins of society and there undergo a liminal experience to find his sense of self and thus realize (often with the aid of mediating figures) symbolic power through victory in his tasks. This attainment of power makes possible the status change which is realized upon his reentry into society. The parallel between the hero's career pattern and the pattern of status change in rites of passage as described by Arnold van Gennep and Victor Turner is patent. But it is precisely this serious pattern of status passage which is perverted in the total extension and elaboration of liminality into a rhythm of "continuous disintegration" characteristic of picaresque narrative. Liminality with all its "betwixt and between" aspects is perhaps the most important distinctive feature of this countergenre.[9]

The picaro's parentage, in contrast to the hero's, is low and "marginal" (e.g., Don Pablos' father in the classic *El Buscón* is a thief, his mother a witch)—if it is specified at all. If the picaro is not orphaned through the agency of jail or execution, he orphans himself by disowning his parents (or parent) at an early age. In so rendering himself fatherless and statusless, he inverts the hero's pattern of loss of patrimony through the agency of society—what Wicks calls the "ejection motif." This symbolic social suicide is comically exemplified in *Huckleberry Finn* when Huck frees himself from father and society by faking his own murder. More recently, *Easy Rider* expresses an even more radical deracination: there is no mention of Captain America's or Billy's homes or families; all we know is that they "come from L.A." This canceling of connections is underlined by "a stranger" they meet who, when asked where he's from, replies "It's hard to say. . . . A city" (Hardin and Schlossberg 1969:72-73), and by the rejection and mockery of his All-American past by the drunken lawyer, George Hanson.

Once the picaro has been ejected or has ejected himself from society, he sets out to eliminate economic and status privation by ingratiating himself to a noble friend, continuing his formal education as a manservant (as in *El Buscón*), or by apprenticing himself to a series of "masters" and learning a "trade" to make his way in the world (as in *Lazarillo*), or by doing both. In any case, there is a mockery if not an explicit inversion of the educational system, the system of mentorship, the master-servant relationship,[10] and, I should add, of the benevolent mediating figures of romance.[11] In contrast to the latter, the picaro's preceptors present an appearance of virtue and a reality of corruption (see Guedj 1968:83). Even if not a servant to many masters in recent renderings, the picaro encounters a number of collective conditions; through his naive and uncomprehending initial response he exposes basic hypocrisy and duplicity. He soon becomes accomplished in the art of deceit and deception, outwits his masters, and sets out on his own to "live by his wits." In contrast, however, to the marked urban-rural contrast in the exile of the romance, the picaro seems to hang on the fringes of the city, for when he goes "on the road" he encounters only a greater variety of marginal types. He attains only the special power of the art of deceit. The only status change attendant upon his return is the transition from deceived to deceiver. These changes occur *within* the city context (urban renewal, as it were); unlike the romance and the pastoral, the rural excursions of the picaresque are mere placebos, confirmations in roguery (Wadlington 1973).

This perversion of the hero's education is repeatedly illustrated in the satire of religion endemic to the picaresque. That religion is singled out is not surprising given its predominance as a cultural system and its control of education in early modern Europe. For instance, Lazarillo de Tormes' second master is a priest who "presented a living portrait of the utmost niggardliness" (Flores 1957:41). He hypocritically preaches temperance in eating and drinking and virtually starves Lazarillo to death. Lazarillo, in turn, begins to pray for people to die, for only at funeral feasts does he truly eat, or, as he says, "in nothing could I find relief except in death." From a tinker (who is traditionally a marginal, wandering figure endowed with dangerous powers, but is described by Lazarillo as an "angel sent by God"), the starving Lazarillo obtains a key to the priest's chest or *arca* (also meaning Holy Ark) in which are kept the loaves of communion bread. The ironies and inversions continue to multiply.[12] Finally the priest suspects mice and boards up the chest, but "necessity is a wondrous sharpener of wits" (Flores 1957:48), and what the priest does by day Lazarillo undoes by night and vice versa. One night the priest beats the "snake" to which he now attributes the desecration and discovers that the mouse/snake is Lazarillo, whom he turns out to suffer an ever worse master, an impoverished hidalgo.

This first picaresque novel establishes a pattern of desacrementalization that virtually every narrative in the picaresque mode repeats. Even in one of the more recent renderings, *Easy Rider*, a meal in New Orleans during Mardi Gras becomes a mass; a church becomes a brothel; a whore, Mary; LSD, the sacred host; and a cemetary, the place of conversion—"turning on." And in addition to such inversions of the sacred and the profane, there is a transvaluation of the more general religious and moral categories of good and evil which I will discuss later.

Rather than inheriting a place in society, experiencing a temporary period of liminality and exile, and rejoining the social order in a new and improved status, the picaro is born into what Victor Turner calls a position of "structural inferiority" (1974:234). He declines to climb the social ladder through the formula of hard work and reward (inverting through trickery the customary work-play distinction), and opts for the truly marginal position of being a "half-outsider" who can neither join nor reject his fellow-men (Guillén 1971:80).[13] The marginal man is condemned and condemns himself "to live, at the same time, in two worlds and (is compelled to assume), in relation to the worlds in which he lives, the role of cosmopolitan and stranger" (Stonequist 1937:xvii). In short, he exploits and makes permanent the liminal state of being "betwixt and between all fixed points in a status sequence" (Turner 1974:232).

One of the major differences between the picaro and the hero, which is central to the former's maintenance of marginality, is his refusal or inability to reintegrate himself socially through marriage. He is either exposed in his attempt to marry (as in *El Buscón*) or his marriage (like Lazarillo's) is based on false premises and self-delusion. The picaro's behavior regarding marriage is indicative, moreover, of his general inability to form any abiding relationships, most especially with women, whom he uses and abuses. Despite his much touted sexuality the picaro ultimately fails to perform.[14] This experience of a number of missed connections is echoed structurally in the "dance pattern" of "meetings and remeetings, . . . one character quickly slipping from another" (Miller 1967:14,17). And as Allan Janik notes, "the very point of the 'dance' motif [is that] sex without love is a meaningless, mechanical ritual" (Janik and Toulmin 1973:64).

In yet another contrast to the idealized and spiritualized realm of romance, the picaresque stresses the material level of existence. The monsters of the picaro's world are all too real and all too human, and he uses his wits as well as his religion simply to survive—physically and immediately—rather than toward some greater end. Beyond the subsistence level, the picaro, unlike the hero of spiritual pursuit, is a lover and pursuer of things found only in this world—the immediate gratification of material things, physical comforts, and delights of the flesh. The very processes of signifying in such narratives express both the extreme materiality and the lack of connectedness in the picaro's world: there is a proliferation of signifiers and a relative poverty of signification, of meaning (Guedj 1968:82-83).[15] This too contributes to the meaninglessness or the reversibility of meaning of his experience, for those things which he covets have meaning only within a system which he has rejected.

The oft-repeated phrase "he lives by his wits" expresses yet another paradox of the picaro's existence. In this sense, too, he lives outside the ordinary feelings of the community: the hypertrophy of his practical intelligence replaces a full emotional development. Ironically, he usually just "takes over available patterns of feelings, and these are most likely to be conventional or orthodox" (Heilman 1958:549). In both a positive and negative sense the picaresque experience is an exercise of mind, a reveling in the mind as conqueror, a relishing of power through purely mental rather than physical or political or social means. Although necessity gives birth to the picaro's trickery and sharpens his wits, there is a point in every picaresque narrative beyond which trickery is indulged in for trickery's sake. In *El Buscón,* for example, Don Pablos joins and enjoys the band of "gentlemen" thieves despite the inheritance in his pocket. But, as Robert Heilman has pointed out: "In all literature that deals with the wit-conducted life there is, ultimately, ambiguity. Perhaps only detective stories naively exploit the passion for the mind's control of existence. Tragedy and picaresque set this passion in play; yet . . . both are penetrated by a sense of failure of mind alone. Picaresque heroes, at their best almost infinitely clever, nonetheless fall prey to . . . the irrationalities of circumstance" (1958:557-558). This ambiguity both delights and threatens us, for we cannot escape the fact that the picaro's intellectual virtue is also his vice, that his "shallowness" is both a disadvantage and an advantage.

Just as the picaro as protagonist has been criticized by literary commentators for his "shallowness," "flatness," and lack of self-awareness, so too the picaro as narrator is criticized for his limited and distorted perspective. While this is usually pointed out as a flaw—another instance of the rudimentary nature of this type of narrative—this convention of limited or restricted perspective is actually one of the virtues of the genre and is essential to its total inverse effect. This particular limitation is both a distinctive feature and a source of the vitality of the narrative form. Were the narrator-protagonist aware of his defects,

much of the humor, irony, and ambiguity would be diminished, contaminated by dull and explicit social criticism or the typical self-righteousness of the satirist. The picaro's defects create an equivocal perspective which functions as an unknown, unexpected source of vitality to constantly repair the solvent effects of a critical attitude within the narrative itself.

In this regard, it is no accident that almost every picaresque narrative presents itself as a first-person autobiographical reminiscence. This mode of narration underlines the picaro's isolation and estrangement as well as the narrative's questioning, if not rejection, of norms, of authority, of objective reality. As Guillén points out, the use of the first person is "more than a formal frame. It means that not only are the hero and his actions picaresque, but everything *else* in the story is colored with the sensibility, or filtered through the mind, of the picaro-narrator" (1971:81).

The first-person point of view, which is split between an experiencing "I" and a narrating "I," calls our attention to the radical estrangement between inner and outer man and inserts the tale into "a double perspective of self-concealment and self-revelation" (Guillén 1971:82).[16] This difference between narrative attitude and events narrated is the major structural irony of the genre: he (narrator) who tells the reader to trust the credibility of his tale then describes himself (protagonist) as the master of deception and deceit. The narrator's statement to the reader about his narrative and his seeming contradiction of it, like the meta-communicative statement, "this is play," "generates a paradox of the Russellian or Epimenides type—a negative statement containing an implicit negative metastatement" (Bateson 1972:179-180). The liar's assertion that "this is not an *un*true story" establishes a paradoxical frame comparable to Epimenides' "Liar" paradox: "All Cretans are liars. I am a Cretan" (Colie 1966:6). Like all paradoxes, the paradox of the picaresque is both a direct criticism of itself as narrative statement and an oblique criticism of absolute judgement or absolute convention in general. Ultimately, of course, the reader, like the picaro himself and his other victims, is taken in, caught in the vertigo of infinite reflection and the play with human understanding. The first-person prevarication of the picaresque is intimately connected with the charges of formlessness, for it is almost impossible not to confuse the paradoxical and "unreliable" mode of presentation with the events that are presented, and hence to regard them and their organization as improbable and illogical. How else, when language has become the instrument of dissimulation and irony (Guillén 1971:81)?

There is yet another irony in the double perspective of first-person reminiscence if we think of "remembered" in the literal sense of the presumptuous autobiographical remembering of something which is basically dismembered and disjointed. For, as Oskar Seidlin has pointed out, there is an ironic discrepancy between the lowly, marginal picaro and the effrontery with which he dares to say "I," to reconstruct his life and adventures, and to offer them to the public with high moral seriousness (Seidlin 1951:191).

It is significant, therefore, that this public revelation may become even more self-conscious—the picaro finding his fullest expression of self as a performer-illusionist, either as one who identifies himself as a maker of illusions or as one who throws himself into a world of illusion in which misrule (or at least poetic license) is the rule. In *El Buscón* Don Pablos' career culminates in the profession of actor and playwright; in Thomas Mann's novel, Felix Krull is identified as an artist; and in *Easy Rider* the destination of Captain America and Billy is New Orleans' Mardi Gras. Mardi Gras is, of course, carnival, the period of license before Lent, and is defined in terms of masking, transformation, and inversion of norms and perceptions. The repeated identification of picaro and artist in modern expressions of the genre indicate that the preceding examples are not simply episodes or temporary professions in the life of the picaro, but synecdoches or base metaphors representing the entirety of the picaresque pattern in life and in art—fiction as a way of life.[17] That this lowlife delinquent is a master of many masks should not surprise us, for it is very likely that there is a positive correlation between marginality and fantasy. "Maybe groups and individuals who are cut out of the benefits of a given society are the ones who most often dream about another, and sometimes act to bring it about" (Cox 1970:64). We can at least say with certainty that in the picaresque, "fantasy thrives among the dissatisfied" (Cox 1970:64).[18]

Ultimately, the effect of such masking, transformation, and inversion as is characteristic of the picaresque is to render ambiguous or "nondisjunctive" (as Kristeva terms it) primary categories which are usually distinguished, such as good and evil, fidelity and treason, sacred and profane, life and death, and "high" and "low" style, and to negate these disjunctions as they are commonly maintained in the older genres of epic and romance.[19] When such basic discretions are inverted, the absolute separation of the discretion is called into question and, in terms of perception and behavior, a continuum of indistinction is created. Thus the utility, if not the validity, of such distinctions becomes a matter of debate. In *El Buscón,* for example, evil is initially equated with unreality and deception, and good with the real and the normal. But, as T. E. May points out, the "reality" that young Pablos confronts is so grotesque and deformed that he can only cope with this evil by assuming a role which is not a true one, by opting for "unreality" or inauthenticity (1950:322). Through this nondisjunction Quevedo raises the moral or metaphysical question, "What does it mean to choose unreality with one's eyes open?" Such transvaluations of values are characteristic of what happens when the hero of a novel must define his rebellion, his alienation from society, in terms which take their meaning from the very authorities he has come to reject (Poirier 1968:101). A reversibility of meaning is both the cause and the effect of a discontinuous world.

Nondisjunction both of meaning and of formal generic constraints—that is, the coexistence of two or more metacode signals and thus of several sets of expectations—also

contributes to the "problematic" ending characteristic of the picaresque. Simply stated, the problem is this: If you don't have a developmental and an end-determined plot, if you parody the conventions and narrative structure of other literary forms, and if you deny the validity of all either-or categories, how *do* you conclude the picaro's life and adventures and yet maintain the novel's fundamental ambiguity? The narratives I have discussed here offer three alternatives:[20] (1) the picaro reenters society, sometimes through marriage, and is apparently reintegrated into the social structure; (2) the picaro is killed or punished; and (3) the picaro's adventures are "to be continued."

The first of these alternatives is the expected end of the romance or comic pattern. It is an unsatisfactory conclusion to the picaresque which has in other respects parodied and inverted the romance pattern. Unless the author has depicted a society which offers alternatives and the possibility of change, or evidence of an official culture that has an historical dignity, which the picaresque does *not,* reaggregation is not a viable or credible conclusion (Poirier 1968:101). When a picaresque narrative does end with reintegration, it is based upon false premises or self-delusion: for example, Lazarillo de Tormes marries the priest's whore and deludes himself regarding her fidelity as well as the importance of his social role as towncrier; Huck Finn is "reborn" in the form of Tom Sawyer and then uses the latter's literary lies to secure Jim's freedom. Such perversions of the romance ending result in little more than a deceptive and temporary restoration of equilibrium. It won't be long until Huck "lights out for the territories."

The second alternative expresses another vector of formal influence: the violation-punishment pattern of melodrama and tragedy in which the individual who violates social and human boundaries is punished, the social order preserved through "the sacrificial principle of victimage," and the victim elevated as martyr. Since picaresque narrative intermittently mocks this very pattern and is itself based on a violation of boundaries, this conclusion is also unsatisfactory if not gratuitous, as illustrated in the violent ending of *Easy Rider.*

Fonda's comments about his movie, its ending, and what he regards as the audience's misinterpretation, are illustrative of the problems of picaresque conclusions:

My movie is about the *lack* of freedom, not about freedom. My heroes are not right, they're wrong. The only thing I can end up doing is killing my character. I end up committing suicide; that's what I'm saying that America is doing. People go in and they think, "Look at those terrible rednecks, they killed those two free souls, who needed to love, blah, blah, blah." That's something we have to put up with.

We don't give out any information through dialogue. We have a very loose plot, nothing you can follow. You can't predict what's going to happen, and that puts everybody off. People want it predicted for them, they want violence to happen when they expect it to happen, so they can deal with it, they want sex to be a certain way and drugs to be a certain way and death to be a certain way. And it ain't. Neither is freedom. "Easy Rider" is a Southern term for a whore's old man, not a pimp, but the dude who lives with a chick. Because he's got the easy ride. Well, that's what happened to America, man. Liberty's become a whore, and we're all taking an easy ride.

[Hardin and Schlossberg 1969:28]

In terms of picaresque conventions, Fonda's interpretation, the typical audience interpretation, and the ending are all in error in that they deny or cannot tolerate the fundamental ambiguity of the genre—they want things "to be a certain way"—which the movie *does* set up in its sympathetic and humorous treatment of antisocial characters and values. His movie is about *both* freedom *and* the lack of freedom; his heroes are *both* right *and* wrong, and we would have gotten that message had the film ended with that penultimate bit of dialogue, "We've done it" "No, we blew it," rather than motorized sacrifice.

This third alternative, the inconclusive conclusion exemplified in *El Buscón*'s "to be continued," is appropriate to the formal and ideological "openness" of picaresque narrative; it is also the logically probable ending of a first-person account of one's life and adventures.[21] In this sense, it doesn't really matter that Thomas Mann never finished *Felix Krull*. Further, I would suggest that "to be continued" is a conventional exit formula for any symbolic process or literary structure based on inversion and on formal and moral nondisjunction. The refusal to end maintains the ambiguity and the vitality of the form but, in most cases, is not meant to be taken literally. And yet, paradoxically, with the picaresque as with all "play" forms (see Bateson 1972) it doesn't work unless we do take the threat of inversion and the violation of boundaries seriously, seeing it in this case as a realistic reflection of the underlife of the group. As Frank Kermode has pointed out in *The Sense of an Ending*: "Men . . . make considerable imaginative investments in coherent patterns which, by the provision of an end, make possible a satisfying consonance with the origins and with the middle. . . . But they also, when awake and sane, feel the need to show a marked respect for things as they are; so that there is a recurring need for adjustments in the interests of reality as well as of control" (1967:17)—a need which the openness and infinite possibilities of picaresque structure fulfills. The absence of plot in Aristotle's sense is the result neither of carelessness nor of ineptitude, for there is, as Howell once said, "an art to not arriving."

To question why we continue to write and to read and to enjoy the picaresque pattern of inversion is tantamount to asking why are there always "social bandits"? Perhaps the old brigand had the last word when he said, "We are sad, it is true, but that is because we have always been persecuted. The gentry use the pen, we the gun" (Hobsbawm 1969:13). Or, as Vita Sackville-West said of Virginia Woolf when she called her gamekeeper's coat a

poacher's, "The poacher would naturally be dearer to her mind than the gamekeeper" (Noble 1972:136). Such literary poachers remind us that even the gamekeeper's laws are man-made fictions.

Notes

1. I am indebted to my colleagues Avrom Fleishman, Anthony Hilfer, Gordon Mills, Warwick Wadlington, and Susan Wittig, all of whom read an earlier version of this paper and made extensive and valuable criticisms and suggestions. And to Roger Abrahams, I owe thanks for criticism, encouragement, and moral support.

2. For discussions of the uses and abuses of the concept of the picaresque see especially Frohock 1967:43-52, Dooley 1957-1958:363-377, Wicks 1972:153-216, and Guillén 1971:71-106. The last two essays are especially important efforts to redefine picaresque and to restore its usefulness as a critical concept.

3. My concept of the picaresque as a synchronic narrative pattern is closely related to Guillén's concept of "picaresque myth" and Wicks' notion of "picaresque mode" (derived from Scholes' modal perspective) as developed in the essays cited above. Wicks' essay appeared when I was in the final stages of revision, and I have indicated those places in which we seem to agree on the description of the genre.

4. See, for example, Chandler 1899 from which succeeding similar criticisms of formlessness largely derive. The low regard for episodic narrative generally derives from Aristotle, who remarked in the *Poetics* that "of all plots and actions the episodic [i.e., without probable or necessary sequence] are the worst."

5. The concept of the dance pattern is developed by Miller 1967:13-20. This structuring has ideological significance with regard to the quality of the picaro's social relationships, especially his relations with women, which I will discuss later in this essay.

6. The term "metacode" is derived from Roman Jakobson's six-element model of a speech act, which he sees as consisting of: sender, receiver, message, code, channel, and context (1960). What literary critics term a "generic pattern of expectation" may be defined in Jakobson's terms as the "code" of a given type of narrative. A metacode signal is a statement which explicitly refers to the code or generic pattern(s) being used and manipulated, e.g., "This incredible story is a true confession."

7. For reasons of time and space, I have limited the discussion that follows to the picaresque's inversions of the romance. For an historical discussion of the picaresque's emergence in counterdistinction to the romance *and* the pastoral, see Guillén 1971:135-158. His concept of "countergenre"—and his statement that these negative impacts or *influences à rebours*,

through which a norm is dialectically surpassed (and assimilated) by another, or a genre by a countergenre, constitute one of the main ways in which a literary model acts upon a writer (pp. 146-147)—is especially relevant to the present discussion.

8. For a discussion of the exile-and-return, quest-and-test pattern of romance, see Rank 1914 and Lord Raglan 1936.

9. If, as Victor Turner suggests in his commentary in this volume, we reserve the use of the terms "liminal" and "liminality" for *ritual* proper and use the term "liminoid" for nontribal, modern industrial leisure-time genres, then the perpetual betwixt-and-between situation of the picaresque would more properly be defined as an extended liminoid state.

10. This particular inversion has ideological implications that go beyond the scope of this essay, and yet are ultimately relevant thereto. Hegel's classic discussion (1964: 228-267) of the inversion of the master-servant relationship, the process of self-enfranchisement, and the resultant "unhappy consciousness" is especially pertinent to the situation in the picaresque.

11. On the basis of her work with medieval romance, my colleague Susan Wittig has speculated that what we have in the hero-preceptor or hero-mediator dyad is a latent *avuncular* relationship. The fact that the hero usually marries his "uncle's" daughter implies a *cross-cousin* marriage, which medieval European culture explicitly denied but implicitly allowed. This suggests that in the picaresque the protagonist who refuses to marry, refuses to live within the community's kinship patterns and is outcast for his refusal. Thus this inversion of the educational system may imply a more profound inversion of kinship rules.

12. For a brilliant discussion of the innumerable ironies and inversions generated by the controlling inversion of the meaning of life and death in *Lazarillo,* see Gilman 1966:149-166.

13. In addition to Guillén, see Kolakowski 1962 on the jester's similar relationship to society and Cox's discussion of a "theology of opposition" and Christ as jester (1962:133-138).

14. This failure to perform sexually and to establish lasting, meaningful relationships with women together with the picaro's assumption of female roles and clothes among his many masks connotes both transvestism and homosexuality. In several novels, moreover, the protagonist is a *picara*. This creative androgyny characteristic of trickster types finds its fullest expression in Virginia Woolf's neopicaresque *Orlando,* in which the title character changes sex every century.

15. In another essay, "The Novel and the Carnival World (1974), I have discussed the uses and effects of a "surplus of signifiers" in symbolic processes, notably as an inversion, a mockery of the mode of signification of serious discourse.

16. See also Wicks 1974:244-245.

17. On the art of illusionism and manipulation as a vital part of the picaresque tradition, and the picaro as a man of imagination who "handles experience much the say an artist handles the materials of his art," and so on, see Alter 1965:126-132.

18. The connection between fantasy and marginality is of course exemplified in the tales and myths of the Trickster, and the picaresque could be regarded as the written version of this in the modern Western world. For further discussion of the correlation between the marginal and the creative, see my "'A Tolerated Margin of Mess': The Trickster and His Tales Reconsidered" (1975). This creativity is notably expressed in the marginal's delight in the activity of disguise, his quick-change artistry denying the garment as a fixed symbol of class and the fixity of the social system (see Alter 1965:41-44).

19. Kristeva (1970) sees just such nondisjunction of values and of generic patterns of expectation as essential to the development of complex prose fiction in the form of the realistic novel. With regard to the Spanish picaresque novel in particular, Whitbourne (1974:1-24) regards moral ambiguity as "one of its most essential and persistent characteristics, and which may account in some measure for its considerable popularity" (p. 16).

20. There are at least three other possible endings: (1) the wanderer reenters society but refuses to abandon his antisocial, antinormative behavior, in which case he is incarcerated in jail or the insane asylum—the modern version of banishment; (2) the deviant returns and remakes the society which expelled him—the pattern of idealistic, revolutionary narrative; and (3) the exile in his wanderings finds a society structured according to his own values, or returns home to find that the society he left has been transformed—the pattern of utopian literature. In all three cases there is a triumph of *one* set of values which reduces the ambiguous nondisjunction of social and antisocial values upon which the picaresque is predicated.

21. On the impossibility of ending a picaresque novel, see Alter 1965:33-34.

References

Alter, Robert. 1965. *Rogue's Progress: Studies in the Picaresque Novel.* Cambridge: Harvard University Press.

Anon. 1554. *Lazarillo de Tormes* (trans.). In Flores, pp. 25-84.

Babcock-Abrahams, Barbara. 1974. "The Carnivalization of the Novel." *Modern Language Notes* 89:911-937.

————. 1975. "'A Tolerated Margin of Mess': The Trickster and His Tales Reconsidered." *Journal of the Folklore Institute* 11:147-186.

Bataillon, M. 1931. *Le roman picaresque.* Paris: La Renaissance du livre.

Bateson, Gregory. 1972. "A Theory of Play and Fantasy." In *Steps to an Ecology of Mind.* San Francisco: Chandler. Pp. 177-200.

Chandler, F. W. 1899. *Romances of Roguery: An Episode in the History of the Novel.* Part I, *The Picaresque Novel in Spain.* New York: Macmillan.

Colie, Rosalie Little. 1966. *Paradoxia Epidemia: The Renaissance Tradition of Paradox.* Princeton: Princeton University Press.

Cox, Harvey. 1970. *The Feast of Fools: A Theological Essay on Festivity and Fantasy.* New York: Harper & Row.

Dooley, D. J. 1957-1958. "Some Uses and Mutations of the Picaresque." *Dalhousie Review* 37:363-377.

Flores, Angel, ed. 1957. *Masterpieces of the Spanish Golden Age.* New York: Holt, Rinehart & Winston.

Frohock, W. M. 1967. "The Idea of the Picaresque." *Yearbook of Comparative and General Literature* 16:43-52.

————. 1969. "The Falling Center: Recent Fiction and the Picaresque Tradition." *Novel* 3:62-69.

Ghose, Zulfikar. 1972. *The Incredible Brazilian.* New York: Holt, Rinehart & Winston.

Gilman, Stephen. 1966. "The Death of Lazarillo de Tormes." *PMLA* 81:149-166.

Guedj, Aimé. 1968. "Structure du monde picaresque." *Linguistique et littérature.* La nouvelle critique, Numéro spécial, Colloque de Cluny, 16-17 April. Pp. 82-87.

Guillén, Claudio. 1971. *Literature as System: Essays toward a Theory of Literary History.* Princeton: Princeton University Press.

Hardin, Nancy, and Marilyn Schlossberg, eds. 1969. *Easy Rider: Original Screenplay by Peter Fonda, Dennis Hopper, Terry Southern.* New York: New American Library.

Hegel, G. W. F. 1964. *The Phenomenology of Mind.* Trans. James Baillie. New York: Humanities Press.

Heilman, Robert B. 1958. "Felix Krull: Variations on Picaresque." *Sewanee Review* 66:547-577.

Hobsbawm, Eric. 1969. *Bandits.* New York: Dell.

Jakobson, Roman. 1960. "Closing Statement: Linguistics and Poetics." In Thomas A. Sebeok, ed., *Style in Language.* Cambridge: M.I.T. Press.

Janik, Allan, and Stephen Toulmin. 1973. *Wittgenstein's Vienna.* New York: Simon and Schuster.

Kermode, Frank. 1967. *The Sense of an Ending: Studies in the Theory of Fiction.* New York: Oxford.

Kolakowski, Leszek. 1962. "The Priest and the Jester." *Dissent* 9:215-235.

Kristeva, Julia. 1970. *Le texte du roman: Approche sémiologique d'une structure discursive transformationnelle.* The Hague: Mouton.

Mann, Thomas, 1955. *Confessions of Felix Krull, Confidence Man: The Early Years.* New York: Vintage.

May, T. E. 1950. "Good and Evil in the Buscón: A Survey." *Modern Language Review* 45:319-335.

Miller, Stuart. 1967. *The Picaresque Novel.* Cleveland, London: Case Western Reserve University Press.

Noble, Joan Russell, ed. 1972. *Recollections of Virginia Woolf.* London: Owen.

Parker, A. A. 1967. *Literature and the Delinquent: The Picaresque Novel in Spain and Europe, 1599-1753.* Edinburgh: Edinburgh University Press.

Poirier, Richard. 1968. "Huck Finn and the Metaphors of Society." In Claude M. Simpson, ed., *Twentieth Century Interpretations of "The Adventures of Huckleberry Finn."* Englewood Cliffs, N.J.: Prentice-Hall. Pp. 92-101.

de Quevedo, Francisco. 1626. *The Life and Adventures of Don Pablos the Sharper* (trans.). In Flores, pp. 85-234.

Raglan, Lord. 1936. *The Hero: A Study in Tradition, Myth, and Drama.* London: Methuen.

Rank, Otto. 1957. *The Myth of the Birth of the Hero.* Trans. F. Robbins and Smith Ely Jelliffe. New York: R. Brunner.

Seidlin, Oskar. 1951. "Picaresque Elements in Thomas Mann's Work." *Modern Language Quarterly* 12:183-200.

Stonequist, E. V. 1937. *The Marginal Man: A Study in Personality and Culture Conflict.* New York: Scribner's.

Turner, Victor. 1967. *The Forest of Symbols: Aspects of Ndembu Ritual.* Ithaca, N.Y.: Cornell University Press.

————. 1969. *The Ritual Process: Structure and Anti-Structure.* Chicago: Aldine.

————. 1974. "Passages, Margins, and Poverty: Religious Symbols of Communitas." In *Dramas, Fields, and Metaphors.* Ithaca, N.Y.: Cornell University Press. Pp. 231-271.

van Gennep, Arnold. 1960. *The Rites of Passage.* Chicago: University of Chicago Press.

Wadlington, Warwick P. 1973. Personal communication.

Weightman, John. 1969. "The Outsider Rides Again." *Encounter* 33:46-50.

Whitbourne, Christine J., ed. 1974. *Knaves and Swindlers: Essays on the Picaresque Novel in Europe.* London: Oxford University Press.

Wicks, Ulrich. 1972. "Picaro, Picaresque: The Picaresque in Literary Scholarship." *Genre* 5:153-216.

————. 1974. "The Nature of Picaresque Narrative: A Modal Approach." *PMLA* 89:240-249.

Woolf, Virginia. 1928. *Orlando: A Biography.* New York: Harcourt Brace Jovanovich.

Joseph W. Meeker (essay date 1997)

SOURCE: Meeker, Joseph W. "The Pastoral and the Picaresque." In *The Comedy of Survival: Literary Ecology and a Play Ethic,* pp. 50-73. Tucson: University of Arizona Press, 1997.

[*In this essay, Meeker considers the character of the picaro from the vantage point of the pastoral tradition in literature.*]

The world has often seemed like a scary place for people. Ours is not the first period in history to notice that there is much corruption in social and political structures, that conventional moralities do not address our real problems, that there are too many people for comfort, that the technologies that promised us ease have also damaged our lives and environments, and that crime and violence are escalating. It is not that the world is itself malevolent or that the gods are angry, for most modern people are well aware that the threats to human well-being are of our own making.

As people have invented their unhappiness, so they have invented means for relief. Since the Renaissance began to unfold the new ages of humanism and technology, Western culture has sought to evade their destructive consequences by using a variety of psychological and intellectual devices. Pastoral and picaresque literature represent two important patterns of response to an unacceptable world. Both terms are commonly applied to conventional literary genres, but both also identify modes of human behavior and systems of human values. Both are currently in use as models for human responses to contemporary social, intellectual, and natural environments. The choice between them is therefore of some usefulness in deciding what to do about the difficult world around us.

The pastoral tradition is the older of the two, and its historical credentials are impressive. Some find its roots in the Genesis account of the Garden of Eden, where the proper human environment appears as a fertile and pleasant natural setting characterized by peace and innocence. But the Roman poet Virgil of the first century B.C. gets credit for perfecting the literary form of the pastoral poem with its conventions of sylvan glades, peaceful animals, and happy shepherds who live in love and kinship with nature. Virgil's pastoral was revived at the Renaissance and has since been the model for countless literary works and a major influence upon modern attitudes toward both nature and human society.

The picaresque tradition has no such classical pedigree. Scholars differ over its literary origins, its definition, and the kind of evidence that might be needed to interpret it. There is general agreement that the term derives from the Spanish *picaro,* "rogue," and that the genre comprises tales about socially deprived people. The first clear example of the form is the anonymous little book *Lazarillo de Tormes,* which appeared in Spain in 1554. *Lazarillo* is the story of a young man's adventures as he struggles to survive in a hostile world that seems bent upon destroying him. To endure, he must adapt himself somehow to the given conditions of his environment, however many rules of decorum and ethics must be ignored in the process. The picaresque, at its origins, is a mode of survival against odds in a world that is hostile or indifferent.

Simply put, escape from the mad world or adaptation to its conditions are the choices offered by the pastoral and picaresque modes. Both presuppose some necessary relationship between human social and biological environments, but differ in their assessment of that relationship. The pastoral looks longingly at biological nature as an alternative to society, while the picaresque sees society itself as a natural environment—a wilderness. Civilization has been in a perpetual state of social and biological crisis at least since the Renaissance. Perhaps these two literary traditions can help to reveal whether they are in fact two different crises, or only one.

THE PASTORAL FANTASY

The pastoral tradition is rooted in imperial Rome, although it has significant antecedents in Hellenistic Greece and is reinforced by weighty influences from the Hebrew Old Testament. It was Virgil, however, who set the pastoral tone of greatest influence. Virgil's *Eclogues,* published in 37 B.C., reflects the weariness of sensitive Romans to the excesses and injustices of their society and their quest for solace and sense in a rural setting. "Lo, to what wretched pass has civil discord brought us," exclaims Meliboeus in the first *Eclogue.*[1] Expelled from his farm by war and its political aftermath, he laments the future and admires his friend who has managed to retain land to grow old on: "Happy in thy old age, here, amid familiar streams and holy springs thou wilt woo the coolness of the shade."[2] Rural repose is contrasted throughout the *Eclogues* with "the thankless town," the symbol of anxiety and misery. Virgil's pastorals show people being oppressed by urban life, but comforted by nature.

Rome inspired many besides Virgil to seek relief on the farm, and for many of the same reasons that move modern urbanites to take refuge in the country. Romans of the first and second centuries often found in their city the same features that cause New Yorkers and Los Angelenos to dream of pastoral settings. The Roman satirist Decimus Junius Juvenalis, in his *Third Satire* (ca. A.D. 110-130), presents a familiar catalogue of urban ills: degrading poverty in the ghettos, high taxes, inflated prices for poor goods and services, corrupt government, crime and vice in the streets, poor schools and wicked teachers, pressures of social conformity, traffic congestion, police brutality, and environmental pollution. "Rome, the great sewer" seems to Juvenal beyond redemption, and his only solution is to go back to the farm:

> Tear yourself from the games, and get a place
>   in the country!
> One little Latian town, like Sora, say,

or Frusino,
Offers a choice of homes, at a price you pay here,
  in one year,
Renting some hole in the wall. Nice houses, too,
  with a garden,
Springs bubbling up from the grass, no need for
  windlass or bucket,
Plenty to water your flowers, if they need it,
  without any trouble.
Live there, fond of your hoe, an independent
  producer,
Willing and able to feed a hundred good vegetarians.
Isn't it something, to feel, wherever you are,
  how far off,
You are a monarch? At least, lord of a
  single lizard.[3]

Juvenal's rhetoric, like that of contemporary suburban real estate developers, stresses the goodness of life in the country, and the final lines reveal another familiar motivation: It is better to be lord of a single lizard than a victim of urban exploitation. The city degrades people and the country restores their sense of power and dignity; in the city we are controlled, but in the country we control. A rural setting symbolizes both the purity of nature and the power of people, a conjunction whose paradoxes were present two thousand years ago. Juvenal was hardly a pastoral poet, although he did share Virgil's belief that amid flocks and fields, trees and birds, one might find both the spiritual peace and the personal satisfaction that cities couldn't offer.

The pastoral goal has always been to find in rural nature an alternative to the ills of civilization. With the decline of Rome, pastoral literature and its attitudes became scarce, perhaps for lack of oppressive cities from which escape was needed. But when the cities arose again with the early Renaissance, pastoral values were revived to meet the needs of harried humanists. Both the pastoral literary genre perfected by Virgil and the antiurban conventions of jaded Romans such as Juvenal seemed to express perfectly the sentiments of many of the new people of the Renaissance.

Disease was one of the more dramatic evils of city life in late medieval and Renaissance Europe. Epidemics of black plague were environmental disasters partly attributable to environmental pollution, humanly induced ecological imbalance, and overcrowding in the newly great cities. When the plague struck Florence in 1348, the aristocratic young men and women of Giovanni Boccaccio's collection of tales, the *Decameron,* sought refuge from death and social disorder in a genteel tour of the Italian countryside where they told one another risqué stories to pass the time. Although the *Decameron* is not properly a pastoral tale, its framework shows the pastoral motivation to flee from the pain and danger of the city to the solace and pleasure of rural life.

Boccaccio's introduction paints a grim picture of the diseased city where "everyone felt doomed and had abandoned his property," where "the authority of human and divine laws almost disappeared," and where "people

cared no more for dead men than we care for dead goats."[4] The alternative to all this misery, sought out by Boccaccio's young people, is a rural garden described in traditional pastoral images: "The sight of this garden, of its beautiful plan, of the plants, and the fountain and the little streams flowing from it, so much pleased the ladies and three young men that they said, if Paradise could be formed on earth, it could be given no other form than that of this garden, nor could any further beauty be added to it."[5] The young people weave garlands from the garden plants, listen to the twenty different birds who serenade them, and delight in the hundreds of beautiful rabbits, goats, deer, and "many other kinds of harmless animals running about as if they were tame."[6] To the classical image of a domesticated rural landscape composed of beautiful plants and harmless animals, the Renaissance can add the dimension of moral innocence that derives from the biblical Garden of Eden and the medieval view of heaven as a divinely created pastoral scene. To the pastoral eye, society is bewilderingly complicated and dangerous while nature is beautifully simple and congenial.

The pastoral flourishes in times of urban crisis, or in those periods often called decadent, when traditional forms and rituals of society have become inappropriate but continue to hold the allegiance of large numbers of people who can find no alternative. One result is a general sense, especially among privileged and intellectual people, that the world is unmanageable, unintelligible, and doomed to self-destruction. Those who have the means to escape begin to look for places to hide from the foreseeable apocalypse, either in a new physical setting or in their fantasies. The pastoral tradition provides both.

Rural life seems rational at such times because it is thought to be governed by natural rather than human laws. Crops sprout, mature, and are harvested for human sustenance in dependable cycles. Animals graze placidly in their pastures without all the jostling and conflicts generated among people who crowd the marketplaces. And the rustic farmer who supervises nature's nourishing processes appears to be a contributing part of the sensible system surrounding him, unlike his socially alienated urban brother. To a tired and frustrated aristocrat, agriculture is a symbol of tranquility and order, God's image of what life should be like everywhere.

Nostalgia for a lost Golden Age is satisfied in part by the discovery in the present of simplified forms of order in agriculture and gardening. Agriculture becomes symbolic of both structural integrity and moral innocence. Eden, after all, was merely a small farm characterized by abundance, purity, and simplicity until its agrarian tenants noticed the existence of some awkwardly polarized contradictions, like good and evil, male and female, obedience and rebellion, and as a result were sent off to build cities where such conflicts belong. The pastoral hope is to reclaim that lost simplicity by escaping present complexity, whether its imagery is that of a classical Golden Age, a biblical garden, a rural landscape, a national park, or merely a suburban lawn with its small vegetable and flower garden to represent the good and natural life in contrast to the evils of civilization.

The pastoral impulse is utopian in its assumption that suffering and chaos are unnecessary and that strategies that will overcome such ills are possible, indeed natural. Adam's unfortunate choice to leave the garden behind was also an abandonment of reason, of common sense, and of orderly administrative structure, but God has generously permitted vestiges of the original plan to persist in the form of farms and gardens that people may imitate in order to regain Eden. If society can only be organized according to the proper principles of organic gardening, peace and stability will surely follow. The utopian vision, like the pastoral, sees nature at work in agriculture and seeks to reproduce the fertility, peacefulness, durability, simplicity, and moral innocence of gardens among the social structures of humanity.

Ebenezer Howard, the influential nineteenth-century English landscape architect and city planner, built his utopian Garden City upon a pastoral foundation:

> The key to the problem how to restore the people to the land—that beautiful land of ours, with its canopy of sky, the air that blows upon it, the sun that warms it, the rain and dew that moisten it—the very embodiment of Divine love for man—is indeed a *Master Key,* for it is the key to a portal through which, even when scarce ajar, will be seen to pour a flood of light on the problems of intemperance, of excessive toil, of restless anxiety, of grinding poverty—the true limits of Governmental interference, ay, and even the relations of man to the Supreme Power.[7]

Howard's alternative to the pain and degradation of city life, like Juvenal's, is the garden. The difference is that Howard wants to rebuild cities to incorporate the virtues of gardens, not merely to escape from the city. Howard had hope for humanity. He was confident that the influence of the garden upon the city would provide a solution to psychological, social, political, and even theological problems common to urban environments. His utopian vision sought relief in fantasies of future gardens, not merely in a change of geography or a return to a previous golden-age garden.

The United States may be the world's largest-scale utopian experiment in creating a nation on the model of a pastoral garden. Many of its earliest settlers looked upon the new land as a green refuge from the oppression they had suffered in European cities. The American pastoral ideal has been studied in detail by Leo Marx in his book *The Machine in the Garden.* Marx traces the pervasive pastoral strain in American thought and shows the painful contradictions that developed as the American garden was gradually transformed into an industrialized farm, then into a national factory: "Beginning in Jefferson's time, the cardinal image of American aspirations was a rural landscape, a well-ordered green garden magnified to continental size."[8] An agricultural America must be both beautiful and morally pure, for, according to Jefferson, "those who labor in the earth are the chosen people of God . . . whose breasts he has made his peculiar deposit for substantial and genuine virtue."[9] Marx also shows that the snake of industrialism that was to corrupt the garden was also known to Jefferson. Foreign competition and the War of 1812 forced America to abandon its gardening project in order to defend itself. Jefferson knew that the garden would never be the same again: "Our enemy has indeed the consolation of Satan on removing our first parents from Paradise: from a peaceable and agricultural nation, he makes us a military and manufacturing one."[10] With the machine in power, the garden was doomed.

The conflict between the pastoral garden and the industrial machine is a fundamental polarity of American thought that has tormented Americans from the beginning. As the machine has achieved greater dominance, the American garden has gradually disappeared, and with it American hopes for realizing a pastoral utopia of peace and purity.

Unfortunately, pastoral gardens are usually made by the same machines that will eventually destroy them. In order to maintain the human dominance and safety required by pastoral values, it is necessary to assert human technological advantage over nature. Predatory or dangerous animal competitors must be exterminated or expelled; poisonous, ugly, or inedible plants must be rooted out; land must be cultivated and sown to nourishing crops or used as pasture for fattening human sources of meat. Whether the machine is the hoe that Juvenal's Roman is so fond of, the rifle and railroad that cleared the prairies of buffalo, or the bulldozers, chemicals, and irrigation systems of modern farming, the machine is an indispensable part of the pastoral garden, for it alone gives people the power to civilize nature. Gardens are not images of nature, but of the human management of nature.

When anthropologists talk about "the pastoral age" they are not referring to a poetic period, but to the stage of human evolution when plants and animals were domesticated, thus encouraging permanent settlements and changing humanity's nutritional relationship with the environment. That kind of pastoralism freed people from the need to hunt and pick berries, and made it possible to pay attention to such things as theology, politics, philosophy, art, and science. Pastoral poetry expresses a longing for this early stage of civilization when agriculture had given people leisure and sufficiency, but before the development of elaborate social and political structures. What the pastoral tradition calls "nature" is merely simplified civilization. No pastoral poet ever gets nostalgic thinking about Paleolithic hunters or australopithecine apes, nor does he long for unimproved wilderness or for violent aspects of natural processes.

The pastoral symphony is a thoroughly domesticated score orchestrated solely around human themes. Its central images—farm, garden, pasture—show nature at the service of the farmer and husbandman. Pastoral scenes include plants valuable for their nutritional or ornamental qualities and animals that have been tamed for human use, such as sheep, cattle, and dogs. The only wild animals are noncompetitors, like songbirds whose music is assumed to be designed for human entertainment. Dangerous or competitive plants and animals are strictly excluded. The pastoral landscape does not permit thistles or loco weed, wolves, lions, eagles, vultures, mosquitos, or poisonous spiders. And when a snake appears in such a garden, it is a sign that the place has been corrupted already. Pastoral values glorify anthropocentric agriculture and rigidly reject the possibility that wild nature has any independent integrity.

Pastoral literature demonstrates the futility that must result from the full exploration of pastoral motives. The pastoral hero is never an image of human success or greatness, and he never achieves what he has been longing for. As his career begins in fear, self-pity, or self-indulgence, so in the end we are likely to see him "either dead or totally alienated from society, alone and powerless, like the evicted shepherd of Virgil's eclogue."[11] The pastoral epiphany is a recognition that neither human society nor wilderness is a suitable environment for people, and that the garden, trying to mediate between the two, merely separates us from other humans and from nature.

Inherent contradictions in pastoral values lead typically to frustration and despair. The sensitive aristocrat who turns toward Arcadia and away from Rome often discovers that Rome is really within him. Although he can leave behind the fearsome environment of civilization and its cities, yet the psyche of civilization remains to guide his responses to nature. He cannot reject civilization without rejecting his own humanness, so he seeks a compromise in the halfway house of a pastoral Arcadia, somewhere midway between the horrors of wilderness and the horrors of the city. His choice of the garden-farm is this exact midpoint, a place of mediation between nature and civilization, but also the point where the two worlds make contact and where both continually tug at him. His fear of wilderness is as intense as his fear of cities, and the garden merely intensifies the contrast without providing a resolution. In his total alienation from both worlds, his only response is self-pity and despair at ever resolving the contradictions that he has now discovered to be internal as well as environmental. He cannot even achieve tragedy, for he has not risked enough. The end of the pastoral cycle is pathos.

PICARESQUE STRATEGIES

The picaresque world is a natural system in which humans are one of the animal species. The picaro suffers from no conflict between society and nature simply because he sees society as one of the many forms of natural order. He objects to the society into which he is born no more than wolves or ants or whales object to theirs, and like these animals, he tries merely to adapt himself to his circumstances in the interest of his own survival. He does not

altruistically strive for the welfare of all humanity, but merely lives his life as well as he can with little regard for distant idealisms. He is so completely absorbed as a participant in life that it never occurs to him to be a critic of it, or to escape into fantasies.

Picaresque nature is not a garden, but a wilderness. Its most obvious features are multiplicity and diversity, for within the picaresque world everything is tied to everything else according to complex interdependencies that defy simplification. Pain and pleasure are equally real, as are birth and death, peace and war, hunger and a full belly, love and hate. To attend to only one side of these polarities while rejecting the other would be to distort the truth, which the picaro knows he must not do if he hopes to endure. Instead, he takes each as it comes (often they come mixed) and deals with it according to its demands, enjoying the pleasant and enduring the painful as best he can. His world is an ecosystem and he is but one small organism within it. How he fits into the whole or what its purpose may be are beyond him, but he doesn't worry much about such questions.

The picaro's birth is generally obscure, often illegitimate, suggesting both his lack of social status and the absence of any sense of continuity with the past. The chaotic social environment in which he grows up has no niche prepared for him, and he soon discovers that he must create whatever success he can from the rawest of materials at hand. Early in life he goes on his own. His experiences quickly awaken him to the realization that no one will help him, that there is no obvious plan or order in the world, and that his survival or failure will depend upon his own inventiveness.

Lazarillo de Tormes, the Spanish novel already mentioned, is the prototype for later picaresque novels. Its hero, Lazarillo, is tricked and beaten by his first master and promptly achieves the realization that defines the picaresque perspective: "It is full time for me to open mine eyes, yea, and to provide and seek mine own advantage, considering that I am alone without any help."[12] Eyes wide open upon the world around him, looking to avoid danger and to exploit advantages, the picaro lives life as an infinite game played with the world, the only prizes for which are more life and an occasional hearty laugh. Lazarillo and the picaresque nonheroes modeled upon him live in risky play with their surrounding social order.

The picaresque hero perceives that the world is particularly dangerous to those who are poor, weak, or defenseless. The high moral and cultural values mouthed by powerful people are merely platitudes that do not in fact govern their actions and so they cannot be taken seriously. Those who live within the established social order are well fed, pious, educated in abstractions but often stupid in practical matters, and vindictive to all who do not conform to their ideals. The picaro is an outsider to this system, practical, clever, amoral, self-sufficient, and dedicated to making do by the best means available. Staying alive is his most important purpose, and having a good time comes second. He does not rebel against his society, nor does he try to reform it or escape from it. Rather, he looks for weaknesses and loopholes in the system that he can use to his own advantage.

The picaro notes the chaotic complexity of society as keenly as his pastoral counterpart, but he reasons that he must meet it by becoming more complex himself, not by seeking simplicity. He learns early in his career that the elaborate mechanisms of social order do not serve his basic human needs, but that does not lead him to hate society. It simply means that he will have to assume full responsibility for his own welfare and that he can expect no help from others. The picaro is alone, not in the lofty and self-indulgent way of the pastoral hero, but in the modest manner of one who simply assumes that no one really cares about him. The problems around him seem too great to be solved or even understood, but since they were not of his making he need not feel guilty. He does need to live in the world that is defined by these problems, however, so he needs intelligence and wit.

William Faulkner's novel *The Reivers* is marginally a picaresque novel. A statement made by the narrator of that story could serve as a definition of picaresque intelligence: "I rate mules second only to rats in intelligence, the mule followed in order by cats, dogs, and horses last—assuming of course that you accept my definition of intelligence: which is the ability to cope with environment yet still retain at least something of personal liberty."[13] The intelligence of mules, rats, and picaresque heroes is directed not toward puzzling out the rational elegance of pastoral utopias, but toward coping with the given circumstances of daily life. There is little room for nostalgia, fantasy, or abstract intellectual speculation in the mind of the picaro, for he is occupied with present actions and events, and with the maintenance of his own precarious liberty.

The picaro (or occasionally, picara) is thus an opportunist rather than an escapist, a person of wit rather than of contemplation, a realist rather than an idealist. His commitment to endure must often be served by breaking or ignoring the laws and rules of his society. He is often an outlaw and vulgar in the eyes of society's aristocrats.

Defensive Strategies

The world in which the picaro must make his way is often at war. Two picaresque war novels from different historical periods will illustrate the consistency of the picaresque genre: *Simplicius Simplicissimus* by the seventeenth-century German writer Johann Jacob Christoffel von Grimmelshausen, and *Catch-22* by the twentieth-century American novelist Joseph Heller. Grimmelshausen's *Simplicissimus* and Heller's *Catch-22* represent typical picaresque responses to the questions that war always raises: How can one live in a time of total social disruption, and what is one to do about the omnipresent threat of injury and death? The picaresque answers are always the same: Adapt to circumstances and take evasive action.

What the black plague was to Boccaccio, the Thirty Years' War was to Grimmelshausen. All Europe suffered near total collapse of civilized amenities, ostensibly over the resolution of religious differences between Protestants and Catholics. Grimmelshausen's picaresque novel begins with scenes of carnage and brutality that define the world in which young Simplicius must make his way. "This introductory entertainment almost spoiled my desire to see the world," remarks Simplicius after witnessing the brutal destruction of his village by a cavalry troop: "If this is the way things are, the wilderness is far more attractive."[14] Although he tries to hide in the forest, events always force him back into human company, where he begins to learn the tricks of survival.

Like most picaresque novels, *Simplicissimus* represents a young man's initiation and education. Simplicius's first teacher is a minister whose message is that "the foolish world wants to be fooled. Use what intelligence they have left you . . . for your own advantage" (80). Intelligence in service of deception is the picaro's basic strategy for survival. But the picaro deceives only so that he may save himself, never intentionally to injure others. Simplicius adopts whatever disguises seem appropriate in order to avoid trouble. His protective coloring makes him into a court jester, a minister, a soldier, a doctor, or an animal as his situation warrants. Each role saves him from some danger, and each teaches him something new by providing a fresh perspective upon events. Although he deceives others, he never gives in to the temptation to take his own disguises seriously.

The picaro does not treat his fantasies as if they were realities, as pastoral heroes tend to do, but regards each new role as one possibility out of the many available to him, useful for solving a particular problem and perhaps interesting for the new insight it may offer, but in no way a limitation to be accepted. Picaresque life is not lived in search of the One True Way, but is rather an endless series of roles to be played in response to ever-changing circumstances.

Simplicius often compares himself to animals and even adopts animal disguises. He becomes a goose to avoid punishment, and later enjoys for some time the role of calf. As a talking animal he lectures his masters on the virtues of animals, praising them for their moderation, responsiveness to environment, and peacefulness compared to humans. Animals are congenial images to the picaro, for like him they live in the present and are not subject to self-deceptive illusions. Superior human mentality merely permits the picaro to become a better animal, not to transcend his animality.

The metaphysics of the picaresque world is relativistic and fluid. Simplicius early perceives that "nothing in the world is more constant than inconstancy" (84). Uncertainty and continuous change are not, however, oppressive to the picaro, for he does not expect or admire permanence. Change means that the world consists of endlessly varied opportunities for new roles to be played and new advantages to be gained. Change may of course work to the picaro's disadvantage, as when Simplicius is transformed by smallpox from a handsome courtier admired by all the ladies to a pock-marked pariah, "so ugly that dogs would pee on me" (153). Neither condition is assumed to be definitive of his destiny or identity; each is merely one more condition that must be explored for its potential. Simplicius simply accepts his ugliness and learns to make his way by begging and fraud rather than by the seduction of wealthy ladies. Picaresque behavior is governed by an internalized acceptance of universal flux as the basic nature of the world. The picaro's philosophy is thus "to go with the times and make use of the inevitable" (215).

War is so often the setting for picaresque novels because its conditions intensify the problems to which the picaro must always adapt himself: rapid change, social disorder, irrationality, and constant threat of injury or death. War merely exaggerates normal social conditions. It matters little whether it is the Thirty Years' War or World War II, for in either case the personal problems of the picaro are the same. Joseph Heller's modern picaro, Yossarian, faces the same challenge as his counterpart Simplicius three centuries earlier: "It was all a sensible young gentleman like himself could do to maintain his perspective amid so much madness. And it was urgent that he did, for he knew his life was in danger."[15]

Yossarian struggles for survival in a world of aerial bombing rather than cavalry charges, but this merely means that his strategy must be more complex and quicker than that of Simplicius. Its principles are the same. Yossarian rejects the heroics expected of him in his role as a bombardier, preferring to survive as a coward: "He had decided to live forever or die in the attempt, and his only mission each time he went up was to come down alive" (30). He becomes a consummate master of the art of "evasive action," the erratic maneuvering of an airplane to avoid antiaircraft fire. Evasive action becomes a way of life for Yossarian whether on a bombing mission or on the ground, for threats are everywhere: "The enemy . . . is anybody who's going to get you killed, no matter *which* side he's on" (24). The American generals who plan bombing missions are as great a threat to his welfare as the German gunners who try to shoot him down. Questions of right and wrong, good and evil, friends and enemies dissolve into irrelevancy before the demanding task of survival in a world at war.

Evasive action means that Yossarian chooses to avoid danger rather than to destroy its source. In the picaresque manner, he assumes the state of his world to be a given condition that is beyond his power to improve. He accepts the irrational rules of war even when they change with every mission, and he tries to survive within them. He lives from minute to minute, limiting his vision of the world to the cockpit or whorehouse or briefing room, each with its own threat to his welfare and challenge to his ingenuity. Whatever the threat, he must adapt himself to

its conditions with no hope of achieving peace and no idealistic delusions about his own capacity to triumph over adversity.

Ironically, Yossarian's evasions and fears are taken to be signs of his *failure* to adapt to the traditions of his culture. "You've been unable to adjust to the idea of war," his psychiatrist tells him. Yossarian agrees, then listens to a further exposition of the kind of adaptation that his society expects of him:

> "You have a morbid aversion to dying. You probably resent the fact that you're at war and might get your head blown off any second."
>
> "I more than resent it, sir. I'm absolutely incensed."
>
> "You have deep-seated survival anxieties. And you don't like bigots, bullies, snobs, or hypocrites. Subconsciously there are many people you hate."
>
> "Consciously, sir, consciously," Yossarian corrected in an effort to help. "I hate them consciously."
>
> "You're antagonistic to the idea of being robbed, exploited, degraded, humiliated, or deceived. Misery depresses you. Ignorance depresses you. Persecution depresses you. Violence depresses you. Slums depress you. Greed depresses you. Crime depresses you. Corruption depresses you. You know, it wouldn't surprise me if you're a manic-depressive!"
>
> "Yes, sir. Perhaps I am."
>
> "Don't try to deny it."
>
> "I'm not denying it, sir," said Yossarian, pleased with the miraculous rapport that finally existed between them. "I agree with all you've said."
>
> "Then you admit you're crazy, do you?"
>
> "Crazy?" Yossarian was shocked. "What are you talking about? Why am I crazy? You're the one who's crazy!"
>
> (312)

Picaresque sanity is recognition of the world's madness, not approval or emulation of it. The picaro cannot join forces with the agents of disaster and misery, for he does not share their ideologies, but neither does he seek to destroy them. Rather than hating the source of evil, he has compassion for its victims, among whom he numbers himself. He is thus out of step with the dominant power structure, in relation to which his actions seem insane. The picaro is a rogue partly because he refuses to endorse the ideologies of his time or their destructive consequences.

Yossarian is a responsible man, but not to the abstract values to which his corrupt society professes allegiance. Dignity, honor, morality, and patriotism are to the picaro the empty words behind which people hide their greed, vice, and treachery. Yossarian in the end runs away from the war and its pretenses of heroic nobility, choosing instead to save his own life and to help another victim of violence, the kid sister of a Roman whore. When he is condemned as an escapist for evading his patriotic duties, Yossarian insists: "I'm not running *away* from my responsibilities, I'm running *to* them. There's nothing negative about running away to save my life. You know who the escapists are, don't you?" (461). The escapists, of course, are the people who lie to themselves about human perfectibility, the righteousness of warfare, the importance of their own egos, and the sanctity of conventional morality.

The picaresque evasion of pain is radically different from the pastoral retreat in search of peace. Picaresque peace is merely a temporary avoidance of danger, never the permanent security sought in pastoral literature. As Yossarian prepares to desert from the army at the end of *Catch-22,* his friends caution him that "no one will ever be on your side, and you'll always live in danger of betrayal." "I live that way now," replies Yossarian (463). His future will be as dangerous as his past, but more on his own terms and with a better likelihood of survival than can be found within the war. Yossarian's life henceforth will be a calculated risk. When last seen, he is still running to avoid death.

Such inconclusive conclusions are typical of picaresque novels. The world's problems are never solved, no enemies are defeated, no new truth is realized, no peace is attained. In the course of the picaro's career he has gained only greater competence at survival, acceptance of responsibility for his own life, and a clearer understanding of the many threats surrounding him.

PICARESQUE ARTISTRY

Picaresque action is not always defensive, but sometimes becomes highly creative. The wit necessary to save the picaro's life in time of war is applicable to the creation of beauty in times of relative peace. As a master manipulator and creator of illusions, the picaro has much in common with the artist, a conjunction that is explored by the twentieth-century German novelist Thomas Mann in his picaresque novel, *Confessions of Felix Krull, Confidence Man.*

As a young man, Felix Krull ponders the implications of various available perspectives upon the world. Great heroes and empire builders, he reasons, must see the world as a small place, like a chessboard upon which they expect to win their identity by managing the various pieces. The world of saints and hermits must also be a small and insignificant place from which it is best to withdraw in the hope of discovering a better one through mental fantasy or religious transcendence. Krull prefers to see the world as "a great and infinitely enticing phenomenon, offering priceless satisfactions and worthy in the highest degree of all my efforts and solicitude."[16] The vastness and complexity of the world is for Krull an endless source of opportunity for exploring his own potentials and talents. His motive is neither mastery of the world nor escape from its conditions, but the full utilization of his own talents to create a life rivaling the world itself in variety and excellence.

"He who really loves the world shapes himself to please it" is Krull's motto (65), and this defines his strategy as a member of society and as an artist. Adaptation to the given conditions of reality becomes more than the defensive technique of wartime picaros, for Krull regards himself as material to be shaped according to the potential richness and beauty of his circumstances. It is not the world that must be made to suit human pleasures, but humans to suit the world's. This does not just mean meeting the expectations of others, for Krull's conception of the world is not bounded by his contemporary society but includes the total context of natural and human history. The world he seeks to please includes both humanity and nature.

In order to please this larger world, it is often necessary to disappoint the expectations of contemporary society. Krull bends and breaks the conventions of his social context when they prevent him from exploiting his potential for creative experimentation. His idea of aristocracy, for instance, is based upon the observation that nature provides a graded hierarchy of beings according to innate gifts of talent and beauty. He early perceives that nature has endowed him with both: "I could not conceal from myself that I was made of superior stuff" (11). Yet his modest social position does not conform to his natural gifts, for society grades its members according to the artificial criteria of wealth and family, both of which are accidental. In order to bring his social position into agreement with his innate superiority, therefore, he must acquire money and rank by means of theft and deception.

There is no rancor or greed involved in these acts, and Krull takes pains to be sure that no one is hurt by them. His technique is to make himself so pleasing and attractive to others that they are moved to give him favors and gifts; while he profits, others feel no loss but give to him willingly. His fortune is acquired from a wealthy woman, slightly perverse, who gets a sexual thrill from being robbed of her jewels by a handsome young man like Krull, and his aristocratic rank is bestowed upon him by a profligate marquis whose identity Krull takes over in order to leave the young nobleman free to pursue anonymously his love affair with an actress. In spite of his unfortunately obscure birth, Krull thus earns the social credentials of superiority that correspond to his innate excellence.

When Krull finds social standards to be false, he corrects them—not for everyone, for that would produce equal falsity—but for himself. Krull is consistent with the picaresque code in his acceptance of the given social order, and in his belief that rank and order are natural hierarchical systems, not false social conventions. He rejects, for instance, the notion that nudity is democratic in that it abolishes the social ranks established by clothing styles. On the contrary, he argues, "Nakedness can only be called just in so far as it proclaims the naturally unjust constitution of the human race, unjust in that it is aristocratic" (90). Clothing displays false social status; its absence abolishes only the falsity and proclaims the natural rank order based upon beauty and agility of body.

The picaro is never a rebel against society, but merely a manipulator of its conditions for his own welfare in accordance with the principles of nature. When asked if he is a socialist, Krull answers, "No, indeed! . . . I find society enchanting just as it is and am on fire to earn its good opinion" (90). Of course he earns society's admiration by deception and illusion, thus earning the title "rogue," but his deceptions resemble those of art more than those of crime. He is an actor portraying the roles appropriate to his immediate context: "I seemed not only able to put on whatever social rank or personal characteristics I chose, but could actually adapt myself to any given period or century" (22). His social roles as elevator boy, waiter, pimp, and nobleman are played in order to fulfill the potential inherent in each role, not only to serve Krull's personal needs. He is a professional illusionist glorying in his adaptive skill.

Yet for all his admiration of society, his life remains by choice alone and isolated. Isolation is a necessary condition of picaresque action that emphasizes the dependence of the picaro upon his own devices. And it is not a cause for sorrow, as it is for the pastoral hero, but rather an opportunity. The picaro takes pride in his independence, even though it requires some sacrifice of personal intimacy. Krull accepts the fact that "close associations, friendship, and companionship were not to be my lot, but that I should instead be inescapably compelled to follow my strange path alone, dependent entirely upon myself, rigorously self-sufficient" (106). Although he remains on a congenial footing with those around him and even proves to be a master lover with women, Krull never permits intimacy to progress to the point of a dependency that might restrict his freedom to respond to new threats or opportunities.

Picaresque life is animal existence augmented by the imaginative and adaptive powers of the human mind. Unlike the pastoral mode, in which the mind is used to create alternatives to a dangerous present reality, the picaresque mode expresses acceptance of the present and adaptation to its conditions without concern for abstract ideologies or sentimental moralities. The comparison of the hero to animals, an almost universal feature of picaresque fiction, emphasizes the picaro's acceptance of biological limitations that define the nature of life and suggest the proper purposes that should govern the human use of intellect. Faulkner's rats and mules, Grimmelshausen's calf and goose, and the many other animals that recur in picaresque literary art are most often used as models of appropriate action rather than as images of debased life that threaten some conventional standard of human dignity.

The final chapters of Mann's *Felix Krull* are devoted to the hero's exploration of his own relationship to animal and biological existence as he is conducted through the Lisbon Museum of Natural History by its director. The first animal Krull sees inside the museum is a magnificent white stag mounted against a forest background. He enjoys the likeness between himself and the stag, not only because both are well-formed and beautiful, but also because of

their common attitude toward their environments. Stag and Krull are "dignified and alert . . . calm yet wary," and ready to "disappear at a bound into the darkness" at the slightest sign of danger (298). The stag is a handsome picaro, adept at evasive action like his human counterpart Felix Krull.

The record of evolution displayed in the museum further shows Krull his kinship with the animals as well as his separation from them. He sees "the contrast between my own fineness and elegance and the primitive crudity of many of the uncanny-looking fossils, the primitive crustaceans, cephalopods, brachiopods, tremendously ancient sponges and entrail-less lily-stars. . . . These first beginnings, however absurd and lacking in dignity and usefulness, were preliminary moves in the direction of me—that is, of Man" (301). Higher evolutionary forms, mammals and primates, further confirm Krull's joy at his newfound unity with all animal life: "In the end they all prefigured me, even though disguised as in some sorry jest" (304). When his tour brings him to the displays of early humans, his pleasure in evolutionary continuity is further confirmed, for in primitive people he sees "what had been striving toward me from the grey reaches of antiquity" (304). He is confirmed in the perception that he had earlier derived from his conversations with the museum director: "Men are descended from animals in just about the same way that the organic is descended from the inorganic. Something was added" (271). Consciousness was added, the gift that augments the process of evolution but does not separate humanity from that process.

Consciousness permits people to enjoy their animal powers and beauties more than the other animals can. As Krull sees it, people do by will only what other animals do by instinct, and so people become responsible for what they are. Unattractive animals cannot be blamed for their ugliness, but among people it is "culpable to be ugly." Krull finds ugliness "a kind of carelessness" that offends him and that contrasts sharply with his own artistic attitude toward himself: "Out of innate consideration for the world that was awaiting me, I took care while I was being formed that I should not offend its eyes. . . . I'd call it a kind of self-discipline" (317). Krull has here restated the law of creative picaresque behavior with which his career began: "He who really loves the world shapes himself to please it."

Consciousness, intelligence, language, imagination—these are to the picaro the means for artistic adaptation to his environment. He uses his gifts for self-defense, but also for playing with others and with his surroundings. Dominance over his environment is not a goal, nor does he use imaginative powers for the creation of idealistic fantasies. Accepting the accidents of natural and social history that have produced him and the environment that defines his possibilities, the picaro applies his intelligence toward making the best of whatever the world may offer.

Rogues and Saints

The roots of pastoral and picaresque go deeply into Western cultural traditions, the collective psyche, and perhaps into human evolutionary origins. It is not easy to tell whether the two modes reflect differences in human temperament and personality or are expressions of beliefs that people hold. The pastoral mode looks something like an ideology, for pastoral writers often claim to know how people should live and expect them to mend their ways; they often assume life to be perfectible, however great their despair at discovering that people often reject their chances for perfection. The picaresque, on the other hand, is more descriptive than prescriptive. Picaresque stories are not much help in the search for what ought to be because they are concerned only with what is. They offer a mirror of behavior, not a model for imitation.

The pastoral hero is born an aristocrat, socially superior to others and highly sophisticated. His anthropocentric world exists for the purpose of perfecting human welfare and elevating the human spirit. Confident that he is at the center of creation, he yet sees the failure of his fellow humans to achieve their potential and he is oppressed by this discovery. He regretfully turns away from his society and its unnecessary miseries, accepts his isolation as a painful consequence, and looks for renewal from an agricultural version of nature. Nature, he hopes, will renew human nobility through her pastoral hero.

The picaro begins life with no credentials of dignity or status. Neither his social status nor his metaphysics supports a claim to superiority over anything. His main concern is with survival. He quickly learns that survival is a tricky process requiring that he attend closely to his immediate environment for both threats and opportunities. Since the world has no plans for him, he is free to become whatever seems appropriate or interesting. He lives as an intelligent animal, interested in the present, and ready to play when the opportunity arises.

Morality is a cornerstone of pastoral life. People are assumed to be naturally good, and if they nevertheless seem corrupt, it must be because the institutions of civilization have made them so. The experience of nature is seen as therapeutic, restoring people to the natural goodness with which they began. Pastoral literature loves noble savages, and urges people to regain the purity that has been sacrificed to civilization.

The picaresque vision usually discovers early that exalted moral postures can quickly lead to someone's death or undoing. Morality is often dangerous to the picaro, either because it limits his flexibility, or because he runs the risk of suffering from the rigidities of others. The picaro is skeptical of moral abstractions, and he rarely thinks about good or evil. If survival is a moral principle, he is enthusiastically in favor of it.

Pastoral emotions tend toward the melodramatic. Self-pity is a common beginning for a pastoral narrative. The hero is despondent because the world has not treated him as well as he deserves. He finds solace in nostalgic fantasies about the good old days of his own youth or of humanity's in the Garden of Eden. His belief that life has been beautiful inspires him with hope that it can be good again if only he can restore the proper conditions. The pastoral quest is a sentimental journey away from present pain in search of past peace. It is never a successful quest. The emotional cycle of pastoral experience normally moves from nostalgia to hope, to disillusionment, to final despair.

Compassion for suffering may be the most serious emotion experienced by picaresque heroes. The picaro makes little distinction between his own misfortune and that of others, treating both with solicitude and resignation. He sees pain as the consequence of his own errors rather than evidence of the world's malice, so he is more likely to be self-mocking than self-pitying. He more often laughs at the world's absurdities than cries over its inequities. As he has no hope, he need never suffer despair. His career does not proceed in a cycle, but is merely an ongoing account of his increasingly adept durability as he responds to a series of surprises. Picaresque narratives do not reach neat conclusions and their heroes never achieve either fulfillment or discovery, for the picaresque mode presents life as a continuous process, perhaps meaningless but compellingly interesting.

Pastoral life is polarized, presenting mutually exclusive alternatives between which a choice must be made. The good must be achieved, the evil rooted out; peace is excellent, war is hell; elegant simplicity is preferable to fearful complexity; purity is our goal, pollution our punishment; society is corrupt but nature is sinless. Pastoral motivation is always in the direction of positive goals that are believed to be attainable if only their opposites can be avoided. The pastoral world is a battleground between God and Satan, and the pastoral hero is enlisted among the angels. He is, to be sure, a rear-echelon angel not involved in the battle itself, but he prays fervently for God's side to win.

The picaro does not positively search for peace but merely hopes to avoid war. He is rarely able to distinguish between good and evil except in their most basic forms, pleasure and pain—and even these are often mixed. His world is systemic rather than polar. Many gods, many Satans, and many beings of indeterminate moral status contend before his eyes, all holding both threats and promises. He does not expect the world to meet his conditions, but he will do all he can to meet its. His constant motivation is to blend into the system where he finds himself.

Images of environment and metaphors of behavior reflect the separate value systems of the pastoral and the picaresque. Garden and farm are the dominant figures in the pastoral mode, while wilderness and the city are the basic images of the picaresque. These images have carried far beyond their literary origins and have become influential habits of the modern mind.

Botany dominates the pastoral scene. Plants symbolize the kind of life most desired by pastoral seekers: rooted, placid, beautiful. The only animals admitted to pastoral landscapes are those domestic creatures whose behavior is similarly calm; nervous and aggressive animals are fenced out. The pastoral psyche yearns for the peace of vegetative life. The typical stages of pastoral narrative begin with the desire to retreat to a simpler life, followed by recognition of helplessness before the world's cruelty, and ending in sad resignation or despair. The attempt to achieve the values of the garden—nourishment, beauty, peacefulness, stability—leads inevitably to disappointment in a perverse and competitive world.

The picaresque wilderness, of course, leads to no great goals either, but since the picaro has no expectations he can hardly be disappointed about that. Picaresque literature does not express the kind of hopelessness implied by tragedy or existential despair, for these traditions seem to hold the world responsible for being reasonable and just to humans and regard its failures as somehow an affront to humanity. The picaro is hopeless only in the sense that he sees hope to be an irrelevant concept, an unjustifiable expectation of the future that offers no help in dealing with present problems. The picaro's only "hope" is that he may succeed at the day-to-day business of keeping himself alive; if a wolf can be said to hope for a meal each day and the avoidance of trappers who want his pelt, then the picaro can be said to hope. In the picaresque tradition, people are shown living as other animals live, confronting the present defensively and opportunistically, without expectations or illusions, proud of strength but accurately aware of limitations, mistrustful but not cynical or malicious, and above all adaptive to the immediate environment.

Perhaps the major difference between pastoral and picaresque lies in the application each makes of human intelligence. The pastoral intellect uses the rational capacity of the mind to criticize the inadequacies of present experience and its imaginative talents to create alternatives to the present. It is characterized by abstract ideas—truth, justice, goodness, love—intended to lead toward a fulfillment of human potential at some future time. The picaresque intellect instead concentrates upon the study of immediate reality, and its imagination upon the creation of strategies for survival. Picaresque liberty is not escape from misfortune, but confidence in one's ability to persist in spite of it.

Modern cities, like ancient Rome, are messy, expensive, chaotic, and dangerous. Those who flee them in search of rural peace and quiet are following a pastoral way that Western culture has endorsed since Virgil. The pastoral tradition also makes it plain that this quest is likely to fail, for the seeker of peace and simplicity is likely to carry inner conflict and anger, and these will govern his or her life more than the rural environment will. Escape into fantasies is not a workable solution to urban and existential ills.

What the picaresque tradition lacks in dignity and respectability, it makes up for in clear-eyed practicality. In the picaresque eye, cities and wild places are all full of both

danger and opportunity, and wherever one finds oneself is the place where life must be lived as well as possible. Picaresque life is infinite play, with no hope of winning much, but endless enthusiasm for keeping the play alive.

Notes

1. *Works of Virgil,* trans. J. W. MacKail (New York: Random House, 1950), 267.

2. Virgil, 266.

3. *Satires of Juvenal,* trans. Rolfe Humphries (Bloomington: Indiana University Press, 1958), 42.

4. Boccaccio, *Decameron,* trans. Richard Aldington (New York: Dell, 1962), 32, 35.

5. Boccaccio, 173.

6. Boccaccio, 174.

7. Ebenezer Howard, *Garden Cities of To-morrow* (1898; reprint, Cambridge: MIT Press, 1965), 44.

8. Leo Marx, *The Machine in the Garden: Technology and the Pastoral Ideal in America* (New York: Oxford University Press, 1964), 141.

9. Thomas Jefferson, *Notes on the State of Virginia,* Query 19, quoted in Marx, 124.

10. Jefferson to William Short, November 28, 1814, quoted in Marx, 144.

11. Marx, 364.

12. *The Pleasaunte Historie of Lazarillo de Tormes,* trans. David Rowland (London, 1586), ed. J.E.V. Crofts (Oxford: Basil Blackwell, 1924), 11.

13. William Faulkner, *The Reivers* (New York: Random House, 1962), 121.

14. Johann von Grimmelshausen, *Simplicius Simplicissimus,* trans. George Schulz-Behrend (Indianapolis: Bobbs-Merrill, 1965), 27; further references are cited parenthetically in the text.

15. Joseph Heller, *Catch-22* (New York: Dell, 1955), 21; further references in text.

16. Thomas Mann, *Confessions of Felix Krull, Confidence Man,* trans. Denver Lindley (New York: Alfred Knopf, 1955), 13; further references in text.

THE PICARA

Edward H. Friedman (essay date 1987)

SOURCE: Friedman, Edward H. "The Voiceless Narrator: The Spanish Feminine Picaresque and Unliberated Discourse." In *The Antiheroine's Voice: Narrative Discourse and Transformation of the Picaresque,* pp. 69-94. Columbia: University of Missouri Press, 1987.

[*In the excerpt which follows, Friedman focuses on* La lozana andaluza *and* La pícara Justina *as examples of the distinct type of picaresque narrative that features female heroes.*]

Men, in determining the "acceptable" values and assumptions (which include the inferior status of women), subject women to experiences that men are not subjected to; but men's language structure does not include the ready means for women to express the thoughts and behavior that result from their subjugation.

Cheris Kramarae, *Women and Men Speaking*

A salient feature of narrative is its paradoxical resistance to historicist principles. As narrative forms proceed historically through time, they both expand the recourses of earlier texts and validate the presence of the new—the novel—in their predecessors. *Don Quijote* stands as a monument to the synchronic backdrop of intertextuality and to the defiant chronology of narrative development. The absurd and counterhistoric temporal scope of Cervantes's novel underscores, perhaps precognitively, the interplay between history and fiction and the powers and limitations of the verbal sign. *Don Quijote* erects barriers between the real and the imaginary; it establishes categories of experience and writing before theories of history and literature legitimize such distinctions. *Don Quijote* reacts to nineteenth-century narrative realism over two centuries before European literary realism takes hold, and it challenges narrative presuppositions from the perspective of author, narrator, character, and reader. Practice encompasses theory, and theory raises rather than answers questions. The problem of truth and the amplification of perspective foreground the self-conscious literary object as a microcosm turned macrocosm, a system of devices that uses artifice to seek essence. By placing himself in the work—by fictionalizing himself—Cervantes acknowledges the comprehensive nature and the inverted hierarchy of his narrative performance. The irony of his vision points forward to twentieth-century skepticism and backward to the discursive strategies of picaresque narrative, in which an implied authorial presence directs language and event. The feminine variations of the picaresque offer new patterns of discourse while forming the basis for further transformations of the model. Quite fittingly, they also anticipate the dialectical discourse and rhetorical effects of the picaresque archetypes.

Borrowing from the tension between stated intention and uncompliant text (and between the author and his alter ego) in the *Libro de Buen Amor,* the early writers of picaresque fiction project ambiguity on various levels of narration. The doubling of the author and narrator in the prologue of *Lazarillo de Tormes* initiates the relationship between implied author and narrator/protagonist that regulates the irony of the text proper. The prologue speaks, without transition, of a book to be judged by a reading public and an explanatory manuscript with a readership of one. Lázaro himself is both man and boy, writer and character, participant and observer. From the standpoint of discourse, he is unreliable and reliable, because the authorial figure encodes the text with fixed patterns of irony and revelations of truth that betray Lázaro's defensive rhetoric. *Guzmán de Alfarache* heightens rhetoric and defense by moving the explanation to a spiritual plane. Guzmán's text

is a confession in the double sense, the story of a professed conversion presented through the discourse of a repressed individual. The separation of episode and moral digression establishes the opposing sides of a narrative competition in which the reader may accept or reject the penitential stance. To read *Guzmán de Alfarache* is to determine priorities, to validate the narrator's redemption or to expose the unredeemed self. Authorial control becomes more prominent in *El Buscón*. The intensification of language, the identifying sign of a baroque stylist rather than of a narrative novice, finds an analogue in the incriminating discourse and fatalistic events of the text. Quevedo announces his presence verbally, in technical and rhetorical terms; neither the words nor their message belong entirely to Pablos. The idiolect, the negative determinism, and the implicit denial of upward mobility mark the intrusion of the creator in his creation, to oppose and ultimately to silence the narrator.

Just as *Don Quijote* makes the process of composition a part of the narrative product, the archetypal picaresque novels allow particular strategies of storytelling to guide message production. The markers of discursive play set opposing systems into motion. The dual direction of the prologue in *Lazarillo de Tormes,* the division between narrative and commentary in *Guzmán de Alfarache,* and linguistic self-consciousness in *El Buscón* suggest a dialectical chain of connections that unite discourse, story, and signification. The premise of each work—Lázaro's explanation of the case, Guzmán's indictment of sin following his conversion, and Pablos's record of his entry into the world of crime—leads to a possible counterargument that would redefine the focus of the work. Lázaro's ascent in society may, in fact, be a descent into complacent depravity, Guzmán may be a hypocrite instead of a convert, and Pablos may adopt a bold tone to camouflage his shame. The narrators as pawns of the authors, real and implied, function as analogues of the individual at the mercy of a regimented society, but the literary space grants the narrator a forum that society does not provide and that an author cannot completely dominate. The discursive structure ironically features variations on the theme of silence, specifically attempts on the part of the narrator to conceal the truth and on the part of the (implied) author to discredit or render problematic the words of the speaker. The ironic consequence is a duplication of narrative voice, which adds a richness of ambiguity and a subtext for speech and social acts.

The earliest of the male picaresque forms secularize the spiritual confession to delineate a character who confronts society and the blank page. Lázaro breaks a protective silence to publicize his disgrace, as the speaker in the first part of the prologue alludes to honor attained in the pursuit of the arts. While boasting of his newly acquired prosperity, Lázaro stresses the importance of silence (and figurative blindness) in the honor-obsessed Spain of his time. Rather than remove him from the preoccupations of his countrymen, his words seem to concede his faith in the power of illusion. The narrative continually reiterates the contradictory force of its existence. Unity comes not so much from the execution of the narrative premises as from the ironic correspondences and "unconscious" revelations of the text. Guzmán links the sacred and the profane in an attempt to negate a sinful past through contrast with a calculatedly exemplary present. To give credence to the earnestness of Guzmán's conversion, the reader must take him at his word and ignore to some extent the comprehensive impact of his words. The discourse of *Guzmán de Alfarache* subtly belies the stated intention and the avowed repentance. Between the adventures of the *pícaro* and the moral lessons of the reformed sinner lie the thoughts (made public) of one made bitter by his rejection by God and his fellow man. This psychic middle ground disrupts the balance created by the textual division to favor the sinner over the would-be saint and a rhetoric of discord and resentment over a language of inner peace. In *El Buscón,* the extended verbal conceits announce the presence of an extranarrative mediator who makes his way into the story by controlling causality as well as discourse. Pablos publicizes his dishonor through words not fully his own, and a fate guided by the implied author conspires to deny him escape from the past. The connecting threads of the narrative relate to the superstructure of linguistic and situational determinism.

The doubling effect, characterized by irony of discourse and circumstance, brings into question the concept of an objective reality or of absolute values. The narrative mirrors the dilemma of man before nature, society, and fate, only partially in control of the events that beset him. While the literary vehicle privileges him, the authorial figure compromises his autonomy at every turn. Message systems interact and at times contradict each other, finding an order of sorts in the evasive syntheses and ironic patterns of narration. When a female protagonist replaces the male, the distance between empathy and contrivance increases. Women do not necessarily sound like women, nor do authors always give them a voice in the narrative. The precariousness and inequality of their social roles are reflected in literary works that often reduce feminism to the status of motif. Male authors bring women into the domain of the picaresque without giving them freedom of speech and without liberating them from the constraints of their social inferiority. The female rogues achieve a degree of success by plotting against men, but society at large, if not the individual, avenges their deviation from behavioral norms. The *pícaras* face despair, unhappy marriages, and even death for their tricks and for their rebellion. The texts that portray their lives marginate them from discourse. Their stories are immoral yet entertaining interludes in the male-oriented scheme of things, and their creators undermine their words as society undermines their actions. Like their male counterparts, the female protagonists achieve an identity in spite of the factors that work against them, and some manage to escape the silence that threatens their discursive authority.

A beauty and an enigma of the picaresque trajectory is the generic consciousness of writers, narrators, readers, and critics, ranging from mythic to socio-historical, from moral

and conceptual to purely formal considerations. The feminine picaresque, with its inherent need for modification of the model, lends itself to the study of the "readings" (and anticipation) of the picaresque archetypes by those authors who choose to present antiheroines. The *pícara* is an orphan, an outsider, a trickster, whose story relies on an episodic structure and a system of poetic justice based on the social status quo. The incipient psychological realism of the *Lazarillo,* the *Guzmán,* and the *Buscón* counts less in these readings than the re-creation of antisocial events to conform to the female characters. Discursive mediation becomes more evident in the presentation of women's lives. The external self—the male view of the opposite sex—dominates the narratives, which nonetheless bespeak woman's place in society and in the text. The discourse contains a number of voices, one of which belongs to the protagonist. Her confrontation with competing voices offers a key to the production of meaning, as well as a social statment.

The dialogic format of Francisco Delicado's *La lozana andaluza* links the work to the tradition of Fernando de Rojas's *La Celestina* (1499, 1502), with its emphasis on verbal portraiture and social panorama. Significantly, however, *La lozana andaluza* points forward to the picaresque mode through an ambiguous prologue, rich in moral intention and challenged by the text proper, and through a doubling of the author, who becomes a character and commentator in Lozana's story. As the object of story and discourse, the protagonist acts and interacts with those around her. As a participant in the dialogue, she develops a voice to complement (and perhaps to rectify) the descriptive and narrative components of the text. In *La pícara Justina,* Francisco López de Ubeda foreshadows the linguistic intricacies of Quevedo's *Buscón* with a voice-over that puts morality at the service of the written word. The baroque idiolect subordinates self-revelation to diversion, accentuating the role of the implied author over the delineation of Justina's inner being. The intertextual motive for the artistic display—and the target of López de Ubeda's moral indolence—is Alemán's *Guzmán de Alfarache.* In Alonso Jerónimo de Salas Barbadillo's *La hija de Celestina,* the authorial figure once again becomes the agent of morality. The narrative commentary, the chronology, and the intervention of fate adhere to a moral order that occupies more narrative space than weight of conviction. Death looms in the background (and in the foreground of narration) for Elena the sinner, the victim of an ignoble heredity, a corrupt environment, and a third-person narrator who gives her little opportunity to speak for herself.

The movement from *La lozana andaluza* to *La hija de Celestina* gives priority to entertainment, instruction, and feminism, generally in that order. The carnivalesque world of inversion and wish-fulfillment informs the feminine picaresque, despite its antifeminist subtext of social hierarchies and male superiority. Alonso de Castillo Solórzano draws on the picaresque models for plot and form, while avoiding a certain ambivalence of discourse. The archetypes are models rather than myths, and discourse is no longer an end in itself. The evidence is a first-person perspective in *Teresa de Manzanares* that changes only slightly in the shift to the third person in *La garduña de Sevilla*. As a unit, the antiheroines' narratives cover the discursive range of their brother works. They become counterfictions when the differentiated voices of the texts convey a sense of variation and sexual consciousness, when the female presence begins to affect the production of meaning. The semiotic (and economic) system associated with these women is the body, a visual and sexual commodity. Their tricks and their words depend on desirability, and the transition from object to subject illustrates the tenuous interiority of the female character. To a degree the texts define identity in negative terms or in terms of what is left unsaid. Discourse becomes a literary response to a social question.

La Lozana Andaluza

Lozana: Mirá, dolorido, que de aquí adelante que "sé cómo se baten las calderas," no quiero de noche que ninguno duerma conmigo sino vos, y de día, comer de todo, y d'esta manera engordaré, y vos procurá de arcarme la lana si queréis que teja cintas de cuero. Andá, entrá, y empleá vuestra garrocha. Entrá en coso, que yo's veo que venís "como estudiante que durmió en duro, que contaba las estrellas."

Look here, heartsick boy, as of now "I know how to stir the cauldron," and I don't want anybody to sleep with me at night but you, and in the daytime, I want to eat some of everything, and in this way I'll fatten myself up, and you'd better check out the territory if you want me to get some hides under my belt. Come on, enter, and employ your spear. Enter the ring, for I can see that you're approaching "like the student who slept on a hard bed, the one who was reaching for the stars."

The Spanish feminine picaresque both addresses itself to the male archetypes and prefigures the dialectical narrative of the models. *La lozana andaluza,* published twenty-six years before *Lazarillo de Tormes*, strives to reproduce reality through the devices of fiction, in a portrait that brings the artist into his work. Expanding the role of the *auctor* from sentimental romances such as Juan Rodríguez del Padrón's *Siervo libre de amor* (*Free Slave of Love*, mid-fifteenth century) and Diego de San Pedro's *Cárcel de Amor* (*Prison of Love,* 1492),[1] Delicado populates his literary creation with characters from an identifiable real world and places them in authentic settings, notably in the holy and corrupt city of Rome. He escapes the fantasy realm of idealistic fiction by concentrating on the lower elements of society and the baser instincts of humanity. The author fictionalizes himself to add credence to the portrait and in doing so gains control of the text from both sides of the figurative canvas. He is a writer, an observer, and an actor who influences events and calls attention to the task of composition. He is not only author as character but also character as author. The literary product becomes the macrocosm, subjecting the elements of reality to the conventions of art. The author manipulates the material from within and beyond the text, while Lozana derives her

power as the focal point of the discourse and as a speaker. The progression of the text is panoramic rather than emotional, but Delicado does include a final moment of disillusionment for his protagonist and with it the possibility of redemption. The individual and morality lie within the portrait, which places extension over depth. As in every portrait, the center carries a privileged status, and at the center of *La lozana andaluza* stands a woman with a well-defined past and an ingenious talent for reaping rewards in the present. She is an unabashedly sensual product of her time and milieu, artistically enriched by the complementary facets of the portrait, one of which is a voice of her own.

In his dedication to an illustrious personage, Delicado stresses the pleasure derived from things related to love, "que deleitan a todo hombre" (which delight every man),[2] especially in the case of so expert a practitioner as the subject of the portrait. Alluding to Juvenal's skill at observation, he purports to reveal only what he has heard and seen. A faithful rendering of events in a less than exemplary moral climate necessitates a degree of poetic license for the sake of reader satisfaction: "Mi intención fue mezclar natura con bemol" (p. 34; My purpose was to mix nature with sweetness), to soften the truth in order to heighten the enjoyment. Delicado modifies the Horatian dichotomy of the sweet and useful, aiming for authenticity over instruction, or perhaps for instruction through an accurate portrayal of life. Morality and didacticism are at the service of art, an art that establishes an order for quotidian reality.[3] For those who would question his motives, Delicado comments, "Si, por tiempo, alguno se maravillare que me puse a escribir semejante materia, respondo por entonces que *epistola enim non erubescit*, y asimismo que es pasado el tiempo que estimaban los que trabajaban en cosas meritorias" (pp. 33-34; If, in time, someone were to wonder that I would bring myself to write such things, I would reply then that a letter does not blush, and likewise that the time is past when they respected those who busied themselves in worthy matters). The ambiguity of this passage, with its debt to Cicero, sets the tone of the work. In unpraiseworthy times, literary scruples cede to verisimilitude, as art reflects life in a double sense. If the *Libro de Buen Amor* rationalizes its carnal obsession under the rubric of negative exemplarity, *La lozana andaluza* relates its scurrilous episodes and vulgarities of language to fidelity in the artistic representation of nature.

Following the dedication, the author offers a brief description of the materials contained in the text. He once again emphasizes the completeness of the portrait and its faithfulness to nature, while using classical sources to justify the need for an artistic arrangement of events and a "dressing up" of the material for the cause of creativity.[4] Thus, in the story Lozana will come to be much wiser than her real-life model ("verná en fábula muncho más sabia la Lozana que no mostraba," p. 36), remade to enter the literary tableau. The analogy to painting expresses the tension between natural phenomena and their transference to another medium, between absolute truth and truth in art. Artistic creation involves re-creation according to the principles of the chosen mode. Delicado acknowledges this distinction, despite repeated references to his accurate rendering of the life around him, by foregrounding his own role in the creative process and later by entering the fictional world. In the preliminary sections of this precursor of *Lazarillo de Tormes* and *Don Quijote,* the author notes, whether consciously or unconsciously, the ongoing dialectic of fiction. Unmediated reality provides multiple options. The writer designs a model, selects some elements at the expense of others, and asks the real to comply with the norms of the imaginary. The contradictions inherent in a verbal approach to reality—standard features of the picaresque and a motivating force of *Don Quijote*—direct the self-consciousness of *La lozana andaluza.* The more the author and his alter ego ponder the act of writing, the more obvious their imposition on reality becomes. By transforming himself, Delicado punctuates the transformation of reality. By defending the veracity of his portrait, he illustrates the pervasive influence of literary artifice.

La lozana andaluza reflects the trope of synecdoche, which centers on the representative part to symbolize the whole. The sinful existence of a courtesan corresponds to the decaying morality of the Roman populace, avenged by Spanish and German soldiers in the 1527 sack of Rome. The portrait is not art for art's sake but art with a foreboding of doom. The historical moment is as significant a part of the structure as setting, character, and speech. The sack of Rome is determined by political, social, and (for Delicado) ethical factors and predetermined by history. As exposition and warning, the text exists in an ironic present and in a parabolic atemporality. Lozana's story evokes a precognitive or precocious determinism, a combination of her *converso* background, her sex, and her exposure to poverty, crime, and sin. Delicado presents the stages of her decline in a systematic fashion. He begins with her birth and ignoble lineage, follows her along the path of destruction, and ends with a spiritual solution to discontentment. The vision of the lower depths, so to speak, offers an early form of naturalism that takes into account the desires, instincts, and motives of the characters. The realistic view of society seen from below builds on the exploration of multiple social levels in *La Celestina* and precedes the anti-idealistic tenor and focus on the individual in *Lazarillo de Tormes. La lozana andaluza* works from the isolated subject to a segment of society to society and humanity at large. Lozana's destiny relates to circumstances beyond her control, as well as to her conscious choices. The author supplies a family portrait to complement the panorama of Rome, allowing descriptive voices to take the place of the introspection that will mark subsequent narrative discourse. As the mediating presence within the unmediated form of dialogue, the author in his dual role sets the terms and the boundaries of Lozana's story.[5]

La lozana andaluza is divided into three parts containing sixty-six *mamotretos,* or memoranda, and several closing pieces. The first *mamotreto* gives a brief biographical introduction, while the second initiates the dialogue form sustained throughout the text, interrupted only by infre-

quent commentary by the author (outside his role as actor). Perhaps unwittingly, given his zeal for realistic depiction, Delicado questions the narrative devices he employs. The author who in the dedication attests to having seen and heard the events portrayed in the text cannot have seen and heard everything, nor could his recounting of the dialogue be exact. Like Cide Hamete Benengeli in the *Quijote,* he claims to be a witness to events he could not possibly have observed. Note, for example, the author's remark in *mamotreto* 14 concerning Lozana and her servant/procurer Rampín, with whom she has just spent the night: "Quisiera saber escribir un par de ronquidos, a los cuales despertó él y, queriéndola besar, despertó ella" (p. 76; I wish I knew how to write down a couple of snores, which woke him up, and when he tried to kiss her, she woke up). The statements supporting the validity of the text underscore their implausibility. The author at work within his fiction—a fiction that applauds its historicity—embraces and opposes a reality perceived by the senses and modified by words. Realism's loss is literature's gain. Delicado exposes what Cervantes exploits: the writing process itself, the creative distance between signifier and signified, the inversion of microcosm and macrocosm. The figure of the author in *La lozana andaluza* makes problematic the elements that he attempts to clarify. Objective reality becomes subjective, absolute truth yields to poetic license, and the poet reveals the tools (and the tricks) of his creative trade.[6]

The author provides a moralizing voice in the text, to the point of confronting Lozana herself on the issue of God's omnipresence and omnipotence (*mamotreto* 42), a passage that places the creator in a superior position to his creation. The moral stance of the author as character approximates narrative perspective, setting up a type of analogy between the historical veracity and moral validity of the text and the credibility of Lozana's penitent attitude at the end of her story. The discrepancy between a moral position and a profane text and between a historical position and an artistic text may predispose a somewhat skeptical reaction to the change of heart, overshadowed by a volume of sinful acts. The quantitative imbalance resembles that of the *Libro de Buen Amor,* in which the rhetoric of bad love proves a formidable combatant to the doctrine of good love. An important difference, however, is the presentation in *La lozana andaluza* of family origins and the origins of antisocial behavior, leading to sin and eventually to despair. Just as Don Quijote and the authorial figure(s) share the spotlight in Cervantes's novel, Lozana and her author(s) command attention in Delicado's work. The author establishes the terms of the socio-biographical account, placing himself within the narrative to report, comment, and interact. Lozana performs mimetically to substantiate his case and to offer her own.

Born in Córdoba to New Christians, Aldonza (later renamed Lozana for her feminine ripeness) travels throughout southern Spain with her widowed mother. The author hints of early sexual encounters and a free-spiritedness that increases on her mother's death. In

Sevilla, Lozana's aunt introduces her to a successful merchant, Diomedes, whose mistress she becomes. She journeys toward Italy with Diomedes and barely escapes death at the hands of his irate father, who imprisons Diomedes and arranges to kill Lozana. The protagonist makes her way to Rome, where she settles in the section known as Pozo Blanco, largely populated by Spanish *conversos*. She finds a kindred spirit in the women of Pozo Blanco, many of whom specialize in the cosmetic arts. Through them she meets a Neapolitan woman whose son Rampín becomes a guide, companion, and sexual partner. Trigo, a wealthy member of the Jewish community, sets Lozana up in a house, where she uses her sexual and economic expertise to profit from her clients. She also practices her skills in the treatment of venereal diseases. At the end of part 1, she comes to the aid of a canon and his pregnant mistress, and at the beginning of part 2, the author discovers that Lozana herself will bear a child by the canon.

The events of what may be termed Lozana's pre-history greatly affect her story, as do the circumstances of her early years. Her impurity of blood, her unstable family life, her status as an orphan, her emerging sexuality, and her mistreatment at the hands of men rob her of youth, innocence, and dignity. Fate brings her to Rome and to Pozo Blanco, where she finds the comfort of group identity and a continuity of ostracism. She becomes the queen of whores in a society that denies her respectability, and the text does not reveal that she would wish it otherwise. The dialogue form gives Lozana an active role in the literary structure, and she has reached a discursive maturity before she begins to speak in the text. She is hardened, cynical, and adept at linguistic as well as sexual expression. The Renaissance predilection for physical beauty customarily manifests itself in paeans to the female form, in works such as Juan del Encina's *Egloga de Plácida y Vitoriano* (*Eclogue of Plácida and Vitoriano*). When Lozana sees Diomedes for the first time, she reacts excitedly to his physical charms, shattering the model (and decorum) to acknowledge feminine sexual urges. In Rome, she recalls her successes: "Fui festejada de cuantos hijos de caballeros hubo en Córdoba, que de aquello me holgaba yo. Y esto puedo jurar, que desde chiquita me comía lo mío, y en ver hombre se me desperezaba, y me quisiera ir con alguno, sin que no me lo daba la edad" (p. 49; I was courted by as many gentlemen's sons as there were in Córdoba, which gave me great satisfaction. And I swear that from the time I was a young girl I could feel the cravings of my sex, and just seeing a man stirred me up, and I would have liked to go off with one of them, but age got in my way). Whether to satisfy her desires or to repay men for their abuse, Lozana—whose name suggests her maturity—thrives as a prostitute, swindling her patrons as she gratifies their desires.

Lozana is the antithesis of the ethereal, virginal, elusive beauty, and she is far removed from the aesthetically erotic love objects of idealistic fiction. She shows little concern for the children she has borne Diomedes, she sleeps with Rampin on their first night together, and she combines prostitution with theft. Like Pablos of *El Buscón,* she is a retrogressive over-achiever, the most flagrant of courtesans, as he is the most flagrant of delinquents. While she deals in cosmetology and legerdemain—arts of illusion—her language reflects the directness of her approach to lovemaking. Her tastes are natural, her needs immediate, her actions shameless, and her discourse is graphic, colloquial, and to the point. When a headwaiter who requires her services approaches her, Lozana says, "'Señor, dijo el ciego que deseaba ver'" (p. 96; "Sir, the blind man said that he wanted to see," that is, "Put your money on the table"). She refers openly to sins past and present, to syphilis and other consequences of these sins, and to sexual topics in general, lying only when the deception of the moment demands it. The following passage, in which Lozana addresses a group of Spanish women living in Rome, illustrates her lack of discursive restraint: "¡Ay, señoras! Contaros he maravillas. Dejáme ir a verter aguas que, como eché aquellas putas viejas alcoholadas por las escaleras abajo, no me paré a mis necesidades, y estaba allí una beata de Lara, el coño puto y el ojo ladrón, que creo hizo pasto a cuantos brunetes van por el mar Océano" (p. 50; Oh, ladies, do I have things to tell you! Just let me make water, since because I had to push through all those old painted whores downstairs, I couldn't stop to answer my needs, and among them was a pious hypocrite from Lara, with her smelly cunt and thieving eyes, who I think has rolled in the hay with every sailor who sails the high seas). Lozana's goal of independence extends to her lexicon. Her language, like her lifestyle, is consciously rebellious, unladylike, and worthy of the basest profligate, male or female.[7]

Delicado's depiction of Lozana is an analogue within an analogue. The antiheroine becomes a symbol of the depravity that is Rome, as Rome itself is a symbol of the triumph of evil. Language, event, and attitude mark a type of semiotic consistency, as all signs lead to sin. Vulgarity is intrinsic to the portrait and to its message, even though the seriousness of the message remains a subtext in a text that seems to take its scandalousness quite seriously. The author forges (or forces) his way into this world, sharing its language and partaking of its temptations yet aware of retributive justice. In *mamotreto* 4, he describes Lozana as "muy contenta, viendo en su caro amador Diomedes todos los géneros y partes de gentilhombre, y de hermosura en todos sus miembros" (p. 43; very happy, discovering in her dear lover Diomedes all the goods and parts of a gentleman, and with beauty in all his members). Later, in *mamotreto* 17, he discusses the wayward life with Rampín as one who knows from where he speaks but who knows, as well, the wages of sin. Lozana, for her part, concentrates on the here and now of a commercial venture that unites sexual passion with financial security.

The author as character takes a more active role in part 2, separating himself to a certain degree from both the extratextual author and the intratextual biographer and commentator. A companion provides the exposition of Lozana's affairs, of her victories over men and their pocketbooks, after which the author speaks directly to the protagonist. He is now a lovesick gentleman, she a consultant in matters of the heart. Lozana advises the author to eat sage with his mistress, but prescribes another remedy—monetary in nature—for the companion, who is in love with her. The first *mamotreto* (24) of part 2 presents Lozana in action among three men, including the author, who praise her beauty and ingenuity, avail themselves of her multiple talents, and finally judge her licentiousness as symptomatic of the ills that beset Rome. In the sections that follow, Lozana pursues all manner of meretricious business, giving counsel and giving of herself. In *mamotreto* 31, she tells of a dream in which Rampín falls into the river, and she fears for his safety. Immediately afterward, the chief constable apprehends the servant for robbing a grocer. On his release, Rampín ironically validates the dream by falling into a latrine. The dream vision and its actualization relate to the impending disaster and to the importance of Lozana's dream in *mamotreto* 66, the last memorandum, a dream that may lead to her salvation. In part 2, however, the emphasis is on destruction, personal and communal. Lozana advances as a deceiver of men, and Rome moves toward defeat. In *mamotreto* 34, a squire echoes Silvio's earlier warning of the danger facing Rome, while Lozana disregards the warning and the future to seize the day.

Part 3, which promises to be more entertaining than the preceding parts,[8] gives greater space to the individual and brings the author into the dramatic events and Lozana into the commentary. The protagonist has periodically evaluated her course of action, and she continues to do so, finally realizing that slight modifications cannot benefit her, that the change must be radical. The text devotes little attention to the crisis of conscience and none to the penitence itself. The diversion comes from further variations of Lozana's craft and craftiness. In a lengthy soliloquy at the beginning of part 3, Lozana expresses a desire to separate herself from the prostitute population in order to have greater control over her destiny: "Ya no quiero andar tras el rabo de putas. Hasta agora no he perdido nada; de aquí adelante quiero que ellas me busquen. No quiero que de mí se diga 'puta de todo trance, alcatara a la fin.' Yo quiero de aquí adelante mirar por mi honra, que, como dicen: 'a los audaces la fortuna les ayuda'" (p. 172; I don't want to follow behind whores' tails any more. Up to now I haven't lost anything; from here on I want them to come after me. I don't want it said of me, "a whore all along, a beggar in the end." From here on I want to watch out for my honor, for, as they say, "fortune comes to the aid of the bold"). Even allowing for honor among thieves, there is a certain boldness in Lozana's words. More than honor, what she apparently wants is status within the demimonde. She is the ultimate pragmatist, willing to do anything to stay one step ahead of her neighbor. The road to redemption is thus far the road not taken.

Mamotreto 42 features a debate between Lozana and the author on the legitimacy of her strategies for survival. Lozana elaborates the various branches of her practice, which include paramedical and pseudoreligious rites and the interpretation of dreams. The author chides her for profiteering from the fears and the superstitions of her customers, cautioning her against playing God. Lozana counters that she performs a service by satisfying the needs of the people and that her prognostication is based on fact and common sense. Having observed those around her, she predicts great carnage in Rome. The author recants, ending the polemic by restating his adversary's case: "Y digo que es verdad un dicho que munchas veces leí, que, *quidquid agunt homines, intentio salvat omnes*. Donde se ve claro que vuestra intención es buscar la vida en diversas maneras, de tal modo que otro cría las gallinas y vos coméis los pollos sin perjudicio ni sin fatiga. Felice Lozana, que no habría putas si no hubiese rufianas que las injiriesen a las buenas con las malas" (p. 178; And I maintain as true a saying I read many times, that "whatever men do, their intention saves them." Whence it seems clear that your intention is searching for life in diverse ways, such that another raises hens and you eat chickens, without prejudice and without causing trouble. Fortunate Lozana, there would be no whores if there were no bawds to mix the good with the bad). The dialogue puts the protagonist's activities into moral and practical contexts. Along with the author, the reader discovers the range of Lozana's enterprises and a logical—as well as rhetorical—force that rivals that of Celestina. In spite of his argument to the contrary, the author accepts the instinctive, self-serving rationale of his forensic opponent. Both recognize, nonetheless, that men and women must answer to a higher authority for their conduct. The author looks to the hereafter and Lozana to an imminent hell on earth.

The debate between the fictionalized creator and his creation attests to the persuasive and multiperspectivist capabilities of the literary work and to an emerging self-consciousness on the part of the artist. Just as the character Miguel de Unamuno allows Augusto Pérez to present a superior argument centuries later in the climactic confrontation of *Niebla*,[9] Delicado gives his protagonist the final word in the debate, using his foreknowledge of the sack of Rome to justify her prophetic claims. Rhetoric triumphs over absolute values, self-preservation over virtue. *La lozana andaluza* offers no psychological progression, but the author's position in the debate conveys an understanding of the protagonist's social predicament. Lozana builds from weakness, using her marginated identity to survive in a hostile world. She becomes mistress of the illegitimate, specialist in the unholy, advisor/confessor in cases of love. Alienated from social acceptability, she inverts the hierarchies of society to control fragmented (and errant) souls. The author places himself in the role of the reader, and his reaction to Lozana's speech guides the reader of the text to a more sympathetic response to her antisocial behavior. Because of his involvement in Lozana's story—he is, in fact, one of the errant souls—the author achieves a dual credibility, as director and participant. By allowing Lozana to "outvoice" him, he gives a victory of sorts to the female outsider and to the evolution of narrative discourse.

The foregrounding of Lozana in the debate serves the transition to her withdrawal from the world, an escape that the text presents as her own decision. *Mamotreto* 44 sustains the ambivalent portrait of Lozana and of the prostitute in general by addressing the issue of security. As an active member of the community within a community, Lozana lives "better than the Pope," yet her unceremonious language suggests a concern for and kinship with the older prostitutes whose days of glory have come to an end. She dares to recommend that society provide for the former ladies of pleasure in order to ensure continuity among the ranks. She defends this stance with a traditional argument in favor of prostitution: "Cuando a las perdidas o lisiadas y pobres y en senetud constitutas, no les dan el premio o mérito que merecen, serán causa que no vengan munchas que vinieran a relevar a las naturales las fatigas y cansancios y combates, . . . y de aquí redundará que los galanes requieran a las casadas y a las vírgenes d'esta tierra" (p. 184; When the lost and crippled and poor and elderly don't receive the recompense or recognition they deserve, it will turn out that many who would have come to relieve the regulars from their weariness and toil and conflicts won't come, . . . and from this it will follow that gentlemen will court the married women and virgins of this land). Human interest competes with sin, and scruples with logic, in a speech that has greater impact because it follows Lozana's case (with the author's endorsement) for resourcefulness and survival at any cost. The presentation of the problem by Lozana herself stresses the importance of perspective on message production. The prostitutes are agents of sin and guardians of purity; by corrupting themselves, they save others from corruption.

In the debate, the author offers a compassionate and socially advanced affirmation of Lozana's views. Here and in the following memoranda, he gives the antiheroine a voice to identify and elicit sympathy for her sisters in sin. As a character, he yields the floor to Lozana's rhetoric of self-defense. As manipulator of the text, he fosters the cause of the underdog while vacillating slightly in the area of feminine discourse. It is implicit in the statements concerning sexual roles that women fall into one of two categories. They are either good (chaste or married) or bad (prostitutes). Men, in contrast, can have it both ways. Their sexual activities do not affect their honor or their social status. When Delicado has a prostitute rationalize the benefits of her profession for society as a whole, he bestows a somewhat suspicious magnanimity on the figure of the scapegoat. Although he may be accused of putting words into the speaker's mouth, one must note that the double standard has endured far beyond the early sixteenth century and that Lozana's voice, however contrived, has a significant function in the text.

In the concluding sections, Lozana labors as a sexual and medical counselor and cosmetics specialist, mixing with all types from pimps to jurists. She is aggressive, cynical, ready to compete for business. More mature and more pensive than in the preceding parts of the text, she continues to seek notoriety in the margins of society. *Ma-*

motreto 51 represents a turning point in the protagonist's life, as the deceiver of men becomes the trickster tricked, duped into giving her affection for nothing. She takes this as a personal affront, and her speech to that effect contains numerous linguistic signs of her rage. The episode forms part of a progression toward her total disenchantment with the things of this world and toward the decision to isolate herself from the past. While Delicado's structure has a beginning, a middle, and an end, the order of events does not reflect a calculated building of momentum. After the deception, it is business as usual for Lozana until she registers dissatisfaction with her earthly existence in the final memorandum. *La lozana andaluza* is an outline rather than a manifestation of psychological realism. The text provides a compendium of scenes, a portrait of Lozana's enterprises and of her environment, and a re-creation of her speech. The transformation, be it spiritual or self-serving, is a fitting culmination to the material presented in the text. The rigors of her profession, which have a cumulative force in the work, take their toll on Lozana, and she determines to pursue the road to eternity.

Delicado returns to the motif of the dream to inspire Lozana's reformed outlook. Lozana's dream in *mamotreto* 66 draws images from mythology, legend, and astrology to conclude that "'el hombre apercibido medio combatido'" (p. 244; "forewarned is forearmed"). From the tree of human destiny, she will reach for the fruit that will lead her to paradise. The vision allows her to put her present existence into perspective: "Ya estoy harta de meter barboquejos a putas y poner jáquimas de mi casa, y pues he visto mi ventura y desgracia, y he tenido modo y manera y conversación para saber vivir, y veo que mi trato y plática ya me dejan, que [no] corren como solían, haré como hace la Paz, que huye a las islas, y como no la buscan, duerme quieta y sin fastidio" (p. 245; I'm tired of putting chin straps on whores and applying home-made depilatories, and since I've seen my fortune and misfortune, and I've had the ways and means and conversation to know how to live, and I see that style and repartee now leave me, for those things don't flow forth the way they used to, I will do as Peace does, which is to flee to the islands, and since they don't seek it out, it sleeps tranquilly and with no burdens). Lozana will retire to the island of Lipari, leaving behind the vanities of her life in Rome, in the hope that a new setting may calm her troubled soul. The author closes with the wish that his portrait may lead its readers to peace, as he has led the protagonist to righteousness. If the resolution is abrupt, the motive is worthy. Lozana laments her age and fading beauty, neither of which has an earthly remedy, and the dream gives her an extramundane alternative that begins with atonement. The reader may applaud the intention and hope for the best or consider Pablos's closing words in *El Buscón,* published a century later, to the effect that a change of locale does not bring a change of habits.

La lozana andaluza ends with several short compositions, including an apology, an explanation, an epilogue, two letters (one an epistle written by Lozana), and a digression.

In the apology, the author answers possible objections to his work. He refers to the moral intention evoked in the dedication to remind the reader what the text proposes. He cites modesty and verisimilitude to justify its imperfections, its crudeness of episode and language. The apology advances the story by stating that Lozana did, in fact, go to live on the island, where she changed her name to signify her change in attitude. The author mentions that he composed the work—which he calls "estas vanidades," this nonsense—to pass the time while recuperating from a grave and lengthy illness. He closes with an admonition to the reader to place the spirit above the body, as those of the portrait do not, to win God's approval and salvation. The explanation defines *mamotreto* as a book that contains diverse arguments, in this case secular, thus emphasizing the idea of multiple items of interest and multiple perspectives. Delicado gives the background of Lipari, traditionally a home of condemned criminals, and notes that Lozana's three names (Aldonza, Lozana, and Vellida) all derive from words meaning exuberance and beauty. He adds, "Por tanto, digo que para gozar d'este retrato y para murmurar del autor, que primero lo deben bien leer y entender, *sed non legatur in escolis*" (pp. 250-51; Therefore, I say that in order to enjoy this portrait and to criticize the author, they first ought to read and comprehend it well, but "it should not be read in school"). The apology and the explanation, along with the introductory materials, offer a literary frame (and moral framework) for the portrait of Lozana.

In the "Letter of Excommunication against a Cruel Maiden in Good Health," the author presents the suffering of love from the viewpoint of a gentleman overcome by the fire of passion, a lover who laments his lost freedom and blames the ungrateful woman (described in courtly detail) responsible for his metaphorical demise. Significantly, the speaker here is Cupid, a figure whose effect on humanity informs *La lozana andaluza*. Sixteenth-century Rome rejects Christian doctrine to worship the pagan deity of love, and moral chaos and destruction follow. Lozana's epistle deals directly with the sack of Rome. Addressing her sisters in love, she points out that sin, the cause of the devastation, must now yield to reconstruction, for the prostitutes have only past glories to celebrate. Delicado's digression, written in Venice, places the sack of Rome in the context of divine retribution for mortal errors. On a more personal level, the author recounts the situation that brings him to have his manuscript (which he does not count among his "legitimate" writings) printed in Venice. In addition to the dual culmination—the sack of Rome and the publication of the text—the digression asserts the authority of Delicado's voice in the dialogue, bringing the "real" author into his work to validate his fictional counterpart. The result may be an inversion of this principle; the touted diversity of the memoranda may include the fragmentation of the author.

La lozana andaluza creates verbal portraits of an antiheroine and her milieu with a consciousness of history, causality, and the act of composition. The protagonist is an outcast among outcasts, poor, foreign, a New Christian, and a woman who works as a prostitute in a Jewish quarter of Rome. The precocious naturalism of the text relates to Delicado's conception of portraiture as a detailed rendering of reality and to his analogical vision of corruption as a prelude to disaster. The portrait "freezes" a moment to present its richness and its historical irony. Lozana is an agent of sin and a product of the society that ostracizes her. Her position in the portrait is genetically and socially determined, a testimony to the importance of bloodlines for social respectability and responsibility. Up to the final memorandum, Lozana is a character without a conscience and without a sense of the hereafter.[10] Disillusioned at last, she retires to Lipari as a form of penitence, thereby abetting the author in his claim of a moral intention. The same author seems to relish the freedom that Lozana's licentiousness gives him to convert her negative energy into a justifiably scatological text. The tension between the expressed purpose and the direction of the text typifies the interplay of author and narrator in the later picaresque models. The dialogue format of *La lozana andaluza* effects a unique strategy of authority that nonetheless points the way to succeeding fictions.

By projecting himself into the text, the author brings the real world into the realm of fiction while pretending to do precisely the opposite. He is artist and character. He interacts with Lozana and her associates and develops a portrait according to the conventions of literature. He respects truth but subjects his work to the criteria of poetic truth and artistic unity. He makes the writing process a part of the product. One can distinguish between the several faces (or voices) of the author as creator, participant, witness, and mediator. His presence heightens the verisimilitude of the events and at the same time puts narrative reliability into question. The direct discourse calls for exact reproduction, and the privacy of a number of scenes precludes the intrusion of a witness. The author must approximate, must create new realities from old, and must reinvent the world to conform to the demands and the limitations of fiction. The arguments for literary realism and the divided self indicate the distance between the world and the work of art. Literary reality is faithful to its source in an analogical, symbolic way, a fact lost neither on the picaresque authors nor on Cervantes. Self-consciousness turns restrictions into assets by expanding the horizons of literature, by incorporating the problematic relation between life and art into the text. Delicado seems to intuit both the delicate balance and the means of using it to his advantage through the author's multiple functions in *La lozana andaluza*. As in the later forms, realistic and counterrealistic tendencies coexist.

The fragmentation of the authorial figure and the use of dialogue make possible a variety of perspectives. Several characters describe the protagonist, and she completes the portrait by acting and speaking in the text. Through her, Delicado seeks a discursive correlative for immoral behavior in a richly indecent speech. *La lozana andaluza* is a display of colloquial and dialectal speech, proverbs, classical *sententiae*, lists, literary allusions, maledictions, and the sexual lexicon of its period. The antiheroine is the principal informant, a storehouse of linguistic data. Because she offers counsel on beauty and carnal matters, her discourse provides not only a vocabulary but also a state of the art, and perhaps an experiential statement about the author. Discourse reflects character, as the wayward Lozana freely expresses her emotions, with little or no concern for polite society. Language becomes a form of release, a means of decrying social inequity, a verbal analogue of promiscuity. The author's discourse mirrors the ambiguity of intention by uniting moral insertions with vulgar speech. His language alternately places him above the characters he depicts and makes him one of them. He pleads for piety in an age of sin but shows compassion for the sinner, fights for spiritual ideals but defends the tactics of survival in this life, shows the protagonist on the road to hell but leads her toward peace. Using a non-narrative form, he fashions a multiperspectivist object in which the author interacts with the antiheroine and discourse parallels story. Lozana's language, like her lifestyle, is unrestrained, yet she is free only in a relative sense. A higher authority regulates her conduct and her discourse.

Considered historically, *La lozana andaluza* points to the subtle interplay between author and narrator/protagonist in the picaresque. As is often the case in the archetypal novels, the more the speaker (here, the author as character) says, the wider the distance between the expressed intention and the messages produced by the text itself. Discourse works ironically to shatter the foundations of a positive or moral purpose. Speech intervenes when only silence will protect secrets or serve didacticism. Lozana's discourse hardly progresses toward the change of attitude reflected in the final memorandum. The linguistic consistency conveys a pattern of thought and behavior. Lozana is as much a product of heredity and environment at the end of the work as she is at the beginning. The text does not prepare the reader for a conversion, so that the shift from sin to repentance may carry a note of skepticism. The intervention of the author in the work, as both moralizer and womanizer, intensifies the system of mixed messages. The anonymous author of *Lazarillo de Tormes* announces his presence in the prologue and within the text as the manipulator of irony. Alemán extends the interpretive possibilities in *Guzmán de Alfarache* by allowing the allegedly reformed sinner to describe his errors and provide moral commentary. When the inner thoughts conflict with the outward stance, Guzmán may reveal more than he intends. Like his author, he may accept morality as a necessary premise while responding more fully to the world of feeling and spontaneity. Quevedo's *Buscón* unites stylized discourse with a coercive story to acknowledge the intrusion of the author into his fiction. Published between *Guzmán de Alfarache* and *El Buscón*, *La pícara Justina* has a different historical (and intertextual) role than *La lozana andaluza*. Borrowing a gloss of morality from Alemán and offering a prelude to the linguistic achievement of Quevedo, López de Ubeda forges a new direction for the picaresque.[11]

LA PÍCARA JUSTINA

> No quiero, pluma mía, que vuestras manchas cubran las de mi vida, que (si es que mi historia ha de ser retrato verdadero, sin tener que retratar de lo mentido), siendo pícara, es forzoso pintarme con manchas y mechas.
>
> I don't wish, my pen, to have your stains cover those of my life, for—if my story is to be a valid drawing, without having to withdraw from deceptive events—being a *pícara,* it's essential to paint myself with stains and threads showing.

La pícara Justina opens with a dedication, two prologues, and a general introduction. In the dedication to his patron Don Rodrigo Calderón, López de Ubeda puts forth certain facts "out of character." He emphasizes the diversity of the material and its great entertainment value, which will give respite from the grave issues of state that concern Don Rodrigo. In the prologue to the reader, written in a comically sycophantic tone, he recognizes that a totally playful book should not be published and that a totally solemn one would not be read, and so he opts for leisure reading with a message. To the frivolous adventures of a free woman he has appended moral messages in the style of the fabulists. The author claims to avoid the love plot of *La Celestina* by focusing on the greater evil of deception for financial purposes. He replaces a carnal structure with a commercial structure that incorporates all manner of sin. For every crime there is an implied punishment and for every punishment a lesson: "En este libro hallará la doncella el conocimiento de su perdición, los peligros en que se pone una libre mujer que no se rinde al consejo de otros; aprenderán las casadas los inconvenientes de los malos ejemplos y mala crianza de sus hijas; . . . y finalmente, todos los hombres, de cualquier calidad y estado, aprenderán los enredos de que se han de librar, los peligros que han de huir, los pecados que les pueden saltear las almas . . . pues no hay en él número ni capítulo que no se aplique a la reformación espiritual" (In this book, the maiden will find knowledge of her perdition, the danger into which a woman who will not heed the counsel of others places herself; married women will learn the consequences of bad examples and inadequate rearing of their daughters; and finally, all men, of every rank and status, will learn the snares from which they must free themselves, the dangers that they must flee, the sins that may rob them of their souls, since there is in it no item nor chapter that does not apply to spiritual reformation).[12] The second prologue uses the words of the protagonist, directed to her fiancé Guzmán de Alfarache, to summarize the major episodes of the text through epithets that collectively affirm her protean nature.

In the three parts of the general introduction, Justina Díez addresses herself to the act of writing. The point of departure is a reaction to a hair on her pen. In an apostrophe to the writing instrument, she wonders if the hair has appeared to cover her blemishes or rather to show that hair will never cover her blemishes, an allusion to the loss of hair from venereal disease. Submitting that artful treatment may make an ugly object valuable, she will present a truthful picture of herself and hope that, as in other creatures of nature, the spots will enhance her worth. She plays on the verb *confesar*, to confess, and her status as *confesa*, converted Jew, to synthesize the writing process with its social implications. In the second part of the introduction, Justina again works with variations of the word *mancha* (spot, blemish) as she complains of the ink stains she has received in removing the hair from her pen. Attempting to remove the stains, she gets ink on her skirt, a situation treated as emblematic. In the third part, the narrator reacts to the small snake that serves as watermark on her paper, at first fearing the symbol and then indicating its positive qualities. Similarly, negative incidents may have illuminating results, and her book will allow readers to see the light as it entertains them. Thus, with pen and paper in order, the composition may begin.

The writing process has, of course, already begun. The introduction defines the goals and the parameters of Justina's text and establishes the direction of the discourse. The author enters the text to frame the narrator's story with a verse resumé at the beginning of each section and moral commentary (*aprovechamiento*, application) at the end. The commentaries represent a concession to didacticism, with a special nod to the digressions of *Guzmán de Alfarache*. Despite their prominent position in the text, the concluding passages register as truthful but uninventive adages competing against the resourceful and sophisticated discourse of the antiheroine. *La pícara Justina* is a static work from the perspective of psychological or ethical development. The protagonist liberates herself from the dictates of society to pursue monetary rewards. She knows that she is wrong to place wealth and pleasure above all else, but she chooses to obey the mandates of pocketbook and heart over the admonitions of Christian dogma and conscience. The text alternately celebrates this freedom and condemns it, placing entertainment in the context of final judgment and reminding the reader that freedom abused is license. As an object unto itself, *La pícara Justina* prioritizes a lack of restraint in deed and discourse, while the *aprovechamientos* link the text to the world and make the present moment part of an eternal scheme. The narrator justifies her work as entertainment without fully convincing the reader of its enlightened vision. As a self-consciously conventional gesture, the author coats the wanton account with studied virtue.

The introduction presents a framework for the text and a format for the relation between author and narrator, and it foregrounds Justina's linguistic skills. Here, as throughout the narrative, one discovers a mistress of the word whose art becomes a type of structure of consciousness. If *Guzmán de Alfarache* alternates story with moral digression, Justina does little but digress at every phase of storytelling. The hair of the first section, for example, leads to word plays, symbolic interpretations, historical and mythological allusions, fables, rhetorical analogies, refrains, and hieroglyphic or emblematic representation.[13] Blowing on the hair, she stains herself and her clothing

and thereby progresses into a new set of verbal tricks. From there, she finds additional digressive possibilities in the watermark. The obsession with hair illustrates the inevitable suffering for sins of the past, as her crowning glory falls prey to syphilis. The constant shifts aid the cause of multiperspectivism, for Justina devotedly complements the bad with the good, the bitter with the sweet, and the sweet with the useful. Within this miscellany of free association, Justina speaks of the exemplary nature of her manuscript, of her current social and physical status, and of the picaresque life. There is method in her tangents. The salient features of her discourse are its directness, its commitment to honesty at the expense of modesty, and its virtuosity. Her willingness to push self-examination to the limit may denote the presence of a male author who takes every opportunity to criticize and to satirize her actions or to make her the mouthpiece of such criticism. Justina is quick, perhaps too quick, to make her impure blood, her infirmities, and her calamitous existence the object of verbal abuse. There are signs to indicate that the author does not withdraw from the text between the opening verses and the closing admonition, and that he controls the irony of Justina's discourse.

Whatever subtextual strategies may be discerned from the discourse of *La pícara Justina*, it is important to note that López de Ubeda creates a protagonist who recounts her life from birth to her first marriage (with the promise of a sequel) in a consistent style and with a literary sensibility. While the author has the last word in each section, Justina has the major voice, even if it is not entirely her own. López de Ubeda makes the antiheroine a specialist in proverbs, tales, historical and geographical data, and symbolic meanings. Justina ventures into the realm of the senses—debatably from the male perspective—to discuss general feminine psychology. The judgment of her own actions comes primarily from the author's commentaries as opposed to narrative introspection. More dedicated to details than to motives, Justina moves chronologically (and tangentially) from one episode to the next. In her role as narrator, she periodically considers the ramifications of her deceptions. As a character, she has little regard for the future and little regret for her errant ways. The four books of *La pícara Justina* share a common ground in Justina's greed and tricks to ensure economic security, in a figurative and literal return to her roots, and in the discursive plan. To comply with his moral aim, the author employs the narrator as speaker in the introduction to undermine the success and the self-determination of the young protagonist. In the text proper, he assumes the task of guardian of morality, while, at least quantitatively, Justina dominates the discourse. The interdependence of author and narrator marks an impressive collaboration that nonetheless precludes discursive freedom for Justina.

Book 1, "La pícara montañesa" (from the mountains, where most people have pure blood), begins with the narrator's comments on writing and with a defense of her endeavor. She has barely started to write when her first critic appears. Perlícaro ridicules the presumptuousness of her act. Is her story holy or significant? Is she a legitimate artist? Does posterity require the thoughts and deeds of a lowly, untrained, and undesirable woman? This case of devil's advocacy on the part of the author confronts the question of justification. Justina devotes far more space to answering Perlícaro's charge that she is old than to answering his condemnation of her literary enterprise, but the implied argument, based on fables and verbal emblems, is to let the book speak for itself and to judge it after the fact. The author comes into the text to censure Justina's vanity and humanity's inclination to use words for evil rather than for good. The antiheroine's discourse has detractors before her story commences.

The narrator maintains that the picaresque nature is hereditary, a premise supported by her family tree. The none-too-impressive ancestry leads to her parents, shrewd and unscrupulous innkeepers who give Justina a practical, if not pious, education. Justina's grief at the loss of her parents is shortlived. Of her lack of tears upon her mother's death, she notes, "Hay veces que, aunque un hombre se sangre de la vena cebollera, no quiere salir gota de agua por los ojos, que las lágrimas andan con los tiempos, y aquél debía de ser estío de lágrimas, y aun podré decir que unas lagrimitas que se me rezumaron salían a tragantones. ¿Qué mucho? Vía que ya yo me podía criar sin madre, y también que ella me dejó enseñada desde el mortuorio de mi padre a hacer entierros enjutos y de poca costa" (pp. 144-45; There are times when, although a man may even resort to peeling onions, not a drop of water will come from his eyes, for tears are at the mercy of the occasion, and this must have been the summer of tears, and I can even say that some little tears that did leak out came out in gulps. Indeed, I saw that I could get along without a mother, and she herself taught me on my father's death how to bring off a dry and cheap funeral). The passage shows an inherited insensitivity and an acquired self-sufficiency, as well as a comic and colloquial form of expression. The *pícara* is now an orphan who must fend for herself. She leaves her village to see the world and conquer.

Book 2, "La pícara romera," takes its title from the practice of making pilgrimages in memory of loved ones. Justina's adventures in the town of Arenillas are more secular than spiritual, as is logical of one whose goals are to dance and to travel. Justina has an extremely brief career as a religious devotee, then finds herself pursued by a zealous suitor, a bacon and pork dealer. Escaping him through deception, she participates in a celebration with acquaintances whose envy and ill treatment force her to move on. She meets up with a group of student-rogues dressed in religious habits and involved in mock-religious celebrations. The captain or "bishop" of the company, called Pero Grullo after a character in folklore, takes a liking to Justina and wants to add her to his flock. The rogues kidnap her and prepare for her seduction by their leader. Using reason, her feminine wiles, and a great deal of wine, Justina manages to outwit them and to hold them up to ridicule. To complete her revenge, she leads them to Mansilla, accuses

them of robbery, and watches in delight as they flee. Home again, she enjoys the notoriety of her triumph. Having set out to complete a holy mission, she falls in with an unholy alliance. She prays only when Pero Grullo threatens to violate her, yet her salvation hardly makes her more devout. Her escape is not a moral victory but a demonstration of her ability to trick the trickster. The townspeople praise her as chaste, astute, and brave. The author denounces her as loose-living, lazy, and hypocritical.

Justina confesses that she has never felt any particular affection for the men of her village. Now that she has risen above the rustic life, she departs for León. Her journey marks the beginning of the second part of book 2. The author remarks, "Pondera, el lector, que los males crecen a palmos, pues esta mujer, la cual, la primera vez que salió de su casa, tomó achaque de que iba a romería, ahora, la segunda vez, sale sin otro fin ni ocasión más que gozar su libertad, ver y ser vista, sin reparar en el qué dirán" (p. 224; Ponder, if you will, reader, that evil grows by leaps and bounds, for if this woman, when she left home the first time, used the pretext that she was going on a pilgrimage, now, the second time, she goes without any other end or reason than to enjoy her freedom, to see and to be seen, without any regard for what people will say). In the midst of the holy activities of the cathedral city of León, Justina may observe the religious sites, but her mind is on money and men. An episode with a student-cardsharper shows Justina blinding her admirer with love only to defraud him of a gold crucifix, a symbol of the sacred ideals that she is rejecting. The (implied) author cleverly juxtaposes this episode with Justina's commentary on why hypocrites are abhorrent, based on an encounter with a thief dressed in hermit's garb. The protagonist is, of course, not beyond duping the hypocrite of his money.

Never quite devoted to her role as pilgrim, Justina covers herself with a cloak and places herself at a church door to beg for alms. Shortly after the account of her experience as a mendicant, she delivers a "sermon" on the glories of virtue, which ends, "No predico ni tal uso, como sabes, sólo repaso mi vida y digo que tengo esperanza de ser buena algún día y aun alguna noche, ca, pues me acerco a la sombra del árbol de la virtud, algún día comeré fruta, y si Dios me da salud, verás lo que pasa en el último tomo, en que diré mi conversión. Basta de seso, pues. Quédese aquí. Voy a mi cuento" (p. 303; It's not my custom to preach, as you know, for I'm only reviewing my life, and I tell you that I have hopes of being good someday and even some night, for I'm approaching the shade of the tree of virtue and someday I'll partake of its fruit, and if God gives me strength, you will see what happens in the last volume, where I'll tell of my conversion. Enough food for thought, now. Let's leave it here, and I'll get on with my story). She is still some distance away from the tree of virtue. She tricks a student, a widow, a barber who has helped her rob the widow, and others before a second triumphal return to Mansilla.

Book 2 of *La pícara Justina* sustains the format of book 1, differing only in the intensification of story and discourse.

The tricks become more complex, with several cases of repeated crimes against the same victim. There is greater emphasis on role-playing and disguise and on the sacrilegious nature of Justina's behavior. She is an insincere pilgrim who uses León as her base of operations and nominal religious practice as a means to financial ends. Her contact with clerical figures is economically rather than divinely inspired, and she prays for the success of her sinful ventures. Just as Justina exploits those around her, the author forces his narrator to sermonize against the very transgressions that typify her behavior. Neither her promised conversion nor his promised sequel materializes, a fact that consciously or unconsciously adds to the irony. The successful homecoming is a return to the sins of the past and a prelude to those of the future. The motif of inheritance appropriately dominates the third book of the narrative. Throughout the text, Justina Díez acts according to a parental and ethnic legacy, a public notoriety, and an ironic code of self-betrayal inherited from her picaresque predecessors.

In book 3, "La pícara pleitista" (litigant), Justina quarrels with her siblings over the estate of their parents and is disinherited: "Para mí fue la justicia justicia, para mis hermanas misericordia" (p. 391; For me the court of justice was just, while for my sisters it was compassionate). To avenge the decision of the magistrate, she convinces a roguish admirer to rob the family coffers, and, with the newly acquired wealth, she departs for the town of Ríoseco. There she uses the stolen money to renew her claims. A "perverse" solicitor enters a suit but consumes her resources in the process. With finances depleted but spirit intact, she endears herself to three spinners—having changed her costume to fit the enterprise—whom she relieves of wool and profits. Justina meets her match in an elderly Moorish woman, a sorceress whom she calls "great-grandmother of Celestina." During the time that Justina resides with the old crone, she finds her ingenuity (formerly termed "grandiose," she informs the reader) of little avail. Fate intervenes, however. The old woman dies, and Justina claims to be her granddaughter and only heir. Her acting achieves what her legitimate defense does not; a constable grants her the rights of inheritance. After resisting the "importunate" sacristan who handles the burial, Justina once more returns to Mansilla. Motivated by pride and encouraged by prosperity, she appeals the earlier judgment and obtains a favorable sentence. Now that she has resolved the problems of the past, she turns to domestic possibilities for the future.

Book 4, "La pícara novia" (bride), traces Justina's steps to the altar and, in the process, allows the narrator (and the implied author) to satirize some members of male society. The first of the suitors is Maximino de Umenos, a turner with illusions of grandeur. Ironically, or hypocritically, Justina rejects him for pretending to be more than he is. The next candidate is an equally presumptuous washerwoman's son who appears as a flagellant to woo Justina. In the third chapter of book 4, the narrator catalogs the aspirants to marriage, emphasizing vices that range from

insincerity, egotism, ostentation, and rustic impropriety to excessive gravity. For Justina, the bottom line in courtship is the economic status of the suitor: "Gustamos las damas que haya pasajeros por nuestra puerta, que no es buen bodegón donde no cursan muchos. Pero no es ese el *finis terrae,* que ya la gallardía, gravedad, señorío—y aun el gusto y el amor—, por pragmática usual se ha reducido a sólo el dar. . . . El amor se declina por sólo dos casos, conviene a saber: dativo y genitivo. El primero por antes de casarse y el segundo por postre. ¡El diablo soy, que hasta los nominativos se me encajaron!" (p. 448; We women like to have travelers pass by our door, for a tavern can't be any good if few frequent it. But this isn't the be all and end all, since gallantry, seriousness, distinction—and even pleasure and love—as a general rule have been reduced to only giving. Love is declined in only two cases, to wit, the dative and the genitive. Devil that I am, even nominatives cramped my style!). Justina sacrifices some of her illusions to marry Lozano, a soldier given to gambling and defender of her estate in the suit against her brothers and sisters. She concludes the text with a description of the wedding ceremony and wedding night, then alludes briefly to her second marriage to a wealthy old man named Santolaja and a third and blissful marriage to none other than Guzmán de Alfarache.

In *La pícara Justina,* López de Ubeda creates a loquacious, irreverent, and intelligent narrator full of misdirected energy. Justina's verbosity is a family trait, her delinquency a product of heredity and environment, and her knowledge a synthesis of reading (a collection of works left in her parents' inn) and experience. The misdirected energy is the synthesis of a synthesis; the craving for financial security is the logical final stage of her upbringing and marginated position in society. Lineage and circumstances work against her, so she must fight on her own behalf. Unlike the defensive tenor of Lazarillo de Tormes or the confessional air of Guzmán de Alfarache, Justina's account carries no apologetic overtones. The narrator/protagonist follows the way of the world by differentiating theory from practice, by making action and diction functions of situation rather than of doctrine. She states boldly, "Ya ves que hago alarde de mis males, no a lo devoto, por no espantar la caza, sino a lo gracioso, por ver si puedo hacer buena pecadora" (p. 401; So you see I make a show of my wrongdoing, not in a devout manner, so as not to spoil my prospects, but in an amusing manner, to see if I can make a good sinner). Fully conscious of her picaresque tendencies—and given to dropping forms of the word *pícaro*—Justina relishes her noncomformist performance on the stage of life and on the pages of her manuscript as one who has nothing to lose. It is the author, not she, who professes to make a moral point.

The author superimposes himself on the structure of the narrative, poetically at the beginning of each section and morally at the end. In the poems, he strives for variety and a touch of humor. In the *aprovechamientos,* he appends instructive but commonplace adages to a blatantly antisocial text to remove *La pícara Justina* from the threat of inquisitorial stricture. The benefits are reciprocal in that the author enjoys moral superiority over his creation and the narrator enjoys a certain freedom of speech. From the opposing perspective, equally reciprocal, the author's presence in the text proper seems evident and Justina's liberated discourse may be an illusion. The depth of information, literary and otherwise, contained in the work suggests a background far more diverse than Justina's. The autobiographical thread belongs to the narrator, while the great quantity of non-narrative material—descriptions, judgments, anecdotes, customs, emblems—bears witness to the educational and experiential range of the author. The treatment of hypocrisy reflects an ironic strategy in which the narrator betrays herself by condemning others for a sin that she continually commits; this is the author's discursive version of tricking the trickster. In terms of plot, López de Ubeda builds unity around the themes of freedom, deception, and inheritance, with special emphasis on the latter. Justina is a product, perhaps victim, of biological and socio-historical factors that dominate her existence. She responds to and pursues the family legacy, fighting her closest blood relations and fighting the discrimination caused by her blood. Her means of survival in an inimical world is deception, just as the only power she can achieve is wealth. Criminality is freedom only in the most relative sense, and Justina is subject to control from without, both in society and in the text.

Following the lead of Delicado's Lozana, Justina flouts the rules of proper (feminine) speech, as well as the social proprieties. López de Ubeda makes a concerted effort to include what may be termed women's topics in *La pícara Justina,* but the series of observations bespeaks a male viewpoint. The manipulation of the female voice to evoke antifeminist (or pre-feminist) responses signals the inversion of perspective characteristic of the picaresque variations. In book 1, chapter 1, number 2, Justina discusses the basic generic roles: "El hombre fue hecho para enseñar y gobernar, en lo cual las mujeres ni damos ni tomamos. La mujer fue hecha principalmente para ayudarle (no a este oficio, sino a otros de a ratos, conviene a saber:) a la propagación del linaje humano y a cuidar de la familia" (p. 98; Man was made to instruct and govern, in which we women have no give or take. Woman was made primarily to help him [not in this duty but in others from time to time, namely:] the propagation of the human race and looking after the family). In book 2, she provides male-oriented theories as to why women are restless, why women respond to rejection, why women favor possessions over the welfare of men (an inheritance from Eve) and why they are vain about their beauty.[14] Justina also credits her sex with the invention of false stories and stratagems: "La primera que oyó ficciones en el mundo fue la mujer. . . . La primera que buscó aparentes remedios para persuadirse que en un daño claro había remedio infalible, fue mujer. La primera que con dulces palabras hizo a un hombre, de padre amoroso, padrastro tirano, y de madre de vivos, abuela de todos los muertos, fue una mujer. En fin, la primera que falseó el bien y la naturaleza, fue mujer" (p. 345; The first in the world to hear falsehoods was

woman. The first to seek outward cures to persuade herself that a clear injury had an infallible cure was woman. The first to use sweet words to turn a man from loving father to tyrannical stepfather and a mother of the living to grandmother of all the dead was a woman. In sum, the first to falsify goodness and nature was woman). Few readers, it seems, would deem this unqualified freedom of expression for the *pícara.*

In the throes of courtship and imminent marriage, the narrator further examines the nature of male-female relations in book 4. In chapter 4 ("On the Obligations of Love"), she declares that there are three reasons why a woman loves. The first is wealth, which she places above honor. The second is to preserve, albeit temporarily, the natural order and have man submissive to her as a slave of love. Justina notes that women react against dominion and subjection "although it is natural and for our own good" ("aunque sea natural y para nuestro bien," p. 455). The third reason stems from woman's nature to please ("dar gusto"). Wishing to make the best match possible and yet not disappoint anyone, women respond most strongly to the men who are most persistent. True to her sex, Justina yields to interest, presumption, and persistence in agreeing to marry Lozano. Idealized love and honor have no place in this pragmatic approach to holy matrimony. López de Ubeda transforms the sexual reprobate of *La lozana andaluza* into a virgin sinner. Justina's body is a selling point, but not for sale; she takes men's money and escapes before they can abuse her. On her wedding night, she laments her lack of education in the wifely duties and faces the nuptial couch with a certain degree of modesty. At the end of the narrative, Justina alludes to future volumes that will include accounts of her widowhood and a second and unfortunate marriage to Santolaja, which nonetheless leaves her with property she may share with Guzmán de Alfarache. She refers somewhat ambiguously to her current happiness ("el felice estado que ahora poseo," p. 465) while saying that she will be called the poor one ("la pobre," p. 466) in the fourth volume of her account. In any event, the interest from her second marriage presumably allows her to modify the criteria for selection of a third partner, a love match with the infamous Guzmán.

Early in the narrative, Justina mentions that she wrote the manuscript quite a while before ("Mil años ha que hice esta obrecilla," p. 79), so one must assume that the narrating voice is a composite of past and present. The text barely reflects the dual temporal scheme, however. There is no interplay between an unreflective past and a reflective present nor a dialectic of experience and contemplation, and there is only negligible difference between the Justina of the introduction and the Justina of book 4. For all her loquacity, insights, and data, the narrator resists self-examination, stressing detail and cross-reference over the implications of events. A dubious prosperity, reminiscent of *Lazarillo de Tormes,* marks an ending that shifts from the first wedding ceremony to the third marriage. A conversion that would link the work to *Guzmán de Alfarache* is conspicuous by its absence, with the exception of a fleeting remark. López de Ubeda responds parodically to Alemán's novel, retaining the moral lessons but separating them from the narrator/protagonist and greatly reducing their quantitative impact.[15] The *aprovechamientos* vindicate the author from negative reaction to story and discourse, while the associative thinking of the narrator justifies unlimited interpolations. Justina provides the reprehensible examples, the author provides a rhetoric of righteousness. Alemán and later Quevedo create protagonists who fight to deny their heritage, whereas Lopéz de Ubeda shows Justina's struggles to attain her birthright. With no facade of piety and no defensive maneuvers, she moves doggedly forward to reach her objective, as the author recasts her temerity in the framework of eternity, or of eternal damnation. The intricate use of language, exhaustive range of materials, and ironic exposure of hypocrisy proclaim an authorial presence who combines invention with subversion. *La pícara Justina* heralds the linguistic flourishes and discursive intrusions of *El Buscón* and the narrative syntheses of Salas Barbadillo and Castillo Solórzano.

Notes

1. See Barbara F. Weissberger, "'Habla el auctor': *L'Elegia di Madonna Fiammetta* as a Source for the *Siervo libre de amor*," *Journal of Hispanic Philology* 4 (1980): 203-36. The intertext for the feminine variations of the picaresque would include the autobiography of Leonor López de Córdoba, written early in the fifteenth century. See Reinaldo Ayerbe-Chaux, "Las memorias de doña Leonor López de Córdoba," *Journal of Hispanic Philology* 2 (1977): 11-33; Randolph D. Pope, *La autobiografía española hasta Torres Villarroel* (Frankfurt: Peter Lang, 1974), pp. 14-24; and Alan Deyermond, "Spain's First Women Writers," in *Women in Hispanic Literature: Icons and Fallen Idols*, ed. Beth Miller (Berkeley and Los Angeles: University of California Press, 1983), pp. 27-52.

2. Francisco Delicado, *La lozana andaluza*, ed. Bruno Damiani (Madrid: Editorial Castalia, 1969), p. 33. All subsequent quotations from *La lozana andaluza* will refer to this edition, and page numbers will be indicated in parentheses. See Francisco Delicado, *Retrato de la loçana andaluza*, ed. Bruno M. Damiani and Giovanni Allegra (Madrid: Ediciones José Porrúa Turanzas, 1975). M. Louise Salstad treats the narratives discussed in this chapter in *The Presentation of Women in Spanish Golden Age Literature: An Annotated Bibliography* (Boston: G. K. Hall, 1980). For background material in the European context, see Ian MacLean, *The Renaissance Notion of Woman* (Cambridge: Cambridge University Press, 1980).

3. José María Díez Borque, in "Francisco Delicado, autor y personaje de *La lozana andaluza*," *Prohemio* 3 (1972): 455-66; Bruno M. Damiani, in *Francisco Delicado* (New York: Twayne Publishers, 1974); and José A. Hernández Ortiz, in *La génesis artística de La lozana andaluza* (Madrid: Editorial Aguilera,

1974) argue for a moral intention in *La lozana andaluza*. See also Juan Goytisolo, "Notas sobre *La lozana andaluza*," *Triunfo*, no. 689 (10 April 1976): 50-55; and Augusta E. Foley, *Delicado: La Lozana andaluza* (London: Grant and Cutler, 1977).

4. See Bruce W. Wardropper, "La novela como retrato: El arte de Francisco Delicado," *Nueva Revista de Filología Hispánica* 7 (1953): 475-88; and Valeria Scorpioni, "Un ritratto a due facce: *La loçana andaluza* di F. Delicado," *Annali Istituto Universitario Orientale, Napoli: Sezione Romanza* 22 (1980): 441-76. For studies of the portrait with Rome as backdrop, see Segundo Serrano Poncela, "Aldonza la andaluza lozana en Roma," *Cuadernos Americanos* 122 (1962): 117-32, and Lilia Ferrara de Orduna, "Algunas observaciones sobre *La Lozana andaluza*," *Archivum* 23 (1973): 105-15; and for a relation of the portrait to literary theory, see José M. Domínguez, "La teoría literaria en la época de Francisco Delgado [Delicado], c. 1474-c. 1536," *Explicación de Textos Literarios* 6, 1 (1977): 93-96.

5. On the use of the dialogue form, see Claude Allaigre, "A propos des dialogues de la *Lozana andaluza*: La Pelegrina du mamotreto LXIII," in *Essais sur le dialogue*, intro. Jean Lavédrine (Grenoble: Publications de l'Université des Langues et Lettres, 1980), pp. 103-14; and Augusta Espantoso Foley, "Técnica audio-visual del diálogo y retrato de *La lozana andaluza*," in *Actas del Sexto Congreso Internacional de Hispanistas*, ed. Alan M. Gordon and Evelyn Rugg (Toronto: University of Toronto, 1980), pp. 258-60.

6. For views on the role of the author, see Díez Borque, in "Francisco Delicado"; Hernández Ortiz, in *La génesis artística*, esp. pp. 119-27; and Peter N. Dunn, "A Postscript to *La lozana andaluza*: Life and Poetry," *Romanische Forschungen* 88 (1976): 355-60. Addressing himself to a great extent to Delicado himself, as opposed to his textual alter ego, Dunn writes, "The sack of Rome is read in light of a code which is also a theodicy: wicked peoples and nations are punished by God in exemplary fashion. Lozana, learning to read the signs of Providence, rewrites her life on the pattern of St. Mary of Egypt: she retires to an island and becomes a pious recluse. For his part, the author protests his serious purpose; afflicted now with disease and the onset of age, he reads his own life and its involvement with Lozana as a sign. All that careless fornication and insouciant indulgence, and the seemingly gratuitous note-taking for the unmotivated 'portrait' of Lozana, appear as if directed by the same finger of Providence which points to the catastrophic punishment that is to come. He writes his book at the convergence of life (his own and Lozana's) and myth" (p. 356).

7. For linguistic considerations of *La lozana andaluza*, see Manuel Criado de Val, "Antífrasis y contaminaciones de sentido erótico en *La lozana andaluza*," in

Studia Philologica: Homenaje ofrecido a Dámaso Alonso, vol. 1 (Madrid: Editorial Gredos, 1960), pp. 431-57, and Damiani, in the introduction to *Retrato de la loçana andaluza,* esp. pp. 33-51.

8. The title of *mamotreto* 41 begins, "Aquí comienza la tercera parte del retrato, y serán más graciosas cosas que lo pasado" (p. 171).

9. In chapter 31 of Unamuno's novel *Niebla (Mist,* 1914), the fictionalized author debates the question of authenticity with the protagonist, Augusto Pérez. In the climactic confrontation, Augusto uses Unamuno's own words against him.

10. Bruno Damiani speaks of a "spirit of the Renaissance" in *La lozana andaluza.* The protagonist "takes pride in asserting her dignity and merit and her right to use the physical and intellectual attributes in full to enjoy what the world has to offer. The concomitant effect of this attribute is the formation of a strong individualism and a notable social amorality. Although this amorality existed without any sense of guilt, in the ethical sense of the word, it created, nevertheless, a milieu for the inevitable disenchantment man felt with worldly things" (*Francisco Delicado,* pp. 90-91).

11. For general studies of *La pícara Justina,* see Marcel Bataillon, *Pícaros y picaresca* (Madrid: Taurus Ediciones, 1969); Bruno M. Damiani, *Francisco López de Ubeda* (New York: Twayne Publishers, 1977), "Aspectos barrocos de *La pícara Justina,*" in *Actas del Sexto Congreso Internacional de Hispanistas,* ed. Alan M. Gordon and Evelyn Rugg, pp. 198-202, and "Notas sobre lo grotesco en *La pícara Justina,*" *Romance Notes* 22 (1982): 341-47; Luz Rodríguez, "Aspectos de la primera variante femenina de la picaresca española," *Explicación de Textos Literario* 8 (1979-1980): 175-81; Antonio Rey Hazas, "La compleja faz de una pícara: Hacia una interpretación de *La pícara Justina,*" *Revista de Literatura* 45 (1983): 87-109. Peter N. Dunn treats "The Pícara: The Rogue Female" from *La pícara Justina* to the narratives of Castillo Solórzano in *The Spanish Picaresque Novel* (Boston: Twayne Publishers, 1979), pp. 113-33. See also Thomas Hanrahan, S. J., *La mujer en la novela picaresca española,* vol. 2 (Madrid: José Porrúa Turanzas, 1967), pp. 195-261; Richard Bjornson, *The Picaresque Hero in European Fiction* (Madison: The University of Wisconsin Press, 1977), pp. 87-96; Pablo J. Ronquillo, *Retrato de la pícara: La protagonista de la picaresca española del XVII* (Madrid: Playor, 1980); and José María Alegre, "Las mujeres en el *Lazarillo de Tormes,*" *Arbor* 117, 460 (1984): 23-35.

12. [Francisco López de Ubeda,] *La pícara Justina,* ed. Bruno Mario Damiani (Madrid: José Porrúa Turanzas, 1982), pp. 44-45. All subsequent quotations from *La pícara Justina* will refer to this edition.

13. Joseph Jones studies "'Hieroglyphics' in *La pícara Justina,*" in *Estudios literarios de hispanistas norteamericanos dedicados a Helmut Hatzfeld con motivo de su 80 aniversario,* ed. Josep Sola-Solé, Alessandro S. Crisafulli, and Bruno M. Damiani (Barcelona: Hispam, 1974), pp. 415-29. For a study of semantic layering, see Claude Allaigre and René Cotrait, "'La escribana fisgada': Estratos de significación en un pasaje de *La pícara Justina,*" in *Hommage des hispanistes français a Noël Salomon,* intro. Henry Bonneville (Barcelona: LAIA, 1979), pp. 27-47.

14. See, respectively, book 2 (first part), chapter 1, number 1, pp. 154-55; book 2 (second part), chapter 1, number 2, pp. 225-26; and book 2 (second part), chapter 4, number 3, pp. 294-96.

15. Bataillon (*Pícaros y picaresca,* esp. pp. 175-99) and Damiani (*Francisco López de Ubeda,* esp. pp. 49-60) discuss the influence of *Guzmán de Alfarache* on *La pícara Justina.* Alexander A. Parker, in *Literature and the Delinquent: The Picaresque Novel in Spain and Europe, 1599-1753* (Edinburgh: The University Press, 1967), states, "It seems to me that Ubeda . . . honestly thought that *Guzmán* was not the way to write a work of entertainment combining pleasure and profit, that a low-life theme should not be treated seriously, and that the tone of realistic fiction should therefore be lowered. Ubeda's extraordinary language can be considered an intentional travesty of the 'low style' in order to counter the solemnity of Alemán. His aim was to make the new *genre* laughable, which is why the title page does not offer the 'Life' of the heroine, but a 'Book of Entertainment' concerning her" (p. 50).

Anne K. Kaler (essay date 1991)

SOURCE: Kaler, Anne K. "Literary Origins of the Picaro and the Picara." In *Picara: From Hera to Fantasy Heroine,* pp. 21-41. Bowling Green, Ohio: Bowling Green State University Press, 1991.

[*In this excerpt, Kaler discusses the early picaras in Spanish literature, focusing on their autonomy.*]

Imagine that, after all the primary colors that the picaro left us are blended into crude figures, the artist introduces a true blinding white which is laid on top of all the other shades to highlight prominent points.

Autonomy is such a white—a brighter, larger, obtrusive, awkward, unpredictable, crystalline, visible, shattering white. For it is around and about and in and through her autonomy that the picara takes her distinctive literary form, separate from the subdued shades of earlier literary forms. If her autonomy clarifies her picaresque traits, autonomy also magnifies the shapes and colors of the earlier picaresque forms. Asserting that her autonomy is her distinctive characteristic, this part of the chapter will seek to prove that her existence not only precedes the emergence of the literary picaro in time, but also that her picaresque traits diverge sharply enough from that of the picaro to force us to look beyond him for their cause. For, where Lazarillo, Simplicius, and Guzman are more affected by their society than affecting it, the picara adapts the brilliance of her autonomy to survive in her society. She controls her own destiny. The picaros might serve masters but the picara is never a mistress—that is, she is never a mistress unless it will profit her.

The assertion of her autonomy over her sexuality brings the picara to the notice of Western literature: the Greek *hetaira,* the desert harlot, and the Renaissance courtesan, all possessed autonomy over men by bestowing their sexual favors. While the Song of Songs might praise women's breasts as apples and the images of Eve's tempting apple and of Israel as the unfaithful bride of the covenant might pervade the Scriptures, Christianity found sexual autonomy, such as the Lilith myth demanded, too dangerous a tool for women. While Christ's teachings upgraded the status of women by giving them the protection of marriage, some church fathers rejected feminine sexuality in their misogynist list of evil women. While the Church lauded Mary of Nazareth for her obedient submission to the will of God, it ignored her autonomy over her own destiny in choosing to be the bearer of Christ; she could have said "no" but her *Fiat* became the hallmark of acceptance of her feminine role and the model for all women. In contrast, Eve's apple is a borrowing from the cult of Aphrodite and her sin of "disobedience" was thought to be a sexual one akin to that of Lilith—a sin of rampant feminine sexuality gone wild. In iconography, Mary's crushing the head of the serpent with the apple of Eve's temptation still in his mouth exemplified the defeat of the spiritual over the material powers.

If the white of the picara's autonomy highlights the vivid green of her prostitution, the yellow of her courtesanship, and the dark green of her bawdry, her entrance point into literature is marked by her emergence, not by her sexual role as a prostitute, but by her role as the bawd. What characterizes her first is her avaricious greed. When the sin of usury prohibited Christians from the charging of interest because money should not beget money—Mammon should not beget Mammon—the bawd's major sin was her avarice, not her prostitution. While her traffic in fornication was serious enough, her more serious sin was that she profited from prostitution. Ironically, she is an early entrepreneur investing her capital—her time, experience, and efforts—in her prostitutes and living from the rewards of their labors: as Lynne Lawner in her *Lives of the Courtesans* notes, "the courtesan is one of the first examples of modern woman achieving a relatively autonomous economic position" (4). The later mercantile society chastised her for encouraging men's wastefulness and the lack of good stewardship; like coins debased with inferior metals, the man who frequented prostitutes wasted his efforts since no children resulted. So repugnant was this unproductive form of sexuality that the bawd was as-

signed to be the gatekeeper to hell, further tying her with the devil of Mammon. It took the satirical humor of Spanish literature to characterize the bawd as a woman worthy of notice.

In Spanish literature, as early as the fourteenth century, the bawd is the "sempi-eternal figure of Spanish literature" (Cohen 15). Prefigured as the go-between and the duenna in the *Roman de la Rose,* the bawd figure first entered into the tapestry of the young lovers in the Archpriest of Hita Juan Ruiz's 1330-43 tale of *El libro de buen amor* or the *Book of Good Love.* Often compared with the realism of *The Canterbury Tales* of his contemporary Chaucer, Ruiz's tale resembles the Wyf of Bath's Tale with the wandering knight who must marry the old hag when she gives him the correct answer as to what women want most—sovereignty. The hero of the *Book of Good Love* calls on Venus and the bawd to aid his amatory conquests. Using a twelfth century dramatic remnant of Terence and Plautus' comedies as a basis, Ruiz popularized the bawd under the title of "Trotaconventos" whose name describes her function, a woman who "trots" between convents or religious events to secure assignations for her clients. While Trotaconventos obtains for the narrator the object of his desire, Dona Endrina, the young widow is disgraced while the picaro narrator lives to bed a series of ugly shepherdesses (or cowherds), Moorish girls, and chaste nuns before Trotaconventos dies and he ends the book. That a bawd would have religious implications is not unexpected in a country like Spain where religious events were also social events and where church services provided a natural trysting place for women secluded by family and custom.

Such a mixture of religious and secular themes places Ruiz's book among goliardic or juglaresque literatures for his love songs jostle elbows with his hymns to Mary, his comic touches abut his serious moralizations, his autobiographical style compliments his misery at his imprisonment. He categorizes and castigates love in all its forms, rendering the nature of the book closer to *carpe diem* verses of goliardic literature in its celebration of wine, women and song. The narrator is a wandering cleric who writes for the wandering artists, actors, journalists of his time, for "blind men, for begging scholars, for Jews and Moors and wise women and serenading lovers" (Brenan 83). While all of these characters types are found in picaresque literature in some form and all contribute to the picara, so many literary genres are used by the author that the work becomes a satire on literary forms and pretensions of his day. The theatre, for example, is a natural environment for the picara and the drama a natural way to express herself. The church's use of *auto sacramentales* or religious drama heightened the use of dialogue as a worthy medium of literary exchange, as appears in the *debat* form of psychomachia of later literatures and in the later *La Celestina.* Ruiz's book contains drama in the *debat* between Dona Quaresma (Lent) and Don Carnal (Feast or Carnival), with Don Amor welcomed as a conqueror over Dona Quaresma. Still, the author creates the character of the memorable bawd with a gentle and humorous understanding of her necessary position in his society.

A century later, the 1438 work of another churchman presented the darker green-black view of the bawd. Nicknamed the *Corbacho* the work of the Arciprete de Talavera Alfonso Martinez de Toledo solidified the medieval litany of evil women by embroidering on the bawd of Boccaccio's *Carbaccio* until the bawd became a fit ancestress to Celestina. Unlike Ruiz, Martinez de Toledo introduced a lower form of dialogue to characterize his bawd, a form which continues into *La Celestina.* So intent is Martinez de Toledo's work that Chandler and Schwartz claim that the author made "misogyny a studied art" (165) in his indictment of types of evil women.

In the 1528 picaresque work of another churchman Francisco Delicado, *Retrato de la lozana andaluza,* the Andaluzian girl Lozana travels to Rome where she becomes an eavesdropper on courtesan life in her occupation as beautician. Lozana's autonomy appears in her recording that the Renaissance courtesans were exalted as *cortesanae honestae* or honorable whores in their roles as the personification of earthly beauty of Eros in contrast with the spiritual beauty. As Lawner in her work details, Rome was the "city of celibates" and of Renaissance artists where the "theoretical Neoplatonism idealizing the female figure as 'heaven on earth'—literally the stepping stone to, or shadowy copy of, divine beauty—converged with a practical epicureanism to allow a quite concrete image of the desirable woman to emerge" (4). Entrepreneurs to a woman, the courtesans used portraiture as an advertising medium to increase belief in their role as necessary deities in the Roman society much as their later descendents used pictures to lure clients. As women who lived in secluded houses and attracted only the highest quality of clients, the courtesans' solemnity in their portraits shows the seriousness of their vocation.

Many of the picaresque traits are imitated in stories of these courtesans—they adopt fanciful names, change lovers, seek money; in Lozana's case, she travels from her home to Rome and from lover to lover, combining two major traits of the picara. While not quite knowing what to call her—Chandler and Schwartz settle for the term of "anti-heroine" (181)—they admit that she is the first of the picaras. What is of interest is the fact that the term "Lazarillo" for a beggar is mentioned in connection with her, proving that the name was in existence as a type long before Lazarillo became the literary picaro.

The most famous Spanish bawd, however, appears in the 1499 closet drama of Fernando de Rojas' *La Celestina* which achieved such popularity that more than sixty editions and even more imitations were produced in the century following its publication. While Rojas probably wrote the piece in 1499, the first act differs from the rest of the play in so many particulars that critics feel that it preceded the play by as much as a quarter of a century. In a letter accompanying the 1501 edition, Rojas claims to have reworked an old "auto" or interlude he found while on vacation from its one-act concentration on Celestina the bawd into the romantic story of Calisto and Melibea.

The Spanish *auto sacramentales* (short skits used as moral teaching devices akin to the Corpus Christi miracle and mystery plays of the English stage) employed the one-act structure of the morality play, personified vices and virtues, and were usually performed within a procession. For example, the "ship of fools" which convention appeared in Gil Vincente's 1519 *Barca de la gloria,* an "auto" based on the medieval *danse macabre,* was a familiar theme to a society who held the bawd as the gatekeeper of hell and who had sin and death as the children of the devil. Akin to the story of Dame Siriz in the "Interludum de Clerico et Puella," *Celestina* was adapted by confreres of St. Thomas More as an interlude between the courses of banquets where it served the same purpose as a morality lesson to warn society of the evils of procuresses. Because the drama and the tale both come from similar sources of oral tradition, to find the same story in two genres is not any more unusual than to find the story of Tevye in a short story or in a musical comedy or a movie.

Critics agree that Celestina is actually a novel; Chandler and Schwartz refuse to place it in drama and insert it under the novel because it "was obviously never intended to be acted" (72-3). Yet the dramatic structure increases the play's connection with the picaresque novel. "What is gained by the use of uninterrupted dialogue is a condensation [with] no description of places or situations, which arbitrarily change. Everything is conveyed by conversation, stifled asides, and soliloquy," J. M. Cohen claims in his introduction to his 1964 Penguin translation entitled *The Spanish Bawd* (9). Such paucity of details, such concentration on episodic action, such interchange of dialogue rather than description is characteristic of the picaresque tale and becomes the mainstay of picaresque novels.

Celestina is a bawd who, like Lazarillo, lives near a Spanish river with her two prostitutes Elicia and Areusa and two servants Sempronio and Parmeno. As a peddler of notions and potions she has access to the women at church services and in their homes. When Parmeno suggests that his master Calisto used Celestina's services to obtain the secluded Melibea, Celestina's professional skills become a *tour de force,* justifying her existence as a bawd. When she is successful, her servants kill her in an argument about the reward she has received for arranging the assignation between Calisto and Melibea. These star-crossed lovers are unfortunate; during one of their meetings, Calisto is killed in a fall from the ladder and Melibea throws herself from a tower in mourning.

Cohen asserts that Celestina's origins can be traced back to the lighthearted madam and bawd of Plautus and Terence because the names are Latin rather than Spanish in their origins (9). Monteser claims that in Plautus' parasites are early picaros and that in *Truculentus* the courtesan Phronesium is "clearly a sister-at-heart of Celestina, and therein is to be found a direct connection between Rome and the *Siglo de Oro*" (35). So popular was Rojas' combination of the bawd figure with the sentimental and romantic story of Calisto and Melibea that it was first translated into English as early as 1526. James Mabbe's famous translation entitled *The Spanish Bawd* in 1631 brought Celestina into prominence, prefiguring Shakespeare's combining the love story of Romeo and Juliet with Juliet's nurse as the bawd. Chandler and Schwartz claim that Shakespeare used an Italian edition to form his Juliet's nurse (172); as a descendant of Celestina, the nurse's practical, i.e. non-romantic comments, on the interchangeability of lovers shows her basic survival trait. Count Paris is as attractive as Romeo and he is available, she reasons the nurse's husband exists for no other reason than to provide lewd remarks to Juliet. This bawdic callousness in the face of love flaunts the convention of romance and is typically picaresque; love does not pay the rent nor buy the bread. By defying the traditional concept that marriages were arranged for the society's good and not for the individual's pleasure, Romeo and Juliet plunge into modern romanticism. Similarly, Celestina exemplifies the old morals while Calisto and Melibea employ the new romanticism of the individual. The entire play/novel can be read as a moral lesson on how unbridled passions of the individuals can lead to their deaths and to the rupture of society's communal growth.

While Celestina's tale remains a truncated picaresque morality play, in the hands of Rojas, however, the major love story develops leisurely in dialogue before it expands into a social commentary on the hostility of Spanish culture to its Jewish "conversos." Because recent critics believed Rojas may have been such a "converso," Cohen argues that the union between the lovers cannot take place because they are of different castes, religions, and social status, citing "the lack of Christian language in the speeches of Melibea and her father" (13), the superior attitude of Calisto, and Rojas' initial hesitation in acknowledging authorship as the signs of a "certain nervousness" (13) about censorship. Indeed, the anonymity of much Spanish literature, even *Lazarillo des Tormes,* Cohen claims, may stem from the fear of censorship that forced Rojas to include his name in an acrostic in the 1502 edition. For example, the same is not true of Celestina's story which remains an undeveloped and functionally picaresque tale of the bawd who dies for greed whereas the time and leisure of play's dialogue allows the lover's characters and backgrounds to develop; of special note is the fact that the story of Celestina dominates the first edition with the love story being expanded in later editions.

The picara is often accused of being a witch because she practices herbal or folk medicine under her cover as a seamstress. Celestina's witchcraft is associated with the prostitute/picara's occupation of cloth and sewing when she pictures herself as a peddler who deals in needles and thread. Parmeno the servant claims that she "had six trades in all. She was a seamstress, a perfumer, a master hand at making up cosmetics and patching maidenheads, a procuress, and a bit of a witch. Her first trade was a cover for the rest" (37). For over a hundred lines, Rojas details Celestina's lists of medicinal compounds and love potions

with which she would "paint letters on their palms in saffron or vermilion, or give them wax hearts stuck full of broken needles [or] draw figures on the ground and recite spells" (39). Furthermore at the end of the third act, Celestina's list of ingredients would put Macbeth's witches to shame as she conjures up the dark forces of classical hell of "melancholy Pluto [to] wind this thread around you, and do not let it go till the time comes for Melibea to buy it. Then remain so tangled in it that the longer she gazes at it . . . she will forget her modesty, reveal herself to me, and reward me for my labours" (68). Ironically, Parmeno delivers a diabolic litany of her titles, the proudest of which is "old bawd" (36). As a witch and a procuress, she is a social outcast, her house "on the edge of town . . . stands a bit back from the road, near the tanneries and beside the river. It is a tumbledown place, in poor repair and badly furnished." (37).

While Celestina harkens back to the personified Vice of Avarice in playing the archetypically greedy old woman, she is uniquely autonomous even in Spanish picaresque literature where she is worth of recognition in a society that is obsessed with servants and servitude. Whereas the later European derivatives of the picaros are usually free men and women, the Spanish picaro is a servant while the picara is not. Whatever her status, Celestina is a manipulator of people and industrious in her own cause, an independent entrepreneur who must adopt a servile guise but one who has "lived an honourable life, as everybody knows. I'm a person of note" (63). Like her avaricious sister-picaras, she demands and gets one hundred crowns to secure Melibea for Calisto by seducing Parmeno from his innocence into greed, counteracting his "I don't want ill gotten gains" with her own statement, "I'm for gains by fair means or foul" (48).

While Celestina adds the green of procuress and seamstress to the picaresque colors, the character of *La Picara Justina* adds the moon-silver of the wandering rogue to the nature of the Spanish picara. Where Trotaconventos trotted between lovers and Celestina went between the houses of the lovers, Justina moves from city to city, not in pursuit of love or lovers but for adventure and fun. Justina, Parker claims, "adds nothing new to the exploration of delinquency, but it does add a new element to the literary material of delinquency by the creation of a female rogue" (50-1). She is the first of the picara rogue/tricksters without being a bawd or prostitute herself.

Controversy still exists about Justina's authorship with most critics accepting Francisco de Ubeda as the author, although Frank Chandler claims that a Dominican friar Andres Perez of Leon wrote the work during his student years and used Ubeda as a frontman. Written in 1603, the story was classified with other picaresque tales, quickly passed into other European languages, and finally was condensed under its English subtitle of *The Country Jilt* with tales of Celestina and other minor picaros and published in 1707 by John Stevens.

As a literary work, Justina is perhaps more conscious of its literary style, although most critics see it as a *roman a clef* of Ubeda's court scene; it has three prologues and four books, an introductory preface, and little literary merit for its interest lies in its relationship to the other picaras and picaros. The subtitles of the books indicate the author's use of cultural and social customs in the different types of picaros and picaras: Justina is a *picara montanesa* whose concern with a high place in society implies the denial of Jewish or Moorish blood, a *picara romera* or pilgrim rogue, a *picara plietista* or deceiving rogue, and a *picara novia* or engaged rogue (Sieber 27-8). She compares herself to Celestina, Lazarillo, and other lesser picaros in the description she sends to Guzman prior to their marriage. For example, in the fourth book, Justina marries a soldier named Lozana, the same name as the first Spanish picara; in the promised but never delivered sequel, Justina was to marry Aleman's Guzman de Alfarache. In fact, Frank Chandler notes that the frontispiece of the first publications of *Justina* shows Celestina and Guzman accompanying Justina toward the Port of Death with Lazarillo in a neighboring boat (428).

Well aware of her position in such august company of the picaros and picaras, Justina is closer to the trickster-picaro than to the bawd Celestina. Justina is an anti-heroine to the romantic heroines as much as Lazarillo is an anti-hero to the knights errant. Like Lazarillo, she is much more of a trickster who seeks her identity and her inheritance by her cunning ways. What the world will not give her, she takes through chicanery. She has made the step from the hunger theme to the avarice theme because she needs money or goods rather than food itself to survive; in a sense, she feeds off the thrill of the adventure itself. As Frank Chandler points out, "the picara thus secured inevitably greater freedom of movement than the picaro, and through her was to come the evolution of the rogue novel to a higher stage, where the theme was not so much the classes in society as individual adventures and aspects of life" (239).

After establishing her picaresque genealogy, "for a rogue should prove roguery a heritage" (Chandler 235), and the death of her innkeeper parents, Justina wanders to the Spanish cities, joining with occasional con men to pull off tricks, returning home to Mansilla at the end of each book, marrying finally, and leaving her readers at that point. Because she is not a courtesan, Justina does not follow the picaresque exchange of masters; because she is not a beggar, she is never a picaresque parasite; because she is seldom a servant, she is not subservient. "Justina herself had but one mistress, the *Morisca,* and thereafter, down to Moll Flanders, the women of the romances of roguery were treated rather according to their lovers and their personal exploits than according to their changes of service" (Chandler 239). The picara had begun to wrest autonomy from a reluctant society.

Spain contributed other picaras, all of whom are variations on the same themes—courtesan, trickster, romantic heroine, adventuress—all of whom push the picara into the criminal/trickster image. The titles alone give a hint to their contents. In 1631, Castillo Solorzano wrote *Las harpias en Madrid y coche de las estafas,* a collection of four novellas about four fatherless girls who use a coach from a deceased admirer to defraud hapless suitors and to acquire wealth. The four retire to Granada, promising new adventures. His romances include *Teresa del Manzanares* [Teresa, the Child of Frauds] in which Teresa follows the sharpster tricks of Justina in defrauding and satirizing society. She joins the theatrical troupe, marries four times, and settles down, promising to "a new volume to treat of the avarice of his [her husband's] and her family" (Chandler 314). Solorzano's other novels are about the picaro Trapaza (whose name means deceit) and his daughter Rufina whose story in *La graduna de Sevilla* in 1642 gave rise to many translations and imitations; Scarron used it in his 1651 *Roman Comique;* John Davies printed *La Picara or the Triumph of Female Subtilty* in 1665 which was later titled *The Life of Donna Rosina;* in 1717, *The Spanish Pole-Cat: or the Adventure of Senora Rufina* appeared.

Influenced by the lists of evil women prevalent in the writings of church fathers, the picara acquired the darker shades of the villainess so that every evil woman becomes a picara. For example, Salas Barbadillo's 1612 novel *La hija de Celestina,* known also as *La Ingeniosa Elena,* departs from the picaresque genre into that of the murder mystery in which the heroine is executed for her crimes. Confusing the sordid reputation of Helen of Troy with the contemporary picaras, critics agree that Elena has strayed into the realm of villainesses: to Chandler and Schwartz, she is "the typical evil, vice-ridden woman . . . the most depraved of all the picaras" (186) and the tale of such a picara has deteriorated so that it is "no longer communicating with the birth of the rogue, and dispensing entirely with the service of masters, its observation of low life was only such as would contribute to the working of the plot, the intrigue standing out as supremely important" (Chandler 291).

Written within seventy years of each other, the early picaras' stories contribute additional colors to the basic formula: Lozana is a wanderer; Celestina is a full-time bawd, Justina is a trickster. While French and Italian authors never developed the picara beyond her Spanish origins, the German Grimmelshausen constructed his picara Courage as a countervoice to his picaro Simplicius. Hans Speier claims that it is unlikely that Grimmelshausen consciously used *Celestina* or *Justina* as sources of his picara while Monteser claims that "*Trutz Simplex* was probably based" on the French version of Justina, *La Narquoise Justine* (31). Indeed, while she does imitate the other picaras, Courage is very much her own individual; her contribution to the tapestry is the sparkling blue of the adventuress and the purple of the warrior.

Her name is intimately tied with her vice. When she is the daughter of an unidentified Bohemian nobleman, she is called Libuschka; when she is the military serving boy, she is Janco; when she is revealed as a woman, her captain names her Courage because, in her fight to resist discovery of her true sex, she refers to her opponent's grabbing her "between the legs because he wanted to get hold of the tool [male genitals] that I did not have" (99). Just as the name Lazarillo delineates his character, the various translations of Courage's name and subtitles color the reader's view of her. For example, Speier's translation refers to her as the "adventuress," a word used by G.B. Shaw for his female heroines. Yet an "adventuress" is somehow less than an "adventurer" who is defined by Webster's as "one who engages in new and perilous enterprises" and "a soldier of fortune" while an "adventuress," on the other hand, is a lesser being, a "female adventurer; a woman who seeks position or livelihood by equivocal means." The older translation of George Schulz-Behrend's calls her the "Runagate" Courage, a word which confuses the Latin word "to deny" or "renegade" with the Middle English words "to run" and "agate" or "on the way." Monteser calls her by the first German words of the manuscript— "Trutz Simplex"—"to spite Simplex" because he feels that it best describes Grimmelshausen's intent to weave Courage into his ten-novel series as a female rogue and antithetical contrast to Simplicimus. Most critics call her a picara.

Courage's life story, interwoven as it is with that of the picaros Simplicimus and Skipinthefield, ultimately revolves around the Thirty Years War. Because of the constant war, she adds a dimension not used by the Spanish picaras like Celestina and Justina; where their survival efforts center on wresting food from their reluctant societies, Courage's survival is even more basic because she is constantly uprooted by the chaos of war; it is not surprising to find her as a warrior of sorts. However, Speier notes that, while Courage is "as much an amazon as a harlot," she also "has many of the quantities of the heroines in the idealistic novels of the baroque era . . . a manlike, vigorous creature, a virago . . . the ideal of the Renaissance, fashioned after illustrious ancient models" (32-3). He cites the several contemporary German baroque novels which helped form Courage but maintains that she has several picaresque elements which set her apart.

One of those elements is the variable final status of the picaras: Celestina is murdered; Justina survives to marry happily; Courage survives but at a lesser status as she is reduced from being the daughter of a nobleman to the "Madam General" or queen of the wandering gypsies. Within her military career, she is increasingly less fortunate as she is reduced from an actual combatant and plunderer, to her trade as a sutler, to a lesser position as dealer in minor tobacco and brandy, finally to a psuedo-military leader of a raid for stolen food from peasants. Fortune is often flexibility for the picara and what autonomy Courage has is linked with her military career as it parallels the Germany's war-ravaged destiny. Her picaresque nature allows her to move as easily within military ranks as she can in civilian life. While she cannot control the actions of war, she can control her participation in it as a combatant, plunderer, sutler, camp follower, or soldier of fortune; her fortune may decrease but Fortune still protects her.

In her marriages, her career is equally downward as she starts with marriage to a cavalry captain, descends to a infantry captain, to a lieutenant, to a sutler, to a musketeer (Skipinthefield), and ends up with a gypsy husband. Despite her checkered career, she outwits Fortune by her survival in the face of the horrors of war. At the end of the novel, she claims that she and the gypsies are "of no use to God or man and do not want to serve either of them, but to the detriment of both the country folk and the great, whom we relieve of many a head of game, [we] live on nothing but lies, fraud, and theft." (223). The operative word here is "live" because she does survive into her seventies. Even then, as the wife of the gypsy lieutenant, blackened by "goose drippings and various salves for lice on my skin and from the use of unguents to dye my hair," Courage is "so struck by the change I had undergone that I had to laugh at myself out loud" (216-6). Change, growth, Fortune, chance, chaos—all color the tapestry with their hues but the grim black-red of war dominates Courage's story.

The streaked black and red of the chaos of war are the natural foil for an autonomous picara; war and social change establish the disordered universe of the early picaras which later novel picaras use merely as backgrounds while many fantasy picaras adopt it as integral to their character as warriors. Parker claims that war is the ultimate delinquency derived from pride or the inability to submit the individual will to the common good (135), a vestige of the primal capital sin of pride. Courage prides herself in gaining revenge on Simplicius by abandoning a child for him to raise and on various lovers for their ill-treatment of her. Her pride leads to her concern with vanity about her loss of beauty which in turn might lead to a loss of money and an attack of avarice, the second deadly sin. She accuses herself of other faults—anger, indolence, melancholy, wantonness, lust—to construct her own version of the seven deadly sins that are so much a part of the makeup of Celestina and other Spanish picaras.

Courage uses the military aspect of war as a secondary source of her two vices: avarice and sexuality. She is aware of these as faults as she mentions in her first chapter: speaking of herself, she claims that "her sauciness and wantonness have subsided, her stricken conscience is anxiously awake, and the listless old age she has reached makes her feel ashamed of keeping on with her excessive follies . . . What I am lacking is repentance, and what I ought to be lacking are avarice and envy" (89-91). Always her chief characteristic is her avarice which drives her to her revenge on Simplicius; her ultimate trick, she claims, is that she has left her maid's child to be brought up at Simplicius' charge. Thus, her avarice is both motivation of her need for survival and a demonstration of her skill of survival. Even when she tries to settle down as a farmer, she is able to gain financially on the soldiers billeted at her house, so that she found that her "prosperity and income exceeded the expenses incurred through the war" (202). Her rapaciousness in accumulating plunder leads first to her dabbling in trade and then to her acquiring goods through tricks and scams; again, there is a downward movement as she participates in legal theft on the battlefield to illegal thievery with gypsies.

Just as the military setting satisfies the restlessness of the picara, so also does it provide a natural environment for her lustfulness. The change of military husbands and lovers serves as the picara's version of the picaro's change of masters, a form of autonomous control. With the help of her nurse, Courage first tries to avoid losing her virginity by disguising herself as a boy; when that disguise is about to be uncovered, she gives herself to the cavalry captain who promises to protect her. Even then she is autonomous because she controls the situation: "I liked the touch of his lascivious hands much better than his fine promises, but I resisted gallantly, not in order to get away from his or to escape his desire, but in order to arouse and excite him to even more fervent efforts" (101). Her assessment of her sexual powers achieves autonomy for her; once she understands that she has a marketable body, she uses it to obtain her survival by marrying and prostituting herself to her financial advantage. Thus, war has satisfied her need for chaos of Fortune, for pride in her military accomplishments, for her avarice in accumulating money, for her lust in sexual endeavors, for her need to travel, and for her general restlessness. Onto the picaro's colored skeins of wandering, hunger, and trickery, the picara laid her colorful skills in bawdry, avarice, and war. The next color to be applied came with the transportation of the picara into English.

The primary colors of these Continental picaros and picaras were muted down into softer shades of the English female rogue, derived partly from life and partly from the prose fiction forms of autobiography (criminal, spiritual), jest biography, joke books, fabliaux, drama. Although the English fictional picara is slashed in the bold outline of the criminal biography, her introduction of humor, literary realism, and social criticism capture the more complex tones and values to define the English picara.

Just as the *epylla* cluster around a central hero to become an epic, so do the stories within a generation center on the most prominent person of that century. In such a mythopoeic process, the subjects of the jest biographies or *Schwankbiographen* could not have created all the tricks and riddles assigned to them any more than Abraham Lincoln could have experienced all the anecdotes attributed to him. In England, the citrus yellow of jest biography— the treasury of jokes, riddles, and anecdotes—tinged the popular mind in various literary forms. Because such books needed justification for their existence, many overlapped characters with Lazarillo and Celestina, Justina and Guzman, frequenting later editions of each other's works. This spin-off effect or "visiting star guest" format is most familiar in television but its purpose is the same as that of the jest book: to provide "a whetstone to mirth" as the prologue of the 1635 edition of *Long Meg of Westminster* does when it compares the heroine's escapades with those of Robin Hood and Bevis of Southampton (Mish 83).

Despite the fact that her biography was entered in the Stationers' Register in 1590 and her story has continued down as an example of the jest biography, debate as to whether Long Meg was an actual living person is still going on. The actual persons mentioned in her biography place her in the early sixteenth century in the time of Henry VIII through Queen Mary's reign in 1557. According to the epitaph by a later writer Gayton, Long Meg of Westminster was buried in the Abbey: "I, Long Meg, once the wonder of the spinsters / was laid, as was my right, i' the best of Minsters" (Burford 47).

Long Meg's name stems from her extreme height of more than seven feet and from the "length of her proportion [where] every limb was so fit to her tallness that she seemed the picture and shape of some tall man cast in a woman's mold" (Mish 84). When she leaves her Lancashire home to London to "serve and to learn city fashions," she is accompanied by several young women. Encouraged to find work as a tavern-maid at the Eagle tavern in Westminster, she is tested by two historical jesters—Will Summers and Doctor Skelton; when she defeats a third man in combat, a Spaniard, Sir James of Castile, she is hired as a "bouncer" for the tavern. That Sir James is a Spanish knight heightens awareness of the picara's origins in the Spanish picaresque, jest books, and anti-romantic spoofs. When this latter *miles gloriosus* again engages her in combat in her male attire, the braggart knight pleads with the disguised Long Meg for his life, declaring that the duel was only "for a woman's matter; spill not my blood" (Mish 91). When Meg agrees to spare his life if he serves as a page at dinner, she reveals herself as a woman and enjoys being "master of the feast, Sir James playing the proper page, and Meg sitting in her majesty" (Mish 92).

While Long Meg's two occupations of soldiering and tavern-keeping seem to lift her above the tradeless picaro, the trades actually precipitate and emphasize the later picara's autonomous abilities. Her original military career is precipitated by her taking the place of her servant. Nowhere is she called a camp follower but rather a "laundress [who caused] her women soldiers to throw down stones and scalding water" (104) on the French soldiers. When Meg is challenged by a braggart Frenchman, she defeats him in single combat and sends his head to her commander. For her military efforts, she is granted lifetime pension by the King of eightpence a day, not an uncommon practice for many of the actual women who soldiered in various wars. (The seventeenth century Christian Davies fought with the British army and was awarded a shilling a day pension (Thompson 69).) In peacetime, Meg also resorts to physical means to defend her business from a persistent constable who tries to count "what guests she had"; she promised to "beswinge you as ever constable was beswinged since Islington stood" (107). She keeps order in her tavern by enforcing a list of rules of conduct yet within her own marriage she gives apparent autonomy to her husband by refusing to fight with him when she is challenged.

The taint of prostitution was so intimately linked with picaresque soldiering and tavern-keeping that Long Meg is accounted as a prostitute everywhere but in her telling of her own tale. The closest the original text comes to prostitution is a reference to her house at Islington where "oftentimes there resorted gentlewomen thither and divers brave courtiers and other men of meaner degree, [so that] her house was spoken of" (107). Even here her soldiering affects her tavern-keeping. While her biography itself does not detail any prostitution, the house she kept at Islington with "lodging and victuals for gentlemen and yeomen . . . surpassed all other victuallers in excess of company" was kept "quiet" (108) and peaceful through a series of posted rules which, while generous to the impoverished, were enforced by Meg's strong arm. The only reference to other women is in one of these house rules where, if a "ruffler [who caused] an alehouse brawl . . . would not manfully . . . fight a bout or two with Long Meg, the maids of the house should dry beat him and so thrust him out of doors" (Mish 108). Whether the maids were prostitutes is not clear, although the assumption in picaresque literature is that any tavern or inn provided maidservants as temporary prostitutes.

Contemporary reports attribute prostitution to her tavern. For example, a tract "The Golden Grove" by William Vaughan assumes that she is a bawd: "It is saide that Long Megg of Westminster kept alwaies twentie Courtezans in her howse, who by their pictures she solde to alle commers" (Burford 47). Mentioning the practice of advertising the prostitutes by their pictures ties Meg with the same practice used by the Renaissance courtesans, the Dutch and Flemish brothels, and by Holland Leaguer's, the most famous brothel of its time. Perhaps her military career may have gotten tangled up with Holland Leaguer's reputation for defending itself against attack by the law. Somewhere after 1562 and before 1578, Long Meg was the alleged owner of the Manor in that area around the Bankside, infamous from its mention in the twelfth century rules laid down for licensed brothels. According to the anonymous 1632 pamphlet, the estate called Holland's Leaguer was known for "the memorie of that famous Amazon, Longa Margarita who had there for manie yeeres kept a famous Infamous House of Open Hospitalitie" (Burford 46).

The autonomy of the English prostitute rests with the strange Elizabethan institution of Holland's Leaguer and again it involves actual people rather than literary ones. Holland's Leaguer was originally the estate known as the Liberty of Old Paris Gardens on the south bank of the river Thames, so called because it provided a natural defensive front with its moat and porticullis. Playwright Shackerley Marmion's tract describes it as "a Fort citadell or Mansion Howse so fortified and envyroned about with al maner [of] fortifications that ere any foe could approach it he must march more than a muskette shotte on a narow banke . . . betwixt two dangerous ditches . . . then a worlde of bulwarks rivers ditches trenches and outworkes" (Burford 53). Holland's Leaguer lay very near the three

major theatres of the day—the Swan, the Globe, and the Hope-Bear-pit—outside the environs of London proper and subject to its own laws because it was an "ancient Liberty with rights of asylum . . . and with very ill-defined means of law enforcement even by the king's officers" (Burford 55). It was called "leaguer" because of the difficulty anyone would have in beleaguering or capturing it. Easily reached by city clients who could walk over London Bridge or ferry across the river, the brothel was equally approachable by the court.

Its uniqueness does not lie with its defensibility alone but in the famous procuress and prostitutes who were sheltered by its walls. E.J. Burford in his *Queen of the Bawds* claims that the majority of information comes from a 1632 tract, possibly by the playwright Shackerley Marmion whose later play uses the house of prostitution, Holland's Leaguer, as it title and the theme. The pamphlet creates an early history from sparse facts to concentrate on the life and adventures of a young London housewife in the 1590s. During the Elizabethan and Jacobean era, the most famous prostitute of her time was Elizabeth Holland or Dona or Madame Brittanica Holland. Lured to London by the glitter of court life, the girl entered into genteel "service" in the household of an city alderman where his pictures of famous classical "curitizans" or courtesans encouraged her that to "synne wysely was to synne safely" (16). Such influences affected her choice of occupations.

Like Aphra Behn's mysterious disappearing husband, Elizabeth Holland's husband apparently contributed only his name before retiring from the arena while his wife started a lucrative brothel in London near the playhouses. While Elizabeth's merchant-husband may actually have been a member of the Holland family who ruled the Elizabethan underworld, there is considerable doubt about which Holland, Elizabeth or otherwise, owned the brothel and, indeed, so many references to Hollands being fined for prostitution during those years may point to the existence of an entire family who governed the vice. While her husband's position as a merchant may have first served to introduce her into the international set in bustling London, her liaison with an Italian courtier Alberto Gentile encouraged Elizabeth to provide a brothel for multi-national foreigners, streaming into prosperous London.

What is of importance is that Elizabeth Holland changed her name to Madame Britannica Hollandia in keeping with the regulations, stemming back to Roman times, that registered prostitutes must adopt a professional name to avoid confusion with street walkers or casual prostitutes. Also, it would hardly be political wisdom for "London's most popular well-known high-class Brothel Queen" (40) to bear the name of the Queen. This change of name allowed Elizabeth to follow the old custom that brothel "madams were either Flemish (including Dutch) or French [and] that whores should bear fancy foreign names, in line with the tradition that continental harlots knew their business better than local British ones" (Burford 40). One contemporary critic complains of the Bankside stews that

"English women disdayned to be Baudes; Froes (women) of Flaunders were women for that purpose" (40). One of Elizabeth's prostitutes was known as Longa Margarita whose name, beside being connected to Long Meg, may have been a variant of the Flemish saint Margaret who died defending her employers' or relatives' tavern from being robbed; many Flemish taverns are named after her.

The connection of the Netherlands, France, and Italy with prostitution is a frequent one in English literature. Burford cites an instance where the apprentices' annual Shrove Tuesday shutting down of the Shoreditch brothels forced a brewer-owner, a Mrs. Leake or Leeke of Flemish heritage, to protest to the courts. According to Burford, Holland's Leaguer in Paris Gardens was the "congregating place for all the Dutch Whores at the end of the 16th century, and was popularly known as Hollands Laager" (119), in imitation of the "famous *'Schoen Majken'* (The lovely Little Maiden) in Brussels, renowned at this time for its excellence in every respect" (73); Holland Leaguer's popularity depended on the business-like atmosphere in which it was conducted, its good food, luxurious surroundings, modern plumbing, medical inspections, clean linens, and high class prostitutes. Thus, the Continental brothels made popular by the Elizabethan poets and sonneteers sported English whores imitating the Dutch or Flemish "froes" imitating Italian Renaissance *cortesanos* imitating Roman courtesans imitating Greeks *hetairai*.

The civil authorities always threatened brothels and Elizabeth, employing her girls in Duke Street, near the docks but within the town walls and jurisdiction, came under the London court's harsh punishments. In 1597 she was imprisoned in the infamous debtor's prison of Newgate charged with running a brothel. While Elizabeth's literary sisters—Moll, Amber—find themselves in the notorious prison as harlots or thieves awaiting the punitive sentence to Bridewell—the prison for rehabilitation or punishment for women—or transportation to the colonies, Elizabeth had enough money to buy a comfortable existence in the Newgate. She paid her fine for running a brothel but escaped the physical punishment and humiliation of a public whipping at a cart's tail by fleeing to sanctuary outside London's jurisdiction. Stung by the law's inroads into her affairs, she swore to fight off any forces which might seek to disrupt her again. Consequently, she leased the estate outside of London and entered history as the Dona Hollandia Britannica, madam of Holland's Leaguer.

Elizabeth's ability to be autonomous is her most outstanding quality in a business where she competed with skilled whoremasters like Henslowe and Edward Alleyn. Frank Chandler, sees her as the "English Celestina, who had taken up her abode on the south shore of the Thames in an establishment impregnable except to her well-wishers and furnishing for the moment the scandal of the town" (147). As the bawd of a thriving brothel, Elizabeth became the major subject of a pamphlet by Nicholas Breton and the minor subject of a play by Marmion, where she is rendered

as a "fierce imperious creature full of defiant spirit" (Burford 89). She is able to defend her house against the law from within; ordered by Privy Council to surrender, she defied the law and abandoned the house without answering any summons with no trace of her being punished or fined. Thus, Holland's Leaguer lived up to its name by withstanding the law's beleaguering to give its mistress time to escape unharmed. Shortly afterwards a balladeer Lawrence Price who wrote in *"News from Holland's Leaguer"* that "Hollands Leaguer is lately broken up / This for Certain is spoken" suggests that disappointed young men keep a lookout for the new brothel "at *Bewdley* where they [prostitutes] keep their musters" (Burford 116).

Burford asserts that King James must have known and probably visited her establishment. This tradition of the courtesan's connection with the king pervades the literature of the picara as the ultimate goal to be achieved, even though the picara's fortunes invariably decline after her liaison with the king. Courage has affairs with the military "king" of her high-ranking captain; Roxana's liaison with the king is a highpoint of her life and her French prince is another. Amber's one-night stand with Charles II frustrates her when she is not called back and Becky's affair with Lord Steyne is the highest she goes in the nobility. Even Scarlett marries Rhett who sets out to be the "king" of Atlanta society so that his daughter can be the "princess." (This concept carries over into the film version where the "King" of movieland, Clark Gable created the role of Rhett Butler.) Liaison with the king does not usually continue into the fantasy picaras, although the created worlds which they inhabit often boast a monarchy of sorts; the fantasy picaras do not sleep their way to fame; either they earn fame themselves or they have affairs with men whom they consider "kingly" by their picara standards.

If the vivid green of Elizabethan courtesans did not clash with the earthier greens of the bawdic imitations of Celestina, the green of English picara broadened to incorporate the subtle camouflage greens of the trickster / confidence women like Justina. For example, Mary Frith was better known as Moll Cutpurse, a term arising from her thieves' jargon as a gangster's woman, a "moll" or a "doll," and from her specific occupation as a pickpocket. Best known through her alleged diary of 1662, Moll was probably a hermaphrodite, according to her biographer C.J.S. Thompson; she was brought up as a girl but soon adopted attire akin to that of the hobby horse—a doublet on the top and a skirt on the bottom. As an actual person, Mary appears in court records for wearing men's clothes for which she had to do public penance in St. Paul's. So disguised she joined a group of thieves or "land pyrates" (21) who preyed on tourists near Covent Garden and the theatrical neighborhoods. She fenced stolen items for a network of thieves and, using her reputation as a fortune-teller and finder of lost items, returned the stolen goods for a reward: "'The world consists of the cheats and the cheated,'" Mary claimed and there was no doubt which side she favored.

Just as Elizabeth Holland was immortalized in drama, so also did actual English female rogues like Mary Frith appear in plays as subjects and possibly as actresses. According to William Macqueen-Pope, "there had been rumours of a woman appearing before at the Fortune Theatre in 1610, in a play by Middleton and Dekker called *The Roaring Girle-or Moll Cutpurse.* Presumably the character was drawn from life for the author in an epilogue promised that Moll herself should appear if the public wanted her to do so" (27). She was also mentioned in Field's 1618 play *Amends for Ladies* and, over a hundred years later, Defoe knew her so well that he referred to her in *Applebee's Journal* of March 23, 1723 and, very possibly, used some of her experiences as a base for Moll Flanders.

Criminal autobiography further formed the English picara. In the life of Mary Moders Carleton, who appears in James Kirkman's 1673 criminal biography, *The Counterfeit Lady Unveil'd,* was so popular that twenty-four books emerged on her between 1663 and 1673, according to Spiro Peterson's introduction to Kirkman. Mary Moders Carleton was a swindler and impersonator who for twenty years bilked unsuspecting dupes. Charged with bigamy, she fled to Germany where she so infatuated an old man that she was able to abscond with his money. Arriving in England again, she posed as an impoverished German princess, swindled several men and was charged with bigamy for her third marriage. In one escapade reminiscent of Defoe and Amber, she and her maid posed as young men to escape with their loot; in another, she pulled the "jealous husband" scam, blackmailing a young lawyer to preserve his reputation. When she was apprehended, she was sent to Newgate, transported to Jamaica, returned to London, arrested again and hanged in January 1673. Her life story reads like a summary of the picara's archetype; her use of male clothes as a disguise to escape prosecution is typical picaresque action; her willingness to deceive by altering her name is also. The German Princess, as she titled herself, possessed the picaresque elements of roguery, vanity, thievery, disguise and deception; so widespread was her influence that Defoe has Roxana title herself the German Princess (271). In fact, critic Ernest Bernbaum, the early editor of the *Mary Carleton Narratives,* sees a foreshadowing of Defoe when he states that "Kirkman maintains the manner commonly associated with Defoe . . . serious moral tone, minute depiction of occurrences, the coherence of plot, the tracing of the motives of the character and the elaborate creation of verisimilitude" (90).

Not all the picaras existed before 1700, however. Another set of more subtle shades influenced by increased realism, the sharper light of criticism, and the color-hungry readers created the picaras of Behn and Defoe, the immediate ancestresses of the novel picaras and the distant ancestresses of the fantasy picaras.

The beginnings of the novel show glimmers of the picara as a subject worth writing about. Nicholas Breton's *The Miseries of Manuilla* lacks the force of character associated with the picara because for, while Manuilla suffers the troubles of a defenseless young woman in a wicked world, she escapes the fate of the disillusioned picara by dying while she is still innocent. Aphra Behn's heroines, on the other hand, present a variety of types from innocent to villainess. Unusually strong in mind and in action, Behn's heroines are determined to pursue their survival. Philadelphia in *A True History* suffers a Clarissa-like brothel imprisonment by her brother, survives, and emerges as a rich and honored widow, capable of choosing her next husband. Arabella in *The Wandering Beauty* escapes from an unwanted marriage by a journey of flight and disguise, finally choosing the husband she wants. The villainesses exhibit the same ferocious feminism. Ardelia in *The Nun: or The Perjured Beauty* is lustful, malicious, and vengeful; Sylvia in *Love Letters* is little better than a nymphomaniac; the heroine of *The Fair Vow-Breaker* is so evil that she murders one man and accidentally kills her husband. The subjects which Behn selects range from an Oedipal incest motif in *The Force of Imagination* to vanity as a reason for murder in *The Fair Jilt.*

Defoe's female heroines are logical steps in the development of the picara from her mythical origins through her counterpart with the picaro. Using the older forms, Defoe is a pivotal writer whose works both reflect his traditions and forecast the future of the novel. Just as Richardson developed *Pamela*'s epistolary style from his books of letters and Fielding developed his comic epic of *Tom Jones* from earlier satires, so did Defoe rework criminal autobiographies as major themes in his novels. With the wealth of picaresque literature at his disposal, Defoe was in the enviable position of creating the first picara who blends the awkward primary colors of the picaresque forms with the subtler shades of the novel heroines, while still remaining very much her own autonomous person.

An innovator seldom perfects the form and Defoe's attempts are not generally considered novels. While each of Defoe's novels is different and each one is *sui generis,* Defoe makes the prefaces of *Robinson Crusoe, Colonel Jacque, Moll Flanders,* and *Roxana* complement each other in their insistence on the autobiographical confessional intent as the sole motive for their writings. *Crusoe* uses a variant of the spiritual pseudo-autobiography: thus, "the story is told with modesty, with seriousness, and with a religious application of events to the uses to which wise men always apply them, viz. to the instruction of others by this example" (n.p.) In *Moll,* Defoe comments that "as the best use is to be made of even the worst story the moral 'tis hoped will keep the reader serious, even where the story might incline him to be otherwise" (3). With *Roxana,* however, Defoe departs from his cautious statement of purpose; although he maintains the facade that the novel is meant for instruction, its fullest impact centers on its entertainment value. Nor apparently did Defoe feel that *Roxana* needed much apology for its existence since, "the advantages of the present Work are so great, and the Virtuous Reader has room for such much Improvement, that we make no Question, the Story however meanly told, will find a Passage to his best Hours; and be read both with Profit and Delight" (2-3).

Although *Moll Flanders* has been accorded the title of Defoe's most picaresque work, his *Roxana* is the stronger example of our argument because she is a full-bodied, full-blooded picara. Critics stress only some of the picaresque traits within *Moll*: Alter calls her an "anti-heroine" (73): Monteser sees Moll as "in the direct tradition of the picara" while Roxana is only one of the "samples of the picaresque romance" (48). As Starr points out in his preface, Moll is closer to a criminal autobiography; he cites several actual persons whose lives may have been the sources for Moll but denies that she is wholly taken from any one person. By limiting her to criminal autobiography, Defoe is able to expand on this familiar theme of what Starr calls the "callousness of society towards the unprotected and the unproductive—orphans, debtors, criminals, single women without trades, and other marginal types" (xiv). Within the larger scope of the picaresque being discussed in this book, Moll comes up a poor second to Roxana as a picara who overrides her genre. This is not to deny that Moll is a picara. She is a fine one but one whose picaresqueness is limited to her ability as a thief, as a wanderer, as a prostitute because, after her picaresque birth and background, Moll's story swerves into conventional marriage and economic problems, with only the second half involving her picaresque journey. Roxana, on the other hand, is immersed in the picaresque from her first memory as an immigrant from France; while the stability of her early upbringing aligns her more with the Continental picara, she is early forced into prostitution and deception for her survival before her autonomy asserts itself. Roxana is a picara; Moll is picaresque.

In developing an updated picara, Defoe did not need to create a character beyond Roxana because he had reached the zenith; this only possibility lay in creating an imaginary heroine and that was too far from the historical and literary realities to suit him. In *Roxana*, Defoe flexes his novelistic muscles into the showmanship of an older genre rather than the creation of a new genre. Having once finished *Roxana*, he had exhausted the genre and Defoe was too practical a man to pursue a dying genre. No matter what critics decide *ex post facto*, Defoe's experience with Roxana did lead him back to expository prose and away from a fictional suitable for a novel. Ironically, as Defoe's last fiction, *Roxana* is his most critically neglected work because his other novels distract from it. Within the history of literature, *Roxana* has been seen from the wrong perspective. The novel is not an example of an early novel—an archetype of the eighteenth century fiction or a prototype of the sentimental heroine's tale of misfortune. *Roxana* is Defoe's version of picaresque novel about a picara and, as such, it exhibits his unique adaptation of all the picaresque traditions.

Yet, *Roxana* has long perplexed critics who felt comfortable with Moll's picaro origins but not with Roxana's picara origins. (One critic even commented that he suspected that Roxana enjoyed being a courtesan. Chandler considers Roxana to be "almost without emotion. She

certainly wins no sympathy . . . with characters so perverse in motive, with personages who are simply puppets, it is only natural that the morality of 'Roxana,' should be external and distorted" (196-7). Maximillan Novak calls her "Defoe's least attractive character" (50); Harrison Steeves sees her as "vain, avaricious, hypocritical, and a ruinous influence" (33). Is it her flagrant sexuality that offends them; is it her feminine approach to the masculine world that disturbs them? Or is it that critics avoid Roxana because they cannot recognize the archetype of autonomy? For our argument, Roxana presents a sharp outline of what the picara has been, should be, and will be.

Departing from the creamy homespun wool and the primitive herbal or vegetable dyes of the early picaresque genres, the colors of the picara in these early novels began to imitate the industrial practices where yarn was spun on mechanical wheels, looms were owned by factory owners, and colors expanded in numbers to over two thousand shades for the tapestry. The subtlety of the picara's figure deepened as new shades of picaresque color were developed in a group of novels classified, for the sake of our argument, as the later "novel" picaras, to separate them from the picaras of Defoe.

Primary among them is Thackeray's *Vanity Fair,* that novel without a hero, which presents another version of the picara, one who has learned how to mingle in society while milking it. Here, the actual actions of the picaresque are masked in the satire of polite society, journeying through the Fair. Just as Becky's hunger theme has been transmuted into her greed for goods and security, Thackeray's Puppet Master device distances the author from his work and gives him a set of impartial archetypal patterns which the picaro, telling his own story, never achieves. Becky is not an autobiographer and the lack of this viewpoint must be assumed by Thackeray as he does when he defends his heroines for their actions. What he admires are Becky's survival techniques and, consequently, he stresses her autonomy. However, Amelia is equally a picara: as the emanation of the Widow of Windsor archetype, doting on her child and her memories, she fights mightily for her autonomy in a mass of sentiment and Thackeray is as critical of her as he is of Becky. But, while Amelia is an economic outsider, Becky is still the emotional outsider who cannot find a place in her society; nor does she care to as long as she has the means to survive. Just as the somber black of Amelia's widows' weeds is a fugitive dye, so also the sharper reds of Becky's villainy that tint her sandy hair pale into insignificant and unobtrusive pink when she achieves some measure of respectability.

In contrast, another redheaded modern picara Scarlett O'Hara in Margaret Mitchell's *Gone with the Wind* marches onto our tapestry, trailing the red clay of Tara in her wake. Critics claim that it is a satire on Mitchell's own culture as well as a reordering of the antebellum South. As a historical romance, it might be expected to end happily as its subsequent bodice-ripping novels do. But, of course, it does not. What Scarlett does is to rise above her literary romance heritage to become an archetype of the strong southern woman who insists on her own way; she is the first picara to become accessible in novel and film, the first to capture the popular imagination, the prime figure in our modern tapestry.

Another novel picara is Amber in Kathleen Winsor's *Forever Amber,* written some ten years after *Gone with the Wind* and in direct imitation of it and of early picaresque forms and novels. Closely derivative of Moll Flanders, Roxana, and Scarlett, Winsor's use of historical details and scandalous liaisons made the book an instant bestseller with its recreation of Restoration England. By alternating chapters of the fictional life of Charles II, the novel differs from later historical novels by featuring a picaresque heroine in opposition to the well-balanced fictional biographies of historical figures such as those written by Jean Plaidy and Antonia Fraser and Norah Lofts. Amber has few morally redeeming values and the book was roundly condemned for its immorality by contemporary critics. So potent was the novel that Winsor carried autobiography to the ultimate by writing another book *Star Money* about her experiences as an author of a bestseller whose character became confused with her author in the eyes of the public. It too was made into successful film.

The last category of the picara is that of the fantasy picara who apparently developed from science fiction heroine. I say apparently because a quick look at the heroines of science fiction disproves this: in science fiction, the heroine is a pale appendage of the hero, the object of desire, usually sexual, the reward for the quest. She has no identity of her own because she seldom acts on her own; she lacks autonomy as she waits to be rescued. Not so the fantasy picara who is an autonomous hero who is a woman rather than a heroine. While she appears to have "ridden the coattails" of science fiction until she gained strength and identity to launch her own sub-genre in fantasy, we have only to look at her origins in the picara to see that such is not the case.

The fantasy picara is both the newest and the oldest picara. Built on the warp threads of the Great Goddess archetype, the picara is never far from any genre; in fantasy, she uses the background colors of the science fiction genre as foils to show off her skills but she is a clearly woven figure of her own. She is more than the feminine version of the hero because her quest is so vitally different; as a woman, she was different goals and different obstacles to overcome; her monsters are society's disapprovals, her mountains are galactic spaces, her hunger is for self-knowledge. The picara simply highlights the existing warp threads underlying her modern design because her autonomy demands full participation in any action involving her life. Furthermore, where science fiction is more hospitable to the nature and needs of science, fantasy includes the overwhelming need of the picara to tell her story.

The increase in women authors of fantasy and in the genre itself has made necessary some investigation as to why the fantasy heroine is a popular species. This leads im-

mediately to the conclusion that the fantasy heroine often partakes of the nature of the picara, intentionally or unintentionally, consciously or unconsciously. The fantasy picara is an imperfect one because she is tinged with a humanism not found in early picaras. While she is motivated by the same needs—survival, hunger, traveling, adventure—as her sister/picaras, she is always subject to compassion. This somewhat limits her, as a fully functioning picara. Because the fantasy picara inhabits a created world and not a real one, she is seldom in science fiction which limits technology to that which is in existence. The fantasy picara can extend into the realm of fantasy in her use of pseudo-scientific psychic powers or magical powers which enable her to cope in a created or unreal world. That she carries over the same worries as a woman in the real world and how she handles them make her a picara. To maintain interest, the authors of fantasy, usually women, must create a sympathetic woman who upholds general moral principles; who does not destroy unnecessarily; who is reluctant to kill but will when forced to; who is an outsider but who does not refuse human companionship when it is offered; who abjures sexual morals for whatever feels good but who is responsible for her actions; who uses but does not abuse people; who judges all according to her standards; who rejects the double standard for sex and for power; who resists slavery of any sort as death to human spirit; who retains her autonomy despite the struggles of her society to remove it from her.

Many of these women authors have created several picaras: Jo Clayton has created Alyetys of the Diadem series of nine novels, Skeen with three novels, Brann of the *Drinker of Souls* series with two, Serroi of *Moonscatter* with three. Sharon Green has created Diana Santee of the *Spaceways* series with two novels, Jalav the Amazon warrior with five novels, Terrilian with five novels; Inky in *The Mists of Ages* series of two novels. Marion Zimmer Bradley has numerous picaras in her many novels of the Darkover planet as well as her Lythande of the short stories and her Zygydiek of the warrior stories. Other authors have one or more: Elizabeth A. Lynn has many picaras in her three Tornor novels and several in other works. Ann Maxwell has Rheba in the three Firedancer novels. Suzy McKee Charnas has Alldera in her two utopian novels. Jan Morris has Estri in the three High Couch of Silistra novels. Joan D. Vinge has a mother/daughter set in her two novels of Tiamet; Pamela Sargent has one in *The Shore of Women* and several others in other novels. Judith Ann Karr has two novels about Thorn and Frostflower; Joanna Russ has Alyx in the Paradise novels and Jan in the Whileaway novels. Vonda McIntyre has one major picara in *Dreamsnake* and lesser ones in *The Exile Waiting*. And there are many other novelists in the mainstream of science fiction/ fantasy genre with others whose heroines are peripherally picaras.

As our investigation of the picaresque elements are defined, identified and classified, different aspects of these novels will be identified as being picaresque. No one single archetypal pattern flashes through every story but the persistence of the pattern in all the stories appears most often in fantasy. We shall trace important traits through the four steps of the picara mentioned—the early, the Puritan, the Victorian, and the fantasy—to attempt to establish the fluctuating presence of the picara. Even before we turn to the literary characteristics, the picara has accumulated her major traits of thievery, deception, disguise, sexual excess and avarice. She has become an autonomous, irascible, financially avaricious bawd who does not beget children nor nourish them, who does not align herself with anything but her own survival.

Autonomy is still the highlighting white which catches and disperses the light in the tapestry. The mix of traits provides a varied palette of colors to use, colors which are more freely mixed to enrich the personal identity of the picara. Restricted by the cultural or religious *mores* of male authors, the picara stands in her glaring yellow shade of the veil that the Renaissance courtesans had to wear. After the passage of time, the individual colors of the tapestry become more muted and more complementary and therefore harder to discern. Trying to explicate one strand of color from an entire tapestry involves touching all other colors forcing many levels of the picara to be discussed in each chapter; trying to give precedence to one color over another is a useless occupation. The patterns and combinations of colors may change but the primary colors of the picaresque blend into the subtle and complex tones of the picara's tapestry.

Each chapter that follows will try to isolate one or more colorful strands of the picaresque traits, identify its picaresque origins, trace its development in all levels of the picara—early, Defoe, novel, and fantasy. Because many traits overlap in time and emphasis, the order of the chapters is somewhat arbitrary as all the colors are needed to see the figure of the picara clearly. Each chapter will present picaresque color-traits which are either complementary or contradictory to each other but which are necessary shades to the tapestry.

Works Cited

Alter, Robert. *The Rogue's Progress: Studies in the Picaresque Novel.* Cambridge: Harvard UP, 1965.

Bernbaum, Ernest. *The Mary Carleton Narratives (1663-73)* Cambridge: Harvard UP, 1914.

Brenan, Gerald. *The Literature of the Spanish People.* New York: Meridian, 1957.

Burford, E. J. *Queen of the Bawds or The True Story of Madame Britannica Hollandia and her House of Obsenitie, Hollands Leaguer.* London: Spearman, 1973.

Chandler, Frank W. *The Literature of Roguery.* 2 volumes New York: Random, 1958.

———*Romances of Roguery.* New York: Franklin, 1899, 1961.

Chandler, Richard E. and Kessel Schwartz. *A New History of Spanish Literature.* Baton Rouge LA: Louisiana UP, 1961.

Grimmelshausen, Hans Jacob Christoffel, von. *Courage the Adventuress and The False Messiah.* Trans. Hans Speier. Princeton: Princeton UP, 1964.

———*Simplicius Simplicissimus.* Trans. George Schulz-Behrend. New York: Bobbs Merrill, 1965.

Lawner, Lynne. *Lives of the Courtesans: Portraits of the Renaissance.* New York: Rizzoli, 1987.

Life of Long Meg of Westminster, The. Anchor Anthology of Short Fiction of the Seventeenth Century, Charles Mish, ed. Garden City NY: Doubleday, 1963.

Macqueen-Pope, William. *Ladies First: The Story of Women's Conquest of the British Stage.* London: Allen, 1952.

Monteser, Frederick. *The Picaresque Element in Western Literature.* Alabama: Alabama UP, 1975.

Novak, Maxmillian E. "Crime and Punishment in Defoe's *Roxana,*" JEGP, LXV (July 1966): 445-65.

Parker, Alexander A. *Literature and the Delinquent: The Picaresque Novel in Spain and Europe 1599-1753.* Edinburgh: Edinburgh UP, 1967.

Rojas, Fernando de. *The Spanish Bawd: La Celestina Being the Tragic-Comedy of Calisto and Melibea.* Trans. J.M. Cohen. Baltimore, MD: Penguin, 1964.

Sieber, Harry. *The Picaresque.* London: Methuen, 1977.

Starr, George A. *Defoe and Spiritual Autobiography.* Princeton: Princeton UP, 1965.

Thackeray, William M. *Vanity Fair.* John W. Dodds, introduction. New York: Holt, Rinehart and Winston, 1955.

Thompson, Bertha. *Sister of the Road.* New York: Macauley, 1937.

FURTHER READING

Bibliography

Wicks, Ulrich. "A Picaresque Bibliography." *Genre* 5, no. 2 (1972): 193-216.

Lists scholarship in both English and Spanish focusing on genre issues. This bibliography is not annotated.

Criticism

Alter, Robert. *Rogue's Progress: Studies in the Picaresque Novel.* Cambridge: Harvard University Press, 1964, 148 p.

Suggests a middle path for defining the picaresque genre as both historically specific and evolving dramatically over time; this study examines picaresque narratives of the eighteenth century and after.

Atkinson, William. "Studies in Literary Decadence." *Bulletin of Hispanic Studies* 4, no. 13 (1927): 19-27.

Suggests social and cultural factors contributing to the rise of the picaresque in sixteenth-century Spain, maintaining that the genre began to falter by the mid-seventeenth century.

Beberfall, Lester. "The *Pícaro* in Context." *Hispania* 37, no. 3 (1954): 288-92.

Argues that the picaro characters in *Guzmán de Alfarache* and *Moll Flanders* are morally redeemed.

Bjornson, Richard. *The Picaresque Hero in European Fiction.* Madison: University of Wisconsin Press, 1977, 308 p.

Places the development of the picaresque novel in the context of the rise of bourgeois individualism, observing that the perspective of the picaro reflects the social and economic evolution of European culture.

Blackburn, Alexander. *The Myth of the Picaro: Continuity and Transformation of the Picaresque Novel, 1554-1954.* Chapel Hill: University of North Carolina Press, 1979, 267 p.

Draws from Guillén's assertion of a picaresque myth to define the picaro, emphasizing historical notions of individualism, the self, and the soul.

Chandler, Frank Wadleigh. *Literature of Roguery.* Boston: Houghton Mifflin, 1907, 584 p.

Traces the development of the rogue character, or anti-hero, in English literature, considering Spanish picaresque narratives as a source.

Chandler, Frank Wadleigh. *Romances of Roguery: An Episode in the History of the Novel.* 2 vols. London, Macmillan, 1899, 483 p.

Focuses on the rogue character primarily in Spanish literature, including the picaresque novel. This study also discusses the role of the picaresque genre in the overall development of fiction.

Chesterton, G. K. "The Romance of a Rascal." In *The Common Man*, pp. 42-9. New York: Sheed and Ward, 1950.

Discusses the evolution of picaresque narratives through the English novel.

Clarke, Henry Butler. "The Spanish Rogue-Story (Novela de Pícaros)." In *Studies in European Literature, Being the Taylorian Lectures, 1889-1899*, pp. 313-49. Oxford: Clarendon Press, 1900.

Reviews the appearance of the rogue, or picaro, character is Spanish literature from *La celestina* through Quevedo's *El buscón*.

Crawford, J. P. Wickersham. "The Picaro in the Spanish Drama of the Sixteenth Century." In *Schelling Anniversary Papers, by His Former Students*, pp. 107-16. New York: The Century Company, 1923.

Examines the comedies of early sixteenth-century Spain to find evidence of the picaro character, considering the influence of *Lazarillo de Tormes* on the Spanish stage of this period.

Dooley, D. J. "Some Uses and Mutations of the Picaresque." *Dalhousie Review* 37, no. 4 (1958): 363-77.

Compares a variety of picaresque novels from the sixteenth century to the present to determine how elements of the picaresque endured and changed over the centuries.

Dunn, Peter N. *Spanish Picaresque Fiction: A New Literary History.* Ithaca, N.Y.: Cornell University Press, 1993, 335 p.

Analysis of the major works of Spanish picaresque narratives in terms of their realism and representation of the self.

———. *The Spanish Picaresque Novel.* Boston: Twayne Publishers, 1979, 166 p.

Surveys the major works of the picaresque canon, focusing on the development of the genre through each text.

Durán, Manuel. "Picaresque Elements in Cervantes' Works." In *The Picaresque: Tradition and Displacement*, edited by Giancarlo Maiorino, pp. 226-47. Minneapolis: University of Minnesota Press, 1996.

Discusses Cervantes's response to the picaresque, including his modification of certain picaresque elements in *Don Quixote*. Durán suggests that Cervantes developed a more sophisticated form of the realism pioneered by the picaresque.

Frohock, W. M. "The Idea of the Picaresque." *Yearbook of Comparative and General Literature* 16 (1967): 43-52.

Addresses the question of genre, suggesting that the term "picaresque" should identify works from any culture or era as long as the meet certain basic criteria, which he narrowly defines.

Grass, Roland. "Morality in the Picaresque Novel." *Hispania* 42, no. 2 (1959): 192-98.

Focuses on the three major picaresques—*Lazarillo*, *Guzmán*, and *El buscón*—to argue that the picaresque does have a moral element.

Miller, Stuart. *The Picaresque Novel.* Cleveland: Case Western Reserve University Press, 1967, 164 p.

Examines formal characteristics of the picaresque—including character, point of view, and plot—as well as discussing the picaresque as a literary genre.

Paulson, Ronald. "Picaresque Narrative: The Servant-Master Relation." In *The Fictions of Satire,* pp. 58-73. Baltimore: Johns Hopkins Press, 1967.

Describes the servant-master relationship as an essential element of picaresque satire.

Rico, Francisco. *The Spanish Picaresque Novel and the Point of View*. Translated by Charles Davis and Harry Sieber. Cambridge: Cambridge University Press, 1984, 148 p.

Discusses the development of point of view in the picaresque through the major Spanish novels.

Rodríguez-Luis, Julio. "*Pícaras*: The Modal Approach to the Picaresque." *Comparative Literature* 31, no. 1 (1979): 32-46.

Argues that early Spanish picaras are not truly picaresque, proposing *Moll Flanders* as the first true female picaresque character.

Sieber, Harry. *The Picaresque*. London, Methuen, 1977, 85 p.

Outlines the development of the picaresque novel from its Spanish origins to its appropriation by English and other European authors.

Smith, Paul Julian. "The Rhetoric of Representation in Picaresque Narrative." In *Writing in the Margin: Spanish Literature of the Golden Age*, pp. 78-126. Oxford: Clarendon Press, 1988.

Analyzes literary representation in *Lazarillo, Guzmán*, and *El buscón* using insights from modern theorists, including Jacques Derrida and Michel Foucault.

Stamm, James R. "The Use and Types of Humor in the Picaresque Novel." *Hispania* 42, no. 4 (1959): 482-87.

Places the humor found in early Spanish picaresques into classifications such as parental humor, folkloric stories, puns and other forms of verbal humor, social satire, and scatological humor.

Whitbourn, Christine J. "Moral Ambiguity in the Spanish Picaresque Tradition." In *Knaves and Swindlers: Essays on the Picaresque Novel in Europe*, edited by Christine J. Whitbourn, pp. 1-24. Oxford: Oxford University Press, 1974.

Looks back to early antecedents of the picaresque novel to demonstrate the centrality of moral ambiguity to the development of the genre, linking this ambiguity the unreliable narrators of picaresque narratives.

Wicks, Ulrich. "Picaro, Picaresque: the Picaresque in Literary Scholarship." *Genre* 5, no. 2 (1972): 153-92.

Outlines contemporary approaches to the problem of the picaresque genre.

——. "Onlyman." *Mosaic* 8, no. 3 (1975): 21-47.

Defines an aspect of the picaresque as the exile or exclusion of the picaro, discussing such modern works as Ralph Ellison's *Invisible Man* as well as the major Spanish picaresque novels.

——. "The Nature of the Picaresque Narrative: A Model Approach." *PMLA* 89, no. 2 (1974): 240-49.

Proposes the concept of a picaresque "mode" to address the difficulties in defining the picaresque as a genre and establishes several criteria for defining the picaresque.

How to Use This Index

The main references

Calvino, Italo
1923-1985 .... CLC **5, 8, 11, 22, 33, 39,**
73; SSC 3

---

list all author entries in the following Gale Literary Criticism series:

BLC = *Black Literature Criticism*
CLC = *Contemporary Literary Criticism*
CLR = *Children's Literature Review*
CMLC = *Classical and Medieval Literature Criticism*
DA = *DISCovering Authors*
DAB = *DISCovering Authors: British*
DAC = *DISCovering Authors: Canadian*
DAM = *DISCovering Authors: Modules*
    DRAM: *Dramatists Module;* *MST:* *Most-Studied Authors Module;*
    MULT: *Multicultural Authors Module;* *NOV:* *Novelists Module;*
    POET: *Poets Module;* *POP:* *Popular Fiction and Genre Authors Module*
DC = *Drama Criticism*
HLC = *Hispanic Literature Criticism*
LC = *Literature Criticism from 1400 to 1800*
NCLC = *Nineteenth-Century Literature Criticism*
NNAL = *Native North American Literature*
PC = *Poetry Criticism*
SSC = *Short Story Criticism*
TCLC = *Twentieth-Century Literary Criticism*
WLC = *World Literature Criticism, 1500 to the Present*

The cross-references

See also CANR 23; CA 85-88;
obituary CA116

---

list all author entries in the following Gale biographical and literary sources:

AAYA = *Authors & Artists for Young Adults*
AITN = *Authors in the News*
BEST = *Bestsellers*
BW = *Black Writers*
CA = *Contemporary Authors*
CAAS = *Contemporary Authors Autobiography Series*
CABS = *Contemporary Authors Bibliographical Series*
CANR = *Contemporary Authors New Revision Series*
CAP = *Contemporary Authors Permanent Series*
CDALB = *Concise Dictionary of American Literary Biography*
CDBLB = *Concise Dictionary of British Literary Biography*
DLB = *Dictionary of Literary Biography*
DLBD = *Dictionary of Literary Biography Documentary Series*
DLBY = *Dictionary of Literary Biography Yearbook*
HW = *Hispanic Writers*
JRDA = *Junior DISCovering Authors*
MAICYA = *Major Authors and Illustrators for Children and Young Adults*
MTCW = *Major 20th-Century Writers*
SAAS = *Something about the Author Autobiography Series*
SATA = *Something about the Author*
YABC = *Yesterday's Authors of Books for Children*

Literary Criticism Series
Cumulative Author Index

20/1631
See Upward, Allen

A/C Cross
See Lawrence, T(homas) E(dward)

Abasiyanik, Sait Faik 1906-1954
See Sait Faik
See also CA 123

Abbey, Edward 1927-1989 .... **CLC 36, 59**
See also ANW; CA 45-48; 128; CANR 2, 41; DA3; DLB 256; MTCW 2; TCWW 2

Abbott, Lee K(ittredge) 1947- .... **CLC 48**
See also CA 124; CANR 51, 101; DLB 130

Abe, Kobo 1924-1993 .... **CLC 8, 22, 53, 81**
See also CA 65-68; 140; CANR 24, 60; DAM NOV; DFS 14; DLB 182; MJW; MTCW 1, 2; SFW 4; TCLC 121

Abe Kobo
See Abe, Kobo

Abelard, Peter c. 1079-c. 1142 ...... **CMLC 11**
See also DLB 115, 208

Abell, Kjeld 1901-1961 .... **CLC 15**
See also CA 191; 111; DLB 214

Abish, Walter 1931- .... **CLC 22; SSC 44**
See also CA 101; CANR 37; CN 7; DLB 130, 227

Abrahams, Peter (Henry) 1919- .... **CLC 4**
See also AFW; BW 1; CA 57-60; CANR 26; CDWLB 3; CN 7; DLB 117, 225; MTCW 1, 2; RGEL 2; WLIT 2

Abrams, M(eyer) H(oward) 1912- ... **CLC 24**
See also CA 57-60; CANR 13, 33; DLB 67

Abse, Dannie 1923- .... **CLC 7, 29; PC 41**
See also CA 53-56; CAAS 1; CANR 4, 46, 74; CBD; CP 7; DAB; DAM POET; DLB 27, 245; MTCW 1

Abutsu 1222(?)-1283 .... **CMLC 46**
See also Abutsu-ni

Abutsu-ni
See Abutsu
See also DLB 203

Achebe, (Albert) Chinua(lumogu)
1930- ...... **CLC 1, 3, 5, 7, 11, 26, 51, 75, 127, 152; BLC 1; WLC**
See also AAYA 15; AFW; BPFB 1; BW 2, 3; CA 1-4R; CANR 6, 26, 47; CDWLB 3; CLR 20; CN 7; CP 7; CWRI 5; DA; DA3; DAB; DAC; DAM MST, MULT, NOV; DLB 117; DNFS 1; EXPN; EXPS; LAIT 2; MAICYA 1, 2; MTCW 1, 2; NFS 2; RGEL 2; RGSF 2; SATA 38, 40; SATA-Brief 38; SSFS 3, 13; WLIT 2

Acker, Kathy 1948-1997 .... **CLC 45, 111**
See also CA 117; 122; 162; CANR 55; CN 7

Ackroyd, Peter 1949- .... **CLC 34, 52, 140**
See also BRWS 6; CA 123; 127; CANR 51, 74, 99; CN 7; DLB 155, 231; HGG; INT 127; MTCW 1; RHW

Acorn, Milton 1923-1986 .... **CLC 15**
See also CA 103; CCA 1; DAC; DLB 53; INT 103

Adamov, Arthur 1908-1970 .... **CLC 4, 25**
See also CA 17-18; 25-28R; CAP 2; DAM DRAM; GFL 1789 to the Present; MTCW 1; RGWL 2

Adams, Alice (Boyd) 1926-1999 .. **CLC 6, 13, 46; SSC 24**
See also CA 81-84; 179; CANR 26, 53, 75, 88; CN 7; CSW; DLB 234; DLBY 1986; INT CANR-26; MTCW 1, 2; SSFS 14

Adams, Andy 1859-1935 .... **TCLC 56**
See also TCWW 2; YABC 1

Adams, Brooks 1848-1927 .... **TCLC 80**
See also CA 123; DLB 47

Adams, Douglas (Noel) 1952-2001 .. **CLC 27, 60**
See also AAYA 4, 33; BEST 89:3; BYA 14; CA 106; 197; CANR 34, 64; CPW; DA3; DAM POP; DLBY 1983; JRDA; MTCW 1; NFS 7; SATA 116; SATA-Obit 128; SFW 4

Adams, Francis 1862-1893 .... **NCLC 33**

Adams, Henry (Brooks)
1838-1918 .... **TCLC 4, 52**
See also AMW; CA 104; 133; CANR 77; DA; DAB; DAC; DAM MST; DLB 12, 47, 189; MTCW 1; NCFS 1

Adams, John 1735-1826 .... **NCLC 106**
See also DLB 31, 183

Adams, Richard (George) 1920- ... **CLC 4, 5, 18**
See also AAYA 16; AITN 1, 2; BPFB 1; BYA 5; CA 49-52; CANR 3, 35; CLR 20; CN 7; DAM NOV; FANT; JRDA; LAIT 5; MAICYA 1, 2; MTCW 1, 2; NFS 11; SATA 7, 69; YAW

Adamson, Joy(-Friederike Victoria)
1910-1980 .... **CLC 17**
See also CA 69-72; 93-96; CANR 22; MTCW 1; SATA 11; SATA-Obit 22

Adcock, Fleur 1934- .... **CLC 41**
See also CA 25-28R, 182; CAAE 182; CAAS 23; CANR 11, 34, 69, 101; CP 7; CWP; DLB 40; FW

Addams, Charles (Samuel)
1912-1988 .... **CLC 30**
See also CA 61-64; 126; CANR 12, 79

Addams, Jane 1860-1945 .... **TCLC 76**
See also AMWS 1; FW

Addison, Joseph 1672-1719 .... **LC 18**
See also BRW 3; CDBLB 1660-1789; DLB 101; RGEL 2; WLIT 3

Adler, Alfred (F.) 1870-1937 .... **TCLC 61**
See also CA 119; 159

Adler, C(arole) S(chwerdtfeger)
1932- .... **CLC 35**
See also AAYA 4, 41; CA 89-92; CANR 19, 40, 101; CLR 78; JRDA; MAICYA 1, 2; SAAS 15; SATA 26, 63, 102, 126; YAW

Adler, Renata 1938- .... **CLC 8, 31**
See also CA 49-52; CANR 95; CN 7; MTCW 1

Adorno, Theodor W(iesengrund)
1903-1969 .... **TCLC 111**
See also CA 89-92; 25-28R; CANR 89; DLB 242

Ady, Endre 1877-1919 .... **TCLC 11**
See also CA 107; CDWLB 4; DLB 215; EW 9

A.E. .... **TCLC 3, 10**
See also Russell, George William
See also DLB 19

Aelfric c. 955-c. 1010 .... **CMLC 46**
See also DLB 146

Aeschines c. 390B.C.-c. 320B.C. .... **CMLC 47**
See also DLB 176

Aeschylus 525(?)B.C.-456(?)B.C. .. **CMLC 11, 51; DC 8; WLCS**
See also AW 1; CDWLB 1; DA; DAB; DAC; DAM DRAM, MST; DFS 5, 10; DLB 176; RGWL 2

Aesop 620(?)B.C.-560(?)B.C. .... **CMLC 24**
See also CLR 14; MAICYA 1, 2; SATA 64

Affable Hawk
See MacCarthy, Sir (Charles Otto) Desmond

Africa, Ben
See Bosman, Herman Charles

Afton, Effie
See Harper, Frances Ellen Watkins

Agapida, Fray Antonio
See Irving, Washington

Agee, James (Rufus) 1909-1955 ...... **TCLC 1, 19**
See also AITN 1; AMW; CA 108; 148; CDALB 1941-1968; DAM NOV; DLB 2, 26, 152; DLBY 1989; LAIT 3; MTCW 1; RGAL 4

Aghill, Gordon
See Silverberg, Robert

Agnon, S(hmuel) Y(osef Halevi)
1888-1970 .... **CLC 4, 8, 14; SSC 30**
See also CA 17-18; 25-28R; CANR 60, 102; CAP 2; MTCW 1, 2; RGSF 2; RGWL 2

Agrippa von Nettesheim, Henry Cornelius
1486-1535 .... **LC 27**

Aguilera Malta, Demetrio 1909-1981
See also CA 111; 124; CANR 87; DAM MULT, NOV; DLB 145; HLCS 1; HW 1

Agustini, Delmira 1886-1914
See also CA 166; HLCS 1; HW 1, 2; LAW

Aherne, Owen
See Cassill, R(onald) V(erlin)
Ai 1947- .... **CLC 4, 14, 69**
See also CA 85-88; CAAS 13; CANR 70;
DLB 120
Aickman, Robert (Fordyce)
1914-1981 .... **CLC 57**
See also CA 5-8R; CANR 3, 72, 100; HGG;
SUFW
Aiken, Conrad (Potter) 1889-1973 .... **CLC 1,**
3, 5, 10, 52; PC 26; SSC 9
See also AMW; CA 5-8R; 45-48; CANR 4,
60; CDALB 1929-1941; DAM NOV,
POET; DLB 9, 45, 102; EXPS; HGG;
MTCW 1, 2; RGAL 4; RGSF 2; SATA 3,
30; SSFS 8
Aiken, Joan (Delano) 1924- .... **CLC 35**
See also AAYA 1, 25; CA 9-12R, 182;
CAAE 182; CANR 4, 23, 34, 64; CLR 1,
19; DLB 161; FANT; HGG; JRDA; MAI-
CYA 1, 2; MTCW 1; RHW; SAAS 1;
SATA 2, 30, 73; SATA-Essay 109; WYA;
YAW
Ainsworth, William Harrison
1805-1882 .... **NCLC 13**
See also DLB 21; HGG; RGEL 2; SATA
24; SUFW
Aitmatov, Chingiz (Torekulovich)
1928- .... **CLC 71**
See also CA 103; CANR 38; MTCW 1;
RGSF 2; SATA 56
Akers, Floyd
See Baum, L(yman) Frank
Akhmadulina, Bella Akhatovna
1937- .... **CLC 53**
See also CA 65-68; CWP; CWW 2; DAM
POET
Akhmatova, Anna 1888-1966 ..... **CLC 11, 25,**
64, 126; PC 2
See also CA 19-20; 25-28R; CANR 35;
CAP 1; DA3; DAM POET; EW 10;
MTCW 1, 2; RGWL 2
Aksakov, Sergei Timofeyvich
1791-1859 .... **NCLC 2**
See also DLB 198
Aksenov, Vassily
See Aksyonov, Vassily (Pavlovich)
Akst, Daniel 1956- .... **CLC 109**
See also CA 161
Aksyonov, Vassily (Pavlovich)
1932- .... **CLC 22, 37, 101**
See also CA 53-56; CANR 12, 48, 77;
CWW 2
Akutagawa Ryunosuke
1892-1927 .... **TCLC 16; SSC 44**
See also CA 117; 154; DLB 180; MJW;
RGSF 2; RGWL 2
Alain 1868-1951 .... **TCLC 41**
See also CA 163; GFL 1789 to the Present
Alain-Fournier .... **TCLC 6**
See also Fournier, Henri Alban
See also DLB 65; GFL 1789 to the Present;
RGWL 2
Alarcon, Pedro Antonio de
1833-1891 .... **NCLC 1**
Alas (y Urena), Leopoldo (Enrique Garcia)
1852-1901 .... **TCLC 29**
See also CA 113; 131; HW 1; RGSF 2
Albee, Edward (Franklin III) 1928- . **CLC 1,**
2, 3, 5, 9, 11, 13, 25, 53, 86, 113; DC
11; WLC
See also AITN 1; AMW; CA 5-8R; CABS
3; CAD; CANR 8, 54, 74; CD 5; CDALB
1941-1968; DA; DA3; DAB; DAC; DAM
DRAM, MST; DFS 2, 3, 8, 10, 13, 14;
DLB 7; INT CANR-8; LAIT 4; MTCW
1, 2; RGAL 4; TUS
Alberti, Rafael 1902-1999 .... **CLC 7**
See also CA 85-88; 185; CANR 81; DLB
108; HW 2; RGWL 2

Albert the Great 1193(?)-1280 ...... **CMLC 16**
See also DLB 115
Alcala-Galiano, Juan Valera y
See Valera y Alcala-Galiano, Juan
Alcayaga, Lucila Godoy
See Godoy Alcayaga, Lucila
Alcott, Amos Bronson 1799-1888 .... **NCLC 1**
See also DLB 1, 223
Alcott, Louisa May 1832-1888 . **NCLC 6, 58,**
83; SSC 27; WLC
See also AAYA 20; AMWS 1; BPFB 1;
BYA 2; CDALB 1865-1917; CLR 1, 38;
DA; DA3; DAB; DAC; DAM MST, NOV;
DLB 1, 42, 79, 223, 239, 242; DLBD 14;
FW; JRDA; LAIT 2; MAICYA 1, 2; NFS
12; RGAL 4; SATA 100; WCH; WYA;
YABC 1; YAW
Aldanov, M. A.
See Aldanov, Mark (Alexandrovich)
Aldanov, Mark (Alexandrovich)
1886(?)-1957 .... **TCLC 23**
See also CA 118; 181
Aldington, Richard 1892-1962 .... **CLC 49**
See also CA 85-88; CANR 45; DLB 20, 36,
100, 149; RGEL 2
Aldiss, Brian W(ilson) 1925- . **CLC 5, 14, 40;**
SSC 36
See also AAYA 42; CA 5-8R; CAAE 190;
CAAS 2; CANR 5, 28, 64; CN 7; DAM
NOV; DLB 14; MTCW 1, 2; SATA 34;
SFW 4
Alegria, Claribel 1924- .... **CLC 75; HLCS 1;**
PC 26
See also CA 131; CAAS 15; CANR 66, 94;
CWW 2; DAM MULT; DLB 145; HW 1;
MTCW 1
Alegria, Fernando 1918- .... **CLC 57**
See also CA 9-12R; CANR 5, 32, 72; HW
1, 2
Aleichem, Sholom .... **TCLC 1, 35; SSC 33**
See also Rabinovitch, Sholem
Aleixandre, Vicente 1898-1984 ... **TCLC 113;**
HLCS 1
See also CANR 81; DLB 108; HW 2;
RGWL 2
Alencon, Marguerite d'
See de Navarre, Marguerite
Alepoudelis, Odysseus
See Elytis, Odysseus
See also CWW 2
Aleshkovsky, Joseph 1929-
See Aleshkovsky, Yuz
See also CA 121; 128
Aleshkovsky, Yuz .... **CLC 44**
See also Aleshkovsky, Joseph
Alexander, Lloyd (Chudley) 1924- ... **CLC 35**
See also AAYA 1, 27; BPFB 1; BYA 5, 6,
7, 9, 10, 11; CA 1-4R; CANR 1, 24, 38,
55; CLR 1, 5, 48; CWRI 5; DLB 52;
FANT; JRDA; MAICYA 1, 2; MAICYAS
1; MTCW 1; SAAS 19; SATA 3, 49, 81,
129; SUFW; WYA; YAW
Alexander, Meena 1951- .... **CLC 121**
See also CA 115; CANR 38, 70; CP 7;
CWP; FW
Alexander, Samuel 1859-1938 .... **TCLC 77**
Alexie, Sherman (Joseph, Jr.)
1966- .... **CLC 96, 154**
See also AAYA 28; CA 138; CANR 95;
DA3; DAM MULT; DLB 175, 206;
MTCW 1; NNAL
Alfau, Felipe 1902-1999 .... **CLC 66**
See also CA 137
Alfieri, Vittorio 1749-1803 .... **NCLC 101**
See also EW 4; RGWL 2
Alfred, Jean Gaston
See Ponge, Francis

Alger, Horatio, Jr. 1832-1899 .... **NCLC 8, 83**
See also DLB 42; LAIT 2; RGAL 4; SATA
16; TUS
Al-Ghazali, Muhammad ibn Muhammad
1058-1111 .... **CMLC 50**
See also DLB 115
Algren, Nelson 1909-1981 ..... **CLC 4, 10, 33;**
SSC 33
See also AMWS 9; BPFB 1; CA 13-16R;
103; CANR 20, 61; CDALB 1941-1968;
DLB 9; DLBY 1981, 1982, 2000; MTCW
1, 2; RGAL 4; RGSF 2
Ali, Ahmed 1908-1998 .... **CLC 69**
See also CA 25-28R; CANR 15, 34
Alighieri, Dante
See Dante
Allan, John B.
See Westlake, Donald E(dwin)
Allan, Sidney
See Hartmann, Sadakichi
Allan, Sydney
See Hartmann, Sadakichi
Allard, Janet .... **CLC 59**
Allen, Edward 1948- .... **CLC 59**
Allen, Fred 1894-1956 .... **TCLC 87**
Allen, Paula Gunn 1939- .... **CLC 84**
See also AMWS 4; CA 112; 143; CANR
63; CWP; DA3; DAM MULT; DLB 175;
FW; MTCW 1; NNAL; RGAL 4
Allen, Roland
See Ayckbourn, Alan
Allen, Sarah A.
See Hopkins, Pauline Elizabeth
Allen, Sidney H.
See Hartmann, Sadakichi
Allen, Woody 1935- .... **CLC 16, 52**
See also AAYA 10; CA 33-36R; CANR 27,
38, 63; DAM POP; DLB 44; MTCW 1
Allende, Isabel 1942- . **CLC 39, 57, 97; HLC**
1; WLCS
See also AAYA 18; CA 125; 130; CANR
51, 74; CDWLB 3; CWW 2; DA3; DAM
MULT, NOV; DLB 145; DNFS 1; FW;
HW 1, 2; INT CA-130; LAIT 5; LAWS
1; MTCW 1, 2; NCFS 1; NFS 6; RGSF
2; SSFS 11; WLIT 1
Alleyn, Ellen
See Rossetti, Christina (Georgina)
Alleyne, Carla D. .... **CLC 65**
Allingham, Margery (Louise)
1904-1966 .... **CLC 19**
See also CA 5-8R; 25-28R; CANR 4, 58;
CMW 4; DLB 77; MSW; MTCW 1, 2
Allingham, William 1824-1889 ...... **NCLC 25**
See also DLB 35; RGEL 2
Allison, Dorothy E. 1949- .... **CLC 78, 153**
See also CA 140; CANR 66, 107; CSW;
DA3; FW; MTCW 1; NFS 11; RGAL 4
Alloula, Malek .... **CLC 65**
Allston, Washington 1779-1843 .... **NCLC 2**
See also DLB 1, 235
Almedingen, E. M. .... **CLC 12**
See also Almedingen, Martha Edith von
See also SATA 3
Almedingen, Martha Edith von 1898-1971
See Almedingen, E. M.
See also CA 1-4R; CANR 1
Almodovar, Pedro 1949(?)- .... **CLC 114;**
HLCS 1
See also CA 133; CANR 72; HW 2
Almqvist, Carl Jonas Love
1793-1866 .... **NCLC 42**
Alonso, Damaso 1898-1990 .... **CLC 14**
See also CA 110; 131; 130; CANR 72; DLB
108; HW 1, 2
Alov
See Gogol, Nikolai (Vasilyevich)

Alta 1942- .... **CLC 19**
    See also CA 57-60

Alter, Robert B(ernard) 1935- .... **CLC 34**
    See also CA 49-52; CANR 1, 47, 100

Alther, Lisa 1944- .... **CLC 7, 41**
    See also BPFB 1; CA 65-68; CAAS 30;
    CANR 12, 30, 51; CN 7; CSW; GLL 2;
    MTCW 1

Althusser, L.
    See Althusser, Louis

Althusser, Louis 1918-1990 .... **CLC 106**
    See also CA 131; 132; CANR 102; DLB
    242

Altman, Robert 1925- .... **CLC 16, 116**
    See also CA 73-76; CANR 43

Alurista
    See Urista, Alberto H.
    See also DLB 82; HLCS 1

Alvarez, A(lfred) 1929- .... **CLC 5, 13**
    See also CA 1-4R; CANR 3, 33, 63, 101;
    CN 7; CP 7; DLB 14, 40

Alvarez, Alejandro Rodriguez 1903-1965
    See Casona, Alejandro
    See also CA 131; 93-96; HW 1

Alvarez, Julia 1950- .... **CLC 93; HLCS 1**
    See also AAYA 25; AMWS 7; CA 147;
    CANR 69, 101; DA3; MTCW 1; NFS 5,
    9; SATA 129; WLIT 1

Alvaro, Corrado 1896-1956 .... **TCLC 60**
    See also CA 163

Amado, Jorge 1912-2001 ... **CLC 13, 40, 106;
    HLC 1**
    See also CA 77-80; 201; CANR 35, 74;
    DAM MULT, NOV; DLB 113; HW 2;
    LAW; LAWS 1; MTCW 1, 2; RGWL 2;
    WLIT 1

Ambler, Eric 1909-1998 .... **CLC 4, 6, 9**
    See also BRWS 4; CA 9-12R; 171; CANR
    7, 38, 74; CMW 4; CN 7; DLB 77; MSW;
    MTCW 1, 2

Ambrose, Stephen E(dward)
    1936- .... **CLC 145**
    See also CA 1-4R; CANR 3, 43, 57, 83,
    105; NCFS 2; SATA 40

Amichai, Yehuda 1924-2000 .. **CLC 9, 22, 57,
    116; PC 38**
    See also CA 85-88; 189; CANR 46, 60, 99;
    CWW 2; MTCW 1

Amichai, Yehudah
    See Amichai, Yehuda

Amiel, Henri Frederic 1821-1881 .... **NCLC 4**
    See also DLB 217

Amis, Kingsley (William)
    1922-1995 ...... **CLC 1, 2, 3, 5, 8, 13, 40,
    44, 129**
    See also AITN 2; BPFB 1; BRWS 2; CA
    9-12R; 150; CANR 8, 28, 54; CDBLB
    1945-1960; CN 7; CP 7; DA; DA3; DAB;
    DAC; DAM MST, NOV; DLB 15, 27,
    100, 139; DLBY 1996; HGG; INT
    CANR-8; MTCW 1, 2; RGEL 2; RGSF 2;
    SFW 4

Amis, Martin (Louis) 1949- .... **CLC 4, 9, 38,
    62, 101**
    See also BEST 90:3; BRWS 4; CA 65-68;
    CANR 8, 27, 54, 73, 95; CN 7; DA3;
    DLB 14, 194; INT CANR-27; MTCW 1

Ammons, A(rchie) R(andolph)
    1926-2001 .... **CLC 2, 3, 5, 8, 9, 25, 57,
    108; PC 16**
    See also AITN 1; AMWS 7; CA 9-12R;
    193; CANR 6, 36, 51, 73, 107; CP 7;
    CSW; DAM POET; DLB 5, 165; MTCW
    1, 2; RGAL 4

Amo, Tauraatua i
    See Adams, Henry (Brooks)

Amory, Thomas 1691(?)-1788 .... **LC 48**
    See also DLB 39

Anand, Mulk Raj 1905- .... **CLC 23, 93**
    See also CA 65-68; CANR 32, 64; CN 7;
    DAM NOV; MTCW 1, 2; RGSF 2

Anatol
    See Schnitzler, Arthur

Anaximander c. 611B.C.-c.
    546B.C. .... **CMLC 22**

Anaya, Rudolfo A(lfonso) 1937- ...... **CLC 23,
    148; HLC 1**
    See also AAYA 20; BYA 13; CA 45-48;
    CAAS 4; CANR 1, 32, 51; CN 7; DAM
    MULT, NOV; DLB 82, 206; HW 1; LAIT
    4; MTCW 1, 2; NFS 12; RGAL 4; RGSF
    2; WLIT 1

Andersen, Hans Christian
    1805-1875 ... **NCLC 7, 79; SSC 6; WLC**
    See also CLR 6; DA; DA3; DAB; DAC;
    DAM MST, POP; EW 6; MAICYA 1, 2;
    RGSF 2; RGWL 2; SATA 100; WCH;
    YABC 1

Anderson, C. Farley
    See Mencken, H(enry) L(ouis); Nathan,
    George Jean

Anderson, Jessica (Margaret) Queale
    1916- .... **CLC 37**
    See also CA 9-12R; CANR 4, 62; CN 7

Anderson, Jon (Victor) 1940- .... **CLC 9**
    See also CA 25-28R; CANR 20; DAM
    POET

Anderson, Lindsay (Gordon)
    1923-1994 .... **CLC 20**
    See also CA 125; 128; 146; CANR 77

Anderson, Maxwell 1888-1959 .... **TCLC 2**
    See also CA 105; 152; DAM DRAM; DLB
    7, 228; MTCW 2; RGAL 4

Anderson, Poul (William)
    1926-2001 .... **CLC 15**
    See also AAYA 5, 34; BPFB 1; BYA 6, 8,
    9; CA 1-4R, 181; 199; CAAE 181; CAAS
    2; CANR 2, 15, 34, 64; CLR 58; DLB 8;
    FANT; INT CANR-15; MTCW 1, 2;
    SATA 90; SATA-Brief 39; SATA-Essay
    106; SCFW 2; SFW 4; SUFW

Anderson, Robert (Woodruff)
    1917- .... **CLC 23**
    See also AITN 1; CA 21-24R; CANR 32;
    DAM DRAM; DLB 7; LAIT 5

Anderson, Roberta Joan
    See Mitchell, Joni

Anderson, Sherwood 1876-1941 ..... **TCLC 1,
    10, 24; SSC 1, 46; WLC**
    See also AAYA 30; AMW; BPFB 1; CA
    104; 121; CANR 61; CDALB 1917-1929;
    DA; DA3; DAB; DAC; DAM MST, NOV;
    DLB 4, 9, 86; DLBD 1; EXPS; GLL 2;
    MTCW 1, 2; NFS 4; RGAL 4; RGSF 2;
    SSFS 4, 10, 11

Andier, Pierre
    See Desnos, Robert

Andouard
    See Giraudoux, Jean(-Hippolyte)

Andrade, Carlos Drummond de ..... **CLC 18**
    See also Drummond de Andrade, Carlos
    See also RGWL 2

Andrade, Mario de .... **TCLC 43**
    See also de Andrade, Mario
    See also LAW; RGWL 2; WLIT 1

Andreae, Johann V(alentin)
    1586-1654 .... **LC 32**
    See also DLB 164

Andreas Capellanus fl. c. 1185- .... **CMLC 45**
    See also DLB 208

Andreas-Salome, Lou 1861-1937 ... **TCLC 56**
    See also CA 178; DLB 66

Andress, Lesley
    See Sanders, Lawrence

Andrewes, Lancelot 1555-1626 .... **LC 5**
    See also DLB 151, 172

Andrews, Cicily Fairfield
    See West, Rebecca

Andrews, Elton V.
    See Pohl, Frederik

Andreyev, Leonid (Nikolaevich)
    1871-1919 .... **TCLC 3**
    See also CA 104; 185

Andric, Ivo 1892-1975 .... **CLC 8; SSC 36**
    See also CA 81-84; 57-60; CANR 43, 60;
    CDWLB 4; DLB 147; EW 11; MTCW 1;
    RGSF 2; RGWL 2

Androvar
    See Prado (Calvo), Pedro

Angelique, Pierre
    See Bataille, Georges

Angell, Roger 1920- .... **CLC 26**
    See also CA 57-60; CANR 13, 44, 70; DLB
    171, 185

Angelou, Maya 1928- ..... **CLC 12, 35, 64, 77,
    155; BLC 1; PC 32; WLCS**
    See also AAYA 7, 20; AMWS 4; BPFB 1;
    BW 2, 3; BYA 2; CA 65-68; CANR 19,
    42, 65; CDALBS; CLR 53; CP 7; CPW;
    CSW; CWP; DA; DA3; DAB; DAC;
    DAM MST, MULT, POET, POP; DLB 38;
    EXPN; EXPP; LAIT 4; MAICYA 2; MAI-
    CYAS 1; MAWW; MTCW 1, 2; NCFS 2;
    NFS 2; PFS 2, 3; RGAL 4; SATA 49;
    WYA; YAW

Angouleme, Marguerite d'
    See de Navarre, Marguerite

Anna Comnena 1083-1153 .... **CMLC 25**

Annensky, Innokenty (Fyodorovich)
    1856-1909 .... **TCLC 14**
    See also CA 110; 155

Annunzio, Gabriele d'
    See D'Annunzio, Gabriele

Anodos
    See Coleridge, Mary E(lizabeth)

Anon, Charles Robert
    See Pessoa, Fernando (Antonio Nogueira)

Anouilh, Jean (Marie Lucien Pierre)
    1910-1987 . **CLC 1, 3, 8, 13, 40, 50; DC
    8**
    See also CA 17-20R; 123; CANR 32; DAM
    DRAM; DFS 9, 10; EW 13; GFL 1789 to
    the Present; MTCW 1, 2; RGWL 2

Anthony, Florence
    See Ai

Anthony, John
    See Ciardi, John (Anthony)

Anthony, Peter
    See Shaffer, Anthony (Joshua); Shaffer,
    Peter (Levin)

Anthony, Piers 1934- .... **CLC 35**
    See also AAYA 11; BYA 7; CA 21-24R;
    CAAE 200; CANR 28, 56, 73, 102; CPW;
    DAM POP; DLB 8; FANT; MAICYA 2;
    MAICYAS 1; MTCW 1, 2; SAAS 22;
    SATA 84; SATA-Essay 129; SFW 4;
    SUFW; YAW

Anthony, Susan B(rownell)
    1820-1906 .... **TCLC 84**
    See also FW

Antoine, Marc
    See Proust, (Valentin-Louis-George-Eugene-
)Marcel

Antoninus, Brother
    See Everson, William (Oliver)

Antonioni, Michelangelo 1912- .... **CLC 20,
    144**
    See also CA 73-76; CANR 45, 77

Antschel, Paul 1920-1970
    See Celan, Paul
    See also CA 85-88; CANR 33, 61; MTCW
    1

Anwar, Chairil 1922-1949 .... **TCLC 22**
    See also CA 121

Anzaldua, Gloria (Evanjelina) 1942-
See also CA 175; CSW; CWP; DLB 122;
FW; HLCS 1; RGAL 4

Apess, William 1798-1839(?) .... **NCLC 73**
See also DAM MULT; DLB 175, 243;
NNAL

Apollinaire, Guillaume 1880-1918 .. **TCLC 3, 8, 51; PC 7**
See also CA 152; DAM POET; DLB 258;
EW 9; GFL 1789 to the Present; MTCW
1; RGWL 2; WP

Apollonius of Rhodes
See Apollonius Rhodius
See also AW 1; RGWL 2

Apollonius Rhodius c. 300B.C.-c.
220B.C. .... **CMLC 28**
See also Apollonius of Rhodes
See also DLB 176

Appelfeld, Aharon 1932- ... **CLC 23, 47; SSC 42**
See also CA 112; 133; CANR 86; CWW 2;
RGSF 2

Apple, Max (Isaac) 1941- .... **CLC 9, 33; SSC 50**
See also CA 81-84; CANR 19, 54; DLB
130

Appleman, Philip (Dean) 1926- .... **CLC 51**
See also CA 13-16R; CAAS 18; CANR 6,
29, 56

Appleton, Lawrence
See Lovecraft, H(oward) P(hillips)

Apteryx
See Eliot, T(homas) S(tearns)

Apuleius, (Lucius Madaurensis)
125(?)-175(?) .... **CMLC 1**
See also AW 2; CDWLB 1; DLB 211;
RGWL 2; SUFW

Aquin, Hubert 1929-1977 .... **CLC 15**
See also CA 105; DLB 53

Aquinas, Thomas 1224(?)-1274 ..... **CMLC 33**
See also DLB 115; EW 1

Aragon, Louis 1897-1982 .... **CLC 3, 22**
See also CA 69-72; 108; CANR 28, 71;
DAM NOV, POET; DLB 72, 258; EW 11;
GFL 1789 to the Present; GLL 2; MTCW
1, 2; RGWL 2

Arany, Janos 1817-1882 .... **NCLC 34**

Aranyos, Kakay 1847-1910
See Mikszath, Kalman

Arbuthnot, John 1667-1735 .... **LC 1**
See also DLB 101

Archer, Herbert Winslow
See Mencken, H(enry) L(ouis)

Archer, Jeffrey (Howard) 1940- .... **CLC 28**
See also AAYA 16; BEST 89:3; BPFB 1;
CA 77-80; CANR 22, 52, 95; CPW; DA3;
DAM POP; INT CANR-22

Archer, Jules 1915- .... **CLC 12**
See also CA 9-12R; CANR 6, 69; SAAS 5;
SATA 4, 85

Archer, Lee
See Ellison, Harlan (Jay)

Archilochus c. 7th cent. B.C.- .... **CMLC 44**
See also DLB 176

Arden, John 1930- .... **CLC 6, 13, 15**
See also BRWS 2; CA 13-16R; CAAS 4;
CANR 31, 65, 67; CBD; CD 5; DAM
DRAM; DFS 9; DLB 13, 245; MTCW 1

Arenas, Reinaldo 1943-1990 .. **CLC 41; HLC 1**
See also CA 124; 128; 133; CANR 73, 106;
DAM MULT; DLB 145; GLL 2; HW 1;
LAW; LAWS 1; MTCW 1; RGSF 2;
WLIT 1

Arendt, Hannah 1906-1975 .... **CLC 66, 98**
See also CA 17-20R; 61-64; CANR 26, 60;
DLB 242; MTCW 1, 2

Aretino, Pietro 1492-1556 .... **LC 12**
See also RGWL 2

Arghezi, Tudor -1967 .... **CLC 80**
See also Theodorescu, Ion N.
See also CA 167; CDWLB 4; DLB 220

Arguedas, Jose Maria 1911-1969 .... **CLC 10, 18; HLCS 1**
See also CA 89-92; CANR 73; DLB 113;
HW 1; LAW; RGWL 2; WLIT 1

Argueta, Manlio 1936- .... **CLC 31**
See also CA 131; CANR 73; CWW 2; DLB
145; HW 1

Arias, Ron(ald Francis) 1941-
See also CA 131; CANR 81; DAM MULT;
DLB 82; HLC 1; HW 1, 2; MTCW 2

Ariosto, Ludovico 1474-1533 .... **LC 6**
See also EW 2; RGWL 2

Aristides
See Epstein, Joseph

Aristophanes 450B.C.-385B.C. .... **CMLC 4, 51; DC 2; WLCS**
See also AW 1; CDWLB 1; DA; DA3;
DAB; DAC; DAM DRAM, MST; DFS
10; DLB 176; RGWL 2

Aristotle 384B.C.-322B.C. .... **CMLC 31; WLCS**
See also AW 1; CDWLB 1; DA; DA3;
DAB; DAC; DAM MST; DLB 176;
RGEL 2

Arlt, Roberto (Godofredo Christophersen)
1900-1942 .... **TCLC 29; HLC 1**
See also CA 123; 131; CANR 67; DAM
MULT; HW 1, 2; LAW

Armah, Ayi Kwei 1939- .... **CLC 5, 33, 136; BLC 1**
See also AFW; BW 1; CA 61-64; CANR
21, 64; CDWLB 3; CN 7; DAM MULT,
POET; DLB 117; MTCW 1; WLIT 2

Armatrading, Joan 1950- .... **CLC 17**
See also CA 114; 186

Arnette, Robert
See Silverberg, Robert

**Arnim, Achim von (Ludwig Joachim von
Arnim)** 1781-1831 ..... **NCLC 5; SSC 29**
See also DLB 90

Arnim, Bettina von 1785-1859 .... **NCLC 38**
See also DLB 90; RGWL 2

Arnold, Matthew 1822-1888 ..... **NCLC 6, 29, 89; PC 5; WLC**
See also BRW 5; CDBLB 1832-1890; DA;
DAB; DAC; DAM MST, POET; DLB 32,
57; EXPP; PAB; PFS 2; WP

Arnold, Thomas 1795-1842 .... **NCLC 18**
See also DLB 55

Arnow, Harriette (Louisa) Simpson
1908-1986 .... **CLC 2, 7, 18**
See also BPFB 1; CA 9-12R; 118; CANR
14; DLB 6; FW; MTCW 1, 2; RHW;
SATA 42; SATA-Obit 47

Arouet, Francois-Marie
See Voltaire

Arp, Hans
See Arp, Jean

Arp, Jean 1887-1966 .... **CLC 5**
See also CA 81-84; 25-28R; CANR 42, 77;
EW 10; TCLC 115

Arrabal
See Arrabal, Fernando

Arrabal, Fernando 1932- ... **CLC 2, 9, 18, 58**
See also CA 9-12R; CANR 15

Arreola, Juan Jose 1918-2001 .... **CLC 147; HLC 1; SSC 38**
See also CA 113; 131; 200; CANR 81;
DAM MULT; DLB 113; DNFS 2; HW 1,
2; LAW; RGSF 2

Arrian c. 89(?)-c. 155(?) .... **CMLC 43**
See also DLB 176

Arrick, Fran .... **CLC 30**
See also Gaberman, Judie Angell
See also BYA 6

Artaud, Antonin (Marie Joseph)
1896-1948 .... **TCLC 3, 36; DC 14**
See also CA 104; 149; DA3; DAM DRAM;
DLB 258; EW 11; GFL 1789 to the
Present; MTCW 1; RGWL 2

Arthur, Ruth M(abel) 1905-1979 ..... **CLC 12**
See also CA 9-12R; 85-88; CANR 4; CWRI
5; SATA 7, 26

Artsybashev, Mikhail (Petrovich)
1878-1927 .... **TCLC 31**
See also CA 170

Arundel, Honor (Morfydd)
1919-1973 .... **CLC 17**
See also CA 21-22; 41-44R; CAP 2; CLR
35; CWRI 5; SATA 4; SATA-Obit 24

Arzner, Dorothy 1900-1979 .... **CLC 98**

Asch, Sholem 1880-1957 .... **TCLC 3**
See also CA 105; GLL 2

Ash, Shalom
See Asch, Sholem

Ashbery, John (Lawrence) 1927- .. **CLC 2, 3, 4, 6, 9, 13, 15, 25, 41, 77, 125; PC 26**
See also Berry, Jonas
See also AMWS 3; CA 5-8R; CANR 9, 37,
66, 102; CP 7; DA3; DAM POET; DLB
5, 165; DLBY 1981; INT CANR-9;
MTCW 1, 2; PAB; PFS 11; RGAL 4; WP

Ashdown, Clifford
See Freeman, R(ichard) Austin

Ashe, Gordon
See Creasey, John

Ashton-Warner, Sylvia (Constance)
1908-1984 .... **CLC 19**
See also CA 69-72; 112; CANR 29; MTCW
1, 2

Asimov, Isaac 1920-1992 ..... **CLC 1, 3, 9, 19, 26, 76, 92**
See also AAYA 13; BEST 90:2; BPFB 1;
BYA 4, 6, 7, 9; CA 1-4R; 137; CANR 2,
19, 36, 60; CLR 12, 79; CMW 4; CPW;
DA3; DAM POP; DLB 8; DLBY 1992;
INT CANR-19; JRDA; LAIT 5; MAICYA
1, 2; MTCW 1, 2; RGAL 4; SATA 1, 26,
74; SCFW 2; SFW 4; YAW

Assis, Joaquim Maria Machado de
See Machado de Assis, Joaquim Maria

Astell, Mary 1666-1731 .... **LC 68**
See also DLB 252; FW

Astley, Thea (Beatrice May) 1925- .. **CLC 41**
See also CA 65-68; CANR 11, 43, 78; CN
7

Astley, William 1855-1911
See Warung, Price

Aston, James
See White, T(erence) H(anbury)

Asturias, Miguel Angel 1899-1974 .... **CLC 3, 8, 13; HLC 1**
See also CA 25-28; 49-52; CANR 32; CAP
2; CDWLB 3; DA3; DAM MULT, NOV;
DLB 113; HW 1; LAW; MTCW 1, 2;
RGWL 2; WLIT 1

Atares, Carlos Saura
See Saura (Atares), Carlos

Athanasius c. 295-c. 373 .... **CMLC 48**

Atheling, William
See Pound, Ezra (Weston Loomis)

Atheling, William, Jr.
See Blish, James (Benjamin)

Atherton, Gertrude (Franklin Horn)
1857-1948 .... **TCLC 2**
See also CA 104; 155; DLB 9, 78, 186;
HGG; RGAL 4; SUFW; TCWW 2

Atherton, Lucius
See Masters, Edgar Lee

Atkins, Jack
See Harris, Mark

Atkinson, Kate .... **CLC 99**
See also CA 166; CANR 101

Attaway, William (Alexander)
1911-1986 .... **CLC 92; BLC 1**
See also BW 2, 3; CA 143; CANR 82;
DAM MULT; DLB 76

Atticus
See Fleming, Ian (Lancaster); Wilson,
(Thomas) Woodrow

Atwood, Margaret (Eleanor) 1939- ... **CLC 2,
3, 4, 8, 13, 15, 25, 44, 84, 135; PC 8;
SSC 2, 46; WLC**
See also AAYA 12; BEST 89:2; BPFB 1;
CA 49-52; CANR 3, 24, 33, 59, 95; CN
7; CP 7; CPW; CWP; DA; DA3; DAB;
DAC; DAM MST, NOV, POET; DLB 53,
251; EXPN; FW; INT CANR-24; LAIT
5; MTCW 1, 2; NFS 4, 12, 13, 14; PFS 7;
RGSF 2; SATA 50; SSFS 3, 13; YAW

Aubigny, Pierre d'
See Mencken, H(enry) L(ouis)

Aubin, Penelope 1685-1731(?) .... **LC 9**
See also DLB 39

Auchincloss, Louis (Stanton) 1917- .. **CLC 4,
6, 9, 18, 45; SSC 22**
See also AMWS 4; CA 1-4R; CANR 6, 29,
55, 87; CN 7; DAM NOV; DLB 2, 244;
DLBY 1980; INT CANR-29; MTCW 1;
RGAL 4

Auden, W(ystan) H(ugh) 1907-1973 . **CLC 1,
2, 3, 4, 6, 9, 11, 14, 43, 123; PC 1;
WLC**
See also AAYA 18; AMWS 2; BRW 7;
BRWR 1; CA 9-12R; 45-48; CANR 5, 61,
105; CDBLB 1914-1945; DA; DA3;
DAB; DAC; DAM DRAM, MST, POET;
DLB 10, 20; EXPP; MTCW 1, 2; PAB;
PFS 1, 3, 4, 10; WP

Audiberti, Jacques 1900-1965 .... **CLC 38**
See also CA 25-28R; DAM DRAM

Audubon, John James 1785-1851 . **NCLC 47**
See also ANW; DLB 248

Auel, Jean M(arie) 1936- .... **CLC 31, 107**
See also AAYA 7; BEST 90:4; BPFB 1; CA
103; CANR 21, 64; CPW; DA3; DAM
POP; INT CANR-21; NFS 11; RHW;
SATA 91

Auerbach, Erich 1892-1957 .... **TCLC 43**
See also CA 118; 155

Augier, Emile 1820-1889 .... **NCLC 31**
See also DLB 192; GFL 1789 to the Present

August, John
See De Voto, Bernard (Augustine)

Augustine, St. 354-430 .... **CMLC 6; WLCS**
See also DA; DA3; DAB; DAC; DAM
MST; DLB 115; EW 1; RGWL 2

Aunt Belinda
See Braddon, Mary Elizabeth

Aunt Weedy
See Alcott, Louisa May

Aurelius
See Bourne, Randolph S(illiman)

Aurelius, Marcus 121-180 .... **CMLC 45**
See also Marcus Aurelius
See also RGWL 2

Aurobindo, Sri
See Ghose, Aurabinda

Austen, Jane 1775-1817 ...... **NCLC 1, 13, 19,
33, 51, 81, 95; WLC**
See also AAYA 19; BRW 4; BRWR 2; BYA
3; CDBLB 1789-1832; DA; DA3; DAB;
DAC; DAM MST, NOV; DLB 116;
EXPN; LAIT 2; NFS 1, 14; WLIT 3;
WYAS 1

Auster, Paul 1947- .... **CLC 47, 131**
See also CA 69-72; CANR 23, 52, 75;
CMW 4; CN 7; DA3; DLB 227; MTCW
1

Austin, Frank
See Faust, Frederick (Schiller)
See also TCWW 2

Austin, Mary (Hunter) 1868-1934 . **TCLC 25**
See also Stairs, Gordon
See also ANW; CA 109; 178; DLB 9, 78,
206, 221; FW; TCWW 2

Averroes 1126-1198 .... **CMLC 7**
See also DLB 115

Avicenna 980-1037 .... **CMLC 16**
See also DLB 115

Avison, Margaret 1918- .... **CLC 2, 4, 97**
See also CA 17-20R; CP 7; DAC; DAM
POET; DLB 53; MTCW 1

Axton, David
See Koontz, Dean R(ay)

Ayckbourn, Alan 1939- ...... **CLC 5, 8, 18, 33,
74; DC 13**
See also BRWS 5; CA 21-24R; CANR 31,
59; CBD; CD 5; DAB; DAM DRAM;
DFS 7; DLB 13, 245; MTCW 1, 2

Aydy, Catherine
See Tennant, Emma (Christina)

Ayme, Marcel (Andre) 1902-1967 ... **CLC 11;
SSC 41**
See also CA 89-92; CANR 67; CLR 25;
DLB 72; EW 12; GFL 1789 to the Present;
RGSF 2; RGWL 2; SATA 91

Ayrton, Michael 1921-1975 .... **CLC 7**
See also CA 5-8R; 61-64; CANR 9, 21

Azorin .... **CLC 11**
See also Martinez Ruiz, Jose
See also EW 9

Azuela, Mariano 1873-1952 .. **TCLC 3; HLC
1**
See also CA 104; 131; CANR 81; DAM
MULT; HW 1, 2; LAW; MTCW 1, 2

Baastad, Babbis Friis
See Friis-Baastad, Babbis Ellinor

Bab
See Gilbert, W(illiam) S(chwenck)

Babbis, Eleanor
See Friis-Baastad, Babbis Ellinor

Babel, Isaac
See Babel, Isaak (Emmanuilovich)
See also EW 11; SSFS 10

Babel, Isaak (Emmanuilovich)
1894-1941(?) .... **TCLC 2, 13; SSC 16**
See also Babel, Isaac
See also CA 104; 155; MTCW 1; RGSF 2;
RGWL 2

Babits, Mihaly 1883-1941 .... **TCLC 14**
See also CA 114; CDWLB 4; DLB 215

Babur 1483-1530 .... **LC 18**

Babylas 1898-1962
See Ghelderode, Michel de

Baca, Jimmy Santiago 1952- .... **PC 41**
See also CA 131; CANR 81, 90; CP 7;
DAM MULT; DLB 122; HLC 1; HW 1, 2

Baca, Jose Santiago
See Baca, Jimmy Santiago

Bacchelli, Riccardo 1891-1985 .... **CLC 19**
See also CA 29-32R; 117

Bach, Richard (David) 1936- .... **CLC 14**
See also AITN 1; BEST 89:2; BPFB 1; BYA
5; CA 9-12R; CANR 18, 93; CPW; DAM
NOV, POP; FANT; MTCW 1; SATA 13

Bache, Benjamin Franklin
1769-1798 .... **LC 74**
See also DLB 43

Bachman, Richard
See King, Stephen (Edwin)

Bachmann, Ingeborg 1926-1973 .... **CLC 69**
See also CA 93-96; 45-48; CANR 69; DLB
85; RGWL 2

Bacon, Francis 1561-1626 .... **LC 18, 32**
See also BRW 1; CDBLB Before 1660;
DLB 151, 236, 252; RGEL 2

Bacon, Roger 1214(?)-1294 .... **CMLC 14**
See also DLB 115

Bacovia, George 1881-1957 .... **TCLC 24**
See also Vasiliu, Gheorghe
See also CDWLB 4; DLB 220

Badanes, Jerome 1937- .... **CLC 59**

Bagehot, Walter 1826-1877 .... **NCLC 10**
See also DLB 55

Bagnold, Enid 1889-1981 .... **CLC 25**
See also BYA 2; CA 5-8R; 103; CANR 5,
40; CBD; CWD; CWRI 5; DAM DRAM;
DLB 13, 160, 191, 245; FW; MAICYA 1,
2; RGEL 2; SATA 1, 25

Bagritsky, Eduard 1895-1934 .... **TCLC 60**

Bagryana, Elisaveta
See Belcheva, Elisaveta Lyubomirova

Bagryana, Elisaveta -1991 .... **CLC 10**
See also Belcheva, Elisaveta Lyubomirova
See also CA 178; CDWLB 4; DLB 147

Bailey, Paul 1937- .... **CLC 45**
See also CA 21-24R; CANR 16, 62; CN 7;
DLB 14; GLL 2

Baillie, Joanna 1762-1851 .... **NCLC 71**
See also DLB 93; RGEL 2

Bainbridge, Beryl (Margaret) 1934- . **CLC 4,
5, 8, 10, 14, 18, 22, 62, 130**
See also BRWS 6; CA 21-24R; CANR 24,
55, 75, 88; CN 7; DAM NOV; DLB 14,
231; MTCW 1, 2

Baker, Carlos (Heard)
1909-1987 .... **TCLC 119**
See also CA 5-8R; 122; CANR 3, 63; DLB
103

Baker, Elliott 1922- .... **CLC 8**
See also CA 45-48; CANR 2, 63; CN 7

Baker, Jean H. .... **TCLC 3, 10**
See also Russell, George William

Baker, Nicholson 1957- .... **CLC 61**
See also CA 135; CANR 63; CN 7; CPW;
DA3; DAM POP; DLB 227

Baker, Ray Stannard 1870-1946 .... **TCLC 47**
See also CA 118

Baker, Russell (Wayne) 1925- .... **CLC 31**
See also BEST 89:4; CA 57-60; CANR 11,
41, 59; MTCW 1, 2

Bakhtin, M.
See Bakhtin, Mikhail Mikhailovich

Bakhtin, M. M.
See Bakhtin, Mikhail Mikhailovich

Bakhtin, Mikhail
See Bakhtin, Mikhail Mikhailovich

Bakhtin, Mikhail Mikhailovich
1895-1975 .... **CLC 83**
See also CA 128; 113; DLB 242

Bakshi, Ralph 1938(?)- .... **CLC 26**
See also CA 112; 138; IDFW 3

Bakunin, Mikhail (Alexandrovich)
1814-1876 .... **NCLC 25, 58**

Baldwin, James (Arthur) 1924-1987 . **CLC 1,
2, 3, 4, 5, 8, 13, 15, 17, 42, 50, 67, 90,
127; BLC 1; DC 1; SSC 10, 33; WLC**
See also AAYA 4, 34; AFAW 1, 2; AMWS
1; BW 1; CA 1-4R; 124; CABS 1; CAD;
CANR 3, 24; CDALB 1941-1968; CPW;
DA; DA3; DAB; DAC; DAM MST,
MULT, NOV, POP; DFS 11; DLB 2, 7,
33, 249; DLBY 1987; EXPS; LAIT 5;
MTCW 1, 2; NFS 4; RGAL 4; RGSF 2;
SATA 9; SATA-Obit 54; SSFS 2

Bale, John 1495-1563 .... **LC 62**
See also DLB 132; RGEL 2

Ball, Hugo 1886-1927 .... **TCLC 104**

Ballard, J(ames) G(raham) 1930- . **CLC 3, 6,
14, 36, 137; SSC 1, 53**
See also AAYA 3; BRWS 5; CA 5-8R;
CANR 15, 39, 65, 107; CN 7; DA3; DAM
NOV, POP; DLB 14, 207; HGG; MTCW
1, 2; NFS 8; RGEL 2; RGSF 2; SATA 93;
SFW 4

Balmont, Konstantin (Dmitriyevich)
1867-1943 .... **TCLC 11**
See also CA 109; 155

Baltausis, Vincas 1847-1910
See Mikszath, Kalman

Balzac, Honore de 1799-1850 ... **NCLC 5, 35,**
53; SSC 5; WLC
See also DA; DA3; DAB; DAC; DAM
MST, NOV; DLB 119; EW 5; GFL 1789
to the Present; RGSF 2; RGWL 2; SSFS
10; SUFW

Bambara, Toni Cade 1939-1995 ...... **CLC 19,**
88; BLC 1; SSC 35; WLCS
See also AAYA 5; AFAW 2; BW 2, 3; BYA
12, 14; CA 29-32R; 150; CANR 24, 49,
81; CDALBS; DA; DA3; DAC; DAM
MST, MULT; DLB 38, 218; EXPS;
MTCW 1, 2; RGAL 4; RGSF 2; SATA
112; SSFS 4, 7, 12; TCLC 116

Bamdad, A.
See Shamlu, Ahmad

Banat, D. R.
See Bradbury, Ray (Douglas)

Bancroft, Laura
See Baum, L(yman) Frank

Banim, John 1798-1842 .... **NCLC 13**
See also DLB 116, 158, 159; RGEL 2

Banim, Michael 1796-1874 .... **NCLC 13**
See also DLB 158, 159

Banjo, The
See Paterson, A(ndrew) B(arton)

Banks, Iain
See Banks, Iain M(enzies)

Banks, Iain M(enzies) 1954- .... **CLC 34**
See also CA 123; 128; CANR 61, 106; DLB
194; HGG; INT 128; SFW 4

Banks, Lynne Reid .... **CLC 23**
See also Reid Banks, Lynne
See also AAYA 6; BYA 7

Banks, Russell 1940- .... **CLC 37, 72; SSC 42**
See also AMWS 5; CA 65-68; CAAS 15;
CANR 19, 52, 73; CN 7; DLB 130; NFS
13

Banville, John 1945- .... **CLC 46, 118**
See also CA 117; 128; CANR 104; CN 7;
DLB 14; INT 128

Banville, Theodore (Faullain) de
1832-1891 .... **NCLC 9**
See also DLB 217; GFL 1789 to the Present

Baraka, Amiri 1934- . **CLC 1, 2, 3, 5, 10, 14,**
33, 115; BLC 1; DC 6; PC 4; WLCS
See also Jones, LeRoi
See also AFAW 1, 2; AMWS 2; BW 2, 3;
CA 21-24R; CABS 3; CAD; CANR 27,
38, 61; CD 5; CDALB 1941-1968; CP 7;
CPW; DA; DA3; DAC; DAM MST,
MULT, POET, POP; DFS 3, 11; DLB 5,
7, 16, 38; DLBD 8; MTCW 1, 2; PFS 9;
RGAL 4; WP

Baratynsky, Evgenii Abramovich
1800-1844 .... **NCLC 103**
See also DLB 205

Barbauld, Anna Laetitia
1743-1825 .... **NCLC 50**
See also DLB 107, 109, 142, 158; RGEL 2

Barbellion, W. N. P. .... **TCLC 24**
See also Cummings, Bruce F(rederick)

Barber, Benjamin R. 1939- .... **CLC 141**
See also CA 29-32R; CANR 12, 32, 64

Barbera, Jack (Vincent) 1945- .... **CLC 44**
See also CA 110; CANR 45

Barbey d'Aurevilly, Jules-Amedee
1808-1889 .... **NCLC 1; SSC 17**
See also DLB 119; GFL 1789 to the Present

Barbour, John c. 1316-1395 .... **CMLC 33**
See also DLB 146

Barbusse, Henri 1873-1935 .... **TCLC 5**
See also CA 105; 154; DLB 65; RGWL 2

Barclay, Bill
See Moorcock, Michael (John)

Barclay, William Ewert
See Moorcock, Michael (John)

Barea, Arturo 1897-1957 .... **TCLC 14**
See also CA 111; 201

Barfoot, Joan 1946- .... **CLC 18**
See also CA 105

Barham, Richard Harris
1788-1845 .... **NCLC 77**
See also DLB 159

Baring, Maurice 1874-1945 .... **TCLC 8**
See also CA 105; 168; DLB 34; HGG

Baring-Gould, Sabine 1834-1924 ... **TCLC 88**
See also DLB 156, 190

Barker, Clive 1952- .... **CLC 52; SSC 53**
See also AAYA 10; BEST 90:3; BPFB 1;
CA 121; 129; CANR 71; CPW; DA3;
DAM POP; HGG; INT 129; MTCW 1, 2

Barker, George Granville
1913-1991 .... **CLC 8, 48**
See also CA 9-12R; 135; CANR 7, 38;
DAM POET; DLB 20; MTCW 1

Barker, Harley Granville
See Granville-Barker, Harley
See also DLB 10

Barker, Howard 1946- .... **CLC 37**
See also CA 102; CBD; CD 5; DLB 13,
233

Barker, Jane 1652-1732 .... **LC 42**
See also DLB 39, 131

Barker, Pat(ricia) 1943- ...... **CLC 32, 94, 146**
See also BRWS 4; CA 117; 122; CANR 50,
101; CN 7; INT 122

Barlach, Ernst (Heinrich)
1870-1938 .... **TCLC 84**
See also CA 178; DLB 56, 118

Barlow, Joel 1754-1812 .... **NCLC 23**
See also AMWS 2; DLB 37; RGAL 4

Barnard, Mary (Ethel) 1909- .... **CLC 48**
See also CA 21-22; CAP 2

Barnes, Djuna 1892-1982 .... **CLC 3, 4, 8, 11,**
29, 127; SSC 3
See Steptoe, Lydia
See also AMWS 3; CA 9-12R; 107; CAD;
CANR 16, 55; CWD; DLB 4, 9, 45; GLL
1; MTCW 1, 2; RGAL 4

Barnes, Julian (Patrick) 1946- . **CLC 42, 141**
See also BRWS 4; CA 102; CANR 19, 54;
CN 7; DAB; DLB 194; DLBY 1993;
MTCW 1

Barnes, Peter 1931- .... **CLC 5, 56**
See also CA 65-68; CAAS 12; CANR 33,
34, 64; CBD; CD 5; DFS 6; DLB 13, 233;
MTCW 1

Barnes, William 1801-1886 .... **NCLC 75**
See also DLB 32

Baroja (y Nessi), Pio 1872-1956 ..... **TCLC 8;**
HLC 1
See also CA 104; EW 9

Baron, David
See Pinter, Harold

Baron Corvo
See Rolfe, Frederick (William Serafino
Austin Lewis Mary)

Barondess, Sue K(aufman)
1926-1977 .... **CLC 8**
See also Kaufman, Sue
See also CA 1-4R; 69-72; CANR 1

Baron de Teive
See Pessoa, Fernando (Antonio Nogueira)

Baroness Von S.
See Zangwill, Israel

Barres, (Auguste-)Maurice
1862-1923 .... **TCLC 47**
See also CA 164; DLB 123; GFL 1789 to
the Present

Barreto, Afonso Henrique de Lima
See Lima Barreto, Afonso Henrique de

Barrett, Andrea 1954- .... **CLC 150**
See also CA 156; CANR 92

Barrett, Michele .... **CLC 65**

Barrett, (Roger) Syd 1946- .... **CLC 35**

Barrett, William (Christopher)
1913-1992 .... **CLC 27**
See also CA 13-16R; 139; CANR 11, 67;
INT CANR-11

Barrie, J(ames) M(atthew)
1860-1937 .... **TCLC 2**
See also BRWS 3; BYA 4, 5; CA 104; 136;
CANR 77; CDBLB 1890-1914; CLR 16;
CWRI 5; DA3; DAB; DAM DRAM; DFS
7; DLB 10, 141, 156; FANT; MAICYA 1,
2; MTCW 1; SATA 100; SUFW; WCH;
WLIT 4; YABC 1

Barrington, Michael
See Moorcock, Michael (John)

Barrol, Grady
See Bograd, Larry

Barry, Mike
See Malzberg, Barry N(athaniel)

Barry, Philip 1896-1949 .... **TCLC 11**
See also CA 109; 199; DFS 9; DLB 7, 228;
RGAL 4

Bart, Andre Schwarz
See Schwarz-Bart, Andre

Barth, John (Simmons) 1930- ... **CLC 1, 2, 3,**
5, 7, 9, 10, 14, 27, 51, 89; SSC 10
See also AITN 1, 2; AMW; BPFB 1; CA
1-4R; CABS 1; CANR 5, 23, 49, 64; CN
7; DAM NOV; DLB 2, 227; FANT;
MTCW 1; RGAL 4; RGSF 2; RHW;
SSFS 6

Barthelme, Donald 1931-1989 ... **CLC 1, 2, 3,**
5, 6, 8, 13, 23, 46, 59, 115; SSC 2
See also AMWS 4; BPFB 1; CA 21-24R;
129; CANR 20, 58; DA3; DAM NOV;
DLB 2, 234; DLBY 1980, 1989; FANT;
MTCW 1, 2; RGAL 4; RGSF 2; SATA 7;
SATA-Obit 62; SSFS 3

Barthelme, Frederick 1943- ...... **CLC 36, 117**
See also CA 114; 122; CANR 77; CN 7;
CSW; DLB 244; DLBY 1985; INT CA-
122

Barthes, Roland (Gerard)
1915-1980 .... **CLC 24, 83**
See also CA 130; 97-100; CANR 66; EW
13; GFL 1789 to the Present; MTCW 1, 2

Barzun, Jacques (Martin) 1907- ..... **CLC 51,**
145
See also CA 61-64; CANR 22, 95

Bashevis, Isaac
See Singer, Isaac Bashevis

Bashkirtseff, Marie 1859-1884 .... **NCLC 27**

Basho, Matsuo
See Matsuo Basho
See also RGWL 2; WP

Basil of Caesaria c. 330-379 .... **CMLC 35**

Bass, Kingsley B., Jr.
See Bullins, Ed

Bass, Rick 1958- .... **CLC 79, 143**
See also ANW; CA 126; CANR 53, 93;
CSW; DLB 212

Bassani, Giorgio 1916-2000 .... **CLC 9**
See also CA 65-68; 190; CANR 33; CWW
2; DLB 128, 177; MTCW 1; RGWL 2

Bastian, Ann .... **CLC 70**

Bastos, Augusto (Antonio) Roa
See Roa Bastos, Augusto (Antonio)

Bataille, Georges 1897-1962 .... **CLC 29**
See also CA 101; 89-92

Bates, H(erbert) E(rnest)
1905-1974 .... **CLC 46; SSC 10**
See also CA 93-96; 45-48; CANR 34; DA3;
DAB; DAM POP; DLB 162, 191; EXPS;
MTCW 1, 2; RGSF 2; SSFS 7

Bauchart
See Camus, Albert

Baudelaire, Charles 1821-1867 . **NCLC 6, 29, 55; PC 1; SSC 18; WLC**
See also DA; DA3; DAB; DAC; DAM MST, POET; DLB 217; EW 7; GFL 1789 to the Present; RGWL 2

Baudouin, Marcel
See Peguy, Charles (Pierre)

Baudouin, Pierre
See Peguy, Charles (Pierre)

Baudrillard, Jean 1929- .... **CLC 60**

Baum, L(yman) Frank 1856-1919 ... **TCLC 7**
See also CA 108; 133; CLR 15; CWRI 5; DLB 22; FANT; JRDA; MAICYA 1, 2; MTCW 1, 2; NFS 13; RGAL 4; SATA 18, 100; WCH

Baum, Louis F.
See Baum, L(yman) Frank

Baumbach, Jonathan 1933- .... **CLC 6, 23**
See also CA 13-16R; CAAS 5; CANR 12, 66; CN 7; DLBY 1980; INT CANR-12; MTCW 1

Bausch, Richard (Carl) 1945- .... **CLC 51**
See also AMWS 7; CA 101; CAAS 14; CANR 43, 61, 87; CSW; DLB 130

Baxter, Charles (Morley) 1947- . **CLC 45, 78**
See also CA 57-60; CANR 40, 64, 104; CPW; DAM POP; DLB 130; MTCW 2

Baxter, George Owen
See Faust, Frederick (Schiller)

Baxter, James K(eir) 1926-1972 .... **CLC 14**
See also CA 77-80

Baxter, John
See Hunt, E(verette) Howard, (Jr.)

Bayer, Sylvia
See Glassco, John

Baynton, Barbara 1857-1929 .... **TCLC 57**
See also DLB 230; RGSF 2

Beagle, Peter S(oyer) 1939- .... **CLC 7, 104**
See also BPFB 1; BYA 9, 10; CA 9-12R; CANR 4, 51, 73; DA3; DLBY 1980; FANT; INT CANR-4; MTCW 1; SATA 60, 130; SUFW; YAW

Bean, Normal
See Burroughs, Edgar Rice

Beard, Charles A(ustin)
1874-1948 .... **TCLC 15**
See also CA 115; 189; DLB 17; SATA 18

Beardsley, Aubrey 1872-1898 .... **NCLC 6**

Beattie, Ann 1947- ..... **CLC 8, 13, 18, 40, 63, 146; SSC 11**
See also AMWS 5; BEST 90:2; BPFB 1; CA 81-84; CANR 53, 73; CN 7; CPW; DA3; DAM NOV, POP; DLB 218; DLBY 1982; MTCW 1, 2; RGAL 4; RGSF 2; SSFS 9

Beattie, James 1735-1803 .... **NCLC 25**
See also DLB 109

Beauchamp, Kathleen Mansfield 1888-1923
See Mansfield, Katherine
See also CA 104; 134; DA; DA3; DAC; DAM MST; MTCW 2

Beaumarchais, Pierre-Augustin Caron de
1732-1799 .... **LC 61; DC 4**
See also DAM DRAM; DFS 14; EW 4; GFL Beginnings to 1789; RGWL 2

Beaumont, Francis 1584(?)-1616 .... **LC 33; DC 6**
See also BRW 2; CDBLB Before 1660; DLB 58

Beauvoir, Simone (Lucie Ernestine Marie Bertrand) de 1908-1986 .... **CLC 1, 2, 4, 8, 14, 31, 44, 50, 71, 124; SSC 35; WLC**
See also BPFB 1; CA 9-12R; 118; CANR 28, 61; DA; DA3; DAB; DAC; DAM MST, NOV; DLB 72; DLBY 1986; EW 12; FW; GFL 1789 to the Present; MTCW 1, 2; RGSF 2; RGWL 2

Becker, Carl (Lotus) 1873-1945 ..... **TCLC 63**
See also CA 157; DLB 17

Becker, Jurek 1937-1997 .... **CLC 7, 19**
See also CA 85-88; 157; CANR 60; CWW 2; DLB 75

Becker, Walter 1950- .... **CLC 26**

Beckett, Samuel (Barclay)
1906-1989 .. **CLC 1, 2, 3, 4, 6, 9, 10, 11, 14, 18, 29, 57, 59, 83; SSC 16; WLC**
See also BRWR 1; BRWS 1; CA 5-8R; 130; CANR 33, 61; CBD; CDBLB 1945-1960; DA; DA3; DAB; DAC; DAM DRAM, MST, NOV; DFS 2, 7; DLB 13, 15, 233; DLBY 1990; GFL 1789 to the Present; MTCW 1, 2; RGSF 2; RGWL 2; WLIT 4

Beckford, William 1760-1844 .... **NCLC 16**
See also BRW 3; DLB 39, 213; HGG; SUFW

Beckman, Gunnel 1910- .... **CLC 26**
See also CA 33-36R; CANR 15; CLR 25; MAICYA 1, 2; SAAS 9; SATA 6

Becque, Henri 1837-1899 .... **NCLC 3**
See also DLB 192; GFL 1789 to the Present

Becquer, Gustavo Adolfo
1836-1870 .... **NCLC 106; HLCS 1**
See also DAM MULT

Beddoes, Thomas Lovell
1803-1849 .... **NCLC 3; DC 15**
See also DLB 96

Bede c. 673-735 .... **CMLC 20**
See also DLB 146

Bedford, Donald F.
See Fearing, Kenneth (Flexner)

Beecher, Catharine Esther
1800-1878 .... **NCLC 30**
See also DLB 1, 243

Beecher, John 1904-1980 .... **CLC 6**
See also AITN 1; CA 5-8R; 105; CANR 8

Beer, Johann 1655-1700 .... **LC 5**
See also DLB 168

Beer, Patricia 1924- .... **CLC 58**
See also CA 61-64; 183; CANR 13, 46; CP 7; CWP; DLB 40; FW

Beerbohm, Max
See Beerbohm, (Henry) Max(imilian)

Beerbohm, (Henry) Max(imilian)
1872-1956 .... **TCLC 1, 24**
See also BRWS 2; CA 104; 154; CANR 79; DLB 34, 100; FANT

Beer-Hofmann, Richard
1866-1945 .... **TCLC 60**
See also CA 160; DLB 81

Beg, Shemus
See Stephens, James

Begiebing, Robert J(ohn) 1946- .... **CLC 70**
See also CA 122; CANR 40, 88

Behan, Brendan 1923-1964 ...... **CLC 1, 8, 11, 15, 79**
See also BRWS 2; CA 73-76; CANR 33; CBD; CDBLB 1945-1960; DAM DRAM; DFS 7; DLB 13, 233; MTCW 1, 2

Behn, Aphra 1640(?)-1689 .... **LC 1, 30, 42; DC 4; PC 13; WLC**
See also BRWS 3; DA; DA3; DAB; DAC; DAM DRAM, MST, NOV, POET; DLB 39, 80, 131; FW; WLIT 3

Behrman, S(amuel) N(athaniel)
1893-1973 .... **CLC 40**
See also CA 13-16; 45-48; CAD; CAP 1; DLB 7, 44; IDFW 3; RGAL 4

Belasco, David 1853-1931 .... **TCLC 3**
See also CA 104; 168; DLB 7; RGAL 4

Belcheva, Elisaveta Lyubomirova
1893-1991 .... **CLC 10**
See also Bagryana, Elisaveta

Beldone, Phil ''Cheech''
See Ellison, Harlan (Jay)

Beleno
See Azuela, Mariano

Belinski, Vissarion Grigoryevich
1811-1848 .... **NCLC 5**
See also DLB 198

Belitt, Ben 1911- .... **CLC 22**
See also CA 13-16R; CAAS 4; CANR 7, 77; CP 7; DLB 5

Bell, Gertrude (Margaret Lowthian)
1868-1926 .... **TCLC 67**
See also CA 167; DLB 174

Bell, J. Freeman
See Zangwill, Israel

Bell, James Madison 1826-1902 ... **TCLC 43; BLC 1**
See also BW 1; CA 122; 124; DAM MULT; DLB 50

Bell, Madison Smartt 1957- ...... **CLC 41, 102**
See also AMWS 10; BPFB 1; CA 111, 183; CAAE 183; CANR 28, 54, 73; CN 7; CSW; DLB 218; MTCW 1

Bell, Marvin (Hartley) 1937- .... **CLC 8, 31**
See also CA 21-24R; CAAS 14; CANR 59, 102; CP 7; DAM POET; DLB 5; MTCW 1

Bell, W. L. D.
See Mencken, H(enry) L(ouis)

Bellamy, Atwood C.
See Mencken, H(enry) L(ouis)

Bellamy, Edward 1850-1898 ...... **NCLC 4, 86**
See also DLB 12; RGAL 4; SFW 4

Belli, Gioconda 1949-
See also CA 152; CWW 2; HLCS 1

Bellin, Edward J.
See Kuttner, Henry

Belloc, (Joseph) Hilaire (Pierre Sebastien Rene Swanton) 1870-1953 ...... **TCLC 7, 18; PC 24**
See also CA 106; 152; CWRI 5; DAM POET; DLB 19, 100, 141, 174; MTCW 1; SATA 112; WCH; YABC 1

Belloc, Joseph Peter Rene Hilaire
See Belloc, (Joseph) Hilaire (Pierre Sebastien Rene Swanton)

Belloc, Joseph Pierre Hilaire
See Belloc, (Joseph) Hilaire (Pierre Sebastien Rene Swanton)

Belloc, M. A.
See Lowndes, Marie Adelaide (Belloc)

Bellow, Saul 1915- . **CLC 1, 2, 3, 6, 8, 10, 13, 15, 25, 33, 34, 63, 79; SSC 14; WLC**
See also AITN 2; AMW; BEST 89:3; BPFB 1; CA 5-8R; CABS 1; CANR 29, 53, 95; CDALB 1941-1968; CN 7; DA; DA3; DAB; DAC; DAM MST, NOV, POP; DLB 2, 28; DLBD 3; DLBY 1982; MTCW 1, 2; NFS 4, 14; RGAL 4; RGSF 2; SSFS 12

Belser, Reimond Karel Maria de 1929-
See Ruyslinck, Ward
See also CA 152

Bely, Andrey .... **TCLC 7; PC 11**
See also Bugayev, Boris Nikolayevich
See also EW 9; MTCW 1

Belyi, Andrei
See Bugayev, Boris Nikolayevich
See also RGWL 2

Benary, Margot
See Benary-Isbert, Margot

Benary-Isbert, Margot 1889-1979 .... **CLC 12**
See also CA 5-8R; 89-92; CANR 4, 72; CLR 12; MAICYA 1, 2; SATA 2; SATA-Obit 21

Benavente (y Martinez), Jacinto
1866-1954 .... **TCLC 3; HLCS 1**
See also CA 106; 131; CANR 81; DAM DRAM, MULT; GLL 2; HW 1, 2; MTCW 1, 2

Benchley, Peter (Bradford) 1940- .. **CLC 4, 8**
See also AAYA 14; AITN 2; BPFB 1; CA
17-20R; CANR 12, 35, 66; CPW; DAM
NOV, POP; HGG; MTCW 1, 2; SATA 3,
89

Benchley, Robert (Charles)
1889-1945 .... **TCLC 1, 55**
See also CA 105; 153; DLB 11; RGAL 4

Benda, Julien 1867-1956 .... **TCLC 60**
See also CA 120; 154; GFL 1789 to the
Present

Benedict, Ruth (Fulton)
1887-1948 .... **TCLC 60**
See also CA 158; DLB 246

Benedikt, Michael 1935- .... **CLC 4, 14**
See also CA 13-16R; CANR 7; CP 7; DLB
5

Benet, Juan 1927-1993 .... **CLC 28**
See also CA 143

Benet, Stephen Vincent 1898-1943 . **TCLC 7;
SSC 10**
See also CA 104; 152; DA3; DAM POET;
DLB 4, 48, 102, 249; DLBY 1997; HGG;
MTCW 1; RGAL 4; RGSF 2; SUFW;
WP; YABC 1

Benet, William Rose 1886-1950 ..... **TCLC 28**
See also CA 118; 152; DAM POET; DLB
45; RGAL 4

Benford, Gregory (Albert) 1941- ... **CLC 52**
See also BPFB 1; CA 69-72, 175; CAAE
175; CAAS 27; CANR 12, 24, 49, 95;
CSW; DLBY 1982; SCFW 2; SFW 4

Bengtsson, Frans (Gunnar)
1894-1954 .... **TCLC 48**
See also CA 170

Benjamin, David
See Slavitt, David R(ytman)

Benjamin, Lois
See Gould, Lois

Benjamin, Walter 1892-1940 .... **TCLC 39**
See also CA 164; DLB 242; EW 11

Benn, Gottfried 1886-1956 .. **TCLC 3; PC 35**
See also CA 106; 153; DLB 56; RGWL 2

Bennett, Alan 1934- .... **CLC 45, 77**
See also CA 103; CANR 35, 55, 106; CBD;
CD 5; DAB; DAM MST; MTCW 1, 2

Bennett, (Enoch) Arnold
1867-1931 .... **TCLC 5, 20**
See also BRW 6; CA 106; 155; CDBLB
1890-1914; DLB 10, 34, 98, 135; MTCW
2

Bennett, Elizabeth
See Mitchell, Margaret (Munnerlyn)

Bennett, George Harold 1930-
See Bennett, Hal
See also BW 1; CA 97-100; CANR 87

Bennett, Hal .... **CLC 5**
See also Bennett, George Harold
See also DLB 33

Bennett, Jay 1912- .... **CLC 35**
See also AAYA 10; CA 69-72; CANR 11,
42, 79; JRDA; SAAS 4; SATA 41, 87;
SATA-Brief 27; WYA; YAW

Bennett, Louise (Simone) 1919- ...... **CLC 28;
BLC 1**
See also BW 2, 3; CA 151; CDWLB 3; CP
7; DAM MULT; DLB 117

Benson, E(dward) F(rederic)
1867-1940 .... **TCLC 27**
See also CA 114; 157; DLB 135, 153;
HGG; SUFW

Benson, Jackson J. 1930- .... **CLC 34**
See also CA 25-28R; DLB 111

Benson, Sally 1900-1972 .... **CLC 17**
See also CA 19-20; 37-40R; CAP 1; SATA
1, 35; SATA-Obit 27

Benson, Stella 1892-1933 .... **TCLC 17**
See also CA 117; 155; DLB 36, 162; FANT

Bentham, Jeremy 1748-1832 .... **NCLC 38**
See also DLB 107, 158, 252

Bentley, E(dmund) C(lerihew)
1875-1956 .... **TCLC 12**
See also CA 108; DLB 70; MSW

Bentley, Eric (Russell) 1916- .... **CLC 24**
See also CA 5-8R; CAD; CANR 6, 67;
CBD; CD 5; INT CANR-6

Beranger, Pierre Jean de
1780-1857 .... **NCLC 34**

Berdyaev, Nicolas
See Berdyaev, Nikolai (Aleksandrovich)

Berdyaev, Nikolai (Aleksandrovich)
1874-1948 .... **TCLC 67**
See also CA 120; 157

Berdyayev, Nikolai (Aleksandrovich)
See Berdyaev, Nikolai (Aleksandrovich)

Berendt, John (Lawrence) 1939- ...... **CLC 86**
See also CA 146; CANR 75, 93; DA3;
MTCW 1

Beresford, J(ohn) D(avys)
1873-1947 .... **TCLC 81**
See also CA 112; 155; DLB 162, 178, 197;
SFW 4; SUFW

Bergelson, David 1884-1952 .... **TCLC 81**

Berger, Colonel
See Malraux, (Georges-)Andre

Berger, John (Peter) 1926- .... **CLC 2, 19**
See also BRWS 4; CA 81-84; CANR 51,
78; CN 7; DLB 14, 207

Berger, Melvin H. 1927- .... **CLC 12**
See also CA 5-8R; CANR 4; CLR 32;
SAAS 2; SATA 5, 88; SATA-Essay 124

Berger, Thomas (Louis) 1924- .. **CLC 3, 5, 8,
11, 18, 38**
See also BPFB 1; CA 1-4R; CANR 5, 28,
51; CN 7; DAM NOV; DLB 2; DLBY
1980; FANT; INT CANR-28; MTCW 1,
2; RHW; TCWW 2

Bergman, (Ernst) Ingmar 1918- ...... **CLC 16,
72**
See also CA 81-84; CANR 33, 70; DLB
257; MTCW 2

Bergson, Henri(-Louis) 1859-1941 . **TCLC 32**
See also CA 164; EW 8; GFL 1789 to the
Present

Bergstein, Eleanor 1938- .... **CLC 4**
See also CA 53-56; CANR 5

Berkeley, George 1685-1753 .... **LC 65**
See also DLB 101, 252

Berkoff, Steven 1937- .... **CLC 56**
See also CA 104; CANR 72; CBD; CD 5

Berlin, Isaiah 1909-1997 .... **TCLC 105**
See also CA 85-88; 162

Bermant, Chaim (Icyk) 1929-1998 ... **CLC 40**
See also CA 57-60; CANR 6, 31, 57, 105;
CN 7

Bern, Victoria
See Fisher, M(ary) F(rances) K(ennedy)

Bernanos, (Paul Louis) Georges
1888-1948 .... **TCLC 3**
See also CA 104; 130; CANR 94; DLB 72;
GFL 1789 to the Present; RGWL 2

Bernard, April 1956- .... **CLC 59**
See also CA 131

Berne, Victoria
See Fisher, M(ary) F(rances) K(ennedy)

Bernhard, Thomas 1931-1989 ..... **CLC 3, 32,
61; DC 14**
See also CA 85-88; 127; CANR 32, 57; CD-
WLB 2; DLB 85, 124; MTCW 1; RGWL
2

Bernhardt, Sarah (Henriette Rosine)
1844-1923 .... **TCLC 75**
See also CA 157

Bernstein, Charles 1950- .... **CLC 142,**
See also CA 129; CAAS 24; CANR 90; CP
7; DLB 169

Berriault, Gina 1926-1999 .... **CLC 54, 109;
SSC 30**
See also CA 116; 129; 185; CANR 66; DLB
130; SSFS 7,11

Berrigan, Daniel 1921- .... **CLC 4**
See also CA 33-36R; CAAE 187; CAAS 1;
CANR 11, 43, 78; CP 7; DLB 5

Berrigan, Edmund Joseph Michael, Jr.
1934-1983
See Berrigan, Ted
See also CA 61-64; 110; CANR 14, 102

Berrigan, Ted .... **CLC 37**
See also Berrigan, Edmund Joseph Michael,
Jr.
See also DLB 5, 169; WP

Berry, Charles Edward Anderson 1931-
See Berry, Chuck
See also CA 115

Berry, Chuck .... **CLC 17**
See also Berry, Charles Edward Anderson

Berry, Jonas
See Ashbery, John (Lawrence)
See also GLL 1

Berry, Wendell (Erdman) 1934- ... **CLC 4, 6,
8, 27, 46; PC 28**
See also AITN 1; AMWS 10; ANW; CA
73-76; CANR 50, 73, 101; CP 7; CSW;
DAM POET; DLB 5, 6, 234; MTCW 1

Berryman, John 1914-1972 ... **CLC 1, 2, 3, 4,
6, 8, 10, 13, 25, 62**
See also AMW; CA 13-16; 33-36R; CABS
2; CANR 35; CAP 1; CDALB 1941-1968;
DAM POET; DLB 48; MTCW 1, 2; PAB;
RGAL 4; WP

Bertolucci, Bernardo 1940- ...... **CLC 16, 157**
See also CA 106

Berton, Pierre (Francis Demarigny)
1920- .... **CLC 104**
See also CA 1-4R; CANR 2, 56; CPW;
DLB 68; SATA 99

Bertrand, Aloysius 1807-1841 .... **NCLC 31**
See also Bertrand, Louis oAloysiusc

Bertrand, Louis oAloysiusc
See Bertrand, Aloysius
See also DLB 217

Bertran de Born c. 1140-1215 .... **CMLC 5**

Besant, Annie (Wood) 1847-1933 ..... **TCLC 9**
See also CA 105; 185

Bessie, Alvah 1904-1985 .... **CLC 23**
See also CA 5-8R; 116; CANR 2, 80; DLB
26

Bethlen, T. D.
See Silverberg, Robert

Beti, Mongo .... **CLC 27; BLC 1**
See also Biyidi, Alexandre
See also AFW; CANR 79; DAM MULT;
WLIT 2

Betjeman, John 1906-1984 ...... **CLC 2, 6, 10,
34, 43**
See also BRW 7; CA 9-12R; 112; CANR
33, 56; CDBLB 1945-1960; DA3; DAB;
DAM MST, POET; DLB 20; DLBY 1984;
MTCW 1, 2

Bettelheim, Bruno 1903-1990 .... **CLC 79**
See also CA 81-84; 131; CANR 23, 61;
DA3; MTCW 1, 2

Betti, Ugo 1892-1953 .... **TCLC 5**
See also CA 104; 155; RGWL 2

Betts, Doris (Waugh) 1932- ..... **CLC 3, 6, 28;
SSC 45**
See also CA 13-16R; CANR 9, 66, 77; CN
7; CSW; DLB 218; DLBY 1982; INT
CANR-9; RGAL 4

Bevan, Alistair
See Roberts, Keith (John Kingston)

Bey, Pilaff
See Douglas, (George) Norman

Bialik, Chaim Nachman
　　1873-1934 .... **TCLC 25**
　　See also CA 170
Bickerstaff, Isaac
　　See Swift, Jonathan
Bidart, Frank 1939- .... **CLC 33**
　　See also CA 140; CANR 106; CP 7
Bienek, Horst 1930- .... **CLC 7, 11**
　　See also CA 73-76; DLB 75
Bierce, Ambrose (Gwinett)
　　1842-1914(?) ..... **TCLC 1, 7, 44; SSC 9;**
　　WLC
　　　　See also AMW; BYA 11; CA 104; 139;
　　　　CANR 78; CDALB 1865-1917; DA;
　　　　DA3; DAC; DAM MST; DLB 11, 12, 23,
　　　　71, 74, 186; EXPS; HGG; LAIT 2; RGAL
　　　　4; RGSF 2; SSFS 9; SUFW
Biggers, Earl Derr 1884-1933 .... **TCLC 65**
　　See also CA 108; 153
Billings, Josh
　　See Shaw, Henry Wheeler
Billington, (Lady) Rachel (Mary)
　　1942- .... **CLC 43**
　　See also AITN 2; CA 33-36R; CANR 44;
　　CN 7
Binchy, Maeve 1940- .... **CLC 153**
　　See also BEST 90:1; BPFB 1; CA 127; 134;
　　CANR 50, 96; CN 7; CPW; DA3; DAM
　　POP; INT CA-134; MTCW 1; RHW
Binyon, T(imothy) J(ohn) 1936- .... **CLC 34**
　　See also CA 111; CANR 28
Bion 335B.C.-245B.C. .... **CMLC 39**
Bioy Casares, Adolfo 1914-1999 ... **CLC 4, 8,**
　　13, 88; HLC 1; SSC 17
　　　　See also Casares, Adolfo Bioy; Miranda,
　　　　Javier; Sacastru, Martin
　　　　See also CA 29-32R; 177; CANR 19, 43,
　　　　66; DAM MULT; DLB 113; HW 1, 2;
　　　　LAW; MTCW 1, 2
Birch, Allison .... **CLC 65**
Bird, Cordwainer
　　See Ellison, Harlan (Jay)
Bird, Robert Montgomery
　　1806-1854 .... **NCLC 1**
　　See also DLB 202; RGAL 4
Birkerts, Sven 1951- .... **CLC 116**
　　See also CA 128; 133, 176; CAAE 176;
　　CAAS 29; INT 133
Birney, (Alfred) Earle 1904-1995 .. **CLC 1, 4,**
　　6, 11
　　　　See also CA 1-4R; CANR 5, 20; CP 7;
　　　　DAC; DAM MST, POET; DLB 88;
　　　　MTCW 1; PFS 8; RGEL 2
Biruni, al 973-1048(?) .... **CMLC 28**
Bishop, Elizabeth 1911-1979 ..... **CLC 1, 4, 9,**
　　13, 15, 32; PC 3, 34
　　　　See also AMWS 1; CA 5-8R; 89-92; CABS
　　　　2; CANR 26, 61, 108; CDALB 1968-
　　　　1988; DA; DA3; DAC; DAM MST,
　　　　POET; DLB 5, 169; GLL 2; MAWW;
　　　　MTCW 1, 2; PAB; PFS 6, 12; RGAL 4;
　　　　SATA-Obit 24; TCLC 121; WP
Bishop, John 1935- .... **CLC 10**
　　See also CA 105
Bishop, John Peale 1892-1944 ..... **TCLC 103**
　　See also CA 107; 155; DLB 4, 9, 45; RGAL
　　4
Bissett, Bill 1939- .... **CLC 18; PC 14**
　　See also CA 69-72; CAAS 19; CANR 15;
　　CCA 1; CP 7; DLB 53; MTCW 1
Bissoondath, Neil (Devindra)
　　1955- .... **CLC 120**
　　See also CA 136; CN 7; DAC
Bitov, Andrei (Georgievich) 1937- ... **CLC 57**
　　See also CA 142
Biyidi, Alexandre 1932-
　　See Beti, Mongo
　　See also BW 1, 3; CA 114; 124; CANR 81;
　　DA3; MTCW 1, 2

Bjarme, Brynjolf
　　See Ibsen, Henrik (Johan)
Bjoernson, Bjoernstjerne (Martinius)
　　1832-1910 .... **TCLC 7, 37**
　　See also CA 104
Black, Robert
　　See Holdstock, Robert P.
Blackburn, Paul 1926-1971 .... **CLC 9, 43**
　　See also CA 81-84; 33-36R; CANR 34;
　　DLB 16; DLBY 1981
Black Elk 1863-1950 .... **TCLC 33**
　　See also CA 144; DAM MULT; MTCW 1;
　　NNAL; WP
Black Hobart
　　See Sanders, (James) Ed(ward)
Blacklin, Malcolm
　　See Chambers, Aidan
Blackmore, R(ichard) D(oddridge)
　　1825-1900 .... **TCLC 27**
　　See also CA 120; DLB 18; RGEL 2
Blackmur, R(ichard) P(almer)
　　1904-1965 .... **CLC 2, 24**
　　See also AMWS 2; CA 11-12; 25-28R;
　　CANR 71; CAP 1; DLB 63
Black Tarantula
　　See Acker, Kathy
Blackwood, Algernon (Henry)
　　1869-1951 .... **TCLC 5**
　　See also CA 105; 150; DLB 153, 156, 178;
　　HGG; SUFW
Blackwood, Caroline 1931-1996 .... **CLC 6, 9,**
　　100
　　　　See also CA 85-88; 151; CANR 32, 61, 65;
　　　　CN 7; DLB 14, 207; HGG; MTCW 1
Blade, Alexander
　　See Hamilton, Edmond; Silverberg, Robert
Blaga, Lucian 1895-1961 .... **CLC 75**
　　See also CA 157; DLB 220
Blair, Eric (Arthur) 1903-1950
　　See Orwell, George
　　See also CA 104; 132; DA; DA3; DAB;
　　DAC; DAM MST, NOV; MTCW 1, 2;
　　SATA 29
Blair, Hugh 1718-1800 .... **NCLC 75**
Blais, Marie-Claire 1939- .... **CLC 2, 4, 6, 13,**
　　22
　　　　See also CA 21-24R; CAAS 4; CANR 38,
　　　　75, 93; DAC; DAM MST; DLB 53; FW;
　　　　MTCW 1, 2
Blaise, Clark 1940- .... **CLC 29**
　　See also AITN 2; CA 53-56; CAAS 3;
　　CANR 5, 66, 106; CN 7; DLB 53; RGSF
　　2
Blake, Fairley
　　See De Voto, Bernard (Augustine)
Blake, Nicholas
　　See Day Lewis, C(ecil)
　　See also DLB 77; MSW
Blake, William 1757-1827 .... **NCLC 13, 37,**
　　57; PC 12; WLC
　　　　See also BRW 3; BRWR 1; CDBLB 1789-
　　　　1832; CLR 52; DA; DA3; DAB; DAC;
　　　　DAM MST, POET; DLB 93, 163; EXPP;
　　　　MAICYA 1, 2; PAB; PFS 2, 12; SATA
　　　　30; WCH; WLIT 3; WP
Blanchot, Maurice 1907- .... **CLC 135**
　　See also CA 117; 144; DLB 72
Blasco Ibanez, Vicente 1867-1928 . **TCLC 12**
　　See also BPFB 1; CA 110; 131; CANR 81;
　　DA3; DAM NOV; EW 8; HW 1, 2;
　　MTCW 1
Blatty, William Peter 1928- .... **CLC 2**
　　See also CA 5-8R; CANR 9; DAM POP;
　　HGG
Bleeck, Oliver
　　See Thomas, Ross (Elmore)
Blessing, Lee 1949- .... **CLC 54**
　　See also CAD; CD 5

Blight, Rose
　　See Greer, Germaine
Blish, James (Benjamin) 1921-1975 . **CLC 14**
　　See also BPFB 1; CA 1-4R; 57-60; CANR
　　3; DLB 8; MTCW 1; SATA 66; SCFW 2;
　　SFW 4
Bliss, Reginald
　　See Wells, H(erbert) G(eorge)
Blixen, Karen (Christentze Dinesen)
　　1885-1962
　　　　See Dinesen, Isak
　　　　See also CA 25-28; CANR 22, 50; CAP 2;
　　　　DA3; DLB 214; MTCW 1, 2; SATA 44
Bloch, Robert (Albert) 1917-1994 .... **CLC 33**
　　See also AAYA 29; CA 5-8R, 179; 146;
　　CAAE 179; CAAS 20; CANR 5, 78;
　　DA3; DLB 44; HGG; INT CANR-5;
　　MTCW 1; SATA 12; SATA-Obit 82; SFW
　　4; SUFW
Blok, Alexander (Alexandrovich)
　　1880-1921 .... **TCLC 5; PC 21**
　　See also CA 104; 183; EW 9; RGWL 2
Blom, Jan
　　See Breytenbach, Breyten
Bloom, Harold 1930- .... **CLC 24, 103**
　　See also CA 13-16R; CANR 39, 75, 92;
　　DLB 67; MTCW 1; RGAL 4
Bloomfield, Aurelius
　　See Bourne, Randolph S(illiman)
Blount, Roy (Alton), Jr. 1941- .... **CLC 38**
　　See also CA 53-56; CANR 10, 28, 61;
　　CSW; INT CANR-28; MTCW 1, 2
Bloy, Leon 1846-1917 .... **TCLC 22**
　　See also CA 121; 183; DLB 123; GFL 1789
　　to the Present
Bluggage, Oranthy
　　See Alcott, Louisa May
Blume, Judy (Sussman) 1938- .... **CLC 12, 30**
　　See also AAYA 3, 26; BYA 1, 8, 12; CA 29-
　　32R; CANR 13, 37, 66; CLR 2, 15, 69;
　　CPW; DA3; DAM NOV, POP; DLB 52;
　　JRDA; MAICYA 1, 2; MAICYAS 1;
　　MTCW 1, 2; SATA 2, 31, 79; WYA; YAW
Blunden, Edmund (Charles)
　　1896-1974 .... **CLC 2, 56**
　　See also BRW 6; CA 17-18; 45-48; CANR
　　54; CAP 2; DLB 20, 100, 155; MTCW 1;
　　PAB
Bly, Robert (Elwood) 1926- .... **CLC 1, 2, 5,**
　　10, 15, 38, 128; PC 39
　　　　See also AMWS 4; CA 5-8R; CANR 41,
　　　　73; CP 7; DA3; DAM POET; DLB 5;
　　　　MTCW 1, 2; RGAL 4
Boas, Franz 1858-1942 .... **TCLC 56**
　　See also CA 115; 181
Bobette
　　See Simenon, Georges (Jacques Christian)
Boccaccio, Giovanni 1313-1375 ... **CMLC 13;**
　　SSC 10
　　See also EW 2; RGSF 2; RGWL 2
Bochco, Steven 1943- .... **CLC 35**
　　See also AAYA 11; CA 124; 138
Bode, Sigmund
　　See O'Doherty, Brian
Bodel, Jean 1167(?)-1210 .... **CMLC 28**
Bodenheim, Maxwell 1892-1954 .... **TCLC 44**
　　See also CA 110; 187; DLB 9, 45; RGAL 4
Bodker, Cecil 1927- .... **CLC 21**
　　See also CA 73-76; CANR 13, 44; CLR 23;
　　MAICYA 1, 2; SATA 14
Bodker, Cecil 1927-
　　See Bodker, Cecil
Boell, Heinrich (Theodor)
　　1917-1985 ..... **CLC 2, 3, 6, 9, 11, 15, 27,**
　　32, 72; SSC 23; WLC
　　　　See also Boll, Heinrich
　　　　See also CA 21-24R; 116; CANR 24; DA;
　　　　DA3; DAB; DAC; DAM MST, NOV;
　　　　DLB 69; DLBY 1985; MTCW 1, 2

Boerne, Alfred
See Doeblin, Alfred

Boethius c. 480-c. 524 .... **CMLC 15**
See also DLB 115; RGWL 2

Boff, Leonardo (Genezio Darci)
1938- .... **CLC 70; HLC 1**
See also CA 150; DAM MULT; HW 2

Bogan, Louise 1897-1970 .... **CLC 4, 39, 46,
93; PC 12**
See also AMWS 3; CA 73-76; 25-28R;
CANR 33, 82; DAM POET; DLB 45, 169;
MAWW; MTCW 1, 2; RGAL 4

Bogarde, Dirk
See Van Den Bogarde, Derek Jules Gaspard
Ulric Niven
See also DLB 14

Bogosian, Eric 1953- .... **CLC 45, 141**
See also CA 138; CAD; CANR 102; CD 5

Bograd, Larry 1953- .... **CLC 35**
See also CA 93-96; CANR 57; SAAS 21;
SATA 33, 89; WYA

Boiardo, Matteo Maria 1441-1494 .... **LC 6**

Boileau-Despreaux, Nicolas 1636-1711 . **LC 3**
See also EW 3; GFL Beginnings to 1789;
RGWL 2

Bojer, Johan 1872-1959 .... **TCLC 64**
See also CA 189

Bok, Edward W. 1863-1930 .... **TCLC 101**
See also DLB 91; DLBD 16

Boland, Eavan (Aisling) 1944- .. **CLC 40, 67,
113**
See also BRWS 5; CA 143; CANR 61; CP
7; CWP; DAM POET; DLB 40; FW;
MTCW 2; PFS 12

Boll, Heinrich
See Boell, Heinrich (Theodor)
See also BPFB 1; CDWLB 2; EW 13;
RGSF 2; RGWL 2

Bolt, Lee
See Faust, Frederick (Schiller)

Bolt, Robert (Oxton) 1924-1995 .... **CLC 14**
See also CA 17-20R; 147; CANR 35, 67;
CBD; DAM DRAM; DFS 2; DLB 13,
233; LAIT 1; MTCW 1

Bombal, Maria Luisa 1910-1980 ...... **SSC 37;
HLCS 1**
See also CA 127; CANR 72; HW 1; LAW;
RGSF 2

Bombet, Louis-Alexandre-Cesar
See Stendhal

Bomkauf
See Kaufman, Bob (Garnell)

Bonaventura .... **NCLC 35**
See also DLB 90

Bond, Edward 1934- .... **CLC 4, 6, 13, 23**
See also BRWS 1; CA 25-28R; CANR 38,
67, 106; CBD; CD 5; DAM DRAM; DFS
3,8; DLB 13; MTCW 1

Bonham, Frank 1914-1989 .... **CLC 12**
See also AAYA 1; BYA 1, 3; CA 9-12R;
CANR 4, 36; JRDA; MAICYA 1, 2;
SAAS 3; SATA 1, 49; SATA-Obit 62;
TCWW 2; YAW

Bonnefoy, Yves 1923- .... **CLC 9, 15, 58**
See also CA 85-88; CANR 33, 75, 97;
CWW 2; DAM MST, POET; DLB 258;
GFL 1789 to the Present; MTCW 1, 2

Bontemps, Arna(ud Wendell)
1902-1973 .... **CLC 1, 18; BLC 1**
See also BW 1; CA 1-4R; 41-44R; CANR
4, 35; CLR 6; CWRI 5; DA3; DAM
MULT, NOV, POET; DLB 48, 51; JRDA;
MAICYA 1, 2; MTCW 1, 2; SATA 2, 44;
SATA-Obit 24; WCH; WP

Booth, Martin 1944- .... **CLC 13**
See also CA 93-96; CAAE 188; CAAS 2;
CANR 92

Booth, Philip 1925- .... **CLC 23**
See also CA 5-8R; CANR 5, 88; CP 7;
DLBY 1982

Booth, Wayne C(layson) 1921- .... **CLC 24**
See also CA 1-4R; CAAS 5; CANR 3, 43;
DLB 67

Borchert, Wolfgang 1921-1947 .... **TCLC 5**
See also CA 104; 188; DLB 69, 124

Borel, Petrus 1809-1859 .... **NCLC 41**
See also DLB 119; GFL 1789 to the Present

Borges, Jorge Luis 1899-1986 ... **CLC 1, 2, 3,
4, 6, 8, 9, 10, 13, 19, 44, 48, 83; HLC 1;
PC 22, 32; SSC 4, 41; WLC**
See also AAYA 26; BPFB 1; CA 21-24R;
CANR 19, 33, 75, 105; CDWLB 3; DA;
DA3; DAB; DAC; DAM MST, MULT;
DLB 113; DLBY 1986; DNFS 1, 2; HW
1, 2; LAW; MSW; MTCW 1, 2; RGSF 2;
RGWL 2; SFW 4; SSFS 4, 9; TCLC 109;
WLIT 1

Borowski, Tadeusz 1922-1951 .... **TCLC 9;
SSC 48**
See also CA 106; 154; CDWLB 4, 4; DLB
215; RGSF 2; SSFS 13

Borrow, George (Henry)
1803-1881 .... **NCLC 9**
See also DLB 21, 55, 166

Bosch (Gavino), Juan 1909-2001
See also CA 151; DAM MST, MULT; DLB
145; HLCS 1; HW 1, 2

Bosman, Herman Charles
1905-1951 .... **TCLC 49**
See also Malan, Herman
See also CA 160; DLB 225; RGSF 2

Bosschere, Jean de 1878(?)-1953 ... **TCLC 19**
See also CA 115; 186

Boswell, James 1740-1795 ... **LC 4, 50; WLC**
See also BRW 3; CDBLB 1660-1789; DA;
DAB; DAC; DAM MST; DLB 104, 142;
WLIT 3

Bottomley, Gordon 1874-1948 ..... **TCLC 107**
See also CA 120; 192; DLB 10

Bottoms, David 1949- .... **CLC 53**
See also CA 105; CANR 22; CSW; DLB
120; DLBY 1983

Boucicault, Dion 1820-1890 .... **NCLC 41**

Boucolon, Maryse
See Conde, Maryse

Bourget, Paul (Charles Joseph)
1852-1935 .... **TCLC 12**
See also CA 107; 196; DLB 123; GFL 1789
to the Present

Bourjaily, Vance (Nye) 1922- .... **CLC 8, 62**
See also CA 1-4R; CAAS 1; CANR 2, 72;
CN 7; DLB 2, 143

Bourne, Randolph S(illiman)
1886-1918 .... **TCLC 16**
See also AMW; CA 117; 155; DLB 63

Bova, Ben(jamin William) 1932- ...... **CLC 45**
See also AAYA 16; CA 5-8R; CAAS 18;
CANR 11, 56, 94; CLR 3; DLBY 1981;
INT CANR-11; MAICYA 1, 2; MTCW 1;
SATA 6, 68; SFW 4

Bowen, Elizabeth (Dorothea Cole)
1899-1973 . **CLC 1, 3, 6, 11, 15, 22, 118;
SSC 3, 28**
See also BRWS 2; CA 17-18; 41-44R;
CANR 35, 105; CAP 2; CDBLB 1945-
1960; DA3; DAM NOV; DLB 15, 162;
EXPS; FW; HGG; MTCW 1, 2; NFS 13;
RGSF 2; SSFS 5; SUFW; WLIT 4

Bowering, George 1935- .... **CLC 15, 47**
See also CA 21-24R; CAAS 16; CANR 10;
CP 7; DLB 53

Bowering, Marilyn R(uthe) 1949- .... **CLC 32**
See also CA 101; CANR 49; CP 7; CWP

Bowers, Edgar 1924-2000 .... **CLC 9**
See also CA 5-8R; 188; CANR 24; CP 7;
CSW; DLB 5

Bowie, David .... **CLC 17**
See also Jones, David Robert

Bowles, Jane (Sydney) 1917-1973 ..... **CLC 3,
68**
See also CA 19-20; 41-44R; CAP 2

Bowles, Paul (Frederick) 1910-1999 . **CLC 1,
2, 19, 53; SSC 3**
See also AMWS 4; CA 1-4R; 186; CAAS
1; CANR 1, 19, 50, 75; CN 7; DA3; DLB
5, 6, 218; MTCW 1, 2; RGAL 4

Bowles, William Lisle 1762-1850 . **NCLC 103**
See also DLB 93

Box, Edgar
See Vidal, Gore
See also GLL 1

Boyd, James 1888-1944 .... **TCLC 115**
See also CA 186; DLB 9; DLBD 16; RGAL
4; RHW

Boyd, Nancy
See Millay, Edna St. Vincent
See also GLL 1

Boyd, Thomas (Alexander)
1898-1935 .... **TCLC 111**
See also CA 111; 183; DLB 9; DLBD 16

Boyd, William 1952- .... **CLC 28, 53, 70**
See also CA 114; 120; CANR 51, 71; CN
7; DLB 231

Boyle, Kay 1902-1992 .... **CLC 1, 5, 19, 58,
121; SSC 5**
See also CA 13-16R; 140; CAAS 1; CANR
29, 61; DLB 4, 9, 48, 86; DLBY 1993;
MTCW 1, 2; RGAL 4; RGSF 2; SSFS 10,
13, 14

Boyle, Mark
See Kienzle, William X(avier)

Boyle, Patrick 1905-1982 .... **CLC 19**
See also CA 127

Boyle, T. C.
See Boyle, T(homas) Coraghessan
See also AMWS 8

Boyle, T(homas) Coraghessan
1948- .... **CLC 36, 55, 90; SSC 16**
See also Boyle, T. C.
See also BEST 90:4; BPFB 1; CA 120;
CANR 44, 76, 89; CN 7; CPW; DA3;
DAM POP; DLB 218; DLBY 1986;
MTCW 2; SSFS 13

Boz
See Dickens, Charles (John Huffam)

Brackenridge, Hugh Henry
1748-1816 .... **NCLC 7**
See also DLB 11, 37; RGAL 4

Bradbury, Edward P.
See Moorcock, Michael (John)
See also MTCW 2

Bradbury, Malcolm (Stanley)
1932-2000 .... **CLC 32, 61**
See also CA 1-4R; CANR 1, 33, 91, 98;
CN 7; DA3; DAM NOV; DLB 14, 207;
MTCW 1, 2

Bradbury, Ray (Douglas) 1920- .... **CLC 1, 3,
10, 15, 42, 98; SSC 29, 53; WLC**
See also AAYA 15; AITN 1, 2; AMWS 4;
BPFB 1; BYA 4, 5, 11; CA 1-4R; CANR
2, 30, 75; CDALB 1968-1988; CN 7;
CPW; DA; DA3; DAB; DAC; DAM MST,
NOV, POP; DLB 2, 8; EXPN; EXPS;
HGG; LAIT 3, 5; MTCW 1, 2; NFS 1;
RGAL 4; RGSF 2; SATA 11, 64, 123;
SCFW 2; SFW 4; SSFS 1; SUFW; YAW

Braddon, Mary Elizabeth
1837-1915 .... **TCLC 111**
See also Aunt Belinda
See also CA 108; 179; CMW 4; DLB 18,
70, 156; HGG

Bradford, Gamaliel 1863-1932 .... **TCLC 36**
See also CA 160; DLB 17

Bradford, William 1590-1657 .... **LC 64**
See also DLB 24, 30; RGAL 4

Bradley, David (Henry), Jr. 1950- ... **CLC 23, 118; BLC 1**
See also BW 1, 3; CA 104; CANR 26, 81; CN 7; DAM MULT; DLB 33

Bradley, John Ed(mund, Jr.) 1958- . **CLC 55**
See also CA 139; CANR 99; CN 7; CSW

Bradley, Marion Zimmer
1930-1999 .... **CLC 30**
See also Chapman, Lee; Dexter, John; Gardner, Miriam; Ives, Morgan; Rivers, Elfrida
See also AAYA 40; BPFB 1; CA 57-60; 185; CAAS 10; CANR 7, 31, 51, 75, 107; CPW; DA3; DAM POP; DLB 8; FANT; FW; MTCW 1, 2; SATA 90; SATA-Obit 116; SFW 4; YAW

Bradshaw, John 1933- .... **CLC 70**
See also CA 138; CANR 61

Bradstreet, Anne 1612(?)-1672 ...... **LC 4, 30; PC 10**
See also AMWS 1; CDALB 1640-1865; DA; DA3; DAC; DAM MST, POET; DLB 24; EXPP; FW; PFS 6; RGAL 4; WP

Brady, Joan 1939- .... **CLC 86**
See also CA 141

Bragg, Melvyn 1939- .... **CLC 10**
See also BEST 89:3; CA 57-60; CANR 10, 48, 89; CN 7; DLB 14; RHW

Brahe, Tycho 1546-1601 .... **LC 45**

Braine, John (Gerard) 1922-1986 . **CLC 1, 3, 41**
See also CA 1-4R; 120; CANR 1, 33; CDBLB 1945-1960; DLB 15; DLBY 1986; MTCW 1

Bramah, Ernest 1868-1942 .... **TCLC 72**
See also CA 156; CMW 4; DLB 70; FANT

Brammer, William 1930(?)-1978 ...... **CLC 31**
See also CA 77-80

Brancati, Vitaliano 1907-1954 .... **TCLC 12**
See also CA 109

Brancato, Robin F(idler) 1936- .... **CLC 35**
See also AAYA 9; BYA 6; CA 69-72; CANR 11, 45; CLR 32; JRDA; MAICYA 2; MAICYAS 1; SAAS 9; SATA 97; WYA; YAW

Brand, Max
See Faust, Frederick (Schiller)
See also BPFB 1; TCWW 2

Brand, Millen 1906-1980 .... **CLC 7**
See also CA 21-24R; 97-100; CANR 72

Branden, Barbara .... **CLC 44**
See also CA 148

Brandes, Georg (Morris Cohen)
1842-1927 .... **TCLC 10**
See also CA 105; 189

Brandys, Kazimierz 1916-2000 .... **CLC 62**

Branley, Franklyn M(ansfield)
1915- .... **CLC 21**
See also CA 33-36R; CANR 14, 39; CLR 13; MAICYA 1, 2; SAAS 16; SATA 4, 68

Brathwaite, Edward Kamau 1930- . **CLC 11; BLCS**
See also BW 2, 3; CA 25-28R; CANR 11, 26, 47, 107; CDWLB 3; CP 7; DAM POET; DLB 125

Brathwaite, Kamau
See Brathwaite, Edward Kamau

Brautigan, Richard (Gary)
1935-1984 ..... **CLC 1, 3, 5, 9, 12, 34, 42**
See also BPFB 1; CA 53-56; 113; CANR 34; DA3; DAM NOV; DLB 2, 5, 206; DLBY 1980, 1984; FANT; MTCW 1; RGAL 4; SATA 56

Brave Bird, Mary
See Crow Dog, Mary (Ellen)
See also NNAL

Braverman, Kate 1950- .... **CLC 67**
See also CA 89-92

Brecht, (Eugen) Bertolt (Friedrich)
1898-1956 ..... **TCLC 1, 6, 13, 35; DC 3; WLC**
See also CA 104; 133; CANR 62; CDWLB 2; DA; DA3; DAB; DAC; DAM DRAM, MST; DFS 4, 5, 9; DLB 56, 124; EW 11; IDTP; MTCW 1, 2; RGWL 2

Brecht, Eugen Berthold Friedrich
See Brecht, (Eugen) Bertolt (Friedrich)

Bremer, Fredrika 1801-1865 .... **NCLC 11**
See also DLB 254

Brennan, Christopher John
1870-1932 .... **TCLC 17**
See also CA 117; 188; DLB 230

Brennan, Maeve 1917-1993 .... **CLC 5**
See also CA 81-84; CANR 72, 100

Brent, Linda
See Jacobs, Harriet A(nn)

Brentano, Clemens (Maria)
1778-1842 .... **NCLC 1**
See also DLB 90; RGWL 2

Brent of Bin Bin
See Franklin, (Stella Maria Sarah) Miles (Lampe)

Brenton, Howard 1942- .... **CLC 31**
See also CA 69-72; CANR 33, 67; CBD; CD 5; DLB 13; MTCW 1

Breslin, James 1930-
See Breslin, Jimmy
See also CA 73-76; CANR 31, 75; DAM NOV; MTCW 1, 2

Breslin, Jimmy .... **CLC 4, 43**
See also Breslin, James
See also AITN 1; DLB 185; MTCW 2

Bresson, Robert 1901(?)-1999 .... **CLC 16**
See also CA 110; 187; CANR 49

Breton, Andre 1896-1966 .. **CLC 2, 9, 15, 54; PC 15**
See also CA 19-20; 25-28R; CANR 40, 60; CAP 2; DLB 65, 258; EW 11; GFL 1789 to the Present; MTCW 1, 2; RGWL 2; WP

Breytenbach, Breyten 1939(?)- .. **CLC 23, 37, 126**
See also CA 113; 129; CANR 61; CWW 2; DAM POET; DLB 225

Bridgers, Sue Ellen 1942- .... **CLC 26**
See also AAYA 8; BYA 7, 8; CA 65-68; CANR 11, 36; CLR 18; DLB 52; JRDA; MAICYA 1, 2; SAAS 1; SATA 22, 90; SATA-Essay 109; WYA; YAW

Bridges, Robert (Seymour)
1844-1930 .... **TCLC 1; PC 28**
See also BRW 6; CA 104; 152; CDBLB 1890-1914; DAM POET; DLB 19, 98

Bridie, James .... **TCLC 3**
See also Mavor, Osborne Henry
See also DLB 10

Brin, David 1950- .... **CLC 34**
See also AAYA 21; CA 102; CANR 24, 70; INT CANR-24; SATA 65; SCFW 2; SFW 4

Brink, Andre (Philippus) 1935- . **CLC 18, 36, 106**
See also AFW; BRWS 6; CA 104; CANR 39, 62, 109; CN 7; DLB 225; INT CA-103; MTCW 1, 2; WLIT 2

Brinsmead, H. F(ay)
See Brinsmead, H(esba) F(ay)

Brinsmead, H. F.
See Brinsmead, H(esba) F(ay)

Brinsmead, H(esba) F(ay) 1922- ...... **CLC 21**
See also CA 21-24R; CANR 10; CLR 47; CWRI 5; MAICYA 1, 2; SAAS 5; SATA 18, 78

Brittain, Vera (Mary) 1893(?)-1970 . **CLC 23**
See also CA 13-16; 25-28R; CANR 58; CAP 1; DLB 191; FW; MTCW 1, 2

Broch, Hermann 1886-1951 .... **TCLC 20**
See also CA 117; CDWLB 2; DLB 85, 124; EW 10; RGWL 2

Brock, Rose
See Hansen, Joseph
See also GLL 1

Brod, Max 1884-1968 .... **TCLC 115**
See also CA 5-8R; 25-28R; CANR 7; DLB 81

Brodkey, Harold (Roy) 1930-1996 ... **CLC 56**
See also CA 111; 151; CANR 71; CN 7; DLB 130

Brodskii, Iosif
See Brodsky, Joseph
See also RGWL 2

Brodsky, Iosif Alexandrovich 1940-1996
See Brodsky, Joseph
See also AITN 1; CA 41-44R; 151; CANR 37, 106; DA3; DAM POET; MTCW 1, 2

Brodsky, Joseph . **CLC 4, 6, 13, 36, 100; PC 9**
See also Brodsky, Iosif Alexandrovich
See also AMWS 8; CWW 2; MTCW 1

Brodsky, Michael (Mark) 1948- .... **CLC 19**
See also CA 102; CANR 18, 41, 58; DLB 244

Brodzki, Bella ed. .... **CLC 65**

Brome, Richard 1590(?)-1652 .... **LC 61**
See also DLB 58

Bromell, Henry 1947- .... **CLC 5**
See also CA 53-56; CANR 9

Bromfield, Louis (Brucker)
1896-1956 .... **TCLC 11**
See also CA 107; 155; DLB 4, 9, 86; RGAL 4; RHW

Broner, E(sther) M(asserman)
1930- .... **CLC 19**
See also CA 17-20R; CANR 8, 25, 72; CN 7; DLB 28

Bronk, William (M.) 1918-1999 .... **CLC 10**
See also CA 89-92; 177; CANR 23; CP 7; DLB 165

Bronstein, Lev Davidovich
See Trotsky, Leon

Bronte, Anne 1820-1849 ..... **NCLC 4, 71, 102**
See also BRW 5; BRWR 1; DA3; DLB 21, 199

Bronte, (Patrick) Branwell
1817-1848 .... **NCLC 109**

Bronte, Charlotte 1816-1855 ...... **NCLC 3, 8, 33, 58, 105; WLC**
See also AAYA 17; BRW 5; BRWR 1; BYA 2; CDBLB 1832-1890; DA; DA3; DAB; DAC; DAM MST, NOV; DLB 21, 159, 199; EXPN; LAIT 2; NFS 4; WLIT 4

Bronte, Emily (Jane) 1818-1848 ... **NCLC 16, 35; PC 8; WLC**
See also AAYA 17; BPFB 1; BRW 5; BRWR 1; BYA 3; CDBLB 1832-1890; DA; DA3; DAB; DAC; DAM MST, NOV, POET; DLB 21, 32, 199; EXPN; LAIT 1; WLIT 3

Brontes
See Bronte, Anne; Bronte, Charlotte; Bronte, Emily (Jane)

Brooke, Frances 1724-1789 .... **LC 6, 48**
See also DLB 39, 99

Brooke, Henry 1703(?)-1783 .... **LC 1**
See also DLB 39

Brooke, Rupert (Chawner)
1887-1915 ..... **TCLC 2, 7; PC 24; WLC**
See also BRWS 3; CA 104; 132; CANR 61; CDBLB 1914-1945; DA; DAB; DAC; DAM MST, POET; DLB 19, 216; EXPP; GLL 2; MTCW 1, 2; PFS 7

Brooke-Haven, P.
See Wodehouse, P(elham) G(renville)

Brooke-Rose, Christine 1926(?)- ...... **CLC 40**
See also BRWS 4; CA 13-16R; CANR 58;
CN 7; DLB 14, 231; SFW 4

Brookner, Anita 1928- .. **CLC 32, 34, 51, 136**
See also BRWS 4; CA 114; 120; CANR 37,
56, 87; CN 7; CPW; DA3; DAB; DAM
POP; DLB 194; DLBY 1987; MTCW 1,
2

Brooks, Cleanth 1906-1994 . **CLC 24, 86, 110**
See also CA 17-20R; 145; CANR 33, 35;
CSW; DLB 63; DLBY 1994; INT CANR-
35; MTCW 1, 2

Brooks, George
See Baum, L(yman) Frank

Brooks, Gwendolyn (Elizabeth)
1917-2000 .. **CLC 1, 2, 4, 5, 15, 49, 125;**
BLC 1; PC 7; WLC
See also AAYA 20; AFAW 1, 2; AITN 1;
AMWS 3; BW 2, 3; CA 1-4R; 190; CANR
1, 27, 52, 75; CDALB 1941-1968; CLR
27; CP 7; CWP; DA; DA3; DAC; DAM
MST, MULT, POET; DLB 5, 76, 165;
EXPP; MAWW; MTCW 1, 2; PFS 1,
4, 6; RGAL 4; SATA 6; SATA-Obit 123;
WP

Brooks, Mel .... **CLC 12**
See also Kaminsky, Melvin
See also AAYA 13; DLB 26

Brooks, Peter (Preston) 1938- .... **CLC 34**
See also CA 45-48; CANR 1, 107

Brooks, Van Wyck 1886-1963 .... **CLC 29**
See also AMW; CA 1-4R; CANR 6; DLB
45, 63, 103

Brophy, Brigid (Antonia)
1929-1995 .... **CLC 6, 11, 29, 105**
See also CA 5-8R; 149; CAAS 4; CANR
25, 53; CBD; CN 7; CWD; DA3; DLB
14; MTCW 1, 2

Brosman, Catharine Savage 1934- .... **CLC 9**
See also CA 61-64; CANR 21, 46

Brossard, Nicole 1943- .... **CLC 115**
See also CA 122; CAAS 16; CCA 1; CWP;
CWW 2; DLB 53; FW; GLL 2

Brother Antoninus
See Everson, William (Oliver)

The Brothers Quay
See Quay, Stephen; Quay, Timothy

Broughton, T(homas) Alan 1936- ..... **CLC 19**
See also CA 45-48; CANR 2, 23, 48

Broumas, Olga 1949- .... **CLC 10, 73**
See also CA 85-88; CANR 20, 69; CP 7;
CWP; GLL 2

Broun, Heywood 1888-1939 .... **TCLC 104**
See also DLB 29, 171

Brown, Alan 1950- .... **CLC 99**
See also CA 156

Brown, Charles Brockden
1771-1810 .... **NCLC 22, 74**
See also AMWS 1; CDALB 1640-1865;
DLB 37, 59, 73; FW; HGG; RGAL 4

Brown, Christy 1932-1981 .... **CLC 63**
See also BYA 13; CA 105; 104; CANR 72;
DLB 14

Brown, Claude 1937-2002 ... **CLC 30; BLC 1**
See also AAYA 7; BW 1, 3; CA 73-76;
CANR 81; DAM MULT

Brown, Dee (Alexander) 1908- ... **CLC 18, 47**
See also AAYA 30; CA 13-16R; CAAS 6;
CANR 11, 45, 60; CPW; CSW; DA3;
DAM POP; DLBY 1980; LAIT 2; MTCW
1, 2; SATA 5, 110; TCWW 2

Brown, George
See Wertmueller, Lina

Brown, George Douglas
1869-1902 .... **TCLC 28**
See also Douglas, George
See also CA 162

Brown, George Mackay 1921-1996 ... **CLC 5,**
48, 100
See also BRWS 6; CA 21-24R; 151; CAAS
6; CANR 12, 37, 67; CN 7; CP 7; DLB
14, 27, 139; MTCW 1; RGSF 2; SATA 35

Brown, (William) Larry 1951- .... **CLC 73**
See also CA 130; 134; CSW; DLB 234; INT
133

Brown, Moses
See Barrett, William (Christopher)

Brown, Rita Mae 1944- .... **CLC 18, 43, 79**
See also BPFB 1; CA 45-48; CANR 2, 11,
35, 62, 95; CN 7; CPW; CSW; DA3;
DAM NOV, POP; FW; INT CANR-11;
MTCW 1, 2; NFS 9; RGAL 4

Brown, Roderick (Langmere) Haig-
See Haig-Brown, Roderick (Langmere)

Brown, Rosellen 1939- .... **CLC 32**
See also CA 77-80; CAAS 10; CANR 14,
44, 98; CN 7

Brown, Sterling Allen 1901-1989 ...... **CLC 1,**
23, 59; BLC 1
See also AFAW 1, 2; BW 1, 3; CA 85-88;
127; CANR 26; DA3; DAM MULT,
POET; DLB 48, 51, 63; MTCW 1, 2;
RGAL 4; WP

Brown, Will
See Ainsworth, William Harrison

Brown, William Wells 1815-1884 ... **NCLC 2,**
89; BLC 1; DC 1
See also DAM MULT; DLB 3, 50, 183,
248; RGAL 4

Browne, (Clyde) Jackson 1948(?)- ... **CLC 21**
See also CA 120

Browning, Elizabeth Barrett
1806-1861 ... **NCLC 1, 16, 61, 66; PC 6;**
WLC
See also BRW 4; CDBLB 1832-1890; DA;
DA3; DAB; DAC; DAM MST, POET;
DLB 32, 199; EXPP; PAB; PFS 2; WLIT
4; WP

Browning, Robert 1812-1889 . **NCLC 19, 79;**
PC 2; WLCS
See also BRW 4; BRWR 2; CDBLB 1832-
1890; DA; DA3; DAB; DAC; DAM MST,
POET; DLB 32, 163; EXPP; PAB; PFS 1;
RGEL 2; TEA; WLIT 4; WP; YABC 1

Browning, Tod 1882-1962 .... **CLC 16**
See also CA 141; 117

Brownmiller, Susan 1935- .... **CLC 159**
See also CA 103; CANR 35, 75; DAM
NOV; FW; MTCW 1, 2

Brownson, Orestes Augustus
1803-1876 .... **NCLC 50**
See also DLB 1, 59, 73, 243

Bruccoli, Matthew J(oseph) 1931- ... **CLC 34**
See also CA 9-12R; CANR 7, 87; DLB 103

Bruce, Lenny .... **CLC 21**
See also Schneider, Leonard Alfred

Bruin, John
See Brutus, Dennis

Brulard, Henri
See Stendhal

Brulls, Christian
See Simenon, Georges (Jacques Christian)

Brunner, John (Kilian Houston)
1934-1995 .... **CLC 8, 10**
See also CA 1-4R; 149; CAAS 8; CANR 2,
37; CPW; DAM POP; MTCW 1, 2; SCFW
2; SFW 4

Bruno, Giordano 1548-1600 .... **LC 27**
See also RGWL 2

Brutus, Dennis 1924- ... **CLC 43; BLC 1; PC**
24
See also AFW; BW 2, 3; CA 49-52; CAAS
14; CANR 2, 27, 42, 81; CDWLB 3; CP
7; DAM MULT, POET; DLB 117, 225

Bryan, C(ourtlandt) D(ixon) B(arnes)
1936- .... **CLC 29**
See also CA 73-76; CANR 13, 68; DLB
185; INT CANR-13

Bryan, Michael
See Moore, Brian
See also CCA 1

Bryan, William Jennings
1860-1925 .... **TCLC 99**

Bryant, William Cullen 1794-1878 . **NCLC 6,**
46; PC 20
See also AMWS 1; CDALB 1640-1865;
DA; DAB; DAC; DAM MST, POET;
DLB 3, 43, 59, 189, 250; EXPP; PAB;
RGAL 4

Bryusov, Valery Yakovlevich
1873-1924 .... **TCLC 10**
See also CA 107; 155; SFW 4

Buchan, John 1875-1940 .... **TCLC 41**
See also CA 108; 145; CMW 4; DAB;
DAM POP; DLB 34, 70, 156; HGG;
MSW; MTCW 1; RGEL 2; RHW; YABC
2

Buchanan, George 1506-1582 .... **LC 4**
See also DLB 132

Buchanan, Robert 1841-1901 .... **TCLC 107**
See also CA 179; DLB 18, 35

Buchheim, Lothar-Guenther 1918- .... **CLC 6**
See also CA 85-88

Buchner, (Karl) Georg 1813-1837 . **NCLC 26**
See also CDWLB 2; DLB 133; EW 6;
RGSF 2; RGWL 2

Buchwald, Art(hur) 1925- .... **CLC 33**
See also AITN 1; CA 5-8R; CANR 21, 67,
107; MTCW 1, 2; SATA 10

Buck, Pearl S(ydenstricker)
1892-1973 .... **CLC 7, 11, 18, 127**
See also AAYA 42; AITN 1; AMWS 2;
BPFB 1; CA 1-4R; 41-44R; CANR 1, 34;
CDALBS; DA; DA3; DAB; DAC; DAM
MST, NOV; DLB 9, 102; LAIT 3; MTCW
1, 2; RGAL 4; RHW; SATA 1, 25

Buckler, Ernest 1908-1984 .... **CLC 13**
See also CA 11-12; 114; CAP 1; CCA 1;
DAC; DAM MST; DLB 68; SATA 47

Buckley, Vincent (Thomas)
1925-1988 .... **CLC 57**
See also CA 101

Buckley, William F(rank), Jr. 1925- . **CLC 7,**
18, 37
See also AITN 1; BPFB 1; CA 1-4R; CANR
1, 24, 53, 93; CMW 4; CPW; DA3; DAM
POP; DLB 137; DLBY 1980; INT CANR-
24; MTCW 1, 2; TUS

Buechner, (Carl) Frederick 1926- . **CLC 2, 4,**
6, 9
See also BPFB 1; CA 13-16R; CANR 11,
39, 64; CN 7; DAM NOV; DLBY 1980;
INT CANR-11; MTCW 1, 2

Buell, John (Edward) 1927- .... **CLC 10**
See also CA 1-4R; CANR 71; DLB 53

Buero Vallejo, Antonio 1916-2000 ... **CLC 15,**
46, 139
See also CA 106; 189; CANR 24, 49, 75;
DFS 11; HW 1; MTCW 1, 2

Bufalino, Gesualdo 1920(?)-1990 ...... **CLC 74**
See also CWW 2; DLB 196

Bugayev, Boris Nikolayevich
1880-1934 .... **TCLC 7; PC 11**
See also Bely, Andrey; Belyi, Andrei
See also CA 104; 165; MTCW 1

Bukowski, Charles 1920-1994 ... **CLC 2, 5, 9,**
41, 82, 108; PC 18; SSC 45
See also CA 17-20R; 144; CANR 40, 62,
105; CPW; DA3; DAM NOV, POET;
DLB 5, 130, 169; MTCW 1, 2

Bulgakov, Mikhail (Afanas'evich)
1891-1940 .... **TCLC 2, 16; SSC 18**
See also BPFB 1; CA 105; 152; DAM DRAM, NOV; NFS 8; RGSF 2; RGWL 2; SFW 4

Bulgya, Alexander Alexandrovich
1901-1956 .... **TCLC 53**
See also Fadeyev, Alexander
See also CA 117; 181

Bullins, Ed 1935- ... **CLC 1, 5, 7; BLC 1; DC 6**
See also BW 2, 3; CA 49-52; CAAS 16; CAD; CANR 24, 46, 73; CD 5; DAM DRAM, MULT; DLB 7, 38, 249; MTCW 1, 2; RGAL 4

Bulwer-Lytton, Edward (George Earle Lytton) 1803-1873 .... **NCLC 1, 45**
See also DLB 21; RGEL 2; SFW 4; SUFW

Bunin, Ivan Alexeyevich
1870-1953 .... **TCLC 6; SSC 5**
See also CA 104; RGSF 2; RGWL 2

Bunting, Basil 1900-1985 ...... **CLC 10, 39, 47**
See also BRWS 7; CA 53-56; 115; CANR 7; DAM POET; DLB 20; RGEL 2

Bunuel, Luis 1900-1983 ... **CLC 16, 80; HLC 1**
See also CA 101; 110; CANR 32, 77; DAM MULT; HW 1

Bunyan, John 1628-1688 ..... **LC 4, 69; WLC**
See also BRW 2; BYA 5; CDBLB 1660-1789; DA; DAB; DAC; DAM MST; DLB 39; RGEL 2; WCH; WLIT 3

Buravsky, Alexandr .... **CLC 59**

Burckhardt, Jacob (Christoph)
1818-1897 .... **NCLC 49**
See also EW 6

Burford, Eleanor
See Hibbert, Eleanor Alice Burford

Burgess, Anthony . **CLC 1, 2, 4, 5, 8, 10, 13, 15, 22, 40, 62, 81, 94**
See also Wilson, John (Anthony) Burgess
See also AAYA 25; AITN 1; BRWS 1; CDBLB 1960 to Present; DAB; DLB 14, 194; DLBY 1998; MTCW 1; RGEL 2; RHW; SFW 4; YAW

Burke, Edmund 1729(?)-1797 .... **LC 7, 36; WLC**
See also BRW 3; DA; DA3; DAB; DAC; DAM MST; DLB 104, 252; RGEL 2

Burke, Kenneth (Duva) 1897-1993 ... **CLC 2, 24**
See also AMW; CA 5-8R; 143; CANR 39, 74; DLB 45, 63; MTCW 1, 2; RGAL 4

Burke, Leda
See Garnett, David

Burke, Ralph
See Silverberg, Robert

Burke, Thomas 1886-1945 .... **TCLC 63**
See also CA 113; 155; CMW 4; DLB 197

Burney, Fanny 1752-1840 .... **NCLC 12, 54, 107**
See also BRWS 3; DLB 39; RGEL 2

Burney, Frances
See Burney, Fanny

Burns, Robert 1759-1796 ... **LC 3, 29, 40; PC 6; WLC**
See also BRW 3; CDBLB 1789-1832; DA; DA3; DAB; DAC; DAM MST, POET; DLB 109; EXPP; PAB; RGEL 2; WP

Burns, Tex
See L'Amour, Louis (Dearborn)
See also TCWW 2

Burnshaw, Stanley 1906- .... **CLC 3, 13, 44**
See also CA 9-12R; CP 7; DLB 48; DLBY 1997

Burr, Anne 1937- .... **CLC 6**
See also CA 25-28R

Burroughs, Edgar Rice 1875-1950 . **TCLC 2, 32**
See also AAYA 11; BPFB 1; BYA 4, 9; CA 104; 132; DA3; DAM NOV; DLB 8; FANT; MTCW 1, 2; RGAL 4; SATA 41; SCFW 2; SFW 4; YAW

Burroughs, William S(eward)
1914-1997 .. **CLC 1, 2, 5, 15, 22, 42, 75, 109; WLC**
See also Lee, William; Lee, Willy
See also AITN 2; AMWS 3; BPFB 1; CA 9-12R; 160; CANR 20, 52, 104; CN 7; CPW; DA; DA3; DAB; DAC; DAM MST, NOV, POP; DLB 2, 8, 16, 152, 237; DLBY 1981, 1997; HGG; MTCW 1, 2; RGAL 4; SFW 4; TCLC 121

Burton, Sir Richard F(rancis)
1821-1890 .... **NCLC 42**
See also DLB 55, 166, 184

Burton, Robert 1577-1640 .... **LC 74**
See also DLB 151; RGEL 2

Busch, Frederick 1941- ... **CLC 7, 10, 18, 47**
See also CA 33-36R; CAAS 1; CANR 45, 73, 92; CN 7; DLB 6, 218

Bush, Ronald 1946- .... **CLC 34**
See also CA 136

Bustos, F(rancisco)
See Borges, Jorge Luis

Bustos Domecq, H(onorio)
See Bioy Casares, Adolfo; Borges, Jorge Luis

Butler, Octavia E(stelle) 1947- .... **CLC 38, 121; BLCS**
See also AAYA 18; AFAW 2; BPFB 1; BW 2, 3; CA 73-76; CANR 12, 24, 38, 73; CLR 65; CPW; DA3; DAM MULT, POP; DLB 33; MTCW 1, 2; NFS 8; SATA 84; SCFW 2; SFW 4; SSFS 6; YAW

Butler, Robert Olen, (Jr.) 1945- .... **CLC 81**
See also BPFB 1; CA 112; CANR 66; CSW; DAM POP; DLB 173; INT CA-112; MTCW 1; SSFS 11

Butler, Samuel 1612-1680 .... **LC 16, 43**
See also DLB 101, 126; RGEL 2

Butler, Samuel 1835-1902 .... **TCLC 1, 33; WLC**
See also BRWS 2; CA 143; CDBLB 1890-1914; DA; DA3; DAB; DAC; DAM MST, NOV; DLB 18, 57, 174; RGEL 2; SFW 4; TEA

Butler, Walter C.
See Faust, Frederick (Schiller)

Butor, Michel (Marie Francois)
1926- .... **CLC 1, 3, 8, 11, 15**
See also CA 9-12R; CANR 33, 66; DLB 83; EW 13; GFL 1789 to the Present; MTCW 1, 2

Butts, Mary 1890(?)-1937 .... **TCLC 77**
See also CA 148; DLB 240

Buxton, Ralph
See Silverstein, Alvin; Silverstein, Virginia B(arbara Opshelor)

Buzo, Alexander (John) 1944- .... **CLC 61**
See also CA 97-100; CANR 17, 39, 69; CD 5

Buzzati, Dino 1906-1972 .... **CLC 36**
See also CA 160; 33-36R; DLB 177; RGWL 2; SFW 4

Byars, Betsy (Cromer) 1928- .... **CLC 35**
See also AAYA 19; BYA 3; CA 33-36R, 183; CAAE 183; CANR 18, 36, 57, 102; CLR 1, 16, 72; DLB 52; INT CANR-18; JRDA; MAICYA 1, 2; MAICYAS 1; MTCW 1; SAAS 1; SATA 4, 46, 80; SATA-Essay 108; WYA; YAW

Byatt, A(ntonia) S(usan Drabble)
1936- .... **CLC 19, 65, 136**
See also BPFB 1; BRWS 4; CA 13-16R; CANR 13, 33, 50, 75, 96; DA3; DAM NOV, POP; DLB 14, 194; MTCW 1, 2; RGSF 2; RHW

Byrne, David 1952- .... **CLC 26**
See also CA 127

Byrne, John Keyes 1926-
See Leonard, Hugh
See also CA 102; CANR 78; INT CA-102

Byron, George Gordon (Noel)
1788-1824 ..... **NCLC 2, 12, 109; PC 16; WLC**
See also BRW 4; CDBLB 1789-1832; DA; DA3; DAB; DAC; DAM MST, POET; DLB 96, 110; EXPP; PAB; PFS 1, 14; RGEL 2; WLIT 3; WP

Byron, Robert 1905-1941 .... **TCLC 67**
See also CA 160; DLB 195

C. 3. 3.
See Wilde, Oscar (Fingal O'Flahertie Wills)

Caballero, Fernan 1796-1877 .... **NCLC 10**

Cabell, Branch
See Cabell, James Branch

Cabell, James Branch 1879-1958 .... **TCLC 6**
See also CA 105; 152; DLB 9, 78; FANT; MTCW 1; RGAL 4; SUFW

Cabeza de Vaca, Alvar Nunez
1490-1557(?) .... **LC 61**

Cable, George Washington
1844-1925 .... **TCLC 4; SSC 4**
See also CA 104; 155; DLB 12, 74; DLBD 13; RGAL 4

Cabral de Melo Neto, Joao
1920-1999 .... **CLC 76**
See also CA 151; DAM MULT; LAW; LAWS 1

Cabrera Infante, G(uillermo) 1929- . **CLC 5, 25, 45, 120; HLC 1; SSC 39**
See also CA 85-88; CANR 29, 65; CDWLB 3; DA3; DAM MULT; DLB 113; HW 1, 2; LAW; LAWS 1; MTCW 1, 2; RGSF 2; WLIT 1

Cade, Toni
See Bambara, Toni Cade

Cadmus and Harmonia
See Buchan, John

Caedmon fl. 658-680 .... **CMLC 7**
See also DLB 146

Caeiro, Alberto
See Pessoa, Fernando (Antonio Nogueira)

Caesar, Julius .... **CMLC 47**
See also Julius Caesar
See also AW 1; RGWL 2

Cage, John (Milton, Jr.) 1912-1992 . **CLC 41**
See also CA 13-16R; 169; CANR 9, 78; DLB 193; INT CANR-9

Cahan, Abraham 1860-1951 .... **TCLC 71**
See also CA 108; 154; DLB 9, 25, 28; RGAL 4

Cain, G.
See Cabrera Infante, G(uillermo)

Cain, Guillermo
See Cabrera Infante, G(uillermo)

Cain, James M(allahan) 1892-1977 .. **CLC 3, 11, 28**
See also AITN 1; BPFB 1; CA 17-20R; 73-76; CANR 8, 34, 61; CMW 4; DLB 226; MSW; MTCW 1; RGAL 4

Caine, Hall 1853-1931 .... **TCLC 97**
See also RHW

Caine, Mark
See Raphael, Frederic (Michael)

Calasso, Roberto 1941- .... **CLC 81**
See also CA 143; CANR 89

Calderon de la Barca, Pedro
1600-1681 .... **LC 23; DC 3; HLCS 1**
See also EW 2; RGWL 2

Caldwell, Erskine (Preston)
1903-1987 .... **CLC 1, 8, 14, 50, 60; SSC 19**
See also AITN 1; AMW; BPFB 1; CA 1-4R; 121; CAAS 1; CANR 2, 33; DA3; DAM NOV; DLB 9, 86; MTCW 1, 2; RGAL 4; RGSF 2; TCLC 117

Caldwell, (Janet Miriam) Taylor (Holland)
1900-1985 .... **CLC 2, 28, 39**
See also BPFB 1; CA 5-8R; 116; CANR 5;
DA3; DAM NOV, POP; DLBD 17; RHW

Calhoun, John Caldwell
1782-1850 .... **NCLC 15**
See also DLB 3, 248

Calisher, Hortense 1911- ..... **CLC 2, 4, 8, 38,**
134; SSC 15
See also CA 1-4R; CANR 1, 22, 67; CN 7;
DA3; DAM NOV; DLB 2, 218; INT
CANR-22; MTCW 1, 2; RGAL 4; RGSF
2

Callaghan, Morley Edward
1903-1990 .... **CLC 3, 14, 41, 65**
See also CA 9-12R; 132; CANR 33, 73;
DAC; DAM MST; DLB 68; MTCW 1, 2;
RGEL 2; RGSF 2

Callimachus c. 305B.C.-c.
240B.C. .... **CMLC 18**
See also AW 1; DLB 176; RGWL 2

Calvin, Jean
See Calvin, John
See also GFL Beginnings to 1789

Calvin, John 1509-1564 .... **LC 37**
See also Calvin, Jean

Calvino, Italo 1923-1985 .... **CLC 5, 8, 11, 22,**
33, 39, 73; SSC 3, 48
See also CA 85-88; 116; CANR 23, 61;
DAM NOV; DLB 196; EW 13; MTCW 1,
2; RGSF 2; RGWL 2; SFW 4; SSFS 12

Camden, William 1551-1623 .... **LC 77**
See also DLB 172

Cameron, Carey 1952- .... **CLC 59**
See also CA 135

Cameron, Peter 1959- .... **CLC 44**
See also CA 125; CANR 50; DLB 234;
GLL 2

Camoens, Luis Vaz de 1524(?)-1580
See also EW 2; HLCS 1

Camoes, Luis de 1524(?)-1580 .... **LC 62;**
HLCS 1; PC 31
See also RGWL 2

Campana, Dino 1885-1932 .... **TCLC 20**
See also CA 117; DLB 114

Campanella, Tommaso 1568-1639 .... **LC 32**
See also RGWL 2

Campbell, John W(ood, Jr.)
1910-1971 .... **CLC 32**
See also CA 21-22; 29-32R; CANR 34;
CAP 2; DLB 8; MTCW 1; SCFW; SFW 4

Campbell, Joseph 1904-1987 .... **CLC 69**
See also AAYA 3; BEST 89:2; CA 1-4R;
124; CANR 3, 28, 61, 107; DA3; MTCW
1, 2

Campbell, Maria 1940- .... **CLC 85**
See also CA 102; CANR 54; CCA 1; DAC;
NNAL

Campbell, Paul N. 1923-
See hooks, bell
See also CA 21-24R

Campbell, (John) Ramsey 1946- ..... **CLC 42;**
SSC 19
See also CA 57-60; CANR 7, 102; HGG;
INT CANR-7; SUFW

Campbell, (Ignatius) Roy (Dunnachie)
1901-1957 .... **TCLC 5**
See also AFW; CA 104; 155; DLB 20, 225;
MTCW 2; RGEL 2

Campbell, Thomas 1777-1844 .... **NCLC 19**
See also DLB 93, 144; RGEL 2

Campbell, Wilfred .... **TCLC 9**
See also Campbell, William

Campbell, William 1858(?)-1918
See Campbell, Wilfred
See also CA 106; DLB 92

Campion, Jane .... **CLC 95**
See also AAYA 33; CA 138; CANR 87

Campion, Thomas 1567-1620 .... **LC 78**
See also CDBLB Before 1660; DAM POET;
DLB 58, 172; RGEL 2

Camus, Albert 1913-1960 ...... **CLC 1, 2, 4, 9,**
11, 14, 32, 63, 69, 124; DC 2; SSC 9;
WLC
See also AAYA 36; AFW; BPFB 1; CA 89-
92; DA; DA3; DAB; DAC; DAM DRAM,
MST, NOV; DLB 72; EW 13; EXPN;
EXPS; GFL 1789 to the Present; MTCW
1, 2; NFS 6; RGSF 2; RGWL 2; SSFS 4

Canby, Vincent 1924-2000 .... **CLC 13**
See also CA 81-84; 191

Cancale
See Desnos, Robert

Canetti, Elias 1905-1994 .. **CLC 3, 14, 25, 75,**
86
See also CA 21-24R; 146; CANR 23, 61;
79; CDWLB 2; CWW 2; DA3; DLB 85,
124; EW 12; MTCW 1, 2; RGWL 2

Canfield, Dorothea F.
See Fisher, Dorothy (Frances) Canfield

Canfield, Dorothea Frances
See Fisher, Dorothy (Frances) Canfield

Canfield, Dorothy
See Fisher, Dorothy (Frances) Canfield

Canin, Ethan 1960- .... **CLC 55**
See also CA 131; 135

Cankar, Ivan 1876-1918 .... **TCLC 105**
See also CDWLB 4; DLB 147

Cannon, Curt
See Hunter, Evan

Cao, Lan 1961- .... **CLC 109**
See also CA 165

Cape, Judith
See Page, P(atricia) K(athleen)
See also CCA 1

Capek, Karel 1890-1938 .... **TCLC 6, 37; DC**
1; SSC 36; WLC
See also CA 104; 140; CDWLB 4; DA;
DA3; DAB; DAC; DAM DRAM, MST,
NOV; DFS 7, 11 !**; DLB 215; EW 10;
MTCW 1; RGSF 2; RGWL 2; SCFW 2;
SFW 4

Capote, Truman 1924-1984 . **CLC 1, 3, 8, 13,**
19, 34, 38, 58; SSC 2, 47; WLC
See also AMWS 3; BPFB 1; CA 5-8R; 113;
CANR 18, 62; CDALB 1941-1968; CPW;
DA; DA3; DAB; DAC; DAM MST, NOV,
POP; DLB 2, 185, 227; DLBY 1980,
1984; EXPS; GLL 1; LAIT 3; MTCW 1,
2; NCFS 2; RGAL 4; RGSF 2; SATA 91;
SSFS 2

Capra, Frank 1897-1991 .... **CLC 16**
See also CA 61-64; 135

Caputo, Philip 1941- .... **CLC 32**
See also CA 73-76; CANR 40; YAW

Caragiale, Ion Luca 1852-1912 ...... **TCLC 76**
See also CA 157

Card, Orson Scott 1951- .... **CLC 44, 47, 50**
See also AAYA 11, 42; BPFB 1; BYA 5, 8;
CA 102; CANR 27, 47, 73, 102, 106;
CPW; DA3; DAM POP; FANT; INT
CANR-27; MTCW 1, 2; NFS 5; SATA
83, 127; SCFW 2; SFW 4; YAW

Cardenal, Ernesto 1925- ... **CLC 31; HLC 1;**
PC 22
See also CA 49-52; CANR 2, 32, 66; CWW
2; DAM MULT, POET; HW 1, 2; LAWS
1; MTCW 1, 2; RGWL 2

Cardozo, Benjamin N(athan)
1870-1938 .... **TCLC 65**
See also CA 117; 164

Carducci, Giosue (Alessandro Giuseppe)
1835-1907 .... **TCLC 32**
See also CA 163; EW 7; RGWL 2

Carew, Thomas 1595(?)-1640 . **LC 13; PC 29**
See also BRW 2; DLB 126; PAB; RGEL 2

Carey, Ernestine Gilbreth 1908- ...... **CLC 17**
See also CA 5-8R; CANR 71; SATA 2

Carey, Peter 1943- .... **CLC 40, 55, 96**
See also CA 123; 127; CANR 53, 76; CN
7; INT CA-127; MTCW 1, 2; RGSF 2;
SATA 94

Carleton, William 1794-1869 .... **NCLC 3**
See also DLB 159; RGEL 2; RGSF 2

Carlisle, Henry (Coffin) 1926- .... **CLC 33**
See also CA 13-16R; CANR 15, 85

Carlsen, Chris
See Holdstock, Robert P.

Carlson, Ron(ald F.) 1947- .... **CLC 54**
See also CA 105; CAAE 189; CANR 27;
DLB 244

Carlyle, Thomas 1795-1881 ..... **NCLC 22, 70**
See also BRW 4; CDBLB 1789-1832; DA;
DAB; DAC; DAM MST; DLB 55, 144,
254; RGEL 2

Carman, (William) Bliss
1861-1929 .... **TCLC 7; PC 34**
See also CA 104; 152; DAC; DLB 92;
RGEL 2

Carnegie, Dale 1888-1955 .... **TCLC 53**

Carossa, Hans 1878-1956 .... **TCLC 48**
See also CA 170; DLB 66

Carpenter, Don(ald Richard)
1931-1995 .... **CLC 41**
See also CA 45-48; 149; CANR 1, 71

Carpenter, Edward 1844-1929 .... **TCLC 88**
See also CA 163; GLL 1

Carpentier (y Valmont), Alejo
1904-1980 . **CLC 8, 11, 38, 110; HLC 1;**
SSC 35
See also CA 65-68; 97-100; CANR 11, 70;
CDWLB 3; DAM MULT; DLB 113; HW
1, 2; LAW; RGSF 2; RGWL 2; WLIT 1

Carr, Caleb 1955(?)- .... **CLC 86**
See also CA 147; CANR 73; DA3

Carr, Emily 1871-1945 .... **TCLC 32**
See also CA 159; DLB 68; FW; GLL 2

Carr, John Dickson 1906-1977 .... **CLC 3**
See also Fairbairn, Roger
See also CA 49-52; 69-72; CANR 3, 33,
60; CMW 4; MSW; MTCW 1, 2

Carr, Philippa
See Hibbert, Eleanor Alice Burford

Carr, Virginia Spencer 1929- .... **CLC 34**
See also CA 61-64; DLB 111

Carrere, Emmanuel 1957- .... **CLC 89**

Carrier, Roch 1937- .... **CLC 13, 78**
See also CA 130; CANR 61; CCA 1; DAC;
DAM MST; DLB 53; SATA 105

Carroll, James P. 1943(?)- .... **CLC 38**
See also CA 81-84; CANR 73; MTCW 1

Carroll, Jim 1951- .... **CLC 35, 143**
See also AAYA 17; CA 45-48; CANR 42

Carroll, Lewis ... **NCLC 2, 53; PC 18; WLC**
See also Dodgson, Charles L(utwidge)
See also AAYA 39; BRW 5; BYA 5, 13; CD-
BLB 1832-1890; CLR 2, 18; DLB 18,
163, 178; DLBY 1998; EXPN; EXPP;
FANT; JRDA; LAIT 1; NFS 7; PFS 11;
RGEL 2; SUFW; WCH

Carroll, Paul Vincent 1900-1968 ...... **CLC 10**
See also CA 9-12R; 25-28R; DLB 10;
RGEL 2

Carruth, Hayden 1921- ..... **CLC 4, 7, 10, 18,**
84; PC 10
See also CA 9-12R; CANR 4, 38, 59; CP 7;
DLB 5, 165; INT CANR-4; MTCW 1, 2;
SATA 47

Carson, Rachel Louise 1907-1964 .... **CLC 71**
See also AMWS 9; ANW; CA 77-80; CANR
35; DA3; DAM POP; FW; LAIT 4;
MTCW 1, 2; NCFS 1; SATA 23

Carter, Angela (Olive) 1940-1992 ...... **CLC 5, 41, 76; SSC 13**
See also BRWS 3; CA 53-56; 136; CANR 12, 36, 61, 106; DA3; DLB 14, 207; EXPS; FANT; FW; MTCW 1, 2; RGSF 2; SATA 66; SATA-Obit 70; SFW 4; SSFS 4, 12; WLIT 4

Carter, Nick
See Smith, Martin Cruz

Carver, Raymond 1938-1988 ..... **CLC 22, 36, 53, 55, 126; SSC 8, 51**
See also AMWS 3; BPFB 1; CA 33-36R; 126; CANR 17, 34, 61, 103; CPW; DA3; DAM NOV; DLB 130; DLBY 1984, 1988; MTCW 1, 2; RGAL 4; RGSF 2; SSFS 3, 6, 12, 13; TCWW 2

Cary, Elizabeth, Lady Falkland 1585-1639 .... **LC 30**

Cary, (Arthur) Joyce (Lunel) 1888-1957 .... **TCLC 1, 29**
See also BRW 7; CA 104; 164; CDBLB 1914-1945; DLB 15, 100; MTCW 2; RGEL 2

Casanova de Seingalt, Giovanni Jacopo 1725-1798 .... **LC 13**

Casares, Adolfo Bioy
See Bioy Casares, Adolfo
See also RGSF 2

Casas, Bartolome de las 1474-1566
See Las Casas, Bartolome de
See also WLIT 1

Casely-Hayford, J(oseph) E(phraim) 1866-1903 .... **TCLC 24; BLC 1**
See also BW 2; CA 123; 152; DAM MULT

Casey, John (Dudley) 1939- .... **CLC 59**
See also BEST 90:2; CA 69-72; CANR 23, 100

Casey, Michael 1947- .... **CLC 2**
See also CA 65-68; CANR 109; DLB 5

Casey, Patrick
See Thurman, Wallace (Henry)

Casey, Warren (Peter) 1935-1988 .... **CLC 12**
See also CA 101; 127; INT 101

Casona, Alejandro .... **CLC 49**
See also Alvarez, Alejandro Rodriguez

Cassavetes, John 1929-1989 .... **CLC 20**
See also CA 85-88; 127; CANR 82

Cassian, Nina 1924- .... **PC 17**
See also CWP; CWW 2

Cassill, R(onald) V(erlin) 1919- ... **CLC 4, 23**
See also CA 9-12R; CAAS 1; CANR 7, 45; CN 7; DLB 6, 218

Cassiodorus, Flavius Magnus c. 490(?)-c. 583(?) .... **CMLC 43**

Cassirer, Ernst 1874-1945 .... **TCLC 61**
See also CA 157

Cassity, (Allen) Turner 1929- .... **CLC 6, 42**
See also CA 17-20R; CAAS 8; CANR 11; CSW; DLB 105

Castaneda, Carlos (Cesar Aranha) 1931(?)-1998 .... **CLC 12, 119**
See also CA 25-28R; CANR 32, 66, 105; DNFS 1; HW 1; MTCW 1

Castedo, Elena 1937- .... **CLC 65**
See also CA 132

Castedo-Ellerman, Elena
See Castedo, Elena

Castellanos, Rosario 1925-1974 .... **CLC 66; HLC 1; SSC 39**
See also CA 131; 53-56; CANR 58; CD-WLB 3; DAM MULT; DLB 113; FW; HW 1; LAW; MTCW 1; RGSF 2; RGWL 2

Castelvetro, Lodovico 1505-1571 .... **LC 12**

Castiglione, Baldassare 1478-1529 ...... **LC 12**
See also Castiglione, Baldesar
See also RGWL 2

Castiglione, Baldesar
See Castiglione, Baldassare
See also EW 2

Castillo, Ana (Hernandez Del) 1953- .... **CLC 151**
See also AAYA 42; CA 131; CANR 51, 86; CWP; DLB 122, 227; DNFS 2; FW; HW 1

Castle, Robert
See Hamilton, Edmond

Castro (Ruz), Fidel 1926(?)-
See also CA 110; 129; CANR 81; DAM MULT; HLC 1; HW 2

Castro, Guillen de 1569-1631 .... **LC 19**

Castro, Rosalia de 1837-1885 ... **NCLC 3, 78; PC 41**
See also DAM MULT

Cather, Willa (Sibert) 1873-1947 .... **TCLC 1, 11, 31, 99; SSC 2, 50; WLC**
See also AAYA 24; AMW; AMWR 1; BPFB 1; CA 104; 128; CDALB 1865-1917; DA; DA3; DAB; DAC; DAM MST, NOV; DLB 9, 54, 78, 256; DLBD 1; EXPN; EXPS; LAIT 3; MAWW; MTCW 1, 2; NFS 2; RGAL 4; RGSF 2; RHW; SATA 30; SSFS 2, 7; TCWW 2

Catherine II
See Catherine the Great
See also DLB 150

Catherine the Great 1729-1796 .... **LC 69**
See also Catherine II

Cato, Marcus Porcius 234B.C.-149B.C. .... **CMLC 21**
See also Cato the Elder

Cato the Elder
See Cato, Marcus Porcius
See also DLB 211

Catton, (Charles) Bruce 1899-1978 . **CLC 35**
See also AITN 1; CA 5-8R; 81-84; CANR 7, 74; DLB 17; SATA 2; SATA-Obit 24

Catullus c. 84B.C.-54B.C. .... **CMLC 18**
See also AW 2; CDWLB 1; DLB 211; RGWL 2

Cauldwell, Frank
See King, Francis (Henry)

Caunitz, William J. 1933-1996 .... **CLC 34**
See also BEST 89:3; CA 125; 130; 152; CANR 73; INT 130

Causley, Charles (Stanley) 1917- .... **CLC 7**
See also CA 9-12R; CANR 5, 35, 94; CLR 30; CWRI 5; DLB 27; MTCW 1; SATA 3, 66

Caute, (John) David 1936- .... **CLC 29**
See also CA 1-4R; CAAS 4; CANR 1, 33, 64; CBD; CD 5; CN 7; DAM NOV; DLB 14, 231

Cavafy, C(onstantine) P(eter) ... **TCLC 2, 7; PC 36**
See also Kavafis, Konstantinos Petrou
See also CA 148; DA3; DAM POET; EW 8; MTCW 1; RGWL 2; WP

Cavallo, Evelyn
See Spark, Muriel (Sarah)

Cavanna, Betty .... **CLC 12**
See also Harrison, Elizabeth (Allen) Cavanna
See also JRDA; MAICYA 1; SAAS 4; SATA 1, 30

Cavendish, Margaret Lucas 1623-1673 .... **LC 30**
See also DLB 131, 252; RGEL 2

Caxton, William 1421(?)-1491(?) .... **LC 17**
See also DLB 170

Cayer, D. M.
See Duffy, Maureen

Cayrol, Jean 1911- .... **CLC 11**
See also CA 89-92; DLB 83

Cela, Camilo Jose 1916-2002 .... **CLC 4, 13, 59, 122; HLC 1**
See also BEST 90:2; CA 21-24R; CAAS 10; CANR 21, 32, 76; DAM MULT; DLBY 1989; EW 13; HW 1; MTCW 1, 2; RGSF 2; RGWL 2

Celan, Paul -1970 .... **CLC 10, 19, 53, 82; PC 10**
See also Antschel, Paul
See also CDWLB 2; DLB 69; RGWL 2

Celine, Louis-Ferdinand .. **CLC 1, 3, 4, 7, 9, 15, 47, 124**
See also Destouches, Louis-Ferdinand
See also DLB 72; EW 11; GFL 1789 to the Present; RGWL 2

Cellini, Benvenuto 1500-1571 .... **LC 7**

Cendrars, Blaise .... **CLC 18, 106**
See also Sauser-Hall, Frederic
See also DLB 258; GFL 1789 to the Present; RGWL 2; WP

Centlivre, Susanna 1669(?)-1723 .... **LC 65**
See also DLB 84; RGEL 2

Cernuda (y Bidon), Luis 1902-1963 . **CLC 54**
See also CA 131; 89-92; DAM POET; DLB 134; GLL 1; HW 1; RGWL 2

Cervantes, Lorna Dee 1954- .... **PC 35**
See also CA 131; CANR 80; CWP; DLB 82; EXPP; HLCS 1; HW 1

Cervantes (Saavedra), Miguel de 1547-1616 .... **LC 6, 23; HLCS; SSC 12; WLC**
See also BYA 1, 14; DA; DAB; DAC; DAM MST, NOV; EW 2; LAIT 1; NFS 8; RGSF 2; RGWL 2

Cesaire, Aime (Fernand) 1913- . **CLC 19, 32, 112; BLC 1; PC 25**
See also BW 2, 3; CA 65-68; CANR 24, 43, 81; DA3; DAM MULT, POET; GFL 1789 to the Present; MTCW 1, 2; WP

Chabon, Michael 1963- .... **CLC 55, 149**
See also CA 139; CANR 57, 96

Chabrol, Claude 1930- .... **CLC 16**
See also CA 110

Challans, Mary 1905-1983
See Renault, Mary
See also CA 81-84; 111; CANR 74; DA3; MTCW 2; SATA 23; SATA-Obit 36

Challis, George
See Faust, Frederick (Schiller)
See also TCWW 2

Chambers, Aidan 1934- .... **CLC 35**
See also AAYA 27; CA 25-28R; CANR 12, 31, 58; JRDA; MAICYA 1, 2; SAAS 12; SATA 1, 69, 108; WYA; YAW

Chambers, James 1948-
See Cliff, Jimmy
See also CA 124

Chambers, Jessie
See Lawrence, D(avid) H(erbert Richards)
See also GLL 1

Chambers, Robert W(illiam) 1865-1933 .... **TCLC 41**
See also CA 165; DLB 202; HGG; SATA 107; SUFW

Chamisso, Adelbert von 1781-1838 .... **NCLC 82**
See also DLB 90; RGWL 2; SUFW

Chandler, Raymond (Thornton) 1888-1959 .... **TCLC 1, 7; SSC 23**
See also AAYA 25; AMWS 4; BPFB 1; CA 104; 129; CANR 60, 107; CDALB 1929-1941; CMW 4; DA3; DLB 226, 253; DLBD 6; MSW; MTCW 1, 2; RGAL 4

Chang, Eileen 1921-1995 .... **SSC 28**
See also CA 166; CWW 2

Chang, Jung 1952- .... **CLC 71**
See also CA 142

Chang Ai-Ling
See Chang, Eileen

Channing, William Ellery
1780-1842 .... **NCLC 17**
See also DLB 1, 59, 235; RGAL 4

Chao, Patricia 1955- .... **CLC 119**
See also CA 163

Chaplin, Charles Spencer
1889-1977 .... **CLC 16**
See also Chaplin, Charlie
See also CA 81-84; 73-76

Chaplin, Charlie
See Chaplin, Charles Spencer
See also DLB 44

Chapman, George 1559(?)-1634 .... **LC 22**
See also BRW 1; DAM DRAM; DLB 62,
121; RGEL 2

Chapman, Graham 1941-1989 .... **CLC 21**
See also Monty Python
See also CA 116; 129; CANR 35, 95

Chapman, John Jay 1862-1933 .... **TCLC 7**
See also CA 104; 191

Chapman, Lee
See Bradley, Marion Zimmer
See also GLL 1

Chapman, Walker
See Silverberg, Robert

Chappell, Fred (Davis) 1936- ..... **CLC 40, 78**
See also CA 5-8R; CAAE 198; CAAS 4;
CANR 8, 33, 67; CN 7; CP 7; CSW; DLB
6, 105; HGG

Char, Rene(-Emile) 1907-1988 .... **CLC 9, 11,
14, 55**
See also CA 13-16R; 124; CANR 32; DAM
POET; DLB 258; GFL 1789 to the
Present; MTCW 1, 2; RGWL 2

Charby, Jay
See Ellison, Harlan (Jay)

Chardin, Pierre Teilhard de
See Teilhard de Chardin, (Marie Joseph)
Pierre

Chariton fl. 1st cent. (?)- .... **CMLC 49**

Charlemagne 742-814 .... **CMLC 37**

Charles I 1600-1649 .... **LC 13**

Charriere, Isabelle de 1740-1805 .. **NCLC 66**

Chartier, Emile-Auguste
See Alain

Charyn, Jerome 1937- .... **CLC 5, 8, 18**
See also CA 5-8R; CAAS 1; CANR 7, 61,
101; CMW 4; CN 7; DLBY 1983; MTCW
1

Chase, Adam
See Marlowe, Stephen

Chase, Mary (Coyle) 1907-1981 .... **DC 1**
See also CA 77-80; 105; CAD; CWD; DFS
11; DLB 228; SATA 17; SATA-Obit 29

Chase, Mary Ellen 1887-1973 .... **CLC 2**
See also CA 13-16; 41-44R; CAP 1; SATA
10

Chase, Nicholas
See Hyde, Anthony
See also CCA 1

Chateaubriand, Francois Rene de
1768-1848 .... **NCLC 3**
See also DLB 119; EW 5; GFL 1789 to the
Present; RGWL 2

Chatterje, Sarat Chandra 1876-1936(?)
See Chatterji, Saratchandra
See also CA 109

Chatterji, Bankim Chandra
1838-1894 .... **NCLC 19**

Chatterji, Saratchandra .... **TCLC 13**
See also Chatterje, Sarat Chandra
See also CA 186

Chatterton, Thomas 1752-1770 .... **LC 3, 54**
See also DAM POET; DLB 109; RGEL 2

Chatwin, (Charles) Bruce
1940-1989 .... **CLC 28, 57, 59**
See also AAYA 4; BEST 90:1; BRWS 4;
CA 85-88; 127; CPW; DAM POP; DLB
194, 204

Chaucer, Daniel
See Ford, Ford Madox
See also RHW

Chaucer, Geoffrey 1340(?)-1400 .. **LC 17, 56;
PC 19; WLCS**
See also BRW 1; BRWR 2; CDBLB Before
1660; DA; DA3; DAB; DAC; DAM MST,
POET; DLB 146; LAIT 1; PAB; PFS 14;
RGEL 2; WLIT 3; WP

Chavez, Denise (Elia) 1948-
See also CA 131; CANR 56, 81; DAM
MULT; DLB 122; FW; HLC 1; HW 1, 2;
MTCW 2

Chaviaras, Strates 1935-
See Haviaras, Stratis
See also CA 105

Chayefsky, Paddy .... **CLC 23**
See also Chayefsky, Sidney
See also CAD; DLB 7, 44; DLBY 1981;
RGAL 4

Chayefsky, Sidney 1923-1981
See Chayefsky, Paddy
See also CA 9-12R; 104; CANR 18; DAM
DRAM

Chedid, Andree 1920- .... **CLC 47**
See also CA 145; CANR 95

Cheever, John 1912-1982 ..... **CLC 3, 7, 8, 11,
15, 25, 64; SSC 1, 38; WLC**
See also AMWS 1; BPFB 1; CA 5-8R; 106;
CABS 1; CANR 5, 27, 76; CDALB 1941-
1968; CPW; DA; DA3; DAB; DAC;
DAM MST, NOV, POP; DLB 2, 102, 227;
DLBY 1980, 1982; EXPS; INT CANR-5;
MTCW 1, 2; RGAL 4; RGSF 2; SSFS 2,
14

Cheever, Susan 1943- .... **CLC 18, 48**
See also CA 103; CANR 27, 51, 92; DLBY
1982; INT CANR-27

Chekhonte, Antosha
See Chekhov, Anton (Pavlovich)

Chekhov, Anton (Pavlovich)
1860-1904 . **TCLC 3, 10, 31, 55, 96; DC
9; SSC 2, 28, 41, 51; WLC**
See also BYA 14; CA 104; 124; DA; DA3;
DAB; DAC; DAM DRAM, MST; DFS 1,
5, 10, 12; EW 7; EXPS; LAIT 3; RGSF
2; RGWL 2; SATA 90; SSFS 5, 13, 14

Cheney, Lynne V. 1941- .... **CLC 70**
See also CA 89-92; CANR 58

Chernyshevsky, Nikolai Gavrilovich
See Chernyshevsky, Nikolay Gavrilovich
See also DLB 238

Chernyshevsky, Nikolay Gavrilovich
1828-1889 .... **NCLC 1**
See also Chernyshevsky, Nikolai Gavrilov-
ich

Cherry, Carolyn Janice 1942-
See Cherryh, C. J.
See also CA 65-68; CANR 10

Cherryh, C. J. .... **CLC 35**
See also Cherry, Carolyn Janice
See also AAYA 24; BPFB 1; DLBY 1980;
FANT; SATA 93; SCFW 2; SFW 4; YAW

Chesnutt, Charles W(addell)
1858-1932 . **TCLC 5, 39; BLC 1; SSC 7**
See also AFAW 1, 2; BW 1, 3; CA 106;
125; CANR 76; DAM MULT; DLB 12,
50, 78; MTCW 1, 2; RGAL 4; RGSF 2;
SSFS 11

Chester, Alfred 1929(?)-1971 .... **CLC 49**
See also CA 196; 33-36R; DLB 130

Chesterton, G(ilbert) K(eith)
1874-1936 . **TCLC 1, 6, 64; PC 28; SSC
1, 46**
See also BRW 6; CA 104; 132; CANR 73;
CDBLB 1914-1945; CMW 4; DAM NOV,
POET; DLB 10, 19, 34, 70, 98, 149, 178;
FANT; MSW; MTCW 1, 2; RGEL 2;
RGSF 2; SATA 27; SUFW

Chiang, Pin-chin 1904-1986
See Ding Ling
See also CA 118

Ch'ien, Chung-shu 1910-1998 .... **CLC 22**
See also CA 130; CANR 73; MTCW 1, 2

Chikamatsu Monzaemon 1653-1724 ... **LC 66**
See also RGWL 2

Child, L. Maria
See Child, Lydia Maria

Child, Lydia Maria 1802-1880 .. **NCLC 6, 73**
See also DLB 1, 74, 243; RGAL 4; SATA
67

Child, Mrs.
See Child, Lydia Maria

Child, Philip 1898-1978 .... **CLC 19, 68**
See also CA 13-14; CAP 1; DLB 68; RHW;
SATA 47

Childers, (Robert) Erskine
1870-1922 .... **TCLC 65**
See also CA 113; 153; DLB 70

Childress, Alice 1920-1994 .. **CLC 12, 15, 86,
96; BLC 1; DC 4**
See also AAYA 8; BW 2, 3; BYA 2; CA 45-
48; 146; CAD; CANR 3, 27, 50, 74; CLR
14; CWD; DA3; DAM DRAM, MULT,
NOV; DFS 2, 8, 14; DLB 7, 38, 249;
JRDA; LAIT 5; MAICYA 1, 2; MAIC-
YAS 1; MTCW 1, 2; RGAL 4; SATA 7,
48, 81; TCLC 116; WYA; YAW

Chin, Frank (Chew, Jr.) 1940- ...... **CLC 135;
DC 7**
See also CA 33-36R; CANR 71; CD 5;
DAM MULT; DLB 206; LAIT 5; RGAL
4

Chin, Marilyn (Mei Ling) 1955- .... **PC 40**
See also CA 129; CANR 70; CWP

Chislett, (Margaret) Anne 1943- ...... **CLC 34**
See also CA 151

Chitty, Thomas Willes 1926- .... **CLC 11**
See also Hinde, Thomas
See also CA 5-8R; CN 7

Chivers, Thomas Holley
1809-1858 .... **NCLC 49**
See also DLB 3, 248; RGAL 4

Choi, Susan .... **CLC 119**

Chomette, Rene Lucien 1898-1981
See Clair, Rene
See also CA 103

Chomsky, (Avram) Noam 1928- ..... **CLC 132**
See also CA 17-20R; CANR 28, 62; DA3;
DLB 246; MTCW 1, 2

Chopin, Kate .. **TCLC 5, 14; SSC 8; WLCS**
See also Chopin, Katherine
See also AAYA 33; AMWS 1; CDALB
1865-1917; DA; DAB; DLB 12, 78;
EXPN; EXPS; FW; LAIT 3; MAWW;
NFS 3; RGAL 4; RGSF 2; SSFS 2, 13

Chopin, Katherine 1851-1904
See Chopin, Kate
See also CA 104; 122; DA3; DAC; DAM
MST, NOV

Chretien de Troyes c. 12th cent. - . **CMLC 10**
See also DLB 208; EW 1; RGWL 2

Christie
See Ichikawa, Kon

Christie, Agatha (Mary Clarissa)
1890-1976 .. **CLC 1, 6, 8, 12, 39, 48, 110**
See also AAYA 9; AITN 1, 2; BPFB 1;
BRWS 2; CA 17-20R; 61-64; CANR 10,
37, 108; CBD; CDBLB 1914-1945; CMW
4; CPW; CWD; DA3; DAB; DAC; DAM
NOV; DFS 2; DLB 13, 77, 245; MSW;
MTCW 1, 2; NFS 8; RGEL 2; RHW;
SATA 36; YAW

Christie, Philippa .... **CLC 21**
See also Pearce, Philippa
See also BYA 5; CANR 109; CLR 9; DLB
161; MAICYA 1; SATA 1, 67, 129

Christine de Pizan 1365(?)-1431(?) .... **LC 9**
    See also DLB 208; RGWL 2
Chubb, Elmer
    See Masters, Edgar Lee
Chulkov, Mikhail Dmitrievich
    1743-1792 .... **LC 2**
    See also DLB 150
Churchill, Caryl 1938- .... **CLC 31, 55, 157;**
    DC 5
    See also BRWS 4; CA 102; CANR 22, 46,
    108; CBD; CWD; DFS 12; DLB 13; FW;
    MTCW 1; RGEL 2
Churchill, Charles 1731-1764 .... **LC 3**
    See also DLB 109; RGEL 2
Churchill, Sir Winston (Leonard Spencer)
    1874-1965 .... **TCLC 113**
    See also BRW 6; CA 97-100; CDBLB
    1890-1914; DA3; DLB 100; DLBD 16;
    LAIT 4; MTCW 1, 2
Chute, Carolyn 1947- .... **CLC 39**
    See also CA 123
Ciardi, John (Anthony) 1916-1986 . **CLC 10,**
    40, 44, 129
    See also CA 5-8R; 118; CAAS 2; CANR 5,
    33; CLR 19; CWRI 5; DAM POET; DLB
    5; DLBY 1986; INT CANR-5; MAICYA
    1, 2; MTCW 1, 2; RGAL 4; SAAS 26;
    SATA 1, 65; SATA-Obit 46
Cibber, Colley 1671-1757 .... **LC 66**
    See also DLB 84; RGEL 2
Cicero, Marcus Tullius
    106B.C.-43B.C. .... **CMLC 3**
    See also AW 1; CDWLB 1; DLB 211;
    RGWL 2
Cimino, Michael 1943- .... **CLC 16**
    See also CA 105
Cioran, E(mil) M. 1911-1995 .... **CLC 64**
    See also CA 25-28R; 149; CANR 91; DLB
    220
Cisneros, Sandra 1954- .. **CLC 69, 118; HLC**
    1; SSC 32
    See also AAYA 9; AMWS 7; CA 131;
    CANR 64; CWP; DA3; DAM MULT;
    DLB 122, 152; EXPN; FW; HW 1, 2;
    LAIT 5; MAICYA 2; MTCW 2; NFS 2;
    RGAL 4; RGSF 2; SSFS 3, 13; WLIT 1;
    YAW
Cixous, Helene 1937- .... **CLC 92**
    See also CA 126; CANR 55; CWW 2; DLB
    83, 242; FW; GLL 2; MTCW 1, 2
Clair, Rene .... **CLC 20**
    See also Chomette, Rene Lucien
Clampitt, Amy 1920-1994 .... **CLC 32; PC 19**
    See also AMWS 9; CA 110; 146; CANR
    29, 79; DLB 105
Clancy, Thomas L., Jr. 1947-
    See Clancy, Tom
    See also CA 125; 131; CANR 62, 105;
    DA3; INT CA-131; MTCW 1, 2
Clancy, Tom .... **CLC 45, 112**
    See also Clancy, Thomas L., Jr.
    See also AAYA 9; BEST 89:1, 90:1; BPFB
    1; BYA 10, 11; CMW 4; CPW; DAM
    NOV, POP; DLB 227
Clare, John 1793-1864 .. **NCLC 9, 86; PC 23**
    See also DAB; DAM POET; DLB 55, 96;
    RGEL 2
Clarin
    See Alas (y Urena), Leopoldo (Enrique
    Garcia)
Clark, Al C.
    See Goines, Donald
Clark, (Robert) Brian 1932- .... **CLC 29**
    See also CA 41-44R; CANR 67; CBD; CD
    5
Clark, Curt
    See Westlake, Donald E(dwin)

Clark, Eleanor 1913-1996 .... **CLC 5, 19**
    See also CA 9-12R; 151; CANR 41; CN 7;
    DLB 6
Clark, J. P.
    See Clark Bekederemo, J(ohnson) P(epper)
    See also CDWLB 3; DLB 117
Clark, John Pepper
    See Clark Bekederemo, J(ohnson) P(epper)
    See also AFW; CD 5; CP 7; RGEL 2
Clark, M. R.
    See Clark, Mavis Thorpe
Clark, Mavis Thorpe 1909-1999 ...... **CLC 12**
    See also CA 57-60; CANR 8, 37, 107; CLR
    30; CWRI 5; MAICYA 1, 2; SAAS 5;
    SATA 8, 74
Clark, Walter Van Tilburg
    1909-1971 .... **CLC 28**
    See also CA 9-12R; 33-36R; CANR 63;
    DLB 9, 206; LAIT 2; RGAL 4; SATA 8
Clark Bekederemo, J(ohnson) P(epper)
    1935- .... **CLC 38; BLC 1; DC 5**
    See also Clark, J. P.; Clark, John Pepper
    See also BW 1; CA 65-68; CANR 16, 72;
    DAM DRAM, MULT; DFS 13; MTCW 1
Clarke, Arthur C(harles) 1917- .... **CLC 1, 4,**
    13, 18, 35, 136; SSC 3
    See also AAYA 4, 33; BPFB 1; BYA 13;
    CA 1-4R; CANR 2, 28, 55, 74; CN 7;
    CPW; DA3; DAM POP; JRDA; LAIT 5;
    MAICYA 1, 2; MTCW 1, 2; SATA 13,
    70, 115; SCFW; SFW 4; SSFS 4; YAW
Clarke, Austin 1896-1974 .... **CLC 6, 9**
    See also CA 29-32; 49-52; CAP 2; DAM
    POET; DLB 10, 20; RGEL 2
Clarke, Austin C(hesterfield) 1934- .. **CLC 8,**
    53; BLC 1; SSC 45
    See also BW 1; CA 25-28R; CAAS 16;
    CANR 14, 32, 68; CN 7; DAC; DAM
    MULT; DLB 53, 125; DNFS 2; RGSF 2
Clarke, Gillian 1937- .... **CLC 61**
    See also CA 106; CP 7; CWP; DLB 40
Clarke, Marcus (Andrew Hislop)
    1846-1881 .... **NCLC 19**
    See also DLB 230; RGEL 2; RGSF 2
Clarke, Shirley 1925-1997 .... **CLC 16**
    See also CA 189
Clash, The
    See Headon, (Nicky) Topper; Jones, Mick;
    Simonon, Paul; Strummer, Joe
Claudel, Paul (Louis Charles Marie)
    1868-1955 .... **TCLC 2, 10**
    See also CA 104; 165; DLB 192, 258; EW
    8; GFL 1789 to the Present; RGWL 2
Claudian 370(?)-404(?) .... **CMLC 46**
    See also RGWL 2
Claudius, Matthias 1740-1815 .... **NCLC 75**
    See also DLB 97
Clavell, James (duMaresq)
    1925-1994 .... **CLC 6, 25, 87**
    See also BPFB 1; CA 25-28R; 146; CANR
    26, 48; CPW; DA3; DAM NOV, POP;
    MTCW 1, 2; NFS 10; RHW
Clayman, Gregory .... **CLC 65**
Cleaver, (Leroy) Eldridge
    1935-1998 .... **CLC 30, 119; BLC 1**
    See also BW 1, 3; CA 21-24R; 167; CANR
    16, 75; DA3; DAM MULT; MTCW 2;
    YAW
Cleese, John (Marwood) 1939- .... **CLC 21**
    See also Monty Python
    See also CA 112; 116; CANR 35; MTCW 1
Cleishbotham, Jebediah
    See Scott, Sir Walter
Cleland, John 1710-1789 .... **LC 2, 48**
    See also DLB 39; RGEL 2

Clemens, Samuel Langhorne 1835-1910
    See Twain, Mark
    See also CA 104; 135; CDALB 1865-1917;
    DA; DA3; DAB; DAC; DAM MST, NOV;
    DLB 12, 23, 64, 74, 186, 189; JRDA;
    MAICYA 1, 2; SATA 100; YABC 2
Clement of Alexandria
    150(?)-215(?) .... **CMLC 41**
Cleophil
    See Congreve, William
Clerihew, E.
    See Bentley, E(dmund) C(lerihew)
Clerk, N. W.
    See Lewis, C(live) S(taples)
Cliff, Jimmy .... **CLC 21**
    See also Chambers, James
    See also CA 193
Cliff, Michelle 1946- .... **CLC 120; BLCS**
    See also BW 2; CA 116; CANR 39, 72; CD-
    WLB 3; DLB 157; FW; GLL 2
Clifford, Lady Anne 1590-1676 .... **LC 76**
    See also DLB 151
Clifton, (Thelma) Lucille 1936- .... **CLC 19,**
    66; BLC 1; PC 17
    See also AFAW 2; BW 2, 3; CA 49-52;
    CANR 2, 24, 42, 76, 97; CLR 5; CP 7;
    CSW; CWP; CWRI 5; DA3; DAM MULT,
    POET; DLB 5, 41; EXPP; MAICYA 1, 2;
    MTCW 1, 2; PFS 1, 14; SATA 20, 69,
    128; WP
Clinton, Dirk
    See Silverberg, Robert
Clough, Arthur Hugh 1819-1861 ... **NCLC 27**
    See also BRW 5; DLB 32; RGEL 2
Clutha, Janet Paterson Frame 1924-
    See Frame, Janet
    See also CA 1-4R; CANR 2, 36, 76; MTCW
    1, 2; SATA 119
Clyne, Terence
    See Blatty, William Peter
Cobalt, Martin
    See Mayne, William (James Carter)
Cobb, Irvin S(hrewsbury)
    1876-1944 .... **TCLC 77**
    See also CA 175; DLB 11, 25, 86
Cobbett, William 1763-1835 .... **NCLC 49**
    See also DLB 43, 107, 158; RGEL 2
Coburn, D(onald) L(ee) 1938- .... **CLC 10**
    See also CA 89-92
Cocteau, Jean (Maurice Eugene Clement)
    1889-1963 ...... **CLC 1, 8, 15, 16, 43; DC**
    17; WLC
    See also CA 25-28; CANR 40; CAP 2; DA;
    DA3; DAB; DAC; DAM DRAM, MST,
    NOV; DLB 65, 258; EW 10; GFL 1789 to
    the Present; MTCW 1, 2; RGWL 2; TCLC
    119
Codrescu, Andrei 1946- .... **CLC 46, 121**
    See also CA 33-36R; CAAS 19; CANR 13,
    34, 53, 76; DA3; DAM POET; MTCW 2
Coe, Max
    See Bourne, Randolph S(illiman)
Coe, Tucker
    See Westlake, Donald E(dwin)
Coen, Ethan 1958- .... **CLC 108**
    See also CA 126; CANR 85
Coen, Joel 1955- .... **CLC 108**
    See also CA 126
The Coen Brothers
    See Coen, Ethan; Coen, Joel
Coetzee, J(ohn) M(ichael) 1940- ...... **CLC 23,**
    33, 66, 117
    See also AAYA 37; AFW; BRWS 6; CA 77-
    80; CANR 41, 54, 74; CN 7; DA3; DAM
    NOV; DLB 225; MTCW 1, 2; WLIT 2
Coffey, Brian
    See Koontz, Dean R(ay)

Coffin, Robert P(eter) Tristram
1892-1955 .... **TCLC 95**
See also CA 123; 169; DLB 45

Cohan, George M(ichael)
1878-1942 .... **TCLC 60**
See also CA 157; DLB 249; RGAL 4

Cohen, Arthur A(llen) 1928-1986 ...... **CLC 7, 31**
See also CA 1-4R; 120; CANR 1, 17, 42; DLB 28

Cohen, Leonard (Norman) 1934- ...... **CLC 3, 38**
See also CA 21-24R; CANR 14, 69; CN 7; CP 7; DAC; DAM MST; DLB 53; MTCW 1

Cohen, Matt(hew) 1942-1999 .... **CLC 19**
See also CA 61-64; 187; CAAS 18; CANR 40; CN 7; DAC; DLB 53

Cohen-Solal, Annie 19(?)- .... **CLC 50**

Colegate, Isabel 1931- .... **CLC 36**
See also CA 17-20R; CANR 8, 22, 74; CN 7; DLB 14, 231; INT CANR-22; MTCW 1

Coleman, Emmett
See Reed, Ishmael

Coleridge, Hartley 1796-1849 .... **NCLC 90**
See also DLB 96

Coleridge, M. E.
See Coleridge, Mary E(lizabeth)

Coleridge, Mary E(lizabeth)
1861-1907 .... **TCLC 73**
See also CA 116; 166; DLB 19, 98

Coleridge, Samuel Taylor
1772-1834 ...... **NCLC 9, 54, 99, 111; PC 11, 39; WLC**
See also BRW 4; BRWR 2; BYA 4; CDBLB 1789-1832; DA; DA3; DAB; DAC; DAM MST, POET; DLB 93, 107; EXPP; PAB; PFS 4, 5; RGEL 2; WLIT 3; WP

Coleridge, Sara 1802-1852 .... **NCLC 31**
See also DLB 199

Coles, Don 1928- .... **CLC 46**
See also CA 115; CANR 38; CP 7

Coles, Robert (Martin) 1929- .... **CLC 108**
See also CA 45-48; CANR 3, 32, 66, 70; INT CANR-32; SATA 23

Colette, (Sidonie-Gabrielle)
1873-1954 .... **TCLC 1, 5, 16; SSC 10**
See also Willy, Colette
See also CA 104; 131; DA3; DAM NOV; DLB 65; EW 9; GFL 1789 to the Present; MTCW 1, 2; RGWL 2

Collett, (Jacobine) Camilla (Wergeland)
1813-1895 .... **NCLC 22**

Collier, Christopher 1930- .... **CLC 30**
See also AAYA 13; BYA 2; CA 33-36R; CANR 13, 33, 102; JRDA; MAICYA 1, 2; SATA 16, 70; WYA; YAW 1

Collier, James Lincoln 1928- .... **CLC 30**
See also AAYA 13; BYA 2; CA 9-12R; CANR 4, 33, 60, 102; CLR 3; DAM POP; JRDA; MAICYA 1, 2; SAAS 21; SATA 8, 70; WYA; YAW 1

Collier, Jeremy 1650-1726 .... **LC 6**

Collier, John 1901-1980 .... **SSC 19**
See also CA 65-68; 97-100; CANR 10; DLB 77, 255; FANT; SUFW

Collingwood, R(obin) G(eorge)
1889(?)-1943 .... **TCLC 67**
See also CA 117; 155

Collins, Hunt
See Hunter, Evan

Collins, Linda 1931- .... **CLC 44**
See also CA 125

Collins, (William) Wilkie
1824-1889 .... **NCLC 1, 18, 93**
See also BRWS 6; CDBLB 1832-1890; CMW 4; DLB 18, 70, 159; MSW; RGEL 2; RGSF 2; SUFW; WLIT 4

Collins, William 1721-1759 .... **LC 4, 40**
See also BRW 3; DAM POET; DLB 109; RGEL 2

Collodi, Carlo .... **NCLC 54**
See also Lorenzini, Carlo
See also CLR 5; WCH

Colman, George
See Glassco, John

Colonna, Vittoria 1492-1547 .... **LC 71**
See also RGWL 2

Colt, Winchester Remington
See Hubbard, L(afayette) Ron(ald)

Colter, Cyrus 1910-2002 .... **CLC 58**
See also BW 1; CA 65-68; CANR 10, 66; CN 7; DLB 33

Colton, James
See Hansen, Joseph
See also GLL 1

Colum, Padraic 1881-1972 .... **CLC 28**
See also BYA 4; CA 73-76; 33-36R; CANR 35; CLR 36; CWRI 5; DLB 19; MAICYA 1, 2; MTCW 1; RGEL 2; SATA 15; WCH

Colvin, James
See Moorcock, Michael (John)

Colwin, Laurie (E.) 1944-1992 .... **CLC 5, 13, 23, 84**
See also CA 89-92; 139; CANR 20, 46; DLB 218; DLBY 1980; MTCW 1

Comfort, Alex(ander) 1920-2000 .... **CLC 7**
See also CA 1-4R; 190; CANR 1, 45; CP 7; DAM POP; MTCW 1

Comfort, Montgomery
See Campbell, (John) Ramsey

Compton-Burnett, I(vy)
1892(?)-1969 .... **CLC 1, 3, 10, 15, 34**
See also BRW 7; CA 1-4R; 25-28R; CANR 4; DAM NOV; DLB 36; MTCW 1; RGEL 2

Comstock, Anthony 1844-1915 ...... **TCLC 13**
See also CA 110; 169

Comte, Auguste 1798-1857 .... **NCLC 54**

Conan Doyle, Arthur
See Doyle, Sir Arthur Conan
See also BPFB 1; BYA 4, 5, 11

Conde (Abellan), Carmen 1901-1996
See also CA 177; DLB 108; HLCS 1; HW 2

Conde, Maryse 1937- ..... **CLC 52, 92; BLCS**
See also BW 2, 3; CA 110; CAAE 190; CANR 30, 53, 76; CWW 2; DAM MULT; MTCW 1

Condillac, Etienne Bonnot de
1714-1780 .... **LC 26**

Condon, Richard (Thomas)
1915-1996 .... **CLC 4, 6, 8, 10, 45, 100**
See also BEST 90:3; BPFB 1; CA 1-4R; 151; CAAS 1; CANR 2, 23; CMW 4; CN 7; DAM NOV; INT CANR-23; MTCW 1, 2

Confucius 551B.C.-479B.C. .... **CMLC 19; WLCS**
See also DA; DA3; DAB; DAC; DAM MST

Congreve, William 1670-1729 . **LC 5, 21; DC 2; WLC**
See also BRW 2; CDBLB 1660-1789; DA; DAB; DAC; DAM DRAM, MST, POET; DFS 14; DLB 39, 84; RGEL 2; WLIT 3

Connell, Evan S(helby), Jr. 1924- . **CLC 4, 6, 45**
See also AAYA 7; CA 1-4R; CAAS 2; CANR 2, 39, 76, 97; CN 7; DAM NOV; DLB 2; DLBY 1981; MTCW 1, 2

Connelly, Marc(us Cook) 1890-1980 . **CLC 7**
See also CA 85-88; 102; CANR 30; DFS 12; DLB 7; DLBY 1980; RGAL 4; SATA-Obit 25

Connor, Ralph .... **TCLC 31**
See also Gordon, Charles William
See also DLB 92; TCWW 2

Conrad, Joseph 1857-1924 .... **TCLC 1, 6, 13, 25, 43, 57; SSC 9; WLC**
See also AAYA 26; BPFB 1; BRW 6; BRWR 2; BYA 2; CA 104; 131; CANR 60; CDBLB 1890-1914; DA; DA3; DAB; DAC; DAM MST, NOV; DLB 10, 34, 98, 156; EXPN; EXPS; LAIT 2; MTCW 1, 2; NFS 2; RGEL 2; RGSF 2; SATA 27; SSFS 1, 12; WLIT 4

Conrad, Robert Arnold
See Hart, Moss

Conroy, (Donald) Pat(rick) 1945- ... **CLC 30, 74**
See also AAYA 8; AITN 1; BPFB 1; CA 85-88; CANR 24, 53; CPW; CSW; DA3; DAM NOV, POP; DLB 6; LAIT 5; MTCW 1, 2

Constant (de Rebecque), (Henri) Benjamin
1767-1830 .... **NCLC 6**
See also DLB 119; EW 4; GFL 1789 to the Present

Conway, Jill K(er) 1934- .... **CLC 152**
See also CA 130; CANR 94

Conybeare, Charles Augustus
See Eliot, T(homas) S(tearns)

Cook, Michael 1933-1994 .... **CLC 58**
See also CA 93-96; CANR 68; DLB 53

Cook, Robin 1940- .... **CLC 14**
See also AAYA 32; BEST 90:2; BPFB 1; CA 108; 111; CANR 41, 90, 109; CPW; DA3; DAM POP; HGG; INT CA-111

Cook, Roy
See Silverberg, Robert

Cooke, Elizabeth 1948- .... **CLC 55**
See also CA 129

Cooke, John Esten 1830-1886 .... **NCLC 5**
See also DLB 3, 248; RGAL 4

Cooke, John Estes
See Baum, L(yman) Frank

Cooke, M. E.
See Creasey, John

Cooke, Margaret
See Creasey, John

Cooke, Rose Terry 1827-1892 ...... **NCLC 110**
See also DLB 12, 74

Cook-Lynn, Elizabeth 1930- .... **CLC 93**
See also CA 133; DAM MULT; DLB 175; NNAL

Cooney, Ray .... **CLC 62**
See also CBD

Cooper, Douglas 1960- .... **CLC 86**

Cooper, Henry St. John
See Creasey, John

Cooper, J(oan) California (?)- .... **CLC 56**
See also AAYA 12; BW 1; CA 125; CANR 55; DAM MULT; DLB 212

Cooper, James Fenimore
1789-1851 .... **NCLC 1, 27, 54**
See also AAYA 22; AMW; BPFB 1; CDALB 1640-1865; DA3; DLB 3, 183, 250, 254; LAIT 1; NFS 9; RGAL 4; SATA 19; WCH

Coover, Robert (Lowell) 1932- ...... **CLC 3, 7, 15, 32, 46, 87; SSC 15**
See also AMWS 5; BPFB 1; CA 45-48; CANR 3, 37, 58; CN 7; DAM NOV; DLB 2, 227; DLBY 1981; MTCW 1, 2; RGAL 4; RGSF 2

Copeland, Stewart (Armstrong)
1952- .... **CLC 26**

Copernicus, Nicolaus 1473-1543 .... **LC 45**

Coppard, A(lfred) E(dgar)
1878-1957 .... **TCLC 5; SSC 21**
See also CA 114; 167; DLB 162; HGG; RGEL 2; RGSF 2; SUFW; YABC 1

Coppee, Francois 1842-1908 .... **TCLC 25**
  See also CA 170; DLB 217
Coppola, Francis Ford 1939- ... **CLC 16, 126**
  See also AAYA 39; CA 77-80; CANR 40,
  78; DLB 44
Corbiere, Tristan 1845-1875 .... **NCLC 43**
  See also DLB 217; GFL 1789 to the Present
Corcoran, Barbara (Asenath)
  1911- .... **CLC 17**
  See also AAYA 14; CA 21-24R; CAAE 191;
  CAAS 2; CANR 11, 28, 48; CLR 50;
  DLB 52; JRDA; MAICYA 2; MAICYAS
  1; RHW; SAAS 20; SATA 3, 77, 125
Cordelier, Maurice
  See Giraudoux, Jean(-Hippolyte)
Corelli, Marie .... **TCLC 51**
  See also Mackay, Mary
  See also DLB 34, 156; RGEL 2; SUFW
Corman, Cid .... **CLC 9**
  See also Corman, Sidney
  See also CAAS 2; DLB 5, 193
Corman, Sidney 1924-
  See Corman, Cid
  See also CA 85-88; CANR 44; CP 7; DAM
  POET
Cormier, Robert (Edmund)
  1925-2000 .... **CLC 12, 30**
  See also AAYA 3, 19; BYA 1, 2, 6, 8, 9;
  CA 1-4R; CANR 5, 23, 76, 93; CDALB
  1968-1988; CLR 12, 55; DA; DAB; DAC;
  DAM MST, NOV; DLB 52; EXPN; INT
  CANR-23; JRDA; LAIT 5; MAICYA 1,
  2; MTCW 1, 2; NFS 2; SATA 10, 45, 83;
  SATA-Obit 122; WYA; YAW
Corn, Alfred (DeWitt III) 1943- .... **CLC 33**
  See also CA 179; CAAE 179; CAAS 25;
  CANR 44; CP 7; CSW; DLB 120; DLBY
  1980
Corneille, Pierre 1606-1684 .... **LC 28**
  See also DAB; DAM MST; EW 3; GFL
  Beginnings to 1789; RGWL 2
Cornwell, David (John Moore)
  1931- .... **CLC 9, 15**
  See also le Carre, John
  See also CA 5-8R; CANR 13, 33, 59, 107;
  DA3; DAM POP; MTCW 1, 2
Cornwell, Patricia (Daniels) 1956- . **CLC 155**
  See also AAYA 16; BPFB 1; CA 134;
  CANR 53; CMW 4; CPW; CSW; DAM
  POP; MSW; MTCW 1
Corso, (Nunzio) Gregory 1930-2001 . **CLC 1,
  11; PC 33**
  See also CA 5-8R; 193; CANR 41, 76; CP
  7; DA3; DLB 5, 16, 237; MTCW 1, 2;
  WP
Cortazar, Julio 1914-1984 ... **CLC 2, 3, 5, 10,
  13, 15, 33, 34, 92; HLC 1; SSC 7**
  See also BPFB 1; CA 21-24R; CANR 12,
  32, 81; CDWLB 3; DA3; DAM MULT,
  NOV; DLB 113; EXPS; HW 1, 2; LAW;
  MTCW 1, 2; RGSF 2; RGWL 2; SSFS 3;
  WLIT 1
Cortes, Hernan 1485-1547 .... **LC 31**
Corvinus, Jakob
  See Raabe, Wilhelm (Karl)
Corvo, Baron
  See Rolfe, Frederick (William Serafino
  Austin Lewis Mary)
  See also GLL 1; RGEL 2
Corwin, Cecil
  See Kornbluth, C(yril) M.
Cosic, Dobrica 1921- .... **CLC 14**
  See also CA 122; 138; CDWLB 4; CWW
  2; DLB 181
Costain, Thomas B(ertram)
  1885-1965 .... **CLC 30**
  See also BYA 3; CA 5-8R; 25-28R; DLB 9;
  RHW

Costantini, Humberto 1924(?)-1987 . **CLC 49**
  See also CA 131; 122; HW 1
Costello, Elvis 1955- .... **CLC 21**
Costenoble, Philostene 1898-1962
  See Ghelderode, Michel de
Costenoble, Philostene 1898-1962
  See Ghelderode, Michel de
Cotes, Cecil V.
  See Duncan, Sara Jeannette
Cotter, Joseph Seamon Sr.
  1861-1949 .... **TCLC 28; BLC 1**
  See also BW 1; CA 124; DAM MULT; DLB
  50
Couch, Arthur Thomas Quiller
  See Quiller-Couch, Sir Arthur (Thomas)
Coulton, James
  See Hansen, Joseph
Couperus, Louis (Marie Anne)
  1863-1923 .... **TCLC 15**
  See also CA 115; RGWL 2
Coupland, Douglas 1961- .... **CLC 85, 133**
  See also AAYA 34; CA 142; CANR 57, 90;
  CCA 1; CPW; DAC; DAM POP
Court, Wesli
  See Turco, Lewis (Putnam)
Courtenay, Bryce 1933- .... **CLC 59**
  See also CA 138; CPW
Courtney, Robert
  See Ellison, Harlan (Jay)
Cousteau, Jacques-Yves 1910-1997 .. **CLC 30**
  See also CA 65-68; 159; CANR 15, 67;
  MTCW 1; SATA 38, 98
Coventry, Francis 1725-1754 .... **LC 46**
Coverdale, Miles c. 1487-1569 .... **LC 77**
  See also DLB 167
Cowan, Peter (Walkinshaw) 1914- .... **SSC 28**
  See also CA 21-24R; CANR 9, 25, 50, 83;
  CN 7; RGSF 2
Coward, Noel (Peirce) 1899-1973 . **CLC 1, 9,
  29, 51**
  See also AITN 1; BRWS 2; CA 17-18; 41-
  44R; CANR 35; CAP 2; CDBLB 1914-
  1945; DA3; DAM DRAM; DFS 3, 6;
  DLB 10, 245; IDFW 3, 4; MTCW 1, 2;
  RGEL 2
Cowley, Abraham 1618-1667 .... **LC 43**
  See also BRW 2; DLB 131, 151; PAB;
  RGEL 2
Cowley, Malcolm 1898-1989 .... **CLC 39**
  See also AMWS 2; CA 5-8R; 128; CANR
  3, 55; DLB 4, 48; DLBY 1981, 1989;
  MTCW 1, 2
Cowper, William 1731-1800 ..... **NCLC 8, 94;
  PC 40**
  See also BRW 3; DA3; DAM POET; DLB
  104, 109; RGEL 2
Cox, William Trevor 1928-
  See Trevor, William
  See also CA 9-12R; CANR 4, 37, 55, 76,
  102; DAM NOV; INT CANR-37; MTCW
  1, 2
Coyne, P. J.
  See Masters, Hilary
Cozzens, James Gould 1903-1978 . **CLC 1, 4,
  11, 92**
  See also AMW; BPFB 1; CA 9-12R; 81-84;
  CANR 19; CDALB 1941-1968; DLB 9;
  DLBD 2; DLBY 1984, 1997; MTCW 1,
  2; RGAL 4
Crabbe, George 1754-1832 .... **NCLC 26**
  See also BRW 3; DLB 93; RGEL 2
Crace, Jim 1946- .... **CLC 157**
  See also CA 128; 135; CANR 55, 70; CN
  7; DLB 231; INT CA-135
Craddock, Charles Egbert
  See Murfree, Mary Noailles
Craig, A. A.
  See Anderson, Poul (William)

Craik, Mrs.
  See Craik, Dinah Maria (Mulock)
  See also RGEL 2
Craik, Dinah Maria (Mulock)
  1826-1887 .... **NCLC 38**
  See also Craik, Mrs.; Mulock, Dinah Maria
  See also DLB 35, 163; MAICYA 1, 2;
  SATA 34
Cram, Ralph Adams 1863-1942 ..... **TCLC 45**
  See also CA 160
Crane, (Harold) Hart 1899-1932 .... **TCLC 2,
  5, 80; PC 3; WLC**
  See also AMW; CA 104; 127; CDALB
  1917-1929; DA; DA3; DAB; DAC; DAM
  MST, POET; DLB 4, 48; MTCW 1, 2;
  RGAL 4
Crane, R(onald) S(almon)
  1886-1967 .... **CLC 27**
  See also CA 85-88; DLB 63
Crane, Stephen (Townley)
  1871-1900 ...... **TCLC 11, 17, 32; SSC 7;
  WLC**
  See also AAYA 21; AMW; BPFB 1; BYA 3;
  CA 109; 140; CANR 84; CDALB 1865-
  1917; DA; DA3; DAB; DAC; DAM MST,
  NOV, POET; DLB 12, 54, 78; EXPN;
  EXPS; LAIT 2; NFS 4; PFS 9; RGAL 4;
  RGSF 2; SSFS 4; WYA; YABC 2
Cranshaw, Stanley
  See Fisher, Dorothy (Frances) Canfield
Crase, Douglas 1944- .... **CLC 58**
  See also CA 106
Crashaw, Richard 1612(?)-1649 .... **LC 24**
  See also BRW 2; DLB 126; PAB; RGEL 2
Craven, Margaret 1901-1980 .... **CLC 17**
  See also BYA 2; CA 103; CCA 1; DAC;
  LAIT 5
Crawford, F(rancis) Marion
  1854-1909 .... **TCLC 10**
  See also CA 107; 168; DLB 71; HGG;
  RGAL 4; SUFW
Crawford, Isabella Valancy
  1850-1887 .... **NCLC 12**
  See also DLB 92; RGEL 2
Crayon, Geoffrey
  See Irving, Washington
Creasey, John 1908-1973 .... **CLC 11**
  See also Marric, J. J.
  See also CA 5-8R; 41-44R; CANR 8, 59;
  CMW 4; DLB 77; MTCW 1
Crebillon, Claude Prosper Jolyot de (fils)
  1707-1777 .... **LC 1, 28**
  See also GFL Beginnings to 1789
Credo
  See Creasey, John
Credo, Alvaro J. de
  See Prado (Calvo), Pedro
Creeley, Robert (White) 1926- .. **CLC 1, 2, 4,
  8, 11, 15, 36, 78**
  See also AMWS 4; CA 1-4R; CAAS 10;
  CANR 23, 43, 89; CP 7; DA3; DAM
  POET; DLB 5, 16, 169; DLBD 17;
  MTCW 1, 2; RGAL 4; WP
Crevecoeur, Hector St. John de
  See Crevecoeur, Michel Guillaume Jean de
  See also ANW
Crevecoeur, Michel Guillaume Jean de
  1735-1813 .... **NCLC 105**
  See also Crevecoeur, Hector St. John de
  See also AMWS 1; DLB 37
Crevel, Rene 1900-1935 .... **TCLC 112**
  See also GLL 2
Crews, Harry (Eugene) 1935- ..... **CLC 6, 23,
  49**
  See also AITN 1; BPFB 1; CA 25-28R;
  CANR 20, 57; CN 7; CSW; DA3; DLB 6,
  143, 185; MTCW 1, 2; RGAL 4

Crichton, (John) Michael 1942- .... **CLC 2, 6, 54, 90**
See also AAYA 10; AITN 2; BPFB 1; CA 25-28R; CANR 13, 40, 54, 76; CMW 4; CN 7; CPW; DA3; DAM NOV, POP; DLBY 1981; INT CANR-13; JRDA; MTCW 1, 2; SATA 9, 88; SFW 4; YAW

Crispin, Edmund .... **CLC 22**
See also Montgomery, (Robert) Bruce
See also DLB 87; MSW

Cristofer, Michael 1945(?)- .... **CLC 28**
See also CA 110; 152; CAD; CD 5; DAM DRAM; DLB 7

Croce, Benedetto 1866-1952 .... **TCLC 37**
See also CA 120; 155; EW 8

Crockett, David 1786-1836 .... **NCLC 8**
See also DLB 3, 11, 183, 248

Crockett, Davy
See Crockett, David

Crofts, Freeman Wills 1879-1957 .. **TCLC 55**
See also CA 115; 195; CMW 4; DLB 77; MSW

Croker, John Wilson 1780-1857 .... **NCLC 10**
See also DLB 110

Crommelynck, Fernand 1885-1970 .. **CLC 75**
See also CA 189; 89-92

Cromwell, Oliver 1599-1658 .... **LC 43**

Cronenberg, David 1943- .... **CLC 143**
See also CA 138; CCA 1

Cronin, A(rchibald) J(oseph)
1896-1981 .... **CLC 32**
See also BPFB 1; CA 1-4R; 102; CANR 5; DLB 191; SATA 47; SATA-Obit 25

Cross, Amanda
See Heilbrun, Carolyn G(old)
See also BPFB 1; CMW; CPW; MSW

Crothers, Rachel 1878-1958 .... **TCLC 19**
See also CA 113; 194; CAD; CWD; DLB 7; RGAL 4

Croves, Hal
See Traven, B.

Crow Dog, Mary (Ellen) (?)- .... **CLC 93**
See also Brave Bird, Mary
See also CA 154

Crowfield, Christopher
See Stowe, Harriet (Elizabeth) Beecher

Crowley, Aleister .... **TCLC 7**
See also Crowley, Edward Alexander
See also GLL 1

Crowley, Edward Alexander 1875-1947
See Crowley, Aleister
See also CA 104; HGG

Crowley, John 1942- .... **CLC 57**
See also BPFB 1; CA 61-64; CANR 43, 98; DLBY 1982; SATA 65; SFW 4

Crud
See Crumb, R(obert)

Crumarums
See Crumb, R(obert)

Crumb, R(obert) 1943- .... **CLC 17**
See also CA 106; CANR 107

Crumbum
See Crumb, R(obert)

Crumski
See Crumb, R(obert)

Crum the Bum
See Crumb, R(obert)

Crunk
See Crumb, R(obert)

Crustt
See Crumb, R(obert)

Crutchfield, Les
See Trumbo, Dalton

Cruz, Victor Hernandez 1949- .... **PC 37**
See also BW 2; CA 65-68; CAAS 17; CANR 14, 32, 74; CP 7; DAM MULT, POET; DLB 41; DNFS 1; EXPP; HLC 1; HW 1, 2; MTCW 1; WP

Cryer, Gretchen (Kiger) 1935- .... **CLC 21**
See also CA 114; 123

Csath, Geza 1887-1919 .... **TCLC 13**
See also CA 111

Cudlip, David R(ockwell) 1933- .... **CLC 34**
See also CA 177

Cullen, Countee 1903-1946 .... **TCLC 4, 37; BLC 1; PC 20; WLCS**
See also AFAW 2; AMWS 4; BW 1; CA 108; 124; CDALB 1917-1929; DA; DA3; DAC; DAM MST, MULT, POET; DLB 4, 48, 51; EXPP; MTCW 1, 2; PFS 3; RGAL 4; SATA 18; WP

Cum, R.
See Crumb, R(obert)

Cummings, Bruce F(rederick) 1889-1919
See Barbellion, W. N. P.
See also CA 123

Cummings, E(dward) E(stlin)
1894-1962 .. **CLC 1, 3, 8, 12, 15, 68; PC 5; WLC**
See also AAYA 41; AMW; CA 73-76; CANR 31; CDALB 1929-1941; DA; DA3; DAB; DAC; DAM MST, POET; DLB 4, 48; EXPP; MTCW 1, 2; PAB; PFS 1, 3, 12, 13; RGAL 4; WP

Cunha, Euclides (Rodrigues Pimenta) da
1866-1909 .... **TCLC 24**
See also CA 123; LAW; WLIT 1

Cunningham, E. V.
See Fast, Howard (Melvin)

Cunningham, J(ames) V(incent)
1911-1985 .... **CLC 3, 31**
See also CA 1-4R; 115; CANR 1, 72; DLB 5

Cunningham, Julia (Woolfolk)
1916- .... **CLC 12**
See also CA 9-12R; CANR 4, 19, 36; CWRI 5; JRDA; MAICYA 1, 2; SAAS 2; SATA 1, 26

Cunningham, Michael 1952- .... **CLC 34**
See also CA 136; CANR 96; GLL 2

Cunninghame Graham, R. B.
See Cunninghame Graham, Robert (Gallnigad) Bontine

Cunninghame Graham, Robert (Gallnigad) Bontine 1852-1936 .... **TCLC 19**
See also Graham, R(obert) B(ontine) Cunninghame
See also CA 119; 184

Currie, Ellen 19(?)- .... **CLC 44**

Curtin, Philip
See Lowndes, Marie Adelaide (Belloc)

Curtis, Price
See Ellison, Harlan (Jay)

Cutrate, Joe
See Spiegelman, Art

Cynewulf c. 770- .... **CMLC 23**
See also DLB 146; RGEL 2

Cyrano de Bergerac, Savinien de
1619-1655 .... **LC 65**
See also GFL Beginnings to 1789; RGWL 2

Czaczkes, Shmuel Yosef Halevi
See Agnon, S(hmuel) Y(osef Halevi)

Dabrowska, Maria (Szumska)
1889-1965 .... **CLC 15**
See also CA 106; CDWLB 4; DLB 215

Dabydeen, David 1955- .... **CLC 34**
See also BW 1; CA 125; CANR 56, 92; CN 7; CP 7

Dacey, Philip 1939- .... **CLC 51**
See also CA 37-40R; CAAS 17; CANR 14, 32, 64; CP 7; DLB 105

Dagerman, Stig (Halvard)
1923-1954 .... **TCLC 17**
See also CA 117; 155; DLB 259

D'Aguiar, Fred 1960- .... **CLC 145**
See also CA 148; CANR 83, 101; CP 7; DLB 157

Dahl, Roald 1916-1990 .... **CLC 1, 6, 18, 79**
See also AAYA 15; BPFB 1; BRWS 4; BYA 5; CA 1-4R; 133; CANR 6, 32, 37, 62; CLR 1, 7, 41; CPW; DA3; DAB; DAC; DAM MST, NOV, POP; DLB 139, 255; HGG; JRDA; MAICYA 1, 2; MTCW 1, 2; RGSF 2; SATA 1, 26, 73; SATA-Obit 65; SSFS 4; YAW

Dahlberg, Edward 1900-1977 .. **CLC 1, 7, 14**
See also CA 9-12R; 69-72; CANR 31, 62; DLB 48; MTCW 1; RGAL 4

Daitch, Susan 1954- .... **CLC 103**
See also CA 161

Dale, Colin .... **TCLC 18**
See also Lawrence, T(homas) E(dward)

Dale, George E.
See Asimov, Isaac

Dalton, Roque 1935-1975(?) .... **PC 36**
See also CA 176; HLCS 1; HW 2

Daly, Elizabeth 1878-1967 .... **CLC 52**
See also CA 23-24; 25-28R; CANR 60; CAP 2; CMW 4

Daly, Maureen 1921- .... **CLC 17**
See also AAYA 5; BYA 6; CANR 37, 83, 108; JRDA; MAICYA 1, 2; SAAS 1; SATA 2, 129; WYA; YAW

Damas, Leon-Gontran 1912-1978 .... **CLC 84**
See also BW 1; CA 125; 73-76

Dana, Richard Henry Sr.
1787-1879 .... **NCLC 53**

Daniel, Samuel 1562(?)-1619 .... **LC 24**
See also DLB 62; RGEL 2

Daniels, Brett
See Adler, Renata

Dannay, Frederic 1905-1982 .... **CLC 11**
See also Queen, Ellery
See also CA 1-4R; 107; CANR 1, 39; CMW 4; DAM POP; DLB 137; MTCW 1

D'Annunzio, Gabriele 1863-1938 ... **TCLC 6, 40**
See also CA 104; 155; EW 8; RGWL 2

Danois, N. le
See Gourmont, Remy(-Marie-Charles) de

Dante 1265-1321 .... **CMLC 3, 18, 39; PC 21; WLCS**
See also DA; DA3; DAB; DAC; DAM MST, POET; EFS 1; EW 1; LAIT 1; RGWL 2; WP

d'Antibes, Germain
See Simenon, Georges (Jacques Christian)

Danticat, Edwidge 1969- .... **CLC 94, 139**
See also AAYA 29; CA 152; CAAE 192; CANR 73; DNFS 1; EXPS; MTCW 1; SSFS 1; YAW

Danvers, Dennis 1947- .... **CLC 70**

Danziger, Paula 1944- .... **CLC 21**
See also AAYA 4, 36; BYA 6, 7, 14; CA 112; 115; CANR 37; CLR 20; JRDA; MAICYA 1, 2; SATA 36, 63, 102; SATA-Brief 30; WYA; YAW

Da Ponte, Lorenzo 1749-1838 .... **NCLC 50**

Dario, Ruben 1867-1916 ... **TCLC 4; HLC 1; PC 15**
See also CA 131; CANR 81; DAM MULT; HW 1, 2; LAW; MTCW 1, 2; RGWL 2

Darley, George 1795-1846 .... **NCLC 2**
See also DLB 96; RGEL 2

Darrow, Clarence (Seward)
1857-1938 .... **TCLC 81**
See also CA 164

Darwin, Charles 1809-1882 .... **NCLC 57**
See also BRWS 7; DLB 57, 166; RGEL 2; WLIT 4

Darwin, Erasmus 1731-1802 .... **NCLC 106**
See also DLB 93; RGEL 2

Daryush, Elizabeth 1887-1977 ...... **CLC 6, 19**
See also CA 49-52; CANR 3, 81; DLB 20

Dasgupta, Surendranath
1887-1952 .... **TCLC 81**
See also CA 157

**Dashwood, Edmee Elizabeth Monica de la
Pasture** 1890-1943
See Delafield, E. M.
See also CA 119; 154

Daudet, (Louis Marie) Alphonse
1840-1897 .... **NCLC 1**
See also DLB 123; GFL 1789 to the Present;
RGSF 2

Daumal, Rene 1908-1944 .... **TCLC 14**
See also CA 114

Davenant, William 1606-1668 .... **LC 13**
See also DLB 58, 126; RGEL 2

Davenport, Guy (Mattison, Jr.)
1927- .... **CLC 6, 14, 38; SSC 16**
See also CA 33-36R; CANR 23, 73; CN 7;
CSW; DLB 130

David, Robert
See Nezval, Vitezslav

Davidson, Avram (James) 1923-1993
See Queen, Ellery
See also CA 101; 171; CANR 26; DLB 8;
FANT; SFW 4; SUFW

Davidson, Donald (Grady)
1893-1968 .... **CLC 2, 13, 19**
See also CA 5-8R; 25-28R; CANR 4, 84;
DLB 45

Davidson, Hugh
See Hamilton, Edmond

Davidson, John 1857-1909 .... **TCLC 24**
See also CA 118; DLB 19; RGEL 2

Davidson, Sara 1943- .... **CLC 9**
See also CA 81-84; CANR 44, 68; DLB
185

Davie, Donald (Alfred) 1922-1995 .... **CLC 5,
8, 10, 31; PC 29**
See also BRWS 6; CA 1-4R; 149; CAAS 3;
CANR 1, 44; CP 7; DLB 27; MTCW 1;
RGEL 2

Davie, Elspeth 1919-1995 .... **SSC 52**
See also CA 120; 126; 150; DLB 139

Davies, Ray(mond Douglas) 1944- ... **CLC 21**
See also CA 116; 146; CANR 92

Davies, Rhys 1901-1978 .... **CLC 23**
See also CA 9-12R; 81-84; CANR 4; DLB
139, 191

Davies, (William) Robertson
1913-1995 .... **CLC 2, 7, 13, 25, 42, 75,
91; WLC**
See also Marchbanks, Samuel
See also BEST 89:2; BPFB 1; CA 33-36R;
150; CANR 17, 42, 103; CN 7; CPW;
DA; DA3; DAB; DAC; DAM MST, NOV,
POP; DLB 68; HGG; INT CANR-17;
MTCW 1, 2; RGEL 2

Davies, Walter C.
See Kornbluth, C(yril) M.

Davies, William Henry 1871-1940 ... **TCLC 5**
See also CA 104; 179; DLB 19, 174; RGEL
2

Da Vinci, Leonardo 1452-1519 ..... **LC 12, 57,
60**
See also AAYA 40

Davis, Angela (Yvonne) 1944- .... **CLC 77**
See also BW 2, 3; CA 57-60; CANR 10,
81; CSW; DA3; DAM MULT; FW

Davis, B. Lynch
See Bioy Casares, Adolfo; Borges, Jorge
Luis

Davis, Gordon
See Hunt, E(verette) Howard, (Jr.)

Davis, H(arold) L(enoir) 1896-1960 . **CLC 49**
See also ANW; CA 178; 89-92; DLB 9,
206; SATA 114

Davis, Rebecca (Blaine) Harding
1831-1910 .... **TCLC 6; SSC 38**
See also CA 104; 179; DLB 74, 239; FW;
NFS 14; RGAL 4

Davis, Richard Harding
1864-1916 .... **TCLC 24**
See also CA 114; 179; DLB 12, 23, 78, 79,
189; DLBD 13; RGAL 4

Davison, Frank Dalby 1893-1970 ..... **CLC 15**
See also CA 116

Davison, Lawrence H.
See Lawrence, D(avid) H(erbert Richards)

Davison, Peter (Hubert) 1928- .... **CLC 28**
See also CA 9-12R; CAAS 4; CANR 3, 43,
84; CP 7; DLB 5

Davys, Mary 1674-1732 .... **LC 1, 46**
See also DLB 39

Dawson, Fielding 1930-2002 .... **CLC 6**
See also CA 85-88; CANR 108; DLB 130

Dawson, Peter
See Faust, Frederick (Schiller)
See also TCWW 2, 2

Day, Clarence (Shepard, Jr.)
1874-1935 .... **TCLC 25**
See also CA 108; DLB 11

Day, John 1574(?)-1640(?) .... **LC 70**
See also DLB 62, 170; RGEL 2

Day, Thomas 1748-1789 .... **LC 1**
See also DLB 39; YABC 1

Day Lewis, C(ecil) 1904-1972 . **CLC 1, 6, 10;
PC 11**
See also Blake, Nicholas
See also BRWS 3; CA 13-16; 33-36R;
CANR 34; CAP 1; CWRI 5; DAM POET;
DLB 15, 20; MTCW 1, 2; RGEL 2

Dazai Osamu .... **TCLC 11; SSC 41**
See also Tsushima, Shuji
See also CA 164; DLB 182; MJW; RGSF
2; RGWL 2

de Andrade, Carlos Drummond
See Drummond de Andrade, Carlos

de Andrade, Mario 1892-1945
See Andrade, Mario de
See also CA 178; HW 2

Deane, Norman
See Creasey, John

Deane, Seamus (Francis) 1940- ...... **CLC 122**
See also CA 118; CANR 42

**de Beauvoir, Simone (Lucie Ernestine Marie
Bertrand)**
See Beauvoir, Simone (Lucie Ernestine
Marie Bertrand) de

de Beer, P.
See Bosman, Herman Charles

de Brissac, Malcolm
See Dickinson, Peter (Malcolm)

de Campos, Alvaro
See Pessoa, Fernando (Antonio Nogueira)

de Chardin, Pierre Teilhard
See Teilhard de Chardin, (Marie Joseph)
Pierre

Dee, John 1527-1608 .... **LC 20**
See also DLB 136, 213

Deer, Sandra 1940- .... **CLC 45**
See also CA 186

De Ferrari, Gabriella 1941- .... **CLC 65**
See also CA 146

Defoe, Daniel 1660(?)-1731 .. **LC 1, 42; WLC**
See also AAYA 27; BRW 3; BRWR 1; BYA
4; CDBLB 1660-1789; CLR 61; DA;
DA3; DAB; DAC; DAM MST, NOV;
DLB 39, 95, 101; JRDA; LAIT 1; MAI-
CYA 1, 2; NFS 9, 13; RGEL 2; SATA 22;
WCH; WLIT 3

de Gourmont, Remy(-Marie-Charles)
See Gourmont, Remy(-Marie-Charles) de

de Hartog, Jan 1914- .... **CLC 19**
See also CA 1-4R; CANR 1; DFS 12

de Hostos, E. M.
See Hostos (y Bonilla), Eugenio Maria de

de Hostos, Eugenio M.
See Hostos (y Bonilla), Eugenio Maria de

Deighton, Len .... **CLC 4, 7, 22, 46**
See also Deighton, Leonard Cyril
See also AAYA 6; BEST 89:2; BPFB 1; CD-
BLB 1960 to Present; CMW 4; CN 7;
CPW; DLB 87

Deighton, Leonard Cyril 1929-
See Deighton, Len
See also CA 9-12R; CANR 19, 33, 68;
DA3; DAM NOV, POP; MTCW 1, 2

Dekker, Thomas 1572(?)-1632 ..... **LC 22; DC
12**
See also CDBLB Before 1660; DAM
DRAM; DLB 62, 172; RGEL 2

Delafield, E. M. .... **TCLC 61**
See also Dashwood, Edmee Elizabeth
Monica de la Pasture
See also DLB 34; RHW

de la Mare, Walter (John)
1873-1956 . **TCLC 4, 53; SSC 14; WLC**
See also CA 163; CDBLB 1914-1945; CLR
23; CWRI 5; DA3; DAB; DAC; DAM
MST, POET; DLB 19, 153, 162, 255;
EXPP; HGG; MAICYA 1, 2; MTCW 1;
RGEL 2; RGSF 2; SATA 16; SUFW;
WCH

Delaney, Franey
See O'Hara, John (Henry)

Delaney, Shelagh 1939- .... **CLC 29**
See also CA 17-20R; CANR 30, 67; CBD;
CD 5; CDBLB 1960 to Present; CWD;
DAM DRAM; DFS 7; DLB 13; MTCW 1

Delany, Martin Robison
1812-1885 .... **NCLC 93**
See also DLB 50; RGAL 4

Delany, Mary (Granville Pendarves)
1700-1788 .... **LC 12**

Delany, Samuel R(ay), Jr. 1942- . **CLC 8, 14,
38, 141; BLC 1**
See also AAYA 24; AFAW 2; BPFB 1; BW
2, 3; CA 81-84; CANR 27, 43; DAM
MULT; DLB 8, 33; MTCW 1, 2; RGAL
4; SCFW

De La Ramee, (Marie) Louise 1839-1908
See Ouida
See also SATA 20

de la Roche, Mazo 1879-1961 .... **CLC 14**
See also CA 85-88; CANR 30; DLB 68;
RGEL 2; RHW; SATA 64

De La Salle, Innocent
See Hartmann, Sadakichi

Delbanco, Nicholas (Franklin)
1942- .... **CLC 6, 13**
See also CA 17-20R; CAAE 189; CAAS 2;
CANR 29, 55; DLB 6, 234

del Castillo, Michel 1933- .... **CLC 38**
See also CA 109; CANR 77

Deledda, Grazia (Cosima)
1875(?)-1936 .... **TCLC 23**
See also CA 123; RGWL 2

Deleuze, Gilles 1925-1995 .... **TCLC 116**

Delgado, Abelardo (Lalo) B(arrientos) 1930-
See also CA 131; CAAS 15; CANR 90;
DAM MST, MULT; DLB 82; HLC 1; HW
1, 2

Delibes, Miguel .... **CLC 8, 18**
See also Delibes Setien, Miguel

Delibes Setien, Miguel 1920-
See Delibes, Miguel
See also CA 45-48; CANR 1, 32; HW 1;
MTCW 1

DeLillo, Don 1936- ..... **CLC 8, 10, 13, 27, 39,
54, 76, 143**
See also AMWS 6; BEST 89:1; BPFB 1;
CA 81-84; CANR 21, 76, 92; CN 7; CPW;
DA3; DAM NOV, POP; DLB 6, 173;
MTCW 1, 2; RGAL 4

de Lisser, H. G.
See De Lisser, H(erbert) G(eorge)
See also DLB 117

De Lisser, H(erbert) G(eorge)
1878-1944 .... **TCLC 12**
See also de Lisser, H. G.
See also BW 2; CA 109; 152

Deloire, Pierre
See Peguy, Charles (Pierre)

Deloney, Thomas 1543(?)-1600 .... **LC 41**
See also DLB 167; RGEL 2

Deloria, Vine (Victor), Jr. 1933- ...... **CLC 21, 122**
See also CA 53-56; CANR 5, 20, 48, 98; DAM MULT; DLB 175; MTCW 1; NNAL; SATA 21

Del Vecchio, John M(ichael) 1947- .. **CLC 29**
See also CA 110; DLBD 9

de Man, Paul (Adolph Michel)
1919-1983 .... **CLC 55**
See also CA 128; 111; CANR 61; DLB 67; MTCW 1, 2

DeMarinis, Rick 1934- .... **CLC 54**
See also CA 57-60, 184; CAAE 184; CAAS 24; CANR 9, 25, 50; DLB 218

Dembry, R. Emmet
See Murfree, Mary Noailles

Demby, William 1922- .... **CLC 53; BLC 1**
See also BW 1, 3; CA 81-84; CANR 81; DAM MULT; DLB 33

de Menton, Francisco
See Chin, Frank (Chew, Jr.)

Demetrius of Phalerum c.
307B.C.- .... **CMLC 34**

Demijohn, Thom
See Disch, Thomas M(ichael)

Deming, Richard 1915-1983
See Queen, Ellery
See also CA 9-12R; CANR 3, 94; SATA 24

Democritus c. 460B.C.-c. 370B.C. . **CMLC 47**

de Montherlant, Henry (Milon)
See Montherlant, Henry (Milon) de

Demosthenes 384B.C.-322B.C. ...... **CMLC 13**
See also AW 1; DLB 176; RGWL 2

de Natale, Francine
See Malzberg, Barry N(athaniel)

de Navarre, Marguerite 1492-1549 ..... **LC 61**
See also Marguerite d'Angouleme; Marguerite de Navarre

Denby, Edwin (Orr) 1903-1983 .... **CLC 48**
See also CA 138; 110

Denham, John 1615-1669 .... **LC 73**
See also DLB 58, 126; RGEL 2

Denis, Julio
See Cortazar, Julio

Denmark, Harrison
See Zelazny, Roger (Joseph)

Dennis, John 1658-1734 .... **LC 11**
See also DLB 101; RGEL 2

Dennis, Nigel (Forbes) 1912-1989 ...... **CLC 8**
See also CA 25-28R; 129; DLB 13, 15, 233; MTCW 1

Dent, Lester 1904(?)-1959 .... **TCLC 72**
See also CA 112; 161; CMW 4; SFW 4

De Palma, Brian (Russell) 1940- ...... **CLC 20**
See also CA 109

De Quincey, Thomas 1785-1859 ..... **NCLC 4, 87**
See also BRW 4; CDBLB 1789-1832; DLB 110, 144; RGEL 2

Deren, Eleanora 1908(?)-1961
See Deren, Maya
See also CA 192; 111

Deren, Maya .... **CLC 16, 102**
See also Deren, Eleanora

Derleth, August (William)
1909-1971 .... **CLC 31**
See also BPFB 1; BYA 9, 10; CA 1-4R; 29-32R; CANR 4; CMW 4; DLB 9; DLBD 17; HGG; SATA 5; SUFW

Der Nister 1884-1950 .... **TCLC 56**

de Routisie, Albert
See Aragon, Louis

Derrida, Jacques 1930- .... **CLC 24, 87**
See also CA 124; 127; CANR 76, 98; DLB 242; MTCW 1

Derry Down Derry
See Lear, Edward

Dersonnes, Jacques
See Simenon, Georges (Jacques Christian)

Desai, Anita 1937- .... **CLC 19, 37, 97**
See also BRWS 5; CA 81-84; CANR 33, 53, 95; CN 7; CWRI 5; DA3; DAB; DAM NOV; DNFS 2; FW; MTCW 1, 2; SATA 63, 126

Desai, Kiran 1971- .... **CLC 119**
See also CA 171

de Saint-Luc, Jean
See Glassco, John

de Saint Roman, Arnaud
See Aragon, Louis

Desbordes-Valmore, Marceline
1786-1859 .... **NCLC 97**
See also DLB 217

Descartes, Rene 1596-1650 .... **LC 20, 35**
See also EW 3; GFL Beginnings to 1789

De Sica, Vittorio 1901(?)-1974 .... **CLC 20**
See also CA 117

Desnos, Robert 1900-1945 .... **TCLC 22**
See also CA 121; 151; CANR 107; DLB 258

Destouches, Louis-Ferdinand
1894-1961 .... **CLC 9, 15**
See also Celine, Louis-Ferdinand
See also CA 85-88; CANR 28; MTCW 1

de Tolignac, Gaston
See Griffith, D(avid Lewelyn) W(ark)

Deutsch, Babette 1895-1982 .... **CLC 18**
See also BYA 3; CA 1-4R; 108; CANR 4, 79; DLB 45; SATA 1; SATA-Obit 33

Devenant, William 1606-1649 .... **LC 13**

Devkota, Laxmiprasad 1909-1959 . **TCLC 23**
See also CA 123

De Voto, Bernard (Augustine)
1897-1955 .... **TCLC 29**
See also CA 113; 160; DLB 9, 256

De Vries, Peter 1910-1993 ..... **CLC 1, 2, 3, 7, 10, 28, 46**
See also CA 17-20R; 142; CANR 41; DAM NOV; DLB 6; DLBY 1982; MTCW 1, 2

Dewey, John 1859-1952 .... **TCLC 95**
See also CA 114; 170; DLB 246; RGAL 4

Dexter, John
See Bradley, Marion Zimmer
See also GLL 1

Dexter, Martin
See Faust, Frederick (Schiller)
See also TCWW 2

Dexter, Pete 1943- .... **CLC 34, 55**
See also BEST 89:2; CA 127; 131; CPW; DAM POP; INT 131; MTCW 1

Diamano, Silmang
See Senghor, Leopold Sedar

Diamond, Neil 1941- .... **CLC 30**
See also CA 108

Diaz del Castillo, Bernal 1496-1584 .. **LC 31; HLCS 1**
See also LAW

di Bassetto, Corno
See Shaw, George Bernard

Dick, Philip K(indred) 1928-1982 ... **CLC 10, 30, 72**
See also AAYA 24; BPFB 1; BYA 11; CA 49-52; 106; CANR 2, 16; CPW; DA3; DAM NOV, POP; DLB 8; MTCW 1, 2; NFS 5; SCFW; SFW 4

Dickens, Charles (John Huffam)
1812-1870 .... **NCLC 3, 8, 18, 26, 37, 50, 86, 105; SSC 17, 49; WLC**
See also AAYA 23; BRW 5; BYA 1, 2, 3, 13, 14; CDBLB 1832-1890; CMW 4; DA; DA3; DAB; DAC; DAM MST, NOV; DLB 21, 55, 70, 159, 166; EXPN; HGG; JRDA; LAIT 1, 2; MAICYA 1, 2; NFS 4, 5, 10, 14; RGEL 2; RGSF 2; SATA 15; SUFW; WCH; WLIT 4; WYA

Dickey, James (Lafayette)
1923-1997 ...... **CLC 1, 2, 4, 7, 10, 15, 47, 109; PC 40**
See also AITN 1, 2; AMWS 4; BPFB 1; CA 9-12R; 156; CABS 2; CANR 10, 48, 61, 105; CDALB 1968-1988; CP 7; CPW; CSW; DA3; DAM NOV, POET, POP; DLB 5, 193; DLBD 7; DLBY 1982, 1993, 1996, 1997, 1998; INT CANR-10; MTCW 1, 2; NFS 9; PFS 6, 11; RGAL 4

Dickey, William 1928-1994 .... **CLC 3, 28**
See also CA 9-12R; 145; CANR 24, 79; DLB 5

Dickinson, Charles 1951- .... **CLC 49**
See also CA 128

Dickinson, Emily (Elizabeth)
1830-1886 ... **NCLC 21, 77; PC 1; WLC**
See also AAYA 22; AMW; AMWR 1; CDALB 1865-1917; DA; DA3; DAB; DAC; DAM MST, POET; EXPP; MAWW; PAB; PFS 1, 2, 3, 4, 5, 6, 8, 10, 11, 13; RGAL 4; SATA 29; WP; WYA

Dickinson, Mrs. Herbert Ward
See Phelps, Elizabeth Stuart

Dickinson, Peter (Malcolm) 1927- .. **CLC 12, 35**
See also AAYA 9; BYA 5; CA 41-44R; CANR 31, 58, 88; CLR 29; CMW 4; DLB 87, 161; JRDA; MAICYA 1, 2; SATA 5, 62, 95; SFW 4; WYA; YAW

Dickson, Carr
See Carr, John Dickson

Dickson, Carter
See Carr, John Dickson

Diderot, Denis 1713-1784 .... **LC 26**
See also EW 4; GFL Beginnings to 1789; RGWL 2

Didion, Joan 1934- . **CLC 1, 3, 8, 14, 32, 129**
See also AITN 1; AMWS 4; CA 5-8R; CANR 14, 52, 76; CDALB 1968-1988; CN 7; DA3; DAM NOV; DLB 2, 173, 185; DLBY 1981, 1986; MAWW; MTCW 1, 2; NFS 3; RGAL 4; TCWW 2

Dietrich, Robert
See Hunt, E(verette) Howard, (Jr.)

Difusa, Pati
See Almodovar, Pedro

Dillard, Annie 1945- .... **CLC 9, 60, 115**
See also AAYA 6, 43; AMWS 6; ANW; CA 49-52; CANR 3, 43, 62, 90; DA3; DAM NOV; DLBY 1980; LAIT 4, 5; MTCW 1, 2; NCFS 5; RGAL 4; SATA 10

Dillard, R(ichard) H(enry) W(ilde)
1937- .... **CLC 5**
See also CA 21-24R; CAAS 7; CANR 10; CP 7; CSW; DLB 5, 244

Dillon, Eilis 1920-1994 .... **CLC 17**
See also CA 9-12R, 182; 147; CAAE 182; CAAS 3; CANR 4, 38, 78; CLR 26; MAICYA 1, 2; MAICYAS 1; SATA 2, 74; SATA-Essay 105; SATA-Obit 83; YAW

Dimont, Penelope
See Mortimer, Penelope (Ruth)

Dinesen, Isak .... **CLC 10, 29, 95; SSC 7**
See also Blixen, Karen (Christentze Dinesen)
See also EW 10; EXPS; FW; HGG; LAIT 3; MTCW 1; NCFS 2; NFS 9; RGSF 2; RGWL 2; SSFS 3, 6, 13; WLIT 2

Ding Ling .... **CLC 68**
See also Chiang, Pin-chin

Diphusa, Patty
See Almodovar, Pedro

Disch, Thomas M(ichael) 1940- ... **CLC 7, 36**
See also AAYA 17; BPFB 1; CA 21-24R; CAAS 4; CANR 17, 36, 54, 89; CLR 18; CP 7; DA3; DLB 8; HGG; MAICYA 1, 2; MTCW 1, 2; SAAS 15; SATA 92; SCFW; SFW 4

Disch, Tom
See Disch, Thomas M(ichael)

d'Isly, Georges
See Simenon, Georges (Jacques Christian)

Disraeli, Benjamin 1804-1881 ... **NCLC 2, 39, 79**
See also BRW 4; DLB 21, 55; RGEL 2

Ditcum, Steve
See Crumb, R(obert)

Dixon, Paige
See Corcoran, Barbara (Asenath)

Dixon, Stephen 1936- .... **CLC 52; SSC 16**
See also CA 89-92; CANR 17, 40, 54, 91; CN 7; DLB 130

Doak, Annie
See Dillard, Annie

Dobell, Sydney Thompson 1824-1874 .... **NCLC 43**
See also DLB 32; RGEL 2

Doblin, Alfred .... **TCLC 13**
See also Doeblin, Alfred
See also CDWLB 2; RGWL 2

Dobrolyubov, Nikolai Alexandrovich 1836-1861 .... **NCLC 5**

Dobson, Austin 1840-1921 .... **TCLC 79**
See also DLB 35, 144

Dobyns, Stephen 1941- .... **CLC 37**
See also CA 45-48; CANR 2, 18, 99; CMW 4; CP 7

Doctorow, E(dgar) L(aurence) 1931- .... **CLC 6, 11, 15, 18, 37, 44, 65, 113**
See also AAYA 22; AITN 2; AMWS 4; BEST 89:3; BPFB 1; CA 45-48; CANR 2, 33, 51, 76, 97; CDALB 1968-1988; CN 7; CPW; DA3; DAM NOV, POP; DLB 2, 28, 173; DLBY 1980; LAIT 3; MTCW 1, 2; NFS 6; RGAL 4; RHW

Dodgson, Charles L(utwidge) 1832-1898
See Carroll, Lewis
See also CLR 2; DA; DA3; DAB; DAC; DAM MST, NOV, POET; MAICYA 1, 2; SATA 100; YABC 2

Dodson, Owen (Vincent) 1914-1983 .... **CLC 79; BLC 1**
See also BW 1; CA 65-68; 110; CANR 24; DAM MULT; DLB 76

Doeblin, Alfred 1878-1957 .... **TCLC 13**
See also Doblin, Alfred
See also CA 110; 141; DLB 66

Doerr, Harriet 1910- .... **CLC 34**
See also CA 117; 122; CANR 47; INT 122

Domecq, H(onorio Bustos)
See Bioy Casares, Adolfo

Domecq, H(onorio) Bustos
See Bioy Casares, Adolfo; Borges, Jorge Luis

Domini, Rey
See Lorde, Audre (Geraldine)
See also GLL 1

Dominique
See Proust, (Valentin-Louis-George-Eugene-)Marcel

Don, A
See Stephen, Sir Leslie

Donaldson, Stephen R(eeder) 1947- .... **CLC 46, 138**
See also AAYA 36; BPFB 1; CA 89-92; CANR 13, 55, 99; CPW; DAM POP; FANT; INT CANR-13; SATA 121; SFW 4; SUFW

Donleavy, J(ames) P(atrick) 1926- .... **CLC 1, 4, 6, 10, 45**
See also AITN 2; BPFB 1; CA 9-12R; CANR 24, 49, 62, 80; CBD; CD 5; CN 7; DLB 6, 173; INT CANR-24; MTCW 1, 2; RGAL 4

Donne, John 1572-1631 ..... **LC 10, 24; PC 1; WLC**
See also BRW 1; BRWR 2; CDBLB Before 1660; DA; DAB; DAC; DAM MST, POET; DLB 121, 151; EXPP; PAB; PFS 2, 11; RGEL 2; WLIT 3; WP

Donnell, David 1939(?)- .... **CLC 34**
See also CA 197

Donoghue, P. S.
See Hunt, E(verette) Howard, (Jr.)

Donoso (Yanez), Jose 1924-1996 ... **CLC 4, 8, 11, 32, 99; HLC 1; SSC 34**
See also CA 81-84; 155; CANR 32, 73; CD-WLB 3; DAM MULT; DLB 113; HW 1, 2; LAW; LAWS 1; MTCW 1, 2; RGSF 2; WLIT 1

Donovan, John 1928-1992 .... **CLC 35**
See also AAYA 20; CA 97-100; 137; CLR 3; MAICYA 1, 2; SATA 72; SATA-Brief 29; YAW

Don Roberto
See Cunninghame Graham, Robert (Gallnigad) Bontine

Doolittle, Hilda 1886-1961 . **CLC 3, 8, 14, 31, 34, 73; PC 5; WLC**
See also H. D.
See also AMWS 1; CA 97-100; CANR 35; DA; DAC; DAM MST, POET; DLB 4, 45; FW; GLL 1; MAWW; MTCW 1, 2; PFS 6; RGAL 4

Doppo, Kunikida .... **TCLC 99**
See also Kunikida Doppo

Dorfman, Ariel 1942- .... **CLC 48, 77; HLC 1**
See also CA 124; 130; CANR 67, 70; CWW 2; DAM MULT; DFS 4; HW 1, 2; INT CA-130; WLIT 1

Dorn, Edward (Merton) 1929-1999 .... **CLC 10, 18**
See also CA 93-96; 187; CANR 42, 79; CP 7; DLB 5; INT 93-96; WP

Dor-Ner, Zvi .... **CLC 70**

Dorris, Michael (Anthony) 1945-1997 .... **CLC 109**
See also AAYA 20; BEST 90:1; BYA 12; CA 102; 157; CANR 19, 46, 75; CLR 58; DA3; DAM MULT, NOV; DLB 175; LAIT 5; MTCW 2; NFS 3; NNAL; RGAL 4; SATA 75; SATA-Obit 94; TCWW 2; YAW

Dorris, Michael A.
See Dorris, Michael (Anthony)

Dorsan, Luc
See Simenon, Georges (Jacques Christian)

Dorsange, Jean
See Simenon, Georges (Jacques Christian)

Dos Passos, John (Roderigo) 1896-1970 ... **CLC 1, 4, 8, 11, 15, 25, 34, 82; WLC**
See also AMW; BPFB 1; CA 1-4R; 29-32R; CANR 3; CDALB 1929-1941; DA; DA3; DAB; DAC; DAM MST, NOV; DLB 4, 9; DLBD 1, 15; DLBY 1996; MTCW 1, 2; NFS 14; RGAL 4

Dossage, Jean
See Simenon, Georges (Jacques Christian)

Dostoevsky, Fedor Mikhailovich 1821-1881 . **NCLC 2, 7, 21, 33, 43; SSC 2, 33, 44; WLC**
See also Dostoevsky, Fyodor
See also AAYA 40; DA; DA3; DAB; DAC; DAM MST, NOV; EW 7; EXPN; NFS 3, 8; RGSF 2; RGWL 2; SSFS 8

Dostoevsky, Fyodor
See Dostoevsky, Fedor Mikhailovich
See also DLB 238

Doughty, Charles M(ontagu) 1843-1926 .... **TCLC 27**
See also CA 115; 178; DLB 19, 57, 174

Douglas, Ellen .... **CLC 73**
See also Haxton, Josephine Ayres; Williamson, Ellen Douglas
See also CN 7; CSW

Douglas, Gavin 1475(?)-1522 .... **LC 20**
See also DLB 132; RGEL 2

Douglas, George
See Brown, George Douglas
See also RGEL 2

Douglas, Keith (Castellain) 1920-1944 .... **TCLC 40**
See also BRW 7; CA 160; DLB 27; PAB; RGEL 2

Douglas, Leonard
See Bradbury, Ray (Douglas)

Douglas, Michael
See Crichton, (John) Michael

Douglas, (George) Norman 1868-1952 .... **TCLC 68**
See also BRW 6; CA 119; 157; DLB 34, 195; RGEL 2

Douglas, William
See Brown, George Douglas

Douglass, Frederick 1817(?)-1895 .. **NCLC 7, 55; BLC 1; WLC**
See also AFAW 1, 2; AMWS 3; CDALB 1640-1865; DA; DA3; DAC; DAM MST, MULT; DLB 1, 43, 50, 79, 243; FW; LAIT 2; NCFS 2; RGAL 4; SATA 29

Dourado, (Waldomiro Freitas) Autran 1926- .... **CLC 23, 60**
See also CA 25-28R, 179; CANR 34, 81; DLB 145; HW 2

Dourado, Waldomiro Autran
See Dourado, (Waldomiro Freitas) Autran
See also CA 179

Dove, Rita (Frances) 1952- .... **CLC 50, 81; BLCS; PC 6**
See also AMWS 4; BW 2; CA 109; CAAS 19; CANR 27, 42, 68, 76, 97; CDALBS; CP 7; CSW; CWP; DA3; DAM MULT, POET; DLB 120; EXPP; MTCW 1; PFS 1; RGAL 4

Doveglion
See Villa, Jose Garcia

Dowell, Coleman 1925-1985 .... **CLC 60**
See also CA 25-28R; 117; CANR 10; DLB 130; GLL 1

Dowson, Ernest (Christopher) 1867-1900 .... **TCLC 4**
See also CA 105; 150; DLB 19, 135; RGEL 2

Doyle, A. Conan
See Doyle, Sir Arthur Conan

Doyle, Sir Arthur Conan 1859-1930 .... **TCLC 7; SSC 12; WLC**
See also Conan Doyle, Arthur
See also AAYA 14; BRWS 2; CA 104; 122; CDBLB 1890-1914; CMW 4; DA; DA3; DAB; DAC; DAM MST, NOV; DLB 18, 70, 156, 178; EXPS; HGG; LAIT 2; MSW; MTCW 1, 2; RGEL 2; RGSF 2; RHW; SATA 24; SCFW 2; SFW 4; SSFS 2; WCH; WLIT 4; WYA; YAW

Doyle, Conan
See Doyle, Sir Arthur Conan

Doyle, John
See Graves, Robert (von Ranke)

Doyle, Roddy 1958(?)- .... **CLC 81**
See also AAYA 14; BRWS 5; CA 143; CANR 73; CN 7; DA3; DLB 194

Doyle, Sir A. Conan
See Doyle, Sir Arthur Conan

Dr. A
See Asimov, Isaac; Silverstein, Alvin; Silverstein, Virginia B(arbara Opshelor)

Drabble, Margaret 1939- ...... **CLC 2, 3, 5, 8, 10, 22, 53, 129**
See also BRWS 4; CA 13-16R; CANR 18, 35, 63; CDBLB 1960 to Present; CN 7; CPW; DA3; DAB; DAC; DAM MST, NOV, POP; DLB 14, 155, 231; FW; MTCW 1, 2; RGEL 2; SATA 48

Drapier, M. B.
See Swift, Jonathan

Drayham, James
See Mencken, H(enry) L(ouis)

Drayton, Michael 1563-1631 .... **LC 8**
See also DAM POET; DLB 121; RGEL 2

Dreadstone, Carl
See Campbell, (John) Ramsey

Dreiser, Theodore (Herman Albert)
1871-1945 .... **TCLC 10, 18, 35, 83; SSC 30; WLC**
See also AMW; CA 106; 132; CDALB 1865-1917; DA; DA3; DAC; DAM MST, NOV; DLB 9, 12, 102, 137; DLBD 1; LAIT 2; MTCW 1, 2; NFS 8; RGAL 4

Drexler, Rosalyn 1926- .... **CLC 2, 6**
See also CA 81-84; CAD; CANR 68; CD 5; CWD

Dreyer, Carl Theodor 1889-1968 ...... **CLC 16**
See also CA 116

Drieu la Rochelle, Pierre(-Eugene)
1893-1945 .... **TCLC 21**
See also CA 117; DLB 72; GFL 1789 to the Present

Drinkwater, John 1882-1937 .... **TCLC 57**
See also CA 109; 149; DLB 10, 19, 149; RGEL 2

Drop Shot
See Cable, George Washington

Droste-Hulshoff, Annette Freiin von
1797-1848 .... **NCLC 3**
See also CDWLB 2; DLB 133; RGSF 2; RGWL 2

Drummond, Walter
See Silverberg, Robert

Drummond, William Henry
1854-1907 .... **TCLC 25**
See also CA 160; DLB 92

Drummond de Andrade, Carlos
1902-1987 .... **CLC 18**
See also Andrade, Carlos Drummond de
See also CA 132; 123; LAW

Drury, Allen (Stuart) 1918-1998 .... **CLC 37**
See also CA 57-60; 170; CANR 18, 52; CN 7; INT CANR-18

Dryden, John 1631-1700 ..... **LC 3, 21; DC 3; PC 25; WLC**
See also BRW 2; CDBLB 1660-1789; DA; DAB; DAC; DAM DRAM, MST, POET; DLB 80, 101, 131; EXPP; IDTP; RGEL 2; TEA; WLIT 3

Duberman, Martin (Bauml) 1930- ..... **CLC 8**
See also CA 1-4R; CAD; CANR 2, 63; CD 5

Dubie, Norman (Evans) 1945- .... **CLC 36**
See also CA 69-72; CANR 12; CP 7; DLB 120; PFS 12

Du Bois, W(illiam) E(dward) B(urghardt)
1868-1963 ... **CLC 1, 2, 13, 64, 96; BLC 1; WLC**
See also AAYA 40; AFAW 1, 2; AMWS 2; BW 1, 3; CA 85-88; CANR 34, 82; CDALB 1865-1917; DA; DA3; DAC;

DAM MST, MULT, NOV; DLB 47, 50, 91, 246; EXPP; LAIT 2; MTCW 1, 2; NCFS 1; PFS 13; RGAL 4; SATA 42

Dubus, Andre 1936-1999 ..... **CLC 13, 36, 97; SSC 15**
See also AMWS 7; CA 21-24R; 177; CANR 17; CN 7; CSW; DLB 130; INT CANR-17; RGAL 4; SSFS 10

Duca Minimo
See D'Annunzio, Gabriele

Ducharme, Rejean 1941- .... **CLC 74**
See also CA 165; DLB 60

Duchen, Claire .... **CLC 65**

Duclos, Charles Pinot- 1704-1772 .... **LC 1**
See also GFL Beginnings to 1789

Dudek, Louis 1918- .... **CLC 11, 19**
See also CA 45-48; CAAS 14; CANR 1; CP 7; DLB 88

Duerrenmatt, Friedrich 1921-1990 ... **CLC 1, 4, 8, 11, 15, 43, 102**
See also Durrenmatt, Friedrich
See also CA 17-20R; CANR 33; CMW 4; DAM DRAM; DLB 69, 124; MTCW 1, 2

Duffy, Bruce 1953(?)- .... **CLC 50**
See also CA 172

Duffy, Maureen 1933- .... **CLC 37**
See also CA 25-28R; CANR 33, 68; CBD; CN 7; CP 7; CWD; CWP; DLB 14; FW; MTCW 1

Du Fu
See Tu Fu
See also RGWL 2

Dugan, Alan 1923- .... **CLC 2, 6**
See also CA 81-84; CP 7; DLB 5; PFS 10

du Gard, Roger Martin
See Martin du Gard, Roger

Duhamel, Georges 1884-1966 .... **CLC 8**
See also CA 81-84; 25-28R; CANR 35; DLB 65; GFL 1789 to the Present; MTCW 1

Dujardin, Edouard (Emile Louis)
1861-1949 .... **TCLC 13**
See also CA 109; DLB 123

Dulles, John Foster 1888-1959 .... **TCLC 72**
See also CA 115; 149

Dumas, Alexandre (pere)
1802-1870 .... **NCLC 11, 71; WLC**
See also AAYA 22; BYA 3; DA; DA3; DAB; DAC; DAM MST, NOV; DLB 119, 192; EW 6; GFL 1789 to the Present; LAIT 1, 2; NFS 14; RGWL 2; SATA 18; WCH

Dumas, Alexandre (fils)
1824-1895 .... **NCLC 9; DC 1**
See also DLB 192; GFL 1789 to the Present; RGWL 2

Dumas, Claudine
See Malzberg, Barry N(athaniel)

Dumas, Henry L. 1934-1968 .... **CLC 6, 62**
See also BW 1; CA 85-88; DLB 41; RGAL 4

du Maurier, Daphne 1907-1989 .. **CLC 6, 11, 59; SSC 18**
See also AAYA 37; BPFB 1; BRWS 3; CA 5-8R; 128; CANR 6, 55; CMW 4; CPW; DA3; DAB; DAC; DAM MST, POP; DLB 191; HGG; LAIT 3; MSW; MTCW 1, 2; NFS 12; RGEL 2; RGSF 2; RHW; SATA 27; SATA-Obit 60; SSFS 14

Du Maurier, George 1834-1896 ..... **NCLC 86**
See also DLB 153, 178; RGEL 2

Dunbar, Paul Laurence 1872-1906 . **TCLC 2, 12; BLC 1; PC 5; SSC 8; WLC**
See also AFAW 1, 2; AMWS 2; BW 1, 3; CA 104; 124; CANR 79; CDALB 1865-1917; DA; DA3; DAC; DAM MST, MULT, POET; DLB 50, 54, 78; EXPP; RGAL 4; SATA 34

Dunbar, William 1460(?)-1520(?) .... **LC 20**
See also DLB 132, 146; RGEL 2

Duncan, Dora Angela
See Duncan, Isadora

Duncan, Isadora 1877(?)-1927 .... **TCLC 68**
See also CA 118; 149

Duncan, Lois 1934- .... **CLC 26**
See also AAYA 4, 34; BYA 6, 8; CA 1-4R; CANR 2, 23, 36; CLR 29; JRDA; MAICYA 1, 2; MAICYAS 1; SAAS 2; SATA 1, 36, 75; WYA; YAW

Duncan, Robert (Edward)
1919-1988 .... **CLC 1, 2, 4, 7, 15, 41, 55; PC 2**
See also CA 9-12R; 124; CANR 28, 62; DAM POET; DLB 5, 16, 193; MTCW 1, 2; PFS 13; RGAL 4; WP

Duncan, Sara Jeannette
1861-1922 .... **TCLC 60**
See also CA 157; DLB 92

Dunlap, William 1766-1839 .... **NCLC 2**
See also DLB 30, 37, 59; RGAL 4

Dunn, Douglas (Eaglesham) 1942- .... **CLC 6, 40**
See also CA 45-48; CANR 2, 33; CP 7; DLB 40; MTCW 1

Dunn, Katherine (Karen) 1945- .... **CLC 71**
See also CA 33-36R; CANR 72; HGG; MTCW 1

Dunn, Stephen (Elliott) 1939- .... **CLC 36**
See also CA 33-36R; CANR 12, 48, 53, 105; CP 7; DLB 105

Dunne, Finley Peter 1867-1936 ...... **TCLC 28**
See also CA 108; 178; DLB 11, 23; RGAL 4

Dunne, John Gregory 1932- .... **CLC 28**
See also CA 25-28R; CANR 14, 50; CN 7; DLBY 1980

Dunsany, Lord .... **TCLC 2, 59**
See also Dunsany, Edward John Moreton Drax Plunkett
See also DLB 77, 153, 156, 255; FANT; IDTP; RGEL 2; SFW 4; SUFW

Dunsany, Edward John Moreton Drax Plunkett 1878-1957
See Dunsany, Lord
See also CA 104; 148; DLB 10; MTCW 1

du Perry, Jean
See Simenon, Georges (Jacques Christian)

Durang, Christopher (Ferdinand)
1949- .... **CLC 27, 38**
See also CA 105; CAD; CANR 50, 76; CD 5; MTCW 1

Duras, Marguerite 1914-1996 . **CLC 3, 6, 11, 20, 34, 40, 68, 100; SSC 40**
See also BPFB 1; CA 25-28R; 151; CANR 50; CWW 2; DLB 83; GFL 1789 to the Present; IDFW 4; MTCW 1, 2; RGWL 2

Durban, (Rosa) Pam 1947- .... **CLC 39**
See also CA 123; CANR 98; CSW

Durcan, Paul 1944- .... **CLC 43, 70**
See also CA 134; CP 7; DAM POET

Durkheim, Emile 1858-1917 .... **TCLC 55**

Durrell, Lawrence (George)
1912-1990 ..... **CLC 1, 4, 6, 8, 13, 27, 41**
See also BPFB 1; BRWS 1; CA 9-12R; 132; CANR 40, 77; CDBLB 1945-1960; DAM NOV; DLB 15, 27, 204; DLBY 1990; MTCW 1, 2; RGEL 2; SFW 4

Durrenmatt, Friedrich
See Duerrenmatt, Friedrich
See also CDWLB 2; EW 13; RGWL 2

Dutt, Toru 1856-1877 .... **NCLC 29**
See also DLB 240

Dwight, Timothy 1752-1817 .... **NCLC 13**
See also DLB 37; RGAL 4

Dworkin, Andrea 1946- .... **CLC 43, 123**
See also CA 77-80; CAAS 21; CANR 16, 39, 76, 96; FW; GLL 1; INT CANR-16; MTCW 1, 2

Dwyer, Deanna
See Koontz, Dean R(ay)

Dwyer, K. R.
See Koontz, Dean R(ay)

Dwyer, Thomas A. 1923- .... **CLC 114**
See also CA 115

Dybek, Stuart 1942- .... **CLC 114**
See also CA 97-100; CANR 39; DLB 130

Dye, Richard
See De Voto, Bernard (Augustine)

Dyer, Geoff 1958- .... **CLC 149**
See also CA 125; CANR 88

Dylan, Bob 1941- .... **CLC 3, 4, 6, 12, 77; PC 37**
See also CA 41-44R; CANR 108; CP 7; DLB 16

Dyson, John 1943- .... **CLC 70**
See also CA 144

E. V. L.
See Lucas, E(dward) V(errall)

Eagleton, Terence (Francis) 1943- .. **CLC 63, 132**
See also CA 57-60; CANR 7, 23, 68; DLB 242; MTCW 1, 2

Eagleton, Terry
See Eagleton, Terence (Francis)

Early, Jack
See Scoppettone, Sandra
See also GLL 1

East, Michael
See West, Morris L(anglo)

Eastaway, Edward
See Thomas, (Philip) Edward

Eastlake, William (Derry)
1917-1997 .... **CLC 8**
See also CA 5-8R; 158; CAAS 1; CANR 5, 63; CN 7; DLB 6, 206; INT CANR-5; TCWW 2

Eastman, Charles A(lexander)
1858-1939 .... **TCLC 55**
See also CA 179; CANR 91; DAM MULT; DLB 175; NNAL; YABC 1

Eberhart, Richard (Ghormley)
1904- .... **CLC 3, 11, 19, 56**
See also AMW; CA 1-4R; CANR 2; CDALB 1941-1968; CP 7; DAM POET; DLB 48; MTCW 1; RGAL 4

Eberstadt, Fernanda 1960- .... **CLC 39**
See also CA 136; CANR 69

Echegaray (y Eizaguirre), Jose (Maria Waldo) 1832-1916 .... **TCLC 4; HLCS 1**
See also CA 104; CANR 32; HW 1; MTCW 1

Echeverria, (Jose) Esteban (Antonino)
1805-1851 .... **NCLC 18**
See also LAW

Echo
See Proust, (Valentin-Louis-George-Eugene-)Marcel

Eckert, Allan W. 1931- .... **CLC 17**
See also AAYA 18; BYA 2; CA 13-16R; CANR 14, 45; INT CANR-14; MAICYA 2; MAICYAS 1; SAAS 21; SATA 29, 91; SATA-Brief 27

Eckhart, Meister 1260(?)-1327(?) ... **CMLC 9**
See also DLB 115

Eckmar, F. R.
See de Hartog, Jan

Eco, Umberto 1932- .... **CLC 28, 60, 142**
See also BEST 90:1; BPFB 1; CA 77-80; CANR 12, 33, 55; CPW; CWW 2; DA3; DAM NOV, POP; DLB 196, 242; MSW; MTCW 1, 2

Eddison, E(ric) R(ucker)
1882-1945 .... **TCLC 15**
See also CA 109; 156; DLB 255; FANT; SFW 4; SUFW

Eddy, Mary (Ann Morse) Baker
1821-1910 .... **TCLC 71**
See also CA 113; 174

Edel, (Joseph) Leon 1907-1997 .. **CLC 29, 34**
See also CA 1-4R; 161; CANR 1, 22; DLB 103; INT CANR-22

Eden, Emily 1797-1869 .... **NCLC 10**

Edgar, David 1948- .... **CLC 42**
See also CA 57-60; CANR 12, 61; CBD; CD 5; DAM DRAM; DLB 13, 233; MTCW 1

Edgerton, Clyde (Carlyle) 1944- ...... **CLC 39**
See also AAYA 17; CA 118; 134; CANR 64; CSW; INT 134; YAW

Edgeworth, Maria 1768-1849 .... **NCLC 1, 51**
See also BRWS 3; DLB 116, 159, 163; FW; RGEL 2; SATA 21; WLIT 3

Edmonds, Paul
See Kuttner, Henry

Edmonds, Walter D(umaux)
1903-1998 .... **CLC 35**
See also BYA 2; CA 5-8R; CANR 2; CWRI 5; DLB 9; LAIT 1; MAICYA 1, 2; RHW; SAAS 4; SATA 1, 27; SATA-Obit 99

Edmondson, Wallace
See Ellison, Harlan (Jay)

Edson, Russell 1935- .... **CLC 13**
See also CA 33-36R; DLB 244; WP

Edwards, Bronwen Elizabeth
See Rose, Wendy

Edwards, G(erald) B(asil)
1899-1976 .... **CLC 25**
See also CA 201; 110

Edwards, Gus 1939- .... **CLC 43**
See also CA 108; INT 108

Edwards, Jonathan 1703-1758 .... **LC 7, 54**
See also AMW; DA; DAC; DAM MST; DLB 24; RGAL 4

Efron, Marina Ivanovna Tsvetaeva
See Tsvetaeva (Efron), Marina (Ivanovna)

Egoyan, Atom 1960- .... **CLC 151**
See also CA 157

Ehle, John (Marsden, Jr.) 1925- ...... **CLC 27**
See also CA 9-12R; CSW

Ehrenbourg, Ilya (Grigoryevich)
See Ehrenburg, Ilya (Grigoryevich)

Ehrenburg, Ilya (Grigoryevich)
1891-1967 .... **CLC 18, 34, 62**
See also CA 102; 25-28R

Ehrenburg, Ilyo (Grigoryevich)
See Ehrenburg, Ilya (Grigoryevich)

Ehrenreich, Barbara 1941- .... **CLC 110**
See also BEST 90:4; CA 73-76; CANR 16, 37, 62; DLB 246; FW; MTCW 1, 2

Eich, Guenter 1907-1972 .... **CLC 15**
See also Eich, Gunter
See also CA 111; 93-96; DLB 69, 124

Eich, Gunter
See Eich, Guenter
See also RGWL 2

Eichendorff, Joseph 1788-1857 .... **NCLC 8**
See also DLB 90; RGWL 2

Eigner, Larry .... **CLC 9**
See also Eigner, Laurence (Joel)
See also CAAS 23; DLB 5; WP

Eigner, Laurence (Joel) 1927-1996
See Eigner, Larry
See also CA 9-12R; 151; CANR 6, 84; CP 7; DLB 193

Einhard c. 770-840 .... **CMLC 50**
See also DLB 148

Einstein, Albert 1879-1955 .... **TCLC 65**
See also CA 121; 133; MTCW 1, 2

Eiseley, Loren Corey 1907-1977 .... **CLC 7**
See also AAYA 5; ANW; CA 1-4R; 73-76; CANR 6; DLBD 17

Eisenstadt, Jill 1963- .... **CLC 50**
See also CA 140

Eisenstein, Sergei (Mikhailovich)
1898-1948 .... **TCLC 57**
See also CA 114; 149

Eisner, Simon
See Kornbluth, C(yril) M.

Ekeloef, (Bengt) Gunnar
1907-1968 .... **CLC 27; PC 23**
See also Ekelof, (Bengt) Gunnar
See also CA 123; 25-28R; DAM POET

Ekelof, (Bengt) Gunnar 1907-1968
See Ekeloef, (Bengt) Gunnar
See also DLB 259; EW 12

Ekelund, Vilhelm 1880-1949 .... **TCLC 75**
See also CA 189

Ekwensi, C. O. D.
See Ekwensi, Cyprian (Odiatu Duaka)

Ekwensi, Cyprian (Odiatu Duaka)
1921- .... **CLC 4; BLC 1**
See also AFW; BW 2, 3; CA 29-32R; CANR 18, 42, 74; CDWLB 3; CN 7; CWRI 5; DAM MULT; DLB 117; MTCW 1, 2; RGEL 2; SATA 66; WLIT 2

Elaine .... **TCLC 18**
See also Leverson, Ada

El Crummo
See Crumb, R(obert)

Elder, Lonne III 1931-1996 .... **DC 8**
See also BLC 1; BW 1, 3; CA 81-84; 152; CAD; CANR 25; DAM MULT; DLB 7, 38, 44

Eleanor of Aquitaine 1122-1204 ... **CMLC 39**

Elia
See Lamb, Charles

Eliade, Mircea 1907-1986 .... **CLC 19**
See also CA 65-68; 119; CANR 30, 62; CDWLB 4; DLB 220; MTCW 1; SFW 4

Eliot, A. D.
See Jewett, (Theodora) Sarah Orne

Eliot, Alice
See Jewett, (Theodora) Sarah Orne

Eliot, Dan
See Silverberg, Robert

Eliot, George 1819-1880 ...... **NCLC 4, 13, 23, 41, 49, 89; PC 20; WLC**
See also BRW 5; BRWR 2; CDBLB 1832-1890; CN 7; CPW; DA; DA3; DAB; DAC; DAM MST, NOV; DLB 21, 35, 55; RGEL 2; RGSF 2; SSFS 8; WLIT 3

Eliot, John 1604-1690 .... **LC 5**
See also DLB 24

Eliot, T(homas) S(tearns)
1888-1965 ...... **CLC 1, 2, 3, 6, 9, 10, 13, 15, 24, 34, 41, 55, 57, 113; PC 5, 31; WLC**
See also AAYA 28; AMW; AMWR 1; BRW 7; BRWR 2; CA 5-8R; 25-28R; CANR 41; CDALB 1929-1941; DA; DA3; DAB; DAC; DAM DRAM, MST, POET; DFS 4, 13; DLB 7, 10, 45, 63, 245; DLBY 1988; EXPP; LAIT 3; MTCW 1, 2; PAB; PFS 1, 7; RGAL 4; RGEL 2; WLIT 4; WP

Elizabeth 1866-1941 .... **TCLC 41**

Elkin, Stanley L(awrence)
1930-1995 .. **CLC 4, 6, 9, 14, 27, 51, 91; SSC 12**
See also AMWS 6; BPFB 1; CA 9-12R; 148; CANR 8, 46; CN 7; CPW; DAM NOV, POP; DLB 2, 28, 218; DLBY 1980; INT CANR-8; MTCW 1, 2; RGAL 4

Elledge, Scott .... **CLC 34**

Elliot, Don
See Silverberg, Robert

Elliott, Don
See Silverberg, Robert

Elliott, George P(aul) 1918-1980 .... **CLC 2**
See also CA 1-4R; 97-100; CANR 2; DLB 244

Elliott, Janice 1931-1995 .... **CLC 47**
See also CA 13-16R; CANR 8, 29, 84; CN 7; DLB 14; SATA 119

Elliott, Sumner Locke 1917-1991 ..... **CLC 38**
See also CA 5-8R; 134; CANR 2, 21

Elliott, William
See Bradbury, Ray (Douglas)

Ellis, A. E. .... **CLC 7**

Ellis, Alice Thomas .... **CLC 40**
See also Haycraft, Anna (Margaret)
See also DLB 194; MTCW 1

Ellis, Bret Easton 1964- ...... **CLC 39, 71, 117**
See also AAYA 2, 43; CA 118; 123; CANR 51, 74; CN 7; CPW; DA3; DAM POP; HGG; INT CA-123; MTCW 1; NFS 11

Ellis, (Henry) Havelock
1859-1939 .... **TCLC 14**
See also CA 109; 169; DLB 190

Ellis, Landon
See Ellison, Harlan (Jay)

Ellis, Trey 1962- .... **CLC 55**
See also CA 146; CANR 92

Ellison, Harlan (Jay) 1934- ... **CLC 1, 13, 42, 139; SSC 14**
See also AAYA 29; BPFB 1; BYA 14; CA 5-8R; CANR 5, 46; CPW; DAM POP; DLB 8; HGG; INT CANR-5; MTCW 1, 2; SCFW 2; SFW 4; SSFS 13, 14; SUFW

Ellison, Ralph (Waldo) 1914-1994 .... **CLC 1, 3, 11, 54, 86, 114; BLC 1; SSC 26; WLC**
See also AAYA 19; AFAW 1, 2; AMWS 2; BPFB 1; BW 1, 3; BYA 2; CA 9-12R; 145; CANR 24, 53; CDALB 1941-1968; CSW; DA; DA3; DAB; DAC; DAM MST, MULT, NOV; DLB 2, 76, 227; DLBY 1994; EXPN; EXPS; LAIT 4; MTCW 1, 2; NCFS 3; NFS 2; RGAL 4; RGSF 2; SSFS 1, 11; YAW

Ellmann, Lucy (Elizabeth) 1956- ..... **CLC 61**
See also CA 128

Ellmann, Richard (David)
1918-1987 .... **CLC 50**
See also BEST 89:2; CA 1-4R; 122; CANR 2, 28, 61; DLB 103; DLBY 1987; MTCW 1, 2

Elman, Richard (Martin)
1934-1997 .... **CLC 19**
See also CA 17-20R; 163; CAAS 3; CANR 47

Elron
See Hubbard, L(afayette) Ron(ald)

Eluard, Paul .... **TCLC 7, 41; PC 38**
See also Grindel, Eugene
See also GFL 1789 to the Present; RGWL 2

Elyot, Thomas 1490(?)-1546 .... **LC 11**
See also DLB 136; RGEL 2

Elytis, Odysseus 1911-1996 .... **CLC 15, 49, 100; PC 21**
See also Alepoudelis, Odysseus
See also CA 102; 151; CANR 94; CWW 2; DAM POET; EW 13; MTCW 1, 2; RGWL 2

Emecheta, (Florence Onye) Buchi
1944- .... **CLC 14, 48, 128; BLC 2**
See also AFW; BW 2, 3; CA 81-84; CANR 27, 81; CDWLB 3; CN 7; CWRI 5; DA3; DAM MULT; DLB 117; FW; MTCW 1, 2; NFS 12, 14; SATA 66; WLIT 2

Emerson, Mary Moody
1774-1863 .... **NCLC 66**

Emerson, Ralph Waldo 1803-1882 . **NCLC 1, 38, 98; PC 18; WLC**
See also AMW; ANW; CDALB 1640-1865; DA; DA3; DAB; DAC; DAM MST,

POET; DLB 1, 59, 73, 183, 223; EXPP; LAIT 2; NCFS 3; PFS 4; RGAL 4; WP

Eminescu, Mihail 1850-1889 .... **NCLC 33**

Empedocles 5th cent. B.C.- .... **CMLC 50**
See also DLB 176

Empson, William 1906-1984 ... **CLC 3, 8, 19, 33, 34**
See also BRWS 2; CA 17-20R; 112; CANR 31, 61; DLB 20; MTCW 1, 2; RGEL 2

Enchi, Fumiko (Ueda) 1905-1986 ..... **CLC 31**
See also Enchi Fumiko
See also CA 129; 121; FW; MJW

Enchi Fumiko
See Enchi, Fumiko (Ueda)
See also DLB 182

Ende, Michael (Andreas Helmuth)
1929-1995 .... **CLC 31**
See also BYA 5; CA 118; 124; 149; CANR 36; CLR 14; DLB 75; MAICYA 1, 2; MAICYAS 1; SATA 61, 130; SATA-Brief 42; SATA-Obit 86

Endo, Shusaku 1923-1996 ..... **CLC 7, 14, 19, 54, 99; SSC 48**
See also Endo Shusaku
See also CA 29-32R; 153; CANR 21, 54; DA3; DAM NOV; MTCW 1, 2; RGSF 2; RGWL 2

Endo Shusaku
See Endo, Shusaku
See also DLB 182

Engel, Marian 1933-1985 .... **CLC 36**
See also CA 25-28R; CANR 12; DLB 53; FW; INT CANR-12

Engelhardt, Frederick
See Hubbard, L(afayette) Ron(ald)

Engels, Friedrich 1820-1895 .... **NCLC 85**
See also DLB 129

Enright, D(ennis) J(oseph) 1920- .. **CLC 4, 8, 31**
See also CA 1-4R; CANR 1, 42, 83; CP 7; DLB 27; SATA 25

Enzensberger, Hans Magnus
1929- .... **CLC 43; PC 28**
See also CA 116; 119; CANR 103

Ephron, Nora 1941- .... **CLC 17, 31**
See also AAYA 35; AITN 2; CA 65-68; CANR 12, 39, 83

Epicurus 341B.C.-270B.C. .... **CMLC 21**
See also DLB 176

Epsilon
See Betjeman, John

Epstein, Daniel Mark 1948- .... **CLC 7**
See also CA 49-52; CANR 2, 53, 90

Epstein, Jacob 1956- .... **CLC 19**
See also CA 114

Epstein, Jean 1897-1953 .... **TCLC 92**

Epstein, Joseph 1937- .... **CLC 39**
See also CA 112; 119; CANR 50, 65

Epstein, Leslie 1938- .... **CLC 27**
See also CA 73-76; CAAS 12; CANR 23, 69

Equiano, Olaudah 1745(?)-1797 .... **LC 16; BLC 2**
See also AFAW 1, 2; CDWLB 3; DAM MULT; DLB 37, 50; WLIT 2

Erasmus, Desiderius 1469(?)-1536 ...... **LC 16**
See also DLB 136; EW 2; RGWL 2

Erdman, Paul E(mil) 1932- .... **CLC 25**
See also AITN 1; CA 61-64; CANR 13, 43, 84

Erdrich, Louise 1954- .... **CLC 39, 54, 120**
See also AAYA 10; AMWS 4; BEST 89:1; BPFB 1; CA 114; CANR 41, 62; CDALBS; CN 7; CP 7; CPW; CWP; DA3; DAM MULT, NOV, POP; DLB 152, 175, 206; EXPP; LAIT 5; MTCW 1; NFS 5; NNAL; PFS 14; RGAL 4; SATA 94; SSFS 14; TCWW 2

Erenburg, Ilya (Grigoryevich)
See Ehrenburg, Ilya (Grigoryevich)

Erickson, Stephen Michael 1950-
See Erickson, Steve
See also CA 129; SFW 4

Erickson, Steve .... **CLC 64**
See also Erickson, Stephen Michael
See also CANR 60, 68

Ericson, Walter
See Fast, Howard (Melvin)

Eriksson, Buntel
See Bergman, (Ernst) Ingmar

Ernaux, Annie 1940- .... **CLC 88**
See also CA 147; CANR 93; NCFS 3

Erskine, John 1879-1951 .... **TCLC 84**
See also CA 112; 159; DLB 9, 102; FANT

Eschenbach, Wolfram von
See Wolfram von Eschenbach

Eseki, Bruno
See Mphahlele, Ezekiel

Esenin, Sergei (Alexandrovich)
1895-1925 .... **TCLC 4**
See also CA 104; RGWL 2

Eshleman, Clayton 1935- .... **CLC 7**
See also CA 33-36R; CAAS 6; CANR 93; CP 7; DLB 5

Espriella, Don Manuel Alvarez
See Southey, Robert

Espriu, Salvador 1913-1985 .... **CLC 9**
See also CA 154; 115; DLB 134

Espronceda, Jose de 1808-1842 ..... **NCLC 39**

Esquivel, Laura 1951(?)- ... **CLC 141; HLCS 1**
See also AAYA 29; CA 143; CANR 68; DA3; DNFS 2; LAIT 3; MTCW 1; NFS 5; WLIT 1

Esse, James
See Stephens, James

Esterbrook, Tom
See Hubbard, L(afayette) Ron(ald)

Estleman, Loren D. 1952- .... **CLC 48**
See also AAYA 27; CA 85-88; CANR 27, 74; CMW 4; CPW; DA3; DAM NOV, POP; DLB 226; INT CANR-27; MTCW 1, 2

Etherege, Sir George 1636-1692 .... **LC 78**
See also BRW 2; DAM DRAM; DLB 80; PAB; RGEL 2

Euclid 306B.C.-283B.C. .... **CMLC 25**

Eugenides, Jeffrey 1960(?)- .... **CLC 81**
See also CA 144

Euripides c. 484B.C.-406B.C. .... **CMLC 23, 51; DC 4; WLCS**
See also AW 1; CDWLB 1; DA; DA3; DAB; DAC; DAM DRAM, MST; DFS 1, 4, 6; DLB 176; LAIT 1; RGWL 2

Evan, Evin
See Faust, Frederick (Schiller)

Evans, Caradoc 1878-1945 ... **TCLC 85; SSC 43**
See also DLB 162

Evans, Evan
See Faust, Frederick (Schiller)
See also TCWW 2

Evans, Marian
See Eliot, George

Evans, Mary Ann
See Eliot, George

Evarts, Esther
See Benson, Sally

Everett, Percival
See Everett, Percival L.
See also CSW

Everett, Percival L. 1956- .... **CLC 57**
See also Everett, Percival
See also BW 2; CA 129; CANR 94

Everson, R(onald) G(ilmour)
1903-1992 .... **CLC 27**
See also CA 17-20R; DLB 88

Everson, William (Oliver)
1912-1994 .... **CLC 1, 5, 14**
See also CA 9-12R; 145; CANR 20; DLB
5, 16, 212; MTCW 1

Evtushenko, Evgenii Aleksandrovich
See Yevtushenko, Yevgeny (Alexandrovich)
See also RGWL 2

Ewart, Gavin (Buchanan)
1916-1995 .... **CLC 13, 46**
See also BRWS 7; CA 89-92; 150; CANR
17, 46; CP 7; DLB 40; MTCW 1

Ewers, Hanns Heinz 1871-1943 ..... **TCLC 12**
See also CA 109; 149

Ewing, Frederick R.
See Sturgeon, Theodore (Hamilton)

Exley, Frederick (Earl) 1929-1992 .... **CLC 6,
11**
See also AITN 2; BPFB 1; CA 81-84; 138;
DLB 143; DLBY 1981

Eynhardt, Guillermo
See Quiroga, Horacio (Sylvestre)

Ezekiel, Nissim 1924- .... **CLC 61**
See also CA 61-64; CP 7

Ezekiel, Tish O'Dowd 1943- .... **CLC 34**
See also CA 129

Fadeyev, A.
See Bulgya, Alexander Alexandrovich

Fadeyev, Alexander .... **TCLC 53**
See also Bulgya, Alexander Alexandrovich

Fagen, Donald 1948- .... **CLC 26**

Fainzilberg, Ilya Arnoldovich 1897-1937
See Ilf, Ilya
See also CA 120; 165

Fair, Ronald L. 1932- .... **CLC 18**
See also BW 1; CA 69-72; CANR 25; DLB
33

Fairbairn, Roger
See Carr, John Dickson

Fairbairns, Zoe (Ann) 1948- .... **CLC 32**
See also CA 103; CANR 21, 85; CN 7

Fairfield, Flora
See Alcott, Louisa May

Fairman, Paul W. 1916-1977
See Queen, Ellery
See also CA 114; SFW 4

Falco, Gian
See Papini, Giovanni

Falconer, James
See Kirkup, James

Falconer, Kenneth
See Kornbluth, C(yril) M.

Falkland, Samuel
See Heijermans, Herman

Fallaci, Oriana 1930- .... **CLC 11, 110**
See also CA 77-80; CANR 15, 58; FW;
MTCW 1

Faludi, Susan 1959- .... **CLC 140**
See also CA 138; FW; MTCW 1; NCFS 3

Faludy, George 1913- .... **CLC 42**
See also CA 21-24R

Faludy, Gyoergy
See Faludy, George

Fanon, Frantz 1925-1961 .... **CLC 74; BLC 2**
See also BW 1; CA 116; 89-92; DAM
MULT; WLIT 2

Fanshawe, Ann 1625-1680 .... **LC 11**

Fante, John (Thomas) 1911-1983 ..... **CLC 60**
See also CA 69-72; 109; CANR 23, 104;
DLB 130; DLBY 1983

Farah, Nuruddin 1945- .. **CLC 53, 137; BLC
2**
See also AFW; BW 2, 3; CA 106; CANR
81; CDWLB 3; CN 7; DAM MULT; DLB
125; WLIT 2

Fargue, Leon-Paul 1876(?)-1947 .... **TCLC 11**
See also CA 109; CANR 107; DLB 258

Farigoule, Louis
See Romains, Jules

Farina, Richard 1936(?)-1966 .... **CLC 9**
See also CA 81-84; 25-28R

Farley, Walter (Lorimer)
1915-1989 .... **CLC 17**
See also BYA 14; CA 17-20R; CANR 8,
29, 84; DLB 22; JRDA; MAICYA 1, 2;
SATA 2, 43; YAW

Farmer, Philip Jose 1918- .... **CLC 1, 19**
See also AAYA 28; BPFB 1; CA 1-4R;
CANR 4, 35; DLB 8; MTCW 1; SATA
93; SCFW 2; SFW 4

Farquhar, George 1677-1707 .... **LC 21**
See also BRW 2; DAM DRAM; DLB 84;
RGEL 2

Farrell, J(ames) G(ordon)
1935-1979 .... **CLC 6**
See also CA 73-76; 89-92; CANR 36; DLB
14; MTCW 1; RGEL 2; RHW; WLIT 4

Farrell, James T(homas) 1904-1979 . **CLC 1,
4, 8, 11, 66; SSC 28**
See also AMW; BPFB 1; CA 5-8R; 89-92;
CANR 9, 61; DLB 4, 9, 86; DLBD 2;
MTCW 1, 2; RGAL 4

Farrell, Warren (Thomas) 1943- ...... **CLC 70**
See also CA 146

Farren, Richard J.
See Betjeman, John

Farren, Richard M.
See Betjeman, John

Fassbinder, Rainer Werner
1946-1982 .... **CLC 20**
See also CA 93-96; 106; CANR 31

Fast, Howard (Melvin) 1914- ... **CLC 23, 131**
See also AAYA 16; BPFB 1; CA 1-4R, 181;
CAAE 181; CAAS 18; CANR 1, 33, 54,
75, 98; CMW 4; CN 7; CPW; DAM NOV;
DLB 9; INT CANR-33; MTCW 1; RHW;
SATA 7; SATA-Essay 107; TCWW 2;
YAW

Faulcon, Robert
See Holdstock, Robert P.

Faulkner, William (Cuthbert)
1897-1962 .... **CLC 1, 3, 6, 8, 9, 11, 14,
18, 28, 52, 68; SSC 1, 35, 42; WLC**
See also AAYA 7; AMW; AMWR 1; BPFB
1; BYA 5; CA 81-84; CANR 33; CDALB
1929-1941; DA; DA3; DAB; DAC; DAM
MST, NOV; DLB 9, 11, 44, 102; DLBD
2; DLBY 1986, 1997; EXPN; EXPS;
LAIT 2; MTCW 1, 2; NFS 4, 8, 13;
RGAL 4; RGSF 2; SSFS 2, 5, 6, 12

Fauset, Jessie Redmon
1882(?)-1961 .... **CLC 19, 54; BLC 2**
See also AFAW 2; BW 1; CA 109; CANR
83; DAM MULT; DLB 51; FW; MAWW

Faust, Frederick (Schiller)
1892-1944(?) .... **TCLC 49**
See also Austin, Frank; Brand, Max; Challis, George; Dawson, Peter; Dexter, Martin; Evans, Evan; Frederick, John; Frost,
Frederick; Manning, David; Silver, Nicholas
See also CA 108; 152; DAM POP; DLB
256

Fawkes, Guy
See Benchley, Robert (Charles)

Fearing, Kenneth (Flexner)
1902-1961 .... **CLC 51**
See also CA 93-96; CANR 59; CMW 4;
DLB 9; RGAL 4

Fecamps, Elise
See Creasey, John

Federman, Raymond 1928- .... **CLC 6, 47**
See also CA 17-20R; CAAS 8; CANR 10,
43, 83, 108; CN 7; DLBY 1980

Federspiel, J(uerg) F. 1931- .... **CLC 42**
See also CA 146

Feiffer, Jules (Ralph) 1929- ...... **CLC 2, 8, 64**
See also AAYA 3; CA 17-20R; CAD; CANR
30, 59; CD 5; DAM DRAM; DLB 7, 44;
INT CANR-30; MTCW 1; SATA 8, 61,
111

Feige, Hermann Albert Otto Maximilian
See Traven, B.

Feinberg, David B. 1956-1994 .... **CLC 59**
See also CA 135; 147

Feinstein, Elaine 1930- .... **CLC 36**
See also CA 69-72; CAAS 1; CANR 31,
68; CN 7; CP 7; CWP; DLB 14, 40;
MTCW 1

Feke, Gilbert David .... **CLC 65**

Feldman, Irving (Mordecai) 1928- ..... **CLC 7**
See also CA 1-4R; CANR 1; CP 7; DLB
169

Felix-Tchicaya, Gerald
See Tchicaya, Gerald Felix

Fellini, Federico 1920-1993 .... **CLC 16, 85**
See also CA 65-68; 143; CANR 33

Felsen, Henry Gregor 1916-1995 ..... **CLC 17**
See also CA 1-4R; 180; CANR 1; SAAS 2;
SATA 1

Felski, Rita .... **CLC 65**

Fenno, Jack
See Calisher, Hortense

Fenollosa, Ernest (Francisco)
1853-1908 .... **TCLC 91**

Fenton, James Martin 1949- .... **CLC 32**
See also CA 102; CANR 108; CP 7; DLB
40; PFS 11

Ferber, Edna 1887-1968 .... **CLC 18, 93**
See also AITN 1; CA 5-8R; 25-28R; CANR
68, 105; DLB 9, 28, 86; MTCW 1, 2;
RGAL 4; RHW; SATA 7; TCWW 2

Ferdowsi, Abu'l Qasem 940-1020 . **CMLC 43**
See also RGWL 2

Ferguson, Helen
See Kavan, Anna

Ferguson, Niall 1964- .... **CLC 134**
See also CA 190

Ferguson, Samuel 1810-1886 .... **NCLC 33**
See also DLB 32; RGEL 2

Fergusson, Robert 1750-1774 .... **LC 29**
See also DLB 109; RGEL 2

Ferling, Lawrence
See Ferlinghetti, Lawrence (Monsanto)

Ferlinghetti, Lawrence (Monsanto)
1919(?)- ..... **CLC 2, 6, 10, 27, 111; PC 1**
See also CA 5-8R; CANR 3, 41, 73;
CDALB 1941-1968; CP 7; DA3; DAM
POET; DLB 5, 16; MTCW 1, 2; RGAL 4;
WP

Fern, Fanny
See Parton, Sara Payson Willis

Fernandez, Vicente Garcia Huidobro
See Huidobro Fernandez, Vicente Garcia

Fernandez-Armesto, Felipe .... **CLC 70**

Fernandez de Lizardi, Jose Joaquin
See Lizardi, Jose Joaquin Fernandez de

Ferre, Rosario 1942- ...... **CLC 139; HLCS 1;
SSC 36**
See also CA 131; CANR 55, 81; CWW 2;
DLB 145; HW 1, 2; LAWS 1; MTCW 1;
WLIT 1

Ferrer, Gabriel (Francisco Victor) Miro
See Miro (Ferrer), Gabriel (Francisco
Victor)

Ferrier, Susan (Edmonstone)
1782-1854 .... **NCLC 8**
See also DLB 116; RGEL 2

Ferrigno, Robert 1948(?)- .... **CLC 65**
See also CA 140

Ferron, Jacques 1921-1985 .... **CLC 94**
See also CA 117; 129; CCA 1; DAC; DLB 60

Feuchtwanger, Lion 1884-1958 .... **TCLC 3**
See also CA 104; 187; DLB 66

Feuillet, Octave 1821-1890 .... **NCLC 45**
See also DLB 192

Feydeau, Georges (Leon Jules Marie)
1862-1921 .... **TCLC 22**
See also CA 113; 152; CANR 84; DAM DRAM; DLB 192; GFL 1789 to the Present; RGWL 2

Fichte, Johann Gottlieb
1762-1814 .... **NCLC 62**
See also DLB 90

Ficino, Marsilio 1433-1499 .... **LC 12**

Fiedeler, Hans
See Doeblin, Alfred

Fiedler, Leslie A(aron) 1917- .. **CLC 4, 13, 24**
See also CA 9-12R; CANR 7, 63; CN 7; DLB 28, 67; MTCW 1, 2; RGAL 4

Field, Andrew 1938- .... **CLC 44**
See also CA 97-100; CANR 25

Field, Eugene 1850-1895 .... **NCLC 3**
See also DLB 23, 42, 140; DLBD 13; MAICYA 1, 2; RGAL 4; SATA 16

Field, Gans T.
See Wellman, Manly Wade

Field, Michael 1915-1971 .... **TCLC 43**
See also CA 29-32R

Field, Peter
See Hobson, Laura Z(ametkin)
See also TCWW 2

Fielding, Helen 1959(?)- .... **CLC 146**
See also CA 172; DLB 231

Fielding, Henry 1707-1754 .. **LC 1, 46; WLC**
See also BRW 3; BRWR 1; CDBLB 1660-1789; DA; DA3; DAB; DAC; DAM DRAM, MST, NOV; DLB 39, 84, 101; RGEL 2; WLIT 3

Fielding, Sarah 1710-1768 .... **LC 1, 44**
See also DLB 39; RGEL 2

Fields, W. C. 1880-1946 .... **TCLC 80**
See also DLB 44

Fierstein, Harvey (Forbes) 1954- ..... **CLC 33**
See also CA 123; 129; CAD; CD 5; CPW; DA3; DAM DRAM, POP; DFS 6; GLL

Figes, Eva 1932- .... **CLC 31**
See also CA 53-56; CANR 4, 44, 83; CN 7; DLB 14; FW

Finch, Anne 1661-1720 .... **LC 3; PC 21**
See also DLB 95

Finch, Robert (Duer Claydon)
1900-1995 .... **CLC 18**
See also CA 57-60; CANR 9, 24, 49; CP 7; DLB 88

Findley, Timothy 1930- .... **CLC 27, 102**
See also CA 25-28R; CANR 12, 42, 69, 109; CCA 1; CN 7; DAC; DAM MST; DLB 53; FANT; RHW

Fink, William
See Mencken, H(enry) L(ouis)

Firbank, Louis 1942-
See Reed, Lou
See also CA 117

Firbank, (Arthur Annesley) Ronald
1886-1926 .... **TCLC 1**
See also BRWS 2; CA 104; 177; DLB 36; RGEL 2

Fish, Stanley
See Fish, Stanley Eugene

Fish, Stanley E.
See Fish, Stanley Eugene

Fish, Stanley Eugene 1938- .... **CLC 142**
See also CA 112; 132; CANR 90; DLB 67

Fisher, Dorothy (Frances) Canfield
1879-1958 .... **TCLC 87**
See also CA 114; 136; CANR 80; CLR 71,; CWRI 5; DLB 9, 102; MAICYA 1, 2; YABC 1

Fisher, M(ary) F(rances) K(ennedy)
1908-1992 .... **CLC 76, 87**
See also CA 77-80; 138; CANR 44; MTCW 1

Fisher, Roy 1930- .... **CLC 25**
See also CA 81-84; CAAS 10; CANR 16; CP 7; DLB 40

Fisher, Rudolph 1897-1934 .. **TCLC 11; BLC 2; SSC 25**
See also BW 1, 3; CA 107; 124; CANR 80; DAM MULT; DLB 51, 102

Fisher, Vardis (Alvero) 1895-1968 ...... **CLC 7**
See also CA 5-8R; 25-28R; CANR 68; DLB 9, 206; RGAL 4; TCWW 2

Fiske, Tarleton
See Bloch, Robert (Albert)

Fitch, Clarke
See Sinclair, Upton (Beall)

Fitch, John IV
See Cormier, Robert (Edmund)

Fitzgerald, Captain Hugh
See Baum, L(yman) Frank

FitzGerald, Edward 1809-1883 .... **NCLC 9**
See also BRW 4; DLB 32; RGEL 2

Fitzgerald, F(rancis) Scott (Key)
1896-1940 . **TCLC 1, 6, 14, 28, 55; SSC 6, 31; WLC**
See also AAYA 24; AITN 1; AMW; AMWR 1; BPFB 1; CA 110; 123; CDALB 1917-1929; DA; DA3; DAB; DAC; DAM MST, NOV; DLB 4, 9, 86, 219; DLBD 1, 15, 16; DLBY 1981, 1996; EXPN; EXPS; LAIT 3; MTCW 1, 2; NFS 2; RGAL 4; RGSF 2; SSFS 4

Fitzgerald, Penelope 1916-2000 . **CLC 19, 51, 61, 143**
See also BRWS 5; CA 85-88; 190; CAAS 10; CANR 56, 86; CN 7; DLB 14, 194; MTCW 2

Fitzgerald, Robert (Stuart)
1910-1985 .... **CLC 39**
See also CA 1-4R; 114; CANR 1; DLBY 1980

FitzGerald, Robert D(avid)
1902-1987 .... **CLC 19**
See also CA 17-20R; RGEL 2

Fitzgerald, Zelda (Sayre)
1900-1948 .... **TCLC 52**
See also AMWS 9; CA 117; 126; DLBY 1984

Flanagan, Thomas (James Bonner)
1923- .... **CLC 25, 52**
See also CA 108; CANR 55; CN 7; DLBY 1980; INT 108; MTCW 1; RHW

Flaubert, Gustave 1821-1880 .... **NCLC 2, 10, 19, 62, 66; SSC 11; WLC**
See also DA; DA3; DAB; DAC; DAM MST, NOV; DLB 119; EW 7; EXPS; GFL 1789 to the Present; LAIT 2; NFS 14; RGSF 2; RGWL 2; SSFS 6

Flavius Josephus
See Josephus, Flavius

Flecker, Herman Elroy
See Flecker, (Herman) James Elroy

Flecker, (Herman) James Elroy
1884-1915 .... **TCLC 43**
See also CA 109; 150; DLB 10, 19; RGEL 2

Fleming, Ian (Lancaster) 1908-1964 . **CLC 3, 30**
See also AAYA 26; BPFB 1; CA 5-8R; CANR 59; CDBLB 1945-1960; CMW 4; CPW; DA3; DAM POP; DLB 87, 201; MSW; MTCW 1, 2; RGEL 2; SATA 9; YAW

Fleming, Thomas (James) 1927- ...... **CLC 37**
See also CA 5-8R; CANR 10, 102; INT CANR-10; SATA 8

Fletcher, John 1579-1625 .... **LC 33; DC 6**
See also BRW 2; CDBLB Before 1660; DLB 58; RGEL 2

Fletcher, John Gould 1886-1950 .... **TCLC 35**
See also CA 107; 167; DLB 4, 45; RGAL 4

Fleur, Paul
See Pohl, Frederik

Flooglebuckle, Al
See Spiegelman, Art

Flora, Fletcher 1914-1969
See Queen, Ellery
See also CA 1-4R; CANR 3, 85

Flying Officer X
See Bates, H(erbert) E(rnest)

Fo, Dario 1926- .... **CLC 32, 109; DC 10**
See also CA 116; 128; CANR 68; CWW 2; DA3; DAM DRAM; DLBY 1997; MTCW 1, 2

Fogarty, Jonathan Titulescu Esq.
See Farrell, James T(homas)

Follett, Ken(neth Martin) 1949- .... **CLC 18**
See also AAYA 6; BEST 89:4; BPFB 1; CA 81-84; CANR 13, 33, 54, 102; CMW 4; CPW; DA3; DAM NOV, POP; DLB 87; DLBY 1981; INT CANR-33; MTCW 1

Fontane, Theodor 1819-1898 .... **NCLC 26**
See also CDWLB 2; DLB 129; EW 6; RGWL 2

Fontenot, Chester .... **CLC 65**

Foote, Horton 1916- .... **CLC 51, 91**
See also CA 73-76; CAD; CANR 34, 51; CD 5; CSW; DA3; DAM DRAM; DLB 26; INT CANR-34

Foote, Mary Hallock 1847-1938 .. **TCLC 108**
See also DLB 186, 188, 202, 221

Foote, Shelby 1916- .... **CLC 75**
See also AAYA 40; CA 5-8R; CANR 3, 45, 74; CN 7; CPW; CSW; DA3; DAM NOV, POP; DLB 2, 17; MTCW 2; RHW

Forbes, Cosmo
See Lewton, Val

Forbes, Esther 1891-1967 .... **CLC 12**
See also AAYA 17; BYA 2; CA 13-14; 25-28R; CAP 1; CLR 27; DLB 22; JRDA; MAICYA 1, 2; RHW; SATA 2, 100; YAW

Forche, Carolyn (Louise) 1950- .... **CLC 25, 83, 86; PC 10**
See also CA 109; 117; CANR 50, 74; CP 7; CWP; DA3; DAM POET; DLB 5, 193; INT CA-117; MTCW 1; RGAL 4

Ford, Elbur
See Hibbert, Eleanor Alice Burford

Ford, Ford Madox 1873-1939 ... **TCLC 1, 15, 39, 57**
See also Chaucer, Daniel
See also BRW 6; CA 104; 132; CANR 74; CDBLB 1914-1945; DA3; DAM NOV; DLB 34, 98, 162; MTCW 1, 2; RGEL 2

Ford, Henry 1863-1947 .... **TCLC 73**
See also CA 115; 148

Ford, John 1586-1639 .... **LC 68; DC 8**
See also BRW 2; CDBLB Before 1660; DA3; DAM DRAM; DFS 7; DLB 58; IDTP; RGEL 2

Ford, John 1895-1973 .... **CLC 16**
See also CA 187; 45-48

Ford, Richard 1944- .... **CLC 46, 99**
See also AMWS 5; CA 69-72; CANR 11, 47, 86; CN 7; CSW; DLB 227; MTCW 1; RGAL 4; RGSF 2

Ford, Webster
See Masters, Edgar Lee

Foreman, Richard 1937- .... **CLC 50**
See also CA 65-68; CAD; CANR 32, 63; CD 5

Forester, C(ecil) S(cott) 1899-1966 ... **CLC 35**
  See also CA 73-76; 25-28R; CANR 83;
  DLB 191; RGEL 2; RHW; SATA 13

Forez
  See Mauriac, Francois (Charles)

Forman, James
  See Forman, James D(ouglas)

Forman, James D(ouglas) 1932- .... **CLC 21**
  See also AAYA 17; CA 9-12R; CANR 4,
  19, 42; JRDA; MAICYA 1, 2; SATA 8,
  70; YAW

Fornes, Maria Irene 1930- . **CLC 39, 61; DC 10; HLCS 1**
  See also CA 25-28R; CAD; CANR 28, 81;
  CD 5; CWD; DLB 7; HW 1, 2; INT
  CANR-28; MTCW 1; RGAL 4

Forrest, Leon (Richard) 1937-1997 .. **CLC 4; BLCS**
  See also AFAW 2; BW 2; CA 89-92; 162;
  CAAS 7; CANR 25, 52, 87; CN 7; DLB
  33

Forster, E(dward) M(organ)
  1879-1970 ...... **CLC 1, 2, 3, 4, 9, 10, 13, 15, 22, 45, 77; SSC 27; WLC**
  See also AAYA 2, 37; BRW 6; BRWR 2;
  CA 13-14; 25-28R; CANR 45; CAP 1;
  CDBLB 1914-1945; DA; DA3; DAB;
  DAC; DAM MST, NOV; DLB 34, 98,
  162, 178, 195; DLBD 10; EXPN; LAIT
  3; MTCW 1, 2; NCFS 1; NFS 3, 10, 11;
  RGEL 2; RGSF 2; SATA 57; SUFW;
  WLIT 4

Forster, John 1812-1876 .... **NCLC 11**
  See also DLB 144, 184

Forster, Margaret 1938- .... **CLC 149**
  See also CA 133; CANR 62; CN 7; DLB
  155

Forsyth, Frederick 1938- .... **CLC 2, 5, 36**
  See also BEST 89:4; CA 85-88; CANR 38,
  62; CMW 4; CN 7; CPW; DAM NOV,
  POP; DLB 87; MTCW 1, 2

Forten, Charlotte L. 1837-1914 .... **TCLC 16; BLC 2**
  See also Grimke, Charlotte L(ottie) Forten
  See also DLB 50, 239

Foscolo, Ugo 1778-1827 .... **NCLC 8, 97**
  See also EW 5

Fosse, Bob .... **CLC 20**
  See also Fosse, Robert Louis

Fosse, Robert Louis 1927-1987
  See Fosse, Bob
  See also CA 110; 123

Foster, Hannah Webster
  1758-1840 .... **NCLC 99**
  See also DLB 37, 200; RGAL 4

Foster, Stephen Collins
  1826-1864 .... **NCLC 26**
  See also RGAL 4

Foucault, Michel 1926-1984 . **CLC 31, 34, 69**
  See also CA 105; 113; CANR 34; DLB 242;
  EW 13; GFL 1789 to the Present; GLL 1;
  MTCW 1, 2

Fouque, Friedrich (Heinrich Karl) de la Motte 1777-1843 .... **NCLC 2**
  See also DLB 90; RGWL 2; SUFW

Fourier, Charles 1772-1837 .... **NCLC 51**

Fournier, Henri Alban 1886-1914
  See Alain-Fournier
  See also CA 104; 179

Fournier, Pierre 1916- .... **CLC 11**
  See also Gascar, Pierre
  See also CA 89-92; CANR 16, 40

Fowles, John (Robert) 1926- . **CLC 1, 2, 3, 4, 6, 9, 10, 15, 33, 87; SSC 33**
  See also BPFB 1; BRWS 1; CA 5-8R;
  CANR 25, 71, 103; CDBLB 1960 to
  Present; CN 7; DA3; DAB; DAC; DAM
  MST; DLB 14, 139, 207; HGG; MTCW
  1, 2; RGEL 2; RHW; SATA 22; WLIT 4

Fox, Paula 1923- .... **CLC 2, 8, 121**
  See also AAYA 3, 37; BYA 3, 8; CA 73-76;
  CANR 20, 36, 62, 105; CLR 1, 44; DLB
  52; JRDA; MAICYA 1, 2; MTCW 1; NFS
  12; SATA 17, 60, 120; WYA; YAW

Fox, William Price (Jr.) 1926- .... **CLC 22**
  See also CA 17-20R; CAAS 19; CANR 11;
  CSW; DLB 2; DLBY 1981

Foxe, John 1517(?)-1587 .... **LC 14**
  See also DLB 132

Frame, Janet .. **CLC 2, 3, 6, 22, 66, 96; SSC 29**
  See also Clutha, Janet Paterson Frame
  See also CN 7; CWP; RGEL 2; RGSF 2

France, Anatole .... **TCLC 9**
  See also Thibault, Jacques Anatole Francois
  See also DLB 123; GFL 1789 to the Present;
  MTCW 1; RGWL 2; SUFW

Francis, Claude .... **CLC 50**
  See also CA 192

Francis, Dick 1920- .... **CLC 2, 22, 42, 102**
  See also AAYA 5, 21; BEST 89:3; BPFB 1;
  CA 5-8R; CANR 9, 42, 68, 100; CDBLB
  1960 to Present; CMW 4; CN 7; DA3;
  DAM POP; DLB 87; INT CANR-9;
  MSW; MTCW 1, 2

Francis, Robert (Churchill)
  1901-1987 .... **CLC 15; PC 34**
  See also AMWS 9; CA 1-4R; 123; CANR
  1; EXPP; PFS 12

Francis, Lord Jeffrey
  See Jeffrey, Francis
  See also DLB 107

Frank, Anne(lies Marie)
  1929-1945 .... **TCLC 17; WLC**
  See also AAYA 12; BYA 1; CA 113; 133;
  CANR 68; DA; DA3; DAB; DAC; DAM
  MST; LAIT 4; MAICYA 2; MAICYAS 1;
  MTCW 1, 2; NCFS 2; SATA 87; SATA-
  Brief 42; WYA; YAW

Frank, Bruno 1887-1945 .... **TCLC 81**
  See also CA 189; DLB 118

Frank, Elizabeth 1945- .... **CLC 39**
  See also CA 121; 126; CANR 78; INT 126

Frankl, Viktor E(mil) 1905-1997 ...... **CLC 93**
  See also CA 65-68; 161

Franklin, Benjamin
  See Hasek, Jaroslav (Matej Frantisek)

Franklin, Benjamin 1706-1790 .... **LC 25; WLCS**
  See also AMW; CDALB 1640-1865; DA;
  DA3; DAB; DAC; DAM MST; DLB 24,
  43, 73, 183; LAIT 1; RGAL 4; TUS

**Franklin, (Stella Maria Sarah) Miles
  (Lampe)** 1879-1954 .... **TCLC 7**
  See also CA 104; 164; DLB 230; FW;
  MTCW 2; RGEL 2; TWA

Fraser, George MacDonald 1925- ...... **CLC 7**
  See also CA 45-48; 180; CAAE 180; CANR
  2, 48, 74; MTCW 1; RHW

Fraser, Sylvia 1935- .... **CLC 64**
  See also CA 45-48; CANR 1, 16, 60; CCA
  1

Frayn, Michael 1933- .... **CLC 3, 7, 31, 47**
  See also BRWS 7; CA 5-8R; CANR 30, 69;
  CBD; CD 5; CN 7; DAM DRAM, NOV;
  DLB 13, 14, 194, 245; FANT; MTCW 1,
  2; SFW 4

Fraze, Candida (Merrill) 1945- .... **CLC 50**
  See also CA 126

Frazer, Andrew
  See Marlowe, Stephen

Frazer, J(ames) G(eorge)
  1854-1941 .... **TCLC 32**
  See also BRWS 3; CA 118

Frazer, Robert Caine
  See Creasey, John

Frazer, Sir James George
  See Frazer, J(ames) G(eorge)

Frazier, Charles 1950- .... **CLC 109**
  See also AAYA 34; CA 161; CSW

Frazier, Ian 1951- .... **CLC 46**
  See also CA 130; CANR 54, 93

Frederic, Harold 1856-1898 .... **NCLC 10**
  See also AMW; DLB 12, 23; DLBD 13;
  RGAL 4

Frederick, John
  See Faust, Frederick (Schiller)
  See also TCWW 2

Frederick the Great 1712-1786 .... **LC 14**

Fredro, Aleksander 1793-1876 .... **NCLC 8**

Freeling, Nicolas 1927- .... **CLC 38**
  See also CA 49-52; CAAS 12; CANR 1,
  17, 50, 84; CMW 4; CN 7; DLB 87

Freeman, Douglas Southall
  1886-1953 .... **TCLC 11**
  See also CA 109; 195; DLB 17; DLBD 17

Freeman, Judith 1946- .... **CLC 55**
  See also CA 148; DLB 256

Freeman, Mary E(leanor) Wilkins
  1852-1930 .... **TCLC 9; SSC 1, 47**
  See also CA 106; 177; DLB 12, 78, 221;
  EXPS; FW; HGG; MAWW; RGAL 4;
  RGSF 2; SSFS 4, 8; SUFW; TUS

Freeman, R(ichard) Austin
  1862-1943 .... **TCLC 21**
  See also CA 113; CANR 84; CMW 4; DLB
  70

French, Albert 1943- .... **CLC 86**
  See also BW 3; CA 167

French, Marilyn 1929- .... **CLC 10, 18, 60**
  See also BPFB 1; CA 69-72; CANR 3, 31;
  CN 7; CPW; DAM DRAM, NOV, POP;
  FW; INT CANR-31; MTCW 1, 2

French, Paul
  See Asimov, Isaac

Freneau, Philip Morin 1752-1832 .. **NCLC 1, 111**
  See also AMWS 2; DLB 37, 43; RGAL 4

Freud, Sigmund 1856-1939 .... **TCLC 52**
  See also CA 115; 133; CANR 69; EW 8;
  MTCW 1, 2; NCFS 3

Freytag, Gustav 1816-1895 .... **NCLC 109**
  See also DLB 129

Friedan, Betty (Naomi) 1921- .... **CLC 74**
  See also CA 65-68; CANR 18, 45, 74; DLB
  246; FW; MTCW 1, 2

Friedlander, Saul 1932- .... **CLC 90**
  See also CA 117; 130; CANR 72

Friedman, B(ernard) H(arper)
  1926- .... **CLC 7**
  See also CA 1-4R; CANR 3, 48

Friedman, Bruce Jay 1930- ...... **CLC 3, 5, 56**
  See also CA 9-12R; CAD; CANR 25, 52,
  101; CD 5; CN 7; DLB 2, 28, 244; INT
  CANR-25

Friel, Brian 1929- .... **CLC 5, 42, 59, 115; DC 8**
  See also BRWS 5; CA 21-24R; CANR 33,
  69; CBD; CD 5; DFS 11; DLB 13; MTCW
  1; RGEL 2

Friis-Baastad, Babbis Ellinor
  1921-1970 .... **CLC 12**
  See also CA 17-20R; 134; SATA 7

Frisch, Max (Rudolf) 1911-1991 ... **CLC 3, 9, 14, 18, 32, 44**
  See also CA 85-88; 134; CANR 32, 74; CD-
  WLB 2; DAM DRAM, NOV; DLB 69,
  124; EW 13; MTCW 1, 2; RGWL 2;
  TCLC 121

Fromentin, Eugene (Samuel Auguste)
  1820-1876 .... **NCLC 10**
  See also DLB 123; GFL 1789 to the Present

Frost, Frederick
  See Faust, Frederick (Schiller)
  See also TCWW 2

Frost, Robert (Lee) 1874-1963 .. **CLC 1, 3, 4, 9, 10, 13, 15, 26, 34, 44; PC 1, 39; WLC**
See also AAYA 21; AMW; AMWR 1; CA 89-92; CANR 33; CDALB 1917-1929; CLR 67; DA; DA3; DAB; DAC; DAM MST, POET; DLB 54; DLBD 7; EXPP; MTCW 1, 2; PAB; PFS 1, 2, 3, 4, 5, 6, 7, 10, 13; RGAL 4; SATA 14; WP; WYA

Froude, James Anthony
1818-1894 .... **NCLC 43**
See also DLB 18, 57, 144

Froy, Herald
See Waterhouse, Keith (Spencer)

Fry, Christopher 1907- .... **CLC 2, 10, 14**
See also BRWS 3; CA 17-20R; CAAS 23; CANR 9, 30, 74; CBD; CD 5; CP 7; DAM DRAM; DLB 13; MTCW 1, 2; RGEL 2; SATA 66

Frye, (Herman) Northrop
1912-1991 .... **CLC 24, 70**
See also CA 5-8R; 133; CANR 8, 37; DLB 67, 68, 246; MTCW 1, 2; RGAL 4

Fuchs, Daniel 1909-1993 .... **CLC 8, 22**
See also CA 81-84; 142; CAAS 5; CANR 40; DLB 9, 26, 28; DLBY 1993

Fuchs, Daniel 1934- .... **CLC 34**
See also CA 37-40R; CANR 14, 48

Fuentes, Carlos 1928- .. **CLC 3, 8, 10, 13, 22, 41, 60, 113; HLC 1; SSC 24; WLC**
See also AAYA 4; AITN 2; BPFB 1; CA 69-72; CANR 10, 32, 68, 104; CDWLB 3; CWW 2; DA; DA3; DAB; DAC; DAM MST, MULT, NOV; DLB 113; DNFS 2; HW 1, 2; LAIT 3; LAW; LAWS 1; MTCW 1, 2; NFS 8; RGSF 2; RGWL 2; WLIT 1

Fuentes, Gregorio Lopez y
See Lopez y Fuentes, Gregorio

Fuertes, Gloria 1918-1998 .... **PC 27**
See also CA 178, 180; DLB 108; HW 2; SATA 115

Fugard, (Harold) Athol 1932- . **CLC 5, 9, 14, 25, 40, 80; DC 3**
See also AAYA 17; AFW; CA 85-88; CANR 32, 54; CD 5; DAM DRAM; DFS 3, 6, 10; DLB 225; DNFS 1, 2; MTCW 1; RGEL 2; WLIT 2

Fugard, Sheila 1932- .... **CLC 48**
See also CA 125

Fukuyama, Francis 1952- .... **CLC 131**
See also CA 140; CANR 72

Fuller, Charles (H., Jr.) 1939- .... **CLC 25; BLC 2; DC 1**
See also BW 2; CA 108; 112; CAD; CANR 87; CD 5; DAM DRAM, MULT; DFS 8; DLB 38; INT CA-112; MTCW 1

Fuller, Henry Blake 1857-1929 .... **TCLC 103**
See also CA 108; 177; DLB 12; RGAL 4

Fuller, John (Leopold) 1937- .... **CLC 62**
See also CA 21-24R; CANR 9, 44; CP 7; DLB 40

Fuller, Margaret
See Ossoli, Sarah Margaret (Fuller)
See also AMWS 2; DLB 183, 223, 239

Fuller, Roy (Broadbent) 1912-1991 ... **CLC 4, 28**
See also BRWS 7; CA 5-8R; 135; CAAS 10; CANR 53, 83; CWRI 5; DLB 15, 20; RGEL 2; SATA 87

Fuller, Sarah Margaret
See Ossoli, Sarah Margaret (Fuller)

Fuller, Sarah Margaret
See Ossoli, Sarah Margaret (Fuller)
See also DLB 1, 59, 73

Fulton, Alice 1952- .... **CLC 52**
See also CA 116; CANR 57, 88; CP 7; CWP; DLB 193

Furphy, Joseph 1843-1912 .... **TCLC 25**
See also CA 163; DLB 230; RGEL 2

Fuson, Robert H(enderson) 1927- .... **CLC 70**
See also CA 89-92; CANR 103

Fussell, Paul 1924- .... **CLC 74**
See also BEST 90:1; CA 17-20R; CANR 8, 21, 35, 69; INT CANR-21; MTCW 1, 2

Futabatei, Shimei 1864-1909 .... **TCLC 44**
See also Futabatei Shimei
See also CA 162; MJW

Futabatei Shimei
See Futabatei, Shimei
See also DLB 180

Futrelle, Jacques 1875-1912 .... **TCLC 19**
See also CA 113; 155; CMW 4

Gaboriau, Emile 1835-1873 .... **NCLC 14**
See also CMW 4; MSW

Gadda, Carlo Emilio 1893-1973 .... **CLC 11**
See also CA 89-92; DLB 177

Gaddis, William 1922-1998 ... **CLC 1, 3, 6, 8, 10, 19, 43, 86**
See also AMWS 4; BPFB 1; CA 17-20R; 172; CANR 21, 48; CN 7; DLB 2; MTCW 1, 2; RGAL 4

Gaelique, Moruen le
See Jacob, (Cyprien-)Max

Gage, Walter
See Inge, William (Motter)

Gaines, Ernest J(ames) 1933- ...... **CLC 3, 11, 18, 86; BLC 2**
See also AAYA 18; AFAW 1, 2; AITN 1; BPFB 2; BW 2, 3; BYA 6; CA 9-12R; CANR 6, 24, 42, 75; CDALB 1968-1988; CLR 62; CN 7; CSW; DA3; DAM MULT; DLB 2, 33, 152; DLBY 1980; EXPN; LAIT 5; MTCW 1, 2; NFS 5, 7; RGAL 4; RGSF 2; RHW; SATA 86; SSFS 5; YAW

Gaitskill, Mary 1954- .... **CLC 69**
See also CA 128; CANR 61; DLB 244

Galdos, Benito Perez
See Perez Galdos, Benito
See also EW 7

Gale, Zona 1874-1938 .... **TCLC 7**
See also CA 105; 153; CANR 84; DAM DRAM; DLB 9, 78, 228; RGAL 4

Galeano, Eduardo (Hughes) 1940- . **CLC 72; HLCS 1**
See also CA 29-32R; CANR 13, 32, 100; HW 1

Galiano, Juan Valera y Alcala
See Valera y Alcala-Galiano, Juan

Galilei, Galileo 1564-1642 .... **LC 45**

Gallagher, Tess 1943- .... **CLC 18, 63; PC 9**
See also CA 106; CP 7; CWP; DAM POET; DLB 120, 212, 244

Gallant, Mavis 1922- . **CLC 7, 18, 38; SSC 5**
See also CA 69-72; CANR 29, 69; CCA 1; CN 7; DAC; DAM MST; DLB 53; MTCW 1, 2; RGEL 2; RGSF 2

Gallant, Roy A(rthur) 1924- .... **CLC 17**
See also CA 5-8R; CANR 4, 29, 54; CLR 30; MAICYA 1, 2; SATA 4, 68, 110

Gallico, Paul (William) 1897-1976 ..... **CLC 2**
See also AITN 1; CA 5-8R; 69-72; CANR 23; DLB 9, 171; FANT; MAICYA 1, 2; SATA 13

Gallo, Max Louis 1932- .... **CLC 95**
See also CA 85-88

Gallois, Lucien
See Desnos, Robert

Gallup, Ralph
See Whitemore, Hugh (John)

Galsworthy, John 1867-1933 .... **TCLC 1, 45; SSC 22; WLC**
See also BRW 6; CA 104; 141; CANR 75; CDBLB 1890-1914; DA; DA3; DAB; DAC; DAM DRAM, MST, NOV; DLB 10, 34, 98, 162; DLBD 16; MTCW 1; RGEL 2; SSFS 3

Galt, John 1779-1839 .... **NCLC 1, 110**
See also DLB 99, 116, 159; RGEL 2; RGSF 2

Galvin, James 1951- .... **CLC 38**
See also CA 108; CANR 26

Gamboa, Federico 1864-1939 .... **TCLC 36**
See also CA 167; HW 2; LAW

Gandhi, M. K.
See Gandhi, Mohandas Karamchand

Gandhi, Mahatma
See Gandhi, Mohandas Karamchand

Gandhi, Mohandas Karamchand
1869-1948 .... **TCLC 59**
See also CA 121; 132; DA3; DAM MULT; MTCW 1, 2

Gann, Ernest Kellogg 1910-1991 ..... **CLC 23**
See also AITN 1; BPFB 2; CA 1-4R; 136; CANR 1, 83; RHW

Garber, Eric 1943(?)-
See Holleran, Andrew
See also CANR 89

Garcia, Cristina 1958- .... **CLC 76**
See also CA 141; CANR 73; DNFS 1; HW 2

Garcia Lorca, Federico 1898-1936 . **TCLC 1, 7, 49; DC 2; HLC 2; PC 3; WLC**
See also Lorca, Federico Garcia
See also CA 104; 131; CANR 81; DA; DA3; DAB; DAC; DAM DRAM, MST, MULT, POET; DFS 10; DLB 108; HW 1, 2; MTCW 1, 2

Garcia Marquez, Gabriel (Jose)
1928- .... **CLC 2, 3, 8, 10, 15, 27, 47, 55, 68; HLC 1; SSC 8; WLC**
See also AAYA 3, 33; BEST 89:1, 90:4; BPFB 2; BYA 12; CA 33-36R; CANR 10, 28, 50, 75, 82; CDWLB 3; CPW; DA; DA3; DAB; DAC; DAM MST, MULT, NOV, POP; DLB 113; DNFS 1, 2; EXPN; EXPS; HW 1, 2; LAIT 2; LAW; LAWS 1; MTCW 1, 2; NCFS 3; NFS 1, 5, 10; RGSF 2; RGWL 2; SSFS 1, 6; WLIT 1

Garcilaso de la Vega, El Inca 1503-1536
See also HLCS 1; LAW

Gard, Janice
See Latham, Jean Lee

Gard, Roger Martin du
See Martin du Gard, Roger

Gardam, Jane (Mary) 1928- .... **CLC 43**
See also CA 49-52; CANR 2, 18, 33, 54, 106; CLR 12; DLB 14, 161, 231; MAICYA 1, 2; MTCW 1; SAAS 9; SATA 39, 76, 130; SATA-Brief 28; YAW

Gardner, Herb(ert) 1934- .... **CLC 44**
See also CA 149; CAD; CD 5

Gardner, John (Champlin), Jr.
1933-1982 ... **CLC 2, 3, 5, 7, 8, 10, 18, 28, 34; SSC 7**
See also AITN 1; AMWS 6; BPFB 2; CA 65-68; 107; CANR 33, 73; CDALBS; CPW; DA3; DAM NOV, POP; DLB 2; DLBY 1982; FANT; MTCW 1; NFS 3; RGAL 4; RGSF 2; SATA 40; SATA-Obit 31; SSFS 8

Gardner, John (Edmund) 1926- .... **CLC 30**
See also CA 103; CANR 15, 69; CMW 4; CPW; DAM POP; MTCW 1

Gardner, Miriam
See Bradley, Marion Zimmer
See also GLL 1

Gardner, Noel
See Kuttner, Henry

Gardons, S. S.
See Snodgrass, W(illiam) D(e Witt)

Garfield, Leon 1921-1996 .... **CLC 12**
See also AAYA 8; BYA 1, 3; CA 17-20R; 152; CANR 38, 41, 78; CLR 21; DLB 161; JRDA; MAICYA 1, 2; MAICYAS 1; SATA 1, 32, 76; SATA-Obit 90; WYA; YAW

Garland, (Hannibal) Hamlin
   1860-1940 .... TCLC 3; SSC 18
   See also CA 104; DLB 12, 71, 78, 186;
   RGAL 4; RGSF 2; TCWW 2

Garneau, (Hector de) Saint-Denys
   1912-1943 .... TCLC 13
   See also CA 111; DLB 88

Garner, Alan 1934- .... CLC 17
   See also AAYA 18; BYA 3, 5; CA 73-76,
   178; CAAE 178; CANR 15, 64; CLR 20;
   CPW; DAB; DAM POP; DLB 161;
   FANT; MAICYA 1, 2; MTCW 1, 2; SATA
   18, 69; SATA-Essay 108; SUFW; YAW

Garner, Hugh 1913-1979 .... CLC 13
   See also Warwick, Jarvis
   See also CA 69-72; CANR 31; CCA 1; DLB
   68

Garnett, David 1892-1981 .... CLC 3
   See also CA 5-8R; 103; CANR 17, 79; DLB
   34; FANT; MTCW 2; RGEL 2; SFW 4;
   SUFW

Garos, Stephanie
   See Katz, Steve

Garrett, George (Palmer) 1929- .. CLC 3, 11,
   51; SSC 30
   See also AMWS 7; BPFB 2; CA 1-4R;
   CAAS 5; CANR 1, 42, 67, 109; CN 7;
   CP 7; CSW; DLB 2, 5, 130, 152; DLBY
   1983

Garrick, David 1717-1779 .... LC 15
   See also DAM DRAM; DLB 84, 213;
   RGEL 2

Garrigue, Jean 1914-1972 .... CLC 2, 8
   See also CA 5-8R; 37-40R; CANR 20

Garrison, Frederick
   See Sinclair, Upton (Beall)

Garro, Elena 1920(?)-1998
   See also CA 131; 169; CWW 2; DLB 145;
   HLCS 1; HW 1; LAWS 1; WLIT 1

Garth, Will
   See Hamilton, Edmond; Kuttner, Henry

Garvey, Marcus (Moziah, Jr.)
   1887-1940 .... TCLC 41; BLC 2
   See also BW 1; CA 120; 124; CANR 79;
   DAM MULT

Gary, Romain .... CLC 25
   See also Kacew, Romain
   See also DLB 83

Gascar, Pierre .... CLC 11
   See also Fournier, Pierre

Gascoyne, David (Emery)
   1916-2001 .... CLC 45
   See also CA 65-68; 200; CANR 10, 28, 54;
   CP 7; DLB 20; MTCW 1; RGEL 2

Gaskell, Elizabeth Cleghorn
   1810-1865 .... NCLC 5, 70, 97; SSC 25
   See also BRW 5; CDBLB 1832-1890; DAB;
   DAM MST; DLB 21, 144, 159; RGEL 2;
   RGSF 2

Gass, William H(oward) 1924- . CLC 1, 2, 8,
   11, 15, 39, 132; SSC 12
   See also AMWS 6; CA 17-20R; CANR 30,
   71, 100; CN 7; DLB 2, 227; MTCW 1, 2;
   RGAL 4

Gassendi, Pierre 1592-1655 .... LC 54
   See also GFL Beginnings to 1789

Gasset, Jose Ortega y
   See Ortega y Gasset, Jose

Gates, Henry Louis, Jr. 1950- .... CLC 65;
   BLCS
   See also BW 2, 3; CA 109; CANR 25, 53,
   75; CSW; DA3; DAM MULT; DLB 67;
   MTCW 1; RGAL 4

Gautier, Theophile 1811-1872 .. NCLC 1, 59;
   PC 18; SSC 20
   See also DAM POET; DLB 119; EW 6;
   GFL 1789 to the Present; RGWL 2;
   SUFW

Gawsworth, John
   See Bates, H(erbert) E(rnest)

Gay, John 1685-1732 .... LC 49
   See also BRW 3; DAM DRAM; DLB 84,
   95; RGEL 2; WLIT 3

Gay, Oliver
   See Gogarty, Oliver St. John

Gay, Peter (Jack) 1923- .... CLC 158
   See also CA 13-16R; CANR 18, 41, 77;
   INT CANR-18

Gaye, Marvin (Pentz, Jr.)
   1939-1984 .... CLC 26
   See also CA 195; 112

Gebler, Carlo (Ernest) 1954- .... CLC 39
   See also CA 119; 133; CANR 96

Gee, Maggie (Mary) 1948- .... CLC 57
   See also CA 130; CN 7; DLB 207

Gee, Maurice (Gough) 1931- .... CLC 29
   See also AAYA 42; CA 97-100; CANR 67;
   CLR 56; CN 7; CWRI 5; MAICYA 2;
   RGSF 2; SATA 46, 101

Gelbart, Larry (Simon) 1928- .... CLC 21, 61
   See also Gelbart, Larry
   See also CA 73-76; CANR 45, 94

Gelbart, Larry 1928-
   See Gelbart, Larry (Simon)
   See also CAD; CD 5

Gelber, Jack 1932- .... CLC 1, 6, 14, 79
   See also CA 1-4R; CAD; CANR 2; DLB 7,
   228

Gellhorn, Martha (Ellis)
   1908-1998 .... CLC 14, 60
   See also CA 77-80; 164; CANR 44; CN 7;
   DLBY 1982, 1998

Genet, Jean 1910-1986 .. CLC 1, 2, 5, 10, 14,
   44, 46
   See also CA 13-16R; CANR 18; DA3;
   DAM DRAM; DFS 10; DLB 72; DLBY
   1986; EW 13; GFL 1789 to the Present;
   GLL 1; MTCW 1, 2; RGWL 2

Gent, Peter 1942- .... CLC 29
   See also AITN 1; CA 89-92; DLBY 1982

Gentile, Giovanni 1875-1944 .... TCLC 96
   See also CA 119

Gentlewoman in New England, A
   See Bradstreet, Anne

Gentlewoman in Those Parts, A
   See Bradstreet, Anne

Geoffrey of Monmouth c.
   1100-1155 .... CMLC 44
   See also DLB 146

George, Jean
   See George, Jean Craighead

George, Jean Craighead 1919- .... CLC 35
   See also AAYA 8; BYA 2, 4; CA 5-8R;
   CANR 25; CLR 1; 80; DLB 52; JRDA;
   MAICYA 1, 2; SATA 2, 68, 124; WYA;
   YAW

George, Stefan (Anton) 1868-1933 . TCLC 2,
   14
   See also CA 104; 193; EW 8

Georges, Georges Martin
   See Simenon, Georges (Jacques Christian)

Gerhardi, William Alexander
   See Gerhardie, William Alexander

Gerhardie, William Alexander
   1895-1977 .... CLC 5
   See also CA 25-28R; 73-76; CANR 18;
   DLB 36; RGEL 2

Gerson, Jean 1363-1429 .... LC 77
   See also DLB 208

Gersonides 1288-1344 .... CMLC 49
   See also DLB 115

Gerstler, Amy 1956- .... CLC 70
   See also CA 146; CANR 99

Gertler, T. .... CLC 134
   See also CA 116; 121

Ghalib .... NCLC 39, 78
   See also Ghalib, Asadullah Khan

Ghalib, Asadullah Khan 1797-1869
   See Ghalib
   See also DAM POET; RGWL 2

Ghelderode, Michel de 1898-1962 ..... CLC 6,
   11; DC 15
   See also CA 85-88; CANR 40, 77; DAM
   DRAM; EW 11

Ghiselin, Brewster 1903-2001 .... CLC 23
   See also CA 13-16R; CAAS 10; CANR 13;
   CP 7

Ghose, Aurabinda 1872-1950 .... TCLC 63
   See also CA 163

Ghose, Zulfikar 1935- .... CLC 42
   See also CA 65-68; CANR 67; CN 7; CP 7

Ghosh, Amitav 1956- .... CLC 44, 153
   See also CA 147; CANR 80; CN 7

Giacosa, Giuseppe 1847-1906 .... TCLC 7
   See also CA 104

Gibb, Lee
   See Waterhouse, Keith (Spencer)

Gibbon, Lewis Grassic .... TCLC 4
   See also Mitchell, James Leslie
   See also RGEL 2

Gibbons, Kaye 1960- .... CLC 50, 88, 145
   See also AAYA 34; AMWS 10; CA 151;
   CANR 75; CSW; DA3; DAM POP;
   MTCW 1; NFS 3; RGAL 4; SATA 117

Gibran, Kahlil 1883-1931 . TCLC 1, 9; PC 9
   See also CA 104; 150; DA3; DAM POET,
   POP; MTCW 2

Gibran, Khalil
   See Gibran, Kahlil

Gibson, William 1914- .... CLC 23
   See also CA 9-12R; CAD 2; CANR 9, 42,
   75; CD 5; DA; DAB; DAC; DAM
   DRAM, MST; DFS 2; DLB 7; LAIT 2;
   MTCW 2; SATA 66; YAW

Gibson, William (Ford) 1948- ... CLC 39, 63;
   SSC 52
   See also AAYA 12; BPFB 2; CA 126; 133;
   CANR 52, 90, 106; CN 7; CPW; DA3;
   DAM POP; DLB 251; MTCW 2; SCFW
   2; SFW 4

Gide, Andre (Paul Guillaume)
   1869-1951 ..... TCLC 5, 12, 36; SSC 13;
   WLC
   See also CA 104; 124; DA; DA3; DAB;
   DAC; DAM MST, NOV; DLB 65; EW 8;
   GFL 1789 to the Present; MTCW 1, 2;
   RGSF 2; RGWL 2

Gifford, Barry (Colby) 1946- .... CLC 34
   See also CA 65-68; CANR 9, 30, 40, 90

Gilbert, Frank
   See De Voto, Bernard (Augustine)

Gilbert, W(illiam) S(chwenck)
   1836-1911 .... TCLC 3
   See also CA 104; 173; DAM DRAM, POET;
   RGEL 2; SATA 36

Gilbreth, Frank B(unker), Jr.
   1911-2001 .... CLC 17
   See also CA 9-12R; SATA 2

Gilchrist, Ellen (Louise) 1935- .. CLC 34, 48,
   143; SSC 14
   See also BPFB 2; CA 113; 116; CANR 41,
   61, 104; CN 7; CPW; CSW; DAM POP;
   DLB 130; EXPS; MTCW 1, 2; RGAL 4;
   RGSF 2; SSFS 9

Giles, Molly 1942- .... CLC 39
   See also CA 126; CANR 98

Gill, Eric 1882-1940 .... TCLC 85

Gill, Patrick
   See Creasey, John

Gillette, Douglas .... CLC 70

Gilliam, Terry (Vance) 1940- .... CLC 21, 141
   See also Monty Python
   See also AAYA 19; CA 108; 113; CANR
   35; INT 113

Gillian, Jerry
   See Gilliam, Terry (Vance)

Gilliatt, Penelope (Ann Douglass)
1932-1993 .... **CLC 2, 10, 13, 53**
See also AITN 2; CA 13-16R; 141; CANR 49; DLB 14

Gilman, Charlotte (Anna) Perkins (Stetson)
1860-1935 ..... **TCLC 9, 37, 117; SSC 13**
See also BYA 11; CA 106; 150; DLB 221; EXPS; FW; HGG; LAIT 2; MAWW; MTCW 1; RGAL 4; RGSF 2; SFW 4; SSFS 1

Gilmour, David 1946- .... **CLC 35**

Gilpin, William 1724-1804 .... **NCLC 30**

Gilray, J. D.
See Mencken, H(enry) L(ouis)

Gilroy, Frank D(aniel) 1925- .... **CLC 2**
See also CA 81-84; CAD; CANR 32, 64, 86; CD 5; DLB 7

Gilstrap, John 1957(?)- .... **CLC 99**
See also CA 160; CANR 101

Ginsberg, Allen 1926-1997 .... **CLC 1, 2, 3, 4, 6, 13, 36, 69, 109; PC 4; WLC**
See also AAYA 33; AITN 1; AMWS 2; CA 1-4R; 157; CANR 2, 41, 63, 95; CDALB 1941-1968; CP 7; DA; DA3; DAB; DAC; DAM MST, POET; DLB 5, 16, 169, 237; GLL 1; MTCW 1, 2; PAB; PFS 5; RGAL 4; TCLC 120; WP

Ginzburg, Eugenia .... **CLC 59**

Ginzburg, Natalia 1916-1991 .... **CLC 5, 11, 54, 70**
See also CA 85-88; 135; CANR 33; DFS 14; DLB 177; EW 13; MTCW 1, 2; RGWL 2

Giono, Jean 1895-1970 .... **CLC 4, 11**
See also CA 45-48; 29-32R; CANR 2, 35; DLB 72; GFL 1789 to the Present; MTCW 1; RGWL 2

Giovanni, Nikki 1943- .... **CLC 2, 4, 19, 64, 117; BLC 2; PC 19; WLCS**
See also AAYA 22; AITN 1; BW 2, 3; CA 29-32R; CAAS 6; CANR 18, 41, 60, 91; CDALBS; CLR 6, 73; CP 7; CSW; CWP; CWRI 5; DA; DA3; DAB; DAC; DAM MST, MULT, POET; DLB 5, 41; EXPP; INT CANR-18; MAICYA 1, 2; MTCW 1, 2; RGAL 4; SATA 24, 107; YAW

Giovene, Andrea 1904-1998 .... **CLC 7**
See also CA 85-88

Gippius, Zinaida (Nikolayevna) 1869-1945
See Hippius, Zinaida
See also CA 106

Giraudoux, Jean(-Hippolyte)
1882-1944 .... **TCLC 2, 7**
See also CA 104; 196; DAM DRAM; DLB 65; EW 9; GFL 1789 to the Present; RGWL 2

Gironella, Jose Maria 1917-1991 ..... **CLC 11**
See also CA 101; RGWL 2

Gissing, George (Robert)
1857-1903 ...... **TCLC 3, 24, 47; SSC 37**
See also BRW 5; CA 105; 167; DLB 18, 135, 184; RGEL 2

Giurlani, Aldo
See Palazzeschi, Aldo

Gladkov, Fyodor (Vasilyevich)
1883-1958 .... **TCLC 27**
See also CA 170

Glanville, Brian (Lester) 1931- .... **CLC 6**
See also CA 5-8R; CAAS 9; CANR 3, 70; CN 7; DLB 15, 139; SATA 42

Glasgow, Ellen (Anderson Gholson)
1873-1945 .... **TCLC 2, 7; SSC 34**
See also AMW; CA 104; 164; DLB 9, 12; MAWW; MTCW 2; RGAL 4; RHW; SSFS 9

Glaspell, Susan 1882(?)-1948 . **TCLC 55; DC 10; SSC 41**
See also AMWS 3; CA 110; 154; DFS 8; DLB 7, 9, 78, 228; MAWW; RGAL 4; SSFS 3; TCWW 2; YABC 2

Glassco, John 1909-1981 .... **CLC 9**
See also CA 13-16R; 102; CANR 15; DLB 68

Glasscock, Amnesia
See Steinbeck, John (Ernst)

Glasser, Ronald J. 1940(?)- .... **CLC 37**

Glassman, Joyce
See Johnson, Joyce

Gleick, James (W.) 1954- .... **CLC 147**
See also CA 131; 137; CANR 97; INT CA-137

Glendinning, Victoria 1937- .... **CLC 50**
See also CA 120; 127; CANR 59, 89; DLB 155

Glissant, Edouard 1928- .... **CLC 10, 68**
See also CA 153; CWW 2; DAM MULT

Gloag, Julian 1930- .... **CLC 40**
See also AITN 1; CA 65-68; CANR 10, 70; CN 7

Glowacki, Aleksander
See Prus, Boleslaw

Gluck, Louise (Elisabeth) 1943- .. **CLC 7, 22, 44, 81, 160; PC 16**
See also AMWS 5; CA 33-36R; CANR 40, 69, 108; CP 7; CWP; DA3; DAM POET; DLB 5; MTCW 2; PFS 5; RGAL 4

Glyn, Elinor 1864-1943 .... **TCLC 72**
See also DLB 153; RHW

Gobineau, Joseph-Arthur
1816-1882 .... **NCLC 17**
See also DLB 123; GFL 1789 to the Present

Godard, Jean-Luc 1930- .... **CLC 20**
See also CA 93-96

Godden, (Margaret) Rumer
1907-1998 .... **CLC 53**
See also AAYA 6; BPFB 2; BYA 2, 5; CA 5-8R; 172; CANR 4, 27, 36, 55, 80; CLR 20; CN 7; CWRI 5; DLB 161; MAICYA 1, 2; RHW; SAAS 12; SATA 3, 36; SATA-Obit 109

Godoy Alcayaga, Lucila
1899-1957 .... **TCLC 2; HLC 2; PC 32**
See also Mistral, Gabriela
See also BW 2; CA 104; 131; CANR 81; DAM MULT; DNFS; HW 1, 2; MTCW 1, 2

Godwin, Gail (Kathleen) 1937- ..... **CLC 5, 8, 22, 31, 69, 125**
See also BPFB 2; CA 29-32R; CANR 15, 43, 69; CN 7; CPW; CSW; DA3; DAM POP; DLB 6, 234; INT CANR-15; MTCW 1, 2

Godwin, William 1756-1836 .... **NCLC 14**
See also CDBLB 1789-1832; CMW 4; DLB 39, 104, 142, 158, 163; HGG; RGEL 2

Goebbels, Josef
See Goebbels, (Paul) Joseph

Goebbels, (Paul) Joseph
1897-1945 .... **TCLC 68**
See also CA 115; 148

Goebbels, Joseph Paul
See Goebbels, (Paul) Joseph

Goethe, Johann Wolfgang von
1749-1832 ... **NCLC 4, 22, 34, 90; PC 5; SSC 38; WLC**
See also CDWLB 2; DA; DA3; DAB; DAC; DAM DRAM, MST, POET; DLB 94; EW 5; RGWL 2

Gogarty, Oliver St. John
1878-1957 .... **TCLC 15**
See also CA 109; 150; DLB 15, 19; RGEL 2

Gogol, Nikolai (Vasilyevich)
1809-1852 .... **NCLC 5, 15, 31; DC 1; SSC 4, 29, 52; WLC**
See also DA; DAB; DAC; DAM DRAM, MST; DFS 12; DLB 198; EW 6; EXPS; RGSF 2; RGWL 2; SSFS 7

Goines, Donald 1937(?)-1974 . **CLC 80; BLC 2**
See also AITN 1; BW 1, 3; CA 124; 114; CANR 82; CMW 4; DA3; DAM MULT, POP; DLB 33

Gold, Herbert 1924- ... **CLC 4, 7, 14, 42, 152**
See also CA 9-12R; CANR 17, 45; CN 7; DLB 2; DLBY 1981

Goldbarth, Albert 1948- .... **CLC 5, 38**
See also CA 53-56; CANR 6, 40; CP 7; DLB 120

Goldberg, Anatol 1910-1982 .... **CLC 34**
See also CA 131; 117

Goldemberg, Isaac 1945- .... **CLC 52**
See also CA 69-72; CAAS 12; CANR 11, 32; HW 1; WLIT 1

Golding, William (Gerald)
1911-1993 ..... **CLC 1, 2, 3, 8, 10, 17, 27, 58, 81; WLC**
See also AAYA 5; BPFB 2; BRWR 1; BRWS 1; BYA 2; CA 5-8R; 141; CANR 13, 33, 54; CDBLB 1945-1960; DA; DA3; DAB; DAC; DAM MST, NOV; DLB 15, 100, 255; EXPN; HGG; LAIT 4; MTCW 1, 2; NFS 2; RGEL 2; RHW; SFW 4; WLIT 4; YAW

Goldman, Emma 1869-1940 .... **TCLC 13**
See also CA 110; 150; DLB 221; FW; RGAL 4

Goldman, Francisco 1954- .... **CLC 76**
See also CA 162

Goldman, William (W.) 1931- ...... **CLC 1, 48**
See also BPFB 2; CA 9-12R; CANR 29, 69, 106; CN 7; DLB 44; FANT; IDFW 3, 4

Goldmann, Lucien 1913-1970 .... **CLC 24**
See also CA 25-28; CAP 2

Goldoni, Carlo 1707-1793 .... **LC 4**
See also DAM DRAM; EW 4; RGWL 2

Goldsberry, Steven 1949- .... **CLC 34**
See also CA 131

Goldsmith, Oliver 1730-1774 .. **LC 2, 48; DC 8; WLC**
See also BRW 3; CDBLB 1660-1789; DA; DAB; DAC; DAM DRAM, MST, NOV, POET; DFS 1; DLB 39, 89, 104, 109, 142; IDTP; RGEL 2; SATA 26; TEA; WLIT 3

Goldsmith, Peter
See Priestley, J(ohn) B(oynton)

Gombrowicz, Witold 1904-1969 .... **CLC 4, 7, 11, 49**
See also CA 19-20; 25-28R; CANR 105; CAP 2; CDWLB 4; DAM DRAM; DLB 215; EW 12; RGWL 2

Gomez de Avellaneda, Gertrudis
1814-1873 .... **NCLC 111**
See also LAW

Gomez de la Serna, Ramon
1888-1963 .... **CLC 9**
See also CA 153; 116; CANR 79; HW 1, 2

Goncharov, Ivan Alexandrovich
1812-1891 .... **NCLC 1, 63**
See also DLB 238; EW 6; RGWL 2

Goncourt, Edmond (Louis Antoine Huot) de
1822-1896 .... **NCLC 7**
See also DLB 123; EW 7; GFL 1789 to the Present; RGWL 2

Goncourt, Jules (Alfred Huot) de
1830-1870 .... **NCLC 7**
See also DLB 123; EW 7; GFL 1789 to the Present; RGWL 2

Gongora (y Argote), Luis de
1561-1627 .... **LC 72**
See also RGWL 2

Gontier, Fernande 19(?)- .... **CLC 50**

Gonzalez Martinez, Enrique
1871-1952 .... **TCLC 72**
See also CA 166; CANR 81; HW 1, 2

Goodison, Lorna 1947- .... **PC 36**
See also CA 142; CANR 88; CP 7; CWP;
DLB 157

Goodman, Paul 1911-1972 ..... **CLC 1, 2, 4, 7**
See also CA 19-20; 37-40R; CAD; CANR
34; CAP 2; DLB 130, 246; MTCW 1;
RGAL 4

Gordimer, Nadine 1923- ...... **CLC 3, 5, 7, 10,
18, 33, 51, 70, 123, 160; SSC 17;
WLCS**
See also AAYA 39; AFW; BRWS 2; CA
5-8R; CANR 3, 28, 56, 88; CN 7; DA;
DA3; DAB; DAC; DAM MST, NOV;
DLB 225; EXPS; INT CANR-28; MTCW
1, 2; NFS 4; RGEL 2; RGSF 2; SSFS 2,
14; WLIT 2; YAW

Gordon, Adam Lindsay
1833-1870 .... **NCLC 21**
See also DLB 230

Gordon, Caroline 1895-1981 . **CLC 6, 13, 29,
83; SSC 15**
See also AMW; CA 11-12; 103; CANR 36;
CAP 1; DLB 4, 9, 102; DLBD 17; DLBY
1981; MTCW 1, 2; RGAL 4; RGSF 2

Gordon, Charles William 1860-1937
See Connor, Ralph
See also CA 109

Gordon, Mary (Catherine) 1949- .... **CLC 13,
22, 128**
See also AMWS 4; BPFB 2; CA 102;
CANR 44, 92; CN 7; DLB 6; DLBY
1981; FW; INT CA-102; MTCW 1

Gordon, N. J.
See Bosman, Herman Charles

Gordon, Sol 1923- .... **CLC 26**
See also CA 53-56; CANR 4; SATA 11

Gordone, Charles 1925-1995 .. **CLC 1, 4; DC
8**
See also BW 1, 3; CA 93-96; 180; 150;
CAAE 180; CAD; CANR 55; DAM
DRAM; DLB 7; INT 93-96; MTCW 1

Gore, Catherine 1800-1861 .... **NCLC 65**
See also DLB 116; RGEL 2

Gorenko, Anna Andreevna
See Akhmatova, Anna

Gorky, Maxim .... **TCLC 8; SSC 28; WLC**
See also Peshkov, Alexei Maximovich
See also DAB; DFS 9; EW 8; MTCW 2

Goryan, Sirak
See Saroyan, William

Gosse, Edmund (William)
1849-1928 .... **TCLC 28**
See also CA 117; DLB 57, 144, 184; RGEL
2

Gotlieb, Phyllis Fay (Bloom) 1926- .. **CLC 18**
See also CA 13-16R; CANR 7; DLB 88,
251; SFW 4

Gottesman, S. D.
See Kornbluth, C(yril) M.; Pohl, Frederik

Gottfried von Strassburg fl. c.
1170-1215 .... **CMLC 10**
See also CDWLB 2; DLB 138; EW 1;
RGWL 2

Gould, Lois 1932(?)-2002 .... **CLC 4, 10**
See also CA 77-80; CANR 29; MTCW 1

Gourmont, Remy(-Marie-Charles) de
1858-1915 .... **TCLC 17**
See also CA 109; 150; GFL 1789 to the
Present; MTCW 2

Govier, Katherine 1948- .... **CLC 51**
See also CA 101; CANR 18, 40; CCA 1

Gower, John c. 1330-1408 .... **LC 76**
See also BRW 1; DLB 146; RGEL 2

Goyen, (Charles) William
1915-1983 .... **CLC 5, 8, 14, 40**
See also AITN 2; CA 5-8R; 110; CANR 6,
71; DLB 2, 218; DLBY 1983; INT
CANR-6

Goytisolo, Juan 1931- .... **CLC 5, 10, 23, 133;
HLC 1**
See also CA 85-88; CANR 32, 61; CWW
2; DAM MULT; GLL 2; HW 1, 2; MTCW
1, 2

Gozzano, Guido 1883-1916 .... **PC 10**
See also CA 154; DLB 114

Gozzi, (Conte) Carlo 1720-1806 .... **NCLC 23**

Grabbe, Christian Dietrich
1801-1836 .... **NCLC 2**
See also DLB 133; RGWL 2

Grace, Patricia Frances 1937- .... **CLC 56**
See also CA 176; CN 7; RGSF 2

Gracian y Morales, Baltasar
1601-1658 .... **LC 15**

Gracq, Julien .... **CLC 11, 48**
See also Poirier, Louis
See also CWW 2; DLB 83; GFL 1789 to
the Present

Grade, Chaim 1910-1982 .... **CLC 10**
See also CA 93-96; 107

Graduate of Oxford, A
See Ruskin, John

Grafton, Garth
See Duncan, Sara Jeannette

Graham, John
See Phillips, David Graham

Graham, Jorie 1951- .... **CLC 48, 118**
See also CA 111; CANR 63; CP 7; CWP;
DLB 120; PFS 10

Graham, R(obert) B(ontine) Cunninghame
See Cunninghame Graham, Robert
(Gallnigad) Bontine
See also DLB 98, 135, 174; RGEL 2; RGSF
2

Graham, Robert
See Haldeman, Joe (William)

Graham, Tom
See Lewis, (Harry) Sinclair

Graham, W(illiam) S(idney)
1918-1986 .... **CLC 29**
See also BRWS 7; CA 73-76; 118; DLB 20;
RGEL 2

Graham, Winston (Mawdsley)
1910- .... **CLC 23**
See also CA 49-52; CANR 2, 22, 45, 66;
CMW 4; CN 7; DLB 77; RHW

Grahame, Kenneth 1859-1932 .... **TCLC 64**
See also BYA 5; CA 108; 136; CANR 80;
CLR 5; CWRI 5; DA3; DAB; DLB 34,
141, 178; FANT; MAICYA 1, 2; MTCW
2; RGEL 2; SATA 100; WCH; YABC 1

Granger, Darius John
See Marlowe, Stephen

Granin, Daniil .... **CLC 59**

Granovsky, Timofei Nikolaevich
1813-1855 .... **NCLC 75**
See also DLB 198

Grant, Skeeter
See Spiegelman, Art

Granville-Barker, Harley
1877-1946 .... **TCLC 2**
See also Barker, Harley Granville
See also CA 104; DAM DRAM; RGEL 2

Granzotto, Gianni
See Granzotto, Giovanni Battista

Granzotto, Giovanni Battista
1914-1985 .... **CLC 70**
See also CA 166

Grass, Guenter (Wilhelm) 1927- ... **CLC 1, 2,
4, 6, 11, 15, 22, 32, 49, 88; WLC**
See also BPFB 2; CA 13-16R; CANR 20,
75, 93; CDWLB 2; DA; DA3; DAB;
DAC; DAM MST, NOV; DLB 75, 124;
EW 13; MTCW 1, 2; RGWL 2

Gratton, Thomas
See Hulme, T(homas) E(rnest)

Grau, Shirley Ann 1929- .... **CLC 4, 9, 146;
SSC 15**
See also CA 89-92; CANR 22, 69; CN 7;
CSW; DLB 2, 218; INT CA-89-92;
CANR-22; MTCW 1

Gravel, Fern
See Hall, James Norman

Graver, Elizabeth 1964- .... **CLC 70**
See also CA 135; CANR 71

Graves, Richard Perceval
1895-1985 .... **CLC 44**
See also CA 65-68; CANR 9, 26, 51

Graves, Robert (von Ranke)
1895-1985 .. **CLC 1, 2, 6, 11, 39, 44, 45;
PC 6**
See also BPFB 2; BRW 7; BYA 4; CA 5-8R;
117; CANR 5, 36; CDBLB 1914-1945;
DA3; DAB; DAC; DAM MST, POET;
DLB 20, 100, 191; DLBD 18; DLBY
1985; MTCW 1, 2; NCFS 2; RGEL 2;
RHW; SATA 45

Graves, Valerie
See Bradley, Marion Zimmer

Gray, Alasdair (James) 1934- .... **CLC 41**
See also CA 126; CANR 47, 69, 106; CN
7; DLB 194; HGG; INT CA-126; MTCW
1, 2; RGSF 2

Gray, Amlin 1946- .... **CLC 29**
See also CA 138

Gray, Francine du Plessix 1930- ..... **CLC 22,
153**
See also BEST 90:3; CA 61-64; CAAS 2;
CANR 11, 33, 75, 81; DAM NOV; INT
CANR-11; MTCW 1, 2

Gray, John (Henry) 1866-1934 ...... **TCLC 19**
See also CA 119; 162; RGEL 2

Gray, Simon (James Holliday)
1936- .... **CLC 9, 14, 36**
See also AITN 1; CA 21-24R; CAAS 3;
CANR 32, 69; CD 5; DLB 13; MTCW 1;
RGEL 2

Gray, Spalding 1941- ..... **CLC 49, 112; DC 7**
See also CA 128; CAD; CANR 74; CD 5;
CPW; DAM POP; MTCW 2

Gray, Thomas 1716-1771 .... **LC 4, 40; PC 2;
WLC**
See also BRW 3; CDBLB 1660-1789; DA;
DA3; DAB; DAC; DAM MST; DLB 109;
EXPP; PAB; PFS 9; RGEL 2; WP

Grayson, David
See Baker, Ray Stannard

Grayson, Richard (A.) 1951- .... **CLC 38**
See also CA 85-88; CANR 14, 31, 57; DLB
234

Greeley, Andrew M(oran) 1928- ...... **CLC 28**
See also BPFB 2; CA 5-8R; CAAS 7;
CANR 7, 43, 69, 104; CMW 4; CPW;
DA3; DAM POP; MTCW 1, 2

Green, Anna Katharine
1846-1935 .... **TCLC 63**
See also CA 112; 159; CMW 4; DLB 202,
221; MSW

Green, Brian
See Card, Orson Scott

Green, Hannah
See Greenberg, Joanne (Goldenberg)

Green, Hannah 1927(?)-1996 .... **CLC 3**
See also CA 73-76; CANR 59, 93; NFS 10

Green, Henry .... **CLC 2, 13, 97**
See also Yorke, Henry Vincent
See also BRWS 2; CA 175; DLB 15; RGEL
2

Green, Julian (Hartridge) 1900-1998
See Green, Julien
See also CA 21-24R; 169; CANR 33, 87;
DLB 4, 72; MTCW 1

Green, Julien .... CLC 3, 11, 77
See also Green, Julian (Hartridge)
See also GFL 1789 to the Present; MTCW
2

Green, Paul (Eliot) 1894-1981 .... CLC 25
See also AITN 1; CA 5-8R; 103; CANR 3;
DAM DRAM; DLB 7, 9, 249; DLBY
1981; RGAL 4

Greenaway, Peter 1942- .... CLC 159
See also CA 127

Greenberg, Ivan 1908-1973
See Rahv, Philip
See also CA 85-88

Greenberg, Joanne (Goldenberg)
1932- .... CLC 7, 30
See also AAYA 12; CA 5-8R; CANR 14,
32, 69; CN 7; SATA 25; YAW

Greenberg, Richard 1959(?)- .... CLC 57
See also CA 138; CAD; CD 5

Greenblatt, Stephen J(ay) 1943- ...... CLC 70
See also CA 49-52

Greene, Bette 1934- .... CLC 30
See also AAYA 7; BYA 3; CA 53-56; CANR
4; CLR 2; CWRI 5; JRDA; LAIT 4; MAI-
CYA 1, 2; NFS 10; SAAS 16; SATA 8,
102; WYA; YAW

Greene, Gael .... CLC 8
See also CA 13-16R; CANR 10

Greene, Graham (Henry)
1904-1991 .... CLC 1, 3, 6, 9, 14, 18, 27,
37, 70, 72, 125; SSC 29; WLC
See also AITN 2; BPFB 2; BRWR 2; BRWS
1; BYA 3; CA 13-16R; 133; CANR 35,
61; CBD; CDBLB 1945-1960; CMW 4;
DA; DA3; DAB; DAC; DAM MST, NOV;
DLB 13, 15, 77, 100, 162, 201, 204;
DLBY 1991; MSW; MTCW 1, 2; RGEL
2; SATA 20; SSFS 14; WLIT 4

Greene, Robert 1558-1592 .... LC 41
See also DLB 62, 167; IDTP; RGEL 2; TEA

Greer, Germaine 1939- .... CLC 131
See also AITN 1; CA 81-84; CANR 33, 70;
FW; MTCW 1, 2

Greer, Richard
See Silverberg, Robert

Gregor, Arthur 1923- .... CLC 9
See also CA 25-28R; CAAS 10; CANR 11;
CP 7; SATA 36

Gregor, Lee
See Pohl, Frederik

Gregory, Lady Isabella Augusta (Persse)
1852-1932 .... TCLC 1
See also BRW 6; CA 104; 184; DLB 10;
IDTP; RGEL 2

Gregory, J. Dennis
See Williams, John A(lfred)

Grekova, I. .... CLC 59

Grendon, Stephen
See Derleth, August (William)

Grenville, Kate 1950- .... CLC 61
See also CA 118; CANR 53, 93

Grenville, Pelham
See Wodehouse, P(elham) G(renville)

Greve, Felix Paul (Berthold Friedrich)
1879-1948
See Grove, Frederick Philip
See also CA 104; 141; 175; CANR 79;
DAC; DAM MST

Grey, Zane 1872-1939 .... TCLC 6
See also BPFB 2; CA 104; 132; DA3; DAM
POP; DLB 9, 212; MTCW 1, 2; RGAL 4;
TCWW 2

Grieg, (Johan) Nordahl (Brun)
1902-1943 .... TCLC 10
See also CA 107; 189

Grieve, C(hristopher) M(urray)
1892-1978 .... CLC 11, 19
See also MacDiarmid, Hugh; Pteleon
See also CA 5-8R; 85-88; CANR 33, 107;
DAM POET; MTCW 1; RGEL 2

Griffin, Gerald 1803-1840 .... NCLC 7
See also DLB 159; RGEL 2

Griffin, John Howard 1920-1980 ..... CLC 68
See also AITN 1; CA 1-4R; 101; CANR 2

Griffin, Peter 1942- .... CLC 39
See also CA 136

Griffith, D(avid Lewelyn) W(ark)
1875(?)-1948 .... TCLC 68
See also CA 119; 150; CANR 80

Griffith, Lawrence
See Griffith, D(avid Lewelyn) W(ark)

Griffiths, Trevor 1935- .... CLC 13, 52
See also CA 97-100; CANR 45; CBD; CD
5; DLB 13, 245

Griggs, Sutton (Elbert)
1872-1930 .... TCLC 77
See also CA 123; 186; DLB 50

Grigson, Geoffrey (Edward Harvey)
1905-1985 .... CLC 7, 39
See also CA 25-28R; 118; CANR 20, 33;
DLB 27; MTCW 1, 2

Grillparzer, Franz 1791-1872 . NCLC 1, 102;
DC 14; SSC 37
See also CDWLB 2; DLB 133; EW 5;
RGWL 2

Grimble, Reverend Charles James
See Eliot, T(homas) S(tearns)

Grimke, Charlotte L(ottie) Forten
1837(?)-1914
See Forten, Charlotte L.
See also BW 1; CA 117; 124; DAM MULT,
POET

Grimm, Jacob Ludwig Karl
1785-1863 .... NCLC 3, 77; SSC 36
See also DLB 90; MAICYA 1, 2; RGSF 2;
RGWL 2; SATA 22; WCH

Grimm, Wilhelm Karl 1786-1859 .. NCLC 3,
77; SSC 36
See also CDWLB 2; DLB 90; MAICYA 1,
2; RGSF 2; RGWL 2; SATA 22; WCH

**Grimmelshausen, Hans Jakob Christoffel
von**
See Grimmelshausen, Johann Jakob Christoffel von
See also RGWL 2

**Grimmelshausen, Johann Jakob Christoffel
von** 1621-1676 .... LC 6
See also Grimmelshausen, Hans Jakob
Christoffel von
See also CDWLB 2; DLB 168

Grindel, Eugene 1895-1952
See Eluard, Paul
See also CA 104; 193

Grisham, John 1955- .... CLC 84
See also AAYA 14; BPFB 2; CA 138;
CANR 47, 69; CMW 4; CN 7; CPW;
CSW; DA3; DAM POP; MSW; MTCW 2

Grossman, David 1954- .... CLC 67
See also CA 138; CWW 2

Grossman, Vasily (Semenovich)
1905-1964 .... CLC 41
See also CA 124; 130; MTCW 1

Grove, Frederick Philip .... TCLC 4
See also Greve, Felix Paul (Berthold
Friedrich)
See also DLB 92; RGEL 2

Grubb
See Crumb, R(obert)

Grumbach, Doris (Isaac) 1918- . CLC 13, 22,
64
See also CA 5-8R; CAAS 2; CANR 9, 42,
70; CN 7; INT CANR-9; MTCW 2

Grundtvig, Nicolai Frederik Severin
1783-1872 .... NCLC 1

Grunge
See Crumb, R(obert)

Grunwald, Lisa 1959- .... CLC 44
See also CA 120

Guare, John 1938- .... CLC 8, 14, 29, 67
See also CA 73-76; CAD; CANR 21, 69;
CD 5; DAM DRAM; DFS 8, 13; DLB 7,
249; MTCW 1, 2; RGAL 4

Gubar, Susan (David) 1944- .... CLC 145
See also CA 108; CANR 45, 70; FW;
MTCW 1; RGAL 4

Gudjonsson, Halldor Kiljan 1902-1998
See Laxness, Halldor
See also CA 103; 164; CWW 2

Guenter, Erich
See Eich, Guenter

Guest, Barbara 1920- .... CLC 34
See also CA 25-28R; CANR 11, 44, 84; CP
7; CWP; DLB 5, 193

Guest, Edgar A(lbert) 1881-1959 ... TCLC 95
See also CA 112; 168

Guest, Judith (Ann) 1936- .... CLC 8, 30
See also AAYA 7; CA 77-80; CANR 15,
75; DA3; DAM NOV, POP; EXPN; INT
CANR-15; LAIT 5; MTCW 1, 2; NFS 1

Guevara, Che .... CLC 87; HLC 1
See also Guevara (Serna), Ernesto

Guevara (Serna), Ernesto
1928-1967 .... CLC 87; HLC 1
See also Guevara, Che
See also CA 127; 111; CANR 56; DAM
MULT; HW 1

Guicciardini, Francesco 1483-1540 ..... LC 49

Guild, Nicholas M. 1944- .... CLC 33
See also CA 93-96

Guillemin, Jacques
See Sartre, Jean-Paul

Guillen, Jorge 1893-1984 . CLC 11; HLCS 1;
PC 35
See also CA 89-92; 112; DAM MULT,
POET; DLB 108; HW 1; RGWL 2

Guillen, Nicolas (Cristobal)
1902-1989 .... CLC 48, 79; BLC 2; HLC
1; PC 23
See also BW 2; CA 116; 125; 129; CANR
84; DAM MST, MULT, POET; HW 1;
LAW; RGWL 2; WP

Guillen y Alavarez, Jorge
See Guillen, Jorge

Guillevic, (Eugene) 1907-1997 .... CLC 33
See also CA 93-96; CWW 2

Guillois
See Desnos, Robert

Guillois, Valentin
See Desnos, Robert

Guimaraes Rosa, Joao
See Rosa, Joao Guimaraes
See also LAW

Guimaraes Rosa, Joao 1908-1967
See also CA 175; HLCS 2; LAW; RGSF 2;
RGWL 2

Guiney, Louise Imogen
1861-1920 .... TCLC 41
See also CA 160; DLB 54; RGAL 4

Guinizelli, Guido c. 1230-1276 ...... CMLC 49

Guiraldes, Ricardo (Guillermo)
1886-1927 .... TCLC 39
See also CA 131; HW 1; LAW; MTCW 1

Gumilev, Nikolai (Stepanovich)
1886-1921 .... TCLC 60
See also CA 165

Gunesekera, Romesh 1954- .... CLC 91
See also CA 159; CN 7

Gunn, Bill .... CLC 5
See also Gunn, William Harrison
See also DLB 38

Gunn, Thom(son William) 1929- .. **CLC 3, 6, 18, 32, 81; PC 26**
See also BRWS 4; CA 17-20R; CANR 9, 33; CDBLB 1960 to Present; CP 7; DAM POET; DLB 27; INT CANR-33; MTCW 1; PFS 9; RGEL 2

Gunn, William Harrison 1934(?)-1989
See Gunn, Bill
See also AITN 1; BW 1, 3; CA 13-16R; 128; CANR 12, 25, 76

Gunn Allen, Paula
See Allen, Paula Gunn

Gunnars, Kristjana 1948- .... **CLC 69**
See also CA 113; CCA 1; CP 7; CWP; DLB 60

Gurdjieff, G(eorgei) I(vanovich)
1877(?)-1949 .... **TCLC 71**
See also CA 157

Gurganus, Allan 1947- .... **CLC 70**
See also BEST 90:1; CA 135; CN 7; CPW; CSW; DAM POP; GLL 1

Gurney, A(lbert) R(amsdell), Jr.
1930- .... **CLC 32, 50, 54**
See also AMWS 5; CA 77-80; CAD; CANR 32, 64; CD 5; DAM DRAM

Gurney, Ivor (Bertie) 1890-1937 ... **TCLC 33**
See also BRW 6; CA 167; PAB; RGEL 2

Gurney, Peter
See Gurney, A(lbert) R(amsdell), Jr.

Guro, Elena 1877-1913 .... **TCLC 56**

Gustafson, James M(oody) 1925- ... **CLC 100**
See also CA 25-28R; CANR 37

Gustafson, Ralph (Barker)
1909-1995 .... **CLC 36**
See also CA 21-24R; CANR 8, 45, 84; CP 7; DLB 88; RGEL 2

Gut, Gom
See Simenon, Georges (Jacques Christian)

Guterson, David 1956- .... **CLC 91**
See also CA 132; CANR 73; MTCW 2; NFS 13

Guthrie, A(lfred) B(ertram), Jr.
1901-1991 .... **CLC 23**
See also CA 57-60; 134; CANR 24; DLB 6, 212; SATA 62; SATA-Obit 67

Guthrie, Isobel
See Grieve, C(hristopher) M(urray)

Guthrie, Woodrow Wilson 1912-1967
See Guthrie, Woody
See also CA 113; 93-96

Guthrie, Woody .... **CLC 35**
See also Guthrie, Woodrow Wilson
See also LAIT 3

Gutierrez Najera, Manuel 1859-1895
See also HLCS 2; LAW

Guy, Rosa (Cuthbert) 1925- .... **CLC 26**
See also AAYA 4, 37; BW 2; CA 17-20R; CANR 14, 34, 83; CLR 13; DLB 33; DNFS 1; JRDA; MAICYA 1, 2; SATA 14, 62, 122; YAW

Gwendolyn
See Bennett, (Enoch) Arnold

H. D. .... **CLC 3, 8, 14, 31, 34, 73; PC 5**
See also Doolittle, Hilda

H. de V.
See Buchan, John

Haavikko, Paavo Juhani 1931- .. **CLC 18, 34**
See also CA 106

Habbema, Koos
See Heijermans, Herman

Habermas, Juergen 1929- .... **CLC 104**
See also CA 109; CANR 85; DLB 242

Habermas, Jurgen
See Habermas, Juergen

Hacker, Marilyn 1942- . **CLC 5, 9, 23, 72, 91**
See also CA 77-80; CANR 68; CP 7; CWP; DAM POET; DLB 120; FW; GLL 2

Hadrian 76-138 .... **CMLC 52**

Haeckel, Ernst Heinrich (Philipp August)
1834-1919 .... **TCLC 83**
See also CA 157

Hafiz c. 1326-1389(?) .... **CMLC 34**
See also RGWL 2

Haggard, H(enry) Rider
1856-1925 .... **TCLC 11**
See also BRWS 3; BYA 4, 5; CA 108; 148; DLB 70, 156, 174, 178; FANT; MTCW 2; RGEL 2; RHW; SATA 16; SCFW; SFW 4; SUFW; WLIT 4

Hagiosy, L.
See Larbaud, Valery (Nicolas)

Hagiwara, Sakutaro 1886-1942 .... **TCLC 60; PC 18**
See also CA 154

Haig, Fenil
See Ford, Ford Madox

Haig-Brown, Roderick (Langmere)
1908-1976 .... **CLC 21**
See also CA 5-8R; 69-72; CANR 4, 38, 83; CLR 31; CWRI 5; DLB 88; MAICYA 1, 2; SATA 12

Hailey, Arthur 1920- .... **CLC 5**
See also AITN 2; BEST 90:3; BPFB 2; CA 1-4R; CANR 2, 36, 75; CCA 1; CN 7; CPW; DAM NOV, POP; DLB 88; DLBY 1982; MTCW 1, 2

Hailey, Elizabeth Forsythe 1938- ..... **CLC 40**
See also CA 93-96; CAAE 188; CAAS 1; CANR 15, 48; INT CANR-15

Haines, John (Meade) 1924- .... **CLC 58**
See also CA 17-20R; CANR 13, 34; CSW; DLB 5, 212

Hakluyt, Richard 1552-1616 .... **LC 31**
See also DLB 136; RGEL 2

Haldeman, Joe (William) 1943- .... **CLC 61**
See also Graham, Robert
See also AAYA 38; CA 53-56; 179; CAAE 179; CAAS 25; CANR 6, 70, 72; DLB 8; INT CANR-6; SCFW 2; SFW 4

Hale, Sarah Josepha (Buell)
1788-1879 .... **NCLC 75**
See also DLB 1, 42, 73, 243

Halevy, Elie 1870-1937 .... **TCLC 104**

Haley, Alex(ander Murray Palmer)
1921-1992 .... **CLC 8, 12, 76; BLC 2**
See also AAYA 26; BPFB 2; BW 2, 3; CA 77-80; 136; CANR 61; CDALBS; CPW; CSW; DA; DA3; DAB; DAC; DAM MST, MULT, POP; DLB 38; LAIT 5; MTCW 1, 2; NFS 9

Haliburton, Thomas Chandler
1796-1865 .... **NCLC 15**
See also DLB 11, 99; RGEL 2; RGSF 2

Hall, Donald (Andrew, Jr.) 1928- ...... **CLC 1, 13, 37, 59, 151**
See also CA 5-8R; CAAS 7; CANR 2, 44, 64, 106; CP 7; DAM POET; DLB 5; MTCW 1; RGAL 4; SATA 23, 97

Hall, Frederic Sauser
See Sauser-Hall, Frederic

Hall, James
See Kuttner, Henry

Hall, James Norman 1887-1951 ..... **TCLC 23**
See also CA 123; 173; LAIT 1; RHW 1; SATA 21

Hall, (Marguerite) Radclyffe
1880-1943 .... **TCLC 12**
See also BRWS 6; CA 110; 150; CANR 83; DLB 191; MTCW 2; RGEL 2; RHW

Hall, Rodney 1935- .... **CLC 51**
See also CA 109; CANR 69; CN 7; CP 7

Hallam, Arthur Henry
1811-1833 .... **NCLC 110**
See also DLB 32

Halleck, Fitz-Greene 1790-1867 .... **NCLC 47**
See also DLB 3, 250; RGAL 4

Halliday, Michael
See Creasey, John

Halpern, Daniel 1945- .... **CLC 14**
See also CA 33-36R; CANR 93; CP 7

Hamburger, Michael (Peter Leopold)
1924- .... **CLC 5, 14**
See also CA 5-8R; CAAE 196; CAAS 4; CANR 2, 47; CP 7; DLB 27

Hamill, Pete 1935- .... **CLC 10**
See also CA 25-28R; CANR 18, 71

Hamilton, Alexander
1755(?)-1804 .... **NCLC 49**
See also DLB 37

Hamilton, Clive
See Lewis, C(live) S(taples)

Hamilton, Edmond 1904-1977 .... **CLC 1**
See also CA 1-4R; CANR 3, 84; DLB 8; SATA 118; SFW 4

Hamilton, Eugene (Jacob) Lee
See Lee-Hamilton, Eugene (Jacob)

Hamilton, Franklin
See Silverberg, Robert

Hamilton, Gail
See Corcoran, Barbara (Asenath)

Hamilton, Mollie
See Kaye, M(ary) M(argaret)

Hamilton, (Anthony Walter) Patrick
1904-1962 .... **CLC 51**
See also CA 176; 113; DLB 10, 191

Hamilton, Virginia (Esther)
1936-2002 .... **CLC 26**
See also AAYA 2, 21; BW 2, 3; BYA 1, 2, 8; CA 25-28R; CANR 20, 37, 73; CLR 1, 11, 40; DAM MULT; DLB 33, 52; DLBY 01; INT CANR-20; JRDA; LAIT 5; MAICYA 1, 2; MAICYAS 1; MTCW 1, 2; SATA 4, 56, 79, 123; WYA; YAW

Hammett, (Samuel) Dashiell
1894-1961 .... **CLC 3, 5, 10, 19, 47; SSC 17**
See also AITN 1; AMWS 4; BPFB 2; CA 81-84; CANR 42; CDALB 1929-1941; CMW 4; DA3; DLB 226; DLBD 6; DLBY 1996; LAIT 3; MSW; MTCW 1, 2; RGAL 4; RGSF 2

Hammon, Jupiter 1720(?)-1800(?) . **NCLC 5; BLC 2; PC 16**
See also DAM MULT, POET; DLB 31, 50

Hammond, Keith
See Kuttner, Henry

Hamner, Earl (Henry), Jr. 1923- ...... **CLC 12**
See also AITN 2; CA 73-76; DLB 6

Hampton, Christopher (James)
1946- .... **CLC 4**
See also CA 25-28R; CD 5; DLB 13; MTCW 1

Hamsun, Knut .... **TCLC 2, 14, 49**
See also Pedersen, Knut
See also EW 8; RGWL 2

Handke, Peter 1942- .... **CLC 5, 8, 10, 15, 38, 134; DC 17**
See also CA 77-80; CANR 33, 75, 104; CWW 2; DAM DRAM, NOV; DLB 85, 124; MTCW 1, 2

Handy, W(illiam) C(hristopher)
1873-1958 .... **TCLC 97**
See also BW 3; CA 121; 167

Hanley, James 1901-1985 ..... **CLC 3, 5, 8, 13**
See also CA 73-76; 117; CANR 36; CBD; DLB 191; MTCW 1; RGEL 2

Hannah, Barry 1942- .... **CLC 23, 38, 90**
See also BPFB 2; CA 108; 110; CANR 43, 68; CN 7; CSW; DLB 6, 234; INT CA-110; MTCW 1; RGSF 2

Hannon, Ezra
See Hunter, Evan

Hansberry, Lorraine (Vivian)
1930-1965 ... **CLC 17, 62; BLC 2; DC 2**
See also AAYA 25; AFAW 1, 2; AMWS 4;
BW 1, 3; CA 109; 25-28R; CABS 3;
CANR 58; CDALB 1941-1968; DA;
DA3; DAB; DAC; DAM DRAM, MST,
MULT; DFS 7, 38; FW; LAIT 4;
MTCW 1, 2; RGAL 4

Hansen, Joseph 1923- .... **CLC 38**
See also Brock, Rose; Colton, James
See also BPFB 2; CA 29-32R; CAAS 17;
CANR 16, 44, 66; CMW 4; DLB 226;
GLL 1; INT CANR-16

Hansen, Martin A(lfred)
1909-1955 .... **TCLC 32**
See also CA 167; DLB 214

Hansen and Philipson eds. .... **CLC 65**

Hanson, Kenneth O(stlin) 1922- ...... **CLC 13**
See also CA 53-56; CANR 7

Hardwick, Elizabeth (Bruce) 1916- . **CLC 13**
See also AMWS 3; CA 5-8R; CANR 3, 32,
70, 100; CN 7; CSW; DA3; DAM NOV;
DLB 6; MAWW; MTCW 1, 2

Hardy, Thomas 1840-1928 .. **TCLC 4, 10, 18,
32, 48, 53, 72; PC 8; SSC 2; WLC**
See also BRW 6; BRWR 1; CA 104; 123;
CDBLB 1890-1914; DA; DA3; DAB;
DAC; DAM MST, NOV; DLB 18,
19, 135; EXPN; EXPP; LAIT 2; MTCW
1, 2; NFS 3, 11; PFS 3, 4; RGEL 2; RGSF
2; WLIT 4

Hare, David 1947- .... **CLC 29, 58, 136**
See also BRWS 4; CA 97-100; CANR 39,
91; CBD; CD 5; DFS 4, 7; DLB 13;
MTCW 1

Harewood, John
See Van Druten, John (William)

Harford, Henry
See Hudson, W(illiam) H(enry)

Hargrave, Leonie
See Disch, Thomas M(ichael)

Harjo, Joy 1951- .... **CLC 83; PC 27**
See also CA 114; CANR 35, 67, 91; CP 7;
CWP; DAM MULT; DLB 120, 175;
MTCW 2; NNAL; RGAL 4

Harlan, Louis R(udolph) 1922- .... **CLC 34**
See also CA 21-24R; CANR 25, 55, 80

Harling, Robert 1951(?)- .... **CLC 53**
See also CA 147

Harmon, William (Ruth) 1938- .... **CLC 38**
See also CA 33-36R; CANR 14, 32, 35;
SATA 65

Harper, F. E. W.
See Harper, Frances Ellen Watkins

Harper, Frances E. W.
See Harper, Frances Ellen Watkins

Harper, Frances E. Watkins
See Harper, Frances Ellen Watkins

Harper, Frances Ellen
See Harper, Frances Ellen Watkins

Harper, Frances Ellen Watkins
1825-1911 ..... **TCLC 14; BLC 2; PC 21**
See also AFAW 1, 2; BW 1, 3; CA 111; 125;
CANR 79; DAM MULT, POET; DLB 50,
221; MAWW; RGAL 4

Harper, Michael S(teven) 1938- ... **CLC 7, 22**
See also AFAW 2; BW 1; CA 33-36R;
CANR 24, 108; CP 7; DLB 41; RGAL 4

Harper, Mrs. F. E. W.
See Harper, Frances Ellen Watkins

Harpur, Charles 1813-1868 .... **NCLC 113**
See also DLB 230; RGEL 2

Harris, Christie (Lucy) Irwin
1907-2002 .... **CLC 12**
See also CA 5-8R; CANR 6, 83; CLR 47;
DLB 88; JRDA; MAICYA 1, 2; SAAS 10;
SATA 6, 74; SATA-Essay 116

Harris, Frank 1856-1931 .... **TCLC 24**
See also CA 109; 150; CANR 80; DLB 156,
197; RGEL 2

Harris, George Washington
1814-1869 .... **NCLC 23**
See also DLB 3, 11, 248; RGAL 4

Harris, Joel Chandler 1848-1908 ... **TCLC 2;
SSC 19**
See also CA 104; 137; CANR 80; CLR 49;
DLB 11, 23, 42, 78, 91; LAIT 2; MAI-
CYA 1, 2; RGSF 2; SATA 100; WCH;
YABC 1

**Harris, John (Wyndham Parkes Lucas)
Beynon** 1903-1969
See Wyndham, John
See also CA 102; 89-92; CANR 84; SATA
118; SFW 4

Harris, MacDonald .... **CLC 9**
See also Heiney, Donald (William)

Harris, Mark 1922- .... **CLC 19**
See also CA 5-8R; CAAS 3; CANR 2, 55,
83; CN 7; DLB 2; DLBY 1980

Harris, Norman .... **CLC 65**

Harris, (Theodore) Wilson 1921- .... **CLC 25,
159**
See also BRWS 5; BW 2, 3; CA 65-68;
CAAS 16; CANR 11, 27, 69; CDWLB 3;
CN 7; CP 7; DLB 117; MTCW 1; RGEL
2

Harrison, Barbara Grizzuti 1934- . **CLC 144**
See also CA 77-80; CANR 15, 48; INT
CANR-15

Harrison, Elizabeth (Allen) Cavanna
1909-2001
See Cavanna, Betty
See also CA 9-12R; 200; CANR 6, 27, 85,
104; MAICYA 2; YAW

Harrison, Harry (Max) 1925- .... **CLC 42**
See also CA 1-4R; CANR 5, 21, 84; DLB
8; SATA 4; SCFW 2; SFW 4

Harrison, James (Thomas) 1937- ...... **CLC 6,
14, 33, 66, 143; SSC 19**
See also Harrison, Jim
See also CA 13-16R; CANR 8, 51, 79; CN
7; CP 7; DLBY 1982; INT CANR-8

Harrison, Jim
See Harrison, James (Thomas)
See also AMWS 8; RGAL 4; TCWW 2

Harrison, Kathryn 1961- .... **CLC 70, 151**
See also CA 144; CANR 68

Harrison, Tony 1937- .... **CLC 43, 129**
See also BRWS 5; CA 65-68; CANR 44,
98; CBD; CD 5; CP 7; DLB 40, 245;
MTCW 1; RGEL 2

Harriss, Will(ard Irvin) 1922- .... **CLC 34**
See also CA 111

Harson, Sley
See Ellison, Harlan (Jay)

Hart, Ellis
See Ellison, Harlan (Jay)

Hart, Josephine 1942(?)- .... **CLC 70**
See also CA 138; CANR 70; CPW; DAM
POP

Hart, Moss 1904-1961 .... **CLC 66**
See also CA 109; 89-92; CANR 84; DAM
DRAM; DFS 1; DLB 7; RGAL 4

Harte, (Francis) Bret(t)
1836(?)-1902 .... **TCLC 1, 25; SSC 8;
WLC**
See also AMWS 2; CA 104; 140; CANR
80; CDALB 1865-1917; DA; DA3; DAC;
DAM MST; DLB 12, 64, 74, 79, 186;
EXPS; LAIT 2; RGAL 4; RGSF 2; SATA
26; SSFS 3

Hartley, L(eslie) P(oles) 1895-1972 ... **CLC 2,
22**
See also BRWS 7; CA 45-48; 37-40R;
CANR 33; DLB 15, 139; HGG; MTCW
1, 2; RGEL 2; RGSF 2; SUFW

Hartman, Geoffrey H. 1929- .... **CLC 27**
See also CA 117; 125; CANR 79; DLB 67

Hartmann, Sadakichi 1869-1944 ... **TCLC 73**
See also CA 157; DLB 54

Hartmann von Aue c. 1170-c.
1210 .... **CMLC 15**
See also CDWLB 2; DLB 138; RGWL 2

Haruf, Kent 1943- .... **CLC 34**
See also CA 149; CANR 91

Harwood, Ronald 1934- .... **CLC 32**
See also CA 1-4R; CANR 4, 55; CBD; CD
5; DAM DRAM, MST; DLB 13

Hasegawa Tatsunosuke
See Futabatei, Shimei

Hasek, Jaroslav (Matej Frantisek)
1883-1923 .... **TCLC 4**
See also CA 104; 129; CDWLB 4; DLB
215; EW 9; MTCW 1, 2; RGSF 2; RGWL
2

Hass, Robert 1941- .... **CLC 18, 39, 99; PC 16**
See also AMWS 6; CA 111; CANR 30, 50,
71; CP 7; DLB 105, 206; RGAL 4; SATA
94

Hastings, Hudson
See Kuttner, Henry

Hastings, Selina .... **CLC 44**

Hathorne, John 1641-1717 .... **LC 38**

Hatteras, Amelia
See Mencken, H(enry) L(ouis)

Hatteras, Owen .... **TCLC 18**
See also Mencken, H(enry) L(ouis); Nathan,
George Jean

Hauptmann, Gerhart (Johann Robert)
1862-1946 .... **TCLC 4; SSC 37**
See also CA 104; 153; CDWLB 2; DAM
DRAM; DLB 66, 118; EW 8; RGSF 2;
RGWL 2

Havel, Vaclav 1936- ..... **CLC 25, 58, 65, 123;
DC 6**
See also CA 104; CANR 36, 63; CDWLB
4; CWW 2; DA3; DAM DRAM; DFS 10;
DLB 232; MTCW 1, 2

Haviaras, Stratis .... **CLC 33**
See also Chaviaras, Strates

Hawes, Stephen 1475(?)-1529(?) .... **LC 17**
See also DLB 132; RGEL 2

Hawkes, John (Clendennin Burne, Jr.)
1925-1998 .. **CLC 1, 2, 3, 4, 7, 9, 14, 15,
27, 49**
See also BPFB 2; CA 1-4R; 167; CANR 2,
47, 64; CN 7; DLB 2, 7, 227; DLBY
1980, 1998; MTCW 1, 2; RGAL 4

Hawking, S. W.
See Hawking, Stephen W(illiam)

Hawking, Stephen W(illiam) 1942- . **CLC 63,
105**
See also AAYA 13; BEST 89:1; CA 126;
129; CANR 48; CPW; DA3; MTCW 2

Hawkins, Anthony Hope
See Hope, Anthony

Hawthorne, Julian 1846-1934 .... **TCLC 25**
See also CA 165; HGG

Hawthorne, Nathaniel 1804-1864 ... **NCLC 2,
10, 17, 23, 39, 79, 95; SSC 3, 29, 39;
WLC**
See also AAYA 18; AMW; AMWR 1; BPFB
2; BYA 3; CDALB 1640-1865; DA; DA3;
DAB; DAC; DAM MST, NOV; DLB 1,
74, 183, 223; EXPN; EXPS; HGG; LAIT
1; NFS 1; RGAL 4; RGSF 2; SSFS 1, 7,
11; SUFW; WCH; YABC 2

Haxton, Josephine Ayres 1921-
See Douglas, Ellen
See also CA 115; CANR 41, 83

Hayaseca y Eizaguirre, Jorge
See Echegaray (y Eizaguirre), Jose (Maria
Waldo)

Hayashi, Fumiko 1904-1951 .... **TCLC 27**
See also Hayashi Fumiko
See also CA 161

Hayashi Fumiko
See Hayashi, Fumiko
See also DLB 180

Haycraft, Anna (Margaret) 1932-
See Ellis, Alice Thomas
See also CA 122; CANR 85, 90; MTCW 2

Hayden, Robert E(arl) 1913-1980 . **CLC 5, 9, 14, 37; BLC 2; PC 6**
See also AFAW 1, 2; AMWS 2; BW 1, 3; CA 69-72; 97-100; CABS 2; CANR 24, 75, 82; CDALB 1941-1968; DA; DAC; DAM MST, MULT, POET; DLB 5, 76; EXPP; MTCW 1, 2; PFS 1; RGAL 4; SATA 19; SATA-Obit 26; WP

Hayek, F(riedrich) A(ugust von) 1899-1992 .... **TCLC 109**
See also CA 93-96; 137; CANR 20; MTCW 1, 2

Hayford, J(oseph) E(phraim) Casely
See Casely-Hayford, J(oseph) E(phraim)

Hayman, Ronald 1932- .... **CLC 44**
See also CA 25-28R; CANR 18, 50, 88; CD 5; DLB 155

Hayne, Paul Hamilton 1830-1886 . **NCLC 94**
See also DLB 3, 64, 79, 248; RGAL 4

Haywood, Eliza (Fowler) 1693(?)-1756 .... **LC 1, 44**
See also DLB 39; RGEL 2

Hazlitt, William 1778-1830 ...... **NCLC 29, 82**
See also BRW 4; DLB 110, 158; RGEL 2

Hazzard, Shirley 1931- .... **CLC 18**
See also CA 9-12R; CANR 4, 70; CN 7; DLBY 1982; MTCW 1

Head, Bessie 1937-1986 .... **CLC 25, 67; BLC 2; SSC 52**
See also AFW; BW 2, 3; CA 29-32R; 119; CANR 25, 82; CDWLB 3; DA3; DAM MULT; DLB 117, 225; EXPS; FW; MTCW 1, 2; RGSF 2; SSFS 5, 13; WLIT 2

Headon, (Nicky) Topper 1956(?)- ..... **CLC 30**

Heaney, Seamus (Justin) 1939- ..... **CLC 5, 7, 14, 25, 37, 74, 91; PC 18; WLCS**
See also BRWR 1; BRWS 2; CA 85-88; CANR 25, 48, 75, 91; CDBLB 1960 to Present; CP 7; DA3; DAB; DAM POET; DLB 40; DLBY 1995; EXPP; MTCW 1, 2; PAB; PFS 2, 5, 8; RGEL 2; WLIT 4

Hearn, (Patricio) Lafcadio (Tessima Carlos) 1850-1904 .... **TCLC 9**
See also CA 105; 166; DLB 12, 78, 189; HGG; RGAL 4

Hearne, Vicki 1946-2001 .... **CLC 56**
See also CA 139; 201

Hearon, Shelby 1931- .... **CLC 63**
See also AITN 2; AMWS 8; CA 25-28R; CANR 18, 48, 103; CSW

Heat-Moon, William Least .... **CLC 29**
See also Trogdon, William (Lewis)
See also AAYA 9

Hebbel, Friedrich 1813-1863 .... **NCLC 43**
See also CDWLB 2; DAM DRAM; DLB 129; EW 6; RGWL 2

Hebert, Anne 1916-2000 .... **CLC 4, 13, 29**
See also CA 85-88; 187; CANR 69; CCA 1; CWP; CWW 2; DA3; DAC; DAM MST, POET; DLB 68; GFL 1789 to the Present; MTCW 1, 2

Hecht, Anthony (Evan) 1923- ...... **CLC 8, 13, 19**
See also AMWS 10; CA 9-12R; CANR 6, 108; CP 7; DAM POET; DLB 5, 169; PFS 6; WP

Hecht, Ben 1894-1964 .... **CLC 8**
See also CA 85-88; DFS 9; DLB 7, 9, 25, 26, 28, 86; FANT; IDFW 3, 4; RGAL 4; TCLC 101

Hedayat, Sadeq 1903-1951 .... **TCLC 21**
See also CA 120; RGSF 2

Hegel, Georg Wilhelm Friedrich 1770-1831 .... **NCLC 46**
See also DLB 90

Heidegger, Martin 1889-1976 .... **CLC 24**
See also CA 81-84; 65-68; CANR 34; MTCW 1, 2

Heidenstam, (Carl Gustaf) Verner von 1859-1940 .... **TCLC 5**
See also CA 104

Heifner, Jack 1946- .... **CLC 11**
See also CA 105; CANR 47

Heijermans, Herman 1864-1924 .... **TCLC 24**
See also CA 123

Heilbrun, Carolyn G(old) 1926- .... **CLC 25**
See also Cross, Amanda
See also CA 45-48; CANR 1, 28, 58, 94; FW

Hein, Christoph 1944- .... **CLC 154**
See also CA 158; CANR 108; CDWLB 2; CWW 2; DLB 124

Heine, Heinrich 1797-1856 .... **NCLC 4, 54; PC 25**
See also CDWLB 2; DLB 90; EW 5; RGWL 2

Heinemann, Larry (Curtiss) 1944- .. **CLC 50**
See also CA 110; CAAS 21; CANR 31, 81; DLBD 9; INT CANR-31

Heiney, Donald (William) 1921-1993
See Harris, MacDonald
See also CA 1-4R; 142; CANR 3, 58; FANT

Heinlein, Robert A(nson) 1907-1988 . **CLC 1, 3, 8, 14, 26, 55**
See also AAYA 17; BPFB 2; BYA 4, 13; CA 1-4R; 125; CANR 1, 20, 53; CLR 75; CPW; DA3; DAM POP; DLB 8; EXPS; JRDA; LAIT 5; MAICYA 1, 2; MTCW 1, 2; RGAL 4; SATA 9, 69; SATA-Obit 56; SCFW; SFW 4; SSFS 7; YAW

Helforth, John
See Doolittle, Hilda

Heliodorus fl. 3rd cent. - .... **CMLC 52**

Hellenhofferu, Vojtech Kapristian z
See Hasek, Jaroslav (Matej Frantisek)

Heller, Joseph 1923-1999 . **CLC 1, 3, 5, 8, 11, 36, 63; WLC**
See also AAYA 24; AITN 1; AMWS 4; BPFB 2; BYA 1; CA 5-8R; 187; CABS 1; CANR 8, 42, 66; CN 7; CPW; DA; DA3; DAB; DAC; DAM MST, NOV, POP; DLB 2, 28, 227; DLBY 1980; EXPN; INT CANR-8; LAIT 4; MTCW 1, 2; NFS 1; RGAL 4; YAW

Hellman, Lillian (Florence) 1906-1984 .. **CLC 2, 4, 8, 14, 18, 34, 44, 52; DC 1**
See also AITN 1, 2; AMWS 1; CA 13-16R; 112; CAD; CANR 33; CWD; DA3; DAM DRAM; DFS 1, 3, 14; DLB 7, 228; DLBY 1984; FW; LAIT 3; MAWW; MTCW 1, 2; RGAL 4; TCLC 119

Helprin, Mark 1947- .... **CLC 7, 10, 22, 32**
See also CA 81-84; CANR 47, 64; CDALBS; CPW; DA3; DAM NOV, POP; DLBY 1985; FANT; MTCW 1, 2

Helvetius, Claude-Adrien 1715-1771 .. **LC 26**

Helyar, Jane Penelope Josephine 1933-
See Poole, Josephine
See also CA 21-24R; CANR 10, 26; CWRI 5; SATA 82

Hemans, Felicia 1793-1835 ...... **NCLC 29, 71**
See also DLB 96; RGEL 2

Hemingway, Ernest (Miller) 1899-1961 .... **CLC 1, 3, 6, 8, 10, 13, 19, 30, 34, 39, 41, 44, 50, 61, 80; SSC 1, 25, 36, 40; WLC**
See also AAYA 19; AMW; AMWR 1; BPFB 2; BYA 2, 3, 13; CA 77-80; CANR 34; CDALB 1917-1929; DA; DA3; DAB; DAC; DAM MST, NOV; DLB 4, 9, 102, 210; DLBD 1, 15, 16; DLBY 1981, 1987, 1996, 1998; EXPN; EXPS; LAIT 3, 4; MTCW 1, 2; NFS 1, 5, 6, 14; RGAL 4; RGSF 2; SSFS 1, 6, 8, 9, 11; TCLC 115; WYA

Hempel, Amy 1951- .... **CLC 39**
See also CA 118; 137; CANR 70; DA3; DLB 218; EXPS; MTCW 2; SSFS 2

Henderson, F. C.
See Mencken, H(enry) L(ouis)

Henderson, Sylvia
See Ashton-Warner, Sylvia (Constance)

Henderson, Zenna (Chlarson) 1917-1983 .... **SSC 29**
See also CA 1-4R; 133; CANR 1, 84; DLB 8; SATA 5; SFW 4

Henkin, Joshua .... **CLC 119**
See also CA 161

Henley, Beth .... **CLC 23; DC 6, 14**
See also Henley, Elizabeth Becker
See also CABS 3; CAD; CD 5; CSW; CWD; DFS 2; DLBY 1986; FW

Henley, Elizabeth Becker 1952-
See Henley, Beth
See also CA 107; CANR 32, 73; DA3; DAM DRAM, MST; MTCW 1, 2

Henley, William Ernest 1849-1903 .. **TCLC 8**
See also CA 105; DLB 19; RGEL 2

Hennissart, Martha
See Lathen, Emma
See also CA 85-88; CANR 64

Henry VIII 1491-1547 .... **LC 10**
See also DLB 132

Henry, O. .... **TCLC 1, 19; SSC 5, 49; WLC**
See also Porter, William Sydney
See also AAYA 41; AMWS 2; EXPS; RGAL 4; RGSF 2; SSFS 2

Henry, Patrick 1736-1799 .... **LC 25**
See also LAIT 1

Henryson, Robert 1430(?)-1506(?) ...... **LC 20**
See also BRWS 7; DLB 146; RGEL 2

Henschke, Alfred
See Klabund

Hentoff, Nat(han Irving) 1925- .... **CLC 26**
See also AAYA 4, 42; BYA 6; CA 1-4R; CAAS 6; CANR 5, 25, 77; CLR 1, 52; INT CANR-25; JRDA; MAICYA 1, 2; SATA 42, 69; SATA-Brief 27; WYA; YAW

Heppenstall, (John) Rayner 1911-1981 .... **CLC 10**
See also CA 1-4R; 103; CANR 29

Heraclitus c. 540B.C.-c. 450B.C. ... **CMLC 22**
See also DLB 176

Herbert, Frank (Patrick) 1920-1986 .... **CLC 12, 23, 35, 44, 85**
See also AAYA 21; BPFB 2; BYA 4, 14; CA 53-56; 118; CANR 5, 43; CDALBS; CPW; DAM POP; DLB 8; INT CANR-5; LAIT 5; MTCW 1, 2; SATA 9, 37; SATA-Obit 47; SCFW 2; SFW 4; YAW

Herbert, George 1593-1633 .... **LC 24; PC 4**
See also BRW 2; BRWR 2; CDBLB Before 1660; DAB; DAM POET; DLB 126; EXPP; RGEL 2; WP

Herbert, Zbigniew 1924-1998 .... **CLC 9, 43**
See also CA 89-92; 169; CANR 36, 74; CDWLB 4; CWW 2; DAM POET; DLB 232; MTCW 1

Herbst, Josephine (Frey)
1897-1969 .... **CLC 34**
See also CA 5-8R; 25-28R; DLB 9

Herder, Johann Gottfried von
1744-1803 .... **NCLC 8**
See also DLB 97; EW 4

Heredia, Jose Maria 1803-1839
See also HLCS 2; LAW

Hergesheimer, Joseph 1880-1954 ... **TCLC 11**
See also CA 109; 194; DLB 102, 9; RGAL 4

Herlihy, James Leo 1927-1993 .... **CLC 6**
See also CA 1-4R; 143; CAD; CANR 2

Hermogenes fl. c. 175- .... **CMLC 6**

Hernandez, Jose 1834-1886 .... **NCLC 17**
See also LAW; RGWL 2; WLIT 1

Herodotus c. 484B.C.-c. 420B.C. .. **CMLC 17**
See also AW 1; CDWLB 1; DLB 176; RGWL 2

Herrick, Robert 1591-1674 .... **LC 13; PC 9**
See also BRW 2; DA; DAB; DAC; DAM MST, POP; DLB 126; EXPP; PFS 13; RGAL 4; RGEL 2; WP

Herring, Guilles
See Somerville, Edith Oenone

Herriot, James 1916-1995 .... **CLC 12**
See also Wight, James Alfred
See also AAYA 1; BPFB 2; CA 148; CANR 40; CLR 80; CPW; DAM POP; LAIT 3; MAICYA 2; MAICYAS 1; MTCW 2; SATA 86; YAW

Herris, Violet
See Hunt, Violet

Herrmann, Dorothy 1941- .... **CLC 44**
See also CA 107

Herrmann, Taffy
See Herrmann, Dorothy

Hersey, John (Richard) 1914-1993 .... **CLC 1, 2, 7, 9, 40, 81, 97**
See also AAYA 29; BPFB 2; CA 17-20R; 140; CANR 33; CDALBS; CPW; DAM POP; DLB 6, 185; MTCW 1, 2; SATA 25; SATA-Obit 76

Herzen, Aleksandr Ivanovich
1812-1870 .... **NCLC 10, 61**

Herzl, Theodor 1860-1904 .... **TCLC 36**
See also CA 168

Herzog, Werner 1942- .... **CLC 16**
See also CA 89-92

Hesiod c. 8th cent. B.C.- .... **CMLC 5**
See also AW 1; DLB 176; RGWL 2

Hesse, Hermann 1877-1962 ... **CLC 1, 2, 3, 6, 11, 17, 25, 69; SSC 9, 49; WLC**
See also AAYA 43; BPFB 2; CA 17-18; CAP 2; CDWLB 2; DA; DA3; DAB; DAC; DAM MST, NOV; DLB 66; EW 9; EXPN; LAIT 1; MTCW 1, 2; NFS 6; RGWL 2; SATA 50

Hewes, Cady
See De Voto, Bernard (Augustine)

Heyen, William 1940- .... **CLC 13, 18**
See also CA 33-36R; CAAS 9; CANR 98; CP 7; DLB 5

Heyerdahl, Thor 1914-2002 .... **CLC 26**
See also CA 5-8R; CANR 5, 22, 66, 73; LAIT 4; MTCW 1, 2; SATA 2, 52

Heym, Georg (Theodor Franz Arthur)
1887-1912 .... **TCLC 9**
See also CA 106; 181

Heym, Stefan 1913- .... **CLC 41**
See also CA 9-12R; CANR 4; CWW 2; DLB 69

Heyse, Paul (Johann Ludwig von)
1830-1914 .... **TCLC 8**
See also CA 104; DLB 129

Heyward, (Edwin) DuBose
1885-1940 .... **TCLC 59**
See also CA 108; 157; DLB 7, 9, 45, 249; SATA 21

Heywood, John 1497(?)-1580(?) .... **LC 65**
See also DLB 136; RGEL 2

Hibbert, Eleanor Alice Burford
1906-1993 .... **CLC 7**
See also Holt, Victoria
See also BEST 90:4; CA 17-20R; 140; CANR 9, 28, 59; CMW 4; CPW; DAM POP; MTCW 2; RHW; SATA 2; SATA-Obit 74

Hichens, Robert (Smythe)
1864-1950 .... **TCLC 64**
See also CA 162; DLB 153; HGG; RHW; SUFW

Higgins, George V(incent)
1939-1999 .... **CLC 4, 7, 10, 18**
See also BPFB 2; CA 77-80; 186; CAAS 5; CANR 17, 51, 89, 96; CMW 4; CN 7; DLB 2; DLBY 1981, 1998; INT CANR-17; MSW; MTCW 1

Higginson, Thomas Wentworth
1823-1911 .... **TCLC 36**
See also CA 162; DLB 1, 64, 243

Higgonet, Margaret ed. .... **CLC 65**

Highet, Helen
See MacInnes, Helen (Clark)

Highsmith, (Mary) Patricia
1921-1995 .... **CLC 2, 4, 14, 42, 102**
See also Morgan, Claire
See also BRWS 5; CA 1-4R; 147; CANR 1, 20, 48, 62, 108; CMW 4; CPW; DA3; DAM NOV, POP; MSW; MTCW 1, 2

Highwater, Jamake (Mamake)
1942(?)-2001 .... **CLC 12**
See also AAYA 7; BPFB 2; BYA 4; CA 65-68; 199; CAAS 7; CANR 10, 34, 84; CLR 17; CWRI 5; DLB 52; DLBY 1985; JRDA; MAICYA 1, 2; SATA 32, 69; SATA-Brief 30

Highway, Tomson 1951- .... **CLC 92**
See also CA 151; CANR 75; CCA 1; CD 5; DAC; DAM MULT; DFS 2; MTCW 2; NNAL

Hijuelos, Oscar 1951- .... **CLC 65; HLC 1**
See also AAYA 25; AMWS 8; BEST 90:1; CA 123; CANR 50, 75; CPW; DA3; DAM MULT, POP; DLB 145; HW 1, 2; MTCW 2; RGAL 4; WLIT 1

Hikmet, Nazim 1902(?)-1963 .... **CLC 40**
See also CA 141; 93-96

Hildegard von Bingen 1098-1179 . **CMLC 20**
See also DLB 148

Hildesheimer, Wolfgang 1916-1991 .. **CLC 49**
See also CA 101; 135; DLB 69, 124

Hill, Geoffrey (William) 1932- ...... **CLC 5, 8, 18, 45**
See also BRWS 5; CA 81-84; CANR 21, 89; CDBLB 1960 to Present; CP 7; DAM POET; DLB 40; MTCW 1; RGEL 2

Hill, George Roy 1921- .... **CLC 26**
See also CA 110; 122

Hill, John
See Koontz, Dean R(ay)

Hill, Susan (Elizabeth) 1942- ...... **CLC 4, 113**
See also CA 33-36R; CANR 29, 69; CN 7; DAB; DAM MST, NOV; DLB 14, 139; HGG; MTCW 1; RHW

Hillard, Asa G. III .... **CLC 70**

Hillerman, Tony 1925- .... **CLC 62**
See also AAYA 40; BEST 89:1; BPFB 2; CA 29-32R; CANR 21, 42, 65, 97; CMW 4; CPW; DA3; DAM POP; DLB 206; MSW; RGAL 4; SATA 6; TCWW 2; YAW

Hillesum, Etty 1914-1943 .... **TCLC 49**
See also CA 137

Hilliard, Noel (Harvey) 1929-1996 ... **CLC 15**
See also CA 9-12R; CANR 7, 69; CN 7

Hillis, Rick 1956- .... **CLC 66**
See also CA 134

Hilton, James 1900-1954 .... **TCLC 21**
See also CA 108; 169; DLB 34, 77; FANT; SATA 34

Himes, Chester (Bomar) 1909-1984 .. **CLC 2, 4, 7, 18, 58, 108; BLC 2**
See also AFAW 2; BPFB 2; BW 2; CA 25-28R; 114; CANR 22, 89; CMW 4; DAM MULT; DLB 2, 76, 143, 226; MSW; MTCW 1, 2; RGAL 4

Hinde, Thomas .... **CLC 6, 11**
See also Chitty, Thomas Willes

Hine, (William) Daryl 1936- .... **CLC 15**
See also CA 1-4R; CAAS 15; CANR 1, 20; CP 7; DLB 60

Hinkson, Katharine Tynan
See Tynan, Katharine

Hinojosa(-Smith), Rolando (R.) 1929-
See also CA 131; CAAS 16; CANR 62; DAM MULT; DLB 82; HLC 1; HW 1, 2; MTCW 2; RGAL 4

Hinton, S(usan) E(loise) 1950- .. **CLC 30, 111**
See also AAYA 2, 33; BPFB 2; BYA 2, 3; CA 81-84; CANR 32, 62, 92; CDALBS; CLR 3, 23; CPW; DA; DA3; DAB; DAC; DAM MST, NOV; JRDA; LAIT 5; MAI-CYA 1, 2; MTCW 1, 2; NFS 5, 9; SATA 19, 58, 115; WYA; YAW

Hippius, Zinaida .... **TCLC 9**
See also Gippius, Zinaida (Nikolayevna)

Hiraoka, Kimitake 1925-1970
See Mishima, Yukio
See also CA 97-100; 29-32R; DA3; DAM DRAM; MTCW 1, 2

Hirsch, E(ric) D(onald), Jr. 1928- .... **CLC 79**
See also CA 25-28R; CANR 27, 51; DLB 67; INT CANR-27; MTCW 1

Hirsch, Edward 1950- .... **CLC 31, 50**
See also CA 104; CANR 20, 42, 102; CP 7; DLB 120

Hitchcock, Alfred (Joseph)
1899-1980 .... **CLC 16**
See also AAYA 22; CA 159; 97-100; SATA 27; SATA-Obit 24

Hitchens, Christopher (Eric)
1949- .... **CLC 157**
See also CA 149; CANR 89

Hitler, Adolf 1889-1945 .... **TCLC 53**
See also CA 117; 147

Hoagland, Edward 1932- .... **CLC 28**
See also ANW; CA 1-4R; CANR 2, 31, 57, 107; CN 7; DLB 6; SATA 51; TCWW 2

Hoban, Russell (Conwell) 1925- ... **CLC 7, 25**
See also BPFB 2; CA 5-8R; CANR 23, 37, 66; CLR 3, 69; CN 7; CWRI 5; DAM NOV; DLB 52; FANT; MAICYA 1, 2; MTCW 1, 2; SATA 1, 40, 78; SFW 4

Hobbes, Thomas 1588-1679 .... **LC 36**
See also DLB 151, 252; RGEL 2

Hobbs, Perry
See Blackmur, R(ichard) P(almer)

Hobson, Laura Z(ametkin)
1900-1986 .... **CLC 7, 25**
See also Field, Peter
See also BPFB 2; CA 17-20R; 118; CANR 55; DLB 28; SATA 52

Hoccleve, Thomas c. 1368-c. 1437 ...... **LC 75**
See also DLB 146; RGEL 2

Hoch, Edward D(entinger) 1930-
See Queen, Ellery
See also CA 29-32R; CANR 11, 27, 51, 97; CMW 4; SFW 4

Hochhuth, Rolf 1931- .... **CLC 4, 11, 18**
See also CA 5-8R; CANR 33, 75; CWW 2; DAM DRAM; DLB 124; MTCW 1, 2

Hochman, Sandra 1936- .... **CLC 3, 8**
See also CA 5-8R; DLB 5

Hochwaelder, Fritz 1911-1986 .... **CLC 36**
See also Hochwalder, Fritz
See also CA 29-32R; 120; CANR 42; DAM
DRAM; MTCW 1

Hochwalder, Fritz
See Hochwaelder, Fritz
See also RGWL 2

Hocking, Mary (Eunice) 1921- .... **CLC 13**
See also CA 101; CANR 18, 40

Hodgins, Jack 1938- .... **CLC 23**
See also CA 93-96; CN 7; DLB 60

Hodgson, William Hope
1877(?)-1918 .... **TCLC 13**
See also CA 111; 164; CMW 4; DLB 70,
153, 156, 178; HGG; MTCW 2; SFW 4;
SUFW

Hoeg, Peter 1957- .... **CLC 95, 156**
See also CA 151; CANR 75; CMW 4; DA3;
DLB 214; MTCW 2

Hoffman, Alice 1952- .... **CLC 51**
See also AAYA 37; AMWS 10; CA 77-80;
CANR 34, 66, 100; CN 7; CPW; DAM
NOV; MTCW 1, 2

Hoffman, Daniel (Gerard) 1923- . **CLC 6, 13,
23**
See also CA 1-4R; CANR 4; CP 7; DLB 5

Hoffman, Stanley 1944- .... **CLC 5**
See also CA 77-80

Hoffman, William 1925- .... **CLC 141**
See also CA 21-24R; CANR 9, 103; CSW;
DLB 234

Hoffman, William M(oses) 1939- ..... **CLC 40**
See also CA 57-60; CANR 11, 71

Hoffmann, E(rnst) T(heodor) A(madeus)
1776-1822 .... **NCLC 2; SSC 13**
See also CDWLB 2; DLB 90; EW 5; RGSF
2; RGWL 2; SATA 27; SUFW; WCH

Hofmann, Gert 1931- .... **CLC 54**
See also CA 128

Hofmannsthal, Hugo von
1874-1929 .... **TCLC 11; DC 4**
See also CA 106; 153; CDWLB 2; DAM
DRAM; DFS 12; DLB 81, 118; EW 9;
RGWL 2

Hogan, Linda 1947- .... **CLC 73; PC 35**
See also AMWS 4; ANW; BYA 12; CA 120;
CANR 45, 73; CWP; DAM MULT; DLB
175; NNAL; TCWW 2

Hogarth, Charles
See Creasey, John

Hogarth, Emmett
See Polonsky, Abraham (Lincoln)

Hogg, James 1770-1835 .... **NCLC 4, 109**
See also DLB 93, 116, 159; HGG; RGEL 2;
SUFW

Holbach, Paul Henri Thiry Baron
1723-1789 .... **LC 14**

Holberg, Ludvig 1684-1754 .... **LC 6**
See also RGWL 2

Holcroft, Thomas 1745-1809 .... **NCLC 85**
See also DLB 39, 89, 158; RGEL 2

Holden, Ursula 1921- .... **CLC 18**
See also CA 101; CAAS 8; CANR 22

Holderlin, (Johann Christian) Friedrich
1770-1843 .... **NCLC 16; PC 4**
See also CDWLB 2; DLB 90; EW 5; RGWL
2

Holdstock, Robert
See Holdstock, Robert P.

Holdstock, Robert P. 1948- .... **CLC 39**
See also CA 131; CANR 81; FANT; HGG;
SFW 4

Holinshed, Raphael fl. 1580- .... **LC 69**
See also DLB 167; RGEL 2

Holland, Isabelle 1920- .... **CLC 21**
See also AAYA 11; CA 21-24R, 181; CAAE
181; CANR 10, 25, 47; CLR 57; CWRI
5; JRDA; LAIT 4; MAICYA 1, 2; SATA
8, 70; SATA-Essay 103; WYA

Holland, Marcus
See Caldwell, (Janet Miriam) Taylor
(Holland)

Hollander, John 1929- .... **CLC 2, 5, 8, 14**
See also CA 1-4R; CANR 1, 52; CP 7; DLB
5; SATA 13

Hollander, Paul
See Silverberg, Robert

Holleran, Andrew 1943(?)- .... **CLC 38**
See also Garber, Eric
See also CA 144; GLL 1

Holley, Marietta 1836(?)-1926 .... **TCLC 99**
See also CA 118; DLB 11

Hollinghurst, Alan 1954- .... **CLC 55, 91**
See also CA 114; CN 7; DLB 207; GLL 1

Hollis, Jim
See Summers, Hollis (Spurgeon, Jr.)

Holly, Buddy 1936-1959 .... **TCLC 65**

Holmes, Gordon
See Shiel, M(atthew) P(hipps)

Holmes, John
See Souster, (Holmes) Raymond

Holmes, John Clellon 1926-1988 ...... **CLC 56**
See also CA 9-12R; 125; CANR 4; DLB
16, 237

Holmes, Oliver Wendell, Jr.
1841-1935 .... **TCLC 77**
See also CA 114; 186

Holmes, Oliver Wendell
1809-1894 .... **NCLC 14, 81**
See also AMWS 1; CDALB 1640-1865;
DLB 1, 189, 235; EXPP; RGAL 4; SATA
34

Holmes, Raymond
See Souster, (Holmes) Raymond

Holt, Victoria
See Hibbert, Eleanor Alice Burford
See also BPFB 2

Holub, Miroslav 1923-1998 .... **CLC 4**
See also CA 21-24R; 169; CANR 10; CD-
WLB 4; CWW 2; DLB 232

Homer c. 8th cent. B.C.- .... **CMLC 1, 16; PC
23; WLCS**
See also AW 1; CDWLB 1; DA; DA3;
DAB; DAC; DAM MST, POET; DLB
176; EFS 1; LAIT 1; RGWL 2; WP

Hongo, Garrett Kaoru 1951- .... **PC 23**
See also CA 133; CAAS 22; CP 7; DLB
120; EXPP; RGAL 4

Honig, Edwin 1919- .... **CLC 33**
See also CA 5-8R; CAAS 8; CANR 4, 45;
CP 7; DLB 5

Hood, Hugh (John Blagdon) 1928- . **CLC 15,
28; SSC 42**
See also CA 49-52; CAAS 17; CANR 1,
33, 87; CN 7; DLB 53; RGSF 2

Hood, Thomas 1799-1845 .... **NCLC 16**
See also BRW 4; DLB 96; RGEL 2

Hooker, (Peter) Jeremy 1941- .... **CLC 43**
See also CA 77-80; CANR 22; CP 7; DLB
40

hooks, bell .... **CLC 94**
See also Watkins, Gloria Jean
See also DLB 246

Hope, A(lec) D(erwent) 1907-2000 .... **CLC 3,
51**
See also BRWS 7; CA 21-24R; 188; CANR
33, 74; MTCW 1, 2; PFS 8; RGEL 2

Hope, Anthony 1863-1933 .... **TCLC 83**
See also CA 157; DLB 153, 156; RGEL 2;
RHW

Hope, Brian
See Creasey, John

Hope, Christopher (David Tully)
1944- .... **CLC 52**
See also AFW; CA 106; CANR 47, 101;
CN 7; DLB 225; SATA 62

Hopkins, Gerard Manley
1844-1889 .... **NCLC 17; PC 15; WLC**
See also BRW 5; BRWR 2; CDBLB 1890-
1914; DA; DA3; DAB; DAC; DAM MST,
POET; DLB 35, 57; EXPP; PAB; RGEL
2; WP

Hopkins, John (Richard) 1931-1998 .. **CLC 4**
See also CA 85-88; 169; CBD; CD 5

Hopkins, Pauline Elizabeth
1859-1930 .... **TCLC 28; BLC 2**
See also AFAW 2; BW 2, 3; CA 141; CANR
82; DAM MULT; DLB 50

Hopkinson, Francis 1737-1791 .... **LC 25**
See also DLB 31; RGAL 4

Hopley-Woolrich, Cornell George 1903-1968
See Woolrich, Cornell
See also CA 13-14; CANR 58; CAP 1;
CMW 4; DLB 226; MTCW 2

Horace 65B.C.-8B.C. .... **CMLC 39**
See also AW 2; CDWLB 1; DLB 211;
RGWL 2

Horatio
See Proust, (Valentin-Louis-George-Eugene-
)Marcel

**Horgan, Paul (George Vincent
O'Shaughnessy)** 1903-1995 .. **CLC 9, 53**
See also BPFB 2; CA 13-16R; 147; CANR
9, 35; DAM NOV; DLB 102, 212; DLBY
1985; INT CANR-9; MTCW 1, 2; SATA
13; SATA-Obit 84; TCWW 2

Horn, Peter
See Kuttner, Henry

Hornem, Horace Esq.
See Byron, George Gordon (Noel)

**Horney, Karen (Clementine Theodore
Danielsen)** 1885-1952 .... **TCLC 71**
See also CA 114; 165; DLB 246; FW

Hornung, E(rnest) W(illiam)
1866-1921 .... **TCLC 59**
See also CA 108; 160; CMW 4; DLB 70

Horovitz, Israel (Arthur) 1939- .... **CLC 56**
See also CA 33-36R; CAD; CANR 46, 59;
CD 5; DAM DRAM; DLB 7

Horton, George Moses
1797(?)-1883(?) .... **NCLC 87**
See also DLB 50

Horvath, Odon von 1901-1938 .... **TCLC 45**
See also von Horvath, Oedoen
See also CA 118; 194; DLB 85, 124; RGWL
2

Horvath, Oedoen von -1938
See Horvath, Odon von

Horwitz, Julius 1920-1986 .... **CLC 14**
See also CA 9-12R; 119; CANR 12

Hospital, Janette Turner 1942- .... **CLC 42,
145**
See also CA 108; CANR 48; CN 7; RGSF
2

Hostos, E. M. de
See Hostos (y Bonilla), Eugenio Maria de

Hostos, Eugenio M. de
See Hostos (y Bonilla), Eugenio Maria de

Hostos, Eugenio Maria
See Hostos (y Bonilla), Eugenio Maria de

Hostos (y Bonilla), Eugenio Maria de
1839-1903 .... **TCLC 24**
See also CA 123; 131; HW 1

Houdini
See Lovecraft, H(oward) P(hillips)

Hougan, Carolyn 1943- .... **CLC 34**
See also CA 139

Household, Geoffrey (Edward West)
1900-1988 .... **CLC 11**
See also CA 77-80; 126; CANR 58; CMW
4; DLB 87; SATA 14; SATA-Obit 59

Housman, A(lfred) E(dward)
1859-1936 ... **TCLC 1, 10; PC 2; WLCS**
See also BRW 6; CA 104; 125; DA; DA3;
DAB; DAC; DAM MST, POET; DLB 19;
EXPP; MTCW 1, 2; PAB; PFS 4, 7;
RGEL 2; WP

Housman, Laurence 1865-1959 .... **TCLC 7**
See also CA 106; 155; DLB 10; FANT;
RGEL 2; SATA 25

Howard, Elizabeth Jane 1923- ..... **CLC 7, 29**
See also CA 5-8R; CANR 8, 62; CN 7

Howard, Maureen 1930- .... **CLC 5, 14, 46, 151**
See also CA 53-56; CANR 31, 75; CN 7;
DLBY 1983; INT CANR-31; MTCW 1, 2

Howard, Richard 1929- .... **CLC 7, 10, 47**
See also AITN 1; CA 85-88; CANR 25, 80;
CP 7; DLB 5; INT CANR-25

Howard, Robert E(rvin)
1906-1936 .... **TCLC 8**
See also BPFB 2; BYA 5; CA 105; 157;
FANT; SUFW

Howard, Warren F.
See Pohl, Frederik

Howe, Fanny (Quincy) 1940- .... **CLC 47**
See also CA 117; CAAE 187; CAAS 27;
CANR 70; CP 7; CWP; SATA-Brief 52

Howe, Irving 1920-1993 .... **CLC 85**
See also AMWS 6; CA 9-12R; 141; CANR
21, 50; DLB 67; MTCW 1, 2

Howe, Julia Ward 1819-1910 .... **TCLC 21**
See also CA 117; 191; DLB 1, 189, 235;
FW

Howe, Susan 1937- .... **CLC 72, 152**
See also AMWS 4; CA 160; CP 7; CWP;
DLB 120; FW; RGAL 4

Howe, Tina 1937- .... **CLC 48**
See also CA 109; CAD; CD 5; CWD

Howell, James 1594(?)-1666 .... **LC 13**
See also DLB 151

Howell, W. D.
See Howells, William Dean

Howells, William D.
See Howells, William Dean

Howells, William Dean 1837-1920 .. **TCLC 7, 17, 41; SSC 36**
See also AMW; CA 104; 134; CDALB
1865-1917; DLB 12, 64, 74, 79, 189;
MTCW 2; RGAL 4

Howes, Barbara 1914-1996 .... **CLC 15**
See also CA 9-12R; 151; CAAS 3; CANR
53; CP 7; SATA 5

Hrabal, Bohumil 1914-1997 .... **CLC 13, 67**
See also CA 106; 156; CAAS 12; CANR
57; CWW 2; DLB 232; RGSF 2

Hrotsvit of Gandersheim c. 935-c.
1000 .... **CMLC 29**
See also DLB 148

Hsi, Chu 1130-1200 .... **CMLC 42**

Hsun, Lu
See Lu Hsun

Hubbard, L(afayette) Ron(ald)
1911-1986 .... **CLC 43**
See also CA 77-80; 118; CANR 52; CPW;
DA3; DAM POP; FANT; MTCW 2; SFW
4

Huch, Ricarda (Octavia)
1864-1947 .... **TCLC 13**
See also CA 111; 189; DLB 66

Huddle, David 1942- .... **CLC 49**
See also CA 57-60; CAAS 20; CANR 89;
DLB 130

Hudson, Jeffrey
See Crichton, (John) Michael

Hudson, W(illiam) H(enry)
1841-1922 .... **TCLC 29**
See also CA 115; 190; DLB 98, 153, 174;
RGEL 2; SATA 35

Hueffer, Ford Madox
See Ford, Ford Madox

Hughart, Barry 1934- .... **CLC 39**
See also CA 137; FANT; SFW 4

Hughes, Colin
See Creasey, John

Hughes, David (John) 1930- .... **CLC 48**
See also CA 116; 129; CN 7; DLB 14

Hughes, Edward James
See Hughes, Ted
See also DA3; DAM MST, POET

Hughes, (James) Langston
1902-1967 .... **CLC 1, 5, 10, 15, 35, 44, 108; BLC 2; DC 3; PC 1; SSC 6; WLC**
See also AAYA 12; AFAW 1, 2; AMWR 1;
AMWS 1; BW 1, 3; CA 1-4R; 25-28R;
CANR 1, 34, 82; CDALB 1929-1941;
CLR 17; DA; DA3; DAB; DAC; DAM
DRAM, MST, MULT, POET; DLB 4, 7,
48, 51, 86, 228; EXPP; EXPS; JRDA;
LAIT 3; MAICYA 1, 2; MTCW 1, 2;
PAB; PFS 1, 3, 6, 10; RGAL 4; RGSF 2;
SATA 4, 33; SSFS 4, 7; WCH; WP; YAW

Hughes, Richard (Arthur Warren)
1900-1976 .... **CLC 1, 11**
See also CA 5-8R; 65-68; CANR 4; DAM
NOV; DLB 15, 161; MTCW 1; RGEL 2;
SATA 8; SATA-Obit 25

Hughes, Ted 1930-1998 . **CLC 2, 4, 9, 14, 37, 119; PC 7**
See Hughes, Edward James
See also BRWR 2; BRWS 1; CA 1-4R; 171;
CANR 1, 33, 66, 108; CLR 3; CP 7;
DAB; DAC; DLB 40, 161; EXPP; MAI-
CYA 1, 2; MTCW 1, 2; PAB; PFS 4;
RGEL 2; SATA 49; SATA-Brief 27;
SATA-Obit 107; YAW

Hugo, Richard
See Huch, Ricarda (Octavia)

Hugo, Richard F(ranklin)
1923-1982 .... **CLC 6, 18, 32**
See also AMWS 6; CA 49-52; 108; CANR
3; DAM POET; DLB 5, 206; RGAL 4

Hugo, Victor (Marie) 1802-1885 .... **NCLC 3, 10, 21; PC 17; WLC**
See also AAYA 28; DA; DA3; DAB; DAC;
DAM DRAM, MST, NOV, POET; DLB
119, 192, 217; EFS 2; EW 6; EXPN; GFL
1789 to the Present; LAIT 1, 2; NFS 5;
RGWL 2; SATA 47

Huidobro, Vicente
See Huidobro Fernandez, Vicente Garcia
See also LAW

Huidobro Fernandez, Vicente Garcia
1893-1948 .... **TCLC 31**
See also Huidobro, Vicente
See also CA 131; HW 1

Hulme, Keri 1947- .... **CLC 39, 130**
See also CA 125; CANR 69; CN 7; CP 7;
CWP; FW; INT 125

Hulme, T(homas) E(rnest)
1883-1917 .... **TCLC 21**
See also BRWS 6; CA 117; DLB 19

Hume, David 1711-1776 .... **LC 7, 56**
See also BRWS 3; DLB 104, 252

Humphrey, William 1924-1997 .... **CLC 45**
See also AMWS 9; CA 77-80; 160; CANR
68; CN 7; CSW; DLB 6, 212, 234;
TCWW 2

Humphreys, Emyr Owen 1919- .... **CLC 47**
See also CA 5-8R; CANR 3, 24; CN 7;
DLB 15

Humphreys, Josephine 1945- ..... **CLC 34, 57**
See also CA 121; 127; CANR 97; CSW;
INT 127

Huneker, James Gibbons
1860-1921 .... **TCLC 65**
See also CA 193; DLB 71; RGAL 4

Hungerford, Hesba Fay
See Brinsmead, H(esba) F(ay)

Hungerford, Pixie
See Brinsmead, H(esba) F(ay)

Hunt, E(verette) Howard, (Jr.)
1918- .... **CLC 3**
See also AITN 1; CA 45-48; CANR 2, 47,
103; CMW 4

Hunt, Francesca
See Holland, Isabelle

Hunt, Howard
See Hunt, E(verette) Howard, (Jr.)

Hunt, Kyle
See Creasey, John

Hunt, (James Henry) Leigh
1784-1859 .... **NCLC 1, 70**
See also DAM POET; DLB 96, 110, 144;
RGEL 2; TEA

Hunt, Marsha 1946- .... **CLC 70**
See also BW 2, 3; CA 143; CANR 79

Hunt, Violet 1866(?)-1942 .... **TCLC 53**
See also CA 184; DLB 162, 197

Hunter, E. Waldo
See Sturgeon, Theodore (Hamilton)

Hunter, Evan 1926- .... **CLC 11, 31**
See also McBain, Ed
See also AAYA 39; BPFB 2; CA 5-8R;
CANR 5, 38, 62, 97; CMW 4; CN 7;
CPW; DAM POP; DLBY 1982; INT
CANR-5; MSW; MTCW 1; SATA 25;
SFW 4

Hunter, Kristin 1931-
See Lattany, Kristin (Elaine Eggleston)
Hunter

Hunter, Mary
See Austin, Mary (Hunter)

Hunter, Mollie 1922- .... **CLC 21**
See also McIlwraith, Maureen Mollie
Hunter
See also AAYA 13; BYA 6; CANR 37, 78;
CLR 25; DLB 161; JRDA; MAICYA 1,
2; SAAS 7; SATA 54, 106; WYA; YAW

Hunter, Robert (?)-1734 .... **LC 7**

Hurston, Zora Neale 1891-1960 .. **CLC 7, 30, 61; BLC 2; DC 12; SSC 4; WLCS**
See also AAYA 15; AFAW 1, 2; AMWS 6;
BW 1, 3; BYA 12; CA 85-88; CANR 61;
CDALBS; DA; DA3; DAC; DAM MST,
MULT, NOV; DFS 6; DLB 51, 86; EXPN;
EXPS; FW; LAIT 3; MAWW; MTCW 1,
2; NFS 3; RGAL 4; RGSF 2; SSFS 1, 6,
11; TCLC 121; YAW

Husserl, E. G.
See Husserl, Edmund (Gustav Albrecht)

Husserl, Edmund (Gustav Albrecht)
1859-1938 .... **TCLC 100**
See also CA 116; 133

Huston, John (Marcellus)
1906-1987 .... **CLC 20**
See also CA 73-76; 123; CANR 34; DLB
26

Hustvedt, Siri 1955- .... **CLC 76**
See also CA 137

Hutten, Ulrich von 1488-1523 .... **LC 16**
See also DLB 179

Huxley, Aldous (Leonard)
1894-1963 .... **CLC 1, 3, 4, 5, 8, 11, 18, 35, 79; SSC 39; WLC**
See also AAYA 11; BPFB 2; BRW 7; CA
85-88; CANR 44, 99; CDBLB 1914-1945;
DA; DA3; DAB; DAC; DAM MST, NOV;
DLB 36, 100, 162, 195, 255; EXPN;
LAIT 5; MTCW 1, 2; NFS 6; RGEL 2;
SATA 63; SCFW 2; SFW 4; YAW

Huxley, T(homas) H(enry)
1825-1895 .... **NCLC 67**
See also DLB 57

Huysmans, Joris-Karl 1848-1907 ... **TCLC 7, 69**
See also CA 104; 165; DLB 123; EW 7;
GFL 1789 to the Present; RGWL 2

Hwang, David Henry 1957- .. **CLC 55; DC 4**
See also CA 127; 132; CAD; CANR 76;
CD 5; DA3; DAM DRAM; DFS 11; DLB
212, 228; INT CA-132; MTCW 2; RGAL
4

Hyde, Anthony 1946- .... **CLC 42**
See also Chase, Nicholas
See also CA 136; CCA 1

Hyde, Margaret O(ldroyd) 1917- ..... **CLC 21**
See also CA 1-4R; CANR 1, 36; CLR 23;
JRDA; MAICYA 1, 2; SAAS 8; SATA 1,
42, 76

Hynes, James 1956(?)- .... **CLC 65**
See also CA 164; CANR 105

Hypatia c. 370-415 .... **CMLC 35**

Ian, Janis 1951- .... **CLC 21**
See also CA 105; 187

Ibanez, Vicente Blasco
See Blasco Ibanez, Vicente

Ibarbourou, Juana de 1895-1979
See also HLCS 2; HW 1; LAW

Ibarguengoitia, Jorge 1928-1983 ...... **CLC 37**
See also CA 124; 113; HW 1

Ibsen, Henrik (Johan) 1828-1906 ... **TCLC 2,
8, 16, 37, 52; DC 2; WLC**
See also CA 104; 141; DA; DA3; DAB;
DAC; DAM DRAM, MST; DFS 1, 6, 8,
10, 11; EW 7; LAIT 2; RGWL 2

Ibuse, Masuji 1898-1993 .... **CLC 22**
See also Ibuse Masuji
See also CA 127; 141; MJW

Ibuse Masuji
See Ibuse, Masuji
See also DLB 180

Ichikawa, Kon 1915- .... **CLC 20**
See also CA 121

Ichiyo, Higuchi 1872-1896 .... **NCLC 49**
See also MJW

Idle, Eric 1943-2000 .... **CLC 21**
See also Monty Python
See also CA 116; CANR 35, 91

Ignatow, David 1914-1997 .... **CLC 4, 7, 14,
40; PC 34**
See also CA 9-12R; 162; CAAS 3; CANR
31, 57, 96; CP 7; DLB 5

Ignotus
See Strachey, (Giles) Lytton

Ihimaera, Witi 1944- .... **CLC 46**
See also CA 77-80; CN 7; RGSF 2

Ilf, Ilya .... **TCLC 21**
See also Fainzilberg, Ilya Arnoldovich

Illyes, Gyula 1902-1983 .... **PC 16**
See also CA 114; 109; CDWLB 4; DLB
215; RGWL 2

Immermann, Karl (Lebrecht)
1796-1840 .... **NCLC 4, 49**
See also DLB 133

Ince, Thomas H. 1882-1924 .... **TCLC 89**
See also IDFW 3, 4

Inchbald, Elizabeth 1753-1821 ...... **NCLC 62**
See also DLB 39, 89; RGEL 2

Inclan, Ramon (Maria) del Valle
See Valle-Inclan, Ramon (Maria) del

Infante, G(uillermo) Cabrera
See Cabrera Infante, G(uillermo)

Ingalls, Rachel (Holmes) 1940- .... **CLC 42**
See also CA 123; 127

Ingamells, Reginald Charles
See Ingamells, Rex

Ingamells, Rex 1913-1955 .... **TCLC 35**
See also CA 167

Inge, William (Motter) 1913-1973 ..... **CLC 1,
8, 19**
See also CA 9-12R; CDALB 1941-1968;
DA3; DAM DRAM; DFS 1, 5, 8; DLB 7,
249; MTCW 1, 2; RGAL 4

Ingelow, Jean 1820-1897 .... **NCLC 39, 107**
See also DLB 35, 163; FANT; SATA 33

Ingram, Willis J.
See Harris, Mark

Innaurato, Albert (F.) 1948(?)- ... **CLC 21, 60**
See also CA 115; 122; CAD; CANR 78;
CD 5; INT CA-122

Innes, Michael
See Stewart, J(ohn) I(nnes) M(ackintosh)
See also MSW

Innis, Harold Adams 1894-1952 .... **TCLC 77**
See also CA 181; DLB 88

Ionesco, Eugene 1912-1994 ... **CLC 1, 4, 6, 9,
11, 15, 41, 86; DC 12; WLC**
See also CA 9-12R; 144; CANR 55; CWW
2; DA; DA3; DAB; DAC; DAM DRAM,
MST; DFS 4, 9; EW 13; GFL 1789 to the
Present; MTCW 1, 2; RGWL 2; SATA 7;
SATA-Obit 79

Iqbal, Muhammad 1877-1938 .... **TCLC 28**

Ireland, Patrick
See O'Doherty, Brian

Irenaeus St. 130- .... **CMLC 42**

Iron, Ralph
See Schreiner, Olive (Emilie Albertina)

Irving, John (Winslow) 1942- ... **CLC 13, 23,
38, 112**
See also AAYA 8; AMWS 6; BEST 89:3;
BPFB 2; CA 25-28R; CANR 28, 73; CN
7; CPW; DA3; DAM NOV, POP; DLB 6;
DLBY 1982; MTCW 1, 2; NFS 12, 14;
RGAL 4

Irving, Washington 1783-1859 . **NCLC 2, 19,
95; SSC 2, 37; WLC**
See also AMW; CDALB 1640-1865; DA;
DA3; DAB; DAC; DAM MST; DLB 3,
11, 30, 59, 73, 74, 183, 186, 250, 254;
EXPS; LAIT 1; RGAL 4; RGSF 2; SSFS
1, 8; SUFW; WCH; YABC 2

Irwin, P. K.
See Page, P(atricia) K(athleen)

Isaacs, Jorge Ricardo 1837-1895 ... **NCLC 70**
See also LAW

Isaacs, Susan 1943- .... **CLC 32**
See also BEST 89:1; BPFB 2; CA 89-92;
CANR 20, 41, 65; CPW; DA3; DAM
POP; INT CANR-20; MTCW 1, 2

Isherwood, Christopher (William Bradshaw)
1904-1986 .... **CLC 1, 9, 11, 14, 44**
See also BRW 7; CA 13-16R; 117; CANR
35, 97; DA3; DAM DRAM, NOV; DLB
15, 195; DLBY 1986; IDTP; MTCW 1, 2;
RGAL 4; RGEL 2; WLIT 4

Ishiguro, Kazuo 1954- .. **CLC 27, 56, 59, 110**
See also BEST 90:2; BPFB 2; BRWS 4;
CA 120; CANR 49, 95; CN 7; DA3;
DAM NOV; DLB 194; MTCW 1, 2; NFS
13; WLIT 4

Ishikawa, Hakuhin
See Ishikawa, Takuboku

Ishikawa, Takuboku
1886(?)-1912 .... **TCLC 15; PC 10**
See also CA 113; 153; DAM POET

Iskander, Fazil 1929- .... **CLC 47**
See also CA 102

Isler, Alan (David) 1934- .... **CLC 91**
See also CA 156; CANR 105

Ivan IV 1530-1584 .... **LC 17**

Ivanov, Vyacheslav Ivanovich
1866-1949 .... **TCLC 33**
See also CA 122

Ivask, Ivar Vidrik 1927-1992 .... **CLC 14**
See also CA 37-40R; 139; CANR 24

Ives, Morgan
See Bradley, Marion Zimmer
See also GLL 1

Izumi Shikibu c. 973-c. 1034 .... **CMLC 33**

J .... **CLC 8**
See also CA 33-36R; CANR 28, 67; CN 7;
DLB 2, 28, 218; DLBY 1980

J. R. S.
See Gogarty, Oliver St. John

Jabran, Kahlil
See Gibran, Kahlil

Jabran, Khalil
See Gibran, Kahlil

Jackson, Daniel
See Wingrove, David (John)

Jackson, Helen Hunt 1830-1885 .... **NCLC 90**
See also DLB 42, 47, 186, 189; RGAL 4

Jackson, Jesse 1908-1983 .... **CLC 12**
See also BW 1; CA 25-28R; 109; CANR
27; CLR 28; CWRI 5; MAICYA 1, 2;
SATA 2, 29; SATA-Obit 48

Jackson, Laura (Riding) 1901-1991
See Riding, Laura
See also CA 65-68; 135; CANR 28, 89;
DLB 48

Jackson, Sam
See Trumbo, Dalton

Jackson, Sara
See Wingrove, David (John)

Jackson, Shirley 1919-1965 . **CLC 11, 60, 87;
SSC 9, 39; WLC**
See also AAYA 9; AMWS 9; BPFB 2; CA
1-4R; 25-28R; CANR 4, 52; CDALB
1941-1968; DA; DA3; DAC; DAM MST;
DLB 6, 234; EXPS; HGG; LAIT 4;
MTCW 2; RGAL 4; RGSF 2; SATA 2;
SSFS 1; SUFW

Jacob, (Cyprien-)Max 1876-1944 .... **TCLC 6**
See also CA 104; 193; GFL 1789 to the
Present; GLL 2; RGWL 2

Jacobs, Harriet A(nn)
1813(?)-1897 .... **NCLC 67**
See also AFAW 1, 2; DLB 239; FW; LAIT
2; RGAL 4

Jacobs, Jim 1942- .... **CLC 12**
See also CA 97-100; INT 97-100

Jacobs, W(illiam) W(ymark)
1863-1943 .... **TCLC 22**
See also CA 121; 167; DLB 135; EXPS;
HGG; RGEL 2; RGSF 2; SSFS 2; SUFW

Jacobsen, Jens Peter 1847-1885 .... **NCLC 34**

Jacobsen, Josephine 1908- .... **CLC 48, 102**
See also CA 33-36R; CAAS 18; CANR 23,
48; CCA 1; CP 7; DLB 244

Jacobson, Dan 1929- .... **CLC 4, 14**
See also AFW; CA 1-4R; CANR 2, 25, 66;
CN 7; DLB 14, 207, 225; MTCW 1;
RGSF 2

Jacqueline
See Carpentier (y Valmont), Alejo

Jagger, Mick 1944- .... **CLC 17**

Jahiz, al- c. 780-c. 869 .... **CMLC 25**

Jakes, John (William) 1932- .... **CLC 29**
See also AAYA 32; BEST 89:4; BPFB 2;
CA 57-60; CANR 10, 43, 66; CPW; CSW;
DA3; DAM NOV, POP; DLBY 1983;
FANT; INT CANR-10; MTCW 1, 2;
RHW; SATA 62; SFW 4; TCWW 2

James I 1394-1437 .... **LC 20**
See also RGEL 2

James, Andrew
See Kirkup, James

James, C(yril) L(ionel) R(obert)
1901-1989 .... **CLC 33; BLCS**
See also BW 2; CA 117; 125; 128; CANR
62; DLB 125; MTCW 1

James, Daniel (Lewis) 1911-1988
See Santiago, Danny
See also CA 174; 125

James, Dynely
See Mayne, William (James Carter)

James, Henry Sr. 1811-1882 .... **NCLC 53**

James, Henry 1843-1916 ..... **TCLC 2, 11, 24, 40, 47, 64; SSC 8, 32, 47; WLC**
   See also AMW; AMWR 1; BPFB 2; BRW 6; CA 104; 132; CDALB 1865-1917; DA; DA3; DAB; DAC; DAM MST, NOV; DLB 12, 71, 74, 189; DLBD 13; EXPS; HGG; LAIT 2; MTCW 1, 2; NFS 12; RGAL 4; RGEL 2; RGSF 2; SSFS 9; SUFW

James, M. R.
   See James, Montague (Rhodes)
   See also DLB 156, 201

James, Montague (Rhodes)
   1862-1936 .... **TCLC 6; SSC 16**
   See also James, M. R.
   See also CA 104; HGG; RGEL 2; RGSF 2; SUFW

James, P. D. .... **CLC 18, 46, 122**
   See also White, Phyllis Dorothy James
   See also BEST 90:2; BPFB 2; BRWS 4; CDBLB 1960 to Present; DLB 87; DLBD 17; MSW

James, Philip
   See Moorcock, Michael (John)

James, Samuel
   See Stephens, James

James, Seumas
   See Stephens, James

James, Stephen
   See Stephens, James

James, William 1842-1910 .... **TCLC 15, 32**
   See also AMW; CA 109; 193; RGAL 4

Jameson, Anna 1794-1860 .... **NCLC 43**
   See also DLB 99, 166

Jameson, Fredric (R.) 1934- .... **CLC 142**
   See also CA 196; DLB 67

Jami, Nur al-Din 'Abd al-Rahman
   1414-1492 .... **LC 9**

Jammes, Francis 1868-1938 .... **TCLC 75**
   See also CA 198; GFL 1789 to the Present

Jandl, Ernst 1925-2000 .... **CLC 34**
   See also CA 200

Janowitz, Tama 1957- .... **CLC 43, 145**
   See also CA 106; CANR 52, 89; CN 7; CPW; DAM POP

Japrisot, Sebastien 1931- .... **CLC 90**
   See also Rossi, Jean Baptiste
   See also CMW 4

Jarrell, Randall 1914-1965 .... **CLC 1, 2, 6, 9, 13, 49; PC 41**
   See also AMW; BYA 5; CA 5-8R; 25-28R; CABS 2; CANR 6, 34; CDALB 1941-1968; CLR 6; CWRI 5; DAM POET; DLB 48, 52; EXPP; MAICYA 1, 2; MTCW 1, 2; PAB; PFS 2; RGAL 4; SATA 7

Jarry, Alfred 1873-1907 .... **TCLC 2, 14; SSC 20**
   See also CA 104; 153; DA3; DAM DRAM; DFS 8; DLB 192, 258; EW 9; GFL 1789 to the Present; RGWL 2

Jarvis, E. K.
   See Silverberg, Robert

Jawien, Andrzej
   See John Paul II, Pope

Jaynes, Roderick
   See Coen, Ethan

Jeake, Samuel, Jr.
   See Aiken, Conrad (Potter)

Jean Paul 1763-1825 .... **NCLC 7**

Jefferies, (John) Richard
   1848-1887 .... **NCLC 47**
   See also DLB 98, 141; RGEL 2; SATA 16; SFW 4

Jeffers, (John) Robinson 1887-1962 .. **CLC 2, 3, 11, 15, 54; PC 17; WLC**
   See also AMWS 2; CA 85-88; CANR 35; CDALB 1917-1929; DA; DAC; DAM MST, POET; DLB 45, 212; MTCW 1, 2; PAB; PFS 3, 4; RGAL 4

Jefferson, Janet
   See Mencken, H(enry) L(ouis)

Jefferson, Thomas 1743-1826 . **NCLC 11, 103**
   See also ANW; CDALB 1640-1865; DA3; DLB 31, 183; LAIT 1; RGAL 4

Jeffrey, Francis 1773-1850 .... **NCLC 33**
   See also Francis, Lord Jeffrey

Jelakowitch, Ivan
   See Heijermans, Herman

Jellicoe, (Patricia) Ann 1927- .... **CLC 27**
   See also CA 85-88; CBD; CD 5; CWD; CWRI 5; DLB 13, 233; FW

Jemyma
   See Holley, Marietta

Jen, Gish .... **CLC 70**
   See also Jen, Lillian

Jen, Lillian 1956(?)-
   See Jen, Gish
   See also CA 135; CANR 89

Jenkins, (John) Robin 1912- .... **CLC 52**
   See also CA 1-4R; CANR 1; CN 7; DLB 14

Jennings, Elizabeth (Joan)
   1926-2001 .... **CLC 5, 14, 131**
   See also BRWS 5; CA 61-64; 200; CAAS 5; CANR 8, 39, 66; CP 7; CWP; DLB 27; MTCW 1; SATA 66

Jennings, Waylon 1937- .... **CLC 21**

Jensen, Johannes V. 1873-1950 ...... **TCLC 41**
   See also CA 170; DLB 214

Jensen, Laura (Linnea) 1948- .... **CLC 37**
   See also CA 103

Jerome, Jerome K(lapka)
   1859-1927 .... **TCLC 23**
   See also CA 119; 177; DLB 10, 34, 135; RGEL 2

Jerrold, Douglas William
   1803-1857 .... **NCLC 2**
   See also DLB 158, 159; RGEL 2

Jewett, (Theodora) Sarah Orne
   1849-1909 .... **TCLC 1, 22; SSC 6, 44**
   See also AMW; CA 108; 127; CANR 71; DLB 12, 74, 221; EXPS; FW; MAWW; RGAL 4; RGSF 2; SATA 15; SSFS 4

Jewsbury, Geraldine (Endsor)
   1812-1880 .... **NCLC 22**
   See also DLB 21

Jhabvala, Ruth Prawer 1927- . **CLC 4, 8, 29, 94, 138**
   See also BRWS 5; CA 1-4R; CANR 2, 29, 51, 74, 91; CN 7; DAB; DAM NOV; DLB 139, 194; IDFW 3, 4; INT CANR-29; MTCW 1, 2; RGSF 2; RGWL 2; RHW

Jibran, Kahlil
   See Gibran, Kahlil

Jibran, Khalil
   See Gibran, Kahlil

Jiles, Paulette 1943- .... **CLC 13, 58**
   See also CA 101; CANR 70; CWP

Jimenez (Mantecon), Juan Ramon
   1881-1958 .... **TCLC 4; HLC 1; PC 7**
   See also CA 104; 131; CANR 74; DAM MULT, POET; DLB 134; EW 9; HW 1; MTCW 1, 2; RGWL 2

Jimenez, Ramon
   See Jimenez (Mantecon), Juan Ramon

Jimenez Mantecon, Juan
   See Jimenez (Mantecon), Juan Ramon

Jin, Ha .... **CLC 109**
   See also Jin, Xuefei
   See also CA 152; DLB 244

Jin, Xuefei 1956-
   See Jin, Ha
   See also CANR 91

Joel, Billy .... **CLC 26**
   See also Joel, William Martin

Joel, William Martin 1949-
   See Joel, Billy
   See also CA 108

John, Saint 107th cent. -100 .... **CMLC 27**

John of the Cross, St. 1542-1591 .... **LC 18**
   See also RGWL 2

John Paul II, Pope 1920- .... **CLC 128**
   See also CA 106; 133

Johnson, B(ryan) S(tanley William)
   1933-1973 .... **CLC 6, 9**
   See also CA 9-12R; 53-56; CANR 9; DLB 14, 40; RGEL 2

Johnson, Benjamin F., of Boone
   See Riley, James Whitcomb

Johnson, Charles (Richard) 1948- .... **CLC 7, 51, 65; BLC 2**
   See also AFAW 2; AMWS 6; BW 2, 3; CA 116; CAAS 18; CANR 42, 66, 82; CN 7; DAM MULT; DLB 33; MTCW 2; RGAL 4

Johnson, Denis 1949- .... **CLC 52, 160**
   See also CA 117; 121; CANR 71, 99; CN 7; DLB 120

Johnson, Diane 1934- .... **CLC 5, 13, 48**
   See also BPFB 2; CA 41-44R; CANR 17, 40, 62, 95; CN 7; DLBY 1980; INT CANR-17; MTCW 1

Johnson, Eyvind (Olof Verner)
   1900-1976 .... **CLC 14**
   See also CA 73-76; 69-72; CANR 34, 101; DLB 259; EW 12

Johnson, J. R.
   See James, C(yril) L(ionel) R(obert)

Johnson, James Weldon
   1871-1938 . **TCLC 3, 19; BLC 2; PC 24**
   See also AFAW 1, 2; BW 1, 3; CA 104; 125; CANR 82; CDALB 1917-1929; CLR 32; DA3; DAM MULT, POET; DLB 51; EXPP; MTCW 1, 2; PFS 1; RGAL 4; SATA 31

Johnson, Joyce 1935- .... **CLC 58**
   See also CA 125; 129; CANR 102

Johnson, Judith (Emlyn) 1936- .... **CLC 7, 15**
   See also Sherwin, Judith Johnson
   See also CA 25-28R; 153; CANR 34

Johnson, Lionel (Pigot)
   1867-1902 .... **TCLC 19**
   See also CA 117; DLB 19; RGEL 2

Johnson, Marguerite (Annie)
   See Angelou, Maya

Johnson, Mel
   See Malzberg, Barry N(athaniel)

Johnson, Pamela Hansford
   1912-1981 .... **CLC 1, 7, 27**
   See also CA 1-4R; 104; CANR 2, 28; DLB 15; MTCW 1, 2; RGEL 2

Johnson, Paul (Bede) 1928- .... **CLC 147**
   See also BEST 89:4; CA 17-20R; CANR 34, 62, 100

Johnson, Robert .... **CLC 70**

Johnson, Robert 1911(?)-1938 .... **TCLC 69**
   See also BW 3; CA 174

Johnson, Samuel 1709-1784 .... **LC 15, 52; WLC**
   See also BRW 3; BRWR 1; CDBLB 1660-1789; DA; DAB; DAC; DAM MST; DLB 39, 95, 104, 142, 213; RGEL 2; TEA

Johnson, Uwe 1934-1984 .. **CLC 5, 10, 15, 40**
   See also CA 1-4R; 112; CANR 1, 39; CD-WLB 2; DLB 75; MTCW 1; RGWL 2

Johnston, George (Benson) 1913- .... **CLC 51**
   See also CA 1-4R; CANR 5, 20; CP 7; DLB 88

Johnston, Jennifer (Prudence)
1930- .... **CLC 7, 150**
See also CA 85-88; CANR 92; CN 7; DLB 14

Joinville, Jean de 1224(?)-1317 ..... **CMLC 38**

Jolley, (Monica) Elizabeth 1923- ..... **CLC 46; SSC 19**
See also CA 127; CAAS 13; CANR 59; CN 7; RGSF 2

Jones, Arthur Llewellyn 1863-1947
See Machen, Arthur
See also CA 104; 179; HGG

Jones, D(ouglas) G(ordon) 1929- ..... **CLC 10**
See also CA 29-32R; CANR 13, 90; CP 7; DLB 53

Jones, David (Michael) 1895-1974 .... **CLC 2, 4, 7, 13, 42**
See also BRW 6; BRWS 7; CA 9-12R; 53-56; CANR 28; CDBLB 1945-1960; DLB 20, 100; MTCW 1; PAB; RGEL 2

Jones, David Robert 1947-
See Bowie, David
See also CA 103; CANR 104

Jones, Diana Wynne 1934- .... **CLC 26**
See also AAYA 12; BYA 6, 7, 9, 11, 13; CA 49-52; CANR 4, 26, 56; CLR 23; DLB 161; FANT; JRDA; MAICYA 1, 2; SAAS 7; SATA 9, 70, 108; SFW 4; YAW

Jones, Edward P. 1950- .... **CLC 76**
See also BW 2, 3; CA 142; CANR 79; CSW

Jones, Gayl 1949- .... **CLC 6, 9, 131; BLC 2**
See also AFAW 1, 2; BW 2, 3; CA 77-80; CANR 27, 66; CN 7; CSW; DA3; DAM MULT; DLB 33; MTCW 1, 2; RGAL 4

Jones, James 1931-1978 ...... **CLC 1, 3, 10, 39**
See also AITN 1, 2; BPFB 2; CA 1-4R; 69-72; CANR 6; DLB 2, 143; DLBD 17; DLBY 1998; MTCW 1; RGAL 4

Jones, John J.
See Lovecraft, H(oward) P(hillips)

Jones, LeRoi .... **CLC 1, 2, 3, 5, 10, 14**
See Baraka, Amiri
See also MTCW 2

Jones, Louis B. 1953- .... **CLC 65**
See also CA 141; CANR 73

Jones, Madison (Percy, Jr.) 1925- ...... **CLC 4**
See also CA 13-16R; CAAS 11; CANR 7, 54, 83; CN 7; CSW; DLB 152

Jones, Mervyn 1922- .... **CLC 10, 52**
See also CA 45-48; CAAS 5; CANR 1, 91; CN 7; MTCW 1

Jones, Mick 1956(?)- .... **CLC 30**

Jones, Nettie (Pearl) 1941- .... **CLC 34**
See also BW 2; CA 137; CAAS 20; CANR 88

Jones, Preston 1936-1979 .... **CLC 10**
See also CA 73-76; 89-92; DLB 7

Jones, Robert F(rancis) 1934- .... **CLC 7**
See also CA 49-52; CANR 2, 61

Jones, Rod 1953- .... **CLC 50**
See also CA 128

Jones, Terence Graham Parry
1942- .... **CLC 21**
See also Jones, Terry; Monty Python
See also CA 112; 116; CANR 35, 93; INT 116; SATA 127

Jones, Terry
See Jones, Terence Graham Parry
See also SATA 67; SATA-Brief 51

Jones, Thom (Douglas) 1945(?)- .... **CLC 81**
See also CA 157; CANR 88; DLB 244

Jong, Erica 1942- .... **CLC 4, 6, 8, 18, 83**
See also AITN 1; AMWS 5; BEST 90:2; BPFB 2; CA 73-76; CANR 26, 52, 75; CN 7; CP 7; CPW; DA3; DAM NOV, POP; DLB 2, 5, 28, 152; FW; INT CANR-26; MTCW 1, 2

Jonson, Ben(jamin) 1572(?)-1637 .. **LC 6, 33; DC 4; PC 17; WLC**
See also BRW 1; BRWR 1; CDBLB Before 1660; DA; DAB; DAC; DAM DRAM, MST, POET; DFS 4, 10; DLB 62, 121; RGEL 2; WLIT 3

Jordan, June 1936- .... **CLC 5, 11, 23, 114; BLCS; PC 38**
See also Meyer, June
See also AAYA 2; AFAW 1, 2; BW 2, 3; CA 33-36R; CANR 25, 70; CLR 10; CP 7; CWP; DAM MULT, POET; DLB 38; GLL 2; LAIT 5; MAICYA 1, 2; MTCW 1; SATA 4; YAW

Jordan, Neil (Patrick) 1950- .... **CLC 110**
See also CA 124; 130; CANR 54; CN 7; GLL 2; INT 130

Jordan, Pat(rick M.) 1941- .... **CLC 37**
See also CA 33-36R

Jorgensen, Ivar
See Ellison, Harlan (Jay)

Jorgenson, Ivar
See Silverberg, Robert

Joseph, George Ghevarughese .... **CLC 70**

Josephson, Mary
See O'Doherty, Brian

Josephus, Flavius c. 37-100 .... **CMLC 13**
See also AW 2; DLB 176

Josiah Allen's Wife
See Holley, Marietta

Josipovici, Gabriel (David) 1940- ...... **CLC 6, 43, 153**
See also CA 37-40R; CAAS 8; CANR 47, 84; CN 7; DLB 14

Joubert, Joseph 1754-1824 .... **NCLC 9**

Jouve, Pierre Jean 1887-1976 .... **CLC 47**
See also CA 65-68; DLB 258

Jovine, Francesco 1902-1950 .... **TCLC 79**

Joyce, James (Augustine Aloysius)
1882-1941 ... **TCLC 3, 8, 16, 35, 52; DC 16; PC 22; SSC 3, 26, 44; WLC**
See also AAYA 42; BRW 7; BRWR 1; BYA 11, 13; CA 104; 126; CDBLB 1914-1945; DA; DA3; DAB; DAC; DAM MST, NOV, POET; DLB 10, 19, 36, 162, 247; EXPN; EXPS; LAIT 3; MTCW 1, 2; NFS 7; RGSF 2; SSFS 1; WLIT 4

Jozsef, Attila 1905-1937 .... **TCLC 22**
See also CA 116; CDWLB 4; DLB 215

Juana Ines de la Cruz, Sor
1651(?)-1695 ...... **LC 5; HLCS 1; PC 24**
See also FW; LAW; RGWL 2; WLIT 1

Juana Inez de La Cruz, Sor
See Juana Ines de la Cruz, Sor

Judd, Cyril
See Kornbluth, C(yril) M.; Pohl, Frederik

Juenger, Ernst 1895-1998 .... **CLC 125**
See also Junger, Ernst
See also CA 101; 167; CANR 21, 47, 106; DLB 56

Julian of Norwich 1342(?)-1416(?) . **LC 6, 52**
See also DLB 146

Julius Caesar 100B.C.-44B.C.
See Caesar, Julius
See also CDWLB 1; DLB 211

Junger, Ernst
See Juenger, Ernst
See also CDWLB 2; RGWL 2

Junger, Sebastian 1962- .... **CLC 109**
See also AAYA 28; CA 165

Juniper, Alex
See Hospital, Janette Turner

Junius
See Luxemburg, Rosa

Just, Ward (Swift) 1935- .... **CLC 4, 27**
See also CA 25-28R; CANR 32, 87; CN 7; INT CANR-32

Justice, Donald (Rodney) 1925- .. **CLC 6, 19, 102**
See also AMWS 7; CA 5-8R; CANR 26, 54, 74; CP 7; CSW; DAM POET; DLBY 1983; INT CANR-26; MTCW 2; PFS 14

Juvenal c. 60-c. 130 .... **CMLC 8**
See also AW 2; CDWLB 1; DLB 211; RGWL 2

Juvenis
See Bourne, Randolph S(illiman)

Kabakov, Sasha .... **CLC 59**

Kacew, Romain 1914-1980
See Gary, Romain
See also CA 108; 102

Kadare, Ismail 1936- .... **CLC 52**
See also CA 161

Kadohata, Cynthia .... **CLC 59, 122**
See also CA 140

Kafka, Franz 1883-1924 . **TCLC 2, 6, 13, 29, 47, 53, 112; SSC 5, 29, 35; WLC**
See also AAYA 31; BPFB 2; CA 105; 126; CDWLB 2; DA; DA3; DAB; DAC; DAM MST, NOV; DLB 81; EW 9; EXPS; MTCW 1, 2; NFS 7; RGSF 2; RGWL 2; SFW 4; SSFS 3, 7, 12

Kahanovitsch, Pinkhes
See Der Nister

Kahn, Roger 1927- .... **CLC 30**
See also CA 25-28R; CANR 44, 69; DLB 171; SATA 37

Kain, Saul
See Sassoon, Siegfried (Lorraine)

Kaiser, Georg 1878-1945 .... **TCLC 9**
See also CA 106; 190; CDWLB 2; DLB 124; RGWL 2

Kaledin, Sergei .... **CLC 59**

Kaletski, Alexander 1946- .... **CLC 39**
See also CA 118; 143

Kalidasa fl. c. 400-455 .... **CMLC 9; PC 22**
See also RGWL 2

Kallman, Chester (Simon)
1921-1975 .... **CLC 2**
See also CA 45-48; 53-56; CANR 3

Kaminsky, Melvin 1926-
See Brooks, Mel
See also CA 65-68; CANR 16

Kaminsky, Stuart M(elvin) 1934- ..... **CLC 59**
See also CA 73-76; CANR 29, 53, 89; CMW 4

Kandinsky, Wassily 1866-1944 .... **TCLC 92**
See also CA 118; 155

Kane, Francis
See Robbins, Harold

Kane, Henry 1918-
See Queen, Ellery
See also CA 156; CMW 4

Kane, Paul
See Simon, Paul (Frederick)

Kanin, Garson 1912-1999 .... **CLC 22**
See also AITN 1; CA 5-8R; 177; CAD; CANR 7, 78; DLB 7; IDFW 3, 4

Kaniuk, Yoram 1930- .... **CLC 19**
See also CA 134

Kant, Immanuel 1724-1804 ..... **NCLC 27, 67**
See also DLB 94

Kantor, MacKinlay 1904-1977 .... **CLC 7**
See also CA 61-64; 73-76; CANR 60, 63; DLB 9, 102; MTCW 2; RHW; TCWW 2

Kanze Motokiyo
See Zeami

Kaplan, David Michael 1946- .... **CLC 50**
See also CA 187

Kaplan, James 1951- .... **CLC 59**
See also CA 135

Karageorge, Michael
See Anderson, Poul (William)

Karamzin, Nikolai Mikhailovich
1766-1826 .... NCLC **3**
See also DLB 150; RGSF 2

Karapanou, Margarita 1946- .... CLC **13**
See also CA 101

Karinthy, Frigyes 1887-1938 .... TCLC **47**
See also CA 170; DLB 215

Karl, Frederick R(obert) 1927- .... CLC **34**
See also CA 5-8R; CANR 3, 44

Kastel, Warren
See Silverberg, Robert

Kataev, Evgeny Petrovich 1903-1942
See Petrov, Evgeny
See also CA 120

Kataphusin
See Ruskin, John

Katz, Steve 1935- .... CLC **47**
See also CA 25-28R; CAAS 14, 64; CANR
12; CN 7; DLBY 1983

Kauffman, Janet 1945- .... CLC **42**
See also CA 117; CANR 43, 84; DLB 218;
DLBY 1986

Kaufman, Bob (Garnell) 1925-1986 . CLC **49**
See also BW 1; CA 41-44R; 118; CANR
22; DLB 16, 41

Kaufman, George S. 1889-1961 ...... CLC **38**;
DC **17**
See also CA 108; 93-96; DAM DRAM;
DFS 1, 10; DLB 7; INT CA-108; MTCW
2; RGAL 4

Kaufman, Sue .... CLC **3, 8**
See also Barondess, Sue K(aufman)

Kavafis, Konstantinos Petrou 1863-1933
See Cavafy, C(onstantine) P(eter)
See also CA 104

Kavan, Anna 1901-1968 .... CLC **5, 13, 82**
See also BRWS 7; CA 5-8R; CANR 6, 57;
DLB 255; MTCW 1; RGEL 2; SFW 4

Kavanagh, Dan
See Barnes, Julian (Patrick)

Kavanagh, Julie 1952- .... CLC **119**
See also CA 163

Kavanagh, Patrick (Joseph)
1904-1967 .... CLC **22**; PC **33**
See also BRWS 7; CA 123; 25-28R; DLB
15, 20; MTCW 1; RGEL 2

Kawabata, Yasunari 1899-1972 ..... CLC **2, 5,
9, 18, 107**; SSC **17**
See also Kawabata Yasunari
See also CA 93-96; 33-36R; CANR 88;
DAM MULT; MJW; MTCW 2; RGSF 2;
RGWL 2

Kawabata Yasunari
See Kawabata, Yasunari
See also DLB 180

Kaye, M(ary) M(argaret) 1909- .... CLC **28**
See also CA 89-92; CANR 24, 60, 102;
MTCW 1, 2; RHW; SATA 62

Kaye, Mollie
See Kaye, M(ary) M(argaret)

Kaye-Smith, Sheila 1887-1956 .... TCLC **20**
See also CA 118; DLB 36

Kaymor, Patrice Maguilene
See Senghor, Leopold Sedar

Kazakov, Yuri Pavlovich 1927-1982 . SSC **43**
See also CA 5-8R; CANR 36; MTCW 1;
RGSF 2

Kazan, Elia 1909- .... CLC **6, 16, 63**
See also CA 21-24R; CANR 32, 78

Kazantzakis, Nikos 1883(?)-1957 .... TCLC **2,
5, 33**
See also BPFB 2; CA 105; 132; DA3; EW
9; MTCW 1, 2; RGWL 2

Kazin, Alfred 1915-1998 ..... CLC **34, 38, 119**
See also AMWS 8; CA 1-4R; CAAS 7;
CANR 1, 45, 79; DLB 67

Keane, Mary Nesta (Skrine) 1904-1996
See Keane, Molly
See also CA 108; 114; 151; CN 7; RHW

Keane, Molly .... CLC **31**
See also Keane, Mary Nesta (Skrine)
See also INT 114

Keates, Jonathan 1946(?)- .... CLC **34**
See also CA 163

Keaton, Buster 1895-1966 .... CLC **20**
See also CA 194

Keats, John 1795-1821 ... NCLC **8, 73**; PC **1**;
WLC
See also BRW 4; BRWR 1; CDBLB 1789-
1832; DA; DA3; DAB; DAC; DAM MST,
POET; DLB 96, 110; EXPP; PAB; PFS 1,
2, 3, 9; RGEL 2; WLIT 3; WP

Keble, John 1792-1866 .... NCLC **87**
See also DLB 32, 55; RGEL 2

Keene, Donald 1922- .... CLC **34**
See also CA 1-4R; CANR 5

Keillor, Garrison .... CLC **40, 115**
See also Keillor, Gary (Edward)
See also AAYA 2; BEST 89:3; BPFB 2;
DLBY 1987; SATA 58

Keillor, Gary (Edward) 1942-
See Keillor, Garrison
See also CA 111; 117; CANR 36, 59; CPW;
DA3; DAM POP; MTCW 1, 2

Keith, Carlos
See Lewton, Val

Keith, Michael
See Hubbard, L(afayette) Ron(ald)

Keller, Gottfried 1819-1890 .... NCLC **2**; SSC
26
See also CDWLB 2; DLB 129; EW; RGSF
2; RGWL 2

Keller, Nora Okja 1965- .... CLC **109**
See also CA 187

Kellerman, Jonathan 1949- .... CLC **44**
See also AAYA 35; BEST 90:1; CA 106;
CANR 29, 51; CMW 4; CPW; DA3;
DAM POP; INT CANR-29

Kelley, William Melvin 1937- .... CLC **22**
See also BW 1; CA 77-80; CANR 27, 83;
CN 7; DLB 33

Kellogg, Marjorie 1922- .... CLC **2**
See also CA 81-84

Kellow, Kathleen
See Hibbert, Eleanor Alice Burford

Kelly, M(ilton) T(errence) 1947- ...... CLC **55**
See also CA 97-100; CAAS 22; CANR 19,
43, 84; CN 7

Kelly, Robert 1935- .... SSC **50**
See also CA 17-20R; CAAS 19; CANR 47;
CP 7; DLB 5, 130, 165

Kelman, James 1946- .... CLC **58, 86**
See also BRWS 5; CA 148; CANR 85; CN
7; DLB 194; RGSF 2; WLIT 4

Kemal, Yashar 1923- .... CLC **14, 29**
See also CA 89-92; CANR 44; CWW 2

Kemble, Fanny 1809-1893 .... NCLC **18**
See also DLB 32

Kemelman, Harry 1908-1996 .... CLC **2**
See also AITN 1; BPFB 2; CA 9-12R; 155;
CANR 6, 71; CMW 4; DLB 28

Kempe, Margery 1373(?)-1440(?) ... LC **6, 56**
See also DLB 146; RGEL 2

Kempis, Thomas a 1380-1471 .... LC **11**

Kendall, Henry 1839-1882 .... NCLC **12**
See also DLB 230

Keneally, Thomas (Michael) 1935- ... CLC **5,
8, 10, 14, 19, 27, 43, 117**
See also BRWS 4; CA 85-88; CANR 10,
50, 74; CN 7; CPW; DA3; DAM NOV;
MTCW 1, 2; RGEL 2; RHW

Kennedy, Adrienne (Lita) 1931- ..... CLC **66**;
BLC **2**; DC **5**
See also AFAW 2; BW 2, 3; CA 103; CAAS
20; CABS 3; CANR 26, 53, 82; CD 5;
DAM MULT; DFS 9; DLB 38; FW

Kennedy, John Pendleton
1795-1870 .... NCLC **2**
See also DLB 3, 248, 254; RGAL 4

Kennedy, Joseph Charles 1929-
See Kennedy, X. J.
See also CA 1-4R; CAAE 201; CANR 4,
30, 40; CP 7; CWRI 5; MAICYA 2; MAI-
CYAS 1; SATA 14, 86; SATA-Essay 130

Kennedy, William 1928- ... CLC **6, 28, 34, 53**
See also AAYA 1; AMWS 7; BPFB 2; CA
85-88; CANR 14, 31, 76; CN 7; DA3;
DAM NOV; DLB 143; DLBY 1985; INT
CANR-31; MTCW 1, 2; SATA 57

Kennedy, X. J. .... CLC **8, 42**
See also Kennedy, Joseph Charles
See also CAAS 9; CLR 27; DLB 5; SAAS
22

Kenny, Maurice (Francis) 1929- ...... CLC **87**
See also CA 144; CAAS 22; DAM MULT;
DLB 175; NNAL

Kent, Kelvin
See Kuttner, Henry

Kenton, Maxwell
See Southern, Terry

Kenyon, Robert O.
See Kuttner, Henry

Kepler, Johannes 1571-1630 .... LC **45**

Ker, Jill
See Conway, Jill K(er)

Kerkow, H. C.
See Lewton, Val

Kerouac, Jack 1922-1969 ...... CLC **1, 2, 3, 5,
14, 29, 61**; WLC
See also Kerouac, Jean-Louis Lebris de
See also AAYA 25; AMWS 3; BPFB 2;
CDALB 1941-1968; CPW; DLB 2, 16,
237; DLBD 3; DLBY 1995; GLL 1;
MTCW 2; NFS 8; RGAL 4; TCLC 117;
WP

Kerouac, Jean-Louis Lebris de 1922-1969
See Kerouac, Jack
See also AITN 1; CA 5-8R; 25-28R; CANR
26, 54, 95; DA; DA3; DAB; DAC; DAM
MST, NOV, POET, POP; MTCW 1, 2

Kerr, Jean 1923- .... CLC **22**
See also CA 5-8R; CANR 7; INT CANR-7

Kerr, M. E. .... CLC **12, 35**
See also Meaker, Marijane (Agnes)
See also AAYA 2, 23; BYA 1, 7, 8; CLR
29; SAAS 1; WYA

Kerr, Robert .... CLC **55**

Kerrigan, (Thomas) Anthony 1918- .. CLC **4,
6**
See also CA 49-52; CAAS 11; CANR 4

Kerry, Lois
See Duncan, Lois

Kesey, Ken (Elton) 1935-2001 ... CLC **1, 3, 6,
11, 46, 64**; WLC
See also AAYA 25; BPFB 2; CA 1-4R;
CANR 22, 38, 66; CDALB 1968-1988;
CN 7; CPW; DA; DA3; DAB; DAC;
DAM MST, NOV, POP; DLB 2, 16, 206;
EXPN; LAIT 4; MTCW 1, 2; NFS 2;
RGAL 4; SATA 66; SATA-Obit 131; YAW

Kesselring, Joseph (Otto)
1902-1967 .... CLC **45**
See also CA 150; DAM DRAM, MST

Kessler, Jascha (Frederick) 1929- ...... CLC **4**
See also CA 17-20R; CANR 8, 48

Kettelkamp, Larry (Dale) 1933- .... CLC **12**
See also CA 29-32R; CANR 16; SAAS 3;
SATA 2

Key, Ellen (Karolina Sofia)
1849-1926 .... TCLC **65**
See also DLB 259

Keyber, Conny
See Fielding, Henry

Keyes, Daniel 1927- .... **CLC 80**
See also AAYA 23; BYA 11; CA 17-20R, 181; CAAE 181; CANR 10, 26, 54, 74; DA; DA3; DAC; DAM MST, NOV; EXPN; LAIT 4; MTCW 2; NFS 2; SATA 37; SFW 4

Keynes, John Maynard
1883-1946 .... **TCLC 64**
See also CA 114; 162, 163; DLBD 10; MTCW 2

Khanshendel, Chiron
See Rose, Wendy

Khayyam, Omar 1048-1131 ... **CMLC 11; PC 8**
See also Omar Khayyam
See also DA3; DAM POET

Kherdian, David 1931- .... **CLC 6, 9**
See also AAYA 42; CA 21-24R; CAAE 192; CAAS 2; CANR 39, 78; CLR 24; JRDA; LAIT 3; MAICYA 1, 2; SATA 16, 74; SATA-Essay 125

Khlebnikov, Velimir .... **TCLC 20**
See also Khlebnikov, Viktor Vladimirovich
See also EW 10; RGWL 2

Khlebnikov, Viktor Vladimirovich 1885-1922
See Khlebnikov, Velimir
See also CA 117

Khodasevich, Vladislav (Felitsianovich)
1886-1939 .... **TCLC 15**
See also CA 115

Kielland, Alexander Lange
1849-1906 .... **TCLC 5**
See also CA 104

Kiely, Benedict 1919- .... **CLC 23, 43**
See also CA 1-4R; CANR 2, 84; CN 7; DLB 15

Kienzle, William X(avier) 1928- .... **CLC 25**
See also CA 93-96; CAAS 1; CANR 9, 31, 59; CMW 4; DA3; DAM POP; INT CANR-31; MSW; MTCW 1, 2

Kierkegaard, Soren 1813-1855 ..... **NCLC 34, 78**
See also EW 6

Kieslowski, Krzysztof 1941-1996 .... **CLC 120**
See also CA 147; 151

Killens, John Oliver 1916-1987 .... **CLC 10**
See also BW 2; CA 77-80; 123; CAAS 2; CANR 26; DLB 33

Killigrew, Anne 1660-1685 .... **LC 4, 73**
See also DLB 131

Killigrew, Thomas 1612-1683 .... **LC 57**
See also DLB 58; RGEL 2

Kim
See Simenon, Georges (Jacques Christian)

Kincaid, Jamaica 1949- ..... **CLC 43, 68, 137; BLC 2**
See also AAYA 13; AFAW 2; AMWS 7; BRWS 7; BW 2, 3; CA 125; CANR 47, 59, 95; CDALBS; CDWLB 3; CLR 63; CN 7; DA3; DAM MULT, NOV; DLB 157, 227; DNFS 1; EXPS; FW; MTCW 2; NCFS 1; NFS 3; SSFS 5, 7; YAW

King, Francis (Henry) 1923- .... **CLC 8, 53, 145**
See also CA 1-4R; CANR 1, 33, 86; CN 7; DAM NOV; DLB 15, 139; MTCW 1

King, Kennedy
See Brown, George Douglas

King, Martin Luther, Jr.
1929-1968 .... **CLC 83; BLC 2; WLCS**
See also BW 2, 3; CA 25-28; CANR 27, 44; CAP 2; DA; DA3; DAB; DAC; DAM MST, MULT; LAIT 5; MTCW 1, 2; SATA 14

King, Stephen (Edwin) 1947- .... **CLC 12, 26, 37, 61, 113; SSC 17**
See also AAYA 1, 17; AMWS 5; BEST 90:1; BPFB 2; CA 61-64; CANR 1, 30, 52, 76; CPW; DA3; DAM NOV, POP;

DLB 143; DLBY 1980; HGG; JRDA; LAIT 5; MTCW 1, 2; RGAL 4; SATA 9, 55; SUFW; WYAS 1; YAW

King, Steve
See King, Stephen (Edwin)

King, Thomas 1943- .... **CLC 89**
See also CA 144; CANR 95; CCA 1; CN 7; DAC; DAM MULT; DLB 175; NNAL; SATA 96

Kingman, Lee .... **CLC 17**
See also Natti, (Mary) Lee
See also CWRI 5; SAAS 3; SATA 1, 67

Kingsley, Charles 1819-1875 .... **NCLC 35**
See also CLR 77; DLB 21, 32, 163, 178, 190; FANT; MAICYA 2; MAICYAS 1; RGEL 2; WCH; YABC 2

Kingsley, Henry 1830-1876 .... **NCLC 107**
See also DLB 21, 230; RGEL 2

Kingsley, Sidney 1906-1995 .... **CLC 44**
See also CA 85-88; 147; CAD; DFS 14; DLB 7; RGAL 4

Kingsolver, Barbara 1955- . **CLC 55, 81, 130**
See also AAYA 15; AMWS 7; CA 129; 134; CANR 60, 96; CDALBS; CPW; CSW; DA3; DAM POP; DLB 206; INT CA-134; LAIT 5; MTCW 2; NFS 5, 10, 12; RGAL 4

Kingston, Maxine (Ting Ting) Hong
1940- .... **CLC 12, 19, 58, 121; AAL; WLCS**
See also AAYA 8; AMWS 5; BPFB 2; CA 69-72; CANR 13, 38, 74, 87; CDALBS; CN 7; DA3; DAM MULT, NOV; DLB 173, 212; DLBY 1980; FW; INT CANR-13; LAIT 5; MAWW; MTCW 1, 2; NFS 6; RGAL 4; SATA 53; SSFS 3

Kinnell, Galway 1927- ..... **CLC 1, 2, 3, 5, 13, 29, 129; PC 26**
See also AMWS 3; CA 9-12R; CANR 10, 34, 66; CP 7; DLB 5; DLBY 1987; INT CANR-34; MTCW 1, 2; PAB; PFS 9; RGAL 4; WP

Kinsella, Thomas 1928- .... **CLC 4, 19, 138**
See also BRWS 5; CA 17-20R; CANR 15; CP 7; DLB 27; MTCW 1, 2; RGEL 2

Kinsella, W(illiam) P(atrick) 1935- . **CLC 27, 43**
See also AAYA 7; BPFB 2; CA 97-100; CAAS 7; CANR 21, 35, 66, 75; CN 7; CPW; DAC; DAM NOV, POP; FANT; INT CANR-21; LAIT 5; MTCW 1, 2; RGSF 2

Kinsey, Alfred C(harles)
1894-1956 .... **TCLC 91**
See also CA 115; 170; MTCW 2

Kipling, (Joseph) Rudyard
1865-1936 .. **TCLC 8, 17; PC 3; SSC 5; WLC**
See also AAYA 32; BRW 6; BYA 4; CA 105; 120; CANR 33; CDBLB 1890-1914; CLR 39, 65; CWRI 5; DA; DA3; DAB; DAC; DAM MST, POET; DLB 19, 34, 141, 156; EXPS; FANT; LAIT 3; MAICYA 1, 2; MTCW 1, 2; RGEL 2; RGSF 2; SATA 100; SFW 4; SSFS 8; SUFW; WCH; WLIT 4; YABC 2

Kirk, Russell (Amos) 1918-1994 .. **TCLC 119**
See also AITN 1; CA 1-4R; 145; CAAS 9; CANR 1, 20, 60; HGG; INT CANR-20; MTCW 1, 2

Kirkland, Caroline M. 1801-1864 . **NCLC 85**
See also DLB 3, 73, 74, 250, 254; DLBD 13

Kirkup, James 1918- .... **CLC 1**
See also CA 1-4R; CAAS 4; CANR 2; CP 7; DLB 27; SATA 12

Kirkwood, James 1930(?)-1989 .... **CLC 9**
See also AITN 2; CA 1-4R; 128; CANR 6, 40; GLL 2

Kirshner, Sidney
See Kingsley, Sidney

Kis, Danilo 1935-1989 .... **CLC 57**
See also CA 109; 118; 129; CANR 61; CD-WLB 4; DLB 181; MTCW 1; RGSF 2; RGWL 2

Kissinger, Henry A(lfred) 1923- ..... **CLC 137**
See also CA 1-4R; CANR 2, 33, 66, 109; MTCW 1

Kivi, Aleksis 1834-1872 .... **NCLC 30**

Kizer, Carolyn (Ashley) 1925- ... **CLC 15, 39, 80**
See also CA 65-68; CAAS 5; CANR 24, 70; CP 7; CWP; DAM POET; DLB 5, 169; MTCW 2

Klabund 1890-1928 .... **TCLC 44**
See also CA 162; DLB 66

Klappert, Peter 1942- .... **CLC 57**
See also CA 33-36R; CSW; DLB 5

Klein, A(braham) M(oses)
1909-1972 .... **CLC 19**
See also CA 101; 37-40R; DAB; DAC; DAM MST; DLB 68; RGEL 2

Klein, Joe
See Klein, Joseph

Klein, Joseph 1946- .... **CLC 154**
See also CA 85-88; CANR 55

Klein, Norma 1938-1989 .... **CLC 30**
See also AAYA 2, 35; BPFB 2; BYA 6, 7, 8; CA 41-44R; 128; CANR 15, 37; CLR 2, 19; INT CANR-15; JRDA; MAICYA 1, 2; SAAS 1; SATA 7, 57; WYA; YAW

Klein, T(heodore) E(ibon) D(onald)
1947- .... **CLC 34**
See also CA 119; CANR 44, 75; HGG

Kleist, Heinrich von 1777-1811 ...... **NCLC 2, 37; SSC 22**
See also CDWLB 2; DAM DRAM; DLB 90; EW 5; RGSF 2; RGWL 2

Klima, Ivan 1931- .... **CLC 56**
See also CA 25-28R; CANR 17, 50, 91; CDWLB 4; CWW 2; DAM NOV; DLB 232

Klimentov, Andrei Platonovich
1899-1951 .... **TCLC 14; SSC 42**
See also CA 108

Klinger, Friedrich Maximilian von
1752-1831 .... **NCLC 1**
See also DLB 94

Klingsor the Magician
See Hartmann, Sadakichi

Klopstock, Friedrich Gottlieb
1724-1803 .... **NCLC 11**
See also DLB 97; EW 4; RGWL 2

Knapp, Caroline 1959-2002 .... **CLC 99**
See also CA 154

Knebel, Fletcher 1911-1993 .... **CLC 14**
See also AITN 1; CA 1-4R; 140; CAAS 3; CANR 1, 36; SATA 36; SATA-Obit 75

Knickerbocker, Diedrich
See Irving, Washington

Knight, Etheridge 1931-1991 . **CLC 40; BLC 2; PC 14**
See also BW 1, 3; CA 21-24R; 133; CANR 23, 82; DAM POET; DLB 41; MTCW 2; RGAL 4

Knight, Sarah Kemble 1666-1727 .... **LC 7**
See also DLB 24, 200

Knister, Raymond 1899-1932 .... **TCLC 56**
See also CA 186; DLB 68; RGEL 2

Knowles, John 1926-2001 ... **CLC 1, 4, 10, 26**
See also AAYA 10; BPFB 2; BYA 3; CA 17-20R; CANR 40, 74, 76; CDALB 1968-1988; CN 7; DA; DAC; DAM MST, NOV; DLB 6; EXPN; MTCW 1, 2; NFS 2; RGAL 4; SATA 8, 89; YAW

Knox, Calvin M.
See Silverberg, Robert

Knox, John c. 1505-1572 .... **LC 37**
  See also DLB 132
Knye, Cassandra
  See Disch, Thomas M(ichael)
Koch, C(hristopher) J(ohn) 1932- .... **CLC 42**
  See also CA 127; CANR 84; CN 7
Koch, Christopher
  See Koch, C(hristopher) J(ohn)
Koch, Kenneth 1925- .... **CLC 5, 8, 44**
  See also CA 1-4R; CAD; CANR 6, 36, 57,
  97; CD 5; CP 7; DAM POET; DLB 5;
  INT CANR-36; MTCW 2; SATA 65; WP
Kochanowski, Jan 1530-1584 .... **LC 10**
  See also RGWL 2
Kock, Charles Paul de 1794-1871 . **NCLC 16**
Koda Rohan
  See Koda Shigeyuki
Koda Rohan
  See Koda Shigeyuki
  See also DLB 180
Koda Shigeyuki 1867-1947 .... **TCLC 22**
  See also Koda Rohan
  See also CA 121; 183
Koestler, Arthur 1905-1983 ... **CLC 1, 3, 6, 8,
  15, 33**
  See also BRWS 1; CA 1-4R; 109; CANR 1,
  33; CDBLB 1945-1960; DLBY 1983;
  MTCW 1, 2; RGEL 2
Kogawa, Joy Nozomi 1935- ...... **CLC 78, 129**
  See also CA 101; CANR 19, 62; CN 7;
  CWP; DAC; DAM MST, MULT; FW;
  MTCW 2; NFS 3; SATA 99
Kohout, Pavel 1928- .... **CLC 13**
  See also CA 45-48; CANR 3
Koizumi, Yakumo
  See Hearn, (Patricio) Lafcadio (Tessima
  Carlos)
Kolmar, Gertrud 1894-1943 .... **TCLC 40**
  See also CA 167
Komunyakaa, Yusef 1947- .... **CLC 86, 94;
  BLCS**
  See also AFAW 2; CA 147; CANR 83; CP
  7; CSW; DLB 120; PFS 5; RGAL 4
Konrad, George
  See Konrad, Gyorgy
  See also CWW 2
Konrad, Gyorgy 1933- .... **CLC 4, 10, 73**
  See also Konrad, George
  See also CA 85-88; CANR 97; CDWLB 4;
  CWW 2; DLB 232
Konwicki, Tadeusz 1926- .... **CLC 8, 28, 54,
  117**
  See also CA 101; CAAS 9; CANR 39, 59;
  CWW 2; DLB 232; IDFW 3; MTCW 1
Koontz, Dean R(ay) 1945- .... **CLC 78**
  See also AAYA 9, 31; BEST 89:3, 90:2; CA
  108; CANR 19, 36, 52, 95; CMW 4;
  CPW; DA3; DAM NOV, POP; HGG;
  MTCW 1; SATA 92; SFW 4; YAW
Kopernik, Mikolaj
  See Copernicus, Nicolaus
Kopit, Arthur (Lee) 1937- ...... **CLC 1, 18, 33**
  See also AITN 1; CA 81-84; CABS 3; CD
  5; DAM DRAM; DFS 7, 14; DLB 7;
  MTCW 1; RGAL 4
Kops, Bernard 1926- .... **CLC 4**
  See also CA 5-8R; CANR 84; CBD; CN 7;
  CP 7; DLB 13
Kornbluth, C(yril) M. 1923-1958 .... **TCLC 8**
  See also CA 105; 160; DLB 8; SFW 4
Korolenko, V. G.
  See Korolenko, Vladimir Galaktionovich
Korolenko, Vladimir
  See Korolenko, Vladimir Galaktionovich
Korolenko, Vladimir G.
  See Korolenko, Vladimir Galaktionovich
Korolenko, Vladimir Galaktionovich
  1853-1921 .... **TCLC 22**
  See also CA 121

Korzybski, Alfred (Habdank Skarbek)
  1879-1950 .... **TCLC 61**
  See also CA 123; 160
Kosinski, Jerzy (Nikodem)
  1933-1991 .... **CLC 1, 2, 3, 6, 10, 15, 53,
  70**
  See also AMWS 7; BPFB 2; CA 17-20R;
  134; CANR 9, 46; DA3; DAM NOV;
  DLB 2; DLBY 1982; HGG; MTCW 1, 2;
  NFS 12; RGAL 4
Kostelanetz, Richard (Cory) 1940- .. **CLC 28**
  See also CA 13-16R; CAAS 8; CANR 38,
  77; CN 7; CP 7
Kotlowitz, Robert 1924- .... **CLC 4**
  See also CA 33-36R; CANR 36
Kotzebue, August (Friedrich Ferdinand) von
  1761-1819 .... **NCLC 25**
  See also DLB 94
Kotzwinkle, William 1938- ..... **CLC 5, 14, 35**
  See also BPFB 2; CA 45-48; CANR 3, 44,
  84; CLR 6; DLB 173; FANT; MAICYA
  1, 2; SATA 24, 70; SFW 4; YAW
Kowna, Stancy
  See Szymborska, Wislawa
Kozol, Jonathan 1936- .... **CLC 17**
  See also CA 61-64; CANR 16, 45, 96
Kozoll, Michael 1940(?)- .... **CLC 35**
Kramer, Kathryn 19(?)- .... **CLC 34**
Kramer, Larry 1935- .... **CLC 42; DC 8**
  See also CA 124; 126; CANR 60; DAM
  POP; DLB 249; GLL 1
Krasicki, Ignacy 1735-1801 .... **NCLC 8**
Krasinski, Zygmunt 1812-1859 .... **NCLC 4**
  See also RGWL 2
Kraus, Karl 1874-1936 .... **TCLC 5**
  See also CA 104; DLB 118
Kreve (Mickevicius), Vincas
  1882-1954 .... **TCLC 27**
  See also CA 170; DLB 220
Kristeva, Julia 1941- .... **CLC 77, 140**
  See also CA 154; CANR 99; DLB 242; FW
Kristofferson, Kris 1936- .... **CLC 26**
  See also CA 104
Krizanc, John 1956- .... **CLC 57**
  See also CA 187
Krleza, Miroslav 1893-1981 .... **CLC 8, 114**
  See also CA 97-100; 105; CANR 50; CD-
  WLB 4; DLB 147; EW 11; RGWL 2
Kroetsch, Robert 1927- .. **CLC 5, 23, 57, 132**
  See also CA 17-20R; CANR 8, 38; CCA 1;
  CN 7; CP 7; DAC; DAM POET; DLB 53;
  MTCW 1
Kroetz, Franz
  See Kroetz, Franz Xaver
Kroetz, Franz Xaver 1946- .... **CLC 41**
  See also CA 130
Kroker, Arthur (W.) 1945- .... **CLC 77**
  See also CA 161
Kropotkin, Peter (Aleksieevich)
  1842-1921 .... **TCLC 36**
  See also CA 119
Krotkov, Yuri 1917-1981 .... **CLC 19**
  See also CA 102
Krumb
  See Crumb, R(obert)
Krumgold, Joseph (Quincy)
  1908-1980 .... **CLC 12**
  See also BYA 1, 2; CA 9-12R; 101; CANR
  7; MAICYA 1, 2; SATA 1, 48; SATA-Obit
  23; YAW
Krumwitz
  See Crumb, R(obert)
Krutch, Joseph Wood 1893-1970 ..... **CLC 24**
  See also ANW; CA 1-4R; 25-28R; CANR
  4; DLB 63, 206
Krutzch, Gus
  See Eliot, T(homas) S(tearns)

Krylov, Ivan Andreevich
  1768(?)-1844 .... **NCLC 1**
  See also DLB 150
Kubin, Alfred (Leopold Isidor)
  1877-1959 .... **TCLC 23**
  See also CA 112; 149; CANR 104; DLB 81
Kubrick, Stanley 1928-1999 .... **CLC 16**
  See also AAYA 30; CA 81-84; 177; CANR
  33; DLB 26; TCLC 112
Kueng, Hans 1928-
  See Kung, Hans
  See also CA 53-56; CANR 66; MTCW 1, 2
Kumin, Maxine (Winokur) 1925- ..... **CLC 5,
  13, 28; PC 15**
  See also AITN 2; AMWS 4; ANW; CA
  1-4R; CAAS 8; CANR 1, 21, 69; CP 7;
  CWP; DA3; DAM POET; DLB 5; EXPP;
  MTCW 1, 2; PAB; SATA 12
Kundera, Milan 1929- . **CLC 4, 9, 19, 32, 68,
  115, 135; SSC 24**
  See also AAYA 2; BPFB 2; CA 85-88;
  CANR 19, 52, 74; CDWLB 4; CWW 2;
  DA3; DAM NOV; DLB 232; EW 13;
  MTCW 1, 2; RGSF 2; SSFS 10
Kunene, Mazisi (Raymond) 1930- ... **CLC 85**
  See also BW 1, 3; CA 125; CANR 81; CP
  7; DLB 117
Kung, Hans .... **CLC 130**
  See also Kueng, Hans
Kunikida Doppo 1869(?)-1908
  See Doppo, Kunikida
  See also DLB 180
Kunitz, Stanley (Jasspon) 1905- .. **CLC 6, 11,
  14, 148; PC 19**
  See also AMWS 3; CA 41-44R; CANR 26,
  57, 98; CP 7; DA3; DLB 48; INT CANR-
  26; MTCW 1, 2; PFS 11; RGAL 4
Kunze, Reiner 1933- .... **CLC 10**
  See also CA 93-96; CWW 2; DLB 75
Kuprin, Aleksander Ivanovich
  1870-1938 .... **TCLC 5**
  See also CA 104; 182
Kureishi, Hanif 1954(?)- .... **CLC 64, 135**
  See also CA 139; CBD; CD 5; CN 7; DLB
  194, 245; GLL 2; IDFW 4; WLIT 4
Kurosawa, Akira 1910-1998 ..... **CLC 16, 119**
  See also AAYA 11; CA 101; 170; CANR
  46; DAM MULT
Kushner, Tony 1957(?)- .... **CLC 81; DC 10**
  See also AMWS 9; CA 144; CAD; CANR
  74; CD 5; DA3; DAM DRAM; DFS 5;
  DLB 228; GLL 1; LAIT 5; MTCW 2;
  RGAL 4
Kuttner, Henry 1915-1958 .... **TCLC 10**
  See also CA 107; 157; DLB 8; FANT;
  SCFW 2; SFW 4
Kuzma, Greg 1944- .... **CLC 7**
  See also CA 33-36R; CANR 70
Kuzmin, Mikhail 1872(?)-1936 ...... **TCLC 40**
  See also CA 170
Kyd, Thomas 1558-1594 .... **LC 22; DC 3**
  See also BRW 1; DAM DRAM; DLB 62;
  IDTP; RGEL 2; TEA; WLIT 3
Kyprianos, Iossif
  See Samarakis, Antonis
Labrunie, Gerard
  See Nerval, Gerard de
La Bruyere, Jean de 1645-1696 .... **LC 17**
  See also EW 3; GFL Beginnings to 1789
Lacan, Jacques (Marie Emile)
  1901-1981 .... **CLC 75**
  See also CA 121; 104
Laclos, Pierre Ambroise Francois
  1741-1803 .... **NCLC 4, 87**
  See also EW 4; GFL Beginnings to 1789;
  RGWL 2
Lacolere, Francois
  See Aragon, Louis

La Colere, Francois
See Aragon, Louis
La Deshabilleuse
See Simenon, Georges (Jacques Christian)
Lady Gregory
See Gregory, Lady Isabella Augusta (Persse)
Lady of Quality, A
See Bagnold, Enid
La Fayette, Marie-(Madelaine Pioche de la Vergne) 1634-1693 .... **LC 2**
See also GFL Beginnings to 1789; RGWL 2
Lafayette, Rene
See Hubbard, L(afayette) Ron(ald)
La Fontaine, Jean de 1621-1695 .... **LC 50**
See also EW 3; GFL Beginnings to 1789; MAICYA 1, 2; RGWL 2; SATA 18
Laforgue, Jules 1860-1887 . **NCLC 5, 53; PC 14; SSC 20**
See also DLB 217; EW 7; GFL 1789 to the Present; RGWL 2
Layamon
See Layamon
See also DLB 146
Lagerkvist, Paer (Fabian) 1891-1974 .... **CLC 7, 10, 13, 54**
See also Lagerkvist, Par
See also CA 85-88; 49-52; DA3; DAM DRAM, NOV; MTCW 1, 2
Lagerkvist, Par .... **SSC 12**
See also Lagerkvist, Paer (Fabian)
See also DLB 259; EW 10; MTCW 2; RGSF 2; RGWL 2
Lagerloef, Selma (Ottiliana Lovisa) 1858-1940 .... **TCLC 4, 36**
See also Lagerlof, Selma (Ottiliana Lovisa)
See also CA 108; MTCW 2; SATA 15
Lagerlof, Selma (Ottiliana Lovisa)
See Lagerloef, Selma (Ottiliana Lovisa)
See also CLR 7; SATA 15
La Guma, (Justin) Alex(ander) 1925-1985 .... **CLC 19; BLCS**
See also AFW; BW 1, 3; CA 49-52; 118; CANR 25, 81; CDWLB 3; DAM NOV; DLB 117, 225; MTCW 1, 2; WLIT 2
Laidlaw, A. K.
See Grieve, C(hristopher) M(urray)
Lainez, Manuel Mujica
See Mujica Lainez, Manuel
See also HW 1
Laing, R(onald) D(avid) 1927-1989 . **CLC 95**
See also CA 107; 129; CANR 34; MTCW 1
Lamartine, Alphonse (Marie Louis Prat) de 1790-1869 .... **NCLC 11; PC 16**
See also DAM POET; DLB 217; GFL 1789 to the Present; RGWL 2
Lamb, Charles 1775-1834 .. **NCLC 10; WLC**
See also BRW 4; CDBLB 1789-1832; DA; DAB; DAC; DAM MST; DLB 93, 107, 163; RGEL 2; SATA 17
Lamb, Lady Caroline 1785-1828 ... **NCLC 38**
See also DLB 116
Lamming, George (William) 1927- ... **CLC 2, 4, 66, 144; BLC 2**
See also BW 2, 3; CA 85-88; CANR 26, 76; CDWLB 3; CN 7; DAM MULT; DLB 125; MTCW 1, 2; RGEL 2
L'Amour, Louis (Dearborn) 1908-1988 .... **CLC 25, 55**
See also Burns, Tex; Mayo, Jim
See also AAYA 16; AITN 2; BEST 89:2; BPFB 2; CA 1-4R; 125; CANR 3, 25, 40; CPW; DA3; DAM NOV, POP; DLB 206; DLBY 1980; MTCW 1, 2; RGAL 4
Lampedusa, Giuseppe (Tomasi) di .... **TCLC 13**
See also Tomasi di Lampedusa, Giuseppe
See also CA 164; EW 11; MTCW 2; RGWL 2

Lampman, Archibald 1861-1899 ... **NCLC 25**
See also DLB 92; RGEL 2
Lancaster, Bruce 1896-1963 .... **CLC 36**
See also CA 9-10; CANR 70; CAP 1; SATA 9
Lanchester, John .... **CLC 99**
See also CA 194
Landau, Mark Alexandrovich
See Aldanov, Mark (Alexandrovich)
Landau-Aldanov, Mark Alexandrovich
See Aldanov, Mark (Alexandrovich)
Landis, Jerry
See Simon, Paul (Frederick)
Landis, John 1950- .... **CLC 26**
See also CA 112; 122
Landolfi, Tommaso 1908-1979 .... **CLC 11, 49**
See also CA 127; 117; DLB 177
Landon, Letitia Elizabeth 1802-1838 .... **NCLC 15**
See also DLB 96
Landor, Walter Savage 1775-1864 .... **NCLC 14**
See also BRW 4; DLB 93, 107; RGEL 2
Landwirth, Heinz 1927-
See Lind, Jakov
See also CA 9-12R; CANR 7
Lane, Patrick 1939- .... **CLC 25**
See also CA 97-100; CANR 54; CP 7; DAM POET; DLB 53; INT 97-100
Lang, Andrew 1844-1912 .... **TCLC 16**
See also CA 114; 137; CANR 85; DLB 98, 141, 184; FANT; MAICYA 1, 2; RGEL 2; SATA 16; WCH
Lang, Fritz 1890-1976 .... **CLC 20, 103**
See also CA 77-80; 69-72; CANR 30
Lange, John
See Crichton, (John) Michael
Langer, Elinor 1939- .... **CLC 34**
See also CA 121
Langland, William 1332(?)-1400(?) ..... **LC 19**
See also BRW 1; DA; DAB; DAC; DAM MST, POET; DLB 146; RGEL 2; WLIT 3
Langstaff, Launcelot
See Irving, Washington
Lanier, Sidney 1842-1881 .... **NCLC 6**
See also AMWS 1; DAM POET; DLB 64; DLBD 13; EXPP; MAICYA 1; PFS 14; RGAL 4; SATA 18
Lanyer, Aemilia 1569-1645 .... **LC 10, 30**
See also DLB 121
Lao-Tzu
See Lao Tzu
Lao Tzu c. 6th cent. B.C.-3rd cent. B.C. .... **CMLC 7**
Lapine, James (Elliot) 1949- .... **CLC 39**
See also CA 123; 130; CANR 54; INT 130
Larbaud, Valery (Nicolas) 1881-1957 .... **TCLC 9**
See also CA 106; 152; GFL 1789 to the Present
Lardner, Ring
See Lardner, Ring(gold) W(ilmer)
See also BPFB 2; CDALB 1917-1929; DLB 11, 25, 86, 171; DLBD 16; RGAL 4; RGSF 2
Lardner, Ring W., Jr.
See Lardner, Ring(gold) W(ilmer)
Lardner, Ring(gold) W(ilmer) 1885-1933 .... **TCLC 2, 14; SSC 32**
See also Lardner, Ring
See also AMW; CA 104; 131; MTCW 1, 2
Laredo, Betty
See Codrescu, Andrei
Larkin, Maia
See Wojciechowska, Maia (Teresa)

Larkin, Philip (Arthur) 1922-1985 ... **CLC 3, 5, 8, 9, 13, 18, 33, 39, 64; PC 21**
See also BRWS 1; CA 5-8R; 117; CANR 24, 62; CDBLB 1960 to Present; DA3; DAB; DAM MST, POET; DLB 27; MTCW 1, 2; PFS 3, 4, 12; RGEL 2
Larra (y Sanchez de Castro), Mariano Jose de 1809-1837 .... **NCLC 17**
Larsen, Eric 1941- .... **CLC 55**
See also CA 132
Larsen, Nella 1893-1963 ...... **CLC 37; BLC 2**
See also AFAW 1, 2; BW 1; CA 125; CANR 83; DAM MULT; DLB 51; FW
Larson, Charles R(aymond) 1938- ... **CLC 31**
See also CA 53-56; CANR 4
Larson, Jonathan 1961-1996 .... **CLC 99**
See also AAYA 28; CA 156
Las Casas, Bartolome de 1474-1566 . **LC 31; HLCS**
See also Casas, Bartolome de las
See also LAW
Lasch, Christopher 1932-1994 .... **CLC 102**
See also CA 73-76; 144; CANR 25; DLB 246; MTCW 1, 2
Lasker-Schueler, Else 1869-1945 ... **TCLC 57**
See also CA 183; DLB 66, 124
Laski, Harold J(oseph) 1893-1950 . **TCLC 79**
See also CA 188
Latham, Jean Lee 1902-1995 .... **CLC 12**
See also AITN 1; BYA 1; CA 5-8R; CANR 7, 84; CLR 50; MAICYA 1, 2; SATA 2, 68; YAW
Latham, Mavis
See Clark, Mavis Thorpe
Lathen, Emma .... **CLC 2**
See also Hennissart, Martha; Latsis, Mary J(ane)
See also BPFB 2; CMW 4
Lathrop, Francis
See Leiber, Fritz (Reuter, Jr.)
Latsis, Mary J(ane) 1927(?)-1997
See Lathen, Emma
See also CA 85-88; 162; CMW 4
Lattany, Kristin
See Lattany, Kristin (Elaine Eggleston) Hunter
Lattany, Kristin (Elaine Eggleston) Hunter 1931- .... **CLC 35**
See also AITN 1; BW 1; BYA 3; CA 13-16R; CANR 13, 108; CLR 3; CN 7; DLB 33; INT CANR-13; MAICYA 1, 2; SAAS 10; SATA 12; YAW
Lattimore, Richmond (Alexander) 1906-1984 .... **CLC 3**
See also CA 1-4R; 112; CANR 1
Laughlin, James 1914-1997 .... **CLC 49**
See also CA 21-24R; 162; CAAS 22; CANR 9, 47; CP 7; DLB 48; DLBY 1996, 1997
Laurence, (Jean) Margaret (Wemyss) 1926-1987 . **CLC 3, 6, 13, 50, 62; SSC 7**
See also BYA 13; CA 5-8R; 121; CANR 33; DAC; DAM MST; DLB 53; FW; MTCW 1, 2; NFS 11; RGEL 2; RGSF 2; SATA-Obit 50; TCWW 2
Laurent, Antoine 1952- .... **CLC 50**
Lauscher, Hermann
See Hesse, Hermann
Lautreamont 1846-1870 .. **NCLC 12; SSC 14**
See also Lautreamont, Isidore Lucien Ducasse
See also GFL 1789 to the Present; RGWL 2
Lautreamont, Isidore Lucien Ducasse
See Lautreamont
See also DLB 217
Laverty, Donald
See Blish, James (Benjamin)

Lavin, Mary 1912-1996 . **CLC 4, 18, 99; SSC 4**
> See also CA 9-12R; 151; CANR 33; CN 7; DLB 15; FW; MTCW 1; RGEL 2; RGSF 2

Lavond, Paul Dennis
> See Kornbluth, C(yril) M.; Pohl, Frederik

Lawler, Raymond Evenor 1922- .... **CLC 58**
> See also CA 103; CD 5; RGEL 2

Lawrence, D(avid) H(erbert Richards) 1885-1930 .... **TCLC 2, 9, 16, 33, 48, 61, 93; SSC 4, 19; WLC**
> See also Chambers, Jessie
> See also BPFB 2; BRW 7; BRWR 2; CA 104; 121; CDBLB 1914-1945; DA; DA3; DAB; DAC; DAM MST, NOV, POET; DLB 10, 19, 36, 98, 162, 195; EXPP; EXPS; LAIT 2, 3; MTCW 1, 2; PFS 6; RGEL 2; RGSF 2; SSFS 2, 6; WLIT 4; WP

Lawrence, T(homas) E(dward) 1888-1935 .... **TCLC 18**
> See also Dale, Colin
> See also BRWS 2; CA 115; 167; DLB 195

Lawrence of Arabia
> See Lawrence, T(homas) E(dward)

Lawson, Henry (Archibald Hertzberg) 1867-1922 .... **TCLC 27; SSC 18**
> See also CA 120; 181; DLB 230; RGEL 2; RGSF 2

Lawton, Dennis
> See Faust, Frederick (Schiller)

Laxness, Halldor .... **CLC 25**
> See also Gudjonsson, Halldor Kiljan
> See also EW 12; RGWL 2

Layamon fl. c. 1200- .... **CMLC 10**
> See also Layamon
> See also RGEL 2

Laye, Camara 1928-1980 ... **CLC 4, 38; BLC 2**
> See also AFW; BW 1; CA 85-88; 97-100; CANR 25; DAM MULT; MTCW 1, 2; WLIT 2

Layton, Irving (Peter) 1912- .... **CLC 2, 15**
> See also CA 1-4R; CANR 2, 33, 43, 66; CP 7; DAC; DAM MST, POET; DLB 88; MTCW 1, 2; PFS 12; RGEL 2

Lazarus, Emma 1849-1887 ...... **NCLC 8, 109**

Lazarus, Felix
> See Cable, George Washington

Lazarus, Henry
> See Slavitt, David R(ytman)

Lea, Joan
> See Neufeld, John (Arthur)

Leacock, Stephen (Butler) 1869-1944 .... **TCLC 2; SSC 39**
> See also CA 104; 141; CANR 80; DAC; DAM MST; DLB 92; MTCW 2; RGEL 2; RGSF 2

Lead, Jane Ward 1623-1704 .... **LC 72**
> See also DLB 131

Lear, Edward 1812-1888 .... **NCLC 3**
> See also BRW 5; CLR 1, 75; DLB 32, 163, 166; MAICYA 1, 2; RGEL 2; SATA 18, 100; WCH; WP

Lear, Norman (Milton) 1922- .... **CLC 12**
> See also CA 73-76

Leautaud, Paul 1872-1956 .... **TCLC 83**
> See also DLB 65; GFL 1789 to the Present

Leavis, F(rank) R(aymond) 1895-1978 .... **CLC 24**
> See also BRW 7; CA 21-24R; 77-80; CANR 44; DLB 242; MTCW 1, 2; RGEL 2

Leavitt, David 1961- .... **CLC 34**
> See also CA 116; 122; CANR 50, 62, 101; CPW; DA3; DAM POP; DLB 130; GLL 1; INT 122; MTCW 2

Leblanc, Maurice (Marie Emile) 1864-1941 .... **TCLC 49**
> See also CA 110; CMW 4

Lebowitz, Fran(ces Ann) 1951(?)- ... **CLC 11, 36**
> See also CA 81-84; CANR 14, 60, 70; INT CANR-14; MTCW 1

Lebrecht, Peter
> See Tieck, (Johann) Ludwig

le Carre, John .... **CLC 3, 5, 9, 15, 28**
> See also Cornwell, David (John Moore)
> See also AAYA 42; BEST 89:4; BPFB 2; BRWS; CDBLB 1960 to Present; CMW 4; CN 7; CPW; DLB 87; MSW; MTCW 2; RGEL 2

Le Clezio, J(ean) M(arie) G(ustave) 1940- .... **CLC 31, 155**
> See also CA 116; 128; DLB 83; GFL 1789 to the Present; RGSF 2

Leconte de Lisle, Charles-Marie-Rene 1818-1894 .... **NCLC 29**
> See also DLB 217; EW 6; GFL 1789 to the Present

Le Coq, Monsieur
> See Simenon, Georges (Jacques Christian)

Leduc, Violette 1907-1972 .... **CLC 22**
> See also CA 13-14; 33-36R; CANR 69; CAP 1; GFL 1789 to the Present; GLL 1

Ledwidge, Francis 1887(?)-1917 .... **TCLC 23**
> See also CA 123; DLB 20

Lee, Andrea 1953- .... **CLC 36; BLC 2**
> See also BW 1, 3; CA 125; CANR 82; DAM MULT

Lee, Andrew
> See Auchincloss, Louis (Stanton)

Lee, Chang-rae 1965- .... **CLC 91**
> See also CA 148; CANR 89

Lee, Don L. .... **CLC 2**
> See also Madhubuti, Haki R.

Lee, George W(ashington) 1894-1976 .... **CLC 52; BLC 2**
> See also BW 1; CA 125; CANR 83; DAM MULT; DLB 51

Lee, (Nelle) Harper 1926- .... **CLC 12, 60; WLC**
> See also AAYA 13; AMWS 8; BPFB 2; BYA 3; CA 13-16R; CANR 51; CDALB 1941-1968; CSW; DA; DA3; DAB; DAC; DAM MST, NOV; DLB 6; EXPN; LAIT 3; MTCW 1, 2; NFS 2; SATA 11; WYA; YAW

Lee, Helen Elaine 1959(?)- .... **CLC 86**
> See also CA 148

Lee, John .... **CLC 70**

Lee, Julian
> See Latham, Jean Lee

Lee, Larry
> See Lee, Lawrence

Lee, Laurie 1914-1997 .... **CLC 90**
> See also CA 77-80; 158; CANR 33, 73; CP 7; CPW; DAB; DAM POP; DLB 27; MTCW 1; RGEL 2

Lee, Lawrence 1941-1990 .... **CLC 34**
> See also CA 131; CANR 43

Lee, Li-Young 1957- .... **PC 24**
> See also CA 153; CP 7; DLB 165; PFS 11

Lee, Manfred B(ennington) 1905-1971 .... **CLC 11**
> See also Queen, Ellery
> See also CA 1-4R; 29-32R; CANR 2; CMW 4; DLB 137

Lee, Shelton Jackson 1957(?)- .... **CLC 105; BLCS**
> See also Lee, Spike
> See also BW 2, 3; CA 125; CANR 42; DAM MULT

Lee, Spike
> See Lee, Shelton Jackson
> See also AAYA 4, 29

Lee, Stan 1922- .... **CLC 17**
> See also AAYA 5; CA 108; 111; INT 111

Lee, Tanith 1947- .... **CLC 46**
> See also AAYA 15; CA 37-40R; CANR 53, 102; FANT; SATA 8, 88; SFW 4; SUFW; YAW

Lee, Vernon .... **TCLC 5; SSC 33**
> See also Paget, Violet
> See also DLB 57, 153, 156, 174, 178; GLL 1; SUFW

Lee, William
> See Burroughs, William S(eward)
> See also GLL 1

Lee, Willy
> See Burroughs, William S(eward)
> See also GLL 1

Lee-Hamilton, Eugene (Jacob) 1845-1907 .... **TCLC 22**
> See also CA 117

Leet, Judith 1935- .... **CLC 11**
> See also CA 187

Le Fanu, Joseph Sheridan 1814-1873 .... **NCLC 9, 58; SSC 14**
> See also CMW 4; DA3; DAM POP; DLB 21, 70, 159, 178; HGG; RGEL 2; RGSF 2; SUFW

Leffland, Ella 1931- .... **CLC 19**
> See also CA 29-32R; CANR 35, 78, 82; DLBY 1984; INT CANR-35; SATA 65

Leger, Alexis
> See Leger, (Marie-Rene Auguste) Alexis Saint-Leger

Leger, (Marie-Rene Auguste) Alexis Saint-Leger 1887-1975 .. **CLC 4, 11, 46; PC 23**
> See also Perse, Saint-John; Saint-John Perse
> See also CA 13-16R; 61-64; CANR 43; DAM POET; MTCW 1

Leger, Saintleger
> See Leger, (Marie-Rene Auguste) Alexis Saint-Leger

Le Guin, Ursula K(roeber) 1929- ..... **CLC 8, 13, 22, 45, 71, 136; SSC 12**
> See also AAYA 9, 27; AITN 1; BPFB 2; BYA 5, 8, 11, 14; CA 21-24R; CANR 9, 32, 52, 74; CDALB 1968-1988; CLR 3, 28; CN 7; CPW; DA3; DAB; DAC; DAM MST, POP; DLB 8, 52, 256; EXPS; FANT; FW; INT CANR-32; JRDA; LAIT 5; MAICYA 1, 2; MTCW 1, 2; NFS 6, 9; SATA 4, 52, 99; SCFW; SFW 4; SSFS 2; SUFW; WYA; YAW

Lehmann, Rosamond (Nina) 1901-1990 .... **CLC 5**
> See also CA 77-80; 131; CANR 8, 73; DLB 15; MTCW 2; RGEL 2; RHW

Leiber, Fritz (Reuter, Jr.) 1910-1992 .... **CLC 25**
> See also BPFB 2; CA 45-48; 139; CANR 2, 40, 86; DLB 8; FANT; HGG; MTCW 1, 2; SATA 45; SATA-Obit 73; SCFW 2; SFW 4; SUFW

Leibniz, Gottfried Wilhelm von 1646-1716 .... **LC 35**
> See also DLB 168

Leimbach, Martha 1963-
> See Leimbach, Marti
> See also CA 130

Leimbach, Marti .... **CLC 65**
> See also Leimbach, Martha

Leino, Eino .... **TCLC 24**
> See also Loennbohm, Armas Eino Leopold

Leiris, Michel (Julien) 1901-1990 ..... **CLC 61**
> See also CA 119; 128; 132; GFL 1789 to the Present

Leithauser, Brad 1953- .... **CLC 27**
> See also CA 107; CANR 27, 81; CP 7; DLB 120

Lelchuk, Alan 1938- .... **CLC 5**
 See also CA 45-48; CAAS 20; CANR 1,
 70; CN 7

Lem, Stanislaw 1921- ..... **CLC 8, 15, 40, 149**
 See also CA 105; CAAS 1; CANR 32;
 CWW 2; MTCW 1; SCFW 2; SFW 4

Lemann, Nancy 1956- .... **CLC 39**
 See also CA 118; 136

Lemonnier, (Antoine Louis) Camille
 1844-1913 .... **TCLC 22**
 See also CA 121

Lenau, Nikolaus 1802-1850 .... **NCLC 16**

L'Engle, Madeleine (Camp Franklin)
 1918- .... **CLC 12**
 See also AAYA 28; AITN 2; BPFB 2; BYA
 2, 4, 5, 7; CA 1-4R; CANR 3, 21, 39, 66,
 107; CLR 1, 14, 57; CPW; CWRI 5; DA3;
 DAM POP; DLB 52; JRDA; MAICYA 1,
 2; MTCW 1, 2; SAAS 15; SATA 1, 27,
 75, 128; SFW 4; WYA; YAW

Lengyel, Jozsef 1896-1975 .... **CLC 7**
 See also CA 85-88; 57-60; CANR 71;
 RGSF 2

Lenin 1870-1924
 See Lenin, V. I.
 See also CA 121; 168

Lenin, V. I. .... **TCLC 67**
 See also Lenin

Lennon, John (Ono) 1940-1980 .. **CLC 12, 35**
 See also CA 102; SATA 114

Lennox, Charlotte Ramsay
 1729(?)-1804 .... **NCLC 23**
 See also DLB 39; RGEL 2

Lentricchia, Frank, (Jr.) 1940- .... **CLC 34**
 See also CA 25-28R; CANR 19, 106; DLB
 246

Lenz, Gunter .... **CLC 65**

Lenz, Siegfried 1926- .... **CLC 27; SSC 33**
 See also CA 89-92; CANR 80; CWW 2;
 DLB 75; RGSF 2; RGWL 2

Leon, David
 See Jacob, (Cyprien-)Max

Leonard, Elmore (John, Jr.) 1925- . **CLC 28,
 34, 71, 120**
 See also AAYA 22; AITN 1; BEST 89:1,
 90:4; BPFB 2; CA 81-84; CANR 12, 28,
 53, 76, 96; CMW 4; CN 7; CPW; DA3;
 DAM POP; DLB 173, 226; INT CANR-
 28; MSW; MTCW 1, 2; RGAL 4; TCWW
 2

Leonard, Hugh .... **CLC 19**
 See Byrne, John Keyes
 See also CBD; CD 5; DFS 13; DLB 13

Leonov, Leonid (Maximovich)
 1899-1994 .... **CLC 92**
 See also CA 129; CANR 74, 76; DAM
 NOV; MTCW 1, 2

Leopardi, (Conte) Giacomo
 1798-1837 .... **NCLC 22; PC 37**
 See also EW 5; RGWL 2; WP

Le Reveler
 See Artaud, Antonin (Marie Joseph)

Lerman, Eleanor 1952- .... **CLC 9**
 See also CA 85-88; CANR 69

Lerman, Rhoda 1936- .... **CLC 56**
 See also CA 49-52; CANR 70

Lermontov, Mikhail Iur'evich
 See Lermontov, Mikhail Yuryevich
 See also DLB 205

Lermontov, Mikhail Yuryevich
 1814-1841 .... **NCLC 5, 47; PC 18**
 See also Lermontov, Mikhail Iur'evich
 See also EW 6; RGWL 2

Leroux, Gaston 1868-1927 .... **TCLC 25**
 See also CA 108; 136; CANR 69; CMW 4;
 SATA 65

Lesage, Alain-Rene 1668-1747 .... **LC 2, 28**
 See also EW 3; GFL Beginnings to 1789;
 RGWL 2

Leskov, N(ikolai) S(emenovich) 1831-1895
 See Leskov, Nikolai (Semyonovich)

Leskov, Nikolai (Semyonovich)
 1831-1895 .... **NCLC 25; SSC 34**
 See also Leskov, Nikolai Semenovich

Leskov, Nikolai Semenovich
 See Leskov, Nikolai (Semyonovich)
 See also DLB 238

Lesser, Milton
 See Marlowe, Stephen

Lessing, Doris (May) 1919- ... **CLC 1, 2, 3, 6,
 10, 15, 22, 40, 94; SSC 6; WLCS**
 See also AFW; BRWS 1; CA 9-12R; CAAS
 14; CANR 33, 54, 76; CD 5; CDBLB
 1960 to Present; CN 7; DA; DA3; DAB;
 DAC; DAM MST, NOV; DLB 15, 139;
 DLBY 1985; EXPS; FW; LAIT 4; MTCW
 1, 2; RGEL 2; RGSF 2; SFW 4; SSFS 1,
 12; WLIT 2, 4

Lessing, Gotthold Ephraim 1729-1781 . **LC 8**
 See also CDWLB 2; DLB 97; EW 4; RGWL
 2

Lester, Richard 1932- .... **CLC 20**

Levenson, Jay .... **CLC 70**

Lever, Charles (James)
 1806-1872 .... **NCLC 23**
 See also DLB 21; RGEL 2

Leverson, Ada 1865(?)-1936(?) .... **TCLC 18**
 See also Elaine
 See also CA 117; DLB 153; RGEL 2

Levertov, Denise 1923-1997 .. **CLC 1, 2, 3, 5,
 8, 15, 28, 66; PC 11**
 See also AMWS 3; CA 1-4R; 178; 163;
 CAAE 178; CAAS 19; CANR 3, 29, 50,
 108; CDALBS; CP 7; CWP; DAM POET;
 DLB 5, 165; EXPP; FW; INT CANR-29;
 MTCW 1, 2; PAB; PFS 7; RGAL 4; WP

Levi, Jonathan .... **CLC 76**
 See also CA 197

Levi, Peter (Chad Tigar)
 1931-2000 .... **CLC 41**
 See also CA 5-8R; 187; CANR 34, 80; CP
 7; DLB 40

Levi, Primo 1919-1987 . **CLC 37, 50; SSC 12**
 See also CA 13-16R; 122; CANR 12, 33,
 61, 70; DLB 177; MTCW 1, 2; RGWL 2;
 TCLC 109

Levin, Ira 1929- .... **CLC 3, 6**
 See also CA 21-24R; CANR 17, 44, 74;
 CMW 4; CN 7; CPW; DA3; DAM POP;
 HGG; MTCW 1, 2; SATA 66; SFW 4

Levin, Meyer 1905-1981 .... **CLC 7**
 See also AITN 1; CA 9-12R; 104; CANR
 15; DAM POP; DLB 9, 28; DLBY 1981;
 SATA 21; SATA-Obit 27

Levine, Norman 1924- .... **CLC 54**
 See also CA 73-76; CAAS 23; CANR 14,
 70; DLB 88

Levine, Philip 1928- .. **CLC 2, 4, 5, 9, 14, 33,
 118; PC 22**
 See also AMWS 5; CA 9-12R; CANR 9,
 37, 52; CP 7; DAM POET; DLB 5; PFS 8

Levinson, Deirdre 1931- .... **CLC 49**
 See also CA 73-76; CANR 70

Levi-Strauss, Claude 1908- .... **CLC 38**
 See also CA 1-4R; CANR 6, 32, 57; DLB
 242; GFL 1789 to the Present; MTCW 1,
 2

Levitin, Sonia (Wolff) 1934- .... **CLC 17**
 See also AAYA 13; CA 29-32R; CANR 14,
 32, 79; CLR 53; JRDA; MAICYA 1, 2;
 SAAS 2; SATA 4, 68, 119; SATA-Essay
 131; YAW

Levon, O. U.
 See Kesey, Ken (Elton)

Levy, Amy 1861-1889 .... **NCLC 59**
 See also DLB 156, 240

Lewes, George Henry 1817-1878 ... **NCLC 25**
 See also DLB 55, 144

Lewis, Alun 1915-1944 .... **TCLC 3; SSC 40**
 See also BRW 7; CA 104; 188; DLB 20,
 162; PAB; RGEL 2

Lewis, C. Day
 See Day Lewis, C(ecil)

Lewis, C(live) S(taples) 1898-1963 .... **CLC 1,
 3, 6, 14, 27, 124; WLC**
 See also AAYA 3, 39; BPFB 2; BRWS 3;
 CA 81-84; CANR 33, 71; CDBLB 1945-
 1960; CLR 3, 27; CWRI 5; DA; DA3;
 DAB; DAC; DAM MST, NOV, POP;
 DLB 15, 100, 160, 255; FANT; JRDA;
 MAICYA 1, 2; MTCW 1, 2; RGEL 2;
 SATA 13, 100; SCFW; SFW 4; SUFW;
 WCH; WYA; YAW

Lewis, Cecil Day
 See Day Lewis, C(ecil)

Lewis, Janet 1899-1998 .... **CLC 41**
 See also Winters, Janet Lewis
 See also CA 9-12R; 172; CANR 29, 63;
 CAP 1; CN 7; DLBY 1987; RHW;
 TCWW 2

Lewis, Matthew Gregory
 1775-1818 .... **NCLC 11, 62**
 See also DLB 39, 158, 178; HGG; RGEL
 2; SUFW

Lewis, (Harry) Sinclair 1885-1951 . **TCLC 4,
 13, 23, 39; WLC**
 See also AMW; BPFB 2; CA 104; 133;
 CDALB 1917-1929; DA; DA3; DAB;
 DAC; DAM MST, NOV; DLB 9, 102;
 DLBD 1; LAIT 3; MTCW 1, 2; RGAL 4

Lewis, (Percy) Wyndham
 1884(?)-1957 .... **TCLC 2, 9, 104; SSC 34**
 See also BRW 7; CA 104; 157; DLB 15;
 FANT; MTCW 2; RGEL 2

Lewisohn, Ludwig 1883-1955 .... **TCLC 19**
 See also CA 107; DLB 4, 9, 28, 102

Lewton, Val 1904-1951 .... **TCLC 76**
 See also CA 199; IDFW 3, 4

Leyner, Mark 1956- .... **CLC 92**
 See also CA 110; CANR 28, 53; DA3;
 MTCW 2

Lezama Lima, Jose 1910-1976 .... **CLC 4, 10,
 101; HLCS 2**
 See also CA 77-80; CANR 71; DAM
 MULT; DLB 113; HW 1, 2; LAW; RGWL
 2

L'Heureux, John (Clarke) 1934- ...... **CLC 52**
 See also CA 13-16R; CANR 23, 45, 88;
 DLB 244

Liddell, C. H.
 See Kuttner, Henry

Lie, Jonas (Lauritz Idemil)
 1833-1908(?) .... **TCLC 5**
 See also CA 115

Lieber, Joel 1937-1971 .... **CLC 6**
 See also CA 73-76; 29-32R

Lieber, Stanley Martin
 See Lee, Stan

Lieberman, Laurence (James)
 1935- .... **CLC 4, 36**
 See also CA 17-20R; CANR 8, 36, 89; CP
 7

Lieh Tzu fl. 7th cent. B.C.-5th cent.
 B.C. .... **CMLC 27**

Lieksman, Anders
 See Haavikko, Paavo Juhani

Li Fei-kan 1904-
 See Pa Chin
 See also CA 105

Lifton, Robert Jay 1926- .... **CLC 67**
 See also CA 17-20R; CANR 27, 78; INT
 CANR-27; SATA 66

Lightfoot, Gordon 1938- .... **CLC 26**
 See also CA 109

Lightman, Alan P(aige) 1948- .... **CLC 81**
 See also CA 141; CANR 63, 105

Ligotti, Thomas (Robert) 1953- ...... **CLC 44; SSC 16**
See also CA 123; CANR 49; HGG

Li Ho 791-817 .... **PC 13**

Liliencron, (Friedrich Adolf Axel) Detlev von 1844-1909 .... **TCLC 18**
See also CA 117

Lilly, William 1602-1681 .... **LC 27**

Lima, Jose Lezama
See Lezama Lima, Jose

Lima Barreto, Afonso Henrique de 1881-1922 .... **TCLC 23**
See also CA 117; 181; LAW

Lima Barreto, Afonso Henriques de
See Lima Barreto, Afonso Henrique de

Limonov, Edward 1944- .... **CLC 67**
See also CA 137

Lin, Frank
See Atherton, Gertrude (Franklin Horn)

Lincoln, Abraham 1809-1865 .... **NCLC 18**
See also LAIT 2

Lind, Jakov .... **CLC 1, 2, 4, 27, 82**
See also Landwirth, Heinz
See also CAAS 4

Lindbergh, Anne (Spencer) Morrow 1906-2001 .... **CLC 82**
See also BPFB 2; CA 17-20R; 193; CANR 16, 73; DAM NOV; MTCW 1, 2; SATA 33; SATA-Obit 125

Lindsay, David 1878(?)-1945 .... **TCLC 15**
See also CA 113; 187; DLB 255; FANT; SFW 4; SUFW

Lindsay, (Nicholas) Vachel 1879-1931 .... **TCLC 17; PC 23; WLC**
See also AMWS 1; CA 114; 135; CANR 79; CDALB 1865-1917; DA; DA3; DAC; DAM MST, POET; DLB 54; EXPP; RGAL 4; SATA 40; WP

Linke-Poot
See Doeblin, Alfred

Linney, Romulus 1930- .... **CLC 51**
See also CA 1-4R; CAD; CANR 40, 44, 79; CD 5; CSW; RGAL 4

Linton, Eliza Lynn 1822-1898 .... **NCLC 41**
See also DLB 18

Li Po 701-763 .... **CMLC 2; PC 29**
See also WP

Lipsius, Justus 1547-1606 .... **LC 16**

Lipsyte, Robert (Michael) 1938- ...... **CLC 21**
See also AAYA 7; CA 17-20R; CANR 8, 57; CLR 23, 76; DA; DAC; DAM MST, NOV; JRDA; LAIT 5; MAICYA 1, 2; SATA 5, 68, 113; WYA; YAW

Lish, Gordon (Jay) 1934- ... **CLC 45; SSC 18**
See also CA 113; 117; CANR 79; DLB 130; INT 117

Lispector, Clarice 1925(?)-1977 .... **CLC 43; HLCS 2; SSC 34**
See also CA 139; 116; CANR 71; CDWLB 3; DLB 113; DNFS 1; FW; HW 2; LAW; RGSF 2; RGWL 2; WLIT 1

Littell, Robert 1935(?)- .... **CLC 42**
See also CA 109; 112; CANR 64; CMW 4

Little, Malcolm 1925-1965
See Malcolm X
See also BW 1, 3; CA 125; 111; CANR 82; DA; DA3; DAB; DAC; DAM MST, MULT; MTCW 1, 2; NCFS 3

Littlewit, Humphrey Gent.
See Lovecraft, H(oward) P(hillips)

Litwos
See Sienkiewicz, Henryk (Adam Alexander Pius)

Liu, E. 1857-1909 .... **TCLC 15**
See also CA 115; 190

Lively, Penelope (Margaret) 1933- .. **CLC 32, 50**
See also BPFB 2; CA 41-44R; CANR 29, 67, 79; CLR 7; CN 7; CWRI 5; DAM NOV; DLB 14, 161, 207; FANT; JRDA; MAICYA 1, 2; MTCW 1, 2; SATA 7, 60, 101

Livesay, Dorothy (Kathleen) 1909-1996 .... **CLC 4, 15, 79**
See also AITN 2; CA 25-28R; CAAS 8; CANR 36, 67; DAC; DAM MST, POET; DLB 68; FW; MTCW 1; RGEL 2

Livy c. 59B.C.-c. 12 .... **CMLC 11**
See also AW 2; CDWLB 1; DLB 211; RGWL 2

Lizardi, Jose Joaquin Fernandez de 1776-1827 .... **NCLC 30**
See also LAW

Llewellyn, Richard
See Llewellyn Lloyd, Richard Dafydd Vivian
See also DLB 15

Llewellyn Lloyd, Richard Dafydd Vivian 1906-1983 .... **CLC 7, 80**
See also Llewellyn, Richard
See also CA 53-56; 111; CANR 7, 71; SATA 11; SATA-Obit 37

Llosa, (Jorge) Mario (Pedro) Vargas
See Vargas Llosa, (Jorge) Mario (Pedro)

Lloyd, Manda
See Mander, (Mary) Jane

Lloyd Webber, Andrew 1948-
See Webber, Andrew Lloyd
See also AAYA 1, 38; CA 116; 149; DAM DRAM; SATA 56

Llull, Ramon c. 1235-c. 1316 .... **CMLC 12**

Lobb, Ebenezer
See Upward, Allen

Locke, Alain (Le Roy) 1886-1954 . **TCLC 43; BLCS**
See also BW 1, 3; CA 106; 124; CANR 79; RGAL 4

Locke, John 1632-1704 .... **LC 7, 35**
See also DLB 101, 213, 252; RGEL 2; WLIT 3

Locke-Elliott, Sumner
See Elliott, Sumner Locke

Lockhart, John Gibson 1794-1854 .. **NCLC 6**
See also DLB 110, 116, 144

Lockridge, Ross (Franklin), Jr. 1914-1948 .... **TCLC 111**
See also CA 108; 145; CANR 79; DLB 143; DLBY 1980; RGAL 4; RHW

Lodge, David (John) 1935- .... **CLC 36, 141**
See also BEST 90:1; BRWS 4; CA 17-20R; CANR 19, 53, 92; CN 7; CPW; DAM POP; DLB 14, 194; INT CANR-19; MTCW 1, 2

Lodge, Thomas 1558-1625 .... **LC 41**
See also DLB 172; RGEL 2

Loewinsohn, Ron(ald William) 1937- .... **CLC 52**
See also CA 25-28R; CANR 71

Logan, Jake
See Smith, Martin Cruz

Logan, John (Burton) 1923-1987 .... **CLC 5**
See also CA 77-80; 124; CANR 45; DLB 5

Lo Kuan-chung 1330(?)-1400(?) .... **LC 12**

Lombard, Nap
See Johnson, Pamela Hansford

Lomotey (editor), Kofi .... **CLC 70**

London, Jack 1876-1916 ..... **TCLC 9, 15, 39; SSC 4, 49; WLC**
See also London, John Griffith
See also AAYA 13; AITN 2; AMW; BPFB 2; BYA 4, 13; CDALB 1865-1917; DLB 8, 12, 78, 212; EXPS; LAIT 3; NFS 8; RGAL 4; RGSF 2; SATA 18; SFW 4; SSFS 7; TCWW 2; TUS; WYA; YAW

London, John Griffith 1876-1916
See London, Jack
See also CA 110; 119; CANR 73; DA; DA3; DAB; DAC; DAM MST, NOV; JRDA; MAICYA 1, 2; MTCW 1, 2

Long, Emmett
See Leonard, Elmore (John, Jr.)

Longbaugh, Harry
See Goldman, William (W.)

Longfellow, Henry Wadsworth 1807-1882 .... **NCLC 2, 45, 101, 103; PC 30; WLCS**
See also AMW; CDALB 1640-1865; DA; DA3; DAB; DAC; DAM MST, POET; DLB 1, 59, 235; EXPP; PAB; PFS 2, 7; RGAL 4; SATA 19; WP

Longinus c. 1st cent. - .... **CMLC 27**
See also AW 2; DLB 176

Longley, Michael 1939- .... **CLC 29**
See also CA 102; CP 7; DLB 40

Longus fl. c. 2nd cent. - .... **CMLC 7**

Longway, A. Hugh
See Lang, Andrew

Lonnrot, Elias 1802-1884 .... **NCLC 53**
See also EFS 1

Lonsdale, Roger ed. .... **CLC 65**

Lopate, Phillip 1943- .... **CLC 29**
See also CA 97-100; CANR 88; DLBY 1980; INT 97-100

Lopez, Barry (Holstun) 1945- .... **CLC 70**
See also AAYA 9; ANW; CA 65-68; CANR 7, 23, 47, 68, 92; DLB 256; INT CANR-7, -23; MTCW 1; RGAL 4; SATA 67

Lopez Portillo (y Pacheco), Jose 1920- .... **CLC 46**
See also CA 129; HW 1

Lopez y Fuentes, Gregorio 1897(?)-1966 .... **CLC 32**
See also CA 131; HW 1

Lorca, Federico Garcia
See Garcia Lorca, Federico
See also DFS 4; EW 11; RGWL 2; WP

Lord, Bette Bao 1938- .... **CLC 23; AAL**
See also BEST 90:3; BPFB 2; CA 107; CANR 41, 79; INT CA-107; SATA 58

Lord Auch
See Bataille, Georges

Lord Byron
See Byron, George Gordon (Noel)

Lorde, Audre (Geraldine) 1934-1992 .. **CLC 18, 71; BLC 2; PC 12**
See also Domini, Rey
See also AFAW 1, 2; BW 1, 3; CA 25-28R; 142; CANR 16, 26, 46, 82; DA3; DAM MULT, POET; DLB 41; FW; MTCW 1, 2; RGAL 4

Lord Houghton
See Milnes, Richard Monckton

Lord Jeffrey
See Jeffrey, Francis

Loreaux, Nichol .... **CLC 65**

Lorenzini, Carlo 1826-1890
See Collodi, Carlo
See also MAICYA 1, 2; SATA 29, 100

Lorenzo, Heberto Padilla
See Padilla (Lorenzo), Heberto

Loris
See Hofmannsthal, Hugo von

Loti, Pierre .... **TCLC 11**
See also Viaud, (Louis Marie) Julien
See also DLB 123; GFL 1789 to the Present

Lou, Henri
See Andreas-Salome, Lou

Louie, David Wong 1954- .... **CLC 70**
See also CA 139

Louis, Father M.
See Merton, Thomas

Lovecraft, H(oward) P(hillips)
1890-1937 .... **TCLC 4, 22; SSC 3, 52**
See also AAYA 14; BPFB 2; CA 104; 133;
CANR 106; DA3; DAM POP; HGG;
MTCW 1, 2; RGAL 4; SCFW; SFW 4;
SUFW

Lovelace, Earl 1935- .... **CLC 51**
See also BW 2; CA 77-80; CANR 41, 72;
CD 5; CDWLB 3; CN 7; DLB 125;
MTCW 1

Lovelace, Richard 1618-1657 .... **LC 24**
See also BRW 2; DLB 131; EXPP; PAB;
RGEL 2

Lowell, Amy 1874-1925 ... **TCLC 1, 8; PC 13**
See also AMW; CA 104; 151; DAM POET;
DLB 54, 140; EXPP; MAWW; MTCW 2;
RGAL 4

Lowell, James Russell 1819-1891 ... **NCLC 2,
90**
See also AMWS 1; CDALB 1640-1865;
DLB 1, 11, 64, 79, 189, 235; RGAL 4

Lowell, Robert (Traill Spence, Jr.)
1917-1977 .... **CLC 1, 2, 3, 4, 5, 8, 9, 11,
15, 37, 124; PC 3; WLC**
See also AMW; CA 9-12R; 73-76; CABS
2; CANR 26, 60; CDALBS; DA; DA3;
DAB; DAC; DAM MST, NOV; DLB 5,
169; MTCW 1, 2; PAB; PFS 6, 7; RGAL
4; WP

Lowenthal, Michael (Francis)
1969- .... **CLC 119**
See also CA 150

Lowndes, Marie Adelaide (Belloc)
1868-1947 .... **TCLC 12**
See also CA 107; CMW 4; DLB 70; RHW

Lowry, (Clarence) Malcolm
1909-1957 .... **TCLC 6, 40; SSC 31**
See also BPFB 2; BRWS 3; CA 105; 131;
CANR 62, 105; CDBLB 1945-1960; DLB
15; MTCW 1, 2; RGEL 2

Lowry, Mina Gertrude 1882-1966
See Loy, Mina
See also CA 113

Loxsmith, John
See Brunner, John (Kilian Houston)

Loy, Mina .... **CLC 28; PC 16**
See also Lowry, Mina Gertrude
See also DAM POET; DLB 4, 54

Loyson-Bridet
See Schwob, Marcel (Mayer Andre)

Lucan 39-65 .... **CMLC 33**
See also AW 2; DLB 211; EFS 2; RGWL 2

Lucas, Craig 1951- .... **CLC 64**
See also CA 137; CAD; CANR 71, 109;
CD 5; GLL 2

Lucas, E(dward) V(errall)
1868-1938 .... **TCLC 73**
See also CA 176; DLB 98, 149, 153; SATA
20

Lucas, George 1944- .... **CLC 16**
See also AAYA 1, 23; CA 77-80; CANR
30; SATA 56

Lucas, Hans
See Godard, Jean-Luc

Lucas, Victoria
See Plath, Sylvia

Lucian c. 125-c. 180 .... **CMLC 32**
See also AW 2; DLB 176; RGWL 2

Lucretius c. 94B.C.-c. 49B.C. .... **CMLC 48**
See also AW 2; CDWLB 1; DLB 211; EFS
2; RGWL 2

Ludlam, Charles 1943-1987 .... **CLC 46, 50**
See also CA 85-88; 122; CAD; CANR 72,
86

Ludlum, Robert 1927-2001 .... **CLC 22, 43**
See also AAYA 10; BEST 89:1, 90:3; BPFB
2; CA 33-36R; 195; CANR 25, 41, 68,
105; CMW 4; CPW; DA3; DAM NOV,
POP; DLBY 1982; MSW; MTCW 1, 2

Ludwig, Ken .... **CLC 60**
See also CA 195; CAD

Ludwig, Otto 1813-1865 .... **NCLC 4**
See also DLB 129

Lugones, Leopoldo 1874-1938 ...... **TCLC 15;
HLCS 2**
See also CA 116; 131; CANR 104; HW 1;
LAW

Lu Hsun .... **TCLC 3; SSC 20**
See also Shu-Jen, Chou

Lukacs, George .... **CLC 24**
See also Lukacs, Gyorgy (Szegeny von)

Lukacs, Gyorgy (Szegeny von) 1885-1971
See Lukacs, George
See also CA 101; 29-32R; CANR 62; CD-
WLB 4; DLB 215, 242; EW 10; MTCW
2

Luke, Peter (Ambrose Cyprian)
1919-1995 .... **CLC 38**
See also CA 81-84; 147; CANR 72; CBD;
CD 5; DLB 13

Lunar, Dennis
See Mungo, Raymond

Lurie, Alison 1926- .... **CLC 4, 5, 18, 39**
See also BPFB 2; CA 1-4R; CANR 2, 17,
50, 88; CN 7; DLB 2; MTCW 1; SATA
46, 112

Lustig, Arnost 1926- .... **CLC 56**
See also AAYA 3; CA 69-72; CANR 47,
102; CWW 2; DLB 232; SATA 56

Luther, Martin 1483-1546 .... **LC 9, 37**
See also CDWLB 2; DLB 179; EW 2;
RGWL 2

Luxemburg, Rosa 1870(?)-1919 ..... **TCLC 63**
See also CA 118

Luzi, Mario 1914- .... **CLC 13**
See also CA 61-64; CANR 9, 70; CWW 2;
DLB 128

L'vov, Arkady .... **CLC 59**

Lyly, John 1554(?)-1606 .... **LC 41; DC 7**
See also BRW 1; DAM DRAM; DLB 62,
167; RGEL 2

L'Ymagier
See Gourmont, Remy(-Marie-Charles) de

Lynch, B. Suarez
See Borges, Jorge Luis

Lynch, David (K.) 1946- .... **CLC 66**
See also CA 124; 129

Lynch, James
See Andreyev, Leonid (Nikolaevich)

Lyndsay, Sir David 1485-1555 .... **LC 20**
See also RGEL 2

Lynn, Kenneth S(chuyler)
1923-2001 .... **CLC 50**
See also CA 1-4R; 196; CANR 3, 27, 65

Lynx
See West, Rebecca

Lyons, Marcus
See Blish, James (Benjamin)

Lyotard, Jean-Francois
1924-1998 .... **TCLC 103**
See also DLB 242

Lyre, Pinchbeck
See Sassoon, Siegfried (Lorraine)

Lytle, Andrew (Nelson) 1902-1995 ... **CLC 22**
See also CA 9-12R; 150; CANR 70; CN 7;
CSW; DLB 6; DLBY 1995; RGAL 4;
RHW

Lyttelton, George 1709-1773 .... **LC 10**
See also RGEL 2

Lytton of Knebworth, Baron
See Bulwer-Lytton, Edward (George Earle
Lytton)

Maas, Peter 1929-2001 .... **CLC 29**
See also CA 93-96; 201; INT CA-93-96;
MTCW 2

Macaulay, Catherine 1731-1791 .... **LC 64**
See also DLB 104

Macaulay, (Emilie) Rose
1881(?)-1958 .... **TCLC 7, 44**
See also CA 104; DLB 36; RGEL 2; RHW

Macaulay, Thomas Babington
1800-1859 .... **NCLC 42**
See also BRW 4; CDBLB 1832-1890; DLB
32, 55; RGEL 2

MacBeth, George (Mann)
1932-1992 .... **CLC 2, 5, 9**
See also CA 25-28R; 136; CANR 61, 66;
DLB 40; MTCW 1; PFS 8; SATA 4;
SATA-Obit 70

MacCaig, Norman (Alexander)
1910-1996 .... **CLC 36**
See also BRWS 6; CA 9-12R; CANR 3, 34;
CP 7; DAB; DAM POET; DLB 27; RGEL
2

MacCarthy, Sir (Charles Otto) Desmond
1877-1952 .... **TCLC 36**
See also CA 167

MacDiarmid, Hugh .... **CLC 2, 4, 11, 19, 63;
PC 9**
See also Grieve, C(hristopher) M(urray)
See also CDBLB 1945-1960; DLB 20;
RGEL 2

MacDonald, Anson
See Heinlein, Robert A(nson)

Macdonald, Cynthia 1928- .... **CLC 13, 19**
See also CA 49-52; CANR 4, 44; DLB 105

MacDonald, George 1824-1905 .... **TCLC 9,
113**
See also BYA 5; CA 106; 137; CANR 80;
CLR 67; DLB 18, 163, 178; FANT; MAI-
CYA 1, 2; RGEL 2; SATA 33, 100; SFW
4; SUFW; WCH

Macdonald, John
See Millar, Kenneth

MacDonald, John D(ann)
1916-1986 .... **CLC 3, 27, 44**
See also BPFB 2; CA 1-4R; 121; CANR 1,
19, 60; CMW 4; CPW; DAM NOV, POP;
DLB 8; DLBY 1986; MSW; MTCW 1, 2;
SFW 4

Macdonald, John Ross
See Millar, Kenneth

Macdonald, Ross ..... **CLC 1, 2, 3, 14, 34, 41**
See also Millar, Kenneth
See also AMWS 4; BPFB 2; DLBD 6;
MSW; RGAL 4

MacDougal, John
See Blish, James (Benjamin)

MacDougal, John
See Blish, James (Benjamin)

MacDowell, John
See Parks, Tim(othy Harold)

MacEwen, Gwendolyn (Margaret)
1941-1987 .... **CLC 13, 55**
See also CA 9-12R; 124; CANR 7, 22; DLB
53, 251; SATA 50; SATA-Obit 55

Macha, Karel Hynek 1810-1846 .... **NCLC 46**

Machado (y Ruiz), Antonio
1875-1939 .... **TCLC 3**
See also CA 104; 174; DLB 108; EW 9;
HW 2; RGWL 2

Machado de Assis, Joaquim Maria
1839-1908 ..... **TCLC 10; BLC 2; HLCS
2; SSC 24**
See also CA 107; 153; CANR 91; LAW;
RGSF 2; RGWL 2; WLIT 1

Machen, Arthur .... **TCLC 4; SSC 20**
See also Jones, Arthur Llewellyn
See also CA 179; DLB 156, 178; RGEL 2;
SUFW

Machiavelli, Niccolo 1469-1527 ..... **LC 8, 36;
DC 16; WLCS**
See also DA; DAB; DAC; DAM MST; EW
2; LAIT 1; NFS 9; RGWL 2

MacInnes, Colin 1914-1976 .... **CLC 4, 23**
See also CA 69-72; 65-68; CANR 21; DLB
14; MTCW 1, 2; RGEL 2; RHW

MacInnes, Helen (Clark)
1907-1985 .... **CLC 27, 39**
See also BPFB 2; CA 1-4R; 117; CANR 1,
28, 58; CMW 4; CPW; DAM POP; DLB
87; MSW; MTCW 1, 2; SATA 22; SATA-
Obit 44

Mackay, Mary 1855-1924
See Corelli, Marie
See also CA 118; 177; FANT; RHW

Mackenzie, Compton (Edward Montague)
1883-1972 .... **CLC 18**
See also CA 21-22; 37-40R; CAP 2; DLB
34, 100; RGEL 2; TCLC 116

Mackenzie, Henry 1745-1831 .... **NCLC 41**
See also DLB 39; RGEL 2

Mackintosh, Elizabeth 1896(?)-1952
See Tey, Josephine
See also CA 110; CMW 4

MacLaren, James
See Grieve, C(hristopher) M(urray)

Mac Laverty, Bernard 1942- .... **CLC 31**
See also CA 116; 118; CANR 43, 88; CN
7; INT CA-118; RGSF 2

MacLean, Alistair (Stuart)
1922(?)-1987 .... **CLC 3, 13, 50, 63**
See also CA 57-60; 121; CANR 28, 61;
CMW 4; CPW; DAM POP; MTCW 1;
SATA 23; SATA-Obit 50; TCWW 2

Maclean, Norman (Fitzroy)
1902-1990 .... **CLC 78; SSC 13**
See also CA 102; 132; CANR 49; CPW;
DAM POP; DLB 206; TCWW 2

MacLeish, Archibald 1892-1982 ... **CLC 3, 8,
14, 68**
See also AMW; CA 9-12R; 106; CAD;
CANR 33, 63; CDALBS; DAM POET;
DLB 4, 7, 45; DLBY 1982; EXPP;
MTCW 1, 2; PAB; PFS 5; RGAL 4

MacLennan, (John) Hugh
1907-1990 .... **CLC 2, 14, 92**
See also CA 5-8R; 142; CANR 33; DAC;
DAM MST; DLB 68; MTCW 1, 2; RGEL
2

MacLeod, Alistair 1936- .... **CLC 56**
See also CA 123; CCA 1; DAC; DAM
MST; DLB 60; MTCW 2; RGSF 2

Macleod, Fiona
See Sharp, William
See also RGEL 2; SUFW

MacNeice, (Frederick) Louis
1907-1963 .... **CLC 1, 4, 10, 53**
See also BRW 7; CA 85-88; CANR 61;
DAB; DAM POET; DLB 10, 20; MTCW
1, 2; RGEL 2

MacNeill, Dand
See Fraser, George MacDonald

Macpherson, James 1736-1796 .... **LC 29**
See also Ossian
See also DLB 109; RGEL 2

Macpherson, (Jean) Jay 1931- .... **CLC 14**
See also CA 5-8R; CANR 90; CP 7; CWP;
DLB 53

Macrobius fl. 430- .... **CMLC 48**

MacShane, Frank 1927-1999 .... **CLC 39**
See also CA 9-12R; 186; CANR 3, 33; DLB
111

Macumber, Mari
See Sandoz, Mari(e Susette)

Madach, Imre 1823-1864 .... **NCLC 19**

Madden, (Jerry) David 1933- ...... **CLC 5, 15**
See also CA 1-4R; CAAS 3; CANR 4, 45;
CN 7; CSW; DLB 6; MTCW 1

Maddern, Al(an)
See Ellison, Harlan (Jay)

Madhubuti, Haki R. 1942- . **CLC 6, 73; BLC
2; PC 5**
See also Lee, Don L.
See also BW 2, 3; CA 73-76; CANR 24,
51, 73; CP 7; CSW; DAM MULT; POET;
DLB 5, 41; DLBD 8; MTCW 2; RGAL 4

Maepenn, Hugh
See Kuttner, Henry

Maepenn, K. H.
See Kuttner, Henry

Maeterlinck, Maurice 1862-1949 ..... **TCLC 3**
See also CA 104; 136; CANR 80; DAM
DRAM; DLB 192; EW 8; GFL 1789 to
the Present; RGWL 2; SATA 66

Maginn, William 1794-1842 .... **NCLC 8**
See also DLB 110, 159

Mahapatra, Jayanta 1928- .... **CLC 33**
See also CA 73-76; CAAS 9; CANR 15,
33, 66, 87; CP 7; DAM MULT

Mahfouz, Naguib (Abdel Aziz Al-Sabilgi)
1911(?)- .... **CLC 153**
See also Mahfuz, Najib (Abdel Aziz al-
Sabilgi)
See also BEST 89:2; CA 128; CANR 55,
101; CWW 2; DA3; DAM NOV; MTCW
1, 2; RGWL 2; SSFS 9

Mahfuz, Najib (Abdel Aziz al-Sabilgi)
.... **CLC 52, 55**
See also Mahfouz, Naguib (Abdel Aziz Al-
Sabilgi)
See also AFW; DLBY 1988; RGSF 2;
WLIT 2

Mahon, Derek 1941- .... **CLC 27**
See also BRWS 6; CA 113; 128; CANR 88;
CP 7; DLB 40

Maiakovskii, Vladimir
See Mayakovski, Vladimir (Vladimirovich)
See also IDTP; RGWL 2

Mailer, Norman 1923- ... **CLC 1, 2, 3, 4, 5, 8,
11, 14, 28, 39, 74, 111**
See also AAYA 31; AITN 2; AMW; BPFB
2; CA 9-12R; CABS 1; CANR 28, 74, 77;
CDALB 1968-1988; CN 7; CPW; DA;
DA3; DAB; DAC; DAM MST, NOV,
POP; DLB 2, 16, 28, 185; DLBD 3;
DLBY 1980, 1983; MTCW 1, 2; NFS 10;
RGAL 4

Maillet, Antonine 1929- .... **CLC 54, 118**
See also CA 115; 120; CANR 46, 74, 77;
CCA 1; CWW 2; DAC; DLB 60; INT
120; MTCW 2

Mais, Roger 1905-1955 .... **TCLC 8**
See also BW 1, 3; CA 105; 124; CANR 82;
CDWLB 3; DLB 125; MTCW 1; RGEL 2

Maistre, Joseph 1753-1821 .... **NCLC 37**
See also GFL 1789 to the Present

Maitland, Frederic William
1850-1906 .... **TCLC 65**

Maitland, Sara (Louise) 1950- .... **CLC 49**
See also CA 69-72; CANR 13, 59; FW

Major, Clarence 1936- . **CLC 3, 19, 48; BLC
2**
See also AFAW 2; BW 2, 3; CA 21-24R;
CAAS 6; CANR 13, 25, 53, 82; CN 7;
CP 7; CSW; DAM MULT; DLB 33; MSW

Major, Kevin (Gerald) 1949- .... **CLC 26**
See also AAYA 16; CA 97-100; CANR 21,
38; CLR 11; DAC; DLB 60; INT CANR-
21; JRDA; MAICYA 1, 2; MAICYAS 1;
SATA 32, 82; WYA; YAW

Maki, James
See Ozu, Yasujiro

Malabaila, Damiano
See Levi, Primo

Malamud, Bernard 1914-1986 .. **CLC 1, 2, 3,
5, 8, 9, 11, 18, 27, 44, 78, 85; SSC 15;
WLC**
See also AAYA 16; AMWS 1; BPFB 2; CA
5-8R; 118; CABS 1; CANR 28, 62;
CDALB 1941-1968; CPW; DA; DA3;

DAB; DAC; DAM MST, NOV, POP;
DLB 2, 28, 152; DLBY 1980, 1986;
EXPS; LAIT 4; MTCW 1, 2; NFS 4, 9;
RGAL 4; RGSF 2; SSFS 8, 13

Malan, Herman
See Bosman, Herman Charles; Bosman,
Herman Charles

Malaparte, Curzio 1898-1957 .... **TCLC 52**

Malcolm, Dan
See Silverberg, Robert

Malcolm X .... **CLC 82, 117; BLC 2; WLCS**
See also Little, Malcolm
See also LAIT 5

Malherbe, Francois de 1555-1628 .... **LC 5**
See also GFL Beginnings to 1789

Mallarme, Stephane 1842-1898 ...... **NCLC 4,
41; PC 4**
See also DAM POET; DLB 217; EW 7;
GFL 1789 to the Present; RGWL 2

Mallet-Joris, Francoise 1930- .... **CLC 11**
See also CA 65-68; CANR 17; DLB 83;
GFL 1789 to the Present

Malley, Ern
See McAuley, James Phillip

Mallowan, Agatha Christie
See Christie, Agatha (Mary Clarissa)

Maloff, Saul 1922- .... **CLC 5**
See also CA 33-36R

Malone, Louis
See MacNeice, (Frederick) Louis

Malone, Michael (Christopher)
1942- .... **CLC 43**
See also CA 77-80; CANR 14, 32, 57

Malory, Sir Thomas 1410(?)-1471(?) . **LC 11;
WLCS**
See also BRW 1; BRWR 2; CDBLB Before
1660; DA; DAB; DAC; DAM MST; DLB
146; EFS 2; RGEL 2; SATA 59; SATA-
Brief 33; WLIT 3

Malouf, (George Joseph) David
1934- .... **CLC 28, 86**
See also CA 124; CANR 50, 76; CN 7; CP
7; MTCW 2

Malraux, (Georges-)Andre
1901-1976 .... **CLC 1, 4, 9, 13, 15, 57**
See also BPFB 2; CA 21-22; 69-72; CANR
34, 58; CAP 2; DA3; DAM NOV; DLB
72; EW 12; GFL 1789 to the Present;
MTCW 1, 2; RGWL 2

Malzberg, Barry N(athaniel) 1939- ... **CLC 7**
See also CA 61-64; CAAS 4; CANR 16;
CMW 4; DLB 8; SFW 4

Mamet, David (Alan) 1947- .. **CLC 9, 15, 34,
46, 91; DC 4**
See also AAYA 3; CA 81-84; CABS 3;
CANR 15, 41, 67, 72; CD 5; DA3; DAM
DRAM; DFS 2, 3, 6, 12; DLB 7; IDFW
4; MTCW 1, 2; RGAL 4

Mamoulian, Rouben (Zachary)
1897-1987 .... **CLC 16**
See also CA 25-28R; 124; CANR 85

Mandelshtam, Osip
See Mandelstam, Osip (Emilievich)
See also EW 10; RGWL 2

Mandelstam, Osip (Emilievich)
1891(?)-1943(?) .... **TCLC 2, 6; PC 14**
See also Mandelshtam, Osip
See also CA 104; 150; MTCW 2

Mander, (Mary) Jane 1877-1949 ... **TCLC 31**
See also CA 162; RGEL 2

Mandeville, Sir John fl. 1350- ...... **CMLC 19**
See also DLB 146

Mandiargues, Andre Pieyre de .... **CLC 41**
See also Pieyre de Mandiargues, Andre
See also DLB 83

Mandrake, Ethel Belle
See Thurman, Wallace (Henry)

Mangan, James Clarence
1803-1849 .... **NCLC 27**
See also RGEL 2

Maniere, J.-E.
See Giraudoux, Jean(-Hippolyte)

Mankiewicz, Herman (Jacob)
1897-1953 .... **TCLC 85**
See also CA 120; 169; DLB 26; IDFW 3, 4

Manley, (Mary) Delariviere
1672(?)-1724 .... **LC 1, 42**
See also DLB 39, 80; RGEL 2

Mann, Abel
See Creasey, John

Mann, Emily 1952- .... **DC 7**
See also CA 130; CAD; CANR 55; CD 5;
CWD

Mann, (Luiz) Heinrich 1871-1950 ... **TCLC 9**
See also CA 106; 164, 181; DLB 66, 118;
EW 8; RGWL 2

Mann, (Paul) Thomas 1875-1955 ... **TCLC 2,
8, 14, 21, 35, 44, 60; SSC 5; WLC**
See also BPFB 2; CA 104; 128; CDWLB 2;
DA; DA3; DAB; DAC; DAM MST, NOV;
DLB 66; EW 9; GLL 1; MTCW 1, 2;
RGSF 2; RGWL 2; SSFS 4, 9

Mannheim, Karl 1893-1947 .... **TCLC 65**

Manning, David
See Faust, Frederick (Schiller)
See also TCWW 2

Manning, Frederic 1887(?)-1935 ... **TCLC 25**
See also CA 124

Manning, Olivia 1915-1980 .... **CLC 5, 19**
See also CA 5-8R; 101; CANR 29; FW;
MTCW 1; RGEL 2

Mano, D. Keith 1942- .... **CLC 2, 10**
See also CA 25-28R; CAAS 6; CANR 26,
57; DLB 6

Mansfield, Katherine ... **TCLC 2, 8, 39; SSC
9, 23, 38; WLC**
See also Beauchamp, Kathleen Mansfield
See also BPFB 2; BRW 7; DAB; DLB 162;
EXPS; FW; GLL 1; RGEL 2; RGSF 2;
SSFS 2, 8, 10, 11

Manso, Peter 1940- .... **CLC 39**
See also CA 29-32R; CANR 44

Mantecon, Juan Jimenez
See Jimenez (Mantecon), Juan Ramon

Mantel, Hilary (Mary) 1952- .... **CLC 144**
See also CA 125; CANR 54, 101; CN 7;
RHW

Manton, Peter
See Creasey, John

Man Without a Spleen, A
See Chekhov, Anton (Pavlovich)

Manzoni, Alessandro 1785-1873 ... **NCLC 29,
98**
See also EW 5; RGWL 2

Map, Walter 1140-1209 .... **CMLC 32**

Mapu, Abraham (ben Jekutiel)
1808-1867 .... **NCLC 18**

Mara, Sally
See Queneau, Raymond

Marat, Jean Paul 1743-1793 .... **LC 10**

Marcel, Gabriel Honore 1889-1973 . **CLC 15**
See also CA 102; 45-48; MTCW 1, 2

March, William 1893-1954 .... **TCLC 96**

Marchbanks, Samuel
See Davies, (William) Robertson
See also CCA 1

Marchi, Giacomo
See Bassani, Giorgio

Marcus Aurelius
See Aurelius, Marcus
See also AW 2

Marguerite
See de Navarre, Marguerite

Marguerite d'Angouleme
See de Navarre, Marguerite
See also GFL Beginnings to 1789

Marguerite de Navarre
See de Navarre, Marguerite
See also RGWL 2

Margulies, Donald 1954- .... **CLC 76**
See also CA 200; DFS 13; DLB 228

Marie de France c. 12th cent. - ..... **CMLC 8;
PC 22**
See also DLB 208; FW; RGWL 2

Marie de l'Incarnation 1599-1672 ...... **LC 10**

Marier, Captain Victor
See Griffith, D(avid Lewelyn) W(ark)

Mariner, Scott
See Pohl, Frederik

Marinetti, Filippo Tommaso
1876-1944 .... **TCLC 10**
See also CA 107; DLB 114; EW 9

Marivaux, Pierre Carlet de Chamblain de
1688-1763 .... **LC 4; DC 7**
See also GFL Beginnings to 1789; RGWL
2

Markandaya, Kamala .... **CLC 8, 38**
See also Taylor, Kamala (Purnaiya)
See also BYA 13; CN 7

Markfield, Wallace 1926- .... **CLC 8**
See also CA 69-72; CAAS 3; CN 7; DLB
2, 28

Markham, Edwin 1852-1940 .... **TCLC 47**
See also CA 160; DLB 54, 186; RGAL 4

Markham, Robert
See Amis, Kingsley (William)

Marks, J
See Highwater, Jamake (Mamake)

Marks, J.
See Highwater, Jamake (Mamake)

Marks-Highwater, J
See Highwater, Jamake (Mamake)

Marks-Highwater, J.
See Highwater, Jamake (Mamake)

Markson, David M(errill) 1927- .... **CLC 67**
See also CA 49-52; CANR 1, 91; CN 7

Marley, Bob .... **CLC 17**
See also Marley, Robert Nesta

Marley, Robert Nesta 1945-1981
See Marley, Bob
See also CA 107; 103

Marlowe, Christopher 1564-1593 ...... **LC 22,
47; DC 1; WLC**
See also BRW 1; BRWR 1; CDBLB Before
1660; DA; DA3; DAB; DAC; DAM
DRAM, MST; DFS 1, 5, 13; DLB 62;
EXPP; RGEL 2; WLIT 3

Marlowe, Stephen 1928- .... **CLC 70**
See also Queen, Ellery
See also CA 13-16R; CANR 6, 55; CMW
4; SFW 4

Marmontel, Jean-Francois 1723-1799 .. **LC 2**

Marquand, John P(hillips)
1893-1960 .... **CLC 2, 10**
See also AMW; BPFB 2; CA 85-88; CANR
73; CMW 4; DLB 9, 102; MTCW 2;
RGAL 4

Marques, Rene 1919-1979 .. **CLC 96; HLC 2**
See also CA 97-100; 85-88; CANR 78;
DAM MULT; DLB 113; HW 1, 2; LAW;
RGSF 2

Marquez, Gabriel (Jose) Garcia
See Garcia Marquez, Gabriel (Jose)

Marquis, Don(ald Robert Perry)
1878-1937 .... **TCLC 7**
See also CA 104; 166; DLB 11, 25; RGAL
4

Marric, J. J.
See Creasey, John
See also MSW

Marryat, Frederick 1792-1848 .... **NCLC 3**
See also DLB 21, 163; RGEL 2; WCH

Marsden, James
See Creasey, John

Marsh, Edward 1872-1953 .... **TCLC 99**

Marsh, (Edith) Ngaio 1899-1982 .. **CLC 7, 53**
See also CA 9-12R; CANR 6, 58; CMW 4;
CPW; DAM POP; DLB 77; MSW;
MTCW 1, 2; RGEL 2

Marshall, Garry 1934- .... **CLC 17**
See also AAYA 3; CA 111; SATA 60

Marshall, Paule 1929- .. **CLC 27, 72; BLC 3;
SSC 3**
See also AFAW 1, 2; BPFB 2; BW 2, 3;
CA 77-80; CANR 25, 73; CN 7; DA3;
DAM MULT; DLB 33, 157, 227; MTCW
1, 2; RGAL 4

Marshallik
See Zangwill, Israel

Marsten, Richard
See Hunter, Evan

Marston, John 1576-1634 .... **LC 33**
See also BRW 2; DAM DRAM; DLB 58,
172; RGEL 2

Martha, Henry
See Harris, Mark

Marti (y Perez), Jose (Julian)
1853-1895 .... **NCLC 63; HLC 2**
See also DAM MULT; HW 2; LAW; RGWL
2; WLIT 1

Martial c. 40-c. 104 .... **CMLC 35; PC 10**
See also AW 2; CDWLB 1; DLB 211;
RGWL 2

Martin, Ken
See Hubbard, L(afayette) Ron(ald)

Martin, Richard
See Creasey, John

Martin, Steve 1945- .... **CLC 30**
See also CA 97-100; CANR 30, 100;
MTCW 1

Martin, Valerie 1948- .... **CLC 89**
See also BEST 90:2; CA 85-88; CANR 49,
89

Martin, Violet Florence
1862-1915 .... **TCLC 51**

Martin, Webber
See Silverberg, Robert

Martindale, Patrick Victor
See White, Patrick (Victor Martindale)

Martin du Gard, Roger
1881-1958 .... **TCLC 24**
See also CA 118; CANR 94; DLB 65; GFL
1789 to the Present; RGWL 2

Martineau, Harriet 1802-1876 .... **NCLC 26**
See also DLB 21, 55, 159, 163, 166, 190;
FW; RGEL 2; YABC 2

Martines, Julia
See O'Faolain, Julia

Martinez, Enrique Gonzalez
See Gonzalez Martinez, Enrique

Martinez, Jacinto Benavente y
See Benavente (y Martinez), Jacinto

Martinez de la Rosa, Francisco de Paula
1787-1862 .... **NCLC 102**

Martinez Ruiz, Jose 1873-1967
See Azorin; Ruiz, Jose Martinez
See also CA 93-96; HW 1

Martinez Sierra, Gregorio
1881-1947 .... **TCLC 6**
See also CA 115

Martinez Sierra, Maria (de la O'LeJarraga)
1874-1974 .... **TCLC 6**
See also CA 115

Martinsen, Martin
See Follett, Ken(neth Martin)

Martinson, Harry (Edmund)
1904-1978 .... **CLC 14**
See also CA 77-80; CANR 34; DLB 259

Martyn, Edward 1859-1923 .... **TCLC 121**
See also CA 179; DLB 10; RGEL 2

Marut, Ret
See Traven, B.
Marut, Robert
See Traven, B.
Marvell, Andrew 1621-1678 .... **LC 4, 43; PC 10; WLC**
See also BRW 2; BRWR 2; CDBLB 1660-1789; DA; DAB; DAC; DAM MST, POET; DLB 131; EXPP; PFS 5; RGEL 2; WP
Marx, Karl (Heinrich) 1818-1883 . **NCLC 17**
See also DLB 129
Masaoka, Shiki .... **TCLC 18**
See also Masaoka, Tsunenori
Masaoka, Tsunenori 1867-1902
See Masaoka, Shiki
See also CA 117; 191
Masefield, John (Edward)
1878-1967 .... **CLC 11, 47**
See also CA 19-20; 25-28R; CANR 33; CAP 2; CDBLB 1890-1914; DAM POET; DLB 10, 19, 153, 160; EXPP; FANT; MTCW 1, 2; PFS 5; RGEL 2; SATA 19
Maso, Carole 19(?)- .... **CLC 44**
See also CA 170; GLL 2; RGAL 4
Mason, Bobbie Ann 1940- ... **CLC 28, 43, 82, 154; SSC 4**
See also AAYA 5, 42; AMWS 8; BPFB 2; CA 53-56; CANR 11, 31, 58, 83; CDALBS; CN 7; CSW; DA3; DLB 173; DLBY 1987; EXPS; INT CANR-31; MTCW 1, 2; NFS 4; RGAL 4; RGSF 2; SSFS 3,8; YAW
Mason, Ernst
See Pohl, Frederik
Mason, Hunni B.
See Sternheim, (William Adolf) Carl
Mason, Lee W.
See Malzberg, Barry N(athaniel)
Mason, Nick 1945- .... **CLC 35**
Mason, Tally
See Derleth, August (William)
Mass, Anna .... **CLC 59**
Mass, William
See Gibson, William
Massinger, Philip 1583-1640 .... **LC 70**
See also DLB 58; RGEL 2
Master Lao
See Lao Tzu
Masters, Edgar Lee 1868-1950 .... **TCLC 2, 25; PC 1, 36; WLCS**
See also AMWS 1; CA 104; 133; CDALB 1865-1917; DA; DAC; DAM MST, POET; DLB 54; EXPP; MTCW 1, 2; RGAL 4; WP
Masters, Hilary 1928- .... **CLC 48**
See also CA 25-28R; CANR 13, 47, 97; CN 7; DLB 244
Mastrosimone, William 19(?)- .... **CLC 36**
See also CA 186; CAD; CD 5
Mathe, Albert
See Camus, Albert
Mather, Cotton 1663-1728 .... **LC 38**
See also AMWS 2; CDALB 1640-1865; DLB 24, 30, 140; RGAL 4
Mather, Increase 1639-1723 .... **LC 38**
See also DLB 24
Matheson, Richard (Burton) 1926- .. **CLC 37**
See also AAYA 31; CA 97-100; CANR 88, 99; DLB 8, 44; HGG; INT 97-100; SCFW 2; SFW 4
Mathews, Harry 1930- .... **CLC 6, 52**
See also CA 21-24R; CAAS 6; CANR 18, 40, 98; CN 7
Mathews, John Joseph 1894-1979 .... **CLC 84**
See also CA 19-20; 142; CANR 45; CAP 2; DAM MULT; DLB 175; NNAL

Mathias, Roland (Glyn) 1915- .... **CLC 45**
See also CA 97-100; CANR 19, 41; CP 7; DLB 27
Matsuo Basho 1644-1694 .... **LC 62; PC 3**
See also Basho, Matsuo
See also DAM POET; PFS 2, 7
Mattheson, Rodney
See Creasey, John
Matthews, (James) Brander
1852-1929 .... **TCLC 95**
See also DLB 71, 78; DLBD 13
Matthews, Greg 1949- .... **CLC 45**
See also CA 135
Matthews, William (Procter III)
1942-1997 .... **CLC 40**
See also AMWS 9; CA 29-32R; 162; CAAS 18; CANR 12, 57; CP 7; DLB 5
Matthias, John (Edward) 1941- .... **CLC 9**
See also CA 33-36R; CANR 56; CP 7
Matthiessen, F(rancis) O(tto)
1902-1950 .... **TCLC 100**
See also CA 185; DLB 63
Matthiessen, Peter 1927- ... **CLC 5, 7, 11, 32, 64**
See also AAYA 6, 40; AMWS 5; ANW; BEST 90:4; BPFB 2; CA 9-12R; CANR 21, 50, 73, 100; CN 7; DA3; DAM NOV; DLB 6, 173; MTCW 1, 2; SATA 27
Maturin, Charles Robert
1780(?)-1824 .... **NCLC 6**
See also DLB 178; HGG; RGEL 2; SUFW
Matute (Ausejo), Ana Maria 1925- .. **CLC 11**
See also CA 89-92; MTCW 1; RGSF 2
Maugham, W. S.
See Maugham, W(illiam) Somerset
Maugham, W(illiam) Somerset
1874-1965 .. **CLC 1, 11, 15, 67, 93; SSC 8; WLC**
See also BPFB 2; BRW 6; CA 5-8R; 25-28R; CANR 40; CDBLB 1914-1945; CMW 4; DA; DA3; DAB; DAC; DAM DRAM, MST, NOV; DLB 10, 36, 77, 100, 162, 195; LAIT 3; MTCW 1, 2; RGEL 2; RGSF 2; SATA 54
Maugham, William Somerset
See Maugham, W(illiam) Somerset
Maupassant, (Henri Rene Albert) Guy de
1850-1893 .... **NCLC 1, 42, 83; SSC 1; WLC**
See also BYA 14; DA; DA3; DAB; DAC; DAM MST; DLB 123; EW 7; EXPS; GFL 1789 to the Present; LAIT 2; RGSF 2; RGWL 2; SSFS 4; SUFW; TWA
Maupin, Armistead (Jones, Jr.)
1944- .... **CLC 95**
See also CA 125; 130; CANR 58, 101; CPW; DA3; DAM POP; GLL 1; INT 130; MTCW 2
Maurhut, Richard
See Traven, B.
Mauriac, Claude 1914-1996 .... **CLC 9**
See also CA 89-92; 152; CWW 2; DLB 83; GFL 1789 to the Present
Mauriac, Francois (Charles)
1885-1970 .... **CLC 4, 9, 56; SSC 24**
See also CA 25-28; CAP 2; DLB 65; EW 10; GFL 1789 to the Present; MTCW 1, 2; RGWL 2
Mavor, Osborne Henry 1888-1951
See Bridie, James
See also CA 104
Maxwell, William (Keepers, Jr.)
1908-2000 .... **CLC 19**
See also AMWS 8; CA 93-96; 189; CANR 54, 95; CN 7; DLB 218; DLBY 1980; INT CA-93-96; SATA-Obit 128
May, Elaine 1932- .... **CLC 16**
See also CA 124; 142; CAD; CWD; DLB 44

Mayakovski, Vladimir (Vladimirovich)
1893-1930 .... **TCLC 4, 18**
See also Maiakovskii, Vladimir; Mayakovsky, Vladimir
See also CA 104; 158; MTCW 2; SFW 4
Mayakovsky, Vladimir
See Mayakovski, Vladimir (Vladimirovich)
See also EW 11; WP
Mayhew, Henry 1812-1887 .... **NCLC 31**
See also DLB 18, 55, 190
Mayle, Peter 1939(?)- .... **CLC 89**
See also CA 139; CANR 64, 109
Maynard, Joyce 1953- .... **CLC 23**
See also CA 111; 129; CANR 64
Mayne, William (James Carter)
1928- .... **CLC 12**
See also AAYA 20; CA 9-12R; CANR 37, 80, 100; CLR 25; FANT; JRDA; MAICYA 1, 2; MAICYAS 1; SAAS 11; SATA 6, 68, 122; YAW
Mayo, Jim
See L'Amour, Louis (Dearborn)
See also TCWW 2
Maysles, Albert 1926- .... **CLC 16**
See also CA 29-32R
Maysles, David 1932-1987 .... **CLC 16**
See also CA 191
Mazer, Norma Fox 1931- .... **CLC 26**
See also AAYA 5, 36; BYA 1, 8; CA 69-72; CANR 12, 32, 66; CLR 23; JRDA; MAICYA 1, 2; SAAS 1; SATA 24, 67, 105; WYA; YAW
Mazzini, Guiseppe 1805-1872 .... **NCLC 34**
McAlmon, Robert (Menzies)
1895-1956 .... **TCLC 97**
See also CA 107; 168; DLB 4, 45; DLBD 15; GLL 1
McAuley, James Phillip 1917-1976 .. **CLC 45**
See also CA 97-100; RGEL 2
McBain, Ed
See Hunter, Evan
See also MSW
McBrien, William (Augustine)
1930- .... **CLC 44**
See also CA 107; CANR 90
McCabe, Patrick 1955- .... **CLC 133**
See also CA 130; CANR 50, 90; CN 7; DLB 194
McCaffrey, Anne (Inez) 1926- .... **CLC 17**
See also AAYA 6, 34; AITN 2; BEST 89:2; BPFB 2; BYA 5; CA 25-28R; CANR 15, 35, 55, 96; CLR 49; CPW; DA3; DAM NOV, POP; DLB 8; JRDA; MAICYA 1, 2; MTCW 1, 2; SAAS 11; SATA 8, 70, 116; SFW 4; WYA; YAW
McCall, Nathan 1955(?)- .... **CLC 86**
See also BW 3; CA 146; CANR 88
McCann, Arthur
See Campbell, John W(ood, Jr.)
McCann, Edson
See Pohl, Frederik
McCarthy, Charles, Jr. 1933-
See McCarthy, Cormac
See also CANR 42, 69, 101; CN 7; CPW; CSW; DA3; DAM POP; MTCW 2
McCarthy, Cormac .... **CLC 4, 57, 59, 101**
See also McCarthy, Charles, Jr.
See also AAYA 41; AMWS 8; BPFB 2; CA 13-16R; CANR 10; DLB 6, 143, 256; TCWW 2
McCarthy, Mary (Therese)
1912-1989 .. **CLC 1, 3, 5, 14, 24, 39, 59; SSC 24**
See also AMW; BPFB 2; CA 5-8R; 129; CANR 16, 50, 64; DA3; DLB 2; DLBY 1981; FW; INT CANR-16; MAWW; MTCW 1, 2; RGAL 4
McCartney, (James) Paul 1942- . **CLC 12, 35**
See also CA 146

McCauley, Stephen (D.) 1955- .... **CLC 50**
See also CA 141

McClaren, Peter .... **CLC 70**

McClure, Michael (Thomas) 1932- ... **CLC 6, 10**
See also CA 21-24R; CAD; CANR 17, 46, 77; CD 5; CP 7; DLB 16; WP

McCorkle, Jill (Collins) 1958- .... **CLC 51**
See also CA 121; CSW; DLB 234; DLBY 1987

McCourt, Frank 1930- .... **CLC 109**
See also CA 157; CANR 97; NCFS 1

McCourt, James 1941- .... **CLC 5**
See also CA 57-60; CANR 98

McCourt, Malachy 1932- .... **CLC 119**
See also SATA 126

McCoy, Horace (Stanley)
1897-1955 .... **TCLC 28**
See also CA 108; 155; CMW 4; DLB 9

McCrae, John 1872-1918 .... **TCLC 12**
See also CA 109; DLB 92; PFS 5

McCreigh, James
See Pohl, Frederik

McCullers, (Lula) Carson (Smith)
1917-1967 .... **CLC 1, 4, 10, 12, 48, 100; SSC 9, 24; WLC**
See also AAYA 21; AMW; BPFB 2; CA 5-8R; 25-28R; CABS 1, 3; CANR 18; CDALB 1941-1968; DA; DA3; DAB; DAC; DAM MST, NOV; DFS 5; DLB 2, 7, 173, 228; EXPS; FW; GLL 1; LAIT 3, 4; MAWW; MTCW 1, 2; NFS 6, 13; RGAL 4; RGSF 2; SATA 27; SSFS 5; YAW

McCulloch, John Tyler
See Burroughs, Edgar Rice

McCullough, Colleen 1938(?)- .. **CLC 27, 107**
See also AAYA 36; BPFB 2; CA 81-84; CANR 17, 46, 67, 98; CPW; DA3; DAM NOV, POP; MTCW 1, 2; RHW

McDermott, Alice 1953- .... **CLC 90**
See also CA 109; CANR 40, 90

McElroy, Joseph 1930- .... **CLC 5, 47**
See also CA 17-20R; CN 7

McEwan, Ian (Russell) 1948- ..... **CLC 13, 66**
See also BEST 90:4; BRWS 4; CA 61-64; CANR 14, 41, 69, 87; CN 7; DAM NOV; DLB 14, 194; HGG; MTCW 1, 2; RGSF 2

McFadden, David 1940- .... **CLC 48**
See also CA 104; CP 7; DLB 60; INT 104

McFarland, Dennis 1950- .... **CLC 65**
See also CA 165

McGahern, John 1934- .... **CLC 5, 9, 48, 156; SSC 17**
See also CA 17-20R; CANR 29, 68; CN 7; DLB 14, 231; MTCW 1

McGinley, Patrick (Anthony) 1937- . **CLC 41**
See also CA 120; 127; CANR 56; INT 127

McGinley, Phyllis 1905-1978 .... **CLC 14**
See also CA 9-12R; 77-80; CANR 19; CWRI 5; DLB 11, 48; PFS 9, 13; SATA 2, 44; SATA-Obit 24

McGinniss, Joe 1942- .... **CLC 32**
See also AITN 2; BEST 89:2; CA 25-28R; CANR 26, 70; CPW; DLB 185; INT CANR-26

McGivern, Maureen Daly
See Daly, Maureen

McGrath, Patrick 1950- .... **CLC 55**
See also CA 136; CANR 65; CN 7; DLB 231; HGG

McGrath, Thomas (Matthew)
1916-1990 .... **CLC 28, 59**
See also AMWS 10; CA 9-12R; 132; CANR 6, 33, 95; DAM POET; MTCW 1; SATA 41; SATA-Obit 66

McGuane, Thomas (Francis III)
1939- .... **CLC 3, 7, 18, 45, 127**
See also AITN 2; BPFB 2; CA 49-52; CANR 5, 24, 49, 94; CN 7; DLB 2, 212; DLBY 1980; INT CANR-24; MTCW 1; TCWW 2

McGuckian, Medbh 1950- ... **CLC 48; PC 27**
See also BRWS 5; CA 143; CP 7; CWP; DAM POET; DLB 40

McHale, Tom 1942(?)-1982 .... **CLC 3, 5**
See also AITN 1; CA 77-80; 106

McIlvanney, William 1936- .... **CLC 42**
See also CA 25-28R; CANR 61; CMW 4; DLB 14, 207

McIlwraith, Maureen Mollie Hunter
See Hunter, Mollie
See also SATA 2

McInerney, Jay 1955- .... **CLC 34, 112**
See also AAYA 18; BPFB 2; CA 116; 123; CANR 45, 68; CN 7; CPW; DA3; DAM POP; INT 123; MTCW 2

McIntyre, Vonda N(eel) 1948- .... **CLC 18**
See also CA 81-84; CANR 17, 34, 69; MTCW 1; SFW 4; YAW

McKay, Claude .... **TCLC 7, 41; BLC 3; PC 2; WLC**
See also McKay, Festus Claudius
See also AFAW 1, 2; AMWS 10; DAB; DLB 4, 45, 51, 117; EXPP; GLL 2; LAIT 3; PAB; PFS 4; RGAL 4; WP

McKay, Festus Claudius 1889-1948
See McKay, Claude
See also BW 1, 3; CA 104; 124; CANR 73; DA; DAC; DAM MST, MULT, NOV, POET; MTCW 1, 2

McKuen, Rod 1933- .... **CLC 1, 3**
See also AITN 1; CA 41-44R; CANR 40

McLoughlin, R. B.
See Mencken, H(enry) L(ouis)

McLuhan, (Herbert) Marshall
1911-1980 .... **CLC 37, 83**
See also CA 9-12R; 102; CANR 12, 34, 61; DLB 88; INT CANR-12; MTCW 1, 2

McMillan, Terry (L.) 1951- .... **CLC 50, 61, 112; BLCS**
See also AAYA 21; BPFB 2; BW 2, 3; CA 140; CANR 60, 104; CPW; DA3; DAM MULT, NOV, POP; MTCW 2; RGAL 4; YAW

McMurtry, Larry (Jeff) 1936- .. **CLC 2, 3, 7, 11, 27, 44, 127**
See also AAYA 15; AITN 2; AMWS 5; BEST 89:2; BPFB 2; CA 5-8R; CANR 19, 43, 64, 103; CDALB 1968-1988; CN 7; CPW; CSW; DA3; DAM NOV, POP; DLB 2, 143, 256; DLBY 1980, 1987; MTCW 1, 2; RGAL 4; TCWW 2

McNally, T. M. 1961- .... **CLC 82**

McNally, Terrence 1939- .... **CLC 4, 7, 41, 91**
See also CA 45-48; CAD; CANR 2, 56; CD 5; DA3; DAM DRAM; DLB 7, 249; GLL 1; MTCW 2

McNamer, Deirdre 1950- .... **CLC 70**

McNeal, Tom .... **CLC 119**

McNeile, Herman Cyril 1888-1937
See Sapper
See also CA 184; CMW 4; DLB 77

McNickle, (William) D'Arcy
1904-1977 .... **CLC 89**
See also CA 9-12R; 85-88; CANR 5, 45; DAM MULT; DLB 175, 212; NNAL; RGAL 4; SATA-Obit 22

McPhee, John (Angus) 1931- .... **CLC 36**
See also AMWS 3; ANW; BEST 90:1; CA 65-68; CANR 20, 46, 64, 69; CPW; DLB 185; MTCW 1, 2

McPherson, James Alan 1943- .. **CLC 19, 77; BLCS**
See also BW 1, 3; CA 25-28R; CAAS 17; CANR 24, 74; CN 7; CSW; DLB 38, 244; MTCW 1, 2; RGAL 4; RGSF 2

McPherson, William (Alexander)
1933- .... **CLC 34**
See also CA 69-72; CANR 28; INT CANR-28

McTaggart, J. McT. Ellis
See McTaggart, John McTaggart Ellis

McTaggart, John McTaggart Ellis
1866-1925 .... **TCLC 105**
See also CA 120

Mead, George Herbert 1873-1958 . **TCLC 89**

Mead, Margaret 1901-1978 .... **CLC 37**
See also AITN 1; CA 1-4R; 81-84; CANR 4; DA3; FW; MTCW 1, 2; SATA-Obit 20

Meaker, Marijane (Agnes) 1927-
See Kerr, M. E.
See also CA 107; CANR 37, 63; INT 107; JRDA; MAICYA 1, 2; MAICYAS 1; MTCW 1; SATA 20, 61, 99; SATA-Essay 111; YAW

Medoff, Mark (Howard) 1940- .... **CLC 6, 23**
See also AITN 1; CA 53-56; CAD; CANR 5; CD 5; DAM DRAM; DFS 4; DLB 7; INT CANR-5

Medvedev, P. N.
See Bakhtin, Mikhail Mikhailovich

Meged, Aharon
See Megged, Aharon

Meged, Aron
See Megged, Aharon

Megged, Aharon 1920- .... **CLC 9**
See also CA 49-52; CAAS 13; CANR 1

Mehta, Ved (Parkash) 1934- .... **CLC 37**
See also CA 1-4R; CANR 2, 23, 69; MTCW 1

Melanter
See Blackmore, R(ichard) D(oddridge)

Melies, Georges 1861-1938 .... **TCLC 81**

Melikow, Loris
See Hofmannsthal, Hugo von

Melmoth, Sebastian
See Wilde, Oscar (Fingal O'Flahertie Wills)

Meltzer, Milton 1915- .... **CLC 26**
See also AAYA 8; BYA 2, 6; CA 13-16R; CANR 38, 92, 107; CLR 13; DLB 61; JRDA; MAICYA 1, 2; SAAS 1; SATA 1, 50, 80, 128; SATA-Essay 124; WYA; YAW

Melville, Herman 1819-1891 ..... **NCLC 3, 12, 29, 45, 49, 91, 93; SSC 1, 17, 46; WLC**
See also AAYA 25; AMW; AMWR 1; CDALB 1640-1865; DA; DA3; DAB; DAC; DAM MST, NOV; DLB 3, 74, 250, 254; EXPN; EXPS; LAIT 1, 2; NFS 7, 9; RGAL 4; RGSF 2; SATA 59; SSFS 3

Members, Mark
See Powell, Anthony (Dymoke)

Membreno, Alejandro .... **CLC 59**

Menander c. 342B.C.-c. 293B.C. .... **CMLC 9, 51; DC 3**
See also AW 1; CDWLB 1; DAM DRAM; DLB 176; RGWL 2

Menchu, Rigoberta 1959- .. **CLC 160; HLCS 2**
See also CA 175; DNFS 1; WLIT 1

Mencken, H(enry) L(ouis)
1880-1956 .... **TCLC 13**
See also AMW; CA 105; 125; CDALB 1917-1929; DLB 11, 29, 63, 137, 222; MTCW 1, 2; RGAL 4

Mendelsohn, Jane 1965- .... **CLC 99**
See also CA 154; CANR 94

Mercer, David 1928-1980 .... **CLC 5**
See also CA 9-12R; 102; CANR 23; CBD; DAM DRAM; DLB 13; MTCW 1; RGEL 2

Merchant, Paul
See Ellison, Harlan (Jay)

Meredith, George 1828-1909 ... **TCLC 17, 43**
See also CA 117; 153; CANR 80; CDBLB 1832-1890; DAM POET; DLB 18, 35, 57, 159; RGEL 2

Meredith, William (Morris) 1919- .... **CLC 4, 13, 22, 55; PC 28**
See also CA 9-12R; CAAS 14; CANR 6, 40; CP 7; DAM POET; DLB 5

Merezhkovsky, Dmitry Sergeyevich
1865-1941 .... **TCLC 29**
See also CA 169

Merimee, Prosper 1803-1870 ... **NCLC 6, 65; SSC 7**
See also DLB 119, 192; EW 6; EXPS; GFL 1789 to the Present; RGSF 2; RGWL 2; SSFS 8; SUFW

Merkin, Daphne 1954- .... **CLC 44**
See also CA 123

Merlin, Arthur
See Blish, James (Benjamin)

Merrill, James (Ingram) 1926-1995 .. **CLC 2, 3, 6, 8, 13, 18, 34, 91; PC 28**
See also AMWS 3; CA 13-16R; 147; CANR 10, 49, 63, 108; DA3; DAM POET; DLB 5, 165; DLBY 1985; INT CANR-10; MTCW 1, 2; PAB; RGAL 4

Merriman, Alex
See Silverberg, Robert

Merriman, Brian 1747-1805 .... **NCLC 70**

Merritt, E. B.
See Waddington, Miriam

Merton, Thomas 1915-1968 ..... **CLC 1, 3, 11, 34, 83; PC 10**
See also AMWS 8; CA 5-8R; 25-28R; CANR 22, 53; DA3; DLB 48; DLBY 1981; MTCW 1, 2

Merwin, W(illiam) S(tanley) 1927- ... **CLC 1, 2, 3, 5, 8, 13, 18, 45, 88**
See also AMWS 3; CA 13-16R; CANR 15, 51; CP 7; DA3; DAM POET; DLB 5, 169; INT CANR-15; MTCW 1, 2; PAB; PFS 5; RGAL 4

Metcalf, John 1938- .... **CLC 37; SSC 43**
See also CA 113; CN 7; DLB 60; RGSF 2

Metcalf, Suzanne
See Baum, L(yman) Frank

Mew, Charlotte (Mary) 1870-1928 .. **TCLC 8**
See also CA 105; 189; DLB 19, 135; RGEL 2

Mewshaw, Michael 1943- .... **CLC 9**
See also CA 53-56; CANR 7, 47; DLBY 1980

Meyer, Conrad Ferdinand
1825-1905 .... **NCLC 81**
See also DLB 129; EW; RGWL 2

Meyer, Gustav 1868-1932
See Meyrink, Gustav
See also CA 117; 190

Meyer, June
See Jordan, June
See also GLL 2

Meyer, Lynn
See Slavitt, David R(ytman)

Meyers, Jeffrey 1939- .... **CLC 39**
See also CA 73-76; CAAE 186; CANR 54, 102; DLB 111

Meynell, Alice (Christina Gertrude Thompson) 1847-1922 .... **TCLC 6**
See also CA 104; 177; DLB 19, 98; RGEL 2

Meyrink, Gustav .... **TCLC 21**
See also Meyer, Gustav
See also DLB 81

Michaels, Leonard 1933- .... **CLC 6, 25; SSC 16**
See also CA 61-64; CANR 21, 62; CN 7; DLB 130; MTCW 1

Michaux, Henri 1899-1984 .... **CLC 8, 19**
See also CA 85-88; 114; DLB 258; GFL 1789 to the Present; RGWL 2

Micheaux, Oscar (Devereaux)
1884-1951 .... **TCLC 76**
See also BW 3; CA 174; DLB 50; TCWW 2

Michelangelo 1475-1564 .... **LC 12**
See also AAYA 43

Michelet, Jules 1798-1874 .... **NCLC 31**
See also EW 5; GFL 1789 to the Present

Michels, Robert 1876-1936 .... **TCLC 88**

Michener, James A(lbert)
1907(?)-1997 .. **CLC 1, 5, 11, 29, 60, 109**
See also AAYA 27; AITN 1; BEST 90:1; BPFB 2; CA 5-8R; 161; CANR 21, 45, 68; CN 7; CPW; DA3; DAM NOV, POP; DLB 6; MTCW 1, 2; RHW

Mickiewicz, Adam 1798-1855 . **NCLC 3, 101; PC 38**
See also EW 5; RGWL 2

Middleton, Christopher 1926- .... **CLC 13**
See also CA 13-16R; CANR 29, 54; CP 7; DLB 40

Middleton, Richard (Barham)
1882-1911 .... **TCLC 56**
See also CA 187; DLB 156; HGG

Middleton, Stanley 1919- .... **CLC 7, 38**
See also CA 25-28R; CAAS 23; CANR 21, 46, 81; CN 7; DLB 14

Middleton, Thomas 1580-1627 .... **LC 33; DC 5**
See also BRW 2; DAM DRAM, MST; DLB 58; RGEL 2

Migueis, Jose Rodrigues 1901- .... **CLC 10**
See also FW

Mikszath, Kalman 1847-1910 .... **TCLC 31**
See also CA 170

Miles, Jack .... **CLC 100**
See also CA 200

Miles, John Russiano
See Miles, Jack

Miles, Josephine (Louise)
1911-1985 .... **CLC 1, 2, 14, 34, 39**
See also CA 1-4R; 116; CANR 2, 55; DAM POET; DLB 48

Militant
See Sandburg, Carl (August)

Mill, Harriet (Hardy) Taylor
1807-1858 .... **NCLC 102**
See also FW

Mill, John Stuart 1806-1873 .... **NCLC 11, 58**
See also CDBLB 1832-1890; DLB 55, 190; FW 1; RGEL 2

Millar, Kenneth 1915-1983 .... **CLC 14**
See also Macdonald, Ross
See also CA 9-12R; 110; CANR 16, 63, 107; CMW 4; CPW; DA3; DAM POP; DLB 2, 226; DLBD 6; DLBY 1983; MTCW 1, 2

Millay, E. Vincent
See Millay, Edna St. Vincent

Millay, Edna St. Vincent
1892-1950 ... **TCLC 4, 49; PC 6; WLCS**
See also Boyd, Nancy
See also AMW; CA 104; 130; CDALB 1917-1929; DA; DA3; DAB; DAC; DAM MST, POET; DLB 45, 249; EXPP; MAWW; MTCW 1, 2; PAB; PFS 3; RGAL 4; WP

Miller, Arthur 1915- ...... **CLC 1, 2, 6, 10, 15, 26, 47, 78; DC 1; WLC**
See also AAYA 15; AITN 1; AMW; CA 1-4R; CABS 3; CAD; CANR 2, 30, 54, 76; CD 5; CDALB 1941-1968; DA; DA3; DAB; DAC; DAM DRAM, MST; DFS 1, 3; DLB 7; LAIT 4; MTCW 1, 2; RGAL 4; WYAS 1

Miller, Henry (Valentine)
1891-1980 .... **CLC 1, 2, 4, 9, 14, 43, 84; WLC**
See also AMW; BPFB 2; CA 9-12R; 97-100; CANR 33, 64; CDALB 1929-1941; DA; DA3; DAB; DAC; DAM MST, NOV; DLB 4, 9; DLBY 1980; MTCW 1, 2; RGAL 4

Miller, Jason 1939(?)-2001 .... **CLC 2**
See also AITN 1; CA 73-76; 197; CAD; DFS 12; DLB 7

Miller, Sue 1943- .... **CLC 44**
See also BEST 90:3; CA 139; CANR 59, 91; DA3; DAM POP; DLB 143

Miller, Walter M(ichael, Jr.)
1923-1996 .... **CLC 4, 30**
See also BPFB 2; CA 85-88; CANR 108; DLB 8; SCFW; SFW 4

Millett, Kate 1934- .... **CLC 67**
See also AITN 1; CA 73-76; CANR 32, 53, 76; DA3; DLB 246; FW; GLL 1; MTCW 1, 2

Millhauser, Steven (Lewis) 1943- .... **CLC 21, 54, 109**
See also CA 110; 111; CANR 63; CN 7; DA3; DLB 2; FANT; INT CA-111; MTCW 2

Millin, Sarah Gertrude 1889-1968 ... **CLC 49**
See also CA 102; 93-96; DLB 225

Milne, A(lan) A(lexander)
1882-1956 .... **TCLC 6, 88**
See also BRWS 5; CA 104; 133; CLR 1, 26; CMW 4; CWRI 5; DA3; DAB; DAC; DAM MST; DLB 10, 77, 100, 160; FANT; MAICYA 1, 2; MTCW 1, 2; RGEL 2; SATA 100; WCH; YABC 1

Milner, Ron(ald) 1938- .... **CLC 56; BLC 3**
See also AITN 1; BW 1; CA 73-76; CAD; CANR 24, 81; CD 5; DAM MULT; DLB 38; MTCW 1

Milnes, Richard Monckton
1809-1885 .... **NCLC 61**
See also DLB 32, 184

Milosz, Czeslaw 1911- .... **CLC 5, 11, 22, 31, 56, 82; PC 8; WLCS**
See also CA 81-84; CANR 23, 51, 91; CD-WLB 4; CWW 2; DA3; DAM MST, POET; DLB 215; EW 13; MTCW 1, 2; RGWL 2

Milton, John 1608-1674 ..... **LC 9, 43; PC 19, 29; WLC**
See also BRW 2; BRWR 2; CDBLB 1660-1789; DA; DA3; DAB; DAC; DAM MST, POET; DLB 131, 151; EFS 1; EXPP; LAIT 1; PAB; PFS 3; RGEL 2; WLIT 3; WP

Min, Anchee 1957- .... **CLC 86**
See also CA 146; CANR 94

Minehaha, Cornelius
See Wedekind, (Benjamin) Frank(lin)

Miner, Valerie 1947- .... **CLC 40**
See also CA 97-100; CANR 59; FW; GLL 2

Minimo, Duca
See D'Annunzio, Gabriele

Minot, Susan 1956- .... **CLC 44, 159**
See also AMWS 6; CA 134; CN 7

Minus, Ed 1938- .... **CLC 39**
See also CA 185

Miranda, Javier
See Bioy Casares, Adolfo
See also CWW 2

Mirbeau, Octave 1848-1917 .... **TCLC 55**
See also DLB 123, 192; GFL 1789 to the Present

Miro (Ferrer), Gabriel (Francisco Victor)
1879-1930 .... **TCLC 5**
See also CA 104; 185

Misharin, Alexandr .... **CLC 59**
Mishima, Yukio ... **CLC 2, 4, 6, 9, 27; DC 1;
SSC 4**
See also Hiraoka, Kimitake
See also BPFB 2; DLB 182; GLL 1; MJW;
MTCW 2; RGSF 2; RGWL 2; SSFS 5, 12
Mistral, Frederic 1830-1914 .... **TCLC 51**
See also CA 122; GFL 1789 to the Present
Mistral, Gabriela
See Godoy Alcayaga, Lucila
See also DNFS 1; LAW; RGWL 2; WP
Mistry, Rohinton 1952- .... **CLC 71**
See also CA 141; CANR 86; CCA 1; CN 7;
DAC; SSFS 6
Mitchell, Clyde
See Ellison, Harlan (Jay); Silverberg, Robert
Mitchell, James Leslie 1901-1935
See Gibbon, Lewis Grassic
See also CA 104; 188; DLB 15
Mitchell, Joni 1943- .... **CLC 12**
See also CA 112; CCA 1
Mitchell, Joseph (Quincy)
1908-1996 .... **CLC 98**
See also CA 77-80; 152; CANR 69; CN 7;
CSW; DLB 185; DLBY 1996
Mitchell, Margaret (Munnerlyn)
1900-1949 .... **TCLC 11**
See also AAYA 23; BPFB 2; BYA 1; CA
109; 125; CANR 55, 94; CDALBS; DA3;
DAM NOV, POP; DLB 9; LAIT 2;
MTCW 1, 2; NFS 9; RGAL 4; RHW;
WYAS 1; YAW
Mitchell, Peggy
See Mitchell, Margaret (Munnerlyn)
Mitchell, S(ilas) Weir 1829-1914 .... **TCLC 36**
See also CA 165; DLB 202; RGAL 4
Mitchell, W(illiam) O(rmond)
1914-1998 .... **CLC 25**
See also CA 77-80; 165; CANR 15, 43; CN
7; DAC; DAM MST; DLB 88
Mitchell, William 1879-1936 .... **TCLC 81**
Mitford, Mary Russell 1787-1855 .... **NCLC 4**
See also DLB 110, 116; RGEL 2
Mitford, Nancy 1904-1973 .... **CLC 44**
See also CA 9-12R; DLB 191; RGEL 2
Miyamoto, (Chujo) Yuriko
1899-1951 .... **TCLC 37**
See also Miyamoto Yuriko
See also CA 170, 174
Miyamoto Yuriko
See Miyamoto, (Chujo) Yuriko
See also DLB 180
Miyazawa, Kenji 1896-1933 .... **TCLC 76**
See also CA 157
Mizoguchi, Kenji 1898-1956 .... **TCLC 72**
See also CA 167
Mo, Timothy (Peter) 1950(?)- ... **CLC 46, 134**
See also CA 117; CN 7; DLB 194; MTCW
1; WLIT 4
Modarressi, Taghi (M.) 1931-1997 ... **CLC 44**
See also CA 121; 134; INT 134
Modiano, Patrick (Jean) 1945- .... **CLC 18**
See also CA 85-88; CANR 17, 40; CWW
2; DLB 83
Mofolo, Thomas (Mokopu)
1875(?)-1948 .... **TCLC 22; BLC 3**
See also AFW; CA 121; 153; CANR 83;
DAM MULT; DLB 225; MTCW 2; WLIT
2
Mohr, Nicholasa 1938- .... **CLC 12; HLC 2**
See also AAYA 8; CA 49-52; CANR 1, 32,
64; CLR 22; DAM MULT; DLB 145; HW
1, 2; JRDA; LAIT 5; MAICYA 2; MAIC-
YAS 1; RGAL 4; SAAS 8; SATA 8, 97;
SATA-Essay 113; WYA; YAW
Mojtabai, A(nn) G(race) 1938- ..... **CLC 5, 9,
15, 29**
See also CA 85-88; CANR 88

Moliere 1622-1673 ..... **LC 10, 28, 64; DC 13;
WLC**
See also DA; DA3; DAB; DAC; DAM
DRAM, MST; DFS 13; EW 3; GFL Begin-
nings to 1789; RGWL 2
Molin, Charles
See Mayne, William (James Carter)
Molnar, Ferenc 1878-1952 .... **TCLC 20**
See also CA 109; 153; CANR 83; CDWLB
4; DAM DRAM; DLB 215; RGWL 2
Momaday, N(avarre) Scott 1934- ...... **CLC 2,
19, 85, 95, 160; PC 25; WLCS**
See also AAYA 11; AMWS 4; ANW; BPFB
2; CA 25-28R; CANR 14, 34, 68;
CDALBS; CN 7; CPW; DA; DA3; DAB;
DAC; DAM MST, MULT, NOV, POP;
DLB 143, 175, 256; EXPP; INT CANR-
14; LAIT 4; MTCW 1, 2; NFS 10; NNAL;
PFS 2, 11; RGAL 4; SATA 48; SATA-
Brief 30; WP; YAW
Monette, Paul 1945-1995 .... **CLC 82**
See also AMWS 10; CA 139; 147; CN 7;
GLL 1
Monroe, Harriet 1860-1936 .... **TCLC 12**
See also CA 109; DLB 54, 91
Monroe, Lyle
See Heinlein, Robert A(nson)
Montagu, Elizabeth 1720-1800 .... **NCLC 7**
See also FW
Montagu, Mary (Pierrepont) Wortley
1689-1762 .... **LC 9, 57; PC 16**
See also DLB 95, 101; RGEL 2
Montagu, W. H.
See Coleridge, Samuel Taylor
Montague, John (Patrick) 1929- ..... **CLC 13,
46**
See also CA 9-12R; CANR 9, 69; CP 7;
DLB 40; MTCW 1; PFS 12; RGEL 2
Montaigne, Michel (Eyquem) de
1533-1592 .... **LC 8; WLC**
See also DA; DAB; DAC; DAM MST; EW
2; GFL Beginnings to 1789; RGWL 2
Montale, Eugenio 1896-1981 ... **CLC 7, 9, 18;
PC 13**
See also CA 17-20R; 104; CANR 30; DLB
114; EW 11; MTCW 1; RGWL 2
Montesquieu, Charles-Louis de Secondat
1689-1755 .... **LC 7, 69**
See also EW 3; GFL Beginnings to 1789
Montessori, Maria 1870-1952 ...... **TCLC 103**
See also CA 115; 147
Montgomery, (Robert) Bruce 1921(?)-1978
See Crispin, Edmund
See also CA 179; 104; CMW 4
Montgomery, L(ucy) M(aud)
1874-1942 .... **TCLC 51**
See also AAYA 12; BYA 1; CA 108; 137;
CLR 8; DA3; DAC; DAM MST; DLB 92;
DLBD 14; JRDA; MAICYA 1, 2; MTCW
2; RGEL 2; SATA 100; WCH; WYA;
YABC 1
Montgomery, Marion H., Jr. 1925- .... **CLC 7**
See also AITN 1; CA 1-4R; CANR 3, 48;
CSW; DLB 6
Montgomery, Max
See Davenport, Guy (Mattison, Jr.)
Montherlant, Henry (Milon) de
1896-1972 .... **CLC 8, 19**
See also CA 85-88; 37-40R; DAM DRAM;
DLB 72; EW 11; GFL 1789 to the Present;
MTCW 1
Monty Python
See Chapman, Graham; Cleese, John
(Marwood); Gilliam, Terry (Vance); Idle,
Eric; Jones, Terence Graham Parry; Palin,
Michael (Edward)
See also AAYA 7

Moodie, Susanna (Strickland)
1803-1885 .... **NCLC 14, 113**
See also DLB 99
Moody, Hiram F. III 1961-
See Moody, Rick
See also CA 138; CANR 64
Moody, Minerva
See Alcott, Louisa May
Moody, Rick .... **CLC 147**
See also Moody, Hiram F. III
Moody, William Vaughan
1869-1910 .... **TCLC 105**
See also CA 110; 178; DLB 7, 54; RGAL 4
Mooney, Edward 1951-
See Mooney, Ted
See also CA 130
Mooney, Ted .... **CLC 25**
See also Mooney, Edward
Moorcock, Michael (John) 1939- ...... **CLC 5,
27, 58**
See also Bradbury, Edward P.
See also AAYA 26; CA 45-48; CAAS 5;
CANR 2, 17, 38, 64; CN 7; DLB 14, 231;
FANT; MTCW 1, 2; SATA 93; SFW 4;
SUFW
Moore, Brian 1921-1999 ... **CLC 1, 3, 5, 7, 8,
19, 32, 90**
See also Bryan, Michael
See also CA 1-4R; 174; CANR 1, 25, 42,
63; CCA 1; CN 7; DAB; DAC; DAM
MST; DLB 251; FANT; MTCW 1, 2;
RGEL 2
Moore, Edward
See Muir, Edwin
See also RGEL 2
Moore, G. E. 1873-1958 .... **TCLC 89**
Moore, George Augustus
1852-1933 .... **TCLC 7; SSC 19**
See also BRW 6; CA 104; 177; DLB 10,
18, 57, 135; RGEL 2; RGSF 2
Moore, Lorrie .... **CLC 39, 45, 68**
See also Moore, Marie Lorena
See also AMWS 10; DLB 234
Moore, Marianne (Craig)
1887-1972 .... **CLC 1, 2, 4, 8, 10, 13, 19,
47; PC 4; WLCS**
See also AMW; CA 1-4R; 33-36R; CANR
3, 61; CDALB 1929-1941; DA; DA3;
DAB; DAC; DAM MST, POET; DLB 45;
DLBD 7; EXPP; MAWW; MTCW 1, 2;
PAB; PFS 14; RGAL 4; SATA 20; WP
Moore, Marie Lorena 1957-
See Moore, Lorrie
See also CA 116; CANR 39, 83; CN 7; DLB
234
Moore, Thomas 1779-1852 .... **NCLC 6, 110**
See also DLB 96, 144; RGEL 2
Moorhouse, Frank 1938- .... **SSC 40**
See also CA 118; CANR 92; CN 7; RGSF
2
Mora, Pat(ricia) 1942-
See also CA 129; CANR 57, 81; CLR 58;
DAM MULT; DLB 209; HLC 2; HW 1,
2; MAICYA 2; SATA 92
Moraga, Cherrie 1952- .... **CLC 126**
See also CA 131; CANR 66; DAM MULT;
DLB 82, 249; FW; GLL 1; HW 1, 2
Morand, Paul 1888-1976 .... **CLC 41; SSC 22**
See also CA 184; 69-72; DLB 65
Morante, Elsa 1918-1985 .... **CLC 8, 47**
See also CA 85-88; 117; CANR 35; DLB
177; MTCW 1, 2; RGWL 2
Moravia, Alberto .... **CLC 2, 7, 11, 27, 46;
SSC 26**
See also Pincherle, Alberto
See also DLB 177; EW 12; MTCW 2;
RGSF 2; RGWL 2
More, Hannah 1745-1833 .... **NCLC 27**
See also DLB 107, 109, 116, 158; RGEL 2

More, Henry 1614-1687 .... **LC 9**
See also DLB 126, 252
More, Sir Thomas 1478(?)-1535 .... **LC 10, 32**
See also BRWS 7; DLB 136; RGEL 2
Moreas, Jean .... **TCLC 18**
See also Papadiamantopoulos, Johannes
See also GFL 1789 to the Present
Moreton, Andrew Esq.
See Defoe, Daniel
Morgan, Berry 1919- .... **CLC 6**
See also CA 49-52; DLB 6
Morgan, Claire
See Highsmith, (Mary) Patricia
See also GLL 1
Morgan, Edwin (George) 1920- .... **CLC 31**
See also CA 5-8R; CANR 3, 43, 90; CP 7;
DLB 27
Morgan, (George) Frederick 1922- .. **CLC 23**
See also CA 17-20R; CANR 21; CP 7
Morgan, Harriet
See Mencken, H(enry) L(ouis)
Morgan, Jane
See Cooper, James Fenimore
Morgan, Janet 1945- .... **CLC 39**
See also CA 65-68
Morgan, Lady 1776(?)-1859 .... **NCLC 29**
See also DLB 116, 158; RGEL 2
Morgan, Robin (Evonne) 1941- .... **CLC 2**
See also CA 69-72; CANR 29, 68; FW;
GLL 2; MTCW 1; SATA 80
Morgan, Scott
See Kuttner, Henry
Morgan, Seth 1949(?)-1990 .... **CLC 65**
See also CA 185; 132
Morgenstern, Christian (Otto Josef
Wolfgang) 1871-1914 .... **TCLC 8**
See also CA 105; 191
Morgenstern, S.
See Goldman, William (W.)
Mori, Rintaro
See Mori Ogai
See also CA 110
Moricz, Zsigmond 1879-1942 .... **TCLC 33**
See also CA 165; DLB 215
Morike, Eduard (Friedrich)
1804-1875 .... **NCLC 10**
See also DLB 133; RGWL 2
Mori Ogai
See Mori Ogai
See also DLB 180
Mori Ogai 1862-1922 .... **TCLC 14**
See also Mori Ogai; Ogai
See also CA 164; TWA
Moritz, Karl Philipp 1756-1793 .... **LC 2**
See also DLB 94
Morland, Peter Henry
See Faust, Frederick (Schiller)
Morley, Christopher (Darlington)
1890-1957 .... **TCLC 87**
See also CA 112; DLB 9; RGAL 4
Morren, Theophil
See Hofmannsthal, Hugo von
Morris, Bill 1952- .... **CLC 76**
Morris, Julian
See West, Morris L(anglo)
Morris, Steveland Judkins 1950(?)-
See Wonder, Stevie
See also CA 111
Morris, William 1834-1896 .... **NCLC 4**
See also BRW 5; CDBLB 1832-1890; DLB
18, 35, 57, 156, 178, 184; FANT; RGEL
2; SFW 4; SUFW
Morris, Wright 1910-1998 .. **CLC 1, 3, 7, 18,
37**
See also AMW; CA 9-12R; 167; CANR 21,
81; CN 7; DLB 2, 206, 218; DLBY 1981;
MTCW 1, 2; RGAL 4; TCLC 107;
TCWW 2

Morrison, Arthur 1863-1945 .... **TCLC 72;
SSC 40**
See also CA 120; 157; CMW 4; DLB 70,
135, 197; RGEL 2
Morrison, Chloe Anthony Wofford
See Morrison, Toni
Morrison, James Douglas 1943-1971
See Morrison, Jim
See also CA 73-76; CANR 40
Morrison, Jim .... **CLC 17**
See also Morrison, James Douglas
Morrison, Toni 1931- . **CLC 4, 10, 22, 55, 81,
87; BLC 3**
See also AAYA 1, 22; AFAW 1, 2; AMWS
3; BPFB 2; BW 2, 3; CA 29-32R; CANR
27, 42, 67; CDALB 1968-1988; CN 7;
CPW; DA; DA3; DAB; DAC; DAM MST,
MULT, NOV, POP; DLB 6, 33, 143;
DLBY 1981; EXPN; FW; LAIT 2, 4;
MAWW; MTCW 1, 2; NFS 1, 6, 8, 14;
RGAL 4; RHW; SATA 57; SSFS 5; YAW
Morrison, Van 1945- .... **CLC 21**
See also CA 116; 168
Morrissy, Mary 1958- .... **CLC 99**
Mortimer, John (Clifford) 1923- ..... **CLC 28,
43**
See also CA 13-16R; CANR 21, 69, 109;
CD 5; CDBLB 1960 to Present; CMW 4;
CN 7; CPW; DA3; DAM DRAM, POP;
DLB 13, 245; INT CANR-21; MSW;
MTCW 1, 2; RGEL 2
Mortimer, Penelope (Ruth)
1918-1999 .... **CLC 5**
See also CA 57-60; 187; CANR 45, 88; CN
7
Mortimer, Sir John
See Mortimer, John (Clifford)
Morton, Anthony
See Creasey, John
Morton, Thomas 1579(?)-1647(?) .... **LC 72**
See also DLB 24; RGEL 2
Mosca, Gaetano 1858-1941 .... **TCLC 75**
Mosher, Howard Frank 1943- .... **CLC 62**
See also CA 139; CANR 65
Mosley, Nicholas 1923- .... **CLC 43, 70**
See also CA 69-72; CANR 41, 60, 108; CN
7; DLB 14, 207
Mosley, Walter 1952- .... **CLC 97; BLCS**
See also AAYA 17; BPFB 2; BW 2; CA
142; CANR 57, 92; CMW 4; CPW; DA3;
DAM MULT, POP; MSW; MTCW 2
Moss, Howard 1922-1987 . **CLC 7, 14, 45, 50**
See also CA 1-4R; 123; CANR 1, 44; DAM
POET; DLB 5
Mossgiel, Rab
See Burns, Robert
Motion, Andrew (Peter) 1952- .... **CLC 47**
See also BRWS 7; CA 146; CANR 90; CP
7; DLB 40
Motley, Willard (Francis)
1912-1965 .... **CLC 18**
See also BW 1; CA 117; 106; CANR 88;
DLB 76, 143
Motoori, Norinaga 1730-1801 .... **NCLC 45**
Mott, Michael (Charles Alston)
1930- .... **CLC 15, 34**
See also CA 5-8R; CAAS 7; CANR 7, 29
Mountain Wolf Woman 1884-1960 .. **CLC 92**
See also CA 144; CANR 90; NNAL
Moure, Erin 1955- .... **CLC 88**
See also CA 113; CP 7; CWP; DLB 60
Mowat, Farley (McGill) 1921- .... **CLC 26**
See also AAYA 1; BYA 2; CA 1-4R; CANR
4, 24, 42, 68, 108; CLR 20; CPW; DAC;
DAM MST; DLB 68; INT CANR-24;
JRDA; MAICYA 1, 2; MTCW 1, 2; SATA
3, 55; YAW
Mowatt, Anna Cora 1819-1870 ..... **NCLC 74**
See also RGAL 4

Moyers, Bill 1934- .... **CLC 74**
See also AITN 2; CA 61-64; CANR 31, 52
Mphahlele, Es'kia
See Mphahlele, Ezekiel
See also AFW; CDWLB 3; DLB 125, 225;
RGSF 2; SSFS 11
Mphahlele, Ezekiel 1919- .... **CLC 25, 133;
BLC 3**
See also Mphahlele, Es'kia
See also BW 2, 3; CA 81-84; CANR 26,
76; CN 7; DA3; DAM MULT; MTCW 2;
SATA 119
Mqhayi, S(amuel) E(dward) K(rune Loliwe)
1875-1945 .... **TCLC 25; BLC 3**
See also CA 153; CANR 87; DAM MULT
Mrozek, Slawomir 1930- .... **CLC 3, 13**
See also CA 13-16R; CAAS 10; CANR 29;
CDWLB 4; CWW 2; DLB 232; MTCW 1
Mrs. Belloc-Lowndes
See Lowndes, Marie Adelaide (Belloc)
M'Taggart, John M'Taggart Ellis
See McTaggart, John McTaggart Ellis
Mtwa, Percy (?)- .... **CLC 47**
Mueller, Lisel 1924- .... **CLC 13, 51; PC 33**
See also CA 93-96; CP 7; DLB 105; PFS 9,
13
Muggeridge, Malcolm (Thomas)
1903-1990 .... **TCLC 120**
See also AITN 1; CA 101; CANR 33, 63;
MTCW 1, 2
Muir, Edwin 1887-1959 .... **TCLC 2, 87**
See also Moore, Edward
See also BRWS 6; CA 104; 193; DLB 20,
100, 191; RGEL 2
Muir, John 1838-1914 .... **TCLC 28**
See also AMWS 9; ANW; CA 165; DLB
186
Mujica Lainez, Manuel 1910-1984 ... **CLC 31**
See also Lainez, Manuel Mujica
See also CA 81-84; 112; CANR 32; HW 1
Mukherjee, Bharati 1940- .... **CLC 53, 115;
AAL; SSC 38**
See also BEST 89:2; CA 107; CANR 45,
72; CN 7; DAM NOV; DLB 60, 218;
DNFS 1, 2; FW; MTCW 1, 2; RGAL 4;
RGSF 2; SSFS 7
Muldoon, Paul 1951- .... **CLC 32, 72**
See also BRWS 4; CA 113; 129; CANR 52,
91; CP 7; DAM POET; DLB 40; INT 129;
PFS 7
Mulisch, Harry 1927- .... **CLC 42**
See also CA 9-12R; CANR 6, 26, 56
Mull, Martin 1943- .... **CLC 17**
See also CA 105
Muller, Wilhelm .... **NCLC 73**
Mulock, Dinah Maria
See Craik, Dinah Maria (Mulock)
See also RGEL 2
Munford, Robert 1737(?)-1783 .... **LC 5**
See also DLB 31
Mungo, Raymond 1946- .... **CLC 72**
See also CA 49-52; CANR 2
Munro, Alice 1931- .... **CLC 6, 10, 19, 50, 95;
SSC 3; WLCS**
See also AITN 2; BPFB 2; CA 33-36R;
CANR 33, 53, 75; CCA 1; CN 7; DA3;
DAC; DAM MST, NOV; DLB 53; MTCW
1, 2; RGEL 2; RGSF 2; SATA 29; SSFS
5, 13
Munro, H(ector) H(ugh) 1870-1916
See Saki
See also CA 104; 130; CANR 104; CDBLB
1890-1914; DA; DA3; DAB; DAC; DAM
MST, NOV; DLB 34, 162; EXPS; MTCW
1, 2; RGEL 2; WLC
Murakami, Haruki 1949- .... **CLC 150**
See also Murakami Haruki
See also CA 165; CANR 102; MJW; SFW 4

Murakami Haruki
See Murakami, Haruki
See also DLB 182

Murasaki, Lady
See Murasaki Shikibu

Murasaki Shikibu 978(?)-1026(?) ... **CMLC 1**
See also EFS 2; RGWL 2

Murdoch, (Jean) Iris 1919-1999 ... **CLC 1, 2, 3, 4, 6, 8, 11, 15, 22, 31, 51**
See also BRWS 1; CA 13-16R; 179; CANR 8, 43, 68, 103; CDBLB 1960 to Present; CN 7; DA3; DAB; DAC; DAM MST, NOV; DLB 14, 194, 233; INT CANR-8; MTCW 1, 2; RGEL 2; WLIT 4

Murfree, Mary Noailles 1850-1922 ... **SSC 22**
See also CA 122; 176; DLB 12, 74; RGAL 4

Murnau, Friedrich Wilhelm
See Plumpe, Friedrich Wilhelm

Murphy, Richard 1927- .... **CLC 41**
See also BRWS 5; CA 29-32R; CP 7; DLB 40

Murphy, Sylvia 1937- .... **CLC 34**
See also CA 121

Murphy, Thomas (Bernard) 1935- ... **CLC 51**
See also CA 101

Murray, Albert L. 1916- .... **CLC 73**
See also BW 2; CA 49-52; CANR 26, 52, 78; CSW; DLB 38

Murray, James Augustus Henry
1837-1915 .... **TCLC 117**

Murray, Judith Sargent
1751-1820 .... **NCLC 63**
See also DLB 37, 200

Murray, Les(lie Allan) 1938- .... **CLC 40**
See also BRWS 7; CA 21-24R; CANR 11, 27, 56, 103; CP 7; DAM POET; DLBY 01; RGEL 2

Murry, J. Middleton
See Murry, John Middleton

Murry, John Middleton
1889-1957 .... **TCLC 16**
See also CA 118; DLB 149

Musgrave, Susan 1951- .... **CLC 13, 54**
See also CA 69-72; CANR 45, 84; CCA 1; CP 7; CWP

Musil, Robert (Edler von)
1880-1942 .... **TCLC 12, 68; SSC 18**
See also CA 109; CANR 55, 84; CDWLB 2; DLB 81, 124; EW 9; MTCW 2; RGSF 2; RGWL 2

Muske, Carol .... **CLC 90**
See also Muske-Dukes, Carol (Anne)

Muske-Dukes, Carol (Anne) 1945-
See Muske, Carol
See also CA 65-68; CANR 32, 70; CWP

Musset, (Louis Charles) Alfred de
1810-1857 .... **NCLC 7**
See also DLB 192, 217; EW 6; GFL 1789 to the Present; RGWL 2; TWA

Mussolini, Benito (Amilcare Andrea)
1883-1945 .... **TCLC 96**
See also CA 116

My Brother's Brother
See Chekhov, Anton (Pavlovich)

Myers, L(eopold) H(amilton)
1881-1944 .... **TCLC 59**
See also CA 157; DLB 15; RGEL 2

Myers, Walter Dean 1937- .. **CLC 35; BLC 3**
See also AAYA 4, 23; BW 2; BYA 6, 8, 11; CA 33-36R; CANR 20, 42, 67, 108; CLR 4, 16, 35; DAM MULT, NOV; DLB 33; INT CANR-20; JRDA; LAIT 5; MAICYA 1, 2; MAICYAS 1; MTCW 2; SAAS 2; SATA 41, 71, 109; SATA-Brief 27; WYA; YAW

Myers, Walter M.
See Myers, Walter Dean

Myles, Symon
See Follett, Ken(neth Martin)

Nabokov, Vladimir (Vladimirovich)
1899-1977 .... **CLC 1, 2, 3, 6, 8, 11, 15, 23, 44, 46, 64; SSC 11; WLC**
See also AMW; AMWR 1; BPFB 2; CA 5-8R; 69-72; CANR 20, 102; CDALB 1941-1968; DA; DA3; DAB; DAC; DAM MST, NOV; DLB 2, 244; DLBD 3; DLBY 1980, 1991; EXPS; MTCW 1, 2; NFS 9; RGAL 4; RGSF 2; SSFS 6; TCLC 108

Naevius c. 265B.C.-201B.C. .... **CMLC 37**
See also DLB 211

Nagai, Kafu .... **TCLC 51**
See also Nagai, Sokichi
See also DLB 180

Nagai, Sokichi 1879-1959
See Nagai, Kafu
See also CA 117

Nagy, Laszlo 1925-1978 .... **CLC 7**
See also CA 129; 112

Naidu, Sarojini 1879-1949 .... **TCLC 80**
See also RGEL 2

Naipaul, Shiva(dhar Srinivasa)
1945-1985 .... **CLC 32, 39**
See also CA 110; 112; 116; CANR 33; DA3; DAM NOV; DLB 157; DLBY 1985; MTCW 1, 2

Naipaul, V(idiadhar) S(urajprasad)
1932- .... **CLC 4, 7, 9, 13, 18, 37, 105; SSC 38**
See also BPFB 2; BRWS 1; CA 1-4R; CANR 1, 33, 51, 91; CDBLB 1960 to Present; CDWLB 3; CN 7; DA3; DAB; DAC; DAM MST, NOV; DLB 125, 204, 207; DLBY 1985, 2001; MTCW 1, 2; RGEL 2; RGSF 2; WLIT 4

Nakos, Lilika 1899(?)- .... **CLC 29**

Narayan, R(asipuram) K(rishnaswami)
1906-2001 . **CLC 7, 28, 47, 121; SSC 25**
See also BPFB 2; CA 81-84; 196; CANR 33, 61; CN 7; DA3; DAM NOV; DNFS 1; MTCW 1, 2; RGEL 2; RGSF 2; SATA 62; SSFS 5

Nash, (Fredric) Ogden 1902-1971 . **CLC 23; PC 21**
See also CA 13-14; 29-32R; CANR 34, 61; CAP 1; DAM POET; DLB 11; MAICYA 1, 2; MTCW 1, 2; RGAL 4; SATA 2, 46; TCLC 109; WP

Nashe, Thomas 1567-1601(?) .... **LC 41**
See also DLB 167; RGEL 2

Nathan, Daniel
See Dannay, Frederic

Nathan, George Jean 1882-1958 .... **TCLC 18**
See also Hatteras, Owen
See also CA 114; 169; DLB 137

Natsume, Kinnosuke
See Natsume, Soseki

Natsume, Soseki 1867-1916 .... **TCLC 2, 10**
See also Natsume Soseki; Soseki
See also CA 104; 195; RGWL 2

Natsume Soseki
See Natsume, Soseki
See also DLB 180

Natti, (Mary) Lee 1919-
See Kingman, Lee
See also CA 5-8R; CANR 2

Navarre, Marguerite de
See de Navarre, Marguerite

Naylor, Gloria 1950- . **CLC 28, 52, 156; BLC 3; WLCS**
See also AAYA 6, 39; AFAW 1, 2; AMWS 8; BW 2, 3; CA 107; CANR 27, 51, 74; CN 7; CPW; DA; DA3; DAC; DAM MST, MULT, NOV, POP; DLB 173; FW; MTCW 1, 2; NFS 4, 7; RGAL 4

Neff, Debra .... **CLC 59**

Neihardt, John Gneisenau
1881-1973 .... **CLC 32**
See also CA 13-14; CANR 65; CAP 1; DLB 9, 54, 256; LAIT 2

Nekrasov, Nikolai Alekseevich
1821-1878 .... **NCLC 11**

Nelligan, Emile 1879-1941 .... **TCLC 14**
See also CA 114; DLB 92

Nelson, Willie 1933- .... **CLC 17**
See also CA 107

Nemerov, Howard (Stanley)
1920-1991 .... **CLC 2, 6, 9, 36; PC 24**
See also AMW; CA 1-4R; 134; CABS 2; CANR 1, 27, 53; DAM POET; DLB 5, 6; DLBY 1983; INT CANR-27; MTCW 1, 2; PFS 10, 14; RGAL 4

Neruda, Pablo 1904-1973 .. **CLC 1, 2, 5, 7, 9, 28, 62; HLC 2; PC 4; WLC**
See also CA 19-20; 45-48; CAP 2; DA; DA3; DAB; DAC; DAM MULT, POET; DNFS 2; HW 1; LAW; MTCW 1, 2; PFS 11; RGWL 2; WLIT 1; WP

Nerval, Gerard de 1808-1855 ... **NCLC 1, 67; PC 13; SSC 18**
See also DLB 217; EW 6; GFL 1789 to the Present; RGSF 2; RGWL 2

Nervo, (Jose) Amado (Ruiz de)
1870-1919 .... **TCLC 11; HLCS 2**
See also CA 109; 131; HW 1; LAW

Nesbit, Malcolm
See Chester, Alfred

Nessi, Pio Baroja y
See Baroja (y Nessi), Pio

Nestroy, Johann 1801-1862 .... **NCLC 42**
See also DLB 133; RGWL 2

Netterville, Luke
See O'Grady, Standish (James)

Neufeld, John (Arthur) 1938- .... **CLC 17**
See also AAYA 11; CA 25-28R; CANR 11, 37, 56; CLR 52; MAICYA 1, 2; SAAS 3; SATA 6, 81; SATA-Essay 131; YAW

Neumann, Alfred 1895-1952 .... **TCLC 100**
See also CA 183; DLB 56

Neumann, Ferenc
See Molnar, Ferenc

Neville, Emily Cheney 1919- .... **CLC 12**
See also BYA 2; CA 5-8R; CANR 3, 37, 85; JRDA; MAICYA 1, 2; SAAS 2; SATA 1; YAW

Newbound, Bernard Slade 1930-
See Slade, Bernard
See also CA 81-84; CANR 49; CD 5; DAM DRAM

Newby, P(ercy) H(oward)
1918-1997 .... **CLC 2, 13**
See also CA 5-8R; 161; CANR 32, 67; CN 7; DAM NOV; DLB 15; MTCW 1; RGEL 2

Newcastle
See Cavendish, Margaret Lucas

Newlove, Donald 1928- .... **CLC 6**
See also CA 29-32R; CANR 25

Newlove, John (Herbert) 1938- .... **CLC 14**
See also CA 21-24R; CANR 9, 25; CP 7

Newman, Charles 1938- .... **CLC 2, 8**
See also CA 21-24R; CANR 84; CN 7

Newman, Edwin (Harold) 1919- .... **CLC 14**
See also AITN 1; CA 69-72; CANR 5

Newman, John Henry 1801-1890 . **NCLC 38, 99**
See also BRWS 7; DLB 18, 32, 55; RGEL 2

Newton, (Sir) Isaac 1642-1727 ...... **LC 35, 53**
See also DLB 252

Newton, Suzanne 1936- .... **CLC 35**
See also BYA 7; CA 41-44R; CANR 14; JRDA; SATA 5, 77

New York Dept. of Ed. .... CLC 70
Nexo, Martin Andersen
      1869-1954 .... TCLC 43
      See also DLB 214
Nezval, Vitezslav 1900-1958 .... TCLC 44
      See also CA 123; CDWLB 4; DLB 215
Ng, Fae Myenne 1957(?)- .... CLC 81
      See also CA 146
Ngema, Mbongeni 1955- .... CLC 57
      See also BW 2; CA 143; CANR 84; CD 5
Ngugi, James T(hiong'o) .... CLC 3, 7, 13
      See also Ngugi wa Thiong'o
Ngugi wa Thiong'o
      See Ngugi wa Thiong'o
      See also DLB 125
Ngugi wa Thiong'o 1938- .... CLC 36; BLC 3
      See also Ngugi, James T(hiong'o); Ngugi
      wa Thiong'o
      See also AFW; BW 2; CA 81-84; CANR
      27, 58; CDWLB 3; DAM MULT, NOV;
      DNFS 2; MTCW 1, 2; RGEL 2
Nichol, B(arrie) P(hillip) 1944-1988 . CLC 18
      See also CA 53-56; DLB 53; SATA 66
Nichols, John (Treadwell) 1940- .... CLC 38
      See also CA 9-12R; CAAE 190; CAAS 2;
      CANR 6, 70; DLBY 1982; TCWW 2
Nichols, Leigh
      See Koontz, Dean R(ay)
Nichols, Peter (Richard) 1927- .... CLC 5, 36,
      65
      See also CA 104; CANR 33, 86; CBD; CD
      5; DLB 13, 245; MTCW 1
Nicholson, Linda ed. .... CLC 65
Ni Chuilleanain, Eilean 1942- .... PC 34
      See also CA 126; CANR 53, 83; CP 7;
      CWP; DLB 40
Nicolas, F. R. E.
      See Freeling, Nicolas
Niedecker, Lorine 1903-1970 ...... CLC 10, 42
      See also CA 25-28; CAP 2; DAM POET;
      DLB 48
Nietzsche, Friedrich (Wilhelm)
      1844-1900 .... TCLC 10, 18, 55
      See also CA 107; 121; CDWLB 2; DLB
      129; EW 7; RGWL 2
Nievo, Ippolito 1831-1861 .... NCLC 22
Nightingale, Anne Redmon 1943-
      See Redmon, Anne
      See also CA 103
Nightingale, Florence 1820-1910 ... TCLC 85
      See also CA 188; DLB 166
Nijo Yoshimoto 1320-1388 .... CMLC 49
      See also DLB 203
Nik. T. O.
      See Annensky, Innokenty (Fyodorovich)
Nin, Anais 1903-1977 ..... CLC 1, 4, 8, 11, 14,
      60, 127; SSC 10
      See also AITN 2; AMWS 10; BPFB 2; CA
      13-16R; 69-72; CANR 22, 53; DAM
      NOV, POP; DLB 2, 4, 152; GLL 2;
      MAWW; MTCW 1, 2; RGAL 4; RGSF 2
Nisbet, Robert A(lexander)
      1913-1996 .... TCLC 117
      See also CA 25-28R; 153; CANR 17; INT
      CANR-17
Nishida, Kitaro 1870-1945 .... TCLC 83
Nishiwaki, Junzaburo 1894-1982 .... PC 15
      See also Nishiwaki, Junzaburo
      See also CA 194; 107; MJW
Nishiwaki, Junzaburo 1894-1982
      See Nishiwaki, Junzaburo
      See also CA 194
Nissenson, Hugh 1933- .... CLC 4, 9
      See also CA 17-20R; CANR 27, 108; CN
      7; DLB 28
Niven, Larry .... CLC 8
      See also Niven, Laurence Van Cott
      See also AAYA 27; BPFB 2; BYA 10; DLB
      8; SCFW 2

Niven, Laurence Van Cott 1938-
      See Niven, Larry
      See also CA 21-24R; CAAS 12; CANR 14,
      44, 66; CPW; DAM POP; MTCW 1, 2;
      SATA 95; SFW 4
Nixon, Agnes Eckhardt 1927- .... CLC 21
      See also CA 110
Nizan, Paul 1905-1940 .... TCLC 40
      See also CA 161; DLB 72; GFL 1789 to the
      Present
Nkosi, Lewis 1936- .... CLC 45; BLC 3
      See also BW 1, 3; CA 65-68; CANR 27,
      81; CBD; CD 5; DAM MULT; DLB 157,
      225
Nodier, (Jean) Charles (Emmanuel)
      1780-1844 .... NCLC 19
      See also DLB 119; GFL 1789 to the Present
Noguchi, Yone 1875-1947 .... TCLC 80
Nolan, Christopher 1965- .... CLC 58
      See also CA 111; CANR 88
Noon, Jeff 1957- .... CLC 91
      See also CA 148; CANR 83; SFW 4
Norden, Charles
      See Durrell, Lawrence (George)
Nordhoff, Charles (Bernard)
      1887-1947 .... TCLC 23
      See also CA 108; DLB 9; LAIT 1; RHW 1;
      SATA 23
Norfolk, Lawrence 1963- .... CLC 76
      See also CA 144; CANR 85; CN 7
Norman, Marsha 1947- .... CLC 28; DC 8
      See also CA 105; CABS 3; CAD; CANR
      41; CD 5; CSW; CWD; DAM DRAM;
      DFS 2; DLBY 1984; FW
Normyx
      See Douglas, (George) Norman
Norris, (Benjamin) Frank(lin, Jr.)
      1870-1902 .... TCLC 24; SSC 28
      See also AMW; BPFB 2; CA 110; 160;
      CDALB 1865-1917; DLB 12, 71, 186;
      NFS 12; RGAL 4; TCWW 2; TUS
Norris, Leslie 1921- .... CLC 14
      See also CA 11-12; CANR 14; CAP 1; CP
      7; DLB 27, 256
North, Andrew
      See Norton, Andre
North, Anthony
      See Koontz, Dean R(ay)
North, Captain George
      See Stevenson, Robert Louis (Balfour)
North, Captain George
      See Stevenson, Robert Louis (Balfour)
North, Milou
      See Erdrich, Louise
Northrup, B. A.
      See Hubbard, L(afayette) Ron(ald)
North Staffs
      See Hulme, T(homas) E(rnest)
Northup, Solomon 1808-1863 ...... NCLC 105
Norton, Alice Mary
      See Norton, Andre
      See also MAICYA 1; SATA 1, 43
Norton, Andre 1912- .... CLC 12
      See also Norton, Alice Mary
      See also AAYA 14; BPFB 2; BYA 4, 10,
      12; CA 1-4R; CANR 68; CLR 50; DLB
      8, 52; JRDA; MAICYA 2; MTCW 1;
      SATA 91; SUFW; YAW
Norton, Caroline 1808-1877 .... NCLC 47
      See also DLB 21, 159, 199
Norway, Nevil Shute 1899-1960
      See Shute, Nevil
      See also CA 102; 93-96; CANR 85; MTCW
      2
Norwid, Cyprian Kamil
      1821-1883 .... NCLC 17
Nosille, Nabrah
      See Ellison, Harlan (Jay)

Nossack, Hans Erich 1901-1978 .... CLC 6
      See also CA 93-96; 85-88; DLB 69
Nostradamus 1503-1566 .... LC 27
Nosu, Chuji
      See Ozu, Yasujiro
Notenburg, Eleanora (Genrikhovna) von
      See Guro, Elena
Nova, Craig 1945- .... CLC 7, 31
      See also CA 45-48; CANR 2, 53
Novak, Joseph
      See Kosinski, Jerzy (Nikodem)
Novalis 1772-1801 .... NCLC 13
      See also CDWLB 2; DLB 90; EW 5; RGWL
      2
Novis, Emile
      See Weil, Simone (Adolphine)
Nowlan, Alden (Albert) 1933-1983 ... CLC 15
      See also CA 9-12R; CANR 5; DAC; DAM
      MST; DLB 53; PFS 12
Noyes, Alfred 1880-1958 ...... TCLC 7; PC 27
      See also CA 104; 188; DLB 20; EXPP;
      FANT; PFS 4; RGEL 2
Nunn, Kem .... CLC 34
      See also CA 159
Nwapa, Flora 1931-1993 .... CLC 133; BLCS
      See also BW 2; CA 143; CANR 83; CD-
      WLB 3; CWRI 5; DLB 125; WLIT 2
Nye, Robert 1939- .... CLC 13, 42
      See also CA 33-36R; CANR 29, 67, 107;
      CN 7; CP 7; CWRI 5; DAM NOV; DLB
      14; FANT; HGG; MTCW 1; RHW; SATA
      6
Nyro, Laura 1947-1997 .... CLC 17
      See also CA 194
Oates, Joyce Carol 1938- .. CLC 1, 2, 3, 6, 9,
      11, 15, 19, 33, 52, 108, 134; SSC 6;
      WLC
      See also AAYA 15; AITN 1; AMWS 2;
      BEST 89:2; BPFB 2; BYA 11; CA 5-8R;
      CANR 25, 45, 74; CDALB 1968-1988;
      CN 7; CP 7; CPW; CWP; DA; DA3;
      DAB; DAC; DAM MST, NOV, POP;
      DLB 2, 5, 130; DLBY 1981; EXPS; FW;
      HGG; INT CANR-25; LAIT 4; MAWW;
      MTCW 1, 2; NFS 8; RGAL 4; RGSF 2;
      SSFS 1, 8
O'Brian, Patrick 1914-2000 .... CLC 152
      See also CA 144; 187; CANR 74; CPW;
      MTCW 2; RHW
O'Brien, Darcy 1939-1998 .... CLC 11
      See also CA 21-24R; 167; CANR 8, 59
O'Brien, E. G.
      See Clarke, Arthur C(harles)
O'Brien, Edna 1936- ..... CLC 3, 5, 8, 13, 36,
      65, 116; SSC 10
      See also BRWS 5; CA 1-4R; CANR 6, 41,
      65, 102; CDBLB 1960 to Present; CN 7;
      DA3; DAM NOV; DLB 14, 231; FW;
      MTCW 1, 2; RGSF 2; WLIT 4
O'Brien, Fitz-James 1828-1862 ..... NCLC 21
      See also DLB 74; RGAL 4; SUFW
O'Brien, Flann .... CLC 1, 4, 5, 7, 10, 47
      See also O Nuallain, Brian
      See also BRWS 2; DLB 231; RGEL 2
O'Brien, Richard 1942- .... CLC 17
      See also CA 124
O'Brien, (William) Tim(othy) 1946- . CLC 7,
      19, 40, 103
      See also AAYA 16; AMWS 5; CA 85-88;
      CANR 40, 58; CDALBS; CN 7; CPW;
      DA3; DAM POP; DLB 152; DLBD 9;
      DLBY 1980; MTCW 2; RGAL 4; SSFS 5
Obstfelder, Sigbjoern 1866-1900 .... TCLC 23
      See also CA 123

O'Casey, Sean 1880-1964 .... **CLC 1, 5, 9, 11, 15, 88; DC 12; WLCS**
See also BRW 7; CA 89-92; CANR 62; CBD; CDBLB 1914-1945; DA3; DAB; DAC; DAM DRAM, MST; DLB 10; MTCW 1, 2; RGEL 2; WLIT 4

O'Cathasaigh, Sean
See O'Casey, Sean

Occom, Samson 1723-1792 .... **LC 60**
See also DLB 175; NNAL

Ochs, Phil(ip David) 1940-1976 .... **CLC 17**
See also CA 185; 65-68

O'Connor, Edwin (Greene) 1918-1968 .... **CLC 14**
See also CA 93-96; 25-28R

O'Connor, (Mary) Flannery 1925-1964 .... **CLC 1, 2, 3, 6, 10, 13, 15, 21, 66, 104; SSC 1, 23; WLC**
See also AAYA 7; AMW; BPFB 3; CA 1-4R; CANR 3, 41; CDALB 1941-1968; DA; DA3; DAB; DAC; DAM MST, NOV; DLB 2, 152; DLBD 12; DLBY 1980; EXPS; LAIT 5; MAWW; MTCW 1, 2; NFS 3; RGAL 4; RGSF 2; SSFS 2, 7, 10

O'Connor, Frank .... **CLC 23; SSC 5**
See also O'Donovan, Michael John
See also DLB 162; RGSF 2; SSFS 5

O'Dell, Scott 1898-1989 .... **CLC 30**
See also AAYA 3; BPFB 3; BYA 1, 2, 3, 5; CA 61-64; 129; CANR 12, 30; CLR 1, 16; DLB 52; JRDA; MAICYA 1, 2; SATA 12, 60; WYA; YAW

Odets, Clifford 1906-1963 ..... **CLC 2, 28, 98; DC 6**
See also AMWS 2; CA 85-88; CAD; CANR 62; DAM DRAM; DFS 3; DLB 7, 26; MTCW 1, 2; RGAL 4

O'Doherty, Brian 1928- .... **CLC 76**
See also CA 105; CANR 108

O'Donnell, K. M.
See Malzberg, Barry N(athaniel)

O'Donnell, Lawrence
See Kuttner, Henry

O'Donovan, Michael John 1903-1966 .... **CLC 14**
See also O'Connor, Frank
See also CA 93-96; CANR 84

Oe, Kenzaburo 1935- .. **CLC 10, 36, 86; SSC 20**
See also Oe Kenzaburo
See also CA 97-100; CANR 36, 50, 74; DA3; DAM NOV; DLBY 1994; MTCW 1, 2

Oe Kenzaburo
See Oe, Kenzaburo
See also CWW 2; DLB 182; EWL 3; MJW; RGSF 2; RGWL 2

O'Faolain, Julia 1932- .... **CLC 6, 19, 47, 108**
See also CA 81-84; CAAS 2; CANR 12, 61; CN 7; DLB 14, 231; FW; MTCW 1; RHW

O'Faolain, Sean 1900-1991 ...... **CLC 1, 7, 14, 32, 70; SSC 13**
See also CA 61-64; 134; CANR 12, 66; DLB 15, 162; MTCW 1, 2; RGEL 2; RGSF 2

O'Flaherty, Liam 1896-1984 .... **CLC 5, 34; SSC 6**
See also CA 101; 113; CANR 35; DLB 36, 162; DLBY 1984; MTCW 1, 2; RGEL 2; RGSF 2; SSFS 5

Ogai
See Mori Ogai
See also MJW

Ogilvy, Gavin
See Barrie, J(ames) M(atthew)

O'Grady, Standish (James) 1846-1928 .... **TCLC 5**
See also CA 104; 157

O'Grady, Timothy 1951- .... **CLC 59**
See also CA 138

O'Hara, Frank 1926-1966 .. **CLC 2, 5, 13, 78**
See also CA 9-12R; 25-28R; CANR 33; DA3; DAM POET; DLB 5, 16, 193; MTCW 1, 2; PFS 8; 12; RGAL 4; WP

O'Hara, John (Henry) 1905-1970 . **CLC 1, 2, 3, 6, 11, 42; SSC 15**
See also AMW; BPFB 3; CA 5-8R; 25-28R; CANR 31, 60; CDALB 1929-1941; DAM NOV; DLB 9, 86; DLBD 2; MTCW 1, 2; NFS 11; RGAL 4; RGSF 2

O Hehir, Diana 1922- .... **CLC 41**
See also CA 93-96

Ohiyesa 1858-1939
See Eastman, Charles A(lexander)

Okigbo, Christopher (Ifenayichukwu) 1932-1967 .... **CLC 25, 84; BLC 3; PC 7**
See also AFW; BW 1, 3; CA 77-80; CANR 74; CDWLB 3; DAM MULT, POET; DLB 125; MTCW 1, 2; RGEL 2

Okri, Ben 1959- .... **CLC 87**
See also AFW; BRWS 5; BW 2, 3; CA 130; 138; CANR 65; CN 7; DLB 157, 231; INT CA-138; MTCW 2; RGSF 2; WLIT 2

Olds, Sharon 1942- .. **CLC 32, 39, 85; PC 22**
See also AMWS 10; CA 101; CANR 18, 41, 66, 98; CP 7; CPW; CWP; DAM POET; DLB 120; MTCW 2

Oldstyle, Jonathan
See Irving, Washington

Olesha, Iurii
See Olesha, Yuri (Karlovich)
See also RGWL 2

Olesha, Yuri (Karlovich) 1899-1960 .. **CLC 8**
See also Olesha, Iurii
See also CA 85-88; EW 11

Oliphant, Mrs.
See Oliphant, Margaret (Oliphant Wilson)
See also SUFW

Oliphant, Laurence 1829(?)-1888 .. **NCLC 47**
See also DLB 18, 166

Oliphant, Margaret (Oliphant Wilson) 1828-1897 .... **NCLC 11, 61; SSC 25**
See also Oliphant, Mrs.
See also DLB 18, 159, 190; HGG; RGEL 2; RGSF 2

Oliver, Mary 1935- .... **CLC 19, 34, 98**
See also AMWS 7; CA 21-24R; CANR 9, 43, 84, 92; CP 7; CWP; DLB 5, 193

Olivier, Laurence (Kerr) 1907-1989 . **CLC 20**
See also CA 111; 150; 129

Olsen, Tillie 1912- ... **CLC 4, 13, 114; SSC 11**
See also BYA 11; CA 1-4R; CANR 1, 43, 74; CDALBS; CN 7; DA; DA3; DAB; DAC; DAM MST; DLB 28, 206; DLBY 1980; EXPS; FW; MTCW 1, 2; RGAL 4; RGSF 2; SSFS 1

Olson, Charles (John) 1910-1970 .. **CLC 1, 2, 5, 6, 9, 11, 29; PC 19**
See also AMWS 2; CA 13-16; 25-28R; CABS 2; CANR 35, 61; CAP 1; DAM POET; DLB 5, 16, 193; MTCW 1, 2; RGAL 4; WP

Olson, Toby 1937- .... **CLC 28**
See also CA 65-68; CANR 9, 31, 84; CP 7

Olyesha, Yuri
See Olesha, Yuri (Karlovich)

Omar Khayyam
See Khayyam, Omar
See also RGWL 2

Ondaatje, (Philip) Michael 1943- .... **CLC 14, 29, 51, 76; PC 28**
See also CA 77-80; CANR 42, 74, 109; CN 7; CP 7; DA3; DAB; DAC; DAM MST; DLB 60; MTCW 2; PFS 8

Oneal, Elizabeth 1934-
See Oneal, Zibby
See also CA 106; CANR 28, 84; MAICYA 1, 2; SATA 30, 82; YAW

Oneal, Zibby .... **CLC 30**
See also Oneal, Elizabeth
See also AAYA 5, 41; BYA 13; CLR 13; JRDA; WYA

O'Neill, Eugene (Gladstone) 1888-1953 ...... **TCLC 1, 6, 27, 49; WLC**
See also AITN 1; AMW; CA 110; 132; CAD; CDALB 1929-1941; DA; DA3; DAB; DAC; DAM DRAM, MST; DFS 9, 11, 12; DLB 7; LAIT 3; MTCW 1, 2; RGAL 4

Onetti, Juan Carlos 1909-1994 ... **CLC 7, 10; HLCS 2; SSC 23**
See also CA 85-88; 145; CANR 32, 63; CDWLB 3; DAM MULT, NOV; DLB 113; HW 1, 2; LAW; MTCW 1, 2; RGSF 2

O Nuallain, Brian 1911-1966
See O'Brien, Flann
See also CA 21-22; 25-28R; CAP 2; DLB 231; FANT

Ophuls, Max 1902-1957 .... **TCLC 79**
See also CA 113

Opie, Amelia 1769-1853 .... **NCLC 65**
See also DLB 116, 159; RGEL 2

Oppen, George 1908-1984 ..... **CLC 7, 13, 34; PC 35**
See also CA 13-16R; 113; CANR 8, 82; DLB 5, 165; TCLC 107

Oppenheim, E(dward) Phillips 1866-1946 .... **TCLC 45**
See also CA 111; CMW 4; DLB 70

Opuls, Max
See Ophuls, Max

Origen c. 185-c. 254 .... **CMLC 19**

Orlovitz, Gil 1918-1973 .... **CLC 22**
See also CA 77-80; 45-48; DLB 2, 5

Orris
See Ingelow, Jean

Ortega y Gasset, Jose 1883-1955 ... **TCLC 9; HLC 2**
See also CA 106; 130; DAM MULT; EW 9; HW 1, 2; MTCW 1, 2

Ortese, Anna Maria 1914- .... **CLC 89**
See also DLB 177

Ortiz, Simon J(oseph) 1941- ..... **CLC 45; PC 17**
See also AMWS 4; CA 134; CANR 69; CP 7; DAM MULT, POET; DLB 120, 175, 256; EXPP; NNAL; PFS 4; RGAL 4

Orton, Joe .... **CLC 4, 13, 43; DC 3**
See also Orton, John Kingsley
See also BRWS 5; CBD; CDBLB 1960 to Present; DFS 3, 6; DLB 13; GLL 1; MTCW 2; RGEL 2; WLIT 4

Orton, John Kingsley 1933-1967
See Orton, Joe
See also CA 85-88; CANR 35, 66; DAM DRAM; MTCW 1, 2

Orwell, George .... **TCLC 2, 6, 15, 31, 51; WLC**
See also Blair, Eric (Arthur)
See also BPFB 3; BRW 7; BYA 5; CDBLB 1945-1960; CLR 68; DAB; DLB 15, 98, 195, 255; EXPN; LAIT 4, 5; NFS 3, 7; RGEL 2; SCFW 2; SFW 4; SSFS 4; WLIT 4; YAW

Osborne, David
See Silverberg, Robert

Osborne, George
See Silverberg, Robert

Osborne, John (James) 1929-1994 .... **CLC 1, 2, 5, 11, 45; WLC**
See also BRWS 1; CA 13-16R; 147; CANR 21, 56; CDBLB 1945-1960; DA; DAB; DAC; DAM DRAM, MST; DFS 4; DLB 13; MTCW 1, 2; RGEL 2

Osborne, Lawrence 1958- .... **CLC 50**
See also CA 189

Osbourne, Lloyd 1868-1947 .... **TCLC 93**

Oshima, Nagisa 1932- .... **CLC 20**
See also CA 116; 121; CANR 78

Oskison, John Milton 1874-1947 ... **TCLC 35**
See also CA 144; CANR 84; DAM MULT; DLB 175; NNAL

Ossian c. 3rd cent. - .... **CMLC 28**
See also Macpherson, James

Ossoli, Sarah Margaret (Fuller)
1810-1850 .... **NCLC 5, 50**
See also Fuller, Margaret; Fuller, Sarah Margaret
See also CDALB 1640-1865; FW; SATA 25

Ostriker, Alicia (Suskin) 1937- .... **CLC 132**
See also CA 25-28R; CAAS 24; CANR 10, 30, 62, 99; CWP; DLB 120; EXPP

Ostrovsky, Alexander 1823-1886 .. **NCLC 30, 57**

Otero, Blas de 1916-1979 .... **CLC 11**
See also CA 89-92; DLB 134

Otto, Rudolf 1869-1937 .... **TCLC 85**

Otto, Whitney 1955- .... **CLC 70**
See also CA 140

Ouida .... **TCLC 43**
See also De La Ramee, (Marie) Louise
See also DLB 18, 156; RGEL 2

Ouologuem, Yambo 1940- .... **CLC 146**
See also CA 111; 176

Ousmane, Sembene 1923- ... **CLC 66; BLC 3**
See also Sembene, Ousmane
See also BW 1, 3; CA 117; 125; CANR 81; CWW 2; MTCW 1

Ovid 43B.C.-17 .... **CMLC 7; PC 2**
See also AW 2; CDWLB 1; DA3; DAM POET; DLB 211; RGWL 2; WP

Owen, Hugh
See Faust, Frederick (Schiller)

Owen, Wilfred (Edward Salter)
1893-1918 ... **TCLC 5, 27; PC 19; WLC**
See also BRW 6; CA 104; 141; CDBLB 1914-1945; DA; DAB; DAC; DAM MST, POET; DLB 20; EXPP; MTCW 2; PFS 10; RGEL 2; WLIT 4

Owens, Rochelle 1936- .... **CLC 8**
See also CA 17-20R; CAAS 2; CAD; CANR 39; CD 5; CP 7; CWD; CWP

Oz, Amos 1939- .... **CLC 5, 8, 11, 27, 33, 54**
See also CA 53-56; CANR 27, 47, 65; CWW 2; DAM NOV; MTCW 1, 2; RGSF 2

Ozick, Cynthia 1928- .... **CLC 3, 7, 28, 62, 155; SSC 15**
See also AMWS 5; BEST 90:1; CA 17-20R; CANR 23, 58; CN 7; CPW; DA3; DAM NOV, POP; DLB 28, 152; DLBY 1982; EXPS; INT CANR-23; MTCW 1, 2; RGAL 4; RGSF 2; SSFS 3, 12

Ozu, Yasujiro 1903-1963 .... **CLC 16**
See also CA 112

Pacheco, C.
See Pessoa, Fernando (Antonio Nogueira)

Pacheco, Jose Emilio 1939-
See also CA 111; 131; CANR 65; DAM MULT; HLC 2; HW 1, 2; RGSF 2

Pa Chin .... **CLC 18**
See also Li Fei-kan

Pack, Robert 1929- .... **CLC 13**
See also CA 1-4R; CANR 3, 44, 82; CP 7; DLB 5; SATA 118

Padgett, Lewis
See Kuttner, Henry

Padilla (Lorenzo), Heberto
1932-2000 .... **CLC 38**
See also AITN 1; CA 123; 131; 189; HW 1

Page, Jimmy 1944- .... **CLC 12**

Page, Louise 1955- .... **CLC 40**
See also CA 140; CANR 76; CBD; CD 5; CWD; DLB 233

Page, P(atricia) K(athleen) 1916- ...... **CLC 7, 18; PC 12**
See also Cape, Judith
See also CA 53-56; CANR 4, 22, 65; CP 7; DAC; DAM MST; DLB 68; MTCW 1; RGEL 2

Page, Stanton
See Fuller, Henry Blake

Page, Stanton
See Fuller, Henry Blake

Page, Thomas Nelson 1853-1922 .... **SSC 23**
See also CA 118; 177; DLB 12, 78; DLBD 13; RGAL 4

Pagels, Elaine Hiesey 1943- .... **CLC 104**
See also CA 45-48; CANR 2, 24, 51; FW

Paget, Violet 1856-1935
See Lee, Vernon
See also CA 104; 166; GLL 1; HGG

Paget-Lowe, Henry
See Lovecraft, H(oward) P(hillips)

Paglia, Camille (Anna) 1947- .... **CLC 68**
See also CA 140; CANR 72; CPW; FW; GLL 2; MTCW 2

Paige, Richard
See Koontz, Dean R(ay)

Paine, Thomas 1737-1809 .... **NCLC 62**
See also AMWS 1; CDALB 1640-1865; DLB 31, 43, 73, 158; LAIT 1; RGAL 4; RGEL 2

Palamas, Kostes 1859-1943 .... **TCLC 5**
See also CA 105; 190; RGWL 2

Palazzeschi, Aldo 1885-1974 .... **CLC 11**
See also CA 89-92; 53-56; DLB 114

Pales Matos, Luis 1898-1959
See Pales Matos, Luis
See also HLCS 2; HW 1; LAW

Paley, Grace 1922- .. **CLC 4, 6, 37, 140; SSC 8**
See also AMWS 6; CA 25-28R; CANR 13, 46, 74; CN 7; CPW; DA3; DAM POP; DLB 28, 218; EXPS; FW; INT CANR-13; MAWW; MTCW 1, 2; RGAL 4; RGSF 2; SSFS 3

Palin, Michael (Edward) 1943- .... **CLC 21**
See also Monty Python
See also CA 107; CANR 35, 109; SATA 67

Palliser, Charles 1947- .... **CLC 65**
See also CA 136; CANR 76; CN 7

Palma, Ricardo 1833-1919 .... **TCLC 29**
See also CA 168; LAW

Pancake, Breece Dexter 1952-1979
See Pancake, Breece D'J
See also CA 123; 109

Pancake, Breece D'J .... **CLC 29**
See also Pancake, Breece Dexter
See also DLB 130

Panchenko, Nikolai .... **CLC 59**

Pankhurst, Emmeline (Goulden)
1858-1928 .... **TCLC 100**
See also CA 116; FW

Panko, Rudy
See Gogol, Nikolai (Vasilyevich)

Papadiamantis, Alexandros
1851-1911 .... **TCLC 29**
See also CA 168

Papadiamantopoulos, Johannes 1856-1910
See Moreas, Jean
See also CA 117

Papini, Giovanni 1881-1956 .... **TCLC 22**
See also CA 121; 180

Paracelsus 1493-1541 .... **LC 14**
See also DLB 179

Parasol, Peter
See Stevens, Wallace

Pardo Bazan, Emilia 1851-1921 .... **SSC 30**
See also FW; RGSF 2; RGWL 2

Pareto, Vilfredo 1848-1923 .... **TCLC 69**
See also CA 175

Paretsky, Sara 1947- .... **CLC 135**
See also AAYA 30; BEST 90:3; CA 125; 129; CANR 59, 95; CMW 4; CPW; DA3; DAM POP; INT CA-129; MSW; RGAL 4

Parfenie, Maria
See Codrescu, Andrei

Parini, Jay (Lee) 1948- .... **CLC 54, 133**
See also CA 97-100; CAAS 16; CANR 32, 87

Park, Jordan
See Kornbluth, C(yril) M.; Pohl, Frederik

Park, Robert E(zra) 1864-1944 ..... **TCLC 73**
See also CA 122; 165

Parker, Bert
See Ellison, Harlan (Jay)

Parker, Dorothy (Rothschild)
1893-1967 .. **CLC 15, 68; PC 28; SSC 2**
See also AMWS 9; CA 19-20; 25-28R; CAP 2; DA3; DAM POET; DLB 11, 45, 86; EXPP; FW; MAWW; MTCW 1, 2; RGAL 4; RGSF 2

Parker, Robert B(rown) 1932- .... **CLC 27**
See also AAYA 28; BEST 89:4; BPFB 3; CA 49-52; CANR 1, 26, 52, 89; CMW 4; CPW; DAM NOV, POP; INT CANR-26; MSW; MTCW 1

Parkin, Frank 1940- .... **CLC 43**
See also CA 147

Parkman, Francis, Jr. 1823-1893 .. **NCLC 12**
See also AMWS 2; DLB 1, 30, 183, 186, 235; RGAL 4

Parks, Gordon (Alexander Buchanan)
1912- .... **CLC 1, 16; BLC 3**
See also AAYA 36; AITN 2; BW 2, 3; CA 41-44R; CANR 26, 66; DA3; DAM MULT; DLB 33; MTCW 2; SATA 8, 108

Parks, Tim(othy Harold) 1954- ...... **CLC 147**
See also CA 126; 131; CANR 77; DLB 231; INT CA-131

Parmenides c. 515B.C.-c.
450B.C. .... **CMLC 22**
See also DLB 176

Parnell, Thomas 1679-1718 .... **LC 3**
See also DLB 95; RGEL 2

Parra, Nicanor 1914- ... **CLC 2, 102; HLC 2; PC 39**
See also CA 85-88; CANR 32; CWW 2; DAM MULT; HW 1; LAW; MTCW 1

Parra Sanojo, Ana Teresa de la 1890-1936
See de la Parra, (Ana) Teresa (Sonojo)
See also HLCS 2; LAW

Parrish, Mary Frances
See Fisher, M(ary) F(rances) K(ennedy)

Parshchikov, Aleksei .... **CLC 59**

Parson, Professor
See Coleridge, Samuel Taylor

Parson Lot
See Kingsley, Charles

Parton, Sara Payson Willis
1811-1872 .... **NCLC 86**
See also DLB 43, 74, 239

Partridge, Anthony
See Oppenheim, E(dward) Phillips

Pascal, Blaise 1623-1662 .... **LC 35**
See also EW 3; GFL Beginnings to 1789; RGWL 2

Pascoli, Giovanni 1855-1912 .... **TCLC 45**
See also CA 170; EW 7

Pasolini, Pier Paolo 1922-1975 .. **CLC 20, 37, 106; PC 17**
See also CA 93-96; 61-64; CANR 63; DLB 128, 177; MTCW 1; RGWL 2

Pasquini
See Silone, Ignazio

Pastan, Linda (Olenik) 1932- .... **CLC 27**
See also CA 61-64; CANR 18, 40, 61; CP 7; CSW; CWP; DAM POET; DLB 5; PFS 8

Pasternak, Boris (Leonidovich) 1890-1960 ...... **CLC 7, 10, 18, 63; PC 6; SSC 31; WLC**
See also BPFB 3; CA 127; 116; DA; DA3; DAB; DAC; DAM MST, NOV, POET; EW 10; MTCW 1, 2; RGSF 2; RGWL 2; WP

Patchen, Kenneth 1911-1972 .... **CLC 1, 2, 18**
See also CA 1-4R; 33-36R; CANR 3, 35; DAM POET; DLB 16, 48; MTCW 1; RGAL 4

Pater, Walter (Horatio) 1839-1894 . **NCLC 7, 90**
See also BRW 5; CDBLB 1832-1890; DLB 57, 156; RGEL 2

Paterson, A(ndrew) B(arton) 1864-1941 .... **TCLC 32**
See also CA 155; DLB 230; RGEL 2; SATA 97

Paterson, Katherine (Womeldorf) 1932- .... **CLC 12, 30**
See also AAYA 1, 31; BYA 1, 2, 7; CA 21-24R; CANR 28, 59; CLR 7, 50; CWRI 5; DLB 52; JRDA; LAIT 4; MAICYA 1, 2; MAICYAS 1; MTCW 1; SATA 13, 53, 92; WYA; YAW

Patmore, Coventry Kersey Dighton 1823-1896 .... **NCLC 9**
See also DLB 35, 98; RGEL 2

Paton, Alan (Stewart) 1903-1988 ...... **CLC 4, 10, 25, 55, 106; WLC**
See also AAYA 26; AFW; BPFB 3; BRWS 2; BYA 1; CA 13-16; 125; CANR 22; CAP 1; DA; DA3; DAB; DAC; DAM MST, NOV; DLB 225; DLBD 17; EXPN; LAIT 4; MTCW 1, 2; NFS 3, 12; RGEL 2; SATA 11; SATA-Obit 56; WLIT 2

Paton Walsh, Gillian 1937- .... **CLC 35**
See also Paton Walsh, Jill; Walsh, Jill Paton
See also AAYA 11; CANR 38, 83; CLR 2, 65; DLB 161; JRDA; MAICYA 1, 2; SAAS 3; SATA 4, 72, 109; YAW

Paton Walsh, Jill
See Paton Walsh, Gillian
See also BYA 1, 8

Patton, George S(mith), Jr. 1885-1945 .... **TCLC 79**
See also CA 189

Paulding, James Kirke 1778-1860 ... **NCLC 2**
See also DLB 3, 59, 74, 250; RGAL 4

Paulin, Thomas Neilson 1949-
See Paulin, Tom
See also CA 123; 128; CANR 98; CP 7

Paulin, Tom .... **CLC 37**
See also Paulin, Thomas Neilson
See also DLB 40

Pausanias c. 1st cent. - .... **CMLC 36**

Paustovsky, Konstantin (Georgievich) 1892-1968 .... **CLC 40**
See also CA 93-96; 25-28R

Pavese, Cesare 1908-1950 .. **TCLC 3; PC 13; SSC 19**
See also CA 104; 169; DLB 128, 177; EW 12; RGSF 2; RGWL 2

Pavic, Milorad 1929- .... **CLC 60**
See also CA 136; CDWLB 4; CWW 2; DLB 181

Pavlov, Ivan Petrovich 1849-1936 . **TCLC 91**
See also CA 118; 180

Payne, Alan
See Jakes, John (William)

Paz, Gil
See Lugones, Leopoldo

Paz, Octavio 1914-1998 . **CLC 3, 4, 6, 10, 19, 51, 65, 119; HLC 2; PC 1; WLC**
See also CA 73-76; 165; CANR 32, 65, 104; CWW 2; DA; DA3; DAB; DAC; DAM MST, MULT, POET; DLBY 1990, 1998; DNFS 1; HW 1, 2; LAW; LAWS 1; MTCW 1, 2; RGWL 2; SSFS 13; WLIT 1

p'Bitek, Okot 1931-1982 ..... **CLC 96; BLC 3**
See also AFW; BW 2, 3; CA 124; 107; CANR 82; DAM MULT; DLB 125; MTCW 1, 2; RGEL 2; WLIT 2

Peacock, Molly 1947- .... **CLC 60**
See also CA 103; CAAS 21; CANR 52, 84; CP 7; CWP; DLB 120

Peacock, Thomas Love 1785-1866 .... **NCLC 22**
See also BRW 4; DLB 96, 116; RGEL 2; RGSF 2

Peake, Mervyn 1911-1968 .... **CLC 7, 54**
See also CA 5-8R; 25-28R; CANR 3; DLB 15, 160, 255; FANT; MTCW 1; RGEL 2; SATA 23; SFW 4

Pearce, Philippa
See Christie, Philippa
See also CA 5-8R; CANR 4, 109; CWRI 5; FANT; MAICYA 2

Pearl, Eric
See Elman, Richard (Martin)

Pearson, T(homas) R(eid) 1956- .... **CLC 39**
See also CA 120; 130; CANR 97; CSW; INT 130

Peck, Dale 1967- .... **CLC 81**
See also CA 146; CANR 72; GLL 2

Peck, John (Frederick) 1941- .... **CLC 3**
See also CA 49-52; CANR 3, 100; CP 7

Peck, Richard (Wayne) 1934- .... **CLC 21**
See also AAYA 1, 24; BYA 1, 6, 8, 11; CA 85-88; CANR 19, 38; CLR 15; INT CANR-19; JRDA; MAICYA 1, 2; SAAS 2; SATA 18, 55, 97; SATA-Essay 110; WYA; YAW

Peck, Robert Newton 1928- .... **CLC 17**
See also AAYA 3, 43; BYA 1, 6; CA 81-84, 182; CAAE 182; CANR 31, 63; CLR 45; DA; DAC; DAM MST; JRDA; LAIT 3; MAICYA 1, 2; SAAS 1; SATA 21, 62, 111; SATA-Essay 108; WYA; YAW

Peckinpah, (David) Sam(uel) 1925-1984 .... **CLC 20**
See also CA 109; 114; CANR 82

Pedersen, Knut 1859-1952
See Hamsun, Knut
See also CA 104; 119; CANR 63; MTCW 1, 2

Peeslake, Gaffer
See Durrell, Lawrence (George)

Peguy, Charles (Pierre) 1873-1914 .... **TCLC 10**
See also CA 107; 193; DLB 258; GFL 1789 to the Present

Peirce, Charles Sanders 1839-1914 .... **TCLC 81**
See also CA 194

Pellicer, Carlos 1900(?)-1977
See also CA 153; 69-72; HLCS 2; HW 1

Pena, Ramon del Valle y
See Valle-Inclan, Ramon (Maria) del

Pendennis, Arthur Esquir
See Thackeray, William Makepeace

Penn, William 1644-1718 .... **LC 25**
See also DLB 24

PEPECE
See Prado (Calvo), Pedro

Pepys, Samuel 1633-1703 ... **LC 11, 58; WLC**
See also BRW 2; CDBLB 1660-1789; DA; DA3; DAB; DAC; DAM MST; DLB 101, 213; RGEL 2; WLIT 3

Percy, Thomas 1729-1811 .... **NCLC 95**
See also DLB 104

Percy, Walker 1916-1990 .... **CLC 2, 3, 6, 8, 14, 18, 47, 65**
See also AMWS 3; BPFB 3; CA 1-4R; 131; CANR 1, 23, 64; CPW; CSW; DA3; DAM NOV, POP; DLB 2; DLBY 1980, 1990; MTCW 1, 2; RGAL 4

Percy, William Alexander 1885-1942 .... **TCLC 84**
See also CA 163; MTCW 2

Perec, Georges 1936-1982 .... **CLC 56, 116**
See also CA 141; DLB 83; GFL 1789 to the Present

Pereda (y Sanchez de Porrua), Jose Maria de 1833-1906 .... **TCLC 16**
See also CA 117

Pereda y Porrua, Jose Maria de
See Pereda (y Sanchez de Porrua), Jose Maria de

Peregoy, George Weems
See Mencken, H(enry) L(ouis)

Perelman, S(idney) J(oseph) 1904-1979 .. **CLC 3, 5, 9, 15, 23, 44, 49; SSC 32**
See also AITN 1, 2; BPFB 3; CA 73-76; 89-92; CANR 18; DAM DRAM; DLB 11, 44; MTCW 1, 2; RGAL 4

Peret, Benjamin 1899-1959 .... **TCLC 20; PC 33**
See also CA 117; 186; GFL 1789 to the Present

Peretz, Isaac Loeb 1851(?)-1915 ... **TCLC 16; SSC 26**
See also CA 109

Peretz, Yitzkhok Leibush
See Peretz, Isaac Loeb

Perez Galdos, Benito 1843-1920 ... **TCLC 27; HLCS 2**
See also Galdos, Benito Perez
See also CA 125; 153; HW 1; RGWL 2

Peri Rossi, Cristina 1941- .. **CLC 156; HLCS 2**
See also CA 131; CANR 59, 81; DLB 145; HW 1, 2

Perlata
See Peret, Benjamin

Perloff, Marjorie G(abrielle) 1931- .... **CLC 137**
See also CA 57-60; CANR 7, 22, 49, 104

Perrault, Charles 1628-1703 ... **LC 2, 56; DC 12**
See also BYA 4; CLR 79; GFL Beginnings to 1789; MAICYA 1, 2; RGWL 2; SATA 25; WCH

Perry, Anne 1938- .... **CLC 126**
See also CA 101; CANR 22, 50, 84; CMW 4; CN 7; CPW

Perry, Brighton
See Sherwood, Robert E(mmet)

Perse, St.-John
See Leger, (Marie-Rene Auguste) Alexis Saint-Leger

Perse, Saint-John
See Leger, (Marie-Rene Auguste) Alexis Saint-Leger
See also DLB 258

Perutz, Leo(pold) 1882-1957 .... **TCLC 60**
See also CA 147; DLB 81

Peseenz, Tulio F.
See Lopez y Fuentes, Gregorio

Pesetsky, Bette 1932- .... **CLC 28**
See also CA 133; DLB 130

Peshkov, Alexei Maximovich 1868-1936
See Gorky, Maxim
See also CA 105; 141; CANR 83; DA; DAC; DAM DRAM, MST, NOV; MTCW 2

Pessoa, Fernando (Antonio Nogueira)
1898-1935 ..... **TCLC 27; HLC 2; PC 20**
See also CA 125; 183; DAM MULT; EW
10; RGWL 2; WP

Peterkin, Julia Mood 1880-1961 ...... **CLC 31**
See also CA 102; DLB 9

Peters, Joan K(aren) 1945- .... **CLC 39**
See also CA 158; CANR 109

Peters, Robert L(ouis) 1924- .... **CLC 7**
See also CA 13-16R; CAAS 8; CP 7; DLB
105

Petofi, Sandor 1823-1849 .... **NCLC 21**
See also RGWL 2

Petrakis, Harry Mark 1923- .... **CLC 3**
See also CA 9-12R; CANR 4, 30, 85; CN 7

Petrarch 1304-1374 .... **CMLC 20; PC 8**
See also DA3; DAM POET; EW 2; RGWL
2

Petronius c. 20-66 .... **CMLC 34**
See also AW 2; CDWLB 1; DLB 211;
RGWL 2

Petrov, Evgeny .... **TCLC 21**
See also Kataev, Evgeny Petrovich

Petry, Ann (Lane) 1908-1997 ... **CLC 1, 7, 18**
See also AFAW 1, 2; BPFB 3; BW 1, 3;
BYA 2; CA 5-8R; 157; CAAS 6; CANR
4, 46; CLR 12; CN 7; DLB 76; JRDA;
LAIT 1; MAICYA 1, 2; MAICYAS 1;
MTCW 1; RGAL 4; SATA 5; SATA-Obit
94; TCLC 112

Petursson, Halligrimur 1614-1674 .... **LC 8**

Peychinovich
See Vazov, Ivan (Minchov)

Phaedrus c. 15B.C.-c. 50 .... **CMLC 25**
See also DLB 211

Phelps (Ward), Elizabeth Stuart
See Phelps, Elizabeth Stuart
See also FW

Phelps, Elizabeth Stuart
1844-1911 .... **TCLC 113**
See also Phelps (Ward), Elizabeth Stuart
See also DLB 74

Philips, Katherine 1632-1664 . **LC 30; PC 40**
See also DLB 131; RGEL 2

Philipson, Morris H. 1926- .... **CLC 53**
See also CA 1-4R; CANR 4

Phillips, Caryl 1958- .... **CLC 96; BLCS**
See also BRWS 5; BW 2; CA 141; CANR
63, 104; CBD; CD 5; CN 7; DA3; DAM
MULT; DLB 157; MTCW 2; WLIT 4

Phillips, David Graham
1867-1911 .... **TCLC 44**
See also CA 108; 176; DLB 9, 12; RGAL 4

Phillips, Jack
See Sandburg, Carl (August)

Phillips, Jayne Anne 1952- .... **CLC 15, 33,
139; SSC 16**
See also BPFB 3; CA 101; CANR 24, 50,
96; CN 7; CSW; DLBY 1980; INT
CANR-24; MTCW 1, 2; RGAL 4; RGSF
2; SSFS 4

Phillips, Richard
See Dick, Philip K(indred)

Phillips, Robert (Schaeffer) 1938- .... **CLC 28**
See also CA 17-20R; CAAS 13; CANR 8;
DLB 105

Phillips, Ward
See Lovecraft, H(oward) P(hillips)

Piccolo, Lucio 1901-1969 .... **CLC 13**
See also CA 97-100; DLB 114

Pickthall, Marjorie L(owry) C(hristie)
1883-1922 .... **TCLC 21**
See also CA 107; DLB 92

Pico della Mirandola, Giovanni
1463-1494 .... **LC 15**

Piercy, Marge 1936- .... **CLC 3, 6, 14, 18, 27,
62, 128; PC 29**
See also BPFB 3; CA 21-24R; CAAE 187;
CAAS 1; CANR 13, 43, 66; CN 7; CP 7;
CWP; DLB 120, 227; EXPP; FW; MTCW
1, 2; PFS 9; SFW 4

Piers, Robert
See Anthony, Piers

Pieyre de Mandiargues, Andre 1909-1991
See Mandiargues, Andre Pieyre de
See also CA 103; 136; CANR 22, 82; GFL
1789 to the Present

Pilnyak, Boris 1894-1938 . **TCLC 23; SSC 48**
See also Vogau, Boris Andreyevich

Pinchback, Eugene
See Toomer, Jean

Pincherle, Alberto 1907-1990 ...... **CLC 11, 18**
See also Moravia, Alberto
See also CA 25-28R; 132; CANR 33, 63;
DAM NOV; MTCW 1

Pinckney, Darryl 1953- .... **CLC 76**
See also BW 2, 3; CA 143; CANR 79

Pindar 518(?)B.C.-438(?)B.C. .... **CMLC 12;
PC 19**
See also AW 1; CDWLB 1; DLB 176;
RGWL 2

Pineda, Cecile 1942- .... **CLC 39**
See also CA 118; DLB 209

Pinero, Arthur Wing 1855-1934 .... **TCLC 32**
See also CA 110; 153; DAM DRAM; DLB
10; RGEL 2

Pinero, Miguel (Antonio Gomez)
1946-1988 .... **CLC 4, 55**
See also CA 61-64; 125; CAD; CANR 29,
90; HW 1

Pinget, Robert 1919-1997 .... **CLC 7, 13, 37**
See also CA 85-88; 160; CWW 2; DLB 83;
GFL 1789 to the Present

Pink Floyd
See Barrett, (Roger) Syd; Gilmour, David;
Mason, Nick; Waters, Roger; Wright, Rick

Pinkney, Edward 1802-1828 .... **NCLC 31**
See also DLB 248

Pinkwater, Daniel
See Pinkwater, Daniel Manus

Pinkwater, Daniel Manus 1941- .... **CLC 35**
See also AAYA 1; BYA 9; CA 29-32R;
CANR 12, 38, 89; CLR 4; CSW; FANT;
JRDA; MAICYA 1, 2; SAAS 3; SATA 8,
46, 76, 114; SFW 4; YAW

Pinkwater, Manus
See Pinkwater, Daniel Manus

Pinsky, Robert 1940- .... **CLC 9, 19, 38, 94,
121; PC 27**
See also AMWS 6; CA 29-32R; CAAS 4;
CANR 58, 97; CP 7; DA3; DAM POET;
DLBY 1982, 1998; MTCW 2; RGAL 4

Pinta, Harold
See Pinter, Harold

Pinter, Harold 1930- .. **CLC 1, 3, 6, 9, 11, 15,
27, 58, 73; DC 15; WLC**
See also BRWR 1; BRWS 1; CA 5-8R;
CANR 33, 65; CBD; CD 5; CDBLB 1960
to Present; DA; DA3; DAB; DAC; DAM
DRAM, MST; DFS 3, 5, 7, 14; DLB 13;
IDFW 3, 4; MTCW 1, 2; RGEL 2

Piozzi, Hester Lynch (Thrale)
1741-1821 .... **NCLC 57**
See also DLB 104, 142

Pirandello, Luigi 1867-1936 ...... **TCLC 4, 29;
DC 5; SSC 22; WLC**
See also CA 104; 153; CANR 103; DA;
DA3; DAB; DAC; DAM DRAM, MST;
DFS 4, 9; EW 8; MTCW 2; RGSF 2;
RGWL 2

Pirsig, Robert M(aynard) 1928- ... **CLC 4, 6,
73**
See also CA 53-56; CANR 42, 74; CPW 1;
DA3; DAM POP; MTCW 1, 2; SATA 39

Pisarev, Dmitry Ivanovich
1840-1868 .... **NCLC 25**

Pix, Mary (Griffith) 1666-1709 .... **LC 8**
See also DLB 80

Pixerecourt, (Rene Charles) Guilbert de
1773-1844 .... **NCLC 39**
See also DLB 192; GFL 1789 to the Present

Plaatje, Sol(omon) T(shekisho)
1878-1932 .... **TCLC 73; BLCS**
See also BW 2, 3; CA 141; CANR 79; DLB
125, 225

Plaidy, Jean
See Hibbert, Eleanor Alice Burford

Planche, James Robinson
1796-1880 .... **NCLC 42**
See also RGEL 2

Plant, Robert 1948- .... **CLC 12**

Plante, David (Robert) 1940- . **CLC 7, 23, 38**
See also CA 37-40R; CANR 12, 36, 58, 82;
CN 7; DAM NOV; DLBY 1983; INT
CANR-12; MTCW 1

Plath, Sylvia 1932-1963 ..... **CLC 1, 2, 3, 5, 9,
11, 14, 17, 50, 51, 62, 111; PC 1, 37;
WLC**
See also AAYA 13; AMWS 1; BPFB 3; CA
19-20; CANR 34, 101; CAP 2; CDALB
1941-1968; DA; DA3; DAB; DAC; DAM
MST, POET; DLB 5, 6, 152; EXPN;
EXPP; FW; LAIT 4; MAWW; MTCW 1,
2; NFS 1; PAB; PFS 1; RGAL 4; SATA
96; WP; YAW

Plato c. 428B.C.-347B.C. ... **CMLC 8; WLCS**
See also AW 1; CDWLB 1; DA; DA3;
DAB; DAC; DAM MST; DLB 176; LAIT
1; RGWL 2

Platonov, Andrei
See Klimentov, Andrei Platonovich

Platt, Kin 1911- .... **CLC 26**
See also AAYA 11; CA 17-20R; CANR 11;
JRDA; SAAS 17; SATA 21, 86; WYA

Plautus c. 254B.C.-c. 184B.C. ...... **CMLC 24;
DC 6**
See also AW 1; CDWLB 1; DLB 211;
RGWL 2

Plick et Plock
See Simenon, Georges (Jacques Christian)

Plieksans, Janis
See Rainis, Janis

Plimpton, George (Ames) 1927- .... **CLC 36**
See also AITN 1; CA 21-24R; CANR 32,
70, 103; DLB 185, 241; MTCW 1, 2;
SATA 10

Pliny the Elder c. 23-79 .... **CMLC 23**
See also DLB 211

Plomer, William Charles Franklin
1903-1973 .... **CLC 4, 8**
See also AFW; CA 21-22; CANR 34; CAP
2; DLB 20, 162, 191, 225; MTCW 1;
RGEL 2; RGSF 2; SATA 24

Plotinus 204-270 .... **CMLC 46**
See also CDWLB 1; DLB 176

Plowman, Piers
See Kavanagh, Patrick (Joseph)

Plum, J.
See Wodehouse, P(elham) G(renville)

Plumly, Stanley (Ross) 1939- .... **CLC 33**
See also CA 108; 110; CANR 97; CP 7;
DLB 5, 193; INT 110

Plumpe, Friedrich Wilhelm
1888-1931 .... **TCLC 53**
See also CA 112

Po Chu-i 772-846 .... **CMLC 24**
Poe, Edgar Allan 1809-1849 ..... **NCLC 1, 16,**
    55, 78, 94, 97; PC 1; SSC 1, 22, 34, 35;
    WLC
    See also AAYA 14; AMW; BPFB 3; BYA 5,
    11; CDALB 1640-1865; CMW 4; DA;
    DA3; DAB; DAC; DAM MST, POET;
    DLB 3, 59, 73, 74, 248, 254; EXPP;
    EXPS; HGG; LAIT 2; MSW; PAB; PFS
    1, 3, 9; RGAL 4; RGSF 2; SATA 23;
    SCFW 2; SFW 4; SSFS 2, 4, 7, 8; SUFW;
    WP; WYA
Poet of Titchfield Street, The
    See Pound, Ezra (Weston Loomis)
Pohl, Frederik 1919- .... **CLC 18; SSC 25**
    See also AAYA 24; CA 61-64; CAAE 188;
    CAAS 1; CANR 11, 37, 81; CN 7; DLB
    8; INT CANR-11; MTCW 1, 2; SATA 24;
    SCFW 2; SFW 4
Poirier, Louis 1910-
    See Gracq, Julien
    See also CA 122; 126; CWW 2
Poitier, Sidney 1927- .... **CLC 26**
    See also BW 1; CA 117; CANR 94
Polanski, Roman 1933- .... **CLC 16**
    See also CA 77-80
Poliakoff, Stephen 1952- .... **CLC 38**
    See also CA 106; CBD; CD 5; DLB 13
Police, The
    See Copeland, Stewart (Armstrong); Sum-
    mers, Andrew James; Sumner, Gordon
    Matthew
Polidori, John William 1795-1821 . **NCLC 51**
    See also DLB 116; HGG
Pollitt, Katha 1949- .... **CLC 28, 122**
    See also CA 120; 122; CANR 66, 108;
    MTCW 1, 2
Pollock, (Mary) Sharon 1936- .... **CLC 50**
    See also CA 141; CD 5; CWD; DAC; DAM
    DRAM, MST; DFS 3; DLB 60; FW
Polo, Marco 1254-1324 .... **CMLC 15**
Polonsky, Abraham (Lincoln)
    1910-1999 .... **CLC 92**
    See also CA 104; 187; DLB 26; INT 104
Polybius c. 200B.C.-c. 118B.C. ...... **CMLC 17**
    See also AW 1; DLB 176; RGWL 2
Pomerance, Bernard 1940- .... **CLC 13**
    See also CA 101; CAD; CANR 49; CD 5;
    DAM DRAM; DFS 9; LAIT 2
Ponge, Francis 1899-1988 .... **CLC 6, 18**
    See also CA 85-88; 126; CANR 40, 86;
    DAM POET; GFL 1789 to the Present;
    RGWL 2
Poniatowska, Elena 1933- . **CLC 140; HLC 2**
    See also CA 101; CANR 32, 66, 107; CD-
    WLB 3; DAM MULT; DLB 113; HW 1,
    2; LAWS 1; WLIT 1
Pontoppidan, Henrik 1857-1943 .... **TCLC 29**
    See also CA 170
Poole, Josephine .... **CLC 17**
    See also Helyar, Jane Penelope Josephine
    See also SAAS 2; SATA 5
Popa, Vasko 1922-1991 .... **CLC 19**
    See also CA 112; 148; CDWLB 4; DLB
    181; RGWL 2
Pope, Alexander 1688-1744 ...... **LC 3, 58, 60,**
    64; PC 26; WLC
    See also BRW 3; BRWR 1; CDBLB 1660-
    1789; DA; DA3; DAB; DAC; DAM MST,
    POET; DLB 95, 101, 213; EXPP; PAB;
    PFS 12; RGEL 2; WLIT 3; WP
Popov, Yevgeny .... **CLC 59**
Porter, Connie (Rose) 1959(?)- .... **CLC 70**
    See also BW 2, 3; CA 142; CANR 90, 109;
    SATA 81, 129
Porter, Gene(va Grace) Stratton .. **TCLC 21**
    See also Stratton-Porter, Gene(va Grace)
    See also BPFB 3; CA 112; CWRI 5; RHW

Porter, Katherine Anne 1890-1980 ... **CLC 1,**
    3, 7, 10, 13, 15, 27, 101; SSC 4, 31, 43
    See also AAYA 42; AITN 2; AMW; BPFB
    3; CA 1-4R; 101; CANR 1, 65; CDALBS;
    DA; DA3; DAB; DAC; DAM MST, NOV;
    DLB 4, 9, 102; DLBD 12; DLBY 1980;
    EXPS; LAIT 3; MAWW; MTCW 1, 2;
    NFS 14; RGAL 4; RGSF 2; SATA 39;
    SATA-Obit 23; SSFS 1, 8, 11
Porter, Peter (Neville Frederick)
    1929- .... **CLC 5, 13, 33**
    See also CA 85-88; CP 7; DLB 40
Porter, William Sydney 1862-1910
    See Henry, O.
    See also CA 104; 131; CDALB 1865-1917;
    DA; DA3; DAB; DAC; DAM MST; DLB
    12, 78, 79; MTCW 1, 2; YABC 2
Portillo (y Pacheco), Jose Lopez
    See Lopez Portillo (y Pacheco), Jose
Portillo Trambley, Estela 1927-1998
    See Trambley, Estela Portillo
    See also CANR 32; DAM MULT; DLB
    209; HLC 2; HW 1
Posse, Abel .... **CLC 70**
Post, Melville Davisson
    1869-1930 .... **TCLC 39**
    See also CA 110; CMW 4
Potok, Chaim 1929- .... **CLC 2, 7, 14, 26, 112**
    See also AAYA 15; AITN 1, 2; BPFB 3;
    BYA 1; CA 17-20R; CANR 19, 35, 64,
    98; CN 7; DA3; DAM NOV; DLB 28,
    152; EXPN; INT CANR-19; LAIT 4;
    MTCW 1, 2; NFS 4; SATA 33, 106; YAW
Potter, Dennis (Christopher George)
    1935-1994 .... **CLC 58, 86, 123**
    See also CA 107; 145; CANR 33, 61; CBD;
    DLB 233; MTCW 1
Pound, Ezra (Weston Loomis)
    1885-1972 .. **CLC 1, 2, 3, 4, 5, 7, 10, 13,**
    18, 34, 48, 50, 112; PC 4; WLC
    See also AMW; AMWR 1; CA 5-8R; 37-
    40R; CANR 40; CDALB 1917-1929; DA;
    DA3; DAB; DAC; DAM MST, POET;
    DLB 4, 45, 63; DLBD 15; EFS 2; EXPP;
    MTCW 1, 2; PAB; PFS 2, 8; RGAL 4;
    WP
Povod, Reinaldo 1959-1994 .... **CLC 44**
    See also CA 136; 146; CANR 83
Powell, Adam Clayton, Jr.
    1908-1972 .... **CLC 89; BLC 3**
    See also BW 1, 3; CA 102; 33-36R; CANR
    86; DAM MULT
Powell, Anthony (Dymoke)
    1905-2000 .... **CLC 1, 3, 7, 9, 10, 31**
    See also BRW 7; CA 1-4R; 189; CANR 1,
    32, 62, 107; CDBLB 1945-1960; CN 7;
    DLB 15; MTCW 1, 2; RGEL 2
Powell, Dawn 1896(?)-1965 .... **CLC 66**
    See also CA 5-8R; DLBY 1997
Powell, Padgett 1952- .... **CLC 34**
    See also CA 126; CANR 63, 101; CSW;
    DLB 234; DLBY 01
Powell, (Oval) Talmage 1920-2000
    See Queen, Ellery
    See also CA 5-8R; CANR 2, 80
Power, Susan 1961- .... **CLC 91**
    See also BYA 14; CA 160; NFS 11
Powers, J(ames) F(arl) 1917-1999 ..... **CLC 1,**
    4, 8, 57; SSC 4
    See also CA 1-4R; 181; CANR 2, 61; CN
    7; DLB 130; MTCW 1; RGAL 4; RGSF
    2
Powers, John J(ames) 1945-
    See Powers, John R.
    See also CA 69-72
Powers, John R. .... **CLC 66**
    See also Powers, John J(ames)
Powers, Richard (S.) 1957- .... **CLC 93**
    See also AMWS 9; BPFB 3; CA 148;
    CANR 80; CN 7

Pownall, David 1938- .... **CLC 10**
    See also CA 89-92; 180; CAAS 18; CANR
    49, 101; CBD; CD 5; CN 7; DLB 14
Powys, John Cowper 1872-1963 ... **CLC 7, 9,**
    15, 46, 125
    See also CA 85-88; CANR 106; DLB 15,
    255; FANT; MTCW 1, 2; RGEL 2; SUFW
Powys, T(heodore) F(rancis)
    1875-1953 .... **TCLC 9**
    See also CA 106; 189; DLB 36, 162; FANT;
    RGEL 2; SUFW
Prado (Calvo), Pedro 1886-1952 ... **TCLC 75**
    See also CA 131; HW 1; LAW
Prager, Emily 1952- .... **CLC 56**
Pratt, E(dwin) J(ohn) 1883(?)-1964 . **CLC 19**
    See also CA 141; 93-96; CANR 77; DAC;
    DAM POET; DLB 92; RGEL 2
Premchand .... **TCLC 21**
    See also Srivastava, Dhanpat Rai
Preussler, Otfried 1923- .... **CLC 17**
    See also CA 77-80; SATA 24
Prevert, Jacques (Henri Marie)
    1900-1977 .... **CLC 15**
    See also CA 77-80; 69-72; CANR 29, 61;
    DLB 258; GFL 1789 to the Present;
    IDFW 3, 4; MTCW 1; RGWL 2; SATA-
    Obit 30
Prevost, (Antoine Francois)
    1697-1763 .... **LC 1**
    See also EW 4; GFL Beginnings to 1789;
    RGWL 2
Price, (Edward) Reynolds 1933- ... **CLC 3, 6,**
    13, 43, 50, 63; SSC 22
    See also AMWS 6; CA 1-4R; CANR 1, 37,
    57, 87; CN 7; CSW; DAM NOV; DLB 2,
    218; INT CANR-37
Price, Richard 1949- .... **CLC 6, 12**
    See also CA 49-52; CANR 3; DLBY 1981
Prichard, Katharine Susannah
    1883-1969 .... **CLC 46**
    See also CA 11-12; CANR 33; CAP 1;
    MTCW 1; RGEL 2; RGSF 2; SATA 66
Priestley, J(ohn) B(oynton)
    1894-1984 .... **CLC 2, 5, 9, 34**
    See also BRW 7; CA 9-12R; 113; CANR
    33; CDBLB 1914-1945; DA3; DAM
    DRAM, NOV; DLB 10, 34, 77, 100, 139;
    DLBY 1984; MTCW 1, 2; RGEL 2; SFW
    4
Prince 1958(?)- .... **CLC 35**
Prince, F(rank) T(empleton) 1912- .. **CLC 22**
    See also CA 101; CANR 43, 79; CP 7; DLB
    20
Prince Kropotkin
    See Kropotkin, Peter (Aleksieevich)
Prior, Matthew 1664-1721 .... **LC 4**
    See also DLB 95; RGEL 2
Prishvin, Mikhail 1873-1954 .... **TCLC 75**
Pritchard, William H(arrison)
    1932- .... **CLC 34**
    See also CA 65-68; CANR 23, 95; DLB
    111
Pritchett, V(ictor) S(awdon)
    1900-1997 ... **CLC 5, 13, 15, 41; SSC 14**
    See also BPFB 3; BRWS 3; CA 61-64; 157;
    CANR 31, 63; CN 7; DA3; DAM NOV;
    DLB 15, 139; MTCW 1, 2; RGEL 2;
    RGSF 2
Private 19022
    See Manning, Frederic
Probst, Mark 1925- .... **CLC 59**
    See also CA 130
Prokosch, Frederic 1908-1989 ...... **CLC 4, 48**
    See also CA 73-76; 128; CANR 82; DLB
    48; MTCW 2
Propertius, Sextus c. 50B.C.-c.
    16B.C. .... **CMLC 32**
    See also AW 2; CDWLB 1; DLB 211;
    RGWL 2

Prophet, The
See Dreiser, Theodore (Herman Albert)
Prose, Francine 1947- .... **CLC 45**
See also CA 109; 112; CANR 46, 95; DLB 234; SATA 101
Proudhon
See Cunha, Euclides (Rodrigues Pimenta) da
Proulx, Annie
See Proulx, E(dna) Annie
Proulx, E(dna) Annie 1935- ...... **CLC 81, 158**
See also AMWS 7; BPFB 3; CA 145; CANR 65; CN 7; CPW 1; DA3; DAM POP; MTCW 2
Proust,
(Valentin-Louis-George-Eugene-)Marcel 1871-1922 .... **TCLC 7, 13, 33; WLC**
See also BPFB 3; CA 104; 120; DA; DA3; DAB; DAC; DAM MST, NOV; DLB 65; EW 8; GFL 1789 to the Present; MTCW 1, 2; RGWL 2
Prowler, Harley
See Masters, Edgar Lee
Prus, Boleslaw 1845-1912 .... **TCLC 48**
See also RGWL 2
Pryor, Richard (Franklin Lenox Thomas) 1940- .... **CLC 26**
See also CA 122; 152
Przybyszewski, Stanislaw 1868-1927 .... **TCLC 36**
See also CA 160; DLB 66
Pteleon
See Grieve, C(hristopher) M(urray)
See also DAM POET
Puckett, Lute
See Masters, Edgar Lee
Puig, Manuel 1932-1990 .... **CLC 3, 5, 10, 28, 65, 133; HLC 2**
See also BPFB 3; CA 45-48; CANR 2, 32, 63; CDWLB 3; DA3; DAM MULT; DLB 113; DNFS 1; GLL 1; HW 1, 2; LAW; MTCW 1, 2; RGWL 2; WLIT 1
Pulitzer, Joseph 1847-1911 .... **TCLC 76**
See also CA 114; DLB 23
Purchas, Samuel 1577(?)-1626 .... **LC 70**
See also DLB 151
Purdy, A(lfred) W(ellington) 1918-2000 .... **CLC 3, 6, 14, 50**
See also CA 81-84; 189; CAAS 17; CANR 42, 66; CP 7; DAC; DAM MST, POET; DLB 88; PFS 5; RGEL 2
Purdy, James (Amos) 1923- .... **CLC 2, 4, 10, 28, 52**
See also AMWS 7; CA 33-36R; CAAS 1; CANR 19, 51; CN 7; DLB 2, 218; INT CANR-19; MTCW 1; RGAL 4
Pure, Simon
See Swinnerton, Frank Arthur
Pushkin, Aleksandr Sergeevich
See Pushkin, Alexander (Sergeyevich)
See also DLB 205
Pushkin, Alexander (Sergeyevich) 1799-1837 .... **NCLC 3, 27, 83; PC 10; SSC 27; WLC**
See also DA; DA3; DAB; DAC; DAM DRAM, MST, POET; EW 5; EXPS; RGSF 2; RGWL 2; SATA 61; SSFS 9
P'u Sung-ling 1640-1715 .... **LC 49; SSC 31**
Putnam, Arthur Lee
See Alger, Horatio, Jr.
Puzo, Mario 1920-1999 .... **CLC 1, 2, 6, 36, 107**
See also BPFB 3; CA 65-68; 185; CANR 4, 42, 65, 99; CN 7; CPW; DA3; DAM NOV, POP; DLB 6; MTCW 1, 2; RGAL 4
Pygge, Edward
See Barnes, Julian (Patrick)

Pyle, Ernest Taylor 1900-1945
See Pyle, Ernie
See also CA 115; 160
Pyle, Ernie .... **TCLC 75**
See also Pyle, Ernest Taylor
See also DLB 29; MTCW 2
Pyle, Howard 1853-1911 .... **TCLC 81**
See also BYA 2, 4; CA 109; 137; CLR 22; DLB 42, 188; DLBD 13; LAIT 1; MAI-CYA 1, 2; SATA 16, 100; WCH; YAW
Pym, Barbara (Mary Crampton) 1913-1980 .... **CLC 13, 19, 37, 111**
See also BPFB 3; BRWS 2; CA 13-14; 97-100; CANR 13, 34; CAP 1; DLB 14, 207; DLBY 1987; MTCW 1, 2; RGEL 2
Pynchon, Thomas (Ruggles, Jr.) 1937- ...... **CLC 2, 3, 6, 9, 11, 18, 33, 62, 72, 123; SSC 14; WLC**
See also AMWS 2; BEST 90:2; BPFB 3; CA 17-20R; CANR 22, 46, 73; CN 7; CPW 1; DA; DA3; DAB; DAC; DAM MST, NOV, POP; DLB 2, 173; MTCW 1, 2; RGAL 4; SFW 4; TUS
Pythagoras c. 582B.C.-c. 507B.C. . **CMLC 22**
See also DLB 176

Q

See Quiller-Couch, Sir Arthur (Thomas)
Qian, Chongzhu
See Ch'ien, Chung-shu
Qian Zhongshu
See Ch'ien, Chung-shu
Qroll
See Dagerman, Stig (Halvard)
Quarrington, Paul (Lewis) 1953- ..... **CLC 65**
See also CA 129; CANR 62, 95
Quasimodo, Salvatore 1901-1968 ..... **CLC 10**
See also CA 13-16; 25-28R; CAP 1; DLB 114; EW 12; MTCW 1; RGWL 2
Quay, Stephen 1947- .... **CLC 95**
See also CA 189
Quay, Timothy 1947- .... **CLC 95**
See also CA 189
Queen, Ellery .... **CLC 3, 11**
See also Dannay, Frederic; Davidson, Avram (James); Deming, Richard; Fairman, Paul W.; Flora, Fletcher; Hoch, Edward D(entinger); Kane, Henry; Lee, Manfred B(ennington); Marlowe, Stephen; Powell, (Oval) Talmage; Sheldon, Walter J(ames); Sturgeon, Theodore (Hamilton); Tracy, Don(ald Fiske); Vance, John Holbrook
See also BPFB 3; CMW 4; MSW; RGAL 4
Queen, Ellery, Jr.
See Dannay, Frederic; Lee, Manfred B(ennington)
Queneau, Raymond 1903-1976 ..... **CLC 2, 5, 10, 42**
See also CA 77-80; 69-72; CANR 32; DLB 72, 258; EW 12; GFL 1789 to the Present; MTCW 1, 2; RGWL 2
Quevedo, Francisco de 1580-1645 .... **LC 23**
Quiller-Couch, Sir Arthur (Thomas) 1863-1944 .... **TCLC 53**
See also CA 118; 166; DLB 135, 153, 190; HGG; RGEL 2; SUFW
Quin, Ann (Marie) 1936-1973 .... **CLC 6**
See also CA 9-12R; 45-48; DLB 14, 231
Quinn, Martin
See Smith, Martin Cruz
Quinn, Peter 1947- .... **CLC 91**
See also CA 197
Quinn, Simon
See Smith, Martin Cruz
Quintana, Leroy V. 1944- .... **PC 36**
See also CA 131; CANR 65; DAM MULT; DLB 82; HLC 2; HW 1, 2

Quiroga, Horacio (Sylvestre) 1878-1937 .... **TCLC 20; HLC 2**
See also CA 117; 131; DAM MULT; HW 1; LAW; MTCW 1; RGSF 2; WLIT 1
Quoirez, Francoise 1935- .... **CLC 9**
See also Sagan, Francoise
See also CA 49-52; CANR 6, 39, 73; CWW 2; MTCW 1, 2
Raabe, Wilhelm (Karl) 1831-1910 . **TCLC 45**
See also CA 167; DLB 129
Rabe, David (William) 1940- .. **CLC 4, 8, 33; DC 16**
See also CA 85-88; CABS 3; CAD; CANR 59; CD 5; DAM DRAM; DFS 3, 8, 13; DLB 7, 228
Rabelais, Francois 1494-1553 .... **LC 5, 60; WLC**
See also DA; DAB; DAC; DAM MST; EW 2; GFL Beginnings to 1789; RGWL 2
Rabinovitch, Sholem 1859-1916
See Aleichem, Sholom
See also CA 104
Rabinyan, Dorit 1972- .... **CLC 119**
See also CA 170
Rachilde
See Vallette, Marguerite Eymery
Racine, Jean 1639-1699 .... **LC 28**
See also DA3; DAB; DAM MST; EW 3; GFL Beginnings to 1789; RGWL 2
Radcliffe, Ann (Ward) 1764-1823 ... **NCLC 6, 55, 106**
See also DLB 39, 178; HGG; RGEL 2; SUFW; WLIT 3
Radclyffe-Hall, Marguerite
See Hall, (Marguerite) Radclyffe
Radiguet, Raymond 1903-1923 ...... **TCLC 29**
See also CA 162; DLB 65; GFL 1789 to the Present; RGWL 2
Radnoti, Miklos 1909-1944 .... **TCLC 16**
See also CA 118; CDWLB 4; DLB 215; RGWL 2
Rado, James 1939- .... **CLC 17**
See also CA 105
Radvanyi, Netty 1900-1983
See Seghers, Anna
See also CA 85-88; 110; CANR 82
Rae, Ben
See Griffiths, Trevor
Raeburn, John (Hay) 1941- .... **CLC 34**
See also CA 57-60
Ragni, Gerome 1942-1991 .... **CLC 17**
See also CA 105; 134
Rahv, Philip .... **CLC 24**
See also Greenberg, Ivan
See also DLB 137
Raimund, Ferdinand Jakob 1790-1836 .... **NCLC 69**
See also DLB 90
Raine, Craig (Anthony) 1944- .. **CLC 32, 103**
See also CA 108; CANR 29, 51, 103; CP 7; DLB 40; PFS 7
Raine, Kathleen (Jessie) 1908- ..... **CLC 7, 45**
See also CA 85-88; CANR 46, 109; CP 7; DLB 20; MTCW 1; RGEL 2
Rainis, Janis 1865-1929 .... **TCLC 29**
See also CA 170; CDWLB 4; DLB 220
Rakosi, Carl .... **CLC 47**
See also Rawley, Callman
See also CAAS 5; CP 7; DLB 193
Ralegh, Sir Walter
See Raleigh, Sir Walter
See also BRW 1; RGEL 2; WP
Raleigh, Richard
See Lovecraft, H(oward) P(hillips)
Raleigh, Sir Walter 1554(?)-1618 .... **LC 31, 39; PC 31**
See also Ralegh, Sir Walter
See also CDBLB Before 1660; DLB 172; EXPP; PFS 14; TEA

Rallentando, H. P.
See Sayers, Dorothy L(eigh)
Ramal, Walter
See de la Mare, Walter (John)
Ramana Maharshi 1879-1950 .... **TCLC 84**
Ramoacn y Cajal, Santiago
1852-1934 .... **TCLC 93**
Ramon, Juan
See Jimenez (Mantecon), Juan Ramon
Ramos, Graciliano 1892-1953 .... **TCLC 32**
See also CA 167; HW 2; LAW; WLIT 1
Rampersad, Arnold 1941- .... **CLC 44**
See also BW 2, 3; CA 127; 133; CANR 81;
DLB 111; INT 133
Rampling, Anne
See Rice, Anne
See also GLL 2
Ramsay, Allan 1686(?)-1758 .... **LC 29**
See also DLB 95; RGEL 2
Ramsay, Jay
See Campbell, (John) Ramsey
Ramuz, Charles-Ferdinand
1878-1947 .... **TCLC 33**
See also CA 165
Rand, Ayn 1905-1982 ...... **CLC 3, 30, 44, 79;**
WLC
See also AAYA 10; AMWS 4; BPFB 3;
BYA 12; CA 13-16R; 105; CANR 27, 73;
CDALBS; CPW; DA; DA3; DAC; DAM
MST, NOV, POP; DLB 227; MTCW 1, 2;
NFS 10; RGAL 4; SFW 4; YAW
Randall, Dudley (Felker) 1914-2000 . **CLC 1,**
135; BLC 3
See also BW 1, 3; CA 25-28R; 189; CANR
23, 82; DAM MULT; DLB 41; PFS 5
Randall, Robert
See Silverberg, Robert
Ranger, Ken
See Creasey, John
Rank, Otto 1884-1939 .... **TCLC 115**
Ransom, John Crowe 1888-1974 .. **CLC 2, 4,**
5, 11, 24
See also AMW; CA 5-8R; 49-52; CANR 6,
34; CDALBS; DA3; DAM POET; DLB
45, 63; EXPP; MTCW 1, 2; RGAL 4
Rao, Raja 1909- .... **CLC 25, 56**
See also CA 73-76; CANR 51; CN 7; DAM
NOV; MTCW 1, 2; RGEL 2; RGSF 2
Raphael, Frederic (Michael) 1931- ... **CLC 2,**
14
See also CA 1-4R; CANR 1, 86; CN 7;
DLB 14
Ratcliffe, James P.
See Mencken, H(enry) L(ouis)
Rathbone, Julian 1935- .... **CLC 41**
See also CA 101; CANR 34, 73
Rattigan, Terence (Mervyn)
1911-1977 .... **CLC 7**
See also BRWS 7; CA 85-88; 73-76; CBD;
CDBLB 1945-1960; DAM DRAM; DFS
8; DLB 13; IDFW 3, 4; MTCW 1, 2;
RGEL 2
Ratushinskaya, Irina 1954- .... **CLC 54**
See also CA 129; CANR 68; CWW 2
Raven, Simon (Arthur Noel)
1927-2001 .... **CLC 14**
See also CA 81-84; 197; CANR 86; CN 7
Ravenna, Michael
See Welty, Eudora (Alice)
Rawley, Callman 1903-
See Rakosi, Carl
See also CA 21-24R; CANR 12, 32, 91
Rawlings, Marjorie Kinnan
1896-1953 .... **TCLC 4**
See also AAYA 20; AMWS 10; ANW;
BPFB 3; BYA 3; CA 104; 137; CANR 74;
CLR 63; DLB 9, 22, 102; DLBD 17;
JRDA; MAICYA 1, 2; MTCW 2; RGAL
4; SATA 100; WCH; YABC 1; YAW

Ray, Satyajit 1921-1992 .... **CLC 16, 76**
See also CA 114; 137; DAM MULT
Read, Herbert Edward 1893-1968 ..... **CLC 4**
See also BRW 6; CA 85-88; 25-28R; DLB
20, 149; PAB; RGEL 2
Read, Piers Paul 1941- .... **CLC 4, 10, 25**
See also CA 21-24R; CANR 38, 86; CN 7;
DLB 14; SATA 21
Reade, Charles 1814-1884 .... **NCLC 2, 74**
See also DLB 21; RGEL 2
Reade, Hamish
See Gray, Simon (James Holliday)
Reading, Peter 1946- .... **CLC 47**
See also CA 103; CANR 46, 96; CP 7; DLB
40
Reaney, James 1926- .... **CLC 13**
See also CA 41-44R; CAAS 15; CANR 42;
CD 5; CP 7; DAC; DAM MST; DLB 68;
RGEL 2; SATA 43
Rebreanu, Liviu 1885-1944 .... **TCLC 28**
See also CA 165; DLB 220
Rechy, John (Francisco) 1934- ...... **CLC 1, 7,**
14, 18, 107; HLC 2
See also CA 5-8R; CAAE 195; CAAS 4;
CANR 6, 32, 64; CN 7; DAM MULT;
DLB 122; DLBY 1982; HW 1, 2; INT
CANR-6; RGAL 4
Redcam, Tom 1870-1933 .... **TCLC 25**
Reddin, Keith .... **CLC 67**
See also CAD
Redgrove, Peter (William) 1932- . **CLC 6, 41**
See also BRWS 6; CA 1-4R; CANR 3, 39,
77; CP 7; DLB 40
Redmon, Anne .... **CLC 22**
See also Nightingale, Anne Redmon
See also DLBY 1986
Reed, Eliot
See Ambler, Eric
Reed, Ishmael 1938- .. **CLC 2, 3, 5, 6, 13, 32,**
60; BLC 3
See also AFAW 1, 2; AMWS 10; BPFB 3;
BW 2, 3; CA 21-24R; CANR 25, 48, 74;
CN 7; CP 7; CSW; DA3; DAM MULT;
DLB 2, 5, 33, 169, 227; DLBD 8; MSW;
MTCW 1, 2; PFS 6; RGAL 4; TCWW 2
Reed, John (Silas) 1887-1920 .... **TCLC 9**
See also CA 106; 195
Reed, Lou .... **CLC 21**
See also Firbank, Louis
Reese, Lizette Woodworth 1856-1935 . **PC 29**
See also CA 180; DLB 54
Reeve, Clara 1729-1807 .... **NCLC 19**
See also DLB 39; RGEL 2
Reich, Wilhelm 1897-1957 .... **TCLC 57**
See also CA 199
Reid, Christopher (John) 1949- .... **CLC 33**
See also CA 140; CANR 89; CP 7; DLB 40
Reid, Desmond
See Moorcock, Michael (John)
Reid Banks, Lynne 1929-
See Banks, Lynne Reid
See also AAYA 6; CA 1-4R; CANR 6, 22, 38, 87;
CLR 24; CN 7; JRDA; MAICYA 1, 2;
SATA 22, 75, 111; YAW
Reilly, William K.
See Creasey, John
Reiner, Max
See Caldwell, (Janet Miriam) Taylor
(Holland)
Reis, Ricardo
See Pessoa, Fernando (Antonio Nogueira)
Remarque, Erich Maria 1898-1970 . **CLC 21**
See also AAYA 27; BPFB 3; CA 77-80; 29-
32R; CDWLB 2; DA; DA3; DAB; DAC;
DAM MST, NOV; DLB 56; EXPN; LAIT
3; MTCW 1, 2; NFS 4; RGWL 2
Remington, Frederic 1861-1909 ..... **TCLC 89**
See also CA 108; 169; DLB 12, 186, 188;
SATA 41

Remizov, A.
See Remizov, Aleksei (Mikhailovich)
Remizov, A. M.
See Remizov, Aleksei (Mikhailovich)
Remizov, Aleksei (Mikhailovich)
1877-1957 .... **TCLC 27**
See also CA 125; 133
Renan, Joseph Ernest 1823-1892 .. **NCLC 26**
See also GFL 1789 to the Present
Renard, Jules 1864-1910 .... **TCLC 17**
See also CA 117; GFL 1789 to the Present
Renault, Mary .... **CLC 3, 11, 17**
See also Challans, Mary
See also BPFB 3; BYA 2; DLBY 1983;
GLL 1; LAIT 1; MTCW 2; RGEL 2;
RHW
Rendell, Ruth (Barbara) 1930- .. **CLC 28, 48**
See also Vine, Barbara
See also BPFB 3; CA 109; CANR 32, 52,
74; CN 7; CPW; DAM POP; DLB 87;
INT CANR-32; MSW; MTCW 1, 2
Renoir, Jean 1894-1979 .... **CLC 20**
See also CA 129; 85-88
Resnais, Alain 1922- .... **CLC 16**
Reverdy, Pierre 1889-1960 .... **CLC 53**
See also CA 97-100; 89-92; DLB 258; GFL
1789 to the Present
Rexroth, Kenneth 1905-1982 .... **CLC 1, 2, 6,**
11, 22, 49, 112; PC 20
See also CA 5-8R; 107; CANR 14, 34, 63;
CDALB 1941-1968; DAM POET; DLB
16, 48, 165, 212; DLBY 1982; INT
CANR-14; MTCW 1, 2; RGAL 4
Reyes, Alfonso 1889-1959 .. **TCLC 33; HLCS**
2
See also CA 131; HW 1; LAW
Reyes y Basoalto, Ricardo Eliecer Neftali
See Neruda, Pablo
Reymont, Wladyslaw (Stanislaw)
1868(?)-1925 .... **TCLC 5**
See also CA 104
Reynolds, Jonathan 1942- .... **CLC 6, 38**
See also CA 65-68; CANR 28
Reynolds, Joshua 1723-1792 .... **LC 15**
See also DLB 104
Reynolds, Michael S(hane)
1937-2000 .... **CLC 44**
See also CA 65-68; 189; CANR 9, 89, 97
Reznikoff, Charles 1894-1976 .... **CLC 9**
See also CA 33-36; 61-64; CAP 2; DLB 28,
45; WP
Rezzori (d'Arezzo), Gregor von
1914-1998 .... **CLC 25**
See also CA 122; 136; 167
Rhine, Richard
See Silverstein, Alvin; Silverstein, Virginia
B(arbara Opshelor)
Rhodes, Eugene Manlove
1869-1934 .... **TCLC 53**
See also CA 198; DLB 256
R'hoone, Lord
See Balzac, Honore de
Rhys, Jean 1894(?)-1979 ...... **CLC 2, 4, 6, 14,**
19, 51, 124; SSC 21
See also BRWS 2; CA 25-28R; 85-88;
CANR 35, 62; CDBLB 1945-1960; CD-
WLB 3; DA3; DAM NOV; DLB 36, 117,
162; DNFS 2; MTCW 1, 2; RGEL 2;
RGSF 2; RHW
Ribeiro, Darcy 1922-1997 .... **CLC 34**
See also CA 33-36R; 156
Ribeiro, Joao Ubaldo (Osorio Pimentel)
1941- .... **CLC 10, 67**
See also CA 81-84
Ribman, Ronald (Burt) 1932- .... **CLC 7**
See also CA 21-24R; CAD; CANR 46, 80;
CD 5
Ricci, Nino 1959- .... **CLC 70**
See also CA 137; CCA 1

Rice, Anne 1941- .... CLC 41, 128
See also Rampling, Anne
See also AAYA 9; AMWS 7; BEST 89:2;
BPFB 3; CA 65-68; CANR 12, 36, 53,
74, 100; CN 7; CPW; CSW; DA3; DAM
POP; GLL 2; HGG; MTCW 2; YAW
Rice, Elmer (Leopold) 1892-1967 ...... CLC 7,
49
See also CA 21-22; 25-28R; CAP 2; DAM
DRAM; DFS 12; DLB 4, 7; MTCW 1, 2;
RGAL 4
Rice, Tim(othy Miles Bindon)
1944- .... CLC 21
See also CA 103; CANR 46; DFS 7
Rich, Adrienne (Cecile) 1929- ... CLC 3, 6, 7,
11, 18, 36, 73, 76, 125; PC 5
See also AMWS 1; CA 9-12R; CANR 20,
53, 74; CDALBS; CP 7; CSW; CWP;
DA3; DAM POET; DLB 5, 67; EXPP;
FW; MAWW; MTCW 1, 2; PAB; RGAL
4; WP
Rich, Barbara
See Graves, Robert (von Ranke)
Rich, Robert
See Trumbo, Dalton
Richard, Keith .... CLC 17
See also Richards, Keith
Richards, David Adams 1950- .... CLC 59
See also CA 93-96; CANR 60; DAC; DLB
53
Richards, I(vor) A(rmstrong)
1893-1979 .... CLC 14, 24
See also BRWS 2; CA 41-44R; 89-92;
CANR 34, 74; DLB 27; MTCW 2; RGEL
2
Richards, Keith 1943-
See Richard, Keith
See also CA 107; CANR 77
Richardson, Anne
See Roiphe, Anne (Richardson)
Richardson, Dorothy Miller
1873-1957 .... TCLC 3
See also CA 104; 192; DLB 36; FW; RGEL
2
Richardson (Robertson), Ethel Florence
Lindesay 1870-1946
See Richardson, Henry Handel
See also CA 105; 190; DLB 230; RHW
Richardson, Henry Handel .... TCLC 4
See Richardson (Robertson), Ethel Flo-
rence Lindesay
See also DLB 197; RGEL 2; RGSF 2
Richardson, John 1796-1852 .... NCLC 55
See also CCA 1; DAC; DLB 99
Richardson, Samuel 1689-1761 ...... LC 1, 44;
WLC
See also BRW 3; CDBLB 1660-1789; DA;
DAB; DAC; DAM MST, NOV; DLB 39;
RGEL 2; WLIT 3
Richler, Mordecai 1931-2001 .... CLC 3, 5, 9,
13, 18, 46, 70
See also AITN 1; CA 65-68; 201; CANR
31, 62; CCA 1; CLR 17; CWRI 5; DAC;
DAM MST, NOV; DLB 53; MAICYA 1,
2; MTCW 1, 2; RGEL 2; SATA 44, 98;
SATA-Brief 27
Richter, Conrad (Michael)
1890-1968 .... CLC 30
See also AAYA 21; BYA 2; CA 5-8R; 25-
28R; CANR 23; DLB 9, 212; LAIT 1;
MTCW 1, 2; RGAL 4; SATA 3; TCWW
2; YAW
Ricostranza, Tom
See Ellis, Trey
Riddell, Charlotte 1832-1906 .... TCLC 40
See also Riddell, Mrs. J. H.
See also CA 165; DLB 156
Riddell, Mrs. J. H.
See Riddell, Charlotte
See also HGG; SUFW

Ridge, John Rollin 1827-1867 .... NCLC 82
See also CA 144; DAM MULT; DLB 175;
NNAL
Ridgeway, Jason
See Marlowe, Stephen
Ridgway, Keith 1965- .... CLC 119
See also CA 172
Riding, Laura .... CLC 3, 7
See also Jackson, Laura (Riding)
See also RGAL 4
Riefenstahl, Berta Helene Amalia 1902-
See Riefenstahl, Leni
See also CA 108
Riefenstahl, Leni .... CLC 16
See also Riefenstahl, Berta Helene Amalia
Riffe, Ernest
See Bergman, (Ernst) Ingmar
Riggs, (Rolla) Lynn 1899-1954 .... TCLC 56
See also CA 144; DAM MULT; DLB 175;
NNAL
Riis, Jacob A(ugust) 1849-1914 ..... TCLC 80
See also CA 113; 168; DLB 23
Riley, James Whitcomb
1849-1916 .... TCLC 51
See also CA 118; 137; DAM POET; MAI-
CYA 1, 2; RGAL 4; SATA 17
Riley, Tex
See Creasey, John
Rilke, Rainer Maria 1875-1926 .. TCLC 1, 6,
19; PC 2
See also CA 104; 132; CANR 62, 99; CD-
WLB 2; DA3; DAM POET; DLB 81; EW
9; MTCW 1, 2; RGWL 2; WP
Rimbaud, (Jean Nicolas) Arthur
1854-1891 .... NCLC 4, 35, 82; PC 3;
WLC
See also DA; DA3; DAB; DAC; DAM
MST, POET; DLB 217; EW 7; GFL 1789
to the Present; RGWL 2; TWA; WP
Rinehart, Mary Roberts
1876-1958 .... TCLC 52
See also BPFB 3; CA 108; 166; RGAL 4;
RHW
Ringmaster, The
See Mencken, H(enry) L(ouis)
Ringwood, Gwen(dolyn Margaret) Pharis
1910-1984 .... CLC 48
See also CA 148; 112; DLB 88
Rio, Michel 1945(?)- .... CLC 43
See also CA 201
Ritsos, Giannes
See Ritsos, Yannis
Ritsos, Yannis 1909-1990 .... CLC 6, 13, 31
See also CA 77-80; 133; CANR 39, 61; EW
12; MTCW 1; RGWL 2
Ritter, Erika 1948(?)- .... CLC 52
See also CD 5; CWD
Rivera, Jose Eustasio 1889-1928 ... TCLC 35
See also CA 162; HW 1, 2; LAW
Rivera, Tomas 1935-1984
See also CA 49-52; CANR 32; DLB 82;
HLCS 2; HW 1; RGAL 4; TCWW 2;
WLIT 1
Rivers, Conrad Kent 1933-1968 .... CLC 1
See also BW 1; CA 85-88; DLB 41
Rivers, Elfrida
See Bradley, Marion Zimmer
See also GLL 1
Riverside, John
See Heinlein, Robert A(nson)
Rizal, Jose 1861-1896 .... NCLC 27
Roa Bastos, Augusto (Antonio)
1917- .... CLC 45; HLC 2
See also CA 131; DAM MULT; DLB 113;
HW 1; LAW; RGSF 2; WLIT 1

Robbe-Grillet, Alain 1922- .... CLC 1, 2, 4, 6,
8, 10, 14, 43, 128
See also BPFB 3; CA 9-12R; CANR 33,
65; DLB 83; EW 13; GFL 1789 to the
Present; IDFW 3, 4; MTCW 1, 2; RGWL
2
Robbins, Harold 1916-1997 .... CLC 5
See also BPFB 3; CA 73-76; 162; CANR
26, 54; DA3; DAM NOV; MTCW 1, 2
Robbins, Thomas Eugene 1936-
See Robbins, Tom
See also CA 81-84; CANR 29, 59, 95; CN
7; CPW; CSW; DA3; DAM NOV, POP;
MTCW 1, 2
Robbins, Tom .... CLC 9, 32, 64
See also Robbins, Thomas Eugene
See also AAYA 32; AMWS 10; BEST 90:3;
BPFB 3; DLBY 1980; MTCW 2
Robbins, Trina 1938- .... CLC 21
See also CA 128
Roberts, Charles G(eorge) D(ouglas)
1860-1943 .... TCLC 8
See also CA 105; 188; CLR 33; CWRI 5;
DLB 92; RGEL 2; RGSF 2; SATA 88;
SATA-Brief 29
Roberts, Elizabeth Madox
1886-1941 .... TCLC 68
See also CA 111; 166; CWRI 5; DLB 9, 54,
102; RGAL 4; RHW; SATA 33; SATA-
Brief 27; WCH
Roberts, Kate 1891-1985 .... CLC 15
See also CA 107; 116
Roberts, Keith (John Kingston)
1935-2000 .... CLC 14
See also CA 25-28R; CANR 46; SFW 4
Roberts, Kenneth (Lewis)
1885-1957 .... TCLC 23
See also CA 109; 199; DLB 9; RGAL 4;
RHW
Roberts, Michele (Brigitte) 1949- ..... CLC 48
See also CA 115; CANR 58; CN 7; DLB
231; FW
Robertson, Ellis
See Ellison, Harlan (Jay); Silverberg, Robert
Robertson, Thomas William
1829-1871 .... NCLC 35
See also Robertson, Tom
See also DAM DRAM
Robertson, Tom
See Robertson, Thomas William
See also RGEL 2
Robeson, Kenneth
See Dent, Lester
Robinson, Edwin Arlington
1869-1935 .... TCLC 5, 101; PC 1, 35
See also AMW; CA 104; 133; CDALB
1865-1917; DA; DAC; DAM MST,
POET; DLB 54; EXPP; MTCW 1, 2;
PAB; PFS 4; RGAL 4; WP
Robinson, Henry Crabb
1775-1867 .... NCLC 15
See also DLB 107
Robinson, Jill 1936- .... CLC 10
See also CA 102; INT 102
Robinson, Kim Stanley 1952- .... CLC 34
See also AAYA 26; CA 126; CN 7; SATA
109; SCFW 2; SFW 4
Robinson, Lloyd
See Silverberg, Robert
Robinson, Marilynne 1944- .... CLC 25
See also CA 116; CANR 80; CN 7; DLB
206
Robinson, Smokey .... CLC 21
See also Robinson, William, Jr.
Robinson, William, Jr. 1940-
See Robinson, Smokey
See also CA 116

Robison, Mary 1949- .... **CLC 42, 98**
  See also CA 113; 116; CANR 87; CN 7;
  DLB 130; INT 116; RGSF 2
Rochester
  See Wilmot, John
  See also RGEL 2
Rod, Edouard 1857-1910 .... **TCLC 52**
Roddenberry, Eugene Wesley 1921-1991
  See Roddenberry, Gene
  See also CA 110; 135; CANR 37; SATA 45;
  SATA-Obit 69
Roddenberry, Gene .... **CLC 17**
  See also Roddenberry, Eugene Wesley
  See also AAYA 5; SATA-Obit 69
Rodgers, Mary 1931- .... **CLC 12**
  See also BYA 5; CA 49-52; CANR 8, 55,
  90; CLR 20; CWRI 5; INT CANR-8;
  JRDA; MAICYA 1, 2; SATA 8, 130
Rodgers, W(illiam) R(obert)
  1909-1969 .... **CLC 7**
  See also CA 85-88; DLB 20; RGEL 2
Rodman, Eric
  See Silverberg, Robert
Rodman, Howard 1920(?)-1985 .... **CLC 65**
  See also CA 118
Rodman, Maia
  See Wojciechowska, Maia (Teresa)
Rodo, Jose Enrique 1871(?)-1917
  See also CA 178; HLCS 2; HW 2; LAW
Rodolph, Utto
  See Ouologuem, Yambo
Rodriguez, Claudio 1934-1999 .... **CLC 10**
  See also CA 188; DLB 134
Rodriguez, Richard 1944- .... **CLC 155; HLC 2**
  See also CA 110; CANR 66; DAM MULT;
  DLB 82, 256; HW 1, 2; LAIT 5; NCFS 3;
  WLIT 1
Roelvaag, O(le) E(dvart) 1876-1931
  See Rolvaag, O(le) E(dvart)
  See also CA 117; 171
Roethke, Theodore (Huebner)
  1908-1963 .... **CLC 1, 3, 8, 11, 19, 46,
  101; PC 15**
  See also AMW; CA 81-84; CABS 2;
  CDALB 1941-1968; DA3; DAM POET;
  DLB 5, 206; EXPP; MTCW 1, 2; PAB;
  PFS 3; RGAL 4; WP
Rogers, Samuel 1763-1855 .... **NCLC 69**
  See also DLB 93; RGEL 2
Rogers, Thomas Hunton 1927- .... **CLC 57**
  See also CA 89-92; INT 89-92
Rogers, Will(iam Penn Adair)
  1879-1935 .... **TCLC 8, 71**
  See also CA 105; 144; DA3; DAM MULT;
  DLB 11; MTCW 2; NNAL
Rogin, Gilbert 1929- .... **CLC 18**
  See also CA 65-68; CANR 15
Rohan, Koda
  See Koda Shigeyuki
Rohlfs, Anna Katharine Green
  See Green, Anna Katharine
Rohmer, Eric .... **CLC 16**
  See also Scherer, Jean-Marie Maurice
Rohmer, Sax .... **TCLC 28**
  See also Ward, Arthur Henry Sarsfield
  See also DLB 70; MSW; SUFW
Roiphe, Anne (Richardson) 1935- .. **CLC 3, 9**
  See also CA 89-92; CANR 45, 73; DLBY
  1980; INT 89-92
Rojas, Fernando de 1475-1541 .... **LC 23;
  HLCS 1**
  See also RGWL 2
Rojas, Gonzalo 1917-
  See also CA 178; HLCS 2; HW 2; LAWS 1
**Rolfe, Frederick (William Serafino Austin
  Lewis Mary)** 1860-1913 .... **TCLC 12**
  See also Corvo, Baron
  See also CA 107; DLB 34, 156; RGEL 2

Rolland, Romain 1866-1944 .... **TCLC 23**
  See also CA 118; 197; DLB 65; GFL 1789
  to the Present; RGWL 2
Rolle, Richard c. 1300-c. 1349 ...... **CMLC 21**
  See also DLB 146; RGEL 2
Rolvaag, O(le) E(dvart) .... **TCLC 17**
  See also Roelvaag, O(le) E(dvart)
  See also DLB 9, 212; NFS 5; RGAL 4
Romain Arnaud, Saint
  See Aragon, Louis
Romains, Jules 1885-1972 .... **CLC 7**
  See also CA 85-88; CANR 34; DLB 65;
  GFL 1789 to the Present; MTCW 1
Romero, Jose Ruben 1890-1952 ...... **TCLC 14**
  See also CA 114; 131; HW 1; LAW
Ronsard, Pierre de 1524-1585 . **LC 6, 54; PC
  11**
  See also EW 2; GFL Beginnings to 1789;
  RGWL 2
Rooke, Leon 1934- .... **CLC 25, 34**
  See also CA 25-28R; CANR 23, 53; CCA
  1; CPW; DAM POP
Roosevelt, Franklin Delano
  1882-1945 .... **TCLC 93**
  See also CA 116; 173; LAIT 3
Roosevelt, Theodore 1858-1919 ..... **TCLC 69**
  See also CA 115; 170; DLB 47, 186
Roper, William 1498-1578 .... **LC 10**
Roquelaure, A. N.
  See Rice, Anne
Rosa, Joao Guimaraes 1908-1967 ... **CLC 23;
  HLCS 1**
  See Guimaraes Rosa, Joao
  See also CA 89-92; DLB 113; WLIT 1
Rose, Wendy 1948- .... **CLC 85; PC 13**
  See also CA 53-56; CANR 5, 51; CWP;
  DAM MULT; DLB 175; NNAL; PFS 13;
  RGAL 4; SATA 12
Rosen, R. D.
  See Rosen, Richard (Dean)
Rosen, Richard (Dean) 1949- .... **CLC 39**
  See also CA 77-80; CANR 62; CMW 4;
  INT CANR-30
Rosenberg, Isaac 1890-1918 .... **TCLC 12**
  See also BRW 6; CA 107; 188; DLB 20,
  216; PAB; RGEL 2
Rosenblatt, Joe .... **CLC 15**
  See also Rosenblatt, Joseph
Rosenblatt, Joseph 1933-
  See Rosenblatt, Joe
  See also CA 89-92; CP 7; INT 89-92
Rosenfeld, Samuel
  See Tzara, Tristan
Rosenstock, Sami
  See Tzara, Tristan
Rosenstock, Samuel
  See Tzara, Tristan
Rosenthal, M(acha) L(ouis)
  1917-1996 .... **CLC 28**
  See also CA 1-4R; 152; CAAS 6; CANR 4,
  51; CP 7; DLB 5; SATA 59
Ross, Barnaby
  See Dannay, Frederic
Ross, Bernard L.
  See Follett, Ken(neth Martin)
Ross, J. H.
  See Lawrence, T(homas) E(dward)
Ross, John Hume
  See Lawrence, T(homas) E(dward)
Ross, Martin 1862-1915
  See Martin, Violet Florence
  See also DLB 135; GLL 2; RGEL 2; RGSF
  2
Ross, (James) Sinclair 1908-1996 ... **CLC 13;
  SSC 24**
  See also CA 73-76; CANR 81; CN 7; DAC;
  DAM MST; DLB 88; RGEL 2; RGSF 2;
  TCWW 2

Rossetti, Christina (Georgina)
  1830-1894 .... **NCLC 2, 50, 66; PC 7;
  WLC**
  See also BRW 5; BYA 4; DA; DA3; DAB;
  DAC; DAM MST, POET; DLB 35, 163,
  240; EXPP; MAICYA 1, 2; PFS 10, 14;
  RGEL 2; SATA 20; WCH
Rossetti, Dante Gabriel 1828-1882 . **NCLC 4,
  77; WLC**
  See also BRW 5; CDBLB 1832-1890; DA;
  DAB; DAC; DAM MST, POET; DLB 35;
  EXPP; RGEL 2
Rossi, Cristina Peri
  See Peri Rossi, Cristina
Rossi, Jean Baptiste 1931-
  See Japrisot, Sebastien
  See also CA 201
Rossner, Judith (Perelman) 1935- . **CLC 6, 9,
  29**
  See also AITN 2; BEST 90:3; BPFB 3; CA
  17-20R; CANR 18, 51, 73; CN 7; DLB 6;
  INT CANR-18; MTCW 1, 2
Rostand, Edmond (Eugene Alexis)
  1868-1918 .... **TCLC 6, 37; DC 10**
  See also CA 104; 126; DA; DA3; DAB;
  DAC; DAM DRAM, MST; DFS 1; DLB
  192; LAIT 1; MTCW 1; RGWL 2
Roth, Henry 1906-1995 ..... **CLC 2, 6, 11, 104**
  See also AMWS 9; CA 11-12; 149; CANR
  38, 63; CAP 1; CN 7; DA3; DLB 28;
  MTCW 1, 2; RGAL 4
Roth, (Moses) Joseph 1894-1939 ... **TCLC 33**
  See also CA 160; DLB 85; RGWL 2
Roth, Philip (Milton) 1933- ... **CLC 1, 2, 3, 4,
  6, 9, 15, 22, 31, 47, 66, 86, 119; SSC
  26; WLC**
  See also AMWS 3; BEST 90:3; BPFB 3;
  CA 1-4R; CANR 1, 22, 36, 55, 89;
  CDALB 1968-1988; CN 7; CPW 1; DA;
  DA3; DAB; DAC; DAM MST, NOV,
  POP; DLB 2, 28, 173; DLBY 1982;
  MTCW 1, 2; RGAL 4; RGSF 2; SSFS 12
Rothenberg, Jerome 1931- .... **CLC 6, 57**
  See also CA 45-48; CANR 1, 106; CP 7;
  DLB 5, 193
Rotter, Pat ed. .... **CLC 65**
Roumain, Jacques (Jean Baptiste)
  1907-1944 .... **TCLC 19; BLC 3**
  See also BW 1; CA 117; 125; DAM MULT
Rourke, Constance (Mayfield)
  1885-1941 .... **TCLC 12**
  See also CA 107; YABC 1
Rousseau, Jean-Baptiste 1671-1741 ...... **LC 9**
Rousseau, Jean-Jacques 1712-1778 .... **LC 14,
  36; WLC**
  See also DA; DA3; DAB; DAC; DAM
  MST; EW 4; GFL Beginnings to 1789;
  RGWL 2
Roussel, Raymond 1877-1933 .... **TCLC 20**
  See also CA 117; 201; GFL 1789 to the
  Present
Rovit, Earl (Herbert) 1927- .... **CLC 7**
  See also CA 5-8R; CANR 12
Rowe, Elizabeth Singer 1674-1737 ..... **LC 44**
  See also DLB 39, 95
Rowe, Nicholas 1674-1718 .... **LC 8**
  See also DLB 84; RGEL 2
Rowlandson, Mary 1637(?)-1678 .... **LC 66**
  See also DLB 24, 200; RGAL 4
Rowley, Ames Dorrance
  See Lovecraft, H(oward) P(hillips)
Rowling, J(oanne) K(athleen)
  1965(?)- .... **CLC 137**
  See also AAYA 34; BYA 13, 14; CA 173;
  CLR 66, 80; SATA 109
Rowson, Susanna Haswell
  1762(?)-1824 .... **NCLC 5, 69**
  See also DLB 37, 200; RGAL 4

Roy, Arundhati 1960(?)- .... **CLC 109**
See also CA 163; CANR 90; DLBY 1997

Roy, Gabrielle 1909-1983 .... **CLC 10, 14**
See also CA 53-56; 110; CANR 5, 61; CCA
1; DAB; DAC; DAM MST; DLB 68;
MTCW 1; RGWL 2; SATA 104

Royko, Mike 1932-1997 .... **CLC 109**
See also CA 89-92; 157; CANR 26; CPW

Rozanov, Vassili 1856-1919 .... **TCLC 104**

Rozewicz, Tadeusz 1921- ..... **CLC 9, 23, 139**
See also CA 108; CANR 36, 66; CWW 2;
DA3; DAM POET; DLB 232; MTCW 1,
2

Ruark, Gibbons 1941- .... **CLC 3**
See also CA 33-36R; CAAS 23; CANR 14,
31, 57; DLB 120

Rubens, Bernice (Ruth) 1923- .... **CLC 19, 31**
See also CA 25-28R; CANR 33, 65; CN 7;
DLB 14, 207; MTCW 1

Rubin, Harold
See Robbins, Harold

Rudkin, (James) David 1936- .... **CLC 14**
See also CA 89-92; CBD; CD 5; DLB 13

Rudnik, Raphael 1933- .... **CLC 7**
See also CA 29-32R

Ruffian, M.
See Hasek, Jaroslav (Matej Frantisek)

Ruiz, Jose Martinez .... **CLC 11**
See also Martinez Ruiz, Jose

Rukeyser, Muriel 1913-1980 . **CLC 6, 10, 15,
27; PC 12**
See also AMWS 6; CA 5-8R; 93-96; CANR
26, 60; DA3; DAM POET; DLB 48; FW;
GLL 2; MTCW 1, 2; PFS 10; RGAL 4;
SATA-Obit 22

Rule, Jane (Vance) 1931- .... **CLC 27**
See also CA 25-28R; CAAS 18; CANR 12,
87; CN 7; DLB 60; FW

Rulfo, Juan 1918-1986 .. **CLC 8, 80; HLC 2;
SSC 25**
See also CA 85-88; 118; CANR 26; CD-
WLB 3; DAM MULT; DLB 113; HW 1,
2; LAW; MTCW 1, 2; RGSF 2; RGWL 2;
WLIT 1

Rumi, Jalal al-Din 1207-1273 .... **CMLC 20**
See also RGWL 2; WP

Runeberg, Johan 1804-1877 .... **NCLC 41**

Runyon, (Alfred) Damon
1884(?)-1946 .... **TCLC 10**
See also CA 107; 165; DLB 11, 86, 171;
MTCW 2; RGAL 4

Rush, Norman 1933- .... **CLC 44**
See also CA 121; 126; INT 126

Rushdie, (Ahmed) Salman 1947- .... **CLC 23,
31, 55, 100; WLCS**
See also BEST 89:3; BPFB 3; BRWS 4;
CA 108; 111; CANR 33, 56, 108; CN 7;
CPW 1; DA3; DAB; DAC; DAM MST,
NOV, POP; DLB 194; FANT; INT CA-
111; MTCW 1, 2; RGEL 2; RGSF 2;
WLIT 4

Rushforth, Peter (Scott) 1945- .... **CLC 19**
See also CA 101

Ruskin, John 1819-1900 .... **TCLC 63**
See also BRW 5; BYA 5; CA 114; 129; CD-
BLB 1832-1890; DLB 55, 163, 190;
RGEL 2; SATA 24; WCH

Russ, Joanna 1937- .... **CLC 15**
See also BPFB 3; CA 5-28R; CANR 11,
31, 65; CN 7; DLB 8; FW; GLL 1;
MTCW 1; SCFW 2; SFW 4

Russell, George William 1867-1935
See A.E.; Baker, Jean H.
See also CA 104; 153; CDBLB 1890-1914;
DAM POET; RGEL 2

Russell, Jeffrey Burton 1934- .... **CLC 70**
See also CA 25-28R; CANR 11, 28, 52

Russell, (Henry) Ken(neth Alfred)
1927- .... **CLC 16**
See also CA 105

Russell, William Martin 1947-
See Russell, Willy
See also CA 164; CANR 107

Russell, Willy .... **CLC 60**
See also Russell, William Martin
See also CBD; CD 5; DLB 233

Rutherford, Mark .... **TCLC 25**
See also White, William Hale
See also DLB 18; RGEL 2

Ruyslinck, Ward .... **CLC 14**
See also Belser, Reimond Karel Maria de

Ryan, Cornelius (John) 1920-1974 ..... **CLC 7**
See also CA 69-72; 53-56; CANR 38

Ryan, Michael 1946- .... **CLC 65**
See also CA 49-52; CANR 109; DLBY
1982

Ryan, Tim
See Dent, Lester

Rybakov, Anatoli (Naumovich)
1911-1998 .... **CLC 23, 53**
See also CA 126; 135; 172; SATA 79;
SATA-Obit 108

Ryder, Jonathan
See Ludlum, Robert

Ryga, George 1932-1987 .... **CLC 14**
See also CA 101; 124; CANR 43, 90; CCA
1; DAC; DAM MST; DLB 60

S. H.
See Hartmann, Sadakichi

S. S.
See Sassoon, Siegfried (Lorraine)

Saba, Umberto 1883-1957 .... **TCLC 33**
See also CA 144; CANR 79; DLB 114;
RGWL 2

Sabatini, Rafael 1875-1950 .... **TCLC 47**
See also BPFB 3; CA 162; RHW

Sabato, Ernesto (R.) 1911- .... **CLC 10, 23;
HLC 2**
See also CA 97-100; CANR 32, 65; CD-
WLB 3; DAM MULT; DLB 145; HW 1,
2; LAW; MTCW 1, 2

Sa-Carniero, Mario de 1890-1916 . **TCLC 83**

Sacastru, Martin
See Bioy Casares, Adolfo
See also CWW 2

Sacher-Masoch, Leopold von
1836(?)-1895 .... **NCLC 31**

Sachs, Marilyn (Stickle) 1927- .... **CLC 35**
See also AAYA 2; BYA 6; CA 17-20R;
CANR 13, 47; CLR 2; JRDA; MAICYA
1, 2; SAAS 2; SATA 3, 68; SATA-Essay
110; WYA; YAW

Sachs, Nelly 1891-1970 .... **CLC 14, 98**
See also CA 17-18; 25-28R; CANR 87;
CAP 2; MTCW 2; RGWL 2

Sackler, Howard (Oliver)
1929-1982 .... **CLC 14**
See also CA 61-64; 108; CAD; CANR 30;
DLB 7

Sacks, Oliver (Wolf) 1933- .... **CLC 67**
See also CA 53-56; CANR 28, 50, 76;
CPW; DA3; INT CANR-28; MTCW 1, 2

Sadakichi
See Hartmann, Sadakichi

Sade, Donatien Alphonse Francois
1740-1814 .... **NCLC 3, 47**
See also EW 4; GFL Beginnings to 1789;
RGWL 2

Sadoff, Ira 1945- .... **CLC 9**
See also CA 53-56; CANR 5, 21, 109; DLB
120

Saetone
See Camus, Albert

Safire, William 1929- .... **CLC 10**
See also CA 17-20R; CANR 31, 54, 91

Sagan, Carl (Edward) 1934-1996 .... **CLC 30,
112**
See also AAYA 2; CA 25-28R; 155; CANR
11, 36, 74; CPW; DA3; MTCW 1, 2;
SATA 58; SATA-Obit 94

Sagan, Francoise .... **CLC 3, 6, 9, 17, 36**
See also Quoirez, Francoise
See also CWW 2; DLB 83; GFL 1789 to
the Present; MTCW 2

Sahgal, Nayantara (Pandit) 1927- .... **CLC 41**
See also CA 9-12R; CANR 11, 88; CN 7

Said, Edward W. 1935- .... **CLC 123**
See also CA 21-24R; CANR 45, 74, 107;
DLB 67; MTCW 2

Saint, H(arry) F. 1941- .... **CLC 50**
See also CA 127

St. Aubin de Teran, Lisa 1953-
See Teran, Lisa St. Aubin de
See also CA 118; 126; CN 7; INT 126

Saint Birgitta of Sweden c.
1303-1373 .... **CMLC 24**

Sainte-Beuve, Charles Augustin
1804-1869 .... **NCLC 5**
See also DLB 217; EW 6; GFL 1789 to the
Present

Saint-Exupery, Antoine (Jean Baptiste
Marie Roger) de 1900-1944 .... **TCLC 2,
56; WLC**
See also BPFB 3; BYA 3; CA 108; 132;
CLR 10; DA3; DAM NOV; DLB 72; EW
12; GFL 1789 to the Present; LAIT 3;
MAICYA 1, 2; MTCW 1, 2; RGWL 2;
SATA 20

St. John, David
See Hunt, E(verette) Howard, (Jr.)

St. John, J. Hector
See Crevecoeur, Michel Guillaume Jean de

Saint-John Perse
See Leger, (Marie-Rene Auguste) Alexis
Saint-Leger
See also EW 10; GFL 1789 to the Present;
RGWL 2

Saintsbury, George (Edward Bateman)
1845-1933 .... **TCLC 31**
See also CA 160; DLB 57, 149

Sait Faik .... **TCLC 23**
See also Abasiyanik, Sait Faik

Saki .... **TCLC 3; SSC 12**
See also Munro, H(ector) H(ugh)
See also BRWS 6; LAIT 2; MTCW 2;
RGEL 2; SSFS 1; SUFW

Sakutaro, Hagiwara
See Hagiwara, Sakutaro

Sala, George Augustus 1828-1895 . **NCLC 46**

Saladin 1138-1193 .... **CMLC 38**

Salama, Hannu 1936- .... **CLC 18**

Salamanca, J(ack) R(ichard) 1922- .. **CLC 4,
15**
See also CA 25-28R; CAAE 193

Salas, Floyd Francis 1931-
See also CA 119; CAAS 27; CANR 44, 75,
93; DAM MULT; DLB 82; HLC 2; HW
1, 2; MTCW 2

Sale, J. Kirkpatrick
See Sale, Kirkpatrick

Sale, Kirkpatrick 1937- .... **CLC 68**
See also CA 13-16R; CANR 10

Salinas, Luis Omar 1937- ... **CLC 90; HLC 2**
See also CA 131; CANR 81; DAM MULT;
DLB 82; HW 1, 2

Salinas (y Serrano), Pedro
1891(?)-1951 .... **TCLC 17**
See also CA 117; DLB 134

Salinger, J(erome) D(avid) 1919- .. **CLC 1, 3,
8, 12, 55, 56, 138; SSC 2, 28; WLC**
See also AAYA 2, 36; AMW; BPFB 3; CA
5-8R; CANR 39; CDALB 1941-1968;
CLR 18; CN 7; CPW 1; DA; DA3; DAB;
DAC; DAM MST, NOV, POP; DLB 2,

102, 173; EXPN; LAIT 4; MAICYA 1, 2;
MTCW 1, 2; NFS 1; RGAL 4; RGSF 2;
SATA 67; WYA; YAW

Salisbury, John
See Caute, (John) David

Salter, James 1925- .... **CLC 7, 52, 59**
See also AMWS 9; CA 73-76; CANR 107;
DLB 130

Saltus, Edgar (Everton) 1855-1921 . **TCLC 8**
See also CA 105; DLB 202; RGAL 4

Saltykov, Mikhail Evgrafovich
1826-1889 .... **NCLC 16**
See also DLB 238:

Saltykov-Shchedrin, N.
See Saltykov, Mikhail Evgrafovich

Samarakis, Antonis 1919- .... **CLC 5**
See also CA 25-28R; CAAS 16; CANR 36

Sanchez, Florencio 1875-1910 .... **TCLC 37**
See also CA 153; HW 1; LAW

Sanchez, Luis Rafael 1936- .... **CLC 23**
See also CA 128; DLB 145; HW 1; WLIT
1

Sanchez, Sonia 1934- .... **CLC 5, 116; BLC 3;
PC 9**
See also BW 2, 3; CA 33-36R; CANR 24,
49, 74; CLR 18; CP 7; CSW; CWP; DA3;
DAM MULT; DLB 41; DLBD 8; MAI-
CYA 1, 2; MTCW 1, 2; SATA 22; WP

Sand, George 1804-1876 ..... **NCLC 2, 42, 57;
WLC**
See also DA; DA3; DAB; DAC; DAM
MST, NOV; DLB 119, 192; EW 6; FW;
GFL 1789 to the Present; RGWL 2

Sandburg, Carl (August) 1878-1967 . **CLC 1,
4, 10, 15, 35; PC 2, 41; WLC**
See also AAYA 24; AMW; BYA 1, 3; CA
5-8R; 25-28R; CANR 35; CDALB 1865-
1917; CLR 67; DA; DA3; DAB; DAC;
DAM MST, POET; DLB 17, 54; EXPP;
LAIT 2; MAICYA 1, 2; MTCW 1, 2;
PAB; PFS 3, 6, 12; RGAL 4; SATA 8;
WCH; WP; WYA

Sandburg, Charles
See Sandburg, Carl (August)

Sandburg, Charles A.
See Sandburg, Carl (August)

Sanders, (James) Ed(ward) 1939- .... **CLC 53**
See also Sanders, Edward
See also CA 13-16R; CAAS 21; CANR 13,
44, 78; CP 7; DAM POET; DLB 16, 244

Sanders, Edward
See Sanders, (James) Ed(ward)
See also DLB 244

Sanders, Lawrence 1920-1998 .... **CLC 41**
See also BEST 89:4; BPFB 3; CA 81-84;
165; CANR 33, 62; CMW 4; CPW; DA3;
DAM POP; MTCW 1

Sanders, Noah
See Blount, Roy (Alton), Jr.

Sanders, Winston P.
See Anderson, Poul (William)

Sandoz, Mari(e Susette) 1900-1966 .. **CLC 28**
See also CA 1-4R; 25-28R; CANR 17, 64;
DLB 9, 212; LAIT 2; MTCW 1, 2; SATA
5; TCWW 2

Saner, Reg(inald Anthony) 1931- .... **CLC 9**
See also CA 65-68; CP 7

Sankara 788-820 .... **CMLC 32**

Sannazaro, Jacopo 1456(?)-1530 .... **LC 8**
See also RGWL 2

Sansom, William 1912-1976 . **CLC 2, 6; SSC
21**
See also CA 5-8R; 65-68; CANR 42; DAM
NOV; DLB 139; MTCW 1; RGEL 2;
RGSF 2

Santayana, George 1863-1952 .... **TCLC 40**
See also AMW; CA 115; 194; DLB 54, 71,
246; DLBD 13; RGAL 4

Santiago, Danny .... **CLC 33**
See also James, Daniel (Lewis)
See also DLB 122

Santmyer, Helen Hooven
1895-1986 .... **CLC 33**
See also CA 1-4R; 118; CANR 15, 33;
DLBY 1984; MTCW 1; RHW

Santoka, Taneda 1882-1940 .... **TCLC 72**

Santos, Bienvenido N(uqui)
1911-1996 .... **CLC 22**
See also CA 101; 151; CANR 19, 46; DAM
MULT; RGAL 4

Sapir, Edward 1884-1939 .... **TCLC 108**
See also DLB 92

Sapper .... **TCLC 44**
See also McNeile, Herman Cyril

Sapphire
See Sapphire, Brenda

Sapphire, Brenda 1950- .... **CLC 99**

Sappho fl. 6256th cent. B.C.- ... **CMLC 3; PC
5**
See also CDWLB 1; DA3; DAM POET;
DLB 176; RGWL 2; WP

Saramago, Jose 1922- ..... **CLC 119; HLCS 1**
See also CA 153; CANR 96

Sarduy, Severo 1937-1993 .... **CLC 6, 97;
HLCS 2**
See also CA 89-92; 142; CANR 58, 81;
CWW 2; DLB 113; HW 1, 2; LAW

Sargeson, Frank 1903-1982 .... **CLC 31**
See also CA 25-28R; 106; CANR 38, 79;
GLL 2; RGEL 2; RGSF 2

Sarmiento, Domingo Faustino 1811-1888
See also HLCS 2; LAW; WLIT 1

Sarmiento, Felix Ruben Garcia
See Dario, Ruben

Saro-Wiwa, Ken(ule Beeson)
1941-1995 .... **CLC 114**
See also BW 2; CA 142; 150; CANR 60;
DLB 157

Saroyan, William 1908-1981 ... **CLC 1, 8, 10,
29, 34, 56; SSC 21; WLC**
See also CA 5-8R; 103; CAD; CANR 30;
CDALBS; DA; DA3; DAB; DAC; DAM
DRAM, MST, NOV; DLB 7, 9, 86; DLBY
1981; LAIT 4; MTCW 1, 2; RGAL 4;
RGSF 2; SATA 23; SATA-Obit 24; SSFS
14

Sarraute, Nathalie 1900-1999 .... **CLC 1, 2, 4,
8, 10, 31, 80**
See also BPFB 3; CA 9-12R; 187; CANR
23, 66; CWW 2; DLB 83; EW 12; GFL
1789 to the Present; MTCW 1, 2; RGWL
2

Sarton, (Eleanor) May 1912-1995 ..... **CLC 4,
14, 49, 91; PC 39**
See also AMWS 8; CA 1-4R; 149; CANR
1, 34, 55; CN 7; CP 7; DAM POET; DLB
48; DLBY 1981; FW; INT CANR-34;
MTCW 1, 2; RGAL 4; SATA 36; SATA-
Obit 86; TCLC 120

Sartre, Jean-Paul 1905-1980 . **CLC 1, 4, 7, 9,
13, 18, 24, 44, 50, 52; DC 3; SSC 32;
WLC**
See also CA 9-12R; 97-100; CANR 21; DA;
DA3; DAB; DAC; DAM DRAM, MST,
NOV; DFS 5; DLB 72; EW 12; GFL 1789
to the Present; MTCW 1, 2; RGSF 2;
RGWL 2; SSFS 9

Sassoon, Siegfried (Lorraine)
1886-1967 .... **CLC 36, 130; PC 12**
See also BRW 6; CA 104; 25-28R; CANR
36; DAB; DAM MST, NOV, POET; DLB
20, 191; DLBD 18; MTCW 1, 2; PAB;
RGEL 2

Satterfield, Charles
See Pohl, Frederik

Satyremont
See Peret, Benjamin

Saul, John (W. III) 1942- .... **CLC 46**
See also AAYA 10; BEST 90:4; CA 81-84;
CANR 16, 40, 81; CPW; DAM NOV;
POP; HGG; SATA 98

Saunders, Caleb
See Heinlein, Robert A(nson)

Saura (Atares), Carlos 1932-1998 .... **CLC 20**
See also CA 114; 131; CANR 79; HW 1

Sauser-Hall, Frederic 1887-1961 ...... **CLC 18**
See also Cendrars, Blaise
See also CA 102; 93-96; CANR 36, 62;
MTCW 1

Saussure, Ferdinand de
1857-1913 .... **TCLC 49**
See also DLB 242

Savage, Catharine
See Brosman, Catharine Savage

Savage, Thomas 1915- .... **CLC 40**
See also CA 126; 132; CAAS 15; CN 7;
INT 132; TCWW 2

Savan, Glenn (?)- .... **CLC 50**

Sayers, Dorothy L(eigh)
1893-1957 .... **TCLC 2, 15**
See also BPFB 3; BRWS 3; CA 104; 119;
CANR 60; CDBLB 1914-1945; CMW 4;
DAM POP; DLB 10, 36, 77, 100; MSW;
MTCW 1, 2; RGEL 2; SSFS 12

Sayers, Valerie 1952- .... **CLC 50, 122**
See also CA 134; CANR 61; CSW

Sayles, John (Thomas) 1950- . **CLC 7, 10, 14**
See also CA 57-60; CANR 41, 84; DLB 44

Scammell, Michael 1935- .... **CLC 34**
See also CA 156

Scannell, Vernon 1922- .... **CLC 49**
See also CA 5-8R; CANR 8, 24, 57; CP 7;
CWRI 5; DLB 27; SATA 59

Scarlett, Susan
See Streatfeild, (Mary) Noel

Scarron 1847-1910
See Mikszath, Kalman

Schaeffer, Susan Fromberg 1941- ..... **CLC 6,
11, 22**
See also CA 49-52; CANR 18, 65; CN 7;
DLB 28; MTCW 1, 2; SATA 22

Schama, Simon (Michael) 1945- ..... **CLC 150**
See also BEST 89:4; CA 105; CANR 39,
91

Schary, Jill
See Robinson, Jill

Schell, Jonathan 1943- .... **CLC 35**
See also CA 73-76; CANR 12

Schelling, Friedrich Wilhelm Joseph von
1775-1854 .... **NCLC 30**
See also DLB 90

Scherer, Jean-Marie Maurice 1920-
See Rohmer, Eric
See also CA 110

Schevill, James (Erwin) 1920- .... **CLC 7**
See also CA 5-8R; CAAS 12; CAD; CD 5

Schiller, Friedrich von
1759-1805 .... **NCLC 39, 69; DC 12**
See also CDWLB 2; DAM DRAM; DLB
94; EW 5; RGWL 2

Schisgal, Murray (Joseph) 1926- .... **CLC 6**
See also CA 21-24R; CAD; CANR 48, 86;
CD 5

Schlee, Ann 1934- .... **CLC 35**
See also CA 101; CANR 29, 88; SATA 44;
SATA-Brief 36

Schlegel, August Wilhelm von
1767-1845 .... **NCLC 15**
See also DLB 94; RGWL 2

Schlegel, Friedrich 1772-1829 .... **NCLC 45**
See also DLB 90; EW 5; RGWL 2

Schlegel, Johann Elias (von)
1719(?)-1749 .... **LC 5**

Schleiermacher, Friedrich
1768-1834 .... **NCLC 107**
See also DLB 90

Schlesinger, Arthur M(eier), Jr.
1917- .... **CLC 84**
See also AITN 1; CA 1-4R; CANR 1, 28, 58, 105; DLB 17; INT CANR-28; MTCW 1, 2; SATA 61

Schmidt, Arno (Otto) 1914-1979 ...... **CLC 56**
See also CA 128; 109; DLB 69

Schmitz, Aron Hector 1861-1928
See Svevo, Italo
See also CA 104; 122; MTCW 1

Schnackenberg, Gjertrud (Cecelia)
1953- .... **CLC 40**
See also CA 116; CANR 100; CP 7; CWP; DLB 120; PFS 13

Schneider, Leonard Alfred 1925-1966
See Bruce, Lenny
See also CA 89-92

Schnitzler, Arthur 1862-1931 ... **TCLC 4; DC 17; SSC 15**
See also CA 104; CDWLB 2; DLB 81, 118; EW 8; RGSF 2; RGWL 2

Schoenberg, Arnold Franz Walter
1874-1951 .... **TCLC 75**
See also CA 109; 188

Schonberg, Arnold
See Schoenberg, Arnold Franz Walter

Schopenhauer, Arthur 1788-1860 .. **NCLC 51**
See also DLB 90; EW 5

Schor, Sandra (M.) 1932(?)-1990 ..... **CLC 65**
See also CA 132

Schorer, Mark 1908-1977 .... **CLC 9**
See also CA 5-8R; 73-76; CANR 7; DLB 103

Schrader, Paul (Joseph) 1946- .... **CLC 26**
See also CA 37-40R; CANR 41; DLB 44

Schreiner, Olive (Emilie Albertina)
1855-1920 .... **TCLC 9**
See also AFW; BRWS 2; CA 105; 154; DLB 18, 156, 190, 225; FW; RGEL 2; WLIT 2

Schulberg, Budd (Wilson) 1914- .. **CLC 7, 48**
See also BPFB 3; CA 25-28R; CANR 19, 87; CN 7; DLB 6, 26, 28; DLBY 1981, 2001

Schulman, Arnold
See Trumbo, Dalton

Schulz, Bruno 1892-1942 .. **TCLC 5, 51; SSC 13**
See also CA 115; 123; CANR 86; CDWLB 4; DLB 215; MTCW 2; RGSF 2; RGWL 2

Schulz, Charles M(onroe)
1922-2000 .... **CLC 12**
See also AAYA 39; CA 9-12R; 187; CANR 6; INT CANR-6; SATA 10; SATA-Obit 118

Schumacher, E(rnst) F(riedrich)
1911-1977 .... **CLC 80**
See also CA 81-84; 73-76; CANR 34, 85

Schuyler, James Marcus 1923-1991 .. **CLC 5, 23**
See also CA 101; 134; DAM POET; DLB 5, 169; INT 101; WP

Schwartz, Delmore (David)
1913-1966 ... **CLC 2, 4, 10, 45, 87; PC 8**
See also AMWS 2; CA 17-18; 25-28R; CANR 35; CAP 2; DLB 28, 48; MTCW 1, 2; PAB; RGAL 4

Schwartz, Ernst
See Ozu, Yasujiro

Schwartz, John Burnham 1965- .... **CLC 59**
See also CA 132

Schwartz, Lynne Sharon 1939- .... **CLC 31**
See also CA 103; CANR 44, 89; DLB 218; MTCW 2

Schwartz, Muriel A.
See Eliot, T(homas) S(tearns)

Schwarz-Bart, Andre 1928- .... **CLC 2, 4**
See also CA 89-92; CANR 109

Schwarz-Bart, Simone 1938- . **CLC 7; BLCS**
See also BW 2; CA 97-100

Schwitters, Kurt (Hermann Edward Karl Julius) 1887-1948 .... **TCLC 95**
See also CA 158

Schwob, Marcel (Mayer Andre)
1867-1905 .... **TCLC 20**
See also CA 117; 168; DLB 123; GFL 1789 to the Present

Sciascia, Leonardo 1921-1989 .. **CLC 8, 9, 41**
See also CA 85-88; 130; CANR 35; DLB 177; MTCW 1; RGWL 2

Scoppettone, Sandra 1936- .... **CLC 26**
See also Early, Jack
See also AAYA 11; BYA 8; CA 5-8R; CANR 41, 73; GLL 1; MAICYA 2; MAICYAS 1; SATA 9, 92; WYA; YAW

Scorsese, Martin 1942- .... **CLC 20, 89**
See also AAYA 38; CA 110; 114; CANR 46, 85

Scotland, Jay
See Jakes, John (William)

Scott, Duncan Campbell
1862-1947 .... **TCLC 6**
See also CA 104; 153; DAC; DLB 92; RGEL 2

Scott, Evelyn 1893-1963 .... **CLC 43**
See also CA 104; 112; CANR 64; DLB 9, 48; RHW

Scott, F(rancis) R(eginald)
1899-1985 .... **CLC 22**
See also CA 101; 114; CANR 87; DLB 88; INT CA-101; RGEL 2

Scott, Frank
See Scott, F(rancis) R(eginald)

Scott, Joan .... **CLC 65**

Scott, Joanna 1960- .... **CLC 50**
See also CA 126; CANR 53, 92

Scott, Paul (Mark) 1920-1978 .... **CLC 9, 60**
See also BRWS 1; CA 81-84; 77-80; CANR 33; DLB 14, 207; MTCW 1; RGEL 2; RHW

Scott, Sarah 1723-1795 .... **LC 44**
See also DLB 39

Scott, Sir Walter 1771-1832 .... **NCLC 15, 69, 110; PC 13; SSC 32; WLC**
See also AAYA 22; BRW 4; BYA 2; CD-BLB 1789-1832; DA; DAB; DAC; DAM MST, NOV, POET; DLB 93, 107, 116, 144, 159; HGG; LAIT 1; RGEL 2; RGSF 2; SSFS 10; SUFW; WLIT 3; YABC 2

Scribe, (Augustin) Eugene
1791-1861 .... **NCLC 16; DC 5**
See also DAM DRAM; DLB 192; GFL 1789 to the Present; RGWL 2

Scrum, R.
See Crumb, R(obert)

Scudery, Georges de 1601-1667 .... **LC 75**
See also GFL Beginnings to 1789

Scudery, Madeleine de 1607-1701 .. **LC 2, 58**
See also GFL Beginnings to 1789

Scum
See Crumb, R(obert)

Scumbag, Little Bobby
See Crumb, R(obert)

Seabrook, John
See Hubbard, L(afayette) Ron(ald)

Sealy, I(rwin) Allan 1951- .... **CLC 55**
See also CA 136; CN 7

Search, Alexander
See Pessoa, Fernando (Antonio Nogueira)

Sebastian, Lee
See Silverberg, Robert

Sebastian Owl
See Thompson, Hunter S(tockton)

Sebestyen, Igen
See Sebestyen, Ouida

Sebestyen, Ouida 1924- .... **CLC 30**
See also AAYA 8; BYA 7; CA 107; CANR 40; CLR 17; JRDA; MAICYA 1, 2; SAAS 10; SATA 39; WYA; YAW

Secundus, H. Scriblerus
See Fielding, Henry

Sedges, John
See Buck, Pearl S(ydenstricker)

Sedgwick, Catharine Maria
1789-1867 .... **NCLC 19, 98**
See also DLB 1, 74, 183, 239, 243, 254; RGAL 4

Seelye, John (Douglas) 1931- .... **CLC 7**
See also CA 97-100; CANR 70; INT 97-100; TCWW 2

Seferiades, Giorgos Stylianou 1900-1971
See Seferis, George
See also CA 5-8R; 33-36R; CANR 5, 36; MTCW 1

Seferis, George .... **CLC 5, 11**
See also Seferiades, Giorgos Stylianou
See also EW 12; RGWL 2

Segal, Erich (Wolf) 1937- .... **CLC 3, 10**
See also BEST 89:1; BPFB 3; CA 25-28R; CANR 20, 36, 65; CPW; DAM POP; DLBY 1986; INT CANR-20; MTCW 1

Seger, Bob 1945- .... **CLC 35**

Seghers, Anna -1983 .... **CLC 7**
See also Radvanyi, Netty
See also CDWLB 2; DLB 69

Seidel, Frederick (Lewis) 1936- .... **CLC 18**
See also CA 13-16R; CANR 8, 99; CP 7; DLBY 1984

Seifert, Jaroslav 1901-1986 .. **CLC 34, 44, 93**
See also CA 127; CDWLB 4; DLB 215; MTCW 1, 2

Sei Shonagon c. 966-1017(?) .... **CMLC 6**

Sejour, Victor 1817-1874 .... **DC 10**
See also DLB 50

Sejour Marcou et Ferrand, Juan Victor
See Sejour, Victor

Selby, Hubert, Jr. 1928- .... **CLC 1, 2, 4, 8; SSC 20**
See also CA 13-16R; CANR 33, 85; CN 7; DLB 2, 227

Selzer, Richard 1928- .... **CLC 74**
See also CA 65-68; CANR 14, 106

Sembene, Ousmane
See Ousmane, Sembene
See also AFW; CWW 2; WLIT 2

Senancour, Etienne Pivert de
1770-1846 .... **NCLC 16**
See also DLB 119; GFL 1789 to the Present

Sender, Ramon (Jose) 1902-1982 ...... **CLC 8; HLC 2**
See also CA 5-8R; 105; CANR 8; DAM MULT; HW 1; MTCW 1; RGWL 2

Seneca, Lucius Annaeus c. 4B.C.-c. 65 .... **CMLC 6; DC 5**
See also AW 2; CDWLB 1; DAM DRAM; DLB 211; RGWL 2

Senghor, Leopold Sedar 1906-2001 . **CLC 54, 130; BLC 3; PC 25**
See also AFW; BW 2; CA 116; 125; CANR 47, 74; DAM MULT, POET; DNFS 2; GFL 1789 to the Present; MTCW 1, 2

Senna, Danzy 1970- .... **CLC 119**
See also CA 169

Serling, (Edward) Rod(man)
1924-1975 .... **CLC 30**
See also AAYA 14; AITN 1; CA 162; 57-60; DLB 26; SFW 4

Serna, Ramon Gomez de la
See Gomez de la Serna, Ramon

Serpieres
See Guillevic, (Eugene)

Service, Robert
See Service, Robert W(illiam)
See also BYA 4; DAB; DLB 92

Service, Robert W(illiam)
1874(?)-1958 .... **TCLC 15; WLC**
See also Service, Robert
See also CA 115; 140; CANR 84; DA;
DAC; DAM MST, POET; PFS 10; RGEL
2; SATA 20

Seth, Vikram 1952- .... **CLC 43, 90**
See also CA 121; 127; CANR 50, 74; CN
7; CP 7; DA3; DAM MULT; DLB 120;
INT 127; MTCW 2

Seton, Cynthia Propper 1926-1982 .. **CLC 27**
See also CA 5-8R; 108; CANR 7

Seton, Ernest (Evan) Thompson
1860-1946 .... **TCLC 31**
See also ANW; BYA 3; CA 109; CLR 59;
DLB 92; DLBD 13; JRDA; SATA 18

Seton-Thompson, Ernest
See Seton, Ernest (Evan) Thompson

Settle, Mary Lee 1918- .... **CLC 19, 61**
See also BPFB 3; CA 89-92; CAAS 1;
CANR 44, 87; CN 7; CSW; DLB 6; INT
89-92

Seuphor, Michel
See Arp, Jean

Sevigne, Marie (de Rabutin-Chantal)
1626-1696 .... **LC 11**
See also GFL Beginnings to 1789

Sewall, Samuel 1652-1730 .... **LC 38**
See also DLB 24; RGAL 4

Sexton, Anne (Harvey) 1928-1974 ..... **CLC 2,
4, 6, 8, 10, 15, 53, 123; PC 2; WLC**
See also AMWS 2; CA 1-4R; 53-56; CABS
2; CANR 3, 36; CDALB 1941-1968; DA;
DA3; DAB; DAC; DAM MST, POET;
DLB 5, 169; EXPP; FW; MAWW;
MTCW 1, 2; PAB; PFS 4, 14; RGAL 4;
SATA 10

Shaara, Jeff 1952- .... **CLC 119**
See also CA 163; CANR 109

Shaara, Michael (Joseph, Jr.)
1929-1988 .... **CLC 15**
See also AITN 1; BPFB 3; CA 102; 125;
CANR 52, 85; DAM POP; DLBY 1983

Shackleton, C. C.
See Aldiss, Brian W(ilson)

Shacochis, Bob .... **CLC 39**
See also Shacochis, Robert G.

Shacochis, Robert G. 1951-
See Shacochis, Bob
See also CA 119; 124; CANR 100; INT 124

Shaffer, Anthony (Joshua)
1926-2001 .... **CLC 19**
See also CA 110; 116; 200; CBD; CD 5;
DAM DRAM; DFS 13; DLB 13

Shaffer, Peter (Levin) 1926- .. **CLC 5, 14, 18,
37, 60; DC 7**
See also BRWS 1; CA 25-28R; CANR 25,
47, 74; CBD; CD 5; CDBLB 1960 to
Present; DA3; DAB; DAM DRAM, MST;
DFS 5, 13; DLB 13, 233; MTCW 1, 2;
RGEL 2

Shakey, Bernard
See Young, Neil

Shalamov, Varlam (Tikhonovich)
1907(?)-1982 .... **CLC 18**
See also CA 129; 105; RGSF 2

Shamlu, Ahmad 1925-2000 .... **CLC 10**
See also CWW 2

Shammas, Anton 1951- .... **CLC 55**
See also CA 199

Shandling, Arline
See Berriault, Gina

Shange, Ntozake 1948- .... **CLC 8, 25, 38, 74,
126; BLC 3; DC 3**
See also AAYA 9; AFAW 1, 2; BW 2; CA
85-88; CABS 3; CAD; CANR 27, 48, 74;
CD 5; CP 7; CWD; CWP; DA3; DAM
DRAM, MULT; DFS 2, 11; DLB 38, 249;
FW; LAIT 5; MTCW 1, 2; NFS 11;
RGAL 4; YAW

Shanley, John Patrick 1950- .... **CLC 75**
See also CA 128; 133; CAD; CANR 83;
CD 5

Shapcott, Thomas W(illiam) 1935- .. **CLC 38**
See also CA 69-72; CANR 49, 83, 103; CP
7

Shapiro, Jane 1942- .... **CLC 76**
See also CA 196

Shapiro, Karl (Jay) 1913-2000 ...... **CLC 4, 8,
15, 53; PC 25**
See also AMWS 2; CA 1-4R; 188; CAAS
6; CANR 1, 36, 66; CP 7; DLB 48; EXPP;
MTCW 1, 2; PFS 3; RGAL 4

Sharp, William 1855-1905 .... **TCLC 39**
See also Macleod, Fiona
See also CA 160; DLB 156; RGEL 2

Sharpe, Thomas Ridley 1928-
See Sharpe, Tom
See also CA 114; 122; CANR 85; INT CA-
122

Sharpe, Tom .... **CLC 36**
See also Sharpe, Thomas Ridley
See also CN 7; DLB 14, 231

Shatrov, Mikhail .... **CLC 59**

Shaw, Bernard
See Shaw, George Bernard
See also DLB 190

Shaw, G. Bernard
See Shaw, George Bernard

Shaw, George Bernard 1856-1950 .. **TCLC 3,
9, 21, 45; WLC**
See also Shaw, Bernard
See also BRW 6; BRWR 2; CA 104; 128;
CDBLB 1914-1945; DA; DA3; DAB;
DAC; DAM DRAM, MST; DFS 1, 3, 6,
11; DLB 10, 57; LAIT 3; MTCW 1, 2;
RGEL 2; WLIT 4

Shaw, Henry Wheeler 1818-1885 .. **NCLC 15**
See also DLB 11; RGAL 4

Shaw, Irwin 1913-1984 .... **CLC 7, 23, 34**
See also AITN 1; BPFB 3; CA 13-16R; 112;
CANR 21; CDALB 1941-1968; CPW;
DAM DRAM, POP; DLB 6, 102; DLBY
1984; MTCW 1, 21

Shaw, Robert 1927-1978 .... **CLC 5**
See also AITN 1; CA 1-4R; 81-84; CANR
4; DLB 13, 14

Shaw, T. E.
See Lawrence, T(homas) E(dward)

Shawn, Wallace 1943- .... **CLC 41**
See also CA 112; CAD; CD 5

Shchedrin, N.
See Saltykov, Mikhail Evgrafovich

Shea, Lisa 1953- .... **CLC 86**
See also CA 147

Sheed, Wilfrid (John Joseph) 1930- . **CLC 2,
4, 10, 53**
See also CA 65-68; CANR 30, 66; CN 7;
DLB 6; MTCW 1, 2

Sheldon, Alice Hastings Bradley
1915(?)-1987
See Tiptree, James, Jr.
See also CA 108; 122; CANR 34; INT 108;
MTCW 1

Sheldon, John
See Bloch, Robert (Albert)

Sheldon, Walter J(ames) 1917-1996
See Queen, Ellery
See also AITN 1; CA 25-28R; CANR 10

Shelley, Mary Wollstonecraft (Godwin)
1797-1851 ...... **NCLC 14, 59, 103; WLC**
See also AAYA 20; BPFB 3; BRW 3;
BRWS 3; BYA 5; CDBLB 1789-1832;
DA; DA3; DAB; DAC; DAM MST, NOV;
DLB 110, 116, 159, 178; EXPN; HGG;
LAIT 1; NFS 1; RGEL 2; SATA 29;
SCFW; SFW 4; WLIT 3

Shelley, Percy Bysshe 1792-1822 .. **NCLC 18,
93; PC 14; WLC**
See also BRW 4; BRWR 1; CDBLB 1789-
1832; DA; DA3; DAB; DAC; DAM MST,
POET; DLB 96, 110, 158; EXPP; PAB;
PFS 2; RGEL 2; WLIT 3; WP

Shepard, Jim 1956- .... **CLC 36**
See also CA 137; CANR 59, 104; SATA 90

Shepard, Lucius 1947- .... **CLC 34**
See also CA 128; 141; CANR 81; HGG;
SCFW 2; SFW 4

Shepard, Sam 1943- .... **CLC 4, 6, 17, 34, 41,
44; DC 5**
See also AAYA 1; AMWS 3; CA 69-72;
CABS 3; CAD; CANR 22; CD 5; DA3;
DAM DRAM; DFS 3, 6, 7, 14; DLB 7,
212; IDFW 3, 4; MTCW 1, 2; RGAL 4

Shepherd, Michael
See Ludlum, Robert

Sherburne, Zoa (Lillian Morin)
1912-1995 .... **CLC 30**
See also AAYA 13; CA 1-4R; 176; CANR
3, 37; MAICYA 1, 2; SAAS 18; SATA 3;
YAW

Sheridan, Frances 1724-1766 .... **LC 7**
See also DLB 39, 84

Sheridan, Richard Brinsley
1751-1816 .... **NCLC 5, 91; DC 1; WLC**
See also BRW 3; CDBLB 1660-1789; DA;
DAB; DAC; DAM DRAM; DFS 4,
14; DLB 89; RGEL 2; WLIT 3

Sherman, Jonathan Marc .... **CLC 55**

Sherman, Martin 1941(?)- .... **CLC 19**
See also CA 116; 123; CANR 86

Sherwin, Judith Johnson
See Johnson, Judith (Emlyn)
See also CANR 85; CP 7; CWP

Sherwood, Frances 1940- .... **CLC 81**
See also CA 146

Sherwood, Robert E(mmet)
1896-1955 .... **TCLC 3**
See also CA 104; 153; CANR 86; DAM
DRAM; DFS 11; DLB 7, 26, 249; IDFW
3, 4; RGAL 4

Shestov, Lev 1866-1938 .... **TCLC 56**

Shevchenko, Taras 1814-1861 .... **NCLC 54**

Shiel, M(atthew) P(hipps)
1865-1947 .... **TCLC 8**
See also Holmes, Gordon
See also CA 106; 160; DLB 153; HGG;
MTCW 2; SFW 4; SUFW

Shields, Carol 1935- .... **CLC 91, 113**
See also AMWS 7; CA 81-84; CANR 51,
74, 98; CCA 1; CN 7; CPW; DA3; DAC;
MTCW 2

Shields, David 1956- .... **CLC 97**
See also CA 124; CANR 48, 99

Shiga, Naoya 1883-1971 ..... **CLC 33; SSC 23**
See also Shiga Naoya
See also CA 101; 33-36R; MJW

Shiga Naoya
See Shiga, Naoya
See also DLB 180

Shilts, Randy 1951-1994 .... **CLC 85**
See also AAYA 19; CA 115; 127; 144;
CANR 45; DA3; GLL 1; INT 127; MTCW
2

Shimazaki, Haruki 1872-1943
See Shimazaki Toson
See also CA 105; 134; CANR 84

Shimazaki Toson .... **TCLC 5**
See also Shimazaki, Haruki
See also DLB 180

Sholokhov, Mikhail (Aleksandrovich)
1905-1984 .... **CLC 7, 15**
See also CA 101; 112; MTCW 1, 2; RGWL
2; SATA-Obit 36

Shone, Patric
See Hanley, James

Shreve, Susan Richards 1939- .... **CLC 23**
See also CA 49-52; CAAS 5; CANR 5, 38, 69, 100; MAICYA 1, 2; SATA 46, 95; SATA-Brief 41

Shue, Larry 1946-1985 .... **CLC 52**
See also CA 145; 117; DAM DRAM; DFS 7

Shu-Jen, Chou 1881-1936
See Lu Hsun
See also CA 104

Shulman, Alix Kates 1932- .... **CLC 2, 10**
See also CA 29-32R; CANR 43; FW; SATA 7

Shusaku, Endo
See Endo, Shusaku

Shuster, Joe 1914-1992 .... **CLC 21**

Shute, Nevil .... **CLC 30**
See also Norway, Nevil Shute
See also BPFB 3; DLB 255; NFS 9; RHW; SFW 4

Shuttle, Penelope (Diane) 1947- .... **CLC 7**
See also CA 93-96; CANR 39, 84, 92, 108; CP 7; CWP; DLB 14, 40

Sidney, Mary 1561-1621 .... **LC 19, 39**
See also Sidney Herbert, Mary

Sidney, Sir Philip 1554-1586 . **LC 19, 39; PC 32**
See also BRW 1; BRWR 2; CDBLB Before 1660; DA; DA3; DAB; DAC; DAM MST, POET; DLB 167; EXPP; PAB; RGEL 2; TEA; WP

Sidney Herbert, Mary
See Sidney, Mary
See also DLB 167

Siegel, Jerome 1914-1996 .... **CLC 21**
See also CA 116; 169; 151

Siegel, Jerry
See Siegel, Jerome

Sienkiewicz, Henryk (Adam Alexander Pius)
1846-1916 .... **TCLC 3**
See also CA 104; 134; CANR 84; RGSF 2; RGWL 2

Sierra, Gregorio Martinez
See Martinez Sierra, Gregorio

Sierra, Maria (de la O'LeJarraga) Martinez
See Martinez Sierra, Maria (de la O'LeJarraga)

Sigal, Clancy 1926- .... **CLC 7**
See also CA 1-4R; CANR 85; CN 7

Sigourney, Lydia H.
See Sigourney, Lydia Howard (Huntley)
See also DLB 73, 183

Sigourney, Lydia Howard (Huntley)
1791-1865 .... **NCLC 21, 87**
See also Sigourney, Lydia H.; Sigourney, Lydia Huntley
See also DLB 1

Sigourney, Lydia Huntley
See Sigourney, Lydia Howard (Huntley)
See also DLB 42, 239, 243

Siguenza y Gongora, Carlos de
1645-1700 .... **LC 8; HLCS 2**
See also LAW

Sigurjonsson, Johann 1880-1919 ... **TCLC 27**
See also CA 170

Sikelianos, Angelos 1884-1951 ...... **TCLC 39; PC 29**
See also RGWL 2

Silkin, Jon 1930-1997 .... **CLC 2, 6, 43**
See also CA 5-8R; CAAS 5; CANR 89; CP 7; DLB 27

Silko, Leslie (Marmon) 1948- .... **CLC 23, 74, 114; SSC 37; WLCS**
See also AAYA 14; AMWS 4; ANW; BYA 12; CA 115; 122; CANR 45, 65; CN 7; CP 7; CPW 1; CWP; DA; DA3; DAC;

DAM MST, MULT, POP; DLB 143, 175, 256; EXPP; EXPS; LAIT 4; MTCW 2; NFS 4; NNAL; PFS 9; RGAL 4; RGSF 2; SSFS 4, 8, 10, 11

Sillanpaa, Frans Eemil 1888-1964 ... **CLC 19**
See also CA 129; 93-96; MTCW 1

Sillitoe, Alan 1928- .. **CLC 1, 3, 6, 10, 19, 57, 148**
See also AITN 1; BRWS 5; CA 9-12R; CAAE 191; CAAS 2; CANR 8, 26, 55; CDBLB 1960 to Present; CN 7; DLB 14, 139; MTCW 1, 2; RGEL 2; RGSF 2; SATA 61

Silone, Ignazio 1900-1978 .... **CLC 4**
See also CA 25-28; 81-84; CANR 34; CAP 2; EW 12; MTCW 1; RGSF 2; RGWL 2

Silone, Ignazione
See Silone, Ignazio

Silver, Joan Micklin 1935- .... **CLC 20**
See also CA 114; 121; INT 121

Silver, Nicholas
See Faust, Frederick (Schiller)
See also TCWW 2

Silverberg, Robert 1935- .... **CLC 7, 140**
See also AAYA 24; BPFB 3; BYA 7, 9; CA 1-4R, 186; CAAE 186; CAAS 3; CANR 1, 20, 36, 85; CLR 59; CN 7; CPW; DAM POP; DLB 8; INT CANR-20; MAICYA 1, 2; MTCW 1, 2; SATA 13, 91; SATA-Essay 104; SCFW 2; SFW 4

Silverstein, Alvin 1933- .... **CLC 17**
See also CA 49-52; CANR 2; CLR 25; JRDA; MAICYA 1, 2; SATA 8, 69, 124

Silverstein, Virginia B(arbara Opshelor)
1937- .... **CLC 17**
See also CA 49-52; CANR 2; CLR 25; JRDA; MAICYA 1, 2; SATA 8, 69, 124

Sim, Georges
See Simenon, Georges (Jacques Christian)

Simak, Clifford D(onald) 1904-1988 . **CLC 1, 55**
See also CA 1-4R; 125; CANR 1, 35; DLB 8; MTCW 1; SATA-Obit 56; SFW 4

Simenon, Georges (Jacques Christian)
1903-1989 .... **CLC 1, 2, 3, 8, 18, 47**
See also BPFB 3; CA 85-88; 129; CANR 35; CMW 4; DA3; DAM POP; DLB 72; DLBY 1989; EW 12; GFL 1789 to the Present; MSW; MTCW 1, 2; RGWL 2

Simic, Charles 1938- .... **CLC 6, 9, 22, 49, 68, 130**
See also AMWS 8; CA 29-32R; CAAS 4; CANR 12, 33, 52, 61, 96; CP 7; DA3; DAM POET; DLB 105; MTCW 2; PFS 7; RGAL 4; WP

Simmel, Georg 1858-1918 .... **TCLC 64**
See also CA 157

Simmons, Charles (Paul) 1924- .... **CLC 57**
See also CA 89-92; INT 89-92

Simmons, Dan 1948- .... **CLC 44**
See also AAYA 16; CA 138; CANR 53, 81; CPW; DAM POP; HGG

Simmons, James (Stewart Alexander)
1933- .... **CLC 43**
See also CA 105; CAAS 21; CP 7; DLB 40

Simms, William Gilmore
1806-1870 .... **NCLC 3**
See also DLB 3, 30, 59, 73, 248, 254; RGAL 4

Simon, Carly 1945- .... **CLC 26**
See also CA 105

Simon, Claude 1913-1984 ... **CLC 4, 9, 15, 39**
See also CA 89-92; CANR 33; DAM NOV; DLB 83; EW 13; GFL 1789 to the Present; MTCW 1

Simon, Myles
See Follett, Ken(neth Martin)

Simon, (Marvin) Neil 1927- ... **CLC 6, 11, 31, 39, 70; DC 14**
See also AAYA 32; AITN 1; AMWS 4; CA 21-24R; CANR 26, 54, 87; CD 5; DA3; DAM DRAM; DFS 2, 6, 12; DLB 7; LAIT 4; MTCW 1, 2; RGAL 4

Simon, Paul (Frederick) 1941(?)- ..... **CLC 17**
See also CA 116; 153

Simonon, Paul 1956(?)- .... **CLC 30**

Simonson, Rick ed. .... **CLC 70**

Simpson, Harriette
See Arnow, Harriette (Louisa) Simpson

Simpson, Louis (Aston Marantz)
1923- .... **CLC 4, 7, 9, 32, 149**
See also AMWS 9; CA 1-4R; CAAS 4; CANR 1, 61; CP 7; DAM POET; DLB 5; MTCW 1, 2; PFS 7, 11, 14; RGAL 4

Simpson, Mona (Elizabeth) 1957- ... **CLC 44, 146**
See also CA 122; 135; CANR 68, 103; CN 7

Simpson, N(orman) F(rederick)
1919- .... **CLC 29**
See also CA 13-16R; CBD; DLB 13; RGEL 2

Sinclair, Andrew (Annandale) 1935- . **CLC 2, 14**
See also CA 9-12R; CAAS 5; CANR 14, 38, 91; CN 7; DLB 14; FANT; MTCW 1

Sinclair, Emil
See Hesse, Hermann

Sinclair, Iain 1943- .... **CLC 76**
See also CA 132; CANR 81; CP 7; HGG

Sinclair, Iain MacGregor
See Sinclair, Iain

Sinclair, Irene
See Griffith, D(avid Lewelyn) W(ark)

Sinclair, Mary Amelia St. Clair 1865(?)-1946
See Sinclair, May
See also CA 104; HGG; RHW

Sinclair, May .... **TCLC 3, 11**
See also Sinclair, Mary Amelia St. Clair
See also CA 166; DLB 36, 135; RGEL 2; SUFW

Sinclair, Roy
See Griffith, D(avid Lewelyn) W(ark)

Sinclair, Upton (Beall) 1878-1968 ..... **CLC 1, 11, 15, 63; WLC**
See also AMWS 5; BPFB 3; BYA 2; CA 5-8R; 25-28R; CANR 7; CDALB 1929-1941; DA; DA3; DAB; DAC; DAM MST, NOV; DLB 9; INT CANR-7; LAIT 3; MTCW 1, 2; NFS 6; RGAL 4; SATA 9; YAW

Singer, Isaac
See Singer, Isaac Bashevis

Singer, Isaac Bashevis 1904-1991 .. **CLC 1, 3, 6, 9, 11, 15, 23, 38, 69, 111; SSC 3, 53; WLC**
See also AAYA 32; AITN 1, 2; AMW; BPFB 3; BYA 1, 4; CA 1-4R; 134; CANR 1, 39, 106; CDALB 1941-1968; CLR 1; CWRI 5; DA; DA3; DAB; DAC; DAM MST, NOV; DLB 6, 28, 52; DLBY 1991; EXPS; HGG; JRDA; LAIT 3; MAICYA 1, 2; MTCW 1, 2; RGAL 4; RGSF 2; SATA 3, 27; SATA-Obit 68; SSFS 2, 12

Singer, Israel Joshua 1893-1944 .... **TCLC 33**
See also CA 169

Singh, Khushwant 1915- .... **CLC 11**
See also CA 9-12R; CAAS 9; CANR 6, 84; CN 7; RGEL 2

Singleton, Ann
See Benedict, Ruth (Fulton)

Singleton, John 1968(?)- .... **CLC 156**
See also BW 2, 3; CA 138; CANR 67, 82; DAM MULT

Sinjohn, John
See Galsworthy, John

Sinyavsky, Andrei (Donatevich)
  1925-1997 .... **CLC 8**
    See also Tertz, Abram
    See also CA 85-88; 159

Sirin, V.
    See Nabokov, Vladimir (Vladimirovich)

Sissman, L(ouis) E(dward)
  1928-1976 .... **CLC 9, 18**
    See also CA 21-24R; 65-68; CANR 13;
      DLB 5

Sisson, C(harles) H(ubert) 1914- .... **CLC 8**
    See also CA 1-4R; CAAS 3; CANR 3, 48,
      84; CP 7; DLB 27

Sitwell, Dame Edith 1887-1964 ..... **CLC 2, 9,
  67; PC 3**
    See also BRW 7; CA 9-12R; CANR 35;
      CDBLB 1945-1960; DAM POET; DLB
      20; MTCW 1, 2; RGEL 2

Siwaarmill, H. P.
    See Sharp, William

Sjoewall, Maj 1935- .... **CLC 7**
    See also Sjowall, Maj
    See also CA 65-68; CANR 73

Sjowall, Maj
    See Sjoewall, Maj
    See also BPFB 3; CMW 4; MSW

Skelton, John 1460(?)-1529 ..... **LC 71; PC 25**
    See also BRW 1; DLB 136; RGEL 2

Skelton, Robin 1925-1997 .... **CLC 13**
    See also Zuk, Georges
    See also AITN 2; CA 5-8R; 160; CAAS 5;
      CANR 28, 89; CCA 1; CP 7; DLB 27, 53

Skolimowski, Jerzy 1938- .... **CLC 20**
    See also CA 128

Skram, Amalie (Bertha)
  1847-1905 .... **TCLC 25**
    See also CA 165

Skvorecky, Josef (Vaclav) 1924- ...... **CLC 15,
  39, 69, 152**
    See also CA 61-64; CAAS 1; CANR 10,
      34, 63, 108; CDWLB 4; DA3; DAC;
      DAM NOV; DLB 232; MTCW 1, 2

Slade, Bernard .... **CLC 11, 46**
    See also Newbound, Bernard Slade
    See also CAAS 9; CCA 1; DLB 53

Slaughter, Carolyn 1946- .... **CLC 56**
    See also CA 85-88; CANR 85; CN 7

Slaughter, Frank G(ill) 1908-2001 ... **CLC 29**
    See also AITN 2; CA 5-8R; 197; CANR 5,
      85; INT CANR-5; RHW

Slavitt, David R(ytman) 1935- ..... **CLC 5, 14**
    See also CA 21-24R; CAAS 3; CANR 41,
      83; CP 7; DLB 5, 6

Slesinger, Tess 1905-1945 .... **TCLC 10**
    See also CA 107; 199; DLB 102

Slessor, Kenneth 1901-1971 .... **CLC 14**
    See also CA 102; 89-92; RGEL 2

Slowacki, Juliusz 1809-1849 .... **NCLC 15**

Smart, Christopher 1722-1771 . **LC 3; PC 13**
    See also DAM POET; DLB 109; RGEL 2

Smart, Elizabeth 1913-1986 .... **CLC 54**
    See also CA 81-84; 118; DLB 88

Smiley, Jane (Graves) 1949- ...... **CLC 53, 76,
  144**
    See also AMWS 6; BPFB 3; CA 104;
      CANR 30, 50, 74, 96; CN 7; CPW 1;
      DA3; DAM POP; DLB 227, 234; INT
      CANR-30

Smith, A(rthur) J(ames) M(arshall)
  1902-1980 .... **CLC 15**
    See also CA 1-4R; 102; CANR 4; DAC;
      DLB 88; RGEL 2

Smith, Adam 1723(?)-1790 .... **LC 36**
    See also DLB 104, 252; RGEL 2

Smith, Alexander 1829-1867 .... **NCLC 59**
    See also DLB 32, 55

Smith, Anna Deavere 1950- .... **CLC 86**
    See also CA 133; CANR 103; CD 5; DFS 2

Smith, Betty (Wehner) 1904-1972 .... **CLC 19**
    See also BPFB 3; BYA 3; CA 5-8R; 33-
      36R; DLBY 1982; LAIT 3; RGAL 4;
      SATA 6

Smith, Charlotte (Turner)
  1749-1806 .... **NCLC 23**
    See also DLB 39, 109; RGEL 2

Smith, Clark Ashton 1893-1961 .... **CLC 43**
    See also CA 143; CANR 81; FANT; HGG;
      MTCW 2; SCFW 2; SFW 4; SUFW

Smith, Dave .... **CLC 22, 42**
    See also Smith, David (Jeddie)
    See also CAAS 7; DLB 5

Smith, David (Jeddie) 1942-
    See Smith, Dave
    See also CA 49-52; CANR 1, 59; CP 7;
      CSW; DAM POET

Smith, Florence Margaret 1902-1971
    See Smith, Stevie
    See also CA 17-18; 29-32R; CANR 35;
      CAP 2; DAM POET; MTCW 1, 2

Smith, Iain Crichton 1928-1998 .... **CLC 64**
    See also CA 21-24R; 171; CN 7; CP 7; DLB
      40, 139; RGSF 2

Smith, John 1580(?)-1631 .... **LC 9**
    See also DLB 24, 30; TUS

Smith, Johnston
    See Crane, Stephen (Townley)

Smith, Joseph, Jr. 1805-1844 .... **NCLC 53**

Smith, Lee 1944- .... **CLC 25, 73**
    See also CA 114; 119; CANR 46; CSW;
      DLB 143; DLBY 1983; INT CA-119;
      RGAL 4

Smith, Martin
    See Smith, Martin Cruz

Smith, Martin Cruz 1942- .... **CLC 25**
    See also BEST 89:4; BPFB 3; CA 85-88;
      CANR 6, 23, 43, 65; CMW 4; CPW;
      DAM MULT, POP; HGG; INT CANR-
      23; MTCW 2; NNAL; RGAL 4

Smith, Mary-Ann Tirone 1944- .... **CLC 39**
    See also CA 118; 136

Smith, Patti 1946- .... **CLC 12**
    See also CA 93-96; CANR 63

Smith, Pauline (Urmson)
  1882-1959 .... **TCLC 25**
    See also DLB 225

Smith, Rosamond
    See Oates, Joyce Carol

Smith, Sheila Kaye
    See Kaye-Smith, Sheila

Smith, Stevie .... **CLC 3, 8, 25, 44; PC 12**
    See also Smith, Florence Margaret
    See also BRWS 2; DLB 20; MTCW 2;
      PAB; PFS 3; RGEL 2

Smith, Wilbur (Addison) 1933- .... **CLC 33**
    See also CA 13-16R; CANR 7, 46, 66;
      CPW; MTCW 1, 2

Smith, William Jay 1918- .... **CLC 6**
    See also CA 5-8R; CANR 44, 106; CP 7;
      CSW; CWRI 5; DLB 5; MAICYA 1, 2;
      SAAS 22; SATA 2, 68

Smith, Woodrow Wilson
    See Kuttner, Henry

Smith, Zadie 1976- .... **CLC 158**
    See also CA 193

Smolenskin, Peretz 1842-1885 .... **NCLC 30**

Smollett, Tobias (George) 1721-1771 ... **LC 2,
  46**
    See also BRW 3; CDBLB 1660-1789; DLB
      39, 104; RGEL 2

Snodgrass, W(illiam) D(e Witt)
  1926- .... **CLC 2, 6, 10, 18, 68**
    See also AMWS 6; CA 1-4R; CANR 6, 36,
      65, 85; CP 7; DAM POET; DLB 5;
      MTCW 1, 2; RGAL 4

Snow, C(harles) P(ercy) 1905-1980 ... **CLC 1,
  4, 6, 9, 13, 19**
    See also BRW 7; CA 5-8R; 101; CANR 28;
      CDBLB 1945-1960; DAM NOV; DLB 15,
      77; DLBD 17; MTCW 1, 2; RGEL 2

Snow, Frances Compton
    See Adams, Henry (Brooks)

Snyder, Gary (Sherman) 1930- . **CLC 1, 2, 5,
  9, 32, 120; PC 21**
    See also AMWS 8; ANW; CA 17-20R;
      CANR 30, 60; CP 7; DA3; DAM POET;
      DLB 5, 16, 165, 212, 237; MTCW 2; PFS
      9; RGAL 4; WP

Snyder, Zilpha Keatley 1927- .... **CLC 17**
    See also AAYA 15; BYA 1; CA 9-12R;
      CANR 38; CLR 31; JRDA; MAICYA 1,
      2; SAAS 2; SATA 1, 28, 75, 110; SATA-
      Essay 112; YAW

Soares, Bernardo
    See Pessoa, Fernando (Antonio Nogueira)

Sobh, A.
    See Shamlu, Ahmad

Sobol, Joshua 1939- .... **CLC 60**
    See also Sobol, Yehoshua
    See also CA 200; CWW 2

Sobol, Yehoshua 1939-
    See Sobol, Joshua
    See also CWW 2

Socrates 470B.C.-399B.C. .... **CMLC 27**

Soderberg, Hjalmar 1869-1941 ...... **TCLC 39**
    See also DLB 259; RGSF 2

Soderbergh, Steven 1963- .... **CLC 154**
    See also AAYA 43

Sodergran, Edith (Irene)
    See Soedergran, Edith (Irene)
    See also DLB 259; EW 11; RGWL 2

Soedergran, Edith (Irene)
  1892-1923 .... **TCLC 31**
    See also Sodergran, Edith (Irene)

Softly, Edgar
    See Lovecraft, H(oward) P(hillips)

Softly, Edward
    See Lovecraft, H(oward) P(hillips)

Sokolov, Raymond 1941- .... **CLC 7**
    See also CA 85-88

Sokolov, Sasha .... **CLC 59**

Solo, Jay
    See Ellison, Harlan (Jay)

Sologub, Fyodor .... **TCLC 9**
    See also Teternikov, Fyodor Kuzmich

Solomons, Ikey Esquir
    See Thackeray, William Makepeace

Solomos, Dionysios 1798-1857 .... **NCLC 15**

Solwoska, Mara
    See French, Marilyn

Solzhenitsyn, Aleksandr I(sayevich)
  1918- .. **CLC 1, 2, 4, 7, 9, 10, 18, 26, 34,
  78, 134; SSC 32; WLC**
    See also AITN 1; BPFB 3; CA 69-72;
      CANR 40, 65; DA; DA3; DAB; DAC;
      DAM MST, NOV; EW 13; EXPS; LAIT
      4; MTCW 1, 2; NFS 6; RGSF 2; RGWL
      2; SSFS 9

Somers, Jane
    See Lessing, Doris (May)

Somerville, Edith Oenone
  1858-1949 .... **TCLC 51**
    See also CA 196; DLB 135; RGEL 2; RGSF
      2

Somerville & Ross
    See Martin, Violet Florence; Somerville,
      Edith Oenone

Sommer, Scott 1951- .... **CLC 25**
    See also CA 106

Sondheim, Stephen (Joshua) 1930- . **CLC 30,
  39, 147**
    See also AAYA 11; CA 103; CANR 47, 67;
      DAM DRAM; LAIT 4

Song, Cathy 1955- .... **PC 21**
See also AAL; CA 154; CWP; DLB 169;
EXPP; FW; PFS 5

Sontag, Susan 1933- .... **CLC 1, 2, 10, 13, 31,
105**
See also AMWS 3; CA 17-20R; CANR 25,
51, 74, 97; CN 7; CPW; DA3; DAM POP;
DLB 2, 67; MAWW; MTCW 1, 2; RGAL
4; RHW; SSFS 10

Sophocles 496(?)B.C.-406(?)B.C. .... **CMLC 2,
47, 51; DC 1; WLCS**
See also AW 1; CDWLB 1; DA; DA3;
DAB; DAC; DAM DRAM, MST; DFS 1,
4, 8; DLB 176; LAIT 1; RGWL 2

Sordello 1189-1269 .... **CMLC 15**

Sorel, Georges 1847-1922 .... **TCLC 91**
See also CA 118; 188

Sorel, Julia
See Drexler, Rosalyn

Sorokin, Vladimir .... **CLC 59**

Sorrentino, Gilbert 1929- .. **CLC 3, 7, 14, 22,
40**
See also CA 77-80; CANR 14, 33; CN 7;
CP 7; DLB 5, 173; DLBY 1980; INT
CANR-14

Soseki
See Natsume, Soseki
See also MJW

Soto, Gary 1952- ... **CLC 32, 80; HLC 2; PC
28**
See also AAYA 10, 37; BYA 11; CA 119;
125; CANR 50, 74, 107; CLR 38; CP 7;
DAM MULT; DLB 82; EXPP; HW 1, 2;
INT CA-125; JRDA; MAICYA 2; MAIC-
YAS 1; MTCW 2; PFS 7; RGAL 4; SATA
80, 120; WYA; YAW

Soupault, Philippe 1897-1990 .... **CLC 68**
See also CA 116; 147; 131; GFL 1789 to
the Present

Souster, (Holmes) Raymond 1921- .... **CLC 5,
14**
See also CA 13-16R; CAAS 14; CANR 13,
29, 53; CP 7; DA3; DAC; DAM POET;
DLB 88; RGEL 2; SATA 63

Southern, Terry 1924(?)-1995 .... **CLC 7**
See also BPFB 3; CA 1-4R; 150; CANR 1,
55, 107; CN 7; DLB 2; IDFW 3, 4

Southey, Robert 1774-1843 .... **NCLC 8, 97**
See also BRW 4; DLB 93, 107, 142; RGEL
2; SATA 54

Southworth, Emma Dorothy Eliza Nevitte
1819-1899 .... **NCLC 26**
See also DLB 239

Souza, Ernest
See Scott, Evelyn

Soyinka, Wole 1934- .... **CLC 3, 5, 14, 36, 44;
BLC 3; DC 2; WLC**
See also AFW; BW 2, 3; CA 13-16R;
CANR 27, 39, 82; CD 5; CDWLB 3; CN
7; CP 7; DA; DA3; DAB; DAC; DAM
DRAM, MST, MULT; DFS 10; DLB 125;
MTCW 1, 2; RGEL 2; WLIT 2

Spackman, W(illiam) M(ode)
1905-1990 .... **CLC 46**
See also CA 81-84; 132

Spacks, Barry (Bernard) 1931- .... **CLC 14**
See also CA 154; CANR 33, 109; CP 7;
DLB 105

Spanidou, Irini 1946- .... **CLC 44**
See also CA 185

Spark, Muriel (Sarah) 1918- ..... **CLC 2, 3, 5,
8, 13, 18, 40, 94; SSC 10**
See also BRWS 1; CA 5-8R; CANR 12, 36,
76, 89; CDBLB 1945-1960; CN 7; CP 7;
DA3; DAB; DAC; DAM MST, NOV;
DLB 15, 139; FW; INT CANR-12; LAIT
4; MTCW 1, 2; RGEL 2; WLIT 4; YAW

Spaulding, Douglas
See Bradbury, Ray (Douglas)

Spaulding, Leonard
See Bradbury, Ray (Douglas)

Spelman, Elizabeth .... **CLC 65**

Spence, J. A. D.
See Eliot, T(homas) S(tearns)

Spencer, Elizabeth 1921- .... **CLC 22**
See also CA 13-16R; CANR 32, 65, 87; CN
7; CSW; DLB 6, 218; MTCW 1; RGAL
4; SATA 14

Spencer, Leonard G.
See Silverberg, Robert

Spencer, Scott 1945- .... **CLC 30**
See also CA 113; CANR 51; DLBY 1986

Spender, Stephen (Harold)
1909-1995 .... **CLC 1, 2, 5, 10, 41, 91**
See also BRWS 2; CA 9-12R; 149; CANR
31, 54; CDBLB 1945-1960; CP 7; DA3;
DAM POET; DLB 20; MTCW 1, 2; PAB;
RGEL 2

Spengler, Oswald (Arnold Gottfried)
1880-1936 .... **TCLC 25**
See also CA 118; 189

Spenser, Edmund 1552(?)-1599 ..... **LC 5, 39;
PC 8; WLC**
See also BRW 1; CDBLB Before 1660; DA;
DA3; DAB; DAC; DAM MST, POET;
DLB 167; EFS 2; EXPP; PAB; RGEL 2;
WLIT 3; WP

Spicer, Jack 1925-1965 .... **CLC 8, 18, 72**
See also CA 85-88; DAM POET; DLB 5,
16, 193; GLL 1; WP

Spiegelman, Art 1948- .... **CLC 76**
See also AAYA 10; CA 125; CANR 41, 55,
74; MTCW 2; SATA 109; YAW

Spielberg, Peter 1929- .... **CLC 6**
See also CA 5-8R; CANR 4, 48; DLBY
1981

Spielberg, Steven 1947- .... **CLC 20**
See also AAYA 8, 24; CA 77-80; CANR
32; SATA 32

Spillane, Frank Morrison 1918-
See Spillane, Mickey
See also CA 25-28R; CANR 28, 63; DA3;
MTCW 1, 2; SATA 66

Spillane, Mickey .... **CLC 3, 13**
See Spillane, Frank Morrison
See also BPFB 3; CMW 4; DLB 226;
MSW; MTCW 2

Spinoza, Benedictus de 1632-1677 .. **LC 9, 58**

Spinrad, Norman (Richard) 1940- ... **CLC 46**
See also BPFB 3; CA 37-40R; CAAS 19;
CANR 20, 91; DLB 8; INT CANR-20;
SFW 4

Spitteler, Carl (Friedrich Georg)
1845-1924 .... **TCLC 12**
See also CA 109; DLB 129

Spivack, Kathleen (Romola Drucker)
1938- .... **CLC 6**
See also CA 49-52

Spoto, Donald 1941- .... **CLC 39**
See also CA 65-68; CANR 11, 57, 93

Springsteen, Bruce (F.) 1949- .... **CLC 17**
See also CA 111

Spurling, Hilary 1940- .... **CLC 34**
See also CA 104; CANR 25, 52, 94

Spyker, John Howland
See Elman, Richard (Martin)

Squires, (James) Radcliffe
1917-1993 .... **CLC 51**
See also CA 1-4R; 140; CANR 6, 21

Srivastava, Dhanpat Rai 1880(?)-1936
See Premchand
See also CA 118; 197

Stacy, Donald
See Pohl, Frederik

Stael
See Stael-Holstein, Anne Louise Germaine
Necker
See also EW 5; RGWL 2

Stael, Germaine de
See Stael-Holstein, Anne Louise Germaine
Necker
See also DLB 119, 192; FW; GFL 1789 to
the Present; TWA

**Stael-Holstein, Anne Louise Germaine
Necker** 1766-1817 .... **NCLC 3, 91**
See also Stael; Stael, Germaine de

Stafford, Jean 1915-1979 .. **CLC 4, 7, 19, 68;
SSC 26**
See also CA 1-4R; 85-88; CANR 3, 65;
DLB 2, 173; MTCW 1, 2; RGAL 4; RGSF
2; SATA-Obit 22; TCWW 2

Stafford, William (Edgar)
1914-1993 .... **CLC 4, 7, 29**
See also CA 5-8R; 142; CAAS 3; CANR 5,
22; DAM POET; DLB 5, 206; EXPP; INT
CANR-22; PFS 2, 8; RGAL 4; WP

Stagnelius, Eric Johan 1793-1823 . **NCLC 61**

Staines, Trevor
See Brunner, John (Kilian Houston)

Stairs, Gordon
See Austin, Mary (Hunter)
See also TCWW 2

Stairs, Gordon 1868-1934
See Austin, Mary (Hunter)

Stalin, Joseph 1879-1953 .... **TCLC 92**

Stancykowna
See Szymborska, Wislawa

Stannard, Martin 1947- .... **CLC 44**
See also CA 142; DLB 155

Stanton, Elizabeth Cady
1815-1902 .... **TCLC 73**
See also CA 171; DLB 79; FW

Stanton, Maura 1946- .... **CLC 9**
See also CA 89-92; CANR 15; DLB 120

Stanton, Schuyler
See Baum, L(yman) Frank

Stapledon, (William) Olaf
1886-1950 .... **TCLC 22**
See also CA 111; 162; DLB 15, 255; SFW
4

Starbuck, George (Edwin)
1931-1996 .... **CLC 53**
See also CA 21-24R; 153; CANR 23; DAM
POET

Stark, Richard
See Westlake, Donald E(dwin)

Staunton, Schuyler
See Baum, L(yman) Frank

Stead, Christina (Ellen) 1902-1983 ... **CLC 2,
5, 8, 32, 80**
See also BRWS 4; CA 13-16R; 109; CANR
33, 40; FW; MTCW 1, 2; RGEL 2; RGSF
2

Stead, William Thomas
1849-1912 .... **TCLC 48**
See also CA 167

Stebnitsky, M.
See Leskov, Nikolai (Semyonovich)

Steele, Sir Richard 1672-1729 .... **LC 18**
See also BRW 3; CDBLB 1660-1789; DLB
84, 101; RGEL 2; WLIT 3

Steele, Timothy (Reid) 1948- .... **CLC 45**
See also CA 93-96; CANR 16, 50, 92; CP
7; DLB 120

Steffens, (Joseph) Lincoln
1866-1936 .... **TCLC 20**
See also CA 117

Stegner, Wallace (Earle) 1909-1993 .. **CLC 9,
49, 81; SSC 27**
See also AITN 1; AMWS 4; ANW; BEST
90:3; BPFB 3; CA 1-4R; 141; CAAS 9;
CANR 1, 21, 46; DAM NOV; DLB 9,
206; DLBY 1993; MTCW 1, 2; RGAL 4;
TCWW 2

Stein, Gertrude 1874-1946 .... TCLC **1, 6, 28, 48; PC 18; SSC 42; WLC**
See also AMW; CA 104; 132; CANR 108; CDALB 1917-1929; DA; DA3; DAB; DAC; DAM MST, NOV, POET; DLB 4, 54, 86, 228; DLBD 15; EXPS; GLL 1; MAWW; MTCW 1, 2; RGAL 4; RGSF 2; SSFS 5; WP

Steinbeck, John (Ernst) 1902-1968 ... CLC **1, 5, 9, 13, 21, 34, 45, 75, 124; SSC 11, 37; WLC**
See also AAYA 12; AMW; BPFB 3; BYA 2, 3; CA 1-4R; 25-28R; CANR 1, 35; CDALB 1929-1941; DA; DA3; DAB; DAC; DAM DRAM, MST, NOV; DLB 7, 9, 212; DLBD 2; EXPS; LAIT 3; MTCW 1, 2; NFS 1, 5, 7; RGAL 4; RGSF 2; RHW; SATA 9; SSFS 3, 6; TCWW 2; WYA; YAW

Steinem, Gloria 1934- .... CLC **63**
See also CA 53-56; CANR 28, 51; DLB 246; FW; MTCW 1, 2

Steiner, George 1929- .... CLC **24**
See also CA 73-76; CANR 31, 67, 108; DAM NOV; DLB 67; MTCW 1, 2; SATA 62

Steiner, K. Leslie
See Delany, Samuel R(ay), Jr.

Steiner, Rudolf 1861-1925 .... TCLC **13**
See also CA 107

Stendhal 1783-1842 .. NCLC **23, 46; SSC 27; WLC**
See also DA; DA3; DAB; DAC; DAM MST, NOV; DLB 119; EW 5; GFL 1789 to the Present; RGWL 2

Stephen, Adeline Virginia
See Woolf, (Adeline) Virginia

Stephen, Sir Leslie 1832-1904 .... TCLC **23**
See also BRW 5; CA 123; DLB 57, 144, 190

Stephen, Sir Leslie
See Stephen, Sir Leslie

Stephen, Virginia
See Woolf, (Adeline) Virginia

Stephens, James 1882(?)-1950 .... TCLC **4; SSC 50**
See also CA 104; 192; DLB 19, 153, 162; FANT; RGEL 2; SUFW

Stephens, Reed
See Donaldson, Stephen R(eeder)

Steptoe, Lydia
See Barnes, Djuna
See also GLL 1

Sterchi, Beat 1949- .... CLC **65**

Sterling, Brett
See Bradbury, Ray (Douglas); Hamilton, Edmond

Sterling, Bruce 1954- .... CLC **72**
See also CA 119; CANR 44; SCFW 2; SFW 4

Sterling, George 1869-1926 .... TCLC **20**
See also CA 117; 165; DLB 54

Stern, Gerald 1925- .... CLC **40, 100**
See also AMWS 9; CA 81-84; CANR 28, 94; CP 7; DLB 105; RGAL 4

Stern, Richard (Gustave) 1928- ... CLC **4, 39**
See also CA 1-4R; CANR 1, 25, 52; CN 7; DLB 218; DLBY 1987; INT CANR-25

Sternberg, Josef von 1894-1969 .... CLC **20**
See also CA 81-84

Sterne, Laurence 1713-1768 .... LC **2, 48; WLC**
See also BRW 3; CDBLB 1660-1789; DA; DAB; DAC; DAM MST, NOV; DLB 39; RGEL 2

Sternheim, (William Adolf) Carl 1878-1942 .... TCLC **8**
See also CA 105; 193; DLB 56, 118; RGWL 2

Stevens, Mark 1951- .... CLC **34**
See also CA 122

Stevens, Wallace 1879-1955 ...... TCLC **3, 12, 45; PC 6; WLC**
See also AMW; AMWR 1; CA 104; 124; CDALB 1929-1941; DA; DA3; DAB; DAC; DAM MST, POET; DLB 54; EXPP; MTCW 1, 2; PAB; PFS 13; RGAL 4; WP

Stevenson, Anne (Katharine) 1933- .. CLC **7, 33**
See also BRWS 6; CA 17-20R; CAAS 9; CANR 9, 33; CP 7; CWP; DLB 40; MTCW 1; RHW

Stevenson, Robert Louis (Balfour) 1850-1894 ...... NCLC **5, 14, 63; SSC 11, 51; WLC**
See also AAYA 24; BPFB 3; BRW 5; BRWR 1; BYA 1, 2, 4, 13; CDBLB 1890-1914; CLR 10, 11; DA; DA3; DAB; DAC; DAM MST, NOV; DLB 18, 57, 141, 156, 174; DLBD 13; HGG; JRDA; LAIT 1, 3; MAICYA 1, 2; NFS 11; RGEL 2; RGSF 2; SATA 100; SUFW; WCH; WLIT 4; WYA; YABC 2; YAW

Stewart, J(ohn) I(nnes) M(ackintosh) 1906-1994 .... CLC **7, 14, 32**
See also Innes, Michael
See also CA 85-88; 147; CAAS 3; CANR 47; CMW 4; MTCW 1, 2

Stewart, Mary (Florence Elinor) 1916- .... CLC **7, 35, 117**
See also AAYA 29; BPFB 3; CA 1-4R; CANR 1, 59; CMW 4; CPW; DAB; FANT; RHW; SATA 12; YAW

Stewart, Mary Rainbow
See Stewart, Mary (Florence Elinor)

Stifle, June
See Campbell, Maria

Stifter, Adalbert 1805-1868 .. NCLC **41; SSC 28**
See also CDWLB 2; DLB 133; RGSF 2; RGWL 2

Still, James 1906-2001 .... CLC **49**
See also CA 65-68; 195; CAAS 17; CANR 10, 26; CSW; DLB 9; DLBY 01; SATA 29; SATA-Obit 127

Sting 1951-
See Sumner, Gordon Matthew
See also CA 167

Stirling, Arthur
See Sinclair, Upton (Beall)

Stitt, Milan 1941- .... CLC **29**
See also CA 69-72

Stockton, Francis Richard 1834-1902
See Stockton, Frank R.
See also CA 108; 137; MAICYA 1, 2; SATA 44; SFW 4

Stockton, Frank R. .... TCLC **47**
See also Stockton, Francis Richard
See also BYA 4, 13; DLB 42, 74; DLBD 13; EXPS; SATA-Brief 32; SSFS 3; SUFW; WCH

Stoddard, Charles
See Kuttner, Henry

Stoker, Abraham 1847-1912
See Stoker, Bram
See also CA 105; 150; DA; DA3; DAC; DAM MST, NOV; HGG; SATA 29

Stoker, Bram .... TCLC **8; WLC**
See also Stoker, Abraham
See also AAYA 23; BPFB 3; BRWS 3; BYA 5; CDBLB 1890-1914; DAB; DLB 36, 70, 178; RGEL 2; SUFW; WLIT 4

Stolz, Mary (Slattery) 1920- .... CLC **12**
See also AAYA 8; AITN 1; CA 5-8R; CANR 13, 41; JRDA; MAICYA 1, 2; SAAS 3; SATA 10, 71; YAW

Stone, Irving 1903-1989 .... CLC **7**
See also AITN 1; BPFB 3; CA 1-4R; 129; CAAS 1; CANR 1, 23; CPW; DA3; DAM POP; INT CANR-23; MTCW 1, 2; RHW; SATA 3; SATA-Obit 64

Stone, Oliver (William) 1946- .... CLC **73**
See also AAYA 15; CA 110; CANR 55

Stone, Robert (Anthony) 1937- ... CLC **5, 23, 42**
See also AMWS 5; BPFB 3; CA 85-88; CANR 23, 66, 95; CN 7; DLB 152; INT CANR-23; MTCW 1

Stone, Zachary
See Follett, Ken(neth Martin)

Stoppard, Tom 1937- ... CLC **1, 3, 4, 5, 8, 15, 29, 34, 63, 91; DC 6; WLC**
See also BRWR 2; BRWS 1; CA 81-84; CANR 39, 67; CBD; CD 5; CDBLB 1960 to Present; DA; DA3; DAB; DAC; DAM DRAM, MST; DFS 2, 5, 8, 11, 13; DLB 13, 233; DLBY 1985; MTCW 1, 2; RGEL 2; WLIT 4

Storey, David (Malcolm) 1933- . CLC **2, 4, 5, 8**
See also BRWS 1; CA 81-84; CANR 36; CBD; CD 5; CN 7; DAM DRAM; DLB 13, 14, 207, 245; MTCW 1; RGEL 2

Storm, Hyemeyohsts 1935- .... CLC **3**
See also CA 81-84; CANR 45; DAM MULT; NNAL

Storm, (Hans) Theodor (Woldsen) 1817-1888 .... NCLC **1; SSC 27**
See also DLB 129; EW

Storm, Theodor 1817-1888 .... SSC **27**
See also CDWLB 2; RGSF 2; RGWL 2

Storni, Alfonsina 1892-1938 .. TCLC **5; HLC 2; PC 33**
See also CA 104; 131; DAM MULT; HW 1; LAW

Stoughton, William 1631-1701 .... LC **38**
See also DLB 24

Stout, Rex (Todhunter) 1886-1975 ..... CLC **3**
See also AITN 2; BPFB 3; CA 61-64; CANR 71; CMW 4; MSW; RGAL 4

Stow, (Julian) Randolph 1935- ... CLC **23, 48**
See also CA 13-16R; CANR 33; CN 7; MTCW 1; RGEL 2

Stowe, Harriet (Elizabeth) Beecher 1811-1896 .... NCLC **3, 50; WLC**
See also AMWS 1; CDALB 1865-1917; DA; DA3; DAB; DAC; DAM MST, NOV; DLB 1, 12, 42, 74, 189, 239, 243; EXPN; JRDA; LAIT 2; MAICYA 1, 2; NFS 6; RGAL 4; YABC 1

Strabo c. 64B.C.-c. 25 .... CMLC **37**
See also DLB 176

Strachey, (Giles) Lytton 1880-1932 .... TCLC **12**
See also BRWS 2; CA 110; 178; DLB 149; DLBD 10; MTCW 2

Strand, Mark 1934- .... CLC **6, 18, 41, 71**
See also AMWS 4; CA 21-24R; CANR 40, 65, 100; CP 7; DAM POET; DLB 5; PAB; PFS 9; RGAL 4; SATA 41

Stratton-Porter, Gene(va Grace) 1863-1924
See Porter, Gene(va Grace) Stratton
See also ANW; CA 137; DLB 221; DLBD 14; MAICYA 1, 2; SATA 15

Straub, Peter (Francis) 1943- ... CLC **28, 107**
See also BEST 89:1; BPFB 3; CA 85-88; CANR 28, 65, 109; CPW; DAM POP; DLBY 1984; HGG; MTCW 1, 2

Strauss, Botho 1944- .... CLC **22**
See also CA 157; CWW 2; DLB 124

Streatfeild, (Mary) Noel 1897(?)-1986 .... CLC **21**
See also CA 81-84; 120; CANR 31; CLR 17; CWRI 5; DLB 160; MAICYA 1, 2; SATA 20; SATA-Obit 48

Stribling, T(homas) S(igismund)
1881-1965 .... **CLC 23**
See also CA 189; 107; CMW 4; DLB 9;
RGAL 4

Strindberg, (Johan) August
1849-1912 ...... **TCLC 1, 8, 21, 47; WLC**
See also CA 104; 135; DA; DA3; DAB;
DAC; DAM DRAM, MST; DFS 4, 9;
DLB 259; EW 7; IDTP; MTCW 2; RGWL
2

Stringer, Arthur 1874-1950 .... **TCLC 37**
See also CA 161; DLB 92

Stringer, David
See Roberts, Keith (John Kingston)

Stroheim, Erich von 1885-1957 ..... **TCLC 71**

Strugatskii, Arkadii (Natanovich)
1925-1991 .... **CLC 27**
See also CA 106; 135; SFW 4

Strugatskii, Boris (Natanovich)
1933- .... **CLC 27**
See also CA 106; SFW 4

Strummer, Joe 1953(?)- .... **CLC 30**

Strunk, William, Jr. 1869-1946 ...... **TCLC 92**
See also CA 118; 164

Stryk, Lucien 1924- .... **PC 27**
See also CA 13-16R; CANR 10, 28, 55; CP
7

Stuart, Don A.
See Campbell, John W(ood, Jr.)

Stuart, Ian
See MacLean, Alistair (Stuart)

Stuart, Jesse (Hilton) 1906-1984 ... **CLC 1, 8,
11, 14, 34; SSC 31**
See also CA 5-8R; 112; CANR 31; DLB 9,
48, 102; DLBY 1984; SATA 2; SATA-
Obit 36

Stubblefield, Sally
See Trumbo, Dalton

Sturgeon, Theodore (Hamilton)
1918-1985 .... **CLC 22, 39**
See also Queen, Ellery
See also BPFB 3; BYA 9, 10; CA 81-84;
116; CANR 32, 103; DLB 8; DLBY 1985;
HGG; MTCW 1, 2; SCFW; SFW 4;
SUFW

Sturges, Preston 1898-1959 .... **TCLC 48**
See also CA 114; 149; DLB 26

Styron, William 1925- .... **CLC 1, 3, 5, 11, 15,
60; SSC 25**
See also AMW; BEST 90:4; BPFB 3; CA
5-8R; CANR 6, 33, 74; CDALB 1968-
1988; CN 7; CPW; CSW; DA3; DAM
NOV, POP; DLB 2, 143; DLBY 1980;
INT CANR-6; LAIT 2; MTCW 1, 2;
NCFS 1; RGAL 4; RHW

Su, Chien 1884-1918
See Su Man-shu
See also CA 123

Suarez Lynch, B.
See Bioy Casares, Adolfo; Borges, Jorge
Luis

Suassuna, Ariano Vilar 1927-
See also CA 178; HLCS 1; HW 2; LAW

Suckling, Sir John 1609-1642 . **LC 75; PC 30**
See also BRW 2; DAM POET; DLB 58,
126; EXPP; PAB; RGEL 2

Suckow, Ruth 1892-1960 .... **SSC 18**
See also CA 193; 113; DLB 9, 102; RGAL
4; TCWW 2

Sudermann, Hermann 1857-1928 .. **TCLC 15**
See also CA 107; 201; DLB 118

Sue, Eugene 1804-1857 .... **NCLC 1**
See also DLB 119

Sueskind, Patrick 1949- .... **CLC 44**
See also Suskind, Patrick

Sukenick, Ronald 1932- .... **CLC 3, 4, 6, 48**
See also CA 25-28R; CAAS 8; CANR 32,
89; CN 7; DLB 173; DLBY 1981

Suknaski, Andrew 1942- .... **CLC 19**
See also CA 101; CP 7; DLB 53

Sullivan, Vernon
See Vian, Boris

Sully Prudhomme, Rene-Francois-Armand
1839-1907 .... **TCLC 31**
See also GFL 1789 to the Present

Su Man-shu .... **TCLC 24**
See also Su, Chien

Summerforest, Ivy B.
See Kirkup, James

Summers, Andrew James 1942- .... **CLC 26**

Summers, Andy
See Summers, Andrew James

Summers, Hollis (Spurgeon, Jr.)
1916- .... **CLC 10**
See also CA 5-8R; CANR 3; DLB 6

**Summers, (Alphonsus Joseph-Mary
Augustus) Montague**
1880-1948 .... **TCLC 16**
See also CA 118; 163

Sumner, Gordon Matthew .... **CLC 26**
See also Police, The; Sting

Surtees, Robert Smith 1805-1864 .. **NCLC 14**
See also DLB 21; RGEL 2

Susann, Jacqueline 1921-1974 .... **CLC 3**
See also AITN 1; BPFB 3; CA 65-68; 53-
56; MTCW 1, 2

Su Shi
See Su Shih
See also RGWL 2

Su Shih 1036-1101 .... **CMLC 15**
See also Su Shi

Suskind, Patrick
See Sueskind, Patrick
See also BPFB 3; CA 145; CWW 2

Sutcliff, Rosemary 1920-1992 .... **CLC 26**
See also AAYA 10; BYA 1, 4; CA 5-8R;
139; CANR 37; CLR 1, 37; CPW; DAB;
DAC; DAM MST, POP; JRDA; MAICYA
1, 2; MAICYAS 1; RHW; SATA 6, 44,
78; SATA-Obit 73; WYA; YAW

Sutro, Alfred 1863-1933 .... **TCLC 6**
See also CA 105; 185; DLB 10; RGEL 2

Sutton, Henry
See Slavitt, David R(ytman)

Suzuki, D. T.
See Suzuki, Daisetz Teitaro

Suzuki, Daisetz T.
See Suzuki, Daisetz Teitaro

Suzuki, Daisetz Teitaro
1870-1966 .... **TCLC 109**
See also CA 121; 111; MTCW 1, 2

Suzuki, Teitaro
See Suzuki, Daisetz Teitaro

Svevo, Italo .... **TCLC 2, 35; SSC 25**
See also Schmitz, Aron Hector
See also EW 8; RGWL 2

Swados, Elizabeth (A.) 1951- .... **CLC 12**
See also CA 97-100; CANR 49; INT 97-
100

Swados, Harvey 1920-1972 .... **CLC 5**
See also CA 5-8R; 37-40R; CANR 6; DLB
2

Swan, Gladys 1934- .... **CLC 69**
See also CA 101; CANR 17, 39

Swanson, Logan
See Matheson, Richard (Burton)

Swarthout, Glendon (Fred)
1918-1992 .... **CLC 35**
See also CA 1-4R; 139; CANR 1, 47; LAIT
5; SATA 26; TCWW 2; YAW

Sweet, Sarah C.
See Jewett, (Theodora) Sarah Orne

Swenson, May 1919-1989 ...... **CLC 4, 14, 61,
106; PC 14**
See also AMWS 4; CA 5-8R; 130; CANR
36, 61; DA; DAB; DAC; DAM MST,
POET; DLB 5; EXPP; GLL 2; MTCW 1,
2; SATA 15; WP

Swift, Augustus
See Lovecraft, H(oward) P(hillips)

Swift, Graham (Colin) 1949- ...... **CLC 41, 88**
See also BRWS 5; CA 117; 122; CANR 46,
71; CN 7; DLB 194; MTCW 2; RGSF 2

Swift, Jonathan 1667-1745 .. **LC 1, 42; PC 9;
WLC**
See also AAYA 41; BRW 3; BRWR 1; BYA
5, 14; CDBLB 1660-1789; CLR 53; DA;
DA3; DAB; DAC; DAM MST, NOV,
POET; DLB 39, 95, 101; EXPN; LAIT 1;
NFS 6; RGEL 2; SATA 19; WCH; WLIT
3

Swinburne, Algernon Charles
1837-1909 ... **TCLC 8, 36; PC 24; WLC**
See also BRW 5; CA 105; 140; CDBLB
1832-1890; DA; DA3; DAB; DAC; DAM
MST, POET; DLB 35, 57; PAB; RGEL 2

Swinfen, Ann .... **CLC 34**

Swinnerton, Frank Arthur
1884-1982 .... **CLC 31**
See also CA 108; DLB 34

Swithen, John
See King, Stephen (Edwin)

Sylvia
See Ashton-Warner, Sylvia (Constance)

Symmes, Robert Edward
See Duncan, Robert (Edward)

Symonds, John Addington
1840-1893 .... **NCLC 34**
See also DLB 57, 144

Symons, Arthur 1865-1945 .... **TCLC 11**
See also CA 107; 189; DLB 19, 57, 149;
RGEL 2

Symons, Julian (Gustave)
1912-1994 .... **CLC 2, 14, 32**
See also CA 49-52; 147; CAAS 3; CANR
3, 33, 59; CMW 4; DLB 87, 155; DLBY
1992; MSW; MTCW 1

Synge, (Edmund) J(ohn) M(illington)
1871-1909 .... **TCLC 6, 37; DC 2**
See also BRW 6; BRWR 1; CA 104; 141;
CDBLB 1890-1914; DAM DRAM; DLB
10, 19; RGEL 2; WLIT 4

Syruc, J.
See Milosz, Czeslaw

Szirtes, George 1948- .... **CLC 46**
See also CA 109; CANR 27, 61; CP 7

Szymborska, Wislawa 1923- .... **CLC 99**
See also CA 154; CANR 91; CDWLB 4;
CWP; CWW 2; DA3; DLB 232; DLBY
1996; MTCW 2

T. O., Nik
See Annensky, Innokenty (Fyodorovich)

Tabori, George 1914- .... **CLC 19**
See also CA 49-52; CANR 4, 69; CBD; CD
5; DLB 245

Tagore, Rabindranath 1861-1941 ... **TCLC 3,
53; PC 8; SSC 48**
See also CA 104; 120; DA3; DAM DRAM,
POET; MTCW 1, 2; RGEL 2; RGSF 2;
RGWL 2

Taine, Hippolyte Adolphe
1828-1893 .... **NCLC 15**
See also EW 7; GFL 1789 to the Present

Talese, Gay 1932- .... **CLC 37**
See also AITN 1; CA 1-4R; CANR 9, 58;
DLB 185; INT CANR-9; MTCW 1, 2

Tallent, Elizabeth (Ann) 1954- .... **CLC 45**
See also CA 117; CANR 72; DLB 130

Tally, Ted 1952- .... **CLC 42**
See also CA 120; 124; CAD; CD 5; INT
124

Talvik, Heiti 1904-1947 .... **TCLC 87**

Tamayo y Baus, Manuel
1829-1898 .... **NCLC 1**

Tammsaare, A(nton) H(ansen)
1878-1940 .... **TCLC 27**
See also CA 164; CDWLB 4; DLB 220

Tam'si, Tchicaya U
See Tchicaya, Gerald Felix

Tan, Amy (Ruth) 1952- .... **CLC 59, 120, 151; AAL**
See also AAYA 9; AMWS 10; BEST 89:3; BPFB 3; CA 136; CANR 54, 105; CDALBS; CN 7; CPW 1; DA3; DAM MULT, NOV, POP; DLB 173; EXPN; FW; LAIT 3, 5; MTCW 2; NFS 1, 13; RGAL 4; SATA 75; SSFS 9; YAW

Tandem, Felix
See Spitteler, Carl (Friedrich Georg)

Tanizaki, Jun'ichiro 1886-1965 ... **CLC 8, 14, 28; SSC 21**
See also Tanizaki Jun'ichiro
See also CA 93-96; 25-28R; MJW; MTCW 2; RGSF 2; RGWL 2

Tanizaki Jun'ichiro
See Tanizaki, Jun'ichiro
See also DLB 180

Tanner, William
See Amis, Kingsley (William)

Tao Lao
See Storni, Alfonsina

Tarantino, Quentin (Jerome)
1963- .... **CLC 125**
See also CA 171

Tarassoff, Lev
See Troyat, Henri

Tarbell, Ida M(inerva) 1857-1944 . **TCLC 40**
See also CA 122; 181; DLB 47

Tarkington, (Newton) Booth
1869-1946 .... **TCLC 9**
See also BPFB 3; BYA 3; CA 110; 143; CWRI 5; DLB 9, 102; MTCW 2; RGAL 4; SATA 17

Tarkovsky, Andrei (Arsenyevich)
1932-1986 .... **CLC 75**
See also CA 127

Tartt, Donna 1964(?)- .... **CLC 76**
See also CA 142

Tasso, Torquato 1544-1595 .... **LC 5**
See also EFS 2; EW 2; RGWL 2

Tate, (John Orley) Allen 1899-1979 .. **CLC 2, 4, 6, 9, 11, 14, 24**
See also AMW; CA 5-8R; 85-88; CANR 32, 108; DLB 4, 45, 63; DLBD 17; MTCW 1, 2; RGAL 4; RHW

Tate, Ellalice
See Hibbert, Eleanor Alice Burford

Tate, James (Vincent) 1943- ..... **CLC 2, 6, 25**
See also CA 21-24R; CANR 29, 57; CP 7; DLB 5, 169; PFS 10; RGAL 4; WP

Tauler, Johannes c. 1300-1361 ...... **CMLC 37**
See also DLB 179

Tavel, Ronald 1940- .... **CLC 6**
See also CA 21-24R; CAD; CANR 33; CD 5

Taviani, Paolo 1931- .... **CLC 70**
See also CA 153

Taylor, Bayard 1825-1878 .... **NCLC 89**
See also DLB 3, 189, 250, 254; RGAL 4

Taylor, C(ecil) P(hilip) 1929-1981 .... **CLC 27**
See also CA 25-28R; 105; CANR 47; CBD

Taylor, Edward 1642(?)-1729 .... **LC 11**
See also AMW; DA; DAB; DAC; DAM MST, POET; DLB 24; EXPP; RGAL 4

Taylor, Eleanor Ross 1920- .... **CLC 5**
See also CA 81-84; CANR 70

Taylor, Elizabeth 1932-1975 ..... **CLC 2, 4, 29**
See also CA 13-16R; CANR 9, 70; DLB 139; MTCW 1; RGEL 2; SATA 13

Taylor, Frederick Winslow
1856-1915 .... **TCLC 76**
See also CA 188

Taylor, Henry (Splawn) 1942- .... **CLC 44**
See also CA 33-36R; CAAS 7; CANR 31; CP 7; DLB 5; PFS 10

Taylor, Kamala (Purnaiya) 1924-
See Markandaya, Kamala
See also CA 77-80; NFS 13

Taylor, Mildred D(elois) 1943- .... **CLC 21**
See also AAYA 10; BW 1; BYA 3, 8; CA 85-88; CANR 25; CLR 9, 59; CSW; DLB 52; JRDA; LAIT 3; MAICYA 1, 2; SAAS 5; SATA 15, 70; WYA; YAW

Taylor, Peter (Hillsman) 1917-1994 .. **CLC 1, 4, 18, 37, 44, 50, 71; SSC 10**
See also AMWS 5; BPFB 3; CA 13-16R; 147; CANR 9, 50; CSW; DLB 218; DLBY 1981, 1994; EXPS; INT CANR-9; MTCW 1, 2; RGSF 2; SSFS 9

Taylor, Robert Lewis 1912-1998 .... **CLC 14**
See also CA 1-4R; 170; CANR 3, 64; SATA 10

Tchekhov, Anton
See Chekhov, Anton (Pavlovich)

Tchicaya, Gerald Felix 1931-1988 .. **CLC 101**
See also CA 129; 125; CANR 81

Tchicaya U Tam'si
See Tchicaya, Gerald Felix

Teasdale, Sara 1884-1933 .... **TCLC 4; PC 31**
See also CA 104; 163; DLB 45; GLL 1; PFS 14; RGAL 4; SATA 32

Tegner, Esaias 1782-1846 .... **NCLC 2**

Teilhard de Chardin, (Marie Joseph) Pierre
1881-1955 .... **TCLC 9**
See also CA 105; GFL 1789 to the Present

Temple, Ann
See Mortimer, Penelope (Ruth)

Tennant, Emma (Christina) 1937- .. **CLC 13, 52**
See also CA 65-68; CAAS 9; CANR 10, 38, 59, 88; CN 7; DLB 14; SFW 4

Tenneshaw, S. M.
See Silverberg, Robert

Tennyson, Alfred 1809-1892 ... **NCLC 30, 65, 113; PC 6; WLC**
See also BRW 4; CDBLB 1832-1890; DA; DA3; DAB; DAC; DAM MST, POET; DLB 32; EXPP; PAB; PFS 1, 2, 4, 11; RGEL 2; WLIT 4; WP

Teran, Lisa St. Aubin de .... **CLC 36**
See also St. Aubin de Teran, Lisa

Terence c. 184B.C.-c. 159B.C. ...... **CMLC 14; DC 7**
See also AW 1; CDWLB 1; DLB 211; RGWL 2

Teresa de Jesus, St. 1515-1582 .... **LC 18**

Terkel, Louis 1912-
See Terkel, Studs
See also CA 57-60; CANR 18, 45, 67; DA3; MTCW 1, 2

Terkel, Studs .... **CLC 38**
See also Terkel, Louis
See also AAYA 32; AITN 1; MTCW 2

Terry, C. V.
See Slaughter, Frank G(ill)

Terry, Megan 1932- .... **CLC 19; DC 13**
See also CA 77-80; CABS 3; CAD; CANR 43; CD 5; CWD; DLB 7, 249; GLL 2

Tertullian c. 155-c. 245 .... **CMLC 29**

Tertz, Abram
See Sinyavsky, Andrei (Donatevich)
See also CWW 2; RGSF 2

Tesich, Steve 1943(?)-1996 .... **CLC 40, 69**
See also CA 105; 152; CAD; DLBY 1983

Tesla, Nikola 1856-1943 .... **TCLC 88**

Teternikov, Fyodor Kuzmich 1863-1927
See Sologub, Fyodor
See also CA 104

Tevis, Walter 1928-1984 .... **CLC 42**
See also CA 113; SFW 4

Tey, Josephine .... **TCLC 14**
See also Mackintosh, Elizabeth
See also DLB 77; MSW

Thackeray, William Makepeace
1811-1863 .... **NCLC 5, 14, 22, 43; WLC**
See also BRW 5; CDBLB 1832-1890; DA; DA3; DAB; DAC; DAM MST, NOV; DLB 21, 55, 159, 163; NFS 13; RGEL 2; SATA 23; WLIT 3

Thakura, Ravindranatha
See Tagore, Rabindranath

Thames, C. H.
See Marlowe, Stephen

Tharoor, Shashi 1956- .... **CLC 70**
See also CA 141; CANR 91; CN 7

Thelwell, Michael Miles 1939- .... **CLC 22**
See also BW 2; CA 101

Theobald, Lewis, Jr.
See Lovecraft, H(oward) P(hillips)

Theocritus c. 310B.C.- .... **CMLC 45**
See also AW 1; DLB 176; RGWL 2

Theodorescu, Ion N. 1880-1967
See Arghezi, Tudor
See also CA 116

Theriault, Yves 1915-1983 .... **CLC 79**
See also CA 102; CCA 1; DAC; DAM MST; DLB 88

Theroux, Alexander (Louis) 1939- .... **CLC 2, 25**
See also CA 85-88; CANR 20, 63; CN 7

Theroux, Paul (Edward) 1941- ..... **CLC 5, 8, 11, 15, 28, 46**
See also AAYA 28; AMWS 8; BEST 89:4; BPFB 3; CA 33-36R; CANR 20, 45, 74; CDALBS; CN 7; CPW 1; DA3; DAM POP; DLB 2, 218; HGG; MTCW 1, 2; RGAL 4; SATA 44, 109

Thesen, Sharon 1946- .... **CLC 56**
See also CA 163; CP 7; CWP

Thespis fl. 6th cent. B.C.- .... **CMLC 51**

Thevenin, Denis
See Duhamel, Georges

Thibault, Jacques Anatole Francois
1844-1924
See France, Anatole
See also CA 106; 127; DA3; DAM NOV; MTCW 1, 2

Thiele, Colin (Milton) 1920- .... **CLC 17**
See also CA 29-32R; CANR 12, 28, 53, 105; CLR 27; MAICYA 1, 2; SAAS 2; SATA 14, 72, 125; YAW

Thomas, Audrey (Callahan) 1935- .... **CLC 7, 13, 37, 107; SSC 20**
See also AITN 2; CA 21-24R; CAAS 19; CANR 36, 58; CN 7; DLB 60; MTCW 1; RGSF 2

Thomas, Augustus 1857-1934 .... **TCLC 97**

Thomas, D(onald) M(ichael) 1935- . **CLC 13, 22, 31, 132**
See also BPFB 3; BRWS 4; CA 61-64; CAAS 11; CANR 17, 45, 75; CDBLB 1960 to Present; CN 7; CP 7; DA3; DLB 40, 207; HGG; INT CANR-17; MTCW 1, 2; SFW 4

Thomas, Dylan (Marlais)
1914-1953 ... **TCLC 1, 8, 45, 105; PC 2; SSC 3, 44; WLC**
See also BRWS 1; CA 104; 120; CANR 65; CDBLB 1945-1960; DA; DA3; DAB; DAC; DAM DRAM, MST, POET; DLB 13, 20, 139; EXPP; LAIT 3; MTCW 1, 2; PAB; PFS 1, 3, 8; RGEL 2; RGSF 2; SATA 60; WLIT 4; WP

Thomas, (Philip) Edward
1878-1917 .... **TCLC 10**
See also BRW 6; BRWS 3; CA 106; 153;
DAM POET; DLB 19, 98, 156, 216; PAB;
RGEL 2

Thomas, Joyce Carol 1938- .... **CLC 35**
See also AAYA 12; BW 2, 3; CA 113; 116;
CANR 48; CLR 19; DLB 33; INT CA-
116; JRDA; MAICYA 1, 2; MTCW 1, 2;
SAAS 7; SATA 40, 78, 123; WYA; YAW

Thomas, Lewis 1913-1993 .... **CLC 35**
See also ANW; CA 85-88; 143; CANR 38,
60; MTCW 1, 2

Thomas, M. Carey 1857-1935 .... **TCLC 89**
See also FW

Thomas, Paul
See Mann, (Paul) Thomas

Thomas, Piri 1928- .... **CLC 17; HLCS 2**
See also CA 73-76; HW 1

Thomas, R(onald) S(tuart)
1913-2000 .... **CLC 6, 13, 48**
See also CA 89-92; 189; CAAS 4; CANR
30; CDBLB 1960 to Present; CP 7; DAB;
DAM POET; DLB 27; MTCW 1; RGEL
2

Thomas, Ross (Elmore) 1926-1995 .. **CLC 39**
See also CA 33-36R; 150; CANR 22, 63;
CMW 4

Thompson, Francis (Joseph)
1859-1907 .... **TCLC 4**
See also BRW 5; CA 104; 189; CDBLB
1890-1914; DLB 19; RGEL 2; TEA

Thompson, Francis Clegg
See Mencken, H(enry) L(ouis)

Thompson, Hunter S(tockton)
1939- .... **CLC 9, 17, 40, 104**
See also BEST 89:1; BPFB 3; CA 17-20R;
CANR 23, 46, 74, 77; CPW; CSW; DA3;
DAM POP; DLB 185; MTCW 1, 2

Thompson, James Myers
See Thompson, Jim (Myers)

Thompson, Jim (Myers)
1906-1977(?) .... **CLC 69**
See also BPFB 3; CA 140; CMW 4; CPW;
DLB 226; MSW

Thompson, Judith .... **CLC 39**
See also CWD

Thomson, James 1700-1748 .... **LC 16, 29, 40**
See also BRWS 3; DAM POET; DLB 95;
RGEL 2

Thomson, James 1834-1882 .... **NCLC 18**
See also DAM POET; DLB 35; RGEL 2

Thoreau, Henry David 1817-1862 .. **NCLC 7,
21, 61; PC 30; WLC**
See also AAYA 42; AMW; ANW; BYA 3;
CDALB 1640-1865; DA; DA3; DAB;
DAC; DAM MST; DLB 1, 183, 223;
LAIT 2; NCFS 3; RGAL 4

Thorndike, E. L.
See Thorndike, Edward L(ee)

Thorndike, Edward L(ee)
1874-1949 .... **TCLC 107**
See also CA 121

Thornton, Hall
See Silverberg, Robert

Thucydides c. 455B.C.-c. 395B.C. . **CMLC 17**
See also AW 1; DLB 176; RGWL 2

Thumboo, Edwin Nadason 1933- .... **PC 30**
See also CA 194

Thurber, James (Grover)
1894-1961 .. **CLC 5, 11, 25, 125; SSC 1,
47**
See also AMWS 1; BPFB 3; BYA 5; CA
73-76; CANR 17, 39; CDALB 1929-1941;
CWRI 5; DA; DA3; DAB; DAC; DAM
DRAM, MST, NOV; DLB 4, 11, 22, 102;
EXPS; FANT; LAIT 3; MAICYA 1, 2;
MTCW 1, 2; RGAL 4; RGSF 2; SATA
13; SSFS 1, 10; SUFW

Thurman, Wallace (Henry)
1902-1934 .... **TCLC 6; BLC 3**
See also BW 1, 3; CA 104; 124; CANR 81;
DAM MULT; DLB 51

Tibullus c. 54B.C.-c. 18B.C. .... **CMLC 36**
See also AW 2; DLB 211; RGWL 2

Ticheburn, Cheviot
See Ainsworth, William Harrison

Tieck, (Johann) Ludwig
1773-1853 .... **NCLC 5, 46; SSC 31**
See also CDWLB 2; DLB 90; EW 5; IDTP;
RGSF 2; RGWL 2; SUFW

Tiger, Derry
See Ellison, Harlan (Jay)

Tilghman, Christopher 1948(?)- .... **CLC 65**
See also CA 159; CSW; DLB 244

Tillich, Paul (Johannes)
1886-1965 .... **CLC 131**
See also CA 5-8R; 25-28R; CANR 33;
MTCW 1, 2

Tillinghast, Richard (Williford)
1940- .... **CLC 29**
See also CA 29-32R; CAAS 23; CANR 26,
51, 96; CP 7; CSW

Timrod, Henry 1828-1867 .... **NCLC 25**
See also DLB 3, 248; RGAL 4

Tindall, Gillian (Elizabeth) 1938- ...... **CLC 7**
See also CA 21-24R; CANR 11, 65, 107;
CN 7

Tiptree, James, Jr. .... **CLC 48, 50**
See Sheldon, Alice Hastings Bradley
See also DLB 8; SCFW 2; SFW 4

Tirso de Molina
See Tirso de Molina
See also RGWL 2

Tirso de Molina 1580(?)-1648 ..... **LC 73; DC
13; HLCS 2**
See also Tirso de Molina

Titmarsh, Michael Angelo
See Thackeray, William Makepeace

**Tocqueville, Alexis (Charles Henri Maurice
Clerel Comte) de** 1805-1859 .. **NCLC 7,
63**
See also EW 6; GFL 1789 to the Present

Tolkien, J(ohn) R(onald) R(euel)
1892-1973 .... **CLC 1, 2, 3, 8, 12, 38;
WLC**
See also AAYA 10; AITN 1; BPFB 3;
BRWS 2; CA 17-18; 45-48; CANR 36;
CAP 2; CDBLB 1914-1945; CLR 56;
CPW 1; CWRI 5; DA; DA3; DAB; DAC;
DAM MST, NOV, POP; DLB 15, 160,
255; EFS 2; FANT; JRDA; LAIT 1; MAI-
CYA 1, 2; MTCW 1, 2; NFS 8; RGEL 2;
SATA 2, 32, 100; SATA-Obit 24; SFW 4;
SUFW; WCH; WYA; YAW

Toller, Ernst 1893-1939 .... **TCLC 10**
See also CA 107; 186; DLB 124; RGWL 2

Tolson, M. B.
See Tolson, Melvin B(eaunorus)

Tolson, Melvin B(eaunorus)
1898(?)-1966 .... **CLC 36, 105; BLC 3**
See also AFAW 1, 2; BW 1, 3; CA 124; 89-
92; CANR 80; DAM MULT, POET; DLB
48, 76; RGAL 4

Tolstoi, Aleksei Nikolaevich
See Tolstoy, Alexey Nikolaevich

Tolstoi, Lev
See Tolstoy, Leo (Nikolaevich)
See also RGSF 2; RGWL 2

Tolstoy, Alexey Nikolaevich
1882-1945 .... **TCLC 18**
See also CA 107; 158; SFW 4

Tolstoy, Leo (Nikolaevich)
1828-1910 .. **TCLC 4, 11, 17, 28, 44, 79;
SSC 9, 30, 45; WLC**
See also Tolstoi, Lev
See also CA 104; 123; DA; DA3; DAB;
DAC; DAM MST, NOV; DLB 238; EFS
2; EW 7; EXPS; IDTP; LAIT 2; NFS 10;
SATA 26; SSFS 5

Tolstoy, Count Leo
See Tolstoy, Leo (Nikolaevich)

Tomasi di Lampedusa, Giuseppe 1896-1957
See Lampedusa, Giuseppe (Tomasi) di
See also CA 111; DLB 177

Tomlin, Lily .... **CLC 17**
See also Tomlin, Mary Jean

Tomlin, Mary Jean 1939(?)-
See Tomlin, Lily
See also CA 117

Tomlinson, (Alfred) Charles 1927- .... **CLC 2,
4, 6, 13, 45; PC 17**
See also CA 5-8R; CANR 33; CP 7; DAM
POET; DLB 40

Tomlinson, H(enry) M(ajor)
1873-1958 .... **TCLC 71**
See also CA 118; 161; DLB 36, 100, 195

Tonson, Jacob
See Bennett, (Enoch) Arnold

Toole, John Kennedy 1937-1969 ..... **CLC 19,
64**
See also BPFB 3; CA 104; DLBY 1981;
MTCW 2

Toomer, Eugene
See Toomer, Jean

Toomer, Eugene Pinchback
See Toomer, Jean

Toomer, Jean 1892-1967 .... **CLC 1, 4, 13, 22;
BLC 3; PC 7; SSC 1, 45; WLCS**
See also AFAW 1, 2; AMWS 3, 9; BW 1;
CA 85-88; CDALB 1917-1929; DA3;
DAM MULT; DLB 45, 51; EXPP; EXPS;
MTCW 1, 2; NFS 11; RGAL 4; RGSF 2;
SSFS 5

Toomer, Nathan Jean
See Toomer, Jean

Toomer, Nathan Pinchback
See Toomer, Jean

Torley, Luke
See Blish, James (Benjamin)

Tornimparte, Alessandra
See Ginzburg, Natalia

Torre, Raoul della
See Mencken, H(enry) L(ouis)

Torrence, Ridgely 1874-1950 .... **TCLC 97**
See also DLB 54, 249

Torrey, E(dwin) Fuller 1937- .... **CLC 34**
See also CA 119; CANR 71

Torsvan, Ben Traven
See Traven, B.

Torsvan, Benno Traven
See Traven, B.

Torsvan, Berick Traven
See Traven, B.

Torsvan, Berwick Traven
See Traven, B.

Torsvan, Bruno Traven
See Traven, B.

Torsvan, Traven
See Traven, B.

Tourneur, Cyril 1575(?)-1626 .... **LC 66**
See also BRW 2; DAM DRAM; DLB 58;
RGEL 2

Tournier, Michel (Edouard) 1924- .... **CLC 6,
23, 36, 95**
See also CA 49-52; CANR 3, 36, 74; DLB
83; GFL 1789 to the Present; MTCW 1,
2; SATA 23

Tournimparte, Alessandra
See Ginzburg, Natalia

Towers, Ivar
See Kornbluth, C(yril) M.

Towne, Robert (Burton) 1936(?)- ..... **CLC 87**
See also CA 108; DLB 44; IDFW 3, 4

Townsend, Sue .... **CLC 61**
See also Townsend, Susan Elaine
See also AAYA 28; CBD; CWD; SATA 55,
93; SATA-Brief 48

Townsend, Susan Elaine 1946-
See Townsend, Sue
See also CA 119; 127; CANR 65, 107; CD
5; CPW; DAB; DAC; DAM MST; INT
127; YAW

Townshend, Peter (Dennis Blandford)
1945- .... **CLC 17, 42**
See also CA 107

Tozzi, Federigo 1883-1920 .... **TCLC 31**
See also CA 160

Tracy, Don(ald Fiske) 1905-1970(?)
See Queen, Ellery
See also CA 1-4R; 176; CANR 2

Trafford, F. G.
See Riddell, Charlotte

Traill, Catharine Parr 1802-1899 .. **NCLC 31**
See also DLB 99

Trakl, Georg 1887-1914 .... **TCLC 5; PC 20**
See also CA 104; 165; EW 10; MTCW 2;
RGWL 2

Transtroemer, Tomas (Goesta)
1931- .... **CLC 52, 65**
See also Transtromer, Tomas
See also CA 117; 129; CAAS 17; DAM
POET

Transtromer, Tomas
See Transtroemer, Tomas (Goesta)
See also DLB 257

Transtromer, Tomas Gosta
See Transtroemer, Tomas (Goesta)

Traven, B. 1882(?)-1969 .... **CLC 8, 11**
See also CA 19-20; 25-28R; CAP 2; DLB
9, 56; MTCW 1; RGAL 4

Trediakovsky, Vasilii Kirillovich
1703-1769 .... **LC 68**
See also DLB 150

Treitel, Jonathan 1959- .... **CLC 70**

Trelawny, Edward John
1792-1881 .... **NCLC 85**
See also DLB 110, 116, 144

Tremain, Rose 1943- .... **CLC 42**
See also CA 97-100; CANR 44, 95; CN 7;
DLB 14; RGSF 2; RHW

Tremblay, Michel 1942- .... **CLC 29, 102**
See also CA 116; 128; CCA 1; CWW 2;
DAC; DAM MST; DLB 60; GLL 1;
MTCW 1, 2

Trevanian .... **CLC 29**
See also Whitaker, Rod(ney)

Trevor, Glen
See Hilton, James

Trevor, William .. **CLC 7, 9, 14, 25, 71, 116;**
SSC 21
See also Cox, William Trevor
See also BRWS 4; CBD; CD 5; CN 7; DLB
14, 139; MTCW 2; RGEL 2; RGSF 2;
SSFS 10

Trifonov, Iurii (Valentinovich)
See Trifonov, Yuri (Valentinovich)
See also RGWL 2

Trifonov, Yuri (Valentinovich)
1925-1981 .... **CLC 45**
See also Trifonov, Iurii (Valentinovich)
See also CA 126; 103; MTCW 1

Trilling, Diana (Rubin) 1905-1996 . **CLC 129**
See also CA 5-8R; 154; CANR 10, 46; INT
CANR-10; MTCW 1, 2

Trilling, Lionel 1905-1975 .... **CLC 9, 11, 24**
See also AMWS 3; CA 9-12R; 61-64;
CANR 10, 105; DLB 28, 63; INT CANR-
10; MTCW 1, 2; RGAL 4

Trimball, W. H.
See Mencken, H(enry) L(ouis)

Tristan
See Gomez de la Serna, Ramon

Tristram
See Housman, A(lfred) E(dward)

Trogdon, William (Lewis) 1939-
See Heat-Moon, William Least
See also CA 115; 119; CANR 47, 89; CPW;
INT CA-119

Trollope, Anthony 1815-1882 .... **NCLC 6, 33,**
101; SSC 28; WLC
See also BRW 5; CDBLB 1832-1890; DA;
DA3; DAB; DAC; DAM MST, NOV;
DLB 21, 57, 159; RGEL 2; RGSF 2;
SATA 22

Trollope, Frances 1779-1863 .... **NCLC 30**
See also DLB 21, 166

Trotsky, Leon 1879-1940 .... **TCLC 22**
See also CA 118; 167

Trotter (Cockburn), Catharine
1679-1749 .... **LC 8**
See also DLB 84, 252

Trotter, Wilfred 1872-1939 .... **TCLC 97**

Trout, Kilgore
See Farmer, Philip Jose

Trow, George W. S. 1943- .... **CLC 52**
See also CA 126; CANR 91

Troyat, Henri 1911- .... **CLC 23**
See also CA 45-48; CANR 2, 33, 67; GFL
1789 to the Present; MTCW 1

Trudeau, G(arretson) B(eekman) 1948-
See Trudeau, Garry B.
See also CA 81-84; CANR 31; SATA 35

Trudeau, Garry B. .... **CLC 12**
See also Trudeau, G(arretson) B(eekman)
See also AAYA 10; AITN 2

Truffaut, Francois 1932-1984 ... **CLC 20, 101**
See also CA 81-84; 113; CANR 34

Trumbo, Dalton 1905-1976 .... **CLC 19**
See also CA 21-24R; 69-72; CANR 10;
DLB 26; IDFW 3, 4; YAW

Trumbull, John 1750-1831 .... **NCLC 30**
See also DLB 31; RGAL 4

Trundlett, Helen B.
See Eliot, T(homas) S(tearns)

Truth, Sojourner 1797(?)-1883 ...... **NCLC 94**
See also DLB 239; FW; LAIT 2

Tryon, Thomas 1926-1991 .... **CLC 3, 11**
See also AITN 1; BPFB 3; CA 29-32R; 135;
CANR 32, 77; CPW; DA3; DAM POP;
HGG; MTCW 1

Tryon, Tom
See Tryon, Thomas

Ts'ao Hsueh-ch'in 1715(?)-1763 .... **LC 1**

Tsushima, Shuji 1909-1948
See Dazai Osamu
See also CA 107

Tsvetaeva (Efron), Marina (Ivanovna)
1892-1941 .... **TCLC 7, 35; PC 14**
See also CA 104; 128; CANR 73; EW 11;
MTCW 1, 2; RGWL 2

Tuck, Lily 1938- .... **CLC 70**
See also CA 139; CANR 90

Tu Fu 712-770 .... **PC 9**
See also Du Fu
See also DAM MULT; WP

Tunis, John R(oberts) 1889-1975 ..... **CLC 12**
See also BYA 1; CA 61-64; CANR 62; DLB
22, 171; JRDA; MAICYA 1, 2; SATA 37;
SATA-Brief 30; YAW

Tuohy, Frank .... **CLC 37**
See also Tuohy, John Francis
See also DLB 14, 139

Tuohy, John Francis 1925-
See Tuohy, Frank
See also CA 5-8R; 178; CANR 3, 47; CN 7

Turco, Lewis (Putnam) 1934- ..... **CLC 11, 63**
See also CA 13-16R; CAAS 22; CANR 24,
51; CP 7; DLBY 1984

Turgenev, Ivan (Sergeevich)
1818-1883 .... **NCLC 21, 37; DC 7; SSC**
7; WLC
See also DA; DAB; DAC; DAM MST,
NOV; DFS 6; DLB 238; EW 6; RGSF 2;
RGWL 2

Turgot, Anne-Robert-Jacques
1727-1781 .... **LC 26**

Turner, Frederick 1943- .... **CLC 48**
See also CA 73-76; CAAS 10; CANR 12,
30, 56; DLB 40

Turton, James
See Crace, Jim

Tutu, Desmond M(pilo) 1931- .... **CLC 80;**
BLC 3
See also BW 1, 3; CA 125; CANR 67, 81;
DAM MULT

Tutuola, Amos 1920-1997 ..... **CLC 5, 14, 29;**
BLC 3
See also AFW; BW 2, 3; CA 9-12R; 159;
CANR 27, 66; CDWLB 3; CN 7; DA3;
DAM MULT; DLB 125; DNFS 2; MTCW
1, 2; RGEL 2; WLIT 2

Twain, Mark .... **TCLC 6, 12, 19, 36, 48, 59;**
SSC 34; WLC
See also Clemens, Samuel Langhorne
See also AAYA 20; AMW; BPFB 3; BYA 2,
3, 11, 14; CLR 58, 60, 66; DLB 11;
EXPN; EXPS; FANT; LAIT 2; NFS 1, 6;
RGAL 4; RGSF 2; SFW 4; SSFS 1, 7;
SUFW; WCH; WYA; YAW

Tyler, Anne 1941- . **CLC 7, 11, 18, 28, 44, 59,**
103
See also AAYA 18; AMWS 4; BEST 89:1;
BPFB 3; BYA 12; CA 9-12R; CANR 11,
33, 53, 109; CDALBS; CN 7; CPW;
CSW; DAM NOV, POP; DLB 6, 143;
DLBY 1982; EXPN; MAWW; MTCW 1,
2; NFS 2, 7, 10; RGAL 4; SATA 7, 90;
YAW

Tyler, Royall 1757-1826 .... **NCLC 3**
See also DLB 37; RGAL 4

Tynan, Katharine 1861-1931 .... **TCLC 3**
See also CA 104; 167; DLB 153, 240; FW

Tyutchev, Fyodor 1803-1873 .... **NCLC 34**

Tzara, Tristan 1896-1963 ..... **CLC 47; PC 27**
See also CA 153; 89-92; DAM POET;
MTCW 2

Uhry, Alfred 1936- .... **CLC 55**
See also CA 127; 133; CAD; CD 5; CSW;
DA3; DAM DRAM, POP; DFS 11; INT
CA-133

Ulf, Harved
See Strindberg, (Johan) August

Ulf, Harved
See Strindberg, (Johan) August

Ulibarri, Sabine R(eyes) 1919- .... **CLC 83;**
HLCS 2
See also CA 131; CANR 81; DAM MULT;
DLB 82; HW 1, 2; RGSF 2

Unamuno (y Jugo), Miguel de
1864-1936 . **TCLC 2, 9; HLC 2; SSC 11**
See also CA 104; 131; CANR 81; DAM
MULT, NOV; DLB 108; EW 8; HW 1, 2;
MTCW 1, 2; RGSF 2; RGWL 2

Undercliffe, Errol
See Campbell, (John) Ramsey

Underwood, Miles
See Glassco, John

Undset, Sigrid 1882-1949 ..... **TCLC 3; WLC**
See also CA 104; 129; DA; DA3; DAB;
DAC; DAM MST, NOV; EW 9; FW;
MTCW 1, 2; RGWL 2

Ungaretti, Giuseppe 1888-1970 ... **CLC 7, 11,**
15
See also CA 19-20; 25-28R; CAP 2; DLB
114; EW 10; RGWL 2

Unger, Douglas 1952- .... **CLC 34**
See also CA 130; CANR 94

Unsworth, Barry (Forster) 1930- .... **CLC 76, 127**
See also BRWS 7; CA 25-28R; CANR 30, 54; CN 7; DLB 194

Updike, John (Hoyer) 1932- . **CLC 1, 2, 3, 5, 7, 9, 13, 15, 23, 34, 43, 70, 139; SSC 13, 27; WLC**
See also AAYA 36; AMW; AMWR 1; BPFB 3; BYA 12; CA 1-4R; CABS 1; CANR 4, 33, 51, 94; CDALB 1968-1988; CN 7; CP 7; CPW 1; DA; DA3; DAB; DAC; DAM MST, NOV, POET, POP; DLB 2, 5, 143, 218, 227; DLBD 3; DLBY 1980, 1982, 1997; EXPP; HGG; MTCW 1, 2; NFS 12; RGAL 4; RGSF 2; SSFS 3

Upshaw, Margaret Mitchell
See Mitchell, Margaret (Munnerlyn)

Upton, Mark
See Sanders, Lawrence

Upward, Allen 1863-1926 .... **TCLC 85**
See also CA 117; 187; DLB 36

Urdang, Constance (Henriette) 1922-1996 .... **CLC 47**
See also CA 21-24R; CANR 9, 24; CP 7; CWP

Uriel, Henry
See Faust, Frederick (Schiller)

Uris, Leon (Marcus) 1924- .... **CLC 7, 32**
See also AITN 1, 2; BEST 89:2; BPFB 3; CA 1-4R; CANR 1, 40, 65; CN 7; CPW 1; DA3; DAM NOV, POP; MTCW 1, 2; SATA 49

Urista, Alberto H. 1947- .... **PC 34**
See also Alurista
See also CA 45-48, 182; CANR 2, 32; HLCS 1; HW 1

Urmuz
See Codrescu, Andrei

Urquhart, Guy
See McAlmon, Robert (Menzies)

Urquhart, Jane 1949- .... **CLC 90**
See also CA 113; CANR 32, 68; CCA 1; DAC

Usigli, Rodolfo 1905-1979
See also CA 131; HLCS 1; HW 1; LAW

Ustinov, Peter (Alexander) 1921- ...... **CLC 1**
See also AITN 1; CA 13-16R; CANR 25, 51; CBD; CD 5; DLB 13; MTCW 2

U Tam'si, Gerald Felix Tchicaya
See Tchicaya, Gerald Felix

U Tam'si, Tchicaya
See Tchicaya, Gerald Felix

Vachss, Andrew (Henry) 1942- .... **CLC 106**
See also CA 118; CANR 44, 95; CMW 4

Vachss, Andrew H.
See Vachss, Andrew (Henry)

Vaculik, Ludvik 1926- .... **CLC 7**
See also CA 53-56; CANR 72; CWW 2; DLB 232

Vaihinger, Hans 1852-1933 .... **TCLC 71**
See also CA 116; 166

Valdez, Luis (Miguel) 1940- ..... **CLC 84; DC 10; HLC 2**
See also CA 101; CAD; CANR 32, 81; CD 5; DAM MULT; DFS 5; DLB 122; HW 1; LAIT 4

Valenzuela, Luisa 1938- .... **CLC 31, 104; HLCS 2; SSC 14**
See also CA 101; CANR 32, 65; CDWLB 3; CWW 2; DAM MULT; DLB 113; FW; HW 1, 2; LAW; RGSF 2

Valera y Alcala-Galiano, Juan 1824-1905 .... **TCLC 10**
See also CA 106

Valery, (Ambroise) Paul (Toussaint Jules) 1871-1945 .... **TCLC 4, 15; PC 9**
See also CA 104; 122; DA3; DAM POET; DLB 258; EW 8; GFL 1789 to the Present; MTCW 1, 2; RGWL 2

Valle-Inclan, Ramon (Maria) del 1866-1936 .... **TCLC 5; HLC 2**
See also CA 106; 153; CANR 80; DAM MULT; DLB 134; EW 8; HW 2; RGSF 2; RGWL 2

Vallejo, Antonio Buero
See Buero Vallejo, Antonio

Vallejo, Cesar (Abraham) 1892-1938 .... **TCLC 3, 56; HLC 2**
See also CA 105; 153; DAM MULT; HW 1; LAW; RGWL 2

Valles, Jules 1832-1885 .... **NCLC 71**
See also DLB 123; GFL 1789 to the Present

Vallette, Marguerite Eymery 1860-1953 .... **TCLC 67**
See also CA 182; DLB 123, 192

Valle Y Pena, Ramon del
See Valle-Inclan, Ramon (Maria) del

Van Ash, Cay 1918- .... **CLC 34**

Vanbrugh, Sir John 1664-1726 .... **LC 21**
See also BRW 2; DAM DRAM; DLB 80; IDTP; RGEL 2

Van Campen, Karl
See Campbell, John W(ood, Jr.)

Vance, Gerald
See Silverberg, Robert

Vance, Jack .... **CLC 35**
See also Vance, John Holbrook
See also DLB 8; FANT; SCFW 2; SFW 4; SUFW

Vance, John Holbrook 1916-
See Queen, Ellery; Vance, Jack
See also CA 29-32R; CANR 17, 65; CMW 4; MTCW 1

Van Den Bogarde, Derek Jules Gaspard Ulric Niven 1921-1999 .... **CLC 14**
See also Bogarde, Dirk
See also CA 77-80; 179

Vandenburgh, Jane .... **CLC 59**
See also CA 168

Vanderhaeghe, Guy 1951- .... **CLC 41**
See also BPFB 3; CA 113; CANR 72

van der Post, Laurens (Jan) 1906-1996 .... **CLC 5**
See also AFW; CA 5-8R; 155; CANR 35; CN 7; DLB 204; RGEL 2

van de Wetering, Janwillem 1931- ... **CLC 47**
See also CA 49-52; CANR 4, 62, 90; CMW 4

Van Dine, S. S. .... **TCLC 23**
See also Wright, Willard Huntington
See also MSW

Van Doren, Carl (Clinton) 1885-1950 .... **TCLC 18**
See also CA 111; 168

Van Doren, Mark 1894-1972 .... **CLC 6, 10**
See also CA 1-4R; 37-40R; CANR 3; DLB 45; MTCW 1, 2; RGAL 4

Van Druten, John (William) 1901-1957 .... **TCLC 2**
See also CA 104; 161; DLB 10; RGAL 4

Van Duyn, Mona (Jane) 1921- ...... **CLC 3, 7, 63, 116**
See also CA 9-12R; CANR 7, 38, 60; CP 7; CWP; DAM POET; DLB 5

Van Dyne, Edith
See Baum, L(yman) Frank

van Itallie, Jean-Claude 1936- .... **CLC 3**
See also CA 45-48; CAAS 2; CAD; CANR 1, 48; CD 5; DLB 7

Van Loot, Cornelius Obenchain
See Roberts, Kenneth (Lewis)

van Ostaijen, Paul 1896-1928 .... **TCLC 33**
See also CA 163

Van Peebles, Melvin 1932- .... **CLC 2, 20**
See also BW 2, 3; CA 85-88; CANR 27, 67, 82; DAM MULT

van Schendel, Arthur(-Francois-Emile) 1874-1946 .... **TCLC 56**

Vansittart, Peter 1920- .... **CLC 42**
See also CA 1-4R; CANR 3, 49, 90; CN 7; RHW

Van Vechten, Carl 1880-1964 .... **CLC 33**
See also AMWS 2; CA 183; 89-92; DLB 4, 9; RGAL 4

van Vogt, A(lfred) E(lton) 1912-2000 . **CLC 1**
See also BPFB 3; BYA 13, 14; CA 21-24R; 190; CANR 28; DLB 8, 251; SATA 14; SATA-Obit 124; SCFW; SFW 4

Varda, Agnes 1928- .... **CLC 16**
See also CA 116; 122

Vargas Llosa, (Jorge) Mario (Pedro) 1936- .... **CLC 3, 6, 9, 10, 15, 31, 42, 85; HLC 2**
See also Llosa, (Jorge) Mario (Pedro) Vargas
See also BPFB 3; CA 73-76; CANR 18, 32, 42, 67; CDWLB 3; DA; DA3; DAB; DAC; DAM MST, MULT, NOV; DLB 145; DNFS 2; HW 1, 2; LAIT 5; LAW; LAWS 1; MTCW 1, 2; RGWL 2; SSFS 14; WLIT 1

Vasiliu, George
See Bacovia, George

Vasiliu, Gheorghe
See Bacovia, George
See also CA 123; 189

Vassa, Gustavus
See Equiano, Olaudah

Vassilikos, Vassilis 1933- .... **CLC 4, 8**
See also CA 81-84; CANR 75

Vaughan, Henry 1621-1695 .... **LC 27**
See also BRW 2; DLB 131; PAB; RGEL 2

Vaughn, Stephanie .... **CLC 62**

Vazov, Ivan (Minchov) 1850-1921 . **TCLC 25**
See also CA 121; 167; CDWLB 4; DLB 147

Veblen, Thorstein B(unde) 1857-1929 .... **TCLC 31**
See also AMWS 1; CA 115; 165; DLB 246

Vega, Lope de 1562-1635 .... **LC 23; HLCS 2**
See also EW 2; RGWL 2

Vendler, Helen (Hennessy) 1933- ... **CLC 138**
See also CA 41-44R; CANR 25, 72; MTCW 1, 2

Venison, Alfred
See Pound, Ezra (Weston Loomis)

Verdi, Marie de
See Mencken, H(enry) L(ouis)

Verdu, Matilde
See Cela, Camilo Jose

Verga, Giovanni (Carmelo) 1840-1922 .... **TCLC 3; SSC 21**
See also CA 104; 123; CANR 101; EW 7; RGSF 2; RGWL 2

Vergil 70B.C.-19B.C. ... **CMLC 9, 40; PC 12; WLCS**
See also Virgil
See also AW 2; DA; DA3; DAB; DAC; DAM MST, POET; EFS 1

Verhaeren, Emile (Adolphe Gustave) 1855-1916 .... **TCLC 12**
See also CA 109; GFL 1789 to the Present

Verlaine, Paul (Marie) 1844-1896 .. **NCLC 2, 51; PC 2, 32**
See also DAM POET; DLB 217; EW 7; GFL 1789 to the Present; RGWL 2

Verne, Jules (Gabriel) 1828-1905 ... **TCLC 6, 52**
See also AAYA 16; BYA 4; CA 110; 131; DA3; DLB 123; GFL 1789 to the Present; JRDA; LAIT 2; MAICYA 1, 2; RGWL 2; SATA 21; SCFW; SFW 4; WCH

Verus, Marcus Annius
See Aurelius, Marcus

Very, Jones 1813-1880 .... **NCLC 9**
    See also DLB 1, 243; RGAL 4
Vesaas, Tarjei 1897-1970 .... **CLC 48**
    See also CA 190; 29-32R; EW 11
Vialis, Gaston
    See Simenon, Georges (Jacques Christian)
Vian, Boris 1920-1959 .... **TCLC 9**
    See also CA 106; 164; DLB 72; GFL 1789
    to the Present; MTCW 2; RGWL 2
Viaud, (Louis Marie) Julien 1850-1923
    See Loti, Pierre
    See also CA 107
Vicar, Henry
    See Felsen, Henry Gregor
Vicker, Angus
    See Felsen, Henry Gregor
Vidal, Gore 1925- ...... **CLC 2, 4, 6, 8, 10, 22, 33, 72, 142**
    See also Box, Edgar
    See also AITN 1; AMWS 4; BEST 90:2;
    BPFB 3; CA 5-8R; CAD; CANR 13, 45,
    65, 100; CD 5; CDALBS; CN 7; CPW;
    DA3; DAM NOV, POP; DFS 2; DLB 6,
    152; INT CANR-13; MTCW 1, 2; RGAL
    4; RHW
Viereck, Peter (Robert Edwin)
    1916- .... **CLC 4; PC 27**
    See also CA 1-4R; CANR 1, 47; CP 7; DLB
    5; PFS 9, 14
Vigny, Alfred (Victor) de
    1797-1863 .... **NCLC 7, 102; PC 26**
    See also DAM POET; DLB 119, 192, 217;
    EW 5; GFL 1789 to the Present; RGWL 2
Vilakazi, Benedict Wallet
    1906-1947 .... **TCLC 37**
    See also CA 168
Villa, Jose Garcia 1914-1997 .... **PC 22**
    See also AAL; CA 25-28R; CANR 12;
    EXPP
Villarreal, Jose Antonio 1924-
    See also CA 133; CANR 93; DAM MULT;
    DLB 82; HLC 2; HW 1; LAIT 4; RGAL
    4
Villaurrutia, Xavier 1903-1950 ...... **TCLC 80**
    See also CA 192; HW 1; LAW
Villehardouin, Geoffroi de
    1150(?)-1218(?) .... **CMLC 38**
Villiers de l'Isle Adam, Jean Marie Mathias
    Philippe Auguste 1838-1889 ... **NCLC 3;**
    SSC 14
    See also DLB 123, 192; GFL 1789 to the
    Present; RGSF 2
Villon, Francois 1431-1463(?) . **LC 62; PC 13**
    See also DLB 208; EW 2; RGWL 2
Vine, Barbara .... **CLC 50**
    See also Rendell, Ruth (Barbara)
    See also BEST 90:4
Vinge, Joan (Carol) D(ennison)
    1948- .... **CLC 30; SSC 24**
    See also AAYA 32; BPFB 3; CA 93-96;
    CANR 72; SATA 36, 113; SFW 4; YAW
Viola, Herman J(oseph) 1938- .... **CLC 70**
    See also CA 61-64; CANR 8, 23, 48, 91;
    SATA 126
Violis, G.
    See Simenon, Georges (Jacques Christian)
Viramontes, Helena Maria 1954-
    See also CA 159; DLB 122; HLCS 2; HW
    2
Virgil
    See Vergil
    See also CDWLB 1; DLB 211; LAIT 1;
    RGWL 2; WP
Visconti, Luchino 1906-1976 .... **CLC 16**
    See also CA 81-84; 65-68; CANR 39
Vittorini, Elio 1908-1966 .... **CLC 6, 9, 14**
    See also CA 133; 25-28R; EW 12; RGWL 2

Vivekananda, Swami 1863-1902 .... **TCLC 88**
Vizenor, Gerald Robert 1934- .... **CLC 103**
    See also CA 13-16R; CAAS 22; CANR 5,
    21, 44, 67; DAM MULT; DLB 175, 227;
    MTCW 2; NNAL; TCWW 2
Vizinczey, Stephen 1933- .... **CLC 40**
    See also CA 128; CCA 1; INT 128
Vliet, R(ussell) G(ordon)
    1929-1984 .... **CLC 22**
    See also CA 37-40R; 112; CANR 18
Vogau, Boris Andreyevich 1894-1937(?)
    See Pilnyak, Boris
    See also CA 123
Vogel, Paula A(nne) 1951- .... **CLC 76**
    See also CA 108; CAD; CD 5; CWD; DFS
    14; RGAL 4
Voigt, Cynthia 1942- .... **CLC 30**
    See also AAYA 3, 30; BYA 1, 3, 6, 7, 8;
    CA 106; CANR 18, 37, 40, 94; CLR 13,
    48; INT CANR-18; JRDA; LAIT 5; MAI-
    CYA 1, 2; MAICYAS 1; SATA 48, 79,
    116; SATA-Brief 33; WYA; YAW
Voigt, Ellen Bryant 1943- .... **CLC 54**
    See also CA 69-72; CANR 11, 29, 55; CP
    7; CSW; CWP; DLB 120
Voinovich, Vladimir (Nikolaevich)
    1932- .... **CLC 10, 49, 147**
    See also CA 81-84; CAAS 12; CANR 33,
    67; MTCW 1
Vollmann, William T. 1959- .... **CLC 89**
    See also CA 134; CANR 67; CPW; DA3;
    DAM NOV, POP; MTCW 2
Voloshinov, V. N.
    See Bakhtin, Mikhail Mikhailovich
Voltaire 1694-1778 ..... **LC 14; SSC 12; WLC**
    See also BYA 13; DA; DA3; DAB; DAC;
    DAM DRAM, MST; EW 4; GFL Begin-
    nings to 1789; NFS 7; RGWL 2
von Aschendrof, Baron Ignatz 1873-1939
    See Ford, Ford Madox
von Daeniken, Erich 1935- .... **CLC 30**
    See also AITN 1; CA 37-40R; CANR 17,
    44
von Daniken, Erich
    See von Daeniken, Erich
von Hartmann, Eduard
    1842-1906 .... **TCLC 96**
von Hayek, Friedrich August
    See Hayek, F(riedrich) A(ugust von)
von Heidenstam, (Carl Gustaf) Verner
    See Heidenstam, (Carl Gustaf) Verner von
von Heyse, Paul (Johann Ludwig)
    See Heyse, Paul (Johann Ludwig von)
von Hofmannsthal, Hugo
    See Hofmannsthal, Hugo von
von Horvath, Odon
    See Horvath, Odon von
von Horvath, Odon
    See Horvath, Odon von
von Horvath, Oedoen
    See Horvath, Odon von
    See also CA 184
von Liliencron, (Friedrich Adolf Axel)
    Detlev
    See Liliencron, (Friedrich Adolf Axel) De-
    tlev von
Vonnegut, Kurt, Jr. 1922- . **CLC 1, 2, 3, 4, 5,**
    8, 12, 22, 40, 60, 111; SSC 8; WLC
    See also AAYA 6; AITN 1; AMWS 2; BEST
    90:4; BPFB 3; BYA 3, 14; CA 1-4R;
    CANR 1, 25, 49, 75, 92; CDALB 1968-
    1988; CN 7; CPW 1; DA; DA3; DAB;
    DAC; DAM MST, NOV, POP; DLB 2, 8,
    152; DLBD 3; DLBY 1980; EXPN;
    EXPS; LAIT 4; MTCW 1, 2; NFS 3;
    RGAL 4; SCFW 4; SFW 4; SSFS 5; TUS;
    YAW
Von Rachen, Kurt
    See Hubbard, L(afayette) Ron(ald)

von Rezzori (d'Arezzo), Gregor
    See Rezzori (d'Arezzo), Gregor von
von Sternberg, Josef
    See Sternberg, Josef von
Vorster, Gordon 1924- .... **CLC 34**
    See also CA 133
Vosce, Trudie
    See Ozick, Cynthia
Voznesensky, Andrei (Andreievich)
    1933- .... **CLC 1, 15, 57**
    See also CA 89-92; CANR 37; CWW 2;
    DAM POET; MTCW 1
Waddington, Miriam 1917- .... **CLC 28**
    See also CA 21-24R; CANR 12, 30; CCA
    1; CP 7; DLB 68
Wagman, Fredrica 1937- .... **CLC 7**
    See also CA 97-100; INT 97-100
Wagner, Linda W.
    See Wagner-Martin, Linda (C.)
Wagner, Linda Welshimer
    See Wagner-Martin, Linda (C.)
Wagner, Richard 1813-1883 .... **NCLC 9**
    See also DLB 129; EW 6
Wagner-Martin, Linda (C.) 1936- .... **CLC 50**
    See also CA 159
Wagoner, David (Russell) 1926- .... **CLC 3, 5,**
    15; PC 33
    See also AMWS 9; CA 1-4R; CAAS 3;
    CANR 2, 71; CN 7; CP 7; DLB 5, 256;
    SATA 14; TCWW 2
Wah, Fred(erick James) 1939- .... **CLC 44**
    See also CA 107; 141; CP 7; DLB 60
Wahloo, Per 1926-1975 .... **CLC 7**
    See also BPFB 3; CA 61-64; CANR 73;
    CMW 4; MSW
Wahloo, Peter
    See Wahloo, Per
Wain, John (Barrington) 1925-1994 . **CLC 2,**
    11, 15, 46
    See also CA 5-8R; 145; CAAS 4; CANR
    23, 54; CDBLB 1960 to Present; DLB 15,
    27, 139, 155; MTCW 1, 2
Wajda, Andrzej 1926- .... **CLC 16**
    See also CA 102
Wakefield, Dan 1932- .... **CLC 7**
    See also CA 21-24R; CAAS 7; CN 7
Wakefield, Herbert Russell
    1888-1965 .... **TCLC 120**
    See also CA 5-8R; CANR 77; HGG; SUFW
Wakoski, Diane 1937- ...... **CLC 2, 4, 7, 9, 11,**
    40; PC 15
    See also CA 13-16R; CAAS 1; CANR 9,
    60, 106; CP 7; CWP; DAM POET; DLB
    5; INT CANR-9; MTCW 2
Wakoski-Sherbell, Diane
    See Wakoski, Diane
Walcott, Derek (Alton) 1930- .... **CLC 2, 4, 9,**
    14, 25, 42, 67, 76, 160; BLC 3; DC 7
    See also BW 2; CA 89-92; CANR 26, 47,
    75, 80; CBD; CD 5; CDWLB 3; CP 7;
    DA3; DAB; DAC; DAM MST, MULT,
    POET; DLB 117; DLBY 1981; DNFS 1;
    EFS 1; MTCW 1, 2; PFS 6; RGEL 2
Waldman, Anne (Lesley) 1945- .... **CLC 7**
    See also CA 37-40R; CAAS 17; CANR 34,
    69; CP 7; CWP; DLB 16
Waldo, E. Hunter
    See Sturgeon, Theodore (Hamilton)
Waldo, Edward Hamilton
    See Sturgeon, Theodore (Hamilton)
Walker, Alice (Malsenior) 1944- ... **CLC 5, 6,**
    9, 19, 27, 46, 58, 103; BLC 3; PC 30;
    SSC 5; WLCS
    See also AAYA 3, 33; AFAW 1, 2; AMWS
    3; BEST 89:4; BPFB 3; BW 2, 3; CA 37-
    40R; CANR 9, 27, 49, 66, 82; CDALB
    1968-1988; CN 7; CPW; CSW; DA; DA3;
    DAB; DAC; DAM MST, MULT, NOV,
    POET, POP; DLB 6, 33, 143; EXPN;

EXPS; FW; INT CANR-27; LAIT 3;
MAWW; MTCW 1, 2; NFS 5; RGAL 4;
RGSF 2; SATA 31; SSFS 2, 11; YAW

Walker, David Harry 1911-1992 ...... **CLC 14**
See also CA 1-4R; 137; CANR 1; CWRI 5;
SATA 8; SATA-Obit 71

Walker, Edward Joseph 1934-
See Walker, Ted
See also CA 21-24R; CANR 12, 28, 53; CP
7

Walker, George F. 1947- .... **CLC 44, 61**
See also CA 103; CANR 21, 43, 59; CD 5;
DAB; DAC; DAM MST; DLB 60

Walker, Joseph A. 1935- .... **CLC 19**
See also BW 1, 3; CA 89-92; CAD; CANR
26; CD 5; DAM DRAM, MST; DFS 12;
DLB 38

Walker, Margaret (Abigail)
1915-1998 .... **CLC 1, 6; BLC; PC 20**
See also AFAW 1, 2; BW 2, 3; CA 73-76;
172; CANR 26, 54, 76; CN 7; CP 7;
CSW; DAM MULT; DLB 76, 152; EXPP;
FW; MTCW 1, 2; RGAL 4; RHW

Walker, Ted .... **CLC 13**
See Walker, Edward Joseph
See also DLB 40

Wallace, David Foster 1962- ..... **CLC 50, 114**
See also AMWS 10; CA 132; CANR 59;
DA3; MTCW 2

Wallace, Dexter
See Masters, Edgar Lee

Wallace, (Richard Horatio) Edgar
1875-1932 .... **TCLC 57**
See also CA 115; CMW 4; DLB 70; MSW;
RGEL 2

Wallace, Irving 1916-1990 .... **CLC 7, 13**
See also AITN 1; BPFB 3; CA 1-4R; 132;
CAAS 1; CANR 1, 27; CPW; DAM NOV,
POP; INT CANR-27; MTCW 1, 2

Wallant, Edward Lewis 1926-1962 ... **CLC 5,
10**
See also CA 1-4R; CANR 22; DLB 2, 28,
143; MTCW 1, 2; RGAL 4

Wallas, Graham 1858-1932 .... **TCLC 91**

Walley, Byron
See Card, Orson Scott

Walpole, Horace 1717-1797 .... **LC 2, 49**
See also BRW 3; DLB 39, 104, 213; HGG;
RGEL 2; SUFW

Walpole, Hugh (Seymour)
1884-1941 .... **TCLC 5**
See also CA 104; 165; DLB 34; HGG;
MTCW 2; RGEL 2; RHW

Walser, Martin 1927- .... **CLC 27**
See also CA 57-60; CANR 8, 46; CWW 2;
DLB 75, 124

Walser, Robert 1878-1956 .... **TCLC 18; SSC
20**
See also CA 118; 165; CANR 100; DLB 66

Walsh, Gillian Paton
See Paton Walsh, Gillian

Walsh, Jill Paton .... **CLC 35**
See also Paton Walsh, Gillian
See also CLR 2, 65; WYA

Walter, Villiam Christian
See Andersen, Hans Christian

Walton, Izaak 1593-1683 .... **LC 72**
See also BRW 2; CDBLB Before 1660;
DLB 151, 213; RGEL 2

Wambaugh, Joseph (Aloysius, Jr.)
1937- .... **CLC 3, 18**
See also AITN 1; BEST 89:3; BPFB 3; CA
33-36R; CANR 42, 65; CMW 4; CPW 1;
DA3; DAM NOV, POP; DLB 6; DLBY
1983; MSW; MTCW 1, 2

Wang Wei 699(?)-761(?) .... **PC 18**

Ward, Arthur Henry Sarsfield 1883-1959
See Rohmer, Sax
See also CA 108; 173; CMW 4; HGG

Ward, Douglas Turner 1930- .... **CLC 19**
See also BW 1; CA 81-84; CAD; CANR
27; CD 5; DLB 7, 38

Ward, E. D.
See Lucas, E(dward) V(errall)

Ward, Mrs. Humphry 1851-1920
See Ward, Mary Augusta
See also RGEL 2

Ward, Mary Augusta 1851-1920 ... **TCLC 55**
See also Ward, Mrs. Humphry
See also DLB 18

Ward, Peter
See Faust, Frederick (Schiller)

Warhol, Andy 1928(?)-1987 .... **CLC 20**
See also AAYA 12; BEST 89:4; CA 89-92;
121; CANR 34

Warner, Francis (Robert le Plastrier)
1937- .... **CLC 14**
See also CA 53-56; CANR 11

Warner, Marina 1946- .... **CLC 59**
See also CA 65-68; CANR 21, 55; CN 7;
DLB 194

Warner, Rex (Ernest) 1905-1986 ...... **CLC 45**
See also CA 89-92; 119; DLB 15; RGEL 2;
RHW

Warner, Susan (Bogert)
1819-1885 .... **NCLC 31**
See also DLB 3, 42, 239, 250, 254

Warner, Sylvia (Constance) Ashton
See Ashton-Warner, Sylvia (Constance)

Warner, Sylvia Townsend
1893-1978 .... **CLC 7, 19; SSC 23**
See also BRWS 7; CA 61-64; 77-80; CANR
16, 60, 104; DLB 34, 139; FANT; FW;
MTCW 1, 2; RGEL 2; RGSF 2; RHW

Warren, Mercy Otis 1728-1814 ..... **NCLC 13**
See also DLB 31, 200; RGAL 4

Warren, Robert Penn 1905-1989 .. **CLC 1, 4,
6, 8, 10, 13, 18, 39, 53, 59; PC 37; SSC
4; WLC**
See also AITN 1; AMW; BPFB 3; BYA 1;
CA 13-16R; 129; CANR 10, 47; CDALB
1968-1988; DA; DA3; DAB; DAC; DAM
MST, NOV, POET; DLB 2, 48, 152;
DLBY 1980, 1989; INT CANR-10;
MTCW 1, 2; NFS 13; RGAL 4; RGSF 2;
RHW; SATA 46; SATA-Obit 63; SSFS 8

Warshofsky, Isaac
See Singer, Isaac Bashevis

Warton, Thomas 1728-1790 .... **LC 15**
See also DAM POET; DLB 104, 109;
RGEL 2

Waruk, Kona
See Harris, (Theodore) Wilson

Warung, Price .... **TCLC 45**
See also Astley, William
See also DLB 230; RGEL 2

Warwick, Jarvis
See Garner, Hugh
See also CCA 1

Washington, Alex
See Harris, Mark

Washington, Booker T(aliaferro)
1856-1915 .... **TCLC 10; BLC 3**
See also BW 1; CA 114; 125; DA3; DAM
MULT; LAIT 2; RGAL 4; SATA 28

Washington, George 1732-1799 .... **LC 25**
See also DLB 31

Wassermann, (Karl) Jakob
1873-1934 .... **TCLC 6**
See also CA 104; 163; DLB 66

Wasserstein, Wendy 1950- .. **CLC 32, 59, 90;
DC 4**
See also CA 121; 129; CABS 3; CAD;
CANR 53, 75; CD 5; CWD; DA3; DAM
DRAM; DFS 5; DLB 228; FW; INT CA-
129; MTCW 2; SATA 94

Waterhouse, Keith (Spencer) 1929- . **CLC 47**
See also CA 5-8R; CANR 38, 67, 109;
CBD; CN 7; DLB 13, 15; MTCW 1, 2

Waters, Frank (Joseph) 1902-1995 .. **CLC 88**
See also CA 5-8R; 149; CAAS 13; CANR
3, 18, 63; DLB 212; DLBY 1986; RGAL
4; TCWW 2

Waters, Mary C. .... **CLC 70**

Waters, Roger 1944- .... **CLC 35**

Watkins, Frances Ellen
See Harper, Frances Ellen Watkins

Watkins, Gerrold
See Malzberg, Barry N(athaniel)

Watkins, Gloria Jean 1952(?)-
See hooks, bell
See also BW 2; CA 143; CANR 87; MTCW
2; SATA 115

Watkins, Paul 1964- .... **CLC 55**
See also CA 132; CANR 62, 98

Watkins, Vernon Phillips
1906-1967 .... **CLC 43**
See also CA 9-10; 25-28R; CAP 1; DLB
20; RGEL 2

Watson, Irving S.
See Mencken, H(enry) L(ouis)

Watson, John H.
See Farmer, Philip Jose

Watson, Richard F.
See Silverberg, Robert

Waugh, Auberon (Alexander)
1939-2001 .... **CLC 7**
See also CA 45-48; 192; CANR 6, 22, 92;
DLB 14, 194

Waugh, Evelyn (Arthur St. John)
1903-1966 .. **CLC 1, 3, 8, 13, 19, 27, 44,
107; SSC 41; WLC**
See also BPFB 3; BRW 7; CA 85-88; 25-
28R; CANR 22; CDBLB 1914-1945; DA;
DA3; DAB; DAC; DAM MST, NOV,
POP; DLB 15, 162, 195; MTCW 1, 2;
NFS 13; RGEL 2; RGSF 2; WLIT 4

Waugh, Harriet 1944- .... **CLC 6**
See also CA 85-88; CANR 22

Ways, C. R.
See Blount, Roy (Alton), Jr.

Waystaff, Simon
See Swift, Jonathan

Webb, Beatrice (Martha Potter)
1858-1943 .... **TCLC 22**
See also CA 117; 162; DLB 190; FW

Webb, Charles (Richard) 1939- .... **CLC 7**
See also CA 25-28R

Webb, James H(enry), Jr. 1946- ...... **CLC 22**
See also CA 81-84

Webb, Mary Gladys (Meredith)
1881-1927 .... **TCLC 24**
See also CA 182; 123; DLB 34; FW

Webb, Mrs. Sidney
See Webb, Beatrice (Martha Potter)

Webb, Phyllis 1927- .... **CLC 18**
See also CA 104; CANR 23; CCA 1; CP 7;
CWP; DLB 53

Webb, Sidney (James) 1859-1947 .. **TCLC 22**
See also CA 117; 163; DLB 190

Webber, Andrew Lloyd .... **CLC 21**
See also Lloyd Webber, Andrew
See also DFS 7

Weber, Lenora Mattingly
1895-1971 .... **CLC 12**
See also CA 19-20; 29-32R; CAP 1; SATA
2; SATA-Obit 26

Weber, Max 1864-1920 .... **TCLC 69**
See also CA 109; 189

Webster, John 1580(?)-1634(?) .... **LC 33; DC
2; WLC**
See also BRW 2; CDBLB Before 1660; DA;
DAB; DAC; DAM DRAM, MST; DLB
58; IDTP; RGEL 2; WLIT 3

Webster, Noah 1758-1843 .... **NCLC 30**
See also DLB 1, 37, 42, 43, 73, 243

Wedekind, (Benjamin) Frank(lin)
1864-1918 .... **TCLC 7**
See also CA 104; 153; CDWLB 2; DAM
DRAM; DLB 118; EW 8; RGWL 2

Wehr, Demaris .... **CLC 65**

Weidman, Jerome 1913-1998 .... **CLC 7**
See also AITN 2; CA 1-4R; 171; CAD;
CANR 1; DLB 28

Weil, Simone (Adolphine)
1909-1943 .... **TCLC 23**
See also CA 117; 159; EW 12; FW; GFL
1789 to the Present; MTCW 2

Weininger, Otto 1880-1903 .... **TCLC 84**

Weinstein, Nathan
See West, Nathanael

Weinstein, Nathan von Wallenstein
See West, Nathanael

Weir, Peter (Lindsay) 1944- .... **CLC 20**
See also CA 113; 123

Weiss, Peter (Ulrich) 1916-1982 .. **CLC 3, 15,
51**
See also CA 45-48; 106; CANR 3; DAM
DRAM; DFS 3; DLB 69, 124; RGWL 2

Weiss, Theodore (Russell) 1916- ... **CLC 3, 8,
14**
See also CA 9-12R; CAAE 189; CAAS 2;
CANR 46, 94; CP 7; DLB 5

Welch, (Maurice) Denton
1915-1948 .... **TCLC 22**
See also CA 121; 148; RGEL 2

Welch, James 1940- .... **CLC 6, 14, 52**
See also CA 85-88; CANR 42, 66, 107; CN
7; CP 7; CPW; DAM MULT, POP; DLB
175, 256; NNAL; RGAL 4; TCWW 2

Weldon, Fay 1931- . **CLC 6, 9, 11, 19, 36, 59,
122**
See also BRWS 4; CA 21-24R; CANR 16,
46, 63, 97; CDBLB 1960 to Present; CN
7; CPW; DAM POP; DLB 14, 194; FW;
HGG; INT CANR-16; MTCW 1, 2; RGEL
2; RGSF 2

Wellek, Rene 1903-1995 .... **CLC 28**
See also CA 5-8R; 150; CAAS 7; CANR 8;
DLB 63; INT CANR-8

Weller, Michael 1942- .... **CLC 10, 53**
See also CA 85-88; CAD; CD 5

Weller, Paul 1958- .... **CLC 26**

Wellershoff, Dieter 1925- .... **CLC 46**
See also CA 89-92; CANR 16, 37

Welles, (George) Orson 1915-1985 .. **CLC 20,
80**
See also AAYA 40; CA 93-96; 117

Wellman, John McDowell 1945-
See Wellman, Mac
See also CA 166; CD 5

Wellman, Mac .... **CLC 65**
See also Wellman, John McDowell; Well-
man, John McDowell
See also CAD; RGAL 4

Wellman, Manly Wade 1903-1986 ... **CLC 49**
See also CA 1-4R; 118; CANR 6, 16, 44;
FANT; SATA 6; SATA-Obit 47; SFW 4;
SUFW

Wells, Carolyn 1869(?)-1942 .... **TCLC 35**
See also CA 113; 185; CMW 4; DLB 11

Wells, H(erbert) G(eorge)
1866-1946 .... **TCLC 6, 12, 19; SSC 6;
WLC**
See also AAYA 18; BPFB 3; BRW 6; CA
110; 121; CDBLB 1914-1945; CLR 64;
DA; DA3; DAB; DAC; DAM MST, NOV;
DLB 34, 70, 156, 178; EXPS; HGG;
LAIT 3; MTCW 1, 2; RGEL 2; RGSF 2;
SATA 20; SCFW; SFW 4; SSFS 3; SUFW;
WCH; WLIT 4; YAW

Wells, Rosemary 1943- .... **CLC 12**
See also AAYA 13; BYA 7, 8; CA 85-88;
CANR 48; CLR 16, 69; CWRI 5; MAI-
CYA 1, 2; SAAS 1; SATA 18, 69, 114;
YAW

Welsh, Irvine 1958- .... **CLC 144**
See also CA 173

Welty, Eudora (Alice) 1909-2001 .. **CLC 1, 2,
5, 14, 22, 33, 105; SSC 1, 27, 51; WLC**
See also AMW; AMWR 1; BPFB 3; CA
9-12R; 199; CABS 1; CANR 32, 65;
CDALB 1941-1968; CN 7; CSW; DA;
DA3; DAB; DAC; DAM MST, NOV;
DLB 2, 102, 143; DLBD 12; DLBY 1987,
2001; EXPS; HGG; LAIT 3; MAWW;
MTCW 1, 2; NFS 13; RGAL 4; RGSF 2;
RHW; SSFS 2, 10

Wen I-to 1899-1946 .... **TCLC 28**

Wentworth, Robert
See Hamilton, Edmond

Werfel, Franz (Viktor) 1890-1945 ... **TCLC 8**
See also CA 104; 161; DLB 81, 124;
RGWL 2

Wergeland, Henrik Arnold
1808-1845 .... **NCLC 5**

Wersba, Barbara 1932- .... **CLC 30**
See also AAYA 2, 30; BYA 6, 12, 13; CA
29-32R; 182; CAAE 182; CANR 16, 38;
CLR 3, 78; DLB 52; JRDA; MAICYA 1,
2; SAAS 2; SATA 1, 58; SATA-Essay 103;
WYA; YAW

Wertmueller, Lina 1928- .... **CLC 16**
See also CA 97-100; CANR 39, 78

Wescott, Glenway 1901-1987 .. **CLC 13; SSC
35**
See also CA 13-16R; 121; CANR 23, 70;
DLB 4, 9, 102; RGAL 4

Wesker, Arnold 1932- .... **CLC 3, 5, 42**
See also CA 1-4R; CAAS 7; CANR 1, 33;
CBD; CD 5; CDBLB 1960 to Present;
DAB; DAM DRAM; DLB 13; MTCW 1;
RGEL 2

Wesley, Richard (Errol) 1945- .... **CLC 7**
See also BW 1; CA 57-60; CAD; CANR
27; CD 5; DLB 38

Wessel, Johan Herman 1742-1785 .... **LC 7**

West, Anthony (Panther)
1914-1987 .... **CLC 50**
See also CA 45-48; 124; CANR 3, 19; DLB
15

West, C. P.
See Wodehouse, P(elham) G(renville)

West, Cornel (Ronald) 1953- .... **CLC 134;
BLCS**
See also CA 144; CANR 91; DLB 246

West, Delno C(loyde), Jr. 1936- .... **CLC 70**
See also CA 57-60

West, Dorothy 1907-1998 .... **TCLC 108**
See also BW 2; CA 143; 169; DLB 76

West, (Mary) Jessamyn 1902-1984 ... **CLC 7,
17**
See also CA 9-12R; 112; CANR 27; DLB
6; DLBY 1984; MTCW 1, 2; RHW;
SATA-Obit 37; YAW

West, Morris L(anglo) 1916-1999 ..... **CLC 6,
33**
See also BPFB 3; CA 5-8R; 187; CANR
24, 49, 64; CN 7; CPW; MTCW 1, 2

West, Nathanael 1903-1940 .... **TCLC 1, 14,
44; SSC 16**
See also AMW; BPFB 3; CA 104; 125;
CDALB 1929-1941; DA3; DLB 4, 9, 28;
MTCW 1, 2; RGAL 4

West, Owen
See Koontz, Dean R(ay)

West, Paul 1930- .... **CLC 7, 14, 96**
See also CA 13-16R; CAAS 7; CANR 22,
53, 76, 89; CN 7; DLB 14; INT CANR-
22; MTCW 2

West, Rebecca 1892-1983 ... **CLC 7, 9, 31, 50**
See also BPFB 3; BRWS 3; CA 5-8R; 109;
CANR 19; DLB 36; DLBY 1983; FW;
MTCW 1, 2; RGEL 2

Westall, Robert (Atkinson)
1929-1993 .... **CLC 17**
See also AAYA 12; BYA 2, 6, 7, 8, 9; CA
69-72; 141; CANR 18, 68; CLR 13;
FANT; JRDA; MAICYA 1, 2; MAICYAS
1; SAAS 2; SATA 23, 69; SATA-Obit 75;
WYA; YAW

Westermarck, Edward 1862-1939 . **TCLC 87**

Westlake, Donald E(dwin) 1933- . **CLC 7, 33**
See also BPFB 3; CA 17-20R; CAAS 13;
CANR 16, 44, 65, 94; CMW 4; CPW;
DAM POP; INT CANR-16; MSW;
MTCW 2

Westmacott, Mary
See Christie, Agatha (Mary Clarissa)

Weston, Allen
See Norton, Andre

Wetcheek, J. L.
See Feuchtwanger, Lion

Wetering, Janwillem van de
See van de Wetering, Janwillem

Wetherald, Agnes Ethelwyn
1857-1940 .... **TCLC 81**
See also DLB 99

Wetherell, Elizabeth
See Warner, Susan (Bogert)

Whale, James 1889-1957 .... **TCLC 63**

Whalen, Philip 1923- .... **CLC 6, 29**
See also CA 9-12R; CANR 5, 39; CP 7;
DLB 16; WP

Wharton, Edith (Newbold Jones)
1862-1937 ... **TCLC 3, 9, 27, 53; SSC 6;
WLC**
See also AAYA 25; AMW; AMWR 1; BPFB
3; CA 104; 132; CDALB 1865-1917; DA;
DA3; DAB; DAC; DAM MST, NOV;
DLB 4, 9, 12, 78, 189; DLBD 13; EXPS;
HGG; LAIT 2, 3; MAWW; MTCW 1, 2;
NFS 5, 11; RGAL 4; RGSF 2; RHW;
SSFS 6, 7; SUFW

Wharton, James
See Mencken, H(enry) L(ouis)

Wharton, William (a pseudonym) . **CLC 18,
37**
See also CA 93-96; DLBY 1980; INT 93-96

Wheatley (Peters), Phillis
1753(?)-1784 .. **LC 3, 50; BLC 3; PC 3;
WLC**
See also AFAW 1; CDALB 1640-1865;
DA; DA3; DAC; DAM MST, MULT,
POET; DLB 31, 50; EXPP; PFS 13;
RGAL 4

Wheelock, John Hall 1886-1978 .... **CLC 14**
See also CA 13-16R; 77-80; CANR 14;
DLB 45

White, Babington
See Braddon, Mary Elizabeth

White, E(lwyn) B(rooks)
1899-1985 .... **CLC 10, 34, 39**
See also AITN 2; AMWS 1; CA 13-16R;
116; CANR 16, 37; CDALBS; CLR 1, 21;
CPW; DA3; DAM POP; DLB 11, 22;
FANT; MAICYA 1, 2; MTCW 1, 2;
RGAL 4; SATA 2, 29, 100; SATA-Obit 44

White, Edmund (Valentine III)
1940- .... **CLC 27, 110**
See also AAYA 7; CA 45-48; CANR 3, 19,
36, 62, 107; CN 7; DA3; DAM POP; DLB
227; MTCW 1, 2

White, Hayden V. 1928- .... **CLC 148**
See also CA 128; DLB 246

White, Patrick (Victor Martindale)
1912-1990 ...... **CLC 3, 4, 5, 7, 9, 18, 65,
69; SSC 39**
See also BRWS 1; CA 81-84; 132; CANR
43; MTCW 1; RGEL 2; RGSF 2; RHW

White, Phyllis Dorothy James 1920-
See James, P. D.
See also CA 21-24R; CANR 17, 43, 65;
CMW 4; CN 7; CPW; DA3; DAM POP;
MTCW 1, 2

White, T(erence) H(anbury)
1906-1964 .... **CLC 30**
See also AAYA 22; BPFB 3; BYA 4, 5; CA
73-76; CANR 37; DLB 160; FANT;
JRDA; LAIT 1; MAICYA 1, 2; RGEL 2;
SATA 12; SUFW; YAW

White, Terence de Vere 1912-1994 ... **CLC 49**
See also CA 49-52; 145; CANR 3

White, Walter
See White, Walter F(rancis)

White, Walter F(rancis)
1893-1955 .... **TCLC 15; BLC 3**
See also BW 1; CA 115; 124; DAM MULT;
DLB 51

White, William Hale 1831-1913
See Rutherford, Mark
See also CA 121; 189

Whitehead, Alfred North
1861-1947 .... **TCLC 97**
See also CA 117; 165; DLB 100

Whitehead, E(dward) A(nthony)
1933- .... **CLC 5**
See also CA 65-68; CANR 58; CBD; CD 5

Whitehead, Ted
See Whitehead, E(dward) A(nthony)

Whitemore, Hugh (John) 1936- .... **CLC 37**
See also CA 132; CANR 77; CBD; CD 5;
INT CA-132

Whitman, Sarah Helen (Power)
1803-1878 .... **NCLC 19**
See also DLB 1, 243

Whitman, Walt(er) 1819-1892 .. **NCLC 4, 31,
81; PC 3; WLC**
See also AAYA 42; AMW; AMWR 1;
CDALB 1640-1865; DA; DA3; DAB;
DAC; DAM MST, POET; DLB 3, 64,
224, 250; EXPP; LAIT 2; PAB; PFS 2, 3,
13; RGAL 4; SATA 20; WP; WYAS 1

Whitney, Phyllis A(yame) 1903- .... **CLC 42**
See also AAYA 36; AITN 2; BEST 90:3;
CA 1-4R; CANR 3, 25, 38, 60; CLR 59;
CMW 4; CPW; DA3; DAM POP; JRDA;
MAICYA 1, 2; MTCW 2; RHW; SATA 1,
30; YAW

Whittemore, (Edward) Reed (Jr.)
1919- .... **CLC 4**
See also CA 9-12R; CAAS 8; CANR 4; CP
7; DLB 5

Whittier, John Greenleaf
1807-1892 .... **NCLC 8, 59**
See also AMWS 1; DLB 1, 243; RGAL 4

Whittlebot, Hernia
See Coward, Noel (Peirce)

Wicker, Thomas Grey 1926-
See Wicker, Tom
See also CA 65-68; CANR 21, 46

Wicker, Tom .... **CLC 7**
See also Wicker, Thomas Grey

Wideman, John Edgar 1941- ...... **CLC 5, 34,
36, 67, 122; BLC 3**
See also AFAW 1, 2; AMWS 10; BPFB 4;
BW 2, 3; CA 85-88; CANR 14, 42, 67,
109; CN 7; DAM MULT; DLB 33, 143;
MTCW 2; RGAL 4; RGSF 2; SSFS 6, 12

Wiebe, Rudy (Henry) 1934- .. **CLC 6, 11, 14,
138**
See also CA 37-40R; CANR 42, 67; CN 7;
DAC; DAM MST; DLB 60; RHW

Wieland, Christoph Martin
1733-1813 .... **NCLC 17**
See also DLB 97; EW 4; RGWL 2

Wiene, Robert 1881-1938 .... **TCLC 56**

Wieners, John 1934- .... **CLC 7**
See also CA 13-16R; CP 7; DLB 16; WP

Wiesel, Elie(zer) 1928- .... **CLC 3, 5, 11, 37;
WLCS**
See also AAYA 7; AITN 1; CA 5-8R; CAAS
4; CANR 8, 40, 65; CDALBS; DA; DA3;
DAB; DAC; DAM MST, NOV; DLB 83;
DLBY 1987; INT CANR-8; LAIT 4;
MTCW 1, 2; NFS 4; SATA 56; YAW

Wiggins, Marianne 1947- .... **CLC 57**
See also BEST 89:3; CA 130; CANR 60

Wiggs, Susan .... **CLC 70**
See also CA 201

Wight, James Alfred 1916-1995
See Herriot, James
See also CA 77-80; SATA 55; SATA-Brief
44

Wilbur, Richard (Purdy) 1921- ..... **CLC 3, 6,
9, 14, 53, 110**
See also AMWS 3; CA 1-4R; CABS 2;
CANR 2, 29, 76, 93; CDALBS; CP 7;
DA; DAB; DAC; DAM MST, POET;
DLB 5, 169; EXPP; INT CANR-29;
MTCW 1, 2; PAB; PFS 11, 12; RGAL 4;
SATA 9, 108; WP

Wild, Peter 1940- .... **CLC 14**
See also CA 37-40R; CP 7; DLB 5

Wilde, Oscar (Fingal O'Flahertie Wills)
1854(?)-1900 ... **TCLC 1, 8, 23, 41; DC
17; SSC 11; WLC**
See also BRW 5; BRWR 2; CA 104; 119;
CDBLB 1890-1914; DA; DA3; DAB;
DAC; DAM DRAM, MST, NOV; DFS 4,
8, 9; DLB 10, 19, 34, 57, 141, 156, 190;
EXPS; FANT; RGEL 2; RGSF 2; SATA
24; SSFS 7; SUFW; TEA; WCH; WLIT 4

Wilder, Billy .... **CLC 20**
See also Wilder, Samuel
See also DLB 26

Wilder, Samuel 1906-2002
See Wilder, Billy
See also CA 89-92

Wilder, Stephen
See Marlowe, Stephen

Wilder, Thornton (Niven)
1897-1975 .. **CLC 1, 5, 6, 10, 15, 35, 82;
DC 1; WLC**
See also AAYA 29; AITN 2; AMW; CA 13-
16R; 61-64; CAD; CANR 40; CDALBS;
DA; DA3; DAB; DAC; DAM DRAM,
MST, NOV; DFS 1, 4; DLB 4, 7, 9, 228;
DLBY 1997; LAIT 3; MTCW 1, 2; RGAL
4; RHW; WYAS 1

Wilding, Michael 1942- ...... **CLC 73; SSC 50**
See also CA 104; CANR 24, 49, 106; CN
7; RGSF 2

Wiley, Richard 1944- .... **CLC 44**
See also CA 121; 129; CANR 71

Wilhelm, Kate .... **CLC 7**
See also Wilhelm, Katie (Gertrude)
See also AAYA 20; CAAS 5; DLB 8; INT
CANR-17; SCFW 2

Wilhelm, Katie (Gertrude) 1928-
See Wilhelm, Kate
See also CA 37-40R; CANR 17, 36, 60, 94;
MTCW 1; SFW 4

Wilkins, Mary
See Freeman, Mary E(leanor) Wilkins

Willard, Nancy 1936- .... **CLC 7, 37**
See also BYA 5; CA 89-92; CANR 10, 39,
68, 107; CLR 5; CWP; CWRI 5; DLB 5,
52; FANT; MAICYA 1, 2; MTCW 1;
SATA 37, 71, 127; SATA-Brief 30

William of Ockham 1290-1349 ..... **CMLC 32**

Williams, Ben Ames 1889-1953 ..... **TCLC 89**
See also CA 183; DLB 102

Williams, C(harles) K(enneth)
1936- .... **CLC 33, 56, 148**
See also CA 37-40R; CAAS 26; CANR 57,
106; CP 7; DAM POET; DLB 5

Williams, Charles
See Collier, James Lincoln

Williams, Charles (Walter Stansby)
1886-1945 .... **TCLC 1, 11**
See also CA 104; 163; DLB 100, 153, 255;
FANT; RGEL 2; SUFW

Williams, (George) Emlyn
1905-1987 .... **CLC 15**
See also CA 104; 123; CANR 36; DAM
DRAM; DLB 10, 77; MTCW 1

Williams, Hank 1923-1953 .... **TCLC 81**

Williams, Hugo 1942- .... **CLC 42**
See also CA 17-20R; CANR 45; CP 7; DLB
40

Williams, J. Walker
See Wodehouse, P(elham) G(renville)

Williams, John A(lfred) 1925- ..... **CLC 5, 13;
BLC 3**
See also AFAW 2; BW 2, 3; CA 53-56;
CAAE 195; CAAS 3; CANR 6, 26, 51;
CN 7; CSW; DAM MULT; DLB 2, 33;
INT CANR-6; RGAL 4; SFW 4

Williams, Jonathan (Chamberlain)
1929- .... **CLC 13**
See also CA 9-12R; CAAS 12; CANR 8,
108; CP 7; DLB 5

Williams, Joy 1944- .... **CLC 31**
See also CA 41-44R; CANR 22, 48, 97

Williams, Norman 1952- .... **CLC 39**
See also CA 118

Williams, Sherley Anne 1944-1999 . **CLC 89;
BLC 3**
See also AFAW 2; BW 2, 3; CA 73-76; 185;
CANR 25, 82; DAM MULT, POET; DLB
41; INT CANR-25; SATA 78; SATA-Obit
116

Williams, Shirley
See Williams, Sherley Anne

Williams, Tennessee 1911-1983 . **CLC 1, 2, 5,
7, 8, 11, 15, 19, 30, 39, 45, 71, 111; DC
4; WLC**
See also AAYA 31; AITN 1, 2; AMW; CA
5-8R; 108; CABS 3; CAD; CANR 31;
CDALB 1941-1968; DA; DA3; DAB;
DAC; DAM DRAM, MST; DFS 1, 3, 7,
12; DLB 7; DLBD 4; DLBY 1983; GLL
1; LAIT 4; MTCW 1, 2; RGAL 4

Williams, Thomas (Alonzo)
1926-1990 .... **CLC 14**
See also CA 1-4R; 132; CANR 2

Williams, William C.
See Williams, William Carlos

Williams, William Carlos
1883-1963 .... **CLC 1, 2, 5, 9, 13, 22, 42,
67; PC 7; SSC 31**
See also AMW; AMWR 1; CA 89-92;
CANR 34; CDALB 1917-1929; DA;
DA3; DAB; DAC; DAM MST, POET;
DLB 4, 16, 54, 86; EXPP; MTCW 1, 2;
PAB; PFS 1, 6, 11; RGAL 4; RGSF 2;
WP

Williamson, David (Keith) 1942- ..... **CLC 56**
See also CA 103; CANR 41; CD 5

Williamson, Ellen Douglas 1905-1984
See Douglas, Ellen
See also CA 17-20R; 114; CANR 39

Williamson, Jack .... **CLC 29**
See also Williamson, John Stewart
See also CAAS 8; DLB 8; SCFW 2

Williamson, John Stewart 1908-
See Williamson, Jack
See also CA 17-20R; CANR 23, 70; SFW 4

Willie, Frederick
See Lovecraft, H(oward) P(hillips)

Willingham, Calder (Baynard, Jr.)
1922-1995 .... **CLC 5, 51**
See also CA 5-8R; 147; CANR 3; CSW;
DLB 2, 44; IDFW 3, 4; MTCW 1

Willis, Charles
See Clarke, Arthur C(harles)

Willy
See Colette, (Sidonie-Gabrielle)
Willy, Colette
See Colette, (Sidonie-Gabrielle)
See also GLL 1
Wilmot, John 1647-1680 .... **LC 75**
See also Rochester
See also BRW 2; DLB 131; PAB
Wilson, A(ndrew) N(orman) 1950- .. **CLC 33**
See also BRWS 6; CA 112; 122; CN 7;
DLB 14, 155, 194; MTCW 2
Wilson, Angus (Frank Johnstone)
1913-1991 . **CLC 2, 3, 5, 25, 34; SSC 21**
See also BRWS 1; CA 5-8R; 134; CANR
21; DLB 15, 139, 155; MTCW 1, 2;
RGEL 2; RGSF 2
Wilson, August 1945- ... **CLC 39, 50, 63, 118;**
BLC 3; DC 2; WLCS
See also AAYA 16; AFAW 2; AMWS 8; BW
2, 3; CA 115; 122; CAD; CANR 42, 54,
76; CD 5; DA; DA3; DAB; DAC; DAM
DRAM, MST, MULT; DFS 3, 7; DLB
228; LAIT 4; MTCW 1, 2; RGAL 4
Wilson, Brian 1942- .... **CLC 12**
Wilson, Colin 1931- .... **CLC 3, 14**
See also CA 1-4R; CAAS 5; CANR 1, 22,
33, 77; CMW 4; CN 7; DLB 14, 194;
HGG; MTCW 1; SFW 4
Wilson, Dirk
See Pohl, Frederik
Wilson, Edmund 1895-1972 .. **CLC 1, 2, 3, 8,**
24
See also AMW; CA 1-4R; 37-40R; CANR
1, 46; DLB 63; MTCW 1, 2; RGAL 4
Wilson, Ethel Davis (Bryant)
1888(?)-1980 .... **CLC 13**
See also CA 102; DAC; DAM POET; DLB
68; MTCW 1; RGEL 2
Wilson, Harriet
See Wilson, Harriet E. Adams
See also DLB 239
Wilson, Harriet E. Adams
1827(?)-1863(?) .... **NCLC 78; BLC 3**
See also Wilson, Harriet
See also DAM MULT; DLB 50, 243
Wilson, John 1785-1854 .... **NCLC 5**
Wilson, John (Anthony) Burgess 1917-1993
See Burgess, Anthony
See also CA 1-4R; 143; CANR 2, 46; DA3;
DAC; DAM NOV; MTCW 1, 2
Wilson, Lanford 1937- .... **CLC 7, 14, 36**
See also CA 17-20R; CABS 3; CAD; CANR
45, 96; CD 5; DAM DRAM; DFS 4, 9,
12; DLB 7
Wilson, Robert M. 1944- .... **CLC 7, 9**
See also CA 49-52; CAD; CANR 2, 41; CD
5; MTCW 1
Wilson, Robert McLiam 1964- .... **CLC 59**
See also CA 132
Wilson, Sloan 1920- .... **CLC 32**
See also CA 1-4R; CANR 1, 44; CN 7
Wilson, Snoo 1948- .... **CLC 33**
See also CA 69-72; CBD; CD 5
Wilson, William S(mith) 1932- .... **CLC 49**
See also CA 81-84
Wilson, (Thomas) Woodrow
1856-1924 .... **TCLC 79**
See also CA 166; DLB 47
Wilson and Warnke eds. .... **CLC 65**
Winchilsea, Anne (Kingsmill) Finch
1661-1720
See Finch, Anne
See also RGEL 2
Windham, Basil
See Wodehouse, P(elham) G(renville)
Wingrove, David (John) 1954- .... **CLC 68**
See also CA 133; SFW 4

Winnemucca, Sarah 1844-1891 ..... **NCLC 79**
See also DAM MULT; DLB 175; NNAL;
RGAL 4
Winstanley, Gerrard 1609-1676 .... **LC 52**
Wintergreen, Jane
See Duncan, Sara Jeannette
Winters, Janet Lewis .... **CLC 41**
See also Lewis, Janet
See also DLBY 1987
Winters, (Arthur) Yvor 1900-1968 .... **CLC 4,**
8, 32
See also AMWS 2; CA 11-12; 25-28R; CAP
1; DLB 48; MTCW 1; RGAL 4
Winterson, Jeanette 1959- .... **CLC 64, 158**
See also BRWS 4; CA 136; CANR 58; CN
7; CPW; DA3; DAM POP; DLB 207;
FANT; FW; GLL 1; MTCW 2; RHW
Winthrop, John 1588-1649 .... **LC 31**
See also DLB 24, 30
Wirth, Louis 1897-1952 .... **TCLC 92**
Wiseman, Frederick 1930- .... **CLC 20**
See also CA 159
Wister, Owen 1860-1938 .... **TCLC 21**
See also BPFB 3; CA 108; 162; DLB 9, 78,
186; RGAL 4; SATA 62; TCWW 2
Witkacy
See Witkiewicz, Stanislaw Ignacy
Witkiewicz, Stanislaw Ignacy
1885-1939 .... **TCLC 8**
See also CA 105; 162; CDWLB 4; DLB
215; EW 10; RGWL 2; SFW 4
Wittgenstein, Ludwig (Josef Johann)
1889-1951 .... **TCLC 59**
See also CA 113; 164; MTCW 2
Wittig, Monique 1935(?)- .... **CLC 22**
See also CA 116; 135; CWW 2; DLB 83;
FW; GLL 1
Wittlin, Jozef 1896-1976 .... **CLC 25**
See also CA 49-52; 65-68; CANR 3
Wodehouse, P(elham) G(renville)
1881-1975 ... **CLC 1, 2, 5, 10, 22; SSC 2**
See also AITN 2; BRWS 3; CA 45-48; 57-
60; CANR 3, 33; CDBLB 1914-1945;
CPW 1; DA3; DAB; DAC; DAM NOV;
DLB 34, 162; MTCW 1, 2; RGEL 2;
RGSF 2; SATA 22; SSFS 10; TCLC 108
Woiwode, L.
See Woiwode, Larry (Alfred)
Woiwode, Larry (Alfred) 1941- ... **CLC 6, 10**
See also CA 73-76; CANR 16, 94; CN 7;
DLB 6; INT CANR-16
Wojciechowska, Maia (Teresa)
1927- .... **CLC 26**
See also AAYA 8; BYA 3; CA 9-12R, 183;
CAAE 183; CANR 4, 41; CLR 1; JRDA;
MAICYA 1, 2; SAAS 1; SATA 1, 28, 83;
SATA-Essay 104; YAW
Wojtyla, Karol
See John Paul II, Pope
Wolf, Christa 1929- .... **CLC 14, 29, 58, 150**
See also CA 85-88; CANR 45; CDWLB 2;
CWW 2; DLB 75; FW; MTCW 1; RGWL
2; SSFS 14
Wolf, Naomi 1962- .... **CLC 157**
See also CA 141; FW
Wolfe, Gene (Rodman) 1931- .... **CLC 25**
See also AAYA 35; CA 57-60; CAAS 9;
CANR 6, 32, 60; CPW; DAM POP; DLB
8; FANT; MTCW 2; SATA 118; SCFW 2;
SFW 4
Wolfe, George C. 1954- .... **CLC 49; BLCS**
See also CA 149; CAD; CD 5
Wolfe, Thomas (Clayton)
1900-1938 ...... **TCLC 4, 13, 29, 61; SSC**
33; WLC
See also AMW; BPFB 3; CA 104; 132;
CANR 102; CDALB 1929-1941; DA;
DA3; DAB; DAC; DAM MST, NOV;
DLB 9, 102, 229; DLBD 2, 16; DLBY
1985, 1997; MTCW 1, 2; RGAL 4

Wolfe, Thomas Kennerly, Jr.
1930- .... **CLC 147**
See also Wolfe, Tom
See also CA 13-16R; CANR 9, 33, 70, 104;
DA3; DAM POP; DLB 185; INT
CANR-9; MTCW 1, 2; TUS
Wolfe, Tom .... **CLC 1, 2, 9, 15, 35, 51**
See also Wolfe, Thomas Kennerly, Jr.
See also AAYA 8; AITN 2; AMWS 3; BEST
89:1; BPFB 3; CN 7; CPW; CSW; DLB
152; LAIT 5; RGAL 4
Wolff, Geoffrey (Ansell) 1937- .... **CLC 41**
See also CA 29-32R; CANR 29, 43, 78
Wolff, Sonia
See Levitin, Sonia (Wolff)
Wolff, Tobias (Jonathan Ansell)
1945- .... **CLC 39, 64**
See also AAYA 16; AMWS 7; BEST 90:2;
BYA 12; CA 114; 117; CAAS 22; CANR
54, 76, 96; CN 7; CSW; DA3; DLB 130;
INT CA-117; MTCW 2; RGAL 4; RGSF
2; SSFS 4, 11
Wolfram von Eschenbach c. 1170-c.
1220 .... **CMLC 5**
See also CDWLB 2; DLB 138; EW 1;
RGWL 2
Wolitzer, Hilma 1930- .... **CLC 17**
See also CA 65-68; CANR 18, 40; INT
CANR-18; SATA 31; YAW
Wollstonecraft, Mary 1759-1797 ..... **LC 5, 50**
See also BRWS 3; CDBLB 1789-1832;
DLB 39, 104, 158, 252; FW; LAIT 1;
RGEL 2; WLIT 3
Wonder, Stevie .... **CLC 12**
See also Morris, Steveland Judkins
Wong, Jade Snow 1922- .... **CLC 17**
See also CA 109; CANR 91; SATA 112
Woodberry, George Edward
1855-1930 .... **TCLC 73**
See also CA 165; DLB 71, 103
Woodcott, Keith
See Brunner, John (Kilian Houston)
Woodruff, Robert W.
See Mencken, H(enry) L(ouis)
Woolf, (Adeline) Virginia
1882-1941 .. **TCLC 1, 5, 20, 43, 56, 101;**
SSC 7; WLC
See also BPFB 3; BRW 7; BRWR 1; CA
104; 130; CANR 64; CDBLB 1914-1945;
DA; DA3; DAB; DAC; DAM MST, NOV;
DLB 36, 100, 162; DLBD 10; EXPS; FW;
LAIT 3; MTCW 1, 2; NCFS 2; NFS 8,
12; RGEL 2; RGSF 2; SSFS 4, 12; WLIT
4
Woollcott, Alexander (Humphreys)
1887-1943 .... **TCLC 5**
See also CA 105; 161; DLB 29
Woolrich, Cornell .... **CLC 77**
See also Hopley-Woolrich, Cornell George
See also MSW
Woolson, Constance Fenimore
1840-1894 .... **NCLC 82**
See also DLB 12, 74, 189, 221; RGAL 4
Wordsworth, Dorothy 1771-1855 .. **NCLC 25**
See also DLB 107
Wordsworth, William 1770-1850 .. **NCLC 12,**
38, 111; PC 4; WLC
See also BRW 4; CDBLB 1789-1832; DA;
DA3; DAB; DAC; DAM MST, POET;
DLB 93, 107; EXPP; PAB; PFS 2; RGEL
2; WLIT 3; WP
Wotton, Sir Henry 1568-1639 .... **LC 68**
See also DLB 121; RGEL 2
Wouk, Herman 1915- .... **CLC 1, 9, 38**
See also BPFB 2, 3; CA 5-8R; CANR 6,
33, 67; CDALBS; CN 7; CPW; DA3;
DAM NOV, POP; DLBY 1982; INT
CANR-6; LAIT 4; MTCW 1, 2; NFS 7

Wright, Charles (Penzel, Jr.) 1935- .. **CLC 6, 13, 28, 119, 146**
See also AMWS 5; CA 29-32R; CAAS 7; CANR 23, 36, 62, 88; CP 7; DLB 165; DLBY 1982; MTCW 1, 2; PFS 10

Wright, Charles Stevenson 1932- ... **CLC 49; BLC 3**
See also BW 1; CA 9-12R; CANR 26; CN 7; DAM MULT, POET; DLB 33

Wright, Frances 1795-1852 .... **NCLC 74**
See also DLB 73

Wright, Frank Lloyd 1867-1959 .... **TCLC 95**
See also AAYA 33; CA 174

Wright, Jack R.
See Harris, Mark

Wright, James (Arlington)
1927-1980 .... **CLC 3, 5, 10, 28; PC 36**
See also AITN 2; AMWS 3; CA 49-52; 97-100; CANR 4, 34, 64; CDALBS; DAM POET; DLB 5, 169; EXPP; MTCW 1, 2; PFS 7, 8; RGAL 4; WP

Wright, Judith (Arundell)
1915-2000 .... **CLC 11, 53; PC 14**
See also CA 13-16R; 188; CANR 31, 76, 93; CP 7; CWP; MTCW 1, 2; PFS 8; RGEL 2; SATA 14; SATA-Obit 121

Wright, L(aurali) R. 1939- .... **CLC 44**
See also CA 138; CMW 4

Wright, Richard (Nathaniel)
1908-1960 .... **CLC 1, 3, 4, 9, 14, 21, 48, 74; BLC 3; SSC 2; WLC**
See also AAYA 5, 42; AFAW 1, 2; AMW; BPFB 3; BW 1; BYA 2; CA 108; CANR 64; CDALB 1929-1941; DA; DA3; DAB; DAC; DAM MST, MULT, NOV; DLB 76, 102; DLBD 2; EXPN; LAIT 3, 4; MTCW 1, 2; NCFS 1; NFS 1, 7; RGAL 4; RGSF 2; SSFS 3, 9; YAW

Wright, Richard B(ruce) 1937- .... **CLC 6**
See also CA 85-88; DLB 53

Wright, Rick 1945- .... **CLC 35**

Wright, Rowland
See Wells, Carolyn

Wright, Stephen 1946- .... **CLC 33**

Wright, Willard Huntington 1888-1939
See Van Dine, S. S.
See also CA 115; 189; CMW 4; DLBD 16

Wright, William 1930- .... **CLC 44**
See also CA 53-56; CANR 7, 23

Wroth, Lady Mary 1587-1653(?) .... **LC 30; PC 38**
See also DLB 121

Wu Ch'eng-en 1500(?)-1582(?) .... **LC 7**

Wu Ching-tzu 1701-1754 .... **LC 2**

Wurlitzer, Rudolph 1938(?)- .... **CLC 2, 4, 15**
See also CA 85-88; CN 7; DLB 173

Wyatt, Sir Thomas c. 1503-1542 . **LC 70; PC 27**
See also BRW 1; DLB 132; EXPP; RGEL 2; TEA

Wycherley, William 1640-1716 .... **LC 8, 21**
See also BRW 2; CDBLB 1660-1789; DAM DRAM; DLB 80; RGEL 2

Wylie, Elinor (Morton Hoyt)
1885-1928 .... **TCLC 8; PC 23**
See also AMWS 1; CA 105; 162; DLB 9, 45; EXPP; RGAL 4

Wylie, Philip (Gordon) 1902-1971 ... **CLC 43**
See also CA 21-22; 33-36R; CAP 2; DLB 9; SFW 4

Wyndham, John .... **CLC 19**
See also Harris, John (Wyndham Parkes Lucas) Beynon
See also DLB 255; SCFW 2

Wyss, Johann David Von
1743-1818 .... **NCLC 10**
See also JRDA; MAICYA 1, 2; SATA 29; SATA-Brief 27

Xenophon c. 430B.C.-c. 354B.C. ... **CMLC 17**
See also AW 1; DLB 176; RGWL 2

Yakumo Koizumi
See Hearn, (Patricio) Lafcadio (Tessima Carlos)

Yamamoto, Hisaye 1921- .... **SSC 34; AAL**
See also DAM MULT; LAIT 4; SSFS 14

Yanez, Jose Donoso
See Donoso (Yanez), Jose

Yanovsky, Basile S.
See Yanovsky, V(assily) S(emenovich)

Yanovsky, V(assily) S(emenovich)
1906-1989 .... **CLC 2, 18**
See also CA 97-100; 129

Yates, Richard 1926-1992 .... **CLC 7, 8, 23**
See also CA 5-8R; 139; CANR 10, 43; DLB 2, 234; DLBY 1981, 1992; INT CANR-10

Yeats, W. B.
See Yeats, William Butler

Yeats, William Butler 1865-1939 .... **TCLC 1, 11, 18, 31, 93, 116; PC 20; WLC**
See also BRW 6; BRWR 1; CA 104; 127; CANR 45; CDBLB 1890-1914; DA; DA3; DAB; DAC; DAM DRAM, MST, POET; DLB 10, 19, 98, 156; EXPP; MTCW 1, 2; NCFS 3; PAB; PFS 1, 2, 5, 7, 13; RGEL 2; WLIT 4; WP

Yehoshua, A(braham) B. 1936- .. **CLC 13, 31**
See also CA 33-36R; CANR 43, 90; RGSF 2

Yellow Bird
See Ridge, John Rollin

Yep, Laurence Michael 1948- .... **CLC 35**
See also AAYA 5, 31; BYA 7; CA 49-52; CANR 1, 46, 92; CLR 3, 17, 54; DLB 52; FANT; JRDA; MAICYA 1, 2; MAICYAS 1; SATA 7, 69, 123; WYA; YAW

Yerby, Frank G(arvin) 1916-1991 . **CLC 1, 7, 22; BLC 3**
See also BPFB 3; BW 1, 3; CA 9-12R; 136; CANR 16, 52; DAM MULT; DLB 76; INT CANR-16; MTCW 1; RGAL 4; RHW

Yesenin, Sergei Alexandrovich
See Esenin, Sergei (Alexandrovich)

Yevtushenko, Yevgeny (Alexandrovich)
1933- ...... **CLC 1, 3, 13, 26, 51, 126; PC 40**
See also Evtushenko, Evgenii Aleksandrovich
See also CA 81-84; CANR 33, 54; CWW 2; DAM POET; MTCW 1

Yezierska, Anzia 1885(?)-1970 .... **CLC 46**
See also CA 126; 89-92; DLB 28, 221; FW; MTCW 1; RGAL 4

Yglesias, Helen 1915- .... **CLC 7, 22**
See also CA 37-40R; CAAS 20; CANR 15, 65, 95; CN 7; INT CANR-15; MTCW 1

Yokomitsu, Riichi 1898-1947 .... **TCLC 47**
See also CA 170

Yonge, Charlotte (Mary)
1823-1901 .... **TCLC 48**
See also CA 109; 163; DLB 18, 163; RGEL 2; SATA 17; WCH

York, Jeremy
See Creasey, John

York, Simon
See Heinlein, Robert A(nson)

Yorke, Henry Vincent 1905-1974 ..... **CLC 13**
See also Green, Henry
See also CA 85-88; 49-52

Yosano Akiko 1878-1942 .... **TCLC 59; PC 11**
See also CA 161

Yoshimoto, Banana .... **CLC 84**
See also Yoshimoto, Mahoko
See also NFS 7

Yoshimoto, Mahoko 1964-
See Yoshimoto, Banana
See also CA 144; CANR 98

Young, Al(bert James) 1939- . **CLC 19; BLC 3**
See also BW 2, 3; CA 29-32R; CANR 26, 65, 109; CN 7; CP 7; DAM MULT; DLB 33

Young, Andrew (John) 1885-1971 ...... **CLC 5**
See also CA 5-8R; CANR 7, 29; RGEL 2

Young, Collier
See Bloch, Robert (Albert)

Young, Edward 1683-1765 .... **LC 3, 40**
See also DLB 95; RGEL 2

Young, Marguerite (Vivian)
1909-1995 .... **CLC 82**
See also CA 13-16; 150; CAP 1; CN 7

Young, Neil 1945- .... **CLC 17**
See also CA 110; CCA 1

Young Bear, Ray A. 1950- .... **CLC 94**
See also CA 146; DAM MULT; DLB 175; NNAL

Yourcenar, Marguerite 1903-1987 ... **CLC 19, 38, 50, 87**
See also BPFB 3; CA 69-72; CANR 23, 60, 93; DAM NOV; DLB 72; DLBY 1988; EW 12; GFL 1789 to the Present; GLL 1; MTCW 1, 2; RGWL 2

Yuan, Chu 340(?)B.C.-278(?)B.C. . **CMLC 36**

Yurick, Sol 1925- .... **CLC 6**
See also CA 13-16R; CANR 25; CN 7

Zabolotsky, Nikolai Alekseevich
1903-1958 .... **TCLC 52**
See also CA 116; 164

Zagajewski, Adam 1945- .... **PC 27**
See also CA 186; DLB 232

Zalygin, Sergei -2000 .... **CLC 59**

Zamiatin, Evgenii
See Zamyatin, Evgeny Ivanovich
See also RGSF 2; RGWL 2

Zamiatin, Yevgenii
See Zamyatin, Evgeny Ivanovich

Zamora, Bernice (B. Ortiz) 1938- .. **CLC 89; HLC 2**
See also CA 151; CANR 80; DAM MULT; DLB 82; HW 1, 2

Zamyatin, Evgeny Ivanovich
1884-1937 .... **TCLC 8, 37**
See also Zamiatin, Evgenii
See also CA 105; 166; EW 10; SFW 4

Zangwill, Israel 1864-1926 ... **TCLC 16; SSC 44**
See also CA 109; 167; CMW 4; DLB 10, 135, 197; RGEL 2

Zappa, Francis Vincent, Jr. 1940-1993
See Zappa, Frank
See also CA 108; 143; CANR 57

Zappa, Frank .... **CLC 17**
See also Zappa, Francis Vincent, Jr.

Zaturenska, Marya 1902-1982 ..... **CLC 6, 11**
See also CA 13-16R; 105; CANR 22

Zeami 1363-1443 .... **DC 7**
See also DLB 203; RGWL 2

Zelazny, Roger (Joseph) 1937-1995 . **CLC 21**
See also AAYA 7; BPFB 3; CA 21-24R; 148; CANR 26, 60; CN 7; DLB 8; FANT; MTCW 1, 2; SATA 57; SATA-Brief 39; SCFW; SFW 4; SUFW

Zhdanov, Andrei Alexandrovich
1896-1948 .... **TCLC 18**
See also CA 117; 167

Zhukovsky, Vasilii Andreevich
See Zhukovsky, Vasily (Andreevich)
See also DLB 205

Zhukovsky, Vasily (Andreevich)
1783-1852 .... **NCLC 35**
See also Zhukovsky, Vasilii Andreevich

Ziegenhagen, Eric .... **CLC 55**

Zimmer, Jill Schary
See Robinson, Jill

Zimmerman, Robert
See Dylan, Bob

Zindel, Paul 1936- .... **CLC 6, 26; DC 5**
See also AAYA 2, 37; BYA 2, 3, 8, 11, 14;
CA 73-76; CAD; CANR 31, 65, 108; CD
5; CDALBS; CLR 3, 45; DA; DA3; DAB;
DAC; DAM DRAM, MST, NOV; DFS
12; DLB 7, 52; JRDA; LAIT 5; MAICYA
1, 2; MTCW 1, 2; NFS 14; SATA 16, 58,
102; WYA; YAW

Zinov'Ev, A. A.
See Zinoviev, Alexander (Aleksandrovich)

Zinoviev, Alexander (Aleksandrovich)
1922- .... **CLC 19**
See also CA 116; 133; CAAS 10

Zoilus
See Lovecraft, H(oward) P(hillips)

Zola, Emile (Edouard Charles Antoine)
1840-1902 ...... **TCLC 1, 6, 21, 41; WLC**
See also CA 104; 138; DA; DA3; DAB;
DAC; DAM MST, NOV; DLB 123; EW
7; GFL 1789 to the Present; IDTP; RGWL
2

Zoline, Pamela 1941- .... **CLC 62**
See also CA 161; SFW 4

Zoroaster 628(?)B.C.-551(?)B.C. ... **CMLC 40**

Zorrilla y Moral, Jose 1817-1893 .... **NCLC 6**

Zoshchenko, Mikhail (Mikhailovich)
1895-1958 .... **TCLC 15; SSC 15**
See also CA 115; 160; RGSF 2

Zuckmayer, Carl 1896-1977 .... **CLC 18**
See also CA 69-72; DLB 56, 124; RGWL 2

Zuk, Georges
See Skelton, Robin
See also CCA 1

Zukofsky, Louis 1904-1978 ... **CLC 1, 2, 4, 7,**
11, 18; PC 11
See also AMWS 3; CA 9-12R; 77-80;
CANR 39; DAM POET; DLB 5, 165;
MTCW 1; RGAL 4

Zweig, Paul 1935-1984 .... **CLC 34, 42**
See also CA 85-88; 113

Zweig, Stefan 1881-1942 .... **TCLC 17**
See also CA 112; 170; DLB 81, 118

Zwingli, Huldreich 1484-1531 .... **LC 37**
See also DLB 179

Literary Criticism Series
Cumulative Topic Index

This index lists all topic entries in Gale's *Classical and Medieval Literature Criticism, Contemporary Literary Criticism, Drama Criticism, Literature Criticism from 1400 to 1800, Nineteenth-Century Literature Criticism,* and *Twentieth-Century Literary Criticism.*

The Aesopic Fable LC 51: 1-100
the British Aesopic Fable, 1-54
the Aesopic tradition in non-English-speaking cultures, 55-66
political uses of the Aesopic fable, 67-88
the evolution of the Aesopic fable, 89-99

Age of Johnson LC 15: 1-87
Johnson's London, 3-15
aesthetics of neoclassicism, 15-36
"age of prose and reason," 36-45
clubmen and bluestockings, 45-56
printing technology, 56-62
periodicals: "a map of busy life," 62-74
transition, 74-86

Age of Spenser LC 39: 1-70
overviews and general studies, 2-21
literary style, 22-34
poets and the crown, 34-70

AIDS in Literature CLC 81: 365-416

Alcohol and Literature TCLC 70: 1-58
overview, 2-8
fiction, 8-48
poetry and drama, 48-58

American Abolitionism NCLC 44: 1-73
overviews and general studies, 2-26
abolitionist ideals, 26-46
the literature of abolitionism, 46-72

American Autobiography TCLC 86: 1-115
overviews and general studies, 3-36
American authors and autobiography, 36-82
African-American autobiography, 82-114

American Black Humor Fiction TCLC 54: 1-85
characteristics of black humor, 2-13
origins and development, 13-38
black humor distinguished from related literary trends, 38-60
black humor and society, 60-75
black humor reconsidered, 75-83

American Civil War in Literature NCLC 32: 1-109
overviews and general studies, 2-20
regional perspectives, 20-54
fiction popular during the war, 54-79
the historical novel, 79-108

American Frontier in Literature NCLC 28: 1-103
definitions, 2-12
development, 12-17
nonfiction writing about the frontier, 17-30
frontier fiction, 30-45
frontier protagonists, 45-66
portrayals of Native Americans, 66-86
feminist readings, 86-98
twentieth-century reaction against frontier literature, 98-100

American Humor Writing NCLC 52: 1-59
overviews and general studies, 2-12
the Old Southwest, 12-42
broader impacts, 42-5
women humorists, 45-58

American Mercury, The TCLC 74: 1-80

American Popular Song, Golden Age of TCLC 42: 1-49
background and major figures, 2-34
the lyrics of popular songs, 34-47

American Proletarian Literature TCLC 54: 86-175
overviews and general studies, 87-95
American proletarian literature and the American Communist Party, 95-111
ideology and literary merit, 111-7
novels, 117-36
Gastonia, 136-48
drama, 148-54
journalism, 154-9
proletarian literature in the United States, 159-74

American Romanticism NCLC 44: 74-138
overviews and general studies, 74-84
sociopolitical influences, 84-104
Romanticism and the American frontier, 104-15
thematic concerns, 115-37

American Western Literature TCLC 46: 1-100
definition and development of American Western literature, 2-7
characteristics of the Western novel, 8-23
Westerns as history and fiction, 23-34
critical reception of American Western literature, 34-41
the Western hero, 41-73
women in Western fiction, 73-91
later Western fiction, 91-9

American Writers in Paris TCLC 98: 1-156
overviews and general studies, 2-155

Anarchism NCLC 84: 1-97
overviews and general studies, 2-23
the French anarchist tradition, 23-56
Anglo-American anarchism, 56-68
anarchism: incidents and issues, 68-97

Animals in Literature TCLC 106: 1-120
overviews and general studies, 2-8
animals in American literature, 8-45
animals in Canadian literature, 45-57
animals in European literature, 57-100
animals in Latin American literature, 100-06
animals in women's literature, 106-20

Antebellum South, Literature of the NCLC 112:1-188
overviews, 4-55
culture of the Old South, 55-68
antebellum fiction: pastoral and heroic romance, 68-120
role of women: a subdued rebellion, 120-59
slavery and the slave narrative, 159-85

The Apocalyptic Movement TCLC 106: 121-69

Aristotle CMLC 31:1-397
philosophy, 3-100
poetics, 101-219
rhetoric, 220-301
science, 302-397

Art and Literature TCLC 54: 176-248
overviews and general studies, 176-93
definitions, 193-219
influence of visual arts on literature, 219-31
spatial form in literature, 231-47

Arthurian Literature CMLC 10: 1-127
historical context and literary beginnings, 2-27
development of the legend through Malory, 27-64
development of the legend from Malory to the Victorian Age, 65-81
themes and motifs, 81-95
principal characters, 95-125

Arthurian Revival NCLC 36: 1-77
overviews and general studies, 2-12
Tennyson and his influence, 12-43
other leading figures, 43-73
the Arthurian legend in the visual arts, 73-6

Australian Literature TCLC 50: 1-94
origins and development, 2-21

characteristics of Australian literature, 21-33
historical and critical perspectives, 33-41
poetry, 41-58
fiction, 58-76
drama, 76-82
Aboriginal literature, 82-91

Beat Generation, Literature of the TCLC 42: 50-102
overviews and general studies, 51-9
the Beat generation as a social phenomenon, 59-62
development, 62-5
Beat literature, 66-96
influence, 97-100

The Bell Curve Controversy CLC 91: 281-330

Bildungsroman **in Nineteenth-Century Literature** NCLC 20: 92-168
surveys, 93-113
in Germany, 113-40
in England, 140-56
female *Bildungsroman,* 156-67

Bloomsbury Group TCLC 34: 1-73
history and major figures, 2-13
definitions, 13-7
influences, 17-27
thought, 27-40
prose, 40-52
and literary criticism, 52-4
political ideals, 54-61
response to, 61-71

The Blues in Literature TCLC 82: 1-71

Bly, Robert, *Iron John: A Book about Men and Men's Work* CLC 70: 414-62

The Book of J CLC 65: 289-311

British Ephemeral Literature LC 59: 1-70
overviews and general studies, 1-9
broadside ballads, 10-40
chapbooks, jestbooks, pamphlets, and newspapers, 40-69

Buddhism and Literature TCLC 70: 59-164
eastern literature, 60-113
western literature, 113-63

Businessman in American Literature TCLC 26: 1-48
portrayal of the businessman, 1-32
themes and techniques in business fiction, 32-47

The Calendar LC 55: 1-92
overviews and general studies, 2-19
measuring time, 19-28
calendars and culture, 28-60
calendar reform, 60-92

Catholicism in Nineteenth-Century American Literature NCLC 64: 1-58
3-14
polemical literature, 14-46
Catholicism in literature, 47-57

Celtic Mythology CMLC 26: 1-111
overviews and general studies, 2-22
Celtic myth as literature and history, 22-48
Celtic religion: Druids and divinities, 48-80
Fionn MacCuhaill and the Fenian cycle, 80-111

Celtic Twilight See Irish Literary Renaissance

Chartist Movement and Literature, The NCLC 60: 1-84
overview: nineteenth-century working-class fiction, 2-19
Chartist fiction and poetry, 19-73
the Chartist press, 73-84

Child Labor in Nineteenth-Century Literature NCLC 108: 1-133
overviews, 3-10
climbing boys and chimney sweeps, 10-16
the international traffic in children, 16-45
critics and reformers, 45-82
fictional representations of child laborers, 83-132

Children's Literature, Nineteenth-Century NCLC 52: 60-135
overviews and general studies, 61-72
moral tales, 72-89
fairy tales and fantasy, 90-119
making men/making women, 119-34

Christianity in Twentieth-Century Literature TCLC 110: 1-79
overviews and general studies, 2-31
Christianity in twentieth-century fiction, 31-78

The City and Literature TCLC 90: 1-124
overviews and general studies, 2-9
the city in American literature, 9-86
the city in European literature, 86-124

Civic Critics, Russian NCLC 20: 402-46
principal figures and background, 402-9
and Russian Nihilism, 410-6
aesthetic and critical views, 416-45

The Cockney School NCLC 68: 1-64
overview, 2-7
Blackwood's Magazine and the contemporary critical response, 7-24
the political and social import of the Cockneys and their critics, 24-63

Colonial America: The Intellectual Background LC 25: 1-98
overviews and general studies, 2-17
philosophy and politics, 17-31
early religious influences in Colonial America, 31-60
consequences of the Revolution, 60-78
religious influences in post-revolutionary America, 78-87
colonial literary genres, 87-97

Colonialism in Victorian English Literature NCLC 56: 1-77
overviews and general studies, 2-34
colonialism and gender, 34-51
monsters and the occult, 51-76

Columbus, Christopher, Books on the Quincentennial of His Arrival in the New World CLC 70: 329-60

Comic Books TCLC 66: 1-139
historical and critical perspectives, 2-48
superheroes, 48-67
underground comix, 67-88
comic books and society, 88-122
adult comics and graphic novels, 122-36

Connecticut Wits NCLC 48: 1-95
overviews and general studies, 2-40
major works, 40-76
intellectual context, 76-95

Crime in Literature TCLC 54: 249-307
evolution of the criminal figure in literature, 250-61
crime and society, 261-77
literary perspectives on crime and punishment, 277-88
writings by criminals, 288-306

The Crusades CMLC 38: 1-144
history of the Crusades, 3-60
literature of the Crusades, 60-116
the Crusades and the people: attitudes and influences, 116-44

Cyberpunk TCLC 106: 170-366

overviews and general studies, 171-88
feminism and cyberpunk, 188-230
history and cyberpunk, 230-70
sexuality and cyberpunk, 270-98
social issues and cyberpunk, 299-366

Czechoslovakian Literature of the Twentieth Century TCLC 42:103-96
through World War II, 104-35
de-Stalinization, the Prague Spring, and contemporary literature, 135-72
Slovak literature, 172-85
Czech science fiction, 185-93

Dadaism TCLC 46: 101-71
background and major figures, 102-16
definitions, 116-26
manifestos and commentary by Dadaists, 126-40
theater and film, 140-58
nature and characteristics of Dadaist writing, 158-70

Darwinism and Literature NCLC 32: 110-206
background, 110-31
direct responses to Darwin, 131-71
collateral effects of Darwinism, 171-205

Death in American Literature NCLC 92: 1-170
overviews and general studies, 2-32
death in the works of Emily Dickinson, 32-72
death in the works of Herman Melville, 72-101
death in the works of Edgar Allan Poe, 101-43
death in the works of Walt Whitman, 143-70

Death in Nineteenth-Century British Literature NCLC 68: 65-142
overviews and general studies, 66-92
responses to death, 92-102
feminist perspectives, 103-17
striving for immortality, 117-41

Death in Literature TCLC 78:1-183
fiction, 2-115
poetry, 115-46
drama, 146-81

de Man, Paul, Wartime Journalism of CLC 55: 382-424

Detective Fiction, Nineteenth-Century NCLC 36: 78-148
origins of the genre, 79-100
history of nineteenth-century detective fiction, 101-33
significance of nineteenth-century detective fiction, 133-46

Detective Fiction, Twentieth-Century TCLC 38: 1-96
genesis and history of the detective story, 3-22
defining detective fiction, 22-32
evolution and varieties, 32-77
the appeal of detective fiction, 77-90

Dime Novels NCLC 84: 98-168
overviews and general studies, 99-123
popular characters, 123-39
major figures and influences, 139-52
socio-political concerns, 152-167

Disease and Literature TCLC 66: 140-283
overviews and general studies, 141-65
disease in nineteenth-century literature, 165-81
tuberculosis and literature, 181-94
women and disease in literature, 194-221
plague literature, 221-53
AIDS in literature, 253-82

El Dorado, The Legend of See Legend of El Dorado, The

The Double in Nineteenth-Century Litera-ture NCLC 40: 1-95
genesis and development of the theme, 2-15
the double and Romanticism, 16-27
sociological views, 27-52
psychological interpretations, 52-87
philosophical considerations, 87-95

Dramatic Realism NCLC 44: 139-202
overviews and general studies, 140-50
origins and definitions, 150-66
impact and influence, 166-93
realist drama and tragedy, 193-201

Drugs and Literature TCLC 78: 184-282
overviews and general studies, 185-201
pre-twentieth-century literature, 201-42
twentieth-century literature, 242-82

Eastern Mythology CMLC 26: 112-92
heroes and kings, 113-51
cross-cultural perspective, 151-69
relations to history and society, 169-92

Eighteenth-Century British Periodicals LC 63: 1-123
rise of periodicals, 2-31
impact and influence of periodicals, 31-64
periodicals and society, 64-122

Eighteenth-Century Travel Narratives LC 77: 252-355
overviews and general studies, 254-79
eighteenth-century European travel narra-tives, 279-334
non-European eighteenth-century travel narratives, 334-55

Electronic "Books": Hypertext and Hyper-fiction CLC 86: 367-404
books vs. CD-ROMS, 367-76
hypertext and hyperfiction, 376-95
implications for publishing, libraries, and the public, 395-403

Eliot, T. S., Centenary of Birth CLC 55: 345-75

Elizabethan Drama LC 22: 140-240
origins and influences, 142-67
characteristics and conventions, 167-83
theatrical production, 184-200
histories, 200-12
comedy, 213-20
tragedy, 220-30

Elizabethan Prose Fiction LC 41: 1-70
overviews and general studies, 1-15
origins and influences, 15-43
style and structure, 43-69

Enclosure of the English Common NCLC 88: 1-57
overviews and general studies, 1-12
early reaction to enclosure, 12-23
nineteenth-century reaction to enclosure, 23-56

The Encyclopedists LC 26: 172-253
overviews and general studies, 173-210
intellectual background, 210-32
views on esthetics, 232-41
views on women, 241-52

English Caroline Literature LC 13: 221-307
background, 222-41
evolution and varieties, 241-62
the Cavalier mode, 262-75
court and society, 275-91
politics and religion, 291-306

English Decadent Literature of the 1890s NCLC 28: 104-200
fin de siècle: the Decadent period, 105-19
definitions, 120-37
major figures: "the tragic generation," 137-50

French literature and English literary Decadence, 150-7
themes, 157-61
poetry, 161-82
periodicals, 182-96

English Essay, Rise of the LC 18: 238-308
definitions and origins, 236-54
influence on the essay, 254-69
historical background, 269-78
the essay in the seventeenth century, 279-93
the essay in the eighteenth century, 293-307

English Mystery Cycle Dramas LC 34: 1-88
overviews and general studies, 1-27
the nature of dramatic performances, 27-42
the medieval worldview and the mystery cycles, 43-67
the doctrine of repentance and the mystery cycles, 67-76
the fall from grace in the mystery cycles, 76-88

The English Realist Novel, 1740-1771 LC 51: 102-98
overviews and general studies, 103-22
from Romanticism to Realism, 123-58
women and the novel, 159-175
the novel and other literary forms, 176-197

English Revolution, Literature of the LC 43: 1-58
overviews and general studies, 2-24
pamphlets of the English Revolution, 24-38
political sermons of the English Revolu-tion, 38-48
poetry of the English Revolution, 48-57

English Romantic Hellenism NCLC 68: 143-250
overviews and general studies, 144-69
historical development of English Romantic Hellenism, 169-91
influence of Greek mythology on the Romantics, 191-229
influence of Greek literature, art, and culture on the Romantics, 229-50

English Romantic Poetry NCLC 28: 201-327
overviews and reputation, 202-37
major subjects and themes, 237-67
forms of Romantic poetry, 267-78
politics, society, and Romantic poetry, 278-99
philosophy, religion, and Romantic poetry, 299-324

The Epistolary Novel LC 59: 71-170
overviews and general studies, 72-96
women and the Epistolary novel, 96-138
principal figures: Britain, 138-53
principal figures: France, 153-69

Espionage Literature TCLC 50: 95-159
overviews and general studies, 96-113
espionage fiction/formula fiction, 113-26
spies in fact and fiction, 126-38
the female spy, 138-44
social and psychological perspectives, 144-58

European Debates on the Conquest of the Americas LC 67: 1-129
overviews and general studies, 3-56
major Spanish figures, 56-98
English perceptions of Native Americans, 98-129

European Romanticism NCLC 36: 149-284
definitions, 149-77
origins of the movement, 177-82
Romantic theory, 182-200
themes and techniques, 200-23
Romanticism in Germany, 223-39
Romanticism in France, 240-61
Romanticism in Italy, 261-4

Romanticism in Spain, 264-8
impact and legacy, 268-82

Exile in Literature TCLC 122: 1-129
overviews and general studies, 2-33
exile in fiction, 33-92
German literature in exile, 92-129

Existentialism and Literature TCLC 42: 197-268
overviews and definitions, 198-209
history and influences, 209-19
Existentialism critiqued and defended, 220-35
philosophical and religious perspectives, 235-41
Existentialist fiction and drama, 241-67

Familiar Essay NCLC 48: 96-211
definitions and origins, 97-130
overview of the genre, 130-43
elements of form and style, 143-59
elements of content, 159-73
the Cockneys: Hazlitt, Lamb, and Hunt, 173-91
status of the genre, 191-210

The Faust Legend LC 47: 1-117

Fear in Literature TCLC 74: 81-258
overviews and general studies, 81
pre-twentieth-century literature, 123
twentieth-century literature, 182

Feminism in the 1990s: Commentary on Works by Naomi Wolf, Susan Faludi, and Camille Paglia CLC 76: 377-415

Feminist Criticism in 1990 CLC 65: 312-60

Fifteenth-Century English Literature LC 17: 248-334
background, 249-72
poetry, 272-315
drama, 315-23
prose, 323-33

Film and Literature TCLC 38: 97-226
overviews and general studies, 97-119
film and theater, 119-34
film and the novel, 134-45
the art of the screenplay, 145-66
genre literature/genre film, 167-79
the writer and the film industry, 179-90
authors on film adaptations of their works, 190-200
fiction into film: comparative essays, 200-23

Finance and Money as Represented in Nineteenth-Century Literature NCLC 76: 1-69
historical perspectives, 2-20
the image of money, 20-37
the dangers of money, 37-50
women and money, 50-69

Folklore and Literature TCLC 86: 116-293
overviews and general studies, 118-144
Native American literature, 144-67
African-American literature, 167-238
folklore and the American West, 238-57
modern and postmodern literature, 257-91

Food in Literature TCLC 114: 1-133
food and children's literature, 2-14
food as a literary device, 14-32
rituals invloving food, 33-45
food and social and ethnic identity, 45-90
women's relationship with food, 91-132

Food in Nineteenth-Century Literature NCLC 108: 134-288
overviews, 136-74
food and social class, 174-85
food and gender, 185-219
food and love, 219-31
food and sex, 231-48

eating disorders, 248-70
vegetarians, carnivores, and cannibals, 270-87

French Drama in the Age of Louis XIV LC 28: 94-185
overview, 95-127
tragedy, 127-46
comedy, 146-66
tragicomedy, 166-84

French Enlightenment LC 14: 81-145
the question of definition, 82-9
le siècle des lumières, 89-94
women and the salons, 94-105
censorship, 105-15
the philosophy of reason, 115-31
influence and legacy, 131-44

French New Novel TCLC 98: 158-234
overviews and general studies, 158-92
influences, 192-213
themes, 213-33

French Realism NCLC 52: 136-216
origins and definitions, 137-70
issues and influence, 170-98
realism and representation, 198-215

French Revolution and English Literature NCLC 40: 96-195
history and theory, 96-123
romantic poetry, 123-50
the novel, 150-81
drama, 181-92
children's literature, 192-5

Futurism, Italian TCLC 42: 269-354
principles and formative influences, 271-9
manifestos, 279-88
literature, 288-303
theater, 303-19
art, 320-30
music, 330-6
architecture, 336-9
and politics, 339-46
reputation and significance, 346-51

Gaelic Revival See Irish Literary Renaissance

Gates, Henry Louis, Jr., and African-American Literary Criticism CLC 65: 361-405

Gay and Lesbian Literature CLC 76: 416-39

German Exile Literature TCLC 30: 1-58
the writer and the Nazi state, 1-10
definition of, 10-4
life in exile, 14-32
surveys, 32-50
Austrian literature in exile, 50-2
German publishing in the United States, 52-7

German Expressionism TCLC 34: 74-160
history and major figures, 76-85
aesthetic theories, 85-109
drama, 109-26
poetry, 126-38
film, 138-42
painting, 142-7
music, 147-53
and politics, 153-8

The Gilded Age NCLC 84: 169-271
popular themes, 170-90
Realism, 190-208
Aestheticism, 208-26
socio-political concerns, 226-70

Glasnost **and Contemporary Soviet Literature** CLC 59: 355-97

Gothic Novel NCLC 28: 328-402
development and major works, 328-34
definitions, 334-50
themes and techniques, 350-78
in America, 378-85

in Scotland, 385-91
influence and legacy, 391-400

The Governess in Nineteenth-Century Literature NCLC 104: 1-131
overviews and general studies, 3-28
social roles and economic conditions, 28-86
fictional governesses, 86-131

Graphic Narratives CLC 86: 405-32
history and overviews, 406-21
the "Classics Illustrated" series, 421-2
reviews of recent works, 422-32

Graveyard Poets LC 67: 131-212
origins and development, 131-52
major figures, 152-75
major works, 175-212

Greek Historiography CMLC 17: 1-49

Greek Mythology CMLC 26: 193-320
overviews and general studies, 194-209
origins and development of Greek mythology, 209-29
cosmogonies and divinities in Greek mythology, 229-54
heroes and heroines in Greek mythology, 254-80
women in Greek mythology, 280-320

Greek Theater CMLC 51: 1-58
criticism, 2-58

Hard-Boiled Fiction TCLC 118: 1-109
overviews and general studies, 2-39
major authors, 39-76
women and hard-boiled fiction, 76-109

Harlem Renaissance TCLC 26: 49-125
principal issues and figures, 50-67
the literature and its audience, 67-74
theme and technique in poetry, fiction, and drama, 74-115
and American society, 115-21
achievement and influence, 121-2

Havel, Václav, Playwright and President CLC 65: 406-63

Historical Fiction, Nineteenth-Century NCLC 48: 212-307
definitions and characteristics, 213-36
Victorian historical fiction, 236-65
American historical fiction, 265-88
realism in historical fiction, 288-306

Hollywood and Literature TCLC 118: 110-251
overviews and general studies, 111-20
adaptations, 120-65
socio-historical and cultural impact, 165-206
theater and hollywood, 206-51

Holocaust and the Atomic Bomb: Fifty Years Later CLC 91: 331-82
the Holocaust remembered, 333-52
Anne Frank revisited, 352-62
the atomic bomb and American memory, 362-81

Holocaust Denial Literature TCLC 58: 1-110
overviews and general studies, 1-30
Robert Faurisson and Noam Chomsky, 30-52
Holocaust denial literature in America, 52-71
library access to Holocaust denial literature, 72-5
the authenticity of Anne Frank's diary, 76-90
David Irving and the "normalization" of Hitler, 90-109

Holocaust, Literature of the TCLC 42: 355-450
historical overview, 357-61
critical overview, 361-70
diaries and memoirs, 370-95

novels and short stories, 395-425
poetry, 425-41
drama, 441-8

Homosexuality in Nineteenth-Century Literature NCLC 56: 78-182
defining homosexuality, 80-111
Greek love, 111-44
trial and danger, 144-81

Hungarian Literature of the Twentieth Century TCLC 26: 126-88
surveys of, 126-47
Nyugat and early twentieth-century literature, 147-56
mid-century literature, 156-68
and politics, 168-78
since the 1956 revolt, 178-87

Hysteria in Nineteenth-Century Literature NCLC 64: 59-184
the history of hysteria, 60-75
the gender of hysteria, 75-103
hysteria and women's narratives, 103-57
hysteria in nineteenth-century poetry, 157-83

Imagism TCLC 74: 259-454
history and development, 260
major figures, 288
sources and influences, 352
Imagism and other movements, 397
influence and legacy, 431

Immigrants in Nineteenth-Century Literature, Representation of NCLC 112: 188-298
overview, 189-99
immigrants in America, 199-223
immigrants and labor, 223-60
immigrants in England, 260-97

Incest in Nineteenth-Century American Literature NCLC 76: 70-141
overview, 71-88
the concern for social order, 88-117
authority and authorship, 117-40

Incest in Victorian Literature NCLC 92: 172-318
overviews and general studies, 173-85
novels, 185-276
plays, 276-84
poetry, 284-318

Indian Literature in English TCLC 54: 308-406
overview, 309-13
origins and major figures, 313-25
the Indo-English novel, 325-55
Indo-English poetry, 355-67
Indo-English drama, 367-72
critical perspectives on Indo-English literature, 372-80
modern Indo-English literature, 380-9
Indo-English authors on their work, 389-404

The Industrial Revolution in Literature NCLC 56: 183-273
historical and cultural perspectives, 184-201
contemporary reactions to the machine, 201-21
themes and symbols in literature, 221-73

The Irish Famine as Represented in Nineteenth-Century Literature NCLC 64: 185-261
overviews and general studies, 187-98
historical background, 198-212
famine novels, 212-34
famine poetry, 234-44
famine letters and eye-witness accounts, 245-61

Irish Literary Renaissance TCLC 46: 172-287
    overview, 173-83
    development and major figures, 184-202
    influence of Irish folklore and mythology, 202-22
    Irish poetry, 222-34
    Irish drama and the Abbey Theatre, 234-56
    Irish fiction, 256-86

Irish Nationalism and Literature NCLC 44: 203-73
    the Celtic element in literature, 203-19
    anti-Irish sentiment and the Celtic response, 219-34
    literary ideals in Ireland, 234-45
    literary expressions, 245-73

Irish Novel, The NCLC 80: 1-130
    overviews and general studies, 3-9
    principal figures, 9-22
    peasant and middle class Irish novelists, 22-76
    aristocratic Irish and Anglo-Irish novelists, 76-129

Israeli Literature TCLC 94: 1-137
    overviews and general studies, 2-18
    Israeli fiction, 18-33
    Israeli poetry, 33-62
    Israeli drama, 62-91
    women and Israeli literature, 91-112
    Arab characters in Israeli literature, 112-36

Italian Futurism See Futurism, Italian

Italian Humanism LC 12: 205-77
    origins and early development, 206-18
    revival of classical letters, 218-23
    humanism and other philosophies, 224-39
    humanism and humanists, 239-46
    the plastic arts, 246-57
    achievement and significance, 258-76

Italian Romanticism NCLC 60: 85-145
    origins and overviews, 86-101
    Italian Romantic theory, 101-25
    the language of Romanticism, 125-45

Jacobean Drama LC 33: 1-37
    the Jacobean worldview: an era of transition, 2-14
    the moral vision of Jacobean drama, 14-22
    Jacobean tragedy, 22-3
    the Jacobean masque, 23-36

Jazz and Literature TCLC 102: 3-124

Jewish-American Fiction TCLC 62: 1-181
    overviews and general studies, 2-24
    major figures, 24-48
    Jewish writers and American life, 48-78
    Jewish characters in American fiction, 78-108
    themes in Jewish-American fiction, 108-43
    Jewish-American women writers, 143-59
    the Holocaust and Jewish-American fiction, 159-81

Jews in Literature TCLC 118: 252-417
    overviews and general studies, 253-97
    representing the Jew in literature, 297-351
    the Holocaust in literature, 351-416

Journals of Lewis and Clark, The NCLC 100: 1-88
    overviews and general studies, 4-30
    journal-keeping methods, 30-46
    Fort Mandan, 46-51
    the Clark journal, 51-65
    the journals as literary texts, 65-87

Kabuki LC 73: 118-232
    overviews and general studies, 120-40
    the development of Kabuki, 140-65
    major works, 165-95
    Kabuki and society, 195-231

Kit-Kat Club, The LC 71: 66-112
    overviews and general studies, 67-88
    major figures, 88-107
    attacks on the Kit-Kat Club, 107-12

Knickerbocker Group, The NCLC 56: 274-341
    overviews and general studies, 276-314
    Knickerbocker periodicals, 314-26
    writers and artists, 326-40

Lake Poets, The NCLC 52: 217-304
    characteristics of the Lake Poets and their works, 218-27
    literary influences and collaborations, 227-66
    defining and developing Romantic ideals, 266-84
    embracing Conservatism, 284-303

Larkin, Philip, Controversy CLC 81: 417-64

Latin American Literature, Twentieth-Century TCLC 58: 111-98
    historical and critical perspectives, 112-36
    the novel, 136-45
    the short story, 145-9
    drama, 149-60
    poetry, 160-7
    the writer and society, 167-86
    Native Americans in Latin American literature, 186-97

Legend of El Dorado, The LC 74: 248-350
    overviews, 249-308
    major explorations for El Dorado, 308-50

The Levellers LC 51: 200-312
    overviews and general studies, 201-29
    principal figures, 230-86
    religion, political philosophy, and pamphleteering, 287-311

Literary Prizes TCLC 122: 130-203
    overviews and general studies, 131-34
    the Nobel Prize in Literature, 135-83
    the Pulitzer Prize, 183-203

Literature and Millenial Lists CLC 119: 431-67
    The Modern Library list, 433
    The Waterstone list, 438-439

Literature of the American Cowboy NCLC 96: 1-60
    overview, 3-20
    cowboy fiction, 20-36
    cowboy poetry and songs, 36-59

Literature of the California Gold Rush NCLC 92: 320-85
    overviews and general studies, 322-24
    early California Gold Rush fiction, 324-44
    Gold Rush folklore and legend, 344-51
    the rise of Western local color, 351-60
    social relations and social change, 360-385

Living Theatre, The DC 16: 154-214

Madness in Nineteenth-Century Literature NCLC 76: 142-284
    overview, 143-54
    autobiography, 154-68
    poetry, 168-215
    fiction, 215-83

Madness in Twentieth-Century Literature TCLC 50: 160-225
    overviews and general studies, 161-71
    madness and the creative process, 171-86
    suicide, 186-91
    madness in American literature, 191-207
    madness in German literature, 207-13
    madness and feminist artists, 213-24

Magic Realism TCLC 110: 80-327
    overviews and general studies, 81-94
    magic realism in African literature, 95-110
    magic realism in American literature, 110-32

    magic realism in Canadian literature, 132-46
    magic realism in European literature, 146-66
    magic realism in Asian literature, 166-79
    magic realism in Latin-American literature, 179-223
    magic realism in Israeli literature and the novels of Salman Rushdie, 223-38
    magic realism in literature written by women, 239-326

The Masque LC 63: 124-265
    development of the masque, 125-62
    sources and structure, 162-220
    race and gender in the masque, 221-64

Medical Writing LC 55: 93-195
    colonial America, 94-110
    enlightenment, 110-24
    medieval writing, 124-40
    sexuality, 140-83
    vernacular, 185-95

Memoirs of Trauma CLC 109: 419-466
    overview, 420
    criticism, 429

Metaphysical Poets LC 24: 356-439
    early definitions, 358-67
    surveys and overviews, 367-92
    cultural and social influences, 392-406
    stylistic and thematic variations, 407-38

Missionaries in the Nineteenth-Century, Literature of NCLC 112: 299-392
    history and development, 300-16
    uses of ethnography, 316-31
    sociopolitical concerns, 331-82
    David Livingstone, 382-91

Modern Essay, The TCLC 58: 199-273
    overview, 200-7
    the essay in the early twentieth century, 207-19
    characteristics of the modern essay, 219-32
    modern essayists, 232-45
    the essay as a literary genre, 245-73

Modern French Literature TCLC 122: 205-359
    overviews and general studies, 207-43
    French theater, 243-77
    gender issues and French women writers, 277-315
    ideology and politics, 315-24
    modern French poetry, 324-41
    resistance literature, 341-58

Modern Irish Literature TCLC 102: 125-321
    overview, 129-44
    dramas, 144-70
    fiction, 170-247
    poetry, 247-321

Modern Japanese Literature TCLC 66: 284-389
    poetry, 285-305
    drama, 305-29
    fiction, 329-61
    western influences, 361-87

Modernism TCLC 70: 165-275
    definitions, 166-184
    Modernism and earlier influences, 184-200
    stylistic and thematic traits, 200-229
    poetry and drama, 229-242
    redefining Modernism, 242-275

Muckraking Movement in American Journalism TCLC 34: 161-242
    development, principles, and major figures, 162-70
    publications, 170-9
    social and political ideas, 179-86
    targets, 186-208
    fiction, 208-19

decline, 219-29
impact and accomplishments, 229-40

Multiculturalism in Literature and Education CLC 70: 361-413

Music and Modern Literature TCLC 62: 182-329
overviews and general studies, 182-211
musical form/literary form, 211-32
music in literature, 232-50
the influence of music on literature, 250-73
literature and popular music, 273-303
jazz and poetry, 303-28

Native American Literature CLC 76: 440-76

Natural School, Russian NCLC 24: 205-40
history and characteristics, 205-25
contemporary criticism, 225-40

Naturalism NCLC 36: 285-382
definitions and theories, 286-305
critical debates on Naturalism, 305-16
Naturalism in theater, 316-32
European Naturalism, 332-61
American Naturalism, 361-72
the legacy of Naturalism, 372-81

Negritude TCLC 50: 226-361
origins and evolution, 227-56
definitions, 256-91
Negritude in literature, 291-343
Negritude reconsidered, 343-58

New Criticism TCLC 34: 243-318
development and ideas, 244-70
debate and defense, 270-99
influence and legacy, 299-315

The New World in Renaissance Literature LC 31: 1-51
overview, 1-18
utopia vs. terror, 18-31
explorers and Native Americans, 31-51

New York Intellectuals and *Partisan Review* TCLC 30: 117-98
development and major figures, 118-28
influence of Judaism, 128-39
Partisan Review, 139-57
literary philosophy and practice, 157-75
political philosophy, 175-87
achievement and significance, 187-97

The New Yorker TCLC 58: 274-357
overviews and general studies, 274-95
major figures, 295-304
New Yorker style, 304-33
fiction, journalism, and humor at *The New Yorker*, 333-48
the new *New Yorker*, 348-56

Newgate Novel NCLC 24: 166-204
development of Newgate literature, 166-73
Newgate Calendar, 173-7
Newgate fiction, 177-95
Newgate drama, 195-204

Nigerian Literature of the Twentieth Century TCLC 30: 199-265
surveys of, 199-227
English language and African life, 227-45
politics and the Nigerian writer, 245-54
Nigerian writers and society, 255-62

Nihilism and Literature TCLC 110: 328-93
overviews and general studies, 328-44
European and Russian nihilism, 344-73
nihilism in the works of Albert Camus, Franz Kafka, and John Barth, 373-92

Nineteenth-Century Captivity Narratives NCLC 80:131-218
overview, 132-37
the political significance of captivity narratives, 137-67
images of gender, 167-96
moral instruction, 197-217

Nineteenth-Century Euro-American Literary Representations of Native Americans NCLC 104: 132-264
overviews and general studies, 134-53
Native American history, 153-72
the Indians of the Northeast, 172-93
the Indians of the Southeast, 193-212
the Indians of the West, 212-27
Indian-hater fiction, 227-43
the Indian as exhibit, 243-63

Nineteenth-Century Native American Autobiography NCLC 64: 262-389
overview, 263-8
problems of authorship, 268-81
the evolution of Native American autobiography, 281-304
political issues, 304-15
gender and autobiography, 316-62
autobiographical works during the turn of the century, 362-88

Norse Mythology CMLC 26: 321-85
history and mythological tradition, 322-44
Eddic poetry, 344-74
Norse mythology and other traditions, 374-85

Northern Humanism LC 16: 281-356
background, 282-305
precursor of the Reformation, 305-14
the Brethren of the Common Life, the Devotio Moderna, and education, 314-40
the impact of printing, 340-56

Novel of Manners, The NCLC 56: 342-96
social and political order, 343-53
domestic order, 353-73
depictions of gender, 373-83
the American novel of manners, 383-95

Novels of the Ming and Early Ch'ing Dynasties LC 76: 213-356
overviews and historical development, 214-45
major works—overview, 245-85
genre studies, 285-325
cultural and social themes, 325-55

Nuclear Literature: Writings and Criticism in the Nuclear Age TCLC 46: 288-390
overviews and general studies, 290-301
fiction, 301-35
poetry, 335-8
nuclear war in Russo-Japanese literature, 338-55
nuclear war and women writers, 355-67
the nuclear referent and literary criticism, 367-88

Occultism in Modern Literature TCLC 50: 362-406
influence of occultism on literature, 363-72
occultism, literature, and society, 372-87
fiction, 387-96
drama, 396-405

Opium and the Nineteenth-Century Literary Imagination NCLC 20:250-301
original sources, 250-62
historical background, 262-71
and literary society, 271-9
and literary creativity, 279-300

Orientalism NCLC 96: 149-364
overviews and general studies, 150-98
Orientalism and imperialism, 198-229
Orientalism and gender, 229-59
Orientalism and the nineteenth-century novel, 259-321
Orientalism in nineteenth-century poetry, 321-63

The Oxford Movement NCLC 72: 1-197
overviews and general studies, 2-24
background, 24-59
and education, 59-69
religious responses, 69-128

literary aspects, 128-178
political implications, 178-196

The Parnassian Movement NCLC 72: 198-241
overviews and general studies, 199-231
and epic form, 231-38
and positivism, 238-41

Pastoral Literature of the English Renaissance LC 59: 171-282
overviews and general studies, 172-214
principal figures of the Elizabethan period, 214-33
principal figures of the later Renaissance, 233-50
pastoral drama, 250-81

Periodicals, Nineteenth-Century British NCLC 24: 100-65
overviews and general studies, 100-30
in the Romantic Age, 130-41
in the Victorian era, 142-54
and the reviewer, 154-64

Picaresque Literature of the Sixteenth and Seventeenth Centuries LC 78: 223-355
context and development, 224-71
genre, 271-98
the picaro, 299-326
the picara, 326-53

Plath, Sylvia, and the Nature of Biography CLC 86: 433-62
the nature of biography, 433-52
reviews of *The Silent Woman*, 452-61

Political Theory from the 15th to the 18th Century LC 36: 1-55
overview, 1-26
natural law, 26-42
empiricism, 42-55

Polish Romanticism NCLC 52: 305-71
overviews and general studies, 306-26
major figures, 326-40
Polish Romantic drama, 340-62
influences, 362-71

Politics and Literature TCLC 94: 138-61
overviews and general studies, 139-96
Europe, 196-226
Latin America, 226-48
Africa and the Caribbean, 248-60

Popular Literature TCLC 70: 279-382
overviews and general studies, 280-324
"formula" fiction, 324-336
readers of popular literature, 336-351
evolution of popular literature, 351-382

The Portrayal of Jews in Nineteenth-Century English Literature NCLC 72: 242-368
overviews and general studies, 244-77
Anglo-Jewish novels, 277-303
depictions by non-Jewish writers, 303-44
Hebraism versus Hellenism, 344-67

The Portrayal of Mormonism NCLC 96: 61-148
overview, 63-72
early Mormon literature, 72-100
Mormon periodicals and journals, 100-10
women writers, 110-22
Mormonism and nineteenth-century literature, 122-42
Mormon poetry, 142-47

Postcolonialism TCLC 114: 134-239
overviews and general studies, 135-153
African postcolonial writing, 153-72
Asian/Pacific literature, 172-78
postcolonial literary theory, 178-213
postcolonial women's writing, 213-38

Postmodernism TCLC 90:125-307
overview, 126-166
criticism , 166-224
fiction, 224-282

poetry, 282-300
drama, 300-307

Pre-Raphaelite Movement NCLC 20: 302-401
overview, 302-4
genesis, 304-12
Germ and *Oxford and Cambridge Magazine,* 312-20
Robert Buchanan and the "Fleshly School of Poetry," 320-31
satires and parodies, 331-4
surveys, 334-51
aesthetics, 351-75
sister arts of poetry and painting, 375-94
influence, 394-9

Pre-romanticism LC 40: 1-56
overviews and general studies, 2-14
defining the period, 14-23
new directions in poetry and prose, 23-45
the focus on the self, 45-56

Pre-Socratic Philosophy CMLC 22: 1-56
overviews and general studies, 3-24
the Ionians and the Pythagoreans, 25-35
Heraclitus, the Eleatics, and the Atomists, 36-47
the Sophists, 47-55

Protestant Reformation, Literature of the LC 37: 1-83
overviews and general studies, 1-49
humanism and scholasticism, 49-69
the reformation and literature, 69-82

Psychoanalysis and Literature TCLC 38: 227-338
overviews and general studies, 227-46
Freud on literature, 246-51
psychoanalytic views of the literary process, 251-61
psychoanalytic theories of response to literature, 261-88
psychoanalysis and literary criticism, 288-312
psychoanalysis as literature/literature as psychoanalysis, 313-34

The Quarrel between the Ancients and the Moderns LC 63: 266-381
overviews and general studies, 267-301
Renaissance origins, 301-32
Quarrel between the Ancients and the Moderns in France, 332-58
Battle of the Books in England, 358-80

Rap Music CLC 76: 477-50

Renaissance Natural Philosophy LC 27: 201-87
cosmology, 201-28
astrology, 228-54
magic, 254-86

Representations of the Devil in Nineteenth-Century Literature NCLC 100: 89-223
overviews and general studies, 90-115
the Devil in American fiction, 116-43
English Romanticism: the satanic school, 143-89
Luciferian discourse in European literature, 189-222

Restoration Drama LC 21: 184-275
general overviews and general studies, 185-230
Jeremy Collier stage controversy, 230-9
other critical interpretations, 240-75

Revenge Tragedy LC 71: 113-242
overviews and general studies, 113-51
Elizabethan attitudes toward revenge, 151-88
the morality of revenge, 188-216
reminders and remembrance, 217-41

Revising the Literary Canon CLC 81: 465-509

Revising the Literary Canon TCLC 114: 240-84
overviews and general studies, 241-85
canon change in American literature, 285-339
gender and the literary canon, 339-59
minority and third-world literature and the canon, 359-84

Revolutionary Astronomers LC 51: 314-65
overviews and general studies, 316-25
principal figures, 325-51
Revolutionary astronomical models, 352-64

Robin Hood, Legend of LC 19: 205-58
origins and development of the Robin Hood legend, 206-20
representations of Robin Hood, 220-44
Robin Hood as hero, 244-56

Rushdie, Salman, *Satanic Verses* Controversy CLC 55: 214-63; 59:404-56

Russian Nihilism NCLC 28: 403-47
definitions and overviews, 404-17
women and Nihilism, 417-27
literature as reform: the Civic Critics, 427-33
Nihilism and the Russian novel: Turgenev and Dostoevsky, 433-47

Russian Thaw TCLC 26: 189-247
literary history of the period, 190-206
theoretical debate of socialist realism, 206-11
Novy Mir, 211-7
Literary Moscow, 217-24
Pasternak, *Zhivago,* and the Nobel prize, 224-7
poetry of liberation, 228-31
Brodsky trial and the end of the Thaw, 231-6
achievement and influence, 236-46

Salem Witch Trials LC 38: 1-145
overviews and general studies, 2-30
historical background, 30-65
judicial background, 65-78
the search for causes, 78-115
the role of women in the trials, 115-44

Salinger, J. D., Controversy Surrounding *In Search of J. D. Salinger* CLC 55: 325-44

Science and Modern Literature TCLC 90: 308-419
overviews and general studies, 295-333
fiction, 333-95
poetry, 395-405
drama, 405-19

Science in Nineteenth-Century Literature NCLC 100: 224-366
overviews and general studies, 225-65
major figures, 265-336
sociopolitical concerns, 336-65

Science Fiction, Nineteenth-Century NCLC 24: 241-306
background, 242-50
definitions of the genre, 251-56
representative works and writers, 256-75
themes and conventions, 276-305

Scottish Chaucerians LC 20: 363-412

Scottish Poetry, Eighteenth-Century LC 29: 95-167
overviews and general studies, 96-114
the Scottish Augustans, 114-28
the Scots Vernacular Revival, 132-63
Scottish poetry after Burns, 163-66

Sea in Literature, The TCLC 82: 72-191
drama, 73-9
poetry, 79-119
fiction, 119-91

Sea in Nineteenth-Century English and American Literature, The NCLC 104: 265-362
overviews and general studies, 267-306
major figures in American sea fiction—Cooper and Melville, 306-29
American sea poetry and short stories, 329-45
English sea literature, 345-61

Sensation Novel, The NCLC 80: 219-330
overviews and general studies, 221-46
principal figures, 246-62
nineteenth-century reaction, 262-91
feminist criticism, 291-329

Sentimental Novel, The NCLC 60: 146-245
overviews and general studies, 147-58
the politics of domestic fiction, 158-79
a literature of resistance and repression, 179-212
the reception of sentimental fiction, 213-44

Sex and Literature TCLC 82: 192-434
overviews and general studies, 193-216
drama, 216-63
poetry, 263-87
fiction, 287-431

Sherlock Holmes Centenary TCLC 26: 248-310
Doyle's life and the composition of the Holmes stories, 248-59
life and character of Holmes, 259-78
method, 278-79
Holmes and the Victorian world, 279-92
Sherlockian scholarship, 292-301
Doyle and the development of the detective story, 301-19
Holmes's continuing popularity, 307-09

The Silver Fork Novel NCLC 88: 58-140
criticism, 59-139

Slave Narratives, American NCLC 20: 1-91
background, 2-9
overviews and general studies, 9-24
contemporary responses, 24-7
language, theme, and technique, 27-70
historical authenticity, 70-5
antecedents, 75-83
role in development of Black American literature, 83-8

The Slave Trade in British and American Literature LC 59: 283-369
overviews and general studies, 284-91
depictions by white writers, 291-331
depictions by former slaves, 331-67

Social Conduct Literature LC 55: 196-298
overviews and general studies, 196-223
prescriptive ideology in other literary forms, 223-38
role of the press, 238-63
impact of conduct literature, 263-87
conduct literature and the perception of women, 287-96
women writing for women, 296-98

Socialism NCLC 88: 141-237
origins, 142-54
French socialism, 154-83
Anglo-American socialism, 183-205
Socialist-Feminism, 205-36

Southern Literature of the Reconstruction NCLC 108: 289-369
overview, 290-91
reconstruction literature: the consequences of war, 291-321
old south to new: continuities in southern culture, 321-68

Spanish Civil War Literature TCLC 26: 311-85
topics in, 312-33
British and American literature, 333-59

French literature, 359-62
Spanish literature, 362-73
German literature, 373-75
political idealism and war literature, 375-83

Spanish Golden Age Literature LC 23: 262-332
overviews and general studies, 263-81
verse drama, 281-304
prose fiction, 304-19
lyric poetry, 319-31

Spasmodic School of Poetry NCLC 24: 307-52
history and major figures, 307-21
the Spasmodics on poetry, 321-7
Firmilian and critical disfavor, 327-39
theme and technique, 339-47
influence, 347-51

Sports in Literature TCLC 86: 294-445
overviews and general studies, 295-324
major writers and works, 324-402
sports, literature, and social issues, 402-45

Steinbeck, John, Fiftieth Anniversary of *The Grapes of Wrath* CLC 59: 311-54

Sturm und Drang NCLC 40: 196-276
definitions, 197-238
poetry and poetics, 238-58
drama, 258-75

Supernatural Fiction in the Nineteenth Century NCLC 32: 207-87
major figures and influences, 208-35
the Victorian ghost story, 236-54
the influence of science and occultism, 254-66
supernatural fiction and society, 266-86

Supernatural Fiction, Modern TCLC 30: 59-116
evolution and varieties, 60-74
"decline" of the ghost story, 74-86
as a literary genre, 86-92
technique, 92-101
nature and appeal, 101-15

Surrealism TCLC 30: 334-406
history and formative influences, 335-43
manifestos, 343-54
philosophic, aesthetic, and political principles, 354-75
poetry, 375-81
novel, 381-6
drama, 386-92
film, 392-8
painting and sculpture, 398-403
achievement, 403-5

Symbolism, Russian TCLC 30: 266-333
doctrines and major figures, 267-92
theories, 293-8
and French Symbolism, 298-310
themes in poetry, 310-4
theater, 314-20
and the fine arts, 320-32

Symbolist Movement, French NCLC 20: 169-249
background and characteristics, 170-86
principles, 186-91
attacked and defended, 191-7
influences and predecessors, 197-211
and Decadence, 211-6
theater, 216-26
prose, 226-33
decline and influence, 233-47

Television and Literature TCLC 78: 283-426
television and literacy, 283-98
reading vs. watching, 298-341
adaptations, 341-62
literary genres and television, 362-90

television genres and literature, 390-410
children's literature/children's television, 410-25

Theater of the Absurd TCLC 38: 339-415
"The Theater of the Absurd," 340-7
major plays and playwrights, 347-58
and the concept of the absurd, 358-86
theatrical techniques, 386-94
predecessors of, 394-402
influence of, 402-13

Tin Pan Alley See American Popular Song, Golden Age of

Tobacco Culture LC 55: 299-366
social and economic attitudes toward tobacco, 299-344
tobacco trade between the old world and the new world, 344-55
tobacco smuggling in Great Britain, 355-66

Transcendentalism, American NCLC 24: 1-99
overviews and general studies, 3-23
contemporary documents, 23-41
theological aspects of, 42-52
and social issues, 52-74
literature of, 74-96

Travel Writing in the Nineteenth Century NCLC 44: 274-392
the European grand tour, 275-303
the Orient, 303-47
North America, 347-91

Travel Writing in the Twentieth Century TCLC 30: 407-56
conventions and traditions, 407-27
and fiction writing, 427-43
comparative essays on travel writers, 443-54

Tristan and Isolde Legend CMLC 42: 311-404

True-Crime Literature CLC 99: 333-433
history and analysis, 334-407
reviews of true-crime publications, 407-23
writing instruction, 424-29
author profiles, 429-33

***Ulysses* and the Process of Textual Reconstruction** TCLC 26:386-416
evaluations of the new *Ulysses,* 386-94
editorial principles and procedures, 394-401
theoretical issues, 401-16

Utilitarianism NCLC 84: 272-340
J. S. Mill's Utilitarianism: liberty, equality, justice, 273-313
Jeremy Bentham's Utilitarianism: the science of happiness, 313-39

Utopianism NCLC 88: 238-346
overviews: Utopian literature, 239-59
Utopianism in American literature, 259-99
Utopianism in British literature, 299-311
Utopianism and Feminism, 311-45

Utopian Literature, Nineteenth-Century NCLC 24: 353-473
definitions, 354-74
overviews and general studies, 374-88
theory, 388-408
communities, 409-26
fiction, 426-53
women and fiction, 454-71

Utopian Literature, Renaissance LC 32: 1-63
overviews and general studies, 2-25
classical background, 25-33
utopia and the social contract, 33-9
origins in mythology, 39-48
utopia and the Renaissance country house, 48-52
influence of millenarianism, 52-62

Vampire in Literature TCLC 46: 391-454
origins and evolution, 392-412
social and psychological perspectives, 413-44
vampire fiction and science fiction, 445-53

Vernacular Bibles LC 67: 214-388
overviews and general studies, 215-59
the English Bible, 259-355
the German Bible, 355-88

Victorian Autobiography NCLC 40: 277-363
development and major characteristics, 278-88
themes and techniques, 289-313
the autobiographical tendency in Victorian prose and poetry, 313-47
Victorian women's autobiographies, 347-62

Victorian Fantasy Literature NCLC 60: 246-384
overviews and general studies, 247-91
major figures, 292-366
women in Victorian fantasy literature, 366-83

Victorian Hellenism NCLC 68: 251-376
overviews and general studies, 252-78
the meanings of Hellenism, 278-335
the literary influence, 335-75

Victorian Novel NCLC 32: 288-454
development and major characteristics, 290-310
themes and techniques, 310-58
social criticism in the Victorian novel, 359-97
urban and rural life in the Victorian novel, 397-406
women in the Victorian novel, 406-25
Mudie's Circulating Library, 425-34
the late-Victorian novel, 434-51

Vietnamese Literature TCLC 102: 322-386

Vietnam War in Literature and Film CLC 91: 383-437
overview, 384-8
prose, 388-412
film and drama, 412-24
poetry, 424-35

Violence in Literature TCLC 98: 235-358
overviews and general studies, 236-74
violence in the works of modern authors, 274-358

Vorticism TCLC 62: 330-426
Wyndham Lewis and Vorticism, 330-8
characteristics and principles of Vorticism, 338-65
Lewis and Pound, 365-82
Vorticist writing, 382-416
Vorticist painting, 416-26

Well-Made Play, The NCLC 80: 331-370
overviews and general studies, 332-45
Scribe's style, 345-56
the influence of the well-made play, 356-69

Women's Autobiography, Nineteenth Century NCLC 76: 285-368
overviews and general studies, 287-300
autobiographies concerned with religious and political issues, 300-15
autobiographies by women of color, 315-38
autobiographies by women pioneers, 338-51
autobiographies by women of letters, 351-68

Women's Diaries, Nineteenth-Century NCLC 48: 308-54
overview, 308-13
diary as history, 314-25
sociology of diaries, 325-34
diaries as psychological scholarship, 334-43

diary as autobiography, 343-8
diary as literature, 348-53

Women in Modern Literature TCLC 94: 262-425
    overviews and general studies, 263-86
    American literature, 286-304
    other national literatures, 304-33
    fiction, 333-94
    poetry, 394-407
    drama, 407-24

Women Writers, Seventeenth-Century LC 30: 2-58
    overview, 2-15
    women and education, 15-9
    women and autobiography, 19-31
    women's diaries, 31-9
    early feminists, 39-58

World War I Literature TCLC 34: 392-486
    overview, 393-403
    English, 403-27
    German, 427-50

    American, 450-66
    French, 466-74
    and modern history, 474-82

Yellow Journalism NCLC 36: 383-456
    overviews and general studies, 384-96
    major figures, 396-413

Young Playwrights Festival
    1988 CLC 55: 376-81
    1989 CLC 59: 398-403
    1990 CLC 65: 444-8

Topic Index

LC Cumulative Nationality Index

AFGHAN

Babur **18**

AMERICAN

Bache, Benjamin Franklin **74**
Bradford, William **64**
Bradstreet, Anne **4, 30**
Edwards, Jonathan **7, 54**
Eliot, John **5**
Franklin, Benjamin **25**
Hathorne, John **38**
Henry, Patrick **25**
Hopkinson, Francis **25**
Knight, Sarah Kemble **7**
Mather, Cotton **38**
Mather, Increase **38**
Morton, Thomas **72**
Munford, Robert **5**
Occom, Samson **60**
Penn, William **25**
Rowlandson, Mary **66**
Sewall, Samuel **38**
Stoughton, William **38**
Taylor, Edward **11**
Washington, George **25**
Wheatley (Peters), Phillis **3, 50**
Winthrop, John **31**

BENINESE

Equiano, Olaudah **16**

CANADIAN

Marie de l'Incarnation **10**

CHINESE

Lo Kuan-chung **12**
P'u Sung-ling **3, 49**
Ts'ao Hsueh-ch'in **1**
Wu Ch'eng-en **7**
Wu Ching-tzu **2**

DANISH

Holberg, Ludvig **6**
Wessel, Johan Herman **7**

DUTCH

Erasmus, Desiderius **16**
Lipsius, Justus **16**
Spinoza, Benedictus de **9, 58**

ENGLISH

Addison, Joseph **18**
Amory, Thomas **48**
Andrewes, Lancelot **5**
Arbuthnot, John **1**
Astell, Mary **68**
Aubin, Penelope **9**
Bacon, Francis **18, 32**
Bale, John **62**
Barker, Jane **42**

Beaumont, Francis **33**
Behn, Aphra **1, 30, 42**
Boswell, James **4, 50**
Bradstreet, Anne **4, 30**
Brome, Richard **61**
Brooke, Frances **6, 48**
Bunyan, John **4, 69**
Burke, Edmund **7, 36**
Burton, Robert **74**
Butler, Samuel **16, 43**
Camden, William **77**
Campion, Thomas **78**
Carew, Thomas **13**
Cary, Elizabeth, Lady Falkland **30**
Cavendish, Margaret Lucas **30**
Caxton, William **17**
Centlivre, Susanna **65**
Chapman, George **22**
Charles I **13**
Chatterton, Thomas **3, 54**
Chaucer, Geoffrey **17, 56**
Churchill, Charles **3**
Cibber, Colley **66**
Cleland, John **2, 48**
Clifford, Anne **76**
Collier, Jeremy **6**
Collins, William **4, 40**
Congreve, William **5, 21**
Coventry, Francis **46**
Coverdale, Myles **77**
Crashaw, Richard **24**
Daniel, Samuel **24**
Davenant, William **13**
Davys, Mary **1, 46**
Day, John **70**
Day, Thomas **1**
Dee, John **20**
Defoe, Daniel **1, 42**
Dekker, Thomas **22**
Delany, Mary (Granville Pendarves) **12**
Deloney, Thomas **41**
Denham, John **73**
Dennis, John **11**
Devenant, William **13**
Donne, John **10, 24**
Drayton, Michael **8**
Dryden, John **3, 21**
Elyot, Thomas **11**
Equiano, Olaudah **16**
Etherege, George **78**
Fanshawe, Ann **11**
Farquhar, George **21**
Fielding, Henry **1, 46**
Fielding, Sarah **1, 44**
Finch, Anne **3**
Fletcher, John **33**
Ford, John **68**
Foxe, John **14**
Garrick, David **15**
Gay, John **49**
Gower, John **76**
Gray, Thomas **4, 40**
Greene, Robert **41**

Hakluyt, Richard **31**
Hawes, Stephen **17**
Haywood, Eliza (Fowler) **1, 44**
Henry VIII **10**
Herbert, George **24**
Herrick, Robert **13**
Heywood, John **65**
Hobbes, Thomas **36**
Hoccleve, Thomas **75**
Holinshed, Raphael **69**
Howell, James **13**
Hunter, Robert **7**
Johnson, Samuel **15, 52**
Jonson, Ben(jamin) **6, 33**
Julian of Norwich **6, 52**
Kempe, Margery **6, 56**
Killigrew, Anne **4, 73**
Killigrew, Thomas **57**
Kyd, Thomas **22**
Langland, William **19**
Lanyer, Aemilia **10, 30**
Lead, Jane Ward **72**
Lilly, William **27**
Locke, John **7, 35**
Lodge, Thomas **41**
Lovelace, Richard **24**
Lyly, John **41**
Lyttelton, George **10**
Macaulay, Catherine **64**
Malory, Thomas **11**
Manley, (Mary) Delariviere **1, 42**
Marlowe, Christopher **22, 47**
Marston, John **33**
Marvell, Andrew **4, 43**
Massinger, Philip **70**
Middleton, Thomas **33**
Milton, John **9, 43**
Montagu, Mary (Pierrepont) Wortley **9, 57**
More, Henry **9**
More, Thomas **10, 32**
Nashe, Thomas **41**
Newton, Isaac **35, 52**
Parnell, Thomas **3**
Pepys, Samuel **11, 58**
Philips, Katherine **30**
Pix, Mary (Griffith) **8**
Pope, Alexander **3, 58, 60, 64**
Prior, Matthew **4**
Purchas, Samuel **70**
Raleigh, Walter **31, 39**
Reynolds, Joshua **15**
Richardson, Samuel **1, 44**
Roper, William **10**
Rowe, Nicholas **8**
Sheridan, Frances **7**
Sidney, Mary **19, 39**
Sidney, Philip **19, 39**
Skelton, John **71**
Smart, Christopher **3**
Smith, John **9**
Spenser, Edmund **5, 39**
Steele, Richard **18**
Suckling, John **75**

Swift, Jonathan **1, 42**
Tourneur, Cyril **66**
Trotter (Cockburn), Catharine **8**
Vanbrugh, John **21**
Vaughan, Henry **27**
Walpole, Horace **2, 49**
Walton, Izaak **72**
Warton, Thomas **15**
Webster, John **33**
Wilmot, John **75**
Winstanley, Gerrard **52**
Wollstonecraft, Mary **5, 50**
Wotton, Henry **68**
Wroth, Mary **30**
Wyatt, Thomas **70**
Wycherley, William **8, 21**
Young, Edward **3, 40**

FRENCH

Beaumarchais, Pierre-Augustin Caron de **61**
Boileau-Despréaux, Nicolas **3**
Calvin, John **37**
Christine de Pizan **9**
Condillac, Etienne Bonnot de **26**
Corneille, Pierre **28**
Crébillon, Claude Prosper Jolyot de (fils) **1, 28**
Cyrano de Bergerac, Savinien de **65**
de Navarre, Marguerite **61**
Descartes, René **20, 35**
Diderot, Denis **26**
Duclos, Charles Pinot- **1**
Gassendi, Pierre **54**
Gerson, Jean **77**
Helvetius, Claude-Adrien **26**
Holbach, Paul Henri Thiry Baron **14**
La Bruyère, Jean de **17**
La Fayette, Marie-(Madelaine Pioche de la Vergne) **2**
La Fontaine, Jean de **50**
Lesage, Alain-René **2, 28**
Malherbe, François de **5**
Marat, Jean Paul **10**
Marie de l'Incarnation **10**
Marivaux, Pierre Carlet de Chamblain de **4**
Marmontel, Jean-Francois **2**
Molière **10, 28, 64**
Montaigne, Michel (Eyquem) de **8**
Montesquieu, Charles-Louis de Secondat **7, 69**
Nostradamus **27**
Pascal, Blaise **35**
Perrault, Charles **2, 56**
Prévost, (Antoine François) **1**
Rabelais, François **5, 60**
Racine, Jean **28**
Ronsard, Pierre de **6, 54**
Rousseau, Jean-Baptiste **9**
Rousseau, Jean-Jacques **14, 36**
Scudery, Georges de **75**
Scudéry, Madeleine de **2, 58**

Sévigné, Marie (de Rabutin-Chantal) **11**
Turgot, Anne-Robert-Jacques **26**
Villon, François **62**
Voltaire **14**

GERMAN

Agrippa von Nettesheim, Henry Cornelius **27**
Andreae, Johann V(alentin) **32**
Beer, Johann **5**
Grimmelshausen, Johann Jakob Christoffel von **6**
Hutten, Ulrich von **16**
Kempis, Thomas a **11**
Lessing, Gotthold Ephraim **8**
Luther, Martin **9, 37**
Moritz, Karl Philipp **2**
Schlegel, Johann Elias (von) **5**

ICELANDIC

Petursson, Halligrimur **8**

IRANIAN

Jami, Nur al-Din 'Abd al-Rahman **9**

IRISH

Berkeley, George **65**
Brooke, Henry **1**
Burke, Edmund **7, 36**
Denham, John **73**
Farquhar, George **21**
Goldsmith, Oliver **2, 48**
Sterne, Laurence **2, 48**
Swift, Jonathan **1, 42**

ITALIAN

Aretino, Pietro **12**
Ariosto, Ludovico **6**
Boiardo, Matteo Maria **6**
Bruno, Giordano **27**
Campanella, Tommaso **32**
Casanova de Seingalt, Giovanni Jacopo **13**
Castelvetro, Lodovico **12**
Castiglione, Baldassare **12**
Cellini, Benvenuto **7**
Colonna, Vittoria **71**
Da Vinci, Leonardo **12, 57, 60**
Ficino, Marsilio **12**
Goldoni, Carlo **4**
Guicciardini, Francesco **49**
Machiavelli, Niccolò **8, 36**
Michelangelo **12**
Pico della Mirandola, Giovanni **15**
Sannazaro, Jacopo **8**
Tasso, Torquato **5**

JAPANESE

Chikamatsu Monzaemon **66**
Matsuo Bashō **62**

MEXICAN

Juana Inés de la Cruz **5**
Sigüenza y Gongora, Carlos de **8**

NORWEGIAN

Holberg, Ludvig **6**
Wessel, Johan Herman **7**

POLISH

Kochanowski, Jan **10**

PORTUGUESE

Camões, Luís de **62**

RUSSIAN

Catherine the Great **69**
Chulkov, Mikhail Dmitrievich **2**
Frederick the Great **14**
Ivan IV **17**
Trediakovsky, Vasilii Kirillovich **68**

SCOTTISH

Boswell, James **4, 50**
Buchanan, George **4**
Burns, Robert **3, 29, 40**
Douglas, Gavin **20**
Dunbar, William **20**
Henryson, Robert **20**
Hume, David **7, 56**
James I **20**
Knox, John **37**
Lyndsay, David **20**
Smollett, Tobias (George) **2, 46**
Thomson, James **16, 29, 40**

SPANISH

Cabeza de Vaca, Alvar Nunez **61**
Calderón de la Barca, Pedro **23**
Castro, Guillen de **19**
Cervantes (Saavedra), Miguel de **6, 23**
Cortes, Hernan **31**
Díaz del Castillo, Bernal **31**
Góngora (y Argote), Luis de **72**
Gracian y Morales, Baltasar **15**
John of the Cross **18**
Las Casas, Bartolomé de **31**
de Molina, Tirso **73**
Quevedo, Francisco de **23**
Rojas, Fernando de **23**
Teresa de Jesus, St. **18**
Vega, Lope de **23**

SWISS

Paracelsus **14**
Rousseau, Jean-Jacques **14, 36**
Zwingli, Huldreich **37**

WELSH

Vaughan, Henry **27**

An Account of the Rejoicing at the Diet of Ratisbon (Etherege) **78**:105

"Ad Thamesin (de Hyspanorum fuga)" (Campion) **78**:4, 34, 42-3, 85

The Airs that were sung and played at Brougham Castle in the King's Entertainment (Campion) **78**:6, 28, 33

"And would you see my Mistris face or Followe thy faire sunne" (Campion) **78**:26

"Another Dialogue, to be sung at the same time" (Campion) **78**:29

"Argumentum" (Campion) **78**:42-3

"As by the streames of Babilon" (Campion) **78**:62

"Author of light" (Campion) **78**:16-17, 62-3

"Awake, awake, thou heavy spright" (Campion) **78**:63

"Awake, thou spring of speaking grace! mute rest becomes not thee!" (Campion) **78**:5, 65, 72-3

"A Ballad" (Campion) **78**:31

"Beauty is but a painted hell" (Campion) **78**:77

A Book of Ayres, Set foorth to be song to the Lute, Orpherian, and Base Violl (Campion) **78**:4-6, 10-11, 19, 22, 38-9, 43, 50-1, 54, 58-9, 61, 65, 75-6

"Bravely deckt" (Campion) **78**:62-3

"Bring away this Sacred Tree" (Campion) **78**:92

"Canto Primo" (Campion) **78**:4

"Canto Secundo" (Campion) **78**:4

Cavendish House Entertainment (Campion) **78**:29

The Caversham Entertainment (Campion) **78**:5, 90

"Come, cheerful day, part of my life to me" (Campion) **78**:5, 63

"Come, let us sound with melody" (Campion) **78**:19, 23-4

"Come away" (Campion) **78**:86

"Come follow me my wandring mates" (Campion) **78**:31

"Come you pretty false-ey'd wanton" (Campion) **78**:64

The Comical Revenge: or, Love in a Tub (Etherege) **78**:97-8, 104, 107-11, 116-19, 127, 129, 136, 141, 151, 154, 157-58, 160, 162, 172, 179-80, 184-92, 194, 198, 207, 211

"Could my heart more tongues imploy" (Campion) **78**:65, 77

"The Dance" (Campion) **78**:31-2

"De regis reditu e Scotia" (Campion) **78**:28

"A Dialogue sung the first night, the King being at Supper" (Campion) **78**:29

"Dido was the Carthage Queen" (Campion) **78**:33

"An Elegie" (Campion) **78**:56-7

Eppigramatum Libri II (Campion)
See *Thoma Campiani Epigrammatum Libri II*

"Faine would I my love disclose" (Campion) **78**:77

"The Farewell Song" (Campion) **78**:29, 31, 33

The First Booke of Ayres (Campion) **78**:59, 61, 63, 65, 67, 69

"Follow thy fair sun" (Campion) **78**:17

"Follow Your Saint" (Campion) **78**:22, 24-5, 27-8

The Fourth Booke of Ayres (Campion) **78**:55, 66, 69, 74

"Fragmentum Umbrae" (Campion) **78**:42

"Goe, happy man, like th'Evening Starre" (Campion) **78**:92

"Good men, shew, if you can tell" (Campion) **78**:64

"Grace and Bountie" (Campion) **78**:92

"Harke, al you ladies" (Campion) **78**:5, 72-3, 75

"How easl'y wert thou chained" (Campion) **78**:61

"I must complain" (Campion) **78**:77

"If any hath the heart to kill" (Campion) **78**:69

"If Love loves truth" (Campion) **78**:66

"It fell on a sommers day" (Campion) **78**:18, 70-2, 76

"Kinde are her answers" (Campion) **78**:66, 77

"The Kings Good-night" (Campion) **78**:29, 31

Lady of Pleasure (Etherege) **78**:106

The Letterbrook (Etherege) **78**:116, 123-24, 126, 137

"The Libertine" (Etherege) **78**:138

"Lift up to heav'n" (Campion) **78**:60

Light Conceits of Lovers (Campion) **78**:5

"Lighten, heavy heart thy spright" (Campion) **78**:63

"Loe when backe mine eyes" (Campion) **78**:63

The Lord Hay's Masque (Campion) **78**:5, 84, 93

The Lords' Masque (Campion) **78**:5, 85-6, 89-90, 93

"The Lords Welcome, sung before the Kings Good-night" (Campion) **78**:29, 31

Love in a Tub (Etherege)
See *The Comical Revenge: or, Love in a Tub*

Madam Nelly's Complaint (Etherege) **78**:106

"The man of life upright" (Campion) **78**:20, 23, 25, 27, 62

The Man of Mode, or Sir Fopling Flutter (Etherege) **78**:98, 100-02, 104, 106, 109, 112, 120-24, 127, 132, 136-37, 147, 150-51, 161, 167, 171, 185, 189-90, 194-95, 200-03, 206-9

Masque for Lord Knowles (Campion) **78**:5

Masque for the Marriage of the Earl of Somerset (Campion)
See *The Caversham Entertainment*

Masque in Honour of Lord Hayes and his Bride (Campion)
See *The Lord Hay's Masque*

Masque of Proteus and the Adamantine Rock (Campion) **78**:83

"Maydes are simple" (Campion) **78**:65

"Mistris, since you so much desire" (Campion) **78**:73

"Move now with measured sound" (Campion) **78**:83

"My sweetest Lesbia" (Campion) **78**:61, 70

"Never love unlesse you can" (Campion) **78**:66

"Never weather-beaten Saile" (Campion) **78**:5, 21, 23, 25, 59-60, 62-3

A New Way for making Four Parts in Counterpoint (Campion) **78**:6

"Now let her change" (Campion) **78**:65

"Now winter nights enlarge" (Campion) **78**:5, 21, 23-4, 65

"O, what unhop't for sweet supply" (Campion) **78**:63

"O deare, that I with thee might live" (Campion) **78**:64

"O griefe, O spight" (Campion) **78**:65

Observations in the Art of English Poesie (Campion) **78**:3-4, 6-11, 19, 21-2, 24, 27, 39, 51

"Of Neptune's empire let us sing" (Campion) **78**:6

"Oft have I sigh'd" (Campion) **78**:65

"Out of my soules deapth" (Campion) **78**:62, 67

"The Peacefull westerne winde" (Campion) **78**:5, 82

"Pin'd I am, and like to die" (Campion) **78**:64

Poemata (Campion)
See *Thomæ Campiani Poemata*

"Queen Dido" (Campion) **78**:32

"Robin is a lovely lad" (Campion) **78**:6

"The Ronde" (Campion) **78**:36

"Rose-Cheekt Lawra" (Campion) **78**:19, 22-5

The Second Booke of Ayres (Campion) **78**:58-61, 63, 65, 82

"A secret love or two" (Campion) **78**:64, 77

"Seeke the Lord" (Campion) **78**:62-3

"The shadowes dark'ning our intents" (Campion) **78**:31, 33

"Shall I come, sweet love, to thee?" (Campion) **78**:5

"Shall I then hope when faith is fled" (Campion) **78**:66

She Would if She Could (Etherege) **78**:97-8, 104, 109, 111, 117, 119-20, 127-28, 130, 136, 144, 147, 151, 157-61, 190-94, 196, 200, 208, 211-19

"Sing a song of joy" (Campion) **78**:62, 67-8

"Sing Io, Hymen: Io, Io, Hymen" (Campion) **78**:81-2

"Sleep wayward thoughts" (Campion) **78**:72

"Sleepe, angry beauty" (Campion) **78**:72

"So many loves have I neglected" (Campion) **78**:64, 77

"So tyr'd are all my thoughts" (Campion) **78**:65, 77

The Somerset Masque (Campion) **78**:91

"Song of transformation" (Campion) **78**:82

Songs of Mourning (Campion) **78**:5, 56

The Squires' Masque (Campion) **78**:30, 90-1, 93

"Sweet, exclude me not" (Campion) **78**:64

"The Sypres curten of the night is spread" (Campion) **78**:72

"There is none, O none but you" (Campion) **78**:5

The Third and Fourth Bookes of Ayres (Campion) **78**:5

The Third Booke of Ayres (Campion) **78**:5, 21, 55, 58, 65-6

Thoma Campiani Epigrammatum Libri II (Campion) **78**:6, 34, 39-40

Thomæe Campiani Poemata (Campion) **78**:5, 34, 39-40, 42

"Thou art not faire" (Campion) **78**:77

"Though your strangenesse" (Campion) **78**:64

"Thrice toss these oaken ashes in the air" (Campion) **78**:5

"Thus I resolve" (Campion) **78**:77

"To a lady, asking him how long he would love her" (Etherege) **78**:139

"To Musicke bent is my retyred minde" (Campion) **78**:5, 61-2

"Tune thy Musicke to thy heart" (Campion) **78**:5, 26, 62

Two Bookes of Ayres (Campion) **78**:5, 20-1, 28

"Umbra" (Campion) **78**:34, 40, 42, 85

"Vaine men, whose follies" (Campion) **78**:61, 63, 77

"View mee, Lord" (Campion) **78**:63

"Welcome, welcome king of guests" (Campion) **78**:31

"Were my hart" (Campion) **78**:65

"What harvest half so sweet is" (Campion) **78**:5

"What if a day, or a month, or a year?" (Campion) **78**:6

"What is it all" (Campion) **78**:65

"What is our life?" (Campion) **78**:17

"When the God of merrie love" (Campion) **78**:26

"When thou must home to shades of underground" (Campion) **78**:5, 26, 61, 74-6

"When to her lute Corinna sings" (Campion) **78**:16

"Where are all thy beauties, now, all hearts enchaining?" (Campion) **78**:5

"While dancing rests" (Campion) **78**:92

The Works of Sir George Etherege (Etherege) **78**:116

The Works of Thomas Campion (Campion) **78**:50, 56, 80-92

ISBN 0-7876-5992-4

90000

9 780787 659929